THE NORTH REPORTS
THE CIVIL WAR

The North Reports the Civil War

J. CUTLER ANDREWS

University of Pittsburgh Press

Published by the University of Pittsburgh Press, Pittsburgh, Pa., 15260

Feffer and Simons, Inc., London
Manufactured in the United States of America

Paperback reprint 1985

Library of Congress Cataloging in Publication Data

Andrews, J. Cutler, 1908–1972
The North reports the Civil War.

Reprint. Originally published: Pittsburgh, Pa.: University of Pittsburgh Press, 1955.
Bibliography: p. 761
Includes index.
1. United States—History—Civil War, 1861–1865—Journalists. I. Title.
E609.A6 1985 973.7 84-22087
ISBN 0-8229-5370-6 (pbk.)

To Kenneth, Malcolm, and Sharon

Contents

Foreword

SINCE the publication in 1873 of Frederic Hudson's *Journalism in the United States* many books of varying value have treated aspects of the history of American newspapering. The vast majority, however, have stressed the role of the editors and of the editorial function, leaving largely untold the story of the actual men who collected, wrote, and sent in the news.

In *The North Reports the Civil War,* Dr. Andrews, professor of history at the Pennsylvania College for Women, repairs this defect. He has written a scholarly, readable, comprehensive narrative of the war correspondents on the Northern side of the great sectional conflict. He describes their trials and tribulations in transmitting dispatches to their home offices. He conveys through the reporters' eyes much of the drama of the fighting. But the reader sees also the officers in their tents, the men about the campfires, and desperate action on land and water.

For no other war in modern times, European or American, has the news reporting been analyzed so exhaustively. Besides the printed dispatches from the field, the author has consulted more than fifty manuscript collections scattered through the United States, some of them still in private hands, and delved into numerous published and unpublished government documents, as well as countless books and magazine articles. The sixty newspaper files include some in the South and in Europe.

Thanks to painstaking research, extending over more than a decade, Professor Andrews has established the identity of many reporters, some previously unknown even to specialists in the field. Moreover, he sheds new light on the relationship to the press of leading generals and admirals. Of particular interest perhaps is the instance of Union General George Gordon Meade, whose cavalier treatment of a Philadelphia *Inquirer* correspondent during the Wilderness Campaign helped to frustrate his presidential aspirations.

The North Reports the Civil War

This book demonstrates that the Civil War was of decisive importance in developing the techniques of modern war correspondence. It was in this struggle that the transmission of news by telegraph first occurred on a large scale. During the first two years the leading New York newspapers averaged annually from $60,000 to $100,000 for this purpose. Between 1861 and 1865 the *Herald* alone spent more than $500,000 for newsgathering at the front.

As Dr. Andrews shows, the campaigns in the East received the best coverage, although at times of military defeat official censorship prevented truthful accounts even there. Much of the inaccuracy of the reporting, he points out, was accidental or at any rate unintentional. The reporter could hardly be better than his news sources, and these often proved of gross unreliability. Yet, operating nearer to the battle line than has been possible for correspondents in most wars, the "specials" of the Northern press supplied a surprisingly realistic picture of events.

Professor Andrews, author of *Pittsburgh's Post-Gazette,* which was his first venture in newspaper history, has written a work which will interest not only historians and students of journalism but also the general public.

Arthur M. Schlesinger
July, 1954

CIVIL WAR—EASTERN THEATER

1861 - 1865

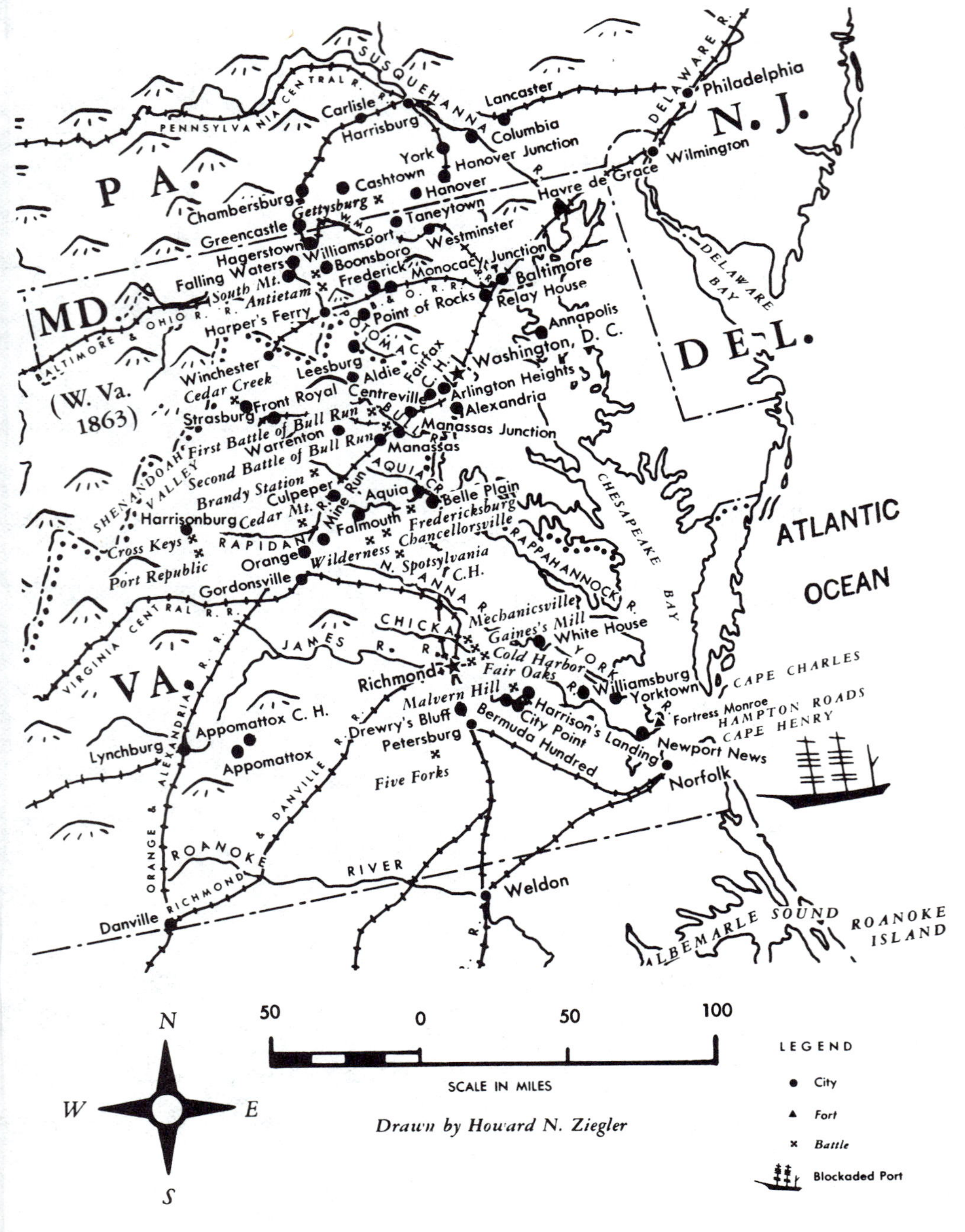

Drawn by Howard N. Ziegler

Civil War Theatre, 1861-1865

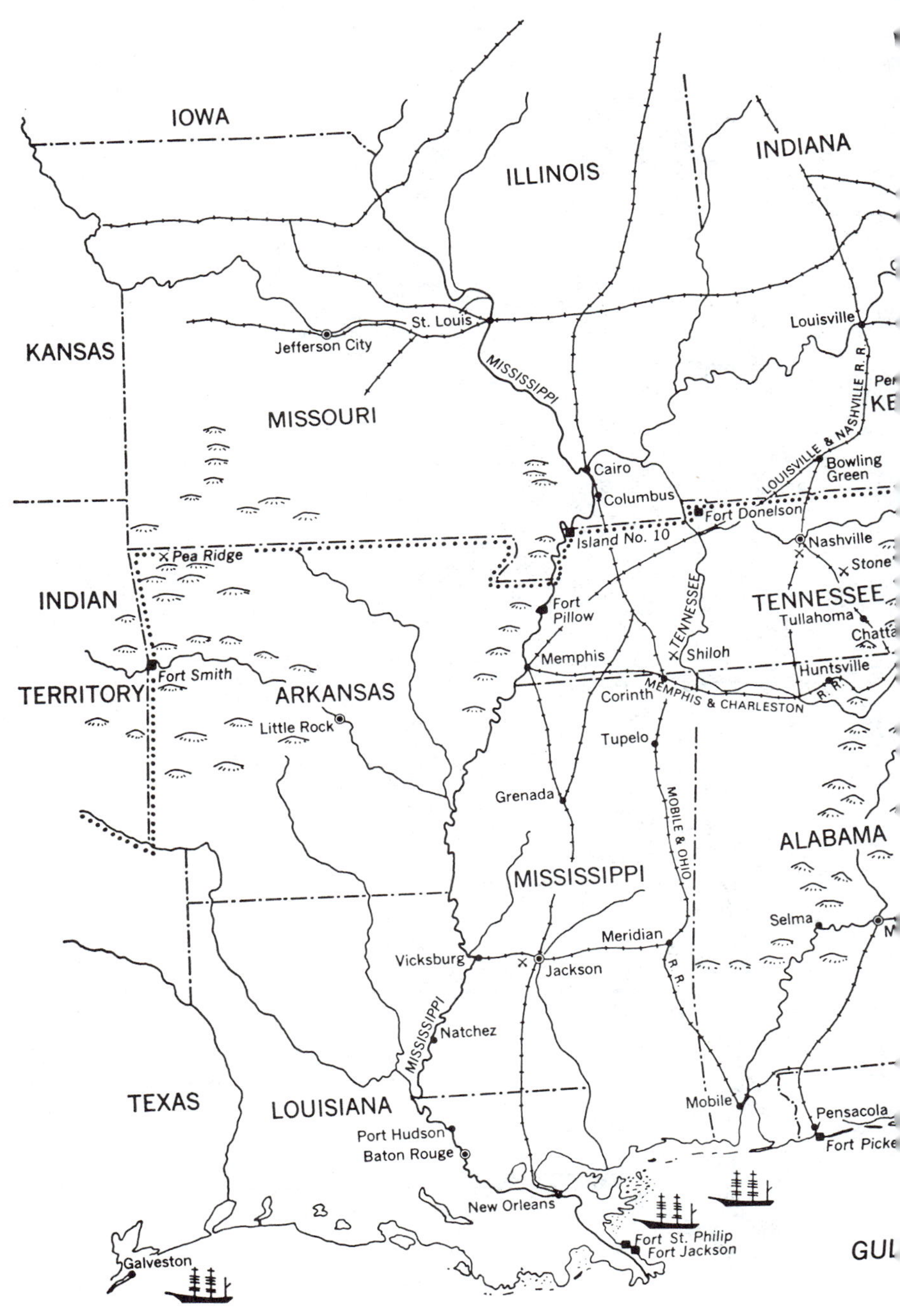

PENNSYLVANIA
Pittsburgh
Harrisburg
Philadelphia
NEW JERSEY
Gettysburg
OHIO
MD.
Baltimore
Harper's Ferry
Frederick
POTOMAC
Winchester
Washington
D.C.
DELAWARE
SHENANDOAH VALLEY
CHESAPEAKE BAY
Cincinnati
(WEST VIRGINIA ADMITTED 1863)
Fredericksburg
RAPPAHANNOCK
Gordonsville
VIRGINIA
JAMES
ankfort
Richmond
Petersburg
Fortress Monroe
Lynchburg
Norfolk
CKY
VIRGINIA & EAST TENNESSEE R.R.
ROANOKE ISLAND
CUMBERLAND GAP
Raleigh
Goldsboro
CAPE HATTERAS
NORTH
CAROLINA
Charlotte
Wilmington
Dalton
Fort Fisher
Columbia
SOUTH
CAROLINA
Atlanta
Augusta
Charleston
ATLANTIC
Milledgeville
Fort Sumter
Macon
GEORGIA
OCEAN
Savannah
Fort McAllister
ery
N
W
E
S
State Capital
Confederate Forts
Battle
Blockaded Port
FLORIDA
F
MEXICO
Drawn by Howard N. Ziegler
0
80
160
MILES

THE NORTH REPORTS THE CIVIL WAR

1

The Reporter and the Fort

IT was shortly after five o'clock in the afternoon of Thursday, April 11, 1861. Abraham Lincoln had been in the White House for thirty-eight days. Two days earlier the Associated Press had made the public aware for the first time of extensive military and naval preparations "intended for defensive purposes only."[1] Only a few moments before, Reporter Bradley Sillick Osbon of the New York *World* had climbed up into the main crosstrees of the U. S. revenue cutter "Harriet Lane," just outside the harbor of Charleston, South Carolina. Seated beside the coast pilot, he surveyed the harbor with deep interest. This was his first view of it, at the end of a rough three-day trip down the coast from New York.

Since the weather had cleared, Osbon could easily make out with the aid of his spy-glass the landmarks in Charleston Harbor. He looked first at the lighthouse and the Cumings Point battery a little to the west of it. Then he caught a glimpse, farther up the harbor, of the pentagonal-shaped fort which had figured so prominently in the news during the last three and a half months.

Although several small craft were anchored near the Cumings Point battery, no vessel was near Fort Sumter. But over the walls of the fort, sixty feet high from the water's edge to the parapet, was flying the flag of the United States. Inside the walls, committed to the defense of that flag, was Major Robert Anderson with nine officers and about seventy men of the First United States Artillery. As yet Osbon had no way of knowing that Anderson had refused, less than an hour before, a demand for the fort's surrender from Brigadier General Pierre G. T. Beauregard, the Confederate commander in the Charleston area.

Night came on. By seven-thirty it was completely dark except for a few stars which imperfectly shone through the dim overcast that had now appeared. All was still except the dip of the paddles that were kept revolving at sufficient speed to enable the ship to maintain her position outside the Charleston bar. Blue lights, rockets, and Roman candles were in readiness in case any of the other members of the Sumter relief expedition hove in view during the night.

Osbon retired to his hammock around midnight, but there was no sleep for him. At three-thirty in the morning a large vessel bore down on the cutter.

"Steamer, ahoy! Is that the 'Harriet Lane'?" asked the stranger.

"Aye, aye, sir."

"Is Fort Sumter evacuated?"

"I cannot tell. I arrived here at six o'clock, but did not notice anything unusual."

"Will you please send a boat to us, and I will come on board. Our boats are too heavy to be lowered away."

"Aye, aye, sir. I will send my boat."[2]

The newcomer proved to be the U. S. S. "Baltic," the troop and store ship of the expedition. Within a few moments, Captain Gustavus V. Fox, who had charge of the relief expedition, came aboard. Osbon dozed off, to be awakened again by a sound which brought him to his feet. It was the boom of a gun. Standing beside the ironclad battery on Morris Island, a venerable Virginia planter named Edmund Ruffin had just fired the opening shot of the Civil War. By the time Osbon reached the deck, Fort Sumter was ringed by fire issuing from every battery in the harbor. It was then shortly after 4:30 A.M., Friday, April 12.

Within the city of Charleston the opening of the bombardment created the most intense excitement. The wind was from the east that morning, so the sound of the guns blasting away across the harbor could be heard in all parts of the city. Wharves, roofs, church steeples, and second-story windows were alive with spectators who followed the progress of the action by the flashes of the guns. At daybreak the crowd which had gathered along the Battery took shelter from a rain shower. But after sunrise they reappeared. To a New York *Times* reporter who had been aroused from his sleep that morning by the misleading announcement, "Wake up, sir, they have been firing all night!" the faces of the watchers appeared "sad, anxious, preoccupied."[3] Yet one of the spectators, a decrepit old gentleman more than seventy years old, told a correspondent of the Charleston *Courier* that although he had five sons on Morris Island, "I would not utter one murmur while standing over their graves if they died fighting to-day."[4]

All day long the cannons thundered through the gloom. Standing on the wheelhouse and other high points for a better view of the action, the crewmen of the "Harriet Lane" raved, screamed, and swore as they demanded that they be led against the assailants of their flag. Throughout the day, however, the fleet remained outside the bar, taking no part in the fighting. Two of the most important units of the expedition were still missing[5] and the others were without tugs to tow their launches into the harbor.

His responsibilities as clerk and signal officer of the "Harriet Lane" did not prevent Reporter Osbon from obtaining a good view of the cannonading. From the time he ran away from boarding school as a boy of eleven to work on a canal boat, Osbon had spent the greater part of his life at sea. During this time his life had been as full of adventures as a novel. In one stretch of five years and eight months during which he was completely out of touch with his family in Brooklyn, he had taken part in whaling operations in the Pacific and Antarctic oceans, engaged in hand-to-hand encounters with Chinese pirates as a member of the Anglo-Chinese navy, spent eight anxious months on board an ice-bound trading vessel north of the Arctic Circle, and narrowly missed death when his ship was caught in an East Indian cyclone. Subsequently, as an officer in the Argentine navy, he had taken part in some of the hardest fighting he had seen up to that time. These experiences were to be of service to him now in reporting fleet operations.

As he watched the shells exploding above Sumter and observed with a practiced eye the effects of the Confederate gunnery, Osbon could hardly have foreseen what all this was to mean for him and many others. As the Civil War's outstanding naval reporter, he was destined to be under fire no less than twenty-seven times and be wounded in action on seven different occasions.[6] But not knowing about this, he remained on deck until 11:30 that night, watching the illuminated tracework of the mortar shells across the sky and feeling very much as if "the end of the world was about due."[7]

Official information of the attack on Sumter did not reach Washington until seven o'clock that evening, although rumors and private telegrams reporting the progress of the attack and Anderson's heroic defense streamed into the White House from an early hour that day.[8] Newspaper dispatches received at Washington gave the public to understand that Fox's supply ships had entered Charleston Harbor without resistance and were presumably landing their cargoes. Lincoln was quoted as saying that if these dispatches were correct (and he hoped they might be true) the whole question had been settled without firing a gun and the crisis was ended.[9]

With the approach of dawn on Saturday morning the Confederates began a brisk cannonade which soon exceeded the tempo of that of the day before. By noon Osbon could plainly see from the "Harriet Lane" a red sheet of flame rising twenty feet above the walls of the fort. Within an hour's time the guns of Sumter became silent. And not long after, a silence descended upon the vessels of the fleet as they saw a white flag waving above the fort. But not until seven o'clock that night did a flag-of-truce boat return with definite information that Anderson and his men had surrendered.

The news of Sumter's surrender reached Washington that evening, shortly after the regular edition of the *Evening Star* had been distributed. In some parts of the North there were still lingering doubts for several days as to whether Anderson had really surrendered and, assuming that he had, whether he had not acted the part of a traitor. The New York *Times* commented:

> Strange to say the more "news" the public receives the more incredulous they become, owing to the contradictory, absurd and evidently *one-sided* character of many of the dispatches which come over the wires. That the rebels, ten thousand strong, had opened their half dozen batteries upon the single beleaguered fortress and its seventy brave defenders was fully credited, and that Major Anderson was replying with his guns to the attack, but that the fleet lay quietly at anchor outside, taking no part in the action; that a granite bomb proof shelter should be on fire, and the flames bursting out through all the port-holes; that a raft should have been constructed and launched, to enable the men to procure *water* to put out the fire, thus subjecting the poor fellows to "terrible slaughter," when there are full water-tanks *in* the fort, and ample pumps to flood the place; that Major Anderson had displayed his flag at half-mast, as a "signal of distress;" that he was *gradually* blowing up the fort, with the supposed intention of escaping seaward—these and like announcements created a general belief that the dispatches were bogus, or at least the mere result of random conjecture, entitling them to no confidence.[10]

On Sunday, April 14, Anderson and his men evacuated the fort and went on board the "Baltic" to go back to New York. So that he might be on the same ship with Major Anderson, Osbon made arrangements to be transferred to the "Baltic," where he began at once to write his story of the fight. As the only newspaperman with the Sumter expedition the *World* reporter had in his grasp an important news beat.

Osbon remained with Anderson throughout the voyage, reading to him while he was ill and acting as his secretary. As the expedition neared Sandy Hook, the Major handed the *World* man a three-hundred word draft of his official report for any additions that he might suggest. With the sick officer's approval, Osbon condensed it to one hundred fifty words and placed it inside a tin box which was hermetically sealed for delivery to the government messengers.[11]

Since the relief expedition had proved a failure, everyone connected with it anticipated a chilly reception when they reached New York. Certainly they had never expected to be regarded as heroes. To their surprise they found upon arriving at New York that they were covered with glory simply because they had been witnesses of Anderson's brave struggle. At the *World* office, which was understandably proud of its reporter's great beat, Osbon was the lion of the hour. At the insistence of the editor and the crowd that swirled about the office Osbon was hoisted on to the counter and persuaded to tell everyone within the range of his voice the glorious story of Sumter. Years later he expressed the opinion that he had never seen "a wilder fever of excitement than throbbed and billowed among those listening men."[12]

There was one disagreeable feature about his homecoming. Before the expedition docked at New York, Captain Fox had requested a special favor from Osbon. Anticipating adverse criticism because of his part in planning the relief operation, Fox asked the *World* reporter to make no mention of his name in reporting the operation. Osbon sympathetically complied. Then when the public reaction proved otherwise than expected, Fox realized that he had made a mistake. In his chagrin, he charged that Osbon had acted on his own initiative in withholding mention of the Captain. To protect his standing as a journalist Osbon made clear the real reason for his reticence, and in the process angered the other man still more. As Assistant Secretary of the Navy under Gideon Welles, Fox had abundant opportunity before the war was over to even the score with this troublesome reporter.

2

The Press Girds for the Conflict

THE journalism of antebellum days was geared to the leisurely pace of an age in which the stagecoach, the horse car, and the sailing ship were still being used in varying degrees. By and large, the American people of that day were more accustomed to being regaled with somebody else's opinion of what had happened the week before than with the news of the previous twenty-four hours. During the eighteen-fifties the morning papers regularly went to press at about 10:00 P.M., and their copy was usually on hand well before that.

In spite of the fact that almost fifty thousand miles of telegraph line, belonging to a half dozen different companies, crisscrossed the area between the eastern border of Kansas and the Atlantic in 1860,[1] the telegraph was being used for newsgathering only to a very limited extent. Even in the East, newspaper managers regarded the telegraph rates as virtually prohibitive. Only in rare cases were more than fifteen hundred words a day received by wire in the newspaper offices of the West and South.[2] When Sumter fell many newspapers used the headline, "By Telegraph," as if that, in itself, were more impressive than the fact that the opening guns of a great civil war had just sounded.

During the Civil War, for the first time in American history, the transmission of war news by telegraph was undertaken on a large scale. Newspapers which had previously printed not more than two or three columns of telegraph news a day were now printing two or three pages of it and were frequently keeping open for telegraphic news until one o'clock in the morning or later. The telegraphing of reports was one of the largest items of newspaper expenditure. The *Herald,* for example, paid at the rate of two hundred fifty dollars a column for its telegraphic account of the Battle of Chickamauga, and the transmission of the story of the capture of New Orleans cost the same newspaper no less than a thousand dollars.[3]

At the time the telegraph was first introduced the larger newspapers were eager to use the wires to any extent, regardless of cost. However, the policy of "first come, first served" instituted by the telegraph companies soon resulted in a variety of abuses. To hold the wire until they were ready to send their dispatches, reporters would sometimes instruct the operator to tap out various chapters of the Bible, beginning with Genesis. On one occasion the weary operator was well on the way through Leviticus before the reporter's copy was in proper shape for transmission. In some cases reporters would not surrender the wire until they were reasonably sure of having an exclusive story. Reprisals were to be expected from rival reporters, who occasionally cut the wires when they were unable to get the line. Such practices led to the imposition by the telegraph companies of the "fifteen-minute system" whereby no reporter was allowed to hold the wire for more than fifteen minutes at a time.[4]

Even as late as 1861 the telegraph had many technical deficiencies. Although the copper wire used at first had generally been replaced by iron wire, which was less likely to break under adverse weather conditions, most of the telegraph lines were poorly insulated. The glass insulators then commonly used were mere bureau-drawer knobs that were hard to keep on the pins and were easily damaged. There was some experimentation with vulcanized rubber insulators during the late fifties, but their use was abandoned after it was discovered that the rubber was easily fouled by dust and moisture.[5] During storms the current frequently became so weak that messages would fail to come through. On October 7, 1861, the Chicago *Tribune* commented on the fact that for "three nights in succession" the telegraph had failed to supply the *Tribune* with its customary budget of news "on account of prevailing storms." Similar complaints appeared from time to time in other newspapers.[6]

Small-scale enterprise characterized the newspaper world of 1861. On July 1 of that year the New York *Courier and Enquirer,* which had played a notable part in American journalism in pre-Civil War days, was sold to the New York *World* for exactly one hundred thousand dollars. Even so, the selling price of the *Courier and Enquirer* was quadruple the figure obtained for the Chicago *Times* when it was sold to Wilbur F. Storey in June, 1861.[7] Few newspapers on the eve of the Civil War netted their owners more than twenty-five thousand dollars a year. At the time, newspaper offices were generally rented buildings.

The old New York *Herald* office at the corner of Fulton and Nassau streets consisted of a half dozen houses taken over one by one as the business of the paper grew. The floors were not on the same level, and the random structure was a veritable rattletrap.[8]

The newspapers of that day were printed on separate sheets, which were placed by hand, one at a time, between revolving cylinders and then fed in again some hours later to print the other side. They were then inserted in similar fashion into machines where each sheet was folded to make four pages, at that time the standard size of most dailies. The front page of the average newspaper, outside of the larger cities, was given over to advertising. Newspapers on the whole contained little display, no comics, no cartoons, no illustrations of any kind except occasional woodcuts. The headlines were limited to a column's width and frequently totaled only two or three column inches. Often they were the same from one day to the next. Judged by present-day standards, the format was decidedly monotonous.

Newspaper work was poorly paid,[9] and for some it seemed hardly less dull than the format. Some such impression is given by the following extract from a letter written by a member of the New York *Tribune* staff in the year of the Dred Scott decision:

> I still work from 8 to 3 on the average rising from 10 to 12 and breakfasting at noon. My work continues to be substantially as I sketched it—not very inspiriting always. Shall I say it—there is drudgery connected with my work, a good deal of drudgery, a very little real hearty work, which leaves one better than it finds him. Drudgery in reading newspapers and scissoring them for things of no earthly interest to myself but of supposed interest to others; drudgery in looking over the telegraph & saying what shall be in this type & what in that; drudgery in fixing up other people's bad English & no special apparent utility in either of these branches of labor; an occasional pleasure in turning a paragraph relative to the news, or "Ed. Head," as we call it, but oftenest drudgery therein also; and a climax of drudgery in hanging around the "forms," deciding what shall go in, out of several things.[10]

Nevertheless, by 1861 New York was generally conceded to be the hub of American newspaperdom. In earlier days Boston, Philadelphia, or Washington had at one time or another been in the lead. Boston, where the first regular newspaper, the *News-Letter,* had made its bow to the public as far back as 1704, had been the cradle of American journalism. Philadelphia had given birth to America's first daily newspaper during the decade which followed the American Revolution. For some forty years before the invention of the telegraph in 1844, the Washington press had enjoyed a virtual monopoly of the news from the national capital. By 1861, however, the situation was radically different. At that time, New York with seventeen daily newspapers dominated the newspaper field as she did most others.

A strangely assorted quartet of New York journalists were the leaders in their city's domination of the American newspaper scene. The members of this little group were the amiable, sometimes irascible, frequently eccentric editor of the New York *Tribune,* Horace Greeley; Greeley's "Little Villain," Henry J. Raymond, who had served his apprenticeship under the *Tribune* editor before he became the founder and first editor of the New York *Times;* the austere and dignified William Cullen Bryant, whose reputation as one of the nation's leading poets has obscured his long and distinguished career as editor of the New York *Evening Post;* and finally, James Gordon Bennett of the New York *Herald,* who was not simply the father of "yellow journalism," but in some respects the greatest newspaper man of them all.

Greeley's career contained many of the elements of the American success story. He had first come to New York in the fall of 1831, a lad of Irish ancestry, barely twenty years old, with all his personal belongings tied up in his pocket handkerchief. Having already acquired some experience as a small town printer, he worked at the printing trade in New York for a short time and gradually moved over into the field of campaign journalism. In 1841, after a successful experience in editing a campaign newspaper known as the *Log Cabin,* he launched the New York *Tribune* with a capital of about three thousand dollars, one-third of which was borrowed.[11] Within five years it had become the leading Whig daily in New York, and by the late fifties it had acquired a national influence exceeding that of any other American newspaper. Long before 1861, Greeley's name had become inseparably identified in the public mind with that of his newspaper. Many of the *Tribune*'s readers apparently believed that Greeley wrote everything in it. By signing many of its editorials, by addressing his readers in their own language, simply, familiarly, and earnestly, by his candor and integrity, Greeley was able to mold public opinion to an incomparable degree. To the farmers of Northern New York and the Western Reserve district of Northeastern

Ohio, who took their opinions on most political topics ready-made from the weekly *Tribune,* that publication was, in the phraseology of James Ford Rhodes, something of a "political bible."[12]

To his contemporaries Greeley the Man was almost, if not more, interesting than Greeley the Editor. His generosity, his shuffling gait and Pickwickian appearance, his illegible handwriting, his absent-mindedness were proverbial. When Alexander K. McClure, a Pennsylvania editor, met Greeley for the first time at the Whig national convention of 1848, he decided that Greeley's eccentricities had been exaggerated to some extent by the press, even though the *Tribune* editor "impressed all who met him with the fact that the one thing that did not give him much concern was the cut of his coat or the bagginess of his trousers."[13]

Although Greeley was one of the most kind-hearted and philanthropic of men, he was not incapable of bitter feeling. On one occasion during the year 1858 he had a furious exchange of letters with Joseph Medill, one of the proprietors of the Chicago *Tribune,* over the question of whether the advancement of Stephen A. Douglas or Abraham Lincoln would be of greater utility to the anti-slavery cause. At the time Greeley was of the opinion that Douglas would be more effective than Lincoln in bringing about the distintegration of the slave power. As a result of the controversy, Greeley stopped reading the Chicago *Tribune,* and it was a long time before he could bring himself once more to speak well of his colleague in Chicago.[14] By 1860, however, Greeley was coming around to Medill's point of view, and in the Republican national convention of that year he was a powerful factor in effecting the nomination of Lincoln.

One of Henry J. Raymond's outstanding qualities—rare among journalists of that day—was his ability to see both sides of a question and discuss current issues without misrepresentation or abusive epithets. In the first issue of the New York *Times,* Editor Raymond declared, "We do not mean to write as if we were in a passion, unless that shall really be the case; and we shall make it a point to get into a passion as rarely as possible."[15]

From his moderation arose what his biographer, Augustus Maverick, characterized as his "unfortunate tendency to temporize,"[16] a deficiency which was perceived by the reporter George Alfred Townsend when he first met the *Times* editor along the Chickahominy during McClellan's Peninsular Campaign:

> he was a very companionable man, a friendly and helping man, and a practical journalist of the first class; but he was deficient in imagination . . . [and] was governed by his nice tastes too much to make a great politician. He discovered too promptly the drawback to every movement. I compared him to McClellan the first day I saw him. He was always ditching and diking with his untiring pen, but he disliked the moment to come when science, taste and dressed ranks must go into the melee. . . . Raymond was a conservative man, with progressive leanings; but he always conserved too much in progression, and advanced too much for conservatism.[17]

Although in later life Greeley said of Raymond, "Abler and stronger men I may have met; a cleverer, readier, more generally efficient journalist, I never saw,"[18] he apparently made no serious effort to prevent Raymond from leaving the *Tribune* and going over to the *Courier and Enquirer* within two years after Raymond had joined the *Tribune* staff. Subsequently the two men became antagonists. When Greeley was forced to step aside in 1854 and see Raymond nominated for the lieutenant-governorship of New York in his place, he confessed that "No other name could have been . . . so bitterly humbling to me."[19] In later years the animosity between the two men softened, however, and an attitude of mutual respect germinated. Greeley's editorial comment at the time of Raymond's death was, in fact, unusually kindly for him and, in the process, contradicted practically everything that he had written about the *Times* editor over a period of twenty-five years.

Under Raymond's editorial guidance, the *Times* had a definite appeal for those who were equally repelled by the low moral tone of the *Herald* and *Sun* and by Greeley's socialistic ideas. Its excellent news service, which even then devoted special attention to foreign affairs, its stable editorial policy, and its general sobriety of manner attracted a growing number of newspaper readers in and around New York. By the opening of the Civil War it was generally recognized as one of the great newspapers of America.[20]

In 1860, Bryant had passed the zenith of an editorial career, which extended over a period of almost a half century. Few men of his times, as Allan Nevins once remarked, "did half as much to lift journalism from a vulgar calling to a place of high honor and national influence."[21] Although the circulation of the *Evening Post* was slender in comparison with that of the other leading New York dailies, it was edited with better literary taste and in a somewhat more refined tone than most of its competitors. In the early days of his editorial career Bryant had been a supporter of Jackson and a strong low-tariff man. In 1848, however, Bryant broke with the Democratic party over the slavery issue, and eight years later he threw his editorial support to the newly-organized Republican party. When Lincoln made his famous Cooper Union speech in the early part of 1860, it was William Cullen Bryant, widely acclaimed as the "first citizen of New York," who introduced him to his New York audience. Bryant had to share the spotlight with Greeley on this occasion, however. After Lincoln had finished speaking, there were loud calls for a speech from the *Tribune* editor, who came forward and assured the audience that the orator of the evening was "a specimen of what free labor and free expression of ideas could produce."[22]

One of the qualities which made Bryant a great editor was his capacity for hard work. During the fifties he wrote nearly all the *Post's* leading editorials, which, like most newspaper editorials of that day, were consistently longer than those of the present day. Although he could hardly excel Greeley in forceful expression, nevertheless, when writing under the influence of momentous events, his poetic gifts found expression in an eloquence almost unparalleled in the press of that period. Fittingly enough, Bryant reaped a rich reward for his editorial labors on the *Evening Post*. By 1861, the venerable sheet, founded under the auspices of Alexander Hamilton, was already well on the way to becoming a million-dollar property, and Bryant, whose partner, John Bigelow, had retired in 1860 with a fortune of more than $175,000 based on his newspaper earnings, was destined to become the nation's richest poet![23]

The fourth member of this galaxy of editors, the sardonic Bennett, was more directly responsible than any of the others for making news of paramount importance in the journalistic world. Bennett had emigrated to America from Scotland while he was still in his early twenties and had undergone a hard struggle to keep alive before he established himself as a successful journalist in New York during the early eighteen-thirties. Once, in Boston, so the story goes, he went hungry for two days and might have gone without food still longer had he not had the good luck to find a York shilling stuck between two cobblestones on the Common.[24] Before he came to America he had trained at Aberdeen for the priesthood. Once embarked in the field of penny journalism as the editor and publisher of the New York *Herald*, however, he scandalized the church-going element to such an extent that a boycott was organized against his newspaper.

Like Bennett, the *Herald* was by turns flippant, cynical, impudent, and vulgar. For the delectation of the prurient it exploited news of crime and police court trials; dished up reports of private scandals, often without giving the names of those involved; and devoted excessive attention to the seamy side of life in general. What must have seemed its crowning offense against good taste was the signed announcement of Bennett's approaching marriage, which appeared in the editorial columns of the *Herald* on June 1, 1840.

In spite of its low standards of journalistic ethics, the *Herald* was undeniably interesting, and it was primarily a *news*-paper, which was more than could be said of most of the political sheets of the Jacksonian era. To make room for the news on one occasion, the *Herald* editor sliced the editorial column to a single article of five lines.[25] Whereas the other editors of his day—including Bryant, Raymond, and even Greeley to some extent—wrote primarily for the benefit of a class economically and intellectually above the average, Bennett reached out for all classes of readers and, in the process, gave attention to many subjects which newspapers previously had neglected. According to Count Adam Gurowski, the Polish diarist, President Lincoln read no other newspaper than the *Herald*.[26] In Europe also, the *Herald* was more widely read and talked about than any other American newspaper.

Bennett's contemporaries described him as tall, gaunt, and ungainly, with coarse features which competed for attention with his defective eye. When Raymond and he passed each other on Nassau Street, as they often did, the meeting, so far as stature was concerned, was that of David and Goliath. In his published reminiscences, John Russell Young remarked:

> I first saw the elder Bennett one bleak snowy night toward the close of Lincoln's presidency. . . . Hair white and clustering, a smooth face soon to have the comfort of a beard, prominent aquiline nose, a long narrow head with abundant development in perceptive faculties, a keen boring eye which threw arrowy glances . . . a firm masterful jaw . . . .
>
> You felt in his company, the impression of a man of genius. . . . His mind teemed with ideas, which streamed into his talk—saucy phrases, invectives, nick-names, keen bits of narrative surcharged

> with cynical pessimism, which remained, one might fancy, as a legacy of early days of disappointment and trial.[27]

Apart from the contributions of its Washington correspondents, the metropolitan press during the fifties depended for news from the country at large on the brief telegrams of the New York Associated Press, supplemented by copyings from local papers and occasional letters from volunteer correspondents. By 1861 this would no longer suffice. Foreseeing or guessing at the momentous events which were destined to follow Lincoln's election, practically every one of the principal New York papers arranged to have correspondents at important points in the Southern states in order to keep their readers informed of developments. It is altogether possible that their reporting resulted in the North's having a much better idea of public opinion in the South by the time the war came than the South had of Northern public opinion.[28]

Newspapers with Southern leanings such as the *Herald,* which condoned secession up to the very eve of Sumter, made no attempt to conceal the identity of their reporters. So long as newspaper letters from the South spoke in flattering terms of the secessionist movement and its leaders, little interference with their authors was to be expected. As time went on, however, the Southern press began to raise a clamor about these "Lincoln spies" who were prowling around in their midst, picking up facts which might prove vital to the security of the Confederacy. In view of the excitement created by these newspaper attacks, Robert Barnwell Rhett of the Charleston *Mercury* advised one of the editors of the New York *Evening Post* not to send a representative of that newspaper to Charleston to cover the proceedings of the secession convention. Rhett intimated that any representative of the *Evening Post* who came there for such a purpose would "come with his life in his hand, and would probably be hung [sic]."[29] Yet the *Post* did receive unsigned correspondence from Charleston and other Southern cities during the gestation period of the Southern separatist movement.

The Charleston correspondent of the New York *World* was in such a jittery state because of this hostile attitude toward Yankee newspapermen that he wrote to one of the editors of that newspaper to request some sort of statement which he might use for his own protection. The editor to whom he addressed his request promptly wrote a letter to the Charleston *Courier* explaining that the *World* was not a "Lincoln sheet," that not one of its editorial corps had voted for Lincoln, and that far from being hostile to slavery the proprietor of the *World* was not averse to owning a few slaves himself. When the issue of the *Courier* which contained this interesting information arrived in New York it occasioned widespread comment. Moreover, the author of the letter was reprimanded by James R. Spalding, the editor-in-chief of the *World*, and the statements it contained were disavowed.[30]

Even before the election of 1860, some of the New York papers instituted the practice of concealing the identities of their Southern correspondents. One hot afternoon during the late summer of that year, Raymond called an experienced *Times* reporter, George Forrester Williams, into his editorial office and showed him several editorials clipped from Charleston, Savannah, and Atlanta newspapers which were violent in their tone and contained indications that the people of the South were even then making active preparations for war. Williams had previously reported for the *Times* in the campaign of 1857-1858 against the Mormons, and had narrowly escaped execution on a mission to Nicaragua in the company of the famous filibusterer, William Walker. In the opening minutes of that late summer interview in 1860, Editor Raymond confided to Reporter Williams:

> It is these hints of military preparation that have attracted my attention. We may dismiss the fierce political diatribes these articles contain, but the possibility that secret steps are on foot for military organization among the people of the South must be looked upon as a danger to the Republic. I have endeavored to learn the precise facts from our correspondents in the South, but so far they have failed to respond, one way or the other.

"What do you propose to do?" queried the reporter, knowing very well that the other man was leading up to something that he had not yet disclosed. Even so, Raymond's answer must have taken him somewhat by surprise, for it speedily developed that what the New York *Times* editor had in mind was for Williams to make a tour of the Southern states in the disguise of a young English tourist who knew very little about American politics and was presumably visiting the South for the first time. Williams was something of a mimic; moreover, he had a British background, and the idea appealed to him. It was arranged, therefore, that Raymond should procure for him in London a complete outfit, which was to be sent to Port au Prince (Haiti) in a leather portmanteau. At the proper time, Williams arrived at Port au Prince, picked up his outfit, and assumed the cover which had been assigned to him.

The first stop on his journey was Galveston, Texas. From there he went first to New Orleans and then to Memphis, Nashville, Atlanta, Mobile, Savannah, and Charleston, in turn, listening to secessionist harangues and making note of how campaign clubs were being utilized for purposes of recruiting and military training. Successfully aping the English vernacular, Williams plied his Southern acquaintances with questions which were designed to convey his lack of familiarity with American speech and American ways of doing things. Frequently he would ask why Lincoln was always called a "rail-splitter," and on one occasion he was taken out to a beautiful plantation near Macon, Georgia, where he was privileged to watch two Negroes cut down a tree and split it into fence rails for his edification.

It was in Charleston, the hotbed of secession, that he met with suspicion for the first time. By various parties there he was closely questioned; only by virtue of the fact that he was able to mention the names of many well-known men whom he had previously met on his journey was he able to fend off his questioners. He had a particularly close call one evening when he entered a barroom with some casual acquaintances with whom he had gone to the theatre. At one end of the counter was a tall cadaverous-looking man, who was half drunk and looking for trouble. After casting some suspicious glances at Williams, he remarked as he tossed down his five fingers of whiskey that he didn't believe the stranger was an Englishman; more likely he was a "damned Lincoln spy." Fortunately Williams had a few English sovereigns in his pocket, one of which he dropped on the counter in payment for a brandy smash. His tormentor reached over and seized the glittering coin. "That's British, anyhow," he conceded. "Have you any more of them?"

"Enough for another round of drinks," returned Williams boldly, tossing down another sovereign to pay for it. Seizing the first opportunity, he left the barroom and departed from Charleston the next day.

Each of Williams' letters to the New York *Times* went piecemeal to several of his own friends, who then forwarded the enclosures to the *Times* office. To foster concealment, dates were purposely mixed and fictitious names used whenever possible. The greatest difficulty lay in mailing these missives, which he usually did at night at the main post office in the town. Some of these letters appeared in due course in the *Times;* others were held back to be used as a basis for editorials.[31]

The operations of the New York *Tribune* correspondents in the South were fraught with especial danger. No newspaper, with the possible exception of the Knoxville *Whig*, was so thoroughly detested throughout the length and breadth of the South as was the *Tribune*, and the more extreme elements were especially eager to catch up with its representatives. Albert D. Richardson, Charles D. Brigham, Edward H. House, John Williamson Palmer, and Frank Lacey Buxton were some of the *Tribune* men who risked their lives in quest of news from the Southland during the closing months of the Buchanan administration. Brigham was the mysterious Charleston correspondent of the *Tribune* during the winter of 1860-1861.[32] After his departure from Charleston, the *Tribune* rotated his successors in pairs, always keeping one man in reserve to take over if his associate were arrested. Brigham was retained in the home office to retouch their letters sufficiently to make them appear to be the work of one man.[33] Meanwhile, the Charleston press, along with some of its Northern sisters, insisted that the *Tribune*'s Southern correspondence was purely synthetic, being concocted at the home office.[34]

Richardson was sent by the *Tribune* to New Orleans in February, 1861, with instructions to remain there or go elsewhere as he pleased but, if possible, to stay in the South "while the excitement lasts."[35] Before he went to New Orleans, Richardson took the precaution of having a friend who had just returned from there write one or two letters under a New Orleans date line. These were copied with some changes of style and published in the *Tribune* to make it appear that the newspaper's New Orleans correspondence antedated Richardson's arrival there by some two or three weeks. Richardson's letters, transmitted sometimes by mail, sometimes by express, were addressed alternately to a half dozen banking and commercial firms in New York, which in turn forwarded them to the *Tribune* office. Some of the letters from other *Tribune* correspondents in the South reached the newspaper through the medium of Inspector Thomas Thorne of the New York police force, a warm friend of Horace Greeley.[36]

To disguise their real character, Richardson's communications were written like ordinary business letters having to do with trade and financial matters and made large drafts on persons who were purely fictitious. They were also written from the point of view of an old citizen of New Orleans who never before in all his years of residence there had seen such evidences of strong feeling. In reporting day-to-day happenings, Richardson was often obliged to make use of fictitious names, places, and dates, while at the same time he attempted to give a generally accurate picture. Toward the close of his stay, inasmuch as there was no evidence that his correspondence had been tampered with, he gave minute and exact details with the expectation that he would be at a safe distance from New Orleans by the time his letters came back from the North in printed form.

Richardson depended upon an ingenious cipher as an additional safeguard. He had an understanding with the *Tribune* editors that all phrases between certain private marks were to be exactly reversed in printing. "A patriot and an honest man" between brackets became in translation "a demagogue and a scoundrel." Certain other marks indicated material to be omitted. If a paragraph commenced at the very edge of the page, it was to be printed exactly as it stood; if it began half way across the page, it contained material written in cipher.

When the storm finally broke in April, 1861, the Yankee newspaper men who were still in the South became objects of special hatred. George H. C. Salter, whose letters to the New York *Times,* signed "Jasper," had been so friendly toward the South that many Northern readers had asked for his dismissal, was arrested within a few hours after the bombardment of Fort Sumter had begun, relieved of his belongings, and thrust into a dungeon "reeking with bad rum and worse tobacco."[37] As he crouched beneath the window sill of his cell, he could hear the police outside exchanging conjectures about the probability of his being hanged at sunrise the next morning. Even more disturbing was the opinion, voiced by one of the gendarmes, that the South Carolina government intended to make a special example of the New York *Times* correspondent by shooting him from the mouth of a sixty-four-pounder cannon "a la Sepoy." Fortunately for him, the local authorities proved to be more lenient than his fears had led him to believe. The next morning, after being imprisoned for twenty-four hours, he was released from his cell, hustled to the railroad station, and advised to leave the city at once. Not until he reached Wilmington, North Carolina, where he was befriended by the editor of one of the local newspapers, did he regain some of his former self-confidence.

Even the *Herald*'s representatives were not spared. "I escaped with my life only by assuming a disguise," declared Charles H. Farrell, the *Herald* man at Pensacola, in a letter addressed to his newspaper. "Send me instructions how to proceed."[38] Samuel R. Glen, the *Herald* special at Charleston, was placed under arrest on three separate occasions, and efforts were made by mobs to hang a *Herald* correspondent in Richmond.[39] By good fortune all of the *Tribune* correspondents escaped personal harm.

At the Spottswood House in Richmond, the *Times* "English tourist" correspondent Williams was apprised by the careful scrutiny to which he was subjected by the desk clerk that his disguise was no longer proof against detection. He was already on the way to the railroad depot when a man whose face was turned away from him rapidly passed him. "Don't notice me, sir!" said the passer-by hurriedly over his shoulder. "I'm a Union man. You are suspected of being a Yankee newspaper correspondent. Get out of town as quick as you can." Quickening his pace, Williams reached the railroad platform in time to board an eastbound train which was ready to pull out. Since railroad tickets were in those days usually sold by the conductors on the trains, the *Times* reporter had a few minutes' grace in which to formulate his plans. By the time the conductor appeared, he had decided to buy a ticket to Culpeper, Virginia. When the train stopped there, he got off, ordered some fried chicken and coffee at one of the restaurants along the main street, and after his meal was finished strolled back to the station, where he was lucky enough to find a train for Washington just ready to leave. Subsequently he learned that his departure from Richmond had been observed and that the first train which he boarded had been carefully searched at Warrenton Junction. No attention was paid, however, to the train which he boarded at Culpeper, and so he managed to get to Washington without any further difficulty.[40] Another New York *Times* reporter who left Richmond under similar circumstances reached Washington after a perilous journey of eight days' duration, during the course of which he travelled by night as well as by day through the woods and by unfrequented roads and was hidden by friends for two or three days in one of the towns along the route.[41]

From the very beginning of the war, the New York newspapers endeavored to surpass each other in the quantity and quality of their war reports. For this purpose they built up extensive news organizations with representatives not simply at Washington and other cities near the war zone but also in the field and with the fleet. With relays of stenographers, telegraphers, and extra printers they also strove to be ready for all emergencies in the home office. On one occasion, the news of a battle reached the New York *Herald* office at tea time. Twenty engravers were immediately put to work on a map, which they completed in time to make the next morning's edition.[42] During the first two years of the war the principal New York papers spent on the average from sixty thousand to one hundred thousand dollars a year on army correspondence alone, whereas the outlay of the Boston, Philadelphia, and Western newspapers for the same purpose ran between ten thousand and thirty thousand dollars annually.[43] As the war progressed, rising labor costs and increases in the cost of printing materials forced newspaper proprietors to become more economical. Only one New York newspaper, the *Herald,* continued to spend money for war news in the same proportion during the last two years of the war.

To employ an army or navy correspondent cost the paper between one and five thousand dollars a year. Special messengers received smaller wages but were accorded travel allowances which frequently exceeded the salaries of the correspondents. Expenditures for horses and campaign outfits were by no means a negligible item: some correspondents used up as many as a half dozen campaign mounts a year. Furthermore, the transfer of correspondents from one army to another frequently made it necessary for the "special" who was being transferred to abandon his entire campaign outfit and order a completely new one for his new field of duty. Property thus left behind was rarely recovered.

In organizing the *Herald* corps of army and navy correspondents, Bennett was assisted by the outstanding managing editor of his day, Frederic Hudson, who chose nearly all of the war correspondents of the *Herald* and who was highly regarded by many of them.[44] Hudson had joined the *Herald* staff at the age of seventeen at a time when Bennett had but one other assistant. His marked efficiency in securing news, particularly that pertaining to shipping, won him Bennett's confidence, and eventually he became the managing editor of the *Herald,* a position that he held until his retirement in 1866. Although Hudson possessed no marked literary ability, this deficiency was in itself something of an asset in his work as managing editor since it tended to keep down any professional jealousy between him and the men he employed.

Not less than sixty-three correspondents of the New York *Herald* were in the field at one time or another during the war.[45] A representative of that paper accompanied each army division, and, in addition, a *Herald* tent and a *Herald* wagon went with each army corps. In a printed circular which was placed in the hands of each *Herald* reporter, he was given to understand that there was no particular merit in merely keeping up with his rivals. He might expect to be dismissed if he fell behind them, but advancement in rank and salary was dependent upon his coming in "ahead."

Estimates of the *Herald*'s expenditures on war news during the years from 1861 to 1865 ranged from five hundred thousand to three-quarters of a million dollars.[46] James Parton writes in a magazine article published in 1866:

> Never did any journal in any country maintain so vast an expenditure for news. . . . There were no rigid or grudging scrutiny of reporters' drafts; no minute and insulting inquiries respecting the last moments of a horse ridden to death in the service; no grumbling about the precise terms of a steamboat charter, or a special locomotive. A reporter returning from the army laden with information, procured at a lavish expense, was received in the office like a conqueror coming home from a victorious campaign, and he went forth again full of courage and zeal, knowing well that every man employed on the Herald was advancing himself when he served the paper well.[47]

The *Herald* maintained a Southern Department in which all information that came from the South was collected and filed. This department was particularly interested in getting copies of Southern newspapers, and overlooked no possibilities to get them. Runaway Negroes, deserters, prisoners of war were searched for newspapers; abandoned camps and villages were combed for them. From these papers the chief of the Southern Department compiled the very complete roster of the Confederate Army which was published in the *Herald* on September 9, 1863. When a copy of that issue reached Richmond, it caused a shake-up in the Confederate War Office and led to the arrest of several clerks who were accused of having furnished this information to the *Herald*.[48]

On one occasion, a gentleman who had been connected with the Confederate government in an official capacity appeared at the *Herald* office with an article which presented a picture of the operations of the Confederate Commissary Department, showing in particular how supplies for the Confederate Army were being obtained from the North. The article seemed appropriate, and therefore was purchased at the modest figure, set by the author, of eight dollars per column. Bennett was very much pleased with the article when it was brought to his attention and promptly called in the editor who had accepted it. After he had ascertained who its author was, he wanted to know:

"How much did you promise to pay him for it?"

"Eight dollars a column," was the answer.

"How much did it make?"

"Six columns."

After doing some simple mental arithmetic, the editor-in-chief remarked: "Forty-eight dollars—that ain't much. Give him a hundred. He may have something else as good." His foresight was borne out by subsequent events, for the author of the article on the Confederate Commissary soon afterward turned up with another interesting exposé of what was by that time the defunct Confederate government.[49]

Good correspondents were not always easy to find. In June, 1862, the chief correspondent of the *Herald* with the Western army wrote a letter to Bennett, in which he explained the arrangements he had made for obtaining news from Memphis during the temporary absence of the regular Memphis correspondent. After the explanation he added:

> I have been most troubled about some one to send to Halleck's army. I had a man engaged several days ago but he backed out on account of his wife having some absurd prejudice against his going to the army & getting killed. I am now on the track of another man & think I shall be able to nail him. Journalists that are worth an army ration daily are exceedingly scarce in the West at present.[50]

Later that same year, another *Herald* lieutenant explained to Bennett why he had sent a certain Mr. Francis back to New York:

> He is useless here. He seems to have exposed himself to all sorts of hardships but dont [sic] write anything. He is willing perhaps but dont know how to perform the duties of a correspondent. It is difficult to manage correspondents after they get into the field. They become so much absorbed with what they see they forget to relate it. I shall send messengers through the army from time to time to prompt them.[51]

One can imagine Bennett's wry smile as he read that last sentence.

Although the news organization which the New York *Herald* built up during the war was more extensive than that of any other newspaper, it was only a step or two ahead of the competing *Times* and *Tribune*, which often had as many as a score of reporters apiece at various points along the battle line.[52] At the time of the Austro-Sardinian War of 1859, Raymond had acted as war correspondent for his own newspaper. Likewise, during the early campaigns of the Civil War he was often at the front, supervising the activities of the other *Times* correspondents and contributing some letters of his own. His chief assistant in organizing the *Times* war correspondence at the beginning of the war was the managing editor, Alexander C. Wilson, who at one time had been the principal editor of the Philadelphia *Inquirer*. Also prominent on the editorial staff of the *Times* were James R. Spalding, who replaced Wilson as managing editor in 1862, and John Swinton, whose brother William was one of the *Times*'s leading war correspondents. During the last two years of the war, the *Times's* news reports from the field were probably earlier and more ample than those of any other newspaper except the *Herald*. In after years, John Swinton remarked:

> What a busy place the editorial office of *The Times* was! Politicians, office-holders, Colonels, and Government spokesmen came there. We were constantly receiving packages from correspondents at all points of the compass, special dispatches from the front, or from many a front, official documents or advices; covert news from army officers, visits from wire-pullers or pipe layers, information from the departments at Washington, and gratuitous suggestions from men of all sorts and conditions. . . .[53]

The war correspondents of the New York *Tribune* rarely came in close contact with Greeley, who was content to leave the control of the news columns in the able hands of his managing editor, Charles A. Dana. Dana had been connected with the *Tribune* in various capacities for nearly twenty years. Under the impact of war, however, divergences in temperament and point of view developed between the two men and resulted in Dana's resignation in late March, 1862.[54] After Dana left the *Tribune* his duties as managing editor were taken over by his first lieutenant, the kindly and mild-mannered Sydney Howard Gay, who on more than one occasion had shielded a blundering *Tribune* reporter from Dana's majestic wrath. That Gay had, nonetheless, a will of his own is indicated by the fact that he was given credit for maintaining a pro-Administration policy on the part of the *Tribune* during the remainder of the war in spite of the vacillations of his chief.[55]

Both the New York *World* and *Evening Post* also employed professional army correspondents, but not to the extent that the *Herald, Times,* and *Tribune* did. Manton Marble, who became both the editor-in-chief and the proprietor of the *World* in April, 1862, James Spalding, and

David G. Croly were chiefly responsible for the *World's* newsgathering enterprise. Marble had learned the newspaper business in Boston and had been on the staff of the New York *Evening Post* from 1858 to 1860. The news staff of the *Post* was managed throughout the war by Charles Nordhoff, a picturesque figure who had emigrated to the United States from Prussia while he was still only a small boy. Later he ran away to sea. During his eight years before the mast, Nordhoff accumulated some exciting experiences which furnished him with material for a series of adventure tales which he later published. Long after he had left the *Post* the old timers at the newspaper office continued to talk of his executive ability, courage, energy, and shrewdness.[56]

The other New York newspapers had little direct correspondence from the field, and what little they had came sporadically. In the field of war news, the Metropolitan press had to reckon, however, with competition from various other Atlantic Coast cities as well as from leading dailies of the Middle West. Philadelphia's location, a hundred miles nearer than New York to the battlefront in Virginia, was an important advantage in the race to be first with the news. During the Civil War, a Washington telegram cost a Philadelphia paper three cents a word whereas the New York newspapers had to pay five.[57] There was also a differential of several hours by rail, which was significant because the jamming of messages on the war-time telegraph lines north of Washington often caused important news to be sent northward from Washington by mail or express.

For these and other reasons, the outstanding rival of the New York press in the East during the first two years of the war was a Philadelphia newspaper, the *Inquirer,* which had been in the possession of the Harding family for more than thirty years. During most of that time the paper had been operated by Jesper Harding, a Philadelphia printer, who published Bibles on the side and established a reputation for an enterprising but conservative brand of journalism. New life was injected into the enterprise by his son, William W. Harding, who took over the management of the *Inquirer* shortly before the war began and made it the leading newspaper of Philadelphia during the Civil War period. In fulfillment of his pledge to procure news at any cost, young Harding employed a corps of army reporters which in 1862 he claimed to be the largest attached to any American newspaper with one single exception.[58] Through his brother George, an eminent patent lawyer, who had been associated with both Edwin M. Stanton and Lincoln in trying the famous McCormick reaper case during 1856, Harding also had a valuable tie-in with the War Department from 1862 on, which gave his paper an important advantage in getting war news. In Philadelphia, the *Inquirer* was commonly regarded as the organ of Jay Cooke and Salmon P. Chase, both of whom were in a position to keep Harding well posted with respect to the war-time activities of the Treasury Department.[59]

The two other Philadelphia newspapers which made a regular practice of employing war correspondents were the *Evening Bulletin* and the *Press*. The *Bulletin*, a rabid anti-slavery journal, was the political organ of Simon Cameron, Lincoln's first Secretary of War. John W. Forney, the owner of the *Press*, commonly known as "the Colonel" among his "office hands," was a picturesque character of German extraction, curly-haired, big-nosed, and warm-hearted. "He was a creature of the affections," wrote Henry Watterson, who had been one of the Washington correspondents of the *Press* just before the Civil War. "A more lovable, immethodical [sic], unbusinesslike human being never lived."[60] George Alfred Townsend, who also was employed by the *Press* about the same time that Watterson was, viewed Forney somewhat more critically. According to Townsend, he was:

> one of the most timid men that ever filled a dictatorial place like editor. It partly arose from his nursing office-seeking on one knee and a newspaper on the other, and his temperament, which was highly nervous, was excited by the character of his work, particularly by his dictations, for he seldom wrote anything himself, but talked it off to an amanuensis, and by his convivial habits, which were those of a Parliamentary gentleman of the date of Fox and Webster. He smoked very much, liked brandy and champagne, and was such good company that he seldom got any rest from it. . . .
>
> He was of a kind temperament, touched with a suspicion that arose from his excessive timidity and apprehension, and listening to tale-bearers. He was always annoyed by having any complaint made at the office or personally to him of what was contained in the paper. Hence any strong man on his staff had to live in fear of touching "the Colonel's" sensibilities.[61]

Partly because of Forney's absorption in politics and partly because he was not given to lavish expenditures for news, the *Press* did not make a great name for itself in the field of war-reporting. During the war, Forney spent most of his time in Washington performing his duties as

Secretary of the Senate; entertaining celebrities in his commodious quarters at the Mills House on Capitol Hill; giving some attention to supervising a newspaper property which he had founded there; and contributing letters to the *Press* under the pseudonym of "Occasional." In his absence the news columns of the *Press* came under the immediate direction of a scholarly Englishman named R. Shelton Mackenzie, onetime private secretary to Lord Brougham, and of John Russell Young, who made something of a reputation for himself as a war correspondent of the *Press.* If Forney had given as much attention to the newspaper business as he did to his own political advancement, he would probably have accumulated a large fortune. As it was, he died in 1881 a comparatively poor man.

Only one of Baltimore's daily newspapers, the *American,* followed the practice of employing special correspondents to report war news. Some of the best reporting for the *American* was done by its editor, Charles C. Fulton, who had been managing editor of the Baltimore *Sun* for twelve years before he bought into the *American* at the advice of the elder Whig statesman, Henry Clay. Throughout the war, Fulton also performed the duties of Baltimore agent for the Associated Press. Partly because of its extensive news coverage, partly because it was delivered in camp a day ahead of the New York and Philadelphia papers, the *American* had a large circulation in the army.[62]

Boston, like Baltimore, had only one newspaper that was widely known for its reporting of war news. This was Colonel Charles A. Rogers' Boston *Journal,* whose ace correspondent, Charles Carleton Coffin, then in his late thirties, was one of the outstanding war reporters on the Northern side. Three of the *Journal's* six Boston competitors — the *Herald, Post,* and *Traveller*—received occasional correspondence from their paid representatives at the front. Nevertheless, the Boston publishers fell considerably behind their Manhattan brethren in the coverage of war news.

At the beginning of the war, none of Washington's three daily newspapers, the *National Intelligencer,* the *National Republican,* or the *Star,* made any serious pretense of gathering news from outside the national capital. A New York *Times* reporter who was stationed in Washington in the early part of 1861 commented:

> . . . so poor are the newspapers in this city, that they are constrained to take much of their news second-hand from the Northern journals. They are unable to pay reporters and purchase tele-

graphic news, and are consequently generally a day behind the times.[63]

Before the war, public men in Washington had depended almost altogether on the Baltimore papers for general news. In June, 1861, the demand for New York and Philadelphia newspapers at the Capital became so brisk that "pony expresses" were organized by the newsboys to run them over at top speed from the depot to Willard's. During the second year of the war, Forney rejuvenated Washington journalism when he established another daily there, known as the *Chronicle.* By December of that year, a Washington correspondent of the St. Louis *Missouri Republican* had reached the conclusion that "Forney's *Chronicle* is certainly superior to any daily paper published here." The reporter added:

> I'm not speaking of it from a *political* point of view. I've nothing to do with that; but regarding it as a *news*paper, it is nearer the mark than any of its contemporaries.[64]

In May, 1863, a Washington correspondent described in lively fashion the system whereby the itching of Washingtonians for news was satisfied by the press:

> Every morning at 6 o'clock a hundred newsboys begin to peddle the Baltimore dailies—the *American, Sun,* and *Clipper. Intelligencer* and *Chronicle* make their appearance about 7 a.m. or an hour after the Baltimore papers arrive. . . .
>
> At eleven o'clock a.m., the Philadelphia train arrives, bringing the *Press* and *Inquirer,* both of which sell very largely, but the latter considerably the most. These furnish the populace and strangers "food for reflection" until three p.m., when the first edition of the *Republican* and *Star* make their appearance, followed every half hour by a later edition, until the New York train arrives at five p.m. bringing large supplies of the *Herald, Tribune,* and *Times,* and are howled about the streets, depots, landings, camps and hospitals till night; this closes the day's news.[65]

Beyond the Alleghenies, the fountain of news enterprise was Cincinnati, whose location at the northern end of the Louisville and Nashville Railroad made it the logical distributing point for news from the western armies. Cincinnati's leading newspaper during the war was the old *Gazette,* widely held to be the stable, steadfast, Whig organ of the Ohio Valley. Its leading proprietor in Civil War days was Richard Smith, otherwise known as "Deacon" Smith, the name "Deacon" having been applied to him by the *Tribune's* editor Dana. Smith was a smallish, staid, red-haired man of Ulster Irish stock who had never been a "deacon" or indeed a member of any church. He had originally followed the carpenter's trade but had entered the newspaper business because he became interested in market reports while working for the Cincinnati Chamber of Commerce.[66]

The principal competitor of the *Gazette* was the Cincinnati *Commercial,* an ably edited journal, whose moving spirit was Murat Halstead, one of the outstanding journalists of his day. Even before the Civil War, Halstead had become famous as a reporter of political conventions and had added to his reputation by attending and describing for the *Commercial* the hanging of John Brown near Harper's Ferry. During the war, he often left his desk in the old *Commercial* building at the corner of Fourth and Race Streets and went into the field, where he established his reputation as a brilliant war correspondent.[67] Few newspapers were as widely read in the western armies as was the *Commercial;* it was frequently called the "soldier's paper." The *Times* and the *Enquirer* were other Cincinnati papers active in the field of war-reporting.

Four Chicago newspapers, the *Tribune, Times, Journal,* and *Post,* made a regular practice of maintaining paid war correspondents at the front. Chicago's newspaper enterprise, like almost everything else there, was affected by its having the characteristics of a boom town. Middle-aged Chicagoans in 1861 could recall the days when the prairie grass, on the land along Michigan Avenue, had stood as high as a man's shoulders. In July of that year Albert D. Richardson, who stopped off in Chicago for a few days on his way East from reporting the campaign in Missouri, noted that pretentious buildings were springing up everywhere, that as many as sixty railroad trains were arriving and departing daily, and that the hotels were doing a land-office business.[68] Two years later, a traveling reporter for the Buffalo *Commercial Advertiser,* visiting Chicago, styled it "the great metropolis of the West—the Odessa of our Northern Mediterranean seas" and expatiated at some length upon its extensive suburbs, its many spires, the towers of its grain elevators, and its "bustling, struggling, eager, commercial life."[69]

The leading Republican newspaper of Chicago was the *Tribune,* which had played an important part in organizing the Lincoln-for-President boom and which claimed in November, 1861, that it spent more money for news telegrams and correspondence than "any newspaper out of New York."[70] Before the war ended it employed as many as twenty-nine special correspondents throughout the country.[71] During the first two and a half years of the war, the editor-in-chief of the *Tribune* was Charles H. Ray, whom his friend Mark Skinner described to Stanton as a "gentleman of intellectual culture, of fine social qualities, a died-in-the-wool opponent of slavery, and in all respects a gentleman worth knowing."[72] Ray's successor as editor of the *Tribune* was Joseph Medill, who had possessed a financial interest in the paper since 1854 and was one of the more outspoken advocates of a radical course of action on the part of the Administration.

The *Tribune*'s aspirations to be first with the news were effectively challenged by the Chicago *Times,* whose editor, Wilbur F. Storey, like Bennett, was one of the first American journalists to place special emphasis upon telegraphic news.[73] In November, 1863, the *Times* boasted:

> There is not an important point in the country where we do not now maintain one or more special correspondents. We employ the magnetic telegraph at a cost of more than a thousand dollars annually, special messengers at a heavy outlay, and the express and mails only as they can be made useful.[74]

Storey's predilection for news at the expense of everything else is indicated by an order which he is alleged to have sent to one of his war correspondents: "Telegraph fully all news you can get, and when there is no news send rumors."[75]

Editor Storey was apparently a man of great physical courage, possessing a powerful physique and a commanding appearance. During the course of his long newspaper career he was the victim of innumerable libel suits and personal assaults; yet he saw the inside of a jail but once and then only for a few hours. Storey, like Stephen A. Douglas, was a product of the Vermont hills and had seen service with a half dozen different newspapers before he entered the field of Chicago journalism in June, 1861. From Detroit, where he had been for some years editor and sole owner of the *Free Press,* he brought a large part of the staff of that newspaper to work with him on the *Times.*[76]

Storey was an ardent champion of states rights and pro-Southern in spite of his Yankee origin, not so much because of any love for the South as because of his hatred of the abolitionists and the anti-slavery movement. His opposition to the war, which became positively virulent after the issuance of the Emancipation Proclamation, gave rise to so many threats that loaded muskets and hand grenades were kept on hand in the editorial rooms in anticipation of a possible attack, and an ingenious contrivance was installed below by means of which the rooms on the lower floor could be instantly filled with scalding steam in case of an attack.[77] Storey himself rarely went about unarmed. In view of his contempt for public opinion, openly expressed, it is hardly surprising that he possessed few intimate friends or that he remained aloof, for the most part, from the members of his newspaper staff. Nevertheless, it seems he knew every member of his large working force—news, editorial, business, and mechanical.

The *Times* presented an example of a newspaper which seemed to thrive on unpopularity. During the summer of 1863 it was suppressed for two days by order of General Ambrose E. Burnside, commander of the Department of the Northwest, because of its "repeated expression of disloyal and incendiary sentiments." This temporary suppression had the effect of making the *Times,* for a little while, the most talked about newspaper in America, and its circulation mounted accordingly.[78] Another event which greatly increased Storey's notoriety was the attempt made by Lydia Thompson of the "British Blondes," one of the more notorious girl-shows of that period, to horsewhip the *Times* editor because of some disparaging comments which she attributed to him. During the mixup, Storey nearly strangled one of the two women who molested him and almost broke the neck of one of their male auxiliaries, but the story got out that he had been soundly horsewhipped by the irate blonde, and he was never quite able to live it down.[79]

The *Missouri Republican* and the *Missouri Democrat* were the only St. Louis newspapers which employed war correspondents with the Western armies. Strangely enough, the *Republican* was the leading Democratic newspaper in St. Louis, and the *Democrat* was the Republican city organ. To make matters more confusing, the *Republican* had two editors, Nathaniel Paschall and George Knapp, one of whom was a unionist and the other a secessionist. Knapp, because of his age, was accustomed to leave the office around four o'clock in the afternoon after writing a scorching pro-Southern editorial for the next morning's issue. In the evening Paschall would come in, take over as night editor, and compose an equally vigorous pro-Union editorial. The next morning the two editorials would appear side by side, expressing diametrically opposed views. Many of its readers regarded the equivocal editorial policy of the *Republican* as a sign of weakness, and from them the paper got the nickname the "swill-tub."[80]

Those newspapers which could not afford the luxury of having special correspondents found it expedient to receive news from the New York Associated Press. This was an association of seven morning newspapers in New York, founded in 1848, which collected news primarily for the benefit of its own members but sold news to other papers as well. During the war the Associated Press employed a larger staff of war correspondents than did any of its member newspapers, even the *Herald.*[81] The attachés of the AP were called agents, not reporters, and were stationed at almost every important point in the country. Even before the Civil War, the subscriber papers comprised several loosely defined geographical groups, to which news was distributed on a regional basis. These local associations were called by such names as the Philadelphia Associated Press, the New York State Associated Press, the Southern Associated Press, and the Western Associated Press.

During the war years some of the Western publishers became discontented with the "exorbitant demands" of the "Metropolitan News Monopoly" and the generally poor quality of service which it provided. Since the press outside of New York contributed to the New York AP from ten to twelve thousand dollars a week, exclusive of additional charges for special reports, the Western publishers would seem to have had some grounds for their complaints.[82] Finally, in November, 1862, these complaints came to fruition in a meeting of the Western publishers at Indianapolis, which resulted eventually in the incorporation of the Western Associated Press and in arrangements for larger and better prepared news reports from New York.[83]

At this time the policy of the New York Associated Press was set by an executive committee of which Hudson and Raymond were the most active members. Another important member of its strategy board was its general agent, Daniel H. Craig. Craig had operated a private news agency between Halifax and Boston, making use of carrier pigeons, before he acquired his connection with the Associated Press. In many a hard-fought tussle with the telegraph companies and dissident elements of the press this hard-bitten, New Hampshire-bred Yankee rarely came out second best. He was "keen, sharp, persistent, untiring, imperturbable," noted a prominent telegraph executive. Frequently, his methods were high-handed and even dictatorial. In late 1861, Gerard Hallock, the publisher of the New York *Journal of Commerce,* was forced to step down from the presidency of the Associated Press because of difficulties caused by his opposition to the war, but Craig remained at his post until the war's end, beating down competition from a rival news service organized by Henry Villard, and keeping his army correspondents on the move from one war theater to another.[84]

One of the most interesting developments in war journalism was the part played by the weekly pictorials, notably *Harper's Weekly* and *Frank Leslie's Illustrated Newspaper*. A few months before the end of the war, *Frank Leslie's* boasted that during the last four years at least one of its "trained corps of the first artists" had accompanied every important expedition "either by sea or land" and that it had published nearly three thousand pictures of "battles, sieges, bombardments, stormings and other scenes, incidental to war," contributed by more than eighty artists.[85] Since the daily newspapers contained only verbal descriptions of war scenes, these other publications provided a special service in the field of war reporting.

At the beginning of the war the press, along with other forms of business, was affected by the hard times, which culminated in the suspension of specie payments near the end of 1861. Many newspapers reduced their sheet size; there were frequent mergers; some were forced out of business. "Not a day passes that does not announce the suspension of newspapers hitherto supposed to be on a good foundation," stated the St. Louis *Republican* during the last week of June, 1861.[86] Similar plaints came from the East. Horace Greeley said in a letter to a friend written about this time:

> We are all as poor as Job's turkey. Advertisements are scarce as saints, and don't threaten to become plentier. Half the newspapers are broken, *not* including the Tribune; but we shall be glad to just live till the War is over.[87]

In October the *Tribune* expressed doubt that a single daily newspaper in New York had paid its current expenses during the last four months or that as many as a dozen newspapers in the entire country had done so.[88]

By 1862, however, the war boom was well under way, and rising production costs were offset by increased profits.[89] Most of the leading dailies advanced their prices about one cent every twelve months until by the end of the war they were selling at four and five cents a copy.[90] Newspaper circulation also mounted as a result of the public's hunger for war news. Indeed it was not unusual for a large-city newspaper to sell five times its normal quota when the details of a great battle were coming over the wires. The market for newspapers in the army was by no means unimportant. As many as twenty-five thousand copies of a single issue of the Philadelphia *Inquirer* were frequently sold in the camps, and the story was told that during a lull in the fighting at Antietam, rowdy little newsboys scampered along the lines shouting extras of the New York papers.[91]

Increased circulation necessitated improved methods of printing. To meet the demand for papers, publishers bought additional presses containing a larger number of cylinders, and in August, 1861, the New York *Tribune* introduced the process of stereotyping, which had been in use in the field of book printing for many years and which made it possible for the first time to produce from the type form a solid plate the size of an entire page, curved to fit the cylinder.[92] By means of this process printing could be speeded up without adding cylinders to the press. Pages could be duplicated an indefinite number of times, and several presses could be used at the same time to print the same edition of the newspaper. Both the New York *Times* and the *Herald* soon adopted the new process. Another new development in newspaper printing was the web perfecting press which permitted both sides of the paper to be printed from one feeding. The first press of this type was put into use by the Philadelphia *Inquirer* in 1863.[93]

Improvements in typographical equipment and the abnormal appetite of the public for war news brought about changes in newspaper makeup and led to widespread use of Sunday and afternoon editions. Raymond is usually credited with the invention of the display headline in 1856, but such headlines were not in general use before the war. Even during the war they were confined to the limits of a single column with anywhere from six to twelve "decks" according to the importance of the news. During the summer of 1862 the New York *Sun* transferred its modest war headlines from the second to the front page to conform to what was becoming a general practice. Throughout the war, however, the New York *Evening Post* usually carried its headlines on page three, where its telegraphic news appeared. In the construction of its headlines and its makeup, Storey's Chicago *Times* excelled most of the newspapers of that day.

Before the war there was a fairly large number of Sunday papers not associated with a daily edition, and by 1860 there were Sunday editions of regular daily papers in at least four cities. Up to that time, however, Sunday papers had been largely incidental to regular newspaper production. During the war popular prejudice against Sunday newspapers diminished considerably as a result of the public desire for a continuous picture of war events, even though the more orthodox complained of the frequency with which battles were fought on Sunday. Some newspapers, apparently unwilling to risk offending that portion of their readers who were strict Sabbatarians, carried a Sunday date line on the first page and a Monday date line on the third as a sort of compromise.[94]

The demand for an uninterrupted flow of news also brought separate morning and evening editions of the same paper, which inspired a waggish comment to the effect that "They issue those evening editions to contradict the lies that they tell in the morning."[95] In Boston, the *Herald* and the *Journal* instituted the practice of issuing afternoon "extras," which ultimately became regular editions but continued to be called extras. In December, 1861, the Chicago *Tribune* decided to put out three editions, morning, afternoon, and evening. In the process, increased space was given to news from the various battlefronts; in some of the larger New York papers, this frequently filled one-third of an issue.

It is much clearer now than it was even in 1865 that the war had brought about sweeping changes in journalistic practice, changes which may accurately be described as revolutionary. Writing in 1881, the librarian of Harvard, Justin Winsor noted the "prodigious extent" to which "the stimulus of the Civil War" had enlarged the scope of the great newspapers.[96] On its fiftieth anniversary the *Times* concluded:

> it was during the civil war that the New York newspapers gained their first realizing sense of two fundamental principles that have made them what they are to-day—first, the surpassing value of individual, competitive, triumphant enterprise in getting early and exclusive news, and second, the possibility of building up large circulations by striving unceasingly to meet a popular demand for prompt and adequate reports of the day-to-day doings of mankind the world over.[97]

Other writers have reached substantially the same conclusion, among them the author of an article published in the *Journalism Quarterly* some years ago, who listed no less than six major effects of the Civil War on American journalism.[98] Such were the forces set in motion by a new kind of journalism, taking its shape from the abnormal conditions created by the war. Under the leadership of such men as Bennett, Harding, and Storey, journalism came to realize, as it had never before, that the primary requisite of a newspaper is news.

3

"Gentlemen of the Ravenous Pen"

FROM the beginning of the war until its very end the national capital was the focal point of press interest, not simply because it was the seat of the national government but also because Washington got the first reports from the eastern war theater and transmitted them by telegraph to all parts of the country. As one of the *Herald* men phrased it, Washington was "the center of gravity around which the Eastern correspondents revolved."[1] In recognition of the importance of the national capital as a center of war news, the press sent its ablest men there to make the rounds of the government offices, to forward dispatches from the men in the field to the home office, and, in cases of special emergency, to go into the field themselves for more complete news coverage. Before the war was over no less than eighteen separate telegraph wires running north out of Washington connected these Washington reporters with their newspaper offices.[2]

In his day-by-day account of his American experiences, published while the war was still going on, William H. Russell of the London *Times* told of meeting at Willard's Hotel an inquisitive-looking gentleman who identified himself as a correspondent for one of the New York dailies. After the two men had become better acquainted, the Gothamite reporter volunteered the information that he had been the first journalist to be employed as a Washington correspondent for any of the New York papers. To Russell, he confided:

> At first, I merely wrote news, and no one cared much; then I spiced it up, squibbed a bit, and let off stories of my own. Congressmen contradicted me,—issued cards, —said they were not facts. The public attention was attracted, and I was told to go on and so the Washington correspondence became a feature in all the New York papers by degrees.[3]

Russell did not mention the name of his acquaintance, who may have been drawing heavily upon his imagination for the substance of this interesting disclosure. The first Washington correspondents in the first decade of the century were editor-reporters who introduced the practice of journeying to Washington during sessions of Congress to gather material upon which to base editorial or semieditorial comment. Their letters, strongly polemic in tone, generally contained less news than opinion. In the absence of such communications, out-of-town newspapers interested in Washington news had to rely upon occasional letters from their local congressmen or copyings from the *National Intelligencer* and other Washington papers.[4]

About 1825, Washington correspondence as a specialized journalistic function made its initial appearance. Probably the first all-year-round professional correspondent in Washington was a graduate of Brown University named Elias Kingman, whose first letter for publication left the Capital sometime in 1822.[5] Another pioneer journalist in this field was James Gordon Bennett, who represented the New York *Courier and Enquirer* in Washington during part of John Quincy Adams' administration. Bennett attracted considerable attention mainly because of the gossipy style in which he wrote concerning the leading Washington personalities of his day. "On he goes creaking and croaking like an ungreased cartwheel," was the way Bennett characterized a leader of the Adams faction in the Senate. Of Adams himself, Bennett said, his very name "would freeze a pair of the most juicy Potomac ducks."[6] In the *Herald* editor's not entirely unbiased opinion, these piquant letters "changed the whole tone, temper, and style of Washington correspondence."[7] In spite of this promising beginning, even the more enterprising New York papers of the Jacksonian era rarely contained more than a half column of Washington news, including congressional proceedings. For one six-week stretch in 1846 Lawrence A. Gobright was the only newspaper correspondent in Washington, all the others having left town, following the example of Congress. Even as late as 1860, few American newspapers outside of New York made a practice of maintaining regular correspondents at the national capital.[8]

The Washington of pre-Civil War days was a droopy Southern city of less than sixty thousand people, housed for the most part in paltry structures of wood or brick. Squalid Negro quarters lay close to fine old mansions. And reaching above them all was the unfinished dome of the Capitol. The phrase, "city of magnificent distances," which John Randolph had once applied to Washington, was now commonly used as a term of derision, for there was little about Washington other than its extended layout that accurately could be described as "magnificent." Hardly one of its half dozen public buildings was in a finished state. Pennsylvania Avenue, the main thoroughfare, was badly rutted and much in need of repair; none of the other streets was paved; in every direction were empty lots, swamps, creeks, and cypress groves. During the spring and autumn the entire West end of the city was one vast slough of impassable mud. In 1860, Washington was still without an adequate system of sewage disposal: all the kitchen drains were above ground, and all the drinking water used in the city came from wells or small springs nearby. At almost every other street corner stood one of the Capital's peculiar landmarks, a huge wooden pump with a long, ponderous iron handle. From morning until night throughout the city could be heard the incessant creaking of pump handles.

In the days before the war, the best Washington society was made up of retired hotel-keepers, army and navy officers, bookbinders, a few money-lenders, some scientific people and inventors, and many widows who clung to the fringes of the army, navy, or civilian official set. Outside of the government service there were few acceptable business opportunities for a young man of quality. As a result, scions of the best families not infrequently resorted to gambling, and it was by no means uncommon to see father and son engaged in the same faro or "short card" business. It was the custom of these gambling proprietors, many descended from famous old Virginia families, to give a large free dinner just after the adjournment of Congress. After the dinner, judges, Indian agents, land surveyors, visiting statesmen, and others would gather around the gaming tables and play until a late hour.

With the onset of hostilities this overgrown village awoke. Throngs of strangers—soldiers and civilians—from all parts of the North converged upon Washington; long lines of army wagons and artillery rumbled through the streets; countless new regiments of stalwart men, confident of easy victory, marched up Pennsylvania Avenue while the bands blared out the jingling notes of "The Girl I Left Behind Me." Along the heights beyond the Potomac white encampments stretched for miles. A Chicago *Tribune* correspondent, who rode a Fourteenth Street bus out to the camp of the Seventh New York Regiment one bright May afternoon in 1861, marveled that in one of the tents he visited there was "almost everything a New York bachelor clerk would have in his counting house bedroom."[9] To lighten the labors of the

Washington police and to quiet the fears of the Capital's fairer sex, many of whom already had decamped in haste, the military authorities detailed a mounted guard of some one hundred twenty soldiers to act as a night patrol. Despite such precautions, brawling between members of rival regiments was common. On one occasion a Washington correspondent of the New York *Times* sustained minor injuries when he was struck in the back by a stray bullet from the gun of an awkward recruit.[10]

During the second year of the war, as one great battle followed another, trains of wounded, seemingly endless, rolled across the Long Bridge out of Virginia, and Washington became one vast hospital, filled with the maimed and bleeding. Among those who ministered daily to the needs of the wounded was the poet Walt Whitman, a lion in muscle and vitality, who trudged from one hospital ward to another with gifts for the soldiers of oranges, ice cream, and horehound candy. On occasions he wrote letters home for those who were too sick to move; now and then he assisted with dressings and operations. Lacking any regular employment until almost the very end of the war, Whitman supported himself in the meantime by contributing occasional letters to the New York *Times,* the Brooklyn *Eagle,* or any other newspaper that would publish them.[11] During those tragic war days Washingtonians became accustomed to seeing men with arms in slings and men with legs bandaged, or missing, hobbling on crutches along Pennsylvania Avenue or resting on the iron settees in the cool shade of the Capitol grounds.

Wartime Washington provided the reporter or the artist of the illustrated weeklies with other themes, however, than those of heroism and self-sacrifice. A great inflow of consumer goods was necessary to meet the needs of the suddenly increased population brought in by the concentration of a quarter of a million men in and around Washington. As early as October, 1861, when the rest of the country was still in the grip of hard times, the activities of the Washington merchants prompted the editor of the Philadelphia *Inquirer* to remark:

> There is a mimic revolution going on there in trading circles that reminds visitors of the magic changes in San Francisco in the infancy of the Pacific metropolis. Stores are being rented at fabulous prices, and millions of dollars are being invested in stocks of such goods as are of daily consumption and demand by soldiers . . . at prices yielding enormous profits to the dealers and sutlers.[12]

In the course of time some of the shoddy aristocracy amassed considerable fortunes, which made it possible for them to build new homes in the fashionable quarter of the town and to cross the threshold, for the first time, of Washington "society."

As the war progressed, Washington became more and more a kind of Mecca for those who were intent on getting rich quick, as well as for some others who seemed interested mainly in ridding themselves of their new-found riches as fast as they could. Office-seekers and lobbyists, "round, rosy, and rascally," supply contractors, gamblers, stock-jobbers, sharpers, and female camp followers galore frequented the hotel lobbies and bars in search of lucrative contacts. As a Chicago *Times* reporter, writing from Washington in October, 1862, saw it:

> Washington is just now lively beyond all precedent. Three theaters, two circuses, and two hybrid places of amusement known respectively as Canterbury and Olympic Hall, beside a dozen smaller places of enjoyment, are in full blast, and are nightly jammed to repletion. Hacks by the hundreds, filled with pleasure-seeking parties, are incessantly dashing hither and thither; gaily dressed esquestrians canter about the avenues, and dense crowds of happy, richly-dressed pedestrians throng the sidewalks at all hours. . . . the gigantic war affects people as little as if it were being waged between the Hotentots [sic] and Senegambians.[13]

In spite of half-hearted efforts to limit the sale of liquor, it could be bought anywhere, and drunkenness was common among all classes of the community. Every night the provost guard enacted the farce of stopping at each public bar, which at once was closed and then reopened as soon as the guard was out of sight. The principal hotels, Willard's, Brown's, the Kirkwood, and the old National, were doing a land-office business, and the new arrivals in Washington complained of the housing shortage. During the autumn of 1863 a newspaper man from Chicago noted that not a vacant house was to be found anywhere in the city or in Georgetown and that hundreds of people rented houses in Baltimore, from which they were commuting to Washington every day.[14] At Willard's, where the owners and servants alike took advantage of their wartime prosperity to be "as disobliging as possible," the dining hour was a picturesque occasion when young sprigs with fresh epaulets and their feminine companions gathered at the table d'hote to partake of the establishment's sumptuous dishes "while corks popped like so many Chinese crackers, and champagne bubbled up like blood."[15]

Strange new developments were another part of wartime life in the Capital. At the time Sumter was fired on, not a horsecar ran in the city. The only public conveyances available to the commuting population at that time were a few "straggling omnibuses and helter-skelter hacks."[16] Within the next two years this was changed. A railway line to connect Washington with Alexandria was completed during the first year of the war, and by the end of 1862 Washingtonians enjoyed the privilege of riding on not one but several street horsecar lines at five cents a head, while the bus drivers and cabmen cursed the day that this new-fangled contrivance invaded their domain. To some extent their feeling was shared by the fine old aristocrats of the city, who bewailed the fact that the "c'yar box," as they called this new form of transportation, would not come to a halt at the wave of a parasol or the beckoning of a hand, as the omnibuses had long been accustomed to do.

In December, 1861, the Smithsonian Institution permitted its lecture hall to be used for the first series of popular lectures ever held in Washington. One of the celebrities in the Smithsonian's lecture series was the *Tribune* editor, Horace Greeley, who spoke on the broad subject of "The Nation." On the platform that night were President Lincoln and three members of his Cabinet: Bates, Chase, and Welles. Greeley looked at Lincoln when he remarked with telling emphasis that the destruction of slavery was the primary objective of the war. Although many in the audience broke into applause at this point, Lincoln obviously was uncomfortable.[17]

According to General Henry van Ness Boynton, a prominent Washington correspondent in the period after 1865, there were in Washington at various times during the war years approximately fifty newspaper correspondents, who in combination represented all the principal daily newspapers of the North.[18] During the first year of the war the Washington staff of the *Herald* consisted of four or five men working under the immediate supervision of an undistinguished gentleman named Simon P. Hanscom. The New York *Tribune* maintained a somewhat smaller staff in Washington under the direction at first of Fitz-Henry Warren and later of Samuel Wilkeson. Wilkeson had been on the editorial staff of the *Tribune* before he had come to Washington in August, 1861, to replace Warren. James Simonton, Abram S. Mitchell, and James Barrett Swain were the principal New York *Times* reporters in Washington in 1861; George W. Adams and Edmund C. Stedman represented the *World*. One Washington reporter sufficed for each of the afternoon papers of New York: the *Post, Advertiser,* and *Express.* [19] None of the Western newspapers attempted to maintain a large Washington staff at any time during the war. The Chicago *Tribune,* which employed two reporters at Washington in February, 1862, one of them exclusively, the other "to the extent of supplying what news we require at his hands,"[20] probably was fairly representative of the Western press in its Washington news coverage.

In November, 1863, the Washington *Daily National Republican* published what purported to be a correct list of the Washington correspondents of the New York, Philadelphia, Boston, and Western press. It included the names of eighteen different men. Apart from whatever interest such a list might have for the general reader, its publication, the *Republican* explained, was for the purpose of breaking up the practice, carried on by sundry individuals, of representing themselves as newspaper correspondents to obtain free railroad passes and other special favors.[21] In all probability the total number of correspondents in Washington at any one time during the war was not greatly at variance with the *Republican*'s listing for 1863.

During Civil War days it was the common practice of distinguished editors to spend part of their time each year in Washington primarily in the capacity of interested observers of the government in action. Some of these editors at one time had been Washington correspondents and therefore found satisfaction in returning to their old places in the press galleries. Most of them made use of the opportunity to contribute to their papers letters, some of which were even more illuminating than those of the regular correspondents.[22]

Many of the leading Washington correspondents of the Civil War era were comparatively young men whose newspaper careers were just beginning. Adams of the *World* had barely come of age in 1861; Uriah H. Painter of the Philadelphia *Inquirer* and Whitelaw Reid of the Cincinnati *Gazette* were each twenty-four years old when Lincoln issued his first call for volunteers; Horace White of the Chicago *Tribune* was not more than twenty-seven. Adams S. Hill of the New York *Tribune,* a Harvard graduate, was only one year older than White. In his *Memoirs,* published nearly a half century after the war, Henry Villard referred to Hill as a "sharpwitted and indefatigable collector of news" who had previously been connected with the *Tribune* in an editorial job.[23]

The dean in terms of service of the Washington press corps was the

Washington agent of the Associated Press, "Larry" Gobright, who had been a fixture in the newspaper life of the Capital since the days of William Henry Harrison and John Tyler. He was described as "a medium sized gentleman with iron-gray hair and side whiskers, bushy eye-brows and a sharp piercing glance." According to Henry Villard, who was employed as a telegraphic correspondent by the *Herald* during the early part of 1861, the fact that the aging AP man was no longer as vigorous as he had been was well known to his employers. Yet they permitted him to remain at his post throughout the war because of his long years of service in Washington, his reliability, and his wide acquaintanceship among the leading public men at the Capital. Gobright was particularly close to Secretary Seward, who had been his firm friend and patron for twenty years or more.[24]

Another old timer among the Washington press delegation was Ben Perley Poore of the Boston *Journal,* a rugged Yankee of Scottish origin who was easily identified by his large head, his abundant growth of hair, and his scraggly, gray beard. Over more than three decades, during which he contributed to various newspapers under the pseudonym of "Perley," he had acquired the reputation of being one of the most popular of the Washington journalists, partly because of his effervescent spirit and because of his ability as a raconteur. Once, during the presidential campaign of 1856, he agreed to a wager calling for him to wheel a barrel of apples from his native Newburyport to Boston in case one of the candidates, Millard Fillmore, failed to carry Massachusetts. After the election, which went against Fillmore, he made good his promise, covering the route in two days while cheering crowds lined the way.[25] Although from the time he was seven years old Poore had spent most of his life in Washington, during the eighteen-forties he had lived abroad, performing the duties of an attaché at the American Legation in Belgium, collecting historical documents for the Massachusetts legislature, and traveling extensively through Europe and the Near East as the foreign correspondent of the Boston *Atlas.* During the fifties he was the Washington correspondent of a succession of Boston papers. At the beginning of the Civil War the future first president of the Gridiron Club left his newspaper work to serve as a major in the Sixth Massachusetts Regiment under General Benjamin F. Butler. He was not physically suited, however, for the hardships of a soldier's life, and after a three-month tour of duty with the army in Maryland, he came back to report Washington news for the *Journal* throughout the war.[26]

One of the more interesting representatives of the New York press in Washington was Sam Wilkeson of the *Tribune,* a vigorous character of lusty humor with unusual powers of story-telling and description. Something of the quality of Wilkeson emerges from a story about one of his many visits to the army. Francis C. Long, an army reporter for the *Tribune,* related that on this particular occasion Wilkeson wished to go to a signal corps observatory, which provided an advantageous view of the Confederate lines. Unfortunately, Wilkeson did not have a pass, but Long was to identify him as a member of the Christian Commission, identification which probably would obtain clearance for him. Before starting out, Wilkeson had fortified himself with a liberal dose of spirits, and as a result his conversation, which was always bright and sparkling, fairly scintillated with wit and intellectual fire. As the two men reached the foot of Pony Mountain, upon which the observatory stood, they were halted by a corporal, who was standing guard by an old, dilapidated gate. "Remember about the Christian Commission," whispered Long to his *Tribune* colleague as he handed his individual pass to the corporal. Upon hearing the other man's explanation concerning Wilkeson's supposed occupation, the corporal called out the sergeant, who in turn summoned the lieutenant from the guard house. By this time the horse of the "Christian Commission man" was becoming excited and displaying obvious signs of uneasiness. But Wilkeson had not forgotten his supposed calling, and much to the astonishment of the lieutenant he began in a stentorian voice: "My son, hearken unto the voice of wisdom; My son, beware of the wine cup; My son, be virtuous (hic) if you would be happy." At this juncture the horse suddenly shied away from the lieutenant, and nearly threw his rider. Forgetting his clerical mission, the lieutenant and everything else, Wilkeson struck the horse over the head with the flat of his hand and roared in an unparsonlike voice: "Whoa-a-a-a! You damned infernal brute!" That settled the matter. Christian Commission or no Christian Commission, Wilkeson was not permitted to climb to the signal station on Pony Mountain.[27]

His family connections and the active part he had taken as a young man in upstate New York politics stood Wilkeson in good stead in the Washington newspaper field. His father had been one of the first settlers of Buffalo, and in recognition of his efforts to bring the Erie Canal to Buffalo, the elder Wilkeson frequently was referred to as the city's founder. Young Sam had spent his boyhood days in the family homestead on Niagara Square, had attended Union College in Schenectady, and had studied law in the office of his future father-in-law, Judge Daniel Cady, one of whose daughters, Elizabeth Cady Stanton, was a leading light in the Woman's Rights movement.

After Wilkeson had practiced law for a few years, however, he decided to take up journalism. It might almost be said that Sam Wilkeson was born a journalist. His school mates still remembered in later life the weekly paper, written with a pen, which he had published every Saturday when he attended Amos Smith's grammar school in New Haven, Connecticut.[28] His first journalistic connection was with the Buffalo *Democracy*, a short-lived publication that was merged with the *Express* in 1855. After the *Democracy* folded up, Wilkeson moved to Albany to become editor and part owner of Thurlow Weed's Albany *Evening Journal.* Some three years later, Wilkeson, having aligned himself with anti-Weed influences, was forced out of the *Journal* by the newspaper's former owner. At the time Wilkeson was suffering from bad health and from the effects of the competition to which the *Journal* was being subjected at the hands of the great metropolitan dailies. Nevertheless, he was keenly resentful of the way in which Weed had "tyrannized over him," and as soon as he recovered his health he was only too happy to accept a position on the staff of a newspaper whose principal editor was the unremitting foe of Thurlow Weed.

Throughout most of the war the former editor of Weed's paper represented the *Tribune* in Washington, although toward the end he was giving an increasing amount of his time to writing persuasive pamphlets which promoted Jay Cooke's bond drives. Through Cooke, Wilkeson became interested in the Northern Pacific Railroad, of which years later he became one of the principal officials.[29]

One of Wilkeson's most interesting sideline activities during the first years of the war was that of preparing federal propaganda for foreign consumption. From October, 1861, to January, 1862, he acted as European telegraphic agent, sending out weekly dispatches to Liverpool for circulation on the Continent and, in some cases, shading reports of events previously mailed or giving them a new interpretation. Occasionally Seward or some other cabinet officer would drop in while he was at work and make suggestions to him as he wrote. When Stanton replaced Cameron as Secretary of War, Wilkeson was dropped abruptly from his job as official reporter.[30] In the files of the War Department is a letter addressed to Stanton by Wilkeson, justifying his employment and enclosing two of his dispatches as specimens of his work.[31]

Among the *Herald* staff were the capable L. A. Whitely, a product of Baltimore journalism, and the tall, spare, distinguished-looking "Chevalier" Henry Wikoff, a social adventurer and a cosmopolite, who first met Bennett on shipboard during one of Bennett's many trips to Europe. None of the Washington correspondents of that day had more bizarre elements in his past than did Wikoff, a wayward son of a wealthy Philadelphia physician. After being expelled from Yale for a trifling offense, Wikoff had studied law and had been at one time or another an American diplomat at the Court of St. James's; an agent of the British foreign office; the manager of the celebrated dancer, Fanny Elsler, over whom he quarreled with Bennett; the friend of Louis Napoleon, at whose escape from the fortress of Ham he claimed to have connived; and the kidnapper of an American heiress to whom he considered himself engaged. As a result of this last escapade Wikoff spent fifteen months in jail. Later he wrote a book, briefly a best seller, about his romantic misfortunes.

During the late eighteen-fifties Wikoff was in Washington from time to time as representative of the *Herald.* Apparently he acted as intermediary between Bennett and Buchanan when the *Herald* shifted its support to Buchanan during the presidential campaign of 1856. To further the wartime interests of the *Herald,* Wikoff attached himself to Mrs. Lincoln, who was apparently greatly flattered by his attentions. It was commonly believed that he received from her an advance copy of President Lincoln's first annual message to Congress. The premature publication in the *Herald* of this message sent Wikoff to jail a second time and ended his usefulness as a White House correspondent.[32]

Another influential New York reporter in Washington was David V. G. (D.W.) Bartlett,[33] who wrote a campaign biography of Lincoln in 1860, contributed letters all through the war to both the New York *Evening Post* and the Springfield *Republican,* and did ghost-writing for members of Congress. Bartlett had the reputation among his colleagues of being particularly close to the War Department.[34]

Few representatives of the opposition press in Washington were more highly regarded than the New York *World*'s "Shad" Adams, an old resident of the District of Columbia, whose reputation as a man of unimpeachable character and veracity rated him high standing among government officials. Even the telegraph censor, Benjamin P. Snyder, frequently permitted Adams to send out dispatches without submitting them for prior examination, simply on the strength of Adams' assurance that the material they contained was "all right."[35] By one of his contemporaries Adams was described as "a plump man with a clean-shaved face, rosy cheeks, twinkling and humorous eyes . . . the very picture of self-content."[36]

The cherubic Adams wrote for the Boston *Herald* and Chicago *Times,* as well as for the *World,* and he employed one assistant and duplicated his copy for the three papers. Apparently his efforts were appreciated by his employers, for his earnings from the three papers netted him an income, princely for those days, of more than ten thousand dollars a year. Although his ethical standards were considerably higher than those of most newspaper men of that era, Adams seems to have had an eye for financial opportunities that came easily to one in his position. On one of his regular trips to the War Department during the early days of the war, he learned that an order for the confiscation of the property of a friend with secessionist leanings was pending and that, in all probability, this same friend was about to be arrested for treason. The friend was prepared to flee as soon as he learned from Adams the fate that was in store for him. In his perplexity he begged Adams to buy his house. At first Adams refused, claiming he could not possibly scrape up more than two thousand dollars for such a purpose. "That is better than losing it entirely," replied the other man, and within a comparatively short time Adams found himself the owner of a property which within a few years was worth somewhere between thirty and forty thousand dollars.[37]

Among the representatives of the Western press who were stationed in Washington at various times during the war were Horace White and Joe K. C. Forrest of the Chicago *Tribune,* William B. Moore of the Columbus *Ohio State Journal,* and Whitelaw Reid of the Cincinnati *Gazette.*

As clerk of the senate committee on military affairs White had one of the best opportunities of any Washington correspondent to get an insight into the secret history of the war. In 1861, he was already an experienced journalist, whose reporting of the Lincoln-Douglas debates for the *Tribune* had given him a national reputation and earned for him the warm friendship of Abraham Lincoln.[38]

In many ways, however, the ablest representative of the Western press in Washington was the youthful Reid, who made his mark as a war correspondent in the field before the Cincinnati *Gazette* sent him to the Capital in June, 1862, to report Washington news. Scarcely had Reid arrived in Washington when he was offered the editorship of the St. Louis *Democrat* at a salary considerably larger than his salary on the *Gazette*. His employer, Richard Smith, promptly met the St. Louis offer by granting him a one-twelfth interest in the *Gazette*, for which he was privileged to pay out of the dividends received from stock. Later that summer Reid began working part-time for the New York *Times*. Subsequently, so long as he remained in Washington, a combination of newspapers, including the Chicago *Tribune*, the St. Louis *Democrat*, the Cleveland *Leader*, the Detroit *Tribune*, and the Pittsburgh *Gazette*, shared with the Cincinnati *Gazette* his voluminous dispatches. Only the *Gazette*, however, received his letters. Further evidence of Reid's success as a Washington journalist appears in a letter to a friend in Cincinnati written during the summer of 1863:

> You & Senator Sherman & all my other friends almost, are doing your best to spoil me about my descriptive writing. I know a great deal better than to put such extravagant estimates on such crude efforts. Still I'm very glad the Public seems to like them. ... If people are gulled into believing what Senator Sherman so extravagantly said, —utterly forgetting Sam Wilkeson & Geo. Wilkes & Bayard Taylor & a dozen others with whom I wouldn't presume for an instant to think of comparing myself—why, I make money by their choosing to be humbugged.[39]

Reid's Washington letters were particularly interesting because of their incisive criticism of military affairs and of their sensitiveness to the undercurrents of Washington political life. From his Covenanter ancestry he derived a certain dour habit of thought which made him always more ready to criticize adversely than to praise, and always more eager to attack than to defend. He was almost unbelievably frank, but although his remarks caused a question of privilege to be raised in the House more than once, he rarely failed to substantiate what he had said.

In spite of his uncomfortable frankness, other Washington public men besides Senator Sherman were attracted to Reid, the dark-haired, handsome young Ohioan who wrote under the pseudonym of "Agate." Through Secretary Chase, his chief sponsor, Reid met Horace Greeley, with whom he established a strong friendship which later resulted in his going to the *Tribune*. Reid also came to know such leading Capital personages as Thaddeus Stevens,[40] whom he profoundly admired; bluff Ben Wade; Lincoln's secretary John Hay, who later joined the *Tribune* staff at Reid's invitation; and Congressman James A. Garfield, who became one of his closest friends. The people he met when he was clerk for the military committee and librarian of the House of Representatives, also facilitated his entrée into congressional circles. Life in Washington, however, was not always easy for Reid. Years later his colleague Bartlett could recall the days when the Cincinnati *Gazette* correspondent, "dead broke," was glad to share Bartlett's room until his fortunes had mended.[41]

There were also several women reporters who helped to cover Washington during the Civil War. Among them was the feminist leader, Jane Grey Swisshelm, who contributed letters to the New York *Tribune* and the St. Cloud (Minnesota) *Democrat* while she worked as a government clerk and volunteer nurse in Washington. Mrs. Swisshelm, a former Pittsburgher, was the first woman (in 1850) to obtain a seat in the Washington press gallery.[42] During the war her journalistic activities were no doubt aided because she was a warm personal friend of Mrs. Lincoln. Another Washington newspaper woman, Sara Jane Lippincott, who used the pseudonym "Grace Greenwood," contributed Washington sketches to both the New York *Times* and *Tribune*.[43] For the most part her writing was a combination of the personal and the political, usually in light vein, sometimes satirical, although she was much less interested in reform than Jane Swisshelm was. A third woman journalist, who made regular contributions to the *Missouri Republican* from Washington under the pen name of "Howard Glyndon," was a Maryland girl, Laura Catherine Redden, whose family had moved to St. Louis while she was still quite young. Although at eleven she had been stricken by a serious illness which deprived her of her hearing and made it difficult for her to speak, her efficiency as a Washington correspondent for the *Republican* does not seem to have been materially impaired by her physical handicaps.[44]

It was common practice at this time for a Washington correspondent of one newspaper to work for several others to increase his earnings. Most Capital newsmen wrote for at least three newspapers, sometimes for as many as a half dozen. Like Reid, some Washington correspondents took advantage of their close association with members of Congress to obtain clerkships of congressional committees, which added to their incomes. Poore, for example, was for some time the clerk of the senate committee on foreign affairs, of which his friend Sumner was chairman; and L. A. Whitely of the New York *Herald* held a sixteen-hundred-dollar clerkship in the Treasury Department until he was ousted from it by Secretary Chase during the latter part of June, 1863.[45] It was also common practice for newspaper men at the Capital to make profitable stock market investments based in large part on early knowledge of tax legislation. During April, 1863, the chief Washington correspondent of the Philadelphia *Inquirer* received a letter from a certain S. C. Chollis in New York which informed him in reproachful terms:

> Your despatch was *ahead* of all the others but one day behind the papers. How was this! I never was so disappointed in my life. Certainly it would have made for you at least $5000—had you sent it sooner.
>
> Allow me to assure you that I am depending on you, and will make you *a pile* if you can get the news in advance when the market is not excited by the same news.[46]

On the other hand, the living expenses of a Washington correspondent were far from cheap. One of the *Herald* correspondents who had a room in a house on Tenth Street and boarded at Willard's during the summer of 1862 was charged the comparatively modest figure of fourteen dollars a week for board and room.[47] Three years later Whitelaw Reid informed his employers on the Cincinnati *Gazette* that his weekly bill for board alone at Willard's amounted to twenty-one dollars and that his combined expenditures for board, lodging, and laundry ran to thirty-five dollars a week. Out of the annual salary of twenty-five hundred dollars, which he received from the *Gazette,* he estimated that he had six hundred and eighty dollars left with which to clothe himself, support his family, and pay for occasional visits to them.[48]

Among the various Washington correspondents considerable rivalry was induced by their newspapers' eagerness to outdo each other in news enterprise. "You will remember how we obtained the Department reports last year," said J. Barclay Harding in a telegram to the chief Washington correspondent of the Philadelphia *Inquirer* shortly before the battle of Fredericksburg. "Be as keen now and we will beat our neighbors."[49] The New York *Tribune* sometimes was alleged to be the beneficiary of official favoritism in departmental news releases. There would seem to have been some ground for such complaints, at least so far as the War Department was concerned, especially after Dana moved from the managing editorship of the *Tribune* into the post of Assistant Secretary of War. These and similar allegations about the *Herald* and other papers finally resulted in an arrangement whereby news releases from the various government departments were to be cleared through the Washington agent of the Associated Press, who, in turn, distributed such items simultaneously to the various out-of-town newspapers.[50]

In spite of the ambition of most correspondents to win distinction by "scoring a beat" over their rivals, considerable camaraderie prevailed among the reporters stationed at the Capital. An undated letter signed "Bartlett" to the Philadelphia *Inquirer* representative stated:

> If Adams does not come back from Annapolis tonight (as he probably will not) and you get hold of any *very important* bit of news won't you send it to the *World* over Adams name. Just a few words is all that is wanted, in case anything *big* is up. I've sent a short dispatch.[51]

To some extent such camaraderie was fostered because the news bureaus maintained by the out-of-town newspapers (one-storied cubby-holes for the most part) were grouped along Fourteenth Street between F Street and Pennsylvania Avenue in what later came to be known as Newspaper Row.[52] Directly across the street, in Willard's Hotel, was the principal Washington office of the American Telegraph Company, where the correspondents filed their dispatches. Of an evening these "gentlemen of the ravenous pen," as Forney picturesquely styled them,[53] gathered in the lobby at Willard's, where they rubbed elbows with army officers, congressmen, and the curious in general, and absorbed their quota of rum, rumors, and tobacco fumes. One of them said:

> If there are any men in Washington who lead dogs' lives, they are the correspondents of the daily papers. From morning to midnight they are on the watch for items, or "points," to use a common term among them, resting not from one week's end to the other, in their weary round of duties, and scarcely able to call one day in the seven their own, indeed, not at all if they are the victims of a Sunday edition.[54]

A Washington correspondent had not done all that was expected of him when he had made the rounds of the government departments. The Washington press corps to which he belonged was a flying squadron, always available for service in the field. The Cincinnati *Commercial* made allusion, not without an admixture of irony, to those "daring youths," the New York reporters at Washington, who:

> ride on horseback over the Long or Chain Bridge, and gallop fearlessly out and beyond the most advanced pickets. They peep from tree tops at rebel camps. They climb to the roof of Ball's

house, and stare around the chimney at the rebel entrenchments. They go up in Lowe's balloon, and attempt anything, feasible or impossible, in their search for news.[55]

What the average day of a Washington correspondent under wartime conditions was like was well described by Swain of the New York *Times* in a letter to his newspaper published during the summer of 1861:

Of course, as usual, the first plunge of a "Special" is for Willard's . . . where . . . men aggregate previous to the diurnal assaults upon "the Departments" and "the White House". . . .

Well, the first man I meet is an old acquaintance from New-York. . . . He takes me cautiously into the soda-shop and inviting me to a smoke, premises that he wants "my candid opinion about that order." "Orders" being as numerous as office-seekers about here, I of course have to ask him what order, and then he explains that, in his opinion, and that "they all say so," the order of the Secretary of War means that Washington is in great danger of a visit . . . from . . . Beauregard and a few thousand of his retainers. It takes some little time to explain to him that a day or two since, my friend "Lew Benedict Jr." of Albany . . . a Lieutenant-Colonel of an embryo regiment . . . had come down to Washington and . . . had suggested that if Government would only sustain the recruits of his regiment while the companies were being filled up, he could very soon have a regiment in the field that would do honor to himself and good service to the Government. . . . The War Department had very little difficulty in . . . giving him the order he desired. And then . . . the Department had concluded that the same order might work well elsewhere, and so had made it general—never dreaming that its promulgation would be taken as a sign of woe that all was lost. . . .

Hardly was this scare disposed of, than a gentleman . . . assured me that "the Confederates . . . had captured two entire companies of our cavalry." "Where," I ask mechanically, and "how," and then "when," and "whose cavalry was it?" Why "they were taken in an ambuscade near Alexandria, last night, and he believed they belonged to the Second Regiment." Pretty definite, that, was it not? But let us wait and see what Gen. Manfield knows about it before we telegraph "another disaster" to the *Times.*

Who is this, coming in such hot haste? Another New-York friend. What do you suppose he has to tell? He comes from "the Department," and of course must have heard something. And so he has—nothing less than that "an order has just gone over to New-York, directing Gen. Sandford to come to Washington by the next train, with the entire First Division." This is important, if true. . . . Of course, as an enterprising "special," I am bound to make a note of this, but do not send it to the *Times*. It has just enough of probability to justify its transmission, but an order that brings 5,000 men out of New-York, must be on the record, and we shall find it in due time at "the Department."

Before I have run the gauntlet at Willard's, another "reliable gentleman" has told me that "Johnston has crossed at Williamsport with 20,000 rebels," and still another informs, very confidentially, that "McClellan and Gen. Scott and all the Cabinet have been in consultation since 9 o'clock". . . .

It would hardly do to go to dinner with all that on one's mind, so the "Special" betakes himself out of the vortex of rumors, and up to the Departments, where Gen. Mansfield tells him that we never had any cavalry at or near Alexandria, and certainly none have been captured by the rebels. The Secretary of War has not heard of Johnston crossing at Williamsport, and Adjutant-Gen. Thomas has no order on his books for Gen. Sandford and the First Division. At the White House, Louis—the gentleman at the door, who decides who shall and who shall not see the President—is very positive that neither Gen. McClellan nor Gen. Scott "have been in to-day," and quite as positive "There has been no meeting of the Cabinet, Sir." So all these bubbles have burst, and the "Special" goes to dinner without even an item for the morning telegram. . . .

The afternoon is but a repetition of the morning. A gentleman of the secesh Press assures me that Hardee, whom we suppose in Missouri commanding 15,000 rebels, is really at Manassas cooperating with Beauregard.

My secesh friend also informs me that Griffin's Battery has joined the rebels. Now, that *is* news indeed. Indeed it will be news to the rebels. It may be true—for with God all things are possible—but I guess I will not venture to send that to the *Times,* even without taking the precaution to go up and ask Capt. Griffin if it is so.

One more illustration of Washington rumors, and I have closed my recital of a day's experience. I am writing upon what I know to be reliable of the day's events, when a transient assistant, who sometimes hangs on the outskirts of Washington life and gathers

> up items for me, rushes in with a terrific report. . . . According to his recital, "it is raining like fury." That I know to be true, feeling it from my damp shoulders clear down to my soaked gaiters. With this promptly admitted truth, he continues that "Johnston is marching on the works on the opposite side of the Potomac; that McClellan has been in the saddle all day, personally directing our men how to dig pitfalls all along the lines from Chain bridge to below Alexandria . . . that while Johnston menaces our front, Beauregard is crossing the Potomac at Occoquan Creek, 20 miles below; that he will turn Fort Washington, and leaving it in the rear, march north on Washington, and after crushing the Excelsior Brigade, will shell the city from the heights where the Insane Asylum stands." My colaborer is assured of "the entire reliability of this statement," for he had it from Lieut. B. . . . and Lieut. B. had further told him, that he had seen an "order" issued from the War Department, commanding the women and children to be gathered away from the country round about the Insane Asylum, which was to be the locale of Gen. Pierre Toutan's assault. . . . The same story, with terrific variations, was repeated to me three times between the White House and the telegraph office.[56]

Much of the correspondence between the heads of the Washington news bureaus and their home offices had to do with the problem of procuring and maintaining the various army correspondents who were attached to the Army of the Potomac. In June, 1864, the chief Washington correspondent of the New York *World* gave a very clear picture of the responsibilities of a Washington correspondent in this regard. In a letter to the editor, in which he expressed his intention of resigning from the *World*, Adams wrote:

> For nearly two years I have endeavored to systematize the army correspondence so far as it has been placed in my hands here and so far as it relates to Washington—with the object in view of securing efficiency and economy. I should have preferred to have had nothing to do with that branch, but as all the correspondents are sent to me I had no alternative. In the first place nearly 18 mos. ago I wrote particularly to the office, and have reiterated at innumerable times not to send any one to Washington for the army until I had obtained passes for them etc.—or that they had secured them before leaving. Right on the heels of this two men were sent to Washington just a year ago without a moment's

> notice to me. They waited here for a long time & finally got off. Nearly $300 passed through my hands to them, which, together with subsequent payments must have amounted to over $400, every cent of which proved a dead loss *to the World*—simply because my request was not adhered to. This thing was kept up until Stillson[57] took hold when he was sent here in just the same way—but fortunately got a pass in due time. He went to work and bought horses and drew on me for money when I had not one dollar to pay. This I protested against much to his (Stillson's) surprise! Still he bought the extra horses on credit, and the result is that the *World* is again the loser of $200—the superfluous horse being left in the army when Stillson left and yesterday I rec'd information that he had been stolen. . . . Stillson had hardly put off Tuesday when who should come along but a Mr. Young also without notice to me, without a pass, and not money enough to more than buy an outfit and with no horse and no experience in the army. I must say that this straw broke my patience—for I saw that it was of no earthly use to try and do anything to save the paper money and secure any news more efficiently and at much less expense—I therefore resolved that if Mr. Croly's "plan was better than my plan," he might carry it out alone, for I was utterly disgusted with the whole matter—after so much fruitful experience.[58]

Evidently the *World* editor, Manton Marble, was able to mollify his exasperated subordinate and persuade him to remain at his post. At any rate, no further correspondence between the two men relating to this subject is to be found in the Marble papers.

Although the White House was a fertile field for news throughout the Civil War period, the only Washington correspondent who was on close personal terms with the President was a jovial Maine reporter named Noah Brooks. Brooks had met Lincoln in Illinois many years before the war, had gone West by ox team to California in the fifties, and had come back East during the second year of the war to represent the Sacramento *Union* in Washington. As an old friend of the President, he became a frequent caller at the White House and often accompanied Lincoln on trips to the front. Although he sometimes functioned in an unofficial capacity as the President's adviser in political matters, he took good care not to presume on the confidential relationship he had with Lincoln.

One great trouble with the press, Lincoln once confided to Brooks, was that it was sure to be "ahead of the hounds, outrunning events, and exciting expectations to be later dashed into disappointment."[59] Most journalists, however, found the President very approachable, even though he held no regular press conferences and granted few interviews, in the sense these terms are used commonly today. Even when Lincoln was in conference, the newspaper men did not hesitate to send in their cards with a request for some desired item of news or for the verification of a rumor. Lincoln would either excuse himself and go outside to tell the representatives of the press what they wished to know, or write the information on the back of the applicant's card and have it delivered to him by messenger.[60] Lincoln once told a correspondent for the *Herald:*

> You gentlemen of the press seem to be pretty much like soldiers, who have to go wherever sent, whatever may be the dangers or difficulties in the way. God forbid I should by any rudeness of speech or manner, make your duties any harder than they are. . . . If I am not afraid of you, it is because I feel you are trustworthy. . . . The press has no better friend than I am—no one who is more ready to acknowledge . . . its tremendous power for both good and evil.[61]

At least one of Lincoln's official family, Secretary Welles, regarded it as an evidence of weakness in the President that "he permits the little newsmongers to come around him and be intimate." He further noted:

> He has great inquisitiveness. Likes to hear all the political gossip as much as Seward. But the President is honest, sincere, and confiding, —traits which are not so prominent in some by whom he is surrounded.[62]

No doubt Welles reacted similarly when he learned, very near the end of the war, that Lincoln's special friend among the Washington newspapermen was about to become his private secretary in place of John G. Nicolay, who was slated to enter the Paris consulate. Lincoln's death occurred, however, before the change could be made. But for a severe cold that kept him at home that night, Brooks would have been in the presidential box at Ford's Theater when the bullet was fired that ended the President's life.[63] In this accidental way, posterity was deprived of an eyewitness account of Lincoln's assassination by an experienced reporter, literally on the spot.[64]

The newspapermen found Secretaries Seward, Cameron, and Chase the most accessible and communicative members of the President's Cabinet. Recognizing that Seward was especially susceptible to flattery, the New York *Herald* made a regular practice of eulogizing him beyond his merits to win favor for its correspondents.[65] Cameron, who was characterized by Villard as "by far the most cordial and talkative of all the secretaries,"[66] was particularly adept in tossing out insinuations and sly remarks to cause the newspaper men to publish things he wished to have said about others without their being attributed to him. Of all the Capital press corps, Cameron seems to have preferred Wilkeson, the *Tribune*'s representative, whose telegrams to the *Tribune* office were permitted to go out without being subjected to the censorship.[67]

Welles and Stanton were much less affable than the other secretaries, and were disliked accordingly by the Washington newspaper men. One of the members of the guild fancied that he detected in Welles's face a resemblance to the famous queen of Louis XVI. Taking their cue from this interesting discovery, the little coterie of Washington correspondents nicknamed the Secretary of the Navy "Marie Antoinette," and sidestepped him in favor of the assistant secretary, Gustavus Fox, whose relations with the press were more cordial.[68]

Stanton, on the other hand, was desperately hated by the newspaper men, some of whom, according to Noah Brooks, looked upon him as a "fiend incarnate."[69] "Stanton absolutely stinks in the nostrils of the people and the army," wrote one of the Washington correspondents of the *Herald* to Frederic Hudson in March, 1863. "His manner has made him offensive to every one who approaches him."[70] The *Herald*'s antipathy toward Stanton, exhibited on every possible occasion, was in marked contrast to its demeanor toward most public men of consequence. To some degree at least, the *Herald*'s attacks on Stanton were the result of the rough treatment accorded by the bearish Secretary of War to Malcolm Ives, of the *Herald*'s Washington staff, soon after Stanton took over the War Department.

Ives was a tall slender man of Italian appearance, from New York City. He had been at one time a clerk in a Philadelphia banking house. Sometime during the late forties he went abroad and was converted to Catholicism in Rome. Following his return to this country, he became a Jesuit priest and was appointed professor of biblical literature in the Catholic college at Milwaukee. He later ran into difficulties with the bishop of his diocese, possibly because of alleged unpriestly behavior in connection with an army officer's wife whom he had met at the Tremont House in Chicago. Ultimately, he found journalistic employment in New York, first with the *Journal of Commerce,* then with the *Times,* and finally (in 1859) with the *Herald.* While he was on the staff of the *Journal of Commerce* he had married a Protestant girl whom he persuaded to turn Catholic; she then left him because her conscience forbade her to remain the wife of a former priest.[71]

Ives first appeared in Washington during the summer of 1861 because of a patent speculation in which he was interested. From that time on he made occasional visits to Washington (up until New Year's time, 1862). Then he joined the Washington staff of the *Herald* and became a regular guest at Willard's. Apparently Ives had been sent to Washington by Bennett to tighten up the *Herald's* news organization at the Capital. Simon P. Hanscom was still the chief Washington correspondent of the *Herald,* and it is hardly surprising, therefore, that ill-feeling speedily arose between the two men. On January 29, 1862, Ives wrote to Bennett complaining:

> Hanscom visited the War Dept. yesterday and told them that I had no connection with the Herald, beyond a local Employ in New York, and that any attempts I made to get news were unauthorized, obtrusive & in opposition to orders.... Wykoff [sic] & Shaw[72] had both represented him as abusing me systematically, and his feeling was confirmed to me by Whitely.

Ten days later Ives placed in Hanscom's hands a letter from Bennett notifying him that his services were no longer required and directing him to turn over his keys and other office effects to Ives. At the time several newspapers carried stories intimating that Hanscom had aroused Bennett's ill-will by carelessly referring to one of Mrs. Lincoln's White House parties as a "social blunder"![73]

On the day after he took over the direction of the *Herald's* Washington office, Ives visited the War Department and obtained an interview with John Tucker, one of Stanton's assistants. In the course of the interview Ives informed Tucker that he expected the *Herald* to be notified in advance of all other newspapers about changes in administration policy, military operations, troop movements, and the like. He stated that he would use his own discretion about withholding such information from the public and made it pretty clear that this was the price the administration must pay for the continued support of the *Herald.* After he had finished speaking with Tucker, the *Herald* man entered the room of Assistant Secretary Peter H. Watson, which adjoined the private office of Secretary Stanton, and was about to walk into Stanton's presence without knocking when he learned from Watson that the Secretary was "engaged." Instead of accepting this rebuff gracefully, Ives created a scene, insisting that he had a perfect right as a representative of the New York *Herald* to enter the Secretary of War's office anytime he thought proper, regardless of who was there before him.[74]

On the evening of the following day, as Ives was giving instructions to some other *Herald* reporters in the lobby of Willard's Hotel, two gentlemen who had been sitting close by stepped up to him and said they had some news for him. They suggested, however, that since strangers were within earshot, perhaps it would be better to go to some private room. A meeting of the *Herald* staff at Willard's was scheduled for 10:00 A.M. the following morning, but the appointed time passed without any sign of Ives. At 2:00 P.M. an order from the War Department announcing the arrest and confinement of Ives in Fort McHenry near Baltimore dispelled the mystery.[75]

Bennett promptly disavowed the action of his officious correspondent, saying that he was not authorized to make threats, but expressed doubts that Ives, as Stanton charged in his order, was a Confederate spy.[76] Meanwhile, the Secretary's action was applauded by a large section of the press as a "stinging rebuke" to the *Herald,* although the *National Intelligencer* was of the opinion that "the long indulgence practiced toward these purveyors of the sensation press has naturally encouraged them to act in a high-handed manner toward public functionaries."[77] Ives remained a prisoner in Fort McHenry until his release in May, 1862,[78] following which he dropped out of sight very quickly.

The only Washington correspondent in whom Stanton confided to any extent was a Quaker youth from West Chester, Pennsylvania, Uriah Hunt Painter, who worked for the Philadelphia *Inquirer.* Painter was a man of strong character, close-mouthed and inclined to concentrate his attention on facts, leaving descriptive writing to others. By his skillful methods of obtaining news and by his proficiency in arriving at correct deductions as to enemy intentions before they became apparent at headquarters, he finally won the confidence of the crusty Secretary of War. From then on, the use of the military telegraph lines and the Secretary's cipher were open to him. According to General Boynton, himself a prominent newspaperman in Washington, there was no one in any department of public life on whose statements Stanton placed greater reliance and by whose information he was more frequently guided.[79]

These were the members of the Capital press corps; these were the men whose portrayal of a nation at war with itself and whose interpretation of events as they mounted to a climax clicked over the wires to all the country: to New Hampshire hill farmers and the quartz miners of California; to the women who drove their reapers on the Illinois prairie and the frock-coated merchants on Wall Street. In their interpretation of the great drama that unrolled before their eyes on the stinking mud flats along the Potomac, they were frequently compelled to rely upon shrewd guesses in the absence of reliable information. Moreover, their judgments inevitably reflected biases that had crystallized during the stormy years of controversy preceding the actual outbreak of war. Much of what they had to say was tinged with gossip or was simply commonplace. The Philadelphia *Press* claimed:

> Nearly all the New-York reporters in Washington, with a few honorable exceptions, use their proprietors for the ventilation of their private griefs against public men. . . . Mr. Bennett, of the *Herald*, is sold out continually. . . . Mr. Greeley, of the *Tribune*, and Mr. Raymond, of the *Times*, often find themselves in embarrassing and conflicting positions, by reason of the mendacity of those who represent them in Washington City.[80]

One must recognize, nonetheless, that many of the shortcomings of the Washington reporters and their reporting were the result of factors over which they had little or no control. Their journalistic activities were circumscribed by a capricious censorship, against which they raged constantly and, in the main, ineffectually. To some extent, the entire corps, made up preponderantly of legitimate and accredited representatives of the leading newspapers, was brought into disrepute by the misconduct of a little band of "newspaper guerrillas" which descended upon Washington soon after the outbreak of hostilities. Many of these "guerrillas" were fakers who paid little attention to facts in their pursuit of news items and over whom the chiefs of the Washington offices had comparatively little control.[81] In spite of the bushwhacking conduct of some of the smaller-fry Washington journalists, the reporting achievements of the more reputable newsmen along Fourteenth Street were by no means insignificant. Public understanding of war issues would have been immeasurably poorer had it not been for the news-gathering efforts, carried on in the midst of the fog of misinformation that continuously surrounded war operations, of these "gentlemen of the ravenous pen."

4

The Men in the Field

THE average field correspondent with the Northern army knew well from personal experience the meaning of the "strenuous life." Day and night, in all weather, he had to be alert to avoid being scooped by rival newsmen. It was his business to go everywhere, to see everything, and to squeeze information out of everybody from the commanding general to the rearmost teamster in the quartermaster's train. Some army reporters made their way to the enemy's picket lines and over a persuasive bottle of whiskey established confidential relations with the enemy pickets. "Early news is expensive news, Mr. Greeley," retorted Charles A. Page of the New York *Tribune* when the *Tribune* editor reproached him as the most expensive reporter the paper ever had employed. "If I have the watermelons and whiskey ready when the officers come along from the fight, I get the news without asking questions."[1]

During the war, more than three hundred correspondents accompanied the Northern armies from one bloody battlefield to another or reported the operations of the fleet.[2] They were a heterogeneous lot. After eighteen months in the field, one of them, from the Philadelphia *Press,* came to the conclusion that twenty-nine out of fifty-three army correspondents whom he knew personally were "well educated, talented, and accomplished gentlemen"; eleven belonged to the "genus blower"; seven, energetic and enterprising though they were, were misfits as army correspondents; the remaining three were "rank Secessionists."[3] In August, 1862, William Painter wrote his brother Uriah from camp:

> that reporter you left here did not go up to Banks for 2 days after you left, and got drunk here before he left. . . . If you have any *Gentlemen* connected with the Inquirer you can send here we would be glad to have them. But we do not want any more blackguards, and you are disgracing me by sending or leaving such men.[4]

Among the newspapermen were former school teachers, lawyers, government clerks, telegraphers, bookkeepers, poets, preachers, and even soldiers. One army reporter had been secretary of the Milwaukee Chamber of Commerce; another had been a stenographer for the Canadian Parliament; another had been a clerk on a Mississippi steamboat. The great majority of the reporters in the field, however, had had some previous newspaper experience. Both Richard C. McCormick and George F. Williams had been war correspondents during the fifties: one during the Crimean War; one during the campaign against the Mormons in 1858. James O. Noyes, the Associated Press correspondent at Fortress Monroe during the first year of the Civil War, had been a foreign correspondent in Turkey, Palestine, and Egypt for the New York *Tribune*, Detroit *Free Press*, and other newspapers. Edward H. House had covered John Brown's Raid in Virginia for the New York *Tribune* shortly before the war.[5]

The average age of the correspondents in the field was somewhere in the late twenties, although at least six were nineteen or less in 1861.[6] On the other hand, the Chicago *Journal's* Benjamin F. Taylor and the New York *Herald's* Samuel R. Glen were in their middle forties at the outbreak of the war. These men came from all parts of the country, although comparatively few were from west of the Mississippi. At least eighteen were born in New York State; of the seventy-eight whose biographical data is known, twenty-one had lived in New England; fifteen were of foreign origin, seven of them Irish.[7]

Many of the reporters were comparatively well educated. Within their ranks were graduates of Harvard, Yale, Columbia, Amherst, Union, Trinity, Williams, University of Vermont, Rensselaer, Hamilton, Beloit, St. Xavier, Mt. Union, Antioch, and Cornell College (Iowa). The Chicago *Tribune's* George P. Upton even had received the master's degree from Brown in 1854. Stephen Ryder Fiske had been a student at Rutgers but had been expelled for writing a novel satirizing the professors.[8] Edmund Clarence Stedman had experienced a similar fate at Yale. Others, such as George Alfred Townsend, Joel Cook, and Ainsworth Spofford, had received a high school education or its equivalent.

Among the reporters a significant number in post-Civil War days were distinguished either in journalism or in other fields. Thomas Bailey Aldrich, Robert Henry Newell, Bayard Taylor, and Stedman were the best known literary men in the field. Aldrich and Taylor were employed by the New York *Tribune*, Stedman was accredited to the *World*, and

Newell to the *Herald.* Other celebrities who collected news items on the battlefield or in the fleet were Henry M. Stanley of "Darkest Africa" fame; James Redpath, of the lyceum movement; George W. Nichols, founder of the Cincinnati College of Music and active in the cultural development of that city; Ainsworth Spofford and John Russell Young, both, at different times, Librarian of Congress; and Henry Villard, who completed the first Northwestern transcontinental railroad, the Northern Pacific, and who during the early eighteen-eighties probably was the most important railway promoter in the United States.

At least ten saw service as war reporters at some time or another during the years that followed Appomattox. Both George W. Smalley and George Alfred Townsend reported the Austro-Prussian War of 1866; Finley Anderson, who was representing the *Herald* in London at that time, cabled to his newspaper, at a cost of sixty-five hundred dollars in gold, the full text of a speech made by the King of Prussia announcing the end of the war. This was said to be the first newspaper report carried by the Atlantic cable.[9] Murat Halstead, William F. G. Shanks, George F. Williams, and John Russell Young were foreign correspondents of American newspapers during the Franco-Prussian War. Williams also saw the Emperor Maximilian executed at Queretaro, and he later campaigned in South America. Other Civil War correspondents who answered the call to arms after 1865 were Samuel R. Glen, who covered the Fenian expedition for the *Herald;* Januarius Aloysius MacGahan, a Civil War correspondent for one of the St. Louis newspapers, who made an outstanding reputation for himself as a war correspondent during the Russo-Turkish War; Jerome Stillson, a New York *Herald* reporter during the Indian campaigns of the early seventies; and Stephen R. Fiske, the companion of Garibaldi in his last campaign against Rome.

Many other members of the newspaper brigade used their Civil War reporting to advance in journalism. The Philadelphia *Press* army reporter, Joel Cook, for example, for many years after the war was financial editor of the Philadelphia *Ledger* and was the American correspondent of the London *Times.* Both Lorenzo Livingston Crounse and De Benneville Randolph Keim became outstanding Washington correspondents for the New York *Times* and for the *Herald.* William Conant Church and his brother Francis P. Church, both former army correspondents of the New York *Times,* were the founders of the *Army and Navy Journal* and then of a magazine called the *Galaxy,* which later was merged with the *Atlantic Monthly.* Henry Watterson, who made claim to having been a correspondent in both armies during the war,[10] likewise made an outstanding reputation for himself as editor of the Louisville *Courier-Journal.* In newspaper publishing after the war were the Cincinnati *Commercial's* enterprising army reporter, William D. Bickham, who was owner of the Dayton (Ohio) *Journal* for more than thirty years; the Philadelphia *Inquirer* reporter, John H. Taggart, who for many years published in Philadelphia the enterprising little *Taggart's Times;* and Henry Villard, who had a controlling interest in the New York *Evening Post.* Another Civil War reporter was Joseph B. McCullagh, later editor of the influential St. Louis *Globe-Democrat.*

Most of the better known army correspondents were attached to the forces operating in the East. Events were concentrated there within a comparatively limited area near the large cities. Reporters billeted with the Army of the Potomac therefore were more conspicuous. In the West, army movements were on a larger scale, in which the individual reporter more easily was lost. Managing editors, however, commonly kept their reporters in continual motion and shifted them about from one part of the war zone to another. After reporting an important battle in Virginia, a correspondent might be transferred to Tennessee or to Louisiana, and then in a few weeks he might be moved again to an entirely different area. He could expect to cover several thousand miles during the course of a campaign or season.

They were a picturesque lot with their fancy vests, their stiff collars, and their beards of all shapes and sizes. The New York *Tribune* took a special pride in having its correspondents outshine those employed by the other papers, and so they commonly wore knickerbockers of the finest corduroy, buckskin jackets, high-topped boots of top grain leather, conspicuous gauntlets, and broad-brimmed hats.[11] Like other correspondents, however, they used the standard equipment of revolver, field glasses, notebook, one or more blankets, a haversack for provisions on the march, and a good horse. Cushioned saddles, portable camp beds, and waterproof clothing were conveniences available only for the few who could carry superfluous baggage. A New York *Times* man, writing to his paper from Falmouth, Virginia, warned:

> If you send out any more correspondents, don't provide them with anything. The best outfit will get scattered in the course of a week. Of my horse, bridle, saddle, blankets, and other accoutrements, I have one spur remaining, and expect to miss that tomorrow morning.[12]

Horses were expensive and difficult to get, even at premium prices. Just before the first Battle of Bull Run, a Washington liveryman demanded that William H. Russell, the London *Times* correspondent, pay him one thousand dollars for a spavined bay horse. He told Russell to "take it or leave it. If you want to see this fight, a thousand dollars is cheap."[13] Army reporters constantly had to be on the lookout for horse thieves, who made off with horses in the night and then remained under cover until pursuit had ended. Charles Carleton Coffin, the Boston *Journal* man, had a showy animal which was stolen frequently. His African factotum often would thrust his head into the tent and awaken his master with the salutation: "Breakfast is ready. Mr. Coffin, your horse is gone again."[14]

Among the outstanding correspondents who saw service mainly in the Eastern war theater were George W. Smalley of the New York *Tribune* and William Swinton and Lorenzo Livingston Crounse of the New York *Times*. Smalley's career as a war correspondent lasted for hardly more than a year, but within that time he achieved what one of his fellow war-correspondents regarded as the greatest single journalistic exploit of the war: his account of Antietam.

Smalley was a graduate of Yale, where he had rowed stroke in the first Yale-Harvard race on Lake Winnepesaukee. Afterwards he had attended the Harvard law school and had practiced law for five years in Boston. There he became interested, through Wendell Phillips, his future father-in-law, in the anti-slavery movement. But for failing eyesight, which compelled him to abandon his legal career, he might never have gone into journalism.

It was through Phillips that Smalley met Sydney Howard Gay of the New York *Tribune* staff. Gay arranged to send Smalley to Port Royal in the autumn of 1861 where he was to do a series of articles on Negro life in South Carolina. After a dull winter there, he was transferred the following spring to the Shenandoah Valley, and saw service with General Fremont's command. In August, as Lee was marching northward, Smalley was shifted again, to the Army of the Potomac. During the battle of South Mountain, he stood only a few feet from General George B. McClellan, and he viewed with some amazement the commanding general's singular air of detachment. At Antietam he served as impromptu aide to General Joseph Hooker and delivered orders for him under fire. Twice during that battle enemy bullets hit his horse and cut his clothing. His account of Antietam, written by the dim light of an oil lamp on the night train to New York, was finer than any other writing of the kind during the whole four years of the conflict.[15]

Swinton and Crounse were the two principal correspondents of the New York *Times* with the Army of the Potomac. Although the distinctive peculiarities of the various newspapers usually were reflected to some extent in the style and deportment of their reporters, these two *Times* men were a study in contrast: Swinton tall and well formed, with eyes large and luminous, and with a well-modulated voice which failed to betray his Scottish birth; Crounse small and dapper, distinguished chiefly by his molasses-candy-colored moustache and goatee.

Swinton had emigrated from Scotland to Canada with his family when he was ten, had prepared for the Presbyterian ministry at Knox College in Toronto and at Amherst, had done some preaching, and had then left the pulpit to teach languages in a female seminary at Greensboro, North Carolina. In 1858 he joined the staff of the New York *Times,* probably with the help of his brother John, already an employee of the paper.

Crounse, on the other hand, had been interested in newspaper work ever since he was twelve. Then he rode thirty miles in the back end of a wagon over Wisconsin country roads to answer an advertisement for a printer's apprentice. Although he was rejected as too young, nevertheless only two years later Crounse was working for the Milwaukee *Free Democrat.* Within eight years he had become one of the editors and proprietors of the paper, and he employed the very man who, a few years before, had thought him too much of a boy to learn the printer's trade. At the beginning of the war, Crounse reported from the field for several Western newspapers before he joined the army staff, first of the *World* and then of the New York *Times.*

Whereas Crounse was deliberate, cautious, and reliable, Swinton discussed military movements and criticized generals with such freedom that he constantly was in difficulties with the military authorities. At one time General Grant stopped Swinton's letters and threatened to have him shot, but Secretary Seward, who was very friendly toward the New York *Times,* countermanded the order and procured Swinton's release. Later Swinton angered General Ambrose E. Burnside, who is said to have issued an order for his execution, but this time it was Grant who suspended the sentence, directing instead that Swinton be expelled from the Army of the Potomac and not be permitted to return.[16]

Crounse's narrow escapes resulted largely from his eagerness to be a witness of the events he was to describe. Twice his horse was shot from under him, and once, in 1862, he was struck in the shoulder by a piece of shell which long left his arm useless. With several other New York newspaper men, he once was captured by Mosby's rangers, who released him and his companions after they had relieved them of their watches and notebooks, turning over the latter to the Richmond press.[17] During much of the fighting Crounse was accompanied by his brother Silas, who was his dispatch bearer. Crounse left the field at the end of 1863 to become night editor of the *Times,* and did the paper an important service when he questioned the authenticity of the famous "bogus proclamation" of May, 1864, invented for its effect on the stock market, which fooled some of the other New York papers.[18]

Although they competed fiercely for news, the Western army correspondents were generally on friendly terms with each other: they usually ate, slept, traveled, smoked together, and not infrequently drank from the same flask with equal relish. On the other hand, the Eastern correspondents of the New York papers with the Army of the Potomac competed so sharply that they hesitated to let others know of their movements. L. A. Whitely of the *Herald,* in a Washington letter of November, 1863, to Frederic Hudson, expressed some surprise that a *Tribune* correspondent had just arrived from the front with a portfolio of dispatches belonging to several different newspapers. Whitely remarked to his chief that:

> It is a rather singular performance for the special correspondent of the *Tribune* to act as bearer of dispatches for the Times, World, and Associated Press, but such a course may suit that paper.[19]

Apart from Whitelaw Reid and Joe McCullagh, already mentioned, the outstanding correspondents with the Western armies were Franc B. Wilkie and Benjamin C. Truman of the New York *Times,* Thomas W. Knox and William F. G. Shanks of the New York *Herald,* Henry Villard and Albert D. Richardson of the New York *Tribune,* William S. Furay of the Cincinnati *Gazette,* Benjamin F. Taylor of the Chicago *Evening Journal,* and Sylvanus Cadwallader of the Chicago *Times.*

Cadwallader, like Crounse, began in Milwaukee journalism. Unlike the majority of his fellow correspondents he was inclined to be distant and unsociable. He was a slender man with dark, mysterious eyes, and he was constantly on the move. With Grant he was an especial favorite, and was able to get news denied other correspondents.

This favoritism stemmed from an incident which occurred near the end of 1862. Grant was planning a movement up the Yazoo River in Northwestern Mississippi. During the early stages of the movement, Grant decided to go up the Yazoo in a small boat and to look over the ground. Cadwallader and one or two other correspondents were permitted to accompany the expedition. The trip was long and tiresome, and, but for the foresight of a staff member, who smuggled aboard a demijohn of whiskey, it might have seemed more so. When the expedition returned to its starting point that evening, Grant plunged ashore the moment the gang plank was run out and mounted his waiting horse with considerable difficulty. Without waiting for his staff, he rode off in the direction of the Federal forces, closely followed by the still-sober Cadwallader.

At a sudden turn in the winding road, Grant, reputed to be one of the most expert horsemen in the service, was thrown from his saddle. Checking his pace, Cadwallader reined up, dismounted, grasped by the shoulders the now quite helpless fallen officer, and dragged him out of sight. Presently the staff cantered by tipsily. The coast clear, Cadwallader rode to camp, got an ambulance, and deposited the casualty of the war with alcohol in his tent without anyone being the wiser. Almost immediately afterward, Cadwallader took a front place among the reporters in Grant's army, and during the siege of Vicksburg he was the only newspaper man allowed on the steamer "Magnolia," Grant's headquarters.[20]

Cadwallader was not the only Civil War correspondent who enjoyed the special confidence of a general. D. B. R. Keim, one of the *Herald* reporters in the West, likewise ingratiated himself into Grant's favor and became a lifelong friend. It even has been claimed that one of Keim's letters to the *Herald,* which described Grant's methods and stressed his ability as a commander, helped to bring about his selection as commander in chief.[21] Other close relationships between generals and reporters were those of Bickham and General William S. Rosecrans, of Smalley and Hooker, of William H. Merriam and Ben Butler, and of Finley Anderson and General Winfield S. Hancock. Even General William T. Sherman, *bête noire* of army reporters, made an exception in the case of Henry Villard.[22]

The extraordinary uses of such favoritism are illustrated by a happening in one of the late campaigns. Merriam, a *Herald* reporter, was attached to the headquarters of General Butler's Army of the James.

Edward A. Pollard, editor of the Richmond *Examiner,* had been captured a short time before that and was a prisoner in the "bull pen" at Butler's headquarters. Merriam, who was highly genial and companionable, decided to relieve Pollard's prison life with a grand dinner. He made all arrangements, except for getting the General's permission for Pollard's temporary release. Not until the guests all had assembled for the spread, did Merriam go to the General's tent and request liberty of the camp for Pollard that night so he could attend the banquet. Had anyone else made this request, he undoubtedly would have been jailed in the "pen" alongside Pollard. Since it was Merriam, however, Butler granted the favor immediately, and Pollard was free for the night. His banquet was an all-night revel, and time and again General Butler sent the guard to suppress the hilarity. Merriam invariably asked the guard to "present my compliments to General Butler, with the hope that he will sleep well, while the North and South continue to clasp hands over the bloody chasm." Not knowing the bond of fellowship between the General and their host, most of the guests expected that the guard's next visit would send all of them to jail![23]

Probably Butler had reasons for his indulgent treatment of the *Herald* correspondent. In a letter written to Frederic Hudson about this same time, William H. Stiner, another army reporter of the *Herald,* reminded Hudson of a promise he and Bennett had made—that nothing derogatory to General Butler should appear in the editorial columns of the *Herald,* and Stiner suggested that this promise be kept in the future.[24] As indicated before, it was a common practice of the *Herald* to praise extravagantly and quite indiscriminately officers holding important commands so that the *Herald*'s army reporters might get news more readily. Usually the reporters of the New York *Herald* and of the New York *Tribune* received preferred treatment from the generals. Along with other favored correspondents, they lived near headquarters and enjoyed the hospitality of some friendly officer's military family. In some instances, they even were equipped at government expense.[25]

One of the principal sources of complaint from other newspaper correspondents was that they had no established position in the army. B. F. Taylor of the Chicago *Evening Journal* observed:

> While "the pen is mightier than the sword" is all very well in the play and among the Scribes, it is very far from being true in a

> wide-awake department of the army, where the scale of being runs downward thus: men, munitions, mules, scribblers; brigades, batteries, bacon, beasts, Bohemians.[26]

To be sure, army reporters commonly received passes from headquarters, and in general were free to come and go as they pleased, but their privileges might be terminated on very short notice. Moreover, as they were not recognized as noncombatants, they were just as liable to attack by the enemy as the enlisted men.[27] When excluded from camp, as they frequently were, they assumed many roles to elude the provost marshal. Some volunteered as hospital stewards; others enlisted as common soldiers; others pursued army news as secretaries or clerks. Frequently army correspondents managed to secure appointments as staff officers and performed both important military and journalistic services.[28]

It was a common experience for army correspondents to be ushered from the presence of a general after a long conference with the parting words, "Do not forget to notice my own personal staff." This was well understood to mean "one word for my staff and two for me." Townsend was once assured by General Hancock, at whose headquarters he was living, that the General wanted no praise for himself or anybody else in his camp. After a short time it became obvious to Townsend that he was no longer welcome at that particular headquarters, and so he found accommodations elsewhere. Later Townsend learned from someone close to the General that it was Townsend's failure to mention Hancock frequently in his correspondence which had cooled the General's hospitality.[29]

Stedman, who represented the New York *World* in Virginia early in the war, had a similar experience, in reverse. Shortly after the Battle of Ball's Bluff, Stedman was called into the office of General Charles T. James, an artillery officer. Some kind words about James's cannon, which Stedman had mentioned in a letter describing the fight, had greatly pleased the General. Would Stedman be willing to accept fifty dollars as a token of appreciation from the General? Apparently Stedman saw nothing irregular in accepting the General's proposition for, relating the incident in a letter to his wife, he stated frankly:

> If ever a man needed $50, it is I. . . . I took his agent's name and shall next week draw for the amount. . . . Of course he expects me

> to keep a lookout for his guns hereafter, and I believe I can do so with a clear conscience.[30]

Naval reporting of the war was not entirely specialized. There was a certain amount of interchange of duty, on land and afloat, for the reporters who saw the war at close range. Charles Carleton Coffin, Henry Villard, Lorenzo L. Crounse, and Thomas M. Cook were some of the better-known press representatives who saw long service at sea during their careers as army reporters. Although the policy of the Navy Department toward the press was more temperate than that of the War Department, the reporters found it even more difficult, in some respects, to do business with the admirals than with the generals. Whereas reporters could browbeat political generals into giving them news tips, and sometimes did, admirals were more closemouthed. Ranking officers of the navy did not look forward to a postwar political career, as numerous major generals did. Moreover, the dissemination of naval operations news was more easily controlled at its source. Unlike their army colleagues, press reporters with the fleet were completely dependent upon the service for a means of getting to the scene, and they had to submit to censorship.[31]

Yet the navy, no less than the army, was under pressure for special privileges from newsmen. That naval officials were by no means impervious to such pressures is indicated by a letter addressed to the managing editor of the *Herald* in 1864 by one of its naval reporters, T. M. Cook. The letter described an interview with the Assistant Secretary of the Navy, Gustavus Fox, which Cook had obtained through the good offices of the paper's Washington news bureau. Cook advised:

> He seemed to be very glad to see me, and was pleased at my assignment to go with the fleet. He thanked me for my Mobile Bay report, which he said was represented by all officers who had come up as a perfectly correct account of the fight. He then gave me a note to Admiral Porter simply to the effect that I wrote the best account of the Mobile Bay fight and was therefore well qualified to give a description of any other fight. I then told him my relations with Porter and that this note would do me no good; what I wanted was to be placed on the Admiral's ship with facilities at my disposal to get away north in advance of the mass of correspondents or any of them. To this he replied that it would not do to put any such permission in writing, but that Porter understood it and everything would be fixed to my satisfaction.

> I urged that I could not be satisfied until I knew what the arrangement was to be, but if it should be satisfactory I could make a report that would be acceptable both to the Admiral and the Department. Fox then said something about Dahlgren getting into a scrape by sending a Tribune correspondent away specially with important news. I insisted that I cared nothing for the scrapes of Dahlgren or the Tribune, but it might be arranged to send me to New York direct twelve hours before the Admiral should send his dispatches to Fortress Monroe and that the affair could be covered up. Fox then promised to go to Fortress Monroe on Saturday night where we could get together with the Admiral and fix up something.
>
> I do not believe they will give me a special boat to get away in; they are afraid to do it; but I am satisfied that I shall be on the flagship exclusively, and then if an opportunity occurs Porter will assist me in giving the other correspondents the slip. . . .
>
> So soon as I get things fixed with the Admiral I shall go to New York to complete arrangements with you. In case of failure to get a special boat from the Navy I believe you will make the grandest strike of the age by sending me down a boat as suggested in my last. The Herald could boast of such a piece of enterprise for years to come. But I yet think the Navy Department could be induced to procure for us an outside vessel which we might call our own were Ashley or some other person who is on confidential terms there authorized to promise Fox that thereafter he and the Department would be exempt from attacks in the columns of the Herald—this hint is, of course, *sub rosa.*[32]

Oscar G. Sawyer of the New York *Herald* and Henry J. Winser of the *Times* were two of the outstanding naval correspondents of the war. Sawyer, the son of a distinguished Universalist clergyman in Massachusetts, was rather exceptional among *Herald* reporters in being reserved and quiet-mannered. At seventeen he entered the service of the *Herald* during the first year of the war as an army correspondent. He became a naval reporter for the *Herald* at the time of the siege of Yorktown and continued to report naval happenings for that newspaper for the remainder of the war. A large proportion of the letters and dispatches sent to the *Herald* from the squadrons commanded by David G. Farragut, Louis M. Goldsborough, David D. Porter, and other famous admirals were composed by this soft-spoken *Herald* reporter. At one time during the war, Sawyer acted as private secretary to Admiral

Farragut, and he was on Farragut's flagship at Mobile Bay at the time of the famous command: "Damn the torpedoes. Full speed ahead."

Winser had been with the *Times* almost from the time it was founded, first as a proofreader and later as a reporter of local news. When war came, he left the newspaper to help Colonel Elmer E. Ellsworth recruit the first regiment of fire Zouaves from the ranks of the fire department of the city of New York. Subsequently, as private secretary, he accompanied Ellsworth to the battlefront. Following Ellsworth's tragic death in Alexandria, Winser went back to newspaper work and soon was commissioned to represent the *Times* on the joint land and sea expedition that captured Port Royal during the autumn of 1861. Possibly his father's having been a British naval officer had something to do with Winser's undertaking to report war news from the quarter-deck of a United States war vessel. During the spring of 1862 he had one of the greatest newspaper triumphs of the war when his account of the naval bombardment of Forts Jackson and St. Philip below New Orleans and the passing of the Forts by Farragut's ships was published in the *Times* in advance of any other newspaper.[33]

Much of the press correspondence published during the war was written in railway cars and on steamboats, on camp chests, on stumps, and even, at one time, if we are to believe one of his fellow reporters, on the broad chest of a slumbering colleague.[34] On the night after a great battle the army correspondents frequently sat up all night to write by the dim light of the camp fire or of the commissary candles. At daybreak they would saddle their horses and gallop off, sparing neither themselves nor their mounts, until the product of their all-night vigil was safely on its way to the newspaper office. Sometimes an army reporter returned from a long ride so exhausted that he physically was unable to write. In such emergencies a shorthand expert often was pressed into service to commit the correspondent's story to writing. Ordinarily the men employed by the larger papers were provided with special messengers who conveyed their letters and dispatches to the nearest post or telegraph office. In the case of a big story, correspondents were under instructions from their employers to act as their own messengers, not simply to gain time but also to superintend the printing and assist in the preparation of appropriate editorial comment.[35] Nevertheless correspondence from the front was seldom less than three or four days old before it was published and sometimes much older than that.[36]

Some of the stratagems utilized by the war correspondents to smuggle news through the lines were exceedingly clever. On one occasion, a Union soldier released from Libby Prison, where he had been confined in the company of several *Herald* correspondents, called at the *Herald* office upon his arrival in New York, cut a button from his military coat, and presented it to the editor. When the button was pried open, a letter written on thin tissue paper was found that described the state of affairs in Richmond. The letter had been handed to the soldier by one of the *Herald* correspondents in Libby. Another correspondent concealed a similar letter wrapped in tin foil within a quid of tobacco which he gave to a soldier about to be exchanged. Before the soldier left the prison, his mouth was examined in a routine search, but, anticipating this procedure, he had removed the quid from his mouth and had avoided detection. Save for a yellow stain or two, the letter reached its destination without mishap.[37]

As a rule, newspaper editors did not require their correspondents to expose themselves to enemy gunfire in the line of duty, but the more enterprising reporters assumed the risks of battle like any soldier, following columns of attack, riding along the lines, and locating themselves at the most strategic points for obtaining a better view of the field. In some cases they even picked up the muskets of fallen soldiers and used them. Fatalities were not uncommon. A Chicago *Journal* reporter was killed outright at the storming of Fort Henry. Another Chicago reporter was struck by a cannon ball and killed while riding with Grant at Shiloh. Arthur B. Fuller, brother of the gifted transcendentalist critic Margaret Fuller and an occasional correspondent of the Boston *Journal*, died at Fredericksburg. Several other newspaper men failed to recover from wounds received in battle, and no less than eight died of camp diseases.

While riding to the front in one battle, David P. Conyngham of the *Herald* was accosted by a general who wanted to know who he was. Upon being informed, the military man remarked with a sneer that he didn't think newspaper correspondents would go far in *that* battle and turned away. Soon they were enveloped by a hot fire in which the general fell, badly wounded. Thereupon Conyngham, who was only a few paces away from his former interlocutor when he fell, coolly remarked, "You see, sir, that correspondents go farther than generals here," and he quietly rode on in search of news.[38]

One of the most tedious and difficult tasks of the correspondent in the field was the collection of casualty statistics. For several days after a great battle the army reporters were kept busy checking names on the regimental rolls. During McClellan's retreat from the Peninsula, the army newspaper men agreed to entrust compilation of accurate casualty lists to the Associated Press. Before the new system had had a fair trial, however, the New York *Tribune* obtained and printed one of the lists before it had been released by the Associated Press. With this, the old competitive system returned.[39]

During the long hiatus between battles, the men in the field, lacking anything more exciting to write about, indulged in speculation concerning future movements, described camp life, discussed such diverse subjects as the army diet, the weather, the physical condition of the troops, the unseemly behavior of Southern women, and, in the absence of other topics, elaborated on "the situation." From time to time, certain bold spirits criticized abuses in army administration, abuses such as vandalism, unsanitary camps, shocking neglect of the wounded by incompetent surgeons, waste in the commissariat, clothing Union troops in Confederate gray uniforms, and many others. The unpopularity of such correspondents at army headquarters readily can be understood.

Some army reporters were very skillful in improvising material for a good news story. At the time the Army of the Potomac was reorganized in March, 1864, Finley Anderson of the New York *Herald* rode over to the headquarters of General William H. French to have a visit with the General, only to find that he and General George Sykes already had left camp after issuing farewell orders to their troops. Anderson then went to see General Alfred Pleasanton, who, he learned, also was to be relieved. Pleasanton, afforded a glimpse of French's farewell remarks by the agreeable *Herald* correspondent, decided to prepare a farewell speech of his own. As both Pleasanton and General John Newton, who also was to be superseded, were leaving for Washington the following morning, Anderson made arrangements to acompany them so that he might forward from Washington an account of the recent changes in command. During the journey, assuming the liberty of an old acquaintance, he asked Newton whether he had issued a farewell address to his troops. The General admitted that he had not as yet done so. Seizing the opportunity, Anderson pointed out that Generals Sykes, French, and Pleasanton each had issued brief addresses, copies of which were in his, Anderson's, possession. "My account would be incomplete without an address from you," he added. After some consideration, Newton agreed to oblige his newspaper friend, and his address later appeared in the *Herald* before anyone in his recent command had any inkling that such a thing had been written.[40]

Such were the day-to-day experiences of the field correspondents. Ubiquitous, irrepressible, observing the letter of military law while taking liberties with its spirit, they roved about from one part of the war zone to another, gathering the details of a battle in the midst of its dangers, bivouacking on the ground in all kinds of weather, and often journeying to the rear through guerrilla-infested country. Few correspondents possessed the stamina to remain in the field continuously; fewer still, perhaps, would have cared to remain. Yet Stedman did not speak for himself alone when, looking back upon his wartime experiences as a reporter from the comfortable distance of several decades, he declared, "They still are what I would not have missed, and what could never occur to me again."[41]

5

The First Fruits of the Censorship

WHILE in London as Minister to the Court of St. James's, Edward Everett once had occasion to discuss the Battle of Waterloo with the Duke of Wellington while both were at a dance in the ballroom of Devonshire House, The Duke had just received a letter from a man who was about to write a description of the battle and was seeking information. The Duke said:

> I answered him that by comparing and studying the almost innumerable printed descriptions of the battle, English, French, and German, a man of sense could acquire a better knowledge of it at the present day than anybody, even the Commander-in-Chief, could get at the time from personal observation. Suppose that anyone should ask us tomorrow morning to describe the position and movements of all the groups of dancers in this small space before us, we should not be able to report anything beyond what concerned a few of the more prominent personages on the floor. Much less can any individual observation extend to the detailed movements of numerous bodies of men extended over several miles.

Everett went on to comment:

> If such was the modest reserve with which so consummate a chief as Wellington habitually spoke of his personal knowledge of the details of the great event of his life, the memorable engagement fought under his own orders—how little can be expected of the most intelligent and active spectator, who necessarily occupies a post of safe observation, who is borne away in a tumultuous retreat, and writes a hurried report by the next mail!

To this theme, journalists often recurred during the trying days which followed the great battles of the Civil War.[1]

The First Fruits of the Censorship

The first Battle of Bull Run furnished the opening major test of the performance of the press in the field. Although some of the best journalists were on hand to describe the fighting, the reporting of Bull Run evinced certain shortcomings which were to become more glaring as the war went on: incomplete information, inaccurate statements, and artificial heightening of the dramatic effect of the narrative. Perhaps the best excuse that could be made for the uneven record of the reporters at Bull Run was that the excited state of the public mind made both press and government feel that it was neither wise nor safe to reveal the exact truth of this disgraceful episode.[2]

Even after the fall of Fort Sumter, few people in the North expected a long-drawn-out war. Most Northerners so thoroughly believed that the South was playing a game of bluster and bluff that they fancied the war still might be won by a display of force and with a minimum of bloodshed. As late as the autumn of 1861, Alexander K. McClure, a prominent Pennsylvania politician, was appalled to hear the prediction from General Burnside that the capture of Richmond would cost the lives of ten thousand soldiers![3] During the fortnight which followed Sumter, however, there was justifiable concern throughout the North because of the exposed and unprotected position of the national capital.

A week after Sumter, on the nineteenth of April, Henry Villard, one of the ablest and most conscientious reporters of that era, started back from New York to the imperiled Capital with the message from Bennett to Lincoln that the *Herald* was ready to throw its support to the administration. As his Washington-bound train clacked along the rails, recollections of the hardships and disappointments which had filled his earlier life well may have passed through Villard's mind.

Difficulties with his father, resulting from his participation in the revolutionary movements of 1848, had caused Villard to leave Germany and to emigrate to America when he was only eighteen and a half. Henry Villard was not his original name. He had been christened Ferdinand Heinrich Gustav Hilgard, Hilgard being the family surname. Fearing, however, that his father would have him returned to Germany and placed in the ranks of the army, young Hilgard decided for his own protection to adopt the name of a former schoolmate, Henri Villard, a name later anglicized to Henry Villard.

From New York, where he landed in 1853 with only twenty dollars in his pocket, and that borrowed on shipboard, Villard proceeded west by easy stages, eventually arriving at the home of relatives in Belleville,

Illinois. He decided that the legal profession offered the best opportunities for advancement, and he sought a legal education by reading law, first in a Belleville, and then in a Peoria, law firm. In both places, however, there was not enough privacy for study. Lacking sufficient means to enter law school, Villard turned from the law to peddling books, to selling real estate, and to other employments. Once he became interested in a scheme for settling Germans in Kansas, and he journeyed to Washington in an unsuccessful effort to secure a federal land donation.

Eventually he turned to newspaper work. During the Panic of 1857, when many similar adventurers literally died of starvation, the unemployed and almost penniless Villard made the rounds of the New York newspaper offices. At the office of the New York *Evening Post* he suggested to John Bigelow that the *Post* send him to India to report the Sepoy Mutiny.[4] Bigelow promised him twenty dollars for every letter that he wrote from that country, but Villard did not go to India. A school-teaching job in a small Pennsylvania Dutch community tided him over the winter, and during the following year, as business conditions began to improve so did his fortunes. Having already acquired some preliminary experience in journalism as editor of a small-town German-language newspaper in Wisconsin during the fall campaign of 1856, Villard found employment as a special correspondent of the New York *Staats Zeitung.*[5] In that capacity he returned to Illinois to report the widely publicized Lincoln-Douglas debates of 1858.

On his previously mentioned trip to Washington, Villard had met Douglas, but this was his first introduction to Lincoln. Although he saw the man from Springfield many times during the course of that historic campaign, a special opportunity to view Lincoln at close range was afforded to Villard as a result of an accidental meeting at a flag railroad station about twenty miles west of Springfield one evening near the end of the summer. While waiting for the train, the two men were compelled by a sudden thunderstorm to take refuge together in an empty freight car on a side track nearby. Huddled together on the floor of the car, they discussed many subjects.

During their conversation, Lincoln frankly admitted that at one time he did not consider himself qualified for the United States Senate. And he still continued to say to himself every day, "It is too big a thing for you; you will never get it." But Lincoln also humorously informed his attentive listener that "Mary [Mrs. Lincoln] insists, however, that I am going to be Senator and President of the United States, too. Just think," exclaimed Lincoln, shaking all over with mirth at his wife's ambition, "of such a sucker as me as President!"[6]

Villard's reporting of the senatorial campaign in Illinois put him in line for other journalistic opportunities. Following the presidential campaign of 1860, which he reported for the St. Louis *Missouri Democrat,* the New York *Tribune,* and the Cincinnati *Commercial,* he was stationed at Springfield, Illinois, by the New York *Herald* to report the day-by-day actions of the President-elect. Villard remained in Springfield until Lincoln departed for Washington, and from Springfield he forwarded to the *Herald* daily dispatches which, under the rules of the Associated Press, were shared with other newspapers throughout the country. Since he also corresponded freely at this time with several of the Western papers, a considerable proportion of the political news given to the public during the critical period from December, 1860, to March, 1861, was supplied by this immigrant youth, who only two years previously had mastered the English language sufficiently to write for the English-language press.

Villard's more immediate difficulties on his trip from New York to Washington began, however, at Perryville, Maryland, some forty miles north of Baltimore, where his train came to an abrupt halt, and the passengers were told that they would have to remain at Perryville at least overnight. Not until the following morning did the *Herald* man learn the reason for this departure from schedule: the bloody riots which had occurred in Baltimore the day before when the Sixth Massachusetts Regiment, hastening to the relief of Washington, attempted to march through the streets of the city. To reach Washington, Villard first had to hire a boat to ferry him across the Susquehanna to Havre de Grace. From there he went on to Baltimore in a planter's buggy, which he managed to hire. At Baltimore he had to post a hundred dollars as security for the loan of a saddle horse to cover the remaining forty miles to the Capital.[7]

For more than a week all communication by rail or telegraph between Washington and the North was suspended. Everyone who could leave the Capital did so. At Willard's, where nearly a thousand guests had been in residence at the time of Lincoln's inauguration, less than forty remained. Not until the arrival on April 25 of the Seventh New York Regiment, which had come by rail from Annapolis after making a wide detour around Baltimore, did loyal Washingtonians breathe easily again. From Havre de Grace on April 27 Villard was able to notify the Chicago

Tribune, which shared his telegrams and letters with the *Herald,* that:

> After a few days interruption, I am again able to supply you with news from Washington. I am obliged to do this, however, in a rather roundabout way owing to the cutting off of all telegraph & railroad facilities between the capital & the North. I have started a courier-line between Perryville (opposite this point on the left bank of the Susquehanna river) the nearest telegraph & mail station beyond the reach of the secessionists & Co. The distance is 78 miles, which the couriers make in ten hours. They will start every morning from *W* & reach here early in the evening —in time for dispatching to morning papers. Their route is by way of Baltimore, but as I employed none but reliable & discreet men, there is no danger of an interruption. In order to insure expeditiousness, I established six relay-stations, working as many horses once daily each way.—The expense is, of course, heavy. But the *Herald* will bear by far the largest portion of it. Your share will not exceed five or six dollars per day—an amount which is hardly more than the saving in the cost of telegraphing by the overland transmission for nearly 80 miles.[8]

Other troop reinforcements now were coming in daily from Northern cities. Within a month, more than the seventy-five thousand troops for which the President originally had asked already had reached Washington, and travel through Baltimore had been resumed. In the face of such a concentration of troops along the Potomac, the public grew impatient for a forward movement, and the press began to clamor for action. "Forward to Richmond! Forward to Richmond!" chanted the New York *Tribune*. "The Rebel Congress must not be allowed to meet there on the 20th of July!"

Shortly before the end of May, Federal troops crossed the Potomac to forestall any Confederate attempt to seize and occupy Arlington Heights. While the movement was in progress, Colonel Elmer E. Ellsworth, who commanded a New York regiment of Fire Zouaves, was shot by the proprietor of a second-class hotel in Alexandria, whose flagpole had flown a secession flag for several days. Among the eyewitnesses of the tragedy were Edward H. House, a representative of the New York *Tribune*, and Ellsworth's military secretary, Lieutenant Henry J. Winser, who caught Ellsworth in his arms as the Colonel fell, mortally wounded.[9] Colonel Ellsworth's funeral received wide publicity in the newspapers, partly because he was the first fatal casualty of the war on the Northern side and also because of his close personal friendship with the President. On the day of the funeral, the solemn procession was halted by an unsubstantiated report that a battle was in progress somewhere in the vicinity of Arlington Heights. The funeral escort dashed off to repel the enemy only to discover that the "battle" was a training exercise of the New York Seventh Regiment![10]

A few days after the affray at Alexandria, the press had an opportunity to needle the military authorities about a check which Major General Benjamin F. Butler's troops had received at Big Bethel, Virginia, a few miles above Fortress Monroe. Two columns of troops had been sent out by Butler to deliver a simultaneous attack at dawn. In the dim starlight one of the commands mistook the other for the enemy and opened fire. Although the mistake was discovered before serious loss had resulted, the morale of the troops was affected seriously. Moreover, the attack on the enemy position at Big Bethel which followed was unsuccessful. Among the casualties was Major Theodore Winthrop, Butler's aide and military secretary, whose story of the march of the New York Seventh Regiment to Washington, published in the *Atlantic Monthly*,[11] had attracted nation-wide attention. The account of the fight at Big Bethel that appeared in the New York *Herald*[12] sought to represent the result as a Federal victory, but as further information became available it was only too clear that someone had blundered. One of the most scathing attacks on the military imbecility exhibited at Big Bethel was written for the Cincinnati *Commercial* by Murat Halstead, who was in Washington at the time and, incidentally, was no particular friend of Ben Butler.[13]

During the early part of June, 1861, Charles Carleton Coffin came to Washington to gather war news for the Boston *Journal*. Coffin had the distinction of being one of the few army correspondents who remained on the job throughout the war.[14] This particular "historian of the war" once had been a New Hampshire farm boy, whose Puritan ancestors had come to America on the eve of the English civil war of the seventeenth century. Although young Coffin attended the district schools and had the advantage of several terms in the local academy at Boscawen, much of his education came from self-directed reading. Particularly influential was a textbook on surveying, upon which he chanced one winter while recovering from a serious illness. From this well-thumbed little volume, Coffin obtained a knowledge of engineering principles that stood him in good stead years later when he was called upon to explain the problems of military strategy to the readers of the Boston *Journal.* Another of his youthful pastimes was listening to the tales of soldier life repeated by veterans of the American Revolutionary War, in which his own grandfather had fought. Perhaps it was these tingling narratives that inspired him at thirteen to troop along after the militia during its musters on the local parade ground and to drill his fellow school boys in the manual of arms.

Before he entered newspaper work in Boston in 1853, Coffin sampled a variety of jobs. He had tried school-teaching, clerking in a grocery store, lumbering, working as a construction engineer for one of the local railroad lines, and contributing articles to some of the newspapers in Concord, New Hampshire. His first newspaper job in Boston was with the *Journal,* with which he served a three-months apprenticeship, without pay. During his "cub" newspaper days, Coffin came to realize that:

> what the public wanted was news in condensed form; that the day for stately editorials was passing away; that short statements and arguments, which went like an arrow straight to the mark, were what the public would be likely to read.[15]

With this in mind he formed an incisive newswriting style of sentences and preponderantly of pithy Anglo-Saxon words. In 1856 he became assistant editor of the Boston *Atlas,* which at one time had been the leading Whig newspaper in Massachusetts. The *Atlas* was in difficulties, however, and during the hard times of 1857 it was merged with the Boston *Traveller.* Coffin had no regular newspaper connection for some time after that, although he continued to do occasional reporting for the *Journal* and for some of the other Boston newspapers.

Perhaps the most exciting experience of Coffin's peacetime newspaper days was attending the Republican National Convention of 1860 in Chicago, where Lincoln edged out Seward for the coveted presidential nomination. After the result had been decided, Coffin went down to Springfield with the committees designated by the Convention to notify Lincoln of the great honor he had just won. Including the newspaper men, there were approximately thirty people aboard the special train that raced southward from Chicago behind one of the Illinois Central Railroad's fastest locomotives. It was after eight o'clock that Saturday evening when the committee called at the Lincoln home and were shown into the parlor on the left side of the front hall. While Lincoln, dressed in a black frock coat, stood self-consciously in front of the fireplace, George Ashmun, the president of the committee, made the formal announcement. The following morning Coffin visited Lincoln's law office, and while Coffin talked about public affairs with Lincoln and his secretary, John G. Nicolay, he observed the plain furnishings of the large square room and its general air of untidiness.[16]

During the campaign that followed, Coffin reported one political meeting after another for the *Journal*. Soon after the election he became night editor of the paper, but lost his job a few months later when the *Journal* began laying off its employees because of the recession. When war came, Coffin tried to join the army but was rejected because of a lame heel, the result of a surveying accident. Thereupon, at the prompting of his old friend, Senator Henry Wilson of Massachusetts, Coffin went to Washington in June, 1861, and began sending letters at his own risk to the *Journal*, which, as it turned out, was only too glad to publish them.

Wherever he went during the next four years, Coffin was heartily welcomed by the generals and the soldiers. They liked him because of his ability, his geniality, his fondness for repartee, and his courage. He did not set himself up as a critic of army movements; instead he described what he saw or knew on good authority to be true. Once, so the story goes, he rode forty miles to ascertain the truth of an important report.[17] While Coffin never avoided the hardships of the march, he found by experience that through remaining near headquarters he was better able to ascertain the plans of the commanding general and thereby to obtain a better understanding of the movements of the army as a whole. He had what amounted to a sixth sense for recognizing the signs of an impending movement: the loading of a barge, the quick departure of an orderly, or the nod of a general's head. Unlike most other correspondents, he made frequent use of diagrams to enable the reader to visualize more readily the movements of the army.

Being a gifted musician, in addition to all his other accomplishments, Coffin soon learned to identify the notes and tones of various types of projectiles: round and conical bullet, globular and case shot, shell or rocket. Standing behind a cannon, he was able to follow the path of the projectile; from the side he observed the short plug of compressed air in front of a ball, which shows up clearly in a photograph. He also noted how a variation in the amount of the powder charge changed the pitch of the ball, and how certain shells with ragged edges did more harm to the morale of the men by their unearthly screams than by the injuries they caused. From long practice in observing the peculiarities in physical appearance, mannerisms, and speech of the men in the various regiments, he usually could tell from what state and even from what locality a regiment had come.

Coffin's personal bravery won for him the respect of those to whom courage was a familiar sight. One soldier remarked:

> He would talk to the commander as no civilian could or would, but Meade usually took it pleasantly, and Grant always welcomed it, and seemed glad to get it.[18]

After he had satisfied his first impulse to discover what it was like to be under fire, Coffin never exposed himself needlessly. But when it was necessary for him to go into the front lines for information, he did not flinch from exposure to danger. Many a soldier, feeling the impulse to turn and run, was heartened by Coffin's cool behavior. Years later, one of the soldiers told how during his first battle he was frightened by the shot flying around him and would have run away if he had dared. Presently he noticed a man standing under a tree some little distance away and writing as methodically as if he were standing at a desk. The soldier inquired who the man was and learned that it was Coffin, the *Journal* correspondent. Said the soldier:

> There he stood, perfectly unconcerned, and I felt easier every time I looked at him. Finally he finished and went off to another place. But that was his reputation among the men all through the war,—perfectly cool, and always at the front.[19]

Soon after his arrival in Washington in June, 1861, Coffin visited Arlington Heights, where he found a number of Union troops encamped under the trees on the Lee estate. Among the debris scattered through the house were several military maps which had been left behind, presumably by "Marse Robert." While the *Journal* reporter was poking about, he suddenly became aware of cannonading, which sounded as if it were only a mile or so away. Hurrying to Alexandria, Coffin discovered that a reconnoitering party of the First Regiment of Ohio Volunteers earlier had run into an ambush at Vienna, along the railroad line between Alexandria and Leesburg.[20] The Ohio boys had sustained minor casualties (five men killed, six wounded, and thirteen missing). Although such a small fracas hardly would have been worthy of mention later in the war, Brigadier General Robert C. Schenck, the ranking officer with the party, received considerable criticism from the press because of his supposed negligence. Newspaper accounts of the ambush also overemphasized the importance of the "masked batteries" of the Confederates, which were to become an even greater bugaboo to the army reporters in the campaign that followed.

On the twenty-ninth of June, 1861, there was a strategy meeting at the White House to which President Lincoln summoned his leading generals. Winfield Scott, the aged commander in chief, then 75, opposed the idea of immediate battle, but he was overruled by the President, who was sensitive to the clamor of the press for action. Brigadier General Irvin McDowell, in charge of field operations, then was asked to present a plan for an attack upon the Confederate position. After a brief discussion the plan was approved, and McDowell was requested to speed up preparations since the enlistments in his regiments were due to expire within a few weeks.[21]

The principal Confederate army of twenty-three thousand men under General Beauregard was encamped near Manassas Junction, the point of intersection of the Orange and Alexandria and the Manassas Gap railroads, about thirty miles southwest of Washington. A second Confederate army of about nine thousand men under Brigadier General Joseph E. Johnston was encamped near Winchester in the Shenandoah Valley, where it faced a slightly larger Union army under Major General Robert Patterson. McDowell's plan was to advance from Washington by way of Fairfax Court House and Centreville and to attack Beauregard while Patterson kept watch on Johnston to prevent a junction of the two Confederate armies. After considerable prodding, McDowell's "Grand Army" of slightly more than thirty thousand men, made up for the most part of three-months volunteers with a sprinkling of regulars and a fair complement of artillery, broke camp on July 16 and moved forward toward Centreville, a town of three to four hundred, twenty-two miles from Washington. Many of McDowell's soldiers were armed with condemned muskets, bought in Europe by agents of the War Department, which may very well have been more dangerous to them than they were to the enemy.[22]

Despite the difficulty of procuring passes, the press was well represented in the field. Editors of small-town papers rubbed elbows with correspondents of metropolitan dailies. To the newspapermen the whole affair was something of a lark. In fact there was considerable speculation among the army scribes whether the Southern bravos after all their loud talk actually would stand up and fight. On the evening of the seventeenth, E. C. Stedman of the New York *World* wrote to his wife:

> I have just time to drop you a line to say that I am very well, though tired, not having slept since yesterday and eating little but corn-cake. To-night I mean to get some sleep on the stoop of a farm-house—though I'm afraid my Secession blankets, captured to-day, will give me the itch or measles.
>
> We had a perfectly magnificent time to-day. I never enjoyed a day so much in my life. Was in the van throughout, at the head of the army, and it was exciting and dramatic beyond measure.[23]

Notably absent from the press corps which accompanied McDowell was the special correspondent of the London *Times,* William H. Russell, who had been in America since March, 1861.[24] During April and May, Russell had made a rapid tour of the Southern states, a tour which led him to believe that there was little possibility of the Union's being restored by force of arms. Subsequently he had gone down to Fortress Monroe to have a look at Butler's command. On the sixteenth of July, the day of the advance, Russell had returned to Washington, but was unable to get either a horse or a conveyance that day.[25]

On the morning of the eighteenth, one of the brigades in General Dan Tyler's division made a reconnaissance along the road between Centreville and Manassas which resulted in an unsuccessful skirmish near Blackburn's Ford. During the fighting three war correspondents—Villard, Stedman, and House—came upon a farm house in the battle area. The door was locked, but in the yard was a cherry tree laden with ripe fruit. While Villard was climbing the tree for some fruit, a rebel brigade concealed in a nearby thicket opened fire. The frightened reporter dropped to the ground and scurried for shelter behind the farm house. House and Stedman were there before him. Years afterwards Villard recalled that the volley which drove him from the cherry tree was as hot as any he experienced in any campaign of the war.[26]

During the melee a rifle bullet, which passed uncomfortably close to his ear, completely unnerved Adams S. Hill, House's assistant. It frightened him so badly that he galloped all the way back to Washington with the report that five hundred men had been killed and that "the press" had fled the field.[27] Actually the total casualties on the Northern side—killed, wounded, and missing—were less than a hundred. That night, after the fighting was over, a group of New York reporters contributed a dollar and a half apiece toward hiring a messenger to deliver their accounts of the skirmish to Washington. Because of the extreme heat, they agreed to recompense their agent for the loss of his horse if the ride should prove fatal.[28]

In a letter to his wife written the following day, one of the New York *Times* correspondents told how:

> We stood on the hill above Bull's Run, and saw the whole affair, and suddenly had the cannon-balls flying among us. I tell you, the first experience of a round shot, whirring over one's head, is a sensation. Every one ducks and *whirr!* they go right over you .... I have written a long account for the "Times." Our men did not act very well, and the enemy were well posted. It was a trap for us. We go to the same point to-day, and will attack them with a larger force. It was the most exciting day of my life, yesterday, and I could hardly sleep, tired as I was.[29]

On the afternoon of the eighteenth, General McDowell arrived at Centreville, where he received word that Tyler had engaged the enemy in spite of orders to the contrary. The Commanding General was considerably annoyed and expressed his annoyance in soldierlike terms. During the next two days, the army remained inactive. At noon on the twentieth, while McDowell still was attempting to determine by reconnaissance the best method of turning Beauregard's left, Johnston slipped away from Patterson and joined Beauregard with the main body of his command. General Scott in Washington received the bad news that same afternoon and promptly telegraphed it to McDowell, but the latter did not see fit to change his plans. At ten o'clock that night it was announced in camp that the army would begin its advance within four hours. One hour later the editor of the New York *Times*, who had come down from Washington to direct the efforts of the *Times* staff in the field, was hard at work writing a letter for his newspaper:

> This is one of the most beautiful nights that the imagination can conceive. The sky is perfectly clear, the moon is full and bright, and the air as still as if it were not within a few hours to be disturbed by the roar of cannon and the shouts of contending men. ... An hour ago I rode back to Gen. McDowell's head-quarters, a mile and a half distant, at the foot of a sloping hill, along and beyond which the ten or fifteen regiments are encamped. As I rose over the crest of the hill, and caught a view of the scene in front, it seemed a picture of enchantment. The bright moon cast the woods which bound the field into deep shadows, through

which the camp-fires shed a clear and brilliant glow. On the extreme right, in the neighborhood of the Fire Zouaves, a party were singing the "Star-Spangled Banner," and from the left rose the sweet strains of a magnificent band, intermingling opera airs ... with the patriotic bursts of "Hail Columbia" and Yankee Doodle. ... Everything here is quiet, save the sounds of the music and the occasional shout of a soldier, or the lowing of the cattle, whose dark forms spot the broad meadow in the rear. ...

I have been very kindly furnished with a saddle-horse by Major Wadsworth, and shall join the General's staff at 3 o'clock.[30]

At 2:00 A.M., Sunday, July 21, the army began to stir. In order to get a good view of the march, *World* correspondent Stedman started at the extreme rear and rode all the way along the line to the front. For a few moments he stopped to talk with Lieutenant Colonel James Haggerty of the Sixty-ninth New York Regiment, who mentioned some newspaper accounts of his death that had been published the day before and who laughingly remarked that he felt very warlike for a dead man.[31] Meanwhile, McDowell's men were having trouble finding their places in the dark, and the various commands were late in getting into position. One of the *Tribune* correspondents thought he noticed even at that hour a lack of unity and purpose among the officers, which could hardly fail to communicate itself to the ranks.[32]

While William A. Croffut of the New York *Tribune* was on his way to the battlefield, he noticed a civilian wearing a long linen duster and carrying a box as large as a beehive strapped to his shoulders. His name was "Napoleon Bonaparte" Brady,[33] he said, and he explained that he was a photographer. As Brady mopped his sweaty brow, he remarked:

> I know well enough that I cannot take a photograph of a battle, but I can get a little glimpse of some corner somewhere that will be worth while. We are making history now, and every picture that we get will be valuable.[34]

Croffut also noticed Senator Henry Wilson of Massachusetts sitting in a top buggy in a field alongside the road and overhead him asking where "Tecumseh" Sherman's brigade was. Staring at his watch, the Senator remarked gloomily to one of the officers, "You are three hours late at this point." It was then exactly eight o'clock.[35] Tyler's artillery already had opened fire at six-fifteen, hurling shells along the Warrenton Turnpike beyond the Stone Bridge across Bull Run. As the Confederate batterymen did not accept the challenge, Tyler spent the next three or four hours pushing his skirmishers and infantry gradually down toward the banks of the stream, intermittently shelling the Confederate positions of the opposite bank. Sometime between half-past ten and eleven o'clock that morning the correspondents with Tyler heard the sound of musketry over on the right, indicating that the flanking column under Colonels David Hunter and Samuel P. Heintzelman was engaging the enemy.[36]

As the battle extended over an area seven or eight miles wide, most of the reporters had only an indistinct impression of what was going on in other parts of the field. The correspondent of the Cincinnati *Gazette* had climbed a tree to get a better view of the Confederate batteries in action, but a few salvos in his direction made him retire to a safer point of observation.[37] Russell, five days after his return from Fortress Monroe, finally on the morning of the battle had driven out from Washington in a carriage with one of the attachés from the British legation. He viewed the fight from the crest of the Centreville Hill, where a large number of spectators, mostly civilians, had gathered.[38] From this point there was a magnificent view of the battlefield for miles. Far to the left was Manassas Junction, the ultimate objective for McDowell's forces. Over on the right was Manassas Gap, a cleft in the distant slopes of the Blue Ridge. Looking straight ahead, Russell could see puffs of smoke from bursting shells and clouds of dust rising above the treetops, but not the movements of the various divisions. Presently Frank Vizetelly, the artist of the *Illustrated London News*, came along with information of what was going on up ahead. He reported that the Union army had had the best of the fight so far, and then he dashed off in search of food and drink for himself and his friends.[39]

In a little Negro cabin at the edge of a woods where the wounded were being cared for, Uriah H. Painter, the Philadelphia *Inquirer* reporter, stopped for a moment to make some notes. There he found J. P. Pryor, a former newspaper editor of Memphis and Vicksburg, who just had been brought in as a prisoner. Although the Confederate journalist seemed downcast, he was not unwilling to talk. In response to Painter's questioning he admitted that the Confederate loss was heavy, but he insisted that even though the South were to lose the battle, it could never be conquered. According to Painter, Pryor had:

> no arms, not even a sword; his pants were miserable cotton stuff with a gold stripe down the sides, and his hat was a Kossuth

fastened up at the sides with a button, on which were arms of the State of Mississippi.[40]

Until midafternoon the Union army fought well. In the early stages of the battle the Confederate left wing was driven back across the Warrenton Turnpike in the direction of Manassas almost to the Henry House Plateau. Here the Union advance was stopped, and McDowell ordered two of his best batteries (Ricketts' and Griffin's) moved forward, without infantry support, to break the enemy line. To the right of McDowell's guns, a regiment of infantry appeared. Their uniforms were unrecognizable, and the Federal battery commanders hesitated to open fire on them. The men drew nearer; their commander said something to them, and their guns shattered the silence. As the smoke lifted, observers noted that the Federal batteries had been almost wiped out. Then the Confederate generals began throwing in their reserves, including the remainder of Johnston's Army of the Shenandoah under Brigadier General Edmund Kirby-Smith which just had reached the battlefield.[41]

About four o'clock, Stedman of the *World*, who was with Tyler's division near the Stone Bridge, saw a body of Confederate cavalry followed by massed infantry come dashing out of the woods that separated Tyler's command in the center from General Israel B. Richardson's brigade on the left. The woods, by somebody's oversight, had been left unguarded, and the quick Confederate maneuver threw the Union troops into confusion. By the time the *World* correspondent had reached the top of a nearby hill, Tyler's men were in headlong flight.

Several of the correspondents, according to their own testimony, strove heroically to stay the panic. U. H. Painter told of seeing Stedman waving the standards of the Fifth Massachusetts Regiment and pleading in vain for the men to rally around him. "We took muskets and threatened to shoot them down if they did not [go back]," continued Painter, "but we might as well have pled with the winds to cease blowing."[42] At that juncture a Union officer came rushing up to Stedman and begged for permission to ride behind him. Before they had gone a hundred yards, a stray bullet struck the officer in the head.[43]

While leading his horse over numerous dead bodies, a *Herald* correspondent came upon a wounded officer with the breast plate of the Mississippi Rifles. The wounded man raised himself slowly upon his elbows and leveled his gun at the correspondent. There was no time to expostulate. The reporter quickly drew his pistol and put a bullet through the officer's head.[44]

Clark Tracy of the Rochester (New York) *Express* narrowly escaped being captured; Congressman Alfred Ely, who was with him at the time, was less fortunate. Ely was hustled off to a Richmond prison where he remained in custody for several months.[45]

John Russell Young, the Philadelphia *Press* correspondent, had left the battlefield before the full extent of the counterattack was apparent. He therefore believed that the conflict had resulted in a Federal victory by a narrow margin, at the very least a drawn battle. As there was no telegraph station in Centreville, he went on to Fairfax, hoping to send his dispatches from there. When he reached Fairfax, it was already dusk. Everyone there also believed that the battle had resulted in a Union victory, but within an hour, a dispatch from General Tyler left no doubt that the Northern army was in retreat. Numerous groups of Federal troops began to straggle in, while rumors spread that a large force of rebels had taken possession of one of the roads beyond Fairfax and were hoping to capture that point and to cut off the retreat of McDowell's army. Several members of the New York press were extremely anxious to leave Fairfax forthwith. One of their number offered his gold watch and his purse to a traveler if he would drive him to Arlington, but the reporter was refused.

Croffut of the New York *Tribune* remained on the battlefield until nearly dark, when it became evident to him that the army was in full retreat. By that time the hospital at Sudley Church where he had been helping with the wounded was already within the Confederate lines. Seizing a Union artillery horse, Croffut conducted his own retreat to Centreville, where he rested for a few hours before resuming his journey to Washington.[46]

Thinking that the retreat would not extend beyond Centreville, both House of the New York *Tribune* and Joe Glenn of the Cincinnati *Gazette* remained there the night after the battle. The next morning they found that Centreville was practically deserted and that the Union army had fallen back to Washington. House went in search of Al Waud, the army artist of *Harper's Weekly*, and the two men hastily decamped together. Fully expecting Beauregard to appear at any moment, Glenn trudged all the way to Washington in a drenching rain.[47]

Probably none of the correspondents was more chagrined at the outcome of the fighting than the New York *Times* editor, Raymond. At two o'clock on Sunday afternoon while the battle was still in progress, he had wired his paper from Centreville that a victory was in the making and that all that remained was for McDowell to march on to Richmond. On the way back to the battlefield for further information, he was confronted by the Federal army in retreat. At first he refused to believe that a defeat had occurred, for all signs had indicated otherwise at the time he left the battlefield, but, finding it impossible to proceed farther, he was forced to turn back. Presently Raymond was overtaken and passed by a horseman as profoundly disgusted as he with the whole affair. It was Russell of the London *Times,* who was making all possible haste to get to Washington.

On the road about a mile east of Centreville, the crowd of fugitives around Raymond panicked, and a great mass of wagons, horses, and men on foot rushed headlong down the hill at a rate which threatened destruction to everything in their path. Raymond's driver attempted to check the speed of the carriage, but it was crushed like an egg shell by an enormous Pennsylvania army wagon. It looked as if the editor of the New York *Times* would have to walk the rest of the way to Washington, but another carriage containing a couple of Congressmen opportunely relieved him from his predicament.[48]

No one in the national capital knew what had happened. Until seven o'clock telegraphic reports unvaryingly had indicated Federal success. About dinner time President Lincoln had felt so much encouraged by what he had heard that he had called for his carriage and gone out for a drive.

At nine o'clock the Associated Press reporter, who had left the field early, arrived at the Washington office of the AP. He was breathless and exhausted from his long ride and too much agitated to write out his own account of the day's events. At the time he had left the field the enemy was in full retreat. He talked, pacing back and forth with the stump of an unlit cigar in his mouth, while Gobright, the Washington agent of the Associated Press, wrote furiously of the supposed Federal victory. By eleven o'clock or shortly after, the AP story was ready to be sent over the wires. Gobright and his reporter then left the office to see if they might not pick up some later news. In front of Brown's Hotel on Pennsylvania Avenue they came upon a hackload of passengers, one of whom had just arrived from the battlefield and was eager to recount his experience. As their informant stood there in the bright moonlight and illustrated the movements of the troops with his cane, Gobright and his companion became more and more excited, for the stage passenger was telling them news of stunning importance: there had been no Union victory. Instead, the Union army had sustained a crushing blow and was at that very moment in full retreat. The two newspaper men hurried back to the telegraph office, ordered it kept open, and rapidly began preparing new dispatches.[49]

Other correspondents began to come in. Russell pulled up in front at Willard's at exactly eleven o'clock, fifty minutes ahead of the Chicago *Tribune* reporter.[50] At midnight Raymond, sun-burned, dusty, and hardly recognizable, reached the Capital. He in turn prepared for the New York *Times*, a brief dispatch, the essential facts of the disaster.[51]

Between 2:00 A.M. and 3:00 A.M. on the twenty-second, Painter and Stedman arrived in Washington together with an exciting story. The Union retreat had been so sudden and unexpected that Painter had been trapped inside the Confederate lines. He had passed himself off as a hospital attendant, however, and then had caught a wounded army horse which came rushing through the woods. Clinging to its mane, Painter had ridden off, and later that night he overtook Stedman. As the two men were approaching the Potomac Heights early the next morning, they met Montgomery Meigs, the Quartermaster General of the Union Army, going out in search of news from the field. Meigs listened in silence to their account of the defeat and then asked Painter where he had obtained his horse. When Meigs learned that the animal was U.S. property, he instructed Painter to turn him in at the Government corral as soon as he reached Washington. The two correspondents rode on, complaining about the surly manners of military men in general and quartermaster generals in particular. Neither of them took Meigs's order very seriously, however, since they thought it highly probable that the enemy would reach Washington before they did.[52]

When the fugitive correspondents did reach Washington, they found that the telegraph office was closed. Painter thereupon decided that the quickest and surest way of getting the news to Philadelphia would be to take it there himself. The first northbound train was scheduled to leave about nine that morning. Since there was not a vacant seat on the train, the wearied correspondent stretched out on the floor of the baggage car and slept all the way into Philadelphia. When he appeared at the *Inquirer* office, there was considerable consternation. What was he doing in Philadelphia? Why was he not with the army on the way to Richmond? At first the editors refused to accept his version of what had happened, but before night there was abundant evidence that what he had said was absolutely true.[53]

Stedman had planned to leave Washington on the same train with Painter, but in the meantime, giving strict orders that he was to be called for seven o'clock breakfast, he stopped at the National Hotel for a hour's sleep. When he awoke, it was quite dark, and the hands on his watch pointed to half-past six. Dressing hastily, he went down to the dining room for breakfast. To his surprise he found that dinner was being served! Finally he realized what had happened. The hotel clerk had failed to call him at the appointed time, and, utterly exhausted, he had slept on for twelve hours! By this time the New York *World* must have been scooped by every paper in the country. Under the circumstances there was nothing he could do but take the night train to New York and prepare a comprehensive account of the battle en route.[54]

Villard did not come within sight of Washington until about five-thirty on Monday morning, the twenty-second of July. On the way out of Centreville the highway was blocked by a train of army wagons, and he had been forced to dismount and to follow a circuitous route through the woods before he could reach the highway again. Near the west end of the Long Bridge across the Potomac, he was halted and not allowed to pass until he could properly identify himself. At that early hour the streets of the Capital were almost deserted. The telegraph office was not expected to open until seven o'clock, so there was time for a quick breakfast at Willard's before Villard could send his dispatch of six hundred words, the maximum length by wire except with special permission from the editor in chief. After his message was sent, Villard slept several hours and then rode on over to General McDowell's headquarters on Arlington Heights to get information for a full report.[55] McDowell's beaten army had been streaming into Washington for several hours, and the wildest stories of the army's being cut to pieces were in circulation. In fact, Beauregard and his victorious Southerners momentarily were expected to appear on Arlington Heights.

News of the defeat had reached Washington in ample time to make all Monday morning editions, but there was no hint of disaster in that morning's newspapers. On Sunday night, for example, the New York press put out extra editions; and these were followed up on Monday morning with flaming headlines of a "glorious Union victory," which furnished the theme for numerous editorials to the effect that Sumter had been avenged.

Government censorship had produced this amazing misapprehension. On the night of April 19, 1861, within a week after the outbreak of hostilities, Secretary of State Seward had ordered stopped the transmission from Washington to Boston of the names of the Massachusetts soldiers who had been wounded in the Baltimore Riot, and a government censor had been detailed to supervise all messages sent out of the Washington telegraph office.[56] Less than two weeks before the July 21 Battle of Bull Run, General Scott had issued another order in an effort to stop the leakage of military information through the press. He forbade the transmission by telegraph from Washington of any dispatches concerning army movements unless those dispatches had been reviewed by the Commanding General.[57] Then a few days later this arrangement was superseded by an agreement between General Scott and the newspaper men, which permitted them to telegraph the "progress and results of all battles actually occurring" without submitting their copy to an army censor. The reporters were bound by the terms of the agreement, however, not to report by telegraph anything having to do with (1) arrivals, departures, or other movements of troops; (2) mutinies or riots among the soldiery; (3) predictions of movements to come. Furthermore, it was understood that a Mr. Burns of the American Telegraph Office was to act in an informal way as a censor to supervise the carrying out of the agreement.[58] This loose form of censorship was in effect on the eve of Bull Run. When General Scott learned, however, that McDowell had been defeated and that his army was in full retreat, Scott promptly imposed a strict censorship on the telegraph. Although the Washington papers were free to print what they would, not a word about the defeat was allowed to go out over the wires until Monday morning.

The first report of the defeat to be received in New York was probably Villard's preliminary telegram, which arrived early Monday morning. The more detailed account which he wired on Monday evening was so severe in its comments on the performance of the New York regiments and their officers that the editor of the *Herald* refused to publish it in its original form. Painter's story of the battle in the Philadelphia *Inquirer* was the first full-length account of the defeat to be printed. So great was the revulsion of feeling it produced, that an indignant crowd gathered along Third Street in Philadelphia outside the newspaper office and threatened to wreck it for spreading "copperhead" news.[59]

As the press and the readers became aware of the way they first had been deceived, a great outcry went up. The New York *Times* stated editorially:

> We desire it to be distinctly understood that we are not in the slightest degree responsible for what, if done deliberately by us, would be branded as a wanton and reckless trifling with the feelings of the public....
>
> It was an agent of the government,—and not the conductors of the *Times,* — who suppressed the facts of this most important case.[60]

Other newspapers voiced similar resentment.

The New York Associated Press, however, used a cunning device to evade Scott's new censorship. While the AP account of Bull Run was being prepared on Sunday night, Gobright arranged to let the proprietor of the Washington *National Republican* copy the AP account, for a specified sum, and on Monday morning the account appeared in the *National Republican.* Since correspondents of the various out-of-town papers were permitted to copy what appeared in the Washington papers and to telegraph it, Gobright clipped from the *National Republican* the AP's account of the battle and sent it on to New York for distribution and printing.[61] The Associated Press also was responsible for a scare story from its assistant agent in Philadelphia, John Hasson, the night of the battle or the following day. This story greatly exaggerated the extent of the Federal defeat, and it spread panic throughout the country. In George Alfred Townsend's opinion, this dispatch:

> was the most startling that ever issued through such an agency to the country or the world and I well remember the gloom I felt reading it on my arrival at Philadelphia from a day's excursion to Delaware City.[62]

In the excitement which followed the battle most of the correspondents were heroes to their friends. "Sted," wrote C. B. Conant, "we're all proud of you. Ludlow[63] just cried when he read of your brave thing with the flag." Richard Grant White wrote in similar vein:

> I congratulate you upon your admirable description of our hapless attack upon Manassas. It is much, very much, the best letter that has yet come from the war.... Its clearness, its scope, its systematic arrangements, and its unpretending picturesqueness are positive qualities in which it is excelled by few letters of the kind....[64]

Other correspondents received similar letters. John Russell Young's friend, G. B. P. Ringwalt, wrote to him from Philadelphia saying that:

> our fears were completely dissipated on Tuesday morning when we had the pleasure of reading your glorious letter in *The Press* —and here let me remark that there was but one expression in regard to it and that was an expression of universal admiration. This expression was by no means confined to those in the office, but at the Central,[65] at the railroad depots and in the streets, it was extensively discussed and highly praised.[66]

In other quarters, however, widespread dissatisfaction with the way the battle had been reported was coupled with an intense desire to know who was responsible for the disaster. The New York *Express* declared that "seldom or never in all our experience of journalism" had the paper experienced so much difficulty in "getting at the truth,"[67] while the St. Louis *Republican* could find very little in the various newspaper accounts, both Northern and Southern, of the Battle of Bull Run except "conflict and contradiction, from which it is impossible to infer anything save that there has been monstrous blundering and monstrous lying on both sides."[68]

Caustic comment on the reporting of the campaign was not confined to newspaper editors. An army correspondent for one of the Cincinnati papers whose account was based on first-hand observation admitted:

> the accounts of the battle given by some of the reporters are . . . embellished and amplified to such a degree as to make them almost unrecognizable. Among the humorous phases of the affair are the "you-tickle-me-and-I'll-tickle-you" statements made by some of these redoubtable individuals, as to the strenuous efforts of each other and certain Senators and Congressmen to rally the retreating troops. The idea of panic struck troops rallying at the appeals of gentlemen in white linen coats whom they never saw before is rather amusing to say the least.[69]

Some of the better accounts of the Battle of Bull Run which appeared in the Northern press were those written by Stedman, George Wilkes (the editor of a racing journal in New York who was also employed by the New York *Tribune*), John Russell Young, Henry J. Raymond, and Charles Carleton Coffin. Stedman's and Wilkes's accounts subsequently were republished in pamphlet form. Probably the most complete story of the battle that was published in a Southern newspaper appeared in the Richmond *Dispatch;* this paper's correspondent was one of the few civilians permitted to witness the battle from the Southern side.

Whereas the Northern clergy generally ascribed the Federal defeat to the battle's having been fought on Sunday, there was a great diversity of opinion among the newspaper fraternity about the causes of the disaster. "The secret of that panic will perhaps never be known," said the *Tribune* reporter, House. "All essay to explain it, and all fail."[70] It was alleged that McDowell's soldiers had been sent into action without adequate food and water; that confusion had resulted from the lack of a regulation uniform; that the army had been filled with overconfidence which was inspired by its unopposed march to Centreville; that Colonel Dixon S. Miles, who commanded the Fifth Division, had been too drunk on the day of the battle to know what he was doing and had failed to bring up the reserve at the time ordered;[71] that McDowell's army had been outnumbered two to one in over-all size (newspaper estimates of the size of the Confederate army ranged anywhere from seventy to one hundred and ten thousand) and was even more hopelessly outclassed by the splendid cavalry and artillery units of the Southerners. Subsequently a humorous story went the rounds of the newspaper exchanges that when the battle was at its height and victory trembled in the balance, the stampede of the officers and their men had been started by a rumor that there were two vacancies in the New York Customs House.[72]

No one could agree on who primarily was to blame for the debacle. "If we are to have any more battles, God save us from such Generals as Schenck," wrote the Philadelphia *Inquirer* reporter, Painter.[73] Some other newspapers placed the responsibility for the defeat on General Patterson, who had failed to prevent the junction of Johnston and Beauregard and who had not marched to the aid of McDowell after the junction. Patterson was particularly unpopular with the newspaper correspondents because he had arrested one of them[74] a few days before the battle and was generally considered unfriendly toward the newspapermen. Both McDowell and Tyler also were roundly censured; it was even alleged that McDowell was helplessly drunk throughout the battle. And the Commissary Department of the army came in for its share of abuse.

On the other hand, the press itself did not escape blame. Horace Greeley in particular was criticized for exerting pressure upon General Scott to advance into Virginia before he was adequately prepared. According to Raymond, the General had stated during a dinner-table conversation on the Tuesday preceding the battle that an advance upon Richmond was not part of his strategic plan; that, on the contrary, he wished to garrison Washington securely, institute a vigorous blockade of the Southern ports, and then sometime in the autumn march an army of eighty thousand men down the Mississippi to New Orleans. Once the Mississippi and the Atlantic were in Northern possession, the capitulation of the South, Scott felt, would be only a question of time.[75]

For the *Tribune*'s part in causing the General to deviate from his great strategic plan, Greeley did full penance in an editorial published in that newspaper on July 25, 1861. Soon afterward Fitz-Henry Warren, who generally was regarded as the originator of the "Forward to Richmond" slogan, resigned his connection with the *Tribune* to undertake a military assignment.[76] Warren did not fail to issue a vigorous counterblast against those who were disposed to make him shoulder the blame for the *Tribune*'s blunder. In a letter published in the St. Louis *Republican* some weeks after this first Battle of Bull Run, Warren denied that the phrase "Forward to Richmond" was original with him but admitted that he still believed in it and did not regret anything that he had written to the *Tribune* from Washington. In Washington he declared:

> I arrived here soon after the interruption of direct communication via Annapolis. Troops were coming in rapidly and on the service [surface] all seemed progressing well.
>
> I was not long here before I saw that under this appearance of doing, nothing was being done. There was no order and no system. Troops came in, and marched in review before the President, and went supperless to bed. They were stowed away in public buildings and private halls, with no regard to health or the modified comfort of a soldier's life. They were neither instructed in the art of war nor made to understand the discipline of the camp. . . .
>
> I have spent more hours in walking to and from the War Department, and waiting there to urge the requisition of regiments, than I have in writing letters, and for days and weeks I spent my strength for naught. I asked, over and over again, why temporary hospitals were not erected for the care of the wounded . . . but without reply. . . .
>
> I cannot go into the details of the last two months. But what shall I say of sending 25,000 men into the massacre of Bull Run? Whose madness was this? . . . No one knew the force or the position. There was no reconnoissance. Men marched into bloody graves as they walked into the doors of the homestead. Batteries blazed out at their feet, of which none but the enemy had the slightest knowledge. One half of the men engaged had nothing

> to eat after supper of the night previous. Many of them marched at double-quick for ten miles, and were under fire for hour after hour, so exhausted by hunger that they could hardly stand. . . . Artillery horses were . . . so weak from want of forage that they could not be beaten into a trot. Do you wish more of this damning testimony to imbecility? If you do, you can have it.[77]

As soon as the first afterglow of excitement was over, the paramount thought in the minds of many people was "What will Russell say?" It was realized clearly in this country that Russell's letters to the London *Times* were reprinted widely in the European press and generally were regarded abroad as an authoritative expression of what was happening in America. Because of the slow mails of that day Russell's account of Bull Run was not published in the London *Times* until August 6, some two weeks and a half after the battle. Two more weeks elapsed before copies of the *Times* containing his account reached the American public.

It is difficult to describe or exaggerate the force of the shock which Russell's letter produced. Although at the outset the American press had reported the battle and the retreat which followed in terms hardly less flattering than those which Russell employed, a reaction soon set in. On July 26, an editorial in the Cincinnati *Gazette* claimed that the panic which followed the battle was chiefly a panic of newspaper reporters who fled for their lives and then enlarged on the disaster to justify their own conduct. By the time Russell's letter reached America the public already was beginning to forget the many harsh things which had been said by its own press. Moreover, it was a blow to the national vanity to have an English newspaperman of Russell's standing write in contemptuous terms of the "disgraceful conduct" and "scandalous behavior" of an American army. From all sides abuse descended upon the correspondent of the London *Times*. It was rumored that "Bull Run" Russell had not even been an eyewitness of the battle. Charles H. Ray, one of the editors of the Chicago *Tribune,* who actually had ridden with Russell for some distance during the retreat, made a public statement accusing Russell of having given a completely false picture of the cowardly behavior of the Union troops in their flight from the battlefield.[78] Even the comic papers entered the fray, and made numerous quips at the expense of "Russell's Running Account."[79]

Northern newspaper readers were in no mood for lengthy post mortems of what the army had done or failed to do. On the whole they were anxious to forget about Bull Run and its tragic aftermath and to look to the future instead for victories yet to be won. Some, no doubt, found encouragement in a *Tribune* editorial published little more than a week after McDowell's undisciplined force came straggling back to Washington. Greeley then admonished his readers:

> It is not characteristic of Americans to sit down despondently after a defeat. . . . Reverses, though stunning at first, by their recoil stimulate and quicken to unwonted exertion, and in the end our achievement is the greater for the temporary rebuff. . . .
>
> Let us go to work, then, with a will. There is no lack of men ready and willing to serve the country in her hour of peril, if we only assure them fair treatment, good fare, immediate acceptance, and thorough instruction in the school of the soldier.[80]

6

The Curtain Slowly Rises

LIFE in the field for the war correspondents of 1861 was far less strenuous during the summer and autumn of that year than it was to be during their later campaigns. Most of the fighting during the first year of the war was in the Eastern border area, comparatively near the centers of metropolitan journalism. Furthermore, editors had little or no previous opportunity to test the performance of their representatives under battle conditions and were themselves mostly inexperienced in gathering war news. They therefore were likely to hold a slack rein on their reporters, although they stressed the importance of maintaining good relations with commanding officers.

With certain notable exceptions, relations between the army and the press were generally cordial. The commanders of the Union armies, especially those who were not professional soldiers, usually were accessible, affable, and cooperative. If they proved otherwise, information not readily available at headquarters might be wormed out of a subordinate officer seeking advancement through favorable press notices. Probably the greatest source of dissatisfaction to the correspondents in the field was the prolonged inactivity of the army, broken only by campaigns of short duration and indecisive result.[1] In a letter, written to his wife during the early fall of 1861, *World* correspondent Edmund C. Stedman groaned:

> The monotony of the encampments is insufferable; one regiment acts, talks and looks just like another—and all like Yankees. When they fight I shall be glad.[2]

Reporting in the Western war zone during 1861 mainly was related to three areas which were organized as separate commands: Western Virginia, Kentucky, and Missouri.

The rugged topography of Western Virginia created problems for the war news-gatherer which differed greatly from those confronting the writers who accompanied McDowell's undisciplined army to Bull Run. The news hawks of the Cincinnati press were first in the field to garner the details of Major General George B. McClellan's campaign in this mountain country. Indeed it was more than a month after the campaign had begun before special correspondents of the New York dailies first made their appearance in this area.[3] In the meantime the Cincinnati newspapers had almost a monopoly of the army news from Western Virginia.

Some of the best reporting of the campaign was contributed to the Cincinnati *Gazette* by the youthful Whitelaw Reid. Reid arrived in the field during the first week of June and wrote his first letters from Grafton, an important junction point on the Baltimore and Ohio Railroad about a hundred miles southeast of Wheeling. Encamped around Grafton at the time were eight regiments of Federal troops which had come by rail from Wheeling and Parkersburg only a few days before, and, before Reid reached camp, already had been involved in a minor skirmish at Philippi, a few miles south of Grafton. During his first few days at Grafton, Reid recorded the usual incidents of camp life and took special note of how little was being done to promote the comfort and well-being of the common soldier. In his first letter to the editor of the *Gazette* Reid enclosed a specimen of the shoddy cloth, consisting of factory clippings and sweepings, from which soldiers' uniforms were being made. "Put it up in the counting room," he suggested, "and let Ohioans see how Ohio troops in the field are clothed."[4] Before long he had the opportunity of observing the kind of shoes that were being issued to the Confederate soldiers, when some enemy prisoners were brought in from Philippi: the soles made of wood, glued to the uppers, and covered with stained paper. Then he realized, with something of a shock, how little difference there was between army contractors on either side.

Like most of the reporters at camp, Reid awaited with some anticipation and no little anixety another clash with the enemy. Near the end of June, Henri Lovie, a campaign artist for *Frank Leslie's*, had a narrow escape when he was sighted roaming, artist-like, over the hills by some Union sentries, who concluded from his erratic behavior that he must be an enemy scout. While he was considering their invitation to come forward and identify himself, a bullet from one of their guns whizzed uncomfortably near. As the frightened artist broke for cover, a fusillade of musket balls clipped off some twigs above his head. Later he observed, to the delight of his comrades, that he had "no objections to running reasonable risks from the enemy, but to be killed by mistake would be damnably unpleasant!"[5]

During the last week of June, Reid noted with some misgiving the arrival at Grafton of the department commander, General McClellan. McClellan was a professional soldier who had been born in Philadelphia and trained at West Point. He had made his mark in the army before leaving it, several years prior to the Civil War, to enter the railroad business. As a business executive McClellan had been as successful as he formerly had been as a soldier. Nevertheless—in spite of his distinguished record as an engineering officer during the Mexican War, in spite of the fact that he had been one of a board of officers sent to Russia during the Crimean War to make a careful study of military operations, and was for this and other reasons highly regarded by his professional colleagues—there must have been some surprise in regular army circles when in May, 1861, he was elevated in a single step from the position of a retired captain to that of a major general in the regular army. At that time he also had been placed in command of the Department of the Ohio, which then included Ohio, Indiana, and Illinois, and to which later were added certain portions of Western Pennsylvania and Virginia.[6]

His personal appearance was not particularly striking if one may judge from a description by a New York *Tribune* correspondent at Cairo, Illinois, a few days before McClellan entered the field in Western Virginia. To the *Tribune* reporter McClellan was:

> a stoutly-built man, somewhat below medium hight [sic], with light hair, blue eyes, and a full, youthful-looking face, with no beard except a brown moustache.

There was nothing about McClellan, the *Tribune* man thought, to cause anyone to select him out of a crowd to hold the highest command in the army next to General Scott. He admitted, however, that the General's manner was "quite devoid of hauteur" and that he was "personally extremely popular" with officers and men.[7]

On June 27, Reid informed his brother by letter that he was on the point of starting for Philippi. He added:

> A battle is expected there in a day or two more important & bloody than any since the beginning of the insurrection. It is utterly impossible for me to predict my future movements. I have

> orders to keep with the advance of the army & hope to be at Richmond before the summer is over. . . .
>
> I go with any of the Generals, as circumstances may dictate. Gen. Morris is the senior Brigadier & will command at the approaching battle, unless Gen. McClellan comes over. In that case I shall be with his staff.[8]

At this time the main body of the enemy under General Robert S. Garnett, comprising some thirty-three hundred men, was posted on Laurel Hill, sixteen miles north of Beverly. McClellan's plan of campaign called for General Morris to push his brigade forward to Philippi in order to menace the enemy position on Laurel Hill and to give the impression that the main attack was to be made there. Meanwhile McClellan was to move with the main body of his troops, consisting of three brigades, from Clarksburg to Beverly via Buckhannon and thence up the Beverly pike to the east side of the Laurel range. Before he could reach Beverly, McClellan was halted by a brigade of thirteen hundred enemy troops, commanded by Lieutenant Colonel John Pegram, which occupied a strongly fortified position on Rich Mountain to the west of Beverly. Since a frontal attack upon this unexpected opponent promised to be costly, McClellan decided to send a detachment of two thousand men under the command of Brigadier General William S. Rosecrans around the left flank of the enemy and at the proper moment execute a simultaneous attack, front and rear. After a stiff fight Rosecrans succeeded in carrying out his part of the program, but the movement failed of complete success because of McClellan's tardiness. As a result, Pegram made his escape from the trap closing around him and fled northward to join General Garnett on Laurel Hill.

After marching for eighteen hours in that direction, the retreating force learned that Garnett had abandoned his position on Laurel Hill and was also in retreat. Thereupon Pegram reversed his course and, finding himself caught once more between two Union commands with no possibility of escape, he surrendered with the remnants of his force to McClellan on the evening of July 12. Garnett's movement proved only slightly less disastrous to the Confederate cause. While retreating southward toward Beverly, the Confederate general received an erroneous report that it had already been occupied by McClellan's troops. Since escape to the southward now appeared to be out of the question, he turned north again to seek refuge in the mountains. At about noon on the thirteenth, the Confederates were overtaken by the pursuit column of General Morris at Carrick's Ford on the Cheat River, about twenty-six miles northwest of Laurel Hill. Sharp fighting ensued, and Garnett himself was killed. Subsequently the remnants of his retreating force made their escape in spite of the efforts of McClellan's other brigade commanders to intercept their flight at West Union, Virginia.[9]

Both Rich Mountain and Carrick's Ford were mere skirmishes in comparison with the first Battle of Bull Run and the great battles of the following year. They, nevertheless, received full attention, fuller no doubt than they deserved, from the press. Probably the most complete account of the Rich Mountain affair was written by William D. Bickham, the Cincinnati *Commercial*'s army representative, who did not fail on this occasion, as on others, to do more than full justice to the generalship of Rosecrans.[10] Some small irritation among the Ohio troops in Rosecrans' command was aroused by a telegram in the Cincinnati *Gazette* which indicated that one of the Indiana regiments had done practically all the fighting on that day. Later the *Gazette* published a letter from Reid in which proper amends were made and full credit given to the other regiments.[11]

Among the reporters who witnessed the action at Carrick's Ford was George P. Buell of the Cincinnati *Times*, who had excited the ridicule of his fellow newspapermen by riding out in advance of the skirmish line during one of the first days of the campaign and nearly losing his life. During the pursuit of Garnett's forces, Buell showed a more practical kind of courage by shouldering a musket and charging into the thickest of the fight with the troops of the Seventh Indiana. At Carrick's Ford he was impressed that the Southern troops as a general rule seemed better equipped for warfare in every respect except for the arms they carried. He observed:

> The round ball of the enemy is much lighter than our minie ball, and the smooth-bored gun from which it is thrown is not comparable to the Springfield rifle . . . which is a terrible weapon at . . .five hundred yards.[12]

Following the engagement at Carrick's Ford, which had taken place on a Saturday afternoon, the army newspapermen who were there began speculating how they might reach the nearest telegraph office at Rowlesburg before midnight on Sunday in order to make the Monday morning editions of their newspapers. Later that day they learned that arrangements had been made to send the body of General Garnett to

Washington via Rowlesburg and that Reid and another correspondent, Florus B. Plympton of the Cincinnati *Commercial*, would be permitted to go along as escorts.

At about noon on Sunday, the funeral party, which included an army major and two mounted soldiers, started its thirty-mile journey to Rowlesburg. At the outset its progress was necessarily slow, not simply because of the rough terrain over which it was passing but also because it had to be on a constant lookout for bands of enemy stragglers. At a farm house alongside the road, Reid came upon a straggler, suffering from an attack of measles, who had been with Garnett's command at Laurel Hill. "We had a mighty poor General at Laurel Hill," the soldier confessed with some disgust, "but wait till you meet Colonel Hardee and General Lee. You will find *them* military men of another stamp."

Beyond St. George, the road rapidly became worse. Grass was growing as thickly along the pike as it was on the mountain side, and at one point the party had to lift the wagon with the body of General Garnett over two enormous trees lying across the road. In some places there was less than six inches between the outer wagon track and the edge of a steep bluff overlooking the Cheat River. At sundown they were sixteen miles from Rowlesburg, and the most dangerous part of the journey was still before them. By this time the mule driver had completely lost his nerve, and so Reid took over the reins. As they came to one of the highest points on the trail, the outer wheels of the wagon slipped off the road. For a moment it seemed as if there were nothing to prevent wagon, corpse, and men from tumbling into the coffee-colored Cheat, hundreds of feet below. They owed their escape from this uncomfortable predicament to the mules, who braced themselves and clung stubbornly to their footholds until cudgeling persuaded them to pull the wagon back onto the road.

Within four miles of Rowlesburg, the party was fired on by some Union pickets unable to recognize them in the darkness. Under the circumstances there was nothing they could do but unhitch their mules, hoist a flag of truce, and seek what rest they could in the woods until morning came. At daybreak they were conducted into the Union lines and permitted to go on to Rowlesburg, too late by several hours to make the Monday morning editions![13]

There was some controversy among the newspapermen who were in Western Virginia at this time about who was responsible for the escape of Garnett's small force. Bickham and several of the other reporters were inclined to place the blame on one of McClellan's brigadiers, General Charles W. Hill, because of his failure to intercept Garnett's fleeing command at West Union. Reid apparently was the only one of the army correspondents to censure McClellan himself. At the very beginning of the campaign the Cincinnati *Gazette* reporter seems to have had some misgivings whether McClellan's promotion to a major generalship "over the heads of majors and colonels and generals who have grown gray in the service" had been a good thing.[14] Subsequently, in an article reviewing the campaign, he made clear that McClellan himself was at fault in letting Garnett's men escape from the Federal trap. Reid concluded acidly:

> And this is the culmination of the brilliant generalship which the journals of the sensational persuasion have been besmearing with such nauseous flattery.[15]

While McClellan was trying to close in on Garnett, a small force of about three thousand men under General Jacob D. Cox had been marching up the Kanawha valley farther south. On July 25, Cox occupied Charleston, which had been evacuated only a few hours before by Confederate troops commanded by former Governor Henry A. Wise. While Cox was at Charleston, preparing to push on into the interior of the mountain country, William Swinton of the New York *Times* and a correspondent of another prominent eastern paper[16] came to Charleston to report army news. According to Cox, the two reporters sought an audience with him as soon as they arrived and wanted to know upon what terms they might accompany his expedition. He told them he would see to it that the quartermaster furnished them with a tent and free transportation but that the letters which they wrote for their newspapers would have to be read by a member of his staff before transmittal. Both Swinton and his colleague objected strenuously to this. Furthermore, they made it clear that they expected to be admitted to the General's mess and to receive appointments as volunteer aides with military rank. When they understood that the Commanding General had no intention of meeting their terms, they left camp in a huff, but not before they had sent letters to their newspapers in which they accused Cox of gross incompetence and pictured his army as a mob of drunken ruffians destroying everything in its path.[17] Drunken ruffians or no, and other evidence points to some lack of discipline among them,[18] by the end of July Cox's troops had driven their adversaries well back into the interior and had brought to a successful conclusion the second phase of the Western Virginia campaign.

In the meantime Reid, soon after his adventurous trip to Rowlesburg, had gone home to Xenia for a rest. By the middle of August he was back at Clarksburg, however, and in letters written from Rosecrans' headquarters, he was criticizing abuses in army administration. In one, he called attention to the fact that the War Department was obliged to purchase hay in Cincinnati at eighteen dollars a ton and transport it all the way to Clarksburg by rail, despite Clarksburg's location in the heart of one of the finest grass-growing regions in the Union, because the local farmers were demanding thirty dollars a ton for their hay, three times the prewar price.[19] Reid also condemned the lavish use of the telegraph by Union army officers, one of whom, he said, had sent a wire to headquarters, four miles away, to request two sheets of paper and one steel pen. Taken together, the pen and paper were worth three cents; the dispatch had cost the government three dollars![20]

By the end of August, a newly organized force under the command of General Robert E. Lee was threatening the Cheat Mountain gaps region. This, coupled with increasing activity on the part of Wise and John B. Floyd, the two other Confederate commanders in Western Virginia, impelled Rosecrans with three brigades to start from Clarksburg on September 3 in the direction of the Gauley River valley. Rosecrans' soldiers for the most part were raw recruits, but Reid was particularly critical of the officers, many of them political appointees. In a letter to the Cincinnati *Gazette* written from the line of march on September 8, he expressed the opinion that:

> the highest boon Heaven could bestow upon our distracted country would still be a supply of officers, even measurably worthy of the men. . . . The honest truth is that not one half of our volunteer officers in this department have yet any adequate conception whatever of the nature and responsibility of their duties. The men are brave enough—as a rule, I believe all men are brave . . . but I believe also that there have been times within the last thirty-six hours, when five hundred regulars, properly handled, would have stampeded our whole force.[21]

Two days later, September 10, Rosecrans' brigades clashed with Floyd's troops at Carnifex Ferry on the Gauley River some fifty miles east of Charleston. Scarcely two thousand out of a total Federal force of 5,887 soldiers actually were engaged. Although these Union men fought bravely, they were handled badly, and they lost about a hundred and fifty men.

In writing of the battle neither Reid nor any of his fellow reporters mentioned Henry W. Benham, who really was responsible for the mishandling. He was in command of Rosecrans' advance brigade on the march to Carnifex Ferry and subsequently was dismissed from the service for incompetence. His troops had plunged ahead through the woods that day without even a skirmish line deployed in front. Then after a preliminary brush with some enemy pickets, Benham blundered upon the main force of the enemy, which was protected by strong earthworks, and exposed himself to a murderous fire at a range of hardly more than fifty yards. Rosecrans undertook to bring up reinforcements, but, although his troops kept up a tremendous fusillade against the enemy's position, their fire did little more than cause the enemy to lie low. After determining the general layout of the enemy's position, Rosecrans then planned an all-out assault, but night fell before he could deliver it.[22] Among the wounded that night was a reporter for the Cincinnati *Enquirer* named John H. Green, who had been acting as private secretary for Colonel William H. Lytle, the commander of one of the regiments in Benham's brigade.[23]

During the battle, Reid and his fellow correspondent, Bickham of the Cincinnati *Commercial,* served as volunteer aides on the staff of General Rosecrans. Both reporters were in the saddle from four o'clock that morning, and they were without food all day, except for a mouthful of coffee and a hard biscuit which Jimmy Bradley, the General's Irish servant, had shoved into their haversacks as they were leaving their tents. By nightfall they were almost completely exhausted and were interested only in finding something to eat and a place to sleep. From Captain William L. Mallory of General Benham's staff, who happened by, they learned that no food was available. One of the enemy regiments had left the field in too great a hurry to carry away all its blankets, however, and Captain Mallory was able to provide the weary reporters with a couple of thin blankets apiece. Reid and Bickham decided to bivouac right where they stood and to run their chances of being caught in a crossfire in case of an enemy sortie. Within a few minutes, however, they were roused by a sentry and told to move on to a safer spot.

Leading their tired horses, they tried in vain to locate the General's headquarters, and in the process received some dubious compliments from the sleepers over whom they stumbled in the darkness. Finally the reporters took shelter beneath a group of ambulances drawn up along the edge of a woods—but not for long. A pair of pawing steeds was hitched to one of the ambulances; presently the wheels began to turn. At this juncture General Rosecrans rode by and reined up suddenly.

"Why, who's here?" he exclaimed. "Bickham? Reid? What do you mean?"

"We mean to sleep, General, if such a thing is possible."

"Well, upon my word, you pick a pretty place for sleeping! We've been changing the position of our lines within the last hour, and you are on exactly the most exposed point in the whole neighborhood! You couldn't miss Floyd's fire or ours either!"

Heartily sick of these repeated cautions against being exposed to sudden death, Reid ventured to inquire: "But General, you don't think they'll make a sortie tonight?"

"I can't tell you, sir, what Floyd may or may not do; but I can tell you that if *I* commanded his army, *I would make a sortie,* and make it tell, too!"

In desperation the two correspondents headed for a log stable converted to hospital use, spread their blankets behind a fence corner in the rear, and slept until the morning sun blazed in their faces. When they awoke, they discovered that the hard place in the ground of which Reid had complained when they settled down for the night was a tremendous Spanish stiff-bit bridle, and that after all their searching the evening before, they finally had selected as their haven of rest a fragrant pile of stable manure![24]

In common with the other army correspondents they experienced further difficulties in forwarding their accounts after the battle. After some discussion the reporters for the various Cincinnati papers decided to prepare a dispatch for the press as a whole. No press dispatch could leave camp without official permission, however, and General Rosecrans was so busy on the day after the battle that the dispatch did not receive clearance until late that evening. To make matters worse, the telegraph operator at Clarksburg changed the date and locality of the message and made certain other unwarranted alterations which further lessened the value of the correspondents' news story.[25] In a letter written to the *Commercial* within a few days of the battle, Bickham gloomed:

> The miseries of a War correspondent are superlative. If we criticise the military or unmilitary conduct of one officer, his superior is apt to regard it as censure of his own orders. If we ridicule or

> condemn the management of any expedition, or department, you offend "the whole general camp, pioneers and all." Therefore we are constrained to distribute adjectives freely, or forever—while we are in the army—hold our peace.[26]

Reid's account of Carnifex Ferry, which he prepared independently of the other reporters for the Cincinnati *Gazette,* was one of his best letters of the campaign,[27] even though in the enthusiasm of the moment, he overestimated the importance of Rosecrans' victory. His later correspondence reflected his disappointment at the failure of the Union commander to obtain any tangible benefits from his success. As he was preparing to return to Cincinnati on September 24, he wrote:

> Never was there a more barren victory. I do not choose now to speak of what *might* have been done at Carnifex's Ferry. The time may come when bepraised generalship will be called upon to explain why a battle was fought at all when simply crossing the Gauley at Hughes' Ferry might have cut off the enemy's supplies, and a single regiment might have prevented his retreat; or why, if, for somebody's reputation, a battle must be fought, it was necessary to plunge troops without dinner and already wearied with an eighteen miles' march, blindfold, upon a fortification whose very position was unknown till the troops were under the fire of its guns.[28]

After the fiasco at Carnifex Ferry, the campaign in Western Virginia virtually was ended. Already the autumn rains were setting in, and the problem of supply was fast becoming insurmountable. After lingering in the vicinity of Beverly for nearly two weeks, Reid and Bickham concluded that nothing further was likely to happen to enable them to "illustrate a brighter page in the history of this not very brilliant campaign."[29] While Reid hurried off to have a look at developments in Kentucky, Bickham accepted an opportunity to accompany enemy prisoners being transported by rail to Columbus, Ohio. After Reid's departure, the Cincinnati *Gazette* was represented at Rosecrans' headquarters by William S. Furay, later its leading army correspondent in the West during some of the principal campaigns of the war.

Having little to write about in the way of military activity, those few army correspondents who still remained with the army in Western Virginia devoted increasing attention in their letters to abuses in army administration. One of the strongest letters on this theme was forwarded to the Cincinnati *Times* early in October by its special correspondent,

William G. Crippen, who wrote under the pseudonym "Invisible Green." Crippen did not mince words in describing the nefarious conduct of the "infernal thieves" with whom, he claimed, the quartermaster and commissary departments of the army were filled. He told of one quartermaster in western Virginia who was reported to have stolen a hundred thousand dollars. He added:

> Complaint after complaint have [sic] been sent to the War Department but he is not disturbed in his depredations. He publicly made this declaration not long since—"Cameron *dare* not turn me out. *I know too much for him.*"[30]

As a result of the newspaper publicity given to the scarcity of warm clothing among the troops, Governor William Dennison of Ohio finally issued a proclamation calling upon the people of that state to contribute blankets and heavy clothing to relieve the suffering of the Ohio troops in the mountain area. Afterwards, however, it become obvious that the press had given an exaggerated picture of the soldiers' distress in Western Virginia.[31]

* * *

In Kentucky, the "Dark and Bloody Ground" of Indian days, there was little military activity for the reporters to write about early in the war. Public sentiment there at first tended to favor neutrality, at least in outward form. As the New York *Tribune* correspondent, Albert D. Richardson paused in Louisville on his way East during the last week of July, he took note of the strange mixture of Union and secessionist feeling in the Falls City. He later wrote:

> At the breakfast table, one looked up from his New York paper . . . to see his nearest neighbor perusing *The Charleston Mercury.* He found *The Louisville Courier* urging the people to take up arms against the Government. *The Journal,* published just across the street, advised Union men to arm themselves, and announced that any of them wanting first-class revolvers could learn something to their advantage by calling upon its editor. In the telegraph-office, the loyal agent of the Associated Press, who made up dispatches for the North, chatted with the Secessionist, who spiced his news for the southern palate.[32]

Following the overwhelming victory of the unionist faction in the August state election, however, Kentucky's neutrality collapsed. Suspecting the uses to which the state militia might be put by Beriah

Magoffin, the secessionist-minded Governor, the Unionist leaders prior to the election had begun to recruit companies of home guards throughout the northern and central part of the state. Although no Federal training camp had been built on Kentucky soil up to the time of the election, mountaineer lads from the upland districts of Kentucky for some time had been drilling at Camp Joe Holt opposite Louisville on the Indiana side of the Ohio River. On the day after the election, even before the result had been decided, the news came that Lieutenant William Nelson, a former U. S. naval officer of Kentucky birth, had established a Federal training center at Camp Dick Robinson on the southern edge of the blue grass country, less than a hundred miles from the Tennessee line.

While the defeated Magoffin was doing everything in his power to keep his state from becoming identified with the Union cause, the war was moving closer to Kentucky from the south. On September 4, 1861, two days after the meeting of the newly elected legislature at Frankfort, a Confederate army under Major General Leonidas Polk crossed into Kentucky from Tennessee and occupied Columbus, the best military position on the Mississippi River between Memphis and Cairo. Within a few days another Confederate army commanded by Brigadier General Felix Zollicoffer surged into eastern Kentucky through Cumberland Gap. Still a third rebel force commanded by General Albert Sidney Johnston entered Kentucky on the fifteenth, seized Bowling Green, and pushed forward an advance guard under Brigadier General Simon B. Buckner to seize Louisville.

Henry Villard was in Louisville at the time of Buckner's push, and was reporting war news for the *Herald*. Villard had arrived during the last week of August after a two-weeks vacation in the North,[33] little more than a fortnight before the Confederate move. In common with the other reporters who had been drawn to the scene by the prospect of active operations, Villard expected heavy fighting to occur and with it opportunities for some interesting work.

The threat to Louisville vanished, however, almost as rapidly as it had arisen. Receiving prompt information concerning Buckner's intentions, Brigadier General Robert Anderson, one-time commander at Fort Sumter, who recently had been placed in charge of the newly organized Department of Kentucky, moved the recruits from Camp Holt and the Louisville home guards to an elevated position south of the city known as Muldraugh's Hill. Writing from army headquarters in the field on September 27, a reporter for the New York *Times* predicted that Muldraugh's Hill would "become as famous in military history as the Alps or the Black Forest."[34] Whatever expectations he or the other reporters may have had of seeing a decisive battle at that point were to come to naught, however. Abashed by the cool reception he was given by the civilian population of central Kentucky, Buckner halted at Elizabethtown, seven miles from Muldraugh's Hill; then learning of the approach of Federal troops, he fell back to Bowling Green. In similar fashion Zollicoffer's advance into eastern Kentucky was checked without a battle by Brigadier General George H. Thomas' command operating from Camp Dick Robinson.

At that point a change of command at Louisville brought to the fore the most unremitting foe of the newspaper men that the war produced. Whereas General Anderson had been on excellent terms with the gentlemen of the press, the new department commander, Brigadier General William T. Sherman, spoke of them as "infamous dogs," "buzzards," "paid spies," and "little whippersnappers . . . too lazy, idle and cowardly to be soldiers," and treated them accordingly.[35]

To Plympton of the Cincinnati *Commercial,* who came to Sherman's headquarters during an early stage of the campaign with letters of introduction from Murat Halstead and Sherman's brother-in-law, Tom Ewing, Jr., the General rasped,

"It's eleven o'clock, the next train for Louisville goes at half-past one. Take that train! Be sure you take it; don't let me see you around here after it's gone!"

"But General! The people are anxious. I'm only after the truth."

"We don't want the truth told about things here—that's what we *don't* want! Truth, eh? No, sir! We don't want the enemy any better informed than he is. Make no mistake about that train!"

For a little while Sherman paced up and down the railroad platform upon which they were standing. Then he broke out again: "See that house? They will feed you—say I sent you—but don't miss that train!"[36]

The army journalists answered Sherman's name-calling with similar epithets; they called him "prejudiced," peevish," "a monomaniac on the subject of journalism." One reporter compared Sherman's manners to those of a Pawnee Indian and when Sherman protested publicly, apologized not to Sherman but to the Indians![37]

The only newspaper men with whom Sherman was on anything like friendly terms at this time were Villard and George W. Tyler, the Associated Press agent in Louisville. Tyler was an elderly man, originally from Massachusetts, and a graduate of Harvard.[38] Every evening about nine o'clock Sherman came to the Associated Press office to find out what news had come over the wire. Often he remained there until the closing hour, three o'clock in the morning, discussing the issues of the day with whoever happened to be there.

Obsessed as he was with the idea that his own forces were greatly outnumbered by those of the enemy, Sherman became increasingly tense and irritable. Watching for a chance to discredit their red-haired tormentor, the army newspapermen saw their opportunity when the Secretary of War stopped in Louisville in mid-October on his way back to Washington from Missouri. In the Secretary's entourage was the *Tribune* correspondent, Sam Wilkeson. Being assured by Secretary Cameron that he could speak freely and not realizing that a newspaperman was present, Sherman told the Secretary that the Union cause in Kentucky was in a low state, that recruits badly needed there were being sent elsewhere, and he said something about an army of two hundred thousand men being required to clear the state of its invaders.[39] Before the Cameron party left Louisville, Wilkeson confided to Villard that the Secretary regarded Sherman as "unbalanced" and that it would not do to leave him in command.[40] When the *Tribune* subsequently published in advance of the other papers an official report of Cameron's tour signed by Adjutant General Lorenzo Thomas, it was believed in some quarters that certain passages in the report insinuating that Sherman was mentally deranged were the work of Wilkeson's pen.[41]

As the press campaign against Sherman gained momentum, he began to talk of barring all newspaper correspondents from his department. There was joy among the army press men, therefore, when, on November 9, they received their first inkling that Brigadier General Don Carlos Buell was on his way east from California to supersede Sherman. On December 11, 1861, while the peppery Ohio General was on leave of absence from the army with his family at Lancaster, the Cincinnati *Commercial* published a sensational article stating flatly that Sherman was insane, that while on duty in Kentucky he had been "stark mad," and that it was for this reason he had been relieved of his command.

The *Commercial's* story, widely reprinted in other newspapers, was, of course, absolutely untrue. Not simply was Sherman's sanity unimpaired; equally false was the statement concerning his removal since he had been relieved at his own request, never having wanted the supreme command in Kentucky in the first place. Investigation by the Sherman family showed that the usually reliable Henry Villard had been a party, innocently perhaps, to the libel. Murat Halstead, the editor of the *Commercial,* told Philemon Ewing, a Sherman relation, that Villard had come to Cincinnati from Louisville with the information that Sherman was crazy although no newspaper man at the front dared write it. According to Halstead, Villard had begged him to make public that Sherman was insane to insure the safety of his army.[42] In later years Villard gave a different version of what had happened, saying that he had given the information to Halstead in a private letter and that the *Commercial* editor "could not resist the temptation of utilizing the sensational information for his paper."[43] However the story originated, the *Commercial* published a statement from Ewing on the thirteenth branding the insanity story false in every particular, but the damage had been done. Many months passed before the nation's confidence in Sherman was restored.

"Crazy" Sherman was not unique among the generals in Kentucky in running into trouble with the war correspondents. Having been criticized by the army "specials" because of his unpopular retreat from Crab Orchard to Lebanon, General Thomas fired them out of his camp.[44] Whitelaw Reid also was banished when some remarks in one of his letters from Camp Nevin concerning defective cartridges furnished to the army and the high percentage of sickness in the Indiana regiments were brought to the attention of Brigadier General Alexander M. McCook.[45] One of the New York *Times* reporters probably expressed the sentiments of most of his colleagues when he complained that "the only energy exhibited thus far by the Kentucky Generals has been in hunting newspaper correspondents."[46]

Whatever might be said concerning the performance of the Kentucky Generals, the reporters themselves did not escape criticism. In its issue of November 22, 1861, the New York *Tribune* printed a letter from a correspondent in Evansville, Indiana, which turned the spotlight on the failure of certain reporters to check their facts:

> I have noticed in the Western correspondence of certain "trustworthy" writers for the New-York press, a statement, when speaking of the military facilities of South Western Kentucky, that there was a railroad from Henderson to Hopkinsville, a fact rendering Buckner's progress to the Ohio River at Henderson an easy matter, unless properly provided against. I observe also in two maps recently issued—one by Frank Leslie and one in *Harper's*

> *Weekly*... both warranted to be perfectly accurate, that such a railroad is fully established.
>
> Now... it may be well to... set the public right by saying, that no such railroad exists, except on the aforesaid maps. It is true, that some ten years ago a charter for one was obtained, a board of Directors elected, a man with a tape-line sent over the route, off and on for seven years, during which time six Presidents or more officiated and a good deal of money was expended, but to this day not a bar of railroad iron has made its appearance....
>
> This may not be a matter requiring especial correction. It is a fair average specimen of the ignorance of the Eastern papers and their readers in regard to Western affairs.

* * *

Of greater interest to the army newspaper men than any of the fighting in Kentucky during 1861 was a clash across the river from Columbus early in November. The fighting was at Belmont, a little camp of shanties eighteen miles below the mouth of the Ohio. Brigadier General Ulysses S. Grant, the Union commander in this engagement, had been in charge of the district of Southeast Missouri with headquarters at Cairo since early September and had built up there a force of twenty thousand men, as yet without battle experience. At this time Grant was practically unknown to the country at large although his relations with the press were favorable, as for the most part they continued to be throughout the war. On orders received from the department commander to make a demonstration against Columbus to prevent Polk from sending reinforcements to the Confederates in Missouri, the future commander in chief of the Union army left Cairo on November 6, 1861, with five regiments, mainly of Illinois volunteers, in four steam transports convoyed by the wooden gunboats "Tyler" and "Lexington."[47]

Grant had no intention at the time he left Cairo of attacking Columbus, which was strongly fortified and defended by a garrison considerably outnumbering his force. Only a few days before his departure a correspondent of the St. Louis *Republican*, William E. Webb, who had accompanied a flag of truce boat to Columbus, had scanned Polk's "Gibraltar" carefully and had come to the conclusion that it would require ten thousand Union troops to reduce it.[48] Learning, however, that Polk, the Confederate commander at Columbus, was sending troops across to Belmont to cut off another Union force operating in southeastern Missouri, Grant decided to attack the Confederate camp at Belmont.

In the early morning hours of November 7, the attacking force landed in a corn field on the west side of the river, posted a guard to protect the transports, and moved against the camp. During the hard four-hour fight that followed, Grant's horse was shot from under him, and one of his subordinates, Brigadier General John A. McClernand, lost three horses.[49] Grant's inexperienced men fought well, however, and by the time the fighting was over had succeeded in driving the Confederates from their camp. The Unionists failed to follow up their victory properly, however, and fell to rummaging through the camp for trophies. At this juncture Confederate reinforcements from Columbus came streaming across the river. Finding themseves the center of a hot fire from the Confederate guns at Columbus, as well as counterattacked, Grant's men had to do some more hard fighting before they were able to cut their way through to the transports and to embark for Cairo. Although the Confederate loss at Belmont (642 men killed, wounded, and missing) slightly exceeded that of their opponents, the retreating Federals had to leave behind 125 wounded men in addition to their dead.[50]

Since very few Northern reporters actually saw the fight and those who did were comparatively inexperienced journalists, the Union newspaper accounts of the action presented a confused picture of what had happened. Readers of the New York *Herald* were told that Grant had won a victory "as clear as ever warriors gained" and that although "our loss was heavy," the Confederates had lost three times as many men. The *Herald* account also contained some fanciful pictures of General Grant "swinging his sword above his head [and] shouting himself hoarse in the thickest of the fire" and of General McClernand "setting his boys an example of heroism by plunging headlong into the rebel ranks and making himself a road of blood."[51]

One of the St. Louis *Republican* reporters on the other hand stated flatly that "we have met the enemy and they are not ours."[52] In the Chicago *Tribune* and some of the other Western newspapers the Belmont fight was pronounced a defeat, "and some," bewailed a Louisville *Journal* reporter, "have gone so far as to proclaim it a rout."[53] Many of the Illinois newspapers gave the impression that Grant had bungled his assignment, which was erroneously assumed to be the capture of Columbus, and that it was McClernand who had saved the day.[54]

* * *

The press probably devoted a greater amount of attention to military developments in Missouri than it did to anything which occurred in either the Kentucky or the Western Virginia areas. This was especially true after the appointment early in July, 1861, of John C. Fremont to the command of what was then known as the Department of the West, with headquarters at St. Louis. At one time or another during the campaign which followed, nearly all the leading newspapers of the country were represented at Fremont's headquarters.

One of the first war correspondents from the East to enter the Missouri war zone prior to Fremont's appointment was Thomas W. Knox of the New York *Herald,* a large, heavy man, "rather clumsy in movement and ungainly in form." Knox was well acquainted with western life,[55] having spent some time in Denver when the Colorado gold rush of 1859 was at its height. With avid interest he watched the unfolding of the drama in which Claiborne F. Jackson, the Southern-minded Governor of Missouri, on the one hand, and Francis P. Blair and Captain Nathaniel Lyon, the leaders of the pro-Union faction, on the other, played the leading parts. At a time when recruits for the Confederate cause openly were being enlisted at the old Berthold mansion in the very heart of St. Louis and when Southern state militia units were being trained at Camp Jackson just outside the city limits, feeling between the two factions ran high. On the day of his arrival in the city, Knox had opportunity to sample this feeling when he encountered quite unexpectedly a former acquaintance, whom he had met in the Rocky Mountains six months before. After some preliminary conversation, the *Herald* correspondent attempted to sound out the political views of his Rocky Mountain acquaintance.

"I am a Union man," was the emphatic response.

"What kind of a Union man are you?" asked Knox.

"I am this kind of a Union man," was the reply as he threw open his coat to display a huge revolver strapped about his waist.[56]

Such an atmosphere invited an armed clash. On the tenth of May, 1861, Lyon, the commander of the St. Louis arsenal, had marched out to Camp Jackson with a force of three hundred regulars and several thousand volunteers, made up in large part of the German-American citizens of St. Louis, and had compelled Jackson's state militiamen to surrender. As the prisoners were being herded through the streets of west St. Louis, bloody fighting ensued between the soldiers and the angry citizenry, and resulted in twenty-eight deaths.[57] Almost a month elapsed, however, before the Governor stalked out of the Planter's House in St. Louis, after a stormy session with Lyon which had left no doubt of the futility of further hopes of compromise.

On the following day, June 13, the *Herald* correspondent accompanied Lyon, recently commissioned a brigadier general, on an expedition up the Missouri River to dislodge Governor Jackson and his supporters from the state capital. Within forty-eight hours the expeditionary force occupied Jefferson City without any opposition from the Governor, who already had fled along with most of the other state officials. At about noon on the sixteenth, Lyon started in pursuit, traveling as before by steamboat. From an enemy scout, who was picked up at one of the boat landings, it was learned that a detachment of state militia, hastily assembled by Jackson and Sterling Price, was preparing to make a stand at Booneville, a little town about fifty miles upstream from Jefferson City. From his bunk on shipboard that evening, Knox watched with considerable foreboding the army surgeons checking over their instruments in preparation for the grim work of the morrow. Many years later he recalled:

> Since that time I have witnessed many a battle, many a scene of preparation and of bloody work with knife and saw and bandage, but I have never experienced a chill like that I felt on that early day of the Rebellion.[58]

The "Battle of Booneville," which took place on June 18, was in reality hardly more than a roadside skirmish. After a sharp fight which lasted only twenty minutes, the state troops were put to flight. Although not more than eleven men on the Union side were either killed or wounded, Knox and a fellow correspondent, Lucien J. Barnes of the St. Louis *Democrat,* had a narrow escape. While viewing the battle from what appeared to them to be a safe distance, they were mistaken for enemy scouts by General Lyon, who ordered his sharpshooters to pick them off. Fortunately they were recognized just in time by Lyon's chief of staff, and the order to fire on them was countermanded.[59] Acting on the principle that "to the victor belongs the spoils," the two reporters freely appropriated whatever they could find in the enemy camp. Knox, whose store of useful articles on the eve of the fight had consisted of a nimble pair of legs, a notebook, and two pieces of bread, emerged from the combat with a horse, an overcoat, a roll of fine blankets, and a pair of well-filled saddle bags! There is no reason to suppose that his fellow correspondent did not fare equally well.

Within three or four days after the Booneville affair, representatives of the New York *Times* and *Tribune* came over on the double from Cairo, thereby increasing the number of camp correspondents to four.[60]

A fifth newspaper man, Julius Shrick of the St. Louis *Republican,* who appeared at Booneville on the twenty-second promptly was placed under arrest, under suspicion of being a spy, as he was forwarding some news dispatches to his paper. Subsequently, he was shipped back to Jefferson City.[61]

As the newspaper men were preparing to accompany Lyon on his advance into the southern part of the state, they learned of Fremont's appointment to supreme command in the Western Department. But it was about the end of July before the new department commander came to St. Louis, where he was greeted with great enthusiasm by the local press. Western editors freely predicted for him at this time achievements quite as spectacular and impossible as those which the New York dailies were currently envisioning for McClellan.

There were elements of the fantastic in the career of this son of a French emigré dancing master, who, as a young army lieutenant, had wooed vivacious Jessie Benton, the brilliant and youthful daughter of Missouri's senior United States Senator. While still a comparatively young man, Fremont had led five successive exploring expeditions into the Great West, winning for himself in the process an international reputation as the "Pathfinder." One of his most striking feats as an explorer had been his crossing of the high Sierras in midwinter, a perilous undertaking even in our own day. While in Mexico during the Mexican War period, Fremont had met further good fortune, acquiring title through a friend to a valuable mining property which made him a millionaire. To one upon whom fortune had smiled so graciously even the Presidency must not have seemed unattainable, and, when in 1856 he received the Republican nomination for that office, his aspirations to be Chief Executive must have seemed well on the way to being realized. Further he had met defeat in an election in which he made a respectable showing even though he failed to receive a single electorial vote south of the Mason-Dixon line. This was the glamorous soldier of fortune, possessing something of the qualities of a dreamer, upon whom Lincoln had conferred a major generalship at the outset of the war and with it carte blanche to devise his own plan of campaign, and to whom Lincoln had said as they parted: "You must use your own judgment and do the best you can. I doubt if the States will ever come back."[62]

While Fremont was laboring hard and in the main with little help from Washington to meet the overwhelming responsibilities of his new command, ominous news flashed over the wires from Southwestern

Missouri, where Lyon with a pitifully weak force was confronted by an army nearly two and a half times as large under the joint command of Price and Ben McCulloch. Lyon had his choice of falling back to Rolla, the nearest point of railroad communication with St. Louis, or of fighting. Against the advice of his officers, he chose to fight. At Wilson Creek, about ten miles south of Springfield, the two armies clashed on August 10 in what turned out to be the hardest fought battle of the campaign.

Knox of the *Herald* was standing beside Captain James Totten's battery as the battle opened. He had just exchanged a few words with the officer in charge of the skirmish line when he became the target of a very hot fire. Speedily he placed himself beyond the range of the enemy's musket fire, but he was still discommoded by the attentions of the Confederate artillery. While he was writing up his notes under a small oak tree in the rear of Totten's battery, he glanced up in time to see a six-pound shot crash through the branches not more than four feet above his head. As he moved toward a safer spot, another shell landed directly beside him, tearing up the ground all around him and covering him with dirt. At that point Knox redoubled his efforts to get to the rear, where he finished his notes.

Throughout the battle, he was unable to rid himself of the illusion of greatly exaggerated distances. "How far are you firing?" Knox inquired of Captain Totten during a short pause between cannonades. "About eight hundred yards, not over that," the Captain told him. Knox shook his head in bewilderment, for to him the shells appeared to be dropping at least sixteen hundred yards away. He also experienced the sensation, not uncommon for those who are taking part in their first battle, of time dragging out interminably. Frequently, upon consulting his watch, he discovered that events were happening within less than a half or a quarter of the time he would have estimated.[63]

As the battle progressed, the outlook became less hopeful for Lyon's command. Before daybreak that morning the Union officer had taken the risk of detaching twelve hundred men under Colonel Franz Sigel to make an assault on the enemy's rear while he, with the main body of his force, attacked in front. Sigel had been repulsed after some initial success, but Lyon succeeded in driving the enemy from their camp and in beating off repeated counterattacks. While rallying his men during a critical phase of the fighting, the intrepid Lyon was shot fatally through the breast. After a hurried consultation, his surviving officers gave the order to retreat. Meanwhile the enemy commanders had arrived at a similar decision and were in the process of withdrawing until they learned of the Federal troop departure.[64]

That night a council of war in the Federal camp determined to evacuate Springfield and to execute a retreat to Rolla, a hundred and twenty miles away. The movement was to begin at daylight. The army journalists—Knox, Franc Wilkie of the New York *Times* and Dubuque (Iowa) *Herald,* Barnes, and an unidentified representative of the New York *Tribune*—likewise held their own council of war and decided on a similar plan. As a precaution in case they were overtaken by an enemy cavalry unit, the newspapermen deleted all references to the strength of the army from their notebooks and destroyed all other records in their possession which might give important information to the enemy. They also agreed that if they were captured they would frankly admit that they were journalists and rely upon their credentials to identify them.[65]

Although their route involved some very rough traveling, much of it through the Ozark mountain country, the reporters managed to cover seventy miles the first day. Wilkie, who had gone without sleep for seventy-two hours before starting the journey, declared:

> The physical agonies of that day were something that I shall never forget. Every joint and muscle quivered with pain at each motion of the animal which I rode. I was "dying for sleep" and fell into deep slumber a thousand times, only to be awakened as often by the pain from the jolting motion.

In Lebanon, midway between Springfield and Rolla, the newspapermen put up for the night at a log tavern, whose proprietor was obviously a secessionist. As they were about to retire for the night, one of the journalists was called aside by a stranger, who warned of a plot by some of the townspeople to rob and possibly to kill them. To their relief, the plot did not materialize. Nevertheless, they were awakened before daylight by their landlord, who assisted them in making their way out of the town by a circuitous route and who placed them safely on the road to Rolla. On the third day of their journey the reporters reached Rolla, where they continued on to St. Louis by rail, and brought there the first authoritative accounts of the defeat and death of Lyon.[66]

On the basis of preliminary information from Springfield and other points, the press already had portrayed the desperate struggle at Wilson's Creek as a "glorious victory" for the Union side in which both Price and McCulloch had shared Lyon's melancholy fate.[67] For days the public was left in doubt as to precisely what had happened. A more detailed account of the fighting which the St. Louis *Republican* carried on August 14 was based almost entirely on a highly inaccurate interview with a Captain Fairchild, who was not even present at the battle.[68] Said a correspondent of the *Republican* more than ten days after the battle:

> The reports which have hitherto come in, although they have generally agreed as to the grand results, have yet greatly differed and been sadly deficient in the details. Everybody has given the battle his own coloring, according as his prejudices and interests and the peculiar point from which he was able to observe dictated. Facts have been distorted, men who deserved no praise have been highly extolled, while others who ought to be held up as models of bravery and noble bearing have been passed over in comparative silence.[69]

Probably the most satisfactory accounts of what the reporters at first referred to as "the Battle of Springfield" appeared in the New York *Herald* and *Tribune*, the Chicago *Post*, and Wilkie's paper, the Dubuque *Herald*.[70] Wilkie had been taken on as a war correspondent of the New York *Times* a month or so before the battle. In the meantime he had addressed several communications to that paper without receiving any acknowledgment. Thinking that there must be some mistake about his connection with the *Times*, Wilkie decided in a spirit of pique not to forward an account of the battle to it. After several days, however, he mailed to the *Times* a marked copy of the issue of the Dubuque *Herald* in which his battle account had appeared, along with a letter in which he gave his reasons for his apparent neglect of duty. Within a very short time he received first a telegram and then a letter from Raymond, in which a check accompanied an urgent request for him to remain in the employment of the *Times*. Except for a mild expression of regret that through an unfortunate misunderstanding the *Times* had failed to obtain an eyewitness account of the battle, the letter contained no reproof.[71] This was the more remarkable because on his way back to St. Louis after the battle, Wilkie had telegraphed to Storey's Chicago *Times* an account of the fighting which provided that paper with its first important news scoop of the war. According to one of the owners of the Chicago paper, it took all the ready money Storey could scrape up to pay the tolls on Wilkie's message, since the telegraph company refused to deviate from its policy of requiring money in advance for every word transmitted over its line.[72]

A Cincinnati *Gazette* reporter, Milton P. McQuillan, was one of the funeral party which entered the Confederate lines at Springfield to bring back Lyon's corpse for burial. In his letter describing the experience, the *Gazette* man wrote:

> those who draw their conceptions of the appearance of rebel soldiery from pictures in Harper's Weekly would hardly recognize one on sight. They are not *uniformed* at all, and generally speaking, it is impossible to distinguish a Colonel from a private.[73]

At about this same time another interesting characterization of the enemy, surprisingly objective, appeared in a letter to the Chicago *Tribune* from its special correspondent in Missouri, G. C. Clark:

> I think by this time the idea of the inhumanity of the enemy must have been exploded. They have been represented as utterly heartless and barbarous, but from all I can hear the [Confederate] forces in Missouri have displayed as much courtesy and humanity as the Union men. . . . They have carried on a mean and tricky warfare at times and used dishonorable deceit, such as displaying Union flags . . . but . . . on the whole, I think their character and actions have been misrepresented.[74]

As the real facts concerning Lyon's sacrifice gradually became known, outspoken criticism of Fremont was voiced by the press. The newspapermen blamed him for his failure to reinforce Lyon in time; and they complained that he was inaccessible, that he lived in "oriental style" in an elegant mansion, for which the government paid a rental of six thousand dollars a year, and that he issued commissions and distributed army contracts in highly irregular fashion.[75] Among the lynx-eyed contractors who danced attendance upon him were a sufficient number of his old California friends to provide substance for slighting remarks about the "California gang."[76] The Pathfinder, however, was not without his defenders. Among them was Lincoln's assistant secretary, John Hay, who visited St. Louis during the latter part of August, saw much of Fremont and his wife, and upon his return to Washington contributed letters to the New York *World* and the *Journal of Commerce*, in which he warmly defended the General's record.[77]

While Wilkie was waiting in St. Louis for active campaigning to resume, he was invited by Colonel Sam Sturgis to accompany a small force being dispatched to northwestern Missouri. After the Battle of

Wilson's Creek, Price had marched north from Springfield with an army of twenty thousand men and had laid siege to a little river town called Lexington, defended by some twenty-five hundred Federal troops under Colonel James A. Mulligan. Within a few miles of Lexington, his relief column, which consisted of only two regiments of infantry without any cavalry or artillery support, abandoned the idea of relieving Mulligan and withdrew. Wilkie was the only reporter who had accompanied the relief column on its march to Lexington, and he was determined not to miss the opportunity of witnessing the final act of the drama. Actuated by a wild idea, born, he admitted, in a drinking bout, he crossed the Missouri River and placed himself in the hands of General Price, requesting that he be given parole status until the battle was over. Price was at first inclined to look upon the New York *Times* correspondent as a spy. He gave orders for Wilkie to be well treated, however, and after the surrender of Mulligan and his "Irish Brigade" on September 21 permitted the *Times* reporter to return to St. Louis with an exclusive account of the surrender.[78]

Wilkie was almost completely without funds by the time he reached St. Louis. In fact, he hardly had sufficient clothing to enable him to present himself at Barnum's Hotel, where his New York newspaper acquaintances, Knox and Richardson, were staying. Knox was away from the hotel when Wilkie arrived, but Richardson, whom the *Times* man disliked, listened attentively to Wilkie's recital.

"I'll tell you what I'll do," said Richardson after a casual inspection of the story which Wilkie had prepared for the *Times*. "This isn't a bad letter, and I don't mind offering you one hundred and twenty-five dollars in gold for it for the use of 'The Tribune'."

This was indeed a tempting offer. In the first place, Wilkie was not under an exclusive contract with the *Times*, and moreover, it would be at least two weeks before he could expect to receive any pay for his article. In the meantime he needed money very badly. Furthermore, he realized that his *Tribune* colleague was offering him more than three times as much for his letter as he would be likely to receive from his own paper.[79] Nevertheless, after considering the matter for a few moments, he flatly refused to accept Richardson's terms, which he well knew would involve a grave breach of faith on his part. As it turned out, his decision did not inconvenience him seriously, for Knox later agreed to act as his banker until he could obtain funds. Moreover, as soon as he learned of what Wilkie had done, Raymond sent a draft for a handsome sum to his wife; raised his salary to a regular weekly amount, "an amount that I had never even dreamed of in my wildest aspirations for journalistic earnings"; agreed to pay all his necessary traveling expenses; and published in the *Times* a half-column editorial highly complimentary to Wilkie.[80] The editorial stated:

> We published [on the previous day] a very interesting letter from one of our correspondents in Missouri, written under circumstances which, we venture to say, cannot be paralleled in the history of journalism in this country or in Europe. Knowing that a battle was going on at Lexington, and being unable to reach the camp of the Union troops, he determined to surrender as a prisoner to the rebels, in order that he might witness the battle and describe it for the *New-York Times*. . . .
>
> We do not believe any instance can be cited of similar courage and devotion on the part of a newspaper correspondent; and we respectfully commend it to those who are so glib in their censure of a class of men who will compare most favorably with any others, not excepting officers in the Army, for the zeal, resolution and self-denying enterprise which they bring to the performance of their arduous and responsible duties.[81]

The news of the surrender at Lexington produced an indignant outcry from the press. Although the two principal St. Louis newspapers stoutly defended Fremont, the *Evening News*, generally regarded as the personal organ of Frank Blair, published an editorial so outspokenly critical that Fremont suppressed the *News* for one day and placed its proprietor, Charles G. Ramsay, under arrest.[82] The New York *Herald*, *Times* and *World*, the Philadelphia *Press*, the Washington *Star*, and even the Chicago *Tribune*, which had been a strong supporter of Fremont, turned against him and clamored for his removal.[83] To avert criticism from the Administration, Fremont felt obliged to strike soon and decisively. To Army Headquarters in Washington on September 23, 1861, he dispatched a telegram:

> I am taking the field myself, and hope to destroy the enemy either before or after the junction of [the] forces under McCulloch. Please notify the President immediately.[84]

While Fremont was concentrating his army near Jefferson City for active campaigning, a sizeable group of reporters representing a cross-section of the country's leading newspapers came together there to write about army movements. Among the new arrivals on the scene were Richart T. Colburn of the New York *World;* Junius H. Browne of the St. Louis *Republican* and George W. Beaman of the rival *Democrat;* Joe Glenn of the Cincinnati *Gazette;* Henri Lovie, the artist, of *Frank Leslie's;* and Alexander Simplot, the artist of *Harper's Weekly.* Just before the army broke camp, Bickham of the *Commercial* came hurrying over from Cincinnati to try reporting under conditions which contrasted strikingly with the theater of action which he had just left. Bickham mused:

> They had a homely, matter-of-fact, old fashioned, business sort of way of operating in Western Virginia, which, although a little slow sometimes, was, on the whole, rather agreeable than otherwise, and quite effective. Since I was landed in St. Louis, I have been in a sort of military maelstrom.[85]

For more than a fortnight the Bohemian Brigade, as this little group of reporters called themselves, remained in Jefferson City waiting for Fremont to pursue Price. During this two-week period they bunked together in a wretched little tavern, with no two rooms on the same level and with no means of getting upstairs except an outside staircase. Since there was very little they could do until the army was ready to move, the Bohemians whiled away the time by discussing the weather, politics, art, and other random topics, and by indulging in boyish pranks. One of them, a huge, good-natured fellow, whom they nicknamed "the Elephant," frequently slept in the daytime, and so, when other amusements lost their attractiveness, someone was likely to suggest that they all go and sleep with "the Elephant." Thereupon eight or ten rowdy Bohemians would crowd into his bed at once and make such a commotion that finally the giant reporter would emerge from the bed covers, throw out his visitors, and then return majestically to slumber.[86]

The reporters' brigade also frequently amused themselves by racing their horses over the roughest kind of terrain. In one of these races, the "Elephant" was thrown from his horse and badly shaken up. Undaunted, he returned to the racing course the next evening and suffered another spill which knocked him unconscious for three or four hours. One of the other correspondents dislocated his shoulder in the race and had to be sent home before the campaign had even begun.

It was a great day for these Bohemians when, during the first week of October, they learned that Fremont's grand army at last was moving forward along the road to Tipton, thirty miles west of Jefferson City. While the first army contingents were moving out, some of the latecomers within the Bohemian Brigade were rushing about in a frantic effort to get themselves horses and field equipment. Beaman of the St. Louis *Democrat* soliloquized:

> If it be true that "the pen is mightier than the sword," Price has shown admirable discretion and tact in getting out of the way of our army as fast as possible, for the number of army correspondents going forward . . . would be enough to annihilate him.[87]

Among the first reporters to leave Jefferson City were the representatives of the St. Louis *Democrat* and the Cincinnati papers, who were attached to Fremont's staff. A second group, made up of the correspondents of the St. Louis *Republican,* the New York *Herald, Tribune,* and *World* and the artist for *Frank Leslie's,* had to wait five days longer for a train.[88]

Few happenings of any importance and no battles occurred during Fremont's march into southwest Missouri. Price previously had evacuated Lexington on September 29, and, although he was encumbered by his long wagon train, he had no difficulty in outdistancing his pursuers. Ironically enough, no correspondent was on hand to report the only skirmish of any importance during the campaign, the reckless charge of Fremont's bodyguard at Springfield.[89]

While the army was at Warsaw, several of the journalists lodged at the home of a widow who had a son in Price's army and who also had a pretty daughter to whom the Bohemians were properly attentive. One evening the daughter invited a young lady friend to her home and introduced the newspaper guests. In an effort to say something complimentary about them, the hostess announced that she did not dislike the Yankees even though she did despise the Dutch and the Black Republicans.

"Do you dislike the Black Republicans very much?" inquired the *Tribune* correspondent blandly.

"Oh! yes, I *hate* them. I wish they were all dead."

"Well," said the *Tribune* man gravely, "we are Black Republicans. I am the blackest of them all."

The widow's daughter was considerably taken aback at this information. She admitted with some chagrin that she had never before seen a Black Republican, and she seemed amazed to find that one looked like any other human being. Apparently the reporters were not greatly troubled by the attitude of their youthful hostess, for, when they left Warsaw they presented her with a handsome volume of Cowper bearing a suitable dedication on the fly leaf with the autographs of the various members of the Bohemian Brigade. Several neighbor women came in to witness their farewell, and as the reporters bowed themselves out of the widow's parlor one of the neighbor women expressed the opinion, more frank than polite, that she believed "any Union man would steal the coppers from a dead nigger's eyes!"[90]

On November 2, Fremont's army was encamped just beyond Springfield in expectation of an immediate advance on the enemy. Then a messenger arrived in camp with an order from President Lincoln relieving Fremont of his command. Although the removal order was dated October 24, instructions had been given that it was to be withheld if at the time of its delivery Fremont already had fought and had won a battle, was actually engaged in battle, or was in the immediate presence of the enemy in expectation of a battle.[91]

Throughout the campaign the press had given publicity to rumors that Fremont was about to be or already had been separated from his command.[92] Lincoln himself had provided some basis for such rumors shortly before mid-October by sending Secretary of War Cameron and Adjutant General Thomas to St. Louis to investigate Fremont's fitness to exercise command. As previously noted, one of the members of the Cameron party was Sam Wilkeson of the New York *Tribune,* who was apparently no friend of Fremont, although the *Tribune* was at the time one of the General's strongest defenders. After spending several days in St. Louis, Cameron visited Fremont's field headquarters with the intention, it seemed, of removing him. After talking to the General, Cameron agreed, however, to suspend any such action, at least until after he returned to Washington. In the meantime Adjutant General Thomas, who belonged to the old regular army crowd with which Fremont had feuded during Mexican War days, after an investigation of his own, wrote a report highly critical of Fremont, which he released to the press when he returned to Washington. Through Wilkeson's efforts, publication of the Thomas Report was a *Tribune* scoop, although the report was held for a week in type at the *Tribune* office and was not published until permission had been obtained from Washington.[93]

Fremont's removal was probably the biggest news story of the campaign. Letters of the army correspondents described movingly the indignation and excitement which ran through the camp when the news of the General's dismissal was made public. The St. Louis *Republican's* correspondent told how the announcement inspired "various threats of mutiny and resignation," and how "it was whispered that the army would not serve under any other commander."[94] In the opinion of the New York *Herald* correspondent, "nothing but General Fremont's urgent endeavors prevented it [the ugly mood of the army] from ripening into general mutiny."[95]

The news of Fremont's dismissal had been made public, however, before his successor arrived in camp. There was great excitement, therefore, when toward evening on November 3, Fremont promised his officers that if his successor, Hunter, did not arrive within the next few hours he himself would lead his army to the attack at dawn. The members of the Bohemian Brigade were apparently napping in their tents at the time this announcement was made. Aroused by the cheers of the officers, they rushed out in time to gather a general idea of what had happened from some bystanders, "which they put to paper in reporters' fashion."[96] To everyone's disappointment, the new commander of the Western Department arrived in camp about ten o'clock that night, whereupon Fremont abdicated his command and began making preparations to leave camp the next day.

Newspaper editors differed widely on Fremont's removal. In a letter to Secretary Chase, the Cincinnati *Gazette* editor, Richard Smith, demanded:

> Is it known to the administration that the West is threatened with a revolution? Could you have been among the people yesterday and . . . seen sober citizens pulling from their walls and trampling under foot the portrait of the President . . . you would, I think, feel as I feel. Is it not time for the President to stop and consider whether . . . it is not unsafe to disregard . . . public sentiment, as has been done in the case of General Fremont?[97]

Even the New York *Times,* which during most of the campaign had been highly critical of Fremont, praised his final order to his troops as being "manly and patriotic" and made reference to "that confidence in his character and ability which is so widely felt throughout the Western States."[98]

In a letter to the *Times,* published in that newspaper soon after his return to St. Louis, Wilkie predicted that an investigation would soon be made of the activities of the Bohemian Brigade during the campaign and added that he thought this would result in some interesting findings. He reported:

> It is charged that these correspondents, or a portion of them, who were so loud in their praises of Fremont and his policy, and who spoke so feelingly of the gloom which succeeded the announcement of his removal, were not merely fed and transported at the public expense, but were the recipients of valuable gifts from those they so sedulously glorified, and [were] also interested in contracts depending for their existence upon the remaining of Fremont & Co. at the head of this Department. These charges are of the gravest character.... The public have a right to know whether the sources of information... afforded by correspondents in this department, have been of that disinterested character which should entitle them to credence, or whether they have simply been those that one would naturally expect from the paid hirelings of knavish contractors.[99]

In reply to such, Browne of the St. Louis *Republican,* who had been accused by the New York *World* of sending dispatches of a highly misleading character to his newspaper,[100] published a defense of his conduct which the *Republican* printed over his signature. He began:

> I will state particularly for the sake of the *Republican* that I never sent any dispatches save those published in your columns.... As respects the riding and living at the expense of the Government, I asked no courtesies whatever, and received none except those invariably accorded to all correspondents and shared alike by all those with the army in Missouri.
>
> Regarding the dispatches to the *Republican,* the officers and soldiers are the best judges of the extent to which they reflected their feelings and opinions. I have not and never had the least interest in advocating or defending Fremont, though I believe and still believe he has been most unjustly treated.... With Gen. Fremont I have no personal acquaintance whatever, never having exchanged a syllable with him in my life, and I am confident he is totally unaware of the existence of so unimportant an individual as myself.[101]

By the end of Fremont's "Hundred Days" the campaign was virtually over. Having received strict orders from the President not to continue the pursuit of Price farther southward, Hunter decided to evacuate

Southwestern Missouri and to fall back to the line of the Pacific railway. When they learned of Hunter's decision, the army reporters, who confidently had expected to witness the decisive battle of the campaign near Springfield, were profoundly disgusted. In his exasperation, Wilkie stigmatized the order to retreat as the last act of one of "the most stupendous and remarkable farces ever exhibited to this or any other public."[102] There was nothing, however, that Wilkie or anyone else could do about it. And so the disgruntled members of the Bohemian Brigade, veterans of many an exciting tiff with avaricious tavern-keepers and tart-tongued "Secesh" women, packed away in their saddlebags their notebooks and other effects and jogged back across the Ozarks to St. Louis.

7

The First Tidings From the Fleet

DURING the spring and summer of 1861 the reporters assigned to the naval branch of the service had little more to write about than did their army brethren. At the beginning of the war the United States Navy was anemic, resulting in no small measure from limited appropriations and the spirit of routine with which it had become thoroughly impregnated. Of the ninety vessels listed in the Navy Register for 1861, more than half were sailing vessels—ships of the line, frigates, sloops, brigs—now, in an age of steam, almost completely obsolete. Five of the forty steamers whose names appeared on the general list were unserviceable for one reason or another, two were nothing more than tugs, and eight were laid up in ordinary.[1] The remaining twenty-four steam vessels, the core of the fighting fleet, were scattered all over the world.

With this inadequate force the navy was expected to perform three general types of service: the ocean service, involving the pursuit and capture of Confederate blockade runners and raiders; the coast service, which called for the maintenance of a blockade of thirty-five hundred miles of difficult seacoast, as well as for lending support to various army operations directed against coastal objectives; and finally the river service, in which the navy had to cooperate with the army in reducing fortified points and maintaining lines of communication along the Mississippi River and its tributaries. Coastal operations, naturally enough, received special attention in the Eastern press; whereas the focus of naval reporting on the part of the Western newspapers was the activity of the various gunboat flotillas that churned up the waters of the Mississippi, the Ohio, the Cumberland, and Tennessee rivers. Probably the smallest amount of news coverage was given to the ocean service, whose extensive cruising did not lend itself to the requirements of up-to-the-minute reporting.

One of the first news stories concerning the navy in action had to do with a small flotilla that had been given the task of acting as a patrol along the Potomac River. In the performance of their duty, the steamers "Freeborn," "Resolute," "Anacostia," "Yankee," and "Pawnee" of the Potomac Flotilla undertook on May 31 and June 1, 1861, to bombard some Confederate fortifications near Aquia Creek in what has been characterized as "the first naval engagement of the war."[2] From the account of the action that appeared in the New York *Tribune*, Captain James H. Ward, the flotilla commander, had been "itching for a fight" and had made the attack on his own responsibility.[3] Apparently the Confederates did not disappoint him, for the New York *Times* correspondent, who watched the encounter from the deck of the "Pawnee," reported that the "Pawnee" was struck several times by rifled shot from one of the shore batteries and that two men on board the "Pawnee" were slightly wounded.[4] Although the results of the action were of trifling importance, this expenditure of gunpowder had a beneficial effect upon the public morale. The press also took notice of the fact that when the flotilla returned to the Washington Navy Yard, President Lincoln went on board the "Freeborn" to compliment the gunners for their bravery. The occasion was not without its comic aspect, for in the midst of the ceremony a soldier watching the President's movements from a nearby pier lost his balance and tumbled into the water.

As the summer progressed, the blockade of the Atlantic and Gulf coasts instituted by Presidential proclamations of April 19 and 27 slowly began to take shape. Letters from newspaper correspondents attached to the blockading squadrons helped to make the public aware of the problems involved in achieving an effective blockade. From reading such letters one derives the impression that life aboard a blockade steamer must have been occasionally hazardous, more often monotonous, and not without privations. A New York *Tribune* correspondent, writing from the steam sloop "Brooklyn" off the mouth of the Mississippi, spoke feelingly of the lack of fresh meats and vegetables aboard the "Brooklyn." Although the ship's machinery was badly in need of repair, the crew was:

> busied excessively at this juncture in overhauling and subjecting to the necessary examination the numerous vessels that daily make this place, designing and hoping to enter the port of New-Orleans. Alarms by night and chasing sails by day seem now to be the usual routine, which gives us an incalculable amount of work, and keeps the entire ship's company in a state of constant excitement.[5]

Another *Tribune* correspondent, who complained of his hard lot aboard a South Atlantic blockade steamer, felt somewhat different after paying a visit to the troop barracks at Fortress Monroe. He confessed:

> I thought I had it rather hard, but I shall not complain any more, for I did not see the least signs of cleanliness all round the fort. The soldiers' tents are nearly black, and their blankets are of the same color. There is scarcely a bit of dirt anywhere about our ship. At 10 o'clock, when we muster, all our hammocks and bedding are quite white, and the men always look clean and neat. I wish I could say as much for the troops I have seen here.[6]

Of particular interest for its description of the daily routine aboard a United States man-of-war was a letter written near the end of the year by a reporter on board the South Atlantic blockading squadron flagship, "Roanoke." The letter explained that the ship's company was divided into two watches, starboard and port, and a group called "idlers," i.e., men who did not stand watch. Then it went on to say:

> At eight bells (4 o'clock a.m.), the reveille is sounded, and all the "idlers" piped up, hammocks lashed, and stowed away in the nettings, decks scrubbed and holystoned down, and at six bells (7 o'clock) the watch below is piped up, and the man that takes more than 12 minutes to lash up and stow away his hammock must look out for "breakers." At 15 minutes before eight bells (8 o'clock), mess-cloths are spread, and at eight bells the drums are rolled off, the Stars and Stripes are flung to the breeze, saluted by the marines presenting arms, and the band playing national airs. Breakfast is then piped, and grog served, at which period those that drink whisky go to the tub when their names are called, which is done by the purser's steward, and they take the quantity allowed, which is a wine-glassfull. At one bell (8½ o'clock), up mess-cloths, when dishes are cleaned and put away. . . . At two bells (9 o'clock) quarters are beat, and every one is expected to be at his station, as if on the eve of a battle. Then come morning prayers, and immediately after the sick list is sounded, when those in need of the advice of the surgeon go to the "sick-bay," a portion of the berth-deck, partitioned off for the use of the sick, and there the surgeon attends to them. At three bells (9½ o'clock) the mechanics and "busy men" are set to work, and at 8 bells (12 o'clock) dinner and grog is rolled. At two bells (1 o'clock) "all hand turn to" is piped again; and at six bells (3 o'clock) is the officers' dinner, at which time we have some fine music by our

> band. At eight bells (4 o'clock) all hands are piped to supper, at which hour all work for the day is over. At sundown the flag is lowered, the band discoursing national airs, and occasionally, when it is pleasant, the men are allowed to dance, as "all work and no play makes Jack a dull boy."[7]

Sometimes, when the occasion seemed to warrant it, these navy letter writers were free with their criticisms. In July, 1861, for example, when the Confederate raider "Sumter" slipped past the blockade squadron below New Orleans, a New York *Times* correspondent on board the "Brooklyn" took the ship's captain severely to task for abandoning the chase at the very moment when they seemed to be rapidly overtaking the raider.[8] And well he might, for under the command of the resourceful Captain Raphael Semmes the "Sumter" was destined to haul in a long list of prizes before she was condemned by a survey in 1862 and converted into a blockade runner.

Still another New York *Times* man, who was quartered on the U.S.S. "Niagara," was accused by a fellow reporter of having stated "the most abominable falsehoods with regard to this vessel [the 'Montgomery'] and its operations on the blockade that could have been invented by the most fertile imagination." The accuser, and champion of the "Montgomery," continued:

> I have only to say, give the officers of this ship the opportunity, and I will guarantee our flag shall not be dishonored, nor the ship that bears it surrendered while she floats. More I cannot say either for officers or men.[9]

One of the most exciting tales concerning blockading operations during the first year of the war, having to do with the destruction of the Confederate schooner "Judah" at Pensacola on the night of September 13, 1861, was told a *Times* reporter. The exploit was performed by a small party of bluejackets and marines, who entered the harbor in launches under the cover of night, boarded the "Judah" in the face of a murderous fire, spiked its guns, and then made their escape after setting the vessel on fire. The reporter told how one of the members of the boarding party, the assistant surgeon, was obliged by the nature of his duties to remain in his launch while the others climbed aboard the schooner. When bullets began to whistle about his ears, however, he snatched up a pistol and leveled it in the direction of the enemy. The caps exploded once, twice, three times, and still a fourth without producing any result. The fourth failure was too much for the valiant surgeon. Throwing down the pistol, he exclaimed in language which must have warmed the reporter's heart, "Damn the pistol! I could do better with a scalpel."[10]

Perhaps the best opportunities for naval reporting during the early months of the war arose in connection with a series of joint army and navy expeditions directed against strategic points along the Atlantic coast. The first of these expeditions emerged from Hampton Roads on the afternoon of August 26 bound for Hatteras Inlet, one of the more important water gaps in the island barrier that fringes the North Carolina Coast. Both Charleston and Savannah had been considered as possible objectives for the expedition, but Hatteras possessed advantages for such an operation which the others lacked. In the first place it was weakly defended by two small forts built mainly out of sand and pine logs. Moreover, the locale would permit troops to be landed nearby so as to isolate the forts if their return fire should prove too hot for the navy's fighting ships. Most important of all, Hatteras Inlet was the key to the whole Albemarle and Pamlico Sound area which bulked importantly in the navy's plans for tightening the Atlantic blockade.

The naval commander of the expedition was Flag Officer[11] Silas H. Stringham, the commander of the Atlantic blockading squadron with a service record of more than a half century behind him. In addition to his flagship, the screw frigate "Minnesota," the naval part of the expedition consisted of the "Minnesota"'s sister ship, the "Wabash"; three sloops of war, the "Cumberland," "Susquehanna," and "Pawnee"; the steamers "Monticello" and "Harriet Lane"; two steam transports, the "Adelaide" and "George Peabody"; and the tug "Fanny."[12] On board the transports were parts of two New York regiments supplemented by marine, coast guard, and artillery units—860 men in all—under the command of Brigadier General Benjamin F. Butler.[13] The little group of news correspondents on the transports assured adequate press coverage.

By nightfall of the twenty-sixth, Stringham's fleet of ferryboats, gunboats, frigates, and transports had passed Cape Henry and was continuing on its way southward under the light of a full moon. A New York *Times* reporter on board the "Adelaide," who stayed on deck most of the night, was impressed, nevertheless, by the fact that nowhere along the shore from Cape Henry to Cape Hatteras were any lights in evidence, "a proof of the dangerous condition in which secession has left the coast."[14]

At half-past nine on the following morning, Cape Hatteras was sighted, and sometime during the afternoon the squadron came to anchor a few miles south of the Cape. Iron surfboats designed to withstand the heavy surf that was to be expected along this stretch of coast were then hoisted out to be in readiness for landing operations the next morning. In the log of the operation which the New York *Tribune* reporter kept as the basis for his newspaper story appeared an entry making allusion to the fact that:

> As everybody knows, there is not on the entire coast a locality so liable to gales and boisterous weather as the particular spot where we are now lying.[15]

This observation could hardly have been more pertinent, for the landing operations on the morning of the twenty-eighth were brought to a halt by the joint action of wind and waves after about three hundred soldiers and marines had gone ashore. Most of the landing craft were destroyed, and the troops on shore were marooned there for the night without food or shelter and in imminent danger of being captured.

It was the bad fortune of the New York *Tribune* correspondent to be in one of the surfboats that was batted about by the waves during the landing operation. Nevertheless, the circumstance made it possible for him to write a lively description of his hair-raising experience. He ruefully asserted:

> To get from the steamer to the hulk was a feat, though how I, with many more, accomplished it, I nevertheless never shall understand. All I remember distinctly is that an indefinite number of men shouted "Jump!" "Now is your time!" "Wait, not now!" I remember that the hulk went up while the boat went down, and that it was only when the right instant came that one . . . could make the leap and not break his neck or land in the water. The transit from the steamer to the hulk was in all conscience bad enough, but the process of getting back was far more difficult. All I remember about it is that with more recklessness than I supposed I could yield to, I gave a leap and landed partly on the side of and partly in a whale boat which the Adelaide had sent out; that in an instant more the boat was tossed fifty feet away; then as she neared again, half a dozen others got aboard in the same way; that the men pulled lustily as the boat rode now on the crest of a huge roller, now in the trough of the sea, with the waves right over you; that we came near the Adelaide where everybody

> shouted "be careful," "keep her off," that some one instructed me to do something about "grapling a rope," which I thought at the time was a feat in gymnastics, that, under ordinary circumstances I should never have aspired to; that neverless [sic] I followed directions . . . that the boat went out from under me; that I came the hand over hand operation in a manner which I supposed at the time was quite creditable; that strong hands seized me, and with an absence of ceremony which, under almost any other circumstances, would have been quite inexcusable, I was landed in the Adelaide.[16]

While the *Tribune* man was being buffeted by the waves, Stringham's war vessels were pounding away at Fort Clark, which commanded the sea approach to Hatteras Inlet. Instead of anchoring, Stringham kept his ships constantly in motion, passing and repassing the batteries at varying distances to keep the Confederate gunners from getting the range. As a result the shot from the fort rarely found their mark, whereas the shells from the ships speedily compelled the gunners to take cover. By 12:25 P.M. the latter were observed to be making off in the direction of Fort Hatteras or taking to their boats.[17] Later in the afternoon the fleet opened fire on the second of the two forts but was unable to silence it before night.

At sunrise the following morning the Union warships renewed their attack, advancing to within a two-mile range of the fort and hammering away with destructive effect. As the morning advanced, the Hatteras gunners were likewise driven from their stations, and since their guns were too light to punish their assailants, further resistance was obviously futile. A little before noon the white flag went up, and while several Confederate gunboats, whose crews had been watching the bombardment from a safe distance, scuttled away into the sound, the garrison surrendered unconditionally. Theirs had been no token resistance, however, for as the New York *Times* reporter summed up the situation:

> Those who were present at Vera Cruz, and had witnessed other attacks from Naval forces, declared that this exceeded anything ever before witnessed by them. The shower of shell was terrific in the extreme.[18]

Coming as it did only a little more than a month after the Bull Run fiasco, the victory at Hatteras Inlet was cheering news, although the enthusiasm of the newspaper editors moderated somewhat when it became apparent that Stringham's victory was not to be followed by a quick thrust into the Sounds.

Another two months elapsed before the navy journalists were given the chance to accompany a second joint operation, in comparison with which the descent upon Hatteras Inlet was hardly more than a realistic rehearsal. This time the objective was a conveniently located harbor farther down the coast where the blockading steamers might undergo repairs and take on coal without having to go all the way up to Hampton Roads. Although the Navy Department took special precautions to conceal the destination of this new armada, there was plenty of newspaper speculation about where the fleet would strike next.

Finally the New York *Herald* sent B. S. Osbon, who had recently come over from the *World* to the *Herald,* to Washington to pick up any hints that he could concerning the fleet's destination and also to make arrangements for accompanying it. While waiting for an interview with Gideon Welles at the Secretary's office, Osbon caught sight of a Coast Survey chart of Port Royal Harbor in South Carolina lying on top of a pile of documents which the Secretary had evidently been examining. "What is uppermost on the pile is uppermost in their minds," concluded the quick-witted *Herald* man, who was likewise aware that, located as it was midway between Charleston and Savannah, Port Royal was a key point for tightening the blockade in that quarter. Moreover, he knew that the harbor facilities of Port Royal were generally regarded as the finest below the Chesapeake. And so, when the Secretary at last appeared, Osbon opened the conversation by requesting that he be provided with a letter to the commanding officer of the expedition that was going to Port Royal. Welles stared at him in amazement.

"How did you know we were sending a fleet to Port Royal?" he demanded. "Nobody but the President, Captain DuPont, General Sherman, and myself know that."

"And me," Osbon reminded him.

"Who told you?" repeated the Secretary.

"You did, Mr. Secretary, just now."

Welles gazed at the reporter very intently. "Well," he said, "you are a good guesser, and you can go with the fleet. But you know what the violation of the Fifty-ninth Article of War means.[19] If you publish or say anything concerning our plans, you will be arrested and tried by court martial. Under the regulations you can be shot."[20]

With this stern warning, Welles terminated the interview although he did not fail to give the *Herald* man a letter of introduction to Captain Samuel F. DuPont, the flag officer of the expedition. Whereas Osbon took good care not to violate the Secretary's confidence, other newspaper men were less discreet. Before the expedition had even sailed, the New York *Times* published a story which, without stating the expedition's objective, gave a detailed account of the number of troops and ships involved. While the *Tribune* and *Herald* cried treason, Captain DuPont wrote bitterly to Fox:

> Everybody is much disturbed here by the publication of the expedition etc. in the New York *Times*... under the villainous assumption that we had sailed. Of course it is all going over the Southern wires by this time and may add some four or five thousand lives to the list of casualties, but what does the *Times* care for that if it can be in advance of rival sheets.[21]

Subsequently a correspondent of the Boston *Journal* picked up at Hilton's Head a copy of a Charleston newspaper in which this same information had been reprinted before the fleet ever got to Port Royal.[22]

Within the naval armada that left Hampton Roads under DuPont's command on Tuesday, October 29, were gathered together nearly fifty ships, the greatest war fleet that the United States had ever assembled.[23] To the newspaper correspondents distributed among the various transports, this great array of ships must have been an impressive sight, strung out as it was over an area approximately four miles long and three miles wide. In the van was a line of gunboats in an inverted V formation. On either side and in the rear were more armed vessels to provide a screen of floating cannon about the unarmed transports, upon which were embarked a force of thirteen thousand soldiers under the command of General Thomas W. Sherman.

During their first evening at sea Osbon came up on deck to have a look at the fleet by night. He subsequently observed:

> ... a more splendid sight it never was my lot to witness. The sky was as clear as a bell, and myriads of bright, twinkling stars bedecked the deep blue canopy which hung high over our heads. A gentle swell rolled over the surface of old ocean, rocking our staunch craft.... On every hand was heard the rumbling paddles of the host of steamers, and a thousand lights loomed up against the darkened background of the horizon. To our left the green lights on the steamers' paddle boxes looked like bright emeralds

set in jet, while to our right the red lights of the steamers bore the resemblance of rubies in a darkened setting. The large passenger steamers, with their cabins brilliantly lighted, looked like a city in the distance, and one could almost imagine himself passing up New York bay. . . .[24]

While the expedition poked along at the pace set by the slower ships, the reporters on board the army headquarters ship, "Atlantic," Mortimer Thompson of the New York *Tribune* and Henry J. Winser of the *Times*, were considerably amused by the whimsical remarks and quaint expressions of the soldiers with whom they shared accommodations. Life on shipboard was a novel experience for these New Hampshire farm boys, few of whom had "ever seen a bigger ship than a canal scow, or a sea more extensive than a mill-pond."[25] Every rope, iron, step, or hatchway was the subject of incessant "guessing" on their part. It was only natural that the sailors should quickly tire of their questions and draw upon their imaginations for droll answers. One of the correspondents could hardly repress a smile when he heard a tough old boatswain explain to an inquisitive soldier that the signal-halyards were the ropes that kept the anchor from blowing over the maintop in an easterly gale![26]

The fine weather that prevailed at the time of their departure continued all day Wednesday, but on Wednesday evening as they were nearing Hatteras some of the more queasy passengers began to complain of a rolling motion of their ships. During the night the transport "Baltic," on which the correspondent of the New York *Evening Post* was traveling, and one of the other transports ran aground. While some of the ships' passengers were exchanging conjectures concerning the name of the shoal on which they had fouled, the lone Englishman in the party (probably the correspondent of the London *News*) accounted for the presence of the reef in their path by conjecturing it to be a "masked shoal of the rebels." Coming as it did from a foreigner, the Englishman's sally was acknowledged by the others as a fair hit at "our national faith in masked batteries."[27]

On Thursday the sea was smooth again, but toward evening the wind rose, and by Friday noon the fleet was in the grip of one of the worst hurricanes that had been known along that coast in years. In such a storm it was impossible to maintain formation; consequently Flag Officer DuPont presently made signal for every vessel to take care of itself. At the time it was fully expected that many of the ships would founder since few of them were constructed for an ocean voyage, two of them being nothing more than New York ferryboats. Although the damage was surprisingly small, the reporters witnessed some thrilling scenes. As the "Atlantic" was lying-to about ten o'clock, Friday evening, she was struck on the port quarter by an enormous wave which demolished the plate glass windows of the salon as if they had been made out of paper and created pandemonium among the soldiers who were berthed in the after part of the ship. A headlong rush for the boats ensued when someone shouted that the ship had run aground, and it was not without considerable effort that the ship's officers were able to restore order.[28]

The steamer "Governor," which contained a battalion of three hundred marines, became completely unseaworthy under the impact of the heavy sea and after exhausting its supply of rockets was finally taken in tow by the frigate "Sabine." Thirty marines from the sinking transport were "whipped" aboard the "Sabine" on a boom made fast between the two vessels. Forty more came aboard after the "Sabine" moved alongside the other vessel with a force that carried away twenty feet of her hurricane deck. In the final phase of the rescue effort, the marines and crew still aboard the "Governor" lined up in military order and one by one leaped into the raging sea to be hauled aboard the small boats sent over from the "Sabine."[29]

By Saturday afternoon the gale had spent its fury. For several days afterwards, however, there was widespread apprehension for the safety of the fleet throughout the North, which was hardly diminished by the exaggerated story of fleet damage in the New York *Herald*. On November 3, Secretary Welles confided to his son Edgar, who was then away at college, that:

> The great storm of yesterday was, of course, very trying to me, as it may have not only made sad havoc with my summer and autumn labors, but may prove calamitous to the country. . . . I have tried to comfort myself with the hope that this was a south easterly storm that did not go beyond Hatteras on the coast, and the fleet I am satisfed was beyond that point when the storm commenced. But it is not necessary to speculate on the subject, for the facts will probably reach you by telegraph before this letter.[30]

On the day after (Monday, November 4), DuPont's flagship, the "Wabash," arrived off Port Royal along with some thirty-six other fleet units. On the following day, while the gunboats were busy marking out the channel for the larger vessels, a half dozen newspaper correspondents, including Osbon, accompanied General Sherman in the "Mercury" on a reconnaissance of the two forts that commanded the entrance of Port Royal Harbor. The reconnaissance disclosed that it would be suicidal to attempt to land troops in advance of a naval bombardment especially since many of the small boats which were to have been used in the landing operation had been lost during the storm. It was, therefore, determined that the forts must first be attacked and silenced by the fleet without assistance from the army. Upon his return from the reconnaissance mission, Osbon went aboard the squadron flagship, where he learned from Captain DuPont that he (DuPont) "intended to fight his ship close in and make a quick job of it."[31]

Unfavorable weather caused the attack to be postponed for another day, however, so that it was not until the morning of November 7 that DuPont joined action with the batteries. The Flag Officer's plan of operation called for the division of his ships into two lines of battle. The main line, containing nine of his best ships, headed by the "Wabash," were to enter the Sound on the Bay Point side in column formation, directing their port broadsides at Fort Walker on Hilton's Head and using their starboard guns on Fort Beauregard until they had reached a point two miles above the fort. Then they were to turn and come down the Roads in the same order, using their bow guns to enfilade Fort Walker as they approached, their starboard guns as they came abreast, and their quarter guns while they were drawing away. After they got back to their starting point they were to repeat this ellipse maneuver until the forts surrendered. Meanwhile a second line of five gunboats was to flank the movements of the main line on the way up the Roads. At the first turning point, two miles above Fort Beauregard, they were to take station to keep the enemy's naval force in check and act at the same time as a screen for the transports.[32]

Under this plan, the attacking force moved into the Sound, coming under fire from the forts just before 9:30 A.M. In his report of the action written on board one of the army transports, the New York *Evening Post* reporter, William C. Church, told how:

> Sweeping up the channel, within eight hundred yards of Fort Beauregard on the right, the two lines delivered their fire from their starboard guns against the batteries on that side as they passed by, and then continuing up the channel came down on the

other side, delivering their fire at Fort Walker on Hilton Head, meanwhile keeping their port guns and the pivot guns at work as they could bring them to bear. The fire was returned from the rebel batteries with the utmost spirit, but during the first round, which occupied about an hour, no one was killed on any of our vessels. For the second time, and again for the third, the fleet swept past the forts, delivering the fire with more certain aim, and a more and more deadly effect; most of the attention being given to Fort Walker, which was the point of attack; the batteries on the opposite side being engaged only so far as was necessary to occupy their attention, and keep our guns fully employed.[33]

A graphic description of the battle at its height was given by Osbon, who was watching the action from the transport, "Matanzas." He reported:

> At about twenty minutes before eleven o'clock the Wabash commenced operations on the Hilton Head battery in good earnest, delivering a broadside at one command. All her gun-deck armament is nine-inch shell guns, with a ten-inch pivot aft and a sixty-eight rifled Dahlgren gun on the forecastle. If you can imagine the scene you can do more than I can describe. The noise was terrific, while the bursting of the shells was as terrific as it was destructive. I counted no less than forty shells bursting at one time, and that right in the battery and in the woods where about eight hundred rebels lay. In addition to this, the Susquehanna, with her tremendous battery, aided by the Bienville, the Pawnee, and half a dozen smaller gunboats, was making the air brown with the sand, while the blue smoke of the explosion went up to make a most magnificent sight. . . . A moment or two elapsed—just time enough to load the guns—and again the scene was enacted afresh. The rebels replied with seven guns, which were worked splendidly, and from appearances they did considerable execution. After the second broadside the firing became less concerted, and it seemed as if each division on all the vessels were endeavoring to out vie each other in the rapidity with which they worked their guns.[34]

What the battle looked like from the Southern point of view becomes apparent from an examination of the battle story that was published in the Charleston *Mercury*. Apart from the fact that the *Mercury's* account made frequent references to the "Minnesota," which was nowhere near Port Royal at the time of battle, it did not differ in essential details from the stories of the Northern reporters. The *Mercury* man frankly admitted that "our firing was . . . less efficient than theirs," the explanation being that "our troops were volunteers—theirs were picked artillerists. . . ." One of the most interesting features of his account was his description of the retreat of the Fort Walker garrison across a stretch of open ground commanded by the guns of the fleet:

> Across this they were ordered to run for their lives, each man for himself, the object being to scatter them as much as possible, so as not to afford a target for the rifled guns of the fleet. . . . Knapsacks were abandoned, but the men retained their muskets. Each of the wounded was placed in a blanket and carried off by four men. . . . And thus the gallant little band quitted the scene of their glory, and scampered off, each one as best he could, toward the woods.[35]

According to DuPont's official report of the action, it was at 1:15 P.M. that the "Ottawa" signaled the flagship that the works at Fort Walker had been abandoned. As continued firing failed to elicit any reply from the forts, Commander John Rodgers, a passenger on the "Wabash," who had been acting during the fight as aide to Captain DuPont, jumped into a flag-of-truce boat and headed for Fort Walker. The fort remained silent as the boat struck the beach and Commander Rodgers went ashore, borne on the backs of his sailors. At precisely three o'clock the Stars and Stripes were hoisted over the fort, and the battle was over, even though Fort Beauregard was not occupied until the following morning. Although every one of the attacking vessels except the "Vandalia" had been more or less injured, the cost of the victory in terms of naval personnel—eight killed and twenty-three wounded[36]—had been comparatively light. For miles around, however, the surface of the harbor was dotted with wooden shell cases, mute testimony to the intensity of the action.

The only casualty among the press delegation was Osbon's luxuriant red beard, which disappeared like magic during a hot stage of the fight when the wadding from one of the artillery charges blew back in his face. This mortifying injury did not prevent the *Herald* man, however, from accompanying Rodgers in the flag-of-truce boat to Fort Walker nor did it interfere with his completion of a two-page battle story published in the *Herald* exactly one week later.

While the reporters were speeding northward on the dispatch steamer

"Bienville" with their exciting eyewitness accounts of DuPont's spectacular victory, the streets of the national capital were already ringing with the treble cries of the newsboys: "Ere's your extry *Chronicle*! Stars and Stripes floating over South Curliny!" On the whole, the capture of Port Royal was well reported by the press, in terms both of the quantity and quality of its coverage. Well might the public feel after reading the graphic, though somewhat gruesome, narratives of Osbon, Winser, Church, and the other fleet reporters that the navy was prepared to give a good account of itself in the campaigns that were yet to come.[37]

* * *

During the last week of July, 1861, while the joint army-navy operation against Hatteras Inlet was being blueprinted, the press was evaluating a new military luminary who had been plucked from the field in Western Virginia to take command of what was thenceforth to be known as the Army of the Potomac. In his Washington column, on the day McClellan arrived in that city, Forney mused:

> I wonder whether the New York papers will give him a fair chance. He has the genius, the courage, and the experience which they say has been lacking in most of our other military chiefs, but he has the misfortune of being a Pennsylvanian, and, what is still worse, the misfortune of being the friend of the Secretary of War, another Pennsylvanian.[38]

One of the first things the new commanding general did upon his arrival in Washington was to invite the local newshawks to come to his headquarters at Nineteenth Street and Pennsylvania Avenue for an interview. Such an invitation, showing McClellan's cordial attitude toward the press, could hardly fail to be accepted by the newspaper men with great alacrity. There must have been considerable curiosity on the part of casual passersby, however, when on the evening of August 1 two huge omnibuses rolled up in front of Willard's to transport the journalists to their rendezvous with "Little Mac." Upon arriving at the General's headquarters, the reporters were ushered into a spacious parlor, where they awaited their first view of the hero of Grafton, Philippi, and Rich Mountain. After a little while, General McClellan appeared in the company of his father-in-law, Colonel Randolph S. Marcy, his face mottled with dust and perspiration from a long ride up the banks of the Potomac. So unprentencious did he appear under the circumstances that many of the reporters were unaware of the General's identity until he was formally presented to them.

McClellan utilized the occasion to make a little talk in which he spoke in flattering terms of the newspaper profession and solicited the cooperation of his listeners during the trying days which lay ahead. This was a time of great crisis, he said; furthermore, the newspaper men assembled there held positions of great influence and could do much good or harm. A few newspaper correspondents, he added, had been his campaign associates in Western Virginia. They had conformed with his wishes, and he had found no reason to regret having made their acquaintance. As for the newspaper men present, they knew much better than he what was appropriate for publication and what was not. He was inclined, therefore, to give them a wide range of responsibility and hoped that they would soon come to an agreement among themselves to eliminate the possibility of any information being published which was likely to be of benefit to the enemy. After some discussion of the problem, a committee of five newspaper men agreed to convey the suggestions of their host to the press as a whole. As the little group of reporters was about to depart, someone ventured the opinion that the pictorial press ought to be roundly censured for having recently published some sketches of military fortfications. General McClellan dismissed the subject, however, by remarking in airy fashion that he thought the pictorial press could safely be let alone, since its drawings were more likely to confuse than to inform the enemy!

Within the next few days extensive accounts of McClellan's meeting with the press were published in newspapers throughout the country.[39] They included detailed descriptions of the General's personal appearance, one of which referred to him as a close-built, compact man, reminding one of Napoleon. This characterization caught the popular fancy, and thereafter the youthful General was commonly referred to in the press as the "young Napoleon."[40]

It soon became apparent, however, that the gentleman's agreement on the part of the Washington correspondents was ineffectual. On August 10, as a protective measure against further leakage of military information, the War Department issued positive orders that nothing having reference to army movements—past, present, or future—could be telegraphed from Washington "except after actual hostilities."[41] Newspaper correspondents were also told that, unless previously authorized by the major general in command, they were forbidden:

> all correspondence and communication, verbally, or by writing, printing, or telegraphing, respecting operations of the Army or military movements on land or water, or respecting the troops, camps, arsenals, intrenchments, or military affairs within the several military districts.

Violators of this order were liable under the fifty-seventh article of war to the death penalty or such other punishment as might be prescribed by a court martial.[42]

During the inactive period of many months which followed McClellan's assumption of the eastern command, the press, no less than the army, made careful preparation for the resumption of active campaigning. From their experience during the Bull Run campaign, the editors of the leading metropolitan dailies had learned certain lessons which they now began to put to use. They had become aware, among other things, of the necessity of testing the professional qualifications of their reporters. Moreover, they now realized to a greater extent than before the importance of mobility on the part of their correspondents in the field and beyond that the necessity of rendering them independent of the uncertain hospitality of the commanding general. For the first time during the war it became the general practice of editors to provide their army reporters with complete campaigning outfits and allowances for current expenses.[43]

Meanwhile, the Confederates had occupied Fairfax Court House within a few days after the Battle of Bull Run, and during the early part of August they advanced their outposts to Munson's Hill within six miles of the Capitol.[44] From its unfinished dome, one could see a line of yellow earthworks on top of a hill on the opposite side of the Potomac, above which the Confederate Stars and Bars waved defiantly. The near approach of the enemy to Washington and the fact that the Federal authorities made no attempt to dislodge them did not pass unnoticed by the press. Returning from an inspection of the picket line one early autumn day, Coffin and a fellow newspaper correspondent overheard one of McClellan's division commanders complaining bitterly about the policy which was being followed by his superior. The division commander, General Israel B. Richardson, using some choice soldierly epithets, groused:

> Here we are seventy thousand men within one hour's march of that hill, where there are not over four thousand Confederates,

> whose nearest supports are at Fairfax Court-house. We could wipe them out in a twinkling, and yet I am ordered to make no demonstration, and if attacked, to fall back under the guns of the fortifications along Arlington Heights.[45]

Nevertheless, the Washington correspondents of the principal New York newspapers continued to titillate their readers day after day with predictions that another great battle in the vicinity of Washington was to be expected at any time.[46] As the weeks passed by without any signs of serious fighting, such statements were denounced as "unmitigated hoaxes" in other quarters of the press.[47] *Vanity Fair*, a popular humor magazine of that day, jibed:

> The Washington Correspondent of the *Herald* [W. B. Shaw] has prophesied every other day for the past two weeks "a battle in twenty four hours," and it has not yet come off. More's the pity for the prophet who, it is generally supposed, has the ear of the War Department. Oh (P)shaw! do better in future.[48]

Press criticism of the strange inactivity of the army was not as yet directed to any extent at McClellan, who was generally supposed, up to the time that he replaced General Scott in the supreme command on November 1, to be acting under the direction of the aged General in Chief.[49] During the first week of October, possibly at McClellan's suggestion, Simon P. Hanscom of the *Herald*'s Washington bureau wrote to Bennett to dispel any notion on the part of his chief that "we have troops enough here when such is not the fact." Whereas the public generally believed that McClellan had between two hundred and fifty thousand and three hundred thousand men under his command, he did not in reality, Hanscom declared, have as many as fifty thousand men to place in the field in case of an attack.[50] Hanscom failed to add (he probably did not know) that the force opposing McClellan did not exceed forty-five thousand.

At this very time, however, there were indications that the forward movement was at last beginning to take shape. On September 28, the Confederates finally abandoned their positions on Munson's Hill; and when, a few days later, Federal troops marched into Lewinsville on the other side of Arlington Heights, a large delegation from the Washington press corps rode out together in the midst of a pelting rainstorm to investigate reports of heavy fighting in that section. With gum elastic ponchos wrapped about them and mounted on a strange assortment of horses, they dodged between the wagons of the government trains and splashed through mud and water. But it was all to no avail. There had in reality been no fighting.[51] Furthermore, when McClellan's army made another advance, on October 17, this time to Fairfax Court House, there was still nothing other than the advance itself for the battle-hungry journalists to report.[52]

Some indication of the train of developments that kept alive the hopes of the army reporters from week to week is afforded by a letter addressed to his employers by a Chicago *Tribune* correspondent sometime during early October:

> I have not been idle though I have but little on paper as yet. I have been busy getting in such connected shape as may be the list of Brigades and regiments. In this, Coffin, of the Boston *Journal* is helping me we exchanging notes. I shall get it complete and send it in advance of any general movement. When this will come, no one knows, but it seems probable that it can not be long delayed. It is certain that forty miles of telegraph wire have been prepared and that the telegraph constructors were ordered to report at Alexandria tomorrow. Gen. King's Brigade yesterday came down from Georgetown and went out beyond Hunter's Chapel near the lines. Army wagons, empty, are pouring over the river by fifties and hundreds. There is a great Cavalry review and inspection of two days continuance on Tuesday and Wednesday, looking to put the cavalry into efficiency and assign them to Brigades. There have many troops been sent to Annapolis for a Coast Expedition, and full trains have been run for two days past. Other regiments from above are being brought down and thrown forward across the river. Immense activity prevails, and amid all Washington is as quiet and well ordered as a country village. . . .
>
> I have talked with Pinkerton[53] fully and he says the great battle of the Union will be fought within forty miles of here in no long time hence unless the rebels withdraw. Their secret service men say Beauregard is in a tight place the public sentiment forcing him to a fight, whether he will it or not. He is now at Centerville, and his lines not two miles from Falls Church. . . .[54]

While the newspaper men and the country at large were still awaiting the news of a general movement, the telegraph gave ominous report of an engagement along the upper Potomac, where Brigadier General Charles P. Stone was in command. For nearly a week the censorship prevented the press from presenting any coherent account of what had happened. Accompanied by his fellow correspondent, Henry M. Smith of the Chicago *Tribune,* Coffin went to McClellan's headquarters in Washington on the afternoon of October 22 to elicit whatever facts might be available. In the anteroom outside the General's office they came upon President Lincoln, waiting to see McClellan. The President, with whom both reporters were well acquainted, greeted them cordially, but they could hardly fail to detect the lines of care and anxiety in his face and his agitated manner.

"Will you please step in here, Mr. President," said an orderly, who thereupon ushered him into an adjoining room where a telegraph instrument was clicking away industriously. After an interval of five minutes or so, Lincoln emerged from McClellan's office with bowed head, obviously quite overcome with grief. As he stepped into the street, he staggered and almost fell. The two reporters sprang from their seats to offer him assistance, but he recovered himself before they could reach him and continued on his way down the street without acknowledging the salute of the sentry who was pacing his beat before the door. A moment later, General McClellan himself appeared.

"I have not much news to give you," he told the reporters. "There has been a movement of troops across the Potomac at Edwards Ferry, under General Stone, and Colonel Baker is reported killed. That is about all I can give you."[55]

Gradually the principal facts concerning the disaster filtered through the censorship. On October 21, it developed, Colonel Edward D. Baker, United States Senator from Oregon and a close personal friend of President Lincoln, had crossed the Potomac near Leesburg with a force comprising portions of three regiments, approximately eighteen hundred men all told. After some preliminary skirmishing, Baker's troops were hemmed in by the Confederates between a declivity known as Ball's Bluff and the river, with little or nothing in the way of transportation facilities to make good their escape to the opposite shore. Baker himself was shot through the head, and the greater part of his command was shot or bayoneted in the water, drowned, or captured.[56]

Probably the most satisfactory newspaper account of the affair was contributed to the New York *World* by Stedman,[57] who happened to be in Washington at the time the actual fighting was going on. As soon as he learned what had happened, the *World* correspondent rode pell-mell to the scene of action, covering forty-five miles on horseback in one day. He traveled forty additional miles the following day, gathering further details concerning the disaster, and then rode back to Washington on the third day, though he was almost incapacitated by an attack of camp fever. In his diary a significant entry appears, dated October 27:

> To-day wrote 6 columns. Only accurate and synthetic account late battle. Wrote with napkin on my head. Now go to bed and be sick.

But his troubles were not yet over, for in a letter to his friend, Richard Henry Stoddard, written two days later, he called the latter's attention to the fact that "Government has stopped the *World* to-night and talks of interfering with me, because I got angry about Ball's Bluff and told the truth."[58]

In spite of Stedman's courageous effort, the truth concerning the Ball's Bluff affair continued to be the subject of controversy for many months afterward. In a comprehensive account of the fighting which he forwarded to the New York *Tribune* more than a week after Stedman's story had appeared in the *World,* the war correspondent George Wilkes vigorously championed the cause of Colonel Baker and ascribed the charges of recklessness on his part to the "deplorable jealousy" between the regular army and volunteer officers "which has been widening for some time." Whereas Baker was not a professional soldier, Stone, his immediate superior, was a graduate of the United States Military Academy. According to Wilkes, the statement erroneously attributed to Baker at the time he received his order from Stone to cross the river—"I'll do it, but it is my death warrant"—was regarded by Stone's regular army friends as "an assault upon their order" and therefore, a good excuse for joining in the hue and cry against Baker.[59] Baker's senatorial colleagues entered the fray at this point and arranged for a protracted investigation of the responsibility for the disaster by the Congressional Joint Committee on the Conduct of the War. On the strength of evidence of the most doubtful character reflecting upon his loyalty, Stone was placed in solitary confinement at Fort Lafayette and kept there for six months until his release was finally brought about by Act of Congress.[60]

Following the Ball's Bluff setback, McClellan's Grand Army relapsed into its former state of coma, much to the displeasure of the newspaper correspondents who fumed the more at the failure of the Federal authorities to do anything about the Confederate blockade of the lower Potomac.[61] On October 27, the St. Louis *Republican* took note of the fact that "the war upon Gen. McClellan is assuming a bold front in the East" and that "all the New York and Philadelphia papers have more or less to say about it." Although the *Republican* expressed the opinion that there was little possibility of such criticism doing the General much harm, the press was already dividing into two mutually antagonistic camps, pro- and anti-McClellan, neither of which seemed capable of making an objective appraisal of his record.

McClellan in turn was becoming more critical of the press on account of the steady flow of information to the enemy through its news columns. When he saw, for example, in the New York *Times* of December 4, 1861, a six-column map showing the location of his lines outside Washington and listing the divisions defending them, he wrote in protest to the Secretary of War describing what the *Times* had done as "a case of treasonable action" and urging the suppression of "this treasonable sheet." Cameron referred the General's complaint to Raymond, who indignantly refuted the accusations. In his own defense, the editor pointed out that the map he had reproduced in the *Times* could be purchased in any capital bookstore and that supplementary data had been obtained from one of McClellan's own General Orders that had been released to the press for publication two months before. "Not a word," stressed Raymond, "was said of the strength of the divisions or of any detail which could prove either new or important to the enemy."[62]

Among the newspaper men who were reporting news from Washington at this time was the poet, Thomas Bailey Aldrich, then in the employment of the New York *Tribune*. In a letter addressed to his mother from Washington near the end of October, he described in lively fashion a recent jaunt into the enemy's country which provided him with an exciting adventure:

> I have been on horseback two days—and two nights, I was going to say, but I did get out of the saddle to sleep. What a strange time I had of it. House of the New York "Tribune" and myself started on a reconnoissance under the wing of General Stapel and staff. We had not ridden an hour through those wonderful Virginia woods when I got separated from the party, and haven't laid eyes on 'em since—excepting Ned House, who has just reached Washington, having given me up for lost. I don't quite know how it was, but suddenly I found myself alone in a tangle of dense forest and unknown roads. Close on the rebel lines, not knowing quite in what direction, without a guide, and nothing to eat—you may imagine that I wished myself on the harmless banks of the Pis-

> cataqua. Well, I did. To crown all, a moonless night was darkening down on the terrible stillness; and as the darkness grew I caught glimpses of lurid camp-fires here and there—a kind of goblin glare which lent an indescribable mystery and unpleasantness to the scene. Whether these were the camp-fires of friend or foe I had no means of telling. I put spurs to my horse and dashed on—now by the black ruins of a burnt farmhouse, now by some shadowy ford where a fight had evidently taken place. . . . I did not feel alone at such places; for my fancy beheld long lines of infantry, and parks of artillery, and squares of cavalry, moving among the shadows, in a noiseless conflict. I wish I'd time to tell you of the ride—how I stole by the sentinels, and at last feeling that I was going straight to Manassas, stopt and held a council of war with T.B.A. It dawned on me that Washington lay in the *east.* The sun was sinking directly before me in the *west,* so I sensibly turned my horse and rode back. . . . To make a long story short, I slept on my horse's neck in the woods, we two lying cosily together, and at sunrise, oh so hungry, I saw far off the dome of the Capitol and the Long Bridge. Here I am, a year older in looks. I have feasted, and after this is mailed shall go to bed and sleep three days.[63]

Although there is some reason to believe that McClellan was pondering the advisability of a large-scale movement as late as the latter part of November,[64] no such movement materialized before the army went into winter quarters. Deprived of anything more exciting to write about than the familiar routine of camp life, punctuated now and then by a parade or review,[65] the army reporters could do little else than consider the possibility of seeking winter quarters of their own and improvise, for the benefit of their editors and readers, endless variations on the current theme, "All quiet along the Potomac."

8

An Affray With General Halleck

SOON after Fremont's departure from Missouri, the press took note of another change in the Western army command. It was on November 18, 1861, that Major General Henry W. Halleck, eastward bound from California, arrived at St. Louis to head the new Department of the Missouri. Wisconsin, Illinois, and the western half of Kentucky, as well as the trans-Mississippi area, were included within the jurisdiction of the newly organized department. Commonly known among the soldiers as "Old Brains," perhaps because of his election to Phi Beta Kappa during college days, Halleck had left the regular army during the fifties to enter on a successful business career along the west coast. In spite of his soldierly bearing, his austere and scholarly temperament better fitted him for the duties of an office general than for the responsibilities of active command in the field. Coffin of the Boston *Journal* wrote at a later stage:

> He has a fine physique, is stout, burly, weighs two hundred avoirdupois, has a round head, is middle aged, black hair filling fast with silver. He walks by the hour in front of his quarters, his thumbs in the arm pits of his vest . . . casting quick looks, now to the right, now to the left, evidently not for the purpose of seeing anything or anybody, but staring into vacancy the while. . . . The army evidently has confidence in its commander, though I doubt if he is known personally to many of the officers, and to very few of the men. I should judge that there was little about him which could impart magnetism for the *elan,* or dash, with which great commanders . . . inspire men to accomplish daring deeds and great results.[1]

Upon his arrival at St. Louis, Halleck held a press conference attended by a large representation of Eastern and Western newspaper correspondents. The new department commander listened very attentively to the remarks of his guests, smiled frequently, and seemed to be quite willing that there should be a complete understanding between himself and the press. The newsmen left with the impression that they had learned all about his plans, but after a day or so none of them could recall anything definite the General had said.[2] On a later occasion the reporters were to find General Halleck even less communicative.

During the second week of January, 1862, the country was electrified by news dispatches from St. Louis announcing that an army of seventy-five thousand men was being massed at Cairo to move up the Tennessee River and strike at the very heart of the Confederacy. Newspaper correspondents from all points of the compass descended upon Cairo, eager to be on hand for the great "forward movement." Richardson of the New York *Tribune* was among the first to arrive, followed by Richard T. Colburn of the New York *World,* Coffin of the Boston *Journal,* and a score of others. Franc Wilkie of the New York *Times* remarked:

> You meet newspaper men at every step; they block up the approaches to headquarters . . . they are constantly demanding passes, horses, saddles, blankets, news, copies of official papers, a look into private correspondence, and things, whose use and extent are only appreciated by omniscience.[3]

The forward movement was slow getting under way, however, and the manner in which it was executed greatly puzzled the correspondents. On January 18, Coffin communicated to his old friend, Senator Henry Wilson of Massachusetts, a black picture of the state of affairs in the West. Coffin wrote:

> If you want to be disgusted just come out here. Last week you were told that a grand expedition of 75,000 men were moving from here. The dispatches were dictated by General Grant himself. He moved with about 14,000 including the force at Paducah. They have been traveling up and down in the mud between here and Mayfield. I was out yesterday and found them scattered like sheep in a pasture. The advance was within six or seven miles of Columbus. Infantry regiments were miles from any support. They were scattered over a territory as large as Essex County, and this in face of 25,000 rebels at Columbus. If Polk had known of their condition he could have picked them all up as a chicken eats corn. What Grant intended to do no one knows.
>
> But to cap the climax Grant returned to Fort Jefferson last

night and the troops are all on the way back. They will all be in tonight.

Things are in a deplorable condition. A letter from Rolla last night says that several regiments there are in a state of mutiny. Curtis is nobody. Sturgis is drunk nearly all the time and gambles with one of the lowest fellows you can find, connected with the N. Y. *Herald.* Halleck has not once left St. Louis. He has not visited one of his divisions. I have not during the three weeks I have been out here seen a regimental drill and but two or three company drills. There is a looseness of discipline unparalleled.

Commodore Foot is all most [sic] in despair. He came to my room last night and we had a long talk. He has not been able to get a single mortar, although there are 38 boats here which cost $8,300 a piece also thirteen steam tugs which cost $11,600 a piece. He wants the mortars very much. He feels that he has been hardly used. The gunboats are nearly ready, but he says that it will be useless to attempt to shell Columbus without the army cooperates.

I do not believe you will see anything done in the West this winter. Buell is still in Louisville seventy-five miles from his army, and there are no signs of any movement there. Commodore Foot says that the rebels are strengthening their works every day; that they are becoming very formidable.

Meanwhile disease is making sad havoc among the men. The hospitals are fast filling up. You may use this information any way you please for it is the truth.[4]

The real purpose of Grant's movement, which was undertaken at General McClellan's orders, was to create doubt on the part of the enemy as to where the main blow was to fall and to prevent the Confederates in western Tennessee and Kentucky from sending reinforcements to General Buckner at Bowling Green, Kentucky. In the meantime, General George H. Thomas from Buell's command[5] advanced upon Zollicoffer in Eastern Kentucky and won a minor success at Mill Springs, whose importance was greatly exaggerated by the press.[6]

None of the correspondents had a good word to speak for Cairo.[7] As the key to the lower Mississippi Valley it was the most important strategic point in the West, but its flat saucerlike terrain, its marshes and flooded streets, and its unhealthful climate provided a never-ending topic for complaint by the visiting journalists. The only hotel of any consequence in the town was the St. Charles, a six-storied structure swarming with officers and civilians of every description. Members of the press were commonly assigned to Room No. 45 on the third floor rear, overlooking a yard filled with refuse and a pool of stagnant water.

"I am a correspondent of the Podunk *Herald*" would announce the newcomer with the air of one who expected the clerk to be prostrated by this stupendous announcement. "I want a first-class room. Can I get one on the front next to the levee and not too high up?"

"Certainly," the genial clerk would reply, and then after a study of checks as if uncertain whether to give the new arrival the front parlor or a suite of rooms on the floor above he would remark, "Yes, here's Room No. 45; just what you want. Here, boy, show the gentleman to No. 45. Any baggage? No? All right. The boy will show you up. The key is in the door."

After waiting some time for the boy to put in his appearance, the correspondent would start off on his own in search of No. 45. Upon entering the room, he received a rough foretaste of the hospitality which the St. Charles was prepared to offer. There were two beds in the room, invariably occupied by one or more jovial Bohemians fully dressed, including their boots, and exhaling a stale alcoholic aroma. The rest of the furniture was in keeping with the general atmosphere of dirt and confusion: a broken chair or two, a cracked looking-glass, a battered pitcher, and pieces of chipped crockery on a tumble-down washstand. Saddles, bridles, and horse blankets were scattered everywhere. Every morning the floor would be covered with boots, hats, coats, and other articles of masculine attire which the earliest risers would appropriate. It was no use to complain; it was 45 or nothing. Gradually the new arrival became resigned to the inevitable and watched for opportunities to better his lot at the expense of his less fortunate rivals.

As a safeguard against the advance of the Union armies the Confederates had established a line over three hundred miles in length from Columbus, Kentucky (26 miles below Cairo), through Bowling Green to Cumberland Gap. Below Columbus were several well-garrisoned forts protecting the all-important Mississippi life line. The Tennessee and Cumberland rivers—both of them important thoroughfares leading to the very heart of the Confederacy—were guarded respectively by two strongholds, Fort Henry and Fort Donelson, located not more than twelve miles apart just south of the Kentucky-Tennessee line. At the end of January, Grant received the signal from Halleck to move up the Tennessee River and attack Fort Henry with support from Flag Officer

Andrew H. Foote's gunboats. On February 2, four ironclad and three wooden gunboats and a number of transports left Cairo with the first part of the expedition. This time no publicity had been given out in advance. As a result, several of the correspondents were left behind and forced to display some agility in overtaking the advance.[8]

In accordance with his plan, Grant disembarked his troops four miles below the fort to try to block the escape of the garrison. Meanwhile the gunboats continued upstream to attack their objective at close quarters. Franc Wilkie, the New York *Times* representative, remained on a dispatch boat, while Richardson and Browne of the New York *Tribune* and several other journalists went ashore with the troops. At this time the Tennessee River was in flood, and much of the ground around Fort Henry was under water. Wading through half-submerged cornfields, crossing swollen streams on slippery logs, and picking their way through the woods, the little party of journalists came in sight of a half dozen log buildings on the summit of a ridge which constituted a rebel outpost. None of its occupants remained; at the approach of the Union armada they had fled in alarm, abandoning all their effects except their weapons and the clothing they wore. The correspondents continued to push on in the direction of the fort, William E. Webb of the St. Louis *Republican* in the van. "Hush! Do you see those men with guns?" cautioned Webb suddenly as he crouched behind a tree. The rest of the group quickly followed his example and focused their glances upon a column of five or six men armed with rifles passing along the next ridge. Fortunately, they proved to be a party of "Jessie Scouts"[9] operating in advance of the main body. Greetings were exchanged, and the correspondents gladly accepted their offer to act as an escort. After advancing a little farther, the members of the newspaper detachment perched on the brow of a hill within a mile of the fort to obtain a better view of the bombardment and picked out various points of observation. Some stood on logs and rocks; some on fences; others looked on from high in the tree tops.[10]

Since the Confederate guns were barely above the water level, they were unable to reply effectively to the damaging fire of Foote's gunboats. Within hardly more than an hour and a quarter the fleet bombardment resulted in the surrender of the fort and what was left of its twenty-eight hundred defenders. Before the attack began, General Lloyd Tilghman, the rebel commandant, had moved all but a hundred of his garrison out of the fort and directed them to retreat to Fort Donelson.

In spite of the escape of most of the garrison, the capture of Fort Henry was an important victory, and the newspapers made the most of it. One of the Chicago reporters, in an attempt to interview General Tilghman, asked him how he spelled his name.

"Sir," the general was quoted as saying, "I do not desire to have my name appear in this matter, in any newspaper connection whatever. If General Grant sees fit to use it in his official dispatches, I have no objection, Sir; but I do not wish to have it in the newspapers."

"I merely asked it," persisted the reporter, "to mention as one among the prisoners captured."

"You will oblige me, Sir," reiterated the General with an air of finality, "by not giving my name in any newspaper connection whatever."

General Tilghman's desire for anonymity was not respected, however, and the account of the interview was widely reprinted.[11]

After the battle Richardson stopped in at General Grant's headquarters to bid him goodbye before he left for New York. Wilkie had managed to get a letter off on the first dispatch-boat, but Richardson had missed it and there would not be another for ten hours.

"You had better wait a day or two," said the General.

"Why?"

"Because I am going over to capture Fort Donelson tomorrow."

"How strong is it?"

"We have not been able to ascertain exactly, but I think we can take it. At all events, we can try."[12]

Richardson did not follow the General's advice, however. Instead, he went down the river on the first steamer, took the train for New York, and wrote his story en route. Although ten hours behind the *Times* correspondent at the start, he was able to make up the difference while in transit so that his account of the battle for the *Tribune* was published on the same morning as was Wilkie's in the *Times*. In his absence, active campaigning had been held up by rain and bad roads so that he was able to get back in time to be on hand for the capture of Fort Donelson.

It was not until the twelfth of February that Grant's army was able to move against the fort. Meanwhile the gunboats had had to return to Cairo, pass up the Ohio as far as Paducah, and then ascend the winding course of the Cumberland in order to give support to the operation. Captain Henry Walke in the "Carondelet" was the first to come within sight of the fort a little after noon of the twelfth. During the night of the thirteenth, Flag Officer Foote came up with the remainder of the gunboat fleet, bringing with him ten thousand additional troops for Grant's army.

It must have seemed obvious to those in command of the Federal forces that Fort Donelson could not easily be reduced. The fort stood on high ground on the west bank of the Cumberland and covered an area of nearly a hundred acres. To the north of it was Hickman's Creek, a tributary of the Cumberland and much larger than ordinary because of the backwater from the river; to the south was another small stream also in flood; on the west was a line of rifle pits extending two miles back from the river at the farthest point and running along a crest of high ground. This formidable position was defended by about nineteen thousand men under General John B. Floyd, once secretary of war in Buchanan's cabinet.

The battle which settled the fate of Donelson lasted for four days (February 12-15) while about a dozen reporters[13] wandered about the field, half-frozen and half-starved. In later years, Browne told of how he and a fellow correspondent of the New York *World* followed the army supply wagons about in order to pick up any pieces of hard tack which might be jolted out.[14]

At the outset Grant planned to use the army to contain the enemy within his lines while the fleet was to silence the enemy guns. Four ironclad vessels — the "St. Louis," "Louisville," "Pittsburgh," and "Carondelet"—and two wooden gunboats, the "Tyler" and "Conestoga," comprised the attacking force.

In the pilot house of the flagship "St. Louis," acting as private secretary to the Flag Officer, was one of the outstanding newspaper correspondents of the war, Joe McCullagh of the Cincinnati *Gazette.* McCullagh was an Irish immigrant, one of sixteen children, who had left the "old country" when he was eleven years old and worked his way to New York in a sailing vessel. He was in Cincinnati when the war broke out, working as a local reporter for the *Gazette.*[15]

While riding along a side road in rural Missouri one autumn day in 1861, a group of army correspondents came upon a slender young chap in Federal uniform mounted on a bony steed of prodigious size. As one of the group later remembered him, the youthful soldier:

> was blond in complexion, with blue-gray eyes, a large flexible mouth . . . a face of enormous mobility, and an utterance of extreme rapidity . . . interjected at brief intervals with colossal oaths.

As he paused to catch his breath after a savage outburst against Fremont and his wife, the correspondents learned that he was a stenographer with the rank of lieutenant on Fremont's staff, that he was functioning at the same time as a reporter for the Cincinnati *Enquirer*, and that his name was Joe McCullagh.[16]

On another occasion, so the story goes, McCullagh was brought to a halt by an inexperienced sentry while he was attempting to enter General Buell's lines near Corinth. McCullagh was well aware that the pass countersigned by General Grant which he was carrying would never pass muster in Buell's army. Moreover, he realized that a newspaperman stood hardly a chance of obtaining a favor, however slight, from the unamiable "Don Carlos." While these unhappy thoughts were running through his mind, the sentry humbly inquired if he were a commissioned officer. The quick-witted McCullagh suddenly saw an escape from his predicament. "Don't you know that none but commissioned officers are allowed to ride gray horses?" he demanded. "No." I never knew that," stammered the frightened sentry as he gazed with increasing respect at McCullagh's iron-gray steed. The "commissioned officer" left him staring there and rode on in a manner befitting the commanding general of the army.[17]

McCullagh once defined the secret of success in journalism as "guessing where Hell will break loose next."[18] At Fort Donelson, as on several other occasions during the Civil War, he demonstrated that he possessed that ability in no small degree. Although Foote and his men went to their task with a will, they met with a blistering reception. One after another the Federal gunboats were disabled by the effective fire of the Fort Donelson artillerists. Just before the "St. Louis" pulled out of line, a shell from the largest rifled gun in the fort came crashing through the wall of the pilot house, wounding every person in the interior except the *Gazette*'s nimble-footed correspondent.[19]

After fighting for more than an hour, the fleet withdrew. Most of the gunboats were badly crippled; Foote's flagship, the "St. Louis," bore the marks of fifty-seven hits, and her pilot wheel had been shot away. Now it was up to the army to show what it could do.

On the following morning while Grant was conferring with Foote on board the "St. Louis," the Confederates came out of their entrenchments in full force and vigorously attacked John A. McClernand's division on the Federal right. Both McClernand and Lew Wallace were pushed back, and by one o'clock the escape route to Nashville was open to the

Confederates. At that juncture the divided counsels of their commanders proved their undoing. Both Floyd and Brigadier General Gideon Pillow, the second in command, were in favor of falling back to the original position; Buckner, on the other hand, wanted to take advantage of the success gained thus far to effect the escape of the army to Nashville. Meanwhile Grant, who had returned to the battlefield, ordered an advance by Brigadier General Charles F. Smith's division against the Confederate right, which had been thinned out to permit the concentration on the left. Taking Jacob G. Lauman's brigade of Iowa and Indiana troops, General Smith began the advance. In the words of the Chicago *Tribune* reporter:

> they moved across the meadow through a little belt of woods, came to the base of the hill, and met the leaden rain. But they paused not a moment. . . . Without firing a shot, without flinching a moment or faltering as their ranks were thinned, they rushed up the hill, regardless of the fire in front or on their flank, jumped upon the rifle pits and drove the rebels down the eastern slope.[20]

Smith s successful movement was followed by a counterattack on the part of Wallace's and McClernand's divisions. By nightfall the Confederates were forced back beyond the line they had occupied that morning.[21]

That evening a stormy council of war was held within Fort Donelson which resulted in a decision to surrender on the best terms possible. Floyd, the commanding officer, and Pillow swore they would rather die than fall into the hands of the Federals so they transferred their commands to Buckner, who was their junior in rank, and made their escape upstream in a small steamboat. Buckner remained behind to arrange the terms of capitulation.

The capture of Fort Donelson with some fifteen thousand prisoners, at least forty pieces of artillery, and a large quantity of military stores was an important victory. Some curious stories were told after the battle, however, concerning the ultraprofessional zeal displayed by certain newspaper correspondents. One of them was alleged to have locked General Buckner in a room at nearby Dover, Tennessee, and to have kept him there in spite of the General's threats until he had completed a pencil sketch of him. Still another was said to have approached a wounded officer of some distinction who was supposed at the time to be mortally wounded and to have begged him not to die yet, for the sake of the newspaper which he (the reporter) had the honor to represent. As a special inducement, the reporter assured the officer that if he had any last words they would appear in the best form in the earliest possible issue of his "widely circulated and highly influential journal."[22]

Following the surrender, several of the correspondents were permitted to circulate among the prisoners so that they might learn their views and get some impressions of Southern morale. Coffin observed a marked difference between the Kentuckians and Tennesseans on the one hand and those from the deep South on the other. He noted:

> Those from the Gulf States were sour, not inclined to talk as a general rule; or if talkative, they at once commenced about the negro and were defiant. The Tennesseans . . . were not much sorry that the result was as it was.[23]

Richardson concluded on the basis of his inquiries that the common people of the South cared very little which way the war terminated as long as it terminated soon, but most of the officers, as distinguished from the privates, he found to be as "spiteful as hornets."[24]

Some of the army correspondents from New York were inclined to poke a great deal of fun at the "Boston man" as they styled Coffin. At this time the New England papers were generally regarded in the metropolis as being slow and antiquated in their methods, but the New York reporters were soon to discover in Coffin a worthy antagonist.

At ten o'clock on the morning after the surrender, the gunboat "Carondelet" eased alongside the wharf at Cairo, bearing the first news of the great victory. One of her sailors leaped ashore and throwing his hat in the air proposed three cheers for Fort Donelson. The crowd which gathered about the landing gazed at him in wonder, but he soon dispelled the mystery by shouting "We've got 'em at last!" Then Captain Walke stepped ashore and confirmed the report that Donelson had fallen. The effect was magical. Within a few moments the crowd had scattered in every direction, and soon the telegraph operator at Cairo, the nearest telegraph station to Fort Donelson, was ticking out the news of the surrender.[25]

Among the passengers on board the "Carondelet" was Coffin, who had taken the first boat from Fort Donelson to Cairo with the intention of writing his story on shipboard. Instead, he had been kept busy throughout the journey ministering to the needs of the wounded, who filled the cabin and staterooms and choked the passageways. After reaching

Cairo, Coffin decided to go on to Chicago by train, writing up his material as he went. By the time he reached there, his story was ready to go out in time to net him a scoop. Although Boston was two hundred miles farther from the battlefield than New York, all New England had read Coffin's story in the *Journal* before any correspondent's letters from Fort Donelson appeared in the newspapers of Manhattan.[26]

None of the newspaper accounts of the battle, with the possible exception of Coffin's, was particularly outstanding. Contrary to the usual practice, the first reports of the battle actually underrated its importance. Moreover, they reflected their authors' confusion as to the positions of the various regiments in the field and showed a tendency to favor certain regiments at the expense of others.[27] Several correspondents, one of whom was irritated with Grant because of being excluded from his headquarters, deliberately omitted his name from their accounts of the battle and made it appear that General Smith was entitled to most of the credit. Still another reporter met at Cairo a staff officer whom Grant had placed under arrest for habitual drunkenness. Snatching at the opportunity to even scores with the General, the staff officer persuaded the reporter to spread the word that Grant was a drunkard.[28]

Nevertheless, the exciting news from Donelson sent the newspaper men in the various parts of the West scurrying in the direction of Grant's army. Whitelaw Reid had hardly entered the Cincinnati *Gazette* office on the morning after the surrender before passes were crammed into his pockets and he was told to take the first train for Cairo and Fort Donelson. He informed his brother:

> How long I'm to be gone I don't know. Everything depends on future movements of the army. We have two correspondents at Fort Donelson now, & two or three more in Divisions that are coming this way. I am instructed to get our *corps* into proper shape, assign them in their duties, supervise them as long as I think advisable, & see to it that the Gazette is first in the news.[29]

The fall of Donelson meant that the road to strategic Nashville was open. Meanwhile, the news of Donelson's surrender had reached there on a Sunday morning while many of its citizens were on the way to church. Straightway a panic seized upon them at the prospect of imminent invasion by the "ruthless northern hordes." Some wandered aimlessly about, adding to the confusion; others loaded their furniture and valuables into wagons and carriages and headed southward in the wake of Major General William Hardee's retreating army. According to the Richmond *Dispatch,* Governor Isham Harris rode at top speed through the streets of the city mounted on horseback, crying out that the papers in the Capitol must be removed. Subsequently, in company with the Tennessee legislators, who had at once assembled, he left Nashville for Memphis by special train.[30]

One of the first of the Yankee invaders to arrive at Nashville was Henry Villard of the New York *Herald,* who had been invited to accompany Brigadier General William Nelson's command. Learning that not a single Confederate soldier remained in the vicinity, Villard set out on foot to explore the town and gather information as to the local events of the last few days. All the stores and most of the better residences were closed up. The State House, only a few days before the scene of anxious deliberation by the legislature, was deserted save for a colored doorkeeper. The American House, the leading hotel, was likewise closed down. "Massa done gone souf" announced a colored man with a broad grin, who appeared after much ringing of the front bell. Villard was not to be put off so easily, however. Assuming a bold front, he prevailed upon the servitor to show him the best rooms in the house. Having made his selection, he hurried back to the boat to pick up his baggage and in less than a half hour was comfortably installed at the hotel. Before noon it was swarming with other correspondents and staff officers. After a few days the proprietor returned, and the hotel was soon in running order again. Communication by mail and telegraph with the North had been established within forty-eight hours after the arrival of General Buell, and so, after a lapse of nearly a year, the Nashville date line again became a familiar sight in the Northern press.[31]

Early in March, the reporters made ready to accompany a combined naval and land expedition to attack the Confederate position at Columbus, Kentucky, which had for some time represented a threat to the Union position at Cairo. In spite of an order from General Halleck forbidding any journalists to accompany the expedition, Coffin, Richardson, and Constantine D. Millar of the Cincinnati *Commercial* were guests of Commodore Foote on his flagship when the gunboat fleet dropped down the Mississippi on March 4, 1862, to attack the Confederate stronghold. Some years later Coffin wrote:

> It was a new and strange experience, that first night on a gunboat. ... By the dim light of the lamp I could see the great gun within six feet of me, and shining cutlasses and gleaming muskets. Looking out of the ward-room, I could see the men in their hammocks asleep, like orioles in their hanging nests. The sentinels paced the deck above, and all was silent but the sound of the great wheel of the steamer turning lazily in the stream, and the gurgling of the water around the bow.[32]

Well before sunrise the men were astir. Hammocks were packed away, and the decks were cleared for action. Through the morning haze the outline of the bluff upon which the enemy guns were mounted could be dimly seen. But what were those colors waving over the enemy fortifications? That was no rebel flag fluttering in the breeze. As the expedition drew closer to the bluff, it was learned that the enemy had withdrawn twelve hours before and that a scouting party of the Second Illinois Cavalry from Paducah had already hoisted the stars and stripes over the town.

At this same time the newspaper men stationed at Cairo were complaining bitterly about the way in which the local censorship was being exercised by Brigadier General George W. Cullum, Halleck's chief of staff. The Cairo correspondent of the Chicago *Tribune* grumbled in a private letter to one of its editors:

> In many directions he lacks ordinary intelligence. He is no more competent for the position of telegraph censor than the veriest old woman. . . . Scarcely a day has passed that I have not been obliged to delay dispatches three or four hours when the work of revision would not have occupied three or four minutes.[33]

Similar complaints were voiced by other reporters. On the same day that Foote's gunboat fleet dropped down the river to capture Columbus, more than a score of the Cairo correspondents held a meeting, at which a committee was appointed to call upon General Halleck in St. Louis to solicit better treatment for their dispatches. Cullum remained at his post in Cairo until after the Battle of Shiloh, however, at which time the duties of telegraph censor were assigned to another officer.[34]

After the evacuation of Columbus, General Polk, the Confederate commander, fell back to another fortified stronghold along the Mississippi opposite New Madrid, Missouri, called Island No. 10. On March 14, after a brief period of refueling and repair, the Union gunboat fleet left Cairo bound for Island No. 10 with representatives of the principal Boston, New York, Philadelphia, Cincinnati, and Chicago newspapers on board. Contrary to public expectation, the operation resulted in a siege which lasted nearly a month. Although the correspondents with the fleet had a fine view of the frequent duels between the gunboats and the Confederate shore batteries, they became greatly exasperated because they could find so little to write about, and some of them finally left before the operation was over in search of a more active theater of hostilities.[35]

During the siege, some of the St. Louis and Chicago newspapers were strongly criticized on account of the leakage of military information through their columns. The worst offender was the St. Louis *Republican*, which on April 6 published a letter from its Cairo correspondent describing in detail Major General John Pope's plan for flanking the Confederate position by cutting a canal through the Arkansas swamps from the head of the Island to New Madrid. Eventually the War Department felt obliged to send an order to Flag Officer Foote directing him to clear his flagship of all reporters.[36] Nevertheless, they spoke in flattering terms of the facilities for obtaining news furnished to them by Foote and his fellow naval officers and of their "uniform courtesy . . . in strong contradistinction to the manners of some of our army officers."[37] On April 7, Island No. 10 at last fell, netting General Pope six thousand prisoners and providing a scoop for George P. Upton of the Chicago *Tribune* staff.[38]

Following the capture of Island No. 10, a prominent officer on General Halleck's staff who had served under Scott in Mexico was given the task of fortifying the captured rebel post. An obscure country newspaper erroneously gave credit to another officer, whereupon the aggrieved engineer sought out the agent of the Associated Press at Halleck's headquarters and remarked:

"By the way, Mr. Weir, I have been carrying a paper in my pocket for several days, but have forgotten to hand it to you. Here it is!"

So saying he produced a manuscript upon which the ink was hardly dry, stating that the island had been fortified under the immediate supervision of himself, the well-known officer of the regular army, who served upon the staff of Lieutenant General Scott during the Mexican War and was at present holding an important position upon the staff of General Halleck.

"I rely upon your sense of justice," said the complainant in an injured tone, "to give this proper publicity."

Without cracking a smile, the Associated Press man sent this long dispatch word for word to the Associated Press with a note appended to the effect that "You may rest assured that this is perfectly reliable, because every word of it was written by the old fool himself!" Weir's confidential note was, of course, left out of the newspapers, but it provided considerable amusement for the telegraphers, who were by no means unaccustomed to private comments of this sort.[39]

While the siege of Island No. 10 was still in progress, Grant's army advanced up the Tennessee River and went into camp at Pittsburg Landing on the west bank of the stream about nine miles south of Savannah, Tennessee. There a steep bluff rose about a hundred feet above the river's low-water level. To the west stretched a broken plateau heavily wooded for the most part but dotted with clearings. Two roads led from the Landing to Corinth, Mississippi, twenty-two miles southwest. Corinth was an important railroad junction and the point where General Albert Sidney Johnston, then in command of all the Confederate troops west of the Allegheny Mountains, had decided to concentrate his forces for a fresh stand.

In spite of the scant distance which separated the two armies, neither Grant nor Halleck seems to have entertained any fear of an attack from that quarter. No attempt had been made to construct entrenchments or establish an effective line of battle. On the morning of the attack Sherman's and Benjamin M. Prentiss' divisions were loosely strung out in front; McClernand's division was slightly to the rear of Sherman's position; Stephen A. Hurlbut's and W. H. L. Wallace's were somewhat farther back; Colonel David Stuart's brigade of Sherman's division was on the far left at Lick Creek with a gap over a half mile wide between his right and Prentiss' left which an alert enemy could hardly fail to detect. Buell with his Army of the Cumberland was advancing from Nashville to establish a junction with Grant, but without haste as he had no information from either Halleck or Grant that the army at Pittsburg Landing was in danger of being attacked.[40]

There is no indication that the press was any better informed. Most of the army correspondents in the Western theater were with the Mississippi Flotilla, reporting the operation at Island No. 10. The correspondents with Grant's army—there were probably less than ten on the eve of Shiloh[41]—apparently expected Johnston to make a stand at or near Corinth, but none of them predicted that the Confederates were about to attempt a major offensive stroke.

Johnston was well aware, however, that Buell was marching to join Grant. Now if ever, he decided, was the time to strike. Grant's position between two creeks with a deep river behind him constituted a natural trap from which there appeared to be no escape. A frontal attack pressed home with vigor might destroy Grant's army before Buell could come to his rescue. Johnston had planned to move his army from Corinth to Pittsburg Landing in two days with the attack scheduled for daybreak on April 5. There were the usual delays, however, resulting from rain, bad roads, and the difficulty of handling inexperienced troops. Not until late in the afternoon of the fifth were the Confederate troops in their prescribed positions. After some consultation Johnston and Beauregard decided that an immediate advance was out of the question and prepared to strike the enemy at daybreak.[42]

The full shock of the next morning's attack fell upon Sherman's and Prentiss' divisions, made up for the most part of inexperienced troops. During the night Colonel Everett Peabody, commanding the first brigade of Prentiss' division, had been unable to sleep. Shortly before daybreak, he rose and led three companies of the Twenty-fifth Missouri out along the Corinth Road to "feel" the enemy and ascertain if he were present in force. Unexpectedly they came upon the skirmish line of Hardee's Corps advancing to the attack and were flung back. About 4:30 A.M. as the Federals in camp were just beginning to cook breakfast, they were startled by the wild cries of the pickets, followed by crashing volleys from the advancing foe.

"George," said Henry Bentley of the Philadelphia *Inquirer* to his colored servant, "those grey coated chaps will soon be in here; you had better let the breakfast go at present and keep at a safe distance from the cotton and rice plantations."

"They never keep me there, sir, if they catch me," piped George tremulously as he headed for the river. Bentley remained behind, was soon trapped along with several others, and hustled to the Confederate rear as a prisoner.[43]

The Confederates advanced to the attack in single parallel lines. Hardee's corps was first, followed by Braxton Bragg, with Polk supporting the left and John C. Breckenridge the right. Their assault forced the Unionists to yield ground steadily all along the line. Prentiss was separated from the greater portion of his troops, and by ten o'clock his division had ceased to function as a unit. By that time, however, the fresh divisions of W. H. L. Wallace and Hurlbut had moved up to help establish a new line.

When the sound of the firing first reached him, Grant was eating breakfast in Savannah, nine miles downstream from the Landing and on the opposite side of the river. Nelson's division, the advance guard of Buell's army, had arrived there the evening before and had received orders from Grant to move up the East bank of the river to a position where it could be ferried over to either Crump's Landing or Pittsburg Landing. Grant needed no more urgent summons. Pausing only long enough to write a note to Buell, whom he was expecting to meet sometime that morning, he boarded the dispatch boat "Tigress" and moved swiftly upstream in the direction of the firing. On the way, he ran in close to Crump's Landing to speak with General Lew Wallace, whose division was guarding the bulk of the army supplies. While Grant was giving Wallace his orders, Whitelaw Reid of the Cincinnati *Gazette* came aboard and accompanied General Grant to Pittsburg Landing. Reid had risen from his sick bed at Wallace's headquarters to go to the field. In later years he took satisfaction in recalling that he had arrived on the battlefield as early as the Commanding General.[44]

Johnston's original plan had been to turn the Union left, cut his adversaries off from the Landing, and then surround them in the angle formed by the river and Owl Creek. In the heat of the conflict this plan was lost sight of, and the Confederates wasted much of their strength in a vain effort to dislodge their battered foes from a position along the crest of a ridge which came to be known as the "Hornet's Nest." Brigade after brigade was hurled against it, only to be thrown back. During one of these assaults General Johnston was struck in the thigh by a piece of shell and in the absence of his personal physician and his staff, allowed to bleed to death. As soon as he was notified, General Beauregard took over the command and gave orders that the news of Johnston's death should be concealed from the men.[45]

Shortly after Johnston received his death wound, the Hornet's Nest was forced, and Prentiss with three of his regiments was captured. Grant's army had now been driven back into a space of not more than four hundred acres on a rolling plateau just above the Landing. Below the bluff were several thousand fugitives from the battlefield who had completely lost whatever fighting spirit they might once have had. Another retreat would drive the army into the Tennessee River. It was at about this time that Henry Villard, coming upstream from Savannah on the same steamboat with General Buell, caught sight of the spectacle near the Landing and exclaimed to Captain James B. Fry, Buell's chief of staff," Oh heavens! Captain, here is Bull Run all over again."[46] While a number of officers attempted to lead the skulkers back into the fight, Villard went ashore with one of Nelson's brigades, which had been ferried across from the opposite bank. Meanwhile, Colonel Joseph D. Webster, Grant's chief of staff, had taken advantage of a lull in the conflict to mount about twenty heavy guns along a ravine on the extreme left of the Federal line. Here the last determined stand was made. While the remnants of Grant's army struggled to hold this position, the gunboats "Tyler" and "Lexington" pulled into the mouth of a nearby creek and lobbed seven-inch shells in the general direction of the enemy. With the failure of this last enemy assault, firing ceased. By this time a driving rain had set in, and Villard decided to return to the boat to find shelter for the night. Learning, however, that the officer in charge could not receive his horse on board again, he made arrangements instead to spend the night at Nelson's headquarters. There he was provided the partial shelter of a rubber blanket hung between two trees near a big log fire and given some hardtack, cold bacon, brandy, and water.[47]

It was midnight when Ned Spencer of the Cincinnati *Times* sat down to write up his account of the battle. All was silent except for cries of distress from the wounded and an occasional broadside from the gunboats directed at the general vicinity of the enemy's camp.

> As I sit tonight, writing this epistle, the dead and wounded are all around me. The knife of the Surgeon is busy at work, and amputated legs and arms lie scattered in every direction. The cries of the suffering victim, and the groans of those who patiently await for medical attendance, are most distressing to any one who has any sympathy with his fellow man. All day long they have been coming in, and they are placed upon the decks and within the cabins of the steamers, and wherever else they can find a resting place. I hope my eyes may never again look upon such sights.[48]

During the night, three divisions of Buell's army (Nelson's, Thomas L. Crittenden's, and McCook's) crossed the river and took up their position along the Union left. Sleep was impossible, and therefore Villard and his friends from Nelson's staff sat around the fire protected from the rain by their waterproofs, discussing the events of the day before and speculating on those of the morrow. At five-thirty, shots were heard, and soon the battle was on again. At first Villard remained in the rear with the ambulances, but owing to the rough ground and the poor visibility resulting from the mixture of rain and dense powder smoke, it was impossible to learn what was going on by remaining in one spot. He mounted and set out in search of Buell's headquarters. There, likewise, he could obtain very little information. At this juncture, however, heavy firing could be heard from the quarter where McCook's division was engaged, so Villard rode off in that direction and arrived just in time to see McCook's men repel a determined attack. By this time weight of numbers was beginning to tell. Beauregard had only twenty thousand men in line of battle to cope with at least thirty-five thousand of whom twenty-five thousand were fresh troops. Steadily the Confederates were driven back beyond Shiloh Church, at which point Grant halted the Federal advance. By 4:00 P.M. the sound of battle had entirely died away.[49]

When the Confederate right wing gave way, a number of the Union prisoners, Bentley of the Philadelphia *Inquirer* among them, dodged into the bushes along the roadside and made good their escape. Bentley claimed that the rebels had robbed him of everything except his pantaloons and his boots. Subsequently he made his way to Cairo, telegraphed ahead the fact that he had first been captured and then escaped, and then continued on to Philadelphia with his version of the battle written from behind the Confederate lines.[50]

Villard spent about two hours after the battle gathering additional details from those who had taken part. Shortly before dark, he headed for the Landing, tired, hungry, and wet. To his delight he came upon an old friend, a division quartermaster, who readily responded to his request for food and shelter. First his horse was turned over to a deck hand, and then he was shown to a stateroom on one of the boats and provided with a good hot supper to which he did full justice. After ten hours rest and a hearty breakfast, he was ready for work again. Up to this time he had accumulated only part of the material which he needed for a complete account of the two-day battle. He went first to Buell's headquarters, where he learned that Wood's two brigades and Sherman's division had been ordered to resume the pursuit of the enemy. The former was already in motion. As he was anxious to obtain Sherman's version of the battle and feared the pursuit might take the General beyond reach, Villard started to search for him. Sherman was just ready to mount as the *Herald* correspondent came up. The two were, of course, well acquainted, and therefore Sherman was willing to speak freely of the part his division had played and to describe the work of the other divisions insofar as they related to his. Villard then resumed his tour of exploration from one division commander to another, continuing until nearly midafternoon. During his wandering he made inquiries as to telegraph and mail facilities at the various headquarters and learned that as yet there were no telegraph facilities and that even after they had been secured they would not be made available for the newspaper correspondents. A mail boat was to leave for Cairo that very evening, however. As it appeared that no fighting would occur for several days at least, Villard decided to save time by going down the river on the first boat, writing his report on the way and mailing it at Cairo upon arrival. He easily secured a permit through his friend the quartermaster, and by four o'clock he was on board a side-wheeler bound for Cairo. Somewhat to his surprise, he learned that Whitelaw Reid of the Cincinnati *Gazette* and another correspondent were also on board. Introductions were exchanged, and the three reporters quickly became acquainted. As Reid and his friend had been with Grant's army and knew very little of Buell's part in the conflict, it proved of mutual advantage to exchange notes.[51]

Wilkie of the New York *Times* was in Cairo, having just come up from Island No. 10, when Reid and his two newspaper companions arrived there. To Wilkie it seemed that:

> the expression of his [Reid's] face suggested an escape from . . . imminent . . . danger. He was no coward, as I have reason to know, and yet . . . there was not only a suggestion of something like fright in his expression, but a good deal of apparent awe, as if he had just been the witness of some tremendous calamity from which he had narrowly escaped.[52]

At Cairo, Reid and his friends learned that they had already been scooped by another *Herald* correspondent, Frank Chapman, a shrewd and not overly scrupulous fellow. Chapman had gone up the river to Fort Henry from Pittsburg Landing with a correspondent of the Cincinnati *Times* on the night after the battle and obtained access to the army telegraph on the pretext that he was a member of Grant's staff.[53] On Wednesday morning, April 9, the order of business in the

United States Senate was suspended immediately, after the Journal of the day before had been read and approved, while Senator Orville H. Browning of Illinois read a summary of a telegraphic dispatch which had been received that morning by the New York *Herald.* The dispatch read:

> The bloodiest battle of modern times just closed, resulting in complete rout of the enemy, who attacked us Sunday morning. Battle lasted until Monday 4.35, p.m., when the enemy commenced their retreat, and are still flying towards Corinth, pursued by large force of our cavalry. Slaughter on both sides immense. Lost in killed, wounded, and missing from eighteen to twenty thousand; that of the enemy is estimated from thirty-five to forty thousand.[54]

Later in the day, Chapman's dispatch was read before the House of Representatives. According to the *Herald,* when Congressman Schuyler Colfax asked permission to read it, he was greeted from all sides of the House with cries, "To the Clerk's desk," and as the House listened to this first report of the bloody struggle, "all hearts were stilled and the very breathing almost suppressed till the last word of the dispatch was read."[55]

The *Herald's* scoop created a considerable sensation, but the inaccuracies of Chapman's dispatch were soon apparent. Both the extent of the victory and his estimate of the losses on both sides were considerably overdrawn.[56] The *Herald* man, moreover, laid himself open to widespread criticism by his heavy-handed attempts to curry favor with General Grant. The obsequious Chapman wrote:

> About three o'clock in the afternoon [of the second day] General Grant rode to the left, where the fresh regiments had been ordered, and finding the rebels wavering, sent a portion of his bodyguard to the head of each of five regiments, and then ordered a charge across the field, himself leading, as he brandished his sword and waved them on to the crowning victory, while cannon balls were falling like hail around him.[57]

What were the real facts of the case? In a Cincinnati *Gazette* editorial published on April 19, Chapman's story of General Grant leading the charge that broke the enemy's line on the second day of the battle was characterized as "pure romance." Three weeks later a soldier correspondent of the Cincinnati *Commercial* admitted that there had been such a charge but denied that Grant had led the charge in person. He maintained:

> Gen. Buell ordered the charge and Gen. Nelson, the true hero of the left wing, led it. *This I saw.* Gen. Grant was not seen on the left wing during the day and in fact had no business there.

In his official report of the battle, written almost immediately afterward, Grant made no mention of the charge or the contribution which he made to its success. In the account of the battle which appears in his autobiography, however, he tells of gathering up "a couple of regiments or parts of regiments" about the middle of the afternoon on the second day and of marching them forward, "going in front myself to prevent premature or long-range firing." The account continues:

> After marching to within musket-range, I stopped and let the troops pass. The command *Charge* was given, and was executed with loud cheers and with a run, when the last of the enemy broke.[58]

There is no reason to suppose that the version presented in Grant's *Memoirs* is willfully inaccurate although Adam Badeau, rather than Grant, appears to have been the real author of the account of Shiloh given in the *Memoirs.*[59] It seems probable, however, that both the *Herald* correspondent and Badeau ascribed greater importance to the charge in affecting the outcome of the fighting of the second day than it really merited.

Probably no battle fought during the Civil War excited a greater amount of controversy than did the Battle of Shiloh, and for this the army correspondents were in no small degree responsible. Lacking precise information in many cases they dashed off long paragraphs, imaginary for the most part, about desperate hand-to-hand fighting that never occurred;[60] circulated wild stories, later demonstrated to be wholly untrue, about Sherman's men being bayoneted in their tents;[61] and exaggerated the extent of both the Union defeat on Sunday and the Union victory on the following day.[62] Shiloh was the first battle of the war in which the faking of eyewitness accounts of the fighting took place on a large scale.[63] Many of the self-styled authors of eye-witness narratives never came any closer to the battlefield than Cairo.[64] As a result of such practices the term "Cairo war correspondent" took on an invidious connotation.

Considerable ill-feeling arose soon after the battle because of the uncomfortably frank statements that appeared in the newspapers, particularly the Chicago newspapers, concerning the behavior of the Ohio troops on the first day of the battle. A soldier correspondent of the Cincinnati *Commercial* wrote:

> For days the people of Ohio lay under the deep mortification and disgrace of her sons. For days Indiana, Illinois and Iowa waded in blood and did the most daring acts, Ohio wearing only the badge of disgrace.[65]

Eventually the Chicago *Tribune* made editorial amends for the injustice that had been done to certain Ohio regiments in the first reports from Pittsburg Landing,[66] but by that time the damage had been done. To remove the stigma of cowardice from the Buckeye troops, prominent Ohio editors and politicians denounced the "criminal negligence" of their generals, Grant in particular.[67]

Such accusations met with prompt refutation. On April 25, Congressman Elihu B. Washburne of Illinois wrote to one of the editors of the Chicago *Tribune,* fuming at:

> the infamous and slanderous article on Grant copied into your paper from the Cincinnati Gazette. It comes with a pretty grace from a paper in Ohio the troops of which State led to the disaster on Sunday by negligence and cowardice to be assailing an Illinois general who as done the only fighting that has been done in this war, who rescued victory from the jaws of defeat on Monday and drove Beauregard howling to his den.[68]

Still another significant comment in defense of Grant appeared in a letter to the *Tribune* written by an army correspondent of the Philadelphia *Press* several weeks after the battle:

> I went to Pittsburg Landing just after the battle as correspondent of an eastern newspaper. I was almost entirely unacquainted in the army; I had no constituency to tickle, no State's runaway troops to find a scapegoat for, no politico-military friends to write up, and no aspirations for a staff appointment. Consequently I . . . found myself differing very materially from the correspondents who sent out those first reports, and who looked through other people's spectacles. I feel convinced that every general on that field has been wickedly, wilfully and maliciously slandered, and that General Grant and General Sherman have

> had more than their share of abuse. I feel convinced too that they were by far the most able men on that field; that through their admirable generalship, an attack of double our force was successfully resisted; and that in all they did they scarcely... did anything which they now wish had been done differently.[69]

Although a letter contributed to the New York *Evening Post* by a member of Halleck's staff has been characterized as the best picture of the Battle of Shiloh that appeared in any newspaper, that praise might perhaps better be given to Whitelaw Reid's account in the Cincinnati *Gazette*.[70] Like most of his newspaper colleagues, Reid was of the opinion that Grant's army had been surprised, although the army denied it to a man. In later years General Sherman took issue with Reid on this point and made certain unwarranted reflections on his veracity.[71] Most of the evidence, however, seems to indicate that Reid was more nearly correct than Sherman.[72]

The most remarkable feature of Reid's account was its comprehensive view of the battle, which appears the more amazing when the lack of any recognizable plan of attack or defense on the part of the Union commanders is taken into consideration. There were dramatic passages in his narrative, too, and colorful anecdotes relating to the conduct of individual officers and their men. Reid told of watching Grant as he sat on horseback surrounded by his staff at the close of the first day's fighting and of hearing him reply to someone who asked if the prospect did not appear gloomy:

> Not at all. They can't force our lines around these batteries to-night—it is too late. Delay counts everything with us. To-morrow we shall attack them with fresh troops and drive them, of course.[73]

The descriptive quality of Reid's report and its general accuracy established his reputation as one of the foremost correspondents of the war. In Cincinnati, where the loss of life resulting from the battle was felt more directly than in the East, there was deep appreciation of his presentation of the facts as he saw them without fear or favor.

The most widely reprinted account of the battle written from the Southern point of view appears to have been the one published in the Savannah *Republican*, which contained a highly interesting narrative of the conversation between Generals Prentiss and Beauregard on the night following Prentiss' capture.[74]

As a result of the controversial aspect of what happened at Shiloh, at least one army reporter got a new job. Following the battle, McCullagh showed what he had written about it—strongly colored by reports of mismanagement and drunkenness on the part of certain high ranking officers—to one of his associates. He was informed by his colleague that the *Gazette* would not publish his letter as it stood. The high-spirited McCullagh promptly retorted that if the paper would not print his letter he would resign—and he carried out his threat. As soon as Murat Halstead of the Cincinnati *Commercial* learned of McCullagh's impetuous action, he made him an offer of twice the amount he had been receiving from the *Gazette,* together with a stipulation that he should be free to write whatever he chose as long as he worked for the *Commercial.* From that time on, McCullagh's war correspondence received publication through the columns of the *Commercial.*[75]

Within a week after the Battle of Shiloh, General Halleck made his appearance at Grant's headquarters at Pittsburg Landing and took over the active direction of the campaign. Approximately ten days later General Pope with an army of twenty thousand men came over from Island No. 10 to join Halleck. This in conjunction with other reinforcements increased the size of Halleck's army to 125,000, the largest number of troops that had yet been assembled at one place under one commander during the war.

In spite of the numerical superiority of the troops under his command, "Old Brains" was painfully deliberate in his movements. His advance upon Corinth, to which Beauregard had retreated after the blood bath at Shiloh, was not begun until the end of April. Even then his army moved forward at an average speed of less than three-quarters of a mile a day, throwing up breastworks at night after each day's march.[76]

During the early stages of the advance, the Federal camp was filled with army newspapermen, who had been trooping into the lines ever since Shiloh to be on hand for the great battle that was expected to take place near Corinth. By May 3, more than thirty special correspondents were attached to Halleck's army. One of them wrote:

> This is the largest representation of the press ever assembled to witness a battle and between them all what the public don't learn about the forthcoming conflict—if come it does—will hardly be worth knowing.[77]

In spite of the dilatory pace of Halleck's "Grand Army," the campaign was far from being a lark for the reporters. In a letter to his newspaper postmarked May 9, Webb of the St. Louis *Republican* wrote:

> It is doubtful if any movements during the war have been as difficult to chronicle correctly as the present ones. Divisions of advance are miles apart, and so separated by impassable roads that each is as completely ignorant of movements in the other as if there were a special order reading: Let not the right wing know what the left one doeth.[78]

Furthermore, Halleck, who had the usual regular army attitude toward newspaper correspondents, was becoming increasingly impatient with the reporters who hung around headquarters wanting to know why, among other things, "we were putting up breastworks every hundred yards between Shiloh and Corinth."[79] He was also under considerable pressure from several of his division commanders and certain staff officers who resented the needling criticisms of the reporters.

A foretaste of what was in store for the newspapermen was received by Warren P. Isham of the Chicago *Times* one fine May morning when he came upon a mounted party of Union soldiers along the highway. Isham was about to ride past on the gallop when he was halted by a peremptory command from a sinister-looking little man who seemed to have worked up a special batch of indignation for this occasion.

"Where are you going?" demanded the irate one with something between a roar and a snarl.

"Nowhere in particular."

"What is your business?"

"Nothing in particular."

"Who are you?"

"Correspondent of the Chicago *Times*."

"You are, hey? By God, I'll see about that. What in hell brought you here?"

"Anybody with ordinary common sense would suppose I came here in pursuit of my legitimate business."

"Hell and damnation. Do you know who I am?"

"It is easy enough to recognize you. Your little peculiarities are in everybody's mouth. You are General Wood.[80] Glad to find you so amicable."

"By God, sir. I'll show you how to ride by my quarters on the gallop. I put you under arrest. There is an order against any damned civilian coming into the lines."

"Never heard of it."

"Everybody knows it. You knew it."

"That is rather complimentary to your officers. I have been in their company three weeks, and I am very certain they did not know it."

"You are under arrest. I'll show you there's a God in Israel."

The General was as good as his word. Isham and his ten-dollar Texas pony were straightway lodged in the guardhouse and were not released until Isham had been hauled before General Halleck to receive a special reprimand.[81]

An order had been issued by General Halleck on April 27 revoking all passes issued previous to that date, unless renewed or countersigned, and excluding all unauthorized civilians from the lines.[82] All but one or two of the army reporters applied for the renewal of their passes and upon presenting the proper credentials were permitted to remain.

On May 13, Halleck issued a second order, more stringent than the first, calling for the expulsion of all "unauthorized hangers on" from his army.[83] Anyone seeking to evade Field Order No. 54 as it was called, was to be put to work on the entrenchments, and the Provost Marshal was instructed to report for summary punishment any officer of whatever rank who neglected to enforce the order or connived at its violation. This second order did not, however, revoke any pass issued since April 27, and it is entirely possible that the ambiguous term "unauthorized hangers on" was deliberately placed in the order by Halleck for the various corps and division commanders to interpret as they saw fit. On the one hand, generals with the newspaper phobia would be inclined to regard it as sufficient justification for hunting down any luckless reporter who might be within the limits of their commands. Others might adopt the point of view that accredited correspondents were anything but "unauthorized hangers on," and in those divisions there would be no trouble.

If this were Halleck's purpose, it was speedily frustrated by General Pope, who had been rather friendly toward the reporters and was determined not to take any action without explicit instructions. Pope first asked the Commanding General what he meant by "unauthorized hangers on." Halleck attempted to parry the question with the answer, "The Regulations fully explain that point." Determined not to be put off so easily, Pope then inquired, "Do you include newspaper correspondents among the unauthorized hangers on?" This time there was no possibility of evasion, and General Halleck was obliged to admit that he did.[84] Even at this late date, the army correspondents were still generally of the opinion that the difficulty might be smoothed over. On May 16, Richard T. Colburn of the New York *World* went to headquarters to have his pass countersigned. Somewhat to his surprise, he learned from the Provost Marshal, Major John M. Key, that no newspaper correspondent could remain in camp and that consequently he, Colburn, must leave at once. As Colburn turned to go, the Provost Marshal added by way of justifying himself that several of the "specials" had been guilty of accepting gratuities from army officers in return for newspaper puffs.[85]

As soon as they learned of Colburn's experience, the newspaper brigade held two meetings in rapid succession. At the first it was agreed to send a deputation to Major Key to request him to expose the offenders so that their names might be published in the newspapers. When approached by the committee of newspapermen, the Major first denied having made the statement attributed to him by Colburn, then became evasive, and finally admitted that he had made the statement but could adduce no evidence to support it.[86] At the second meeting a petition to General Halleck was drawn up, requesting permission to remain in camp and pointing out that the effect of his order would be to exclude the better class of reporters and leave untouched those who had brought disrepute upon their calling. During this meeting a correspondent of the Cincinnati *Times* objected strongly to the idea of presenting such a petition on the ground that it would only cause the signers to be conducted from the lines at once without any further parleying. He was overruled, nevertheless, and the meeting was adjourned so that the journalists might go in a body to headquarters to present their views to General Halleck.[87]

Two interviews were held with Halleck. At the first one the General stated that the presence of enemy spies in camp was definitely established and that in order to make sure of excluding them, he had determined to exclude all civilians.[88] He professed to have no objection to army correspondents as such; on the contrary, he said he was open to suggestions as to a means of removing the difficulty.

After some discussion the spokesmen for the group met with him again and offered to sign a parole similar to that used in the Army of the Potomac at this time. At this second conference the General's manner was considerably less cordial than it had been earlier. Upon reading the resolution which the correspondents had prepared, he announced abruptly that it would not do at all. When it was brought to his attention that two of the correspondents had passes from the War Department authorizing them to go anywhere within the lines of the United States Army, he disclaimed any official knowledge of the issue of such passes and said that in any case he would not be bound by them. The most he would concede was a promise to furnish the correspondents with news if they cared to remain in the rear of the army. Upon further inquiry it was learned that this meant nothing more than giving them access to a bulletin board at Pittsburg Landing seventeen miles in the rear of the army upon which abstracts of the dispatches to the Associated Press were posted. After this second interview the army reporters had no alternative but immediate withdrawal. Consequently, all the regular correspondents except three, one of whom (W. F. G. Shanks of the New York *Herald)* was too sick to leave his bed,[89] left for Cairo in a body on May 19.

More than one competent observer believed that Halleck and his subordinates were not exclusively responsible for the departure of the army newspapermen. Shortly after they returned to Cairo, a letter signed "Outsider" appeared in the Cincinnati *Times* accusing Frank Chapman, Franc B. Wilkie, and several other Eastern reporters of having organized a plot to bring about the expulsion of all the correspondents from Halleck's army except a few connected with the leading papers of New York.[90] Some color was lent to the accusation by the lukewarm reaction of the New York press in comparison with the widespread criticism which the expulsion of the reporters occasioned in the newspapers of Cincinnati, Chicago, and St. Louis.[91] The New York *Tribune,* for example, stated that it would acquiesce most heartily in Halleck's edict if it were enforced impartially against all reporters.[92] The New York *Herald* enthusiastically indorsed Halleck's order—so far as the Chicago and Cincinnati newspapers were concerned—but added mysteriously, "The *Herald's* correspondents will remain with General Halleck."[93] Several months later when most of the Eastern correspondents were expelled from Pope's army on the eve of second Bull Run, Whitelaw Reid called attention to the fact that the New York press was now paying the penalty for its failure to support the Western newspapers when the first move to expel the journalists was made.[94]

Even more significant was the comment of the New York *Times* man, Wilkie, who frankly admitted that he could not find much fault with Halleck's action in driving the correspondents out of his army:

> Almost every third man you meet is the "Reporter of the Something Diurnal." Half of them are individuals who board with some officer, and whose letters invariably inform the world that the gallant Colonel of the regiment preëminently distinguished himself in the late fight, that his men fought a half day's hand-to-hand fight with the enemy, and finally fell back in splendid order some two hours after the——Regiment on the right and the——Battery on the left had disgracefully run away without firing a single shot. . . .
>
> It is the writers of this class who are constantly giving the world information as to our strength and our position; who tell the public that a canal is being dug in order to flank No. 10; that Gen. Pope has so many regiments, so many cannon of certain calibres, and all arranged in a certain manner. They do not hesitate to advise Gen. Halleck, condemn Gen. McClellan, and criticise the operations of the profoundest minds engaged in working out the tremendous problem now submitted to the National Government. They are particularly severe on West Pointers, and are ardent admirers of men in proportion as their early education unfits them for the vast and intricate responsibilities of Generalship. Invariably the officer who is most free with his table, bottle, horses and information is (to them) the greatest soldier. With them a small skirmish is ever a tremendous battle, in which one Federal drives a thousand, and two Federals ten thousand Confederates—a battle proper is a theme upon which they lavish more superlatives, hyperbole, exaggerations and nonsense than they would upon the crash of a dozen worlds butting against each other in space.
>
> For such reasons as these and a thousand additional ones, the profession has been brought into disrepute—a disrepute which has fallen alike on those who deserve it, and those who do not.[95]

Contrary to what Halleck and the reporters had been led to believe, Beauregard did not choose to "fight to the last ditch" in defense of Corinth. It was the prevailing opinion at Halleck's headquarters up until the eve of the evacuation of Corinth that the enemy was preparing to strike another great blow. Beauregard did what he could to foster this amazing misconception. On May 24, taking a leaf from Halleck's notebook, he banished all the newspaper correspondents from his army.[96] Moreover, all through the night of May 29, while the city was being evacuated, the Confederate drummers were kept busy in the front lines beating reveille, and empty trains of cars were shuttled back and forth along the Memphis and Charleston Railroad tracks to give the impression that Beauregard was being reinforced. On the morning of the thirtieth, the Union army marched into Corinth to discover an abandoned camp and a deserted city. The Confederate army had escaped southward with most of its equipment and had burned the remainder to keep it from falling into Federal hands.[97]

Among the ranks of the entering army was a reporter for the Chicago *Tribune* who had managed to persuade a friendly officer belonging to Halleck's bodyguard to lend him the horse, clothing, and arms of a sick trooper. Subsequently he remarked in a letter to his newspaper that:

> Gen. Halleck little knew when he rode down the line, and glanced at his well appointed bodyguard that one of those "d——d newspaper correspondents" looked him right in the eye, from under one of those infernally ugly looking trooper hats.[98]

It may well be surmised that the press derived perverse satisfaction from the success of Beauregard's stratagem. While the Commanding General was asserting in his official dispatches that the enemy's works at Corinth were very strong and could easily have been defended, the Associated Press dispatches insisted that they were very weak and might have been stormed at any time by the Federal army. The Cincinnati *Gazette* reporter declared:

> But a single line of general fortifications had been constructed, and these were actually less formidable than those thrown up by our forces last night, after occupying a new position.[99]

There can be little doubt that the Chicago *Tribune* reporter summed up the general impression in the army when he stated that in taking Corinth, Halleck had achieved "one of the most barren triumphs of the war."[100]

The campaign was now about at an end. Soon afterward, Halleck was summoned to Washington to assume the chief command of the armies of the United States. With the approach of hot weather, moreover, it seemed best to suspend active campaigning in an area which had already proved highly unhealthful for the troops. And so it was decided to return Buell's Army of the Ohio to its department to give attention to enemy movements in Eastern Tennessee while Grant's Army of the Tennessee was being split up to perform garrison duty. By this time the attention of press and public alike was shifting to events of greater moment in the Eastern war theater.

9

The Press Goes to the Peninsula

As the winter of 1861-1862 drew to a close, the reporters along Washington's Fourteenth Street saw indications that the long period of military inactivity in the East was near its end. Under continuous prodding from the President and his civilian advisers, McClellan it seemed was about ready to undertake the forward movement for which the press clamored. To Edwin M. Stanton, who just had replaced the discredited Cameron as Secretary of War, Joseph Medill addressed a letter of congratulation which expressed the opinion that:

> this . . . has been a contractor's war, a war on Chinese principles. It has been a war of horrible grimaces, of shocking expenditure, of sickening blunders, of quasi loyalty, of benumbing inaction. . . . The country looks to you with longing heart to impress vigor, system, honesty and fight into the service.[1]

During the first week of March, a swarm of New York reporters descended upon Washington to be on hand for the opening of the campaign. Among them was the poet-correspondent, Bayard Taylor, who had come home a few evenings previously and told his wife that:

> I have just been at the *Tribune* office, and have been asked to go to Washington as the head correspondent of the paper. A battle is expected there hourly, and I am to report it.[2]

It was the general supposition in Washington that the Army of the Potomac was preparing to advance upon Richmond by the same route that McDowell had taken in the campaign of the previous summer. Those who shared McClellan's confidence knew, however, that he had under consideration a different plan: a movement, by way of the lower Rappahannock, designed to flank the enemy position at Manassas Junction and to compel Johnston, the Confederate commander, to fall back upon Richmond.

While McClellan was concentrating his troops at Fairfax Court House for the proposed movement, he learned from his scouts that the enemy had withdrawn from the Manassas line without firing a shot and had taken a new position along the south bank of the Rappahannock. The army correspondents were thoroughly disgusted by this new development. They had been looking forward to a battle of some kind—even a skirmish would have pleased them. Now they had nothing to serve as a theme for their correspondence except empty barracks and piles of rubbish. In default of news items, they ransacked the deserted fortifications for trophies of various kinds: muskets, bayonets, banners, even unexploded shells. Alfred Waud, the artist of *Harper's Weekly*, sported a red shirt, which some Confederate had left behind, and brandished a captive cavalry lance, flying a small flag or streamer known as a *guidon.*[3]

Upon closer inspection of the field, Taylor of the New York *Tribune* and several other reporters uncovered information which was given wide circulation by the anti-McClellan section of the press. They found some maple logs, camouflaged to look like cannon, projecting from the embrasures in the fortifications along the Centreville ridge. It was obvious that the strength of these fortifications had been greatly exaggerated, and, in Taylor's opinion, they might have been occupied with ease by the Union Army at any time since the previous October. In a widely reprinted letter to his newspaper, Taylor wrote:

> Utterly dispirited, ashamed and humiliated I return from this visit to the Rebel stronghold, feeling that their retreat is *our defeat.* For seven months we have waited, organizing a powerful army, until its drill and equipment should be so complete that we might safely advance against the "Gibraltar" of rebellion; we have forborne to make a single step forward, until perfectly sure that we should not have to step back again; we have allowed the river communication to our Capital to be blockaded, our prestige as a nation to be endangered, the patience of our noble people to be stretched to the utmost, and the wings of our vast line of operations to be weakened, that we might not fail when the long-delayed hour for action came. And now, since we have moved, we see that our enemies, like the Chinese, have frightened us by the sound of gongs and the wearing of devils' masks.[4]

In a letter to his wife written about the same time Taylor told of having:

> just returned from riding two miles beyond Manassas. I got there ahead of McClellan, and 20 hours after the Rebels. I am stiff and sore from riding 70 miles, and sleeping two nights on a bare plank. . . . We found Manassas burning, a dreadful scene of ruin. . . . The fortifications are a damnable humbug and McClellan has been completely fooled.[5]

Some quarters of the press, however, later doubted that the "Quaker guns" were anything more than reportorial imagination. On April 6, 1862, the St. Louis *Republican* expressed the opinion that "the story about some wooden guns, said to have been found in the deserted rebel fortifications at Centreville. . . . is now pretty much exploded." The Chicago *Tribune*, on the other hand, in an editorial published during the same week stated flatly that some thirty or forty specimens of the "Quakers" picked up by curiosity hunters at Manassas had been sent all over the North and placed on exhibit in various large cities.[6]

Even before news of the evacuation of Manassas had reached Washington, President Lincoln had agreed with some misgivings to a revised plan of attack upon Richmond by way of the peninsula formed by the York and James rivers. According to the new plan, Fortress Monroe was to be used as the primary base during the campaign. On March 17 the movement to the Peninsula began. Over a period of nineteen days approximately one hundred thousand men were transported from Alexandria to Fortress Monroe in echelons of ten thousand each, the largest amphibious operation the country had ever seen.[7] On March 22, Bayard Taylor told his wife about having ridden out from Washington that day through "seas of mud" in an effort to locate the division then under the command of General George A. McCall. He noted:

> The Bucktails[8] want me to embark with them, and I shall try to do so. . . . I saw Hawthorne[9], this morning. He, also, is just off for Fortress Monroe, and I hope to meet him there again.[10]

Taylor was still in Washington two days later, however, waiting for authorization to go to the Peninsula. He informed his wife:

> I saw Gen. McDowell last night, and he says: "When three more divisions have gone, get ready!" On Saturday about 10,000 troops left, and probably as many yesterday. We shall have over 100,000 in all, and I scarcely anticipate much fighting. . . . Senator Chandler told me he thought there would be none—that the rebels would not make a stand against so large a force.[11]

Other newspapers were making extensive preparations for full coverage of what promised to be the major campaign of the war. During most of the campaign the New York *Times* staff of army correspondents on the Peninsula was headed by the *Times* editor, Henry J. Raymond, who remained at McClellan's headquarters until it became clear that the General did not relish the critical tone of the editor's letters. According to George Alfred Townsend, the *Herald* had no less than fourteen correspondents with McClellan's army, hardly one of whom, in his opinion, was "fit to describe a fire." He added:

> They were the usual run of forward, uneducated, flimsy-headed, often middle-aged, misplaced people, who had mysteriously gotten on a newspaper. They were capable of plenty of endurance, and would ride up and down, and talk with great confidence, and be familiar with everybody, and then not know how to relate what they saw. . . . Whenever a big battle would start up, the *Herald* man would dash immediately for New York, and there portray a plan of the battlefield he had never seen, with all the worm fences and creeks running the wrong way in it. Instead of placing one or two well-equipped, well-mounted, well-behaved young men with the army, who should feel independent, gain the confidence of the general officers and make the reputation of the newspaper with their own, the work was all cut up, and any forward, tricky fellow could take the credit from all the modest ones —if there were any such. Hence, the correspondents had little or no encouragement from the home office, and instead of some system being arranged to collect their accounts and notes, the usual thing was to dash off from the army to the base of supplies at White House, and have a good time there and a gallop back.[12]

Two letters, forwarded to the Philadelphia *Inquirer* by one of its correspondents at Fortress Monroe while the movement to the Peninsula was still underway, reveal the news-gathering problems of that paper's correspondents. The first letter states:

> I have just got your letter. It has been in the P.O. for several days. Carelessness on the part of the clerks. . . . You cannot get a horse here for love or money. . . . I have hired a horse twice since I have been here—but it is gone. Tom Towne, of the Penn. 3d light Cavalry, is going to get me a horse. . . . We are not allowed to say a word about the army. I may be back in a day or so. Things are taking a tangible shape here. . . . I will walk some 20 miles to-day.

And then again four days later:

> I would have written to you in full—but am debarred from doing so, on account of the severe restrictions placed upon us. I expect we will move from here very soon. . . . Bowers is here—he will be with the fifth corps, Gen. Porter. . . . I have not paid any board since I have been here. I suppose that is all right. You gave me $20, when I started. . . . I paid clerk of steamer for board, &c. $6.00; postage stamps 1.00; boat line 3.00—going out to flags of truce, foreign vessels &c.; newspapers 2.00; horse hire 2.00—to go to camp; expense on reconnoizance 2.00—wagon &c.; newspapers again 1.00; portable inkstand, papers, pencils &c. 1.00; reconnoizance with 3d Pa. cav. 2.00. . . . $5 at hand from Pedrick. Locomotion is very hard about here. Every available means to move around is extravagantly high—you cannot know. . . . If you think I need any more than this $5 to start away with—you had better send it immediately, as I cannot tell how long I may be here.[13]

All newspaper correspondents were under strict orders not to say anything about the movement of McClellan's army to the Peninsula while it was in progress. Even before the March 17 movement began the government had taken additional steps to prevent publication of any information which might prove valuable to the enemy. In February, 1862, management of telegraphic censorship, which had been criticized widely, was transferred from the State Department to the War Department, and all telegraph lines were placed under military control, since the policy adopted the year before of taking control only of those lines radiating from Washington had proved ineffective. Furthermore, the War Department had ordered on February 25 that all newspapers publishing military news "not expressly authorized by the War Department, the general commanding, or the general commanding armies in the field in the several departments" would be deprived of the privilege of receiving news reports by telegraph or of transmitting copies of their publications by rail. It appeared that Stanton's order was aimed primarily at some of the New York newspapers which seemed overly well informed about military plans of the Administration. There was so much editorial opposition to the order, however, that it was modified the very next day to permit the publication of "past facts," providing these facts did not include any details concerning the military forces of the United States from which their number, position, or strength could be inferred.[14]

There was, nevertheless, still some confusion among the newspaper men on how these rules were to be interpreted, and, when on March 25 the Post Office Department issued a similar order "more vague than any of its predecessors," the Washington correspondent of the Chicago *Tribune,* Horace White, hastened to the General Post Office to obtain an explanation of the ruling. To his dismay be learned that John A. Kasson, the First Assistant Postmaster General:

> was equally in the dark with myself—said the order had been issued in conformity with a wish of the Secretary of War, and he presumed that the language adopted was such as Mr. Stanton desired. I observed that it was so indefinite that no two postmasters or publishers could ever construe it alike . . . hence it could be productive only of mischief, and in all probability would fail to secure the object for which it was intended. Mr. K. replied that he could not hope to enlighten me in points which he did not himself comprehend, but he would consult Mr. Blair and Mr. Stanton during the day, and obtain a general answer to the queries likely to be provoked by the order.[15]

In a private letter to Ray, White expressed himself in somewhat stronger language concerning Stanton than was appropriate in a newspaper article:

> I presume you have been amazed at Blair's newspaper order. Capt. Fox says that when he came back from Old Point he found that Stanton had taken possession of the Navy & Post Office Depts & was playing h—l generally—that he (Fox) ejected him from the Navy, but that he had held on to the Postoffice! So it appears. Kasson don't know what the order means—that is he *presumes* it means so & so, but he admits that the language is vague & mischievous, & moreover that the whole thing is illegal. Stanton is a kind of Mephistopheles & the only good thing about him is that he hates McClellan profoundly.[16]

The War Department further had served notice that it was determined to enforce its regulations. On the eve of McClellan's departure for the Peninsula, John Russell Young, then editor of Forney's Washington *Chronicle,* was placed under arrest and was brought before the military governor of the District of Columbia to answer for a news item about the movement of General McCall's division to Alexandria en route to the Peninsula. (Although this was not made known at the time, the real author of the offending paragraph was George Alfred

Townsend, who had come down from Philadelphia only a fortnight before as a war correspondent.) Young attempted to excuse himself by representing that the item had been handed in at a very late hour and had not passed under his personal scrutiny. After some further questioning he was released with a reprimand, coupled with a promise on his part to exercise greater care in the future.[17] Other newspapers received similar warnings. Among them was the Boston *Journal,* whose editor was threatened with a court martial because of a letter, which the *Journal* published, that revealed important information about the Peninsula expedition while it was still in progress.[18]

On April 2 the press was thrown into further confusion by another War Department order revoking all passes to newspaper correspondents with the Army of the Potomac and requiring those who already had gone to Fortress Monroe to return at once under penalty of immediate arrest. Forty-eight hours later the order was revoked with the explanation that it had been framed exclusively to prevent the London *Times* correspondent, William H. Russell, from going to the Peninsula.[19] Apparently the order served its purpose, for, in a letter to Nicolay dated April 3, John Hay confided that "W. H. Russell is hideously outraged because Stanton had him ordered off the ship on which he was going to Fortress Monroe."[20] Subsequently, after an attempt to persuade President Lincoln to overrule Stanton had failed, "Bull Run" Russell telegraphed to New York for a sailing reservation on the next Cunard steamer and was soon on his way back to England.[21]

At the outset of the campaign the censorship exercised by the military authorities at Fortress Monroe was tighter than any to which the news correspondents had been subjected thus far. No message sent by an army reporter, not even a private letter to his editor, could pass through the post office without being inspected by an aide-de-camp on the staff of General John E. Wool. Hardly a week after McClellan's arrival at Yorktown, the Philadelphia *Inquirer* published a dispatch from J. Robly Dunglison, one of its correspondents at Fortress Monroe, which stated that General McClellan had advanced upon the enemy's lines extending across the York Peninsula, and gave a brief account of some skirmishing near Yorktown. As soon as the dispatch was brought to the attention of the War Department, Stanton cancelled the telegraphic privileges of the *Inquirer* and instructed Edward S. Sanford, the military superintendent of the telegraph, to go at once to Fortress Monroe to investigate the incident.[22] Sanford reported that Dunglison's dispatch had been passed by General Wool, the department commander, with some slight alterations and was therefore an authorized dispatch. This was sufficient to clear the *Inquirer,* but Sanford also learned during his investigation that there was considerable dissatisfaction at Fortress Monroe about the way the local censorship was being administered. With Stanton's approval he issued on April 12 an order abolishing the local censorship and replacing it with a parole system, which, in effect, made each correspondent his own censor under certain definite limitations.

The parole was a formidable looking document attached to the pass from the War Department which each correspondent carried. Under the conditions which it prescribed, each correspondent was required to give his word of honor that he was a loyal citizen of the United States and that in the discharge of his duties he would not write, make, or transmit any intelligence, opinion, statement, drawing, or plan that would give or tend to give aid or comfort to the enemy. He further was required to avoid making any reference in his correspondence to the following:

1. The location or change of location of headquarters of generals, as well as the names of generals, regiments, brigades, or divisions in the field "except when engagements have taken place."
2. The number of regiments, brigades, divisions, batteries or pieces of artillery, or the proportion of cavalry in service at any point.
3. The kind of arms or ammunition used or the number of days' rations served.
4. The number of transports used for any movement, the description of any movement, until after its objective had been accomplished or defeated, allusions to the object of movements or suggestions of future movements or attacks.
5. The position or location of camps, pickets, or outposts.
6. Pictorial representations of Federal fortifications or lines of defenses.[23]

These were drastic restrictions. Had they been rigidly enforced, they almost certainly would have reduced the flow of war news from the Peninsula to a trickle. But they were not enforced. Appalled by the sheer length of the parole document, which covered two letter-size printed pages, the guards generally passed anyone who presented the parole rather than take the trouble of reading through it. According to one of the reporters, none of the correspondents on the Peninsula ever was called to account for anything he had written while the parole system was in effect.[24]

To circumvent the telegraphic censorship, the *Herald* used another device. It was the responsibility of one of the *Herald* correspondents at Fortress Monroe to forward the messages of the other members of the *Herald* staff to Baltimore, usually through the stewards on the Old Colony Steamship Line. In case the Baltimore packet failed to make a connection with the New York train, the *Herald* representative in Baltimore was instructed to telegraph his material to New York. When the boat was on time, however, the letters from Fortress Monroe were sent from Baltimore to New York by special messenger, thus saving at least an hour over the mails.[25]

For almost a month after its arrival on the Peninsula, McClellan's army remained in front of Yorktown to conduct a siege operation. Among the news correspondents gathered there, competition for news was brisk. On April 28, Gay, the managing editor of the New York *Tribune*, wrote a letter to one of his correspondents at Yorktown in which he expressed his dissatisfaction with the performance of the *Tribune*'s army staff on the Peninsula. The letter began:

> My Dear Sir—Mr. Sinclair has gone to ye army before Yorktown to make arrangements to get us ye news. He will probably see you, & you will act in conjunction with him.
>
> Your sketch of ye battle-ground of the 16th came just *eight* days after ye battle. Of course it was useless. The corr. of ye Philadelphia *Inquirer* had sent one to that paper, which it had had engraved & published, which I had also had engraved & published, three days before yours reached me. I pray you remember ye *Tribune* is a *daily news*-paper—or meant to be,—& not a historical record of past events. Correspondents to be of any value must be prompt, fresh, & full of facts. I know how difficult it is, under ye censor-ship to write, but there must be facts enough of general interest all about you to make a daily letter. . . . I should like you to write daily, if only a half, a quarter column, so that ye report of all you may tell be continuous. The curiosity & anxiety about Yorktown is feverish, & ye public like ye paper best that is always giving something. If there is absolutely *nothing* to write about, drop a line and tell me that. The *Herald* is constantly ahead of us with Yorktown news. The battle of ye 16th we were compelled to copy from it.[26]

While the Yorktown siege still was going on, the publication of *Harper's Weekly* was suspended by an order of the War Department. The order seemed to have been prompted by a sketch which had appeared in the *Weekly* revealing the position of the Federal troops by brigades and divisions, and the location of the various headquarters, including that of the commanding general. Stanton followed up his suspension order with a telegram in which he requested that some member of the Harper firm be sent to Washington to answer for this shocking breach of security. Upon his arrival at the War Department, Fletcher Harper, to whom this delicate mission had been entrusted, found the Secretary in one of his more belligerent moods. Before Stanton could begin his verbal assault, however, the publisher skillfully contrived to place him on the defensive by bringing up a matter entirely foreign to the object of his visit. As they talked along, Stanton became progressively less bellicose, and by the time the interview was over, his caller had succeeded in persuading him to revoke the suspension order. As Harper was leaving, Stanton, by this time in the best of humor, extended to the publisher his cordial thanks for the support which the *Weekly* had been giving to the policies of the Administration![27]

The evacuation of Yorktown by the Confederates on May 3 took McClellan by surprise. Uriah H. Painter, the well-informed correspondent of the Philadelphia *Inquirer,* had advance information about the evacuation, which he communicated to General Marcy, McClellan's chief of staff. Marcy refused to credit Painter's story, however, inasmuch as the General possessed information of "undoubted accuracy" which led him to believe that the Confederates were prepared to defend Yorktown to the last ditch.[28] Shortly after midnight of May 3, however, the Union pickets reported that they had observed a large fire in the vicinity of the enemy stronghold. McClellan promptly asked Professor Thaddeus S. C. Lowe, the aeronaut, to make a balloon ascension to find out what the enemy was doing. Lowe's reconnaissance disclosed that the enemy's works were completely deserted.

Although a business trip to Washington had prevented the editor of the New York *Times* from witnessing the evacuation of Yorktown, upon his return a few days afterward, he made an inspection of the enemy's deserted works. He then expressed the opinion, considerably wide of the mark, that:

> they [the enemy] have certainly had here more than one hundred and ten thousand men,—which, behind intrenchments as strong

> as theirs were, would be equivalent to three times that number in the open field.[29]

Orders had been given to begin an immediate pursuit of the enemy, while the Union troops were moving into the deserted fortifications, and early on the morning of May 5, Joe Hooker's division overtook the Confederate rear guard near Williamsburg. There they became involved in a Confederate delaying action to give the Southern supply trains an opportunity to escape. Although Hancock's brigade executed a brilliant charge during the action, the Union advance was checked with heavy losses. McClellan did not arrive on the field until the fighting was practically over, to be greeted, as the correspondent of the New York *Evening Post* reported:

> with long and enthusiastic cheering. Regiment after regiment, as he was quickly recognised, gave utterance to a welcome of which Napoleon might have been proud.[30]

At about ten o'clock that evening, L. L. Crounse of the New York *World,* dog-tired, came staggering in from the field to Whitaker's house where he had found lodging along with several other army correspondents. It was hardly comforting to learn then that General McClellan had taken over the house that very day for his own headquarters and had relegated the newspaper corps to the cellar. Since the battle had been fought in the midst of a driving rainstorm, none of the correspondents on the ground had a very clear idea of what had happened. Yet all were busy writing. At about 2:00 A.M. all hands agreed to call it a day. The *Times* and *World* stretched out on a table which they previously had used for a desk; the *Tribune* propped himself up against the wall; the Philadelphia *Inquirer* snored loudly from a bench near the fire.

At daybreak Crounse discovered Wilkeson, the *Tribune* man, out in the yard, rubbing his tired limbs and searching for his horse. A Negro was standing by, watching nonchalantly, and in desperation Wilkeson offered him five dollars if he could produce the missing animal.

"Dunno 'bout findin' *dat ar* horse," replied John. " 'Spec likely could find you *a* horse."

"Very well, *a* horse will do," conceded Wilkeson, and within an hour he possessed a mournful-looking brute which in all probability formerly had belonged to the individual who had stolen his mount.[31]

Widespread dissatisfaction was voiced in the army about the way these correspondents and others had reported the Battle of Williamsburg. The *Herald* was blamed for giving a large share of the credit to a regiment that was not within three miles of the battlefield and of passing over completely the fine work of some of the other regiments.[32] There were also complaints that the Philadelphia *Inquirer* had magnified the charge of Hancock's brigade out of all proportion to its true significance,[33] and the New York *Tribune* was criticized for some statements made by its correspondents reflecting on the valor of two of the New Jersey regiments. In a letter to the *Tribune* the chaplain of one of these regiments wrote:

> I will speak plainly, and trust you will do us the justice we deserve. . . . Your correspondent has, to say the least, erred, or taken his information from rumor or prejudiced second-hand information. . . . I witnessed the whole of the engagement—being actively engaged through the fiercest of it in caring for the wounded and getting them from the field. I can positively affirm that the New-Jersey boys did not give way—nor did they at any time fall into disorder.[34]

In a later publication, Townsend, who by then was working for the *Herald,* claimed that most of the stories of Hancock's celebrated bayonet charge were altogether fictitious. "The musket, not the bayonet, gave him the victory," declared Townsend, but one would never have reached this conclusion from reading newspaper accounts of the battle.[35]

Among the army correspondents who were present at the Battle of Williamsburg was Stedman of the New York *World,* who had left his desk in the Attorney General's office and had gone to Yorktown largely, as he explained in a letter to his brother, because:

> our correspondents were managing affairs there badly, and Marble begged me to get leave of absence and straighten matters out. So Judge Bates gave me two weeks leave from May 1st. I started on the 28th April, rode my horse to Baltimore, took boat for Fort Monroe, and rode to Yorktown, which I reached May 1st. Was at the siege and evacuation, joined the pursuit, was in Sunday's skirmish, next day saw the battle of Williamsburgh . . . all the time had frequent pleasant and confidential intercourse with McClellan. He is developing, you see, those great qualities which I always have claimed for him—although our battles on the Peninsula have not been decisive, and the rebels have hand-

> somely covered their retreat. All the time I lived on hard bread and coffee—slept in the rain and mud—got fat, and felt gloriously. The spirit of the soldiers is splendid, and death and suffering are so constantly on every side that no one cares anything about them.[36]

During the fortnight after Williamsburg, McClellan moved his advance base from Fortress Monroe to White House on the Pamunkey River and marched some forty or fifty miles up the Peninsula without encountering serious opposition. He made slow progress partly because of the poor condition of the roads, and partly because he mistakenly believed that his army was greatly outnumbered by the enemy.

Although they made little or no mention of it in letters at this time to their newspapers, the army correspondents hardly could have been oblivious of the continuing ill-feeling between McClellan and Stanton, which had been accentuated by the withdrawal of McDowell's corps from the Army of the Potomac to serve as a part of the covering force for the protection of Washington. From the letters written to the editor of the New York *World* during the course of the campaign by General Fitz John Porter, McClellan's most trusted subordinate, it almost would appear that McClellan looked upon Stanton rather than Johnston as his principal antagonist.[37]

Meanwhile the press was having difficulties of its own. About a week after the Battle of Williamsburg an order from McClellan's headquarters forbade any newspaper correspondent to go beyond General Headquarters or to accompany the advance guard or any of the advanced divisions on the march.[38] Yet wide publicity had been given to the fact that the first men to enter Norfolk at its occupation were two young newspaper "specials," and a position in the van was regarded by correspondents and their employers alike as a mark of enterprise.[39] On the day the order was published, moreover, the cavalry advance had been full of "specials." That evening a large group of them made arrangements to stay overnight at the plantation home of Lemuel J. Bowden near the front line, and there they were entertained with excellent music by the ladies of the household until a late hour. In the midst of their hilarity, there was a loud rapping at the door, and in walked the general who commanded the cavalry advance. One of the reporters who was masquerading in the uniform of a cavalry captain was especially reprimanded, but the others did not escape. Everyone in the group, in fact, was placed under arrest and was marched back to the rear under military escort through seven miles of mud and darkness. The next morning they were brought before General McClellan, who released them after giving them a mild reproof.[40]

There were probably many more such incidents in what the New York *Times* described as "a little side war going on between the newspaper correspondents and the military."[41] Since they were under strict orders not to report army movements, the newspapermen worked hard to get Richmond newspapers for their employers. Eventually this traffic provoked an order from the commanding general requiring that all Richmond papers which came through the picket line be forwarded to headquarters as soon as they were obtained. Not long after the order was issued an enterprising young reporter succeeded in procuring a copy of one of the Richmond dailies from a Negro he had induced to go through the lines to get it. Much elated, the reporter dashed off in the direction of White House to forward the latest news from Richmond to his newspaper. An ill-natured competitor, however, had learned of his good fortune and had lodged a complaint at the Provost Marshal's office. As a result, a cavalry guard galloped to White House, arrested the delinquent reporter before he could send off the Richmond paper, and threw him in the guard house for forty-eight hours.[42]

Some of the friction between the army and the press was the result of regular army prejudice, which was heightened, as one army correspondent admitted, by "the persistent impertinence of some members of our now unpopular profession."[43] Indeed, on May 27 McClellan wrote a letter to Stanton in which he complained that some of the newspapers:

> frequently published letters from their correspondents with this army, giving important information concerning our movements, positions of troops, &c., in positive violation of your orders.[44]

He went on to suggest that since he could not ascertain with certainty who these "anonymous writers" were, the War Department issue an order holding newspaper editors responsible for any infraction. Subsequently he made heated reference to the fact that:

> my order of the 25th May, directing the order of march from the Chickahominy and the disposition to be made of trains and baggage, is published in full in the Baltimore American of the 2d instant. If any statement could afford more important information to the enemy I am unable to perceive it.[45]

Preceding McClellan's complaint to Stanton, however, on May 20 the advance guard of the Army of the Potomac had crossed the Chickahominy River at Bottom's Ridge, fourteen miles East of Richmond. Five days later Heintzelman's corps was thrown forward in support. Nevertheless, McClellan was proceeding cautiously. The reinforcements for which he never ceased to importune his superiors as yet had failed to materialize, and he was still laboring under the false impression fostered by faulty intelligence reports[46] that his troops were considerably outnumbered by the enemy. Even so, there was an element of risk in dividing his army at a time when a watchful enemy might be presumed to be in readiness to attack.

On the afternoon of May 30, the first of a series of heavy thunderstorms began, and by noon of the next day the Chickahominy River was a torrent. Shortly before that time, masses of gray-clad men appeared along both sides of the Williamsburg Road and struck with crushing force the advance line of the Federal army front and flank. Silas Casey's division of Erasmus D. Keyes's corps, which was drawn up on the right side of the Williamsburg Road and at right angles to it, was driven back upon the position occupied by Darius Couch's division. While struggling to check a large force of the enemy which was making its way around Casey's right flank, four of Couch's regiments were separated from the main body of his division and pressed back toward Fair Oaks Station. Frantic appeals for reinforcements resulted in the dispatch of two brigades from Philip Kearny's division of Heintzelman's corps. But it was the arrival of Edwin V. Sumner, who had crossed the Chickahominy with Richardson's and John Sedgwick's divisions despite the possibility that the bridges spanning the swollen stream might be swept away at any moment, which saved the left wing of the Union army from a crushing defeat. Among the minor casualties of that day's fighting was a New York *Times* correspondent, William C. Church, who was struck in the leg by a bullet.[47] Still another army correspondent, Wilkeson of the *Tribune,* served as a volunteer aide during the battle and received special mention from General Heintzelman for his gallantry and coolness under fire.[48]

On the following day the fighting was resumed, but the Confederates no longer had the advantage of surprise. Moreover, their commanding general, Joseph E. Johnston, had been struck by a shell fragment during the first day's fighting, and his successor, Major General Gustavus W. Smith, was rendered ineffective by illness. During the course of the day the defenders of Richmond were driven back to the positions they had occupied before the battle began. Neither side, however, had achieved a clear-cut victory. As at Shiloh, the Confederates had won a partial success on the first day, only to see their gains erased on the morrow by an all but vanquished foe.[49]

How the New York *Herald* reported the Battle of Fair Oaks was described in flattering terms in an article written after the war by an ex-soldier who had had some newspaper experience:

> The *Herald* men were at my quarters when the first gun was fired at Fair Oaks. "There they go," was the cry, and immediately all was activity. Charles Farrell . . . was the chief on the field at this time. In less time than it takes me to write it orders were issued by him for each one of them to accompany such and such a corps (it was astonishing how well they understood the position of each command), and in a twinkling all had mounted and were off. I suppose they knew where they were to meet again, for I afterwards found them on the south bank of the Chickahominy, in the rear of Heintzelman's headquarters. All were assembled around a pile of cracker boxes and were as busy as nailers writing up the particulars of the fight then going on. As each man finished he passed his manuscript to Farrell and was mounted and had ridden away to some distant part of the field. I had other matters to look after and could not stop to watch them, but I presume they did this all day long, and from the light in the commissary's tent I presume all night long. . . .
>
> For two days I caught only fleeting glimpses of the newspaper correspondents. They were too busy. When all was over Farrell came and brought with him the papers of the day before. There were eight or nine columns of description of the first day's fight, and in the next day's paper was an account nearly as long as the first of the second day's battle. It was not as well written as the first. One could see traces of exhaustion through it, but it was wonderful—wonderful, indeed, to see an account of the battle all the way from New York back on the field in four days. One evening shortly afterward, while smoking a friendly pipe with Farrell, I asked him how he and the others had managed to know so much about the battle and how they could ever write it and get it into the paper with the quickness they had? [sic] "You see," said he, "we have some of our best men here. Each man knows what he is to do and does it with the quickest possible dispatch."

> He then went on to relate how he arranged the manuscripts of each man, put it [sic] into shape, corrected it as far as he was able and then rode with it to the White House, where he chartered a tug-boat and went with it to Fortress Monroe, how he had telegraphed as much as the authorities would allow and then had given his package to the Fortress Monroe correspondent, and within three or four hours had retaken the tug-boat for the White House, and as I saw, was now on the field again. It was a mystery to me then, and has been a mystery to me ever since: a fight to take place four or five hundred miles away without telegraphic communication and the full particulars to be spread before the people at home on the day but one following the occurrence.[50]

That reporting under such circumstances should be completely accurate was too much to expect. During the aftermath of the battle one of the *Herald* correspondents wrote:

> Those who suppose that the labor of a news gatherer upon the battle field is facile and rapid should stroll, as I have, over the ground where the dead yet lie unburied, and the survivors expect momentarily to resume the conflict. Beyond vague and general statements nothing can be learned. The colonel of each regiment takes the whole credit of the victory upon himself, but can give no information as to the number of his missing, the distances traversed or the outlines of the fight . . . . many participants . . . cannot relate anything beyond isolated and unimportant statements, while the whole field stretches before the correspondent, who must glean its particulars in momentary dread of provost guards, between whom and himself the antipathies are vaster than seas.[51]

A New York *Times* reporter who tried to determine the army's losses by questioning the survivors reported that he invariably received as an answer, "O, Sir, our regiment was all cut to pieces—cut to pieces, Sir; nothing left of it."[52]

Among the numerous errors, large and small, which appeared in newspaper accounts of the battle were the following:

1. The New York *Herald* published a map purporting to show the field of action of "the great three days battle of Saturday, Sunday, and Monday."[53] *There was no fighting whatsoever on Monday.*
2. On June 4, 1862, the Boston *Journal* undertook to correct a statement

which had come over the telegraph to the effect that "only *three hundred* of our troops were killed, wounded, and missing after the battles of Saturday and Sunday." Commented the *Journal,* "the numbers ought to have been stated at *three thousand." The total figure of Union casualties as set forth in McClellan's official report of the battle was 5,737.*

3. The Philadelphia *Press* related an imaginary incident concerning a North Carolina regiment which staged a mutiny during the battle, threw down their guns, and surrendered en masse. The *Press* further reported the capture of five thousand Confederate prisoners.[54] *The total number of Confederate casualties—killed, wounded, and missing—was not in excess of 4,500.*
4. The New York *World* reported that General Casey was killed while in the process of rallying his men.[55] *Instead, Casey received a brevet in the regular army for distinguished service at the Battle of Fair Oaks and retired from active service in 1868.*
5. According to the New York *Times,* McClellan was on the battlefield all day Sunday, June 1, and the battle of that day was fought under his immediate supervision.[56] *McClellan did not arrive on the field that day until the battle was over.*
6. The *Herald* reported in all seriousness that the enemy had made use of dams on the upper Chickahominy with which to flood the country in the rear of the Union left wing.[57] The Cincinnati *Commercial* retorted to this:

> The enemy did not dam the river. The only dams of which the army has any knowledge were those constructed by blundering engineers, who fashioned our rude bridges so unskilfully that they formed breakwaters, until the whole valley was overflowed when the bridges were swept away.[58]

7. An Associated Press dispatch claimed that Kearny's division, upon being brought into action on the afternoon of the first day of the battle made a bayonet charge in which they regained all but a half mile of the ground lost earlier in the day.[59] *The truth was that the Union side was hard pressed throughout the day. No lost ground was regained.*

The New York *Tribune* and its Chicago counterpart were apparently the only important Northern newspapers which portrayed the outcome of the battle as a defeat.[60] Even before he received any detailed reports from his correspondents on the Peninsula, Greeley had written a highly controversial editorial entitled "The Reverse before Richmond," which lambasted McClellan for placing his army athwart the Chickahominy, thereby inviting a surprise attack.[61] Later the *Tribune* published a stinging letter from Sam Wilkeson, which described the stampede of General Casey's division in most unflattering terms and questioned the policy of placing in an advanced position a division composed of raw troops in a poor state of discipline and commanded by a general who, he claimed, lacked "youth, enthusiasm, pride, or combativeness."[62] Wilkeson also made statements reflecting upon the conduct of General David B. Birney at Fair Oaks, which involved him in a prolonged and bitter controversy with the General.[63]

For almost a week after the Battle of Fair Oaks, the army correspondents laboriously compiled casualty lists. Meanwhile it rained almost every day, and the Chickahominy River, which the soldiers derisively called "Chicken-and-hominy" and "Hog-and-hominy," was almost continuously in flood. Ten days after the battle, J. E. B. Stuart, the Confederate cavalry leader, emerged from the enemy's left on what was originally intended as a reconnaissance and then, emboldened by his initial success, made a complete circuit of McClellan's army, burning bridges, destroying army supplies, and causing no end of confusion. On the second or third morning after the raid, a twelve-year-old newsboy appeared among the Federal pickets with an armful of copies of the Richmond *Dispatch,* which contained a long and somewhat exaggerated account of the raid. When called upon by Brigadier General Henry W. Slocum to give an account of himself, the newsboy willingly replied that Stuart's exploit had caused jubilation in Richmond and that certain people within the city had induced him to enter the Federal lines to peddle these newspapers among the Yankee soldiers.[64]

For more than three weeks after the battle McClellan's army remained almost stationary. Meanwhile, the Northern press, well aware of the intense interest of its readers in the developments on the Peninsula, continued to report that McClellan had crossed the Chickahominy, that his army was only a few miles from Richmond, and that the decisive hour was at hand. "All eyes and hopes are on the army now in front of Richmond," wrote W. W. Harding to Painter of the Philadelphia *Inquirer* on June 12. "Keep us posted up. I will try to send another reporter or two to you tomorrow." On June 28, an editorial in the Cincinnati *Times* remarked with justifiable sarcasm:

> Arithmetical problems are the Chickahominy letter writers for the New York press. A month ago, they placed McClellan within four miles of Richmond, and have since advanced him, piece by piece, nine miles. They seem to be affected with a strange optical illusion which elongates square feet into full English miles. . . . McClellan is still four miles, and perhaps a few odd inches, from Richmond, and not several miles on the other side of it, as the various reported advances would have us believe.

During this period of inactivity, Townsend of the *Herald* was comfortably billeted in a nine-dollar-a-week room at a farmhouse owned by a Virginia gentleman named Michie on the right bank of the Chickahominy. The Michie house was something of a correspondents' rendezvous, housing at one time as many as twelve representatives of five different newspapers. From the Michie homestead Townsend took daily rides to all parts of the lines and noted on different occasions the headquarters and tents, "so neat and trim, and with such good food, with buckets of champagne and ice in it." Many years later Townsend said:

> They lived very well around McClellan's headquarters. . . . [Yet] I have always felt that McClellan's campaign was a sort of farce. . . . They did not know at headquarters enough about the location of parts and parcels of the army. If you would put a question on that subject to Marcy or some other staff officer, he would have to think and inquire before he could tell you. They were polite people, but there was a sort of feeble aristocratic tone about them . . . instead of that gnarled, nasal, direct reply and address I found in Western men.[65]

While he was staying at Michie's, Townsend shared a bed with the editor of the New York *Times* and engaged in many an evening's conversation with him about the leading New York editors of the day. According to Townsend, Raymond spoke slightingly of his competitors, intimating that Greeley had become envious of him because of his success in being elected to office, and characterizing Bennett as a "monstrous blackguard" and Webb as an "old, inflated sausage." Although Raymond offered Townsend a much larger salary than he was receiving from the *Herald* to join the *Times* staff and to supply it with copies of the Richmond newspapers, for reasons which he later characterized as stemming from "the youthful ideas of fidelity," Townsend declined this tempting offer.[66]

Inactivity ended when, on Wednesday, June 25, McClellan advanced along the Williamsburg Road in a movement preliminary to a series of murderous battles which flung the Union army backward from the gates of Richmond and almost resulted in its complete destruction.[67] General Robert E. Lee, who had been in command of the Confederate army since June 1, had planned to attack in force north of the Chickahominy on the morning of June 26 to overwhelm the Union right, and to cut McClellan off from his supply base at White House. Although McClellan's attack on the twenty-fifth, which was hardly more than a reconnaissance in force, caught Lee off balance, the Confederate general adhered to his plan. Shortly after noon on June 27, after an initial repulse at Mechanicsville on the afternoon of the twenty-sixth, Lee threw fifty-five thousand of his best troops—including those under "Stonewall" Jackson's command, which had been secretly recalled from the Shenandoah Valley for this purpose[68]—against the Union right wing. Porter, who was in command there, handled his troops with considerable skill, even though he was outnumbered two to one and matched against the South's best generalship. During the night of June 27, following the Battle of Gaines's Mill, the shattered remnants of Porter's command were withdrawn to the South bank of the Chickahominy. On the morning of the twenty-eighth, after a conference with his corps commanders, McClellan gave orders for the army to retreat southward to the James River in order to establish a new line of communication.

Townsend rode up to the front that morning in company with another *Herald* correspondent, Finley Anderson, and talked with some of the soldiers who had crossed the Chickahominy during the night. As he later described his experience:

> I went to and fro, obtaining the names of killed, wounded and missing, with incidents of the battle as well as its general plan. These I scrawled upon bits of newspaper, upon envelopes, upon the lining of my hat, and finally upon my shirt wristbands. I was literally filled with notes before noon, and if I had been shot at that time, endeavors to obtain my name would have been extremely difficult.[69]

On the day of McClellan's preliminary feeler, June 25, an order had been published at White House, the army's forward base, prohibiting any civilian from going up to the front.[70] As a result of the order several army correspondents who had gone down to White House to mail their letters were prevented from returning to their posts; some others who tried to slip past the provost guard on their way to the front lines speedily were sent back. After railroad communication with White House ceased, many of the correspondents who were still with the army eagerly attached themselves to the cavalry column which was sent ahead of the main body to open communication with the Federal gunboats on the James River. Panic-stricken as they were by the terrible scenes of death and destruction which they had already witnessed, these reporters largely were responsible for creating an exaggerated impression of the reverse which the army had encountered.

The march to the James was one long nightmare of pain, hunger, heat, and weariness for everyone involved. On June 29, the morning after the retreat began, Townsend came upon a group of reporters who were feeling too depressed to pay any attention to the fighting which was in progress at that very moment in the neighborhood of the Fair Oaks battlefield. One of the reporters, a stoutish gentleman, given to panting and perspiration, was convinced that they were all about to be "gobbled up." He moaned:

> I promised my wife to stay at home after the Burnside business.[71] The Burnside job was very nearly enough for me. In fact I should have quite starved on the Burnside job, if I hadn't took the fever. And the fever kept me so busy that I forgot how hungry I was. . . .
>
> Well, the Burnside job wasn't enough for me; I must come out again. I must follow the young Napoleon. And the young Napoleon has made a pretty mess of it. I never expect to get home any more; I know I shall be gobbled up![72]

A reporter for the Chicago *Times,* who had come down from Washington just two days before the Battle of Mechanicsville, described McClellan's staff officers as "completely worn out, sleeping in their saddles" and declared that:

> as regards our camps and tents, we never expect, when we leave them in the morning, to see them at night. I have lost all my personal baggage, except what I happened to have with me on horseback. . . . A correspondent of the New York *Herald* is in a still worse predicament, having lost his horse, saddle, equipments, pistols, and all his baggage.[73]

Crounse of the New York *World* also lost his horse on the morning after the Battle of Gaines's Mill and, consequently, had to do his retreating on foot. All day Sunday, June 29, and far into the night he kept pace with Porter's Fifth Corps in what the men in the ranks jocularly referred to as the "blind march." Porter's men were executing a semicircular movement, which produced rumors among them that they were marching upon the Confederate capital by the flank. At one stage of the march, Crounse had just raised a canteen of cold coffee to his lips, the first article of food or drink he had tasted that day, when the column was thrown into a sudden panic by a frightened horse which had dashed out of the woods into one of the regimental formations ahead. Although the officers soon managed to restore order, the canteen was knocked out of the reporter's hands, and it could not be found anywhere.

Around midnight, Crounse fell out of line, completely overcome by exhaustion, and sank down by the roadside. When he awoke several hours later, he discovered to his surprise that the same regiment with which he had been the night before was passing by on the countermarch. By this time it was clear to everyone that they were heading for the banks of the James. Their spirits rose; their pace quickened. By nine o'clock Monday morning, as they were filing through a cornfield on the summit of Malvern Hill, they got their first glimpse of the Federal gunboats on the James. That afternoon while the Battle of Frayser's Farm was in progress, Crounse stood on this same hill and watched the long lines of Federal baggage wagons as they descended the steep sides to the river flat below and then made off down the river road through blinding clouds of dust.[74]

Most of the army correspondents had had their fill of martial scenes by this time and were eager to get passage on one of the river boats for Fortress Monroe. Bickham of the Cincinnati *Commercial* managed to smuggle himself aboard a schooner laden with hay, whose captain was not averse to receiving a few dollars in exchange for his hospitality. Crounse and several other newspaper men attached themselves to a hospital transport through the connivance of the captain of the guard, who politely mistook them for a surgeon and a trio of nurses. On the way down to Fortress Monroe the little group of reporters made the rounds of the sick and wounded, having previously agreed to divide the boat into four sections so that each reporter might be responsible for his particular share of the men aboard.[75]

In reporting the Battles of the Seven Days the army newspapermen were subjected to the tightest censorship they had experienced since the beginning of the war. At an early hour on Saturday morning, June 28, rumors of a battle before Richmond began to circulate along Washington's "Newspaper Row." In Philadelphia, the *Press* learned that some members of McClellan's staff had telegraphed to their friends in that city to report that they were well. Why should they be unwell unless there had been a battle?, queried the *Press,* and what were the details of the battle?[76] All day Sunday the nation awaited with mingled hope and dread an authoritative statement from Washington about the fate of McClellan's army. At two o'clock that afternoon the War Department issued a dispatch, solely for the information of the press, stating that as soon as exact information of the state of affairs before Richmond was received it would be made available to the public "whether good or bad."[77] There was nothing further until ten o'clock that evening, when the Washington newspapermen received instructions from Sanford not to telegraph any military news without authorization from the War Department.[78] At midnight there was still nothing official, so the New York and Philadelphia papers went to press without any satisfactory information about the state of affairs on the Peninsula.

Meanwhile, there were exciting developments in Baltimore as a result of the arrival there on the previous (Saturday) night of Charles C. Fulton, the editor of the Baltimore *American,* with an exclusive account of the fighting on the Peninsula up until noon on Saturday. On Sunday morning he telegraphed a synopsis of his story to the War Department and then in response to a summons hastened to Washington to confer with the President and the Secretary of War. Later in the day he went back to Baltimore and began to prepare his material for publication in the Monday morning edition of the *American.* Fulton was also the Baltimore agent of the Associated Press, and therefore at nine o'clock that evening he sent a confidential wire to the New York office of the AP offering to release his story to the members of that organization providing that proper credit was given to the *American.* Before he received any answer to this telegram, he sent off a second (around eleven o'clock) in which he stated that permission to telegraph his story had been refused. As a result of a mistake in the New York office both of these dispatches were released for publication in the various New York newspapers on the following morning. Without waiting for any explanation from Fulton, the War Department issued an order for his arrest, and within a few hours' time he was behind the walls of Fort McHenry.

The news of Fulton's arrest created a furore. His loyalty and integrity were beyond question; moreover, there was nothing in the rather over-optimistic battle account in the Baltimore *American* of June 30 which seemed to warrant such a severe penalty. The explanation for the arrest appears to have been this: In his ill-fated telegram to D. H. Craig, the New York agent of the Associated Press, Fulton had unguardedly stated that his battle report included "facts obtained from Washington, having been sent for by special train to communicate with the President." Although Fulton made no reference to his conference with the President in the account which he published in the *American*, the War Department chose to regard the statement which appeared in the telegram as a "flagrant and outrageous breach of confidence." The arrest was plainly a mistake. The New York *World* pronounced it the "most egregious not to say the most despotic blunder" of which Secretary Stanton had yet been guilty, and a resolution was introduced into the Senate by Senator Morton S. Wilkinson of Minnesota asking the President to state the reasons for the editor's arrest. After forty-eight hours in jail, part of which he spent in the company of a "bevy of rats," Fulton was released and permitted to resume his editorial duties.[79]

During the next few days further details about the fighting on the Peninsula were gradually made public. On July 3, the *Times* scooped the other New York newspapers by publishing thirteen columns of battle news which Elias Smith and one of its other special correspondents had just brought in from McClellan's army. The *Times* account revealed that the Army of the Potomac had met with a serious reverse and indicated that it was still in a condition of extreme peril. That evening a local reporter for the *Times* was present at a gathering in Brooklyn where someone was reading aloud the battle accounts in the *Times* issue of that day to a small group of men. After the reader had finished, one of them remarked that the first reports of a battle usually were exaggerated and it might prove so in this case. At this point a well-known clergyman, who had previously remained silent, took the floor. He said:

> Gentlemen, that letter is signed "E.S.," and is from a man whose probity and veracity are unquestioned.... Whenever I see a

> statement signed by him, I know what to believe, and there is no use in blinking these facts. We are badly whipped. . . .[80]

On that same day a party of army newspapermen, including B. S. Osbon of the *Herald* and the army correspondent of the Associated Press, passed through Baltimore on their way north with accounts of the repulse of the Confederates at Malvern Hill in the concluding phase of the Battles of the Seven Days.[81] The mailboat on which they had come up from Fortress Monroe arrived in Baltimore just in time to permit them to make connections with the train for New York. Much to their annoyance the train had to make frequent stops along the way because of the heavy troop traffic. Shortly before dusk a heavy rainstorm reduced the speed of the train still further. Just outside Philadelphia they collided with a cow, which derailed the train. Since the possibility of their reaching New York that night apparently had been eliminated by this mishap, the newspaper contingent, with one exception, made an agreement among themselves to find some place to stop over night. The man who took no part in the parley was the *Herald* correspondent, Osbon, who started out on foot, gripsack in hand, in the direction of a light which proved to be in a farmhouse about a half mile away. Without revealing that he was a newspaper correspondent, Osbon described the railroad accident to the farmer and his wife and added some imaginary details about a deathbed and a mother anxiously waiting. The farmer finally agreed to hitch up his carriage and drive Osbon through a pelting rainstorm to the railroad station in West Philadelphia. Upon arriving there, Osbon learned that he was too late to catch the night train to New York. A wire to Frederick Hudson in New York, requesting permission to charter a special engine, however, produced a quick affirmative. At Jersey City two carriages from the *Herald* office, containing a small army of printers and compositors, met Osbon, seized his great bundle of copy, and cut it into "takes" as they went across on the ferry. At the *Herald* office extra compositors were on hand, ready for action. Throughout the night they worked. By daylight most of Osbon's story of the bitter fighting on the Peninsula was on the street.[82]

In spite of efforts by some newspaper correspondents to create the impression that the retreat to the James had been a masterly accomplishment and that the army was in a better position to attack Richmond than before, it was nonetheless clear that victory had eluded McClellan.[83] A skeptical correspondent of the Chicago *Tribune*, in a letter written from Washington on July 9, expressed the opinion that:

> The amount of lying that has been sent abroad on the wings of the press and telegraphed to mislead and delude the country is enormous. . . . All the reasons are assigned but the right one, to account for a stunning disaster. And the crowning deceit of the whole column of falsehoods is to call the affair a "great strategic movement." It was just as much a great strategic movement as the battle of Ball's Bluff, and not a whit more.[84]

Although at the time McClellan escaped any personal criticism from the army reporters, later, during a political campaign, one of them sharply criticized the General for remaining on the gunboat "Galena" while his army was fighting for its life at Malvern Hill. The reporter, W. D. Bickham, told of seeing McClellan pass:

> so close under the stern of the steamer James Brooks, while approaching the shore, that we could have pitched a copper into his boat. We shall never forget the look of scorn which two British officers—who had been McClellan guests—exchanged as they saw him passing. They knew that it was his duty to be with his heroic army. . . . McClellan on gunboats during the battle of Malvern Hill was the meanest picture that this bloody rebellion has painted.[85]

Many of the army correspondents, on the other hand—Wilkeson of the New York *Tribune* among them—were convinced that the responsibility for the disaster should be placed at the door of the Administration in Washington. "The refusal to give this army ample re-enforcement, on Friday last, came within a hair's breadth of ruining the nation," asserted Wilkeson in a letter which, in view of their hostility toward McClellan, must have astonished the proprietors of the *Tribune* as greatly as it did everyone else.[86] The letter went on to say:

> I don't care about the question—which legislators, soldiers, and politicians have debated—of this General's fitness to command. The York and James River Peninsula were not the place for that discussion. . . . When loyal New-York regiments, lifted from their feet by the fire of Rebel brigades, cry out of their wounds and death for help; when the choicest of New-England and Michigan and Pennsylvania troops, outnumbered . . . by whole divisions of the enemy, beg for re-enforcements, I say that the blackest crime

> that Power can commit is to stalk upon the field of peril and say, "Soldiers, I have no faith in your commander! Let your martyrdom proceed!" And so says this Army of the Potomac.[87]

The *Tribune* printed Wilkeson's letter in full but appended an editorial note that it was not responsible for his opinions nor could it concur in his strictures upon the Government.[88] Not until later did it become generally known that McClellan's army had been slightly larger than the opposing army and that all the newspaper talk about it being outnumbered two to one was utterly without basis.[89] Inaccurate as well was the statement appearing in some newspaper accounts to the effect that thirty thousand troops from Beauregard's western army had been moved from Corinth to Richmond in time to participate in the fighting of the Seven Days.

Nevertheless, the reporters' letters describing the concluding phase of the Peninsular Campaign contained some vivid battle pictures—pictures of McClellan and his staff holding a council of war beneath an arbor of pine boughs the night after the Battle of Gaines's Mill; pictures of thick-flying bullets whining overhead, of riderless, terrified horses stampeding in every direction, of army supplies going up in smoke; pictures of stragglers, skulkers, frightened sutlers, and incompetent surgeons; pictures of wounded men clinging to the garments of their comrades and hobbling along on crutches rather than run the chance of falling into the hands of the enemy. In terms of their descriptive power the battle accounts contributed to the New York *Tribune* by Wilkeson and Charles A. Page were unsurpassed. Among the more detailed accounts, those of Elias Smith, Crounse, Townsend, and Bickham were probably of greatest merit. Written as they were in the heat of the conflict, they reflected an imperfect comprehension of much that went on, but they breathed a grim pride in the accomplishments of an army whose valor, in their eyes, atoned for any defects in its leadership.[90]

As soon as the crisis was over there was widespread dissatisfaction with the censorship because of the anxiety which it had produced after the Battles of the Seven Days.[91] The press was quick to point out that insofar as the aim of the censorship had been to prevent the news of McClellan's defeat from being prematurely made known abroad it had proven a failure. Even before the full details of the defeat had been communicated to the public in this country, copies of the Richmond papers containing exultant accounts of the Confederate success had been smuggled out of Baltimore and were en route to Confederate agents in London and Paris.[92]

Notwithstanding the great efforts made by the press to insure full coverage of the campaign, the end product had been somewhat disappointing. Henry Villard, who was a good judge of the essentials of reporting, thought that although some very fine letters were written to the press during the Peninsular Campaign, the average value of the reporting was mediocre.[93] Said the St. Louis *Republican* in an editorial published on July 6:

> There has been so much confusion in the reports of correspondents, respecting the movements and plans of our army before Richmond, that great difficulty has been encountered by all who attempted to make clear to themselves its position and the significance of its moves.

To some extent the censorship was a factor; to some extent reportorial deficiencies were attributable to defects in organization and to ill-trained personnel. On the other hand, had the campaign terminated in the fall of Richmond, the verdict on the performance of the reporters might have been considerably different.

10

"Come, Sir, this is no Time for Prayer"

IN many ways 1862 was a banner year for the newspaper men who reported the activities of Uncle Sam's fighting fleet. At Roanoke Island and Fort Henry during the first week of February, they watched the Federal gunboats beat down powerful enemy fortifications. In March the epic struggle between the "Virginia" and the "Monitor" afforded them an unforgettable view of the world's first battle between ironclad warships. Little more than another month had passed before they saw Farragut destroy a Confederate squadron below New Orleans and sweep past two massive Confederate forts in one of the most thrilling naval battles of the war. At Fort Pillow, Island No. 10, and again before Memphis they received further proof of the valor of the navy's gold-braided commodores and its intrepid seamen. Meanwhile, from Fortress Monroe, Port Royal, Key West, Ship Island, and other points along the coast there came a steady flow of newspaper correspondence showing the increasing effectiveness of the blockade.

When the 1200-ton gunboat "State of Georgia" came into the Washington Navy Yard for repairs one bright autumn day in October, 1862, a New York *Tribune* correspondent went aboard to gather material for a letter. From the crew he learned that the "State of Georgia" had been in the blockading service off Wilmington, North Carolina, since the previous November; had taken three prizes during that time; and had collided with another blockading vessel at night on one occasion, since the Blockading Squadron did not carry lights.

In describing the capture of the iron steamer "Sunbeam," the *Tribune* man seized the opportunity to get in a dig at the expense of his paper's long-time enemy. He gloated:

> It is my luck to be always running against *The Herald*'s blunders or fabrications. The capture of the Sunbeam is ascribed in that sheet to the Mystic, whereas the fact is, on the word of Mr. Rogers

> and Mr. White, the commander's aid, both gentlemen of honor, "the State of Georgia captured the Sunbeam, and had a prize crew on board of her before the Mystic came up."[1]

As no one from the "Mystic" disputed this version of the capture, the *Tribune* correspondent had the last word.

Earlier in the year, a fair-sized delegation of the press was on board when the Burnside expedition sailed out of Hampton Roads on its way to Roanoke Island. Among the reporters with the expedition, most of them quartered together on the steam transport "Cossack," were James C. Fitzpatrick and John P. Dunn of the New York *Herald;* Elias Smith of the rival *Times;* Philip Ripley, the correspondent of Bryant's *Evening Post;* Lorenzo L. Crounse, who represented simultaneously the *World,* the Cincinnati *Commercial,* and the Chicago *Tribune;* Henry Bentley of the Philadelphia *Inquirer;* and Nehemiah Stanly of the Boston *Journal.* It was the general impression among the newspapermen that they were bound for Norfolk or some point up the York River. Probably none of them realized that the real purpose of the expedition was to seize Roanoke Island and thus to stop blockade-running in the neighborhood of Albemarle Sound.

Before the army transports left Annapolis for Hampton Roads, the military chief of the expedition, Major General Ambrose E. Burnside, called together the reporters. He assured them that he would cooperate with them in every way possible for obtaining news if they would agree in turn not to publish any information concerning the scope or purpose of the expedition until it had "first struck a blow."[2] Although the newspapermen said they were willing to abide by such an agreement, the expedition was hardly underway before the New York *World* and the Chicago *Tribune* made public detailed information concerning the organization of the fleet and the land force which it was carrying, along with other information of a highly confidential character.[3] Both Burnside and Flag Officer Louis M. Goldsborough, who commanded the naval arm of the expedition, were incensed at this breach of confidence. Among the reporters themselves, whatever friendliness they may have exhibited toward each other at the outset speedily was replaced by suspicion. Eventually they aligned themselves into two groups, whose ill-feeling was such that sentries were kept posted day and night to prevent the rival faction from obtaining exclusive possession of any important news.[4]

The fleet cleared from Hampton Roads on a moonlit Saturday night,

January 11. On board the forty-six transports were twelve thousand soldiers, mainly from the northeastern states. The naval part of the expedition consisted of a motley array of ferryboats, tugs, and river steamers which had been converted into men-of-war on rather short notice. There was not one of them that could not have been put out of action by a single well-directed shot, and even the firing of their own guns subjected them to serious strain.

The first day out the weather was fairly pleasant, although it became so rough toward evening that the sailing vessels which were towed by the steamers had to cut loose and shift for themselves. On Monday the weather took a rapid turn for the worse, although most of the lighter draft vessels succeeded in getting across the bar at Hatteras Inlet before the storm overtook them. By midafternoon the heavier vessels outside the bar were being lashed by a northeasterly gale which blew one transport out to sea, caused several others to run aground, and spread terror among the survivors as the ships ground against each other in their restricted anchorage and tossed heavily upon the swell. One of the New York *Tribune* reporters commented:

> Scarce a steamer in the fleet but has had its guards broken, its paddle-boxes smashed, its decks torn into splinters.

As for the "Cossack," upon which he was berthed, she was:

> battered astern to-day by the broken stump of a brig's bowsprit, until her promenade deck, aft, was half destroyed, and a half dozen state-rooms stripped clean into one. Things got to such a pass that at last Capt. Bennett could stand it no longer, so he went in his gig to take soundings, and we are now anchored in a clear spot, nearly a mile from the flagship.[5]

Probably the greatest catastrophe was the loss of the steam transport "City of New-York," which ran aground with two hundred thousand dollars worth of ordnance stores on board and was dashed to pieces by the hurricane. Not until January 29 did the public learn, however, through the columns of the New York *Times*, that most of the ships in the expedition had safely ridden out the gale and reached Hatteras Inlet.

As the stormy weather slowly moderated, the reporters discovered a new hazard in the form of a shoal variously styled the "swash" or "bulkhead," through which the fleet had to pass to enter Pamlico Sound.

Whereas Goldsborough's men-of-war were through the swash and in readiness to proceed to Roanoke Island by January 19, the army transports, many of them drawing eight or nine feet of water or even more, were at first unable to negotiate a channel affording no more than eight and a half feet at high tide. Five tugs had been chartered at Annapolis at extortionate prices to provide just the kind of assistance that was needed here. When they failed to appear, however, Burnside pressed into service three light-draft tug steamers bound for Port Royal but compelled by the weather to put in at the Inlet.

To the ears of the reporters at this juncture came ominous stories about certain individuals "who from selfish motives have palmed off upon the Government worthless crafts, and deceived about their draft of water."[6] Nosing about the government departments at Washington, the watchful correspondent of the Chicago *Tribune*, Horace White, uncovered a sensational news item. General Burnside, he learned, had just sent a message to the War Department specifying the unfitness of many of the transports that had been consigned to him and bewailing the fact that "the contractors have ruined me."[7] In a private letter to the editors of the *Tribune*, White subsequently expressed the hope that:

> you have not suppressed any thing that I have written concerning *Tucker.*[8] The scoundrel bought the transports, vessels, or a portion of them, that wrecked Burnside. There is a mystery about his confirmation which I cannot write at present. Suffice it that he has not yet got beyond the reach of the Senate, notwithstanding Stanton used his utmost efforts to get him through.[9]

By February 5 all of the transports were safely over the swash and ready to push on to Roanoke Island. Their passage had been a rugged one. Said the New York *Tribune* correspondent:

> Our ships have literally plowed their way through the sandy bottom, and opened a channel for vessels of the passage of which into the Sound there appeared to be not the slightest possibility.[10]

Everybody on board the "Cossack" from the captain down to the cook had been jubilant when the word was passed on the evening of the fourth that sailing time was set for the next morning. Even the "specials," to whom the oft-repeated rumor, "Look out for a movement tomorrow," was humorous, had refilled their pipes and had stared at each other in astonishment.

"O, no," one of them finally had shrugged, "I've heard all that before. Hereafter, I shall believe a thing when I see it, and not before. Note that down."[11]

His skepticism notwithstanding, the signal to get underway was received early the next morning, and presently the boatswain's whistle calling, "Away, away—heave anchor," gave notice of their departure. Northward toward Roanoke Island the expedition moved at a leisurely pace, each steamer towing from one to three schooners and brigs laden with troops and munitions. About two o'clock in the afternoon, the reporters caught their first glimpse of the North Carolina shore on their left, and approximately three hours later the dark low outline of Roanoke Island was sighted directly ahead. Within the next half hour, the entire squadron reached the rendezvous area off Stumpy Point and anchored for the night.

On the following morning, February 6, the fleet prepared to go into action. Almost immediately, however, the weather took a turn for the worse, and the attack had to be postponed for twenty-four hours.

As the fog lifted on the morning of February 7, the gunboats took position around the flagship and prepared to enter Croatan Sound which separates Roanoke Island from the mainland. Next in line were the transports, with the army headquarters ship "Spaulding," carrying the newspapermen, in the van.[12] Behind a double row of piles and sunken vessels placed to obstruct the channel a force of eight Confederate gunboats was drawn up to dispute the passage of these narrow waters.[13] Further opposition was to be expected from four strong fortifications, three of them on the west side of Roanoke Island, the fourth at Redstone Point on the mainland.

At 9:55 A.M. the order to get underway was given, and twenty minutes later Goldsborough hoisted the signal, "This day our country expects that every man will do his duty," practically identical with Lord Nelson's fighting words at Trafalgar.[14] The fleet flagship fired the opening gun soon afterward. At first Goldsborough directed his fire against the Confederate gunboats, which gradually fell back to draw his ships within range of the forts. Meanwhile the Federal gunboats steadily advanced until they reached the obstructions, where they were exposed to a destructive crossfire from the forts. For six consecutive hours the opposing forces kept hammering away at each other at close range.

Fairly early in the contest an eighty-pound rifled shell from one of the land batteries penetrated the engine room of the Union gunboat "Louisiana" and set her on fire. Within a few moments, however, the crew extinguished the flames, and the "Louisiana" was back in the fight.[15] Another Union gunboat, the "Hetzel," was obliged to haul off to repair damage inflicted by a fifty-two-pound round shot. Out of action for an hour and a half, she too resumed her station and again took part in the cannonading.[16] Two of the Confederate gunboats, the flagship "Curlew" and the "Forrest," were disabled about 2:30 P.M., but the others remained in action until their supply of ammunition was exhausted.

On board the transports, which were well in the rear of the bombarding fleet, newspapermen and soldiers alike were fascinated spectators of the action. The New York *Commercial Advertiser*'s correspondent observed:

> Their decks, spars, and rigging were crowded by the soldiers, eagerly watching the progress of the struggle between our vessels and the battery, and cheers were given whenever a well-directed shot was observed to strike. They clung to the rigging like bees to a hive, in clusters as close as they could cling. Their dark figures were clearly defined on the western sky, lighted by the afternoon sun. The water was perfectly still, adding greatly to the striking appearance of the scene.[17]

At about 3:00 P.M., the troops embarked in light steamers and boats for the landing operation. As they were approaching the shore, a large body of enemy troops came up to oppose their landing. Thereupon one of the Union gunboats moved in and dispersed the opposition with shrapnel. Within less than an hour four thousand men were ashore, and by eleven o'clock that night the landing operation was complete except for one Massachusetts regiment which could not be put ashore until the next morning.[18]

At daybreak on the eighth, one of Burnside's three brigades moved forward from the landing and drove in the enemy pickets upon their main body. Near the middle of the island the principal Confederate force was entrenched in a strong position flanked by almost impassable swamps and approachable only by a narrow causeway defended by a battery of three guns.[19] While Brigadier General John G. Foster's brigade attacked the battery on the causeway, the other two brigades, plunging waist-deep through the swamps, executed flanking movements. The New York *Times* reporter, who had landed very early that morning, already had found a road leading to the rear of the enemy's position. He was so near the action that he could hear distinctly the sharp ringing voices of the Union officers urging their men forward through the swamps.[20] This movement occupied several tedious hours, but the enemy was completely surprised when on both flanks the Union troops emerged from terrain which had been regarded as impassable. A New York Zouave regiment volunteered to carry the entrenchment at the point of the bayonet. They charged forward at double quick, shouting their Zouave battle cry, and the enemy broke and ran. The surrender of the entire Confederate land force of over twenty-five hundred men soon followed, and by 5:00 P.M. the Stars and Stripes were flying over Fort Bartow, the southernmost of the three forts on Roanoke Island.[21]

Pushing forward in advance of Burnside's troops who were busy rounding up prisoners, Bentley of the Philadelphia *Inquirer*, accompanied by the artist of *Harper's Weekly*, found one of the other forts completely deserted. Filled with martial enthusiasm and forgetting for the moment that they were noncombatants, the newsmen hauled down the Confederate flag with their own hands.[22] Meanwhile, the gunboats had forced their way through the line of piles which barred the way into Albemarle Sound and had put to flight the remnants of the Confederate naval force. Whereas the Battle of Roanoke Island had resulted in army casualties in excess of two hundred, the navy's loss (six men killed, seventeen wounded, and two missing) was negligible.[23] The Confederate prisoners totaled 2,675, including a reporter for the Richmond *Dispatch*.[24]

After lowering the Confederate flag over Fort Huger, Bentley, together with Elias Smith of the New York *Times*, walked about among the Confederate dead and wounded in one of the captured earthworks. They paused to look at a dark-complexioned man, perhaps thirty years of age, who had placed one hand over his face as if to conceal his features from the reporters. As he appeared to be conscious, Bentley decided to ask him a few questions relative to his condition and injuries.

"Have you had any medical attendance, sir?" he inquired.

"I have been promised it."

"Where is your wound?"

He pointed to his leg below the knee.

"As I am here to give as many particulars concerning this battle as possible, sir, if you have no objection, I would be pleased to know your name and residence, that it may gain publicity and reach your friends," persisted the *Inquirer* man.

The wounded man said that his name was J. Porster of Charleston, Kanawha County, Virginia, commanding the Fifty-ninth Virginia or Second Wise Legion. The reporters soon obtained medical attendance for him, and he was removed to more comfortable quarters.

A little farther on among the bushes and briars, the two reporters came across the body of a well-dressed officer lying with face upturned and eyes partially closed. From a Confederate surgeon, who turned out to be his cousin, they learned that the dead officer was Robert Coles, that he had been in command of a company of Albemarle Guards, and that his parents lived in Philadelphia near the intersection of Spruce and Thirteenth Streets. Touched, the New York *Times* correspondent Smith cut a lock of hair from the dead soldier's head to send on to his parents.[25]

On February 10, the remainder of the Confederate fleet made its last stand near Elizabeth City, where it had been pursued by the Federal gunboats. In an engagement which lasted hardly fifteen minutes, the fleet practically was annihilated, although two Confederate gunboats did escape, reaching Norfolk by way of the Pasquotank River and the Dismal Swamp canal.[26]

Some clever work by its correspondent at Fortress Monroe permitted the Philadelphia *Inquirer* to be first with the news of the Roanoke Island victory. The *Inquirer* man had ingratiated himself into the confidence of General Wool, then in command at Fortress Monroe, and had been appointed a volunteer aide to the General. As luck would have it, he also had been placed in command of the tugboat which was used to exchange the Confederate General Pegram under a flag of truce at Hampton Roads. After the Union boat and a Confederate boat had been lashed together, and the exchange completed, the *Inquirer* reporter determined to find out what he could unofficially about the Burnside expedition.

Approaching the captain of the Confederate flag-of-truce boat, the reporter gave him a recent issue of the New York *Herald*, but received only a "thank you" in return. The possibility that there might be a Southern newspaper in the mail coming aboard proved vain too. Sam, the Negro engineer, however, somehow had obtained a copy of the Norfolk *Day Book*, which he was willing to sell to the reporter for a gold half-eagle. This was progress, but the *Inquirer* man still had not found the information he was looking for. He then struck up a conversation with a French naval officer, who was on his way North after a stay of some duration in the South. The officer was not particularly talkative, but a neatly folded newspaper in his breast pocket excited the reporter's curiosity. After some reflection, he decided that the best approach was a little subtle flattery. Bowing politely, he inquired whether monsieur would permit him to look at his "Paris journal." Affected by this unwonted gallantry on the part of an American, the unsuspecting Frenchman handed the precious object to the correspondent with the comment:

"Non, non; it is nossing but ze Confederate journal from Richmond in mourning for ze Blues!"

The *Inquirer* reporter now had an account of the Union victory at Roanoke Island from Confederate sources, but when he entered the Hygeia House at Old Point Comfort he learned that the submarine cable to Cherrystone was working badly and that nothing but government dispatches were being handled. Since the Baltimore steamer "Adelaide" already had steam up and was about to shove off, however, the reporter hastened on board. There he discovered that Henry J. Raymond of the New York *Times* was to be his traveling companion along with the same French officer who had been so obliging. Fortunately, the latter did not seem to connect the *Inquirer* man with the officer who had been in charge of the flag-of-truce boat. The editor of the New York *Times*, however, after finding the French officer uncommunicative, transferred his attention to the *Inquirer*'s representative and offered to pay him a liberal sum in gold for up-to-the-minute news. Feigning ignorance, the *Inquirer* correspondent gave Raymond the slip as soon as the "Adelaide" discharged its passengers at Baltimore and, without losing any further time, telegraphed to his newspaper an exclusive story which speedily was confirmed from Washington.[27] Later Bentley, also of the *Inquirer*, and Smith of the New York *Times* came up together on the gunboat "Stars and Stripes" bringing with them the first detailed accounts of the victory at Roanoke Island.[28]

* * *

Probably the most dramatic naval news story of the war was that of the four-hour combat between the "Monitor" and the "Virginia" off Newport News on a Sunday morning in March, 1862. The "Virginia," formerly known as the "Merrimack," was a screw frigate of thirty-five hundred tons, which had been scuttled by the Federal authorities when the Norfolk Navy Yard fell into Confederate hands near the beginning of the war. Subsequently she had been raised by the Confederates, placed in drydock, renamed the "Virginia," and over a period of months converted into an ironclad.

From the Navy Department in Washington the press picked up hints from time to time about the rehabilitation of the "Merrimack." Finally the managing editor of the New York *Herald* decided to send the resourceful B. S. Osbon down to Fortress Monroe to get further information about the mysterious ironclad. After making some preliminary inquiries around Old Point Comfort, Osbon secured a sixteen-foot pilot boat in which he managed to slip past the Confederate batteries on Sewall's Point under cover of darkness. Continuing up the Elizabeth River, he came to the Gosport Yard, where the one-time "Merrimack" was still in drydock. Insamuch as it was not a particularly dark night, once the fog had lifted Osbon was able to obtain an excellent view of the great ram, soon to descend upon the Union war vessels anchored in Hampton Roads. After taking notes on what he saw, the *Herald* reporter made off without being discovered. His experience netted him not simply a verbal description of the vessel, which he contributed to the *Herald*, but also a pen-and-ink sketch, subsequently published in *Harper's Weekly*. Emboldened by the success of his coup, Osbon volunteered to lead a boarding party over the same route for the purpose of destroying the "Virginia" while she was still immobile. General Wool, the commandant at Fortress Monroe, however, refused to sanction the foolhardy venture.[29]

A correspondent of the New York *Times* was on board the U.S.S. "Minnesota" off Fortress Monroe when the "Virginia," accompanied by several Confederate gunboats, emerged from her lair on the morning of March 8. He stated:

> We were just preparing to go ashore for a short furlough, when the drums beat suddenly to general quarters. The anchors were taken up, and before we knew what was the cause of the alarm we were under way and standing toward Norfolk.[30]

While a second New York *Times* reporter was watching from the shore, the "Virginia" headed for Newport News Point, off which the wooden sailing vessels "Congress" and "Cumberland" were anchored. The "Virginia" was still three-quarters of a mile away when the "Cumberland" opened fire with her pivot gun, as did the "Congress" shortly afterward. Still the "Virginia" came on, contemptuous of the hailstorm of shot which rebounded from her well-protected sides. Then, in the words of the battle report penned by the second *Times* reporter:

> A trap-door opens in her plated roof like a dormer window, and a billow of white smoke rolls up; then the roar and the crash of

> the 100-pound shell in the wooden wall of the frigate ["Congress"]. . . . Now she nears the *Cumberland* sloop-of-war, silent and still, wierd [sic] and mysterious, like some devilish and superhuman monster, or the horrid creation of a nightmare. Now, but a biscuit toss from the ship, and from the sides of both pour out a living tide of fire and smoke, of solid shot and heavy shell. We see from the ship's scuppers running streams of crimson gore. . . . Now the ram has taken her position bow on, and slowly she moves and horribly upon the doomed vessel. Like a rhinoceros she sinks down her head and frightful horn, and with a dead, soul-rendering crunch she pierces her on the starboard bow, lifting her up as a man does a toy. . . .
>
> There lies the "Infernal Machine" for half an hour, waiting to see if the work is complete, pitching in her shot, and calling for her to surrender. But, thank God, it is not done. The gallant ship, her bow sinking gradually, finally gives a lurch to port, and with a shudder throughout her, goes down by the head with one sudden plunge—carrying dead, living and wounded with her. . . .
>
> Meanwhile, the *Congress* frigate seeing her companion's fate, has slipped her cable, and with one sail set has drifted ashore. The *Merrimac* now follows her, pitches in a couple of shots, and the beloved flag of our country is hauled down. One yell of rage and indignation rises from the soldiers and sailors on shore.[31]

While two of the Confederate gunboats were alongside the "Congress" taking off the wounded and prisoners, they came under such a heavy fire from the shore batteries that they were obliged to haul off before they had completed their task. Unable to take possession of his prize, Flag Officer Franklin Buchanan, the commander of the "Virginia," ordered the "Congress" to be destroyed by hot shot and incendiary shells, and within a short time the old frigate was in flames fore and aft. Then the "Virginia" headed for the "Minnesota," which had run aground about a mile from Newport News while attempting to come to the aid of the "Cumberland" and the "Congress." The "Virginia" 's deep draught prevented her from getting within a mile of the "Minnesota," however, and the Confederate leviathan hauled off at dusk and returned to Norfolk, leaving behind her wreckage and foreboding.

To a New York *Herald* correspondent who was at Fortress Monroe that night the sight of the burning "Congress" lighting up the bay was a "fearful and sublime spectacle." He reported:

> The night was clear and beautiful, the bay without a ripple on its surface. At first the flames appeared in a small body, but gradually they spread aft, and in about two hours' time from the commencement of the conflagration the Congress was one mass of flames. Slowly and gradually did the devouring element encircle the tarred rigging, until every stick of wood and every ply of hemp was environed by the fiery element. . . . The fire raged with great fury until about half-past twelve o'clock Sunday morning, when all at once a shock and explosion, resembling the eruption of a volcano, was heard, shaking the staunch old fort almost to its foundation, and the burning vessel, with everything on board, disappeared forever from view. . . . The explosion had the effect to call all the troops to arms—imagining that a signal gun had been fired. Numerous fragments of the vessel were picked up on the beach three or four miles from the fort, which is a distance of about fourteen miles from where the Congress went to the bottom.[32]

The news of the disaster at Hampton Roads did not reach Washington until early the next day. Throughout the morning excited people thronged the lobby at Willard's. No theory or suggestion, however wild, was too extraordinary for them to accept. A correspondent of the St. Louis *Republican* told of seeing an old gentleman, who had a son with Burnside's expedition, "turn purple with fright" when he heard it predicted that the Confederate war monster's next move would be to sink Goldsborough's fleet at Roanoke Island. The old gentleman seemed to feel much better, however, when someone called to his attention that a vessel drawing twenty-one feet would experience considerable difficulty in water of eight-foot depth![33] Many Washingtonians, including the Secretary of War, expected to see the "Virginia" come steaming up the Potomac and start shelling the capital at any moment. As if to heighten their suspense, the telegraph line to Fortress Monroe failed to work, remaining out of order until four o'clock in the afternoon.[34] By that time the "Virginia" had been fought to a standstill by the first of the new ironclads built by the United States government, the U.S.S. "Monitor," a new arrival.

Although the "Monitor"–"Virginia" affair was a *Herald* beat, possibly the best — certainly one of the most widely reprinted — newspaper accounts of the tussle between the two ironclads appeared in the columns of the Baltimore *American*. It was not an eyewitness account, for

Edward Fulton, the reporter who wrote it, did not leave Baltimore until Sunday evening and did not arrive at Fortress Monroe until the following morning.[35] It was, nevertheless, generally accurate and almost wholly free of excess verbiage. Young Fulton declared:

> Never was a greater hope placed upon apparently more insignificant means, but never was a great hope more triumphantly fulfilled. The Monitor is the reverse of formidable; lying low on the water, with a plain structure amidship, a small pilot-house forward, a diminutive smoke-pipe aft, at a mile's distance she might be taken for a raft, with an army ambulance amidship. It is only when on board that her compact strength and formidable means of offensive warfare are discoverable. . . .
>
> Before daylight on Sunday morning, the Monitor moved up, and took a position alongside the Minnesota lying between the latter ship and the Fortress, where she could not be seen by the rebels, but was ready, with steam up, to slip out.
>
> Up to now, on Sunday, the rebels gave no indication of what were their further designs. The Merrimac laid up toward Craney Island, in view, but motionless. At one o'clock[36] she was observed in motion, and came out, followed by the Yorktown and Jamestown, both crowded with troops. The object of the leniency toward the Minnesota on the previous evening thus became evident. It was the hope of the rebels to bring the ships aboard the Minnesota, overpower her crew by the force of numbers, and capture both vessels and men.
>
> As the rebel flotilla came out from Sewall's Point, the Monitor stood out boldly toward them. It is doubtful if the rebels knew what to make of the strange-looking battery, or if they despised it. Even the Yorktown kept on approaching, until a thirteen shell[37] from the Monitor sent her to the right about. The Merrimac and the Monitor kept on approaching each other, the former waiting until she would choose her distance, and the latter apparently not knowing what to make of her funny-looking antagonist. The first shot from the Monitor was fired when about one hundred yards distant from the Merrimac, and this distance was subsequently reduced to fifty yards, and at no time during the furious cannonading that ensued, were the vessels more than two hundred yards apart.
>
> It is impossible to reproduce the animated descriptions given of this grand contest between two vessels of such formidable

> offensive and defensive powers. The scene was in plain view from Fortress Monroe, and in the main facts all the spectators agree. At first the fight was very furious, and the guns of the Monitor were fired rapidly. As she carries but two guns, whilst the Merrimac has eight,[38] of course she received two or three shots for every one she gave. Finding that her antagonist was much more formidable than she looked, the Merrimac attempted to run her down. The superior speed and quicker turning qualities of the Monitor enabled her to avoid these shocks, and to give the Merrimac, as she passed, a shot. Once the Merrimac struck her near amidships, but only to prove that the battery could not be run down nor shot down. She spun round like a top, and as she got her bearing again, sent one of her formidable missiles into her huge opponent.
>
> The officers of the Monitor, at this time, had gained such confidence in the impregnability of their battery, that they no longer fired at random nor hastily. The fight then assumed its most interesting aspects. The Monitor ran round the Merrimac repeatedly, probing her sides, seeking for weak points, and reserving her fire with coolness, until she had the right spot and the exact range, and made her experiments accordingly. In this way the Merrimac received three shots, which must have seriously damaged her. Neither of these shots rebounded at all, but appeared to cut their way clear through iron and wood into the ship. Soon after receiving the third shot, the Merrimac turned toward Sewell's [sic] Point, and made off at full speed.
>
> The Monitor followed the Merrimac until she got well inside Sewall's Point, and then returned to the Minnesota. It is probable that the pursuit would have been continued still further, but Lieut. Worden, her commander, had previously had his eyes injured, and it was also felt that, as so much depended on the Monitor, it was imprudent to expose her unnecessarily.[39]

Somewhat surprising in view of the general excellence of Fulton's narrative was his failure to mention the part that the "Minnesota," still firmly aground, played in the contest. Sometime around 10:00 A.M. at the very height of the conflict, the "Monitor" hauled off into shoal water for a fifteen-minute spell to replenish the supply of shot in her turret.[40] At this juncture the "Virginia" shifted her attention to the "Minnesota," which thereupon let go a broadside "which would have blown out of water any timber-built ship in the world."[41] The "Virginia" countered with a shell from her rifled bow gun which passed through the chief engineer's stateroom on the "Minnesota," and exploded in the boatswain's room, scattering sparks among the powder bags in the shell room. Only prompt action by the ship's crew averted a serious fire. As the New York *Times* correspondent who was on the ship at the time, said: "It was a narrow and wonderful escape."[42] The "Monitor" reappeared just in time to give the "Minnesota" a respite, but the men on the "Minnesota" were convinced that their final hour had come when the Union ironclad withdrew from the fight a second time shortly before noon to take stock of her injuries. Reported the *Times* man aboard the stricken frigate:

> The excitement was indescribable. Men hurried hither and thither, crowding, shouting and struggling to escape by our ports into the tugs. The officers with drawn swords were endeavoring to restore discipline and force back the crowd that poured up the gangway. . . .
>
> Indeed, preparations were already made to fire the ship and flood the magazine in the last extremity; but that extremity was not yet come, though only *moments* seemed to intervene. In those few moments the tide of battle turned. The *Merrimac,* which seemed settling in the water under the rain of shot she had sustained, drew off, and evidently much damaged retired toward Norfolk, taking with her the *Yorktown* (or the one, at least, whichever it was, that remained unsunk).[43]

Northern and Southern press accounts varied on whether the "Monitor" re-entered the fight before the "Virginia" started for Norfolk. Readers of the New York *Herald* were told that:

> At a quarter before twelve o'clock, noon, Lieutenant Hepburn, the signal officer on the ramparts at Fortress Monroe, reported to General Wool that the Monitor had pierced the sides of the Merrimac, and in a few minutes the latter was in full retreat, heading for Sewall's Point, and chased for a few minutes by the Monitor.[44]

The reporter for the Raleigh *Standard,* on the other hand, was convinced that it was the "Yankee iron monster" which retreated first "with all hands at pumps, in a supposed sinking condition." The "Merrimack," he added, "then took the Patrick Henry and Jamestown in tow, and proceeded to Norfolk."[45]

Although the New York *Tribune* correspondent was of the opinion that "nothing could exceed the accuracy of the firing on both sides,"[46] the victory, as James Phinney Baxter[47] has pointed out, was not so much that of one ironclad over another as it was of armor over guns. Most of the newspaper accounts in fact considerably overestimated the effectiveness of the gunners' efforts. Whereas the greater portion of the "Virginia" 's fire passed completely over her dimunitive adversary, the "Monitor" 's gunnery was, if anything, inferior to that of the Confederate ship. One well-directed shot aimed at her unprotected water line probably would have put the "Virginia" out of action.[48]

Although the "Colossus of Roads," as the *Herald*[49] styled her, reappeared on two subsequent occasions, the "Monitor" refused to accept the challenge to renew the encounter. Apparently the taunting remarks of the Norfolk papers riled the "Monitor" 's crew, if one may judge from a letter they sent their ailing captain whom they hoped speedily would return to active duty:

> . . . we are Waiting very Patiently to engage our Antagonist if we could only get a chance to do so the last time she came out we all thought we would have the Pleasure of Sinking her But we all got Disapointed [sic] for we did not fire one Shot and the Norfolk papers Says we are Coward in the *Monitor* and all we want is a chance to Shew them where it lies with you for our Captain we can teach them who is cowards.[50]

But the "Monitor" and the "Virginia" had met for the last time. Hardly more than a fortnight later, Norfolk was evacuated by the Confederates. Because of her deep draught the "Virginia" was unable to escape up the James River. She was set on fire, and, on the morning after the evacuation of Norfolk, she blew up. The "Monitor" survived her by seven months, to perish in a storm off Hatteras just before the end of 1862.

* * *

It was on a crisp January day in 1862 that the New York *Herald*'s ace naval correspondent, B. S. Osbon, applied for the position of clerk to the newly appointed Flag Officer of the Western Gulf Blockading Squadron. Although articles and maps published in the *Herald* had told the public that if New Orleans were attacked at all it would be from the north,[51] plans had been laid as early as November, 1861, for a movement against the city from below. Osbon was well aware that Captain David G. Farragut, the Flag Officer, was to be the naval commander of that expedition. Fortunately for the reporter, a letter of recommendation from Commander David D. Porter, Farragut's foster brother, clinched the appointment, and when, during the first week of February, Farragut left Hampton Roads on the steam sloop "Hartford," the *Herald* man was aboard ready to act as clerk.[52]

The army commander of the expedition, General Butler, did not sail from Hampton Roads until February 25. Possibly there might have been greater difficulty in obtaining army cooperation if McClellan had not been looking for the opportunity to get rid of Butler, whose penchant for intrigue was well known in army circles by this time.[53] Unaware of the reasons that had prompted the selection of Butler for this new command, the newspapermen spoke in guarded terms about "General Butler's Expedition," thereby profoundly irritating the group of planners at the Navy Department whose brain child the expedition was. An interesting characterization of the General, written by a Philadelphia newspaper reporter after Butler's arrival in Louisiana, indicates the generally favorable reaction toward him on the part of the press. The reporter described him as:

> verging on to fifty years of age, about five feet eight inches high, slightly inclined to corpulency and evidently of strong *physique.* His complexion is florid, face round and beardless, save a chesnut [sic] moustache, the color of his hair; his forehead high and broad; head large, and partially bald; eyes hazel gray, with a strabismus in one, which lends additional fire to the other, and features regular and pleasing. . . . His *chapeau* is a velveteen brown slouch, his garb a blue military frock and pants, neither of which are fresh from the tailors; nor is the scanty lace *very* bright. He wears, on occasion, a red morocco sword belt, which supports his revolver and the steel-hilted scabbard and sword, presented to him by his friends. I confess that I was most agreeably disappointed in my estimate of his character, and reiterate my already expressed opinion that he is eminently fitted for the task of ending the rebellion by taking New Orleans, the Malakoff of the Southern Confederacy.[54]

On his way to Key West, Osbon had little contact with Flag Officer Farragut, who was confined to his cabin with a cold for the greater part of the time. One afternoon just before they arrived at Key West, Farragut summoned the *Herald* correspondent to his cabin and said that he had just learned from the fleet surgeon about Osbon's battle experience in the Argentine navy.[55] At the Flag Officer's prompting, Osbon told him about his experiences at sea, beginning with his tour of duty in the Anglo-Chinese navy and ending with the Port Royal engagement three months before. Not long afterward, the *Herald* man was appointed signal officer of the fleet. Osbon later stated:

> No duty could have been more congenial to my tastes or more suited to my position as correspondent. It brought me into the closest touch with the Flag Officer, and gave me the most intimate knowledge of every movement of the fleet. I thankfully accepted the task, and from that day until we were safely at New Orleans, made every signal that controlled the Western Gulf Blockading Squadron. . . .[56]

From Key West the "Hartford" sailed via Havana to Ship Island, the most important Federal base West of the Florida Keys. At Ship Island, sixty-five miles East of New Orleans and about a hundred miles Northeast of the lower end of the Mississippi, was the rendezvous point for the ships that were to take part in the operation against New Orleans.

For more than a month all hands were kept busy gathering the ships at the heads of the passes. Whereas Porter, who was operating under Farragut's command, brought his mortar schooners through Pass a l'Outre without any great difficulty, Farragut had to take his heavier-draught vessels around to Southwest Pass. Eventually he got them all through except the frigate "Colorado," drawing twenty-two feet, which could not be lightened enough to negotiate the fifteen-foot channel.[57]

At this time reports from the Western Gulf Blockading Squadron required anywhere from two to four weeks to reach Washington. The Richmond newspapers smuggled through the lines consistently gave advance information about the Squadron, although such news often was garbled by Southern telegraph operators or watered down by the Confederate censorship. Indeed it was from the Richmond newspapers that the Navy Department received its first information that Farragut had begun to drag his ships across the shallow delta passes leading into the Mississippi River.[58]

Osbon was not the only reporter with the fleet. How two of his competitors made use of an ingenious device to overcome the difficulties of collecting news was described by the New York *Times* correspondent Winser in a letter published some weeks after New Orleans was taken:

> You know that on war vessels, in war time, everybody is busy, and although I have uniformly received attention, and had all possible

> facilities afforded me in collecting information, yet it has not been convenient at all times for even the most accomodating of officers to place a boat at my disposal. To me a boat is indispensable, and I am glad to say that I have one perfectly adapted to my purpose. The correspondent of the Boston *Journal,* Mr. Hills, is joint owner of it with me, and together we make our rounds in search of information. We are indebted to Capt. Guest of the *Owasco,* for our acquisition, which is known through the fleet as the Press-gig. She is a frail little skiff, picked up in secessia, but wherever she goes she is treated with respect. Her proprietors, I say it flatly, are good oarsmen, and if they were not it would be ridiculous to attempt stemming the rapid current of the Mississippi. 'Tis true our hands have grown slightly pachydermatous, but we prosecute our labors, develop brawn, and feel slightly independent when we want to travel.[59]

About thirty miles above the head of the passes were two powerful forts on opposite sides of the Mississippi, constituting New Orleans' main line of defense against an attack from below. On the Southern or right bank of a kneelike bend of the river stood Fort Jackson, with its star-shaped battlements built of solid masonry, rising twenty-five feet from the bottom of a great ditch extending around the fort. On the opposite bank, a little North, was Fort St. Philip, neither so strongly built nor so heavily armed as its companion fort. Just below Fort Jackson was a barrier across the river, originally made of cypress logs held together by iron cables and later reinforced by a line of schooner hulks securely chained together. Above the forts was a nondescript fleet of perhaps a dozen gunboats and ironclads, the most dangerous of which were the iron-plated ram "Manassas" and an ironclad of the "Virginia"-type, still under construction, the "Louisiana."[60]

From the deck of the "Hartford" Osbon that April watched Commander Porter's mortar boat flotilla go up the river under tow to take position for a preliminary bombardment of the forts. On the morning of April 18, the bombardment opened, and for six days and nights the air resounded with the deafening roar of the thirteen-inch mortars and the enemy's heavy guns. Winser observed:

> At each discharge the vessels shivered and vibrated as if each plank and timber were hung upon hinges, making everything movable dance and clatter, the lateral concussion of the atmosphere being forcible enough to shatter, as it did, bulwarks and

other light woodwork, and striking upon the tympanum with a painful ring, productive of headache and deafness.[61]

The answering fire from the forts was quite as hot as that directed against them. "I never saw such a tremendous fire concentrated on a small fleet of boats in my life," commented Osbon on the second day of the bombardment. He went on to say:

> We are having much difficulty here on account of *a lack of fifteen-second fuse. The fault is not ours. The people at home are to blame*. . . . I suppose they thought at home we were going to do as Dupont did—lay alongside of the fort and blaze away. They forgot we had forts to contend with that were built to defy the navies of the world. We need a Monitor here, also; but the Washington politicians are afraid the rebels would take Washington, and instead of taking Norfolk they keep her there to keep the Merrimac in check. *Why not take her, and then send them both down here?*[62]

Still another hazard were the fire rafts which came down the river at night with flames leaping a hundred feet into the air. The first of these "blazing monsters," according to the correspondent of the New York *Evening Post,* produced great excitement among sailors and reporters alike. A rifled shot from one of the Federal steamers soon "shattered the laborious concern into splinters," however, and thereafter they became "objects of laughter rather than of terror, furnishing targets merely for the practice of our less experienced gunners. . . ."[63]

Neither side was able to do very much damage to the other in spite of their incessant cannonading.[64] On the final day of the bombardment, Porter came aboard the "Hartford" for a serious talk with the Flag Officer. At a particularly warm point in the discussion, Farragut, who had been skeptical all along about the ability of the mortars to silence the fort, told his subordinate: "Look here, David, we'll demonstrate the practical value of mortar work."

Summoning his signal officer, Farragut ordered him to take his station on the mizzen topmasthead with two small flags, a white one and a red one, and signal the results of a test run. In case the mortar shells fell inside Fort Jackson, Osbon was to wave the red flag; if outside, the white one. The flags were made ready, a tallyman selected, and presently the mortar flotilla reopened fire with renewed vigor. When Osbon at last descended from his lofty perch and the tally sheet was totaled, the "outs" had it by a large majority.

"There, David," Farragut told Porter when the latter came aboard a second time, "there's the score. I guess we'll go up the river to-night."[65]

Farragut's original plan had been for the attacking ships to advance in two parallel columns, with the one on the right devoting its attention to Fort St. Philip while the other matched fire with Fort Jackson on the opposite bank. Subsequently the plan was changed to provide for a single column formation, with Captain Theodorus Bailey in the "Cayuga" leading the first division, and with Farragut and Captain Henry H. Bell in charge of the second and third divisions respectively. From the starting point it was about five miles to a point above the forts safely beyond the reach of their guns.

At about six o'clock the evening of April 23, Farragut's seventeen vessels began to take position for the movement upstream. Later that evening, as they were standing together on the quarter-deck, Farragut suddenly turned to his clerk and asked him what he thought their casualties would amount to.

"Flag Officer," replied the *Herald* man, "I have been thinking of that, and I believe we will lose a hundred."

"No more than that?" remarked Farragut with an air of surprise. "How do you calculate on so small a number?"

"Well," rejoined Osbon, "most of us are pretty low in the water, and, being near, the enemy will shoot high. Then, too, we will be moving and it will be dark, with dense smoke. Another thing, gunners ashore are never as accurate as gunners aboard a vessel. I believe a hundred men will cover our loss."

Farragut gazed at his clerk steadily for a moment and then murmured in a sad tone, "I wish I could think so. I wish I could be as sure of it as you are."[66]

On the stroke of two, Osbon hoisted to the mizzen peak of the "Hartford," a pair of red lanterns, the signal to get underway. Before the echoes of the boatswain's whistle had died away, the "Cayuga" had her anchors up to speed off through the darkness. As she neared the chain barrier, which had been breached by a demolition party a few nights before, a blaze of light and an outburst of cannon fire showed that she had been discovered. One by one, the "Pensacola," "Mississippi," "Oneida," and "Varuna," the "Katahdin," "Kineo," and "Wissahickon" followed her through the opening and stormed past the forts. Above the forts eleven enemy gunboats (including the unfinished "Louisiana," the most powerful war vessel projected by the South (or any country) up to this time) awaited them. Then it was the "Hartford" 's turn. As she drew near the forts, her bow gun discharged a nine-inch shell toward Fort Jackson, and within a few minutes the broadside firing commenced.

"In that blinding smoke, and night . . . the only thing we could see," declared Osbon, "was the flash of guns in our faces and the havoc on our own ship."[67] High in the mizzen rigging with his feet on the ratlines and his back against the shrouds stood the intrepid Farragut, watching the contest from above the smoke. Repeatedly Osbon implored him to come down as the enemy's fire came closer and closer to the Flag Officer. Scarcely had Farragut taken his clerk's advice before a shell exploded that cut away most of the rigging upon which he had been standing.

At exactly 4:15 A.M. the "Hartford" ran aground on a shoal almost under the blazing guns of Fort St. Philip. At that moment a Confederate tugboat shoved a fire raft under the port quarter of the flagship, causing flames to shoot through the rigging. Then a shell from Fort St. Philip exploded on the berth deck, lighting another fire. As Osbon knelt down to uncap some shells that he had rolled to the edge of the deck, Farragut came over to see what he was doing.

"Come, sir, this is no time for prayer," said Farragut reprovingly.

"Flag Officer, if you'll wait a second you'll get the quickest answer to prayer ever you heard of."[68]

Osbon rolled the shells into the burning raft where they exploded, tearing out the sides of the raft and causing the tug to back away. For fully twenty minutes the "Hartford" lay abreast of Fort St. Philip while her engineers struggled to extricate her. As she slipped into deep water once more, it was evident to those on deck that the battle was nearly over. Not more than three or four vessels of the opposing fleet were still afloat, and they were disabled or retreating.

Meanwhile, the New York *Times* correspondent had mustered a boat's crew from one of the mortar schooners and had labored upstream "as near to the forts as was prudent." He was unable, however, to get a clear impression of what was happening. All he could see were broad flashes of light which occasionally burst through banks of clouds on the horizon like sheet lightning on a sultry day. He wrote:

> A fire raft cast a lurid glare near Fort St. Philip, and for half an hour the din was terrible. . . . At the end of that time it began to grow lighter, and I soon saw the *Harriet Lane,* with Capt. Porter, and all the vessels of his Division, coming rapidly down the river. . . .

It was now about 5 o'clock, and the mortars, which had kept up their fire incessantly, were signalized to cease. Then a report was spread that the larger part of the squadron had passed beyond the forts, and cheers upon cheers of exultation made the welkin ring. . . .

Between 6 and 7 o'clock, I went on board the *Owasco,* with Capt. Guest, who had been commissioned by Capt. Porter to go with a flag of truce up to the forts and demand their unconditional surrender. We approached Fort St. Philip within a mile, when we were fired upon rapidly five times. I confess that I had anticipated something of this sort, and was not, therefore, unprepared.

We immediately hauled down our flag of truce, returned, but in half an hour afterward a gig came down from the rebel fort, flying the rebel flag astern and a white flag in the bow, and containing a pale young man, with bushy hair, in the uniform coat of a First Lieutenant of artillery. . . . Capt. Guest went to meet our visitor, and their conference lasted a few minutes. . . . We waited after the rebels went back to the fort until they came back with an answer to our demand for surrender. On returning, the rebel was invited on board the *Owasco,* and delivered his message there. . . . He brought word that Col. Higginson, the commander of Fort Philip, considered our terms wholly inadmissible, and that the fort would never surrender. He also offered an apology in behalf of his superior officer, for firing upon the flag of truce, assuring us that it was done by mistake—the color of the flag having been indistinguishable. When the young Lieutenant, whose name, I believe, is Kennedy, of the First Louisiana Artillery, left the vessel, he allowed his boat to drop down a considerable distance into our lines, pretending that his men were unable to row against the current. Undoubtedly his object was to make a reconnoissance of our forces, and as soon as his shrewdness was observed, we ran toward him. Capt. Guest remarked, "I must give you a tow," and passing a rope to the boat, we soon took him nearly up to the fort. In this way we observed as much as he, the river being strewed with wrecks of steamers and half-consumed fire-rafts. It was not long after the rebel answer had been returned to Capt. Porter, before the bombs were again howling in the direction of the forts, and the firing continued until the mortar-fleet was ordered down the river.[69]

Although only one Federal ship, the "Varuna," had been sunk during the passage of the forts, the other ships in the squadron had not gone unscathed. The "Hartford" had received eighteen damaging shots, one of which demolished Osbon's room, scattering his clothing and nearly destroying his manuscript of the preliminary bombardment. The "Brooklyn" had been hit sixteen times; the "Richmond," thirteen; the "Mississippi," eleven; the "Cayuga," forty-two! The casualties among fleet personnel (thirty-seven killed and one hundred forty-nine wounded) were nearly double Osbon's estimate of the evening before.[70] The Philadelphia *Inquirer* correspondent, who was on the gunboat "Pinola," told of seeing:

> one poor fellow . . . cut in two by a cannon shot while at his gun. He was standing within two feet of me, and his blood was thrown upon me from head to foot.[71]

The *Herald* correspondent remained on the "Hartford" as it steamed upstream in the company of eleven other Union war vessels on its way to New Orleans. During a brush with the Chalmette batteries just outside New Orleans on the morning of the twenty-fifth, Osbon was struck by a splinter but was not seriously injured. Following the surrender of the city, he made ready to sail on the "Cayuga," which had been detailed to carry Farragut's report of the action to Washington. Another *Herald* reporter, J. Warren Newcomb, and William Ward, the artist for *Frank Leslie's Illustrated Newspaper,* were with him on the "Cayuga."[72]

At the Quarantine Station they paused while Osbon went ashore to see whether General Butler wished to entrust any messages to them. Since it was late at night, the General already had gone to bed, but the *Herald* man readily gained access to his room. He afterwards recalled:

> I went to the end of the hall, opened the door, and there, stretched in a hospital cot, was a fat man, sleeping noisily. On a chair at his side was a bottle bearing the legend "S.T. 1860.X.," and in the neck a flaring tallow candle, burned almost down to the glass. The sleeper was only partly covered. His head was encased in a red nightcap. I spoke to him, but he did not hear me. Then I called in a loud voice, "General Butler!"
>
> He turned over, fixed that peculiar eye of his on me and said: "Well, who are you?"
>
> "Mr. Osbon," I said, from the *Hartford.* The *Cayuga* is here, going north with despatches. Flag Officer Farragut presents compliments, and has asked me to say that if you have a few letters to write we will wait and carry them North for you."

The General was on his feet in an instant—a picture worthy of canvas. A moment later and the building was in an uproar. He was shouting for clerks and aides, and they came rushing in.... Then with three or four of his clerks seated at different tables he began dictating his own correspondence, walking from one to the other, keeping all the different letters going at once, in a way which to me seemed marvellous.[73]

After Butler had finished his composition, the "Cayuga" went on. Osbon left the dispatch boat at Baltimore and completed his journey to New York by rail, arriving there in time to provide the *Herald* with a three-page story of Farragut's great victory for its issue of May 10, 1862. Although Osbon's battle narrative was the most detailed account of the fighting on the lower Mississippi that appeared in any newspaper, it did not net him a scoop. By paddling more than fifty miles down the river in a leaky dugout to the Southwest Pass, the New York *Times* correspondent Winser had managed to place his dispatches on board a steamer for Havana in advance of any of the other reporters. From Havana his battle story was carried to New York rapidly enough for it to appear in print twenty-four hours before any other eyewitness account.[74]

The first news of Farragut's stunning success, received from enemy sources, appeared in the Northern press four days after the event.[75] The Baltimore *American* received its first information of what had happened from a Petersburg newspaper.[76] Headlining the story "New-Orleans Captured—Our Gunboats Pass Fort Jackson," the New York *Tribune* saw no reason to doubt its accuracy "though it reaches us through Rebel sources."[77] Subsequent newspaper reports produced ill-feeling between some of the commanders of the expedition. In a letter, written over a month later to the Assistant Secretary of the Navy, Porter stated with some bitterness and bad grammar:

> Butler did it all!!! So I see it stated by that blackguard reporter of the Herald who acted as Farragut's Secretary and Signal officer, and who had his nose everywhere.
>
> If you could have seen the trouble I had getting old Butler and his soldiers up to the Forts, to take charge of them (after we took possession) you would laugh at the old fools [sic] pretensions. But he actually asserts that it was his presence (30 miles off) which induced the forts to Surrender, and this Herald fellow tries to make it appear so, and says that no harm was done to the forts and that they were as good as new.[78]

Farragut actually had more reason than Porter for feeling aggrieved by the newspapers. On April 28, the *National Intelligencer* had told its readers that "New Orleans has been captured by the mortar fleet under the command of Commodore Porter," and several newspapers on April 30 and May 1 had reprinted a special dispatch to the Chicago *Times* stating that "New-Orleans is now in Capt. Porter's quiet possession."[79] In a letter to his wife written May 16, the commanding officer of the "Brooklyn" observed that:

> In the quotations from the New York Herald, I see that the city of New Orleans surrendered to General Butler and to Porter's mortar boats. This is all as I suspected it would be, and as I ventured to say more than six weeks ago to Captain Farragut, that it would be. "Porter's mortar boats and Butler's expedition" have been all the talk ever since last November, and one of my remarks when in consultation one night upon the proper mode of attack was "Should we be so fortunate as to succeed, it will appear in all our journals as Commander Porter's victory; but should we unfortunately fail, it will be published as the defeat of the Gulf Squadron, under Flag-Officer Farragut.[80]

However he may have felt about seeing the credit for his achievements attributed to others, Farragut expressed no resentment. "I don't read the papers, except to gain information about the war," he stated in a letter written on April 29.[81] The reporters could take that for a compliment of sorts if they so desired.

* * *

Less than six weeks after the capture of New Orleans, the reporters with the upper Mississippi gunboat flotilla had the privilege of seeing what one of them described as "the most spirited and decisive battle that had occurred on the Mississippi."[82] As a result of the advance of Halleck's army upon Corinth, Fort Pillow, the last important Confederate stronghold above Memphis, fell on June 4, 1862. Steaming cautiously downstream, the flotilla, now under the command of Flag Officer Charles H. Davis, came in sight of Memphis just before dark on the evening of June 5 and anchored for the night about a mile and a half above the city. Over on the Arkansas shore some Union troops, which had been landed from the transports, acted as pickets, while the cannoneers slept by their guns, ready to repel a night attack. The Boston *Journal* correspondent, Coffin, spent the night on the commissary boat, "J. H. Dickey," about four miles upstream from the gunboats.[83]

Coffin was awake early the next morning, but it was already light enough for him to see the five Union gunboats in a line across the river and the steam escaping from their pipes. Presently the tugboat "Jessie Benton," the first tender to the flagship, came alongside.

"The Admiral thinks that the Rebel fleet is below the city, and that we are to have a fight. You can go down if you want to," said the captain.[84]

Coffin was on board in an instant, leaving the other newspapermen asleep. The "Jessie Benton" passed through the fleet and moved slowly downstream, followed by the flagship "Benton" and the "Carondelet." Seated in an armchair on top of the tug, Coffin could see men, women, and children gathering on the levee, on foot, on horseback, in carriages. Suddenly a Confederate gunboat took shape on the wooded shore on the Arkansas side, followed by a second, then a third until there were eight of them ranged in two lines of battle. Davis was not yet ready for action, so the "Benton" and "Carondelet" returned to their original positions and the cooks began serving breakfast. Coffin took his on deck—a cup of coffee, hardtack, and a slice of salt junk—as he did not want to miss any of the fleet movements.

By this time the other newspaper correspondents had selected their points of observation. "Cons" Millar of the Cincinnati *Commercial* was on the upper deck of the "Benton"; Knox of the *Herald* and Webb of the St. Louis *Republican* were on the steam transport "Platte Valley" in the rear of the gunboats; Colburn of the *World* was on the captured steamer "Sovereign." Browne of the New York *Tribune* and Frank Vizitelly of the London *Illustrated News* were together on the "J. H. Dickey," the rendezvous of the correspondents; a second *Herald* correspondent looked on from the pilot house of the gunboat "Cairo."[85] Coffin's unusually favorable opportunity for viewing the forthcoming engagement he owed to his own enterprise, together with the friendly relations he had with the flotilla commander, a fellow New Englander, whose home was in Cambridge, Massachusetts, only a little distance from Harvard College.

While Davis' sailors were still at breakfast, the Confederate fleet began to move upstream. A flag appeared at the head of the "Benton" 's flagstaff. "Round to; head down-stream; keep in line with the flag-ship" was the order which went out to the other Union gunboats. To the rear of the gunboats were Colonel Charles Ellet's fleet of rams, nine old steamboats, carrying no cannon but equipped instead with iron prows, projecting under water, and manned with sharpshooters. The action began with a cannonade at a three-quarter-mile range. This lasted for about twenty minutes, and at the end the two fleets were still more than a half-mile apart. Probably none of the newspaper accounts of the fighting conveyed a more vivid picture of what happened than that of the *Journal* man, Coffin. In his usual incisive style he told how:

> The two fleets had been gradually approaching each other, the Federal boats with their bows up stream. The Little Rebel gave the signal for the battle by firing her bow pivot gun at the Benton. The shot passed over the flagship and over the Jessie Benton sufficiently near to give us a lively appreciation of its music, and struck the water a half mile beyond. Looking at my watch, I noticed it wanted twenty minutes to six o'clock.
>
> The Beauregard followed with a sixty-four pound shot, aimed also at the Benton, which passed to the right, and which was too highly elevated. The rebel gunners had evidently made wrong calculations of distance. They had in all previous practice been accustomed to long range, but we were now at short range. The third shot was from the General Price, better aimed than either of the others. It passed very near the Benton, below the level of the larboard ports, and struck the water abreast of the Jessie, but a few feet distant. It was really getting quite interesting. Up to this moment our guns had been silent. The Cairo being on the shortest chord of the arc, to use a mathematical term, brought her nearest the rebel fleet, besides being on the Arkansas shore, and the Little Rebel near the Tennessee shore—the latter was broadside to the Cairo. Lieut. Bryant, commanding the Cairo, thought that there was an opportunity to be improved, and opened with one of his stern guns.
>
> The shot struck the water close under the hull of the Little Rebel. Immediately the other boats joined in quick succession. On both sides the firing was very rapid. In five minutes the fleets were almost lost to sight in the thick smoke which, from the calmness of the morning, hung over the river. The rapid firing lasted nearly fifteen minutes, when the signal from the Benton was given to round to and prepare for a movement head on. He was not going to have any halfway work, but an engagement at close quarters.
>
> The [rams] Queen of the West and the Monarch had arrived before the appearance of the rebel fleet, and were quietly lying under the Arkansas shore. We were sufficiently near them to hear, in the lull of the cannonade, the engineers' bell for more fire and

for a full head of steam. Immediately black volumes of smoke belched from the chimneys, showing that there was good Pittsburg coal, or resin, or something highly combustible in the furnaces. The sharpshooters were alert, preparing in all haste for their work.

The Queen of the West, Col. Ellett, commanding, was first under way. She came out into the stream in a graceful sweep, those on board waving their hands to us as the Queen passed down between the Carondelet and the Benton. Never moved a queen more determinedly—never one so fleet. Great masses of foam were whirled up by her wheels, and she left a wake behind her which danced the Jessie Benton like a feather. . . .

The rebel fleet up to this moment had advanced; but when they saw the Queen moving with so stately a mein [sic], so swiftly and determinedly through the fleet, past the gunboats, straight on across the intervening space toward them, they came to a stand still. Behind her was the Monarch, following the same path, their progress watched with interest. The intrepidity and daring—the total absence of all manifestation of caution or fear—the determination to be in at close quarters—elicited the applause of the whole fleet, and fired officers and men alike with the highest enthusiasm.

As the Queen approached the rebels seemed to be struck with astonishment. They were dumfounded, and simultaneously there was a movement indicating a retreat. The Beauregard turned his prow toward the Queen, and put on steam, evidently with the intention of avoiding the stroke of the Queen and giving her a butt in her ribs. The pilot of the Queen seeing the movement, avoided the anticipated reception, put his helm hard down, wore round with a graceful curve, which won the admiration of thousands on shore, and with a speed which heeled her over as if she was going to lie on her side, fell like a thunderbolt upon the General Price, crushing her wheel-house as if it had been an eggshell or the thinnest tissue paper.

The Beauregard, when the Queen was within a few feet, discharged her forward pivot gun at her, but, strange to say, the shot missed the steamer, and came screaming over the fleet. When the Queen passed, the gunner of the Beauregard wheeled the gun and poured a shot into her stern, which passed through the bulkwarks, wounding Col. Ellett seriously with a splinter. The Little Rebel also poured in a shot which damaged the machinery. The

Beauregard, improving her opportunity, came upon the Queen in return, struck her forward of her wheel house, disabling her for further action. Upon the arrival of the Monarch she was taken ashore.

The sharpshooters were not idle meanwhile. They fired upon the enemy's gunners and crew, driving them within the casemates, killing and wounding several.

Imitating the glorious intrepidity of her consort, the Monarch came down through the Federal fleet. She steered directly for the Beauregard. The latter was struck forward of her casemate, and an ugly hole knocked in her side. The shock disarranged her machinery, and opened her boilers. Then came a great puff of steam, which scalded those who were between decks. The Monarch backed off to repeat the shock, but a white flag was run up and she hastened to the aid of the General Price, which was in a sinking condition with a large number on board. She towed the rebel boat ashore directly opposite the city, then returned and helped her consort, the Queen, to the shore.

Meanwhile the rebel flag ship, having been struck by two shots, came alongside the Beauregard, which was in a sinking condition, took off a portion of her officers and crew, who made all possible speed for the Arkansas shore. They fled to the woods, leaving the Confederate flag still flying at her stern.

Captain Maynadier, Captain Pike, and Lieut. Glassford of the mortar fleet, seeing the flag still there, bore down in their tugs to obtain it.

We of the Jessie Benton coveted the prize, and there was an exciting race. Unmindful of the shot which hissed past us, the rival tugs pressed on—we to lose the prize by about two feet. I had the mortification to see the halyard grasped by Capt. Pike, when two seconds would have enabled me to have flung it to the breeze below the stars and stripes which wave above *The Journal* office! . . . .

The General Lovell was near the city, where the water runs swiftest and deepest. The river there is about seventy-five feet deep at ordinary stages. The Benton, being on the Memphis side in the advance of the fleet was opposed to the Lovell in the fight. Capt. Phelps opened with one of his fifty-pound rifle guns—himself sighting it. A shot fired by him struck the Lovell below the water line, making an opening into which the water rushed with tremendous force. She sunk in less than five minutes. There was an appaling [sic] spectacle. One man was observed running around the deck with his left arm shattered by a shot, with terror in his countenance, crying "Help! help! God have mercy!" When the boat went down fragments from her upper works floated away.

The terror-stricken crew were struggling in the current. Some sank at once, others seized fragments of the ship and floated till assistance arrived.

Instantly the Benton's boats were lowered and manned. So great was the rush of the crew, eager to go to the rescue of the drowning, that the larboard boat was swamped, and two of the crew narrowly escaped drowning. The tugs of the fleet also went to the assistance of the drowning. But few were saved out of the fifty or more on board. . . .

Three of the rebel gunboats had been sunk and one—the flagship—had been run ashore. The fight had lasted forty minutes. The other rebel boats had been repeatedly hit. The rebel captains were in too close quarters to escape with their boats, with the exception of the Van Dorn, which through the fight had maintained a greater distance than any other rebel boat. They saw that it was useless to contend and the thought alone of escape inspired them.

First, the Jeff Thompson was run upon the Arkansas shore, about a mile below the Little Rebel. The officers and crew took to their heels. Whether any were killed or wounded on board is not known. I noticed, as we passed, that there was a big hole in her wheelhouse where a shot had entered; also several in her hull. We had no time to stop and see the extent of injury but followed the Benton. Before we returned she was on fire.

A mile beyond was the Sumter, also run ashore; and still further down, the General Bragg, both deserted. As the rebels fled, our broadsides opened upon the woods with shell; but they were soon out of sight.

The Van Dorn showed a clean pair of heels. We had no boat equaling her in speed, and it was useless to attempt pursuit. . . . The action, from the firing of the first gun by the Little Rebel to the last shot fired at the Van Dorn, was an hour and three minutes. Not a shot had struck the Federal gunboats, not a man had been injured. The Queen of the West alone had received injury, and that was not serious. Col. Ellett was the only one wounded.[86]

Strangely enough, neither Coffin nor any of the other reporters made any allusion to one of the most interesting incidents of the fight. As the "Monarch" followed the "Queen of the West" toward the Confederate battle line, the rams "Beauregard" and "Price" had made a dash at the "Monarch" from opposite sides. The Union ram had cleverly eluded them, however, and as a result they collided with such force that the "Price" was completely disabled.[87] Commenting on the many versions of the conflict between the rams, from eyewitnesses who had a clear view of the affair, Colonel Ellet found some excuse for their discrepancies in the fact that:

> there were three rebel rams and but two of our own mingled together and crashing against each other, and two other rebel steamers coming up . . . close at hand. In this confusion the different boats were mistaken for others. . . . This uncertainty of view was doubtless increased by the accumulation of smoke from the chimneys of so many boats and the fire of our own gunboats.[88]

Other reporters besides Coffin were amazed at the poor quality of the Confederate gunnery. The New York *Tribune* correspondent observed:

> The enemy fired very wildly, either from excitement or discouragement, and had in some instances, as in the case of the rams, shot at a distance of less than 30 yards without hitting their object. The Rebels never, within my knowledge, fired so poorly.[89]

About eleven o'clock in the forenoon, a brigade of infantry which just had arrived from Fort Pillow went ashore and marched up Monroe Street to the Court House. With the troops were the flotilla reporters, staring at everything about them with the most avid curiosity. As one of the *Herald* correspondents walked down the gangplank, a newsboy offered him the latest issue of one of the Memphis papers, requesting five cents in return. He acknowledged ruefully:

> I had given five dollars in Cairo for the *Avalanche* or *Appeal* two days old, but it was decidedly a new sensation to procure either of those papers not six hours from the press for a hundredth part of that sum.[90]

The streets were crowded with people, some of them "nymphs du pave," who greeted the townspeople with such derisive comments as "The Yankees have got you now" and "You'll all go under the abolitionists pretty soon." Many of these Cyprians were "young and comely" and expensively dressed "frequently with sober and excellent taste."[91] As for the other people on the street, to quote Coffin:

> Some looked exceedingly sour; some disconsolate; a few were defiant, but the mass of people were evidently good natured, though deeply humiliated.[92]

Most of the Northern reporters were amazed to find the city so quiet and to meet so little hostility from the townspeople. During a walk of several hours through the main part of the town, the New York *Tribune* correspondent Browne did not see more than a dozen stores open. He commented, "I am quite sure I have known Sundays much less quiet than this day has been."[93] While in the company of another newspaperman who formerly had lived in Memphis, Coffin met a Memphis editor who in times past had written many a bitter editorial denouncing the Yankee invaders. To the surprise of the reporters he courteously invited them to dine with him. The invitation readily was accepted, and soon they were partaking of an excellent bill of fare in the company of their mellowed host.[94]

During the next few days the Memphis journalists made daily calls on their Northern confreres at the Flotilla or at the latters' headquarters in the city. Frequently they laughed and talked about the gasconade of the South and the failure of its performances to match its mighty promises. Later J. H. Browne wrote:

> One could have seen the *New York Tribune* and the *Memphis Appeal* sitting in pleasing converse over a bottle of champagne, at the dinner-table of the Gayoso; the *Chicago Tribune* and *Memphis Argus* strolling through Court Square, arm-in-arm; and the *Cincinnati Times* and the *Memphis Avalanche*, forgetful of the present, discussing the relative merits of Grisi and Gazzaniga on the lyric stage.[95]

For a short time Knox and Richardson supervised the editorial columns of the *Argus* at the request of the commander at Memphis, Major General Lew Wallace. The owners of the paper, however, were permitted to retain control of the business and the news departments. Subsequently, after a Union paper had been set up in Memphis, they were permitted to resume editorial control of the *Argus*. In view of the fact that Bennett and Greeley were unfriendly at this time, the appointment of representatives of the *Herald* and *Tribune* to a position where they would be obliged to work together produced many jests, not only in Memphis but throughout the country generally. Few people outside the ranks of the reporters realized that Knox and Richardson were old friends, who once jointly had published a newspaper in Jefferson (subsequently Colorado) Territory and had been through many adventurous experiences together.[96] Watching the Mississippi rams in action, fighting mosquitoes, fraternizing with the Memphis journalists, or revising a rabid secessionist sheet—it was all in the day's work.

11

Battle Reporting at its Best

WHILE the reporters with McClellan's army were recording the failure of the Peninsular expedition, and their navy colleagues were covering operations at widely scattered points, a storm was gathering behind the Virginia mountains—a storm destined to break within a few weeks and sweep almost to the gates of Washington. To the north and west of Richmond lies the Shenandoah Valley, which was an ideal route for the invasion of the North. From Lexington in central Virginia the Valley extends in a northeasterly direction to Harper's Ferry, where the Baltimore and Ohio Railroad, the main line of transportation between Washington and the west at the time of the Civil War, crossed the Potomac. The strategic center of the Shenandoah Valley was Winchester, a small town about twenty-six miles southwest of Harper's Ferry. By guarding the passes through the Blue Ridge it was possible for a comparatively small Confederate force to operate in the Valley, reasonably secure and well-screened from observation.

Rarely have the evils of a divided command been more aptly illustrated than in the Valley campaign of 1862. The Union forces that vainly attempted to keep pace with Stonewall Jackson's lightning movements were commanded by three generals operating more or less independently. Stationed in the Valley proper was the "bobbin boy" from Massachusetts, Major General Nathaniel P. Banks, who headed the newly created Department of the Shenandoah. Farther West were the fifteen thousand troops of General Fremont, who, at the insistence of his friends in and out of Congress, had been brought back to supervise affairs in the reorganized Mountain Department. At Fredericksburg, well to the East of the Blue Ridge, was a still larger force under General McDowell, whose primary task was to defend Washington. At a critical stage of the campaign, however, a large portion of his command was shifted to the Valley in the effort to bottle up Jackson.

Banks, who had the primary responsibility for holding Jackson in check, had crossed the Potomac at Harper's Ferry during the last week of February, 1862, and had marched along the line of the railroad into the Valley. The details of the crossing were briefly described in the New York *Herald* of March 1 without any indication that the movement had not been well executed. A letter from the Chicago *Tribune* correspondent in Washington to Joseph Medill presented a different picture, however:

> I wrote an account partially imperfect, this morning to Dr. Ray, of the ridiculous & shameful blundering at Harper's Ferry. I learn now from pretty good authority . . . that McClellan's pontoon boats were built *here* expressly for the purpose of being used at Harper's Ferry, and started up the canal simultaneously with Mac's departure by railroad. Arriving at the first lock above Washington the master of pontoons found that they were all too large to go through the lock—contributing in fact a "dead lock." Mac went on to the Ferry, but no pontoons! Supposing that they would be along soon, he & Banks collected a lot of canal boats & scows, & proceeded to rig a temporary concern, zig-zag & rickety & entirely at the mercy of the swift current, by means of which they succeeded in getting over about 6,000 men in the course of two days, losing a number of horses, drivers & wagons however by drowning. Then the bridge became entirely unmanageable & they could not get any more men over, *nor yet Banks & his army back!* Then it was ascertained that the pontoons down the canal were not strong enough to bear artillery even if they could be got through the locks!
>
> Lincoln swore like a Phillistine [sic] when he learned the upshot of the affair, & there was wailing & gnashing of teeth among the imperial staff. Gurley[1] thinks that McClellan will be immediately superseded. Another informant thinks that Halleck will be summoned here to take command. . . . Inextinguishable laughter has been the result of the grand demonstration on the right wing, not unmixed with fears for the safety of Banks.[2]

At the beginning of May, Banks, with nine thousand men, was at Harrisonburg, Virginia, conducting essentially defensive operations. The army reporters who were attached to his command well may have shared the feelings of the general in command, who bewailed that he was not "included in the active operations of the summer."[3] Already the order had gone out from Washington for Major General James Shields's division of ten thousand men, which had previously been assigned to

Banks, to join McDowell at Fredericksburg.[4] After the departure of Shields, Banks prudently fell back to Strasburg. Marching to Fredericksburg with Shields's column, however, was a loose-lipped correspondent of the Cincinnati *Times* who prematurely imparted the news of this important movement to his newspaper. Although the Confederate high command was already aware of the movement before it was published in the *Times,* such leaks hardly could fail to intensify the ill-feeling against army correspondents which many Union officers entertained.[5]

Toward the end of May, terrifying news from the Valley began to appear in the newspapers. The papers told their readers how on May 23 the redoubtable Stonewall Jackson with sixteen thousand Confederate troopers at his back had appeared at Front Royal, which was inadequately defended by a force of not more than eleven hundred Union soldiers under the command of Colonel John R. Kenly. In the action that followed, Kenly's command was cut to pieces; not one in five of the defenders of Front Royal escaped death or capture.[6] Upon learning that Jackson had picked off the little garrison at Front Royal, Banks retreated up the Valley from Strasburg to Winchester, hotly pursued by Jackson's Graybacks. At Winchester there was another battle on the twenty-fifth, in which Banks was defeated and obliged to continue his retreat northward. The panicky mood of most Washingtonians was well depicted by a New York *Times* correspondent, who told of streets and hotels swarming with people anxiously discussing the news:

> and the one word that you catch, as you pass each group—the unfailing refrain—is "Banks." What will he do? What force has he? What reinforcements have been sent him? How strong is the enemy? Is the movement real, or is it a feint?[7]

On the following day the New York *Herald* along with other newspapers published reports, later shown to be inaccurate, that the whole Southern army was marching on Washington.[8]

The only eyewitness newspaper account of Banks's retreat to the Potomac was written by a correspondent of the New York *World,* who was at Strasburg when the retreat began.[9] In his account he told of being roused at 1:00 A.M. on Saturday morning, May 24, and told to get ready to leave at once. During the first phase of the retreat, the *World* man witnessed the panicking of some of the teamsters which he described as a "miniature Bull Run stampede." At Winchester on the following morning:

> the voices of cannon and the rattle of musketry, coming in through my open window, brought me suddenly to the consciousness that another day must be broken of its peaceful quiet by the fierce and unnatural pursuits of war. I listened to the sounds and saw the smoke which rose from the hills, but three miles distant. . . .
>
> During my breakfast I heard the tramping of horses upon the road, and the heavy rolling of artillery over the pavements. . . .
>
> Presently there was a commotion, a sobbing among the women, and a running to and fro, which brought me to my feet in time to find our forces were started on a hasty retreat; and, as I saw flames rising from the burning buildings not far off, and heavy columns of smoke roll upward from them, I began to realize that we were to abandon Winchester.[10]

This same correspondent wrote that some of the townspeople, the women as well as the men, fired on Banks's men as they were retreating through the streets of Winchester and "killed a great many of them."[11]

The New York *Herald* was deprived of an eyewitness account of Banks's retreat by a misadventure of its army correspondent, George W. Clarke. At the outset of the campaign, Clarke was staying in Front Royal at the home of an aunt of the famous Confederate spy, Belle Boyd. On the morning that Kenly was attacked, Clarke, whose persistent attentions to Miss Boyd she had apparently found distasteful, rushed down the stairs and shouted, "Great Heavens! What is the matter?"

"Nothing to speak of," she replied acidly. "Only the rebels are coming, and you had best prepare yourself for a visit to Libby Prison."

Without another word, the *Herald* correspondent did a rapid about-face and hustled to his room. When Belle Boyd passed his door a little later, she saw that it was open, that the key was on the outside, and that Clarke was inside preparing for a hasty departure. She deliberately shut the door, turned the key in the lock, and then made off in the direction of the advancing Confederates. Although the *Herald* man succeeded in escaping through a window, he later was picked up by Jackson's foot cavalry. Belle herself saw him being led away down the street with some prisoners and heard him shout to her as they passed: "I'll make you rue this. It's your doing that I am a prisoner here."[12]

Meanwhile, the authorities in Washington were doing everything possible to retrieve the situation in the Shenandoah Valley. At four o'clock on May 24, an order from the President was telegraphed to Fremont directing him to move immediately against Jackson at Harrisonburg and to "operate against the enemy in such a way as to relieve Banks."[13] An hour later Lincoln countermanded a previous order calling for McDowell to join McClellan on the Peninsula and instructed him to send twenty thousand men to the Shenandoah Valley to capture Jackson's force. Unfortunately, Fremont, who was having considerable difficulty in supplying his command, bungled the assignment. With something less than complete justice to Fremont, the Washington correspondent of the Chicago *Tribune* described his failure in a private letter to one of the *Tribune* editors on May 28:

> Fremont has "been & done it!" On Sunday night the President ordered him to march from Franklin . . . with his whole force (20,000 men) to Harrisonburg to intercept Jackson, Ewell & Co. The dispatch was sent around via Wheeling. Two hours later a reply came: "On the march; will be there tomorrow noon—John Charles"—To-day the Department was thunderstruck to learn from the Pittsburgh telegraph office that Fremont was [at] *Moorefield* with his whole army, almost due North of Franklin, instead of at Harrisonburg, south east! Of course Jackson escaped. Lincoln is a good deal groveled [sic] by this unaccountable disobedience & cowardice, but I fear he is too irresolute, & too much of a coward himself, to inflict the proper punishment. If Fremont had obeyed orders the whole rebel force under Jackson & Ewell would have been bagged.[14]

Fremont's eccentric movement indeed practically had eliminated the possibility that he could help cut off Jackson, for it was more than twice as far to Strasburg as it was to Harrisonburg and to intercept Jackson it would have been necessary to reach Strasburg two days earlier. Meanwhile, Shields's division was heading for Strasburg from the East, and more troops from McDowell's command were on the way. On June 1, Charles H. Webb of the New York *Times* met McDowell himself and several of his subordinates at Front Royal. He reported they were:

> all determined upon one thing . . . to bag Jackson and recapture the immense train he took from Banks—for you must know that Banks lost over two millions of dollars in property, and, it is said, several thousand prisoners.[15]

Hastening to Strasburg, Webb found the town in possession of the Union troops and learned that the main column was already several miles beyond that point. As he rode out toward the front, the *Times* reporter came up with some troops belonging to Blenker's German division which he characterized as being:

> [as] lawless [a] set as ever pillaged hen roosts or robbed dairymaids of milk and butter. I saw a company of them gutting the cellar of a house, carrying off everything eatable and drinkable, and only replying to the earnest remonstrance of the proprietary widow, and the representation that she had seven children to feed, with a guttural *nix fur stay.*[16]

A correspondent for the New York *Tribune* who tried to reach Strasburg on the afternoon of June 3 was somewhat less fortunate than Webb. Although aware when he left Front Royal that the North Branch of the Shenandoah was in flood and therefore not fordable, the reporter was told by a soldier that "he thought he could carry my horse over the railroad bridge on a small platform car if I would risk it." Being very eager to get to Strasburg, the reporter galloped down to the bridge with the soldier just in time to see it go down with a crash and float away on the flood. Even though the *Tribune* man had to return to Front Royal, he was not completely unlucky, for while he was there he held an interview with the personable Belle Boyd, who by this time was receiving reams of publicity through the columns of the press. Although she admitted to the *Tribune* reporter that most of the charges of conveying information to the enemy which had been made against her were true, she objected strenuously to being described as an "accomplished prostitute," an epithet which had already been applied to her by a reporter for the Associated Press.[17] Her *Tribune* interviewer decided:

> In personal appearance, without being beautiful, she is very attractive. Is quite tall, has a superb figure, an intellectual face, and dresses with much taste. . . . That she has rendered much service to the Rebel army, I have not the least doubt, and why she should be allowed to go at will through our camps, flirt with our officers, and display their notes and cards to her visitors, I am at a loss to know. She is a native of Virginia, but professes to be an ardent South Carolinian at heart—wears a gold palmetto tree beneath her beautiful chin, a Rebel soldier's belt around her waist, and a velvet band across her forehead, with the seven stars of the Confederacy shedding their pale light therefrom. It seemed to me, while listening to her narrative, that the only additional ornament she required to render herself perfectly beautiful, was a Yankee halter encircling her neck.[18]

Within a day or two after the interview, her admirer from the New York *Herald* obtained his release at New Market and forwarded to *his* newspaper an exclusive interview with none other than Stonewall Jackson. Shortly after his capture, so he said, Clarke had been brought before Jackson, who received him very affably, remarking that he was very glad to talk with anyone connected with the "American Thunderer."

"I am very glad to see you under the circumstances, General," answered Clarke, "and I hope you will be good enough to pass me out of your lines as soon as possible."

Jackson was annoyed at this. He said that he didn't have time to attend to the matter just then and rode off. After an interval of several days, during which the captive correspondent was hustled about from place to place, he was brought before Jackson once more. In his letter to the *Herald*, Clarke, probably embroidering the interview, wrote:

> When I was [again] introduced to him, I could perceive that his hazel eye, peeping out from his full bearded face, was eying me attentively. . . . Having shaken hands with me, Jackson said:—"Be seated, sir; will you have a glass of water?" I accepted both, and, after some commonplace civilities, observed:
>
> "General, I suppose you will restore me my horse and my clothes?"
>
> "Oh!" replied he, "it was taken in the camp and must be considered contraband of war."
>
> "But as I was supposed to be a non-combatant I stand as a neutral, and you know it to be a law of nations that a neutral flag covers neutral goods."
>
> "Yes," returned the rebel chieftain, "but the Southern confederacy is not recognized by neutral nations, and, consequently, cannot be bound by neutral laws."
>
> "Do you then mean to make war on all neutrals by seizing their property, General?"

Jackson did not reply to this, but twisted his beard, and after a brief pause, directed the *Herald* man to see him again the next day at 9:00 A.M. Clarke testified:

> Next day I was there at the moment; but, to my great surprise, was informed that Jackson had left at three o'clock in the morning, and that I was then without the lines of his army.[19]

Although the newspapers continued to give the impression that Jackson was being vigorously pursued, his safety was assured once he had passed Strasburg. There were rear-guard actions at Cross Keys, just South of Harrisonburg, on June 8 and at Port Republic, four miles beyond, on the ninth. Fremont was in command at Cross Keys but failed to press the attack vigorously against Jackson's lieutenant, Dick Ewell. Although Lincoln sent his thanks to Fremont, his officers, and men for their "gallant battle," the outcome was pretty clearly a Union repulse. Probably the most honest newspaper account of the action was the one contributed to the New York *Times* by its correspondent Webb:

> Our superiority in artillery was the only thing that went to place us on anything approaching equal terms. If not a victory on our part, it at least was not a defeat. The correspondents of some papers claim it as a victory, and telegraphed that we occupied the battle-ground. These gentlemen, whose feelings and sympathies so influence them that they cannot record faithfully, will have a long account to settle with history some day. It is not the common practice of victors to leave their dead and wounded on the field unattended to over night, and this we did. . . .
>
> Our loss in the fight was heavy, very heavy, considering the numbers engaged and the time the fight lasted. I have sent you by telegraph as complete a list of the casualties as could be obtained on the field. I think you will find it to foot up between five and six hundred. Our Generals incline to estimate the enemy's loss as much greater, and stories are told of three or four hundred of their dead being counted in one pile. Chasing these stories up, I can only find the man who has been told by another man that some one else told him, that at a certain spot in an uncertain field, that number of dead was guessed at. . . . Will not truth and common sense satisfy the popular craving, or is it always necessary to pander to the appetite that demands a victory in all cases, an assurance that the enemy lost at least one more man than we?

Of Fremont, he wrote:

> I have never met Fremont before, and if I never meet him again, I must say that I like him immensely. If you ask me why, now, the reply will be because he looks so splendidly on horseback. He has marched his men well, and managed to keep them in good fighting order without rations; but the campaign, after all, but begins with a battle, and until this is ended I shall not crown any man with a laurel wreath.[20]

It was the Confederates who were the attacking party at Port Republic. For four hours, two small brigades from Shields's division, not more than three thousand men all told, held off Stonewall Jackson's entire command so steadfastly that Confederate officers after the war could hardly believe it when they were told that only half of Shields's division had been in action that day.[21] There was a certain amount of rivalry between the men in Fremont's and Shields's commands, however, and George W. Smalley of the New York *Tribune,* who had been with Fremont during most of the campaign, let himself in for some vigorous rebuttal from Shields's partisans because of the way in which he reported the Battle of Port Republic.[22]

By this time, however, the active phase of the Shenandoah Valley campaign was over. On June 8, believing that all chance of damaging Jackson had vanished, Lincoln had ordered the pursuit stopped.[23] Before many days had passed, Jackson was on his way to the Peninsula to take part in the Battles of the Seven Days before Richmond.[24]

Although less space had been given by the press to the fighting in the Shenandoah Valley than had been accorded the movements of McClellan's army during the same period, the campaign in the Valley was, on the whole, well reported. Probably the most significant news development of the entire campaign was the discovery by the reporters that in Stonewall Jackson the South had produced one of its greatest generals. Already "Old Jack" was becoming a legend. "Jackson's retreat, if retreat it can be called, has been conducted with marvellous skill," admitted a New York *Times* correspondent on June 9.[25] "Unsurpassed by anything in the progress of the war," agreed the Washington correspondent of the Chicago *Tribune.*[26] To a Martinsburg special correspondent of the New York *Tribune* who had gone to some of Jackson's old friends for material to be used in a profile sketch of this new celebrity, Jackson was a man:

> whose prime quality is celerity, quick conclusions, and startling execution; who, as a soldier, is as rapid as he is wary, abounding in surprises, brave almost to rashness, and inventive almost to romance. . . .
>
> Such is the Rebel Napoleon, for whom his people venture to claim that in four weeks he has marched 350 miles, and won four victories—that he has crippled or dispersed the forces of Milroy and Schenck at McDowell, Banks at Front Royal and Winchester, Fremont at Cross Keys, and Shields at Port Republic—that he

holds McDowell in check to take care of Washington and Maryland, and monopolizes, for the amusement of the world, the attention of six distinguished Generals.[27]

* * *

For several weeks after McClellan's retreat from White House to the James River the newspaper correspondents at Fortress Monroe were refused permission to go up the James to Harrison's Landing. Some correspondents seeking to return to the army were stopped as far North as Baltimore and were forbidden to proceed any farther.[28] One correspondent, who managed to ship as a cook aboard a transport schooner going up the James, was three times under fire. When at last he arrived at Berkley, the point of debarkation, he was refused an opportunity to land, and when he attempted to run ashore in a small boat, he was fired upon and forced to return to the schooner. After three days of fruitless waiting he returned to Fortress Monroe, again running the gauntlet of shells.[29]

Another correspondent, representing the New York *World,* who managed to reach the army disguised as a surgeon, found that, instead of the confidence he had been led to believe the officers still reposed in McClellan, "there are mutterings long and loud of his inability to accomplish anything with the forces now here or to be sent here."[30]

Other reporters gradually were coming to the same conclusion. During the last week of July, L. A. Whitely, the chief Washington correspondent of the New York *Herald,* wrote to Bennett. He stated that it was definitely settled that McClellan's army "will not be able to move forward upon Richmond from its present position," and he reported that, according to certain leading army officers, a large part of that army soon was to be transferred to the Shenandoah to take part in a forward movement toward Gordonsville. He continued:

> In view of the preparations for active operations, in the Valley, would it not be well to increase the Herald corps in that direction? We have at present Carpenter with King's division, Chapman at Head Quarters and Buckingham and Townsend to attend to Sigel's and Banks's corps and the part of McDowell's corps that is in the valley, with no one at Winchester. . . . If the forward movement is made there should be two correspondents with each army corps. There ought to be several correspondents off duty who were formerly with McClellan, and it might be well to send some of them into the valley.[31]

At this same time the Washington correspondent of the Chicago *Tribune* claimed that there was not a single regular correspondent of the New York or Philadelphia press in McClellan's army. All the correspondence in the newspapers purporting to come from Harrison's Landing, he declared, "is really manufactured at Fortress Monroe."[32] Whatever justification the policy of the military authorities lent to faking the Harrison's Landing dateline, however, no longer applied after the ban on reporters going up the James was lifted on July 30.[33]

* * *

The real focus of reporting interest, nevertheless, was about to shift northward. On June 26, 1862, the very day that Lee launched his attack on McClellan's right at Mechanicsville, President Lincoln issued an order consolidating the several Union commands in Northern Virginia into the Army of Virginia. Its commander was Major General John Pope, who recently had been transferred to Washington from the Western theater.[34] Pope was a dashing figure but hardly the man to cope with Lee or Jackson. Furthermore, a July 14 order from Pope's headquarters in Washington, making invidious comparison between the performance of the Eastern and Western armies, caused considerable resentment in the Army of the Potomac.[35] Townsend of the New York *Herald* a few days later overheard Pope's quip, in answer to a query from another reporter about headquarters location for the coming campaign: "in the saddle."[36] This boastful remark, repeated by the McClellan clique, produced considerable jesting about the general who had his headquarters where his hindquarters ought to be.[37]

Lee on July 13 already had sent to Gordonsville two divisions under Jackson which were augmented a fortnight later by a third division commanded by Major General A. P. Hill. On August 6, Pope began concentrating his army near Culpeper, pursuant to orders of General Halleck, the new commander in chief. The very next day Jackson crossed the Rapidan with approximately twenty-four thousand men, hoping to crush Pope's army before its scattered elements could be united.[38]

The *Herald* reporter Townsend was at Culpeper that same afternoon of August 7 when the news of Jackson's advance was received at Pope's headquarters. At about three o'clock Townsend galloped out to overtake Brigadier General Samuel W. Crawford's infantry brigade, which had been ordered up to meet the enemy. After riding for an hour at high speed he drew rein at a farmhouse where two men in butternut were chopping wood and asked them if Crawford's brigade had passed that way.

"Who's Crawford?"

"Have no troops gone by today?"

"None since yester mornin'—the Prince William Cavalry."

"Isn't this the way to the Rapidan?"

"Rapidan! You're sot straight for Richmond, and ole Stonewall ain't two miles ahead."[39]

Townsend wheeled his horse about; around five o'clock he came up with Crawford's men, marching in open order roaring out songs and shouting their jokes as they trudged along. A few, he observed, had anxious faces, thinking perhaps of home; a few were silent, mindful of the hazards which lay before them, yet firm and courageous; but the majority "were going to their graves in procession, thoughtless, flippant, and hardened."[40] The next morning, August 8, while preparations for the battle continued, Townsend rode back to Culpeper and watched the troops of Banks and Sigel coming in by different roads: Germans, Celts, tall angular Yankees, and stalwart lumbermen from the Alleghenies and the Adirondacks.

On the afternoon of August 9, Jackson brought up his artillery and opened fire. Banks, who commanded the advance corps of Pope's army (not more than eight thousand men), attacked at once without asking for reinforcements. He rolled back the left of Jackson's line, which was strongly posted on Cedar (Slaughter) Mountain, but A. P. Hill came up with his division in time to save the day for the Confederates. Banks's corps was completely overwhelmed and with great loss was driven back upon the remainder of Pope's army. Both armies remained facing each other for the two following days. Then Jackson retreated across the Rapidan toward Gordonsville; Pope forebore to follow.[41]

Only three army correspondents actually had been present at the battle.[42] When Townsend had reached the field on August 9, the fighting was practically over, and the burial parties were already at work. Removing the bridle from his horse, Townsend tied the animal to a fence rail to let him feed on the fresh clover. While he was asking a number of friends from a Maine regiment about the battle, the rebel artillery suddenly opened up at a short distance with grape and canister, stampeding the horses and producing a full-fledged panic. Townsend leaped for his horse and tried to bridle him, but the animal was wild with fright and could not be disengaged from the fence rail. Finally

Townsend took to his heels, the horse following him, dragging the fence rail between his legs until a small shell burst so close that the horse changed his course and Townsend never saw him again. Everywhere the roads were filled with stragglers and provost guards trying to stop them. Townsend himself was challenged several times but at length reached the turnpike and walked six or seven miles into Culpeper, arriving there about one o'clock in the morning.

After a good night's sleep, he borrowed a horse from a fellow correspondent and rode back to the battlefield around noon on August 10 to get a clearer idea of what had happened. There he found that a short truce had been agreed upon to permit the burial of the dead. While waiting for a conference to begin, Townsend rode forward to a knoll and began to draw a map of the battlefield on the back of an envelope. As he was thus engaged, a horseman in a gray suit with numerous gilt ornaments on his arms, hat, and belt and some insignia on his collar reined up beside him and abruptly asked:

"Are you making a sketch of our position?"

"Not for any military purpose, sir, merely for reference."

"Are you a reporter?"

"Yes, sir."

"You may go on."

The officer then rode over to a fallen tree where several Union officers were sitting, and Townsend learned that his questioner was "Jeb" Stuart, the celebrated cavalryman. Stuart chatted pleasantly with Brigadier General George L. Hartsuff, a classmate at West Point, and laughed heartily over some reminiscences of his raid around McClellan's army on the Peninsula.

"That performance gave me a Major-Generalcy," he remarked, "and my saddle cloth there was sent from Baltimore as a reward by a lady whom I never knew."

A surgeon produced a bottle of whiskey out of which all the generals drank to the prospect of an early peace. "Here's hoping you may fall into our hands," cried Stuart, "we'll treat you well at Richmond!"

"The same to you," said Hartsuff, and they all laughed. For the moment the thought of strife had vanished from their minds. One of Stuart's officers, who was from Maryland, became quite friendly with Townsend and asked that his name appear in the *Herald* so that his friends at home who were not able to hear from him might see it. Townsend said he thought it could be arranged if he were given some information to justify it. After a few words with Stuart, the Maryland officer invited Townsend to visit that part of the Confederate lines where the burial parties were already at work. It was then that Townsend learned for the first time that the commander who had crossed the Rapidan and dealt Pope such a hard blow was none other than "Old Jack."[43]

The evening of August 10 Townsend returned to Culpeper, where he employed some friends to go around and make lists of the wounded men at the hospitals scattered throughout the town. As soon as this data had been gathered, Townsend started for New York, writing up his material on the way, and later handed his letter to the managing editor of the *Herald,* along with the carefully drawn map which he had made under such unusual circumstances. He later reminisced:

> Next morning, to my astonishment, there was [in the *Herald*] a map of the battle-field that had nothing intelligible about it, and my account was distributed in half a dozen places in the paper amongst a lot of rubbish by other persons, and a good deal of it I could not find at all. I told Mr. Hudson that the map he printed was nonsense and that the stream put down there was made to run into its spring instead of toward its mouth.

Townsend also learned that the unintelligible map was the handiwork of the harum-scarum Frank Chapman. Chapman had been transferred to the East after he and other newspaper correspondents had been expelled from Halleck's army, and he had been rewarded for his Shiloh scoop by being placed in charge of the *Herald*'s correspondence from Pope's army. Townsend said of him:

> Not a bad fellow, he had simply defined the loose way things were running on the *Herald,* and had made up his mind to have an easy time and appear to be in at the big events, whether there or not. I do not think he was anywhere near the battle of Cedar mountain.[44]

Not all the reporting of the fighting at Cedar Mountain was as slipshod as Chapman's. A careful student of this campaign recently has stated, "Even the first accounts of the engagement that appeared in Northern papers were, in some cases at least, singularly accurate." Of the New York *Tribune*'s reporting, he added, "Better reporting there could hardly be, and such statements would not have to be revised later to the detriment of the people's confidence and the public morale."[45]

Five days after the Battle of Cedar Mountain, McClellan's army evacuated its position at Harrison's Landing and began marching down the Peninsula to join Pope. This movement originally had been ordered by Halleck on August 3, but McClellan, who was firmly opposed to any such abandonment of his cherished plan of operations below Richmond, did not display any great amount of speed in carrying out the order.[46] To the consternation of the War Department, which had good reason to fear that Lee might overwhelm Pope's army before it could be reinforced by the Army of the Potomac, three important newspapers (two in New York and one in Philadelphia) committed a breach of security. On August 14, "before a tent had been struck, or a division put in column for march," the New York *Tribune* and the Philadelphia *Evening Bulletin* published stories indicating that the Army of the Potomac had evacuated Harrison's Landing and was in the process of shifting to a new base of operations. On the following day the New York *Times* went to press with a similar story.[47]

They might have added that McClellan's men had no time to lose. On August 14, the day before they began their march to Fortress Monroe, Longstreet was dispatched to Gordonsville, and on August 15, Lee took over the command of the Confederate force that now rapidly was moving north from Richmond.[48] To the newspaper correspondents with Pope's army it soon became obvious that that army was in the greatest danger. On August 19, Nathaniel Paige of the New York *Tribune* informed the *Tribune's* Washington office that:

> Maj. Fitzhue Adjutant Genl of the Rebel Gen Stewart was captured in a Barn yesterday by a company of Gen Buford's cav'y. Stewart himself narrowly escaped leaving behind his Sash & Hat.

He then added:

> A person whose Statements are entirely reliable arrived at the Head Quarters of Gen Sigel yesterday direct from Richmond. He says there are but three thousand troops in Richmond—The whole Rebel army is within three hours march of Gen Pope.[49]

Paige neglected to state (perhaps he was unaware of the fact) that on Major Fitzhugh's person a letter was found describing in detail the Confederate plan to overwhelm Pope before McClellan could come to his aid.[50] That same day Smalley notified the *Tribune* that Pope was falling back from the Rapidan to the line of the Rappahannock "and will cross that River [the Rappahannock] today with his whole force."[51]

During the critical week that followed, Lee succeeded in occupying Pope's attention along the Rappahannock while that past master of flanking movements, Stonewall Jackson, worked his way around Pope's left to Manassas Junction. Jackson thus severed Pope's communications with Washington, and cleared a route for his own advance on that city. Worse yet, the Union general's complete plan of operations fell into Lee's hands when Stuart's cavalry on August 22 executed a night attack upon Pope's headquarters at Catlett's Station. Only two reporters were on the spot to witness the raid. One of them, a *Herald* man, was stripped of his personal baggage, including his wedding suit![52] Pope, having executed an about-face, finally caught up with Jackson on the old Bull Run battlefield, but was unable to crush him before Lee rejoined him. There was a hard fight on the twenty-ninth, which Pope claimed as a victory, but the battle was renewed on the thirtieth, and his Army of Virginia, reinforced by three divisions from the Army of the Potomac, was driven from the field.[53]

A week previous, at the height of the campaign, the reportorial brigade had sustained a body blow when General Pope issued an order calling for the expulsion of all newspaper correspondents from his army.[54] Pope already had called in Smalley and had told him in a friendly way that he had received a peremptory order from Halleck to remove all newspaper reporters from his army, stop all telegrams except those from himself, and suspend the transmission of any mail "other than that of official communication." Smalley promised the General that he would leave camp at once, but Pope assured him this would not be necessary as "this is not an official interview" and anyway he had not yet made up his mind to issue such an order.[55]

Various explanations later were given for Halleck's decision. The Washington correspondent of the Chicago *Tribune* connected it with a dispatch:

> transmitted from Pope's headquarters, and suppressed here, in which some account was given of the retreat from Cedar Mountain. The correspondent who sent this telegram affirms that in its general scope it was sanctioned by Pope, and was . . . approved by his chief of staff, who made no other change than to substitute the word "withdrawal" for "retreat," for rosewater purposes.[56]

Other newspapers indicate that the War Department was angry about the premature reports of McClellan's movement from the Peninsula and about some intercepted letters addressed to various Kentuckians, who were advised to "look to this or that Yankee journal for information concerning the enemy's movements."[57] According to the report, printed August 25, from the usually well-informed correspondent of the Philadelphia *Inquirer,* some consideration also was being given at this time to excluding all newspaper correspondents from the various other armies in the field. Apparently the President was opposed to this suggestion of Halleck's. Stanton's position was not clearly defined, although he was believed to share Lincoln's point of view against punishing many judicious army correspondents for the sins of an occasional indiscreet one.[58]

How tightly Pope's order for the exclusion of the newspapermen was enforced is not altogether clear. The statement has been made that only two reporters remained in the field to report the Union defeat at second Bull Run and that one of them was arrested nine times before he left the Federal lines.[59] Franc Wilkie, then in Washington for the Chicago *Times,* however, had a different story. According to him, the day after the first wave of letter-writers from Pope's army straggled back across the Long Bridge, two employees of the New York *Herald* left Washington for Warrenton under the protection of passes issued by none other than General Pope himself![60]

Whatever the real facts were, little or nothing about what was happening in Pope's army could be gleaned from the newspapers during the closing stages of the campaign. Day after day the public was told on the highest authority that Stonewall Jackson almost surely had been bagged. Gradually it became clear that such stories were a product of the most drastic censorship that had yet been imposed during the war.[61]

On August 30, however, the War Department, not yet knowing of Pope's latest defeat, partially relaxed the newspaper embargo. Late that afternoon the Philadelphia *Press* carried the first news of the lifting of the ban. The *Press* gave a vivacious account of how the various reporters in Washington dashed about hurriedly from one livery stable to another, offering fabulous prices for saddle horses, horses and carriages, wagons, buggies, or any other vehicle in which they might ride to the battlefield. In large part their quest was vain, for every means of transport already was demanded to bring in the wounded from second Bull Run. Eventually some of the newspaper men got down to Alexandria and went from there on baggage cars to the seat of war.[62]

Wilkie evidently was not among these fortunate few, for he spent the following day, August 31, gathering material for a letter to the Chicago *Times* and describing the Washington scene with grim gusto:

> Mud-stained orderlies tore through, every instant, at a fierce gallop; long trains of supply wagons, with a noise like muffled thunder, filed incessantly along in the direction of Long Bridge, evidently bound for the field of battle. Towards noon long lines of ambulances began to make their appearance . . . filled with the bruised and shattered victims of the fight; hacks began to come in, and, stopping before some hotel, revealed as their contents pallid, blood-stained officers, whom kindly hands bore tenderly to their rooms; a weary, mud-stained soldier occasionally made his appearance on the street, and was instantly surrounded by crowds, who heard his story that "all of his regiment were cut to pieces save him," and forgot his cowardice in listening to his details of the conflict. . . .

Toward evening Wilkie stopped at the Washington telegraph office where he found a group of anxious journalists swapping anecdotes in low tones. After learning that the authorities would not permit anything to be telegraphed, Wilkie went back to his hotel room, "half convinced that the morrow would witness our complete annihilation."[63]

As yet no reporter even had dared to hint that McClellan's tardiness in moving to the aid of Pope had contributed to the second Bull Run defeat. On September 1, however, there was tremendous excitement in Philadelphia when a special dispatch from the New York *Tribune* was made public, stating that General Banks's army had been cut to pieces and that the President had removed McClellan and denounced him as a traitor. Not until the rumor had been officially denied, and the issue of the *Tribune* which contained it suppressed, did the town quiet down.[64] Yet few could dispute the fundamental accuracy of the opinion expressed by a *Tribune* reporter in a letter which the *Tribune* later published:

> The enemy has had no more men, not so much ordnance, nor provisions, nor transportation facilities, nor nearly so much encumbering baggage but he has outgeneraled us from Slaughter Mountain to Edward's Ferry, and God knows but he will do so hereafter. Make your display of capital headings to your war news, harp upon our driving the enemy a mile this morning, and four rods the day after tomorrow, but take your map and see how that enemy has crowded us miles upon miles, and leagues upon

> leagues, from Culpepper to the very gates of the Capitol. . . . This is the plain, unvarnished truth; we have been whipped by an inferior force of inferior men, better handled than our own.[65]

Meanwhile McClellan had been assigned to the command of the fortifications of Washington despite protests from Stanton and other members of the Cabinet.[66] "What is the meaning of this appointment of a man as commander of the armies whom Mr. Lincoln has said over and over again is incompetent?" asked the managing editor of the New York *Tribune* in a letter to the Washington correspondent of that newspaper. "Will Stanton resign? Will he be put out if he don't?"[67] On September 5 it was announced that Pope had been relieved from command of the Army of Virginia. Now that McClellan was back in command, the confidence of the man in the street revived, the more so as it became apparent that Lee had no immediate intention of attacking Washington.[68] By September 3 there was no sign of Confederate troops in front of Washington; between September 5 and 7, Lee's army crossed the Potomac at the fords above and below Point of Rocks and advanced upon Frederick, Maryland.[69]

Although the Baltimore correspondent of the New York *Herald* had predicted as early as August 21 that after marching to Winchester "with 100,000 men" Jackson would strike for Leesburg and cross the Potomac into Maryland,[70] Uriah H. Painter of the Philadelphia *Inquirer* was the first newspaper correspondent to report that Lee's army actually had crossed into Maryland. Painter had been at Bristow Station when Stuart made his first appearance in Pope's rear, and he had been taken prisoner. Since Painter was wearing civilian clothes, he had managed to escape fairly easily, but not until after he had obtained important information on the movements of Lee's army. As soon as he reached Washington, Painter sent one of the *Inquirer* men up the Potomac to Point of Rocks to watch for signs of a crossing. He also reported to the War Department that the enemy was about to invade Maryland. Little attention was paid to his warning, however, for the authorities were convinced that Lee would follow up the advantage he had gained at second Bull Run by an attack upon Washington. On the morning of September 6, Painter's assistant came in from the upper Potomac with the news that the day before the rebels had crossed the river near Leesburg. As before, Painter turned over the information to the government and also forwarded a dispatch based upon it to his newspaper. Yet the afternoon editions of the Washington papers published semiofficial denials of the dispatch to the *Inquirer,* and it was several days before the authorities in Washington would admit that the movement into Maryland was anything more than a foraging expedition.[71]

McClellan's army began marching north in pursuit of Lee during the night of September 5. Newspaper correspondents were forbidden to accompany the army, but several of them managed to evade the order by subterfuges of various kinds. Smalley was invited to accompany Major General John Sedgwick in the capacity of a voluntary aide-de-camp. Another *Tribune* correspondent had an undated pass from General Burnside which enabled him to pass by the guards without interference.[72] So long as the order of the War Department was not openly violated, no one seemed to care, and the newspaper owners were doing their best to place their men at strategic points to cover the invasion. In a telegram to Painter, W. W. Harding said:

> Babcock will return to Washington tonight unless you telgh for him to go off at Balto. Norcross left in noon train. He will report to you. . . . Work ahead Spare no expense. . . . Reporters are hard to get.

Again, in another telegram of the same date: "Norcross was sent because no other Bird [sic] could be had."[73]

Nevertheless, a tight censorship at Washington was still in effect. On September 10, the Washington correspondent of the *Herald* informed his newspaper:

> You desire that everything in reference to the campaign in *Maryland* shall be sent by telegraph. I have tried in vain to comply with that request and find that all my dispatches, however carefully worded in regard to the position of affairs in Maryland are cut out, and, as the news is important, I have adopted the plan of sending everything of that Kind by mail in order to secure its transmission. . . .
>
> I will arrange, without delay, the plan for private dispatches, suggested through Mr. Sawyer, and will communicate it to Mr. Anderson, who will act independently, on the other side of the enemy, and to Mr. Sawyer who will be at head quarters. It would hardly be prudent to expose it to all the correspondents in the army, as the one at head quarters can report all the facts that could be telegraphed in this manner and the others might disclose it and spoil the whole.[74]

On September 12, McClellan occupied Frederick, less than twenty-four hours after the enemy had evacuated it. Like everyone else, the press had no idea where Lee was going and where he would strike next. Franc Wilkie remarked:

> Even correspondents on the ground do not seem to possess the foresight peculiar to that class of gentlemen. They give us battles and skirmishes without number, but yet no two so far as I have seen have agreed in a single one of these particulars.[75]

Shortly after noon on the thirteenth, two soldiers of the Twenty-seventh Indiana Volunteers appeared before Colonel Silas Colgrove with a document one of them had found wrapped around three cigars which carelessly had been tossed aside by a rebel staff officer.[76] Any one of the army reporters gladly would have exchanged places with the finder, for the document he had picked up was a general order signed by Colonel R. H. Chilton, Lee's adjutant general, and it gave directions for the movements of the entire army of invasion. Thus, by a sheer stroke of luck, Lee's whole plan of campaign was revealed to his chief adversary. McClellan learned two things from this order, both of them of the greatest importance: (1) That Lee had divided his army, sending the greater part across the Potomac to capture Harper's Ferry; (2) After accomplishing the object for which they had been detached, the commands of Generals Jackson, LaFayette, McLaws, and Walker were to rejoin the main body of the army at Boonsboro or Hagerstown. News of this spectacular break shortly reached the public. On September 15 under a Washington dateline the *Herald* ran a story based on the statements of some officers who had left Frederick the morning after the "find." Moreover, McClellan now was moving with what was for him unusual celerity to force his way through the gaps in the Blue Ridge, and to destroy that part of Lee's army which was based at Hagerstown, before Jackson could return from Harper's Ferry.

While McClellan's troops were still at Frederick, however, the army newspaper correspondents were obliged to send their dispatches through to Baltimore on horseback, since railroad service had been suspended. Since a strong picket line also had been thrown out from Baltimore to Ellicott's Mills, a reporter late one evening entered what he supposed to be the Provost Marshal's office in Lisbon (midway between Baltimore and Frederick). There he requested from a seated gentleman in military-looking costume a pass to enable him to get through the picket line. He was informed that he could not be given such a pass, but he might have a note to the Provost Marshal at Ellicott's Mills, who probably would be glad to provide him with the necessary credentials. Within a few minutes he was handed a document which, he found later, according to Lorenzo L. Crounse's recollections, read somewhat as follows:

> Head-Quarters, Lisbon, Maryland
> Sept. 13
>
> *Provost Marshal, Ellicott's Mills:*
> The bearer represents himself as a reporter and messenger for the New York——. From certain suspicious circumstances I am strongly of the opinion that he is nothing but a Baltimore secessionist and spy. He wants a pass, and I have referred him to you; but I think it would be well enough to detain him until he can satisfactorily identify himself.
>
> Yours, etc.,
> Timothy Jones,
> Captain and Provost Marshal.

Armed with this deceitful letter, the correspondent went on his way to Ellicott's Mills, where he presented his letter to the pickets. Immediately he was marched off to jail and detained for a whole day before he could convince his captors that he was the victim of a sharp trick. "Timothy Jones" of course was a rival correspondent who had arrived late and who had improvised this method to avoid being scooped. Later as a matter of fact he did succeed in getting off his story from Frederick before his victim.[77]

On the morning of September 14, the Battle of South Mountain opened with an attack by Brigadier General Alfred Pleasanton's cavalry force on the Confederate position at Turner's Gap. More troops were brought up, and the fight lasted throughout the day. Smalley, the *Tribune* correspondent, stood near General McClellan for some time, watching the battle from a distance. At times the commanding general was almost alone. Occasionally a staff officer rode up, only to be sent off again at once. Presently the General became conscious of the presence of a stranger and asked a question or two. Smalley offered the loan of his field glasses, but McClellan waved them aside, explaining that he could see very well without them. Smalley recalled afterward:

> There was in his appearance something prepossessing if not commanding: something rather scholarly than warlike; amiable, well-

> bred, cold, and yet almost sympathetic. His troops were slowly forcing their way up the steep mountain side upon which we looked. It was, in fact, from a military point of view, a very critical moment, but this general commanding had a singular air of detachment; almost that of a disinterested spectator: or of a general watching manoeuvres.[78]

At about 10:00 P.M. the fighting subsided. By a narrow margin it was a Confederate defeat, although the losses on both sides did not exceed forty-five hundred men.[79] To John Russell Young in Philadelphia, the owner of the *Press* sent a telegram from Washington the following day:

> The victory will render your Mission with Army unnecessary. Do full Justice to McClellan & Halleck. Councel [sic] advancing movements & by all means advise continued reinforcements so that rebellion may be crushed before winter. . . . Give Penna and her Generals and soldiers Justice.[80]

Farther to the south William B. Franklin's corps had forced its way through Crampton Gap after a three-hour fight. Because he had failed to hold the passes of South Mountain, Lee decided to retreat to the south side of the Potomac. At about noon of the fifteenth while he was heading for the fords, he received word from Jackson that Harper's Ferry had fallen and that the latter was on his way to rejoin him. Quickly reversing his decision, Lee determined to concentrate his army at Sharpsburg and to hold the right bank of Antietam Creek against an attack by McClellan. After a hard night march Jackson came in on the morning of the sixteenth. By the following morning, Lee's whole army was reunited, save for the division of A. P. Hill which had been left at Harper's Ferry to complete the arrangements for the surrender.[81]

The news that Harper's Ferry had fallen was withheld from the public for a whole day. Although the surrender took place at eight o'clock on the morning of September 15, nobody in government circles knew anything about it until late that afternoon. As a result of the censorship the Washington correspondents were prevented from telegraphing anything about the surrender until the evening of the sixteenth, and even then they were not permitted to tell the whole story.[82]

Special correspondents of the New York *Times* and *Tribune* had witnessed the three-day fight that preceded the surrender at Harper's Ferry and narrowly had missed being captured themselves. Both reporters insisted that there had been treachery or incompetence on the part of those who were in command of this important position. The *Tribune* man recommended a careful investigation by the proper authorities of the premature abandonment of Maryland Heights, the key to the whole position.[83] Of special interest in the letter of the *Times* correspondent was a description of Stonewall Jackson, riding into Harper's Ferry on the morning of the surrender, "dressed in the coarsest kind of homespun, seedy and dirty at that," wearing an old hat "which any Northern beggar would consider an insult to have offered him. In his general appearance," added the correspondent, he "was in no respect to be distinguished from the mongrel, barefooted crew who follow his fortunes." The same reporter admitted, however, that the victorious Confederates comported themselves "in the most unexceptionable manner from the highest officer down." In the same letter were some interesting fragments of conversation between the *Times* man and his would-be captors which throw some light on the thinking of the men in Lee's army:

> "We have," said a South Carolinian captain, "150,000 men on Maryland soil, but we do not come as an army of invasion. You go your way and we will go ours."
>
> "What do you think about pushing us to the wall, now?" playfully remarked another to me. "How about that 'Onward to Richmond,'" inquired a third. "Cincinnati is ours, and so will Washington soon be," said a Georgian. . . .
>
> Lee they considered their most able General; Jackson the best for speedy marches and dashes. . . .
>
> McClellan's strategy no one feared. "How about that last retreat," they said, has become a by-word with our soldiers. . . .
>
> [How] I asked of a South Carolinian, are you going to keep your Southern Confederacy together on the States right theory?
>
> "Give us a chance and we will show you," he retorted. "If we don't make it work, we may return to the old Union, but not with Abolition Lincoln as President."[84]

Late in the afternoon of Tuesday, September 16, General Hooker opened the Battle of Antietam with a forward movement across Antietam Creek against the Confederate left. After an hour's march the cavalry went forward to reconnoiter. "There will be a cavalry stampede in about five minutes," remarked Smalley to Albert D. Richardson, his *Tribune* colleague. "Let us ride out to the front and see it." As they galloped down the road, they heard three artillery shots in rapid succession and then a shout from a little fifer in a tree nearby, "There they come, like the devil, with the Rebels after them." The troopers soon reappeared, dodging missiles from a Confederate battery which had opened upon them.

Hooker then gave the command to press forward, while McClellan, who had accompanied the expedition thus far, rode back to the rear. Presently on the other side of a narrow belt of woods a long line of men in gray sprang up and were as suddenly obscured by the fire from their muskets and the smoke of the batteries. Both Richardson and Smalley were only a few yards from Hooker, and shells were dropping uncomfortably close by. One plowed up the ground under Richardson's rearing horse; another exploded near Smalley and kicked up a great cloud of dust around both correspondents. Hooker just had hurdled a low fence into an adjacent orchard out of range of the firing; the reporters quickly followed.[85] Night came on; the fighting had been sharp but indecisive. As the firing died away, a reporter for the New York *Times* heard Hooker say: "We are through for tonight . . . but tomorrow we fight the battle that will decide the fate of the Republic."[86]

Nathaniel Paige, another one of the *Tribune* correspondents, spent the night at a farmhouse which commanded a view of the entire field. During the evening, Major John J. Key, the judge advocate of McClellan's staff, stopped at the same house and, being ill, decided to remain there for the night. Key obviously had something on his mind and seemed to be looking for someone to whom he could unburden himself. While Paige listened attentively, Key poured out a story about the low morale of the officers in command, which must have been anything but reassuring to a patriotic Union man on the eve of what might prove to be the decisive battle of the war. Key told of how he had just left a conference of McClellan's officers, during which a majority of them had listened with approval to a plan for marching on Washington and setting up a military dictatorship. Most of the officers present had lost faith in the administration, were tired of continued defeat, and saw no prospect of anything better ahead so long as the same leadership prevailed. According to his own statement, Key had remonstrated with the others, and the conference finally had broken up without any action being taken.[87]

Charles Carleton Coffin of the Boston *Journal* was wakened at daylight the next morning by the booming of cannon. From Parkton, Maryland, to Hanover Junction, to Westminster, to Harrisburg, to Greencastle he had ridden, hoping that he might be lucky enough to be on the spot when Lee and McClellan joined battle. He had spent the night of the sixteenth at Hagerstown. Now he had little enough time to mount and gallop for the battlefield nine miles away. Although he lacked a horse, he was soon able to buy one from a stablekeeper eager to dispose of his animals. "Horseflesh is mighty onsartin these days," said the seller. "The rebels took my best ones, and if they should come here again, I reckon they would clean me out."[88] Coffin's first impulse was to ride down the Sharpsburg turnpike to the rear of the Confederate position, there to enter their lines, and to watch the battle from the Confederate side. "Don't do it, sir," advised a well-wisher. "You can't pass yourself off for a Reb," said another. "They'll see, the instant they set eyes on you, that you are a Yank. They'll gobble you up, and take you to Richmond."[89] This seemed sound advice, so Coffin turned about and made off down the Boonsboro road, reaching the right wing of the Union army just as Hooker's men were forming for attack.

McClellan's plan of battle was to attack Lee's left with Hooker's and Joseph K. F. Mansfield's corps, supported by Sumner. This was to be followed by an assault on the Confederate right by Burnside's corps. If either of these attacks succeeded, McClellan intended to advance with his center.[90] Lee's position was reasonably strong, but could have been made stronger with entrenchments. Its average depth between the creek and the river was only about three miles; in case of disaster there was only one good ford in his rear, about a mile and a half below Shepherdstown, to permit the escape of his army. The Union army moreover was numerically superior. Even if the troops engaged in the Harper's Ferry operations were counted, Lee had less than forty thousand men to face roughly twice that number.[91]

Smalley was in the thick of the fight from the very beginning. During a crisis in the first phase of the battle, Hooker's attention was drawn to a civilian who sat quietly upon his horse in advance of the whole staff, gazing at the battle as steadily as if he were sitting in a theater watching a play. Hooker said afterwards:

> In all the experience which I have had of war, I never saw the most experienced and veteran soldier exhibit more tranquil fortitude and unshaken valor than was exhibited by that young man.[92]

Presently the staff had scattered to perform their various assignments (several had already been killed or wounded), and Hooker found himself quite alone. Looking about for an officer, he again spied Smalley and beckoned to him:

"Who are you?"

Smalley told him.

"Will you take an order for me?"

"Certainly."

But Hooker had not waited for his answer. "Tell the colonel of that regiment to take his men to the front and keep them there."

Smalley transmitted the order and was again met with the question, "Who are you?"

"The order is General Hooker's."

"It must come to me from a staff officer or from my brigade commander."

"Very good, I will report to General Hooker that you decline to obey."

"Oh, for God's sake don't do that! The Rebels are too many for us, but I had rather face them than Hooker."

The regiment moved forward. Smalley returned to Hooker and reported. "Yes," said Hooker, "I see, but don't let the next man talk so much."[93] With that the *Tribune* correspondent was off again on a similar errand. Smalley also was with Hooker when the latter was wounded at about nine o'clock that morning. Mounted on a white horse and dressed in a light blue uniform, the General was followed by bullets wherever he rode. Once Smalley ventured to point this out, but Hooker's only reply was a torrent of curses and contempt. A few moments later, a bullet struck him in the foot. He had to be helped from his horse and carried to the rear on an improvised ambulance. With his departure the attack on the Confederate left lost much of its aggressiveness.

The complete success of McClellan's plan largely depended upon accurate timing. To have been effective, the attacks of Hooker, Mansfield, Sumner, and Burnside should have been simultaneous rather than successive. It was in timing as much as in anything else that the plan miscarried. Mansfield's corps arrived on the field barely in time to stem a Confederate counterattack which had driven Hooker's men back almost to the point where the battle had opened. But Mansfield's attack also was unsupported. Not until after his corps had lost its initial drive and stopped firing altogether did Sumner receive orders to advance. Even then the corps did not attack as a whole. Sedgwick's division was frittered away in a separate attack, while French's and Richardson's divisions were held back for the fourth and final assault on the right.

Five thousand spectators watched the battle from a hill comparatively out of range. McClellan and his staff were on another ridge half a mile in the rear. During the lull which followed Sedgwick's repulse, the Commander in Chief went up to the front lines for a better view of the field. Coffin was sitting astride his horse at the edge of a grove when the General rode up with his staff. The soldiers gazed at their commander in silence. There was no enthusiasm, no hurrah of welcome; there were no cheers for "Little Mac." The General surveyed the field through his glass, closed it, turned his horse about, and rode back to headquarters.[94]

It was about twelve o'clock when arrangements were completed for the advance of William H. French's and Richardson's divisions. The artillery prepared the way for the advance by a tremendous bombardment. From the hill behind Richardson observers could see the enemy crouching to avoid the storm of grapeshot. The two Union divisions moved past a cemetery, across a ravine, and met the first line of the enemy drawn up along a country road or lane which runs into the Hagerstown pike from the East, about a mile south of the Dunker church. Inasmuch as the level of this road was below that of the fields on both sides, it constituted a natural rifle pit. The momentum of the Union advance, however, carried it through and over the enemy's advance line and into a cornfield beyond. There they met a second line of defense, and while the noonday sun beat down, the russet corn leaves slowly turned red. A correspondent who visited this sector when the contest was over estimated that a thousand of the enemy's dead were piled up along "Bloody Lane" and in the adjoining cornfield.[95]

During the lull which followed this last attack, Smalley was approached by one of McClellan's staff officers who wanted him to go to Hooker and ask him to take command of the army. "Most of us think that this battle is only half fought and half won," said the officer uneasily. "There is still time to finish it. But McClellan will do no more." Smalley was astounded at such a request which, as he pointed out to the officer, amounted to nothing less than an act of mutiny in the presence of the enemy. "I know that as well as you do," said the other man. "We all know it, but we know also that it is the only way to crush Lee and end the rebellion and save the country."

After some parleying, Smalley finally consented to see Hooker, but only to make a report on his physical condition. The *Tribune* correspondent found the General in bed at a farmhouse and suffering great pain. The wounded man asked eagerly for news of the battle, and when told that all attacks had failed and that no movement had been made for two hours he became angry and excited and spoke some extremely plain words concerning McClellan. Smalley seized the opportunity of asking him whether his wound would permit him to mount his horse again that day.

"No; it is impossible."

"Or to take command of your corps again in any way—in a carriage, if one could be found?"

"No, no; I cannot move. I am perfectly helpless."

Then all at once sensing a hidden meaning in the correspondent's question, he demanded:

"Why do you ask? What do you mean? Who sent you here?"

Smalley explained that the situation was critical and that some friends of the General were anxious to learn whether in an emergency he could resume his duties. The wounded man groaned and swore and tried to raise himself in bed, but the effort was too much. Smalley glanced at the surgeon, who shook his head vigorously. Again Hooker asked Smalley who had sent him, but the correspondent turned the question aside and excused himself, promising to return when he could. His report as to General Hooker's condition put an end to all schemes at headquarters.[96]

On the left, Burnside's Ninth Corps had been assigned the duty of carrying the stone bridge two miles below the turnpike and of storming the heights of Sharpsburg. Following the first order to attack, not received until sometime around ten o'clock,[97] Burnside made four unsuccessful attacks before he finally secured the bridge shortly after noon. It was not until about three o'clock, however, that his corps was ready for the assault against the heights. When it came, the assault was a brilliant success. The Confederate line was broken and driven into the town. Complete victory appeared to be in Burnside's grasp. At the critical moment, however, a body of troops, three thousand at most, appeared on the Union flank. It was A. P. Hill's division which in seven hours had marched the seventeen miles from Harper's Ferry and had arrived just in time to alter affairs completely. The Federal flank was driven in; several brigades were broken; the remainder drifted back to the neighborhood of the bridge, where they bivouacked for the night. Burnside's repulse by Hill brought the battle to a close. Neither army cared to renew the conflict, for the fighting had been terribly costly. More than twenty thousand men on both sides had fallen during the course of what was probably the bloodiest day of the whole war.[98]

At nightfall the four *Tribune* correspondents who had witnessed the battle met at a little farmhouse, where they prepared their reports by the light of a flickering tallow candle in a room filled with the wounded and dying.[99] It was generally supposed that the battle would be renewed the following day, but from what he knew of McClellan, Smalley doubted that this would happen. In any case he determined to try to get an account of the fighting thus far through to New York as soon as possible. Frederick, thirty miles away, was the nearest town where there was a chance of sending a long telegraph message over the wires. Smalley's horse had two bullets in him, so it was necessary to commandeer another from one of the other *Tribune* men.

It was nine o'clock in the evening before Smalley could leave the field. At three o'clock the next morning he jogged into Frederick, having slept in the saddle most of the way. There he discovered that the telegraph office was closed, and no one could tell him where the operator could be found. At seven the operator appeared and consented to take a short message but declared that he could not guarantee when it would reach New York—if ever. The wires had been taken over by the military authorities, who, of course, would have the last word in a case such as this.

Smalley decided to take the chance. He sat down on a log by the door of the office and began to write, handing his sheets to the operator as he finished until a column or more had been sent. Contrary to his hope, neither the story nor his private message to the *Tribune* notifying it that the story was on the way were forwarded to New York. Instead they were sent directly to the War Department in Washington where the former provided Stanton with the first account of the battle he had received with the exception of General McClellan's brief dispatch announcing a victory. After it had been shown to President Lincoln and other members of the Cabinet, Smalley's dispatch was allowed to pass on to New York in time for an extra edition on Friday morning.

Meanwhile Smalley was making every effort to locate a train for Baltimore so that he might send in a more complete account of the battle from there. But the railroad was in the hands of the military authorities too, and no one would accept the responsibility of sending off a train at such a time. Smalley wired the War Department for permission to engage a special but could obtain no answer. Finally he was informed that he would be permitted to go by the first military train. At about two o'clock in the afternoon it puffed out of the station with the *Tribune* man aboard. Smalley had intended to prepare his full-length report en route between Frederick and Baltimore, but he fell asleep almost immediately after he climbed aboard, and when he reached Baltimore minus a story, detailed or otherwise, he found that he had but ten minutes to catch the Washington express for New York. His decision was quickly made: he would continue on to New York, acting as his own messenger. At that time railroad cars ordinarily were lighted by small oil lamps at each end. While sitting, one could not see to read by them, so Smalley stood directly under one of these flickering oil lights and wrote during most of the night, finishing his account about midway between Philadelphia and New York. The *Tribune*'s editor had been notified that Smalley's story might be expected soon after the regular morning edition had gone to press. Consequently, when the weary correspondent staggered into the *Tribune* office around five o'clock on Friday morning, the composing room was crowded, and the presses were manned and waiting. The compositors went to work on what Smalley characterized as the worst piece of manuscript they had ever seen. By breakfast time on the second morning after the battle, the *Tribune*'s complete story of Antietam was on the street.[100]

Smalley's battle account was not simply a scoop; it was widely acclaimed, by his fellow correspondents and by the press generally, as the best newspaper account of Antietam.[101] Henry Villard and Albert D. Richardson, both good judges of reporting, labeled it the best battle report of the war.[102] Several members of foreign legations resident in Washington were so much impressed that they forwarded copies of it to their home governments.[103]

Coffin's story of the battle in the Boston *Journal* probably was second only to Smalley's in its range and comprehensiveness. Coffin had ridden to Hagerstown on the night after the battle and then had gone on to Boston by train, writing his story en route. His narrative was later republished by the Baltimore *American* in a special edition of several thousand copies for the soldiers.[104]

Both the *Herald* and the Philadelphia *Inquirer* were thoroughly scooped. The chief correspondent of the *Herald* was late in reaching the battlefield;[105] as a result no complete account of the battle appeared in the *Herald* until Sunday morning, forty-eight hours after the *Tribune*'s triumph. The *Inquirer* was even more unlucky. Painter had left Washington a few days before the battle, for Mansfield, Ohio, on what a colleague facetiously described as a "Union mission."[106] While

Painter was taking his matrimonial vows, the *Inquirer* news organization bungled its assignment, and the *Inquirer*'s account of the battle was lost in the mails.[107]

The Northern army correspondents in general—there were some exceptions—were inclined to regard Antietam as a great victory and to praise the generalship of McClellan. James B. Hammond of the New York *World* declared:

> We have beaten them beyond the shadow of suspicion, most completely; not, however, by our superiority in numbers, but by the heroic gallantry of our men and officers, and the splendid management of Gen. McClellan.[108]

Other correspondents were more restrained. Smalley's opinion was that the day had been partially successful, not quite a victory, but at least an advantage for the Union side. Coffin's judgment anticipated the verdict of most modern critics:

> Present evidence is not sufficient to warrant any definite conclusion [as to] whether the battle was to us a victory or a defeat. It will probably be classed as a great indecisive engagement.[109]

Reporters for the Southern newspapers, on the other hand, interpreted the result as a victory for the South, "one of the most complete victories," in the opinion of the Richmond *Enquirer*, "that has yet immortalized the confederate [sic] arms."[110] The able army correspondent of the Charleston *Courier* admitted, however, that "last night [the night after the battle] we were inclined to believe it was a drawn battle." He added, "The Federals fought well and were handled in a masterly manner."[111] In the estimation of the editor of the Richmond *Whig*, the *Courier*'s story of the bloodbath at Antietam contained "the most graphic sketches of the operations of our armies which have appeared in print."[112]

The first hasty Northern accounts of the battle contained the usual number of misstatements of fact. It was reported that Lee's army numbered one hundred and forty thousand men,[113] that Longstreet's division had been captured,[114] that fifteen thousand prisoners had been bagged,[115] and that both Stonewall Jackson and A. P. Hill had been killed.[116] In a letter to his wife written within a fortnight after the battle, Brigadier General George G. Meade made allusion to:

> a brilliant account in Forney's "Press" of the battle of Antietam, in which the writer, confusing Hooker's division with his corps,

> speaks of the gallantry of Generals Patterson and Grover in leading the men. . . .

The truth of the matter was, as Meade pointed out, that Hooker's division was at Alexandria when Grover was with it and Patterson had been for some time in Philadelphia. "But such is history," wearily commented the General.[117]

Meade had had other reasons for being dissatisfied with the reporting of the Antietam campaign. Writing to his wife from the battlefield at Sharpsburg on September 20, he had made the significant comment:

> I am afraid I shall not get the credit for these last battles that I did for those near Richmond, for two reasons: First, I was not wounded; second, old Sam Ringwalt[118] was not there to write letters about me. I find the papers barely mention the Pennsylvania Reserves, call them McCall's troops, never mentioning my name; whereas I was not only in command, but at South Mountain, on the 14th, I was on the extreme right flank, had the conduct of the whole operations, and never saw General Hooker, commanding the corps, after getting his instructions, till the whole affair was over.[119]

Considerable space was given by some of the New York papers to a thrilling charge made at Antietam by the "Irish" brigade, under the leadership of Brigadier General Thomas F. Meagher. Meagher's bravery was the subject of various newspaper paragraphs; the manner in which he was wounded while leading his men up to the very cannon's mouth was minutely described; in short he was depicted as one of the greatest heroes of the war.[120] In a letter to the Cincinnati *Gazette,* published two weeks after the battle, Whitelaw Reid contended that such stories were ridiculous:

> The General in question . . . was not in the charge at all!—did not lead or follow it! He was too drunk to keep the saddle, fell from his horse . . . several times, was once assisted to remount by Gen. Kimball of Indiana, almost immediately fell off again, was too stupidly drunk to answer the simplest question Gen. Kimball put to him about the disposition of his brigade, and was finally taken up on a stretcher, covered with a cloth, and carried off the field—the bearers circulating the story as they went that Gen. Meagher was dangerously wounded.[121]

In spite of such lapses, Antietam appears on the whole to have been a well-reported battle.[122] Those correspondents who were eyewitnesses of the fighting had been forced to display some agility to escape the ban of the War Department. Their task had also been complicated by the fact that Antietam had actually been three battles in one, any one of which might have taxed the energies of any ordinary correspondent. To an untrained observer this battle, even more than most, must have presented the aspect of unmitigated confusion. Samuel Fiske of the Springfield (Massachusetts) *Republican* wrote:

> Troops didn't know what they were expected to do, and sometimes, in the excitement, fired at their own men. Generals were the scarcest imaginable article, plentiful as they are generally supposed to be. We neither saw nor heard any thing of our division commander after starting on our first charge early in the morning, but went in and came out here and there, promiscuously, according to our own ideas, through the whole day.[123]

Yet in spite of all the confusion, in spite of the fact that the reporters in the field to some degree had to operate under cover, in spite of the difficulties of leaving the army and getting dispatches out just after a great battle had been fought, the essential facts of what had occurred were made known to the public through the press within forty-eight hours.

The outcome of the battle disappointed the eager hopes of those who counted on the destruction of Lee's army. On the morning of the eighteenth McClellan had sent to Halleck a dispatch in which he gave the latter reason to suppose that the battle would be renewed that day.[124] The day passed, however, without any sign of further hostilities, and by the next morning it was evident that Lee had made his escape across the Potomac, carrying with him most of the spoils of his Maryland campaign. In a letter written from Harper's Ferry a few days later, a New York *Tribune* correspondent adverted bitterly to that "fatal Thursday" on which occurred "the clean leisurely escape of the foe down into the valley, across the difficult ford, and up the Virginia heights."[125]

Bloody as it had been, Antietam was not destined to be the decisive battle of the war. Before many weeks had passed the army newspapermen would be back in the field again, encountering the perils of march and bivouac in a war whose end was not yet in sight.

12

On the March with Buell and Rosecrans

WHILE the movements of McClellan's army absorbed the attention of the press in the East during the early summer months of 1862, the army newspapermen in the Kentucky-Tennessee war theater found comparatively little to write about. Most of the reporters in that area were below Nashville, advancing eastward with Buell along the line of the Memphis and Charleston Railroad. Among them was the former *Herald* reporter, Henry Villard (now with the New York *Tribune),* William F. G. Shanks of the *Herald,* and William S. Furay of the Cincinnati *Gazette.* To the camp newspapermen the army's advance on Chattanooga must have seemed interminably slow. The railroad, constantly exposed to enemy attack, as constantly had to be repaired. The letters to their newspapers indicate that the reporters thought Buell without dash and perhaps no more eager to bring the war to a speedy conclusion than his good friend McClellan was reputed to be.

Nor was Buell's forbidding personality any help in his dealings with the army correspondents. Although he was an excellent organizer and a disciplinarian and had been cited for gallant and meritorious conduct, the reporters bitterly complained that General Buell "never encouraged them," and they made slighting remarks about his habitual reserve and reticence. Shanks, the *Herald* correspondent, observed:

> He was not too much of a book-worm, but too much of a red tapist. His Alma Mater was not West Point, but that more pitiless school, the adjutant general's office. Thirteen years' constant service in that department of the army made him too systematic—smothered the fire in his heart, the impulsive in his nature, and, like Thomas, he taught himself "not to feel."[1]

Other reporters objected to him on political grounds, accusing him of having been overly lenient with members of the slave-holding class whom he met. Reporter Furay, in a private letter to the editor of the

Cincinnati *Gazette* written from Huntsville, Alabama, early in July, presented a lively picture of the feuding that was going on among Buell's subordinates. He said of Major General Ormsby M. Mitchel:

> God grant he may yet Triumph over his enemies! I was recently inclined to think him indifferent upon the great question of Human Freedom, but I am now certain that all his seeming inconsistency upon that matter arose from the orders of General Buell, who cares more for guarding a rebel cabbage patch, or reenslaving a liberated negro, than he does for gaining a triumph over the enemy. . . . General Buell is so intensely pro-slavery that I have no doubt he would sacrifice every officer in his District, for the sake of returning to bondage a single slave. . . . The army is really in a paroxysm of terror, each man fearing he may be the next one arrested and punished for having offended some scoundrelly traitor. It is a common remark in the army now, that there is not a traitor in Huntsville or vicinity who would not be received at Buell's headquarters with greater consideration and respect than any Union officer.[2]

While Furay's letter was on its way to Cincinnati, the telegraph wires began to hum with reports of the daring John M. Morgan's dash through central Kentucky with his Confederate cavalry. With him, Morgan had a force estimated anywhere from one thousand to three thousand mounted men. Hardly had the excitement over this raid subsided before another Confederate raider, Brigadier General Bedford Forrest, provided more sensational news copy. Appearing at Murfreesboro, thirty miles below Nashville, on July 13, Forrest took the entire garrison of fourteen hundred cavalry and infantry; made off with great quantities of supplies; and so damaged the railroad East of Murfreesboro that almost two weeks elapsed before it was running again![3]

Excited by Forrest's destructive raid, the Nashville correspondent of the New York *Herald*, S. R. Glen, on July 19 wrote a letter stressing the absolute necessity for a large Federal cavalry force in central Tennessee:

> How can infantry, in an extent of country like Middle Tennessee, be expected to contend successfully against a mounted enemy? The Union forces are stationed in small squads along the lines of railroads, at long intervals, and occupy villages in small numbers. The enemy make a dash into these places, commit their depredations and then fly upon fleet horses far beyond the reach of the Union soldiery, whose only means of locomotion are their own legs.[4]

Nashville itself appeared none too safe, as ominous reports of Forrest's presence in the vicinity continued to come in. In another letter to the *Herald* dated July 23, Glen told of having been "on the *qui vive*" for four consecutive nights and of having spent the last night on the floor of one of the rooms in the Capitol building "with a chair turned back and upwards for a pillow." Sharing his vigil were Governor Andrew Johnson, Browning and Lindsley of the Governor's staff, and an army sergeant who during the night had broken one of his arms by falling from an upper story of the Capitol.[5]

News of Forrest's activity around Nashville reached Buell's army at Battle Creek, thirty-one miles from Chattanooga. For nearly four weeks the Army of the Ohio had remained almost stationary at that point while signs of increasing Confederate activity multiplied. On a flying visit to the army during the first week of August, the Philadelphia *Press* correspondent, Ben C. Truman, observed the verbal exchanges between the pickets on opposite sides of the Tennessee River, "the rebels generally being more saucy and defiant than our men." He further noted:

> Both parties exchange newspapers, and we frequently read the Atlanta and Knoxville journals. The *modus operandi* of the exchange is novel, each party swimming to the middle of the river with a newspaper in his mouth. An exchange of coffee and tobacco is often made in somewhat the same manner, the parties always shaking hands before separating.[6]

Finding himself completely cut off from Louisville by continuing guerilla raids, Buell detached General Nelson from the command of his division on August 16 and sent him North to clear the guerillas out of Kentucky. Three days later Major General Braxton Bragg, the new Confederate commander at Chattanooga, sent a column of three or four thousand troops across the river. On the twenty-second Buell learned that Bragg's whole army was north of the Tennessee. Believing that Bragg intended to strike for Nashville, Buell moved his supplies from Stevenson and prepared to concentrate his army at Murfreesboro.[7]

Also, Major General E. Kirby Smith, commanding the Confederate Department of East Tennessee, was moving northward from Knoxville into Kentucky with an army of twelve thousand men. Near Richmond, Kentucky, he encountered two brigades of inexperienced troops, whose commander, General Nelson, when the fighting began, was at Lexington, twenty-seven miles away. After a successful flanking movement, the Confederates put their adversaries to rout. While the retreating Federals were making for the bridge over the Kentucky River, General Nelson appeared on the battlefield in a fine rage. In vain did he attempt to stem the tide by beating his soldiers with the flat side of his sword and shouting at the top of his voice that reinforcements were on the way. Although Nelson himself escaped, his little army was almost completely annihilated, more than two thousand of them being taken prisoners. By September 2, Kirby Smith was at Lexington, in the heart of the Blue Grass country, ready to push on to the Ohio River.[8]

Among the fleeing Unionists who were picked up in the Confederate dragnet following the Battle of Richmond were two newspaper reporters, Joe McCullagh of the Cincinnati *Commercial* and "Telmah" of the Cincinnati *Gazette*. McCullagh and his colleague were riding along on an artillery wagon near the front of the retreating Union column when they overheard the significant order, "Cavalry to the front." McCullagh's reasoning told him that the sentence was incomplete and that the injunction "all others to the rear" should have been added. Within a matter of seconds, the two reporters were on the other side of a neighboring fence, making tracks in the direction from which they had recently come. After running through a number of fields, hunting in vain for some place of concealment, they caught sight of some large haystacks. Taking cover behind them, the fugitives listened with breathless anxiety as the noise of the pursuit became more audible. Finally they heard someone say, "Take down that fence, and fire a few rounds into that haystack." When several shots whistled past their ears, the terrified newspapermen decided that their best move was to come out and make a clean surrender.

As the fugitives emerged from their hiding place, three cavalrymen rode up and told the reporters to come along with them. McCullagh wanted to know if it was their habit to arrest noncombatants.

"Yes, we'll arrest every one we catch with this god damn crowd," was the somewhat disconcerting answer.

In the company of some Union soldiers who had been overhauled nearby, the reporters were marched down the road toward the headquarters of the Confederate commander. As they trudged along, a courier came dashing past with the command to "bring up" and "double quick." Someone had mistaken the flight of a Unionist column for a counterattack. Under the influence of this false report, the cavalrymen "double quicked" the little party of prisoners, until most of them were completely exhausted, and threatened to shoot anyone who failed to keep up with the crowd. After about four miles the marchers were turned into a field which they were told was to be their camping ground for the night.

By this time many of the prisoners had lost their carpet bags and even their coats. The correspondent of the *Gazette,* finding it impossible to keep pace with the others, passed his valise over to one of the mounted guards, who volunteered to carry it for him. As soon as they reached the camping ground the reporter put out his hand to repossess himself of the valise. Just then, however, an officer stuck a pistol in his face, snarling "Go on, God damn you, I'll take care of that." And so ended the story of the valise so far as the owner was concerned.

One of the other members of the squad asked McCullagh if he had a watch. The *Commercial* man informed him that it was then half past five.

"Let me have the watch," said his interrogator with an air of authority.

"It ain't in arms against the Confederacy. What do you want it for?" demanded McCullagh.

"To keep—what the hell do you think?" said the Confederate warrior in a bullying tone. "You are a prisoner, and we'll take everything you've got."

"Why, I thought you were a soldier when I surrendered," persisted the owner of the watch.

"What the devil else do I look like?" the soldier demanded.

"I only meant to say that I surrendered to a soldier and not to a highwayman, I thought," answered McCullagh gamely.

Just then a Confederate officer came along. Learning from the reporter of the guard's request, he stated that if the guard had asked for the watch he "was an infernal thief," and the controversy ended with McCullagh retaining his property.

The prisoners were ordered to fall in for the march to Richmond early the next morning, after passing a restless night when they attempted to sleep in the open air without blankets or sufficient clothing. When they arrived, two hours later, the two reporters were informally released on parole, with instruction to report to General Kirby Smith later in the day. From Lieutenant Colonel W. E. Morgan, to whom they were referred by Kirby Smith, they learned that before they could go North they must be paroled as prisoners of war. McCullagh objected to this. He pointed out that he and his colleague were unarmed at the time of their capture and therefore ought not to be treated as prisoners of war. But his argument did him little good. The Confederate officer replied that newspaper correspondents were "more than in arms against them," that, in fact, they were continually pumping people for information and publishing news about them that gave aid and comfort to the Federals. They had their choice of being paroled or remaining in the Southern Confederacy indefinitely. The newspapermen soon made up their minds to take the oath, obtained their passes, and started out under a broiling August sun for an eighty-mile trek to their newspaper offices.[9]

Both Louisville and Cincinnati were already in a state of panic as a result of the northward march of Kirby Smith. At Cincinnati all business activity was shut down, the city was placed under martial law, and every man who was capable of bearing arms was called to the city's defense. Public excitement was high. On September 4, the Cincinnati *Times,* whose loyalty had not previously been questioned, was temporarily suppressed for printing an article accusing the Government of manufacturing a big scare and ridiculing the efforts to which it had given rise.[10]

Albert D. Richardson of the New York *Tribune,* who arrived in Cincinnati just as the crisis was coming to a head, was impressed by the willingness of everyone he saw, "old and young, the millionaire, and the poorest of poor devils," to "carry the musket or dig in the trench side by side." Richardson promised:

> Cincinnati will not be taken. The Rebels will be driven from the soil of Kentucky. Victory will again become a habit with the troops of the Northwest, and they will sweep down to the Gulf leaving no enemy in their rear. But it will only be after the Government shall place the whole West under some one General of brains and vitality, and no longer leave its various departments at the mercy of respectable and educated imbecility.[11]

Bragg did not get underway from Chattanooga until almost the first of September. Even then his movements were so well screened by the Cumberland Mountains that Buell could not be sure until after the Confederate general had reached Carthage, Tennessee, that he was on his way to join Kirby Smith. When at length it became clear beyond all reasonable doubt that Bragg was on the high road to Kentucky, Buell left Murfreesboro, to which he had previously withdrawn, and marched northward by way of Nashville in a desperate attempt to overtake Bragg.

With Brigadier General Lovell H. Rousseau's division as it left Nashville at midnight on September 7 was the *Herald* reporter, W. F. G.

Shanks. Throughout the Sunday preceding their departure, Shanks had roamed the streets in the company of *Herald* correspondent Glen, keeping tab on the army's preparations for the march and hunting northbound travelers by whom to send letters to his newspaper. Hundreds of Union men from as far away as Northern Alabama were crowding the streets, anxiously inquiring what General Buell intended for the defense of Nashville. Plenty of Confederate sympathizers were likewise in evidence, making little effort to conceal their joy at the prospect of a Yankee evacuation. Everywhere the reporters looked, they could see—peering from windows, on door sills, promenading the streets—young women and girls, decked in gaudy colors, sporting red and white ribbons and flaunting Confederate flags. Shanks could not help feeling considerably relieved when, shortly before midnight, he reached the North bank of the Cumberland River. Under the pale light of a full moon, he rode off at a gallop through Edgefield, dim in the cloud of dust kicked up by the troopers.[12]

On September 13, after marching northwestward through central Tennessee, Bragg reached Glasgow, Kentucky. There he paused with the intention of striking at Bowling Green, Buell's only depot of supplies South of Louisville. As Buell approached, Bragg advanced to Munfordville on the line of the Louisville and Nashville Railroad, where with comparatively little difficulty he picked off a garrison of over two thousand infantry. Louisville might well have been Bragg's had he pressed on from Munfordville without delay. Instead, after remaining there for a day or two, apparently with the idea of resisting Buell's advance, he veered off to the Northeast in the direction of Bardstown, leaving the road to Louisville open to his pursuers.[13]

With McCook's division on the march to Louisville was the *Tribune* correspondent Villard, who had been with that division since the beginning of the campaign. They marched the one hundred twenty miles from Bowling Green to Louisville in seven days, the last three being the hardest. As they came within ten miles of Louisville on September 27, Villard rode on ahead of the troops and reined up in front of the Galt House about ten o'clock at night. So vagabondish was his appearance, full-bearded as he was, that the room clerk failed to recognize him and was about to turn him away. The clerk's tone changed, however, when Villard mentioned his name, and he soon had a good bedroom on the top floor.[14]

From his Louisville friends Villard learned of the excitement which had been current there as a result of the steady approach, nearer and nearer, of Bragg's bare-footed veterans. On the morning of the twenty-second, the situation had looked so critical to the Commanding General, Nelson, that he issued an order calling for the women and children in the city to prepare to leave at once. To make matters worse, this was followed by another order announcing that beginning that afternoon the Jeffersonville ferry across the Ohio, the only avenue of escape, would be used exclusively for military purposes. Within an hour from the time these orders were made public, the streets were filled with "skedaddlers," and a first-class panic was in the making. Among those who left town in a hurry were a fair-sized number of the press, leaving behind them, according to one newspaperman, only the correspondents of the New York *Herald* and *Tribune* and the Chicago *Times*.[15] Apparently the count was not strictly accurate, for a correspondent of the Cincinnati *Gazette* was still in Louisville the next morning for an interview with General Nelson. Nelson assured the *Gazette* man that to the best of his information Bragg "undoubtedly" was marching on Louisville and that he fully expected to see Bragg in front of the city by Thursday morning, September 25.[16]

Much of the "news" emanating from Louisville at this time was based on rumors picked up by reporters from frightened fugitives. The Philadelphia *Inquirer*, for example, was informed by its roving representative that Bragg had summoned Nelson to surrender and that Nelson had refused; was prepared, in fact, to meet his Confederate adversary.[17] Such stories were based on imagination and fed by frequent repetition. Even generals were not always reliable informants. The Louisville correspondent of the New York *Tribune* asserted:

> People have lost all dependence upon the admissions and denials of the "Generals commanding," since their experience in the Munfordville affair, when the makers of our military fortunes positively persisted in discrediting all reports of the surrender, even after parties that had witnessed it had arrived here. Between the tide of rumors and the ebb of facts, your correspondent floats like a craft without a rudder. . . .[18]

On the afternoon of the twenty-third, Joe McCullagh of the Cincinnati *Commercial* and another reporter[19] made arrangements to go down to Elizabethtown, about fifty miles South of Louisville, where McCullagh's companion expected to transact some business connected with the army. A horse and buggy were placed at the service of the two correspondents, and it was decided that McCullagh should act as driver. It was nearly midnight before they got underway. Further delay resulted from the *Commercial* reporter's ignorance of the road and from a parley with some Union pickets who stopped them because they did not know the countersign. There was nothing to do, it appeared, but to return to the Galt House. There the necessary information was obtained from the Assistant Adjutant General in time to permit the reporters to start for Elizabethtown once more, at two o'clock in the morning. This time, they had to pass a cavalry column which extended for more than a mile along the Salt River pike. The road was narrow, and the dust raised by the cavalcade did not make it any easier to see the edge of the road. When at length they had reached the head of the column, they were halted again, this time by Captain Ebenezer Gay, the cavalry commander; but after explaining the urgent nature of their business they were allowed to proceed.

Now that they were outside the Federal lines, for anything either man knew, they might encounter Southern guerillas at any time. It was agreed, therefore, that if they fell into the hands of the bushwhackers they should represent themselves as natives of Louisville on the way to Nashville to avoid induction into the Northern army. To make their story more plausible, the correspondents were prepared to use the names of certain prominent citizens of Nashville with whom they had a fictitious acquaintance. No encounters with guerillas materialized, however. At six o'clock in the morning they stopped at the village tavern in West Point for breakfast, tried in vain to change horses, and continued on their way at a gradually slackening pace.

Shortly before noon the two correspondents beheld the thrilling sight of Buell's advance guard marching on Louisville, with Generals Wood and Thomas L. Crittenden riding at the head of the column. Behind the advance guard, the rest of the army was strung out along the road for more than ten miles, with the army train "which should be measured by miles, rather than counted by wagons" bringing up the rear. To McCullagh's experienced eye Buell's soldiers appeared travel-worn and anything but smart. In his September 30 article in the *Commercial* he wrote:

> They had been on the road ten days, without a change of clothing, traveling through a continuous volume of dust all the time. Some of them had no shoes, others no coats, others no hats. . . . They had not slept in tents for several weeks, and had been on half rations for more than a month.

Just outside Elizabethtown the reporters came upon General Buell riding at the head of General McCook's division and accompanied by his staff and escort. McCullagh's description of Buell in the same article is interesting especially because of the storm about to burst around that worthy gentleman's head:

> His dress was that of a Brigadier instead of a Major General. He wore a shabby straw hat, dusty coat, and had neither belt, sash or sword about him. A majority of the field officers, behind and before him, looked more consequential and dignified than he. Though accompanied by his staff, he was not engaged in conversation with any of them, but rode silently and slowly along, noticing nothing that transpired around him.... Buell is, certainly, the most reserved, distant and unsociable of all the Generals in the army. He never has a word of cheer for his men or his officers; and, in turn, his subordinates care little for him save to obey his orders, as machinery works in response to the bidding of the mechanic. There is in McClellan and Fremont an unaccountable something, that keeps this machinery constantly oiled and easy-running; but Buell's unsympathetic nature makes it "squeak" like the drag wheels of a wagon.

After transacting their business at Elizabethtown, the two reporters were forced to return to Louisville by a roundabout route as the main road was blocked with soldiers and army wagons. By this time the excitement in Louisville had moderated, and those who had been most perturbed the week before were now ready to deny that they had ever felt any great uneasiness. Some people were very critical of the Associated Press for magnifying, as they said, the degree of excitement in Louisville to which the approach of Bragg's army had given rise. At the beginning of the next week, the town was in an uproar once more, however, as a result of the murder of a Federal Major General by one of his fellow officers in the lobby of the Galt House, within full view of a large number of spectators.

Villard had just finished eating his breakfast in the hotel dining room on the morning of September 29 when he heard the sound of a pistol shot in the direction of the large entrance hall nearby. Rushing out into the hall, the *Tribune* correspondent learned from a bystander that Brigadier General Jefferson C. Davis, recently in command of the Home Guards which had been summoned to the defense of Louisville, had just shot General Nelson from a distance of eight or ten feet. There had been bad blood between the two officers for some time as a result of a misunderstanding which had culminated in Davis' suspension from command by Nelson. He had been sent back to Louisville four days later by Brigadier General Horatio C. Wright, the new department commander. Earlier that morning Davis had met Nelson in the lobby and had asked him for an explanation of the causes of his suspension. Turning to Governor Oliver P. Morton of Indiana, with whom he had been conversing, Nelson boomed, "Governor Morton, is this the kind of officers you send to the army to insult me?" Then he raised his arm and struck the Indiana general in the face with the back of his hand. Davis did not return the blow, but instead walked off in the company of a gentleman in a linen duster, who was probably a brother officer. At this point another reporter, Alf Burnett of the Cincinnati *Times*, entered the lobby and catching sight of General Nelson wished him good morning.

"Did you hear that damned insolent scoundrel insult me, Sir?" demanded Nelson of the startled reporter. "I suppose he don't know me, Sir. I'll teach him a lesson, Sir."

While he was expressing these sentiments, the three-hundred-pound General kept moving slowly toward the door leading to the ladies' sitting room. Burnett heard General Davis ask for a weapon, first of a gentleman who was standing near him and then of a certain Captain Gibson, who was just about to enter the dining room. Gibson replied, "I always carry the article," and handed Davis a pistol, remarking as Davis walked toward Nelson, "It is a tranter trigger. Work light." General Nelson had just reached the bottom of the stairway leading to the second floor when Davis called out to him, "Not another step farther," drew his pistol, and fired. With the bullet in his breast, Nelson climbed the staircase and fell in the hall between the head of the stairs and General Buell's room. Several people who had gathered around him carried him into an adjoining room pending the arrival of medical assistance. Among the curious watchers who streamed into the room during the next few minutes was a reporter for the Chicago *Times*, who noted as he left the room that the General was very weak and "sinking fast." At half past eight o'clock, within an hour from the time he was shot, General William Nelson was dead. Although Davis was immediately placed under arrest and subsequently indicted for manslaughter by a local grand jury, he never was brought to trial.[20]

On the morning this shocking affair occurred, one of Halleck's staff officers arrived from Washington with an order relieving Buell of his command and substituting General Thomas.[21] None of the newspaper correspondents was greatly surprised, for they were well aware of the widespread dissatisfaction with Buell in the army and were inclined themselves to regard him as a "slow coach." To the surprise of everyone, however, Thomas declined the honor, requesting instead that Buell be retained in command inasmuch as his preparations to move against the enemy had been completed. Three days later, Buell's Army of the Ohio, fifty-eight thousand men, marched from Louisville after Bragg. Brigadier General Joshua W. Sill was ordered to move on Frankfort with two divisions to hold in check Kirby Smith's force. The remainder of the army, organized in three corps, marched by different routes along roads converging upon Bardstown. During the advance to Bardstown, Villard accompanied McCook's corps, which formed the left wing of the army; McCullagh was with Crittenden; Shanks and Furay were elsewhere in the army.

Now that the Army of the Ohio was in motion again, Buell's journalistic friends became suddenly vocal. The Louisville correspondent of the Chicago *Times* asked:

> Does anyone want a more vigorous campaign than Buell is at present prosecuting against the rebels? In all directions the insurgents are flying in confusion, and in all directions Buell's army is pressing closely upon his heels.

Then proceeding to further superlatives:

> Never in the history of this war has the dissipation of an army been so complete. As an army, Bragg's force has ceased to exist. In front of Buell's advance the country is filled with a fugitive mob, — nothing more; no organization; no concert of action; no plan of campaign; nothing but complete rout and demoralization.[22]

The facts were very much otherwise.

Bragg indeed had been misled into thinking that Buell's main attack was being directed at Frankfort. On October 2, acting under this supposition, he ordered Polk to move northeast from Bardstown via Bloomfield and deliver a flank attack on Sill's marching column. As Buell approached Bardstown from the northwest, both Polk and Bragg saw their mistake. Instead of carrying out Bragg's original order, Polk withdrew from Bardstown the following day and headed eastward from Harrodsburg, where Bragg had now decided to concentrate his forces. On

October 7, Polk with the right wing of Bragg's army reached Harrodsburg, while Hardee with the remainder encamped in front of Perryville, a small town about ten miles west of Harrodsburg. During the night of the seventh, Hardee was so closely pressed by Buell's center that Bragg directed Polk to return to Perryville with Cheatham's division and attack the enemy the next morning.[23]

It was approximately two o'clock the morning of the eighth, as Villard recalled it, that orders from General Buell were received at McCook's headquarters calling for the latter to advance upon Perryville.[24] Between ten and eleven o'clock that morning the line of battle was formed. Jackson's and Rousseau's divisions of McCook's corps comprised the Union left; Brigadier General Charles C. Gilbert's corps, including Albin Schoepf's, Philip H. Sheridan's, and Robert B. Mitchell's divisions, was in the center; Crittenden with three more divisions was on the right. There had been some brisk fighting the evening before in front of Sheridan's division but nothing to compare with the action which developed about 1:30 P.M. on the eighth when Rousseau's division began moving up toward the Chaplin River.

As a result of a failure in communications, McCook's corps was forced to bear the brunt of the fighting; Gilbert was involved to a minor extent; Crittenden not at all. For some reason not adequately explained, Buell did not receive any information concerning the attack on his left before four o'clock in the afternoon. Even then, because of a fall from his horse only two days before, he was unfitted for the responsibilities of active command.[25]

Furay of the Cincinnati *Gazette* was standing beside Captain Peter Simonson's Fifth Indiana battery, which was with Mitchell's division, when the enemy cannonade commenced. While Furay was talking with the battery commander about some of the earlier events of the campaign, a spherical shot buried itself deep in the side of a hill just below them and a half dozen others raised great clouds of dust in the dried-up fields beyond. As the cannonade progressed, the enemy's artillery fire, in Furay's opinion, became less effective. He observed:

> Their missiles struck everywhere except where they intended them to strike, and it actually seemed that the safest points which could be selected for a circuit of two or three miles were in the very midst of our batteries.[26]

Furay was posted in the center of the Union line, which was a comparatively quiet zone. Over on the left where McCook was in command, it was a different story.

Jackson, one of McCook's two division commanders, was killed during the first few minutes of the battle. The situation on the Union left became still more serious when one of Jackson's brigades, made up almost entirely of inexperienced troops, gave way in complete disorder and swept Jackson's other brigade along with them. Following this catastrophe, the full force of the Confederate attack launched by three divisions, some sixteen thousand men all told, fell upon Rousseau's division, sweeping from left to right. To Villard, who watched the course of this fighting for over an hour, the resistance of Rousseau's men was decisive in affecting the outcome of the battle. He later wrote:

> The atmosphere was so clear and the sun shone so brightly that, barring momentary obscuration by the powder smoke, every move of assailants and assailed could be clearly perceived with the naked eye or the field-glass from the commanding point where we stood. . . . We were so near that we heard the peculiar pattering noise of falling bullets. We were all struck with the desperate valor of the rebels. Led by mounted officers, their broad columns came to the attack in quick movement and with death-defying steadiness, uttering wild yells, till, staggered by the sweeping cross fire of our artillery and the volleys from Starkweather's regiments, they fell back to the shelter of corn-fields and breaks of the ground.[27]

In his *Personal Recollections of Distinguished Generals,* published soon after the war, Shanks, who performed in the dual capacity of volunteer aide to General Rousseau and reporter for the New York *Herald* during the Battle of Perryville, gave the impression that General McCook had brought on the engagement without authorization from General Buell. According to Shanks, McCook told Captain James S. Stokes during the course of the battle that he had in his pocket General Buell's orders not to fight. McCook said that if Buell supposed that "Aleck McCook was coming in sight of the enemy without fighting him he was much mistaken in his man."[28] From other sources, however, it would appear that at four o'clock in the afternoon when the attack on Rousseau was at its height McCook was in a very different frame of mind. According to Villard, who saw the General at a farm house in the rear about this time, McCook was utterly appalled by the prospect. His chief of staff told Villard that the whole corps had been assailed by overwhelming numbers, that the center was yielding ground and the right being turned, and that there was imminent danger of a complete rout of his corps.[29]

Toward the end of the day, the pressure on McCook was relieved in some measure by counterattacks made by Gilbert's corps, in which a young brigadier general named Sheridan gave indications of the brilliant leadership which later came to be associated with his name. That evening Buell made arrangements with his corps commanders to bring his whole army into battle the next morning. Between 6:00 A.M. and 7:00 A.M. on October 9, Crittenden's and Gilbert's corps moved forward, only to find that Bragg had left the vicinity during the night. Buell had neglected to dispose his forces so as to block Bragg's line of retreat. By the time Sill had rejoined the main body of Buell's army, effective pursuit of Bragg was out of the question.[30]

On the day after the Battle of Perryville, Alf Burnett of the Cincinnati *Times* and Seward of the Philadelphia *Inquirer* visited an improvised hospital in the rear of the battlefield. There they found some twenty Confederate soldiers who had become separated from their command and were attempting to pass themselves off as sick or wounded in order to escape detection. The two reporters suspected that they were "playing sharp"; they therefore let it be known that they were farmers from Dryfork, nearby, and that they would be glad to send down some coffee and sugar for the "wounded boys." After further conversation, the internees revealed that they were from Hardee's corps, that only one of them was wounded, and that they had used his bloody rags for arm bandages and head bandages whenever "suspicious-looking persons" were around. They were anxious to know how they could get out of the state without being captured; several of the Yanks had already been there, they said, but the "damned fools" were under the impression that they were already paroled. The correspondents assured the fugitives that they would be helped by underground-railroad methods to return to their command. That very afternoon, however, by a strange accident which could hardly have mystified the newspapermen as much as it did the other parties concerned, some Federal prowlers appeared unexpectedly and made prisoners of the wounded men.[31]

Apart from such exploits as these, the reporting of the Perryville campaign was disappointing. The first reports from Louisville, including Associated Press telegrams, indicated that Perryville had been a "great and decisive victory" and gave the impression that Buell had "utterly routed" his adversary. As army letters began to come in from the field, newspaper editors were obliged to backtrack in some measure. "I do now know but that it is called a victory with you, but not so here," averred the Louisville correspondent of the Philadelphia *Inquirer* in a letter published in that newspaper on October 18. In the New York *Times*, Perryville was alleged to be "the most sanguinary battle of the war."[32] Fully ten days after the battle, the Cincinnati *Commercial*, whose army reporter, McCullagh, had not been in a position to see any of the fighting, observed sadly that "particulars of the Battle fought at Perryville, Ky. on the 8th, seem never likely to be had with accuracy and fullness."[33]

Various correspondents—Junius Browne of the Cincinnati *Times* and Bickham of the *Commercial* among them—were much impressed by what they heard of the good behavior of Kirby Smith's men during their stay in the Blue Grass. Browne concluded:

> The superior discipline of the Confederates is not a little remarkable when we consider that they are an inferior class of men; that they are poorly provided for . . . and generally very ignorant. . . .
>
> And yet these miserable fellows fight nobly and have endured heroically in a miserable cause.
>
> Is it true that brutal and ignorant men make better soldiers than those possessed of intelligence and sensibility?[34]

On the Sunday following the Battle of Perryville, word was received in Louisville that another action between Buell and Bragg had taken place that day in comparison with which the affair at Perryville was hardly more than a skirmish. In a letter to the Chicago *Times* "Donelson" said:

> I write you tonight in the midst of the most intense excitement. Everybody is asking everybody else, "What's the news?" and everybody else is replying, "That's just what I was going to ask you". . . . People gather in knots on the street-corners; in crowds in the hotels; in great masses wherever masses of the people can assemble. Churches are deserted.[35]

The "great battle" soon proved to be no more substantial than most of the rumors current at such times. Reports of wholesale neglect of the wounded by army surgeons also proved to have little basis inasmuch as the sanitary commissions from Louisville, Cincinnati, and other points reached Perryville soon after the battle, making it possible for the army surgeons to remain with Buell's army during the pursuit of Bragg.[36]

In the meantime, newspaper criticism of Buell, which had temporarily subsided during his march from Louisville, once more assumed formidable proportions. "Buell is a failure—a contemptible failure," declared the army correspondent of the Chicago *Tribune,* writing from Crab Orchard, Kentucky, on October 16.[37] "Utterly unfit for his position" concurred the New York *Tribune* man.[38] Whitelaw Reid, who had been recalled from a short vacation in Ohio to go on a fact-finding mission to Kentucky, wrote in similar vein to the Cincinnati *Gazette.*[39] Of the Western press only the Louisville papers and the Chicago *Times* continued to champion Buell.

The news of Buell's replacement by Rosecrans, first made public on October 30, was no surprise to the newspapermen. The press generally regarded the army's new commander as a "fighting general," whose victory over Van Dorn at Corinth earlier in the month augured well for his future success. The focus of military and consequently of journalistic activity was about to shift back again to central Tennessee where Nashville virtually had been in a state of siege since the early part of September.

Writing from there on September 24, Ben Truman had informed the *Press:*

> The city is a grand cut-off—cut off from everybody and everything. The Louisville Railroad is "done gone," and its future existence fearfully jeopardized.... The guerillas infest every road, lane, and by-path within two miles of the city, and permit no marketing of account to reach us. The soldiers are on half rations .... and our chances for being starved out are abundant.[40]

Fortunately for him, Truman had been able to command the services of a remarkably efficient courier, a Mr. Riley, who made three successful trips from Nashville to Louisville during September and October. On his fourth trip he was captured by Morgan and sentenced to be shot. He escaped, however, and to confuse his pursuers made off in the opposite direction for Murfreesboro, where he reported to John C. Breckenridge, the Confederate commander at that point. Breckenridge was only too happy to receive from a supposed sympathizer "information" concerning the forts at Nashville and to entrust to his care a number of letters addressed to certain friends of the Confederacy in Nashville, where they were turned over to Governor Johnson.[41]

In a diary which he kept for six months during the latter part of 1862, the *Herald* correspondent, Glen, likewise described in eloquent language the plight of the besieged city. On October 21 he wrote:

> Days, weeks, nay, months, roll round and there seems to be no change for the better in this important city. Cut off from communications with the outer world, our suppliers have become exhausted. . . . We hear that Breckenridge is around us with fifty thousand men; that Anderson, mortified at his defeat at Lavergne, declares that he can and will capture the city; and Forrest, incensed from the same cause, roughly swears that he will have Nashville at all hazards, if he falls himself at the first fire. But those who are in the confidence of Governor Johnson know that the enemy, if they should capture the city, will achieve an empty triumph, amid blackened and crumbling ruins.[42]

Glen was less fortunate than Truman in his attempts to communicate with the outside world. A letter which he had written to the *Herald* containing important information about the strength of Buell's army, not intended for publication, was intercepted by a party of twenty armed Confederates between Tyree Springs and Franklin. The *Herald* took editorial notice of the episode some time later, inquiring of "the guerilla Morgan and his rebels" what they had done:

> with some of our correspondence, sent from Nashville a few months ago, and which fell into their hands? They promised when they stole the mailbag and our correspondent's shirts that they would publish the correspondence in a rebel paper and send on copies. If they will send us the letters they may keep the shirts.[43]

Precarious though his situation was, Negley, whom Buell had left in command at Nashville, hung on stubbornly, and early in November came the cheering news that Rosecrans was on his way to the relief of the Tennessee capital. On November 17, the advance guard of what was thenceforth to be known as the Army of the Cumberland reached the city; Rosecrans himself arrived there a few days later; and on the twenty-sixth, railroad communication with Louisville was restored.[44] Now the *Herald* correspondent could rejoice because:

> Nashville is no longer a fort far into the enemy's country cut off from supplies and held with great trouble. . . . Its garrison has been relieved and reinforced and the character of the position changed.[45]

Meanwhile, having gotten back into Tennessee by way of Cumberland

Gap, about the middle of November Bragg began concentrating his forces at Murfreesboro. Resisting pressure from Washington to move against the Confederate commander without delay, Rosecrans busied himself in regrouping, re-equipping, and disciplining his army and in accumulating a sufficient stockpile of supplies to render it independent of any sudden interruption of railroad communication.[46] At such a time there was very little for the reporters to write about other than reviews and army movements. But the reviews were an old story by this time, and as for the movements, they were "too important to be told before they have developed themselves in results."[47] General Rosecrans did not propose to have his plans exposed to the enemy by an overzealous reporter.

One day early in December, Bickham of the Cincinnati *Commercial* learned that Captain Louis M. Buford of General Crittenden's staff was planning to go out on a flag-of-truce mission and that it would be possible for him to go along. Proceeding at a brisk canter down the Murfreesboro pike with an escort of a dozen cavalry, they soon entered the Confederate lines. While the Captain was transacting his business, the reporter gazed curiously at the adventurous Confederate cavalrymen, whom he was now observing at close range for the first time. He informed his newspaper readers:

> We were chatting with Forrest's men—Alabamians, Kentuckians, Tennesseeans. There was nothing of soldierly uniform about them but the ease, grace and firmness, of their seat in saddle, and their military self possession were unmistakable. Incontestably, these troopers are hell raky fellows—reliable at a pinch under gamey leaders. . . .
>
> They were not prepossessing at all in their everlasting butternut, somber, dingy, threadbare and patched—with their dark visages ambushed in long, ragged beards and tangled locks. They were slight men, mostly thin and narrow in body, but enormously developed about the hips—shapen by exercise like a woman. . . . No insignia distinguished non-commissioned officers from privates. Indeed, I learned there was a Lieutenant in the party, only by inquiry. I saw one sharp eyed fellow in threadbare suit, variegated with strips of new butternut on his arms, which I presumed were chevrons, but he enlightened me by grim assurance that they were nothing but patches. Nevertheless, they were comfortably clad, and had blankets enough on their saddles. They were in marauding order, not groomed for display.[48]

Observing as he thought an "odd sort of stiffness" about the party, Bickham undertook to dispel it by uncapping a bottle of Federal "respects." Soon both officers and men were conversing freely, and to enliven the scene still further, the Confederate Major Prentice, a son of the editor of the Louisville *Journal,* playfully crossed swords with a lieutenant to exhibit his skill in fencing. Presently the Major discovered that Bickham had in his possession a number of late papers, containing accounts of a recent Federal victory in Arkansas, which he was planning to forward to the editor of the Murfreesboro *Rebel Banner.* Major Prentice said he would be happy to send the newspapers to Bragg's headquarters, but he was especially interested in having a look at a recent issue of the Louisville *Journal*—would like in fact to see "what his old dad had to say." They didn't agree in politics. The "old man" was a Federal; the Major was a Confederate. "By the way, tell the old man, when you see him, that I am fat, ragged, saucy and rebellious."

During the last week of December, influenced in part no doubt by the Administration's burning desire for a victory to offset Burnside's disastrous defeat at Fredericksburg,[49] Rosecrans started out from Nashville to find Bragg. At General Headquarters, on Christmas Eve, the practiced eye of *Herald* correspondent Shanks detected the signs of an important movement in the unusual activity of orderlies and messengers. Unable to get any confirmation of his suspicions from the General or anyone else, early the next morning he rode out to the advance camp. As he crossed a ridge of hills running athwart the Franklin pike, he spied one long train after another of white-covered wagons converging upon Nashville along the various roads leading into the city from the South. What could this mean? Was Rosecrans planning to evacuate the "Rock City" and retreat northward? To his great satisfaction, Shanks soon learned from General Thomas's Inspector General that the trains had been ordered to the rear to clear the way for an advance. He eagerly informed the *Herald:*

> The whole force is to be thrown onto the Nolinsville and Murfreesboro pikes, and is going in search of Bragg and his army. . . .
>
> I understand that the army moves without trains, with five days' rations and with their blankets only.[50]

The order for the advance to begin at dawn on Christmas morning had been issued on Christmas Eve, but for reasons best known to himself Rosecrans postponed the movement for twenty-four hours. Subsequently the Cincinnati *Commercial* reporter learned that in a council of war held at General Headquarters on Christmas Night, Rosecrans had urged his generals vehemently to "press them hard; strike fast and sharply; give them no rest."[51]

Throughout the morning of the twenty-sixth, the veterans of Perryville, forty-seven thousand strong, marched southeastward through a steady downpour of rain. Ahead of the main body of the army raced David S. Stanley's cavalry, driving the enemy's pickets before them. Proceeding at a slower pace, the left wing of the army under Crittenden advanced along the Murfreesboro pike. Thomas, in command of the center, moved out to Brentwood along the Franklin pike, crossing over to Nolensville. McCook was on his way to Triune by way of the Nolensville pike, seeking to discover whether General Hardee would offer battle there or retreat.[52]

About a half hour before noon, Bickham left Nashville with General Rosecrans and his staff, intent on catching up with the army. Before they were even out of the city, they could hear the sound of cannon fire in the distance. "Only shelling skirmishers," Bickham was assured, and yet as the thunder of hostile guns grew louder, every rider sat a little straighter in his saddle, and his horse impulsively broke into a sharper trot. Presently the sound of rifle fire could be heard from the right:

> It was obvious that McCook had stirred up the fox, and his pack were opening among the hills in full cry. We were too far away to catch the full scope of the music. Now, however, a whole tone thundered from our own front. We were on the Murfreesboro Pike behind Crittenden. Something appeared brewing for us. The General spurred "Bony" a little, and the long cavalcade stretched out into an apology for a canter. We heard no news from "Crit." Say about three o'clock, the General designated headquarters for the night, and then prepared to see McCook.[53]

At this point Bickham had the option of returning to camp or of accompanying Rosecrans on his cross-country ride. Choosing the latter, he and the other members of the General's party reconnoitered the country for a while and then dashed off in the direction of Nolensville. Around eight o'clock the cavalcade came to a halt in a narrow lane flanked by stone fences, with a gate in front and a barn on the right. With a sinking heart, Bickham realized that they had lost their way. An old woman, whom they encountered just then, proved anything but helpful. She had "never bin three miles any way from thar," she confided and then made her auditors even less comfortable by informing them that "Dick McCann and his cavalree (rebel) had been along this ere way about an hour ago." After a little while, however, one of the staff officers succeeded in routing a tenant of the redoubtable Dick out of his cabin and induced him to act as their guide. Following another hour's ride, they reached General McCook's headquarters at Nolensville, where they tarried for a little while in front of a huge pile of blazing cedars while Rosecrans conferred with McCook.

By ten o'clock the Commanding General was ready to return to his headquarters.

"With the blessing of God, General," McCook told him, "I will whip my friend Hardee tomorrow."

"God bless you!" said Rosecrans, and a moment later the General and his staff were on their way down the pike, so dark that they could hardly make out the outline of their own horses. Three times that night they lost their way, once almost wandering into the Confederate picket line. They reached camp about three o'clock, ravenously hungry and utterly exhausted, having ridden forty-eight miles in fifteen hours without so much as a single bite of food.

During the next three days the army continued to advance slowly, with some sharp fighting. At Lavergne and again at the Stewart's Creek bridge, Crittenden's advance was momentarily checked. McCook had a brisk fight at Nolensville, and the cavalry under Stanley skirmished almost continuously during those three days. In recounting the details of this marching and fighting, Shanks commented none too accurately on the treatment accorded by the enemy to their own dead and wounded. He asserted:

> Where they [the Confederates] fall they are left to die, and the first kindness their wounded receive is at our hands. . . . Dead and wounded alike appear to be stripped of blankets and overcoats. Some of them say that their fellow soldiers told them the Yankees had plenty and would take care of them. This disregard for their dead and wounded is a characteristic feature, not of the rebel soldiers, but of the rebel officers. . . . In every engagement which I have witnessed this fact has been notorious, and only in cases of our signal defeat has a battle been fought which did not leave the rebel wounded to be cared for and the rebel dead to be buried by us. It may be, and probably is, considered a mark of ability in a rebel officer to throw this care upon his enemy; but it is certainly very revolting to the feelings of humanity.[54]

By the twenty-ninth of December, the left and center of the Army of the Cumberland were in position before the enemy near Murfreesboro. That evening, on the basis of faulty intelligence indicating that Bragg had retreated, Rosecrans ordered Crittenden to cross Stone's River and occupy Murfreesboro. In attempting to carry out this order, Crittenden ascertained that the enemy had not retreated, and so the order was countermanded. But an Associated Press reporter, misled no doubt by the same false reports that had deceived Rosecrans, had already sent off to the press via Louisville the interesting information that Murfreesboro had fallen and that the enemy was retreating to Tullahoma.[55]

At half-past three on Tuesday morning, December 30, Rosecrans was awakened by a call from General McCook, who had just come up with his three divisions. He was instructed to rest the left of his corps on the right of Negley's division, but still Rosecrans did not move. Bragg, thinking that Rosecrans expected to attack him that day, held his army in line of battle to meet the attack. The day passed, however, without any serious fighting; that night Bragg determined to take the offensive himself.[56]

Both Rosecrans and Bragg had the same general plan of attack, embodying a concentration of troops on the left to crush the opponent's right and envelope his left and center. The two armies were drawn up along Stone's River, west of Murfreesboro, roughly parallel to each other—the Union army facing almost due East. On the Union right were the three divisions of Brigadier Generals Richard W. Johnson, Jefferson C. Davis, and Sheridan, under the general supervision of McCook. Under Thomas in the center of the line were the divisions of Negley and Rousseau. On the left were the three divisions of John M. Palmer, Wood, and Horatio P. Van Cleve extending across the Nashville pike and the railroad to Stone's River. McCook's line was thinnest of all, for many of his troops had been detached for service under Crittenden on the left, where the main Union effort was to be made.[57]

Rosecrans' plan of attack never had a chance to be tested, for before it could be executed, Bragg's men struck the Union right at daybreak, December 31, with crushing force, rolling it back until the Union line resembled a jackknife half shut.

An eyewitness of the attack on the Union right was Reporter Shanks, whose description of the furious assault was worthy of its subject:

The alarm given by the pickets hardly reached the camp before

> the enemy was upon it. . . . I had messed the night previous with a battery captain in Johnson's division, and at the alarm ran with him to mount.
>
> Here, for the first time, I got a good view of the advancing columns of the enemy. . . . Two columns deep, with a front of at least three-fourths of a mile, the line tolerably preserved, advancing with great rapidity, on came the whole rebel left wing, the bayonets glistening in a bright sun which had broken through the thick fog. The rapidity of the movement struck me with fear for our safety, as the sight had filled me with admiration of its grandeur. General Johnson and his brigade commanders were using every effort to get the troops into line. General Johnson is now blamed for being surprised, and I hear ridiculous stories of his being disgraced by Rosecrans, who is reported having torn his straps from his shoulders. So he was surprised, so were we all surprised; and if one is blamed, look higher and blame others.[58]

Both Johnson's and Davis' divisions made repeated efforts to check the enemy's advance, but they eventually were overwhelmed and forced to fall back to the Nashville road in the rear of the center of the army. Now it was Sheridan's turn to feel the full force of the enemy's assault. The Cincinnati *Gazette* reporter, Furay, declared:

> Never did man labor more faithfully than he to perform his task, and never was a leader seconded by more gallant soldiers. His division formed a kind of pivot upon which the broken right wing turned in its flight, and its perilous condition can easily be imagined, when the flight of Davis' division left it without any protection from the triumphant enemy, who now swarmed upon its front and right flank. But it fought until a fourth of its number lay bleeding and dying upon the field, and till both remaining brigade commanders . . . had met with the same fate as General Sill.[59] Then it gave way, and as in almost every instance of the kind, retreat was changed to rout, only less complete than that of the troops of Johnson and Davis.
>
> All these divisions were now hurled back together into the immense series of cedar thickets which skirt the turnpike, and extend far over to the right. Brigade after brigade, battery after battery, from Palmer's, Negley's, and Rousseau's divisions, were sent into the midst of the thickets to check the progress of the foe and rally the fugitives; but all in turn were either crushed outright by the flying crowds, broken by the impetuosity of the

> foe, and put to confused flight, or compelled to retire and extricate themselves in the best manner that seemed to offer....
>
> The scene at this time was grand and awful as anything that I ever expect to witness until the day of judgment. I stood in the midst and upon the highest point of the somewhat elevated space ... between the turnpike and the railroad ... forming the key to our entire position. Let the rebels once obtain possession of it, and of the immense train of wagons parked along the turnpike, and the Union army was irretrievably ruined. Even its line of retreat would be cut off, and nothing could save it from utter rout, slaughter, capture.[60]

By eleven o'clock most of the extreme right flank of the Union army had been swept away, and the full force of the Confederate assault was now bearing on the Union center. At one stage of the fight the Union line formed three sides of a shaky rectangle with the remnants of Sheridan's division on the right, Negley in front, and Rousseau on the left.[61] During a lull in the fighting which occurred around noon, Shanks passed through some of the regiments in McCook's command gathering material for his battle report. The soldiers to whom he talked were very much dispirited, being of the opinion that their rout was not only disgraceful to them but disastrous to the whole army. Even the appearance of Rosecrans, "looking like the best pleased and most hopeful general alive," failed to elicit any great enthusiasm. Shanks noted:

> Along the whole line there was an outcry against officers. The men said, despondingly, "We'll fight if they will give us officers." Imprecations were heaped upon the heads of McCook and of Johnson.... The *esprit du corps* of the right wing appeared to me to be gone.[62]

All afternoon the fighting continued. While the remnants of McCook's corps dug in, Thomas massed his five brigades in suitable positions to enable him to make a stubborn defense. Meanwhile the divisions of Van Cleve and Wood remained in close reserve. Toward the end of the afternoon it seemed to the Philadelphia *Press* correspondent, Ben Truman, that the enemy was getting the upper hand again. Little by little he forced back the Union line. Truman declared:

> I can assure you, our men prayed for night and darkness.... It was long after dark before the cannonading ceased, and, in fact, quite a lively firing along the whole line was kept up until midnight.[63]

After recovering from their first surprise, the Union troops had fought well. But they owed their deliverance from an overwhelming defeat fully as much to a failure in Confederate intelligence as they did to their own valor. Early that morning, Crittenden had moved Van Cleve's division across Stone's River, only to recall it when Hardee struck the Federal right. Although a body of enemy cavalry reported the crossing to Confederate Headquarters, Van Cleve's withdrawal went unnoticed. As a result, Breckenridge, who commanded the Confederate right, kept four brigades in position most of the day to repel an assault that never materialized.[64]

There was no serious fighting on New Year's Day, although the two armies remained within musket range of each other. To a correspondent of the Cincinnati *Times,* the enemy seemed to be probing the Union position along the entire front from left to right.[65]

On the morning of January 2, a correspondent of the St. Louis *Republican* rode out from Nashville to the battlefield just in time to witness an attack on the Union left wing, which had crossed to the East side of Stone's River the day before. The reporter commented in an article published a week later:

> What a scene of desolation is now presented the whole distance from Nashville to this place. But two or three families now live at their homes . . . on a stretch of twenty-eight miles, through an old settled country. Fences are gone, houses are deserted, and a good share of them have been burned, their works smoldering, and their tall shafts of chimneys yet standing. Not a cornfield but has been stripped and trodden down.

Near Lavergne, about halfway from Nashville to Murfreesboro, the wrecks of some sixty burnt and half burnt wagons and ambulances were strung out along the road, marking two separate attempts by Bragg's cavalry to burn the Federal wagon trains. "Some of the wagons were only partially injured," said the *Republican* man, "a wheel, or the box destroyed—others were literally eaten up by fire, except a mass of bolts, bars, and wheel tires."[66]

The Confederate attack on the Union left was only in division strength. One of the Union brigades was so badly demoralized, however, that Rosecrans and his staff mounted and rode into their midst, brandishing their swords and entreating them to stand firm. Eventually fresh troops were brought up and the attack was halted. There was further fighting on January 3, but it was hardly more than skirmishing. That night, Bragg began his retreat to Tullahoma, leaving the battlefield and the town of Murfreesboro in Rosecrans' hands.[67]

For days, the North was in doubt as to the outcome of the fighting in middle Tennessee. On January 2, the Nashville correspondent of the Chicago *Times* informed his newspaper, "we have been blockaded here for seven days. No mails or telegrams have been received or sent, within that time, between Nashville and Louisville."[68] Moreover, while the battle was in progress, a misunderstanding arose between the Post Office Department and the Louisville and Nashville Railroad, as a result of which mail service was suspended along the line of that railroad.[69] To make matters still worse, a midwestern blizzard on January 4 brought wire service between Louisville and Nashville to a halt and seriously interfered with all telegraph communication west of Buffalo, New York.[70] Faced by such unusual difficulties, the army correspondents in the Nashville area were obliged to make use of special messengers or do as the New York *Herald* reporter did—carry their stories to the newspaper office in person.[71] A Philadelphia *Press* reporter exclaimed:

> Could anything have been more sickening to correspondents than the realization of the fact that a great battle was progressing, and no railroad or direct telegraphic connection with the North? But it was even so, and "trust to luck" was our motto. First of all we had to send on despatches as far as Nashville by courier, who had many chances of never arriving there, as the road, most of the time, was in the possession of guerillas. At that point we left our despatches and letters in the hands of an assistant, and the appearance or non-appearance of such documents in the respective journals for which they were prepared, must be the proofs of his good fortune or the reverse.[72]

In spite of such difficulties, the New York *Tribune* secured a preliminary account of the fighting—reasonably accurate in most of its details. This account was telegraphed through from Nashville to New York in time to make the second edition of that paper's Saturday issue (January 3).[73]

While the country waited for an official statement of the result from Rosecrans, rumors of disaster reached alarming proportions. On the afternoon of January 5, Senator Ira Harris of New York was called from his seat in the Federal Senate Chamber to the rotunda, where he was informed by W. B. Shaw, onetime chief Washington correspondent of the New York *Herald*, that a bulletin just issued in New York stated that

Rosecrans had surrendered with thirty thousand of his officers and men. Leaving the Senators to digest the implications of this appalling information, Shaw journeyed all the way to the other end of Pennsylvania Avenue to communicate this same report to his friends at the War and Navy departments.[74] In view of such reports, it is small wonder that when at length the real truth became known, the press was prone to interpret the outcome of the battle as a victory. In the process, Rosecrans came in for his full share of hero worship. Said the Chicago *Times* in a special dispatch from Murfreesboro printed on January 8:

> It is a fact not heretofore published that, on the night of Wednesday's battle, prominent Generals supposed Gen. Rosecrans would retreat. He never entertained such an idea. After the rebels were gone, he was complimented for his tenacity. "Yes," said he, "I suppose you know Bragg is a good dog, but Holdfast is better." The lads call him "old Holdfast." They will fight for him now even more gloriously than before.

Probably the best newspaper account of the Battle of Murfreesboro was the seven-column letter which Furay forwarded to the Cincinnati *Gazette*.[75] Both the New York *Herald* and the Cincinnati *Commercial* carried full-scale reports of the action.[76] While the North was still wondering what had really happened at Murfreesboro, the New York *Tribune* and the New York *Times* became involved in a controversy over the fact that the *Times* had reprinted the *Tribune*'s telegraphic report of the battle without assigning credit to the *Tribune*. The defense of the *Times* was that in common with the *Herald* and *World* it had paid one-fourth the cost of transmitting this particular telegram from Nashville to New York and was therefore entitled to regard the contents of the telegram as its own property. In the opinion of the *Times*, the *Tribune* was endeavoring to establish a reputation for exclusive enterprise in newsgathering and expecting other newspapers to pay for it. The *Tribune*, on the other hand, chose to regard the behavior of the *Times* in this instance as "a reproach to the profession of journalism."[77] Meanwhile, some indignation was being expressed at Rosecrans' headquarters concerning "ridiculous and somewhat outrageous telegrams" communicated to the Eastern press by correspondents who had never even seen the battlefield. In some cases, it was alleged, these telegrams from Nashville were based on exaggerated statements made by cowardly officers who had fled from the field.[78]

In spite of such deficiencies, the reporting of Murfreesboro was considerably more satisfactory than the reporting of the Perryville campaign had been. Increasing reliance on the telegraph was indicated by the fact that the Chicago *Tribune's* telegraphic report of the battle ran to three and a half columns—"the longest special news dispatch ever sent over the wires in the Northwest."[79] For many days after the battle, Murfreesboro was the Mecca for newspaper reporters, sketchers for the pictorials, and the curious in general. "Send Bowers up at once enroute for Nashville," said a telegram from W. W. Harding to the Philadelphia *Inquirer* bureau in Washington on January 7.[80] A Chicago *Tribune* reporter, who arrived in Nashville on January 9 after a wearisome two-day trip from Louisville, wrote:

> I find myself befogged and confused by the vast crowd of dead, wounded and living soldiers with which the city [Nashville] is filled. . . . Every man has some story of his regiment or his company. He saw just so much of the terrible struggle, and for him it was and is all the history of the fight. He who, from out the thousand stories that float about, attempts to chronicle an accurate account of the affair from first to last, must take days at the task, and work with the perseverence of a beaver. I shall not attempt the job.[81]

Not for many months would the army reporters in Tennessee have the opportunity to see the Army of the Cumberland undergo another great trial of strength. Both sides had lost heavily at Murfreesboro—the Union side more heavily in proportion to the number engaged than the Confederate.[82] Rosecrans himself had seen death come close during the afternoon of the first day's conflict when a shell carried away the head of his chief of staff, bespattering the General with his blood. One reporter—Bickham of the Cincinnati *Commercial*—took advantage of the long period of inactivity that followed the battle to prepare for publication in book form his newspaper account of Murfreesboro. Meanwhile, favorable opportunities for war reporting were in the making in other sectors of the battle zone.

13

"Dont Treat . . . Fredericksburg as a Disaster"

HARPER'S FERRY was the principal rendezvous of the newspaper correspondents with McClellan's army during the early autumn of 1862. On September 26, 1862, one of the *Herald* reporters wrote to Hudson:

> I expected to be at the front yesterday afternoon, but was unable to reach there, because . . . I had to come a round-about way; and, being unable to get a horse, had to foot it a short distance. I will be there this afternoon, and will confer with Mr. Cash.[1] Mr. Ashley[1] is here. He says he is going to Harper's Ferry on Monday where the Herald Headquarters will be, instead of at Frederick.[2]

Ugly stories of disaffection in the army were still current among the newspapermen. To Horace Greeley came a letter from a Scranton, Pennsylvania, newspaper editor describing the bad state of army morale.[3] The editor, F. A. Macartney, who just had returned from a visit to the battlefield of Antietam, was shocked by the lack of discipline and the dangerous sentiments prevalent among the officers. In another letter estimating the effect on the army of the preliminary Emancipation Proclamation which President Lincoln had issued on September 22, the chief Washington correspondent of the *Herald* informed Bennett:

> The army is dissatisfied and the air is thick with revolution. It has been not only thought of but talked of and the question now is where can the man be found. McClellan is idolised but he seems to have no political ambition. The sentiment throughout the whole army seems to be in favor of a change of dynasty. . . . God knows what will be the consequence but at present matters look dark indeed. . . . Slavery is already practically abolished but the Proclamation is a different affair and if it should not be received more Kindly by other Officers of the Army than those whom I

> have seen it will go far towards producing an expression on the part of the Army that will startle the Country and give us a Military Dictator.[4]

Although there was strong pressure upon him to follow Lee into Virginia without delay, McClellan was determined not to advance until his army had been completely reorganized and brought to its full strength. Some evidence of the impatience with which the press viewed the continued inactivity of the Army of the Potomac is shown in a letter which the managing editor of the New York *Tribune,* Sydney H. Gay, addressed to the Washington correspondent of that newspaper on September 25:

> Smalley has come back, and his notion is that it is to be quiet along the Potomac for some time to come. George [McClellan], whom Providence helps according to his nature, has got himself on one side of a ditch [the Potomac River], which Providence had already made for him, with the enemy on the other, and has no idea of moving. Wooden-head [Halleck] at Washington will never think of sending a force through the mountains to attack Lee in the rear, so the two armies will watch each other for nobody knows how many weeks, and we shall have the poetry of war with pickets drinking from the same stream, holding friendly converse and sending newspapers across by various ingenious contrivances.[5]

On the evening of September 28, as he was about to call a meeting of the New York *Times* army staff to talk over ways and means of improving their efficiency, James M. Winchell of the *Times*'s Washington bureau heard a false report that the Army of the Potomac had left camp and was marching on Winchester. Realizing that if this were true it was too late to summon the reporters to Washington for a conference, he hastily drafted a set of instructions for their guidance and forwarded copies to William C. Church for transmittal to the other *Times* correspondents. In the same letter he asked Church to supervise the work of the other reporters and as soon as the army had concentrated to "occupy a position as near as possible to the General in command."[6]

Three days later President Lincoln began an unannounced visit to the army, during which he spent several days going over the battlefields of South Mountain and Antietam and having confidential talks with the army commander. One of the New York *Tribune* correspondents who watched the President review General Sumner's corps reported that

Lincoln looked weary and careworn and that he was unusually taciturn "though manifesting his native cheerfulness of disposition."[7] That evening a dispatch from Harper's Ferry to the *Tribune* commenting on the President's visit was stopped by an order from the War Department. Similar treatment was accorded to a dispatch intended for one of the other New York papers, even though its author had the written permission of the President to send it. Although the object of the President's visit was not revealed to the press, the same *Tribune* correspondent conjectured that he was anxious to examine into the condition of the army for himself and as one of McClellan's friends expressed it to "hurry forward Gen. McClellan."

If that was indeed the President's object, he was to be greatly disappointed. After his return to Washington, a peremptory order went out on October 6, bidding McClellan to cross the Potomac and give battle to the enemy "or drive him South."[8] The General replied on the seventh that he would cross the river within three days and advance up the Shenandoah Valley,[9] but the allotted time passed without any sign of the promised forward movement. Meanwhile, the letters of the army correspondents contained hints of the controversy between McClellan and the War Department over whether the army was adequately equipped for active campaigning. To the managing editor of the *Herald* one of the correspondents of that newspaper confided that the troops were "destitute of blankets, tents and overcoats, in fact of all Kinds of Quartermaster stores."[10] Consequently nothing more than a defensive movement could be expected. Similar allegations with respect to the lack of arms, boots, and shoes were made by a New York *Tribune* correspondent in a letter that the *Tribune* published on October 24. By this time the War Department had become very touchy about the whole matter—if one is to judge from a curt message addressed to the Provost-Marshal General, Simeon Draper, by the managing editor of the *Tribune:*

> Sir, The Secy. of War requests that you be furnished with the name of our correspondent who, in a letter of the "24th," made a statement in relation to the want of arms on the authority of one of the Generals.
>
> There is no such letter of that date, but I presume one of the 21st is referred to. That was written by Mr. N. Paige.
>
> The same writer in a letter of the 26th, received to-day, states, I presume on the same authority, that the arms have since been received.[11]

By this time the cry "On to Richmond" had become an almost universal chorus, rising from abolitionist and conservative alike. "The horror with which all in and out of the army springs from the prospect of winter quarters again for 200,000 men on the Potomac is significant," observed the Washington correspondent of the Chicago *Tribune*.[12] Under the impact of this pressure McClellan, on October 26, gave the long-awaited order to advance, and the Confederates fell back on Winchester as the Union army, one hundred and sixteen thousand strong, plunged across the Potomac.

Preparations for the advance had been made with the greatest secrecy. There was considerable irritation in army circles, therefore, when the Baltimore *American* published the full details of the movement within twenty-four hours after it began. An order for the arrest of the correspondent who had furnished the *American* with this information soon followed, together with a warning that the correspondents of that newspaper would be removed from the army if the offense were repeated.[13]

One of the other reporters who accompanied McClellan's army on the march, William Swinton of the New York *Times*, could not help noticing how unlike the army of popular fancy this one was as he saw the men go "hulking and shuffling along" without the slightest effort to preserve the trim lines and precision of movement so much in evidence on dress parade:

> I cannot doubt that there is among our men plenty of high and patriotic feeling; but the soldier-habits do not encourage its expression. . . . men march to death and to exploits that live in history, frivolous, light-hearted, jocular or morose as their personal moods and idiosyncracies may be.

There was a note of warning in his next remark:

> *One week after the battle of Antietam we could better have marched to Richmond than we can do now with all our clothing and supplies!*[14]

On Saturday, November 8, while McClellan's troops were somewhere in the neighborhood of Warrenton, momentous news spread through the army. At a late hour the evening before, so the reporters learned, an order from Halleck was handed to "Little Mac" relieving him of command of the Army of the Potomac and directing him to turn it over to his loyal friend, General Burnside. McClellan's friends in the army were convinced that Lincoln had waited until the fall election was over to strike their favorite down. Not until many years later did it become known that the President had already made up his mind to change commanders in the event that McClellan permitted Lee to cross the Blue Ridge and to interpose his command between the Army of the Potomac and Richmond. This Lee had done, as the news of Longstreet's arrival at Culpeper, received in Washington on or shortly before November 5, made clear.[15]

Although news of McClellan's removal reached the capital press corps on Saturday, permission to telegraph the story was withheld until midnight, and strict censorship was applied to all telegraphic comments on the President's action—with one exception. By means best known to himself, the *Herald*'s Washington correspondent managed to slip several paragraphs past a substitute censor on Sunday night, indicating that the wildest excitement had been created in the army by the removal of General McClellan and that many officers of high rank were ready to resign unless the order were rescinded. In the newspaper offices along Fourteenth Street the story went the rounds that the erring censor had left the capital with considerable haste to escape the vengeance of the irate Secretary of War.[16]

There is little doubt that the *Herald* man considerably exaggerated the extent of army dissatisfaction at McClellan's removal. It was true, nevertheless, that several drunken staff officers gave vent to their feelings by assaulting Richardson, correspondent of the anti-McClellan *Tribune*, on the day that McClellan said farewell to his army.[17] In contrast to the *Herald*'s story, an army reporter of the New York *Times* assured his newspaper:

> there will be no resignations on account of the removal of Gen. McClellan. . . . Gen. Burnside, I can assure you, takes command of no demoralized or discontented army. . . .

Another *Times* reporter concurred:

> Any attempt of the disaffected partisan or mischievous among the officers or men to stir up mutiny in the army, will recoil upon their own heads. The heart of the army is sound.[18]

The news of Burnside's appointment to succeed McClellan was received by the army correspondents with mixed feelings. "Measured in the order of pure intellect, Burnside has no claims to first rank," declared *Times* correspondent Swinton, who admitted, nevertheless, that the General had "a profound sense of duty, and an intense solicitude touching what is committed to his charge."[19] This was substantially the reaction of Henry Villard, who sometime late in November had replaced Smalley as chief correspondent of the *Tribune* with the Army of the Potomac. Although Villard was impressed favorably by Burnside's "frank, honest, sincere nature," he could observe nothing in the outward appearance of the General or in his conversation to indicate that he possessed anything more than average ability:

> My fears were heightened when I learned, soon after his elevation was made known, that he had at first declined the promotion, on the ground that he was not qualified for the highest command and that McClellan was the only proper man to lead the Eastern army.[20]

Many people (including Hooker himself) had expected "Fighting Joe" Hooker, as he was now commonly referred to in the press,[21] to receive the command.[22] Villard, therefore, soon after his arrival in the army, interviewed Hooker. There was no question about it; the physical appearance of the man was tremendously impressive. He was, the *Tribune* correspondent recalled long afterward:

> fully six feet high, finely proportioned, with a soldierly, erect carriage. . . . he looked, indeed, like the ideal soldier and captain. . . .[23]

To the correspondent's surprise, after a few preliminary remarks the General launched forth into a tirade of criticism of everyone in the army command, including his own immediate superior. Villard declared:

> His language was so severe and, at the same time, so infused with self-assertion as to give rise immediately to a fear on my part that he might be inclined to make use of me for his own glorification and for the detraction of others.[24]

Prudently the *Tribune* man said nothing about his earlier intention of asking permission to remain at Hooker's headquarters.

Nonetheless, the press continued to regard Hooker as the "coming man." Within a week after Villard's experience, William A. Babcock of the Philadelphia *Inquirer* had an off-the-record interview with Hooker in the presence of his friend, Major General Daniel Butterfield. Babcock was apparently convinced as a result of the interview that Hooker was not politically ambitious, that his primary objectives were the preservation of the Union and the speedy termination of the war, and that he cherished the kindliest feelings toward Burnside. The letter in which the *Inquirer* correspondent imparted the essential details of the interview concluded with a request that his letter be destroyed as soon as it had been read by its recipient "for was it known that I had told all this it would ruin my usefulness as a newspaper correspondent."[25]

The replacement of McClellan by Burnside brought about a complete change in the plan of campaign. At the time of his removal McClellan had been preparing to advance along the so-called interior line toward Richmond, keeping close to the base of the Blue Ridge and thereby forcing Lee to fall back or fight. Burnside now suggested to his superiors a plan for a movement along the North bank of the Rappahannock to Falmouth, opposite Fredericksburg, and the establishment of a new base of supplies at Aquia Creek on the Potomac estuary, fifteen miles north of Falmouth. Neither the President nor General Halleck favored this change of program, although Lincoln thought it might succeed "if you [Burnside] move very rapidly; otherwise not."[26] Burnside was permitted, nevertheless, to go ahead as he had planned.

If quick movement had been the only criterion of success, the new army commander might easily have demonstrated the wisdom of his appointment. On November 15, his army left Warrenton and marched to Falmouth in almost record time. On the eighteenth a correspondent of the New York *Tribune* who accompanied the marching column wrote exultantly:

> Officers wont to believe that a great command cannot move more than six miles a day . . . rub their eyes in mute astonishment. . . .
>
> We have changed our base from the Manassas Railroad to Acquia Creek and the Rappahannock. *We have marched from Warrenton, forty miles, in two days and a half.*[27]

It was a pity that no greater fruits were realized from this unexpectedly rapid movement. So swiftly, in fact, had it been carried out that Lee, whose intelligence was usually superior to that of his adversaries, was still in doubt as late as the eighteenth as to where Burnside was or where he was going.[28] Had the pontoon bridges which the Federal commander confidently expected to find awaiting him at Falmouth been there at the time of his arrival, Fredericksburg in all probability would have been in Union hands by the twentieth, and quite possibly the costly sacrifice of a few weeks later might have been averted. The pontoons did not arrive at Falmouth until November 25. By that time

Longstreet had reached Fredericksburg with approximately half of Lee's army; two days later Stonewall Jackson received orders to march from the Shenandoah Valley to Fredericksburg with the remainder of the army and to take his position close to Longstreet.[29]

Army correspondents and soldiers alike were perplexed by the failure of the army to cross the Rappahannock as the last days of November passed. On the twenty-first an army reporter for the New York *Tribune* sent to his newspaper the gist of a dialogue which he had overheard the day before between two pickets on opposite sides of the river:

"Hallo, Secesh!"

"Hallo, Yank!"

"What was the matter with your battery, Tuesday night?"

"You made it too hot. Your shots drove the cannoneers away, and they hav'n't stopped running yet. We infantry men had to come out and withdraw the guns."

"You infantry men will run, too, one of these fine mornings."

"When are you coming over, blue coat?"

"When we get ready, butternut."

"What do you want?"

"Want Fredericksburg."

"Don't you wish you may get it?"[30]

Believing that the army was about to go into winter quarters, some of the army correspondents returned home. On November 27 the War Department put a damper on such talk by denying the further issue of passes to civilians seeking to visit the army.[31] The newspaper correspondents who had accompanied the army on the march from Warrenton and were still at Falmouth were not affected by the order; those wishing to join the army found themselves marooned in Washington.

On the last day of November, Burnside returned to the army after a two-day visit to Washington, during which he had conferred with his superiors concerning his future plans. Any idea he or anyone else may have had that the campaign was over was dispelled by the President and his advisers, who urged him to cross the Rappahannock and to march on Richmond.[32] On December 3 Swinton wrote in a letter to the *Times*:

> Dismiss with contempt all reports you hear of Winter quarters here. They are nonsense. *We are to have an active, vigorous Winter campaign against Richmond.*[33]

He said nothing in this letter about the foreboding which he had confessed a few days earlier of a "new, but far more terrible Ball's Bluff" in the neighborhood of Fredericksburg.[34]

In spite of Stanton's "new order," the reporters' brigade received reinforcements during the next few days. Among the new arrivals in camp was Coffin of the Boston *Journal,* who came down from Washington on the sixth, and Murat Halstead, who turned up at Falmouth four days later to report the impending battle for the Cincinnati *Commercial.*

On the same night that Halstead arrived, a council of war was held at Burnside's headquarters which resulted in the decision to cross the Rappahannock the next morning in three places and to make a determined effort to gain the rear of Lee's army. While the council was still going on, Halstead called upon a colonel who was an old personal friend and found him at work writing out his will in case he were killed in the coming battle. Catching sight of a cartoon of General McClellan hanging over the colonel's fireplace, the editor of the *Commercial* asked his host whether, in his opinion, the stories that had been widely circulated about the attachment of the Army of the Potomac to McClellan were true. The colonel assured him that they were, that the army was very fond of McClellan and longed to have him again for their commander. In fact, he added, many of the soldiers were firmly convinced that it was McClellan's destiny yet to come back and lead the Army of the Potomac to final victory.

Later that evening, Halstead was invited to a gathering of some of the officers in the colonel's brigade, who had come together to celebrate the recent promotions of several of their number. Whiskey punch was circulated freely, and many patriotic songs were sung. Among them was one styled "The Hills of Old New England," which had a special appeal since the celebrants were New Englanders to a man. Another selection they sang with great gusto was entitled "McClellan's Our Leader, So March Along." In spite of their merriment Halstead sensed the feeling on the part of the singers that this was the night before the battle and in all probability the last on earth for some of them. So much was he impressed that he could not get to sleep, but all night lay awake listening to the heavy rumble and deep metallic jar of the artillery trains moving forward and the quick clatter of horses' feet bearing the General's aides from one point to another.[35]

Long before it was light the bugles summoned the men from their sleep. Tents were struck, knapsacks packed, and regimental property placed in readiness for removal. About an hour before daylight two signal guns were heard from the direction of Fredericksburg, and presently the Federal artillery posted along Stafford Heights overlooking the North bank of the river accepted the challenge. Meanwhile, under cover of darkness and fog, the army engineers were working like mad to finish the five pontoon bridges across the Rappahannock. As the morning advanced the engineers at the upper bridges were driven from their task again and again by fire from three thousand Mississippi sharpshooters hidden in the houses along the South river bank. When it became clear that the engineers would be unable to carry out their mission, General Burnside gave the order for a general bombardment, and twenty-nine batteries of one hundred and forty-seven guns boomed out in one of the greatest artillery bombardments of the war.[36] The correspondent of the Boston *Journal,* who witnessed the spectacle, wrote of it afterward:

> The air became thick with the murky clouds. The earth shook beneath the terrific explosions of the shells, which went howling over the river, crashing into the houses, battering down walls, splintering doors, ripping up floors. Sixty solid shot and shells a minute were thrown, and the bombardment was kept up till nine thousand were fired. No hot shot were used, but the explosions set fire to a block of houses, which added terrible grandeur to the scene.[37]

For almost two hours the bombardment went on. Then, as it died away, the fog lifted, and it became apparent that tremendous though the effort had been it had not been entirely successful. The gunners on Stafford Heights were unable to depress the muzzles of their cannon enough to shell the part of the town nearest the river. As a result, the Confederate sharpshooters were almost unharmed. Several regiments of volunteers now were rushed across the stream in pontoons to rout out the enemy snipers so that the engineers might resume their work.[38]

Among the first boatload sent to establish the bridgehead was Swinton, the New York *Times* correspondent. Although he did not venture any great distance into the town, he entered a dozen or more houses which had been badly damaged by the bombardment and talked with several of the townspeople who had taken refuge in their cellars. Later he brought back to Falmouth as a trophy a rifle still loaded, which he had removed from the grasp of a headless corpse.[39] Meanwhile, the advance party had succeeded, after a brisk fight, in dislodging the Confederates from their vantage point, making it possible for the engineers to complete their task. By this time the day was nearly over, and hostilities were suspended until the next morning.

Both Sumner and Franklin crossed the river with their divisions on the morning of the twelfth, while Hooker remained on the North bank in command of the reserve force. The built-up portion of the town extending for not more than a dozen blocks along and perhaps five blocks back from the river was soon overcrowded with masses of infantry, mounted men, guns, and vehicles. Yet the enemy batteries in the rear of Fredericksburg remained ominously silent, and the army correspondents wondered why. One officer ventured the opinion that the enemy had no ammunition to spare. Another thought that the enemy was afraid to provoke reprisals. A third hazarded the guess that General Lee was playing for the sympathies of Europe and was out to capitalize on the moral indignation which Burnside's bombardment of Fredericksburg might excite in European circles. Still a fourth soldier, a private, came nearest to the truth in Halstead's estimation when he remarked with a sprinkling of profanity, "They want us to get in. Getting out won't be quite so smart and easy. You'll see if it will."[40]

Sporadic cannonading took place throughout the day, but no full-scale attack was mounted. During the forenoon a detachment of Confederate cavalry succeeded in cutting the telegraph wires between Fredericksburg and Alexandria, causing a temporary news blackout in the capital.[41] At about ten o'clock that evening, Villard rode to Burnside's headquarters, hoping to pick up some information concerning the program for the next day. There he found a large crowd of general and staff officers in attendance. Some were there to confer with the Commanding General; others were awaiting their orders. Villard deduced from their conversation that a general attack might be expected in the morning, but he was unable to learn the precise hour. For reasons of security this was not announced until shortly before the order of attack was issued.[42]

On Saturday morning, December 13, a thick blue haze hung low over Fredericksburg. Posted on the heights back of the town seventy-two thousand Confederates faced a Union army of approximately one hundred and thirteen thousand. At General Sumner's headquarters in the Phillips Mansion a large number of officers and several reporters were gathered to greet General Burnside when he reined up at about nine o'clock. At about nine-thirty the first gun was fired from the Union left where Major General William B. Franklin was in command.[43] Leaving

Sumner's headquarters, Coffin hurried toward the left, where the battle was about to open. There he saw Franklin's Grand Division in line, with John F. Reynolds' First Corps on the extreme left and Major General William F. Smith, now commanding Franklin's old Sixth Corps, next to it. Descending the hill where General Tyler had his batteries, Coffin crossed the river and observed the familiar signs of the bloody work which had already commenced; the cavalry and lancers drawn up on the bank, the surgeons setting up their hospitals close by, and the provost guard on watch to prevent any stragglers from reaching the opposite side of the river.[44]

Up until eleven o'clock there had been no activity on the right. Burnside had not intended that Sumner should advance against Longstreet until Franklin had occupied the ridge in his front, his primary objective. Now, however, "feeling the importance of haste," the commanding general ordered Sumner to attack Marye's Hill, a nearly impregnable position. The brunt of the attack fell upon Darius Couch's Second Corps. William H. French's division of Couch's corps was the first to issue from the town and advance in column across an open plain toward the enemy lines. Midway in its advance the division crossed a ditch, which carried off the waste water from a canal, and then deployed for the assault at a distance of only three hundred yards from the enemy's front line. At the base of Marye's Hill the attacking column was confronted by a sunken road bordered on each side by a retaining wall, breast high, which provided an admirable protection for the Confederate riflemen.[45]

From the rifle pits studding the slope near the crest, from the batteries tier above tier on the terraces, from the enfilading cannon distributed along the arc of a circle two miles in length burst forth a deadly fire which opened great holes in French's line. Hancock's and Oliver O. Howard's divisions, ordered up to support French, experienced the same fate. Men staggered, dropped, died. In vain the Union artillery attempted to give support to the movement. In his letter to the *Commercial,* Halstead wrote:

> I saw with horror that at least half the shells were bursting behind our own men, and that they were certainly killing more of them than the enemy. Gen. Burnside, I have since learned, sent orders to the battery to cease firing, and it did so.[46]

It should have been apparent from the very beginning that the Confederate position was too strong to be carried by a direct assault, but several more efforts were made. First Sam Sturgis' division of Wilcox's corps was thrown in and then the two splendid divisions of Charles Griffin and Andrew A. Humphreys from Butterfield's corps. But they too were unable to reach the stone barrier, and finally were forced to give way after sustaining fearful losses. Six separate assaults were made before the fighting was over in that quarter of the field.[47] Commented a Southern army correspondent:

> The Yankees had essayed a task which no army . . . could have accomplished. To have driven our men from their position and to have taken it, was a work compared with which the storming of Gibraltar would be as child's play. . . . No other man than Burnside would have attempted so difficult or so foolhardy an adventure.[48]

Reports from the left were hardly more encouraging. Although the Confederate positon at that point was somewhat weaker, Franklin's orders from Burnside led him to attack much less aggressively than the situation called for. Meade's division, supported by John Gibbon's, succeeded in penetrating the enemy's line for about a mile and gained the crest of the hill upon which the enemy was posted, capturing several hundred prisoners. Strong counterattacks were launched against the Federals, however, by Stonewall Jackson, who was in command of the Confederate troops in that quarter of the field. As a result Meade's men were driven back with heavy loss through the ranks of Birney's division, which reformed in turn and pushed the Confederates back to the woods beyond the Richmond, Fredericksburg, and Potomac Railroad. While this was going on, for no apparent reason, Smith's corps, the largest in the entire army, was permitted to remain inactive. In fact, no more than three of Franklins' eight divisions, numbering sixty thousand men altogether, were engaged offensively that day.[49]

Night ended the flaming ordeal. More than twelve thousand Union soldiers—killed, wounded, and missing—had paid the price of the futile assault.

Villard, who had watched most of the fighting on the right from a crest on the plateau above Fredericksburg, left the field at about three-thirty in the afternoon and headed for the rear. At the time he was fearful for the safety of the army, being afraid that the enemy was about to launch a vigorous counterattack against the decimated Union lines on the right. Near some buildings which had been converted into hospitals for the "Irish Brigade" he came upon its commander, General

Meagher, with about three hundred men, some wounded, others in good condition. Villard asked the General what he was doing. Meagher replied, "This is all that is left of my 1200 men, and I am going to take them to the other [the North] side of the river." Later Villard discovered that the leader of the Irish Brigade had left his command that morning while going to the front and had executed a retrograde movement on the pretext that he had a bad knee and was forced to go back for his horse![50]

From conversations with Hooker, Couch, Butterfield, and others, Villard became even more convinced of the seriousness of the situation. At about six o'clock he returned from Fredericksburg to Burnside's headquarters on the North bank of the river to collect reports from his three assistants.[51] The first came in at seven o'clock with a very meager and unsatisfactory account of the fighting on the left. The second put in an appearance at nine with what Villard regarded as a worthless report of happenings in the Center Grand Division of the Army. The performance of the third man, who had been assigned the task of compiling casualty lists, was equally disappointing. Under the circumstances Villard felt obliged to work until nearly midnight gathering further information from the officers who came in to headquarters during the evening. Other newspapermen were experiencing similar difficulties; among them was William A. Babcock of the Philadelphia *Inquirer,* who sent off a telegram from Aquia Creek to Painter in Washington the following day, saying:

> I am back from the front & being unable to find any of our Correspondents can only send a disjointed account. Bowers[52] says nothing had better be sent & wants to know what is to be done with the three correspondents who have acted so shamefully. Heard of Wallington[52] as being out riding.[53]

Meanwhile, Villard had made plans to set out for the capital later that night (December 13) after getting a few hours rest. In the back of his mind was the fear, produced by conversations with some of Burnside's staff officers, that they might not be fully aware of the deadly peril of the army and that they might even advise a renewal of the attack the next morning. The thought occurred to him of going to Burnside and urging him to extricate his army before it was too late. He abandoned this idea, however, when he learned, about eight o'clock in the evening, that the General in Chief had made arrangements to see Generals

Sumner and Hooker and their corps commanders and discuss with them the condition of their commands. It seemed hardly probable that under existing circumstances they would advise the resumption of hostilities. Thus reassured, Villard concluded that it would be best for him to lose no time in heading north with an account of what had happened that day, especially since Burnside had already forbidden the use of the telegraph for conveying news of the defeat. Speed and a fair amount of luck might enable him to achieve a great scoop for the *Tribune* by providing it with exclusive first news.

When he awoke from his nap it was about 3:00 A.M. on Sunday morning and so dark outside that he could hardly see anything beyond his horse's head. The road to Aquia Creek was a trackless mire. Occasionally horse and rider stumbled upon patches of corduroy, but since the logs were loose they only increased the hazards of the journey. Once Villard pitched from his horse into a mudhole. Gradually the sky became lighter, and it was now possible to mark the route by following the debris left by army trains. Villard had hoped to complete the first leg of the journey in three or four hours, but it was nine o'clock before he reached Aquia Creek and sat down to a substantial breakfast given him by the quartermaster at the supply depot. It was cheering to learn that none of his rivals had yet appeared on the scene, but his elation vanished when he learned that the quartermaster had received orders from General Burnside not to allow anyone attached to the army, especially any newspaper correspondent, to proceed North without a special permit from his (Burnside's) headquarters. Villard was still more chagrined when the reporter for the Boston *Journal* stuck his head in the quartermaster's tent just as the weary *Tribune* man was finishing his breakfast. How to circumvent Burnside's order and give Coffin the slip at the same time became a problem of paramount importance. In his perplexity Villard wandered up and down the long dock, pondering various methods of escape.

Finally he caught sight of two Negroes in a fishing boat who were just about to shove off from the dock. It occurred to him that they might be induced to row him out far enough into the Potomac that he might obtain passage on one of the steamboats plying between the capital and Hampton Roads. It would never do, however, for Coffin to become aware of his plan. Returning to the quartermaster's, he discovered to his great satisfaction that the correspondent of the *Journal* was fast asleep on a camp bed. Hurrying back to the landing, Villard hailed the Negroes and enlisted their cooperation. Slowly the small craft, with Villard aboard, moved out into the middle of the stream. Presently a steam vessel carrying freight came in sight. Cupping his hands as they drew alongside, Villard hailed the captain of the freighter and asked to be taken aboard. The captain asked Villard if he had a transportation order, explaining that he was not authorized to carry passengers without one. Foreseeing that he was about to be refused, the *Tribune* correspondent seized a rope hanging from the side of the propeller, pulled himself aboard, and tossed some greenbacks to the oarsmen, bidding them depart as quickly as possible. At first the captain was highly indignant. He calmed down somewhat after he had been shown the correspondent's general pass, however, and had been given to understand that he would be protected if any trouble arose because of his failure to comply with Burnside's order.

Now that he was clearly ahead of all his rivals Villard felt confident again. The boat was making very slow progress against the current, and it appeared likely that it would not reach Washington before seven or eight o'clock that night. At least there was time to clean up, get some sleep, and prepare his notes for transmission by mail or telegraph.[54]

In Washington the optimistic mood based on wire reports received at the capital during the night had not yet given way to doubts and forebodings of disaster. From the reports received at the telegraph office up until noon on Sunday it appeared that Franklin had driven the Confederates a full mile, that Sumner had captured their first line of works, and that Hooker, held in reserve up to this time, would attack that morning. The telegraph also intimated that the army was in good spirits and needed no reinforcement. Even more exciting was a story, originating with the Philadelphia *Press,* which indicated that General Banks had landed with twenty thousand troops on the coast of Eastern North Carolina and was marching on Richmond from the South. To one prominent Washington figure, who visited the War Department that day, such reports were not altogether convincing, however. That evening Gideon Welles confided to his diary:

> When I get nothing clear and explicit at the War Department I have my apprehensions. They fear to admit disastrous truths. Adverse tidings are suppressed, with a deal of fuss and mystery, a shuffling over of papers and maps, and a far-reaching vacant gaze at something undefined and indescribable.[55]

By evening, news flashes indicating that the battle had not been renewed that day and that Sumner, instead of gaining ground, had been repulsed gave grounds for pessimistic doubts to others besides the Secretary of the Navy.

Before he left the boat that evening, Villard pressed a fifty-dollar bill into the captain's hands and thanked him warmly for his kindness. Then, as the vessel eased alongside the wharf he leaped to the dock and ran to the *Tribune*'s Fourteenth Street office, where he learned that under no circumstances would the government censor allow his battle report to pass over the telegraph to New York. Under the circumstances, to send it by special messenger on the night train to New York appeared to be the best course.

To Villard's dismay, the editor of the *Tribune* was afraid to publish his battle account as it stood. Villard had not minced words. His letter stated baldly that the Army of the Potomac had sustained another great defeat, that those in charge of the Army had committed an inexcusable blunder by making a frontal attack upon fortifications of such strength as those on the heights above Fredericksburg, and that the Union cause was threatened with disaster as a result of the perilous situation of the army. To guard against reprisals from the War Department, Villard's story of Fredericksburg was considerably watered down before it was published in a *Tribune* extra on the morning of the fifteenth.[56]

The editor might well have spared himself the trouble of tampering with Villard's battle account, for other army correspondents wrote in similarly strong language about the slaughter which they had witnessed. "In spite of all the glosses of official telegrams which you may receive, it seems here to-night that we have suffered a defeat," wrote the *Times* correspondent, Swinton, adding:

> Never for a moment did we . . . suppose that it [the enemy position] would ever be attempted to be taken by hurling masses of men against those works. We had supposed that the resources of strategy would assuredly afford other means of accomplishing the desired end.[57]

Halstead, in the account of the battle which he contributed to the Cincinnati *Commercial*, wrote:

> It can hardly be in human nature for men to show more valor, or Generals to manifest less judgment, than were perceptible on our side that day. . . . We did not take a battery or silence a gun. We did not reach the crest of the hights [sic] held by the enemy

> in a single place. . . . The occupation of Fredericksburg was a blunder. . . .[58]

After Villard had sent off his account, he went to Willard's Hotel for supper. There he met Senator Henry Wilson of Massachusetts, chairman of the Military Affairs Committee in the Senate, who had the reputation among the local correspondents of being the most persistent newshunter in Washington. As soon as he caught sight of Villard, Wilson bombarded him with questions about the outcome of the battle and the condition of the Army. Villard replied:

> Senator, you know whatever news I have belong to my paper, but, for the sake of the cause, I will tell you in strict confidence that Burnside is defeated, and in such a bad plight that I think you can render no greater service to the country than to go at once to the White House and tell the President, if he does not know what has happened on the Rappahannock, to make an immediate demand for the truth. You can state further to him that, as I believe he knows me to be a truthful man, I do not hesitate to say to him, through you, that, in my deliberate judgment, he ought not to wait for information, but instantly order the army back to the north bank.[59]

After some further conversation, the Senator left for the White House. Villard finished his supper and went back to the *Tribune*'s Washington office. Hardly had he arrived there when Senator Wilson reappeared with the information that President Lincoln wanted him to come to the White House at once. The two men went together to the Executive Mansion and were ushered into the old reception room opposite the landing, where the President greeted them heartily, saying to Villard, "I am much obliged to you for coming, for we are very anxious and have heard very little."[60] The *Tribune* correspondent gave as full an account of what he had seen as he could within a few minutes. During the next half hour the President asked him one question after another, using great care to avoid anything like censure of those concerned, but his face betrayed his growing anxiety. Finally the interview came to a close, and as Villard started to leave he remarked somewhat diffidently to the President that he thought no greater service to the country could be rendered than to order General Burnside to withdraw his army at once to the North bank of the Rappahannock if he had not already done so. Lincoln rejoined with a melancholy smile, "I hope it is not so bad as all that," but displayed no resentment.[61]

Villard did not know that only a few minutes before, after receiving an oral report as to the army's condition from Brigadier General Herman Haupt, Lincoln in fact had requested Halleck to issue such an order. Halleck had demurred, however, on the ground that the general in command of the army was the best judge of "existing conditions,"[62] and so Burnside was permitted to work out his own salvation without interference from Washington. On the morning of the fourteenth Burnside was still in favor of renewing the attack on the same ground and was prepared to lead his old Ninth Corps in person against the Confederate position on Marye's Hill. This idea was vetoed by his subordinates, not one of whom would grant it any chance of success. On the night of the fifteenth, after a forty-eight hour pause, the battered Army of the Potomac recrossed to the North side of the river in what one of the New York *Times* correspondents accurately described as "one of the most adroit and successful military escapades during this eventful war."[63] Meanwhile, as a result of the censorship, the news of the bloody repulse at Fredericksburg had been kept from the public for at least twenty-four hours after it had been known and fully discussed inside Washington.[64]

As soon as the full extent of the disaster became known, a great outcry arose against the inaccurate reporting fostered by the censorship. In an editorial that appeared three days after the battle the editor of the New York *Evening Post* queried:

> Who is it that prepares or supervises the telegraphic reports from the seat of war? Whoever he be, we can assure him that he does his work very imperfectly or very knavishly.[65]

In another blast against the censorship published sometime later, the Washington correspondent of the New York *Times* declared:

> After the recent battle at Fredericksburgh [sic], every effort was made by the correspondents there to transmit the facts speedily to their respective papers; and every effort was made by the Government to prevent them from doing so. The telegraphic wires were forbidden, except to the most meagre statements . . . and reporters were compelled to run a blockade more strict than that of Charleston Harbor, in order to carry through the accounts they had written on the spot.[66]

Almost alone in affecting to regard the censorship as of little consequence was the New York *Herald*, which bragged that it had obtained an abundance of news concerning the Fredericksburg disaster in spite of the obstacles placed in the way of its reporters.[67]

The difficulties which the Associated Press underwent in reporting the battle were well depicted, many years later, by L. A. Gobright, the Washington agent of the AP. According to Gobright, the censor at first refused to permit him to telegraph a word about a battle having been fought at Fredericksburg nor would he even allow a telegram to be sent off stating that wounded men had arrived from the Rappahannock. The most that the AP man was allowed to transmit was the information that "a number of wounded men have arrived here."[68] Several days later the government provided the Associated Press with a careful statement (which had been approved by General Burnside) of the losses suffered by the Army of the Potomac. Then at the last minute one of the censors had a change of heart and ordered the statement suppressed. By accident a correspondent of one of the Baltimore newspapers got a copy of this important document before it had been recalled and forwarded it to his newspaper by mail. The War Department learned of this too late to take action in time, so that in spite of the censorship the official statement of casualties was published in Baltimore five days after the battle![69]

The confusion in the public mind created by the news blackout hardly could have been any greater than that existing within the ranks of the Philadelphia *Inquirer*'s army staff, if one is to judge from a telegram sent four days after the battle to the *Inquirer*'s Washington office from one of its correspondents at Aquia Creek:

> Have telegraphed to Clark.[70] Wallington[70] is here sick. Is coming home in the morning. No lists have been forwarded me of the Penna losses. I cannot hear anything of your brother, do not know where Davis[70] is. By Saturday our forces will be reduced to one man.[71]

Two days earlier the same reporter had been so disgusted with the performance of his colleagues that he was halfway disposed to "shut up shop and come home."[72]

None of the newspaper accounts of the Battle of Fredericksburg could compare with Smalley's stirring story of Antietam or Reid's narrative of Shiloh. Swinton's letter to the New York *Times* probably was the best,[73] although creditable performances were turned in by Villard,[74] Coffin,[75] and Halstead.[76] The description of the battle which appeared in the New York *Times* was so brutally frank that General Burnside completely lost his self-control when he read it. Summoning Swinton to his tent, he threatened to shoot him or run him through with his sword. Fortunately for the *Times* man, the editor of the New York *Times* happened along just then and managed to placate the general.[77]

As usual, the *Herald* reporters greatly exaggerated the size of Lee's army. One of them, in fact, avowed that beyond a doubt the Confederate army at Fredericksburg numbered nearly two hundred thousand men![78] The strength of that army was, in reality, hardly more than one third of the *Herald* man's estimate.

Contemporary opinion of the performance of the *Herald* reporters at Fredericksburg varied. In a letter written four days after the battle General Meade told his wife:

> You must . . . look to the newspapers for the details [of the battle], although as usual they seem to ignore the Pennsylvania Reserves, except the New York *Herald*, which I understand says that we ran scandalously at the first fire of the enemy. This is the harder, because I saw the *Herald* correspondent on the field, and he might have known and indeed did know better. What his object in thus falsifying facts was I cannot imagine, but I would advise him not to show himself in our camp if he values his skin, for the men could not be restrained from tarring and feathering him.[79]

More than a year later, however, General Birney stated in a private letter to James Gordon Bennett:

> the report of your faithful correspondent Mr. Anderson, who was present at Fredericksburg, and saw the repulse of the Pennsylvania Reserves and the conduct of my troops was a very true one.[80]

After they had recovered from the first effects of their disappointment, Radical newspapers, such as the New York *Tribune*, the Chicago *Tribune*, the Philadelphia *Press*, and the Cincinnati *Gazette*, did their best to combat the idea that the battle had proved disastrous. On December 16, Forney sent a wire to the managing editor of the *Press* from Washington saying, "Dont treat the affair at Fredericksburg as a disaster."[81] Accordingly the *Press* informed its readers on the following day that:

> we are gratified beyond measure in being enabled to assure the country . . . that the wild rumors of defeat and disaster are with-

out foundation, and that it [the army] is still anxious and ready to move against the enemy.[82]

Such opposition newspapers as the New York *World, Herald,* and *Express,* on the other hand, bitterly attacked Stanton and Halleck for their "mismanagement" and placed the blame for the failure upon their shoulders.[83] To some extent the ground was cut from under these editorial criticisms by General Burnside, who wrote a letter to General Halleck on December 19 (which the press subsequently published) courageously assuming the blame for the Fredericksburg disaster. So frank was his admission, the newspaper correspondents started a rumor that he had made it under orders.[84] Few people realized at the time that this very quality of transparent honesty largely had been responsible for his elevation to the command of the army.

Meanwhile Villard of the *Tribune* was engaging in a small private skirmish. As though it were not sufficiently annoying to have had his bitterly critical report of Fredericksburg watered down, his expense account, including an item for fifty dollars paid the freighter captain, was questioned. When Villard had presented his accounting to Sam Wilkeson in Washington, Wilkeson became very angry and struck Villard. Villard then, according to Richardson, knocked down Wilkeson two or three times. Wilkeson later apologized, however, and good feeling was restored.[85]

After the Battle of Fredericksburg some of the correspondents returned home; others remained in the great city of log huts which sprang up in the dense forests around Falmouth. To them, as to the discouraged men in the ranks, the end of the war must have seemed more remote than ever, although Lee was assured, upon his return to Richmond, by the Confederate government that "in thirty or forty days we would be recognized and peace proclaimed."[86] For some time at least the principal theme of army news seemed likely to be "All quiet along the Rappahannock."

14

By-Lines by General Order

ON a Thursday evening in the middle of January, 1863, the New York *Times* editor, Henry J. Raymond, received a telegram from the *Times* Bureau in Washington, conveying the sad news that his brother's corpse was at Belle Plain[1] and asking him to come to Washington immediately. Raymond's younger brother James was a soldier in the Army of the Potomac. Knowing that he had been ill, the editor left for Washington at once. When he arrived at the capital the following day, he was unable to find Colonel Swain, the author of the telegram; so he went down to the army without any further delay to make arrangements for his brother's funeral. To his utter consternation no one at Belle Plain could tell him where his brother's body was to be found; in the midst of his perplexity, the brother himself appeared.

In its original form, Swain's telegram had stated that the brother's *corps* was at Belle Plain, and that he wished Raymond to come immediately as he was planning to send a boat there at once. Raymond could thank a stupid clerk in the telegraph office for some anxious moments and for making sure that the editor of the New York *Times* would be with the Army of the Potomac at one of the most critical hours in its and the nation's history.[2]

In the dark days following the disaster at Fredericksburg, the Army of the Potomac seemed to have lost faith in its leadership. Burnside had continued to make plans for another advance, but it was clear that none of his general officers favored such a move. Even Lincoln had advised him to be cautious and not to feel that the government or the country was pushing him. There was some conflict in the statements of the army correspondents as to army morale. Coffin, an invincible optimist, had maintained that the folks back home were more discouraged than the men in the army.[3] Babcock of the Philadelphia *Inquirer* also had asserted that the army was not demoralized, but added:

> . . . that they are anxious, eager, and willing to meet the enemy is *not so.* On the contrary the animosity that once existed between the two armies is fast dying out. Each think well of each other, and the majority of our troops are willing to lay down their arms and make peace upon any terms.[4]

Raymond consequently remained in camp for several days to form his own opinion of army morale and to watch the opening of what was later to be called the "mud campaign." He spent his first night in the army at the headquarters of Major General James S. Wadsworth, from whom he gathered the impression that most of the discontent was manifested by certain officer protegés of McClellan who hoped for his return. On the following day the editor visited the camp of one of the Michigan regiments, which he found to be comfortably housed and anything but anxious to undertake a winter campaign. Their colonel alluded to the lack of confidence in Burnside which was common to both officers and men and added that this was traceable in large part to the General's lack of confidence in himself. Raymond suggested that perhaps this was simply the natural modesty of a capable man, but the colonel could not see it that way. Burnside, the colonel thought, had not simply admitted that he was incompetent; he had sworn to the fact before a Congressional Committee; and therefore the army needed a new head and a complete reorganization.

That evening Raymond rode over to Burnside's headquarters, where he found the General in a hospitable mood and willing to talk about the movement which he originally had planned for the following Tuesday morning, January 20, 1863. Because of objections by several subordinate commanders, Burnside frankly told the editor, the movement had been postponed for twenty-four hours. On the Tuesday morning originally selected for the advance the General and his guest went for a promenade together. Raymond listened sympathetically while Burnside again enlarged on the difficulties he was having with his officers—Generals Franklin and William F. Smith among others—who seemed to think that any movement at this time was predestined to failure. So violent was the opposition of these two that Burnside had considered removing them, but in view of the difficulty of replacing them at this late hour, he finally had decided to order them back to their commands.

That evening a light rain began to fall; then the wind rose, and the rain became a driving sleet. The crossing of the Rappahannock scheduled for daybreak had to be abandoned. Artillery, pontoons, baggage wagons, ambulances—all were hopelessly mired, and everything was at a standstill. Meanwhile Franklin, Hooker, and others continued to object to the General's plan and seemed to be doing everything in their power to thwart it.

The big news at army headquarters on Wednesday morning was an order received from the War Department, calling for the arrest and removal to Washington of Sid Deming, the chief correspondent of the Associated Press with the Army of the Potomac. Deming and Theodore Barnard, his principal assistant, it was said, were guilty of having communicated unsatisfactory accounts of army morale to the press. At least one of their fellow-correspondents, S. M. Carpenter of the *Herald*, believed that Stanton had reasons of his own for taking such drastic action:

> No man more fully enjoyed the confidence of the officers at Headquarters, and a more loyal man I believe does not exist. The Secret of his arrest it is alleged is, that he was too warm an admirer of Gen. McClellan. I believe from what I have seen that such is the case. . . . The head of the war office is framing his own guillotine, and a spirit is breeding in this army that will work mischief with those in authority, unless a change of programme is introduced soon.[5]

On the following morning, after breakfasting with Burnside, Raymond encountered Swinton, the New York *Times* correspondent, who informed him that Hooker had talked very openly about the absurdity of Wednesday's movement. According to Swinton, Hooker had denounced Burnside as incompetent and the government at Washington as "imbecile" and "played out." Hooker was quoted as saying that nothing would go right until we had a dictator and the sooner the better.[6]

At about twelve o'clock Raymond rode forward to the advance line and talked with General Wadsworth and several other officers. His friend Wadsworth seemed cheerful and by no means disposed to abandon the idea of an advance. On returning to headquarters at about five o'clock in the afternoon, the editor learned that, as a result of a telegraphic snub from General Halleck, Burnside had given up his intention of going to Washington that day. After dinner Raymond was called into Burnside's tent, where he found the General in a rage over a paragraph in one of Swinton's newspaper letters. The offense consisted of a statement that Burnside had written his letter assuming full responsibility for the outcome of the Battle of Fredericksburg at the dictation of or in connivance with the Government. General Burnside indignantly denied that he had voiced any untruth at the bidding of the Government or had sought to shield anyone from a responsibility rightfully belonging to such a person. The real facts, he asserted, were as follows:

On December 20, 1862, William Conant Church, one of the New York *Times* correspondents, had returned to the army from Washington with a parcel of newspapers which contained violent attacks on Burnside's superiors, notably Lincoln, Stanton, and Halleck, for having forced him to fight against his better judgment. Burnside said he would put a stop to that sort of thing at once by sending a statement to the Associated Press making clear that he alone was responsible for what had occurred. Several of his staff officers, who thought it was not his place to undertake a defense of the Government, suggested that he consult Lincoln before making any such statement. This he had done; only then had the statement been released to the press with the full approval of the President, who was greatly relieved at having the responsibility for the disaster removed from his shoulders.[7]

On Saturday evening, January 24, Raymond left for Washington with Burnside, traveled all night, and arrived at six o'clock the next morning. In spite of the failure of the "mud campaign," Burnside had made up his mind to remove Hooker, Franklin, and several other insubordinate officers. He already had drafted an order to this effect and was prepared to submit his resignation if the President should not approve the order.

Early that morning Raymond called upon Secretary Chase, who seemed surprised to hear what the editor had to say about Hooker. Chase declared that up to that time he had looked upon Hooker as probably the best qualified man to command the Army of the Potomac, but that obviously no man capable of so much selfish and unprincipled ambition was fit for so great a trust. Later Raymond accompanied Chase to the President's levee and repeated to Lincoln the same opinions he had communicated to Chase. Thereupon Lincoln rejoined, "That is all true—Hooker does talk badly; but the trouble is, he is stronger with the country to-day than any other man." Raymond ventured to ask him how long Hooker would retain that strength when his real conduct and character were revealed. "The country," gloomily replied Lincoln, "would not believe it; they would say it is all a lie."[8]

During the afternoon Raymond called at the State Department, where he was warmly greeted by Secretary Seward, who was very anxious to know what the condition of affairs was in the army. Raymond said he thought the men in the ranks were both loyal and sound and army demoralization was confined to the officers. Seward then asked Raymond if he was satisfied with Burnside as commander of the army. Raymond parried this question by saying that military considerations which he was in no position to understand were involved. But Seward was not to be put off so easily. He insisted that Raymond was as good a judge as he, and he was "obliged" to have an opinion. Raymond then told him that according to his best judgment Burnside ought to be retained in command and at the same time be invested with all the powers requisite to that position. Raymond's advice was destined to be passed over, however, for Lincoln already had made up his mind to relieve Burnside and to replace him with General Hooker. Within a few hours the story of the change in commanders was released to the press in time for the Tuesday morning editions of January 27.

The appointment of "Fighting Joe" Hooker to the command of the Army of the Potomac was a generally popular one, although there were sour notes in some quarters. Said a New York *Times* correspondent:

> The appointment of Gen. Hooker . . . is variously received by the army. To speak truthfully, confidence in the powers at the Capital have become so impaired that the soldiers have come to regard all the changes and plans with indifference. Every one, however, feels that the new General will do one or two things, and that right speedily—destroy the rebel army, or our own.[9]

The chief *Herald* correspondent with the Army of the Potomac, S. M. Carpenter, was equally caustic. In a letter to Frederic Hudson, written only a few days after Hooker had assumed command, he observed that the new commander had estimated that he needed only five days in which to whip Lee and only fifteen days to bring about the capture of Richmond, but:

> Seven days have elapsed, and Lee is unwhipped. Eight days remain for the capture of the rebel Capital, but unless we do some tall marching we shall hardly reach the James by the 10th.[10]

Hooker, like McClellan, was a capable organizer; and as a result of his energetic management the army soon was restored to a healthy fighting condition. A system of furloughs was introduced to meet the problem of desertion. The clumsy grand divisions of the army which had prevailed under Burnside were abolished, and the infantry was organized into seven corps. A cavalry corps of three divisions made its appearance for the first time. By the end of April, 1863, "Fighting Joe" had the largest, best equipped, and best organized army which yet had appeared in the war.[11]

During the first week of April, Noah Brooks, the Washington correspondent of the Sacramento (California) *Union,* accompanied the President, Mrs. Lincoln, and their youngest son, Tad, on a visit to the Army of the Potomac. The trip had been postponed for several days because of bad weather, and as the presidential party left the Washington Navy Yard on its way down the Potomac, a brisk snow storm was in progress. At Aquia Creek, the President and the others left the steamer and climbed aboard an ordinary freight car equipped with rough plank benches but resplendent with flags and bunting. At army headquarters in Falmouth station they were greeted by Major General Daniel Butterfield, Hooker's chief of staff, and were allotted three large hospital tents fitted out in the best army style. While they were guests of Hooker, several grand reviews of the Army of the Potomac were held, that of the entire cavalry corps on April 6 being the most impressive. Later Brooks recalled with sadness the nonchalant attitude which Hooker had displayed on several occasions while in the company of the presidential party. One of his most common expressions was "When I get to Richmond" or "After we have taken Richmond." Observing this, Lincoln remarked quietly to Brooks, "That is the most depressing thing about Hooker. It seems to me that he is over-confident."[12]

One night, when no one else was present, Hooker said to the newspaperman, with a quizzical expression, "The President tells me that you know all about the letter he wrote to me when he put me in command of this army." Brooks replied that Lincoln had in fact read it to him. Thereupon Hooker pulled the letter out of his pocket and asked, "Wouldn't you like to hear it again?" The correspondent admitted that he would, although he remarked that he had been so much impressed upon hearing it for the first time that he believed he could repeat the greater part of it from memory. Hooker nodded. Standing in front of his spacious fireplace with his back to the fire, his bright blue eyes sparkling with animation, he began to read:

> I have placed you at the head of the Army of the Potomac. Of course I have done this upon what appear to me to be sufficient reasons, and yet I think it best for you to know that there are some things in regard to which I am not quite satisfied with you. I believe you to be a brave and skillful soldier, which, of course,

> I like. I also believe you do not mix politics with your profession, in which you are right. You have confidence in yourself, which is a valuable, if not an indispensable, quality. You are ambitious, which, within reasonable bounds, does good rather than harm; but I think during Burnside's command of the army you took counsel of your ambition, and thwarted him as much as you could, in which you did a great wrong to the country and to a most meritorious and honorable brother officer.

At this point Hooker stopped and exclaimed with some heat:

> The President is mistaken. I never thwarted Burnside in any way, shape, or manner. Burnside was preëminently a man of deportment: he fought the battle of Fredericksburg on his deportment; he was defeated on his deportment; and he took his deportment with him out of the Army of the Potomac, thank God!

As he resumed his reading of the President's letter, his tone softened at once, and he obviously was affected by the concluding sentence, "Beware of rashness, but with energy and sleepless vigilance, go forward and give us victories." He folded the document and placed it in his breast pocket, remarking to Brooks as he did so:

> That is just such a letter as a father might write to his son. It is a beautiful letter, and, although I think he was harder on me than I deserved, I will say that I love the man who wrote it.

Following a momentary pause, he added, "After I have got to Richmond, I shall give that letter to you to have published."[13] The letter was published, eventually, but not under the circumstances visualized by Hooker.[14]

Another newspaper man, Edwin F. Denyse of the New York *Herald*, by this time also had met Hooker, but under considerably less favorable circumstances. In a letter published in the *Herald* on March 14 the luckless reporter had written unguardedly of "unmistakeable preparations now being made for a speedy movement of the army" and had stated further that "no one in the army doubts [the movement] will come at the earliest possible moment." On the sixteenth, his letter meanwhile having been called to Hooker's attention, Denyse was clapped under arrest and, after a formal hearing before a military commission, sentenced to six months hard labor in the Quartermaster's Department. Subsequently Hooker commuted the *Herald* man's sentence to transportation outside the lines.[15] There was a pertinent warning in Denyse's experience for any newspaperman who took it upon himself to disclose the plans of the army commander.

* * *

While preparations were being made for the spring campaign of the Army of the Potomac, the editorial offices of the leading newspapers were buzzing with rumors of an impending attack by sea upon Charleston, South Carolina. Many months before, Assistant Secretary of the Navy Fox had helped to lend credence to such talk by his statement to a congressional committee that once the "Virginia" was disposed of, the Navy "would have no hesitation in taking the 'Monitor' right into Charleston."[16] There was no important military or naval objective to be gained by an attack on the "Cradle of Secession." In view of the disastrous effect a steady succession of military defeats had had on the public morale, however, the Government was inclined to regard with favor the new journalistic chant, "On to Charleston."[17]

Under the erroneous supposition that preparations for the attack were nearly complete, the *Tribune* correspondent, Henry Villard, left New York on January 14, 1863, bound for Port Royal, South Carolina. Among his fellow passengers on the slow-paced "Arago" was Major General Hunter, commander of the Department of the South. Hunter, a septuagenarian, who sported a full dark brown wig and a short moustache of the same color, was returning to command after a prolonged absence in Washington. Upon their arrival at Hilton Head, South Carolina, after a rough trip of four days, Villard made it his business to become acquainted with the officers of the fleet who were stationed there, not one of whom he knew. He was especially impressed by Rear Admiral DuPont, then in command of the South Atlantic Blockading Squadron, "one of the stateliest, handsomest, and most polished gentlemen I ever met."[18] During his first visit to DuPont, Villard attempted to find out whether Charleston was soon to be attacked. To this the Admiral cautiously replied that "the fleet was not quite ready for it." His answer was evidently a considerable understatement, for as yet not one of the ironclads to be used against Charleston had reached DuPont's base at Port Royal. During the weeks that followed, the representative of the *Tribune* soon became aware that:

> the key to the confidence of the Admiral and his chief of staff was the strict observance of their injunction not to say anything regarding the condition and purposes of the fleet in my corre-

> spondence, except what they should authorize to be published. I advised the managing editor of my intention to submit to this restriction, and confined myself at first to gathering material for purely descriptive letters.[19]

The supply of material for such letters, he soon discovered, was limited. His first letter to the *Tribune* contained all that could possibly be written about dreary, uninviting Hilton Head, the army headquarters, and the fleet. The only other available news opportunities were occasional steamer excursions between headquarters and other occupied points on the Sea Islands and some reconnoitering trips by armed boats in the direction of the mainland.

Other reporters made their appearance from time to time—among them the *Herald* scribes, B. S. Osbon and S. R. Glen; Winser and Swinton of the rival *Times;* and the Boston *Journal's* roving representative, C. C. Coffin.

While on his way down to Port Royal in February, Swinton had engaged in some counter-espionage activity. Berthed in the same cabin with him on the "Arago" was a native of Savannah, W. H. Gladding, who formerly had been a lieutenant in the United States Navy in command of a revenue cutter which operated along the Georgia coast. During the early part of the war he had achieved considerable success as a Confederate blockade runner, making frequent trips between Nassau and various Southern ports. Eventually his luck ran out on him, however, and he was captured and imprisoned, first at Fort Warren, then at Fort Lafayette. Now he was out on parole and on his way southward again. After talking with him for a while, Swinton became convinced that Gladding was on his way to Port Royal to gather information for the South concerning the expedition against Charleston. As soon as the "Arago" arrived at its destination Swinton communicated his suspicions to General Hunter, who straightway arrested Gladding. Among his papers was found ample evidence to establish that he was a spy.[20]

Writing from St. Helena Island near Port Royal on February 23, Reporter Glen told one of the Herald editors:

> The preparations for an early attack upon Charleston are progressing rapidly. I am officially informed that it cannot long be delayed, but, of course the precise day is not yet decided upon. It will be a grand fight. Ammunition in immense quantities are daily arriving, the troops on this island being daily drilled and exercised, and a grand review of them all is to come off today.[21]

His colleague, Osbon, already had seen action aboard the U.S.S. "Montauk" in the first of a series of trial assaults against Fort McAllister, a coastal fortification at the mouth of the Ogeechee River below Savannah. The "Montauk," whose commanding officer, John L. Worden, was the hero of the "Monitor's" spectacular victory over the "Virginia," had been the first of the new monitors to come down from the North. To Osbon's great satisfaction, he received from Worden an appointment as clerk and signal officer. When he reported to DuPont for special instructions, the Admiral said to Osbon:

> Mr. Osbon, you are aware that Commander Worden's eyesight is defective owing to injuries received on board the *Monitor*. I shall expect you to be his eyes, and as his clerk to aid him in every possible way. The *Montauk* will be tested under heavy fire from earthworks, and we desire full information as to results, for it is our purpose to use this type of vessel in reducing the defenses of Charleston. Keep your eyes open and note all events, and the details of the working of ship and guns.[22]

Life on board a monitor-type vessel, as the *Herald* reporter speedily discovered, was anything but comfortable. Confined in close quarters below the surface of the water, with every kind of explosive packed around them and no air except what came down the turret, the crew amused themselves as best they could listening to the whimsies of their executive officer, a certain Cushman. The mathematically minded Cushman had worked out with painstaking detail the exact lung capacity of every man below deck and was prepared to demonstrate the precise length of time that each man would live if the supply of oxygen suddenly ran out. Osbon and the other crew members soon tired of Cushman's figures, however, and no doubt were considerably relieved when, on the morning of January 27, the "Montauk" began pounding away at Fort McAllister.

Peering through one of the peepholes of the pilot house, Osbon supplied his commanding officer with the ranges and with other information which Worden was unable to ascertain for himself. For four hours the engagement continued, during which shell after shell rattled against the ship's armor, making a terrific din but causing little damage. The monitor on the other hand, it soon became apparent, was unable to inflict any substantial damage on the fort. Returning to Port Royal, Osbon ran afoul of Admiral DuPont, who was determined that nothing should appear in the newspapers about the operations on the Ogeechee until they were completed. In an official letter to Commander Worden, the Admiral explained at some length that he was, of course, aware that Osbon was on board the "Montauk":

> but I did not intend that he should be there as a reporter for his paper until after the operations in Charleston, having refused other reporters at Hilton Head to go on this expedition.
>
> This communication of Mr. Osbon's is objectionable for the following reasons, and can not, therefore, be forwarded by mail:
>
> 1. Because it is written from the ship and would naturally be supposed to come from one of the officers, and is therefore in direct violation of my General Order No. 8, which I have enforced vigorously in this squadron.
>
> 2. Because it gives information which would be of the greatest value to the rebels on many material points, particularly in enabling them to perfect their defenses at Charleston.
>
> 3. That it magnifies the object of the expedition, predicts successes which were not borne out by results.
>
> I have always been liberal to reporters, but I can not permit all our preliminary experiments in view of the attack upon Charleston to be made public—experiments of the utmost value to us, which, however, would be neutralized if published to the enemy beforehand.
>
> It is my purpose when the attack on Charleston is made . . . to permit all the members of the press who desire it and can be accommodated to be present, but even in this case their letters must show that they are written by reporters and not by officers of the Navy.[23]

Osbon was on the "Montauk" four weeks later, however, when she set on fire and completely destroyed the Confederate cruiser "Nashville" under the very guns of Fort McAllister. This time the Admiral placed no obstacles in Reporter Osbon's path. Proceeding north on the "Mary Sanford," he reached New York in time for his account of the thrilling exploit to be published in the New York *Herald* of March 13, precisely two weeks after the event. His story, filling twelve columns of the *Herald,* was widely reprinted in Europe and even was translated into Japanese![24]

Defensively the monitors had stood up well in these tests, but the results indicated that their offensive powers against land defenses were limited. Even before the monitors were given their testing, the *Tribune* correspondent Villard had become aware that none of the officers of the fleet had much confidence in either their offensive capacity or maneuverability. In a letter written to his friend Halstead on February 18, Villard had made it clear that he partly shared the officers' opinions. "As sea-going craft," he maintained, "they [the monitors] are failures, Ericson's [sic] persistent assertions to the contrary notwithstanding." He advised Halstead that his statements were not for publication because:

> the authorities want no speculations on the part of the press in regard to an attack on Charleston, but rather efforts to create the impression that Savannah is the object of the campaign.[25]

At this very time, in fact, the authorities to whom he referred were at odds over the proper method to carry out the Charleston operation. The Secretary of the Navy believed that the monitors were fully capable of entering Charleston Harbor and sailing right on past Sumter and Moultrie, but DuPont favored a joint army-navy operation, with the army assuming primary responsibility for capturing the outer defenses of the harbor. Learning from one of the army commanders that the Admiral had revealed to him the Navy Department's plan of independent operation, Welles, considerably irritated, noted in his diary:

> This indicates what I have lately feared,—that Du Pont shrinks, dreads, the conflict he has sought, yet is unwilling that any other undertake it, is afraid the reputation of Du Pont will suffer. . . . While it is right that he should be circumspect and vigilant, I deplore the signs of misgiving and doubt which have recently come over him,—his shirking policy, getting in with the army, making approaches, etc. It is not what we have talked of, not what we expected of him; is not like the firm and impetuous but sagacious and resolute Farragut.[26]

Becoming aware that only token assistance was to be expected from the army, the Admiral made final preparations for the attack with the not very comfortable feeling that he would have to "batter & pound beyond any precedent in history" to achieve the objective that had been set for him.[27]

It was not until almost the end of March that the last of the ironclads to be used in the Charleston operation reached Port Royal. On April 1, Admiral DuPont and his staff left for the mouth of the North Edisto, about halfway between Port Royal and Charleston, where the fleet already was concentrating. To the delight of the newspaper correspondents who hoped to accompany the expedition General Hunter placed at their disposal an army transport, the "Nantasket," in which they were free to go where they chose. According to the Philadelphia *Inquirer* reporter:

> One of our number acts as captain, and he orders the pilot to steer us wherever the majority decide to go. We provide our own mess, which is by no means an inferior one, and we live in a constant state of excitement, being always on the go in the day time, and anchoring in a safe harbor at night.[28]

On the afternoon of the fifth the ironclad fleet arrived off Charleston bar. During that evening and early the next morning the various units of the fleet crossed the bar and took station in the mainship channel off Morris Island. DuPont had planned to attack that day, but just as everything seemed ready a thick haze settled down over the harbor, causing him to postpone the movement for another day.

At sunrise on Tuesday morning, April 7, the horizon still was ringed with mist. By ten o'clock, however, it all had cleared away, and the fleet began to prepare for action. On board the coast survey steamer "Bibb," where correspondents of the New York *Herald, Times,* and Baltimore *American* had gathered to watch the fight, a mounted telescope of two hundred magnifying power brought batteries, shore, and ships to within a distance of a couple of hundred yards. Even without the telescope the reporters could see Sumter, some three and a half miles away, looming up like a sentinel in the harbor, its guns easily visible, its parapets swarming with defenders. On the roofs and steeples of the distant city hundreds of spectators were plainly to be seen. From the deck of the "Bibb," the sea in every direction looked as smooth as "a surface of burnished steel."[29]

On board the Admiral's flagship was the *Tribune* correspondent Villard, the only newspaperman on any of the ships in the attack column.[30] All the other reporters had declined DuPont's invitation for them to share Villard's perilous station, Coffin demurring on the ground that he had no desire to repeat his "warm experience" in the steamboat fight before Memphis. The ten other members of the reportorial corps, exclusive of the group on the "Bibb," remained outside the Charleston bar on board the "Nantasket."[31]

About the middle of the forenoon the press steamer received a request from General Hunter in the "Ben Deford" hard by to deliver a dispatch to the Admiral. Within a short time the "Nantasket" was alongside the flagship "New Ironsides," whose preparations for the grim work ahead the reporters eyed with considerable interest. Most of the crew were on the upper deck enjoying the fine weather and fresh air, soon to be exchanged for the stifling atmosphere of the gun deck. Under the supervision of their officers some of the men were distributing bales of rawhide and bags of sand along the upper deck to provide added protection against plunging shot. In a little while the Admiral himself came up from below to deliver his reply to Hunter to the dispatch carrier, Captain Henry S. Tafft, the chief army signal officer. Catching sight of the party of newspapermen, he acknowledged their salute by raising his gold-banded cap. The correspondents murmured a fervent "God Speed" for the Admiral and his men as the "Nantasket" drew away.[32]

At 12:30 P.M. the signal to get under way was hoisted to the peak of the "New Ironsides." "Close port-holes!" barked the executive officer, and in a moment the ponderous shutters fell, excluding all daylight for those below, except what came through the hatchways. The next command, "Look out for fore-and-aft shot," placed the gunners on the alert. In the van of the column of nine ironclads was the monitor, "Weehawken," pushing ahead of it a "boot-jack" raft to breach the harbor obstructions. Next in line were the monitors, "Passaic," "Montauk," and "Patapsco," followed by the "New Ironsides," a frigate-type vessel. Behind the flagship came the monitors "Catskill," "Nantucket," and "Nahant," with the twin-turreted Whitney battery[33] "Keokuk" bringing up the rear. Outside the bar were the five wooden war vessels constituting the reserve force, the "Canandaigua," "Housatonic," "Huron," "Unadilla," and "Wissahickon." DuPont's order of battle called for the ironclads to pass the enemy batteries on Morris Island at intervals of a cable's length and to continue up the channel to a point northward and westward of Fort Sumter, where they were to engage the fort at a distance of six hundred to eight hundred yards.[34]

Before the attack column had advanced very far, the "Weehawken" became entangled with the strange contraption she was pushing ahead, and the greater part of an hour elapsed before she could free herself. At 1:15 P.M. the Union armada was once more underway. The preliminary phase of the action was portrayed in fitting style by the New York *Times* correspondent, Swinton:

> Slowly the leading vessel, followed by the other eight iron-clads, moves up the Main Ship Channel . . . the shore of Morris Island, against which from our point of view they seem to rest, forming a fixed point, by which we measure the progress of the fleet. The

> first battery to whose fire it will be exposed is Fort Wagener [sic], and one fixes his eye on it and on the *Weehawken,* approaching nearer and nearer, for the fleet will there undergo its first fiery baptism.
>
> Now then, she comes within range of the fort: no fire. She passes across: still no fire! The second ship comes up, and meets the same silent reception; and so on, one by one, till with the *Keokuk,* the whole nine file by without a single shot from this seemingly formidable work.
>
> Meantime, while the fleet is passing Wagener unmolested, the leading vessel has come up with the next rebel work—Battery Bee. The same silent reception for her; the same silent reception for the whole fleet! What is the meaning of this? The enemy is obviously holding back his fire until he can deliver it with the greatest possible effect.[35]

Heading for the Northeast face of Sumter to pass around its weakest side, the "Weehawken" came in sight of the first line of obstructions, extending northeastward across the channel from Sumter to Fort Moultrie. After a cursory inspection of this new hazard, which appeared to be a tangled mass of fish nets, cables, and lager beer casks, with possible torpedoes in the vicinity, Captain John Rodgers ordered the pilot to turn away. As he did so a torpedo exploded under or very near the vessel without causing any serious damage. The vessels immediately astern the "Weehawken" sheered off as she had done. At that point, approximately 2:50 P.M., the guns of Fort Moultrie opened fire on the "Weehawken." Almost immediately Sumter followed, in unison with the batteries on Sullivan's and Morris Islands.[36]

Initially the brunt of the cannonade fell upon the first four ships in line, the "Weehawken," "Passaic," "Montauk," and "Patapsco." The Confederate aim was accurate, inasmuch as the channel was marked with buoys which gave them the exact ranges. Commented the Baltimore *American* correspondent:

> The shots literally rained around them [the ships], splashing the water up thirty feet in the air, and striking and booming from their decks and turrets.[37]

Meanwhile the flagship "New Ironsides," which had been placed in the middle of the column to permit better communication with the other ships, was having troubles of her own. Caught in the heavy tide with an inexperienced pilot at the helm, she twice refused to obey her rudder and finally drifted off in the direction of Fort Moultrie, fouling the "Catskill" and "Nantucket" in the process. Realizing that his plan of battle had gone completely askew, DuPont signaled to the other ships to disregard the movements of the flagship.[38]

Although they were undergoing a terrific pounding from the Confederate batteries, the diminutive monitors fought back gamely. Swinton commented:

> Could you look through the smoke, and through the flame-lit ports, into one of those revolving towers, a spectacle would meet your eye such as Vulcan's stithy might present. Here are the two huge guns which form the armament of each Monitor—the one 11 and the other 15 inches in diameter of bore. The gunners, begrimed with powder and stripped to the waist, are loading the gun. The charge of powder—thirty-five pounds to each charge—is passed up rapidly from below; the shot, weighing 420 pounds, is hoisted up by mechanical appliances to the muzzle of the gun, and rammed home; the gun is run out to the port, and tightly "compressed;" the port is open for an instant, the Captain of the gun stands behind, lanyard in hand—"Ready, fire!" and the enormous projectile rushes through its huge parabola, with the weight of ten thousand tons, home to its mark.[39]

Peering through his glass during occasional lulls in the strife, Coffin could see "increasing pock marks and discolorations upon the walls [of Fort Sumter], as if there had been a sudden breaking out of cutaneous disease."[40] One particularly effective shot carried away a whole section of Sumter's sea face, but the fort kept on firing.

While the cannonade was at its height the correspondents on board the "Bibb" and "Nantasket" were startled by a rifled shot from one of the batteries on Sullivan's Island, which came screaming diagonally across the "Nantasket" and dropped into the sea about a hundred yards from the bow of the "Ben Deford." A second shot fell just a trifle short of the press boat. As the paddle wheels of the little steamers began to churn furiously, there was a mad scramble for cover by the reporters. One of them later claimed that the press had completely silenced a battery—by getting out of the way![41]

At approximately five o'clock the flagship gave the signal to retire. As soon as she was out of range the hatchways of the "New Ironsides" were opened, making it possible for her crew to have a full view of things once more. As Villard reached the spar-deck he caught sight of the "Keokuk" going past on the starboard side, her sides and turrets showing innumerable holes. She was, he concluded, "evidently used up."[42] A few moments later, the New York *Times* correspondent Henry J. Winser, went on board the Whitney battery to ascertain the full extent of her damage:

> Climbing with difficulty her slippery, slanting sides . . . I found myself among the powder-begrimed crew, who were talking excitedly of the fiery ordeal through which they had just passed. A very cursory examination satisfied me that the vessel was past further service. . . . Her deck and sides were deeply furrowed on almost every yard of space. Both turrets were shattered and perforated, and in the after turret a 150-pound Whitworth projectile still remained after penetrating the armor more than a foot. . . . In almost every instance the iron bolts that secured the plating to the turrets and hull were loose . . . and she was leaking badly through several shot holes just at the water line.[43]

So badly damaged was she that on the following morning she keeled over and sank at her anchorage off Morris Island.

The other vessels in the squadron also had sustained considerable damage. The "Weehawken" had been struck fifty-three times; at one point her side armor had parted, exposing the wood backing underneath. The "Nantucket" had been struck fifty-one times; the "Nahant," thirty-six "heavily." More than a month's time would elapse before the latter vessel's turret would be in satisfactory working order again. The "Passaic" had received thirty-five hits, which had badly injured her pilot house, turret, and gun-carriage.[44] Subsequent examination disclosed that at least five of the new monitors would require further servicing before they were ready to undergo another such test. Winser's newspaper colleague, Swinton, spent the night passing from vessel to vessel in a steam tug gathering this and other information for use in his battle report.[45]

It had been Admiral DuPont's intention at the close of the fighting on the seventh to renew the attack the next morning. As the commanders of the various ironclads came aboard the flagship that night, with their reports of the heavy damage that had been done to their ships, the Admiral reconsidered the matter. The following morning he called his captains together and informed them that he had abandoned the idea of any further attack. DuPont realized only too well that his effort would be looked upon as a failure, and he had little reason to suppose that the press would be any kinder to him in the hour of defeat than it had been to McClellan, Pope, Burnside, or McDowell. To offset unfavorable criticism, he permitted Villard and Swinton to leave on the dispatch steamer "Bibb" three days ahead of the other reporters with stories which presented the result in the most favorable light possible. Coffin and the other reporters, on the other hand, were subjected to a combination of cajolery and threats before they were finally permitted to go north on the "Arago."[46]

With the reporters on board the "Arago" was the chief engineer of the recent expedition, Alban C. Stimers, whose freely-voiced criticisms of the Admiral subsequently resulted in his court martial.[47] From Stimers and other sources, Fulton and Coffin derived material for letters critical of DuPont's failure, which inspired a prolonged newspaper controversy and some temper-charged official correspondence. Said Coffin with his usual directness:

> In the army, where discipline is lax compared with the navy, where men express their opinions freely, there is mortification, chagrin and disgust. The troops of the department have had but few opportunities to meet the enemy. They were ready for the encounter. The siege train was complete, the ordnance ample for offensive operations. All of their expectations have vanished. They see nothing but an inactive summer—a dull campaign, which is a soldier's horror. . . .
>
> The result is not what was hoped or expected. We who watched the contest were not surprised to see the fleet withdrawn, for it had been determined to discontinue the fire at sunset. We were surprised to find no loss of life, so few wounds, no serious damage to the monitors after such a pounding.[48]

Fulton was even more outspoken:

> I have spent nearly two months in this vicinity waiting the slow and tedious movements preparatory to the attack on Charleston, and, though I have hoped for success, I have been convinced from the beginning that this great work has been entrusted to incompetent hands. . . . Two hours and fifteen minutes of bombardment, one man killed, seven wounded, one inferior vessel sunk, and the great effort of the country to retake the forts and public property abandoned as impracticable! Oh, that we had a Farragut here to take command at once, and do what has been so weakly attempted by Admiral Dupont![49]

Fulton could not help feeling that the naval high command had been obsessed by an unreasoning fear of enemy torpedoes, but equally significant in explaining the disappointing result, he believed, was the antipathy of the navy gold braid toward Ericsson and his monitors. "They look upon these vessels," asserted Fulton, "as destined, if successful, to do away with quarter-deck grandeur and the dignity of high rank."[50]

DuPont was so exasperated by Fulton's criticisms, which he was not permitted by service regulations to answer in the press, that he made them the subject of a special communication to the Secretary of the Navy on April 22, 1863. Fulton's article, the Admiral maintained, was injurious to himself, unjust to his officers, derogatory to the reputation of the naval service, and "utterly false" in its most important particulars. Moreover, he said, he had been given to understand by Captain Charles O. Boutelle of the "Bibb" that Fulton had cleared his story with Assistant Secretary Fox before it was published in the *American:*[51]

> An editor and correspondent of an influential newspaper, domiciled with the permission of the Department on board a steamer under its control, and submitting his letters to the inspection of one of its highest officials, is, manifestly, in a different position from ordinary correspondents of the press. . . .[52]

When questioned by Welles concerning Boutelle's allegation, Fox stoutly denied that the article in question had been brought to his attention either before or after publication, "nor have I seen Mr. Fulton since the day he applied for the pass, nor have I held any correspondence with him. . . ."[53] Secretary Welles, nevertheless, was too much dissatisfied with the result at Charleston to offer any sympathy to the Admiral. On the contrary, he informed DuPont that the press had been "generally lenient and indulgent" toward him and that in spite of the great disappointment resulting from his failure:

> the censures . . . have been comparatively few. . . . Newspaper animadversion and criticism, though often annoying and erroneous, can not be prevented, nor do I know that it is desirable they should be, for the public crave information and will comment on what so much concerns them.[54]

A gloating comment on the reporting of the battle, written from the Southern point of view, appeared in a letter by a Confederate artillery officer several weeks afterward:

> It appears from the Yankee accounts that we injured their iron-clads more than we thought we did. Some of their accounts are mostly true, interspersed here and there with some awful lies. There was no breach made in the fort at all. Two of their shots ... did come through, but they hit in weak places.... As for knocking two embrasures into one—all humbug. Equally so about any of their boats getting entangled in the obstructions—they did not go within 500 yards of them....[55]

He might have added that several of the Yankee reporters considerably overestimated the strength of the harbor obstructions, the number of guns employed by the Confederates, and the number of shots fired from these guns.[56]

Neither was there any truth in the statement of the Baltimore *American* correspondent that the guns on board the ironclad ships were "fired with much rapidity."[57] The "New Ironsides," which possessed one half the offensive armament of the fleet,[58] fired only one broadside of eight guns during the entire battle. As for the monitors, their fifteen-inch guns could be discharged only at seven-minute intervals; the fire of their eleven-inch partners was hardly more rapid. Indeed, only one hundred thirty-nine shots were fired by the entire squadron during an engagement lasting more than two hours.[59]

The Confederate artillery officer was not alone in his criticism of the way in which DuPont's failure had been reported by the press. In a *Harper's* article discussing war reporting in general, the managing editor of the New York *Evening Post* said of the attack on Fort Sumter:

> Here, for instance ... is ... one of the greatest events in the history of modern warfare. There have been some ambitious descriptions of it, but none satisfactory to the man who wants to know not only the facts, but the spirit of it. The *Tribune*'s correspondent wrote from on board the *Ironsides*, and his account is the only one worth reading. It presents such details as satisfy so far as they go; it has the smoke of battle about it; it left upon my mind an impression that there, in that ungainly hulk, were brave men, entering with unfaltering hearts upon a great experiment, in which, with untried means, they were to assault a place of unknown strength—of men who bore themselves as American seamen always have—most bravely and nobly. In the other accounts which I have seen you read only of smoke and clap bang, and lay the paper down as wise as when you took it up.... Even the *Tribune* writer, who clearly has the spirit and ability,

> is content with his one letter; and all that we so want to know, and have the world know, of the conduct of our men, of the behavior of our ships, of the fierce and dreadful trial which both came out of unharmed, is likely to be lost.[60]

Whatever others might think of their performance, the reporters off Charleston were more concerned by the fact that they saw little prospect for active campaigning in that area for some time to come. Villard and Coffin, along with most of the others, decided to go home on furloughs. After a short stay in New York, Swinton returned to the Army of the Potomac, which, after three months of preparation, was apparently on the eve of another clash with Lee.

* * *

By the middle of April, the press representatives with Hooker were making ready for the advance. In a letter to Forney dated the fourteenth of that month, the New York *Tribune* correspondent, Thomas M. Newbould, noted:

> 12000 cavalry started yesterday morning in the direction of that part of the Rappahannock where the Rapidan debouches. Gen Stoneman's staff followed, and passed these headquarters about noon. He had sealed orders, which he was not to open until today. Pontoons for seven bridges are lying near Banks Ford, 3 miles above Falmouth, and the 15th engineers finished the work yesterday of preparing roads in the neighborhood. . . . It seems as if a flank movement were immediately to be made. This corps is likely to move tomorrow. I go this morning to general headquarters. If I obtain anything further in time for this mail, I will inform you.[61]

Newbould's guess that a flanking movement was in prospect was exactly right. Hooker's plan of campaign, relatively simple though it was, offered distinct possibilities for success. With an army of one hundred and twenty thousand men, roughly double that of Lee's, he proposed to push three corps of infantry across the Rappahannock, twenty-seven miles above Fredericksburg, to turn Lee's left flank. Meanwhile the First, Third, and Sixth Corps under Sedgwick were to cross below Fredericksburg and to make a demonstration against the Confederate right. The Second Corps was to hold the center at Bank's Ford and at Falmouth. If Lee dispatched any large part of his force toward his left flank, Sedgwick was expected to carry the Fredericksburg heights at all costs and to press forward against the Confederate commander's flank and rear. Simultaneous with the advance of the flanking column, Major General George Stoneman's cavalry corps was to cross the Rappahannock farther upstream and to sever Lee's line of communications with Richmond.[62]

After several feints, Hooker issued his order for the advance on Monday, April 27, 1863. The small Confederate guard at Kelly's Ford was brushed aside as the Fifth, Eleventh, and Twelfth Corps powered their way across the Rappahannock two days later, under the immediate command of Major General Henry W. Slocum, and headed for the Rapidan. Fording the river about the same time, Stoneman's ten thousand mounted men fanned out along the highways extending in the direction of Gordonsville and Richmond.

Meanwhile Hooker's difficulties with the press were coming to a head. Almost a week before the order for the advance was given, Hooker had written to Stanton demanding an investigation of an important information leak that had appeared in the Washington *Chronicle* of April 17. By means best known to itself, the *Chronicle* had obtained access to a report from the Surgeon General's office which contained accurate indications of the size and organization of the Army of the Potomac. Hooker mourned:

> The chief of my secret service department would have willingly paid $1,000 for such information in regard to the enemy at the commencement of his operations, and even now would give that sum for it to verify the statements which he has been at great labor and trouble to collect and systemize.[63]

The General's blood pressure must have risen considerably several days later when his eye fell upon a story carried by the Philadelphia *Inquirer* and the New York *Times*. A few days previous, these newspapers revealed, a telegraph wire had been discovered on the bank of the Rappahannock. Having touched it and received a slight shock, the finder reported the occurrence to headquarters. Subsequent investigation disclosed that the line was being used to carry information from a house in Falmouth to the enemy's lines on the opposite side of the river. Both newspapers went on to say that the operator, "a rebel," had been taken into custody.

In response to a request for information concerning the perpetrators of the outrage, Stanton informed Hooker:

> You will have to protect yourself by rigid measures against the reporters in your army, and the Department will support you in any measure you are pleased to take on the subject.... I have just been told that detailed, and no doubt exaggerated, reports of the crossing at Kelly's Ford... have been sent to the Times and Herald by mail. Nothing has been allowed to pass by telegraph.[64]

In line with the Secretary's suggestion, Hooker took steps within a few hours to halt any further leakage of important information through the press. That very day, Thursday, April 30, a new regulation, identified as General Order No. 48, was issued from his headquarters requiring all newspaper correspondents attached to the Army of the Potomac "to publish their communications over their own signatures." The reason for the order, as stated in the text of the order itself, was:

> the frequent transmission of false intelligence, and the betrayal of the movements of the army to the enemy, by the publication of injudicious correspondence of an anonymous character....

Erring reporters were further given to understand:

> In case of failure to comply with this order, through their own or their employers' neglect, such correspondents will be excluded from, and the circulation of the journals for which they correspond suppressed within, the lines of this army.
>
> Commanding officers and Provost Marshals are directed to enforce this order, and will keep themselves informed of all the correspondents within the limits of their respective camps, and should any such disregard its requirements, will send them forthwith beyond the lines of this army.[65]

Up to this time most Northern editors had insisted upon the complete anonymity of their correspondents. "I would not allow *any* letter writer to attach his initials to his communications, unless, he was a widely known & influential man like Greeley or Bayard Taylor," said Sam Wilkeson in a letter of August 6, 1862, to Sydney Howard Gay. Moreover, not all the reporters were convinced of the wisdom of having "their names paraded before the public," since they knew that the generals frequently read reporters' letters in the newspapers. Complain about it as they might and did, Hooker's insistence on the use of by-lines proved a blessing in disguise for the reporters, as many of them thus were enabled to win national reputations!

On the same afternoon that the newspaper order was released, the

Fifth, Eleventh, and Twelfth Corps of Hooker's right wing reached Chancellorsville, the Federal point of concentration, where they were joined by two divisions of the Second Corps, which had crossed the Rappahannock at United States Ford. "Fighting Joe" himself arrived at Chancellorsville that evening and established his headquarters at the Chancellor House, a large brick mansion. Meanwhile, Sedgwick's three corps had pontooned across below Fredericksburg according to plan, in order to mask Hooker's flank movement on the right. By evening the initial phase of the movement had been carried out successfully. So elated was the Federal commander that he issued a congratulatory order to his troops in which he boasted, "the enemy must either ingloriously fly, or come out from behind his defenses and give us battle on our own ground, where certain destruction awaits him."[66]

Greatly outnumbered though he was, Lee had no intention of "ingloriously flying." By the same afternoon, April 30, he had come to realize that the object of Hooker's strategy was to turn the Confederate left, and he at once began to make the necessary counter moves. Major General Jubal A. Early he left at Fredericksburg with a force of ten thousand men to contain Sedgwick; the remainder of the Army of Northern Virginia wheeled about and advanced toward Chancellorsville from the East to meet what Lee correctly estimated as the main threat.[67]

Hooker's line of battle that evening extended along the Plank Road from a point about three miles West of Chancellorsville and then in a northeasterly direction from Chancellorsville to the Rappahannock River. To the East lay a stretch of open country in which the Federal general expected to fight his battle.

On the following morning, May 1, Hooker ordered his troops to move forward along the three roads which connected Chancellorsville and Fredericksburg. Some time during the forenoon, the vanguards of the two armies met on two of these roads. Instead of pushing forward vigorously, Hooker ordered his men to fall back and to improvise a line of defense along the edge of the Wilderness, a region of tangled oak and pine thickets extending from about one mile East of Chancellorsville to the Rapidan. In vain did Hooker's corps commanders point out to him the disadvantages of sacrificing the initiative. The Federal commander was confident that he had selected a strong position for defense and that Lee never would venture to attack him there.[68]

The latter assumption was entirely correct. Lee was quick to recognize the futility of a direct attack upon such a position, especially with inferior numbers; but the nature of the country offered Stonewall Jackson, "the great flanker," opportunity for a type of movement which he had made successfully many times in his Shenandoah Valley campaigns. After a conference between Jackson and Lee it was agreed that Jackson should start out the next morning with thirty thousand men on a march around the right flank of Hooker's army.[69]

The movement of large columns of the enemy to the right on Saturday, May 2, plainly could be observed from the Union lines, but Hooker and his generals missed its real significance. Both Hooker and Major General Oliver O. Howard, who commanded the Eleventh Corps on the extreme right, apparently were convinced that the enemy was retreating toward Gordonsville.[70] During the course of the day Lee's men made several threatening demonstrations along the front of Hooker's line. First they thrust in the direction of Couch's Second Corps, which proved to be well entrenched and inclined to put up a strong resistance. Then they struck lightly at Slocum's front and lobbed shells into the clearing at the Chancellor House. Afterward they made menacing gestures along the line still farther to the right.

About noon, during a lull in the fighting, L. A. Hendricks, one of the *Herald* correspondents, rode out toward the right to join one of the other *Herald* correspondents in what he described as a "cold collation." No doubt he cast watchful glances in various directions as he rode along, for it had been less than a week since J. H. Vosburgh, another one of the *Herald* men, had been made prisoner by three enemy soldiers as he was having breakfast with a local clergyman outside the lines.[71] While the two *Herald* correspondents were deriving what satisfaction they could from their unappetizing meal, the sharp rattle of musketry was heard in the distance. Presently it grew louder and seemed to be drawing nearer. Hendricks quickly remounted his horse to rejoin his command and galloped off down the Plank Road, only to discover that he was riding directly in front of the main line of the army and just back of the line of skirmishers. The firing had not yet opened on this part of the line, but it might begin at any moment. Hendricks dug his spurs into his horse's sides in an effort to make greater speed, for he realized that this was truly a ride for life. "Go it, old boy," greeted his ears as he flew by the gleaming bayonets. "Go it, paymaster," shouted others. "Go it, Mephistopheles," called out still others. "It's a *Herald* correspondent, I'll bet," was the freely voiced opinion of several of his watchers.

Intent on preserving his own safety, Hendricks paid no heed to the shouts, although in later years he enjoyed recalling the strange spectacle he must have presented that day, hunched forward over his saddle and riding like mad, his coat tails flapping in the breeze.[72]

Just about the time that Hendricks started forth on his dash across the front line, another veteran war correspondent, Whitelaw Reid of the Cincinnati *Gazette*, arrived at Falmouth, having come from Washington by boat that morning to find out for himself what was going on at the front. Throughout the previous week the telegraphic censorship had prevented any news of what was happening along the Rappahannock from reaching the public. A *Tribune* extra the previous evening, May 1, had given detailed information concerning the river crossing, but there was no information whether or not there had been any serious fighting during the week.

Somewhat to his surprise, Reid found Falmouth almost deserted. To be sure, Assistant Adjutant General Seth Williams was at Hooker's old headquarters, transmitting orders as fast as the telegraph operator could tick them out. Both the quartermaster and the commissary were issuing and taking receipts, but there were no signs of the great army which had been quartered along these hillsides not more than a week before. Reid and two of his friends walked out to the bluff overlooking the river and surveyed the scene. Across the Rappahannock lay Sedgwick's flanking force concealed in a bend of the river. Over in Fredericksburg, plainly visible, were lines of Confederate infantry inside their entrenchments, and, within easy rifle range of the Union pickets, children were swinging by a rope suspended from the limb of an apple tree. From the tallest of the church spires in Fredericksburg they heard an ancient clock striking out the hours in rich full tones just half an hour faster, with their Richmond-regulated time, than the Washington watches of Reid's party. Away to the right, where Hooker was with the main body of his army, the sound of light musket fire was audible. Soon Jackson would emerge from the gray shades of the forest with his indomitable "foot cavalry" in the most crushing surprise attack of the war since Shiloh. Not more than ten miles west of Falmouth the opportunity for one of the greatest battle stories of the war was in the making. But Reid had no way of knowing this. He believed that Hooker's army was in splendid spirits, and he had heard reports that Lee already was retreating from the line of the Rappahannock.[73]

It was at about six o'clock, as the men in Howard's Eleventh Corps were cooking their suppers, that the avalanche in gray burst out of the forest. The first warning of the attack was given by the wild rush of deer and rabbits into the camp ahead of the advancing Confederates. Only one unit (Gilsa's brigade of Brigadier General Charles Devens' division) was facing westward in the direction of the attackers. After two or three assaults it was forced back, and the next brigade to the left, surprised on its flank, broke into a stampede. Tom Cook of the New York *Herald* wrote:

> I must frankly confess that I have no ability to do justice to the scene that followed. It was my lot to be in the centre of that field when the panic burst upon us. May I never be a witness to another such scene. On one hand was a solid column of infantry retreating at double quick from the face of the enemy, who were already crowding their rear; on the other was a dense mass of beings who had lost their reasoning faculties, and were flying from a thousand fancied dangers. . . . On the hill were ten thousand of the enemy, pouring their murderous volleys in upon us, yelling and hooting, to increase the alarm and confusion; hundreds of cavalry horses, left riderless at the first discharge from the rebels, were dashing frantically about in all directions; a score of batteries of artillery were thrown into disorder, some properly manned, seeking to gain positions for effective duty, and others flying from the field; battery wagons, ambulances, horses, men, cannon, caissons, all jumbled and tumbled together in an apparently inextricable mass, and that murderous fire still pouring in upon them.[74]

Nobody at Falmouth had any inkling of the disaster which just had befallen Hooker's right wing. After enjoying a hearty supper, Reid decided to return to Washington. An hour's ride on the train brought him to Aquia Creek, where the boat on which he had come down from Washington that morning had its steam pressure up, ready for the return trip. Through the soft moonlight he steamed up the broad Potomac, arriving in Washington just in time to dash off a letter to the *Gazette* before the last mail closed.[75]

By this time the attack on Hooker's right had spent its first force. The overwhelming success of the Confederates had been dearly bought, for in the deepening twilight Stonewall Jackson had ridden forward beyond his battle line to reconnoiter and had been fired upon by his own men, who mistook him and his escort for a detachment of Union cavalry. In spite of Jackson's wounding, the fighting continued without a break until shortly before midnight. "It was part of Malvern Hill over again," said Hendricks, "moonlight and mournful massacre of men."[76]

Early the next morning, Sunday, May 3, Jackson's men renewed the attack, shouting the name of their wounded commander as they rushed forward. Unnerved by the rout of the Eleventh Corps, Hooker seemed unable to pull himself together and to exercise the responsibilities of supreme command. Some thirty-five thousand fresh troops near at hand and eager for the fray were not even thrown into the fight. Shortly after nine o'clock that morning, while standing on the veranda of the Chancellor House, the Commanding General was knocked senseless by the concussion from a cannon ball which struck a pillar against which he was leaning. Forty-five minutes later General Couch assumed temporary command of the army with instructions from Hooker to contract the center of his line to a position in the rear of the Chancellor House. By noon the retirement had been successfully carried out. Then Hooker, once more in command, settled down to wait for news from Sedgwick.

During the attack on Howard the evening before, Hooker explicitly had ordered Sedgwick to march up the Chancellorsville Road at once and to strike Lee in the rear with all the means at his disposal.[77] At noon on Sunday, Hooker received the good news that Sedgwick had successfully carried out the first part of his assignment. By daylight the commander of the Union left wing had occupied Fredericksburg; had then advanced upon Marye's Heights (where Burnside's troops had been slaughtered the previous December) and had driven Early's graybacks from their position in a brilliant action. In bombastic style the New York *Times* correspondent, David W. Judd, described the storming of those heights by Sedgwick's magnificent veterans:

> At twenty minutes past eleven the lion-hearted men rose from their feet. Every one of the thousand spectators on the hills in the rear held their breath in terrible suspense, expecting to see them all the next moment prostrate in the dust. "Forward!" cried the General, and they dashed forward on the open plain when instantly there was poured upon them a most terrific discharge of grape and cannister [sic]. . . . The rebel guns further to the left are turned upon them. But they falter not. A moment more they have reached the stone wall, scaled its sides, are clambering the green bank of the bluff, and precisely as the City clock struck, they rush over the embrasure of the rebel guns and the Heights are ours. . . . The guns captured proved to be the Washington

> Artillery, the battery so highly complimented by Gen. Lee in his report of the last battle of Fredericksburgh [sic]. . . . "What men are these," was the interrogatory of one of the astonished and terrified members, as our brave boys appeared over the ramparts. "We are Yankees, —— —— you; do you think we will fight now," was the response from one of our men. "Boys," remarked the Commander of the Battery, "you have captured the best battery in the Confederate service."[78]

A Southern army correspondent viewing the same action from the opposite side of the lines was considerably less impressed by the valor of the Federals. On the basis of "unquestionable sources" concerning the identity of which he remained vague, he assured his readers:

> the Yankees were dealt rations of whisky in order to get them up to Marye's Heights, and . . . each hindmost man was ordered to strike down with the drawn bayonet the man in his front who faltered. . . .

Even such precautions, he indicated, were not sufficient to prevent a precipitate retreat on the part of the attackers during the first charge, "some of the men falling back as far as the other side of the river."[79]

By two o'clock that Sunday afternoon, Sedgwick's Sixth Corps was four and a half miles west of Fredericksburg and still advancing against stiffening opposition. Having defeated and practically immobilized Hooker, Lee was now able to divert enough troops to his right to check Sedgwick in the neighborhood of Salem Church during late afternoon.

Monday, May 4, as Hooker's biographer states, "was a day of many dispatches but little fighting on the main front."[80] While Sedgwick with not more than twenty-two thousand men was under increasing pressure from Lee, Hooker with roughly four times that number was plaintively calling for help and entertaining ideas of retreat. As the counterattacking Confederates neared Fredericksburg that morning, the *Times* correspondent, Judd, narrowly missed being trapped in a farmhouse just outside the town. His escape in the main he owed to having in his possession "a fleet horse."[81]

At midnight there was a council of war at Hooker's headquarters to discuss the question of whether to advance or retire. After listening to the varying opinions of his corps commanders, Hooker said he was convinced that the army should withdraw and declared he would assume responsibility for the decision. During that night, with his approval,

Sedgwick extricated his men from their dangerous situation by recrossing the Rappahannock at Scott's Ford.[82]

The retreat of Hooker's disheartened veterans across that same river during the night of the fifth was vividly described by the *Herald* correspondent, Carpenter. That morning, he reported, the hills at Falmouth were crowded with anxious listeners for the opening gun of the expected battle:

> and at noon I left the old headquarters confident of witnessing another engagement and the rout of the rebel army. To my astonishment I met the wagon trains hurrying down from the river, crowding and overturning in the woods, and rushing frantically on wherever the condition of the roads would allow. Long processions of ambulances full of wounded men streamed away towards Potomac creek and Falmouth, stragglers swarmed like ants in the byways, and everything betokened a retreat. But that was impossible. Hearing that the army had cut loose from its base and pushed on after the enemy I hurried on to accompany it but found all quiet at the fords, and the hospitals on the other side empty.
>
> About five o'clock in the afternoon it commenced raining. The water poured down in torrents; cascades leaped from the hill sides; rivers rushed through every ravine. The teams, blinded by the driving storm, staggered like drunken men. Pack mules turned their backs to the tempest and refused to move, and the soldiers crouched beneath their rubber blankets and behind the trunks of the oaks. By and by the storm abated, and, reaching the front, the problem was solved. All along the road, from the earthworks to the ford, there stretched a line of troops, their arms stacked and cartridge boxes hanging on them. Wagons, pack mules, stragglers—all were gone.... Twilight deepened into night, and in the gathering darkness I rode back to the hospitals, found them deserted, and pushed on to the ford. The river was rising rapidly, and fears were already entertained that the pontoons would be destroyed....
>
> At ten o'clock the scene was most impressive. The moon was just coming up, and shed through the clouds a dim, gray light, while the campfires on the river bank, the bonfires and the torches flared in the wind that swept in fitful gusts down the rock-ribbed gulches. The pines swayed restlessly with a sobbing sound, the rain pattered dolefully on the leaves, and the river foamed and lashed its banks, while the logs and floodwood

> drifted by like spectres. There was no noise and confusion of any kind. Occasionally there was a sound of falling boards and hurried shouts down where the lanterns flitted to and fro, and sometimes strange voices seemed to be whispering in the tree tops on the bluffs above; but the work of preparation for the retreat went on, and at midnight it was done.
>
> The gloom and sinking of the heart occasioned by the retreat was soon forgotten in the fear that the enemy would discover our movement and fall upon our rear. Pine brush was strewed upon the bridges to prevent noise and every precaution was taken to secure a safe removal of our army. . . . Steadily and in silence the dark mass surged on, stretching in one unbroken line from the entrenchments through the woods, out upon the hills, down across the river and up again into the almost Egyptian darkness of the gorges among the pines and cedars. Daylight came and still the enemy was quiet. Six o'clock, seven, eight; and still there was no shot to indicate that we were discovered, nothing but the tramp of the soldiers and the rush of the swollen river. Nearly all of the army had crossed before the enemy found out that we were leaving, and then he followed us with a few pieces of artillery. Our cannon on the bluffs drove back his guns, the rear guard hastened over, the pontoons swung around in the current, and the other side was abandoned.[83]

For the time being at least, the Army of the Potomac was safe.

Meanwhile, several army correspondents had accompanied Stoneman on his spectacular excursion in Lee's rear. Among them were Solomon T. Bulkley of the *Herald,* Edward A. Paul of the New York *Times,* and William A. Croffut of the *Tribune.* On the first night out in the midst of a drenching rain, Croffut amused the soldiers of the Fifty-seventh New York regiment by reading stanzas from an old paper-covered copy of Byron which he had picked up in one of the rebel shanties at Manassas that morning. Some one had built a bonfire at the base of a scrub oak tree. As the reading continued, squad after squad of soldiers joined the circle around the camp fire, each bringing its quota of rails as a fire offering in return for the privilege of listening to the *Tribune* man's rendition of "Childe Harold" and "Don Juan." All three correspondents were impressed by the impact which the war had made on the living conditions of the people in northern Virginia. Paul remarked that in nine days' travel he did not see fifty able-bodied men who were not in some way connected with the army.[84] Said Croffut:

> The country was thoroughly desolated. Farms had been plundered of their stock; bridges, depots, and settlements had been burned; the carcasses of thousands of horses tainted the poisoned air while feebly enriching the exhausted fields. Deserted dogs and hungry cats whined after and followed us from barns that had escaped the torch, as if seeking their faithless masters, and here and there rose, like a grim witness, the blackened shaft that two days before had been the centre of a homestead.[85]

Although one of Stoneman's flying columns managed to penetrate within five miles of Richmond, the general results of the raid proved disappointing. In spite of the widespread panic which the raid created, Stoneman failed to sever Lee's line of communication in time to do Hooker any real good. Moreover, his prolonged absence deprived Hooker of his "eyes" at a time when it was vitally important for the Commanding General to keep track of Lee's movements.

Censorship withheld from the public for several days news of the disaster which had befallen Hooker's army. For the first time during the war the Washington papers were refused permission to print any news which the censor also would not allow to go out on the telegraph. To circumvent the censors, the New York papers were forced to smuggle their correspondents out of the army and to have them go direct to New York with their accounts which were published immediately upon their arrival.[86] On Monday, May 4, so the *Tribune* reported, a correspondent for one of the morning papers arrived in New York with an account of a reverse on Saturday, which his paper refused to publish.[87] Both the *Herald* and the *Tribune* issued extras that morning, but neither contained any news which had not been known the day before. The *Herald,* however, printed a rumor to the effect that Lee had retired to the line of the North Anna, leaving only a small force on the Rappahannock to keep Hooker in check. The *Tribune* also mentioned this as a possibility but concluded that Lee's army was more likely to be in front of Hooker. The Philadelphia *Inquirer* of the same date was in receipt of information that Sedgwick had seized the heights behind Fredericksburg; it also reported that General Hooker had been in the thickest of the fight and that "his escapes from bullets are miraculous." The best the *Times* could offer was to promise that it would publish the news of Saturday's operation as soon as "our correspondent, who left the field on the evening of that day, reaches this City, toward which he is hastening."[88]

The *Times* was true to its word. On Tuesday it published a complete story of the fighting on Saturday and Sunday, twenty-four hours in advance of its contemporaries. Both Swinton and Crounse, whose letters formed the basis for the *Times*'s big story, were greeted with praise from all sides for their journalistic achievement. A correspondent of the Philadelphia *Press* even characterized Crounse's story of the fighting on Sunday as "the best battle description yet inspired by the war."[89] Unfortunately, Carl Schurz, whose division Crounse had criticized, did not share the *Press*'s enthusiasm.

By Tuesday afternoon it had become known at the *Tribune* office that Hooker's army had suffered a defeat of disastrous proportions. James R. Gilmore of the *Tribune* editorial staff was sitting in the managing editor's private office when Greeley entered, clutching the latest telegram from the front, which he had just removed from the dispatch box in the outer office. His face was a ghastly color, and his lip fairly trembled as he exclaimed, "My God! it is horrible—horrible; and to think of it, 130,000 magnificent soldiers so cut to pieces by less than 60,000 half-starved ragamuffins."[90]

In neither the *Tribune*'s account nor the accounts of any of the other newspapers published on Wednesday, however, was there anything to indicate that the Union army had sustained a large-scale disaster. The *Herald* reported that on the basis of direct information from the battlefield covering developments as late as six o'clock Sunday afternoon, the situation appeared favorable for General Hooker. Josiah R. Sypher's letter from the army, published in the *Tribune*, likewise concluded with the statement, "The army is in excellent condition and in fine spirits, ready and anxious to march out on the enemy."[91] Such news "shrouded in careful phrase and hopeful terms"[92] was designed to prepare the public for the shock of learning that Hooker had been forced to retreat. In spite of such statements, uneasiness continued to grow all day Wednesday. William W. Harding telegraphed from Philadelphia to his brother in Washington, complaining that:

> We hear very little from you. Where is Painter and Williamson and Cunnington? Williamson's wife sends word that his child is very sick and she wants Williamson home. If he comes tomorrow night send all news by him. Write frequently and telegraph all the censor will allow you even if expense is $200 a day. Circulation is going up splendidly but we seem to have no reporters anywhere. Can you not remedy it?[93]

On Thursday, May 7, censorship restrictions on news sent by telegraph were removed and the country learned what had been common knowledge in Washington since five o'clock the afternoon before:[94] that Hooker had been driven back across the Potomac. While the press wondered how best to explain away the Federal army's defeat, Horace Greeley had some more uneasy moments. On Thursday morning, a letter from Sypher criticizing Hooker in severe terms found its way into a *Tribune* extra "without the sanction of the responsible editors," and by the time they discovered it, part of the edition already had gone to press. Hooker was still the idol of the *Tribune*'s "radical" friends; at the direction of the editors, therefore, the presses were stopped and the offensive passage expunged, but not in time to prevent the Associated Press from telegraphing all over the country the entire critical letter of the *Tribune*'s chief correspondent with the Army of the Potomac.[95]

Sypher had stated frankly in the letter that "there was no time from Friday morning to Monday night but what Hooker could have attacked and defeated Lee's army, but he lacked the ability to give the order."[96] While the *Tribune, Times,* and Forney's Washington *Chronicle*[97] continued to make excuses for Hooker, dissatisfaction appeared in other quarters of the press. As early as May 8, the *Herald* admitted that the campaign was a failure, yet blamed Stanton and Halleck more than it did "Fighting Joe." The Boston *Journal* editor particularly was irritated by the interference on the part of the military authorities with the reporting of the campaign:

> There never has been during the war such an important series of events, about which the public were so imperfectly informed, as the recent operations on the other side of the Rappahannock. The Government transmitted no information whatever. The newspaper correspondents were successively obliged to pick up what intelligence they could in a hurry, and hasten off northward to secure its early publication. Hence, there has been but very little reporting from personal observation, and nothing like a connected account of the week's history. . . .
>
> We do not know what has been the diminution of the strength of the army of the Potomac during the late series of collisions; what injury it has inflicted upon its antagonist; what was the chief difficulty in our plans or in their execution; what is the state of reinforcements on both sides; what Stoneman has really accomplished. and what measures have been taken by Generals

> Keyes and Peck to co-operate with him. And yet we want to know all these things and others. . . .[98]

On May 10, a group of New York gold operators created still greater public confusion by cooking up a story that Hooker had crossed the Rappahannock a second time with his entire army and that Richmond had fallen. A Philadelphia broker in league with the gold operators succeeded in palming off his story on the Philadelphia *Inquirer,* which in turn bulletined the information as coming from a Washington correspondent of the paper. The evening papers in Philadelphia reprinted the *Inquirer*'s news with the added note that it had been confirmed from Washington and contributed several variations based on supposedly "private sources." An attempt then was made to telegraph this interesting fable to New York, but, failing to pass the censorship, it was sent to New York on a late train by special messenger. From there it was telegraphed to Boston over the lines of the Independent Telegraph Company, which for some reason had not received an order from the War Department forbidding its transmission. By the combined use of railroad and telegraph facilities the story spanned the continent and reached San Francisco almost as soon as it did Boston, even though within forty-eight hours it was all too apparent that the story was entirely without basis.[99]

One defect was more or less common to all the newspaper accounts of Chancellorsville: in their efforts to find a scapegoat upon which to fasten responsibility for the failure of that magnificent army and its leader, they enlarged on the misconduct of the "cowardly Dutchmen" of the Eleventh Corps although considerably less than half the men in that corps were Germans. Carl Schurz, one of Howard's division commanders, became so indignant at the abuse which the press directed at him that he wrote to General Hooker demanding that Hendricks of the New York *Herald* and Crounse of the New York *Times* make full amends for their reflections upon the conduct of his division:

> I am willing to bear what blame justly attaches to my Division; but I insist, and you know it well, that Gen. Devins' [sic] division occupied the front on the points of attack, and that Gen. Devins' division threw itself upon mine, demoralizing my men, preventing my regiments, by their impetuous rush, from changing front, and deploying at the right time. It is most unjust that I should have to bear the responsibility for the conduct of a whole corps, only one-third of which was under my command.[100]

Upon receiving a copy of Schurz's letter from the Adjutant General's office, Crounse promptly made a public apology for an error which he insisted was not made without good authority:

> I took especial pains to inquire on the evening of the disaster, and was informed by several officers, as well as by a correspondent of the *Tribune,* who lived in the Eleventh corps, and with whom I compared notes on Sunday morning, that "it was the Third division which first gave way."[101]

Hendricks, however, made no published acknowledgment of his mistake. Moreover, a garbled account of the controversy in the *Herald* made it appear that Schurz's complaint was directed at the correspondents of the *Times* and *Tribune.*[102]

Immediately following the battle, both the *Times* and *Tribune* dispatched their best men to the army to ascertain its condition and to discover the reasons for Hooker's failure. Reaching Falmouth on May 7, the *Times* investigator, Swinton, was unable to find anyone in the army "in any station" who thought Hooker's conduct was "capable either of explanation or of justification." Whereas on his previous visit to the army, the *Times* man had praised the "superb generalship of Hooker" and attributed to him "powers and qualities that have been displayed by no general who has yet commanded this army," he now did a complete about face. After six days of painstaking investigation, Swinton concluded:

> after the first stages, his [Hooker's] course was ill-advised and unfortunate throughout. It was not only bad—it was the worst possible; and in all the cardinal operations, where there were a half-dozen different modes of action, he not only chose a bad course—he chose the *only bad course. . . .*[103]

Before venturing to publish such a blistering indictment, Raymond prudently sent a copy to Lincoln to see whether he would approve. Nevertheless, Swinton's letter was already in type when word was telegraphed from Washington that if it were published the author might expect to find himself in Fort Lafayette the next morning. Under the circumstances the *Times* editor thought it best to suppress Swinton's criticism.[104]

The *Tribune*'s fact-finder, George W. Smalley, presented himself in the first instance to Hooker, who promptly asked him to be his guest. Explaining the nature of his mission, Smalley made the General see that he could not gracefully accept his invitation. Instead of ordering him out of the lines, which, as general commanding, he had every right to do, Hooker rather grimly acquiesced, saying, "If I am to be investigated, it might as well be by you as anybody." For more than a week, Smalley talked to men of all ranks and no rank. Having heard in New York that Hooker was drunk at the time of the battle, the correspondent inquired of everyone he met about this, but "not one witness could testify to having seen General Hooker the worse for whiskey."[105] Of one fact, however, Smalley was convinced: the Army of the Potomac had lost confidence in both itself and Hooker. Plainly a change of commanders was advisable, but whom did the army want for its leader?

The name Smalley heard mentioned more than any other was that of General Meade. Indeed, a number of officers asked the *Tribune* reporter to call on the General and inform him that it was the wish of a majority in the army that he should be the new commander. "I don't know that I ought to listen to you," said Meade when Smalley delicately explained his errand. Yet he did listen, with an impassive face, while the reporter repeated that he was in no sense an ambassador, that he brought no proposals, that Meade's admirers had no intention of asking him to do anything else than listen to their expression of confidence. Having delivered his message, Smalley made off without knowing what impression his remarks had made upon the discreet Pennsylvanian.

Back in New York, Smalley made an oral report of his findings to the *Tribune*'s managing editor and asked him whether he should prepare a statement for publication. Gay, after considering the matter for a while, said:

> No, it is a case where the truth can do only harm. It is not for the public interest that the public should know the army is demoralized, or know that Hooker must go, or know that no successor to him can yet be named. Write an editorial, keep to generalities, and forget most of what you have told me.[106]

Smalley carried out the first part of his instructions to the letter, but he could never forget that trip to the Army of the Potomac in the hour of its defeat. Before many weeks had elapsed—so fast were events moving—his strange interview with the tight-lipped Meade would seem doubly significant.

15

Some "Casualties" Among the Bohemians

FOR more than a year after the fall of Memphis, in June, 1862, operations along the Mississippi continued the dominant theme of war reporting in the West. During the long river campaign many correspondents were captured or were victims of disease and other occupational hazards. Of the better-known correspondents, Knox, Richardson, and Browne were stopped from writing before Vicksburg fell. Finley Anderson's career was interrupted by Confederate imprisonment, although he returned to the field in the spring campaign of 1864. For various professional reasons, Wilkie wrote less and less after the fall of Vicksburg.

Taking the places of these men were new arrivals, among them the *Herald* correspondent D. B. Randolph Keim. The day he reached camp, Keim saw a "plain-looking man" standing outside General Grant's tent. He was wearing a cheap blouse and was chewing an enormous cigar.

"I am a newspaper correspondent, have just arrived in camp, and I want to see Gen. Grant," announced the new *Herald* special.

"This is the general's headquarters," the plain-looking man told him, "and if you will come here tomorrow morning I am sure the general will be glad to see you."

Early the next morning, Keim was on hand to keep his appointment. To his surprise, he discovered that he already had met the General—the unassuming man with the cigar[1]—who now commanded the Department of the Tennessee. After being in a state of temporary eclipse, Grant had been appointed in late October to the command of this newly organized department, embracing the Western portions of Kentucky and Tennessee and Northern Mississippi as well.

Following the capture of Memphis earlier in the year, only two strong points along the river—Vicksburg, Mississippi, and Port Hudson, Louisiana—had remained in Confederate hands. Perched on a high bluff full two hundred feet above the river and almost unapproachable except from the South and East, Vicksburg deserved the name, commonly applied to her in the press, of the "Gibraltar of the West." Her sister strong point, Port Hudson, some two hundred miles downstream, was hardly less formidable. In August, 1862, after an unsuccessful attempt to reduce Vicksburg by naval bombardment, Knox of the *Herald* had written in pessimistic vein to Bennett:

> There is a possibility that late in September or early in October they [the army] may attempt to capture Vicksburg. They can not move there now during the hot weather without suffering a severe loss by sickness. . . . The shores of this river are exceedingly unhealthy & the malaria & the exposure would sweep away our soldiers with great rapidity. The Louisiana shore opposite the town is but little less dangerous as a residence, as those of us who witnessed the siege of Vicksburg can bear ample testimony. . . . Of eight journalists who were there all returned more or less debilitated & three are now confined to their rooms in St. Louis & Cincinnati. . . .
>
> By October the heat will have passed away & we can then resume active operations. I fear we shall be so long talking about it that Van Dorn[2] will muster an immense force to oppose us & thus keep our fleet & land force at bay. We need many more boats than we now have in order to make a successful attack & especially are we deficient in mortars to make a vigorous bombardment.[3]

It took even longer than Knox had anticipated for the second phase of the Vicksburg operation to materialize. Meanwhile, important changes had taken place in the Western command. About the same time that Grant was appointed to command the Department of the Tennessee, Porter, then an acting Rear Admiral, was sent West to head the navy's new Mississippi Squadron. While in Washington, Porter had learned that he was expected to cooperate in bringing about the capture of Vicksburg with an army specially recruited for the purpose by the Honorable John A. McClernand. McClernand was a "political general" and a former Democratic congressman from Lincoln's home district, for whom military success was a means to a political end. Grant, doubting the new general's fitness for the command of the river expedition and animated (so McClernand thought) by "regular army" prejudice, prepared to move on Vicksburg before the President's special friend could arrive on the scene. On December 8, Grant ordered Sherman back to Memphis to make preparations for a river movement against the Confederate Gibraltar. It was Grant's intention, while Sherman's movement was in progress, to push southward along the line of the Mississippi Central Railroad and then to join Sherman on the Yazoo River above Vicksburg.[4]

Edward Betty of the Cincinnati *Gazette* was with Grant's army at the time this operation was being planned. On the eve of Sherman's departure for Memphis, Betty wrote to a member of the *Gazette*'s editorial staff, describing army life as "absolutely damnable" and confiding that "as soon as circumstances admit of a change I will take advantage of a very desirable return to the United States and civilization." He went on to say:

> Junius[5] and I are together in this wing of the army but we occasionally come across other scribblers. We live literally in the field and really suffer much discomfort, but I prefer doing so because whatever news I give I first assure myself to be correct. This cannot be done away from the points where events . . . transpire, and as far as I can see, it seems to be first the object of "old hands at the bellows" to hunt up comfortable quarters, leaving their propinquity to news depots a mere secondary consideration.[6]

On the day before he left Memphis, Sherman issued what was subsequently referred to as General Order No. 8, excluding all civilians from the limits of his command, except those who were actually employed by the army, and specifying that anyone who wrote accounts of the expedition for publication, thereby giving information to the enemy, would be arrested and treated as a spy.[7] In spite of this warning, more than a score of newspaper correspondents attached themselves to the river expedition, among them Franc Wilkie of the New York *Times*, Junius H. Browne of the Cincinnati *Times* and New York *Tribune*, Thomas W. Knox of the *Herald* and Richard T. Colburn of the *World*, Tom Cook of the Chicago *Times*, and F. C. Foster of the rival *Tribune*. When he learned that his attempt to exclude the newspapermen had failed, the General issued a second order, calling upon the Master of Transports to provide him with a list of all the newspaper correspondents with the expedition and directing that they be sent to the front under arrest to "pass powder." This order, like its predecessor, the Chicago *Times* "special" noted:

> was more honored in its breach than in its observance, and the Bohemian Brigade still lives and prospers. True, a few unlucky fellows, caught ashore in pursuit of information, were snapped up by pickets and sentinels, but on one pretense and another managed to get out of the scrape, and not one of them has as yet suffered any great physical inconvenience from the petty prejudice . . . of this doughty General. . . .[8]

To the discomfiture of everyone concerned, this second attempt to pinch off Vicksburg proved no more successful than the previous naval effort. Although the reporters knew nothing about it at the time, Grant was prevented from carrying out his part of the program by an attack upon his line of communications which compelled him to fall back toward Memphis. On the night before Sherman's futile assault against the Confederate position at Haines' Bluff, the correspondents of the New York *Herald* and *Times* made their miry bed in the forest. According to the *Herald* man:

> No fires were allowed, as they might reveal our position to the watchful enemy. The night was cold. Ice formed at the edge of the bayou, and there was a thick frost on the little patches of open ground. A negro who had lived in that region said the swamp usually abounded in moccasins, copperheads, and cane-snakes, in large numbers. An occasional rustling of the leaves at my side led me to imagine these snakes were endeavoring to make my acquaintance.
>
> Laying aside my snake fancies, it was too cold to sleep. As fast as I would fall into a doze, the chill of the atmosphere would steal through my blanket, and remind me of my location. Half-sleeping and half-waking, I dreamed of every thing disagreeable. I had visions of Greenland's icy mountains, of rambles in Siberia, of my long-past midwinter nights in the snow-drifted gorges of Colorado, of shipwreck, and of burning dwellings, and of all moving accidents by flood and field. . . .
>
> Cold and dampness and snakes and fitful dreams were not the only bodily discomforts. A dozen horses were loose in camp, and trotting gayly about. Several times they passed within a yard of my head. . . .
>
> A teamster, who mistook me for a log, led his mules over me. A negro, under the same delusion, attempted to convert me into a chair, and another wanted to break me up for fuel, to be used in making a fire after daylight. . . .

> A little past daylight a shell from the Rebel batteries exploded within twenty yards of my position, and warned me that it was time to rise. To make my toilet, I pulled the sticks and leaves from my hair and beard, and brushed my overcoat with a handful of moss. I breakfasted on a cracker and a spoonful of whisky. I gave my horse a handful of corn and a large quantity of leaves. The former he ate, but the latter he refused to touch. The column began to move, and I was ready to attend upon its fortunes.[9]

Within two or three hours after the combat began, it became obvious to the reporters that Sherman had undertaken an utterly hopeless assignment. After witnessing a futile charge against the lofty bluffs on the extreme Federal left, Knox and Wilkie moved to another part of the field to escape a possible flanking movement. They acted none too soon, for a heavy column of the enemy swept around the left in a very few minutes and closed the gap through which they had passed. During the course of the day they were many times under hot fire from the artillery on the bluffs and from the muskets of the flanking column.[10] The second day's fighting was a repetition of the first. While Sherman pondered his next move, word reached the army that McClernand finally had arrived to take over the command of the river expedition.

Sherman had been thoroughly unpopular with the press ever since the early days of the war, and it was a foregone conclusion, therefore, that he would be blamed for Grant's failure to take Vicksburg. The first detailed account of the reverse at Chickasaw Bayou, which appeared in the St. Louis *Republican,* was hostile. Similarly the correspondent of the St. Louis *Democrat* characterized the attack as "a stupid blunder, and an ignoble attempt to forestal another General's laurels."[11] Other army reporters revived the old canard that Sherman was insane and therefore unfit for command. Ever since the departure of Halleck from the Western theater of war the correspondents in that theater had been becoming bolder. Taking advantage of Grant's laissez faire policy toward the reporters, they discussed strategy with complete freedom from the customary restraints and became steadily more defiant of military authority.

Sherman was very much irritated by their criticism of his repulse. Some time during February, he wrote to his brother John:

> Now, to every army and almost every general a newspaper reporter goes along, filling up our transports, swelling our trains, reporting our progress, guessing at places, picking up dropped

> expressions, inciting jealousy and discontent, and doing infinite mischief....
>
> The press has now killed McClellan, Buell, Fitz-John Porter, Sumner, Franklin, and Burnside. Add my name and I am not ashamed of the association. If the press can govern the country, let them fight the battles.[12]

Convinced that the time had come, as he put it, "for discussion to cease and action to begin," the peppery general decided to make an example of Knox, whose letter to the *Herald* describing the recent debacle had been particularly offensive to him. Knox, he discovered, had boarded the steamer "Continental" below Memphis at the invitation of Major General Frank Blair, one of his own division commanders, and had enjoyed Blair's hospitality while en route to the scene of the battle. For a short time after the expedition disembarked he had remained on board the transport to circumvent an order calling for his arrest. Yet Knox, as previously mentioned, had managed to be present at the Battle of Chickasaw Bayou along with the other reporters. His account of it, addressed to a friend in Cairo, he placed in the mail at Sherman's headquarters only to be victimized by what Wilkie later characterized as the "assault upon the mail bags."[13] One of Sherman's staff officers, Colonel A. H. Markland, who later claimed that he was acting under orders from Sherman, opened and read all the newspaper letters he could find and then retained them in his possession for a week or ten days before he would permit them to be sent on to their destination. Knox's letter was left lying about headquarters for any officer to examine until finally at the correspondent's request it was returned to him, minus two maps which it had originally contained. In this, his first account of the battle, Knox had refrained from anything more than mild criticism of Sherman's generalship, but in a second account which he carried to Cairo in person he expressed his frank disapproval of the way the campaign had been managed.[14]

When he returned from Cairo about two weeks later, Knox was called before General Sherman to answer for his statements, which meanwhile had appeared in the *Herald*. Knox readily admitted that he had written the letter with which he was confronted, but his explanation only infuriated Sherman the more. "Of course, General Sherman, I had no feeling against you personally," drawled the former Yankee schoolmaster, "but you are regarded [as] the enemy of our set, and we must in self-defense write you down."[15] Afterwards, Knox wrote a letter to Sherman[16] in which he admitted that his report of the battle had been substantially incorrect, but his penitence came too late to deflect the General's wrath. Within a few days, orders were issued for his arrest, and he was taken into custody on board the steamboat "Warsaw" as a preliminary step to bringing him before a general court martial.

Since this was the first court martial of a newspaper correspondent, the case was of unusual interest. Beginning on February 6, the trial was held at Young's Point, Louisiana, before a court consisting of a brigadier general, four colonels, and two majors. Sherman explained to Admiral Porter:

> I am going to have the correspondent of the New York *Herald* tried by a court martial as a spy, not that I want the fellow shot, but because I want to establish the principle that such people cannot attend our armies, in violation of orders, and defy us, publishing their garbled statements and defaming officers who are doing their best.[17]

Three charges were preferred against the *Herald* correspondent: (1) giving information to the enemy directly or indirectly, (2) being a spy, and (3) disobedience of orders.

The first charge set forth that Knox had had published in the New York *Herald* of January 18, 1863, an article concerning the operations of the army before Vicksburg which conveyed to the enemy, in direct violation of the Fifty-Seventh Article of War, an approximate estimate of the army's strength.

The second charge specified that Knox had boarded the transport "Continental" at Helena on or about December 21, 1862, and had remained on board until about January 3, 1863, in violation of General Order No. 8, issued at Memphis on December 18, 1862. It further charged that Knox had published in the *Herald* sundry false allegations against officers in the service of the United States calculated to weaken their authority and to give aid and comfort to the enemy.

In support of the third charge it was argued that Knox had knowingly and willfully disobeyed not simply the order of General Sherman but also a general order issued by the War Department on August 26, 1861, which required that all publications concerning the military movements of the army be authorized and sanctioned by the general in command.

Sherman, appearing as the principal witness against Knox, apparently was determined to impose upon him the full penalties prescribed by military law. The *Herald* correspondent conducted a vigorous defense, however, through his counsel, Lieutenant Colonel W. B. Woods. Among his character witnesses were Generals Frederick Steele and Francis P. Blair; Colonel Isaac Shepherd, a former school teacher of Knox's, and William E. Webb of the St. Louis *Republican*, a fellow newspaper correspondent. Blair testified that although the *Herald* was a Democratic and conservative journal, Knox himself was a radical Republican and thoroughly loyal. Shepherd submitted as further evidence of Knox's loyalty the information that Knox was the only newspaper correspondent to whom the late General Nathaniel Lyon had confided his plan of campaign during the summer of 1861.

One of the principal arguments of the defense was that the War Department's general order of August 26, 1861, had been modified by Sanford's "Notice to the Correspondents," issued during the Peninsular Campaign and permitting the correspondents in McClellan's army to give the order of battle after an engagement had taken place. In this connection the defense pointed out that Knox's letter to the *Herald* had been written four days after the repulse at Chickasaw Bayou and not until after Sherman's army had moved some twenty-five miles from the scene of its defeat. With respect to the alleged violation of Sherman's general order, the defense argued that authority to board the steamer "Continental" was conferred upon the correspondent of the *Herald* by a pass, issued to him by General Grant on December 16, 1862, which was in his possession when he went on board.

The weakest point in the case against Knox was the lack of any evidence to indicate that a copy of the issue of the *Herald* containing Knox's Vicksburg letter actually had come into the possession of the enemy. The prosecution, well aware of this, apparently attempted to delay the trial until such evidence could be obtained. The relevancy of efforts made by the prosecution to show that on other occasions Northern newspapers had found their way into enemy hands was strenuously attacked by the defense.

The sessions of the court martial extended over a period of almost a fortnight, and the court's decision was not finally made known until the morning of February 18, 1863. The court then announced that Knox had been acquitted on the first two charges but had been found guilty of the third. After debating for some time whether he might not be let off with an official reprimand, the court ruled that he should be expelled from the lines of the Army of the Tennessee and ordered not to return under penalty of imprisonment. Similar charges preferred against eight other newspaper correspondents subsequently were dropped.[18]

Sherman was far from being satisfied with the decision of the court martial. In a letter to John A. Rawlins, the Assistant Adjutant General, he objected vigorously to the statement of the court that it attached no criminality to the fact that Knox had accompanied the Vicksburg expedition in defiance of the General's orders. He maintained:

> The inference is that a commanding officer has no right to prohibit citizens from accompanying a military expedition, or, if he does, such citizens incur no criminality by disregarding such command.

Sherman also objected to the court's ruling that Knox's letter to the *Herald* did not convey to the enemy an approximate estimate of the strength of his army, saying:

> . . . if to prove the conveyance of indirect information to the enemy it be necessary to follow that information from its source to the very armies arrayed against us, whose country thus far our hundreds of thousands of men have been unable to invade, and yet whose newspapers are made up of extracts from those very Northern papers, then it is fruitless to attempt to conceal from them all the data they could need to make successful resistance to our plans, and to attack our detached parties and lines of communication.[19]

Knox, on the other hand, had powerful friends who were determined to vindicate him if possible. When the news of his sentence reached the Capital, the members of the Washington press corps, headed by Colonel Forney, united in a petition to the President, requesting him to set aside the sentence. The petition asserted that Knox was known to be thoroughly loyal and declared that it had been the general practice since the beginning of the war not to subject newspaper letters to censorship.[20] Lincoln received the petitioners very amiably and exchanged reminiscences with one of their number, Albert D. Richardson, whom he had met in the West before the war when Richardson was reporting for the Boston *Journal.* In answer to the petition, Lincoln told his callers that he was perfectly willing to suspend Knox's sentence if Grant would agree, but he was not prepared to go over the head of his general. The most he would do was to provide Knox with a letter, which in effect left in Grant's hands the question whether the *Herald* man could return to the army. Grant in turn referred the matter to Sherman, whose answer was a foregone conclusion.[21]

To offset friction between Sherman and McClernand, Grant meanwhile had taken over the direct command of the Army of the Tennessee. During February and March, while the army's new head was trying out various expedients for renewing the attack against Vicksburg, considerable sickness developed in the army. Much of it was the result of high water along the river which made soggy ground for pitching tents. Still annoyed with Sherman, however, the army newsmen wrote angry letters, castigating the inefficiency of the army's medical department. In a letter published in the *Times,* Franc Wilkie told of officers occupying all the fine homes in the vicinity of the army while the sick were left to die "in narrow boats and dirty huts, lately used by negroes." Fully 60 per cent, he estimated, of the one hundred deaths occurring daily could be prevented "were it not for the culpability and negligence of those in command."[22] Subsequent investigation by the Sanitary Commission indicated that the press had considerably exaggerated the amount of sickness in the army.[23]

Meanwhile, attempting to get a foothold on the East bank of the Mississippi, Grant had set his men to work digging a canal across the peninsula formed by a bend of the river immediately West of Vicksburg. On March 1, Joe McCullagh wrote to the Cincinnati *Commercial:*

> The Vicksburg canal seems to afford an inexhaustible theme for newspaper letter writers. And there is this singular fact connected with it, that the further north you go, the more favorable is its condition and prospect. For instance, down here the impression is that it is a decided failure (and I claim at least the credit of having been consistent in pronouncing it a failure from the first, and adhering to that opinion ever since); at Memphis it is always progressing slowly but surely; at Cairo, the sensation men usually have it "doing well when last heard from;" but at Chicago and St. Louis there is no middle ground—it is always a "splendid success."[24]

Six weeks after the canal was begun, a sudden rise in the river level destroyed the dam and caused the project to be given up. Unexpected obstacles also had nullified an attempt to exploit a more roundabout route to the South of Vicksburg by way of Lake Providence and the Red River. Similarly a plan to transport Grant's army down the East side of the Mississippi by way of the Yazoo Pass and there to turn the

Confederates' strong position at Haines' Bluff was dropped after it was discovered that earthworks had been erected by the enemy to command the Yazoo Pass approaches.

Even before Grant assumed direct command of the Vicksburg expedition, however, Junius Browne in a letter to the Cincinnati *Times* had expressed grave doubts about his capacity for military leadership.[25] The continuation of the stalemate at Vicksburg and the apparent failure of what McCullagh styled the "frog-pond strategy"[26] led to repeated outcries from the press for Grant's removal. On February 19, 1863, Murat Halstead wrote to Secretary Chase, enclosing a copy of a letter from one of the army correspondents of the *Commercial* which presented a very dismal and not altogether accurate picture of the situation at Vicksburg:

> There never was a more thoroughly disgusted, disheartened, demoralized army than this is, and all because it is under such men as Grant and Sherman. Disease is decimating its ranks, and while hundreds of poor fellows are dying from smallpox and every other conceivable malady, the medical department is afflicted with delirium tremens. In Memphis smallpox patients are made to walk through the streets from camps to hospitals, while drunken doctors ride from bar rooms in government ambulances. How is it that Grant, who was behind at Fort Henry, drunk at Donelson, surprised and whipped at Shiloh, and driven back from Oxford, Miss., is still in command?

To this Halstead added:

> Governor Chase, these things are true. Our noble army of the Mississippi is being wasted by the foolish, drunken, stupid Grant. He can't organize or control or fight an army. . . . There is not among the whole list of retired major generals a man who is not Grant's superior.[27]

Although Lincoln was unmoved by the press's clamor for Grant's removal, he realized that to appraise the work of Grant and others in his command accurately he had need of one who should be in his words "the eyes of the government at the front."[28] For this purpose Secretary Stanton selected a former newspaper editor, Charles A. Dana, to go to Grant's army, ostensibly as a special commissioner of the War Department to investigate the pay service of the Western armies, but actually to give daily reports of military developments and to provide reliable information concerning Grant and those immediately under him. Dana arrived at Millikan's Bend, where Grant's headquarters were then located, during the first week of April, 1863; during the next three months he sent almost daily telegrams to Washington relating what he had seen and heard. His dispatches, written in clear concise English, were excellent examples of objective reporting. Grant seemed rather relieved than otherwise to have Dana with the army, for he did not like letter writing and Dana's daily dispatches to Stanton spared him the necessity of transmitting lengthy reports to Washington.[29]

One of the favorite, and dangerous, pastimes of the newspapermen while the stalemate continued was to take a four-day run up to Cairo on a river steamer. The river banks between Vicksburg and Memphis were the favorite haunt of guerillas, who liked nothing better than to make life miserable for the passengers on the river steamers. The reporters soon learned that the best procedure was to flatten out with the head or feet in the direction of the enemy's fire and so expose as little of the anatomy as possible.[30] While lying there hugging the floor and listening to the sound of shot crashing through the frail upper structure of the vessel, it must have seemed to the bravest soul that the boat was an eternity in getting away.

One of the most adventurous experiences which any of the reporters had during the siege of Vicksburg was the result of an attempt by Admiral Porter to run some vessels past the Vicksburg batteries. Three newspapermen were on board the gunboat-ram "Queen of the West" on the morning of February 2 when she started down the river, shortly before dawn, on her dangerous mission. At least one of the reporters was well aware of the risks he and his companions were running. Finley Anderson informed his managing editor:

> I have come on board the Queen of the West to accompany Colonel Ellet on another excursion. . . . We expect to start this evening. We have only a small number of men on board—not more than twenty-five or thirty. We are going up Red river *to see what there is there.* It is said that there are several fine transports up the river. If they have not escaped down to Port Hudson we will be after them. It is reported that about sixty miles up Red river there is a battery, and a steamship manned with two hundred and fifty men. If we fall in with her she will try to board us, and if she does there will be a desperate fight. . . .
>
> One of the principal considerations which induce [sic] me to

> accompany the Colonel is an opportunity to test my own personal courage. I go with the understanding that it is probable we will have a hand to hand fight with the rebels. I have been in several battles, and sometimes under pretty heavy fire. But that is not enough. I want to see, just for my own gratification, what kind of stuff I am made of.
>
> If anything serious should happen [to] me I hope you will see that my Mother is not left entirely unprovided for.[31]

For a whole hour the little ram, unarmored except at the prow, was within pistol shot range of the powerful Confederate batteries. While twisting her way through the storm of projectiles leveled at her, the "Queen" sighted a Confederate gunboat lying in the river. At Colonel Ellet's command, the pilot ran her down with such force that the "Queen" stuck fast and seemed about to capsize. While McCullagh of the Cincinnati *Commercial* looked on with amazement, Ellet took a burning stick and started for the powder magazine, resolved to blow up his ship rather than let it be captured. Before he could carry out his desperate intention, the ram swung loose from its adversary and floated out of range of the big Confederate guns. Although she had been struck twelve times during the fracas, nobody on board was hurt, and only trifling damage had been done to the vessel.[32]

Accompanied by the tender "De Soto," the "Queen of the West" continued downstream past the mouth of the Big Black River, Grand Gulf, and Natchez. The evening of February 14, while on its way up the Red River, the Union raider came in sight of a small Confederate battery at Gordon's Landing, about seventy miles from the river's mouth. She was within five hundred yards of the fort when her pilot accidentally ran her aground and could not back her off. Unable to bring her broadside guns to bear on the fort, the "Queen" soon was put out of commission. One thirty-two pound shell, fired at point blank range, penetrated her steam chest and filled her with scalding steam.

Albert H. Bodman of the Chicago *Tribune* was in the pilot house at the time. Quick thinking prompted him to drape a coat about his head and prevented him from being badly scalded. Dashing out of the pilot house, he ran to the stern and from a rope's end dropped into a yawl being used to convey Colonel Ellet to the "De Soto." McCullagh already had sortied from the stricken vessel on a cotton bale, and eventually reached the "De Soto" with some assistance from a passing skiff.

Anderson, the *Herald* correspondent, was less fortunate. Thinking that Colonel Ellet would return with the "De Soto" to rescue the remainder of the "Queen" 's crew, he made no effort to escape. His narrative of the experience, published after more than a year spent inside a Confederate prison, told how:

> Standing on the hurricane deck, I watched the De Soto's light, which looked like a star of hope in the surrounding gloom. I watched it for an hour. It was our only hope. But it did not come. . . . Presently Lieutenant Tuthill came up in a boat from the De Soto to take off our wounded sailing master, Thompson, and to burn the Queen. . . . While we were moving Mr. Thompson an excited soldier came rushing from the gun deck into the cabin, shouting, "I saw three boats full of rebels coming to board us on the bow." The poor wounded man was dropped, like a hot potato, on the cabin floor; the word flew through the ship like wildfire that the rebels were boarding us; the little boat which had been brought up for the wounded officer was instantly cut loose, and was soon at the De Soto with the news that we were boarded. I went out on the gundeck to receive the rebels; but not a rebel was there to receive. The abnormal imagination of the excited soldier must have created boats and human beings out of the shadows on the water of overhanging bushes on the shore. . . . It was now impossible for those on board the Queen to get away. . . . Why did I not jump into the river and get upon a cotton bale? Because I was the guest of the commander; because I was every moment expecting him back on the De Soto, and I thought that to stand by his ship till his return was the part of duty and the part of honor. But he did not return, and that was the reason we were captured.[33]

Hotly pursued by the fast Confederate gunboat "Webb," the survivors of the expedition made their escape down the Red River on the "Era" No. 5, a river packet which they had captured on their way upstream. Soon after they entered the Mississippi, they had the good fortune to be hailed by the ironclad "Indianola," which Porter had sent past Vicksburg on the thirteenth. After watching the "Webb" put to flight by the "Indianola" 's eleven-inch guns, McCullagh and Bodman continued upstream on the "Era." Running past the batteries at Warrenton and several other points, they landed safely on the West bank of the river within the Federal picket lines at midnight on February 22.[34]

Meanwhile Farragut had been urging upon Banks, Butler's successor at New Orleans, the importance of occupying Baton Rouge as a base of operations against Port Hudson. On March 5, Thomas M. Cash, the New Orleans correspondent of the *Herald,* notified Frederic Hudson:

> We are on the eve of important movements; Port Hudson is to be attacked in a few days and I am making every arrangement accordingly. Mr. Thompson leaves tomorrow to join the army at Baton Rouge and I think that I shall assume the responsibilty of sending Mr. Slack with the Squadron, as the attack is to be simultaneous by land and water. . . .
>
> I yesterday . . . called on Admiral Farragut, and was by him remarkably well received. He has also extended every facility and permits *a Herald* man to go on board of any ship I may select. Dr. Foltz the fleet surgeon promises to give me *ahead of all others* a full copy of all casualties. I am rapidly effecting the organization of my department in a manner that will I hope, give entire satisfaction to Mr. Bennett and yourself.[35]

By March 14, the energetic Farragut had assembled a force of four heavy ships and three lighter ones to run past the Port Hudson batteries. The loss of the "Queen of the West" had been followed by the capture of the "Indianola" on February 24, and Porter was too busy North of Vicksburg just then to do anything about reestablishing the blockade of the Red River. It was the plan of the Admiral that each of the three larger ships, the "Hartford," "Richmond," and "Monongahela," should lash a gunboat to her port side to provide motive power if anything happened to their boilers during the engagement. The rearmost vessel, the antique side-wheeler "Mississippi," however, was not built to permit a consort alongside, but some assistance in passing the batteries was to be expected from a flotilla of six mortar schooners which were to remain below Port Hudson.[36]

As the squadron was preparing to get underway that evening of March 14 one of the officers on board the "Richmond" asked the *Herald* correspondent where he was going to station himself during the fight.

"Anywhere," replied Slack, "so that I can be out of the way of the men working the guns, and yet see all that is going on."

"Then I recommend you to get up to the main or fore top," suggested the officer.

"But suppose the mast happens to be shot away—such things do happen, you know—where will the *Herald* correspondent and his report be?"

"Well, you must take your chance," was the answer.

"Of course I must," retorted the newsman, "but, don't you see, I have come here, not to fight or be killed, but to describe what is done. Now if I should happen to be killed or badly wounded, I should just like to know how the *Herald* readers are to be enlightened about the battle of Port Hudson."

"Very cogent reasoning," put in the chief engineer at that point. "Therefore, Mr. Slack, you had better come down with me into the engine room."

To this the *Herald* man objected even more decidedly. In the engine room he would not be able to see anything, and besides there was the risk of being scalded to death should a shot enter one of the boilers. Eventually it was arranged that he should view the fight from the topgallant forecastle.

At exactly 9:00 P.M. the signal for all the vessels to weigh anchor was hoisted on the Admiral's flagship. Immediately the fifer began, encouraging the men at the capstan. He started with an old Virginia reel, shifted to something equally lively and ended, according to custom, with "Yankee Doodle." Soon the "Richmond"'s anchor was aweigh, and she was laboring upstream in the wake of the lead ship, "Hartford." At the first tap of the drum beating to quarters, the *Herald* correspondent went topside to the topgallant forecastle and selected a comfortable seat on the "fish davit," a spar running out from the foremast to the port side. As he looked about him, the reporter noted with some satisfaction that there was no wood work in front of him to be broken into splinters, "those fruitful sources of wounds and death in naval warfare."

The Confederate guns on shore remained silent until the cavalcade of ships was within eight hundred yards of them. Then rockets flared, and an eight-inch rifled shot from one of the batteries fractured the silence. Soon the "Richmond" drew within range of the enemy's fire and became the target of a torrent of shot. In gripping style, the *Herald* man described the action:

> While seated on the "fish davit"...—the Hartford and the Richmond blazing away at the time—a most fearful wail arose from the river, first on our port bow, then on the beam. A man was evidently overboard, probably from the Hartford or the Genesee, then just ahead.... "Man overboard," called out Lieutenant Terry; "throw him a rope." But, poor fellow, who could assist him in such a strait? We were in action; every man was at his gun; to lower a boat would be folly.... Consequently, al-

though the man was evidently a good swimmer, to judge by his unfailing cries for help for a long time, nothing could be done to rescue him, and he floated astern of us, still sending up that wailing cry for help, but without effect. The terrible current of the Mississippi was too much for him, and he, without doubt, sank beneath the waves of the mighty river.

Just after this fearful incident firing was heard astern of us, and it was soon ascertained that the Monongahela, with her consort, the Kineo, and the Mississippi, were in action. The Monongahela carries a couple of two hundred-pounder rifled Parrott guns, besides other ticklers. At first I credited the roar of her amiable two hundred-pounders to the "bummers," till I was undeceived, when I recalled my experience in front of Yorktown last spring, and the opening of fire from similar guns from Wormley's creek. All I can say is, the noise was splendid. The action now became general. The roar of cannon was incessant, and the flashes from the guns, together with the flight of the shells from the mortar boats, made up a combination of sound and sight impossible to describe. To add to the horrors of the night, while it contributed towards the enhancement of a certain terrible beauty, dense clouds of smoke began to envelope the river, shutting out from view the several vessels and confounding them with the batteries. It was very difficult to know how to steer to prevent running ashore, perhaps right under a rebel battery or into a consort. Upwards and upwards rolled the smoke, shutting out of view the beautiful stars and obscuring the vision on every side. Then it was that the order was passed, "Boys, don't fire till you see the flash from the enemy's guns." That was our only guide through the "palpable obscurity". . . .

Nearly up to the time when the action became general my eyes were principally cast aloft, watching the flight of the shells thrown by the "bummers"; but I confess that when the fire became concentrated on the Richmond I ceased star-gazing, and directed my anxious glance ahead, or towards the starboard side, although now and then I did cast a furtive look aloft, to see if it were likely that one of the pretty little celestial toys . . . would drop on board of us, as some of them seemed not unlikely to do. Happily for us we escaped the disaster, which, had it happened, would have been a poor way of "backing o' your friends". . . . While thus on the *qui vive* I would occasionally get up and walk about the topgallant forecastle for a change of position. During one of these peregrinations a terrific explosion took place beneath me. A shell had entered the forward port on the starboard side, and exploded right under the gun . . . cutting off the two legs of a boatswain's mate at the knees and . . . shaking the topgallant forecastle as if with an earthquake. I knew nothing of what had taken place till some time afterwards.

This phrase ["muzzle to muzzle"] is familiar to most persons who have read accounts of sea fights that took place about fifty years ago, but it is difficult for the uninitiated to realize all the horrors conveyed in these three words. For the first time I had, last night, an opportunity of knowing what the phrase really meant. Let the reader consult the accompanying map, and it will be seen that the central battery is situated about the middle of the segment of a circle I have already compared to a horseshoe in shape, though it may better be understood by the term "crescent." This battery stands on a bluff so high that a vessel in passing immediately underneath cannot elevate her guns sufficiently to reach those on the battery; neither can the guns on the battery be sufficiently depressed to bear on the passing ship. In this position the rebel batteries on the two horns of the crescent can enfilade the passing vessel, pouring in a terrible cross fire, which the vessel can return, though at a terrible disadvantage, from her bow and stern chasers. We fully realized this last night; for, as we got within short range, the enemy poured into us a terrible fire of grape and canister, which we were not slow to return—our guns being double shotted, each with a stand of both grape and canister. . . . This was the hottest part of the engagement. We were literally muzzle to muzzle, the distance between us and the enemy's guns being not more than twenty yards, though to me it seemed to be only as many feet. In fact, the battle of Port Hudson has been pronounced by officers and seamen who were engaged in it, and who were present at the passage of Fort St. Philip and Fort Jackson, below New Orleans, and had participated in the fights of Fort Donelson, Fort Henry, Island No. 10, Vicksburg, &c, as the severest in the naval history of the present war. . . .

Matters had gone on in this way for nearly an hour and a half —the first gun having been fired at about half past eleven o'clock —when, to my astonishment, I heard some shells whistling over our port side. Did the rebels have batteries on the right bank of the river? was the query that naturally suggested itself to me. To this the response was given that we had turned back. I soon discovered that it was too true. Our return was, of course, more

> rapid than our passage up. The rebels did not molest us much, and I do not believe one of their shots took effect while we were running down rapidly with the current. . . . We had the satisfaction of learning soon afterwards . . . that the Hartford and the Albatross had succeeded in rounding the point above the batteries. All the rest were compelled to return. We soon came to anchor on the west side of Prophet Island, so near to the shore that the poopdeck was strewn with the blossoms and leaves of the budding trees that we brushed back.[37]

Unable to determine by signal what had happened to the rest of his fleet, Farragut steamed northward in the "Hartford" the next morning, reaching the southern approach to Vicksburg on the twentieth. His total casualties had been one hundred and thirteen, thirty-five of whom were killed.[38] The heaviest losses had occurred on the "Mississippi," which ran aground on the point across from the batteries and was abandoned and set on fire by her crew after all attempts to refloat her had failed. J. R. Hamilton, the New York *Times* reporter who had marched up from Baton Rouge with Banks, gloomed:

> I cannot help thinking . . . that instead of a *partial*, we should have had a *complete* success at Port Hudson, had we been less wedded to our old notions of wooden vessels, and more prone to avail ourselves of the resources of modern science in the use of iron clads. . . .
>
> Why have we not used iron vessels? Simply because, I am told, there is a *prejudice* in the navy against them. One brave officer of the *Mississippi*, in conversation with me, actually laughed at the idea of causing Port Hudson to be evacuated by starving them out. Not that he doubted it could be done, and by iron clads safely passing the forts, but he said that was "*no way of making war.*"[39]

By the time Hamilton's letter appeared in print, developments were taking shape to the North that gave a new direction to the river campaign. For months Grant had been pondering the idea of a movement by land to a point below Vicksburg.

One evening shortly before the middle of April, Franc Wilkie strolled into the tent of Major General Fred Steele, whom he had known since the beginning of the war, and asked him if he had any news.

"Well, yes; there is some," he replied with some hesitation.

"It must be something serious. Is it something that you can give me?"

"Yes, I suppose I can. There was a consultation this afternoon among Grant and other officers, at which Grant submitted a plan for a change of base to some point below Vicksburg so that we can unite with Banks at Port Hudson."

"Was the plan agreed to?"

"By no means. On the contrary, every officer present who expressed an opinion opposed the proposition. In fact, some of them did more than merely oppose it; they protested formally against its adoption."[40]

Naval cooperation of course would be essential to cover the ferrying of troops from the Louisiana shore to the East bank of the river. While Porter made ready to transport his fleet below Vicksburg, Grant started McClernand's corps down the West bank of the Mississippi toward New Carthage, Louisiana, thirty miles below their objective. By April 16, Porter had a fleet of seven ironclads and three army transports loaded with forage and rations ready to move down. At ten o'clock that night the naval contingent started on its perilous journey before a large audience of army officers and their wives who had gathered on board a transport to view the spectacle. For more than two hours the ironclad armada was under fire from the batteries, every one of the gunboats being struck many times but not much damaged. The Confederate gunners, however, did succeed in sinking one of the transports and in disabling another, which was taken in tow by one of the gunboats. Since he was the only newspaperman present that night, Wilkie gave the *Times* an exclusive account of Porter's daring movement.[41]

After an unsuccessful attempt by Porter to silence the Confederate batteries at Grand Gulf on the twenty-ninth, Grant moved farther South the following day to land three divisions at Bruinsburg, on the East bank of the river. Misled by Sherman's diversionary movement to the North of Vicksburg, Pemberton, the Confederate commander, failed to realize what was happening until it was too late and even then he did not react vigorously enough. Meanwhile, his adversary pushed on to Port Gibson, twelve miles eastward, against comparatively light opposition, forcing the Confederates to evacuate their strong position at Grand Gulf.

The sudden transfer of Grant's army below Vicksburg brought newspaper correspondents flocking to the scene. Hastening to overtake the advance units of Grant's marching column, the New York *Tribune*'s Richardson and Colburn of the *World* arrived at Milliken's Bend on May 3, where they were joined by Junius Browne. There they learned that two tugs, each with a barge load of supplies, were to have been sent down the river on the night of May 1, but for some reason the trip had been postponed. That very night, however, it was planned that the tug "Sturgis" and two barges were to run the batteries at Vicksburg, Warrenton, and Grand Gulf with four hundred thousand rations and some medical supplies. The three reporters held a caucus. To reach Grant by the overland route would require a three-day ride of some sixty miles through guerilla-infested country. By running the batteries they might expect to reach Grant's headquarters within eight hours and with a minimum of effort. They readily decided to embark as passengers for the trip.

At ten o'clock the barges cast loose under a bright moon, and the little tug led the way out into the channel. Fifteen sharpshooters from the Forty-Seventh Ohio, a surgeon, the tug's crew of eight, four soldiers on the way to join their regiments, and the three newspapermen made up the party. The barges were covered with bales of hay to protect the tug, but the hay was strung about quite loosely, and the ends of the barges were freely exposed. For several hours the diminutive supply echelon glided silently along, moving very little faster than the current of the stream. At about midnight it came within sight of Vicksburg and approximately a half hour later the rebel pickets on the Louisiana shore opened fire. Then a signal rocket shot upward from the city, and the night voyagers soon were subjected to a heavy fire from the Vicksburg batteries.

Since the river forms a loop in front of Vicksburg, the "Sturgis" party had to run by the city under fire and then, continuing around the loop, run past the city a second time at point blank range. "At first," said Colburn, "there were efforts to peer from behind the rampart of hay bales, and duck on perceiving the flash of the rebel guns; but soon the shots were so rapid and from points so widely apart that that exciting amusement was dropped."[42] Browne, however, persisted in standing in an exposed position to watch the approaching shots. Once, as an explosion was heard near at hand, he dropped down heavily among the hay bales. Fortunately he only had slipped and fallen.

After twenty minutes of bombardment the barges still were afloat, and the little tug continued its reassuring "puff, puff." Already the barges had passed the upper batteries; ten minutes more and they would be out of danger. Then at 12:45 A.M., a terrific explosion, accompanied by a haunting shriek, drowned out the bombardment's roar. A plunging ten-inch shot from one of the upper batteries had scored a direct hit on the boiler of the tug, had killed the captain as he stood at the wheel, and had obliterated the tug. Almost immediately the hay bales on the barges were ignited by a shower of glowing coals, and soon the flames were beyond control.

"The play is over," said Richardson with an attempt at jocularity.

"Hand in your checks, boys," exclaimed Colburn.

"A change of base for the Bohemians," commented Browne with the same forced hilarity.

Richardson was the first member of the trio to take to the water. Colburn and Browne remained on board until everyone else had left and then, with only one bale left for both, stripped for the plunge. Just as they were ready to dive in, a solid shot passed between them and plowed up the water below Richardson, rolling him off his bale and ducking him thoroughly. Colburn and Browne then plunged into the muddy flood and made for the Louisiana shore, where they hoped to reach the protection of friendly pickets. Presently a yawl filled with armed men overtook them, and they were hauled over the side to join those other survivors who had already been picked up. Guarded by rebel bayonets and huddled together in the moonlight, the fugitives took stock: sixteen men including the three correspondents, roughly half of the original party, were alive and unharmed; the remainder were killed, wounded, scalded, or missing. Following their arrival at Vicksburg, the prisoners were accorded the doubtful hospitality of the city jail pending the determination of their future status.[43]

It had been Grant's original intention to move South from Grand Gulf to cooperate with Banks in the reduction of Port Hudson before proceeding against Vicksburg. Learning, however, that Banks was considerably behind schedule and that Joe Johnston was on his way to Jackson to organize the defense of Vicksburg, Grant decided instead to swing to the northeast. Writing from Rocky Springs, Mississippi, on May 7, one of the New York *Tribune* correspondents described the slow advance of the army into the heart of Mississippi "with Jackson in front, and Port Gibson eighteen miles behind." One feature of his description was especially striking:

> We frequently come upon residences of rare beauty, with airy verandahs, and gardens of evergreen and May roses; but the stragglers of the army have made complete havoc of everything in the shape of provisions, portable wares of value, and even

> furniture. Frequently, mirrors, sideboards, wardrobes, and libraries are wantonly demolished and trodden under foot. . . .
>
> Notwithstanding the necessities of the army, they cannot justify the wanton vandalism of our soldiery. I have been personally witness to scenes of pillage which would emulate that of the followers of Attila. . . . It is but justice to the troops to add that these outrages are perpetrated principally by stragglers, who belong to the same category with the "vultures" that rifle the dead on the field of battle.[44]

Five days later McPherson soundly whipped the enemy at Raymond after a brisk two-hour fight and then pushed on to Jackson, which he and Sherman occupied on the fifteenth after a clash with Johnston's inferior force. McCullagh's description of the fight at Raymond was roundly criticized by a fellow correspondent, who complained because he referred to it as:

> a hard fought battle, while the battle of Port Gibson he classes as a "heavy skirmish." We lost over double the number, fought three times as long, and took four times the number of prisoners at Port Gibson. Comparatively, was the battle of Raymond more than a *light* skirmish?[45]

In one of his most interesting letters of the campaign, the New York *Times* man Wilkie sketched a graphic picture of street scenes in captured Jackson on the day the Union troops marched in. Like the *Tribune* man he took special note of the plundering carried on by stragglers, assisted by resident Negroes and "poor white citizens":

> Nothing came amiss to these rejoicing Africans; they went around the streets displaying aggregate miles of double-rowed ivory, and bending under an enormous load of French mirrors, boots, shoes, pieces of calico, wash-stands and bowls, hoop skirts, bags of tobacco, parasols, umbrellas, and fifty other articles equally incongruous. I noticed among the crowd several pretty but poorly-dressed white girls, who were delightfully familiar with the soldiers, and who were about equally active in toting off plunder and chewing tobacco.

Among the captured articles which attracted his attention were:

> a large number of mail bags, a majority of which were filled with letters from the Vicksburgh [sic] army to their friends at home. They were of the usual character—ten per cent. of the writers

> unable to spell correctly the name of county and State; seventy per cent commencing: "Dere Companyan i seet miself an taik mi pen in hand" &c., and containing, in equal quantities, abuse of the "Yanks," protestations of affection for wife and children, and particular directions for the treatment of the gray steer; one per cent. written well and spelled correctly; and all, with one single exception, full of valorous brag relative to whipping, annihilating and otherwise "using up" Yankees. The exception was in the case of one writer, who informed "deer jim," in a manner partaking at once of emphasis and truth, that the "Yanks is giveing us h—— everyware."[46]

Learning from an intercepted dispatch that Johnston was planning to cross the Big Black River and reinforce Lieutenant General John C. Pemberton at Vicksburg, Grant now faced about and in a series of swift movements, resulting in clashes at Champion's Hill and Big Black River Bridge, forced Pemberton to retire within the city's defenses. One of the best accounts of the Battle of Champion's Hill was written by Joe McCullagh of the Cincinnati *Commercial*[47]:

> We (the Mule and I) were traveling toward the left, in the immediate rear of Hovey's division, then fighting desperately for the ground on which it stood. Pretty soon Hovey had to fall back. I tried to indicate to my long-eared steed that I wished to do the same, but he evinced a stubborn disposition to advance instead of retreat. I pulled first one rein and then the other, but the mule wouldn't stir. I spurred the animal, but it only made him kick, and I was obliged to desist in prospect of being left on the road side. The rebels were advancing—were already within rifle range—and the bullets were whistling in pursuit of our men, not of me, I thought, for they surely would not hit a non-combatant. And still the mule wouldn't turn back. . . . If I had had a rat tail file, I should have spiked and abandoned him. He then commenced an unearthly bawl, which I interpreted as my funeral dirge, and which would undoubtedly have proven so, had I not dismounted and led him to the rear, arriving there just in time to save myself. I have studiously avoided mules ever since, and intend to do so for three years, or during the war.[48]

Now that Pemberton was penned up in Vicksburg, Grant hoped that it might be possible to carry the Confederate works by direct assault. A preliminary thrust on May 19 was followed by an assault in force on the twenty-second; both attempts were turned back with heavy losses.

Several officers who had been slightly injured in the affair on the nineteenth turned up at Memphis four days later, however, with a report that Vicksburg had fallen. W. G. Fuller, the telegraph manager at Memphis, promptly sent a telegram to Washington via Cleveland on Saturday night, May 23, stating that "The Stars and Stripes are over Vicksburg, and the victory is complete." The Cleveland telegraph office held the message until the following morning, hoping to confirm it and then finally sent it on to Washington, where it was released to the press on Monday morning, May 25. The report that "Vicksburg is ours" was the occasion for the most enthusiastic celebration that the North had witnessed since the victory at Fort Donelson. Not until several days later was it established that the story was completely without basis.[49]

After his failure to take Vicksburg by a frontal assault, Grant was convinced of the necessity for a regular siege. On the land side several mines were dug, and along the river front Porter's mortar-boat flotilla maintained an incessant bombardment of the city. While the siege was in progress, President Lincoln, like everyone else in the North, was keenly interested in what was going on before Vicksburg. Day and night he visited the War Department to hear the latest news and in some cases to telegraph queries to those officers who were nearest the scene of action. One night Gobright, the Washington agent of the Associated Press, called upon Lincoln to inquire about Vicksburg.

"I have nothing new," replied Lincoln. "I am much concerned about affairs; I can't sleep to-night without hearing something. Come. Go with me to the War Department. Perhaps Stanton has something."

As the two men climbed the staircase, a messenger from the telegraph office in the War Department building handed the President a dispatch dated at some point in the Southwest which stated that "A report has reached here that our troops at Vicksburg have been defeated and our army dispersed." As Lincoln read the dispatch, straining his eyes to decipher its contents under the flickering gas light, he betrayed his extreme nervousness. His hands and legs shook violently, and his face was ghastly pale. Turning to Gobright, he read the dispatch in faltering tones and then repeated half to himself, "Bad news, bad news!" Then, recollecting himself, he remarked with some concern: "Don't say anything about this—don't mention it." At this point Gobright asked permission to make a comment.

"Well, sir."

"The dispatch you have received mentions that the communication of disaster is founded on mere 'report.' It does not come from an army officer, or from any known responsible party. It is given as rumor; probably uttered by some deserter as an excuse for leaving the field. At all events, the story lacks confirmation; and please believe, as we all know from observation, if not from experience, that more than one half of war rumors are false. And so it may be in this particular case."[50]

The President appeared to be somewhat relieved by this advice, which turned out to accord with the facts. Actually there was little to report from Grant's army at this time other than the enormous amount of labor performed in the entrenchment and mining operations. As one of the reporters made clear to his readers, the country immediately to the East of Vicksburg was a succession of hills, which were hardly more than two hundred yards apart. Each hill was surmounted by a fort, well flanked by rifle pits along the hillsides and in the ravines below. As fast as Pemberton's men were dislodged from one of these strong points they took refuge in the next one to the rear. One of the best newspaper descriptions of these tortuous operations was the work of a special correspondent of the Cleveland (Ohio) *Herald*:

> Let us climb the parapet and see the siege by moonlight. In front of us, beyond the enemy's works, but hidden from us, lies the city of Vicksburg. Look carefully, and you can distinguish the spires of the courthouse and two or three churches. The rebels had a signal station on the former when we came, but our shells made it too warm for them, and they withdrew. The mortars are playing to-night, and they are well worth seeing. We watch a moment, and in the direction of Young's Point, beyond the city, suddenly up shoots a flash of light, and in a moment the ponderous shell, with its fuse glowing and sparkling, rises slowly from behind the bluffs; up, up, it goes, as though mounting to the zenith, over it comes towards us, down through its flight trajectory into the city, and explodes with a shock that jars the ground for miles. There are women and tender children where those shells fall, but war is war.
>
> Sherman's eight-inch monsters are grumbling far way on the right. Nearer, McPherson's, too, are playing—we can even see the cannoneers beside them at each flash. Our's will open at midnight; then there will be music to your heart's content. Meanwhile, let us go to the front. A hundred yards to the right of where we now are we enter a deep trench. Following this, as it winds down around the hill, we reach the opening of a cave or

mine. The air within is damp and close, like that of a vault. Candles are burning dimly at intervals, and we hear a hum of voices far within and out of sight. We proceed, and presently meet two men carrying a barrow of earth, for our boys are at work night and day. Finally, we reach the moonlight again, and emerge into a wide, deep trench, cut across the line of the covered way. This is open, and filled with troops, who protect the working party. A heavy parapet of cotton bales and earth is built on the side towards the enemy, and we must mount them to look over.

We are now within sociable distance of the chivalry. Those men lying on the ground, ten to thirty yards from us, are our boys, our advance pickets; but that gray fellow, with the bright musket, which glistens so, a few steps beyond, is a "reb.," long-haired and hot-blooded, one of Wall's famous Texas legion—a bull-dog to fight, you may be sure.

Now jump down and enter the mouth of the other mine, which leads towards the salient of the enemy's work. Stumbling along, we reach the end where the men are digging. The candle burns very dimly—the air is almost stifling. Never mind, let us watch them. See that slender, bright-looking fellow swinging that pick. Great beaded drops of perspiration trickle down his face; there is not a dry thread in his coarse, gray shirt; but no matter, the pick swings, and each stroke slices down six inches of the tough subsoil of Mississippi. That fellow was "Jim," once a tender-handed, smooth-faced, nice young man, whose livery-stable, billiard and cigar bills were a sore trial to his worthy governor. Jim says that he used to wear gloves and "store-clothes," and that girls called him good-looking, but that's played out now; he is going for Uncle Sam.

But we return to the fresh air. Look over the parapet again towards the turret, where we saw the rebel picket. Do you see the little gray mounds which cover the hillside so thickly?—ten, twenty, thirty, you can count on a few square rods. Ah, my friend, this is sacred ground you are looking upon. There our boys charged; there they were slain in heaps; but they pressed on, and leaped into the ditch. They climbed the parapet, and rolled back into eternity. Others followed them; their flag was planted, and they sprang over, to meet their certain death. An hour passed, and *one* returned; the rest were dead.[51]

One of the biggest news stories of the concluding phase of the campaign was Grant's order of June 19 removing McClernand from the command of the Thirteenth Army Corps and ordering him back to Springfield, Illinois. From time to time in the letters of the reporters there had been guarded references to his supposed jealousy of General Grant. It also had been noised about that McClernand's was the hidden hand that had inspired the systematic attacks of the reporters upon Sherman. But finally he had made what proved to be a fatal misstep. By releasing to the press without the permission of his superior a fulsome order glorifying his own troops at the expense of Sherman's and McPherson's, McClernand had rendered himself liable for dismissal. His departure met with the general approval of the army reporters. The Chicago *Journal* correspondent alluded in pointed fashion to his failure to carry out Grant's order for launching an assault on May 19; then, thrusting at McClernand's backers, he added a parting note:

> The [Chicago] *Tribune* and *Missouri Republican* have pronounced the statement false, adducing his loss in the assault on the 22d as evidence that he made an assault on the 19th! All that I asserted was true, and it was also true that he made as an excuse that he could "hear nothing from the right and centre," and received as a reply from Grant that "if he could not move his corps into action as ordered, he would lead it himself."[52]

Gradually it became apparent to the beleaguered garrison in Vicksburg that Johnston could not come to their aid. On July 3, after a council of war with his division commanders, Pemberton signified to Grant his desire for a parley. The two commanders, who had been companions in arms during the Mexican War, met on a hillside a few hundred feet from the Confederate lines for an exchange of views. That evening Grant wrote a letter to Pemberton offering terms of capitulation, which were accepted after some little delay. Through the courtesy of General Leggett, who was in charge of the formal arrangements for the surrender, Bodman, the Chicago *Tribune* correspondent, was permitted to pass the picket line in advance of the actual surrender and thus become one of the very first on the Union side to enter the city.[53]

At half past nine o'clock on the morning of July 4, immediately after the surrender had been concluded, Admiral Porter made arrangements to send dispatches from himself and General Grant up the river on the "V. F. Wilson," a fast boat. Grant's messenger was put ashore at Memphis, which was connected with Cairo by a telgraph line operated exclusively by the Government. The line was temporarily out of order at this time, however, so that Admiral Porter's messenger, who continued on to Cairo on board the "Wilson," brought the first news of the fall of Vicksburg to be sent over the wires. Later that day, July 7, the steamer "Niagara" arrived at Cairo with dispatches from General Grant confirming the news of the surrender. One of the passengers on board the "Niagara" was A. F. Woodal, a correspondent of the Cincinnati *Gazette*, who appears to have been the first army correspondent to reach Cairo with an account of the great triumph.[54]

Wilkie had the bad luck to be away on a trip at the time of Vicksburg's surrender. Before he went away, he left instructions with one of his assistants that in case Vicksburg fell during his absence, the assistant was to take the first boat up the river, writing his story as he went, and continue on to New York without stopping until the account had been placed in the hands of the editor of the *Times*. These instructions were repeated several times, and Wilkie was assured that they would be carried out to the letter. The *Times* correspondent also had an assistant on the gunboat "Lafayette" who was under orders to forward at once anything of interest having to do with fleet operations without waiting to communicate with Wilkie. Having taken these precautions, Wilkie left the army almost a week before Vicksburg fell and arrived at his destination on the very day that Pemberton surrendered his sword to Grant.

Anxiously he watched for the issue of the New York *Times* which he expected to contain the story of the surrender. When it arrived, to his disappointment, it contained not a line about the great event. Neither was anything to be found in the next issue or the next. Meanwhile, all the other prominent dailies received their special accounts of the surrender and printed them. Not until some years later did Wilkie learn what had happened to his faithless lieutenant. The latter, according to his own statement, had started for New York as he had agreed to do and had gotten as far as Indianapolis when he decided to leave the train to have a drink. One drink led to another, and it was several days before the messenger had sobered up sufficiently to continue the journey. Wilkie had no better luck with his naval correspondent, who disappeared without a trace.[55]

Most of the newspaper accounts of the surrender of Vicksburg contained a note of surprise, even disappointment, that so little damage had been done to the city by the incessant bombardment which had been going on for weeks. Only a few buildings had been completely demolished, and what damage there was largely had been localized in the Northern part of the city. To be sure, the house which Pemberton had used for his headquarters had been pierced by a shell which left a hole large enough for a mule to walk through. Moreover, the correspondent of the New York *Tribune* told of being invited into the home of the editor of the Vicksburg *Citizen*, who "interspersed his remarks while showing me around with frequent cautions not to tread here and there for fear a shattered piece of flooring would let me through into the cellar. . . ."[56]

The reporters also mentioned the indomitable spirit which the garrison and the townspeople had displayed, the unspeakable privations which they had endured (many of them had been driven to seek protection in caves during the worst of the bombardment), and the friendly spirit on both sides after the surrender had been concluded.

The capture of Port Hudson followed soon afterward. In a July 10 letter to Hudson, the *Herald* correspondent Cash wrote:

> At last I have the pleasure to announce the fall of Port Hudson. It turned out as I expected, the surrender was caused by the fall of Vicksburg, and the credit of its capture is honestly due to General Grant. You will no doubt hear of it first by way of Cairo.[57]

Probably the best account of the capitulation was written by Hamilton of the New York *Times*, who outraced the other reporters to New Orleans and sent his account from there by steamer in time to make the *Times*'s morning edition of July 23.

Although the press was well represented in the field during the closing stage of the campaign, the reporting of the Vicksburg campaign as a whole was spotty. One of the Chicago *Tribune* reporters was of the opinion that:

> There are a few correspondents who go under fire and see with their own eyes what is doing, but the greater number prefer to remain on the steamer at the landing, and trust to such reports of the doings of the army as Dame Rumor may vouchsafe them. . . . To them great is the Goddess of rumor, for she saves them from the imagination, as her budget is ever full, ever varied, and ever exciting.[58]

A correspondent of the Chicago *Journal*, developing the same theme, told how:

> Gens. Carr, Steele, Blair, and other Generals have been killed off by these reporters since the 22d of May, and as often resurrected, until the troops hereabouts experience a feeling of nausea in reading reports of "artists upon the spot," whose effusions are "nothing if not false," and naturally conclude that the reports from other departments are as destitute of truth as those emanating from this section.[59]

Probably the best reporting was done by men like Wilkie and McCullagh, who had won distinction in earlier campaigns and continued to turn out superior writing. Some of the other reporters who performed creditably during this campaign were Edward Betty and Edward Crapsey of the Cincinnati *Gazette,* Bodman of the Chicago *Tribune,* Sylvanus Cadwallader of the *Times,* and Webb of the St. Louis *Republican.* After the departure of Knox, none of the *Herald* correspondents with Grant's army did anything of note. In fact the *Herald* gave greater space during the campaign to the relatively unimportant operations of Banks's army than to those of General Grant.

Sooner than most of his fellow correspondents, Wilkie perceived in Grant the qualities of military greatness that would enable him, before many months had passed, to attain the supreme command. Wilkie's profile sketch of the General was widely copied from the *Times* by other newspapers:

> Almost at any time one can see a small but compactly-built man of about forty-five years of age walking through the camps. He moves with his shoulders thrown a little forward of the perpendicular, his left hand in the pocket of his pantaloons, an unlighted cigar in his mouth, his eyes thrown straight forward, which, from the haze of abstraction that veils them, and a countenance drawn into furrows of thought, would seem to indicate that he is intensely preoccupied. The soldiers observe him coming, and, rising to their feet, gather on each side of the way to see him pass—they do not salute him, they only watch him curiously, with a certain sort of familiar reverence. His abstract air is not so great, while he thus moves along, as to prevent his seeing everything without apparently looking at it; you will see this in the fact, that however dense the crowd in which you stand, if you are an acquaintance, his eye will for an instant rest on yours with a glance of recollection, and with it a grave nod of recognition. A plain blue suit, without scarf, sword, or trappings of any sort, save the double-starred shoulder strap—an indifferently good

> "Kossuth" hat, with the top battered in close to his head; full beard, of a cross between "light" and "sandy;" a square cut face, whose lines and contour indicate extreme endurance and determination, complete the external appearance of this small man, as one sees him passing along, turning and chewing restlessly the end of his unlighted cigar.
>
> His countenance, in rest, has the rigid immobility of cast iron; and, while this indicates the unyielding tenacity of a bulldog, one finds only in his gray eyes the smiles and other evidences of the possession of those softer traits seen upon the lips and over the entire faces of ordinary people. On horseback he loses all the awkwardness which distinguishes him as he moves about on foot. Erect and graceful, he seems a portion of his steed, without which the full effect would be incomplete. He held in early days the reputation of being the best rider in the Academy, and he seems to have lost none of his excellence in this respect. . . .
>
> Of Gen. Grant's ability I need say nothing—he has been so long before the public that all can judge for themselves. The South calls his successes "luck;" we in the West believe that he owes them mostly to the possession of a cautious military judgment, assisted by good advisers, and backed by invincible perseverance, endurance and determination.[60]

In the files of Civil War journalism there is scarcely a more revealing portrait than this of Keim's "plain-looking man."

16

Gettysburg as the Newsmen Saw It

ON June 26, 1863, eight days before Vicksburg fell, C. C. Coffin mailed to his Boston paper an almost inspired prediction of the outcome of the Gettysburg campaign. It was five days before the battle, when he wrote from Baltimore:

> If Lee advances with nearly all his force into Pennsylvania, there must be a collision of the two armies not many miles west of Gettysburg, probably among the rolling hills near the State line, on the head waters of the Monocacy. . . . I believe that Washington and Baltimore will not be harmed. I expect to see Adams, Franklin, Cumberland and York counties run over somewhat by the rebels, and I also expect to see Lee utterly defeated in his plans. His army may not be annihilated. Hooker may not achieve a great, decisive victory. But I fully believe that Lee will gain nothing by this move.[1]

No battle of the Civil War appeals more to the popular imagination than the one which was fought near Gettysburg, Pennsylvania, July 1, 2, and 3, 1863. Apart from the fact that this struggle, unlike most, is comparatively easy for the layman to understand; apart from the fact that it was one of the bloodiest battles in modern times[2]—the Battle of Gettysburg stands forth as a turning point in the history of the Civil War.

The army correspondents who witnessed the three-day battle hardly could visualize all that it was to mean. For nearly two years they had been making excuses for one sorry military performance after another. On the Peninsula, at Fredericksburg, and again at Chancellorsville they had done their best to gloss over the failures of a magnificent army suffering from incompetent leadership and almost compelled to lose faith in itself. Yet the public, in spite of the reporters' well-meant efforts, realized that there was sharp disagreement concerning the situation in

Hooker's army among those who were presumably in a position to know. In a letter to his brother William, written three weeks after the Battle of Chancellorsville and just after a visit to Washington, Joseph Medill confided that he had not lost his faith in Hooker "one particle. He came within one inch of destroying Lee's army and will do it next time."[3] But the mood of the Army of the Potomac was more nearly that of General Hancock as reflected in a letter written to his wife about this same time:

> I do not know what will be the next turn of the wheel of Fortune, or what Providence has in store for this unhappy army. . . . We get the [Washington] *Chronicle* and [Philadelphia] *Inquirer* daily: they are filled with inaccuracies. We are not allowed to have the New York papers. They may not contain more truth, and I suppose they have some attacks against the Government. . . . I have been approached again in connection with the command of the Army of the Potomac. Give yourself no uneasiness—under no conditions would I accept the command. I do not belong to that class of generals whom the Republicans care to bolster up.[4]

Not more than two weeks after Hooker's failure at Chancellorsville, the Baltimore correspondent of the Philadelphia *Inquirer* received information from sources which had proved reliable in the past that Lee was planning another invasion of the North.[5] Early in June the threat materialized. Lee began withdrawing his troops from the Fredericksburg lines on June 3 in preparation for a move into the Shenandoah Valley. Six days later the largest cavalry encounter of the war took place at Brandy Station near Culpeper as the result of a surprise attack launched against Jeb Stuart by the new cavalry leader of the Army of the Potomac, Brigadier General Alfred Pleasanton.[6]

Through the bad luck of its cavalry correspondent Bulkley, who was captured during the engagement, the New York *Herald* missed an eyewitness account of the fight. The *Times*, however, received a four-column account of the battle from its army correspondent, L. L. Crounse, which it printed on June 11 under the heading: "Great Cavalry Fight—The Engagement at Beverley's Ford and Brandy Station—Desperate and Gallant Fighting by Our Forces—The Rebels Driven Back Three Miles—Their Camps Captured and Occupied—Highly Important Information Gained."

Although the Richmond press was quick to criticize Stuart for having been caught off guard,[7] the fight at Brandy Station had very little effect on Lee's invasion timetable. On June 13, Stonewall Jackson's old corps, now commanded by Lieutenant General Richard Ewell, appeared before Winchester, causing a Federal division stationed there under Major General Robert H. Milroy to decamp in great haste. Two days later, Rodes's division of Ewell's corps crossed the Potomac, occupied Hagerstown, and sent a cavalry brigade on ahead into Pennsylvania to gather supplies from the country around Chambersburg. On the morning of June 16 the principal New York and Philadelphia newspapers headlined the news that Chambersburg was in enemy hands.

One of the *Inquirer* correspondents left Baltimore on Wednesday afternoon, June 17, on the way to Frederick and came into Monocacy Junction just as General Milroy and his staff were climbing aboard a special train bound for Harper's Ferry. There were significant winks and shakings of heads by some of the townspeople, for rumors were current that the rebels had crossed the Potomac in force that afternoon at Point of Rocks and were somewhere in the vicinity of the Junction. The General did not seem to be particularly concerned by these rumors, however. Presently he gave the engineer the signal to pull out, just after the *Inquirer* man had secured permission to attach himself to the party. After a three- or four-mile run, the Milroy "special" puffed into Frederick. It was now about nine o'clock in the evening, and the fatigued representative of the *Inquirer* decided to search out the best hotel in town and stop there for the night. At this juncture another press correspondent who was with him cautioned him to "wait a minute. Something's up." Their attention was drawn to a gentleman in a brown linen duster who approached General Milroy and whispered something in his ear. Milroy must have been impressed by what the gentleman had to say, for he lost no time in making preparations for an immediate departure. The two correspondents decided to forego the idea of a warm bed in a comfortable hotel and climbed back on the train. After a little while they rolled into Monocacy Junction again, only to learn that the telegraph to Frederick was no longer working. It was supposed that the enemy had entered Frederick, taken possession, and cut the wires.

As the train pulled out of Monocacy Junction, bound as they thought for Harper's Ferry, the two newspapermen determined to catch some sleep before they arrived at their destination. They agreed philosophically that if the train were attacked en route they would be awakened without any effort on their part or that of anyone else. Between two and three o'clock in the morning, one of the sleepers stirred uneasily as he realized vaguely that the train was still moving.

"It's a long time reaching Harper's Ferry," he muttered.

"Yes," groaned the other. "It is further than I thought."

Soon they saw the lights of a city twinkling in the distance, and after a little while the train eased into a large and spacious depot.

"This is considerable of a place," remarked the *Inquirer* man as he was stretching his limbs upon the platform.

"Yes," replied a stranger, who was standing nearby. "Baltimore is right smart of a place."

"Baltimore!" exclaimed the two reporters in unison. "Why I thought this was Harper's Ferry!" Then they both laughed immoderately as they realized the situation. The truth of the matter was that the Confederates were not at Frederick. The telegraph operator there had simply become frightened by reports that they were approaching and had deserted his post. Anxious for his own safety, Milroy had concluded to run back to Baltimore, and so it was that the two press men found themselves back at their starting place, little the wiser for their excursion into western Maryland.[8]

Not until more than a week after Rodes's footsore veterans appeared at Hagerstown on June 15 did the main body of Lee's army cross into Maryland. Marching by way of Hagerstown and Greencastle, Pennsylvania, Johnson's division of Ewell's corps overtook Rodes at Chambersburg and accompanied him to Carlisle, arriving there on June 27. Meanwhile, Early's division (the third division of Ewell's corps), marching by way of Cashtown, Gettysburg, and Berlin, reached York on June 28. The remaining two corps of Lee's army, Longstreet's and Hill's, had crossed the Potomac on June 24-25 and had continued on to Chambersburg, where they went into camp on June 27.[9]

As soon as he was sure that Lee's movement was something more than a reconnaissance in force, Hooker had left Falmouth and had begun marching North, keeping well to the East of the Blue Ridge to insure the safety of the Capital. In their letters describing the march, the reporters who accompanied Hooker's army spoke in feeling terms of the sickening heat of those June days, of the roads "ankle deep with dust,"[10] of the rapid pace at which the army moved ("Twenty to twenty-three miles per day in such weather is something unheard of heretofore," remarked one correspondent),[11] and of the straggling, to which another reporter referred as the "bane and pest" of the Army of the Potomac. This same reporter, T. C. Grey of the New York *Tribune*, commented:

> A march of five miles cannot be made without a certain number of stragglers and in a day's march it is astonishing to note the depletion of regiments by straggling. The professional straggler is never guilty of being in the ranks on the occasion of a march; he hates military precision, and hasn't the shadow of an idea of his duties and responsibilities as a soldier of the Republic. He is a philosopher in his way; believes in taking everything quietly, and may be seen in every sylvan retreat along the line of march, with hat and coat off and knapsack unslung, gazing with an air of great composure on his passing comrades. Sometimes a group may be seen playing cards or smoking, and frequently a party may be seen bathing in some contiguous stream. . . . Marauding motives induce most of them to lay behind, and every farm-house, barn, orchard, hen-roost and pig sty is sure to receive a visit from them.
>
> For days after the army has reached a given point, thousands of these fellows throng the road leading to camp, and when, after from two to four days, they reach it, and are asked by their officers to account for their absence, some specious excuse is always presented. The booming of cannon in the advance always considerably augments the number of stragglers, many of whom court capture by guerrillas, for the avowed purpose of being paroled and receiving a furlough of indefinite length. But it must not be inferred that all who remain behind are of this character. On the contrary, there are many privates and officers who are physically unable to undergo the fatigues of a long march, and who find themselves, much to their chagrin, under the necessity of keeping company with their more unprincipled associates.[12]

Ever watchful of the press, Hooker had dispatched a confidential message to newspaper editors throughout the country on June 18, advising them that under no circumstances must the location of any corps, division, brigade, or regiment of the Army of the Potomac be published, "and especially is the location of my headquarters never to be named excepting during a fight."[13] His warning was communicated none too soon. The very next day a staff officer placed in his hands a copy of the New York *Herald* of June 18, specifying in startling detail the location of every one of his corps and of the various cavalry commands as well. From Halleck, to whom he complained bitterly of the *Herald*'s damaging disclosure, he received a veiled suggestion to crack down on the press:

> I appreciate as fully as yourself the injury resulting from newspaper publication of the movements, numbers, and position of our troops, but I see no way of preventing it as long as reporters are permitted in our camps. I expelled them all from our lines in Mississippi. Every general must decide for himself what persons he will permit in his camps.[14]

Strangely enough, Hooker chose to make an example, not of any of the *Herald* reporters but of the New York *Tribune* correspondent, Nathan G. Shepherd. By order of the provost marshal, Shepherd was arrested on June 20 for having written a letter disclosing the position of the various army corps a week earlier and was ordered to leave the lines of the army.[15] A few days later, the proprietor of the Washington *Star*, W. D. Wallach, was arrested by order of the War Department and threatened with an indictment for treason. By some means best known to himself he had procured a private letter to the editor of the Philadelphia *Inquirer* containing similar information to that imparted by the *Tribune*[16] and had published it in the columns of his newspaper. Hooker's action, coupled with that of the War Department, proved highly efficacious. During the remainder of the campaign Lee was able to gain very little information about the movements of the Army of the Potomac from the news columns of the Northern press.

Meanwhile, the energies of the cavalry correspondents were being severely taxed to keep the public informed of the almost daily clashes between the mounted warriors of Stuart and Pleasanton. To glean particulars of the cavalry fighting, Thomas M. Newbould of the New York *Tribune* rode out from Fairfax Court House in the direction of the Shenandoah Valley on the morning of June 21. On either side of the excellent macadamized turnpike leading to Aldie lay beautiful, rolling country, dotted with fine old mansions.

"These people have made their money by planting, I suppose," remarked the correspondent to a Negro with whom he had some conversation at Aldie.

"Yes sir, and raising colored people to sell to the South," the Negro told him. "We worked for them for nothing all our lives, and then they sold our wives and children from us."

Pausing briefly to look inside some of these pretentious homes, Newbould noted their "great barn-like interiors"; the wall paper "much in vogue in the early part of this century, depicting historical and foreign scenes"; the antique, cracked piano in almost every parlor; and, smiling down from a canvas, the "portrait of somebody's grandmother, in her youth, costumed in the style of fifty years back." From Aldie, the *Tribune* man rode on two miles beyond Middleburg to the spot where the fighting of that morning had begun. There he recounted:

> Half a dozen dead horses are suddenly seen lying in the road, or in the fields near by. Further on, and more appear. Some of these are of Thursday's fight. Their bodies have already begun to swell, and a few lie on their backs, with legs stiffly projecting in the air. Long streams of blood issue from their noses. Gaps exist in stone walls, kicked over by leaping horses. Both the road and adjacent patches of young corn are torn by traces of innumerable flying hoofs. Flush-faced men with flashing eyes yet linger to the mind's eye, elated by triumph or panic-struck in retreat. Cheers and yells yet ring to the ear, accompanied by oaths. The less fleet are overtaken with a "surrender ye." Perhaps an oath with a pistol shot is received in reply. It may miss fire, when the stubborn resistant receives a ball which speedily topples him over, while his assailant passes on to new struggles. More frequently the answer is a hasty "I surrender," a throwing down of weapons, and a spreading of the arms, to prove themselves defenseless. . . . At no other time is there ever heard so much hard swearing as in a charge. There is a perfect chorus of oaths, from husky base [sic] to frantic treble. This profanity, painful to the ear, is rarely touched on by correspondents, yet no true idea of a fight can be furnished without its abundant incorporation.[17]

Passing by many more telltale signs of the struggle, Newbould, in the vicinity of Upperville, came upon the tired troopers, returning from their fight. Tangling with the enemy had lost its novelty for Pleasanton's cavalrymen. Their remarks concerning the events of the day were therefore few and communicated without eagerness. Nevertheless, Newbould was able to learn from them that they had left Aldie early that morning and had skirmished with the enemy constantly throughout the day:

> There was no difference in the manliness of the combatants. The Southern men are equal to ours in dash and use of the carbine, but are not equally skillful with the saber. Rarely does a party charged wait to receive it, but there were a few instances to-day where the ground was clear and even, and both charged simultaneously upon each other. Yells, cheers and curses intermingled, firearms cracked, sabers gleamed, and horses rose upon their hind feet, borne upward by the pressure. It was but for the

> moment. Each pushed through the ranks of the other, and turned to engage the nearest combatant. It was a thrust and parry or a pistol shot, and a run. Horses joyously entered into the spirit of the scene, and with snorting nostrils, flew to the bridle of their riders. Wounds they did not feel, and dropped only when utterly disabled. . . . The Rebels at last ran, overpowered by skillful maneuvering, or entrained by the example of each other. "I would not give up my commission as a Captain of Cavalry," said an exhilarated young officer, "for anything an infantry regiment could offer me."[18]

At the front with General Kilpatrick throughout the June 21 fight was the *Herald* correspondent, Lynde Walter Buckingham, who came from a prominent Boston family. Buckingham had replaced Bulkley as the chief cavalry correspondent of the *Herald* after Bulkley's capture at Brandy Station. On the afternoon of the twenty-second, while on his way to Washington with an account of the recent cavalry movements, Buckingham was waylaid by a party of Mosby's guerillas about two and a half miles East of Aldie. The reporter's horse wheeled at the first shots and, becoming completely unmanageable, dashed down a steep hill in the direction of Aldie. In its headlong flight, the animal stumbled on some loose stones, throwing its rider to the ground with great force. Some Union pickets carried him to a little brick church, which was being used as a hospital, nearby. His skull was so badly fractured, however, that there was little that anybody could do for him, and on the following morning he was buried just outside the church in a grave dug for him by his friend A. R. Waud, the artist for *Harper's Weekly*.[19]

On June 25 and 26, the Army of the Potomac crossed the river for which it was named and moved on toward Frederick. At this critical moment a controversy arose between Hooker and General Halleck, and Hooker, at his own request, was removed from command and replaced by General Meade. The change came about so unexpectedly that several of the newspaper correspondents learned about it before some of the corps commanders did.[20] How the army reacted to the sudden change of command was perhaps best summed up by the *Herald*'s Hendricks:

> Many liked General Hooker and had faith in him; most believe in the ability of General Meade to fill his place. It may come inopportunely, but I must say that General McClellan is the man the rank and file of the army want at their head. They cannot get over worshipping him, clamoring for him.[21]

At the moment the public was less interested in the identity of Hooker's successor than in discovering where Lee was going and what measures were being used to halt him. Lacking precise information, editors and newspaper reporters were forced to deal in generalities; indeed some did their best to create the impression that they were in possession of important information which it would be imprudent to reveal. A Pittsburgh newspaper commented:

> All understand this. A correspondent generally hastens to blab whatever he knows, and when he lays claim to reticence on account of patriotism, we may be sure he knows no more than he tells.[22]

At the beginning of the campaign it was generally supposed that Lee intended to strike at Baltimore and Washington, but as Ewell moved northward up the Cumberland Valley into Pennsylvania, the threat to the capital, Harrisburg, seemed paramount. Accordingly newspaper correspondents began to entrain for Harrisburg from all points of the compass. Among the first arrivals there were Joseph A. Ware of the Washington *Chronicle,* Charles H. Graffan of the New York *Herald,* and W. H. Whittemore of the *Times,* all seasoned war correspondents. Correspondents of various Pennsylvania newspapers—of the Pittsburgh *Chronicle,* Philadelphia *Press, Inquirer,* and *Evening Bulletin* among others—soon joined them. By June 28, representatives of no less than twenty out-of-town newspapers were in Harrisburg, keeping the telegraph wires hot with the latest news about the approach of the army of invasion.[23]

Taking all the reports of one day from Harrisburg and totaling up the number of Confederates positively said to be at each place named, the New York *Times* correspondent Crounse obtained a figure of no less than two hundred and twenty thousand men! Moreover, this inflated estimate, he humorously pointed out, did not include the corps of Longstreet and Hill:

> This will make the total strength of the enemy not less than five hundred thousand men. One Harrisburgh dispatch, to the effect that the rebels have four thousand pieces of artillery, I think is slightly exaggerated. I do not think the number will exceed thirty-five hundred!!![24]

On June 25, General Couch, who had been placed in charge of the defense of Harrisburg, had issued orders curtailing the privileges of the correspondents there, and had imposed a censorship over all telegrams sent out of Harrisburg. To the post of censor he had assigned Colonel Henry Coppee, a graduate of the U.S. Military Academy who had been teaching rhetoric and English literature at the University of Pennsylvania.[25] Coppee was instructed to prepare two dispatches each day from official sources for distribution to the reporters. Such an arrangement could hardly fail to lead to misunderstanding.

On the first day of the new arrangement the Colonel could not be found; in his absence the Associated Press correspondent, Sid Deming, managed to provide the afternoon papers with the highlights of the day's news. Further attempts to rout out the elusive censor that evening were unsuccessful, and it was not until noon of the twenty-eighth that a delegation of reporters managed to interview him. To their consternation they learned that he had no idea of what General Couch expected of him. He was under the impression, in fact, that he was simply to revise any dispatches which the reporters cared to submit to him. Under no circumstances, he emphasized, would a newspaperman be permitted to deprive him of his rest. Sleep was important to him, and he was determined to retire at ten or eleven o'clock at the latest, news or no news.[26] Greatly to the satisfaction of the reporters, the Colonel was relieved of his duties after four days and replaced by Wayne McVeigh, a former newspaperman, who seems to have rendered the censorship more tolerable than did his predecessor.[27] Meanwhile, an order had been issued by General Couch forbidding any reporter to cross the Susquehanna in search of news. As a result, the correspondents in Harrisburg had to depend upon hearsay reports from refugees and occasional handouts from the censor for information about Lee's movements and lost the opportunity of being on hand to report the Battle of Gettysburg.[28]

Throughout most of the campaign thus far, Lee had been kept in ignorance of the movements of his principal opponent by the prolonged absence of his cavalry. Stuart had left the main body of Lee's command on June 24 on one of those spectacular raids which were his chief delight. Not until the night of the twenty-eighth did the Confederate Commander in Chief receive information from the lips of a trusted spy that Hooker's army had crossed the Potomac and had advanced as far North as Frederick.[29] The receipt of this disturbing intelligence caused Lee to modify his whole plan of campaign, which had called for a general advance on Harrisburg. On the afternoon of June 29, a courier from Lee's headquarters at Chambersburg dashed into Carlisle with orders directing Ewell to move southward to rejoin the rest of Lee's army.[30] Ewell hastily recalled Rodes's division, which was already on the way from Carlisle to Harrisburg, and summoned Early's division from York. Just as Ewell was about to start back to Chambersburg, he received new orders calling for the army to concentrate East of South Mountain in the vicinity of Gettysburg. Another trial of strength between the Army of the Potomac and its great rival was at hand.

The newspaper correspondents at Washington and elsewhere were aware that a great battle was imminent, but none, with the exception of Coffin, had a very clear idea where it was likely to break. On Sunday evening, June 28, Whitelaw Reid had received a wire in Washington from the home office in Cincinnati advising him to hire a horse and equipment and join the army at once.[31] Sam Wilkeson, currently the chief Washington correspondent of the New York *Times,* and Uriah H. Painter of the Philadelphia *Inquirer* had agreed to accompany him, and so at eleven o'clock on Monday morning the trio climbed aboard the train for Baltimore on the way to the field. As they rode along, they observed bands of soldiers along the line guarding against an attack and heard much chattering among the passengers about the possibility of a sudden onslaught by Stuart. At the Relay House, just outside Baltimore, the newspaper expedition came to a sudden halt.

"Am very sorry, gentlemen," said an official of the Baltimore and Ohio Railroad. "Would get you out at once if I could; would gladly run up an extra train for you; but—the rebels cut our road last night, this side of Frederick, and we have no idea when we can run again."

There was no help for it. The correspondents were just one train too late to reach Frederick, and so they decided to return to Washington. On the following morning, June 30, they were off for Baltimore again. This time the railroad agent was able to assure them that service had been resumed between Baltimore and Frederick and that a train would be available some time that afternoon. As the three sauntered along one of the main streets of Baltimore, they came upon an urchin snatching pebbles from a tar barrel to fling at a passing pig.

"Small boy," exclaimed Wilkeson with an air of ponderous dignity. "You must stop that, sir! You are destroying the defenses of Baltimore."

The boy stared at them in amazement. He could not have been expected to know that those tar barrels and sugar hogsheads, half filled with gravel, were intended to serve as barricades in case of a sudden onset by a rebel raiding force.

At noon, the correspondents heard that Meade's army was concentrating at Westminster in preparation to march on York. Westminster could be reached from Baltimore by way of the Western Maryland Railroad. All traffic had been suspended along that line, however, and there was apparently nothing else for the three men to do but hasten to Frederick, mount, and then attempt to overtake the army as it advanced toward Westminster.

Edward A. Paul, the cavalry correspondent of the New York *Times,* was with Kilpatrick's division of Union cavalry at Hanover that day. As one of Kilpatrick's brigades was passing through the East part of the town around midday, Jeb Stuart suddenly appeared from the South and delivered a surprise attack on the rear and right flank of the Union marchers. Nearly four hours of hard fighting elapsed before the attackers were beaten off. Later in the day, Reporter Paul picked up a letter to Stuart from the Confederate cavalry officer, Fitzhugh Lee. The letter contained a very accurate account of Kilpatrick's movements obtained by Lee from a citizen whom he classed as "reliable." Paul showed the letter to a newspaper editor in Hanover, remarking as he did so that the enemy appeared to have a great many sympathizers in the vicinity.

"I don't know as to that," shrugged the editor, "but you see this is a very strong *Democratic* County, and the Democrats were opposed to the removal of McClellan!"[32]

During that same afternoon, the Boston *Journal's* reporter, C. C. Coffin, was riding North from Frederick alongside the weary marchers of the Second and Fifth Corps. Meade's army was proceeding fanwise North from Frederick, with the First Corps on the left of the line, the Eleventh Corps on a parallel road a little farther East, and the Third and Twelfth Corps moving on parallel routes which converged at Taneytown. The Second and Fifth Corps were strung out still farther to the East along the roads to Liberty and Uniontown; the Sixth Corps with Gregg's division of cavalry was on the extreme right of the line bearing toward Westminster.

As Sykes's Fifth Corps passed through the town of Liberty, Coffin noticed a crowd of soldiers gathering around a farm wagon which had just been driven into the town.

"What have you got to sell, old fellow?" asked one of the soldiers as he peered under a white table cloth which was draped over the rear end of the wagon and spied several loaves of fresh bread and a basket of ginger cakes.

"I haven't any to sell," said the farmer with a peculiar expression.

"See here, old fellow, won't ye sell me a hunk of your gingerbread?" demanded the soldier producing an old wallet.

"No," was still the answer. Then as a chorus of boos rose from the assembled crowd, the old farmer climbed up on his wagon seat, removed the table cloth, and announced that he hadn't brought his bread there to sell.

"My wife and daughters sat up all night to bake it for you, and you are welcome to all I've got, and I wish I had ten times as much. Help yourselves, boys."

There were cheers for the old man and his wife and daughters as the "boys" accepted his invitation. The episode was all over in a few minutes, but it exemplified the kind of human interest material that Coffin knew how to utilize so well.[33]

A. Homer Byington, one of the New York *Tribune* correspondents, that same day was at Lancaster, "a better point for news than Harrisburg." Writing from there to his managing editor, Sydney Howard Gay, Byington referred to a long dispatch he had telegraphed the night before:

> not because the news was so very important but because Herald had at least a half dozen men here picking up everything & telegraphing *ad-libitum.* They are the most *drunken,* irresponsible crew that ever squandered a newspapers money—and they use it without sense or reason.

By this time as well, Reid's group had reached Frederick, and had then split up when Wilkeson and Painter decided to return to Baltimore in order to go up to Westminster on a government train. Luckily for him, as it turned out, Reid chose to remain at Frederick. He was convinced of his good fortune when he learned the next morning, July 1, that Meade had established his headquarters at Taneytown instead of Westminster. Meade evidently was not heading for York. His change of course could only mean that an enemy concentration had been detected to the Northwest, and therefore a battle was imminent.

The afternoon was well advanced when the Cincinnati *Gazette* reporter reined up at Meade's headquarters. There on a camp stool in a plain little tent sat the new commander of the Army of the Potomac poring over a map and looking much more like a thoughtful student than a dashing soldier. While Reid was stealing curious glances at the General, another horseman galloped up and hastily dismounted. It was

L. L. Crounse, who was now acting as chief correspondent of the New York *Times* with the Army of the Potomac. Early that morning, Crounse had lost his bearings while out on a scouting mission. Then in an effort to gain the right road, he had stumbled upon one of the Confederate columns advancing through the Cashtown Gap upon Gettysburg. Making good his escape, the *Times* correspondent hurried to General Reynolds, the commander of the First Corps, and informed him that Lee's men were coming that way. In the fight which ensued, Reynolds had been killed, and there were rumors that the Union force had been driven back.[34]

As Reid listened to Crounse's exciting story, he resolved to tarry at headquarters no longer, but to mount and spur for Gettysburg. It was true that he had covered twenty-seven miles on horseback over rough roads that day, and night was coming on, but at least it was comforting to know that this time he was not to repeat his unfortunate experience at Chancellorsville, where he missed the battle entirely. He and Crounse decided to go to Gettysburg together. A few moments were spent on the Taneytown tavern porch preparing dispatches to be sent by special messenger to the telegraph office in Frederick. Then the two men were off. Down the Gettysburg road they galloped, picking their way through the marching columns of infantry and dodging the crowded trains. Presently they began to meet a stream of aides and orderlies coming from the opposite direction, and now and then a quartermaster or surgeon or commissary in search of stores. Crounse seemed to know them all; from each in turn he extracted the latest news.

"Everything splendid; have driven them five or six miles from Gettysburg," was the first information they received.

"Badly cut up, sir, and falling back," shouted another informant.

"D—d Dutchmen of the Eleventh Corps broke and ran like sheep, just as they did at Chancellorsville, and it's going to be another disaster of just the same sort," cried a third man, who was almost breathless with excitement.

After riding a bit farther, the two correspondents turned off the main road into a byway on the right which would bring them out on the Baltimore turnpike several miles beyond. This, they hoped, would be less obstructed by army trains. After a hearty supper at a comfortable-looking "Dutch" house, they continued on until they caught sight of some campfires in the distance and heard the hum of soldiers' talk in the same direction.

"Yes, the army's right down there," volunteered several farmer folk who were sitting on a door step near the roadside. "If you want to stay all night, turn up by the school house. Squire Durboraw's a nice man."

"Right down there" was the post village of Two Taverns, some four and a half miles to the rear of the battle line. Squire Durboraw had been in bed for two or three hours, but he proved a willing host. With great satisfaction the correspondents saw their horses quartered in what Reid described as "one of those great horse palaces that people build for barns" and then retired to the Squire's front room for a few hours of uneasy sleep.

Both reporters were in the saddle soon after daybreak the next morning, July 2, and ready to ride up to the front. Coffin had spent the night at Hanover, twelve miles East of Gettysburg, and was about to head for the Baltimore turnpike in order to approach the battlefield from the South. On the way up the turnpike, Coffin passed the toll gate, from which the keeper had fled, and continued on until he reached the summit of a hill: on the right, the soldiers of the Eleventh Corps were lying prone; on the left, the remnants of the First Corps were crouched behind a stone wall.

Dismounting from his horse, Coffin went up the stairs of the arched gateway to the cemetery and looked over the field where the battle of the day before had been fought: the town of Gettysburg with its red brick houses and its spires and steeples, the white walls of Pennsylvania College north of the town, and the almshouse beyond, where Barlow's division had left its line of dead. "With my glass I could see the prostrate forms lying where they fell."

Coffin came down the gateway stairs and swung himself into the saddle in order to ride into Gettysburg. He had gone only a few paces when he came upon a soldier hunched down behind a picket fence.

"Halt! Where are you going?" demanded the soldier.

"Into Gettysburg," Coffin replied.

"Into Gettysburg! Do you know where you are? I am on the picket line. Do you see that brick house with the window open? That is full of Confederates, and they have been picking us off all the morning, and the quicker you get out of here the better it will be for you."

The soldier evidently meant what he said, and so Coffin turned about and rode back to the cemetery. There he came upon General Howard, who promptly invited him to a breakfast of cold ham, hard biscuit, and coffee. As they ate, the General told the story of the first day's battle and pointed out the positions of the troops. Then he and Coffin rode along the lines and finally stopped at the headquarters of General Meade, where a group of officers were studying some maps which the engineers had hastily prepared. In front of headquarters, a signal officer was waving his flag in response to another on Little Round Top.[35]

Meade had selected a strong position for defense. His line was approximately three miles long and was shaped in the form of a gigantic fishhook, whose eye was on Round Top and whose barbed end pointed in the direction of Baltimore. The chief advantage of the Union position was its convex shape which permitted any part of the line to be rapidly reinforced by moving along a chord of the arc. The enemy, on the other hand, having a concave line of battle, was compelled to move troops much greater distances in order to support an attack or bolster up a weak point. On Culp's Hill at the extreme right of the line was Slocum's Twelfth Corps, anchored on the left by the Eleventh Corps and the First, both of which had been roughly handled in the fighting of the day before. Hancock's Second Corps was in position along the crest of Cemetery Ridge, and Sickles' Third Corps was on the left, somewhat in advance of the position which Meade had intended it to occupy. Apparently none of the army reporters was aware of the fact—none of them made mention of it at least—that Sickles had taken it upon himself to advance his line, thereby precipitating a long-standing controversy with his chief.[36] Neither the Fifth and Sixth Corps nor two brigades of the Third Corps, however, yet had reached the battlefield on that Thursday morning, July 2. Sedgwick's Sixth Corps, the largest in the army, had been at Manchester, thirty-five miles away, the evening before and was not to reach the battlefield until four o'clock in the afternoon.

With the exception of sporadic cannonading and some skirmishing near the Peach Orchard, an unnatural quiet hung over the lines for most of the day. Toward noon, General Meade and General John Newton, who had succeeded Reynolds in command of the First Corps, met and conferred on Cemetery Ridge within visual range of a tall church belfry in Gettysburg. Meade and Newton were so placed that one had his right side toward the belfry, the other his left; their faces were about three feet apart. Only a few paces away from the generals stood George W. Hosmer, a correspondent of the New York *Herald*. Meade and the corps commander had just begun to converse in low tones when they were startled by the sharp zip of a rifle bullet which passed between their faces. Thinking it was a chance shot, they went on with their conference without pausing. High up in the belfry, it so happened, were several sharpshooters, who were watching intently everything that was happening along the Ridge. Hosmer already had spotted the sharpshooter who had fired the "chance shot" and was reasonably sure that he would fire again. Approaching Meade, the *Herald* man pointed out the rifleman in the belfry. The two generals thereupon withdrew to a safer place, well out of range.[37]

About 4:00 P.M., Longstreet threw two divisions against the exposed salient on the Union left. The first assaults were contained, but after prolonged and heavy fighting, Sickles' advanced line was driven in and greatly imperiled. From the summit of Little Round Top, Coffin could see white clouds of smoke issuing from the woods near the Devil's Den and could hear the roll of musketry rising even above the cannonade. The chief engineer of the Army of the Potomac, Major General Gouverneur K. Warren, was first to see the danger to Little Round Top, which was the key to the Union position on the left and which by some strange oversight Meade had neglected to occupy. As the result of quick action by Warren, two brigades were hurried to the summit barely in time to check Hood's men, who were coming up the opposite slope of the hill.

During the worst of the fighting in that portion of the field, General Sickles was struck below the right knee by a shell fragment which shattered his leg so badly that it was left hanging by a mere shred. The General was carried to a wheat field in the rear, and his leg was amputated then and there. When he recovered consciousness, he noticed Tom Cook, the *Herald* correspondent, standing nearby. Sickles was a special protegé of the *Herald*, whose correspondents in turn were in good favor with the General. Beckoning to Cook, the wounded Sickles looked up feebly and remarked with suitable piety, "Cook, in this war a man is but a cypher. God rules and directs all for the best."[38] When Reid saw him the next morning, July 3, however, he was lying "grim and stoical" on a stretcher borne by two stout privates——his cap pulled down over his eyes and a cigar in his mouth![39]

While Longstreet's assault was rising to a grand crescendo, Ewell commenced a vigorous artillery fire on the Union right and followed it up with an assault by one division. Only one brigade (Greene's) of the Twelfth Corps was left on Culp's Hill to oppose it; the other four, along with the division commanders, Geary and Ruger, had been pulled out of the line and sent to the relief of Sickles. Ewell's men seized the abandoned works of Geary and Ruger and penetrated to within a short distance of the Baltimore pike, dangerously close to Meade's rear. Only the gathering darkness kept them from the triumph which lay within their grasp.

At the close of this second day at Gettysburg, July 2, the general feeling among Meade's corps commanders was one of discouragement. In the first day's battle, both the First and Eleventh Corps had been badly cut up; on this day, the Third, Fifth, and part of the Second Corps likewise had been subjected to considerable punishment. Indeed, after two days' fighting, only the Sixth and Twelfth Corps of the Army of the Potomac were still substantially intact. At a conference of war held that evening, Meade asked his corps commanders whether they thought the army should fall back to a stronger position. In spite of the gloomy outlook for the morrow, the majority of the officers questioned told their General that they thought the Army of the Potomac should "stay and fight it out."[40]

As yet very little information concerning the fighting had reached the press. The battle was being fought in a region almost devoid of railroad and telegraph lines; the transmission of news was therefore difficult. In almost every Northern newspaper of July 3, the public read not of the battle but of the withdrawal of the Confederates from Carlisle on July 1, of the occupation of the town by Union troops, of the return of the enemy later in the day, and of a fight which lasted until ten o'clock that night. From Washington at midnight on July 2 came the report that the Government had no official information concerning the fighting at Gettysburg on July 1. It was very likely that Meade's army had been in contact with the enemy on the following day, but if so, the War Department knew nothing about it. Simultaneous with Washington's disclaimer of any knowledge of army activity, Harrisburg reported that heavy firing had been heard from the general area where the armies of Lee and Meade were supposed to be. As Lee's army was between Harrisburg and the putative battlefield, however, nobody in the city knew what had occurred. From Columbia, Pennsylvania, came a special dispatch to the New York *Tribune* of a more specific character. The *Tribune* man at Columbia had heard that a battle had started near Gettysburg on the morning of July 1 with some heavy skirmishing between Ewell's corps and the First and Eleventh Corps of the Army of the Potomac reinforced by Pleasanton's cavalry and that fighting had been resumed on the morning of the second.[41]

Although Stanton claimed that he had no *official* information concerning the battle, the War Department had received at 8:15 P.M. Thursday, July 2, a telegram from Uriah H. Painter in Baltimore. Painter's telegram stated that he had just arrived there and that:

> I have full account of the battle yesterday & partial list of casualties. Can fair & impartial account go to Phila Inquirer.[42]

Evidently the censor passed his story, for the *Inquirer* on the following morning carried a four-column account of the first day's battle, somewhat more optimistic in tone than the facts justified.

The clouds hung low around the hills South of Gettysburg on Friday morning, July 3. Both Coffin and Reid were awakened at 4:00 A.M. by the sound of guns on the Union right. Meade had taken the offensive in an effort to recover the positions on Culp's Hill which had been lost the evening before. Throughout the morning the struggle went on; men fired at each other Indian style from behind trees and boulders. Gradually the Confederates were pushed back. By eleven o'clock the Union line was intact once more from Culp's Hill to Cemetery Hill.[43]

Sam Wilkeson finally had arrived at the battlefield that morning only to learn that his gallant nineteen-year-old son, Lieutenant Bayard Wilkeson had been a casualty of the first day's fighting. At this time, though, the elder Wilkeson did not know whether his son was alive or dead; he knew only that the young man had been wounded in the leg and was still recorded among the missing. Subsequently he learned to his sorrow that young Bayard had been wounded and left to die for want of attention in a building where the surgeons dared not stay.[44]

At headquarters that morning, Meade was, of course, the focus of all eyes. Among the bystanders was Whitelaw Reid, who was fully conscious that this was truly a historic occasion:

> He [Meade] was quick and nervous in his movements, but calm, and as it seemed to me, lit up with the glow of the occasion. He looked more the General, less the Student. Polished, fashionable-looking Pleasanton, riding whip resting in the leg of one of his jack-boots, and neatly fitting kids drawn over his hands, occasionally put in some earnest remark. Warren, calm, absorbed, earnest as ever, was constantly in consultation with the Commander.[45]

Wilkeson and Reid walked around to the East side of the Leister House and stretched out on the grass. There was much talk among those in the yard about probabilities and some gossip about the supposed arrival of Couch's militia from Harrisburg. From over on the right the sound of fighting could still be heard. Headquarters was likewise under a sporadic fire; most of the missiles seemed to come from the left although now and then a stray shot came whizzing across from directly in front. "That," said Wilkeson referring to an unfamiliar sound from some unknown kind of small arm projectile, "is a muffled howl; that's the exact word to describe it." Presently a round shot passed by, not two feet from the door, followed by another and another. "By Jove," exclaimed one of the staff officers, "those fellows on the left have the range of headquarters." Meade now came to the door and advised those outside to go up the slope fifteen or twenty yards to the stable, which was out of range of the firing. Without waiting for a second warning, Reid mounted his horse and galloped down the Taneytown road.

The bombardment which had thus been inaugurated turned out to be one of the most tremendous of the war. It was almost exactly five minutes past one when Lee's artillery on Seminary Ridge—one hundred and fifteen guns in all—opened fire on the Union positions. Lee had determined to silence the Union batteries in preparation for an assault upon Meade's center. Both Wilkeson and Frank Henry remained at the Leister House throughout the whole terrible bombardment. In his letter, later published in the *Times,* Wilkeson observed:

> Every size and form of shell known to British and American gunnery shrieked, whirled, moaned, whistled and wrathfully fluttered over our ground. . . . Not an orderly—not an ambulance—not a straggler was to be seen upon the plain swept by this tempest of orchestral death thirty minutes after it commenced.[46]

Said the New York *World* correspondent:

> The storm broke upon us so suddenly that soldiers and officers—who leaped, as it began, from their tents, or from lazy siestas on the grass—were stricken in their rising with mortal wounds and died, some with cigars between their teeth, some with pieces of food in their fingers, and one at least—a pale young German, from Pennsylvania—with a miniature of his sister in . . . hands, that seemed more meet to grasp an artist's pencil than a musket. Horses fell, shrieking such awful cries as Cooper told of, and writhing themselves about in hopeless agony. . . . The earth, torn up in clouds, blinded the eyes of hurrying men; and through the branches of the trees and among the grave-stones of the cemetery a shower of destruction crashed ceaselessly.[47]

The Confederate bombardment was answered by eighty Union guns which took up the challenge and threw back their fiery retorts. For an hour and a half this raging cannonade continued. Then, the chief of Artillery, Brigadier General Henry J. Hunt, observing that his ammunition was running low, gave the order to cease fire so as to safeguard his supply for the assault which he correctly assumed was to follow. As soon as the fire from the Union batteries slackened, the Confederate troops formed for attack under the delusion that the Union batteries had been silenced. The attacking force of fifteen thousand men, spearheaded by Pickett's division, had nearly a mile of broad valley to cross before it could reach the Union lines. Said L. L. Crounse in his description of the charge:

> The enemy's front was that of one division in line of battle; there were two such lines, and a very heavy line of skirmishers, almost equal to another line of battle. Out of their concealment in the woods they came across the open fields and up the gentle crest, on the top of which was our line—a weak line of men behind a line of defences hastily thrown up and composed partly of stone walls, partly of rifle-pits, and partly of natural projections of soil and rock. The first charge was repulsed; the line broke and fell back before it had reached a point two-thirds the way over.[48]

Then a second line was formed which continued its advance until "expressions of fierce rage" could be distinguished on the faces of the approaching enemy. Coffin wrote:

> Men fire into each other's faces, not five feet apart. There are bayonet-thrusts, sabre-strokes, pistol-shots; cool, deliberate movements on the part of some, — hot, passionate, desperate efforts with others; hand-to-hand contests; recklessness of life; tenacity of purpose; fiery determination; oaths, yells, curses, hurrahs, shoutings; men going down on their hands and knees, spinning round like tops, throwing out their arms, gulping up blood, falling; legless, armless, headless. There are ghastly heaps of dead men. Seconds are centuries; minutes, ages; but the thin line does not break![49]

Lewis A. Armistead, a Confederate brigadier, reached the crest of Cemetery Ridge with a hundred of his men, but their supports had melted away in the face of the devastating fire from the Union batteries. Armistead and his men were soon shot down, and what was left of Pickett's command straggled back across the fields to Seminary Ridge.

Crounse was standing by when several Confederate officers were brought into the Union lines as prisoners of war.

"Where," asked a captive colonel, "are the men who fought us?"

"Here," said a captain.

"My God!" exclaimed the colonel, "if we only had another line we could have whipped you."

Then looking about him with astonishment, he exclaimed emphatically: "By God, we could have whipped you as it was!"[50]

To all intents and purposes the battle was over. Longstreet was sure that Pickett's repulse would be followed by a Federal counterattack, but Meade had no intention of imitating Pickett's costly example. Already his men had been under fire for thirteen hours that day, and his reserves were almost, if not completely, used up. It was nearly eleven o'clock that evening when Coffin rode up to Meade's headquarters, located in a grove East of the Taneytown road. Meade was sitting on a great flat boulder at the time, listening to the reports of his officers as they were brought in by couriers. Shells had been dropping in the vicinity a few hours earlier when Meade himself rode up while a band came marching in over the hillside playing "Hail to the Chief."

"Ah! General Meade," Sam Wilkeson exclaimed, "You're in very great danger of being President of the United States."

"No," put in another well wisher. "Finish well this work so well begun, and the position you have is better and prouder than President!"[51]

As soon as victory was assured, the correspondents began leaving the field to communicate with their newspapers. Meanwhile, one of them, Byington of the New York *Tribune,* had been making preparations for what proved to be one of the biggest news scoops of the war. Byington had reached the battlefield by a circuitous route, which took him around through Harper's Ferry, Baltimore, Philadelphia, Lancaster, York, and finally Hanover. At Hanover, he learned that Stuart had been there before him and had cut the telegraph wires for ten miles around. Byington asked the landlord at the hotel if there was a telegraph operator on the premises.

"Yes," said the landlord, "there he is, over yonder" and pointed to a little hunchback named Tone, who was lying asleep on a bench. Byington wakened the hunchback and asked him where his battery was.

"Home under the bed," was the answer. "Wires all cut everywhere; no use trying to telegraph."

Finally, under prodding from the *Tribune* man, Tone went over to his house and fished out the battery. Byington then procured a hand car and organized a party to go out and repair the gaps in the line. After the wires were hitched together, the battery was put in operation; presently the operator swung his hat in the air and shouted that he had Baltimore. It was immediately arranged that Byington should have a monopoly of the wire for two days along with a Philadelphia Press reporter who had helped in connecting the relays. As soon as this was settled Byington started for the battlefield, about sixteen miles West of Hanover.

Just after he reached the battlefield, he encountered General Howard, who gave him an account of the first day's fight. About this time, Josiah R. Sypher, one of the other *Tribune* men, caught up with him; together they hastened back to Hanover and telegraphed to the *Tribune* shortly before midnight of July 3 a complete story of the fighting during the first two days. Their account was the only one to get through that night, and as a result, sixty-five thousand copies of the *Tribune* extra which featured it were sold on the streets of New York before morning.

Byington had sent his story by way of Washington and had signed his own name to it. Soon a message came back from the White House, "Dispatch about a battle received. Who are you?" The reporter wired back, "Ask Daddy Welles," referring to the Secretary of the Navy. Summoned from his bed at midnight, Welles told the President that Byington was the editor and proprietor of a weekly newspaper in Connecticut "sometimes employed by the *New York Tribune*," and that in his opinion the telegram was reliable.[52] Within a little while another message from Lincoln came over the wires at Hanover requesting the use of the lines for dispatches between the War Department and General Meade. Byington had no choice in the matter—the request was tantamount to a military order—but in return he exacted the promise that his dispatches should be forwarded to the *Tribune* via the White House. During the next few days while other correspondents were galloping all over the surrounding countryside in search of a telegraph station, Byington kept the *Tribune* provided with all the latest military news.[53]

After attempting in vain to keep pace with the *Tribune* by using ten-mile relays of horses, the *Herald* succeeded in establishing a news monopoly of its own. Early in the morning of July 4, the indefatigable Frank Chapman reached Baltimore ahead of the other newspaper correspondents and commenced looking about for the local manager of the American Telegraph Company, with whom the *Herald* had a contract. Unsuccessful, he hurried to the home of James N. Worl, who was superintendent of a rival concern, the Independent Telegraph Company. Chapman roused him from his sleep, and persuaded him to go down to the telegraph office. When Worl opened the wire to New York, he found that the operators at the other end were at their posts, so he began sending Chapman's material through without delay. At the regular opening time, another operator came on duty, whereupon, at Chapman's suggestion, he was placed at the other wire to New York in order to speed up the transmission of the story. Both operators were pounding their keys as hard as they could and slowly diminishing the pile of copy when one of the *Tribune* correspondents, T. C. Grey, came dashing in with his account. Chapman was about to leave the telegraph office for further information when he realized that as soon as his batch of copy was used up, the operators would be obliged to send whatever else was filed in the order of arrival. To forestall his *Tribune* competitor, Chapman pulled out a pocket edition of the Bible and, turning to the first chapter of Genesis, told Worl to "just keep your men busy sending this until I get back."

All day long he kept the wires hot. Whenever copy ran short, the operators worked in pages from the Bible until he came back with more. The other correspondents who had gathered at the telegraph office were infuriated by Chapman's stratagem, but they were powerless.[54]

Reid and Coffin had left the battlefield that same morning after trying in vain to use the army telegraph and had galloped through nearly thirty miles of mud and rain to Westminster. They arrived there around four o'clock, just in time to catch the hospital train for Baltimore. Loaded with wounded soldiers as it was, however, the train spent the whole night backing and hauling on side tracks and switches so that the two correspondents did not reach the city until daylight on Sunday morning, July 5. While passing through a hotel lobby in Baltimore, Coffin was stopped by Congressman Washburne who was anxious to find out what the outcome of the battle had been. Coffin assured him that Meade had won a great victory and that Lee had already begun to retreat. "You lie," burst from the Congressman's lips. His nerves had been under a strain for days, and the excitement was beginning to tell upon him.[55] Later in the forenoon, Coffin telegraphed a half-column story of the battle to Boston and then left for New York on the evening train. Reid likewise had planned to go on in to Cincinnati with his story, but since railroad travel between Baltimore and Harrisburg still was suspended, he had to go west by way of Philadelphia.

Coffin spent all day Monday, July 6, on the train to Boston, writing some of his story as he rode along and wiring leader paragraphs ahead to his paper. When he reached the *Journal* office that evening, he found Boston's Newspaper Row jammed with people waiting for his arrival. While the crowd milled about outside, Coffin locked himself inside a small room at the office and wrote steadily until the *Journal* went to press, admitting only the men who handled the copy. When the last sheet was finished, he threw himself upon a pile of newspapers in the corner of the room and slept for almost twenty-four hours. Even after he had gone to his home in the suburbs, the townspeople gave him no rest. They came after him with a carriage and a brass band and forced him to come out and tell the story of the battle all over again. On Wednesday, the eighth, he left for the front again, picking up his horse at Westminster, and thus completing a round trip of a hundred miles on horseback and eight hundred miles by rail in less than a week.[56]

The *Times* correspondent Wilkeson had written his story of Gettysburg while sitting beside the body of his dead son. There is real pathos in the concluding lines, an apostrophe to the dead who were lying all about:

> Oh, you dead, who at Gettysburgh have baptized with your blood the second birth of Freedom in America, how you are to be envied! I rise from a grave whose wet clay I have passionately kissed, and I look up and see Christ spanning this battle-field with his feet and reaching fraternal and lovingly up to heaven. His right hand opens the gates of Paradise—with his left he beckons to these mutilated, bloody, swollen forms to ascend.[57]

Before the first newspaper stories of Gettysburg had appeared in print, Lee already had begun his retreat, after remaining entrenched on Seminary Ridge all day July 4, and waiting, even hoping, to be attacked. By Tuesday, July 7 he had reached the Potomac at Williamsport, but was unable to cross because of the high water resulting from recent rains. While he waited for the flood water to subside, the Confederate commander concentrated his army West of Hagerstown to cover the river from Williamsport to Falling Waters. Although he sent his cavalry in pursuit of Lee, Meade made no attempt to follow with his main army. Instead he marched South along the Emmettsburg pike to Frederick and then headed West over South Mountain to intercept the Army of Northern Virginia at the Potomac.[58]

Unable to tell what was taking place, the newsmen filled their papers with the wildest rumors. It was reported, among other things, that Longstreet was dead, that twenty thousand Confederate prisoners had been "bagged" by Meade, and that Lee had been driven into the mountains and completely surrounded. One of the worst offenders among the Northern press was the not overly reliable New York *Herald.* On the Monday following the battle, for example, Chapman telegraphed the *Herald* from Baltimore that General Couch's militia had joined Meade and were slaughtering and capturing the enemy by regiments and brigades.[59] Still later the *Herald* published under a Harrisburg date line an account[60] of a desperate battle which was supposed to have taken place near Williamsport on July 7 and which was entirely mythical. At the time it was alleged to have occurred, the Army of the Potomac was not within twenty miles of Williamsport! Meade's irritation with the reporting of the campaign was reflected in a letter to Halleck written near the end of July in which he sought to "remove the impression which newspaper correspondents have given the public that it was only necessary to advance to secure an easy victory."[61]

From its press the South obtained a very different picture of what had happened at Gettysburg. In the Richmond newspapers of July 7 and 8 it was reported jubilantly that the Yankee army had been "all but annihilated," that forty thousand prisoners had fallen into Confederate hands, and that Meade was retreating toward Baltimore with Lee in hot pursuit. From Richmond the joyous tidings sped to Savannah, where the *Republican,* under the heading "The Best News of the War," told how Meade's army had been surrounded on July 5 by "one of the most brilliant movements on record," and nearly every man either killed, wounded, or captured.[62] No doubt the New York *Times* editor expressed the opinion of many when he said that "such systematic and direct lying has not heretofore been known in this war."[63]

During the closing days of the campaign the correspondents of the New York *Herald* continued to make use of ruthless methods of competition to beat out the other newspapermen. Quotations from letters written by the Philadelphia *Inquirer* reporter, J. H. Taggart, at Frederick to Uriah H. Painter in Washington present a vivid picture of the *Herald*'s cutthroat tactics. On July 13 Taggart wrote:

> Friend Painter, I got your Hagerstown despatch last night per Newbold of N.Y. Tribune, and rewrote it, as Kilty, the operator here, pretended he could not read it. This was at 10 P.M. The N.Y. Herald, an hour or 2 later, got copy of Lee's order from Car-

penter, and yet it got through, & ours did not, as I learn this morning. The Herald monopolizes the telegraph line here, and no messages get through without the *permission* of Mr. Chapman, and he, I suppose, examines all the messages for other papers before being forwarded.

The way Chapman manages it is to engage 5,000 or 10,000 words daily & the operator Here says the Herald has control of the line, as long as they choose to use it—

Newbold's despatch did not get off last night either—although it was in office 2 hours before that of Herald—

I am indignant at this infamous affair, and shall go to Washington immediately, & lay the matter before Mr. Sandford, or else we will not be able to get a message through at all from here while the excitement lasts—. . . .

I loaned Cunnington my horse on Saturday, to go to the front & I have learned nothing of him since. We want an intelligent man here and either you or some one of us ought to be here all the time, or we will be beat to death.

I think it best to go to Washington, to stop this Herald monopoly *at once*, as it would take 3 or 4 days to reach Mr. Sandford by letter. . . .

I feel furious at this affair, as the operator promised me solemnly last night your despatch should go through, and I staid up till mid-night looking after it, and then he deceived me.[64]

On the same morning that Taggart wrote this angry letter, Coffin rode over to Meade's headquarters about a mile South of Boonsboro and talked with Adjutant General Seth Williams. The atmosphere at headquarters was charged with excitement, but the officers were confident that Lee was at the end of his tether. Presently General Meade came in, soaking wet from a reconnaissance. He had always been on good terms with Coffin, and in the excitement of the moment, he spoke freely, saying: "We shall have a great battle tomorrow. The reinforcements are coming up, and as soon as they come we shall pitch in."[65]

But Meade had waited too long. By that afternoon of July 13, the river had dropped sufficiently to permit the use of pontoons. First Ewell's Corps, then Longstreet's, and finally Hill's crossed the river without any interference from Meade except for a rear guard action at the very end. By noon of the fourteenth, the movement was complete. That afternoon, Noah Brooks of the Sacramento *Union* rode over to Falling Waters and looked wistfully across into Virginia, where he could see the smoke rising from the enemy's camp fires. In later years Brooks wrote:

> It is impossible now to describe—almost impossible to recall—the feeling of bitterness with which we regarded the sight. Lee's army was gone. In spite of warnings, expostulations, doubts, and fears, it had escaped, and further pursuit was not even to be thought of.

As the reporter started back toward Meade's headquarters, he passed several soldiers who had enlisted for the duration of the war and heard one of them remark wryly, "Well, here goes for two years more."[66]

A second letter from Taggart to Painter, dated July 15, throws further light on the reporting situation at the close of the campaign:

> I went to Baltimore on Monday evening & saw Mr Westbrook, the Superintendent of the Atlantic & Ohio Telegraph Line, & he promised me the matter should be remedied, & that no partiality should be shown any paper.
>
> I returned yest. at noon, leaving Joe Robinson here while I was gone.
>
> Last night at 11 o'clock, Cunnington came in from Williamsport, with full particulars of the escape of Lee's army. Cun. left there yest. morg. about 10 o'clock.
>
> I got the same news early in evening & had telegraphed it, or rather left a desp. in office, but Cunnington having fuller particulars, I saw his despatch in office also, before midnight.
>
> An order was received from Washington yesterday that all newspaper reports sent over line must be sent to War Department for approval, so I dont know yet whether Cunnington's or my despatch got through.
>
> To make sure of it for . . . to-morrow's paper, I went to office this morning at 6 o'clock, and copied Cunnington's whole despatch & sent it to Philadelphia by Joe Robinson, the office boy, who was here doing nothing. I gave him my tickets to go on with.
>
> Cunnington is here to-day. If he had taken the train this morning, he could have been in Phila. this afternoon, in time to have written an extended article for tomorrow's paper. But he is so tired!
>
> Crounse of N.Y. Times I know will do it, as I saw him at midnight last night & he expected to go at once to New York this morning.

> I notice in yesterday's N.Y. Herald a short despatch I left in telegraph office on Sunday night, which was not in Monday's Inquirer, of the edition received here. It may have been published in city edition, but if it was, the Herald has copied it, and put a date to it a day later.
>
> If it was not published at all in the Inquirer, then it was sold to Chapman here, by the operator, or he was permitted to copy it from the despatch I left in the office. I shall ferret it out, & will raise hell about it, for I do think the whole affair here in the telegraph office has been managed most rascally.
>
> Last night, while I was in office, Chapman brought in several loads of copy, 6, 8, & 10 pages, & laid it down before the operator, pretending it was to go. I believe he only does it to occupy the line, & keep other papers from getting despatches through.
>
> I would have gone to Washington on Monday, & seen Mr. Eckert about it, but railroad between Wash & Balt was not running, because of bridge at Laurel being washed away, so I had to go to Baltimore.
>
> Come here as soon as possible. I am played out for money & cant get home to get any as Joe has got my tickets. . . . The game in this quarter is now *blocked* for news. Chapman leaves to-morrow & all the correspondents are leaving.[67]

In spite of the many absurd stories to which the press gave currency during the campaign, the reporting of the Battle of Gettysburg compares favorably with that of the other great battles of the war. From an examination of their battle narratives it is hard to escape the conclusion that with few exceptions the reporters at Gettysburg rose to the occasion in a manner befitting the great spectacle which they witnessed.[68] Three Northern battle accounts were of especial merit: the New York *World*'s story, written by a correspondent who gave no other clue to his identity than the pseudonym "Bonaparte";[69] Coffin's narrative in the Boston *Journal;* and the account which Whitelaw Reid contributed to the Cincinnati *Gazette.* In some respects, Reid's was the best of the three. Its broad sweep, its tense dramatic quality, and its graphic portrayal of the long pauses and sudden outbursts of desperate energy which characterized the struggle marked it as a permanent contribution to the literature of the war.[70] Of the Southern battle narratives, those which appeared in the Richmond *Enquirer* and the Richmond *Sentinel* belonged unquestionably in the first rank.[71]

One of the most interesting descriptions of the activities of the cavalry arm during the campaign was the work of the New York *Times* correspondent, Edward A. Paul. In an eight-column story he graphically delineated the feverish pace of a sixteen-day period in which the cavalry division he accompanied fought fifteen battles, destroyed, so he claimed, one half of Stuart's cavalry force, and thoroughly demoralized the remainder. "This is cavalry fighting," he declared, "the superior of which the world never saw."[72] From a Union cavalry officer who participated in the fighting, there emanated, however, a different opinion. Charles Francis Adams, Jr., told his brother John Quincy:

> Of course you know well enough that your newspapers tell you nothing but lies and that "the cavalry" as depicted by them is all a figment of the poet's brain. If you don't I tell you so now and know it in future. We have done our work decently, but Pleasanton is, next to Hooker, the greatest humbug of the war, and Kilpatrick is a brave injudicious boy, much given to blowing and who will surely come to grief.[73]

One of the other New York *Times* reporters, L. L. Crounse, was strongly criticized for a letter, written soon after the battle, in which he spoke with uncomfortable frankness of the "craven-hearted meanness" of the people of Gettysburg and the vicinity:

> I do not speak hastily. I but write the unanimous sentiments of the whole army—an army which now feels that the doors from which they drove a host of robbers, thieves, and cut-throats, were not worthy of being defended.[74]

According to the *Times* correspondent, the male inhabitants of Gettysburg, for the most part, ran away at the time of the battle, leaving their wives and children to the mercy of the enemy. Furthermore, when they returned, "instead of lending a helping hand to our wounded," they began presenting bills to the military authorities for damages inflicted by both armies during the campaign. These accusations—doubly offensive because of the numerous editorials blasting "Pennsylvania apathy" which had appeared in the New York papers earlier in the campaign—were vigorously denied by a group of Pennsylvania clergymen, mostly from Philadelphia, who wrote in protest to the editor of the *Times*.[75]

In an open letter replying to the clergymen, Crounse hedged a bit. He admitted that since the battle the people of Gettysburg had in general been tender and kind toward the wounded and that likewise the citizens of Adams County, in which Gettysburg is located, had received injurious treatment from both armies. Nevertheless, he stoutly insisted that it would take the statements:

> of even more than twenty clergymen to eradicate the experiences and the undeniable facts which came to my knowledge in Gettysburgh. When the Army of the Potomac votes the citizens of Gettysburgh as gallant, generous and patriotic, then I shall believe it. Not before.[76]

With this, the whole wretched controversy, painful to everyone concerned, terminated.

17

"Shambling Shanks and the Fugacious Furay"

WHILE Grant and Meade were striking sledgehammer blows on opposite ends of the battle line, Rosecrans — to the infinite boredom of the army reporters—procrastinated at Murfreesboro. Bragg, who in January, 1863, after the Murfreesboro battle had retreated southward to Tullahoma, contented himself with cavalry raids on the Federal lines of communication, as Rosecrans for almost six months devoted his energy to fortifying his position, rebuilding his army, and wrangling ceaselessly with the War Department. Stanton had angered the general by a personal letter, written soon after the fight at Murfreesboro, in which he announced his intention to offer a major generalship in the regular army to the first brigadier who won an important victory.

"I never saw him so angry as when he received that letter," one of Rosecrans' aides told James R. Gilmore of the New York *Tribune.*[1]

To Rosecrans it seemed as if the Secretary were seeking to administer the affairs of the army along the lines of a gift enterprise, and he did not hesitate to say as much in his reply. From that time on, Stanton was deaf to the appeals of his touchy subordinate for more troops, equipment, and supplies. To some observers, however, it appeared that the terrible struggle at Stone's River had deprived Rosecrans of his aggressive spirit. Repeated urgings from Washington for him to advance against the enemy produced only endless excuses. As spring of 1863 approached, an outcry arose in the Eastern press against the inertia of the man who had previously been accounted a "fighting general." The Western newspapers in the main, however, continued as his champions.[2]

About the middle of May, another *Tribune* reporter, Henry Villard, appeared at Murfreesboro to find out what was going on in the Army of the Cumberland. Rosecrans received him with great cordiality and almost overwhelmed him with offers of hospitality. Villard already had received the impression from other newspapermen that Rosecrans was trying to use the press for his own personal advancement. Not wishing to forfeit his independence, the *Tribune* reporter declined the General's favors as politely as he could and took up residence instead with General McCook and his staff, who were quartered in an old plantation home just outside Murfreesboro.

Although he was subject to the usual restrictions on the publication of information that might lend "aid and comfort to the enemy," Villard made frequent visits to Rosecrans' headquarters where he never failed to receive a hearty welcome from the General and his chief of staff, future President James A. Garfield. As the *Tribune* man had anticipated, he had no difficulty in getting on a confidential footing with Rosecrans. Villard said:

> In fact, he freely offered his confidence to me of his own accord, and thus enabled me promptly to take a correct measure of the man. He showed at once that his disagreements with the Washington authorities were the uppermost thoughts in his mind, and that it gratified him greatly to express his ill-humor towards them. Indeed, he criticised General Halleck and Secretary Stanton with such freedom—with such a total disregard of official propriety—. . . that it really embarrassed me to listen to him, although, fortunately, he was content to do the talking without expecting sympathetic echoes from me. . . . Nor did he hesitate to expatiate upon his plans for future operations, and this with scarcely concealed self-appreciation. He evidently believed that he was destined to play the most prominent part and reach the greatest distinction among all the Union generals. He unfolded to me his conception of the grand strategy by which the triumph of the North could be assured, coupling it with a broad intimation that Halleck and Stanton would have to be got out of the way, leaving me to infer that, after this was done, the next necessary step was to put him in the former's place. Talk of this kind was so regularly repeated by him that I could not help concluding that he was anxious to impress me with his greatness and to have that impression reflected in the *Tribune*.[3]

The more Rosecrans tried to impress upon Villard that he was the "great and only hope" of the country, the less inclined the *Tribune* correspondent was to build him up in the press. But there were other reporters at this time who were perfectly willing to accept the General at his own valuation. One of them was Bickham of the Cincinnati *Commercial*, who wrote in such flattering terms about "Old Rosey" that Villard scornfully put him down as a "puffer."[4] Yet Villard's colleague Gilmore had come to the army with special instructions from Greeley to sound out Rosecrans as a possible Republican nominee for the presidency.

Gilmore was at headquarters on June 9 when Rosecrans polled his corps and division commanders about the advisability of a forward movement recently ordered by the War Department. There were some twenty-five or thirty men in the General's anteroom, all more or less well known. While they joked among themselves, Garfield told the *Tribune* representative who they were:

> The stout, full-faced, blond-complexioned man leaning against the wall by the window was the "old Russian," General Turchin; the handsome officer seated next to him, with wavy brown hair, and face so much like James Russell Lowell's, was St. Clair Morton, chief of the engineers, who might have been a poet, and was a hero. Leaning against the wall, at his back, the dark man with keen, intense eyes, heavy black beard, and coarse, wiry hair starting up into a sort of pyramid on the top of his head was Jeff C. Davis, who killed General Nelson, and did such great service at Stone River.... Altogether it was a gathering of men worth going a thousand miles to meet.[5]

Presently an unusually quiet, unassuming soldier of rather less than medium height entered the room and seated himself on the window sill beside General David S. Stanley. Gilmore casually observed the soldier's loose sack coat, his plain trousers, and "everyday boots," but could find nothing about him to warrant any special attention except his eye, "a ball of black flame."

"How are you, Phil?" "Good morning, Sheridan!" chorused the other officers. Gilmore hardly needed the assurance from Garfield that this indeed was General Philip H. Sheridan.

"Do you remember, sir, Pope's thirty thousand muskets, and ten thousand prisoners?" asked a young officer who was sitting near the *Tribune* man.

"Yes, very well," replied Gilmore.

"Well, I took the muskets, and Sheridan took the men. How many men were there, Sheridan?"

"I don't remember," muttered the quiet general.

"Well, I remember the muskets. They counted nine hundred and thirty—not one more or less."

"I was with Pope at the second battle of Booneville," put in another officer, "when Sheridan rode up to him, and reported sixty-five prisoners. 'Why don't you say five hundred?' asked Pope. 'There ought to be five hundred,—call them five hundred anyway;' and five hundred they were, but not in Sheridan's report."[6]

The others laughed, but the quiet general said nothing. Soon afterwards the army's three corps commanders came out of Rosecrans' inner sanctum, and the gathering dispersed. The reporters soon learned that the council of war, almost without dissent, had decided against an advance.

About this time another well-known reporter, William Swinton, arrived at Murfreesboro to report war news for the New York *Times.* In the first of his series of letters from the Army of the Cumberland, published on June 15, he commented upon the superb condition of that army and its unlimited confidence in its leader. In a second letter analyzing the "anatomy and physiology" of the army, he wrote at greater length concerning its "contented, victorious, spirited temper," for which he had found no equivalent in the Army of the Potomac. He was impressed likewise by the rigid system of military justice prevailing in Rosecrans' army. "Deserters are *shot;* spies are *hung*—not sent up to Washington to be pardoned. In consequence, desertion is here a thing almost unknown." One feature of the Army of the Cumberland puzzled the *Times* reporter, however—the absence of sharpshooters. With a little practice, he thought, as large a number as could be desired might be obtained, "for with proper discipline the Western hunters are fitted to make the best *tirailleurs* in the world."[7]

On June 23, Villard learned from Garfield that the forward movement, to which Rosecrans finally had agreed, was scheduled to begin the following day. To avoid a frontal attack on Bragg's strong fortifications at Tullahoma, Rosecrans planned to turn the enemy's right and assail his flank and rear. While Stanley's cavalry feinted toward Shelbyville, the three corps of Thomas, Crittenden, and McCook were to swing to the left and advance through a series of mountain gorges to Manchester, twelve miles in the rear of the Confederate line. At Liberty Gap on the first day of the advance, Villard saw some of the roughest fighting of the campaign. About noon it began to rain; the rain turned into a downpour; and by evening the *Tribune* correspondent was soaked. He had to spend the night in his wet clothes, and by morning he was running a high fever. The army surgeon who examined him told him he was suffering from a very severe attack of malarial fever and inflammatory rheumatism, and that it was completely out of the question for him to remain with the army. Before the day was over, Villard was in an ambulance-train on the first leg of the journey back to Louisville![8]

Some of the reporters were having other difficulties. Use of the telegraph was forbidden the press at the very outset, and, according to the Chicago *Times* correspondent, there was some disposition among army authorities "to deny us the privilege of letter writing until the plan of the campaign . . . should have been fully developed."[9] The movement went so well, however, that all restrictions on press use of the telegraph were lifted less than a week after the initial advance.

On the twenty-eighth of June, Stanley's cavalry occupied Shelbyville. Two days later, discovering that the bridges on the Nashville and Chattanooga Railroad were threatened, Bragg pulled out of Tullahoma and withdrew to the South bank of the Elk River. By July 3, the Tullahoma campaign was virtually ended. Within a nine-day period Rosecrans, with a loss of only five hundred and fifty-seven killed and wounded and thirteen captured or missing, had driven Bragg from middle Tennessee.[10]

So important and cheap a victory led the Federal commander to expect some acclaim at least, but the newspapers were too much engrossed with what was happening at Gettysburg and Vicksburg to pay much attention to Rosecrans' success. For nearly a fortnight after the Tullahoma campaign hardly a line about what was happening in middle Tennessee appeared in any of the leading newspapers. This hiatus in the flow of news was not the fault of the reporters in Rosecrans' army. According to the editor of the Cincinnati *Commercial*, the news blackout was caused:

> partly by the interruption of mail communications with Nashville, in consequence of the Morgan raid through Kentucky, and [was] partly owing to the stupidity of management, and supercilious disregard of the interests of the press, by the parties who control the Louisville Telegraph office. During the last few days we have been receiving piles of delayed dispatches and correspondence.[11]

Three weeks after the affair at Liberty Gap, a full list of casualties forwarded to the *Commercial* on the day after the action still was in one of the telegraph offices between Tullahoma and Louisville.

One of the *Herald* correspondents, E. D. Westfall, had an exciting encounter with Morgan on the way back to Louisville, just after the campaign. Near Lebanon Junction, twenty-two miles out of Louisville, the train on which Westfall was riding was halted by two cross ties placed across the track and by the threatening muzzle of a twelve-pounder brass cannon. Some Union soldiers who were on board the train leaped to the ground as the locomotive abruptly checked its speed, and began firing at the Confederate troopers who were streaming out of the woods. The *Herald* correspondent dived to the floor to escape the bullets which came whistling through the cars.

Presently a ferocious-looking Confederate came crouching along the aisle, gun in hand, admonishing everyone to "get out of this; damned quick too." The passengers needed no second invitation. By this time the firing had ceased, and the plundering was ready to begin. In common with the other passengers, the *Herald* man was relieved of his valuables—his gold watch, pocket knife, toilet case, and pistol, everything in fact but his tooth brush! While the transfer of property was being made, one of Morgan's officers invited the correspondent to come along with the raiders, promising that in this way he could obtain "lots of items" and that he (the officer) would notify James Gordon Bennett that "John Morgan's got your mule." Westfall declined the invitation, however, and continued on toward Louisville in a lumber wagon, from which he transferred to a Louisville mail packet at West Point on the Ohio River.[12]

Only one of the army reporters criticized Federal tactics adversely during the Tullahoma campaign. In a letter describing the fight at Liberty Gap on June 24, the *Herald* correspondent Shanks intimated that the movement of McCook's Twentieth Corps had been intended as a feint, not as a real attack, and stigmatized the affair as a "useless slaughter."[13] Subsequently Shanks was called to account by one of McCook's staff officers, who insisted that the movement was not a feint but added that he supposed it was too late for the reporter to make any correction of his mistake. His supposition was wrong, for in a letter subsequently published in the *Herald* Shanks asserted a little stiffly that:

> It is never too late to correct mistakes. I have endeavored to tell the truth, and shall endeavor to do so in all cases, without fear or favor. At this late hour I give General McCook the benefit of his adjutant's statement without admitting that my first statement was wrong. My authority for it was good. Besides, I did not

> give expression to the opinion until General McCook's retirement from Liberty Gap confirmed all that I had heard of the character of his operations. . . . No man is more willing to give justice to or say something favorable of General McCook than myself, the more particularly as I have had occasion to speak unfavorably of him heretofore, and shall very gladly and hastily seize upon any opportunity to chronicle . . . the skill, activity, energy or other military traits of General McCook.[14]

Shanks was probably misinformed although there is some evidence in the official records of the campaign to substantiate his opinion.[15]

Throughout the remainder of July and the early part of August there was a lull in active campaigning in the Tennessee theater while the Army of the Cumberland gathered large supplies of food and ammunition for an advance on Chattanooga. No one at Rosecrans' headquarters knew for certain where Bragg had gone. On July 13, Swinton turned up at Cincinnati, direct from the Army of the Cumberland, with the exciting news that Bragg had evacuated Chattanooga and was retreating southward to Atlanta.[16] Approximately a week later the New York *Tribune* carried a story bearing a Memphis date line that Bragg's army was retreating "precipitately" into Georgia followed by Rosecrans' army and that Rosecrans' advance units were reported to be at Rome, Georgia.[17] This report was promptly contradicted by the Associated Press,[18] and in a letter written from Nashville on July 29, the *Herald* correspondent Shanks expressed surprise that anyone should think that Chattanooga would be thus readily abandoned.[19]

Meanwhile the War Department was becoming impatient with Rosecrans once more because of what Halleck felt were needless delays. The same opinion was expressed in other quarters. Even Rosecrans' chief of staff was dissatisfied with the dilatory tactics of his superior. Many years later, Shanks revealed that at this time:

> He [Garfield] often deprecated to me personally—with no prohibition of publication, although he knew me as a newspaper correspondent—the inactivity of the army. . . .[20]

Garfield's complaints to others, Chase among them, caused him to be accused, perhaps unjustly, of having intrigued to bring about the removal of Rosecrans.[21]

On August 16, 1863, after an angry exchange of telegrams with Halleck, the Federal General finally resumed the offensive. Rosecrans did not plan to strike directly at Chattanooga. Instead, he proposed to march his army in a Southeasterly direction across the Cumberland Mountains to the banks of the Tennessee River. Then, while Crittenden made a noisy pretense of crossing the river above the city and attacking it from the North, the rest of the army was to strike across the Tennessee near Bridgeport, twenty miles to the Southwest, and flank Bragg out of Chattanooga.[22] In preparation for the march, the army was, in the words of its commander, "stripped to the waist." The ponderous Sibley tents used earlier in the campaign had been discarded for light shelter tents, one of which each man was required to carry on his back as part of his equipment. So far as possible, pack mules were substituted for wagons, and all unnecessary impedimenta was left behind. Meanwhile, Burnside was moving out of Kentucky upon Knoxville with an army of twenty thousand to safeguard Rosecrans' left flank.[23]

One evening as the army was crossing the mountains during the first stage of the campaign, Shanks was standing near the entrance of General Rosecrans' headquarters in Stevenson, Alabama, just as the General himself came out. Catching sight of the *Herald* man, Rosecrans remarked in an offhand way that the army correspondents could do the army a service by informing the public of the great obstacles to campaigning in such country:

> Napoleon's passage of the Alps was not more difficult. He had a higher mountain range to cross, it is true, but he had only one, while we have to cross three distinct and separate ranges, the last of which is as difficult of ascent as any part of the Alps. Napoleon had no rivers: we have the wide and rapid Tennessee; he had good Macadamized roads, almost as ancient as the Alps themselves; we have to build our roads as we go. And when he had crossed the Alps Napoleon had a wide, rich valley route to Rome. When we shall have passed Lookout Mountain our route to Rome will be through as rugged and broken and barren mountains as these we have just passed.[24]

Shanks pricked up his ears at that last statement. He knew only too well what it meant to march that army over these rugged mountains. He had seen one wagon hold up a whole line of vehicles extending to the rear for miles along one of those narrow and precipitous mountain roads, and on one occasion he had watched General Wood working alongside his staff and orderlies to build a bridge over a small chasm in the road caused by a single night's rain and the washing away of a large stone.

But Rosecrans had by a slip of the tongue revealed that Rome, Georgia, was the destination of his army. It was hardly surprising that in reporting the General's remarks, Shanks laid more stress on this disclosure than he did upon the obstacles which he was asked to portray.[25]

By August 20, the right and center divisions of the Army of the Cumberland had reached the bank of the Cumberland below Chattanooga and were preparing to cross. So well timed was the feint under Crittenden that Bragg had concentrated the greater part of his command at and above Chattanooga, leaving the crossing of the river by the main portion of Rosecrans' army virtually unopposed. Beginning August 29, the Federal troops bridged the stream at four points and began a wide flanking march eastward and northeastward. By September 4, all the troops were across the river, Crittenden's men bringing up the rear. One of the most interesting newspaper descriptions of the crossing appeared in a letter contributed to the Cincinnati *Commercial* by its special correspondent, Captain Joseph W. Miller.[26] The most dramatic feature of Miller's description was the collapse of the trestle bridge at Bridgeport while one of Brigadier General John M. Brannan's trains was going across it. The reporter went on to tell how the movement was halted for several hours while repairs were effected. Where the bridge had been, there was a corresponding line of partially submerged wagons and mule teams struggling to free themselves from their network of straps and chains. Finally, all the mules except one were cut loose; by hard poling, the wagons were also brought to shore. Then the engineers went to work to restore the bridge, many of them standing in the water up to their armpits. As the crossing was not contested by the enemy, no serious damage resulted from the accident. "The passage of the river is an unequivocal success," Miller wrote, and so it proved.

In every army reporter's mind was the unanswered question, "What will Bragg do now?" At the beginning of the campaign the Confederate commander had believed that Rosecrans intended to cross Walden Ridge North of Chattanooga to establish a junction with Burnside. From a copy of the Chicago *Times* which fell into his hands on or shortly before September 5, he received a somewhat different picture of Federal intentions. This particular issue of the *Times* contained a letter from its special correspondent at Rosecrans' headquarters stating that:

> Crittenden's Corps [had] moved eastward to feel the strength of the enemy, with the intention of crossing the mountains to the north and east of Chattanooga, crossing the Tennessee River at

> a ford some 30 miles above Chattanooga. This crossing safely effected, Crittenden will swing into the rear of Chattanooga, and if possible take the place. . . .
>
> Meanwhile if Crittenden succeeds well in his efforts upon Chattanooga and will not need re-enforcements, Thomas and McCook will move rapidly upon Rome, Ga.[27]

In a letter to the Confederate War Department in Richmond on September 5 enclosing the above information, Bragg called attention to the fact that the exact move of Crittenden had been made up to crossing the river and that Thomas and McCook had likewise crossed "at the point nearest Rome." As the true shape of Rosecrans' strategy became more apparent, the Confederate commander evacuated Chattanooga on the seventh and eighth of September and retreated southward to La Fayette, Georgia, in the valley East of Pigeon Mountain.

Under the erroneous impression that the enemy was completely demoralized, Rosecrans lost no time in organizing a vigorous pursuit. On the same day (September 9) that Crittenden marched into Chattanooga, he received orders from the army commander to leave behind him only a brigade to garrison the town and to press forward after Bragg along the railroad leading South from Chattanooga. Acting under similar instructions, Thomas advanced from Trenton across Lookout Mountain and thence over Pigeon Mountain toward La Fayette, where, unknown to him, the Confederate army was massed, ready to strike. The third Union corps commander, McCook, began marching from Valley Head across the same ridge of Lookout (although farther South) toward Alpine and Summerville.[28]

By thus scattering his forces over fifty miles of hilly, wooded country traversed only by rough country roads, Rosecrans played squarely into Bragg's hands. Situated as he was, with reinforcements on the way from the armies of Lee and Johnston, the Confederate commander had a golden opportunity to destroy the Union army in detail as it issued from the mountain passes below Chattanooga. To delude his adversary still further, Bragg caused "deserters" from his army to drift into the Union lines with plausible tales of the demoralized state of the army which they had just left.[29]

Most of the army correspondents shared Rosecrans' optimistic mood although one or two of them expressed some misgivings. Shanks was of the opinion that the rapid pursuit of Bragg's army would be continued without halt until Atlanta was taken or until a battle resulted in front of that place or at Rome.[30] A correspondent of the New York *World,* on the other hand, wrote to his newspaper on September 12 (one week before the Battle of Chickamauga) that Bragg's army was receiving reinforcements from all departments of the Gulf and Atlantic states and predicted with remarkable accuracy that "one of the hardest fought and decisive battles of the war" would be fought within ten days on the plains of Northern Georgia.[31]

On September 9, the day Chattanooga fell, Benjamin F. Taylor of the Chicago *Journal* was hastening eastward to catch up with the army on a train bound from Nashville to Stevenson. Among his fellow passengers was the Assistant Secretary of War, Charles A. Dana, who was under instructions from Stanton to report the operations of the Army of the Cumberland as he already had reported those of Grant's Army of the Tennessee during the Vicksburg campaign.[32] On the eleventh of September, Dana rode into Chattanooga, having made the journey over the mountains from Bridgeport on horseback.[33] Dana was regarded with considerable suspicion by the army authorities at Chattanooga. It was common talk around headquarters that he was nothing better than a War Department spy and that his real purpose in coming there was to ruin Rosecrans. The commanding general must have had some such fears, for when the Assistant Secretary first reported to him, he burst into a tirade of abuse directed at the government in general and Stanton and Halleck in particular, alleging that they had done everything in their power to prevent his success. Dana replied sternly that he had no authority to listen to such complaints and that his purpose in coming there was to find out what the government could do to help the army. Rosecrans then quieted down somewhat and began to discuss his plans in more lucid fashion. But the representative of the War Department did not fail to observe, as he rode through the camp on his daily trips, that the soldiers shouted after him in mocking tones, "Hey, old sutler! When are you going to open out?"[34]

Meanwhile, Taylor, who had never been South of the Ohio River before, was gathering material for a remarkable series of campaign letters. In a story mailed from Bridgeport on September 12, he communicated an unusually vivid picture of the army at night, exactly one week before the Battle of Chickamauga. He began:

> Ten thousand men are encamped around us. Far up the hills, reddening the cedars, twinkle the campfires; flocks of tents dot the slopes; clusters of mules and horses, tied to trees, present

peripheries of heels everywhere; valleys and hills are tangled in a net-work of paths; fat bacon is complaining from the ends of ramrods; the aroma of coffee struggles with baser odors; perched upon the ledges, at length beneath the trees, under canvas and in open air—everywhere soldiers. Here a boy has just planked the ace and taken the "trick," or finished the letter to the girl he left behind him, or lighted his pipe, or wrung out his shirt, or shaken up his cedar boughs for a shake-down; he is playing the flute; he is drawing the bows short and long; he is talking over Perryville or Murfreesboro. Here, by an inch of candle, a cluster of two heads hangs over a book. There, around a half cord of bread and a pile of russet slabs of bacon, and sacks of sugar and rice, a group is gathered, little, smoky kettle, tin cup, haversack in hand. Somebody eager to see, skips up on somebody's slab of bacon, and the distribution is effected. Over here is a black brigade; over there, a troop of uncouth, flat-bodied Alabamians and Tennesseans stand out in relief in the red firelight, and like snakes change their butternut skins for army blue. Up through the night wails the bugle; along the valley rolls the beat of drums; down from the crags float, "When this cruel war is over," "Oh, take your time, Miss Lucy," and the loud laugh and the tough word.[35]

With Thomas' Fourteenth Corps ascending Lookout Mountain during this time was the Cincinnati *Gazette* reporter, William S. Furay. Near midday of September 10 during a halt in the march, the reporter tied his wearied horse to a tree on the summit of the mountain and strolled along the crest of the ridge, enjoying the fine view of the country below. Starkweather's brigade of Baird's division was encamped nearby, waiting for the remainder of the division to come up. Catching sight of some soldiers of the First Wisconsin, amusing themselves by rolling rocks down the mountain side, Furay stopped to watch. As the fun progressed, the soliders became more daring until finally they succeeded in prying loose a huge fragment weighing at least a dozen tons and started it on its way downward. Three or four hundred feet from the summit, it struck a tree no less than six inches in diameter, snapping it off as if it were a pipestem. Then bounding forward and downward, it burst into a hundred fragments, each of which sought its own individual route to the bottom. With a roguish glance at the correspondent, whom they apparently recognized, one of the frolickers slyly remarked, "How I wish there were an artist present to picture, or a correspondent to describe, this scene—Wisconsin boys in Georgia rolling rocks down Lookout Mountain!"[36]

Furay was on hand the next day when Negley's division, supported by Baird's, suddenly was attacked by superior numbers and forced to fall back to Stevens' Gap. During the action the *Gazette* reporter saw Starkweather's brigade, which was covering the retreat, deliver a "murderous volley" in the face of the advancing Confederates, effectively checking their pursuit. A moment later, General Negley rode up, evidently in high spirits.

"Did they run against a snag?" he laughingly inquired of the correspondent.

Subsequently Furay admitted that "I think I felt as merry as he when I answered in the affirmative." Later that afternoon, the same reporter stood atop a ridge, watching the retreating Union battalions receding into the distance. Just then Captain William G. Kendrick of Colonel Timothy R. Stanley's staff came by. It was already starting to get dark, and for a moment Furay scarcely knew whether Kendrick was a friend or foe. The captain had a good suggestion, however, which the correspondent promptly followed:

"You had better withdraw," said Kendrick. "I see the enemy's sharpshooters creeping up the hill."[37]

By this time Rosecrans had become fully aware that, instead of withdrawing eastward along the railroad as he had first supposed, Bragg had marched southward from Chattanooga behind the next range of hills and was within striking distance of Thomas' corps. It was, Rosecrans now realized, a matter of life and death to concentrate his scattered forces in the shortest possible time. To McCook on September 12, Garfield dispatched an order to "move forward . . . with all dispatch to the support of General Thomas." On the thirteenth, Crittenden was notified that it was Rosecrans' intention to "close General McCook down on Thomas, and both on you as soon as possible, so as to concentrate the weight of our army against the enemy."[38] By noon of September 18, the concentration of the Army of the Cumberland had virtually been completed. In the meantime, Bragg had made repeated attempts to pick off exposed units of that army, but his efforts had been frustrated in large part by the failure of his subordinates to carry out his orders.[39]

Each day of the week, September 13-18, that preceded the Battle of Chickamauga it was becoming clearer that Bragg intended to fight. The army reporters, veterans and novices alike, sensed an uneasy feeling running through the army that the movements of the enemy spelled mischief. Many an old soldier, long since accustomed to read the signs of an approaching battle from afar off, tore up his latest batch of love letters and waited for the enemy to come through the gaps in Pigeon Mountain. Throughout the night of the seventeenth, Miller of the Cincinnati *Commercial* watched the mysterious messages of the signal officers being spelled out by flaming torches from a distant hill top.

The sky overhead was gray, the air chilly, the morning of September 18, the day before the battle. During the forenoon of the eighteenth, Major General Gordon Granger, who commanded the Reserve Corps, crossed the Chickamauga River with two brigades on a reconnaissance. He came back with information (later disclosed to be unreliable) that Longstreet's corps from Lee's army already had joined Bragg.

That night important changes were made in the Union line of battle. Thomas' corps, which had been in the center position, moved to the left, passing behind Crittenden, to protect Rosecrans' line of communication with Chattanooga. Davis' and Sheridan's divisions of McCook's corps also were shifted to the left to connect with the right of Crittenden. Furay of the Cincinnati *Gazette,* who accompanied Thomas' corps on its night march, described the experience as follows:

> A night march of a large body of troops is a solemn thing. The soldiers scarcely speak a word to each other; the animals move with a dull, mechanical motion which hardly resembles life; the rattle of the wagon wheels seems strangely muffled, and almost the only sound you recognize is the heavy, measured *awful* tramp of thousands of living men!
>
> For the first half of the night . . . everything was comfortable enough, but near midnight it turned freezingly cold, and as it was necessary, after passing General Crittenden, for us to feel our way with caution, long, wearisome halts took place, during which skirmishers would scour the woods immediately upon our front and right flank. The boys who were not skirmishing becoming very cold during these halts, began to kindle fires at every stopping place to warm themselves. At first they made these fires of logs of wood and rails taken from the neighboring fences, but afterward they ceased to trouble themselves about removing the rails and set fire to the fences themselves wherever they chanced to stop.

For part of the march, Furay rode alongside the First Michigan battery and conversed in low tones with its commander, Lieutenant George W. Van Pelt.

"Do you think," asked the artillery officer, voicing what must have been the unspoken thoughts of many another in his command, "that we shall engage the enemy?"

"If we can avoid it, I feel pretty sure we will not," replied Furay.

"Why then this movement?" queried Van Pelt.

"Doubtless to prevent the enemy from turning our left flank, which they have all day been threatening to do."

The battery commander darted a curious look at the army newspaperman. "Then you believe they are endeavoring to bring on a battle?"

"I certainly believe they are," Furay assured him.

"Do you know anything of their strength?" continued the officer with a touch of anxiety in his voice.

"Not certainly," said the reporter, "but in addition to Bragg's old army, Longstreet's corps from Virginia, and at least twenty thousand men from Johnston's army are in front of us."

About that time, Brigadier General Absalom Baird, the division commander, came riding by with several members of his staff.

"General," said Furay, "shall we go to Chattanooga tonight?"

"No," was the reply, "We shall go a mile or two further, then take position upon the left, and await the enemy."[40]

There could be no further doubt of the significance of the movement; these preparations meant battle. Shortly before dawn of Saturday, September 19, the marching columns fell into line facing eastward near Kelly's Plantation. About eight o'clock, Thomas ordered his advance (Brannan's) division to drive back a small enemy force which had crossed to the West bank of the Chickamauga River the evening before. Only two of Thomas' divisions were near him at this time. Reynolds was still several miles in the rear; Negley was over on the Federal right, watching the fords of Chickamauga near Crawfish Spring. Bragg's plans were completely upset, however, by Brannan's sudden attack. The Confederate commander had intended to open the battle by moving around Crittenden's left flank to gain possession of the Rossville road and to cut off Rosecrans from Chattanooga. Now he realized that Thomas, not Crittenden, was on the Federal left, overlapping his own right flank by a considerable margin.[41]

When he heard the first sounds of the fighting on the left, Rosecrans and his staff were still at Crawfish Spring, fourteen miles South of Chattanooga, hurrying up McCook's tired troops from the rear. Observing him closely, Shanks was aware of a frigid dignity not like the General's usual good-natured mien. Rosecrans' mind seemed to be far away from what was happening about him; it was obvious to Shanks that he did not regard the approaching battle with any real confidence.[42] While his staff members were going through the morning mail and waiting for the army telegraphers to establish communication with Rossville, an officer from the left rode up at full speed, bringing with him one of Bragg's orderlies, who had just been taken prisoner.

"Where is Bragg?" was the first question flung at the orderly. The latter replied that the Confederate general had left La Fayette early that morning and was now on the battlefield, about four miles from Rossville. How many troops had he there? The answer was obviously an understatement, but that hardly mattered. It was enough to know that Bragg was in the field and evincing aggressive intentions. As the sound of Brannan's guns gave further report of those intentions, Crittenden galloped off to the right and McCook disappeared in another direction. About the same time Rosecrans left for Widow Glenn's log house, two miles North, which he already had selected as his headquarters for that day.

Earlier that morning, Furay had mounted and ridden off toward the extreme left to gain some idea of the disposition of the troops in that part of the field. After he had gone about a mile, he spied a body of men ahead filing into the road from the woods to the East of it. With the aid of his binoculars, he made sure that their uniforms were regulation blue. Presently a hatless courier emerged from their ranks and raced toward Furay. As he drew nearer, a dozen rifle shots from a woods on the other side of a cornfield caused him to bend sharply forward until his body was almost parallel to that of his horse. The reporter halted until the courier came up and then after watching him deliver his dispatches to another horseman, asked him to identify the command to which he was attached. The courier explained that it consisted of two brigades from General Granger's corps which had been skirmishing in the neighborhood of Reid's bridge the day before and were now on the way to join the main army.

Furay was eager to find Granger's men and to gather details of their fighting, so it was agreed that he should accompany the courier on the ride back. As the two men passed the cornfield, the Confederate sharpshooters posted in the woods beyond again opened fire. A bullet clipped the mane of Furay's horse, but neither of the men was injured. Scarcely had they reached their destination when an order was received from Rosecrans directing General Granger to move the two brigades back to Rossville, where they were to remain in readiness to march at a moment's notice. Furay accompanied them to Rossville where he remained until about ten o'clock when the sound of battle on the Union left summoned him to the front. As he rode along the all-important highway for whose possession the two armies were contending, he met a stream of wounded men and fugitives from the battlefield. As usual, their reports of what was happening at the front were completely contradictory. Not until he reached the hospital earmarked for Brannan's division did Furay learn that it had been the first to go into battle that morning.[43]

As Thomas continued to force the fighting on the Confederate right, other divisions, both Union and Confederate, were drawn in, and gradually the conflict became general. Touches of poetic imagery mingle with exaggeration in the account of the Chicago *Journal* correspondent Taylor, who described for his readers the opening phase of the action:

> ... at half-past ten the enemy bore down upon Brannan like a mountain torrent, sweeping away a brigade as if it had been drift wood, only to be scorched back again. I do not think it was five minutes before Reynolds, Baird, Johnson, Brannan—all four—were involved. It was Jura answering to the Alps. But the gray and motley torrent bore back the Federal divisions slowly but surely. The battle spread like a prairie fire, and shot along the line. Palmer and Van Cleve came under the glowing hammer. Beatty's brigade dashed in with a hedge of steel as silent as the hawthorn, as silent as the death it carried, but drifted back before the rebel surge that rolled out of the dismal wood. Our line shut together like a telescope; Wood was absorbed in the human maelstrom; Gordon's Ford was open to the enemy; down moved Sheridan to the Ford; up moved Negley from Owen's Gap to Thomas. And so it went; it was living whole years in an hour or two; it was bringing the blossoms of the almond tree before their time.[44]

Throughout the day, Rosecrans remained at his headquarters, well to the rear of the line of battle, leaving the actual direction of the fighting to his corps commanders. At a large table in the rear of the house sat Garfield and another staff officer writing dispatches while the General, making use of the Widow Glenn as an aide, attempted to guess the possible location of the fighting. Much of the time neither generals nor reporters had a very clear impression of what was going on. Up until early afternoon, Rosecrans mainly had been concerned with the fighting on the left. By 2:30 P.M., however, Crittenden's corps was under serious pressure, and McCook's last remaining units were thrown in to sustain the sagging Union center. Time after time the Confederates advanced, only to be driven back by counterattacks from the new Union divisions thrown successively into the battle. Not until nightfall did the sound of fighting die away in the shadowy woods.

The result of the fighting that day was clearly a drawn battle. A Southern army reporter who had watched the terrific struggle frankly admitted that:

> the battle of Saturday had closed without our having gained any decided advantage, and from the stubborn resistance made by the enemy, our lines were but little advanced.[45]

Bragg's entire army was now across the Chickamauga, however, in a much better position for attack than it had been that morning. Almost one third of his army consisted of fresh troops, and during the night Longstreet himself arrived on the battlefield with two more brigades from Virginia.

The *Herald* correspondent Shanks was at General Rosecrans' headquarters that night when one of Crittenden's division commanders, Major General John M. Palmer, came in to attend a council of war. Shanks had seen Palmer earlier in the day at a time when his troops were scattered.

"Since I saw you this morning," said Palmer, addressing the *Herald* man, "I have got my troops together again. They are in good spirits, and ready for another fight. I have no hesitation in saying to you"—at this point he caught sight of Assistant Secretary Dana at the other end of the telegraphers' table and would have liked to stop. But he had gone too far, and so he added, "and I have no hesitation in saying to *you,* Mr. Dana, that this battle has been lost because we had no supreme head to the army on the field to direct it."[46]

Miller, the Cincinnati *Commercial* correspondent, spent the night near a field hospital, around which hundreds of desperately wounded men lay with their feet to the fire, their moans suggesting to the wakeful correspondent "the plaintive cries of a flock of doves."[47] Shortly before sunrise on Sunday morning, September 20, he rode over to the Widow

Glenn's house, where he found the staff servants rolling up the blankets and the orderlies bridling their horses. Headquarters, he learned, was to be moved farther to the left to a less exposed position. Presently out of the house came General Rosecrans, in blue army overcoat, his pantaloons stuffed into his boots, and an unlit cigar between his teeth. The Cincinnati reporter received much the same impression of Rosecrans in that fleeting moment as Shanks had gotten the morning before. Anxiously he watched the Commanding General mount his dapple-gray horse and ride swiftly down the lane toward the highway with his staff clattering after him.

Contrary to what the army generally expected, the battle did not get underway until the morning of the twentieth was well advanced. Miller had ridden back to a cornfield in the rear of the lines and had just thrown a few ears of corn to his horse when he heard four rapid discharges of cannon fire followed by a heavy volley of musketry. A glance at his watch showed him it was then exactly five minutes before ten.[48]

As on the previous day, the fighting began on the extreme left, where four divisions commanded by Thomas were firmly entrenched, defending the road to Rossville. Even before the fighting began, Thomas had requested that Negley's division be permitted to rejoin him to strengthen his left flank. Disturbed over the nonappearance of Negley, whom McCook had failed to relieve as ordered, Thomas sent message after message to headquarters calling for aid as the fury of the Confederate attack increased. Determined to hold the left at all hazards, Rosecrans issued a series of orders (based on a complete misconception of Thomas' situation) which ultimately wrecked the whole army. Instead of sending Thomas the single division which he had requested, the Federal General ordered three divisions plus one brigade from a fourth to go to Thomas' aid. Then, in the process of changing positions, he gave another order (also based on faulty information), which created a wide gap between the divisions of Brannan and Davis. Unluckily it was about this time that Longstreet, who commanded the Confederate left, unleashed a terrific attack on the Federal right and center. Into the gap created by the withdrawal of Wood's division from the line swarmed eight Confederate brigades, exploiting their advantage to the fullest.[49] From an elevation overlooking that part of the field, the Cincinnati *Gazette* reporter watched the remnants of the Union right and center—five brigades all told—heading for McFarland's Gap, completely disorganized. Said a reporter for a Louisville newspaper:

> The scenes I witnessed here were such as can be but poorly comprehended from description. . . . Men came madly dashing on, careless of curses and entreaties, consternation pictured in their every feature. . . . Guns, knapsacks, blankets, cartridge-boxes, everything that could impede the flight were cast away.[50]

It was Bull Run all over again. To make matters worse, Rosecrans, McCook, and Crittenden were engulfed in the retreat and did not stop until they reached Chattanooga. Having lost contact with the left wing, they believed at that time that the whole army had been routed.

Several of the army correspondents, sharing the General's view, followed the retreating columns of McCook and Crittenden along the Dry Valley road to Rossville and thence to Chattanooga.[51] Both Shanks and Furay remained on the battlefield, however, in a position to witness Thomas' heroic stand against overwhelming odds. Shanks was standing near the General during a lull in the fighting which occurred soon after the retreat of Crittenden and McCook. Well to the rear of the battle line appeared a heavy cloud of dust which might very well mean the approach of enemy cavalry. If it were really the enemy, then both the day and the army were lost. Peering anxiously through his field glass in the direction of the moving mass of men, Shanks saw, or thought he saw, the United States flag.

"Do you think so? Do you think so?" the General kept asking him.

Then Thomas turned to a staff officer who had just ridden up and instructed him to "ride over there and report to me who and what that force is." Tension relaxed as the officer brought back word that the approaching troops were General Gordon Granger's Reserve Corps of eight thousand men hastening from Rossville to Thomas' assistance.[52]

Throughout the afternoon the bloody fight continued along the crest of two small hills facing South, known as Horseshoe Ridge. In no other newspaper was the scene more colorfully described than in the columns of the Chicago *Journal.* Taylor wrote:

> To and fro in their awful "beat" of death the pair of Federal lines kept marching; firing, falling back, lying down, loading, rising, advancing, firing; and so it went, the rebels pressing up the hill in lines of iron and not of flesh; the rebel guns playing on every side but one.
>
> And just now one of those incidents occurred that makes the stoutest heart stand still. About four o'clock word was brought to General Granger that a certain regiment had but one round of

> ammunition. The blessed saltpetre was expected every moment, but it had not come. "But one round of ammunition, have you?" said the General. "Go back and tell them to fix bayonets, to save that one round—to lie down and wait till the rebels are within eight feet, to deliver their fire and give them the balance in cold steel. May I depend on you?" "You may," was the reply, and the trust was well placed, and the pledge was honored. . . .
>
> And what a dash of ILLINOIS there was in it all! . . . Immortal honor to the Federal legions of the hill! Like the stars of the flag, those men were "still there." No provost guard deployed like skirmishers in the rear, that day, to drive men back to duty and death. They came snugly up to the work, and how grandly they did it the world will know when the writer and his readers are forgotten like the rain that falls upon the sea.[53]

Near the close of the afternoon, Thomas, under orders from Rosecrans telegraphed from Chattanooga, abandoned his position on Horseshoe Ridge and fell back to Rossville. Contrary to the expectations of the army correspondents, the fighting was not resumed the following day, Monday, September 21. Instead, Thomas advised Rosecrans to concentrate the army at Chattanooga, and by the morning of the twenty-second the veterans of Horseshoe Ridge had rejoined their comrades. Bragg, on the other hand, was slow to realize the extent of his victory, and his army was apparently not in shape to risk an attack upon the Union entrenchments at Chattanooga.

On the morning following the battle, Shanks stopped in at General Rosecrans' headquarters to obtain his approval for a dispatch intended for the *Herald.* Rosecrans, Garfield, Dana, and one or two aides were at lunch when the *Herald* correspondent arrived. While Garfield was looking over the dispatch, Rosecrans asked the reporter what he was going to say about the battle. Although Shanks was somewhat taken aback by the question, he replied, "The plain, unvarnished truth, I hope." Rosecrans made no further comment, but Dana excused himself from the gathering and followed the *Herald* reporter to the telegraph office. Upon his arrival, the War Department man instructed the telegraph operators to send Shanks's material through without delay, thereby creating the impression in the reporter's mind that he wanted a complete story of everything that had happened to be published in the *Herald.* Before leaving the telegraph office, Shanks overheard one of the operators remarking to another that he believed that Dana and the *Herald* man were in collusion. One of the other operators told Shanks very frankly that it was evident that they (Shanks and Dana) were conniving to blame Rosecrans for the defeat. Shanks was somewhat disturbed by all this. It was true that he had a very low opinion of Rosecrans' ability as a general; on a later occasion he would even refer to Chickamauga as "the worst managed battle of the war." However, he was convinced that his usefulness as a correspondent would be greatly impaired if the impression became widely current that he was working in combination with Dana to ruin Rosecrans. For this reason, he decided to tone down his newspaper story and to publish at some later time what he could not then write.[54]

Shanks and his fellow correspondent Furay left Chattanooga together that same Monday afternoon and rode horseback across the mountains, arriving at Stevenson, thirty-four miles by rail from Chattanooga, early the next morning, September 22. From there they went on to Cincinnati by rail, narrowly missing death in a train accident between Nashville and Bowling Green. Both reporters leaped from the train just before the engineer, a Confederate sympathizer, deliberately brought about a collision with a second train following closely in the rear. Frightened though he was by their narrow escape, Shanks hardly could keep from laughing as he heard the voice of Furay, above the screech of the locomotive, beseeching him not to lose the list of killed and wounded which they had compiled together! At Bowling Green, the reporters voiced their suspicion of the engineer to Brigadier General Mahlon D. Manson, who promptly placed him under arrest and ordered him held for trial.[55] Meanwhile, Shanks and Furay resumed their journey to Cincinnati, arriving there on Thursday morning, September 24.

Up to this time very little detailed information concerning the Battle of Chickamauga had appeared in the Northern newspapers, and that little was alarming. As early as 4:00 P.M., Sunday, September 20, Dana had telegraphed Stanton from Chattanooga that "Chickamauga is as fatal a name in our history as Bull Run" and had represented the disaster as being complete.[56] Although Dana's telegraph was in cipher, the telegraph operator at Nashville discovered its contents, and there is some reason to believe that he may have communicated them to the agent of the Associated Press at Louisville.[57] At any rate, the Louisville AP man released a story to the press that same night which stated in brief that Rosecrans' army had been badly beaten and compelled to fall back to Chattanooga. He added that owing to the press of military business on the telegraph lines, details of the defeat could not be forwarded.[58]

Subsequent reports of what had happened to the Army of the Cumberland were both confusing and contradictory. On Tuesday, September 22, Northern newspapers carried another Associated Press story, based on a dispatch from the New York *Tribune*'s Washington office, stating that Rosecrans had been forced back to Chattanooga by one hundred forty thousand Confederates, comprising the armies of Bragg and Johnston, half of Lee's army, and the remnants of Pemberton's command.[59] In the same issue was a second dispatch from the Associated Press office in Louisville, announcing that military circles were inclined to doubt the report that Rosecrans' army had suffered a serious defeat, thereby implying that its previous dispatch had been in error. This disclaimer produced a strong reaction from some of the Western newspapers. The Chicago *Journal* referred to the Sunday night news report from Louisville as an "infamous dispatch," and the Cincinnati *Gazette* declared that if further investigation disclosed that it was without basis, its author should be hanged:

> We mean precisely this, that he should be hung by the neck until dead. . . . the man who thus trifles with the feelings and interests of the people, is not only unworthy a position of trust . . . but . . . is unworthy of a square inch of standing room on this broad earth.[60]

Subsequently the author of the offending telegram presented a satisfactory explanation to the editor of the *Gazette,* who then publicly acknowledged that his language had been too severe.[61] Probably the clearest picture of the two-day struggle which appeared in print before Shanks and Furay reached Cincinnati was a brief but generally accurate dispatch from Rosecrans' headquarters which had arrived in time for the Tuesday morning editions. The dispatch contained no indication, however, of the fear then uppermost in Rosecrans' mind that he might at any time be forced out of Chattanooga.[62]

The first complete account of the Battle of Chickamauga to appear in print was Furay's narrative, published in the Friday morning edition of the Cincinnati *Gazette.*[63] The editor of the Chicago *Journal* characterized it as a "long, graphic, and interesting account . . . giving especial prominence to the part taken by Ohio troops" and promised that the *Journal* would soon publish "our own correspondent's account, in which the Illinois as well as other troops will have justice done them."[64]

Much to his chagrin, Furay's colleague Shanks arrived at Cincinnati too late to make connections with the morning train for New York and so had to stay over until ten o'clock that Thursday night. Soon after his arrival he learned that the enterprising Henry Villard was at the local Burnet House, where he had been convalescing from the illness which had forced him to leave the army in June. Shanks was afraid that Villard might succeed in obtaining advance sheets from one of the Cincinnati correspondents who had come up from the battlefield and then go on to New York with them that night, doing a fast rewrite job for the *Tribune* on the way.

Although Shanks knew that his *Gazette* friend Furay had gotten through, he was not quite sure whether the *Commercial*'s army correspondent, Joseph W. Miller, had yet reached Cincinnati. While he was at dinner, most of his doubts were removed by an agent of the *Commercial,* who approached him with a request that he furnish an account of the battle to that newspaper. A few moments later, he learned from Murat Halstead, who came to second the request of his emissary, that Miller had not yet come in from the battlefield. Feeling very much relieved, Shanks refused Halstead's offer of one hundred dollars for his story and then hurried over to the *Gazette* office where he informed Richard Smith that he had been approached by the *Gazette*'s chief rival, the *Commercial.* To protect his own interests, Smith readily agreed that the *Gazette* would not furnish Villard any information in advance of publication provided that Shanks remained aloof from the *Commercial.* Shanks stuck to their agreement even though the *Commercial* later raised its original offer to one hundred and fifty dollars! As a result of all this Villard was obliged to remain in Cincinnati until the next morning, when he forwarded to the *Tribune* by wire a story based on the battle account which already had been published in the *Gazette.* Shanks's telegraphic account of the Battle of Chickamauga already had appeared in the *Herald* that morning, and his complete story of the battle was published two days later, following his arrival in New York.[65] Highly elated by the success of its correspondent, the *Herald* extravagantly claimed that his Chickamauga narrative was "the best account written of that battle . . . the best account written of any battle in this war, and . . . the best account written of any battle ever fought."[66]

Although he left Chattanooga on Tuesday, only one day later than Shanks and Furay, the *Commercial*'s army correspondent, Miller, did not arrive in Cincinnati until the following Sunday. Most of his story was written on the train with an inquisitive Southern mountaineer hanging over his shoulder and reading what he wrote.[67] Miller's battle narrative, published in the *Commercial* on Monday, presented a more flattering view of the army's performance than any previously given by the other reporters. He declared that at the time he left Chattanooga the morale of the army was good and that it was well supplied with guns, ammunition, and provisions. In his opinion, the Federal loss in artillery and other equipment had been greatly exaggerated in the battle accounts published by the other newspapers.[68]

From all sides *Herald* man Shanks and his friend Furay received criticism, much of it undeserved, for having interpreted the outcome of the battle as a Federal defeat. In a malicious editorial entitled "Enterprise and Current History—The Shambling Shanks and the Fugacious Furay," the Cincinnati *Commercial* strongly implied that the two reporters had left the battlefield before the fighting was over and had written their narratives in a state of panic of the kind "that usually prevails among teamsters and stragglers."[69] Particularly irritating to some of their newspaper critics was the fact that they had listed fifty pieces of artillery as captured by the enemy, whereas, in his preliminary report to the authorities at Richmond, Bragg had claimed only twenty.[70] Shanks and Furay might fittingly have answered this objection by pointing out that Rosecrans admitted the loss of thirty-six guns in his report to the War Department—and that in his revised report Bragg listed as captured "51 pieces of artillery."[71]

Only five Northern newspapers carried full-length, eyewitness accounts of the Battle of Chickamauga.[72] That they contained numerous misstatements of fact concerning the movements of the army was to be expected. During the course of the battle, regiments and brigades were shifted about so rapidly that it was almost impossible for the army correspondents to record their movements. Even the official reports submitted by officers were not altogether trustworthy. Henry Villard after a careful examination, many years later, of the official records of the Chickamauga campaign, said, "I found them incomplete, incoherent, and contradictory in a greater degree than those of almost any other of the great actions of the Civil War."[73]

In the Southern press, the Battle of Chickamauga was acclaimed as a brilliant Confederate victory. The battle narrative published by the Atlanta *Appeal* was particularly well written; creditable accounts of the battle also appeared in the Richmond *Dispatch*, the Atlanta *Intelligencer*, the Savannah *Republican*, and the Mobile *Tribune*.[74]

In April, 1865, only a few days before the end of the war, Furay obtained a somewhat different impression of the Battle of Chickamauga from a conversation with the Confederate General William W. Loring. At the time of their conversation, the two men were sitting on the deck of a gulf steamer bound for New Orleans. Loring was then a prisoner of war, having been captured the day before at the Battle of Blakely. Inasmuch as Furay undertook to reproduce it verbatim in a newspaper article published almost a quarter of century later, the conversation must have made a remarkable impression upon the reporter.

First the two men discussed the latest news concerning the progress of Grant's and Sherman's armies, and then Loring remarked somewhat fatalistically:

"Our cause is probably lost, but your temporary victories up to the latter part of 1863 had little to do with it. Not a man in the Southern Confederacy felt that you had really accomplished anything until Chattanooga fell."

"You do not mean to say, General," exclaimed Furay, hunching his chair forward, "that Vicksburg and Gettysburg were nothing!"

"The loss of Vicksburg," he replied, "weakened our prestige, contracted our territory, and practically expelled us from the Mississippi River, but it left the body of our power unharmed. As to Gettysburg, that was an experiment; if we had won that battle, the government at Washington would, perhaps, have tendered peace with a recognition of the Confederacy. Our loss of it, except that we could less easily spare the slaughter of veteran soldiers than you could, left us just where we were."

"But in the latter part of 1863 some of your people lost hope?" asked the correspondent.

"Not exactly that," said Loring, "but they experienced then for the first time a diminution of confidence as to the final result."

"And may I ask what it was that occurred then which occasioned this change of feeling?"

"It was the fall of Chattanooga, in consequence of the Chickamauga campaign, and the subsequent total defeat of General Bragg's efforts to recover it."

"Why did you regard Chattanooga as of such importance?" Furay inquired.

"As long as we held it," said the general, 'it was the closed doorway to the interior of our country. When it came into your hands the door stood open, and however rough your progress in the interior might be, it still left you free to march inside."

"But the capture of Chattanooga convinced you that even the real South was vulnerable, did it?"

"Yes," said Loring, "it was then only a question as to whether we could beat back your armies by sheer force of desperate fighting, and as you largely outnumbered us and our resources were every day diminishing, the prospects to the thinking part of our people looked gloomy indeed."

"But, General," said his interviewer, "there are people in the North who regard the Chickamauga campaign as a failure for the Union arms."

"Ah!" replied the other man, "we would gladly have exchanged a dozen of our previous victories for that one failure."[75]

18

Grim Days at Chattanooga

ARMY correspondents were none too popular around Chattanooga after the Federal setback at Chickamauga the third week of September, 1863. There was widespread feeling in the army that the press had woefully misrepresented the bloody struggle. The Chicago *Tribune* reporter, A. H. Bodman, frankly admitted that the battle accounts:

> lately published by Faray [sic], of the Cincinnati *Gazette,* and Shanks of the *Herald,* have excited a feeling of hostility towards the whole profession, and those of us who remain receive the benefit of that feeling. We are snubbed, and told by looks if not by words, "You are not wanted here."[1]

In spite of the unpopularity of the army newspapermen, their employers were well aware that the public was keenly interested in the Army of the Cumberland. To Chattanooga in early October, therefore, they sent a stream of newspaper reporters to find out about the military situation in Eastern Tennessee.

One of the first of the new arrivals was the Cincinnati *Commercial's* Joe McCullagh. At Nashville, where he had stopped over for two days en route, McCullagh could not get any clear idea of what was going on at the front or even what had happened the previous week. The local military authorities were close-lipped. The townspeople seemed to have "resolved themselves into a mutual interrogation society to ask one another 'What's the news?' " And so the *Commercial* representative had checked out of his Nashville hotel, only too glad to leave behind him its impudent clerks, stupid waiters, and bedrooms swarming with bugs. A ten-hour trip on the Nashville and Chattanooga Railroad had brought him to Stevenson. From there he had gone on by wagon train to Bridgeport, ten miles Northeast, in the company of some members of the United States Christian Commission, a welfare organization. The last thirty miles he had made on foot over the mountains, arriving, completely exhausted, at Chattanooga on the morning of September 30, thirty-six hours ahead of the Commission brethren.[2]

McCullagh quickly realized, as did the other newsmen in Chattanooga, the dangerous predicament of Rosecrans' army. From various sources he learned also that Bragg had been slow to follow up his triumph, but that once he had dug in along the high ground extending from Lookout Mountain to the mouth of Chickamauga Creek the Confederate general had been able to reduce to a bare minimum the movement of Federal supplies into Chattanooga. Not only did Bragg hold the railroad line from Bridgeport to Chattanooga; he controlled the river route as well. As a result, Rosecrans was obliged to haul his supplies in wagon trains from Bridgeport over sixty miles of mountain road Northeast through Jasper and across the Sequatchie Valley to the North bank of the Tennessee above Chattanooga. As the fall rains set in, travel by this roundabout route became steadily more difficult, and presently the Union Army in Chattanooga was faced with imminent starvation. The chief sufferers during the siege were the army horses and mules, for thousands of them were turned loose in the mountains to shift for themselves and most of them died of starvation. So ominous was the situation that many of the reporters feared Rosecrans would be forced to evacuate Chattanooga before relief from outside could reach him. The Confederate view of the situation was reflected by a captured rebel who told the *Herald* correspondent E. D. Westfall:

> Talk about your old Rosey, now; Bragg has got you all where he wants you; you can't get out of the scrape, and in a few days you will be a whipped community.[3]

Before the Chickamauga debacle, Grant in Vicksburg had received orders from the War Department to dispatch reinforcements to Rosecrans at once. These orders were delayed in reaching him, however, and furthermore, details of their execution were slow in reaching Washington. It was therefore decided at a midnight conference of Lincoln and his advisers on the night of September 23 to detach two corps (the Eleventh and Twelfth) from the Army of the Potomac and hurry them to Rosecrans' relief.[4] Within eight days the two corps—some twenty-three thousand men—were brought from Culpeper Court House to Washington and thence transported by rail through Wheeling, Columbus, Indianapolis, Louisville, and Nashville to Stevenson and Bridgeport. This was the first time during the Civil War that troops had been withdrawn from the Eastern war theater to reinforce one of the Union armies in the West.[5]

As soon as the decision to carry out this important troop transfer had been made, an officer from the War Department placed before every press correspondent in Washington a request from the President and the Secretary of War that there be no mention of the movement until authorization was given. The Washington correspondents all agreed and telegraphed or wrote to their newspapers asking them not to make any reference to troop movements during the next few days. Washington officials hardly could believe it, therefore, when the news came from New York on the night of September 26 that the *Evening Post,* an Administration newspaper, had just published full particulars of the movement of the Eleventh and Twelfth Corps to Chattanooga. Although the Sunday papers of the following morning copied the story, one of the Philadelphia newspapers, pointing out that the information was highly confidential, expressed the opinion that the editors of the *Evening Post* ought to be thrown into Fort LaFayette for such a flagrant breach of confidence.[6] Despite the fact that Stanton raged and that Lincoln for once was exceedingly angry, no disciplinary action was taken. The *Evening Post* attempted to protect its Washington correspondent by representing that he was in no way responsible for the "rumors" which had appeared in its Saturday edition, but no satisfactory explanation of the leak was given.[7] Fortunately the revelation was not disastrous.

Henry Villard was just about to leave Cincinnati for the Tennessee battle front on September 29 when General Hooker arrived in town accompanied by his chief of staff, General Butterfield. Hooker was in command of the two corps which were being sent to Rosecrans but was traveling southward by an independent route. Although Villard had not seen the General since the Battle of Fredericksburg, Hooker greeted him very heartily and suggested that he join their party. Inasmuch as "Fighting Joe" was traveling by special train, Villard was only too happy to accept his offer. The Hooker special had the right of way, but still nearly two days and a half were necessary for it to make what was normally a fourteen-hour run, since the lines between Louisville and Bridgeport were crowded with trains carrying troops and supplies.

As they lumbered along, Hooker talked in a jaunty manner about past disappointments and about the new honors which he hoped to win for himself in this present venture. It was obvious that he was highly elated by his return to active service after his great failure at Chancellorsville. He had hoped to do some fighting immediately and was therefore very much disconcerted when he received orders to remain at Bridgeport and to use his men to guard the lines of communication between Nashville and Chattanooga. Villard took leave of him there on the afternoon of October 3 and in an ambulance with three officers started at once for Chattanooga. They did not reach Jasper, ten miles Northeast, until after dark. At daylight they started out again over roads so unspeakably bad that their horses gave out, and so they, like McCullagh, were forced to continue their journey on foot. About midnight they reached the bank of the Tennessee River opposite Chattanooga; the rest of the night they spent getting what sleep they could around a camp fire built by some teamsters. The following morning, October 5, they crossed the bridge into Chattanooga, and Villard went to headquarters to present his respects to Rosecrans and Garfield.[8]

Now that Chattanooga had become, in the words of one correspondent, "a dirty, dusty, garrison town,"[9] the great majority of its inhabitants had left the city. Most of the buildings, which were preponderantly red brick, were now being used for military purposes business was almost at a standstill. Along the sidewalks, a Chicago reporter could see only "a ceaseless play of blue legs with an unending procession of blue coats; humanity seems done in indigo, dotted with sutlers, clerks out of livery, correspondents and faded-out natives."[10]

Disregarding the taunts and sneers of those who accused him of misrepresenting the Chickamauga defeat, Shanks of the *Herald* was back in town once more, sharing with Theodore Davis, the *Harper's Weekly* artist, and a free-lance artist named James Walker the dwelling formerly occupied by the Confederate Governor of Tennessee. "Bohemian Headquarters," as they styled their domicile, consisted of a single bedroom, ten by fifteen, with a small window which afforded a view of Missionary Ridge in the distance, a double bed and single cot, three chairs, an empty candlebox for a stool, and a small table. Here the "Bohemian Club" met daily and nightly to discuss the military situation and exchange experiences. To all who would listen, the "Special of the Weekly" gladly would tell the story of Vicksburg all over again, Shanks would explain to his own satisfaction why Rosecrans had been whipped at Chickamauga, and Walker, whose painting of the battle had been hung in the Capitol at Washington, would give his version of the Battle of Chapultepec in the Mexican War.[11]

During the early days of the siege, military censorship along with other factors had prevented the press from letting it be known how critical was the situation of Rosecrans' army. From September 24 to October 11, 1863, Chattanooga had only intermittent telegraphic communication with the outside world.[12] Even after the telegraph was in working order again, newspaper correspondents were unable to use it because of military priorities. In still other ways they were made to feel unwelcome. On one occasion, Bodman of the Chicago *Tribune* told of seeing a group of "unauthorized persons," which included "negroes of both genders" and several well-known writers for metropolitan journals, being herded along at bayonet point to the Provost Marshal's office for proper identification. Some were dismissed after the issue of proper papers; others were committed to the guard house.[13]

To relieve the tedium of the siege and at the same time to make their letters interesting, the reporters resorted to a variety of expedients. Confederate deserters were always good for a story, but the newspapermen rarely had much chance to talk with them as they were usually sent at once to the rear under guard and kept there until the truth or falsity of their statements had been determined.[14]

Excerpts from a Confederate newspaper smuggled through the lines might also be used to round off a letter. Approaching the enemy picket line one day in quest of some news from the deep South, the *Commercial* reporter McCullagh encountered a reception for which he was not fully prepared. While McCullagh was in the process of brandishing a late *Commercial* in an effort to attract the attention of a rusty-looking individual some three hundred yards away, a Confederate officer stepped out from behind a tree and shouted: "What is that? Is it a flag of truce or a newspaper?" McCullagh explained that it was a newspaper and that he wanted to exchange it. "We don't want your damned papers. They're a pack o' lies; an' if you don't get back I'll shoot," bellowed the officer. The *Commercial* man lost no time in acting upon this impolite warning.[15] He probably did not know that an order already had been issued by the Confederate high command to halt the "familiar intercourse" that had existed between the Union and Confederate pickets for some time.[16]

Because of his long-standing acquaintance with most of the ranking generals in the Army of the Cumberland, Villard enjoyed a preferred status among the correspondents in Chattanooga. In view of the controversy which had arisen in the Northern press concerning the Battle of Chickamauga, the *Tribune* reporter determined to make an investigation of what had happened and to write a review of the battle. Both Rosecrans and Garfield expressed their willingness to place at his disposal all the information they had, including the official reports of the corps, division, and brigade commanders and the various orders which were issued before, during, and after the battle. Furthermore, they both spoke very freely about everyone concerned as they seemed to be glad to find some one outside the army in whom they could confide.

Rosecrans was inclined to place the blame for what had happened upon the Washington authorities in general and upon Halleck and Stanton in particular. He announced that he was going to "show up" these two gentlemen in his official report—a threat which he later decided not to carry out. He also spoke in terms of vigorous denunciation of General Wood for his unfortunate blunder which opened a gap in the line on the second day at Chickamauga, of Generals McCook and Crittenden for coming to Chattanooga "without orders," and of General Negley for marching his troops away on his own initiative. To Villard, Rosecrans appeared nervous, vindictive, and irresolute, with little of his former courage and self-reliance remaining.[17]

From Garfield, Villard learned that there was a very strong feeling in the army over the conduct of Rosecrans, McCook, and Crittenden. It was Garfield's opinion that all three probably would be removed from command; he also had grave doubts whether the Union army could hold Chattanooga. Although Garfield was careful to avoid saying so explicitly, Villard was able to gather that his regard for Rosecrans' military ability had been pretty well shattered and that he would not be sorry to return to civilian life.[18]

Villard also visited the headquarters of General McCook and talked with both McCook and Crittenden. Both generals were highly irritated over the criticism they had received from the Northern newspapers and were delighted with the opportunity to air their grievances to an old acquaintance through whom they hoped to obtain a hearing in the press. Even while Villard was discussing their case with them, the blow they anticipated already had fallen. Late that night, Nashville newspapers three days old came into camp bearing the news that the War Department had issued an order dated September 28 relieving Generals McCook and Crittenden from duty and ordering them to be prepared to appear before a court of inquiry. Both generals issued farewell orders to their corps and then left for Indianapolis, accompanied by their staffs, on October 10.[19]

Both Crittenden and McCook blamed the army correspondents—Shanks in particular—for their removal. In his parting address to the Twentieth Corps, McCook referred with biting emphasis to the "news scribblers," whom he accused of having "slandered and maligned" his troops.[20] There could be little doubt that McCook to a much greater degree than the troops had been victimized by false stories from the press. In various newspapers, it had been stated (quite falsely) that McCook had left his command on the first day of the battle and had gone to Chattanooga on Saturday night, remaining there all that fateful Sunday when the army was fighting for survival. An Associated Press story intimating that Rosecrans had censured McCook for his conduct at Chickamauga (subsequently disavowed by Rosecrans) must likewise have contributed to McCook's irritation.[21] Probably both Crittenden and McCook overestimated the influence of the press in bringing about their removal. The complaints of the division commanders who had served under them, together with similar dispatches from Dana, must have had greater weight with Lincoln and Stanton.

Shortly after the middle of October, Rosecrans himself was relieved of his command, and General Thomas was appointed to succeed him. At the same time, Grant was placed in supreme command in the West[22] and was directed to proceed to Chattanooga to supervise military operations at that point. Although Rosecrans had done little since his defeat at Chickamauga to regain the confidence of his military superiors, his removal came as a stunning surprise to the nation at large, as well as to himself. Thomas W. Knox tried to telegraph the news to the *Herald* from Louisville, where he happened to be when the story broke, but the censorship was implacable.[23] As a result of Knox's failure the *Tribune* rather than the *Herald* scored a beat on the nation's press with an exclusive story, published on the morning of October 20, of Rosecrans' removal from command. The *Tribune*'s scoop, for which it was indebted to its Washington office, enabled many people in New York to receive the news of the General's dismissal before it was generally known in the army. In a letter written from Chattanooga on October 21, McCullagh commented that:

> In my army experience, an official act of such significance has never been so little heralded, or so generally kept secret until so late an hour, as the carrying out of the President's order transfer-

> ring the command of this army and department to General Thomas. Up to 7 o'clock on the morning of the 20th, it was not known to twenty persons in this army outside of Gen. Rosecrans' military household. General R. had written his farewell address, and had started for Nashville two hours before the fact of his supersedure became generally known. And when promulgated, it created very little surprise, and no feeling of either joy or sorrow—none that was perceptible to me, at least. The army seemed totally apathetic on the subject, although I had always been led to believe that Rosecrans possessed the esteem and confidence of officers and men to an extent amounting to enthusiasm.[24]

Whereas McCullagh gave no hint of his own reaction, the *Tribune* reporter Villard viewed the departure of Rosecrans from the scene with some misgivings. He noted:

> On the one hand, while I knew his successor [Thomas] well enough, his natural reserve, if not stiffness of manner, his reticence and indifference to the press, precluded such facilities at headquarters as I had enjoyed under the previous régime.[25]

After Rosecrans' retirement therefore, Villard withdrew from Thomas's headquarters and was glad to accept from Brigadier General August Willich, a Prussian artillery officer, an invitation to share his tent and table. Fortunately for Villard, Dana returned to Chattanooga with Grant on October 23. Since Dana formerly had been affiliated with the *Tribune* organization, Villard was able to secure from him confidential information about the plans of the commanding general. Besides, as Villard himself remarked, "the scene of current events was . . . so confined that any occurrence of importance could hardly escape my notice."[26]

In the absence of any official explanation of the reasons for Rosecrans' separation from command, newspaper speculation ran high. About a fortnight after the *Tribune* broke the news—during which tales of drunkenness, epileptic fits, and even opium eating had been reported to the public—Horace Greeley received an interesting letter from the Washington correspondent of the Cincinnati *Gazette,* Whitelaw Reid.[27] Reid again mentioned an offer to furnish the *Tribune* with what might be the inside story of Rosecrans' removal. Reid's article, based on official correspondence which he somehow had seen, appeared in the *Tribune* on November 7, 1863, and was republished in the Cincinnati *Gazette* three days later.[28] In the army, where the article was read with special interest, several of the correspondents took issue with Reid's somewhat labored effort to prove that Rosecrans had been obliged to fight the Battle of Chickamauga in order to occupy Chattanooga.[29]

In the opinion of the Washington *Star*, the circumstances under which the article was published constituted "one of the most disreputable acts ever perpetrated in the profession of journalism." According to the *Star*, the *Gazette* editor forwarded to the newspaper's Washington correspondent sufficient facts garbled from General Rosecrans' files in Cincinnati to constitute at most a weak case against the General and instructed the correspondent to prepare an article, ostensibly reflecting the point of view of the War Department, for publication in the *Tribune* or some other influential Eastern newspaper. Having been among the first to copy the letter, the *Gazette* editor was prepared, the *Star* surmised, to "demolish his own man of straw."[30] Unfortunately the facts did not bear out this bizarre theory. The editor of the *Gazette*, Richard Smith, himself admitted glumly that:

> Agate[31] did a queer thing in sending that letter to Greely [sic] . . . . What he intended I don't know; but it looked as if he sought a quarrel, with a view of quitting the Gazette. . . . Agate, I apprehend, has got the Tribune on the brain; and feels too big for the Gazette. If he leaves us for the Tribune I think he will make a mistake for his sensitive nature will not stand the snubbings he will receive from the many snobs engaged on that Journal.[32]

Although the tone of Reid's article was fairly objective, the article itself was an artful defense of Rosecrans.

Such controversies helped to keep alive the ill feeling in the Army which had resulted from the various changes in the Western command. Franc Wilkie had been in Nashville as a special correspondent for the Chicago *Times* on the evening of October 20 when Grant and his staff arrived there on their way to Chattanooga. As the news spread about the hotel that Grant had come there to supersede Rosecrans, a heated discussion arose among some of the military who were lounging in the lobby within earshot of the correspondent. "What the hell has he [Grant] ever done?" asked a belligerent pair of shoulder straps from the Potomac, directing his question to the newspaperman. Wilkie retorted, citing Grant's performance at Donelson, Belmont, Shiloh, Vicksburg, and a few other places. "Oh, damned nonsense! Mere skirmishes!" exclaimed the disgruntled officer from the East. "You don't call them fights, do you—such fights as we have had at the Potomac." Wilkie agreed that they were *not* such fights, but principally because after each battle Grant had followed the enemy instead of the enemy following him![33]

Whatever the reporters or anyone else might say about his valor, Grant had no intention of permitting Chattanooga to fall into enemy hands. Immediately after Grant's arrival in the city, Sherman was ordered to march to the relief of Chattanooga with his Army of the Tennessee, and plans were made to utilize Hooker's men more effectively. Even before he left the beleaguered city, Rosecrans had given some thought to regaining control of the "river route" in order to alleviate the supply problem. The first step toward realizing this objective was made on the night of October 26 when a force commanded by Brigadier General William B. Hazen was floated quietly down the river on flatboats from Chattanooga and put ashore at Brown's Ferry on the South bank, several miles below the mouth of Lookout Creek. Villard accompanied another force under Brigadier General William F. Smith which marched down the North bank of the river to the same point and waited there for the flotilla to arrive. It was three hours before the boats reached their destination. Meanwhile the *Tribune* correspondent fell asleep leaning against a tree, but he was wakened by the sound of shots as the boats pulled into the opposite bank. Presently Smith's men were ferried across and after a brisk fight helped to establish a fortified position. Villard accompanied the troops and remained with them the next day until a pontoon bridge had been built across the Tennessee. Then recrossing the river, he made his way back to Chattanooga, bearing the news that the movement had been a success.[34]

Meanwhile, under orders from Grant, Hooker had crossed the river at Bridgeport and was moving East toward Lookout Valley and a junction with Smith's men at Brown's Ferry. At Wauhatchie, Hooker's rear guard, commanded by General John Geary, was attacked by one of Longstreet's divisions, whose alert commander had detected that the Federal rear guard was separated by some distance from the main body. The New York *Times* correspondent Crounse, who had come down to the army in mid-October, accompanied the force under Howard which Hooker hurried back to Geary's relief. On their way to Wauhatchie, Howard's marchers came under a strong fire from Confederates posted on the foothills along the river North of the railway. But this time, Crounse noted, no panic sent the men of the Eleventh Corps scurrying in headlong retreat. Instead, they stood their ground and behaved like the veterans they were. Crounse told his readers:

> It was a very clear and bright moonlight night, and the sharp rattle of the musketry and the quite frequent cannonading reminded us all very forcibly of the terrible night attack made upon Stonewall Jackson's forces by Sickles in the persimmon bottoms of Chancellorsville.[35]

Before Howard's men could reach Wauhatchie, the rear guard had succeeded in beating off their attackers. In his description of the night battle, the New York *Tribune* correspondent C. D. Brigham related a humorous incident which affected the battle's outcome. While Geary's men were fighting desperately, two hundred frightened Federal mules broke loose and dashed across an open field in the direction of the Confederate lines. Thinking that the mules were a cavalry charge, a Georgia regiment stampeded, leaving behind them on the battlefield a thousand Enfield rifles of the best quality. "Who," asked Brigham, "will suitably write of this midnight charge of the Mule Brigade? and who of the panic of the Georgia regiment?"[36]

Shanks of the *Herald* also was with Hooker in the operation to open the supply line and was able to report the Battle of Wauhatchie. The reporter owed his favored position to a friendly tip from Grant, whom Shanks had met at Brown's Ferry while on his way to Nashville with dispatches. "Don't mention that you have repeatedly seen me at this place," Grant told him and then added, "Don't go as far away as Nashville. Go only to Bridgeport, and join Hooker there." In accordance with the Commanding General's advice, Shanks joined Hooker's command just three days before the affair at Wauhatchie.[37]

In telling of the opening of the "cracker line," as the soldiers called it, the Northern press reported inaccurately that Hooker had captured Lookout Mountain.[38] The topography of the country around Chattanooga is such that the reporters had confused the heights Hooker had gained between Lookout Mountain and the river with the mountain itself. To Crounse, with whom he was on terms of familiar acquaintance, Hooker wrote later, indicating that he was not only a little amused but also regretful because the New York *Times* man had erred in this connection. He added:

> I say regret, for I was apprehensive that it might impair your character & reputation as a faithful & reliable correspondent.

> How did it happen? It only goes to show that even correspondents are not exempt from the infirmity common to our race.[39]

With the army's supply line to Nashville reasonably secure, the reporters felt free to explain in some detail how critical the situation had been. In a letter from Chattanooga written on November 3, Brigham declared that at the time Rosecrans was relieved it was an open question whether the army could remain there five days longer.[40] But the safety of that army, he indicated, had necessitated not simply the withholding of some part of the truth but also the coloring of that part to which utterance was given.

Even with Thomas in command of the Army of the Cumberland, the army press men still complained of being subjected to close military supervision. During the last week of October, the vivacious McCullagh had been banished from the department because of a newspaper letter in which he had called attention to the arrival of Hooker's forces at Bridgeport and suggested that they were to be used in a flanking movement to bring about the evacuation of Lookout Mountain. The *Commercial* reporter quipped in his own defense that "if there was a man North or South, who had not known of Hooker's arrival two weeks before I published it, he is in great danger of voting for General Jackson for next President."[41] But the order stood, and thenceforth McCullagh was obliged to write about the the operations of the Army of the Cumberland from the safe distance of Nashville.

Within a week after the *Commercial*'s ace reporter left Chattanooga, the army newspapermen were apprised of a new regulation. Thenceforth, they learned, they must provide the Provost Marshal with their local address and report any change thereof under penalty of being sent out of the lines. Furthermore, they had to sign their "full and proper names" to all letters written for publication.[42] This was the first time during the war that signed correspondence was required of the reporters with the Western armies. Several of the journalists left forthwith rather than submit to the new regulations. But the more hardy remained, abandoning their pen names and otherwise adjusting themselves to the requirements of the new regime.

Although the river had been opened to within eight miles of Chattanooga and supplies were coming in rapidly over the greatly shortened wagon route, nevertheless it was still necessary to dislodge the Confederates from the heights South of the city. During the first week of November, Grant learned that Bragg had detached Longstreet's corps from his command for a movement against Knoxville, the headquarters of General Burnside. Now that Bragg had divided his strength by this ill-considered movement, Grant thought of attacking him at once, but at the advice of Generals Thomas and Smith he decided to remain inactive until Sherman, hastening eastward from Memphis, could join him.

While the army correspondents were waiting for an offensive movement to start, Bodman of the Chicago *Tribune* embarked upon an adventure which acquainted him with the primitive living conditions of the Tennessee mountain folk. To relieve the monotony of camp life, he decided to go out on a scout with a young engineer on General Palmer's staff. On the first night of their journey they stopped at the home of a "genuine East Tennessean." The hospitable family consisted of the farmer himself, his wife and infant, two "marriageable daughters," a grown son, and four other children. Yet their dwelling was nothing more than a single room, which combined the functions of parlor, bedroom, kitchen, and dining room. As he looked about, Bodman could not help wondering by what sort of doubling up process everyone might be accommodated. At about nine o'clock, the head of the household, who had fallen asleep in front of the fireplace, awoke with a snort, rubbed his eyes a bit, and then looking around at his guests remarked abruptly, "Wall, strangers, you kin peel!" Then observing that Bodman was staring at him with a troubled expression, he repeated somewhat gruffly, "You kin peel! Me and the old woman wants to tumble in."

This posed an embarrassing dilemma. Were the guests to disrobe in the presence of the old man and his wife, not to speak of the marriageable daughters, or should they "tumble in" fully clothed, regardless of white dimity and feathers? Bodman turned down the coverlid, ran his hand over the downy pillows, and glanced at the snowy sheets. No, it would never do to anger the good housewife. And so, reflecting that if she could stand the consequences, he could, he deliberately kicked off his boots and spurs, laid off his coat and trousers, removed his drawers, and then, with his shirt describing an angle of ninety degrees behind him, made a flying leap into the center of the bed. Captain Steele, his engineer friend, followed his example; likewise the old man, his wife, and the marriageable daughters. How the rest of the family managed Bodman never knew, as he fell asleep almost immediately and was the last of the household to wake the following morning. During the night he dreamed that he was the father of a large family of "marriageable daughters," each of whom had a pair of white cotton wings and floated through the air, hovering from bedside to bedside and finally settling down for the night on a bed of hot coals in a ten-foot fireplace![43]

On November 14, 1863, the gentlemen of the press saw Sherman ride into Chattanooga, where he was warmly greeted by his old companion in arms, who had been anxiously awaiting him. Grant already had come to the conclusion that the Army of the Cumberland was much too dispirited by defeat and the privations of the siege to carry the main burden of the attack. Nor did he think the "Potomac boys" had been sufficiently accustomed to victory to spark the attack. Moreover, he had little confidence in their commander, "Hardtack Joe," whose removal from command he already had requested through Dana.[44] It was upon the Army of the Tennessee, which he had come to view as peculiarly his own, that Grant chiefly relied. While Sherman stared straight ahead at the great amphitheater opening out from Chattanooga, Grant explained his plan. Sherman, he said, was to march the Army of the Tennessee past Lookout Mountain, cross the Tennessee River at Brown's Ferry, and continue along the North bank to the East of Chattanooga. He then would recross the river at night, and fight his way up the Northern end of Missionary Ridge the following morning. Hooker would support this operation by a demonstration against Lookout Mountain. Then with the Confederate army bent back on either flank, Thomas would move against the center. According to Grant's time schedule, Sherman was to be in position to attack on the morning of November 21.[45]

None of the army correspondents in Chattanooga made any effort to interview Sherman during his brief visit at Grant's headquarters. Since the Vicksburg campaign, stories of his antagonism toward the press had multiplied. In a letter written to a publisher, Sherman was reported to have said that he thought praise from a newspaper was contamination and that he would willingly agree to give half his pay to have his name kept out of the newspapers.[46] Under the circumstances, the reporters thought it best to keep away from him.

Try as he might, Sherman was unable to bring up his men in time for an attack on the twenty-first. It was the old story of mud and bad roads. Furthermore, Sherman had blundered by permitting his heavy division trains to be brought along with each division instead of pushing the infantry and artillery on ahead of them. Not until the night of Monday, November 23, did the Army of the Tennessee reach the position from which it proposed to mount its attack. One of Sherman's divisions (Osterhaus's) had been unable to cross at Brown's Ferry because of damage done to the bridge by its predecessors, and so it was left there to operate under Hooker's command.[47]

The army correspondents also had been alerted by preparations for the coming battle. Writing to his newspaper on November 22, H. S. Doggett of the Cincinnati *Times* spoke of "large additions to the newspaper brigade" brought about by "the likelihood of activity here."[48] Among the new arrivals at Chattanooga were "Jep" Doyle of the Cincinnati *Commercial*, Sylvanus Cadwallader of the Chicago *Times*, and J. A. Daugherty of the Louisville *Journal*.[49] Moreover, several reporters who had been planning to spend Thanksgiving with their families decided to remain in camp.

The Sunday before the three-day battle was a day of anxious expectation in Chattanooga. As he walked through the camps of the soldiers that afternoon, Taylor of the Chicago *Journal* could not help feeling that "the boys were a shade less merry than is their wont; the hush of the coming storm was in the air."[50] Night was coming on as the New York *World* correspondent "J.B.W.," from a window near the roadside, watched General Howard's troops slip out of camp to take up new positions. A rebel deserter just had come in with information that Bragg was retreating. In order to determine whether the enemy was still present in strength within his fortified line, Grant decided that Granger's corps, supported by Howard, should advance the next morning to Orchard Knob, a hill rising about one hundred feet above the plain Northeast of the town and about a mile in front of Missionary Ridge. Thinking that the attack would be launched at daybreak, the *World* reporter stayed up almost the entire night, watching troop movements. When morning of November 23 came, he was so weary from loss of sleep that he flung himself down on a blanket at about ten-thirty to catch some rest. He had hardly done so when he was aroused by the cry that the whole army was in motion. Hastily he mounted the parapets of Fort Wood, where Generals Grant, Thomas, Smith, Quartermaster General Meigs, Dana, and scores of staff officers were watching column after column of men filing out and dressing their lines for the assault. Said the *World* correspondent:

> Never before did I witness so grand a spectacle; never do I expect to witness another of equal magnificance. Not a spot of the valley

> for miles around but was spread out like a map below me; not a movement but was distinctly visible.[51]

Less than a quarter of a mile away, the enemy pickets, hands in pockets, could be seen watching what they apparently thought was a review. They were soon undeceived.

It was nearly two o'clock that afternoon when the advance began. As Wood's and Sheridan's divisions of Granger's corps moved across some open ground in the direction of their objective, cannon fire flamed from the heights. Bragg and his men were still there; the deserter had lied.

Now General Howard's corps was in motion. Wheeling to the left, it passed Fort Wood and took position upon the left of Granger's corps. Looking down upon it from the parapet of the fort was Howard himself, "motionless as a marble statue." Furay, the Cincinnati *Gazette* reporter, who was standing nearby, approached the General and addressed him several times without receiving any reply. Finally, touching him upon the elbow, Furay asked him which of his divisions was nearest General Granger's left. Howard turned sharply around as if he had suddenly been aroused from a deep sleep and asked the correspondent to repeat what he had said. Then, after Furay had reiterated his question, he answered politely, adding, "My line yonder does not suit me exactly; I must go and rectify it." With that, he started off, and soon the Eleventh Corps was moving forward, sweeping the enemy from his rifle pits.[52]

By nightfall, the Confederate skirmish lines had been driven in, and the fortified outpost on Orchard Knob had been secured. What had begun as a reconnaissance in force had resulted in the capture of an important position. *Tribune* man Villard, who had accompanied Willich's brigade during the advance, remained at the front that night and slept on a rubber blanket in a hut which had quickly been thrown up after firing had ceased.[53]

The skies were gloomy, threatening rain, on Tuesday morning, November 24. Sherman was up now, however, and simultaneous attacks by Hooker and Sherman at either end of the line were expected hourly. Picking his way across the battlefield of the afternoon before, the Chicago *Journal* correspondent came in sight of a flotilla of soldier-laden small boats drifting down the river and hastened to meet them as they neared the bank for a landing. The soldiers were in high fettle as they tumbled out of their boats, "the inevitable coffee-kettle swinging from their bayonets."

"Well boys—what now?"

"We've put down the pontoon—taken nineteen rebel pickets without firing a gun—run the rebel blockade—drawn a shot—nobody hurt—Sherman's column is half over—bully for Sherman!"[54]

It was the intention of the high command that the brunt of the fighting that day should fall upon Sherman's men. Shanks of the *Herald* eyed them intently as they began their advance, noting that:

> The men looked serious and rather gruffe [sic] and were painfully quiet. They conversed with each other but seldom, and then in under tones. . . . Ever and anon they would glance at the hill which they were approaching, and it was easy to see why they looked serious. Perhaps they compared the hills in their own minds to the Walnut Hills of Vicksburg, but I do not think there was one man there who feared to test the question of victory or defeat there and then.[55]

Sherman's hardy campaigners were not destined, however, to struggle for the possession of Missionary Ridge that day. As the grizzly-bearded Ohioan pushed forward through the drizzling rain, he discovered that the maps which had been given him were wrong. The Ridge was not continuous after all; instead he was faced by a succession of fortified hills. And so he advanced, took the first hill, entrenched, and called for reinforcements.

Over on the right, Hooker was hurling two divisions and a brigade, some ten thousand men in all, against the rocky slopes of Lookout Mountain. It had been about eleven o'clock that morning when the *Journal* man Taylor first detected the rumble of artillery, coming in gusts from the valley West of Lookout. Hooker's task was made easier by the fact that during the night Bragg had withdrawn the greater part of the force defending Lookout to meet what he justifiably regarded as the greater threat, against his right. Hooker's attacking force consequently possessed a numerical advantage of roughly four to one. Even so, the Confederate defense would probably have been more effective had not the defenders been scattered over the summit and the three sides of the mountain at different heights which made difficult reinforcing the point of attack.

Peering through the mist that hovered about the scene, around noon Taylor caught sight of the head of the Federal column, a half-mile line of blue clinging to the brown face of the mountain. Presently the troops advanced in two parallel columns, sweeping the enemy's rifle pits at every fire and drawing nearer to a level plateau nearly two-thirds of the way up, where the Confederates had a strong position. Then they charged across the field in gallant style. When the smoke cleared away, the reporters watching the scene from the city below could see the Stars and Stripes floating over the abandoned works and the enemy retreating in great disorder.

Nevertheless, the fighting continued until several hours after dark. In his battle account, subsequently published in the Cincinnati *Gazette,* Furay told of standing in front of General Thomas's headquarters in Chattanooga that night:

> watching the combat going on, away up there upon that mighty wall of limestone; and the long line of fires which marked the course of our intrenchments; the shouts of the combatants yelling defiance at each other; the fierce jets of flame from the muzzles of a thousand muskets; the spluttering sound of the discharges, muffled by distance; the great brow of the mountain looming dark and awful through the night; the single signal light upon the extreme crest, which, waving to and fro, revealed to the rebel leader on Mission Ridge, the tale of disaster and woe—all these together formed one of the scenes in that wonderful three days' drama, which will linger forever in my memory, haunting even my dreams. The battle that night upon Lookout Mountain! Seen from Chattanooga, it was the realization of olden traditions; and supernatural armies contended in the air![56]

On the following morning the reporters learned that the remnants of the enemy force had fled during the night to join the main body of Bragg's army on Missionary Ridge and that Lookout Mountain, therefore, was in Union hands.

It is quite possible that in their accounts of Hooker's exploit, the army correspondents overdramatized what had happened, although it was Quartermaster General Meigs, rather than they, who first applied to it the fanciful title of "the battle above the clouds."[57] Subsequently, Grant expressed the opinion that:

> the battle of Lookout Mountain is one of the romances of the war. There was no such battle, and no action even worthy to be called a battle on Lookout Mountain. It is all poetry.[58]

Both Shanks and Cadwallader concurred in this opinion, the latter remarking that Hooker's advance:

> was in no sense a battle; it was only a long, protracted, magnificent skirmish from 8 A.M. till dark. Our loss was consequently trifling.[59]

Cadwallader was indebted to Grant on this occasion, as on several others. Immediately following the capture of Lookout Mountain the Chicago *Times* man tried in vain to obtain permission at Thomas's headquarters to telegraph an account of the fighting he had just witnessed. Fortunately for him, Grant was nearby. Not more than thirty minutes after the refusal, the General took from Cadwallader's hands the same dispatch that Thomas's staff censor had refused to clear and, without reading it, endorsed the following: "Send this. U.S. Grant."[60]

At sunrise on Wednesday morning, November 25, any reporters who were awake could have seen the Union flag floating from the twenty-four-hundred-foot summit of Lookout. Yet in Chattanooga there was little to indicate the fact that another day of heavy fighting was about to begin. Taylor remarked:

> The current of regular business was not checked; the play of men's little passions was as lively as ever. Jest and laughter eddied round the street corners, and pepper-and-salt groups of children frolicked in sunny places.[61]

Herald correspondent Shanks had been up late the night before watching the conflict on Lookout Mountain, so that the morning was well advanced before he reached his observation point on Orchard Knob. By that time Sherman had begun a full-scale attack against Tunnel Hill, just South of the elevation which he had occupied the day before and separated from it by a small ravine. While General Wood shouted after him to stay if he would see some of the finest work of the day performed, Shanks clapped spurs to the jackass which he had pressed into service (he had broken down a good horse the day before) and rode off toward the left to see what Sherman was doing.[62]

C. D. Brigham, who together with Villard represented the New York *Tribune* on the field, remained on Orchard Knob and sketched the appearance of the various notables about him as he waited for Thomas's men to go into action. Brigham wrote:

> If I had not before seen Gen. Grant it is not probable that I would have singled him out from the hundred others on the ground as the man whom the country recognizes as having done most . . . to crush the Rebellion by hard blows. . . . Enveloped in

> a rather huge military coat; wearing a slouching hat, which seemed to have a predisposition to turn up before and down behind . . . giving his orders, speaking but little and in a low tone, and with an accent which partook of the slight nervousness, intensity of feeling, yet perfect self-command seen in all his movements, I thought at the time that Gen. Grant might be described best as a little, old man—yet not really old—with a keen eye, who did not intend that anything should escape his observation.

Thomas, on the other hand, appeared to Brigham to be the beau ideal of what a soldier should be. The *Tribune* correspondent remarked:

> I can well see how his presence must inspire confidence in him on the part of the men, when handled by him in battle. I can understand, too, how he is the man to place his back to the wall on the mountainside, and bid defiance to his enemy, though twice his numbers. Among a thousand other men, I think Gen. Thomas would readily be singled out for the man to do that sort of thing—a man who, though not brilliant, is safe, and quite the man for his present position.[63]

From where he was standing near headquarters, Brigham could distinguish signs of impatience on Grant's face as Sherman fought on hour after hour without gaining ground. The slope of Missionary Ridge is so steep that the Confederates on the summit could not depress the muzzles of their cannon sufficiently to check the charging blue coats. The Rebel forces compensated for this, however, by a hot musketry fire and by rolling down heavy boulders wrenched from the mountain side. From his position near the river, Taylor watched Sherman's column twice advance across a stretch of broad, open field against the North end of the Ridge:

> and twice I saw it swept back in bleeding lines before the furnace-blast, until that russet field seemed some strange page ruled thick with blue and red.[64]

Shanks was standing close to General Sherman around 1:30 P.M. when his third and final assault failed. While the veterans of the Army of the Tennessee began to fall back slowly, Shanks watched their peppery commander bite off the end of a cigar, light it, take a puff or two, and then, turning to one of his aides, say, "Tell Lightburn to intrench and go into position."[65] The battle on the left was over.

As Shanks rode back toward Orchard Knob, however, he saw three divisions of the Army of the Cumberland, those same men whose morale Grant had discounted, move out against the enemy center at the base of Missionary Ridge. There were approximately twenty thousand men in the attacking force. Forming in line of battle within a thin strip of woodland, they had to cross an open space of six hundred yards under fire from forty-two big Confederate guns. Against moderate resistance they carried the first line of rifle pits and then in obedience to their orders halted momentarily. As they paused, there issued from the upper Confederate works a punishing fire which stung them into action. Without orders, in fact in spite of orders, the men in those three divisions (Baird's, Wood's, and Sheridan's) went surging up the ridge.

Never before during this war had the Northern army correspondents seen such a spectacle as this. It was the charge of the Light Brigade all over again, albeit with a different ending. Said Taylor, writing to the Chicago *Journal*:

> And now you have before you one of the most startling episodes of the war; I cannot render it in words; dictionaries are beggarly things. But I may tell you they did not storm that mountain as you would think. They dash out a little way, and then slacken; they creep up, hand over hand, loading and firing, and wavering and halting, from the first line of works toward the second; they burst into a charge with a cheer and go over it. Sheets of flame baptize them; plunging shot tear away comrades on left and right; it is no longer shoulder to shoulder; it is *God* for us all. . . . Ten, fifteen, twenty minutes go by like a reluctant century. The batteries roll like a drum; between the second and the last line of works is the torrid zone of the battle; the hill sways up like a wall before them at an angle of forty-five degrees, but our brave mountaineers are clambering steadily on—up—upward still! You may think it strange, but I would not have recalled those men if I could. They would have lifted you, as they lifted me, in full view of the region of heroic grandeur; they seemed to be spurning the dull earth under their feet, and going up to do Homeric battle with the greater gods.[66]

Within an hour after the charge had begun, it was all over. A dozen regiments had reached the crest and planted their flags within a stone's throw of where Bragg's headquarters had been. Meanwhile, the center of the Confederate line had broken into headlong flight. Down in the valley, men flung themselves exhausted upon the ground, laughed, wept, shook hands, embraced. Bragg's army had been driven from the position which it had occupied so long, and the stain of Chickamauga had been wiped out by the very men who had felt it most keenly. In the opinion of the New York *Times* correspondent, the taking of Missionary Ridge by assault "ought according to military rule have cost at least five thousand lives. It did not cost one-fourth of that number."[67]

Now that the battle was over, the silence which followed it seemed oppressive, so greatly did it contrast with the din and confusion inseparable from any battle. That evening while the soldiers were preparing their supper, the New York *World* correspondent left the campfire and wandered out along the ridge to the eastward. In the red-hazed moonlight the shrieks, groans, and piteous appeals of the wounded and dying still rang in his ears. But presently he became aware of a strange new sound, which came floating up from the valley below. It was the distant rumble of an ambulance train hastening to the battlefield to care for the sufferers and to remove them to hospitals in Chattanooga.[68]

The next day, November 26, was Thanksgiving Day. That morning, Furay rode out from Chattanooga for another look at the battlefield. As he passed a group of soldiers on his way up the mountain, one of them remarked, "There goes a correspondent" and then called out, "Don't forget to speak well of the 1st Ohio boys!"[68] Furay assured them that their deeds would not be soon forgotten. He spent an hour or two on the battlefield gazing at the faces of the dead, examining the captured artillery bunched together in piles, and asking questions of those he saw to determine which regiment had first planted its flag on the crest of Missionary Ridge. There was little enough time to gather details for his story. Already the race was on to provide first news of a Federal triumph unmatched as yet in this war.

On the morning before the final assault on Missionary Ridge, the Chicago *Times* reporter Cadwallader had come to the conclusion that the outcome of the battle would be determined that day and had made preparations accordingly. His thoroughbred mare was kept in readiness for an all-night ride. Cadwallader had guessed correctly that he would be the only correspondent who would leave Chattanooga that night for Stevenson, the nearest railroad station. If only he could make Stevenson by six o'clock the next morning, he would be in time to catch the morning train for Nashville and thereby establish a twenty-four hour lead over his rivals.

Therefore he left Chattanooga at ten o'clock the night of November

25, crossed the river on a pontoon bridge, recrossed to the South side again at Brown's Ferry, rode up the Wauhatchie Valley through miles of knee-deep mud, passed around Raccoon Mountain through Whiteside, rode past several Union pickets who were asleep on the road at Shell Mound, was halted at Nickajack and then allowed to proceed, and reached the end of the bridge opposite Bridgeport at three o'clock in the morning. In order to save time, he persuaded the officer of the guard to walk across the bridge with him while he described the battle just fought. By the time they had reached the other end of the bridge, the guard was so excited that he permitted the correspondent to mount and ride away without offering any identification. Cadwallader stopped for a few minutes at the telegraph office, where by "proper persuasion" and a show of authority he succeeded in sending a short dispatch to Louisville. Then at 4:00 A.M., completely ignorant of the roads and the condition of the country, he started for Stevenson, twelve miles distant.

At this point he caught up with a mounted orderly, who consented, for a five dollar fee, to act as his guide. Together they rode over a frozen crust of mud, fetlock- to knee-deep and too thin to hold them up. During the journey, Cadwallader's mare tore off a foreshoe and broke her hoof badly; however, she was able to bear up until they reached Stevenson fifteen minutes before train time. Thus far all had gone well, but unforseen difficulties were in store for the anxious correspondent.

At Anderson, a wreck held up the train for four hours. At War Trace, another sixteen hours were lost for a similar reason. Then, within sight of Nashville, the locomotive broke down, and Cadwallader had to walk the last few miles into the city. His dispatches were soon cleared for transmission at the telegraph office, but as the night train for Louisville already had left, he had to remain overnight in Nashville.

Making the best of his misfortune, the unlucky correspondent ate a good dinner at Donneguana's restaurant, and then settled back in one of the easy chairs in front of the establishment where he could enjoy a good smoke and watch the passersby. While he was sitting there, he noticed a man hurrying up the street. Thinking there was something familiar about the man's gait, Cadwallader realized that it was his good friend Shanks of the New York *Herald.* Shanks was still breathless as he told of how he had left Chattanooga the morning after the battle and had discovered at Bridgeport a dummy engine that just had brought General Logan over from Nashville and was waiting on the track for orders. Seizing at this heaven-sent opportunity, Shanks had convinced the engineer—with the aid of a hundred dollars in greenbacks—that the original orders signified, even required, the engine's immediate return to Nashville. It was settled that the engine should start at once and that it should carry no passenger but Shanks.

As they pulled away from the platform, Shanks said he saw swinging aboard a heavy, dirty, generally disreputable-looking individual, whom he supposed to be the fireman. The engineer noticed him too and assumed that he was an attaché of Shanks. After they had traveled together for a little while, Shanks learned to his dismay that he was paying one hundred dollars in cash to carry a Mr. Woodward of the Cincinnati *Times* from Bridgeport to Nashville. Woodward remained unmoved by persuasions, bribes, or threats and showed every intention of staying where he was. As neither Shanks nor the engineer felt it expedient to pitch the interloper from the locomotive, they subjected him to the silent treatment. When the engine pulled up at the Nashville depot, Shanks eluded his competitor and raced on ahead of him. Having met Cadwallader, Shanks implored him in token of their friendship to intercept the Cincinnati man and to do what he could to delay his dispatches.

In a little while, Woodward, tired and hungry, arrived at the restaurant. Although Cadwallader already had eaten, he ordered a good supper for two and purposely selected dishes that would take time to prepare. After they had eaten, Woodward went to the telegraph office, where he learned that his dispatches first must be approved by General Granger, the post commandant. Disturbed by this setback, the Cincinnati *Times* man rushed back to Cadwallader for advice. Thereupon the latter accompanied him to headquarters, only to find that it was closed for the night. After a search of the hotels, they located the General at the theater, but of course he refused to be troubled with such business at that hour. Woodward then registered at the St. Cloud Hotel and had his name placed on the call list for the Louisville morning train before going to bed. During the night his name was erased from the call list, possibly by accident, although Cadwallader believed that Shanks had paid the call boy a fair-sized greenback to do it. When the Louisville train pulled out the next morning, Shanks and Cadwallader were aboard; Woodward was not.

While leading Woodward on a wild goose chase the night before, Cadwallader had kept watch on the Nashville telegraphers, who were late in sending out his story. At midnight he sent them an elegant hot supper, and at the same time he wired the Louisville operator that he had deposited ten dollars to the operator's account. In return for this, Cadwallader requested that the Louisville operator remain at his instrument until 4:00 A.M. and take advantage of every opportunity to speed the petitioner's dispatches along. Finally, hours later, the operator in Louisville clicked back the message that the last word had been sent. Cadwallader could relax. The end result had repaid the effort; his newspaper was ahead.[70]

Apparently the Southern press thought to withhold comment on Bragg's stunning defeat until some means could be found to counteract the unfavorable effect of the news upon public opinion. On previous occasions, the New York *Tribune* recalled gleefully, the battle accounts written by the reporters on both sides either had reached the Northern press simultaneously or had followed each other in quick succession.[71] Once they had recovered from their initial surprise, however, the Southern newspapers did not minimize the disaster. With blunt frankness, the correspondent of the Richmond *Dispatch* with Bragg's army stated:

> The confederates have sustained to-day [November 25] the most ignominious defeat of the whole war—a defeat for which there is but little excuse or palliation. For the first time during our struggle for national independence, our defeat is chargeable to the troops themselves, and not to the blunders or incompetency of their leaders.[72]

Northern press accounts of the battle tended to support the Richmond reporter's comment on the lackluster performance of the Confederate troops.[73] Moreover, in their enthusiasm, the Northern reporters were inclined to interpret the defeat as being more complete than it really was. The men who took part in a vigorous pursuit of the retreating Confederates knew better. At Ringgold, Georgia, on November 27, Bragg's rear guard severely checked Hooker's pursuing column. Hooker lost more men at Ringgold than in the more-publicized "Battle above the Clouds"—lost caste as well with Grant, who regarded the whole affair as unfortunate.[74]

Smarting at what he regarded as unfair treatment from the Commanding General, Hooker's resentment flared into unreasoning anger when he read what a *Tribune* reporter had to say about the "very grave mistake" he had made at Ringgold. To Crounse he exploded that:

> There is a devil of an attack on me in the Tribune of the 9th over Brigham's name. There is a snake in the grass somewhere. I sent

> to him to furnish me with the name of his critic & . . . if it is not furnished . . . I shall request that he be expelled from the Department.[75]

Failing to obtain satisfaction from Brigham, Hooker addressed a long and somewhat rambling letter to Stanton in which he set forth his grievance in some detail:

> Permit me to call your attention to the above choice gems from the newspaper world. The former was cut from a letter written from here November 29, by C. D. Brigham, and appeared in the New York Tribune of the 9th December, and the latter was kindly sent me from the office of the New York Times, where it had been sent from Washington by the same individual. It is easy to see that they are from the same source. . . . Soon after the appearance of the former I called on this correspondent, Brigham, to furnish me with the name of the individual whom he styles "one who has a right to criticise," intending, if an officer, to bring him before a court-martial; but as he failed to furnish it under various pretexts I conclude that he only made use of that phraseology to give weight to the lie he was telling. Brigham is a stranger to me, and as these articles are intensely malicious I conclude that he is in the employ of some one. On making inquiries I find that his bosom friend while at Chattanooga was Brig. Gen. W. F. Smith. . . . Other reasons exist to establish the relationship between Smith and Brigham. In the correspondence of the latter with the Tribune he has claimed for him the authorship of my advance into Lookout Valley, when it was pointed out to me by the President before I left Washington, and afterward communicated by Rosecrans long before Smith ever saw Chattanooga. . . . The point of all was to shut me out of the fight, Grant's object being to give the éclat to his old army, and Smith's, if he really had anything to do with it, to exclude your humble servant. . . . But to return to Brigham. He appears to be sailing under honest colors, and to have impressed his employer, Greeley, with this belief. I should like to have him disabused. If Dana should be with you, and you have no objection, I should like to have these gems of honesty and truth submitted to him. If Brigham returns to this department I shall request his expulsion from it. There is no art of villainy of which he is not capable.[76]

There is nothing in the Official Records to indicate what action the Secretary took in response to Hooker's complaint. Feuding in the army was fairly notorious at this time; possibly Stanton had heard rumors from other sources accusing Brigham's colleague, Villard, of connivance with a "League of Regular Officers" supposedly seeking to undermine the position of the volunteer officers in the army.[77] On Brigham's side of the story the records are likewise disappointingly silent.

* * *

Although the press gave fullest coverage to the operations around Chattanooga, nevertheless, Knoxville, Charleston, and the Potomac theater figured more or less importantly in the news during the latter part of 1863. Elias Smith of the New York *Tribune* and Edward Crapsey of the Cincinnati *Commercial* were among the little group of reporters who were with Burnside at Knoxville during the siege. Both Smith and Crapsey witnessed Longstreet's failure to take the city by assault on November 29 and were on hand for the raising of the siege five days later as large Federal reinforcements from Chattanooga neared Knoxville. Despite the efforts of the reporters at Knoxville to keep the public informed of developments in Burnside's department, the Knoxville campaign was one of the most poorly reported of the war, largely as a result of communication difficulties. In explaining the handicaps under which he and his brother reporters had labored, the New York *Tribune* correspondent mentioned that:

> A large proportion of all the couriers sent from Cumberland Gap, and dispatched to that point from this place have been captured; so that much that I have sent forward has doubtless fallen into Rebel hands. This danger has obliged me to write with much circumspection to avoid the giving of valuable information to the enemy, so that I have omitted many things which may hereafter be safely communicated to the public.[78]

Following DuPont's repulse at Charleston in April, 1863, the Eastern press gave considerable space to further attempts to penetrate the defenses of the city. In the meantime, a new team of army and navy commanders, Major General Quincy A. Gillmore and Rear Admiral John A. Dahlgren, had replaced the earlier combination of Hunter and DuPont. Learning from Lincoln that Greeley had been largely responsible for his displacement, Hunter wrote a letter to the *Tribune* editor on June 12, 1863, giving sarcastic utterance to the hope that:

> since you have undertaken the attack on Charleston . . . you will be more successful than in your first advance on Richmond, in which you wasted much ink, and other men shed some blood.[79]

Whether through their own failings or as a result of the interference of others, the newspaper correspondents in the Department of the South were none too successful in reporting the slow progress of the operations at Charleston. Even the Chicago *Tribune* could not help remarking, editorially, that:

> correspondents may gloss and cover up the traces with all zeal, the fact will still creep out that there is a want of harmony, a zig-zag conduct of the siege, growing out of bickerings and dissentient efforts on the part of the two branches of the service there brought together.[80]

The hesitation on the part of the reporters to speak frankly about the lack of harmony between Gillmore and Dahlgren was quite understandable. As the Baltimore *American* had put it:

> Those who have spent any time in the Department of the South know full well that when a correspondent located there dares to say one word that is not complimentary to the authorities on land or water, he finds himself suddenly in the guard-house, to await the departure of the next steamer for the North.[81]

In August, 1863, following a news leak of more than ordinary importance, General Gillmore received instructions from Halleck to place under arrest all the war correspondents in his department and send them down to Hilton Head for safekeeping until the campaign was over.[82] Gillmore softened the effect of the secretary's ukase by impounding the newspapermen on Morris Island instead. The order nevertheless remained in effect.

During the autum of 1863, there was increasing criticism of Admiral Dahlgren in the press. The Admiral thought that much of it was instigated, or at least approved, by his Army colleague. With some irritation, Dahlgren noted that "the correspondent of [the] 'Herald' has frequently referred to what I have confidentially written to General Gillmore."[83] From the Army commander in turn, a fortnight later, he received a note to the effect that the correspondent of the Baltimore *American* "the sole member of the press in the squadron," had been transmitting for publication material giving information to the enemy. Dahlgren sent for Fulton, showed him the note, and asked him to see the General, as requested. Subsequently, the Admiral learned from the *American* reporter that "no case could be made out, and the General had to admit it; but . . . the real grievance was, that he had given some credit to the

Navy on some occasion." There was a pathetic note in the comment which the ailing old naval officer inscribed in his diary that day. "If this is so," he wrote with Fulton's explanation in mind, "it is a very mean proceeding on the part of the General, who has a whole corps of correspondents about him, and lets them abuse me. . . ."[84] Subsequently he was informed by another reporter, G. W. Foss of the Philadelphia *Inquirer,* that the correspondent who had abused him so freely:

> did not suppose it was a harm, because all their letters had to be submitted to General Gillmore, who read them and struck out what he chose, and such matter was not thus prohibited.[85]

Meanwhile, the newspaper reporters with the Army of the Potomac were seeing comparatively little activity. After the Gettysburg campaign, Lee had retreated to the South bank of the Rapidan, where he remained until the Eleventh and Twelfth Corps were sent West under Hooker to relieve Rosecrans. Then, in a campaign marked by considerable marching but little fighting, Meade was forced back to the heights of Centreville, almost within sight of the defenses of Washington, only to become the pursuer again as Lee fell back toward Culpeper.

Following a clash which took place at Kelly's Ford during the first week of November, Francis C. Long, one of the New York *Tribune* correspondents, rode from Kelly's Ford to Warrenton Junction on the Orange and Alexandria Railroad in order to catch a train for Washington. A. Homer Byington was at that time chief of the *Tribune* corps in the Army of the Potomac, and he had given Long a dispatch of considerable importance to deliver to Adams S. Hill, then in charge of the *Tribune* office in Washington. The *Tribune* reporters were supplied with scarlet envelopes, and so even after Long had thrust Byington's letter into the pocket of his coat the end of the bright envelope was plainly visible.

Among those on board the Washington train was the waggish Frank Chapman of Shiloh fame.[86] Chapman had seen Long, covered with dust, ride up to the station. With an eye to the main chance, he waited until the guard on the train had examined Long's pass, then went to the officer in charge and ascertained from him that the newcomer was a *Tribune* man, fresh from the front and therefore in all likelihood a bearer of late news. The train was hardly under way before Chapman took a seat beside Long and began pumping him for information about what the army had done at Kelly's Ford. Chapman professed to be the sutler of a Western regiment, but, hail-fellow-well-met though he was, Long suspected that he was really a newspaperman and therefore declined to give him any information. Chapman did not show any particular resentment at this rebuff. Indeed he seemed to be on good terms with everyone on the train and was very liberal in passing out cigars and mysterious-looking black bottles, especially when the officer in charge of the train guard was around.

As the train was pulling in to Alexandria, Chapman disappeared very suddenly, and almost at the same moment Long missed his red envelope. It seemed strongly probable that the inquisitive stranger had removed it from his pocket, but this might be hard to prove. Long was reasonably certain that the local police would not interfere since the envelope had been taken outside of the city limits, and besides Alexandria was under martial law. While he was debating what course to take, the officer in charge of the train guard was relieved, and Long saw him point toward Long himself while talking to his substitute. Presently the new officer walked up to the *Tribune* correspondent and demanded to see his pass. After examining it for a moment, he said that he had serious doubts about its being genuine since it was not on the usual printed form, was written in pencil, and did not much resemble the signature of General Patrick, the Provost Marshal General. He went on to say that he would not permit Long to cross the Potomac on the pass unless it were signed by Colonel Devereux, whose office was close at hand.

Long protested in vain that General Patrick had written the pass on a sheet of paper torn from a note book which Long himself carried. He was obliged at last to leave the train, and before he could arrange to have his pass countersigned by Colonel Devereux the train pulled out, thereby depriving him of his last chance of reaching Washington that evening. The gist of the stolen dispatch appeared in the *Herald* the next day, some parts of it verbatim. Long sent a hastily prepared version of the affair at Kelly's Ford to the *Tribune* by telegraph from Alexandria and tried his best to keep the story of his experience from getting out. But he was soon driven almost to desperation by the jibes and jeers of his newspaper associates, who speedily found out about his misadventure.

As it happened he soon was able to use Chapman's own tactics. During the last week of November, Meade, intending to attack the Confederates in their winter quarters, crossed the Rapidan at Germanna Ford. On the twenty-seventh, General Warren, who led the advance, became hotly engaged with the enemy in the vicinity of Mine Run, a small tributary of the Rapidan. The next morning Long, carrying dispatches for the *Times* and the Associated Press as well as for his own newspaper, started North for Brandy Station. Before he left the army, Byington had made sure that the army authorities had no objections to Long's leaving. Their comment was simply that "our messenger would be a great deal surer to reach Libby Prison than Washington." Indeed the country through which Long passed was fairly swarming with guerillas and Confederate scouting parties, and when he reached Brandy Station, Long found that it was in the possession of the enemy's cavalry. By means of a detour he made his way to Rappahannock Station, a few miles to the East, where he was arrested by Union pickets and only released by the interposition of Secretary Stanton, to whom Long had sent an explanatory telegram. Stanton had received no information of the engagement at Mine Run other than the report that heavy cannonading had been heard in the direction of Orange Court House. He therefore requested Long to forward his dispatches to the War Department by military telegraph, offering in return to transmit them literally to the *Tribune,* provided they contained no information of an objectionable or contraband nature.

After performing his part of the bargain, Long boarded the train at Rappahannock Station. One of the first people he met on the train was the ubiquitous Chapman, who was hungry for news and who set out to get it by offering Long one hundred dollars for the privilege of reading his account of the fighting near Mine Run. When Long refused to accept, Chapman raised his offer, first to two hundred and then to two hundred and fifty dollars. Long still refused, although he was strongly tempted to accept the bribe out of pure spite since the story had already passed over the wires. Instead, he took out his note book in order to set down a memorandum. As he did so, he noticed that Chapman had taken a seat directly behind him, obviously in order to read what he was about to write. This was too good an opportunity to be missed. Affecting not to notice the *Herald* man, Long set to work to compose an imaginary account of a terrible battle which was supposed to have occurred near Chancellorsville the day before. Chapman, rising to the bait, copied page after page of the spurious manuscript. Finally Long completed his masterpiece by drawing from his haversack an old list of casualties which had occurred at Bristow Station and to which he added the fictitious names of several general officers. Within a few days Long had his revenge, for the *Herald's* issue of December 4, 1863, contained a glowing account of a sanguinary battle that was supposed to have occurred near Chancellorsville, together with a list of killed and wounded not to be found on the Adjutant General's muster rolls. And the *Herald* published an elaborate map of the country around Chancellorsville, showing the respective positions of the forces engaged![87]

Long himself had reached Washington the evening before with an exclusive story of the fighting at Mine Run. The *Tribune* of December 2, 1863, was more than jubilant; it fairly crowed over its big beat, and for a few hours Long was the lion of Newspaper Row. The most fitting reply the disappointed Chapman could think of was a hollow diatribe, published in the *Herald,* against the "marplots of the army," by whom he meant his successful competitors of the *Tribune.*[88] Not for some time would he have an opportunity to even the score, for immediately following the Mine Run fiasco, Meade quietly recrossed the Rapidan to remain in winter quarters along the North bank until the following May.

19

Strange Tales from the Red River Country

ON a crisp February day in 1864 the Philadelphia *Press* editor, John Russell Young, hunched over his desk to read a telegram from his superior, Colonel Forney. The Colonel's telegram, referring to plans Young previously had made to represent the *Press* on the Red River expedition to Northern Louisiana, instructed Young to:

> Go to Broad & Prime & meet mail agent Mr. Mount who has Stanton's letter & pass for you, covered by a letter franked by me. He will reach Phila about half past five having left [Washington] at quarter to eleven.[1]

Several nights later, a party of local newspapermen gathered around the table at Price's, a small basement restaurant at the corner of Fourth and Chestnut Streets, for a farewell dinner in honor of their departing confrere. As Young later recalled it, it was a "radiant night," with innumerable toasts of champagne which Price, the Negro proprietor, provided for the occasion.[2] Within a few days, the representative of the *Press* was on the ocean and bound for New Orleans, where he had spent his boyhood. After arriving in Louisiana, Young dispatched to his newspaper on St. Patrick's Day the first of a series of letters in which he described New Orleans and its people, as well as the momentous changes which had been brought about by the war and the regimes of Butler and Banks.[3]

A combined military and naval movement up the Red River had been under consideration by the authorities in Washington ever since Banks had replaced Butler in command of the Department of the Gulf in December, 1862. The foreign intervention in Mexico instigated by Napoleon III had given the U.S. State Department only too good reason to suspect that French intrigues, designed to prevent the return of Texas to the Federal Union, already were afoot. During the summer of 1863, therefore, Banks had received orders from Halleck to occupy one or more points in Texas for "reasons other than military."[4]

In September of 1863 the Department Commander had attempted to carry out these orders by landing five thousand men at weakly defended Sabine Pass, marching them by way of Houston, and attacking Galveston from the land side. While the army looked on from its transports, four of the navy's ancient gunboats had made a futile assault on the Sabine Pass batteries, manned by about four dozen Texans. After this unsuccessful operation, Major General William B. Franklin, Banks's inept field commander, promptly had drawn off and had headed back for Louisiana.

On-the-spot reporting of the Sabine Pass expedition left considerable to be desired. Typical of the way in which a disgraceful failure was magnified into a gallant struggle against overwhelming odds was the statement made by one of the New York specials that "considering the number of the force engaged, it is doubtful if any affair of the whole war can compare with the battle of Sabine Pass in obstinancy of fighting, loss of life and the amount of interest involved."[5] In such special pleading, a competent soldier historian later would detect:

> the same studied glozing of facts which deceived public opinion . . . [through] all the mishaps of Gulf affairs, from the loss of Galveston, on New Year's Day, 1863, to the expulsion of our grand army from the Red River, and from all western Louisiana, before New Year's Day, 1865.[6]

Two months later, a second expedition had succeeded in planting the United States flag at the mouth of the Rio Grande, and for a little while Banks had toyed with the idea of seizing all ports and passes from the Rio Grande to the Sabine. By December 1, 1863, however, he had come back to New Orleans to cooperate with a new plan devised by Halleck for a spring campaign along the line of the Red River. In such a campaign Shreveport, the capital of Confederate Louisiana, would figure as the initial objective, to be used in turn as a base of operation for an advance into East Texas. Although the primary objective of the campaign was military, an incidental purpose was the seizure of two hundred thousand bales of choice Confederate cotton in the Red River district and East Texas.[7]

Early in 1864 arrangements were completed for General Banks to march up through the Teche country from New Orleans with an army of approximately twenty thousand men drawn from the Thirteenth and Nineteenth army corps. Assistance was to be rendered by ten thousand troops from Sherman's command under Brigadier General Andrew J. ("Whitey") Smith, who were to come over from Vicksburg and meet Banks at Alexandria.[8] It was also planned that Major General Frederick Steele, the Federal commander in Arkansas, was to move South from Little Rock with another column of ten thousand soldiers and to join Banks somewhere near Shreveport. The naval arm of the expedition consisted of a fleet of twenty ironclads and gunboats, together with a large number of transports, under the command of Admiral David D. Porter. March 17, 1864, the date of John Russell Young's initial letter from New Orleans, was the day fixed for the forces of Banks, Porter, and Smith to meet at Alexandria.

As late as March 8, 1864, the St. Louis *Republican* still believed that Banks's forces were to be used in conjunction with Farragut's fleet for an attack on Mobile, the only port between Florida and Texas still in Confederate hands. On the twenty-first of that month, however, the same newspaper issued a front-page story that a force of about ten thousand soldiers and a fleet of gunboats had left Vicksburg for "a southern destination." Soon afterward, the New York *Tribune* received a letter from one of its special correspondents, mailed from "Above the mouth of Red River" on the fourteenth, describing the grand rendezvous of the transports and their escorts near that point. "Such little jealousies as may have heretofore had temporary existence between the land and naval forces are forgotten," concluded the *Tribune* man with a burst of misguided enthusiasm, "and they hail each other with the cordiality of brothers in a common cause."[9]

Porter's movement up the Red River began on March 12. On the following day, General Smith's three divisions, comprising elements of the Sixteenth and Seventeenth corps, were landed at Simsport for an overland march to the Confederate Fort de Russy. Some of the newspaper reporters who accompanied Smith's self-named "guerrillas" on the march were disagreeably impressed by the lawless behavior of these troops. A correspondent of the St. Louis *Republican* told of their robbing a house at "Red River Landing" of several thousand dollars in specie and then setting it on fire to destroy the evidence of their crime. Unless such practices were speedily checked, concluded the reporter, there was danger of "our whole noble army degenerating into a band of cut-throats and robbers."[10]

On the afternoon of March 14, Smith's men came within sight of the fort, defended by a skeleton force of about three hundred soldiers, and after some preliminary skirmishing, an infantry charge was ordered. With great gusto, the army correspondents told how the One Hundred and Nineteenth and Eighty-Ninth Indiana and Twenty-Fourth Missouri regiments in the face of galling fire charged over deep ditches and a thick abattis and how the United States flag was hoisted over the fort by an Illinois Color-Sergeant twenty minutes after the charge had begun. According to the New York *Tribune* correspondent, John E. Hayes, the surviving members of the garrison were so exasperated by the capture of the stronghold which they had been fortifying for nearly twelve months that "they screamed in demoniac tones, even after our banners flaunted from their bastions and ramparts."[11] With the capture of Fort de Russy the Confederates no longer could check effectively the gunboats' further progress upstream, and Major General Dick Taylor, the Confederate commander, was obliged to retreat seventy miles through the pine woods. Smith's Western troops were particularly elated that the gunboats had arrived just in time to witness the triumph of the land forces.

From Fort de Russy the fleet pushed upstream to Alexandria and occupied the town on the sixteenth, one day ahead of schedule. Banks, however, was slow to appear. For the time being, his attention was occupied by the election and inauguration of the new officers of the "Free State of Louisiana." General Franklin, who was in temporary command of the marching column, was held back by the condition of the roads so that the advanced cavalry division commanded by Brigadier General Albert L. Lee did not reach Alexandria until March 19. The infantry and artillery followed on the twenty-fifth and twenty-sixth of March.[12]

A correspondent of the New York *Times* accompanied the march of Lee's cavalry from Franklin to Alexandria through the Teche country, famous for its fine estates. At the beginning of the march, he thought he could detect in the faces of Lee's staff officers "a kind of grim delight at the fearful pounding which I was about to get, and the certain wearing away of the seat of my trowsers." In the long run, however, the *Times* correspondent reached Alexandria in as good condition as the cavalry officers and was able to write a newspaper letter which gave a surprisingly vivid picture of what such a march was like:

The march is a succession of pictures. The bugles wake you in the morning, and you look out of your tent upon the canvas city —you breakfast and dine in perpetual picnic—the march is a procession of glittering men and horses, the halts to feed and water are full of variety, and the bivouac fires at night are exciting. Small herds of cattle join the afternoon march, and as the smokes begin to rise, as the negroes describe it:

"Bang goes de guns, and down goes the critters—golly, master."

After supper, in the space in front of the tents, a great fire blazes, and the General and his Staff collect—it so happens that we have some German singers and a large accordeon, and we have music and song—while the firelight shows around us the faces of the negroes and the forms of the guards—all very pretty —and one thinks, after all, war is not so bad a thing.

Of the *horrors of war,* I have experienced one—the dust!— which in this country is of a very superior description; it is a pillar of cloud by day, hiding us from ourselves, if not from the enemy. We touch, taste, see, and snuff it, and yet we live. I think I shall next go to war in rainy weather. One other thing I shall choose, namely: a continent where there are no dogs, for the civilized dog appears to have lost the power of sleep after sunset, and to have devoted his whole mind to barks and howls in every variety of cadence. . . .

The *soldier* is a queer fellow; he is not at all like other white men. Tired, dusty, cold or hungry—no matter, he is always jolly —I find him, under the most adverse circumstances, shouting, singing, skylarking; there is no care or tire in him. These "Yankees" are not at all the creatures here they are at home. There is a universal and uncontrollable desire for chicken in this soldier, and our most pious corporals are not exempt from this love; chickens are gobbled for "hospital purposes"—the laws of war not permitting it for the ordinary carnal uses—and one feels that the sick soldiers must have a tough time of it if obliged to eat some of these crowing patriarchs. . . .

Your principal business on the march is to see that you get bread and meat by day and a place to sleep by night. . . . War is an enormous business. Bravery in the General is all very well, but business is what makes an army.[13]

Within a day or two after the arrival of Lee's cavalry at Alexandria, General A. J. Smith sent forward a brigade of mounted soldiers with two infantry divisions to clear the way across Bayou Rapides. William

Young, a *Herald* reporter, accompanied the cavalry on what he described as a "long, hard and tedious march," during which he did not unsaddle or sleep for two consecutive nights.[14] Under the cover of a heavy rain storm on the night of March 21, Brigadier General Joseph A. Mower, who was in command of the expedition, skillfully surprised the Second Louisiana Regiment, Taylor's entire cavalry force. With only minor losses, Mower captured practically the whole regiment and four guns. It was a brilliant stroke, which elicited effusive compliments from the army newspapermen. In the opinion of the New York *Tribune* special at Alexandria, Mower's expedition was "one of the most successful of the war."[15] The triumph was no less gratifying because a Confederate courier, who supposed Mower to be the Confederate General Walker, had led the Union general straight into Taylor's camp!

Such exploits seem to have attracted less attention, however, from the newspaper public than might have been supposed. On April 2 the New Orleans correspondent of the New York *Tribune* commented:

> It is a remarkable fact that this Red River expedition is not followed by that anxious interest and solicitude which has heretofore attended similar army movements. The success of our troops is looked upon as a matter of course, and the cotton speculators are the only people I can find who are nicely weighing probabilities and chances in connection with the expedition.[16]

On March 25, the day after Banks's arrival in Alexandria, General Smith held a review of his troops for the benefit of the Department Commander. These troops, mostly from the Western states, were not remarkable for their neatness although physically they were a splendid group of men and they possessed soldierly bearing. Following the review, Banks, who was noted for his attention to dress, was overheard to remark: "Those are ragged guerrillas; those are not soldiers. If a general can't dress his troops better than that, he should disband them."[17]

Apparently this unwise comment became common talk among the "ragged guerrillas" and considerably intensified the friction between the Eastern and Western regiments which were associated in the Red River campaign. At the time, however, the army correspondents did not report even the existence of such a feeling. In fact, a New York *Times* reporter, writing from New Orleans to his newspaper on April 2, had stated that there had existed "some time ago" a certain amount of sectional prejudice between the New England and Western troops which had been brought together under the command of General Banks, but in this campaign, he asserted:

> They are fighting side by side for the Union, and the blood they are shedding together will add another bond of eternal friendship between the East and the West.[18]

Only when the ill-feeling between the two groups later was brought into the open by military defeat were the army correspondents unable to ignore it.

The advance of Banks's army beyond Alexandria temporarily was retarded by Banks's political maneuvering.[19] Further, an abnormally low water stage in the Red River prevented the heavier gunboats from proceeding upstream. Just above Alexandria were two rapids, generally known as the Falls of Alexandria, which steamers could pass only in high water. On March 26, a reporter for the New York *World* ascended the Falls in a small boat and gazed with some curiosity at the "Eastport," an ironclad ram which had run aground that very morning and which was stranded there for nearly three days until a rise in the river level eased her off the rocks.[20] The marine hospital steamer, "Woodford," which followed the "Eastport," was wrecked and had to be abandoned. Not until April 3 did the rest of the ships which made up the naval arm of the expedition safely reach the upper end of the Falls.

While Banks was still at Alexandria, some of the army correspondents began to suspect that the whole expedition was, as the New York *World* expressed it, "a mere cotton raid."[21] Although General Banks told the newspaper correspondents that private speculation in cotton would not be permitted and that all cotton taken by the army must be sent to the quartermaster at New Orleans, the reporters hardly could fail to observe that Alexandria was swarming with cotton speculators, many of whom came all the way from Washington with permits to "trade within the enemy's lines." Said a St. Louis reporter:

> I meet quite a number of persons here [Alexandria] who have Gen. Banks' passes, who are dealing in cotton, sugar, &c. In fact, the boat upon which General Banks came to this place, the Black Hawk, brought up 150 coils of rope, and 50 bales of bagging, to be used in baling cotton, ostensibly shipped for the use of the Government; but it is broadly intimated that it is for

private use, as the Government is not in the cotton-growing business at present. . . .[22]

Even before Banks arrived at Alexandria, the navy had begun seizing cotton from the various plantations along the river between Fort de Russy and Alexandria and carrying it off without compensating the owners. In some cases Porter's sailors used wagons to scour the region for cotton as far as six miles on either side of the stream. Orders had been issued not to seize any cotton bales which were not marked C.S.A., which identified the bales as the property of the Confederate government. In many instances, according to the reporters, however, the sailors went ashore with marking pots and stamped the initials C.S.A. on cotton owned by private individuals, some of them Union sympathizers. Then, after crossing out the offensive initials, the sailors placed underneath them the letters U.S.N.[23]

Eventually Porter gave orders that no more cotton should be seized by anyone in his command without special authorization, but this was after considerable antagonism had developed between the army and the navy. The unlimited wagon transportation which the army enjoyed irritated Porter's sailors, while the army was particularly annoyed by the fact that Jack had not restricted his cotton-gathering to specimens which could be picked up along the river, or at least no further than short hauls of fifty to one hundred yards from shore. The New York *Evening Post* reporter spoke frankly about the existence of this bad feeling,[24] and even the *Herald's* representative, William Young, made an oblique reference to it in his Red River correspondence:

> It is not within the province of your correspondent to criticize what has been done by the army or navy; nor will he state occurrences which it may be unpleasant to read.[25]

Attempts to limit the cotton traffic, moreover, were made still more difficult since one firm of speculators, Butler and Casey, had a special permit from President Lincoln which both Banks and Porter felt obliged to honor.[26]

Another story of the troops' misconduct also was reported from Alexandria. The correspondent of the St. Louis *Republican* described at some length how Federal soldiers had gutted three drugstores in Alexandria. In at least one of these instances the correspondent reported the incident to the Provost Marshal, who at once gave orders for the store to be cleared and a squad of soldiers placed at the door to prevent a repetition of the occurence.[27] The New York *World* correspondent at New Orleans likewise enlarged upon the theme of wholesale plunder and abuse by the Red River expedition. Testimony of eyewitnesses was invoked to substantiate statements which told how:

> every mule, every horse, every ox, every cow, every hog, and every sheep have been driven off . . . and even the cabins of the negroes burnt up and their patches and chickencoops robbed of all they contained. . . . The victims do not know whose troops it is who do this destructive work; but it is asserted here that it is all done by the Western men who were out with Sherman in his raid through Mississippi.[28]

On March 27, while Porter's gunboats were still attempting to pass the Falls above Alexandria, the army took up the line of march and proceeded with little or no opposition to Natchitoches, then a dingy little Indian and French settlement of about two thousand people, located on a tributary of the Red River, one hundred and twenty miles upstream from Alexandria. "Natchitoches is as old as Philadelphia," wrote a *Press* correspondent, "and so queer, and quaint, that I would be tempted to write you a letter about it, if the events of this busy time were not so urgent."[29] At Clautiersville, a pretty French village in Natchitoches parish, the newspaper brigade, weary and hungry, rode ahead of the main column of infantry and made arrangements to have dinner at the home of a gentleman who had sons in the Confederate army. His daughters, "refined and intelligent ladies," were not disposed to conceal their sympathy for the cause for which their brothers were fighting. As the correspondents were about to leave, after finishing their dinner, the *Herald* reporter presented his card, together with some postal currency "fresh from the iron safe of the paymaster," to their hostesses. While the young ladies were examining the postal notes with some curiosity, the representatives of the *Herald* remarked that this was probably the last time he would see them as the army was going on to Shreveport and thence across the state line into Texas. "You are mistaken, gentlemen," replied one of the girls, in a tone which left no doubt as to her meaning. "The army will come back this way."[30] Before many days had passed her remark proved strangely prophetic.

On April 2, the day of their arrival at Natchitoches, a party of printers, who had been detailed from General Dudley's brigade, removed the lock from the office door of the Natchitoches *Union,* whose editor had taken to the woods. At daylight the next morning, they issued an extra edition of the newspaper, giving full particulars of the capture of Natchitoches.[31]

It is to be hoped that the news which appeared in the first Yankee edition of the *Union* was more reliable than some of the stories about the Red River expedition which were being printed elsewhere. Most appropriately on April Fool's Day the New Orleans *Era* and *True Delta* had issued extras featuring a tremendous battle along Cane River, in which ten thousand Federal troops were supposed to have routed fourteen thousand Confederates and taken six hundred prisoners. The *True Delta* intimated that it had received its information from certain military officers on board two transports which had arrived at New Orleans the evening before; the *Era* vaguely credited its story to "passengers." The New York *Herald* also printed the story of the Cane River episode, only to have it repudiated later by its New Orleans correspondent, who remarked:

> No such engagement took place on Cane River, and there has been no fighting in which Mower's and Dudley's troops co-operated. All the numerous reports concerning a fight there originated, undoubtedly, from the affair at Henderson's Hill, eighteen miles above Alexandria, where Mower's infantry and Colonel Lucas' cavalry brigade flanked, surprised and captured two hundred and seventy of the enemy and four guns, as correctly reported in the *Herald* of April 10. Even that had been erroneously reported as the battle of Natchitoches, though it was fought sixty miles this side of there, and about a week before our advance—consisting entirely of cavalry—entered Natchitoches.[32]

Still more exciting was a telegraphic story attributed to the New York *Tribune* which indicated that General Steele had entered Shreveport on March 17 after ten hours of fighting. Since Steele did not leave Little Rock until the twenty-third of March, the *Tribune* story was, to say the least, somewhat premature.[33]

Banks's army remained in the neighborhood of Natchitoches for about three days before resuming its advance upon Shreveport, ninety-eight miles away, on April 6. There was need of haste, for Banks had received orders from Grant, the new general in chief, on March 27 that if the capture of Shreveport had not been accomplished by April 10, the expedition must be abandoned.

To the great disappointment of the cotton speculators, the Confederates, acting under orders from their high command, already had burned most of the cotton along both sides of the river all the way up to Shreveport. Estimates of the amount destroyed ranged from two hundred thousand to three hundred thousand bales. This act of destruction generally was ascribed by the war correspondents to the "lawless conduct" of the navy. The destruction of all this cotton at this particular time had nothing to do with the navy's cotton-gathering methods, however, for General Kirby Smith had issued orders to burn the cotton on March 14 when he first learned that Federal troops were on the march up the Red River.[34] Yet some of the reporters seemed to be under the impression that the Confederates had made an arrangement with Banks to exchange their cotton for provisions and military supplies and that Porter had prevented the arrangement from being carried out.[35]

When these and other topics of conversation wore thin, the army correspondents speculated on the outcome of the campaign. On the day that Banks's army left Natchitoches a special correspondent of the St. Louis *Republican* wrote:

> There are many persons here [Grand Ecore] who fancy that we are on the eve of a great battle. I do not share the opinion. The Confederate army is and has been falling back slowly and regularly before us; at the same time we hear that the enemy is concentrating all his available forces. The Confederates may fight, provided they can take a position naturally defended, where they can collect plenty of supplies; not otherwise. . . .[36]

There was no fighting on the sixth; on the night of April 7, after a sharp skirmish with a Texas cavalry brigade, Albert Lee's cavalry bivouacked on Bayou St. Patrice, seven miles beyond their nearest infantry support at Pleasant Hill. The progress of the infantry had been retarded by a heavy storm so that the army was strung out for twenty-five miles along a single narrow road "more like a broad, deep, red-colored ditch than anything else." To at least one of the newspapermen who reported this campaign, northern Louisiana seemed anything but advantageous for the purposes of invasion:

> The topography of Virginia has been assigned as a reason for every defeat of the Army of the Potomac; but Virginia is a garden and a meadow, when compared with the low, flat pine countries that extend from Opelousas . . . to Fort Smith. . . . I have ridden for fifty miles into the heart of this pine country, and from the

beginning to the end of the journey there was nothing but a dense, impenetrable, interminable forest, traversed by a few narrow roads, with no signs of life or civilization beyond occasional log-houses and half-cleared plantations. . . . Such a thing as subsisting an army in a country like this could only be achieved when men and horses can be induced to live on pine trees and resin.[37]

At daylight on April 8, Lee's cavalry column—three brigades in all, supported by a brigade of infantry—resumed its march on Shreveport and after another clash with the retreating Confederates, arrived about noon at the Eastern edge of a large clearing called Sabine Cross Roads, about four miles South of Mansfield. There they encountered the enemy in force, drawn up in line of battle so as to overlap the Union position on both flanks. After several hours of fierce skirmishing, during which the Chicago *Tribune* correspondent passed from one end of the line to the other noting down the positions of the various units in his memorandum book,[38] Dick Taylor launched a crushing attack on the outnumbered Federals. Reinforcements were called for and were brought forward, first a brigade, then a division at a time, but they were of little use. Lee's batteries, placed in the woods, were ineffective, and gradually the hard-pressed bluecoats were forced back. Finally a retreat was ordered, a retreat which became a stampede as the Northern soldiers found their escape route blocked by a confused mass of horses, mules, artillery, and wagons. Said Young of the Philadelphia *Press*, who also was acting as staff officer to General Banks:

> I find it impossible to describe a scene so sudden and bewildering, although I was present, partly an actor, partly a spectator, and saw plainly everything that took place. . . . I was slowly riding along the edge of a wood, conversing with a friend who had just ridden up about the events and prospects of the day. We had drawn into the side of the wood to allow an ammunition wagon to pass, and although many were observed going to the rear, some on foot and some on horseback, we regarded it as an occurrence familiar to every battle, and it occasioned nothing but a passing remark.
>
> I noticed that most of those thus wildly riding to the rear were negroes, hangers-on and serving-men, for now that we have gone so deeply into this slave holding country every non-commissioned officer has a servant, and every servant a mule. These people were the first to show any panic, but their scamper along

> the road only gave amusement to the soldiers, who pelted them with stones, and whipped their flying animals with sticks to increase their speed. Suddenly there was a rush, a shout, the crashing of trees, the breaking down of rails, the rush and scamper of men. It was as sudden as though a thunderbolt had fallen among us, and set the pines on fire. What caused it, or when it commenced, no one knew. I turned to my companion to inquire the reason of this extraordinary proceeding, but before he had the chance to reply, we found ourselves swallowed up, as it were, in a hissing, seething, bubbling whirlpool of agitated men. We could not avoid the current; we could not stem it, and if we hoped to live in that mad company, we must ride with the rest of them. . . . Gen. Banks took off his hat and implored his men to remain; his staff officers did the same, but it was of no avail. Then the General drew his sabre and endeavored to rally his men, but they would not listen. Behind him the rebels were shouting and advancing. Their musket balls filled the air with that strange file-rasping sound that war has made familiar to our fighting men. . . . Bareheaded riders rode with agony in their faces, and for at least ten minutes it seemed as if we were going to destruction together. It was my fortune to see the first battle of Bull Run, and to be among those who made that celebrated midnight retreat towards Washington. The retreat of the 4th Division was as much a rout as that of the first Federal army with the exception that fewer men were engaged, and our men fought here with a valor that was not shown on that serious, sad, mock-heroic day in July. We rode nearly two miles in this madcap way, until on the edge of a ravine, which might formerly have been a bayou, we found Emory's division drawn up in line. Our retreating men fell beyond this line, and Emory prepared to meet the rebels. They came with a rush, and, as the shades of night crept over the treetops, they encountered our men. Emory fired three rounds, and the rebels retreated. This ended the fight, leaving the Federals masters.[39]

One of the greatest blunders of the army command had been the placing of General Albert Lee's immense wagon train in the rear of the cavalry unit, which made a retreat very difficult, almost impossible. Altogether there were some three hundred and twenty to three hundred and fifty wagons in the train. About half of these fell into the hands of the enemy, along with some fourteen or fifteen pieces of artillery and about two thousand prisoners.[40] In the melee William Young, the

Herald correspondent, lost several blankets, a Negro servant, and a silver bugle which he had recently obtained from a captured bugler and which he had intended to send to the *Herald* publisher as a trophy. C. E. H. Bonwill, the artist for *Frank Leslie's*, mourned the loss of some sketches which he had been accumulating over a long period of time and which he valued highly. The New York *Tribune* correspondent W. H. Wells likewise parted company with most of his wearing apparel and "other fixins."[41]

Although none of the reporters was seriously harmed, the losses on both sides were moderately heavy. According to the army correspondent of the St. Louis *Republican*, at least one-half of the Thirteenth Army Corps, which numbered twenty-six hundred at the outbreak of the battle, had been killed, wounded, or captured, "a loss in proportion to the number engaged, which is perhaps without a parallel in the history of this terrible war."[42]

Brigadier General William H. Emory's Nineteenth Corps at nightfall had checked the enemy's advance, but Banks was convinced that there was no hope of reaching Shreveport within the time allowed by Grant. At midnight, therefore, Emory's men started falling back to Pleasant Hill, a distance of twenty miles from Sabine Cross Roads, to join A. J. Smith, and on the following morning General Banks issued orders for the withdrawal of the entire army to Grand Ecore. Nearly the whole of April 9 was required to get the wagon train in motion. Hardly had this been effected when Taylor, who had been reinforced during the night, attacked the Union left with some initial success, but a vigorous counterattack by A. J. Smith's Western troops forced the whole Confederate line to fall back in considerable confusion. Subsequently, Kirby Smith admitted that "our repulse at Pleasant Hill was so complete and our command was so disorganized that had Banks followed up his success vigorously he would have met feeble opposition to his advance on Shreveport."[43] To the New York *Herald* reporter it seemed that this battle "was one of the best appointed and delivered of the war . . . . [reflecting] much credit upon the head of the Army of the Gulf, and . . . to all who were engaged in it."[44]

Emboldened by his success at Pleasant Hill, Banks considered resuming his advance upon Shreveport, but, after consultation with his subordinates, decided to carry out the retreat as previously planned to Grand Ecore, which he reached on April 11, without meeting any interference from the enemy. Whatever the reporters or anyone else might have to say about the unfavorable turn which the campaign had taken, Banks's soldiers had their own ideas. As they trudged southward from Pleasant Hill, they made the pine woods on either side of the narrow road ring with the ditty:

> In 1861, we all skedaddled to Washington,
> In 1864, we all skedaddled to Grand Ecore.

and then added for good measure as the General and his staff rode by, "Napoleon P. Banks!"[45]

Meanwhile, the fleet had continued up the Red River, accompanied by a brigade of twenty-five hundred men under Brigadier General T. Kilby Smith, whose name was a never-ending source of confusion to the newspaper reporters.[46] At sunset on the ninth, the naval arm of the expedition had reached Mansfield Landing, sixteen miles beyond the Federal position at Pleasant Hill, and on the following day, unaware of Bank's disaster, it had steamed on to Loggy Bayou, less than thirty miles from Shreveport. Not until four o'clock on the afternoon of the tenth, did a dispatch boat bearing dispatches from General Banks overtake Porter with the news of the retreat of the army to Grand Ecore. It was almost five days before the fleet was able to return to Grand Ecore since the ships were subjected to an almost continuous rifle fire from sharpshooters posted along the banks of the stream. Porter's withdrawal was rendered even more difficult by the fact that the army had brought along two oversized transports whose captains, in the hope of bringing down cotton, had violated the General's orders. Since these transports ran aground continuously, they hardly could fail to invite guerilla attacks. A reporter for the St. Louis *Democrat* who was with the fleet during these momentous five days, viewed its escape from its extremely precarious position as "one of the most daring, as well as one of the most successful . . . feats of the whole war."[47]

Because of the remote position of Banks's army, news of the reverse at Sabine Cross Roads and Pleasant Hill was slow in reaching the Northern press. The first account of the fighting appeared in the Chicago *Evening Journal* on April 19, 1864, even before the government in Washington had any information about what had happened. From Chicago the *Journal* story was telegraphed to all parts of the country. The St. Louis *Republican* was inclined at first to regard the *Journal's* scoop as a hoax, since the *Republican* was unable to understand why the news should have reached Chicago "sooner than any other place."[48] Not until five days later did full-length accounts of the battles appear in any of the other Northern newspapers.

There was considerable difference of opinion among newspaper correspondents and their editors about the significance of the news from Louisiana. Forney's Philadelphia *Press* expressed the view on April 25 that the reverse suffered by Banks's army had not been of sufficient magnitude to discourage the country or check its faith in the eventual success of the campaign. The New York *Herald* on the same date concluded that by means of this "brilliant victory," General Banks had crushed the hopes of the enemy throughout the trans-Mississippi region and established control over the states of Louisiana, Texas, and Southern Arkansas! The "great victory" won by Banks and Franklin was similarly lauded to the skies by the New Orleans newspapers, which were dependent for their continued existence upon the favor of the Department Commander. To the New York *World* on the other hand it seemed equally clear from its Red River sources of information that the expedition to conquer the trans-Mississippi region:

> has met with a check which will cripple it for some time to come. . . . Most of the letters from that quarter are cooked to suit the northern market.[49]

One of the most interesting army letters of the campaign, in terms of its frank allegations of military mismanagement, was contributed to the New York *Tribune* by its correspondent, J. E. Hayes. Following the retreat from Pleasant Hill, Hayes had volunteered to act as a nurse on board the hospital steamer "Laurel Hill," which left Grand Ecore on April 11 with four hundred and thirty badly wounded men and arrived at New Orleans three days later. In a letter mailed from the steamer "Henry Ames" on April 23, the *Tribune* reporter alluded to the "greatest incompetency . . . manifested in providing for the care of our sick and wounded on the Red River Expedition." Among other things he complained of the failure of Dr. Charles T. Alexander, Medical Director of General Banks's army, to provide another boat for the use of the sick after the loss of the marine hospital steamer near Alexandria. Then he told of how, after the battle, some of the wounded were left at Pleasant Hill "without half a supply of medical stores" while the others were dragged in ambulances, "many of them in commissary and ammunition wagons," to Grand Ecore where they were placed "in miserable sheds and other outbuildings" for transfer to the hospital boats. He went on to say:

> Not one ounce of any sort of medicine was placed on board [the "Laurel Hill"], and there was no supply of bedding, sheets, clothing, or other articles to relieve the suffering on board. Beyond a few rough pine boards which were hastily constructed in the center of the cabin, there was no preparation. Eight or ten staterooms were filled with chairs and other luggage, where two men might have been placed in each stateroom. No suitable cooking apparatus had been placed on board, and on this account but two meals a day were served to the men. There was no salt on board, which the men eagerly cried for, and no soft bread—nothing but hard tack. The only attendance the sick and wounded received was that bestowed by a few soldiers and undisciplined contrabands who were of little use. . . .
>
> Had it not been for the kindness of Edward Mitchell, esq., of New-York, one of the oldest volunteers laboring for the United States Sanitary Commission, the suffering would have been beyond all belief. Immediately upon the arrival of the Laurel Hill at Alexandria, Mr. Mitchell and one of the United States Sanitary Commission agents brought on board a small supply of luxuries for the use of the wounded. . . . Not a soldier on board that boat will probably ever forget the United States Sanitary Commission, for, to this noble Christian charity alone is due all the relief afforded to those patients on the Laurel Hill.
>
> Before concluding this just exposition, let me state that the Laurel Hill brought up a plentiful supply of cotton-baling, twine, rope, and all other material necessary for the protection of cotton. What a pity the time and trouble spent in stowing away such material was not used in loading medical stores and those things requisite for a hospital boat. Several soldiers died on the passage between Grand Ecore and New-Orleans, and it will not be astonishing if many more perish after enduring the horrible privations of that ever-memorable trip.

Then he added for the benefit of those who might think that he was indulging in mere sensationalism:

> Nothing but a desire to awaken public sympathy in behalf of our gallant soldiers, thousands of miles away from home, has prompted the writing of this account. I have witnessed such abuses altogether too often to remain silent any longer on a sub-

ject which is of such vital importance to the loyal people of the country.[50]

In a private letter to the managing editor of his newspaper, Hayes spoke in caustic terms of the "poor Generalship of Genl Banks and the Botany Bay General under him," and of wholesale drunkenness of many of them. Protesting that he was "totally free from predjudice [sic] in this matter," Hayes expressed regret that:

> it becomes my imperative duty to expose the faults of so many men natives to my own State [Massachusetts], but if you were with me to witness all that I have seen you too would exclaim, 'here incompetency reigns supreme'. . . .[51]

On April 27, J. R. Hamilton of the New York *Times* left New Orleans on the "Iberville" to go on a fact-finding mission up the Red River. New Orleans, at the time, was full of conflicting reports: General Steele had been captured, Porter's fleet had been destroyed above Alexandria, and the same fate had overtaken General Banks's army. With the exception of a fight between two drunken Zouaves on the first evening out and a fracas which arose as a result of the brutal treatment of some Negro soldiers by their Irish compeers, the cruise was relatively quiet until the "Iberville" reached the mouth of the Red River. Near that point at sometime during the early part of the forenoon of April 29, a body of guerillas hidden behind trees and stumps opened fire on the Yankee steamer. In his description of the episode, Hamilton observed:

> The saloon of a river steamboat attacked by guerrillas, presents a scene quite as comic as it is exciting. To those who can at all control their nerves, the ludicrous positively banishes all thought of the tragic, to see great big fellows—with and without shoulder-straps—sprawl flat on their bellies behind every conceivable projection of chair or table, at the first rattle of musketry, and going through the absurdly, impossible process of trying to make pancakes of themselves. Near to my cabin door, where I was sitting reading when the alarm commenced, I saw behind the leaves of a table piled up about two feet high, a United States officer . . . lying flat on his face, on top of him a negro waiter, and on top of the latter a gaunt, petrified, long-bearded sutler, whose eyes seemed ready to leap from their sockets. Poor fellow! I know he must have felt as relieved as any of us when we safely reached this place [Alexandria] at 11 P.M. of the 29th, and saw the

> myriad lights of the transports and gunboats reflected in the stream and lighting up the bluffs, giving the appearance of a large and imposing city.[52]

In Alexandria, Hamilton caught a glimpse of General Banks, who, without notifying Porter, had left Grand Ecore with his army on the twenty-second of April and had reached Alexandria on the twenty-fifth after some brisk fighting at Monette's Ferry. At headquarters Hamilton also met a Cincinnati *Gazette* reporter, Dr. Samuel Silsby, who had come up from New Orleans on the "Silver Wave" and had passed through a similar pattern of guerilla fire. Three volleys of fifty shots each had been fired at the "Silver Wave"; four men sitting together on deck—the captain, pilot, watchman, and the government aide—had escaped without a scratch although bullets had passed through their hats and clothes.[53]

In a letter published in the Philadelphia *Press* on June 1, 1864, an army correspondent of that newspaper, John Weik, described the wholesale devastation practiced by A. J. Smith's command on the march from Grand Ecore to Alexandria:

> Not a building, shanty, or chicken-coop was spared. . . . Men as well as officers participated in this outrage. They went miles out of the way to burn and destroy. They made no distinction between Union and rebel officers [sympathizers?]; were heard glorying in styling themselves the cotton-burners of the 16th Corps.

This same correspondent apparently had made an effort to find out why General Banks permitted such outrages, only to learn that A. J. Smith's command was considered independent and as such not subject to the authority of the commander of the Department of the Gulf!

By the end of April, news had reached the press that the campaign in Arkansas had been no more succesful than the movement up the Red River in Louisiana. While still a hundred miles from Shreveport, General Steele had been checked on April 15 at Camden, Arkansas, by Kirby Smith, who took advantage of Banks's retreat to concentrate most of his available forces against Steele. On May 2, Steele was back in Little Rock after what a reporter for the St. Louis *Democrat* described as "a campaign of forty days in which nothing has been gained but defeat, hard blows and poor fare."[54] During those forty days the press had received information about developments in Arkansas over a newly constructed telegraph line which operated in conjunction with an express to bring news from Little Rock to St. Louis via Fort Smith within a period of twelve hours. To the St. Louis *Republican* it was amusing:

> to see the New York *Herald*, only a day or two ago, doubting the correctness of certain news which had been published, because as that paper alleged, it had to come to St. Louis by a wagon road. For its information we would state, that dispatches are daily received here from Little Rock in from twelve to twenty-four hours. The news which we published yesterday in regard to Gen. Steele and his army being still at Camden, was received in this way.[55]

As it became increasingly clear that the campaign in the Southwest had been a failure,[56] the press became more and more interested in fixing the responsibility for it, the New York *Times* being of the opinion that a prompt and rigid investigation of the disaster was necessary.[57] Banks's retreat was variously attributed by the newspaper wiseacres to low water in the Red River; to delays resulting in part from the fact that the army was engaged with too much baggage;[58] to a plethora of major generals; to the existence of too many independent commands in the field; to the fact that General Banks permitted his cavalry to advance beyond easy supporting distance and that the cavalry train was interposed between the cavalry and the infantry, thereby preventing the use of the only road available for the various units to advance or retreat; likewise to the circumstance that reinforcements were sent forward piecemeal, and that the cavalry unit was permitted to bring on a general engagement, instead of being withdrawn to a point where it could be more easily reinforced. As the New York *Tribune* saw it, Banks had committed at Sabine Cross Roads precisely the same error which cost him a victory at Cedar Mountain in October, 1862.[59]

Full publicity was given by the press to the recriminations exchanged by the various officers in command of the expedition. Admiral Porter was quoted by the St. Louis *Democrat* as saying that "General Banks' recent Red River expedition" was a "disastrous failure."[60] Subsequently, the *Democrat* quoted a dispatch from Natchez intimating that General A. L. Lee and nineteen other officers had been placed under arrest in New Orleans for having stated that the Red River expedition was "not for fighting, but for thieving and speculating."[61] Said a Cincinnati *Gazette* reporter writing from New Orleans on May 7:

> Returning army officers complain that the fleet wasted precious time at the outset by landing to collect cotton, and naval officers state, with the usual profane accompaniments, that the army was rotten, from the commander down. Be all this as it may, it certainly is not a good sign that the condition of affairs is so openly discussed and publicly denounced by those who are employed by the Government to uphold its authority and maintain its power on land and water.[62]

Although a certain amount of newspaper criticism was directed at Banks's chief of staff, General Stone,[63] who was deprived of his voluntary commission on the eve of the battle of Sabine Cross Roads, the bulk of the criticism was reserved for Banks himself, whose popularity in the army had almost entirely vanished. On April 13, the St. Louis *Republican*'s correspondent "Central" wrote from Grand Ecore:

> He [Banks] has lost the confidence of the entire army. The privates are ridiculing him. Officers are not loudly but deeply cursing him and civilians are unanimous in condemnation of the commanding general. . . . Personally, General Banks is a perfect gentleman. I have no prejudice against him, for he has invariably treated me with kindness and consideration. But the truth must be told. As a military man he is, as the vernacular has it, "played out."[64]

Further evidence concerning Banks's unpopularity with his men appeared in such leading administration newspapers as the St. Louis *Democrat* and the Cincinnati *Gazette*. The press likewise printed stories about a quarrel between Generals A. J. Smith and Banks at Pleasant Hill which was brought about by Banks's order to retreat and which culminated in Smith's carrying out the order under protest.[65] Subsequently, so the St. Louis *Republican* reported, Smith took it upon himself to denounce publicly Banks's competence as a general.[66]

Among the camp stories which found their way into the newspapers was one about two wagonloads of paper collars which supposedly were captured by the Confederates at the battle of Sabine Cross Roads. According to the St. Louis *Republican*'s version of the tale, General Taylor returned the collars under a flag of truce with a letter to General Banks in which he stated that:

> I have boiled, fried, baked and stewed these things, and can do nothing with them. We cannot eat them. They are a luxury for

> which we have no use, and I would like, therefore, to exchange them for a like quantity of hard-tack.

When the Western troops under General Smith's command, who were especially contemptuous of Banks, marched past Banks's headquarters as they came into Alexandria, they were said to have groaned, jeered, and called aloud, "How about those paper collars?"[67] The significance of the paper collars story as viewed by another army correspondent of the *Republican* was that Banks had taken the field:

> very much in the style of Louis XIV. Perhaps there were no ballet dancers or actresses along, but between political and convivial parties the damage was nearly as great. . . .[68]

Some of the criticism of Banks and his fellow officers by anti-Administration newspapers is to be explained by the fact that 1864 was a campaign year. In the New York *World* appeared information forwarded by one of its correspondents which indicated that the whole campaign had been planned by a "titular colonel" who was sent from Washington to Louisiana, ostensibly as a special agent of the Treasury Department.[69] According to another newspaper version submitted by a reporter of the anti-Administration St. Louis *Republican*, General Kirby Smith had expressed his willingness to sell out to the Federals and retire to Mexico after making a token resistance. As a part of the "deal," two hundred thousand bales of cotton were to be turned over to the Federals who were to pay either in gold or Bank of England notes. The reporter admitted, however, that he was uncertain whether Kirby Smith had acted in good faith.[70]

But not in anti-Administration papers alone were such exposures of Red River skulduggery given publicity. Later that summer, a Chicago *Tribune* correspondent, who had been with the Western armies since the beginning of the war and was thoroughly acquainted with the military and civil operations in the Southwest, published a remarkable tale about this same cotton deal, in which, according to him, Banks, Porter, Kirby Smith, and Taylor all were implicated. Furthermore, said the *Tribune* man, a former Kentucky congressman named Samuel L. Casey and a certain Colonel Floyd, a Louisianan, were the go-betweens in the transaction, acting with the full knowledge and approval of the authorities in Washington, who were unwilling, however, "to make official endorsement of the documents in the affair." Kirby Smith and Taylor, he further stated, had carried out their part of the bargain, including the offering of only a pretense at resistance, until they learned that no remuneration of any kind was being given for the cotton which the Federals were seizing. At that point they clamped down an embargo upon further deliveries of cotton and began making preparations to resist Banks's advance.[71]

Tales such as these had their effect upon public opinion. On April 29, 1864, Senator John B. Henderson of Missouri read on the floor of the United States Senate an extract from an army letter appearing in the St. Louis *Republican* which called attention to the subject of naval cotton seizures and to the misunderstanding which had arisen between General Banks and Admiral Porter. Senator John Conness of California challenged these statements, denouncing them as a "cruel and base slander" upon Admiral Porter.[72] The reporter whom Henderson had quoted commented:

> It so happens that Senator Conness knows nothing about the facts in the case. He was in Washington; I was at Alexandria, and know that my statements are true. If the authorities at Washington would authorize an investigation . . . they, and Senator Conness would find that all I have ever charged, and more too, to be abundantly proved. I hope an investigation will be had.[73]

Banks denied that he had any personal objection to the New York *World's* New Orleans correspondence. It is entirely possible, however, that the hostile criticisms, published in the *World,* of Banks's management of the campaign caused the *World* correspondent Philip Ripley to be expelled from New Orleans even before Banks returned from the Red River country.[74]

At least one newspaper correspondent, Young of the Philadelphia *Press,* was convinced that full justice had not been meted out to Banks in the press. In a letter to the General expressing appreciation for "the many kindnesses you showed me when in your department," Young informed him that upon returning to Philadelphia early in May:

> I found that the most exaggerated and absurd stories had arrived here in reference to your expedition, generally from the Chicago papers. They have gone to England,—and I see the London Times has an absurd article, about all the "headquarters champagne" being lost and other matters of equally ridiculous import. My own account of the battles,—which was the first published, and was copied over the country, has been denounced as unfair

and partisan, and more of an apology than a description, although my own conviction is that if I did any injustice at all, it was to you and your army.

I have written one article on your campaign, in the way of defence which I send you. From the present tone of public opinion and the misinformation that exists about your whole campaign, it is as bold as I could venture to make it. When the facts become more known, I intend to return to the subject for I feel an interest in the Department of the Gulf as great almost, as though I were its commander.[75]

While the storm of newspaper criticism of the Red River expedition descended upon everyone concerned, Porter's gunboats were utilizing every effort to extricate themselves from the trap which had resulted from Banks's precipitate retreat. During the month which had elapsed since the fleet's departure from Alexandria, the river had fallen six feet. By the end of April only three feet and four inches of water was in the channel and the gunboats drew seven feet; moreover, the channel had become extremely narrow.

It was General Franklin's chief engineer, Lieutenant Colonel Joseph Bailey, who rescued Porter from his plight. Bailey's project involved the construction of a number of wing dams across a strip of water seven hundred feet wide to raise the level of the river and to make it possible to float the gunboats over the rapids. Although the magnitude of the operation was such that no private construction company would have undertaken to accomplish it in less than six months, by May 12 the army engineers had constructed the dams to a sufficient height to permit the gunboats to pass below Alexandria. Eyewitness accounts of Bailey's thrilling exploit were published in the New Orleans *Times*,[76] the New Orleans *Era*,[77] and one or two other newspapers. Probably the most widely read story of the exploit, however, was Admiral Porter's official dispatch containing the essential facts, which was released to the press in time for publication on May 28, 1864. By that time most of the newspaper correspondents with Banks already had decided that the outlook for news in the trans-Mississippi theater was unpromising and had been transferred to other points.

Only the representatives of the New Orleans press and a few others remained behind to cover the concluding phase of the Red River expedition. Among them was a New York *Tribune* correspondent who described the disastrous fire which broke out in Alexandria on the morning of May 15, as the rear guard of Banks's army was evacuating the city and which lasted until the entire business district and nearly half of the residences in the town had been reduced to ashes. The *Tribune* correspondent attributed the fire to some "unknown incendiaries" possibly "jayhawkers."[78] From other sources came accusations that the fire had been started in various sections of the city almost simultaneously, by "some of our soldiers, both white and black, as if by general understanding."[79]

Although the banks of the Red River between Alexandria and Fort de Russy were lined with Confederate guerillas, the fleet reached the mouth of the Red River on May 21 without sustaining serious damage. By the time Banks reached Simsport, he already had learned that two days earlier he had been superseded by Major General Edward R. S. Canby, who had been placed in command of all forces West of the Mississippi.

The campaign was now at an end, "a fit sequel," as the St. Louis *Republican* correspondent viewed it, "to a scheme, conceived in politics and brought forth in iniquity."[80] There is little question that the press was substantially correct in viewing the Red River campaign as one of the most futile episodes of the war. It was perhaps fortunate for everyone connected with it that public attention already had been diverted to other subjects by the opening of Grant's Wilderness Campaign and Sherman's advance upon Atlanta while Banks still was retreating from the Red River country. Subsequently, the campaign in the Southwest came under the inquisitorial eye of the Congressional Joint Committee on the Conduct of the War, which concluded its investigation by placing upon Banks the major share of the blame for the disastrous outcome of the expedition.[81] One of the members of the committee, Daniel W. Gooch, however, took issue with the findings of the majority. In his opinion the unfavorable condition of river navigation and the limited time for which Sherman's troops were loaned deprived Banks of any reasonable chance for success.[82] So far as the cotton transactions alluded to by the army reporters were concerned, the report of the Joint Committee was substantially a whitewash job. As Admiral Porter subsequently commented:

> ... when they dug down their spades would strike some skull it was not desirable to disturb, and those who had charge of the investigations got over them as soon as possible.... In the exam-

ination before the committee on the war there was a very considerable amount of evidence and some "tall lying."[83]

During the Red River campaign, the newspaper reporters who accompanied the expedition were seriously handicapped by their lack of knowledge of the precise objects of the campaign and by Banks's hampering instructions. It seems clear that they overestimated the importance of the cotton speculators in bringing about the campaign in the first place. Yet much of the evidence which to them seemed conclusive is by no means insignificant, even though it might have proved inadmissable in a court of law. The press was deficient, however, at least in part, in its coverage of Banks's retreat from Pleasant Hill to Simsport and in its treatment of the naval side of the campaign from the very beginning. Nevertheless, considering the remoteness of the area in which the campaign was conducted and the consequent delays in transmission of news, these deficiencies are less surprising. It was only too clearly revealed by the press that there had been mismanagement in high places, and if newspaper reporters disagreed about who was primarily responsible, it is equally true that history gives a clouded verdict on this controversial affair.[84]

20

Into the Wilderness Again

ON the night of March 8, 1864, a special dispatch to the New York *Tribune* flashed over the wires from Washington to New York with some interesting news for the *Tribune*'s morning edition. At five o'clock the previous afternoon, the dispatch indicated, an officer leading a child by the hand had entered the dining room at Willard's "quietly and modestly" and had seated himself at the table alongside the other diners. A gentleman from New Orleans who recognized the officer had gone over to shake hands, and as if by electric communication the news spread through the dining room that the hero of Belmont, Donelson, and Vicksburg was in the room. Senators, representatives, staid supreme court justices, along with the hundreds of other guests, had sprung from their seats and cheered "in the most tremendous manner" for Lieutenant General Grant. There had been another demonstration when the General left the room after his meal, and the *Tribune*'s dispatch reported that his retreat up the staircase to his room from the great crowd that awaited him in the lower hall was characterized by "most unsoldierly blushing."[1]

The man who inspired this popular demonstration had arrived in Washington only a few hours before to replace Halleck as General in Chief of the Armies of the United States. Long afterward, the Sacramento *Union* correspondent, Noah Brooks, recalled the scene at the White House that night when the new arrival from the Western army appeared at the President's reception:

> So great was the crowd, and so wild the rush to get near the general, that he was obliged at last to mount a sofa, where he could be seen, and where he was secure, at least for a time, from the madness of the multitude. People were caught up and whirled in the torrent which swept through the great East Room. Ladies suffered dire disaster in the crush and confusion; their laces were

torn and crinolines mashed; and many got upon sofas, chairs, and tables to be out of harm's way or to get a better view of the spectacle. It was the only real mob I ever saw in the White House.[2]

Military activity in the East had been nearly at a standstill since the Mine Run fiasco of the previous November. During January, 1864, while the Army of the Potomac was still in winter quarters near Culpeper, an English newspaperman, George A. Sala of the London *Daily Telegraph*, had come down from Washington with a friend who made frequent business trips to the army. The routine of army life had long since ceased to have any interest for most reporters, but Sala, a recent arrival in this country, was considerably impressed by the large amount of railroad rolling stock which had been ruined by the enemy and was left lying about to gather rust; by the enormous number of dead horses scattered about the camp; by the mud, which "seemed to me . . . explanatory of much of the dilatoriness and over-caution attributed to General M'Clellan;" and by the bell tents in which the soldiers slept, "eight or ten under one canvas roof."[3] In outlying military commands, Sala commented, there was a great deal of quiet hanging and shooting of marauders, but not so in the Army of the Potomac, where not even flogging was permitted. In Sala's opinion, this army was too near Washington and the "hydra-headed, Argus-eyed, Dionysius-eared, multi-tongued New York press" to let pass unnoticed such high-handed specimens of justice.[4]

On the day before Grant reached Washington, the New York *Times* had carried an exclusive story, written by its correspondent Edward A. Paul, of the most important news event in the Virginia war theater since the beginning of the year. Paul had been the only newspaper correspondent to accompany General Judson Kilpatrick when he crossed the Rapidan on the night of February 28 with four thousand cavalrymen and a battery of horse artillery and headed straight for the Confederate capital. Kilpatrick had planned to enter Richmond from the North with the main body of his command and to unite with a detachment which was coming up from the South to release the Union captives in the Richmond war prisons. Once this was effected, he was to make tracks for the nearest Federal lines before an effective pursuit could be organized. According to the *Times*, its correspondent had been familiar with the project from the beginning, had taken an active and useful part in making preparations for it, and had seen all the orders, directions, and other papers connected with it.[5]

Although the treachery of a guide defeated the main object of the expedition, Kilpatrick did penetrate the outer defenses of Richmond, damaged some communication and supply lines, and managed to reach Butler's lines on the Peninsula in safety with the greater part of his command. Referring to the publicity which the expedition received before it was well under way, Correspondent Paul remarked:

> It is undoubtedly true that a great many people knew that there was a movement on foot of some kind, but of what kind, or which way it was to go, or its destination, it seems nearly every one was in ignorance. The enemy knew nothing of the matter, and the correspondents in the field and at Washington, from the different publications in the papers, it is quite certain knew but little more than the rebels. One paper recounts, in fearful terms, how that owing to the indiscretion of some nameless person, the enemy had met Kilpatrick in superior force at the very inauguration of the movement, and fears were entertained for the safety of the command. This class of correspondents show how much knowledge they had of the affair by still persisting in the statement that Kilpatrick left Stevensburgh on Saturday evening, when, without much trouble, they might have known that he did not move until Sunday night. . . . So skillfully managed, indeed, was the whole affair, that the announcement of Gen. Kilpatrick crossing the Rapidan was made in the Richmond papers on the very day he arrived before that city.[6]

Now that Grant was in Washington ready to formulate a unified plan of operation for all the armies in the field, the press was eager to know whether Meade would remain in command of the Eastern army. From the Associated Press, the country learned shortly after Grant's arrival that a recent attack of pneumonia would prevent the victor of Gettysburg from undertaking another campaign in the field. Three days later, on March 14, the New York *Times* printed a special dispatch from Washington which stated flatly that:

> notwithstanding the persistent denials, Gen. Meade is to be superseded in command of the Army of the Potomac. The order relieving him, and appointing his successor, will be issued in a few days.[7]

Both the *Times* and the Associated Press were wrong. After conferring with Meade, who seemed perfectly willing to step down, Grant requested him to remain in command of the army—not an altogether satisfactory arrangement since the General in Chief already had decided to accompany the army in person during the coming campaign.

About this time the long-standing feud between the War Department and the press was brought to a head by an order from Secretary Stanton specifying that no civilians other than those already there would be allowed to be at the front.[8] Every correspondent of the New York *Tribune* accredited to the Army of the Potomac happened to be in Washington on the day the order was made public. Unless Stanton chose to reverse himself, the *Tribune* would be deprived of any news coverage from the army for an indefinite period. Sam Wilkeson, chief of the *Tribune*'s Washington bureau once more, was in a fine rage when he heard of the order. He swore that any correspondent who did not furnish him with dispatches from the army within forty-eight hours would be discharged. At first nobody budged. Stanton would certainly place under arrest any man caught violating his decree. Finally, Henry Wing, a reporter from Connecticut who had been recently taken on by the *Tribune* in some subordinate capacity, dared one of the regular correspondents of the paper, T. C. Grey, to run the blockade with him. After a precarious journey of some sixty miles, they slipped through the Union picket line unobserved and found sanctuary in camp. Wing's companion was now perfectly safe, as his credentials were in his pocket, but Wing himself was unaccredited. As soon as Wilkeson learned of his courageous action, however, he appointed Wing a correspondent of the New York *Tribune* with the Army of the Potomac.[9]

On March 26, Grant established his headquarters at Culpeper and began to make preparations for a trial of strength with Lee. Meanwhile, the press was making preparations for its spring campaign. David G. Croly, managing editor of the *World*, on March 21 had written to Manton Marble:

> It is now clear that the great military interest of the ensuing campaign will centre with the Army of the Potomac. I want the World to be well represented while the fighting is going on and one man is certainly not enough especially as he also is employed on another paper. With your consent I would like to send Mr. Stillson[10] to the army. He is willing to go and I am certain it will be the cheapest and most satisfactory arrangement that could be made. He has written some admirable military letters and knows just what we want. . . . My plan is to give him twenty five dollars a week and his expenses, promote Kennett to the temporary night

> editorship at eighteen dollars per week and get Cary to do Kennetts and his own work for Sixteen dollars—one more than he gets at present. . . .
>
> If you think the matter over you will see that it adds only eleven dollars to the present regular expenses while hiring another correspondent would cost at least twenty dollars and then he might not give satisfaction while we *know* Stillson will.[11]

Marble approved Croly's suggestion, and soon Stillson, equipped with a pass signed by General Meade himself, was on his way to the army. By the time the campaign had gotten under way, every one of the leading New York papers, with the possible exception of the *World*, had at least six correspondents, duly accredited or otherwise, with the Army South of the Rapidan.[12]

While Grant and Meade were at work on their plans for the spring campaign, a small army of newspapermen hovered about headquarters, where they hoped to find something of public interest to write about. The members of the reportorial corps were billeted in an old farmhouse near Brandy Station. The owners had gone South to escape the contaminating influence of their uninvited guests, and had left the place in the charge of two servants, whom the Negroes classed as "white trash." Among the journalists who whiled away their time—reading, smoking, singing, and story-telling—at the bedraggled homestead were Francis C. Long of the New York *Herald*, Byington and Page of the *Tribune*, R. D. Francis of the New York *World*, Cunnington, Crapsey, and Bower of the Philadelphia *Inquirer*, and the Boston *Journal* reporter Coffin.[13]

Shortly before the Army left Culpeper to take the field, the War Department issued an order providing that army correspondents must be registered as such at army headquarters.[14] Thenceforth passes were not to be issued prior to such registration, which, it was stipulated, must be done in person. The practical effect of this rule was that even though a reporter had to be in the army to be registered he could not leave Washington to go to the army until he *was* registered. Telegraphic correspondence with provost marshals at the front and queries addressed to officials at the War Department befogged the issue still further. Finally, the problem was submitted to the President himself, who straightway called in a half-dozen reporters, granted unconditional passes to them, and related an appropriate anecdote.[15]

On May 2, 1864, the day before the Army broke camp, Sylvanus Cadwallader, formerly of the Chicago *Times*, reached Culpeper to take over his new duties as chief correspondent of the New York *Herald* with the Army of the Potomac. On the following day he wrote to the managing editor of the *Herald*, reporting that all arrangements for good news coverage had been made insofar as it was possible to make them under existing circumstances. He announced:

> Have bought a horse at what may appear a rather high figure, but he is worth the money, and is beyond dispute the most Stylish horse in the Army of the Potomac. . . . Mr. Chapman came as far as Gen. Meades Hd Qrs today. Mr. Anderson is in Culpepper. Hancock seems to have no *Herald* Cor. with him. Saw Mr. N. Davidson, and Mr. Hendricks this evening. Both are prepared for any emergency.[16]

The afternoon of that same day, the correspondents at headquarters became aware that something was in the wind. They noticed unusual movements among the officers, and every correspondent was alerted to signs of an advance. At about supper time that evening, official notice was given that the army would strike its tents at midnight. The journalistic encampment became a scene of activity and excitement. As Cunnington of the Philadelphia *Inquirer* described it:

> Haversacks were packed and repacked; blankets that had done duty on our cots were torn off and rolled up and strapped into light bundles; note books were put in order; pencils, pens and pen knives were hunted up; whatever articles of food could be obtained were secured and crowded into our pockets or knapsacks; hasty notes and letters to the "loved ones at home" were written and mailed, for no one could tell when the next opportunity to communicate with them would present itself; hearty hand-shakings and expressions of good will and friendship passed between all of us, for we were going on an unknown voyage and knew not what the morrow might bring forth . . . our horses (or those that had them) were brought out and hastily groomed and saddled; the blankets were secured to the saddles and haversacks thrown over our shoulders; our pants were tucked into our army boots; we paid our scores to the man in charge of the old farm house, and mounting our horses we were ready for operations.[17]

All correspondents were under instructions to write nothing for publication until after a battle had been fought.

The Federal commander's main objective in this campaign was Lee's army, not Richmond. Before he came East, Grant had favored a movement upon the Confederate Capital from South of the James River; this would force the enemy to fight for Richmond's all-important lines of communication. Subsequently Grant decided on the overland route instead, which involved crossing the Rapidan to turn Lee's right flank, thereby interposing the Army of the Potomac between the Confederate army and Richmond. The success of such a movement depended upon the speed with which it was executed and the element of surprise. If Grant were able to get across the Rapidan and push through the Wilderness before Lee could strike, he was assured a smashing victory. Meanwhile, according to Grant's plan, Sherman was to move from Chattanooga against Atlanta, Crook in West Virginia was to strike for the Kanawha and the Virginia and Tennessee Railroad, while Sigel was to operate in the Shenandoah Valley, and Butler with thirty thousand men was to ascend the James River from Fortress Monroe, take Petersburg, and press on toward Richmond.[18]

"Phil" Sheridan, with two of his cavalry divisions, led the advance. Then Hancock's second corps, together with Gregg's cavalry division, crossed the Rapidan at Ely's Ford and pushed on to Chancellorsville, arriving there at nine o'clock on Wednesday morning, May 4. A few hours later the Fifth Corps under Warren crossed the river at Germanna Ford and marched to the Old Wilderness Tavern, an important road junction, where the corps remained overnight. Sedgwick's Sixth Corps, following Warren's route, encamped that night just South of the Rapidan. Thus far the movement had been a success; no opposition to the crossing had materialized.

Had not its great wagon train held up the Army of the Potomac, it might have been out of the Wilderness on the morning of the fifth and in a favorable position to meet a possible counter stroke by Lee. Instead, fighting in the dense undergrowth of the Wilderness began the morning of May 5, when Ewell's corps, advancing eastward along the turnpike from Orange Court House, caught sight of Warren's corps crossing the turnpike up ahead. The action developed into a general engagement as Sedgwick fell into line on Warren's right and Hancock came hurrying back from Todd's Tavern to join in the conflict. In the tangled underbrush, artillery was of little use, and maneuvering was impossible; officers were unable to see more than a part of their commands. During the afternoon, Hancock's corps gained a temporary advantage on Lee's right flank, which was weakened by the absence of

Longstreet's corps, but when night fell no decisive advantage had been gained by either side.

Page's *Tribune* battle account, written at nine o'clock that night, gave a vivid picture of what such fighting was like:

> The work was at close range. No room in that jungle for maneuvering; no possibility of a bayonet charge, no help from artillery; no help from cavalry; nothing but close, square, severe, face-to-face volleys of fatal musketry. The wounded stream out, and fresh troops pour in. Stretchers pass out with ghastly burdens, and go back reeking with blood for more. Word is brought that the ammunition is failing. Sixty rounds fired in one steady stand-up fight, and that fight not fought out. Boxes of cartridges are placed on the returning stretchers, and the struggle shall not cease for want of ball and powder. Do the volleys grow nearer, or do our fears make them seem so? It must be so, for a second line is rapidly formed just where we stand, and the bullets slip singing by as they have not done before, while now and then a limb drops from the tree-tops. . . . But we stay them. . . . Yes, we hold them, and the fresh men going in will drive them. I ride back to General Headquarters, and learn that an advance has been ordered an hour ago along the whole line.[19]

While the fighting was still going on, the *Herald* correspondent Cadwallader obtained permission from Colonel Charles F. Johnson, the provost guard commander, to pass among the Confederate prisoners and to learn if possible whether Longstreet had yet come in from his camp South of Gordonsville to reinforce Lee. Cadwallader had acquired a roster of the Confederate army. Once he had learned the regiment and state to which a prisoner belonged, he would be in a position to obtain the information he was looking for without putting the question direct.

While he was interrogating the prisoners, he was discovered by the Provost Marshal General of the Army, a pompous old martinet named Marcellus R. Patrick, who straightway directed a staff officer to arrest Cadwallader. When the *Herald* reporter was brought before Patrick, he scowled at Cadwallader and fairly shouted,

"Who are you, sir? What were you doing among the prisoners?"

"Trying to learn to what commands they belonged," replied the correspondent uneasily.

"Young man, I think you have not been long in this army," orated the general in a patronizing manner.

"Thank God, I have not," blurted out Cadwallader.

"Who gave you permission to go among those prisoners, sir?" thundered the general, who by this time had worked himself up into a fine rage.

Cadwallader explained that Colonel Johnson had authorized him to do so, but Patrick would not believe him, and so the colonel was called over for questioning. When Patrick learned that Johnson really had given Cadwallader the specified permission, he also placed the colonel under arrest. Then, turning to the *Herald* man, Patrick asked him by what authority the reporter was with the army. Cadwallader presented several passes bearing General Grant's signature, but, without examining them, Patrick jammed the passes into his pockets and ordered a file of soldiers to march the correspondent to the "bull pen."

Fortunately for Cadwallader, Colonel William L. Duff, Grant's chief of artillery, was passing by, and the *Herald* correspondent appealed to him. After listening to what the correspondent had to say, Colonel Duff rose in his stirrups and demanded of Patrick with a frown:

"Do you know me, General Patrick?"

"You are Colonel Duff of General Grant's staff," replied the Provost Marshal General sullenly.

"Release this man instantly and return his papers," Duff told him and then rode off without further comment. Patrick complied, for he had no other alternative; Cadwallader, on the other hand, had reason to congratulate himself that he had gotten off so easily.[20]

That night both armies prepared to renew the struggle. Meade was convinced that the main body of Lee's command had fallen back to the North Anna and that the others were simply fighting a delaying action. Nevertheless, Grant had telegraphed Burnside on the afternoon of the fourth to make a forced march to Germanna Ford, and by the night of May 5 three divisions of Burnside's Ninth Corps were across the river and ready to take part in the next day's fighting.

On Friday morning, May 6, Hancock attacked the Confederate right with great force and, inflicting heavy losses, drove it back across the Plank Road. Longstreet's corps arrived just in time to stem the Union advance, however, and Hancock was forced to give ground as Longstreet advanced in turn. Then while the battle line alternately advanced and receded through the briar thickets, Longstreet fell as Jackson had, pierced by the bullets of his own men. Lee came up in a few moments and personally assumed command of the attack, but it was not pressed vigorously. Later in the afternoon Ewell made a similar attack on the Union right and drove Sedgwick's corps from its position shortly before nightfall. On both sides the casualties had been tremendous.

"We've had a most bitterly contested battle—," Byington told Gay in a letter written the following afternoon, "really *worse* than Gettysburg inasmuch as the *bullet* has been more destructive than artillery." During the two-day battle, newsgathering had been fraught with unusual difficulties. This was no open field engagement, such as Gettysburg or the battles on the Peninsula, but, in Coffin's words, "one of the greatest bush fights the world ever saw."[21] In such terrain it was next to impossible to follow the movements of regiments and brigades or even to gather details about an unseen conflict. Several of the army reporters made their rendezvous in a shady little dell in the rear of the Fifth Corps, near the extreme right flank of the battle line. Both mornings they rode toward the shifting front line and spent the day, notebook in hand, gathering what information they could about the fearful struggle. At the end of the day they returned to the same secluded dell, where they exchanged information, and by candlelight, wrote up their accounts for mail and courier transmittal to their newspaper offices.[22] In spite of such difficulties, several creditable newspaper accounts of the fighting in the Wilderness were published, notably those of Coffin, Swinton, and Page.[23] The *Army and Navy Journal* observed editorially:

> If our space permitted, we should reprint other of Mr. Swinton's letters, which deserve publication in some more permanent form than in the columns of a daily newspaper.[24]

Unfortunately, the army high command did not share this good opinion of Mr. Swinton. On the evening following the first (or possibly the second) day's fighting in the Wilderness, General Meade with several of his staff officers came to Grant's headquarters. While the two generals conferred, members of their staffs retired to the campfire some distance from the front of the tent in order to assure privacy for the interview. Then one of the staff officers noticed a man lying on the ground near the entrance to the tent and listening to the conversation of Meade and Grant. The eavesdropper proved to be Swinton of the New York *Times*.

After a vigorous crossexamination he was turned loose with a warning not to repeat the offense.[25]

Although a New York *Tribune* reporter was the first to reach Washington[26] with an account of the fighting in the Wilderness, President Lincoln himself deprived that paper of a scoop.[27] During the first three days which followed the crossing of the Rapidan, no definite information—official or otherwise—about the fate of Grant's army was made public. That army had vanished into the Wilderness without a trace, leaving behind only rumors of disaster to agitate the public mind. On May 5, several New York newspapers issued extras announcing that Burnside's corps had been badly beaten and practically wiped out. Benumbed with anxiety, the public waited for more authentic information. On Friday evening, May 6, President Lincoln stopped in, as he often did, at the telegraph office in the War Department to pick up the latest news. There he learned from the operator that a correspondent of the New York *Tribune* was at Union Mills, about twenty miles out of Washington, and a little while before had telegraphed a request to talk with Dana. Dana was not there at the time, and Stanton had not only denied the reporter permission to send a telegram to the *Tribune* but had demanded that he turn over his message to the War Department instead. The *Tribune* man had refused to do this unless his terms were agreed to in advance. Thoroughly exasperated, Stanton had denounced the reporter as a spy and had ordered him to be shot the next morning.

Lincoln was incredulous. "Ordered him shot?" he repeated.

"Yes, Mr. President," replied the operator.

Lincoln thought a moment, then said, "Ask him if he will talk with the President."

The answer was affirmative. Henry E. Wing, the *Tribune* correspondent, said he would be glad to tell the President what he knew if he might first send one hundred words to the *Tribune*. To this Lincoln agreed, saying, "Write your hundred words and we will send it at once." An hour later, a military train with the Assistant Secretary of War aboard was on the way to Union Mills. After talking with Wing, Dana was to go on through to the army if possible, while Wing proceeded to Washington by special train. In the meantime, the one-hundred word message had been received at the War Department, and by Lincoln's order a summary of it had been made available to the Associated Press in order to alleviate public anxiety.[28]

Into the Wilderness Again

Between one and two o'clock on Saturday morning, May 7, Wing arrived in Washington and went at once to the White House, where he found the Cabinet in session and awaiting his arrival. "You are Henry Wing from Litchfield, are you not?" said Gideon Welles, the Secretary of the Navy, who recognized him as a constituent. A further question was in the mind of each man: when and where had Wing left Grant and what did he have to tell them.

Wing had actually very little more information than he already had communicated in his message. To the assembled Cabinet members he described the crossing of the Rapidan and told how Hancock's corps, which he had accompanied, on Wednesday, May 4, had penetrated near Chancellorsville into open country suitable for a battle. Then Hancock's corps had entrenched, waiting for the other corps to come up. Instead, Lee had come out of his entrenchments on Thursday morning and had attacked while half the Union army was still entangled in the Wilderness. At headquarters that night no one knew exactly how the battle had gone. All that could be said was that the Army of the Potomac was still on the South side of the Rapidan and that Grant had ordered an attack for the next morning, Friday, May 6.

Wing was asked when he had left the battlefield.

"At four o'clock Friday morning," he replied.

"Then you know nothing of what has happened in the last twenty-four hours?" Their disappointment was obvious.

As Wing shook his head slowly, the members of the Cabinet rose and, bowing silently to their chief, filed out of the room. The President looked inquiringly at Wing, who seemed loath to depart.

"You wanted to speak to me?" he asked.

"Yes, Mr. President. I have a message for you—a message from General Grant. He told me I was to give it to you when you were alone."

"Something from Grant to me?"

"Yes," Wing replied without hesitation. "He told me I was to tell you, Mr. President, that there would be no turning back." Grant had led him aside just as he was about to leave headquarters on Friday morning and had charged him with this message.

This was such a message as Lincoln had been waiting for through three long years of war. Impulsively he passed his long arm around Wing's shoulders and kissed his cheek. "Come and tell me about it," he said gently, and indicated a chair near him.

After they sat down, Wing poured out his pent-up feelings. He tried to tell the President all the things he needed to know about that bloody day in the Wilderness—men fighting in little groups, not knowing where they were going; the lack of coordination between Hancock and Warren, and Warren left without support—a day gone wrong from start to finish. He described the scene at headquarters Thursday night where one officer after another indulged in accusations and countercharges. According to Wing, Meade even had proposed that the Army of the Potomac withdraw to the North bank of the Rapidan, but Grant had vetoed the suggestion, saying "we shall attack again in the morning."

Finally about four o'clock that Saturday morning, the President brought the interview to an end with a request that the reporter come back to see him that afternoon. The exhausted Wing stumbled down the street from the White House to the corner of Sixth Street and Pennsylvania Avenue. There, without taking the trouble to undress, he threw himself across one of the National Hotel's beds and fell asleep. Hardly had he closed his eyes, however, when he was awakened by the insistent cries of the newsboys, summoning the world to read the story which he had been at pains to furnish exclusively to the *Tribune.* Wing leaped from the bed, dashed out of the hotel, and raced down Pennsylvania Avenue for the *Tribune* office on Fourteenth Street.

Elbowing his way through the crowd which filled the street in front of the *Tribune* office, Wing saw his chief, Sam Wilkeson, standing on a table and telling everyone within earshot that the news was a "fake," that Wing was not in Washington, and that somebody—possibly a speculator—was trying to fool the public.

"Here I am, Mr. Wilkeson!" shouted Wing as he struggled to reach the front of the crowd. Impulsively, the crowd caught up the diminutive reporter and passed him over their heads to Wilkeson's table. Once more he had to repeat his story, especially his encounter with Stanton and his narrow escape from execution. Even though the *Tribune* had lost its scoop, Wilkeson was pleased to hear that one of his own staff had outwitted Stanton, the archenemy of the newspapermen. The crowd, sharing his feeling, immediately took up a collection to be presented to this new hero.

At the White House later in the day, Wing told Lincoln that he was leaving for Warrenton right away to recover his horse, Jess. Wing had had to leave the horse behind, tied in a thicket, when the guerillas began to close in. By the President's order Wing was provided with a train and escort from Alexandria so that he might make the trip with a reasonable degree of safety.

Even so, hostile scouts fired on the train after it reached Manassas Junction, and from there on the escort had to fight every mile of the way to the point where Wing could begin to search for his horse. Anxiously the *Tribune* correspondent picked his way through the thicket to the place where his calculations told him the horse must be. And there indeed Jess was, as Wing had left him, head erect, watching for the return of his master. It was a happy train party which, triumphantly bearing the horse with them, returned to Washington that night.

Meanwhile, several "gentlemen of the ravenous pen," Reid, Painter, Wilkeson, among others, had planned a big day on Monday in honor of "Jess." The *Tribune* had arranged to present the faithful animal to Wing as his own permanent possession, and money was being raised by popular subscription to purchase for presentation to the correspondent the finest bridle and saddle which the town afforded. At ten o'clock on Monday morning, Lincoln and several members of his Cabinet met on the White House lawn to inspect the famous steed and his new trophies.[29] By this time the news blackout had been lifted. Official information finally had come through from Grant. It was as Wing had indicated: the Army of the Potomac had not turned back; it was still going forward, albeit at a heavy cost of human life.[30]

A mishap which befell two of its reporters deprived the *Herald* of anything more than a very meager account of the two-day struggle in the Wilderness. At three o'clock on Saturday afternoon, May 7, Cadwallader and a fellow *Herald* man, James C. Fitzpatrick, taking with them full reports of the fighting and a complete list of casualties up to that time, left army headquarters for Washington. Near Ely's Ford, they were overtaken by Edward Crapsey of the Philadelphia *Inquirer*, who had heard that they had started for Washington and had determined to ride off after them. At Ely's the trio of reporters learned that no trains of wounded were ready to be sent forward under cavalry escort, so they decided to push on alone for Rappahannock Station, twenty-five miles distant. There they hoped to make rail connections for Washington. At nightfall they were still some distance from their destination, and, as there was no moonlight, the route ahead looked gloomy and forbidding. Thoughts of "rebs," robbers, and Libby Prison flitted through their minds as they jogged wearily along. At a turn in the road, they were hailed by a squad of infantry approaching from the opposite direction. Obeying the order to "halt and advance singly," they breathed somewhat more easily when they learned that their challengers were Union soldiers who had become separated from their command and were pushing ahead to rejoin it. They had seen no rebels along the road, the soldiers said, and did not think there were any in the vicinity.

Not more than fifty yards from the spot where the reporters had parleyed with the infantrymen, however, five mounted men plunged into the road from the thicket that skirted it on either side. "Surrender, give up your arms, speak and you die" was the persuasive advice which the riders gave the frightened reporters. Unarmed and defenseless, the reporters could only stand by while one of the bold riders satisfied himself that they were indeed without weapons. Taking their horses by the reins, he then led the reporters through an open space of ground to some timber in the distance. There they were compelled to dismount and to submit to further examination. Their captors paid little attention to Cadwallader's explanation that they were newspaper correspondents, not belligerents in any sense, and therefore should be allowed to proceed to Washington unmolested. But the Confederate cavalrymen did read eagerly the reports of Thursday's fighting. The capture of these reports they seemed to think most important, and they expressed their astonishment at the amount of labor that had been expended in compiling the lists of casualties.

Later that night, after what seemed an endless ride through dark forests, deep ravines, blind paths, and deserted farms, the newspapermen were permitted to sleep for a few hours at the home of a Mr. Stringfellow near Cold Spring. At breakfast the next morning they learned from the captain of the party that he was going to take them to Fredericksburg and there turn them over to the Confederate general, Fitzhugh Lee. On the way, the cavalcade was stopped about six miles from Fredericksburg by a bushwhacker who informed the cavalrymen that Lee was not at Fredericksburg, but the "Yanks" were! While Stuart's men were pondering where to go next, they became involved in a skirmish with a squad of wounded Union soldiers on their way to Aquia Creek. In the melee, the reporters managed to make their escape, leaving behind them their money, papers, and even part of their clothing. After a long trek across country which taxed their endurance to the limit, they reached the Potomac near Aquia Creek about nine o'clock Monday morning.

Realizing that the vessels passing upstream from Fortress Monroe rarely answered signals from the Virginia side of the river, the fugitive newspapermen set to work constructing a nondescript marine craft. By noon they were embarked on the Potomac, heading northward. An hour or so later, they were overtaken by the government transport "Rebecca Barton" and given free transportation to Washington, where they undertook to reconstruct their battle accounts from memory.[31]

The failure of the *Herald* staff to match Wing's dazzling exploit was peculiarly galling to Bennett. Along Newspaper Row sped the story that the sardonic Scot had telegraphed his Washington correspondent *five* times on the Saturday after Wing's dispatch appeared in the *Tribune*. In a letter written to Gay five days afterward, Byington added the gleeful note:

> ... & the only way they could pacify the old Caledonian was by insisting that it was a *canard*. Phild. Enquirer man told me & says Whiteley said to him he expected to be discharged, though not at all to blame & that *Chapman,* his army man had got to go sure. It hurt him bad enough to be beaten at Gettysburg but to be distanced *four times in succession since,* was more than he could bear!

After the bloody fighting in the Wilderness had subsided, Lee, and probably most of the army correspondents as well, expected Grant and Meade to retreat, as other commanders of the Army of the Potomac had done on similar occasions in the past. Instead, on the morning of May 7, Grant issued orders for the army to execute a night march to Spotsylvania Court House, a strategic point on the direct road to Richmond. This was intended to be a surprise movement, but Lee sensed his adversary's purpose in time. When the vanguard of the Union forces reached Spotsylvania on the morning of the eighth, it found Lee's men already on the ground, barring the way. Once more there was desperate fighting for several days.

On May 9, General Sedgwick was killed in the van of his troops. On the tenth, the Federal losses alone exceeded four thousand men; among the wounded that day was the *Herald* correspondent Finley Anderson, who only three months before had returned from a year's captivity in a Southern prison.[32]

At eleven o'clock the evening of May 10, Coffin reined up in front of Grant's headquarters, dismounted, and entered Grant's tent. There he found the General with his old friend, Congressman Washburne, who had been with the army since the beginning of the campaign. Coffin asked the Commanding General whether he had any comment to make about the fighting that day. Grant replied with his customary frankness:

> We have had hard fighting to-day, and, I am sorry to say, have not accomplished much. We have lost a good many men, and I suppose I shall be blamed for it.

He was silent for a moment and then added:

> I do not know of any way to put down this Rebellion and restore the authority of the Government except by fighting, and fighting means that men must be killed. If the people of this country expect that the war can be conducted to a successful issue in any other way than by fighting, they must get somebody other than myself to command the army.[33]

The first success of any kind was achieved on the morning of May 12 when Hancock launched a surprise assault at the apex of the Bloody Angle, a salient projecting from the center of the Confederate line. Misled by reports that Grant was preparing to make another flank march, Lee had made the almost fatal error of withdrawing a large portion of his artillery from the salient the evening before. During the first stage of Hancock's attack, Johnson's division of Ewell's corps was almost wiped out. Later Johnson himself was captured along with four thousand of his men and twenty cannon.

Recognizing the danger, Lee pulled reinforcements into the salient from both flanks and threw in his reserves. Terrific fighting continued throughout the day and even until after midnight, but Hancock's men failed to achieve a real break-through beyond the captured salient. At noon the following day Swinton wrote:

> Nothing during the war has equaled the savage desperation of this struggle . . . and the scene of the conflict, from which I have just come, presents a spectacle of horror that curdles the blood of the boldest. The angle of the works at which Hancock entered, and for the possession of which the savage fight of the day was made, is a perfect Golgotha. In this angle of death the dead and wounded rebels lie, this morning, literally in piles—men in the

> agonies of death groaning beneath the dead bodies of their comrades. On an area of a few acres in rear of their position, lie not less than a thousand rebel corpses, many literally torn to shreds by hundreds of balls, and several with bayonet thrusts through and through their bodies, pierced on the very margins of the parapet, which they were determined to retake or perish in the attempt. The one exclamation of every man who looks on the spectacle is, "God forbid that I should ever gaze upon such a sight again."[34]

Earlier that morning of May 13, the Philadelphia *Inquirer* reporter, William H. Cunnington, had started for Washington with an account of the previous day's fighting. In order to reach Fredericksburg, the army base, Cunnington had to walk twelve miles through guerilla-infested country. From Fredericksburg he rode fourteen miles farther to Belle Plain, where he caught a North-bound steamer which brought him to the Capital late that night. As soon as the vessel docked, he headed for the wharf and dashed up Seventh Street toward the Washington telegraph office. Fortunately it was still open, and within a few moments his story of Hancock's charge was speeding over the wires to Philadelphia. Cunnington's story fittingly climaxed a historic day in the Washington telegraph office. That day the American Telegraph Company had transmitted fifty-eight thousand seven hundred fifty words to the nation's press, the largest number that had been sent to the press in a single day.

Cunnington then caught the morning train to Philadelphia and busied himself enroute in writing up a supplementary account of the action to be used in a later edition of the *Inquirer.*[35] His report of the first substantial success achieved by the Army of the Potomac since the beginning of the campaign was a considerable scoop. In a telegram to Painter, W. W. Harding said:

> The town [Philadelphia] is more excited today than any day since bull Run, and the victory of inquirer being first to publish the news is as great as the news is splendid & grand. It was a clean, clear, & complete beat of the other papers. . . . Spare no efforts of time or money to keep the Inquirer ahead.[36]

When the newspaper accounts of Hancock's charge were delivered to the army a few days later, the ranks of Barlow's First Division resented the way in which the press had slighted their performance. To General Birney's division, which had been associated with Barlow's men in the attack, the *Herald* gave all the credit for the success.[37] At the request of the soldiers who felt they had been overlooked, Charles A. Page of the New York *Tribune* tried to make it clear that:

> The main assault was made, and the chief success gained by Gen. Barlow's division.
>
> This is from Hancock's own lips, and will appear in his report. Not that there need be any detraction from Birney's work. His division was out next, not attacking so soon and going in on the flank. While it participates in the honor, to Gen. Barlow's Division attaches the highest credit.[38]

Possibly Page was too zealous an advocate, or perhaps Hancock discovered some new facts which were not in his possession when he talked to the *Tribune* correspondent. At any rate, his official report, submitted several months later, contented itself with stating that the two divisions entered the enemy's works "almost at the same moment."[39]

Probably the best account of the Battles of Spotsylvania which appeared anywhere in the Southern press was that written for the London *Morning Herald*. This account was written by the *Herald*'s correspondent, an English civil engineer named M. Butt Hewson, and was published by consent in the Richmond *Enquirer* on May 31, 1864. The editor of the Charleston *Courier* thought Hewson's narrative of the grim carnage at Spotsylvania was the best battle account that had yet appeared during the war.[40]

About this time the correspondents in Grant's army solved a problem which had long bedevilled them. The newspapermen themselves at this stage of the war rarely had difficulty in getting enough to eat, but they found it almost impossible to obtain forage for their horses. What forage there was in the vicinity of the army belonged to the government. Since none of the military received more forage than was barely sufficient to take care of his animals, the reporters had to pay some officer's servant extortionate prices to keep their horses from starving.

One evening in May just after the Battles of Spotsylvania, some of the reporters gathered together to discuss the forage problem. Some one suggested that a committee be formed to wait upon Grant and acquaint him with their difficulty.

That same evening the committee hunted up the General and presented their case to him somewhat as follows:

> General, there are so many newspaper correspondents here with the Army of the Potomac. Every one of them has a horse, and these horses, as a rule, get over more miles per day, and are subjected to harder service, than any others in the army. You know there is no forage down here except what belongs to the government, but you can see from the condition of our horses here, which are fair samples of all of them, that somehow they do get forage. What we have been deputed by all the correspondents to ask of you is that you will issue an order to all the quartermasters in the army to sell us forage, and furnish us transportation for it. We can nearly every evening get back to our source of supply, or know that we can not, and take rations for a day or two strapped behind the saddle.

Grant issued the order that night. From that time on until the end of the war the reporters' steeds fared sumptuously at less than any stable in the North would have charged, for the order permitted the correspondents to buy forage at no more than its cost to the government.[41]

Following the intense fighting on May 12, there had been a lull while Grant rested his men and brought up more troops. Another attack was unleashed on the seventeenth, but this was definitely a failure and was abandoned within two hours after it began. In a letter to Gay, dated the following evening, May 18, the *Tribune* correspondent T. C. Grey confessed that he was becoming discouraged with Grant and expressed the hope that some great and unexpected success might restore his confidence. "*Lee is a great general* and to-day Grant has stood seemingly baffled and undecided what to do."

Grant, however, had decided to discontinue these costly frontal attacks and to head for Hanover Court House, Northeast of Richmond. But once more Lee was too quick for him. Although Hancock had a start of twelve hours, when he reached the North Anna River on the forenoon of the twenty-third, he found the Confederates drawn up behind it and covering Richmond. Lee's position was too strong to attack. On the other hand, he was unwilling to undertake the offensive, for the Federals were strongly entrenched and besides the topography of the area favored the use of their powerful artillery. On May 27, therefore, Grant's army was in motion again, this time for the Pamunkey River and Cold Harbor.

Meanwhile it was becoming increasingly more obvious from the letters of the reporters attached to B. F. Butler's Army of the James that affairs were not going well in that department. After advancing up the

James River to within a few miles of Drewry's Bluff, Butler was attacked by Beauregard on May 15 and was driven back to Bermuda Hundred Neck. There, in General Grant's expressive phrase, he was "as completely shut off from further operations against Richmond as if he had been in a bottle strongly corked."[42] Thus checkmated by the enemy, Butler began quarreling with his corps commanders, Quincy A. Gillmore and W. F. ("Baldy") Smith.

Instead of remaining aloof from these controversies, the reporters took sides, thereby exposing themselves to reprisals. On May 22, the *Herald* correspondent at Fortress Monroe, William H. Stiner, advised the managing editor of his newspaper that:

> Sawyer gives great dissatisfaction & I should not be surprized if he was sent away—He is very unguarded in his language, and says to officers things which are uncalled for. Gilmore is deadly opposed to Butler & Sawyer seems to echo Gilmores sentiments. S. calls the campaign "Butler's blunders." Of course all this is reported at Hdqrs & tends to demoralize the troops.[43]

Since the *Herald* also received complaints from Sawyer about Stiner's "lickspittle style" and "awful lying," however, the newspaper's higher command took away from its representative at Fortress Monroe the function of forwarding to New York the correspondence from Butler's army.[44]

At the same time, moreover, the *Herald,* by an editorial published on May 25, added fresh fuel to the controversy between Butler and his uppish subordinate. From "authentic sources" the *Herald* had learned that Gillmore had advised Butler to "make his position secure by intrenchments" just before the disastrous reverse on the fifteenth and that Butler had replied that he "could not pause for defensive preparation." Suspecting the Tenth Corps commander had had a part in this newspaper attack, Butler sent his chief of staff over to Gillmore's headquarters with an inquiry: had Gillmore authorized the *Herald* story? Gillmore's disclaimer, which Butler promptly released to the press, evoked an interesting comment from Assistant Secretary of the Navy Fox. Fox told Butler:

> I am glad to see that you have brought up all standing—Gillmore's N. York correspondent. He had the same fellow to cry him up and Dahlgren down off Charleston, but Dahlgren did not understand managing such cases.[45]

During the first week or ten days of the Virginia campaign, the tone of the newspaper dispatches decidedly had been overoptimistic. On May 16 the Cincinnati *Gazette* had warned the public to:

> . . . place no credit in the sensational stories telegraphed to New York last night, and distributed by the Associated Press today, that Lee is retreating in wild disorder, that his retreat is becoming a rout, and the like.

A week later, the Washington correspondent of the Chicago *Tribune* called attention to the fact that telegraph dispatches sent all over the country by newspaper reporters in Washington and at the front—most of whom had allowed their imagination to run away with their judgment—had done incalculable harm by creating false hopes for the Army's performance.[46] In a letter published in the Boston *Journal* on May 24, Charles Carleton Coffin exclaimed:

> You have had a surfeit of news. In reading the papers which come to camp, I am completely puzzled. The accounts are confused, contradictory, extravagant, and in many instances incorrect. In the first place, you have all the wild speculations and rumors of Washington; of intelligence from the front *manufactured* by imaginative persons at the capital, who must send something to satisfy the hungry crowd at home. You have the rumors and stories brought from Belle Plain by steamboatmen and passengers, who can hear the distant booming of guns, and who supply all the facts of battle, of which they know nothing. You have the rumors and speculations of the camp; of correspondents who write up what they hear without investigating it. Last Friday I telegraphed you that we had possession of Spottsylvania Court House.
>
> The Assistant Secretary of War, who is with the army, telegraphs under date of May 13, that Lee was retreating and our army was in pursuit. Another correspondent telegraphs that our army is five miles beyond Spottsylvania Court House. None of these despatches were correct. My information was second hand, but I obtained it at headquarters from an official who ought to have known. . . . Instead of retreating as the Assistant Secretary telegraphed, and instead of being five miles beyond the Court House, the army has merely swung round to a new position.

Early in the campaign the War Department did issue daily news bulletins, summarizing the latest information received about the progress of the campaign. These dispatches, based on Dana's telegrams, were signed by Stanton and, although obstensibly addressed to General John A. Dix in New York, were in fact given directly to the Associated Press.[47] Overwhelming approval was the first reaction to this innovation.[48] The *Herald* opined that Stanton would make a first-rate war correspondent and extended him an invitation through its editorial columns to do some reporting for the *Herald* in Mexico after the war was over in case U.S. troops were needed there to expel the French.[49] Only afterwards, when Stanton's communications became less frequent, did press enthusiasm wane somewhat.[50]

As Grant's army was cutting loose from its base on the Rapidan and moving South from Spotsylvania, the problem of transmitting correspondence northward became increasingly more difficult. L. A. Whitely, the Washington correspondent of the *Herald,* reported to Frederic Hudson:

> Nearly all of our dispatches have come late at night or early in the morning, but we have pushed them through hoping they would be available for extras, if not for the regular edition.[51]

The hardships of the campaign, moreover, hardly could fail to lower the reporters' morale. On May 23, Croly informed Manton Marble that:

> Stillson goes back to the army though most unwillingly. I feel quite ashamed of him. After the money the office has spent and the little real good he has done I thought he would want to redeem himself, but he is a selfish fellow as I now see very clearly. He thought the expedition would be a fine frolic but there was more hard work than he bargained for.[52]

On the same day, the Philadelphia *Inquirer* correspondent Bower wrote to Painter from Bowling Green, Virginia, complaining that one of his colleagues had borrowed his horse and left him in exchange another "so baulky that I cannot get along with him unless he is in company with other horses." Bower continued:

> Where in the devil is George.[53] I want a change of clothing. I will not stand this life. I must have the proper support or I will not take the responsibility of getting you the earliest news. If a fight should occur today the Lord only knows how I would get it in.[54]

On June 3, after some preliminary skirmishing, Grant launched a futile attack upon Lee's strongly entrenched position near Cold Harbor.

It was Fredericksburg all over again. The night before the attack, many of the soldiers pinned identification tags to their coats, for they knew full well that they were going to their death the next morning. Within one hour after the signal for attack was given, the attacking force lost nearly six thousand men—killed, wounded, and missing. Swinton, an eyewitness of the battle, later charged that Meade then had ordered the attack renewed but that the men refused to advance because they realized the utter futility of their attempt.[55] This was flatly denied by the Confederate General Edward P. Alexander, also an eyewitness of the battle, who asserted that no such silent defiance of orders or anything like it occurred.[56] In any case, Grant realized that he had blundered, and ever afterward regretted this useless slaughter.[57]

During the second night after the repulse at Cold Harbor, Coffin rode over to Meade's headquarters, where he found the General pacing up and down in front of his tent, and glancing now and then at the flashes of cannonade lighting the Western sky. "These are Smith's batteries, those are Russell's," said Meade reflectively, as the big Federal guns, one after another, rolled out their thunders. "I should like to have them try it every day and every night."

Moving on over to Grant's headquarters, the *Journal* correspondent saw the General in Chief and his staff sitting around a bright camp fire of burning brush. Grant was holding in his hands a half-smoked cigar, which he whiffed occasionally as he read aloud from the Richmond *Examiner* of the day before some pungent criticisms of his generalship. Coffin ruminated:

> Gen. Grant is imperturbable—quite as much so as any man I ever saw. When the right wing gave way in that night attack in the Wilderness battle—when the panic-stricken men of Ricketts' division streamed through the woods—when the tidings of disaster were given from trembling lips, Gen. Grant sat beside a pine tree, whittling, as usual. He looked steadily upon the ground, absorbed in thought, thinking as intently as a geometrician over an abstract problem of his favorite science. His demeanor was in striking contrast to those who stood around him. . . . restless, listening to every sound, and with every faculty awake.[58]

While the Army of the Potomac remained in front of Cold Harbor an incident took place which was destined to have far-reaching effects on General Meade's relations with the press. On May 27, Correspondent

Crapsey had written a letter to the Philadelphia *Inquirer* in which he sought to define the relationship between General Meade, the commander of the Army of the Potomac, and General Grant, the commander of all the Union armies in the field. Meade was a Philadelphian and highly esteemed by his fellow townsmen because of his splendid performance at the Battle of Gettysburg. It was quite natural, therefore, that Crapsey should attempt to satisfy their curiosity about Meade's status, now that Grant had taken the field with the Army of the Potomac. In introducing the subject, Crapsey said:

> Let me break the thread of narrative again, and say a word of Meade's position. He is as much the commander of the Army of the Potomac as he ever was. Grant plans and exercises a supervisory control over the army, but to Meade belongs everything of detail. He is entitled to great credit for the magnificent movements of the army since we left Brandy, for they have been directed by him. In battle he puts troops in action and controls their movements; in a word, he commands the army. General Grant is here only because he deems the present campaign the vital one of the war, and wishes to decide on the spot all questions that would be referred to him as General-in-chief.
>
> History will record, but newspapers cannot that on one eventful night during the present campaign Grant's presence saved the army, and the nation too; not that General Meade was on the point of committing a blunder unwittingly, but his devotion to his country made him loth to risk her last army on what he deemed a chance. Grant assumed the responsibility, and we are still on to Richmond.[59]

Meade lost his temper completely when he saw the second of these two paragraphs in print in the Philadelphia *Inquirer*. Meade's ungovernable temper was notorious in the army.[60] Moreover, he was still sensitive about the charges, aired before the Joint Committee on the Conduct of the War just before the campaign began, that he had counseled retreat after the second day's fighting at Gettysburg.[61] Both Grant and Dana (who was with the army at the time) tried their best to console the testy general. They assured him that Crapsey's story would not be believed and promised that they would at once take prompt measures to contradict it.[62] But Meade was still not satisfied. Even before the campaign began he had been of the opinion that there were too many "damned correspondents" in the army. As soon as he had found out who had written the offending letter, Meade called Crapsey in and demanded to know what the reporter's authority was for his statements. Crapsey replied somewhat lamely that he had simply reported "the talk of the camp." Meade hotly retorted that the story was a "base and wicked lie" and swore that he would make an example of his defamer.

An order calling for the *Inquirer* reporter's expulsion from the army accordingly was drawn up, and General Patrick was empowered to carry it out. The Provost Marshal General performed the duty which had been assigned to him with particular gusto. The very next day, Wednesday, June 8, he mounted Crapsey—face backward, on a sorry-looking mule, attached placards marked "Libeler of the Press" to the reporter's breast and back, paraded him through the army to the tune of the "Rogue's March," and finally escorted him out of the lines.[63]

Following his release, Crapsey returned to Washington and, at a meeting called for that purpose, presented his case to his newspaper friends. At this meeting it was agreed that General Meade's name should never be mentioned again in dispatches by any of the newspaper correspondents present except in connection with a defeat. All future successes of the Army of the Potomac were to be attributed to General Grant, and if a general order was issued it was understood that Meade's name was to be excised before publication. The temper of the correspondents' meeting was well exemplified by a letter, written about this time to the Cincinnati *Gazette* by Whitelaw Reid, which the *Gazette* wisely refrained from publishing. Commenting on the two paragraphs clipped from the *Inquirer* which he enclosed for the editor's information, Reid acidly stated:

> It was for *this,* & for this only, that Maj. Gen. Meade . . . used the accidental power his place as commander of the Army of the Potomac gives him over all within its lines, to seize a gentleman as well born, as respectably connected, as well educated as himself, to placard an infamous slander on his back, to humiliate him by the coarsest & most unfeeling exposure through the lines of the army, & to endeavor to disgrace him in his profession & before the country by using the influence of his office to publish in the widest manner the punishment he had inflicted!
>
> Major Gen. Meade may have the physical courage which bulls & bull-dogs have; but he is as leprous with moral cowardice as the brute that kicks a helpless cripple on the street, or beats his wife at home. He does not care to grapple with newspapers

> that, (in the kindest & most delicate manner) hint at the truth about him; but he can . . . pick up one of their helpless correspondents within his lines, & humiliate him by elaborate insult.
>
> It would, perhaps, have been as well not to mention the fact, the remotest possible allusion to which in Mr. Crapsey's letter, drove Gen. Meade to the crazy brutality of his order. But since he has himself provoked it, I take particular pleasure in assuring him that it is well understood here, that had Gen. Grant permitted him to control the motions of the Army of the Potomac, it would have retreated across the Rapidan after the battles of the Wilderness. Nay, if it will serve at all to allay his frantic excitement on the subject, I can assure him that I know, of my own personal knowledge, that some of the highest officers of the Government firmly believe it. And he will please to remember that it is not of their own choice that the newspapers make it public; but because he himself has seen fit to drag the subject into a blaze of light by his brutal treatment of a gentleman who had made the slightest possible allusion to it.[64]

As a result of the agreement entered into by Crapsey's newspaper friends, the press almost completely ignored Meade for at least six months. Thus Crapsey had his revenge, and whatever political ambitions Meade may have had were pretty thoroughly nullified by this conspiracy of silence. It is just possible that Meade's ill-treatment of Crapsey and the repercussions that followed cost the Philadelphia general the Presidency of the United States.[65]

Following the Battle of Cold Harbor, the New York *Tribune* reporter, Henry Wing, intending to resign as soon as he reached Washington, went North with his dispatches. His crippled leg, a souvenir of Fredericksburg, was racked with pain, and he was still dazed by the dreadful scenes which he had witnessed all the way from the Wilderness to Cold Harbor. After turning in his dispatches, he went to a hotel room to get some rest, but his sleep was haunted by dreams of dying men, lying helpless where they had fallen and looking upward with piteous eyes, their lips parched. Later that afternoon when he stopped back at the *Tribune* bureau, his chief greeted him with the message, "Henry, Mr. Lincoln knows you are here; he wants to see you."

At their last meeting it had been established that, whenever he came to Washington, Wing should report to the President to give him the benefit of first-hand observations on army morale. In his agitation Wing had forgotten to carry out his promise. Now, as he started for the White House, he resolved to tell Lincoln of his intention to resign. It was evening before he was admitted to the President's study; Lincoln was alone, his face drawn and gray, his eyes filled with anguish. The President greeted his visitor kindly, however, and seemed anxious to learn what he had seen and done since his last visit to Washington three weeks before. Under the spell of the President's gaze, Wing talked freely. He spoke of many things which the censorship had not permitted him to write: of men driven to slaughter which was sheer murder; of quarrels between those in high command so jealous of their own prerogatives that they would stop in the midst of a frightful struggle to accuse each other, to threaten, to weaken their own ability by hate and self seeking. Wing went on to picture camps of men sleeping on their arms, attacks on entrenchments which defied the strongest efforts, incessant marching through swamps and across swollen streams in sunlight and during heavy rains. He told of how he had tramped over the battlefield on the night after Cold Harbor, looking for the bodies of the Connecticut boys he knew and taking down messages from the dying for delivery to their loved ones back home.

Lincoln listened intently to this recital and after Wing had concluded exclaimed with considerable feeling:

"And after that you go back to the army—are going back again! Why, boy, you shame me. You've done your part; anybody would say that. You could quit in honor, but you stick. I wonder," he mused thoughtfully, "if I could do that. I don't believe I would. There's many a night, Henry, that I plan to resign. I wouldn't run again now if I didn't know these other fellows couldn't save the Union on their platforms, whatever they say. I can't quit, Henry; I have to stay. But you could, and you don't." The two men had risen; they stood facing each other. Perhaps the President sensed the latent rebellion in the younger man, for he added in a pleading manner, "I reckon we won't quit, will we, Henry?"

"No, Mr. Lincoln," replied Henry, "we won't quit," and so after taking his leave he returned to the army.[66]

During Wing's absence, Grant had made plans to transfer his army to the South side of the James and to strike at Petersburg, which thus far had defied Butler's feeble efforts to capture it.[67] Ever alert to what was going on at headquarters, Coffin already had foreseen the possibility of such a move. In a letter to his newspaper written on June 4, the *Journal* man had spoken of:

> hard work ahead—digging trenches, mounting guns, but not in the Chickahominy swamps. I know nothing whatever of Gen. Grant's plans, or those of Gen. Meade, but the elements of a problem indicate the method of its solution; therefore I expect to see Richmond besieged with James river for a base—supplies close at hand—water transportation for heavy ordnance . . . destruction of rebel communication south—the Appomattox covering the operation—a consequent weakening of rebel strength.[68]

The crossing of the James during June 12-16 was the most successful maneuver Grant had executed since the beginning of the campaign. So skillfully did he conduct the movement that Lee completely lost track of Grant's army for four days.[69] As a result, when the advance guard of the Army of the Potomac arrived in front of Petersburg, the city was defended by a skeleton force under Beauregard of no more than twenty-five hundred men. On June 18, the press carried front-page headlines, based on a news story "authenticated" by the War Department, that Petersburg had fallen. It was soon demonstrated, however, that this was a false report. After capturing a mile and a half of the Petersburg entrenchments on the fourteenth, "Baldy" Smith, the Eighteenth Corps commander, had remained inactive on the following day, waiting for Hancock to come up. Then had occurred a series of poorly synchronized but costly Federal attacks, which were abandoned after it became apparent that Lee had joined Beauregard. Through the tactical deficiencies of his subordinates, the fruits of Grant's strategic success had been frittered away. For many months to come, Petersburg, which Swinton correctly termed "the key to Richmond,"[70] was destined to remain in Confederate hands.

The press once more ran into difficulties with the censorship in attempting to explain why Grant had failed at Petersburg. Before submitting to his newspaper his account of the repulse of the Second Corps, Finley Anderson showed it to Cadwallader. Both reporters agreed that Stanton would not permit even a moderate statement of losses to be published, and so they whittled down Anderson's estimate considerably. But Stanton still was not satisfied. Before he would permit Anderson's report to be published in the *Herald*, he further reduced the figure of Second Corps casualties to two thousand, approximately one-third of the real figure.[71]

Another army reporter, William H. Kent of the New York *Tribune*, also had trouble with the military authorities when he denounced both Meade and Hancock for failing to cooperate with Smith.[72] When Kent's battle account in the *Tribune* was shown to him, Hancock promptly sent a copy of it to Meade, with the passages to which he objected marked for the special attention of the Commanding General. At Meade's insistence, Grant ordered the *Tribune* reporter placed under arrest on charges of "publishing false intelligence for a malicious purpose."[73] But Reporter Kent had no desire to duplicate Crapsey's humiliating experience. By the time the order for his arrest reached Butler's headquarters, to which he was accredited, Kent had left the army and gone North. There, safely out of Meade's reach, he remained until word came to him that his army reporting days were over.

21

"Atlanta is Ours, and Fairly Won"

EVEN when his preparations for the Atlanta campaign were almost completed, Sherman had lost none of his antipathy for the press corps. Before he started on his Meridian raid in February, 1864, Sherman had given orders that if any newspaperman was found accompanying the army he was to be tried by a drumhead court martial and shot before breakfast. Nevertheless, D. B. R. Keim, the *Herald* reporter, decided to find out whether the General meant what he said.

"How about this order of yours?" Keim asked Sherman. "Does it leave me out? Can't I go?"

"I won't have a damned newspaperman on the expedition," rasped Sherman, "not one, but that doesn't apply to you—you are a volunteer aid on General McPherson's staff."

"So I am," acknowledged Keim, "I had nearly forgotten that."

So Keim went along, and the five-column narrative which he forwarded to the *Herald* was the only newspaper account of the Meridian expedition ever printed.[1] In a letter to his wife Sherman expressed great satisfaction at having given the press the slip but made no mention of the exception he had permitted in Keim's case. "Had I tolerated a corps of newspaper men how could I have made that march a success?" he wrote. "Am I not right? And does not the world now see it?"[2]

To other newspaper correspondents Sherman was considerably less agreeable than he had been to Keim. The latter's colleague Shanks was in Sherman's Nashville headquarters one morning in the latter part of April when Assistant Quartermaster General James L. Donnalson came in to report a small increase over the previous day in the number of car shipments to the army. Sherman could not have been more delighted if he had heard the news of a great victory.

"That's good, that's good, Donnalson!" he exclaimed. "We'll be ready for the start." Then changing his mood abruptly, he turned to Shanks and gruffly informed him that no pass over the military railroad to Chattanooga would be issued to him. "You see," he added, "I have as much as I can do to feed my *soldiers*."

The ungracious emphasis which Sherman gave to the word was not lost on the *Herald* correspondent. Nevertheless, he had in his pocket a pass from General Grant permitting him to visit any point in Sherman's department by any route, and so he could afford to laugh at the slur.[3] Still another *Herald* correspondent, T. M. Cook, seeking to escape the ban on civilian travel to the army, managed to obtain an appointment as private secretary to General Sickles, thereby securing the pass he coveted.[4]

Hardly had Sherman's army begun its movement toward Atlanta before the ax fell on one of the best known of the Western army correspondents. For having stated in one of his letters to the Chicago *Journal* that "our lines now extend from Knoxville to Huntsville," Benjamin F. Taylor was the subject of an order from Sherman calling for his immediate arrest as a spy and trial by court martial. Although the order was not fully carried out, Taylor decamped from the army in great haste.[5] Behind him he left the usual number of the Bohemian fraternity under orders from the high command to observe a strict silence regarding army movements. As the army prepared to advance on Dalton, Georgia, Joseph W. Miller of the Cincinnati *Commercial* advised his newspaper that for "specific intelligence" it must for the present rely on enemy news sources, "which not infrequently are more frank and intelligible than what a correspondent under restrictions can send you."[6]

Sherman's invasion force consisted of approximately ninety-nine thousand infantry and artillery and more than ten thousand cavalry, these organized into three armies—the Cumberland, the Tennessee, and the Ohio—commanded respectively by Generals Thomas, McPherson, and John M. Schofield. In command of the Twentieth Corps of the Army of the Cumberland was Fighting Joe Hooker, still intent on achieving personal glory on the battlefield and prone as ever to criticize his military superiors. To L. L. Crounse he had confided in a letter written several months before the campaign opened:

> You must know that I am regarded with more jealousy in this my new sphere of operations than I ever was in the East. It is not

> without reason for it is as certain as any future event can be that I shall be regarded as the best soldier in this Army if I am not now, provided we have a few opportunities to establish our relative merits. An effort of course will be made to prevent this but the result will be likely to be as futile as the last one. I have never yet seen the time that there was no place for a man willing to fight.[7]

Over on the other side of Rocky Face Ridge, barring the way to Dalton, were some sixty thousand Confederates under the command of Bragg's successor, Joseph E. Johnston.

Recognizing that the enemy position at Buzzard Roost Gap was too strong to justify a frontal attack, Sherman sent McPherson with the Army of the Tennessee around the enemy's left wing through Snake Creek Gap, some twelve to fifteen miles South, while Thomas and Schofield applied pressure against the enemy's front. Standing below the crest of a hill near Buzzard Roost to avoid the bullets of the enemy's sharpshooters, the New York *Tribune* reporter Elias Smith excited the suspicion of an officer who had observed him taking notes. A near miss from a rifle bullet just had prompted Smith to head for the rear, when the officer suggested that he had better identify himself. Unfortunately, the *Tribune* correspondent had left his credentials and his permit to follow the army in his valise. Consequently, in the company of an orderly, he was marched back to General Thomas's headquarters where he was rescued by an adjutant who recalled having been with him during the Burnside expedition to North Carolina.[8]

The first word from McPherson, received on the afternoon of May 9, indicated that he was only five miles from Resaca, a railroad town below Dalton, and that success was imminent. But couriers arriving during the night brought different news. Doubting his ability to carry the enemy's works at Resaca by assault, McPherson had fallen back to Snake Creek Gap without cutting the railroad. Leaving Howard's Fourth Corps in front of Buzzard Roost to keep Johnston occupied, Sherman pushed the rest of his army through Snake Creek Gap toward Resaca, hoping to end the campaign at a single stroke. But, on guard, Johnston already had evacuated Dalton and was on his way back to Resaca.

Shanks of the *Herald* was standing alongside a group of generals, Sherman and Thomas among them, at a crossroads near Calhoun ferry on the afternoon of May 13 when an aide from General Howard rode up to report the evacuation of Dalton. The word was given for "Black Jack" Logan's Fifteenth Corps to feel out the strength of the enemy's troop concentration at Resaca. Pushing forward with Osterhaus' division, Shanks reached the top of a hill overlooking Resaca, where to his pained amazement he learned that he had been accompanying the first line of skirmishers. Indeed at that very time the enemy's skirmish line was going down the other side of the hill "popping it to every unlucky fellow who exposed himself."

Presently one of Logan's batteries was wheeled into position to open fire on a fort mounting eight or ten guns on the other side of the river. Shanks had already noticed that all the trees on the summit of the hill had been cut down except a single tall straight oak around which a rude stockade had been formed. What he did not know was that the gunners in the fort at Resaca had been practicing for at least a year by firing at this tree and had calculated the range with such accuracy that the first round of the Federal battery came very near being its last. The first Confederate volley sent the *Herald* man to cover behind a huge oak stump. During the next twenty minutes he lay behind the stump, watching the batteries pounding away and confidently expecting every one of the shots which came skipping along the top of the hill to end his career. Finally a shell from one of the Confederate guns struck directly in front of the stump; plowed up the ground for a distance of ten feet, sending the soil high in the air like spray; then struck the stump and bounding high landed about five feet behind it with a heavy thud. Shanks picked himself up and ran off at full speed. Amid the loud laughter of a whole brigade which rose up to applaud his hasty retreat, he cleared the stockade with a tremendous leap. Not until he was safely out of range of the shell which had given him such a scare did he learn that it had failed to explode.[9]

Somehow the report got out (it apparently originated with the Cincinnati *Commercial*) that Shanks, "the able correspondent of the New-York *Herald*," had been killed instantly in Logan's breastworks near Resaca. Through the columns of the Louisville *Journal*, the subject of this "sad intelligence" took occasion to deny that he had been killed or wounded:

> at the time and in the manner mentioned by the papers of Cincinnati and Louisville (ours excepted) or that he has been killed or wounded at any other time or in any other manner, whatever.

For the benefit of those who might still be skeptical, the *Journal* further noted that Shanks "was in this city yesterday."[10]

For five days of heavy fighting, Johnston had stood off the Federals at Resaca, but then, in another flanking move, Sherman sent one of McPherson's divisions across the Oostanaula River, Southwest of Resaca. This made the Confederate position untenable. On the night of the fifteenth, the defenders of Resaca retreated southward across the river and burned the railroad bridge behind them to delay pursuit. During this fighting the *Herald* correspondent David P. Conyngham had been with the Army of the Ohio. For the gallantry he had displayed on May 14 in carrying dispatches under fire, Conyngham was personally congratulated by General Schofield.[11]

On May 16, the Cincinnati *Commercial* carried the first full-length account of the operations of Sherman's army since the beginning of the campaign. Some of the best reporting of the campaign was to come from the Cincinnati newspapers, but at this time a tight embargo on news was still in effect on the telegraph lines between Nashville and Chattanooga, and the press of these two cities had been warned against publishing war news based on the reports of officers and soldiers recently returned from the front.[12] As late as May 21 the New York *Times* complained that "whatever tidings reach us from the front as yet come through Washington and the War office."

Back in Nashville from the army a few days after the Battle of Resaca, the Philadelphia *Press* correspondent Ben Truman met his old friend Tom Cook of the New York *Herald.*

"When are you going to the front?" Truman asked.

"I am not going to the front," replied Cook. "I am here as volunteer aide on General Sickles's staff. The President has sent him here on an important mission. Can't you guess it?"

Truman admitted that he could not.

"He has come down here to look after Johnson."

"To look after Johnson?" repeated Truman in bewildered fashion.

"Yes, to look after Johnson. To see what he is doing. To look into his habits. The President wants Johnson on the ticket with him if his habits will permit; and the general has been sent here to investigate."

As soon as he could break away from his friend, the Philadelphia *Press* man hastened to Johnson's house to communicate what he had just heard and discuss it with the Governor.

"I want you to leave for Washington to-morrow," said the Governor as soon as he heard what Truman had to tell him. "Go direct to Colonel Forney and repeat to him what you have said to me, and ask him to look out for my interests."

Four days later Truman was with Forney in Philadelphia, helping to lay the groundwork for the nomination of Johnson to the vice-presidency of the United States.[13]

While politics was diverting Truman from reporting battle scenes, Sherman's army was moving ahead at a rapid clip. From Nashville the Federal commander had brought a great stock of bridges with interchangeable parts, prepared according to a standard pattern. Over these he was able to cross the Oostanaula with great rapidity and to push on after Johnston, who had withdrawn to a new line five miles South. On May 19, Johnston announced to his men that the retreat, which had covered twenty-seven miles in ten days, was at an end. Then changing his mind, he ordered another withdrawal to a line between Kingston and Cassville, ten miles southward. There he deployed his troops to enfilade the two principal roads along which he expected the Federal army to advance. But instead of pursuing with massed columns, Sherman came on with wings spread wide so that the would-be trappers were themselves threatened with encirclement. Once more Johnston fell back, and Sherman moved on to Kingston.

No sooner had the Federal troops arrived at Kingston than Sherman issued a circular which was read before the entire army on May 21 and which made the position of newspaper correspondents in that army exceedingly uncomfortable:

> Inasmuch as an impression is afloat that the commanding general has prohibited the mails to and from the army, he takes this method of assuring all officers and men that, on the contrary, he encourages them by all his influence and authority to keep up the most unreserved correspondence with their families and friends wherever they may be. . . . What the commanding general does discourage is the maintenance of that class of men who will not take a musket and fight, but follow an army to pick up news for sale, speculating upon a species of information dangerous to the army and to our cause, and who are more used to bolster up idle and worthless officers than to notice the hard working and meritorious whose modesty is generally equal to

their courage, and who scorn to seek the cheap flattery of the press.[14]

Most of Sherman's staff, including his brother-in-law, General Ewing, disapproved of this inflammatory statement and advised against its issuance at this time. The Cincinnati *Gazette* probably expressed the opinion of many editors when it termed the circular "the most foolish expression that has ever been delivered in all the military fooling with this subject since the war began."[15] The *Herald* reporter Conyngham regarded it as "unworthy of Sherman" and thought the General would have been on firmer ground if he had simply prohibited newspaper correspondents from accompanying the army. But Sherman refrained from doing that, Conyngham thought, because "he knew too well that the war was a matter of history and public interest; that the country . . . would not allow the press to be gagged. . . ."[16] In spite of Sherman's threats and the singular discomforts of the campaign, a small representation of flea-bitten reporters remained with his army and continued to write of what they saw.

By this time the army had reached a section with which Sherman was very familiar. As a young artillery lieutenant, twenty years before, he had ridden over it many times on horseback. From his intimate knowledge of the terrain, he realized that Johnston's position at Allatoona Pass was an unusually strong one. Sherman therefore left the railroad on May 22 and bore off to the right toward Dallas, a village twenty-five miles South of Kingston. From Dallas he intended to march eastward and strike the railroad again near Marietta. At New Hope Church, near Dallas, there was heavy fighting which lasted for several days. Then, finding himself outflanked, Johnston gave up Allatoona and fell back to Kennesaw Mountain. There he occupied a position sufficiently powerful that, with the aid of heavy rains, he was able to hold Sherman in check for twenty-seven days.

At least one of the reporters with Sherman's army feared that the stalemate would continue indefinitely. In a private letter to the editor of his newspaper he announced that:

> We are making no headway. And — (I may be mistaken) I fear the enemy have it in their power to prevent our further advance upon Atlanta. Perhaps we are only threatening that place to hold the Army here from Assisting Lee, and . . . the actual taking of Atlanta is to follow the Capture of Richmond.[17]

Most of the reporters were impressed by the desolation of the country through which they had just passed by the "Foot and Walker's Express." "There is no adult male population in northern Georgia, except a few old men. Nor are there any available negroes," wrote a correspondent of the Chicago *Tribune.*[18] Others chose to comment on the "poor whites," especially the women, "lean, lank, and scrawny," addicted to snuff dipping and tobacco chewing—most of them "intense she-rebels."[19] Conyngham of the *Herald* observed:

> The more I see of the social scale here, the more am I convinced that this is a war of democracy against aristocracy—that it is a war for the emancipation of "the poor white trash" of the South as much as the swarthy nigger.[20]

The same reporter told of going into a house near Big Shanty, Georgia, where an old lady was discussing the war with a soldier whose pipe she was enjoying.

"You'ns fellows don't fight wee'ns fair," the old lady reproached.

"How so?" queried the soldier.

"Why, you'ns fight wid bags, and that's not fair," said the old lady, drawing a very indignant puff from the pipe. "Besides," said she, "You'ns have furriners fightin'."

"Not that I know of."

"O, you'ns can't come over me that way. Wasn't there fellows from a place called New York here to-day?"[21]

Some of the army reporters frankly admitted that the conduct of the Yankee invaders was not above reproach. In a letter from Resaca written on May 18, the *Tribune* correspondent Elias Smith conceded that there had been many acts of vandalism since the beginning of the campaign "which must operate as a lasting stigma upon the Army of 'law and order.' "[22] About the same time, the correspondent of the Chicago *Tribune* told of seeing more than one hundred dollars worth of plug tobacco removed from one house, along with poultry, hogs, flour, and other foodstuffs. In the cellar of another house, the same correspondent saw several molasses barrels which had been tipped over by the soldiers. The heads had been smashed in and the contents covered the cellar floor to a depth of four inches. "What with flour and molasses, [the] boys presented a motley appearance," the reporter decided.[23] Such acts, the reporters claimed, were not performed by the rank and file of Sherman's troops but rather by the "stragglers and hangers on, who bring up the rear of a large army."

In the lobby of the two-storied hotel at Big Shanty, where he had gone with the *Harper's Weekly* artist Theodore Davis, John E. Hayes of the New York *Tribune* beheld an amazing sight. The guard originally posted around the hotel had been removed only a half hour before, and the building was packed with soldiers from every branch of the service, accompanied by a sprinkling of Negro servants—all intent on making high carnival. Around the grand piano in the hotel parlor was a boisterous crowd of soldiers shouting for various tunes, while one of them alternately drummed and played on the instrument. But this was comparatively mild entertainment. Hayes said:

> Look into the entry with me, and see the scrambling of fifty soldiers over a barrel of flour and a barrel of sugar and molasses, while feather beds are torn to pieces. One mischievous fellow has found the dinner-bell, and yells out "Fifteen minutes for dinner." Another has discovered a string of cow-bells, and at once strives to drown the inharmonious sounds of his rivals.
>
> With the drumming of the piano, the striking clock, the blowing of horns, the rattling of dishes, the ringing of cow and dinner-bells, the clatter of a sewing machine, and the wrangling of soldiers over the spoils, the ear was appalled and deafened. Furniture, bedding, cooking utensils, books, pictures, China-ware, ladies' wearing apparel, hoop skirts and bonnets, were thrown together in promiscuous heaps with all sorts of dirty rubbish. For a better description the reader is referred to Mr. Theodore Davis's excellent sketch, which will shortly appear in *Harper's Weekly*, illustrating this raid upon the Big Shanty Hotel.[24]

Perhaps Fletcher Harper thought that the publication of such a sketch might lead to another interview with Stanton. At any rate Davis' portrait of this remarkable scene never appeared in *Harper's Weekly*.

At least such incidents provided diversion from the rigorous campaigning of which the reporters complained unceasingly. In a letter which the newspaper published on June 27, a New York *Times* correspondent told of having listened to the roar of cannon fire for nine straight days, during which "the explosions, slaughter, and tumult of battle have not left us for a day or a night or an hour." While Conyngham was sitting in his tent on the twenty-first of June and composing a letter to his newspaper, a minie ball bursting through the canvas missed him by a slight margin. Later the same correspondent told how:

> another [bullet] struck me lately in the breast, passing through my coat and vest; but, fortunately for me, I had my portfolio full of paper inside, through which it also passed, but did me no serious injury.[25]

W. L. Bearrie of the Cincinnati *Times* and Furay of the Cincinnati *Gazette* had similar tales to tell.

Amid the constant uproar of battle the army newspapermen were kept busy sifting the facts from the medley of rumors which were an inseparable feature of army life. "Each newcomer from the field of battle . . . tells a different story of the same thing to that which was told you only a few minutes since by a different person," grumbled a confused reporter for a Cincinnati newspaper.[26] To make matters worse, the camp correspondents had to contend with the species of "professional liars" in the army, whose function it was to:

> invent all manner of absurd reports, merely for the gratification of hearing them repeated to wondering listeners, or gulped down by credulous reporters and sent forward as racy items for the newspapers.[27]

Among the favorite yarns which made the rounds of the camp was one about the fabulous fifteen-hundred-dollar Whitworth rifle, of a range vastly superior to any Federal firearm, which supposedly was used by the enemy sharpshooters. Still another canard was told of the "fatal tree" near New Hope Church. Beneath the branches eight different soldiers were supposed to have been taken off suddenly and mysteriously. Eventually, so the story went, a signboard labeled "Dangerous" was tacked to the tree. But the sign had been shot away by the Confederates and a Yankee sergeant who took shelter behind the tree soon afterward shared the fate of his predecessors. It was probably one of these same news fakers who palmed off on a Louisville *Journal* reporter the story, widely circulated by the press, that Sherman himself had fired the shot which killed the Confederate General Polk on Pine Mountain on June 14.[28]

On June 27, 1864, the campaign entered a new phase when three Federal divisions, each from a different army corps, were hurled against the strongly fortified Confederate position on Kennesaw Mountain. Sherman at first had been disposed to dislodge Johnston from his position by some method besides frontal assault. Then he changed his mind, as a result, so John A. Logan claimed, of reading a newspaper in which considerable space was given to Grant's battering of Lee's entrenched positions in Virginia. According to Logan, Sherman was convinced that the "whole attention of the country was fixed on the Army of the Potomac and that his army was entirely forgotten."[29] The order for the assault, the only serious mistake during the campaign, was issued on June 25, two days in advance of the time set.

At eight o'clock on the morning of the twenty-seventh, the attacking force raced up the steep, rocky slope of Kennesaw. Describing the action on the Federal left, Miller of the Cincinnati *Commercial* told how:

> In a moment our skirmishers engaged those of the enemy, but without pausing save to kill those who refused to surrender . . . they swept on, behind them the serried lines of our lads, colors flying and the alignments unwavering. The enemy opened fiercely from Big and Little Kinesaw [sic] but the column advanced in superb order until it struck a swampy tract, covered with a clinging thicket of thorny bushes. Through this, in mud knee deep, the brigades forced their impetuous way, and the necessary disorder of the column was speedily retrieved, when it emerged from this fearful bar to success. Through a tempest of iron the advance was resumed, the troops breaking into a cheer and a run, and dashing over the stony sides of Little Kenesaw without faltering. As the difficulties of the ground increased, the fearful clangor from the enemy's trenches was heightened and became more and more prolonged. Over their yellow rifle-pits the blue tufts of musketry danced wildly, and the whirling spheres of vapor from their masked artillery, curled up as tightly as cocoons, seemed to start out hideously from the foliage of the knob. From right and left, down the slopes of big Kenesaw and along the ridges to the west of the point of assault, the enemy poured his forces, emptying his adjacent trenches to confront us at the point of danger. The brigades charging the flanks of the mountain, subjected to a most cruel and destructive cross-fire, after repeated and heroic efforts, failed to reach the crest and retired in comparative disorder to the best cover they could obtain near the base of the hill. The brigade of Giles Smith, however, dashed ahead, no longer a column but a swarm of men, and poured up to the very crest of the hill, passing over the

> enemy's first trenches and abattis, where two color bearers fell; but, alas, to find just as they gained the summit, the enemy in another and stronger line, posted on a slight ridge not perceptible until the plateau of the mountain was reached. The fresh line opened with a volley, and the blast of death swelled into a hurricane. The brigade slowly fell back, while the enemy, attempting to pursue, was met by a heavy artillery fire from our trenches and hastily driven back. About fifty men of this brigade took refuge behind a ledge of rocks, where during the rest of the day they dared not expose so much as a finger. Occasionally one or two would attempt to dash down the hill and run the gauntlet, but of all who attempted this not one escaped. At the same time the enemy was unable to come forth and capture them, for every man was covered by a hundred Federal muskets carefully poised on our trenches for their protection.[30]

Within an hour after it began, Sherman realized that the attack was a failure. Harker and McCook, who had led it, were dying; twenty-five hundred others had been killed or wounded; the enemy still held his lines, with a loss of only eight hundred and eight.[31] With the consent of his division and corps commanders, Sherman abandoned the attempt and returned to the old routine of flanking. There was comparatively little press criticism of this useless expenditure of men although Miller did not hesitate to pronounce it an "unbroken failure."[32] Furay said:

> With regard to the merit of the plan itself or that of the immediate mode of assault in the center . . . I have not a word to say. There are those high in command, in the army, who loudly and openly censure both, especially the latter.[33]

On the morning after the battle, Furay and a rival journalist, J. A. Daugherty of the Louisville *Journal*, started northward with their accounts of the fighting, supplemented by a full list of the killed and wounded. As they were crossing the Cumberland Mountains near Cowan, Tennessee, their train was run into by another train which had left Chattanooga immediately behind them, and the car in which the two correspondents were riding was smashed. Ten minutes after they had extricated themselves from the wreckage, they found each other groping about in the dark. Each was looking for the dead body of the other man and his notes concerning the battle![34]

Before Furay and Daugherty returned to the army, Sherman's skirmishers took possession of Kennesaw on July 3, as the result of a successful flanking maneuver. Six days later, the Confederates, after some noisy but not desperate fighting, retreated across the Chattahoochee River. Sherman was in full possession of its North bank and for the first time in sight of Atlanta.

About this time the *Herald* reporter Keim was victimized by a blunder in the *Herald* office which cost him his job and which might have had more serious consequences. Bennett required that each of his war correspondents once a week should send him a confidential letter, giving such information about the progress of the war as the correspondent was able to get and yet could not print. In one of these letters, Keim told how:

> A short time ago a signal officer by the name of Fluke, if I remember the name rightly, discovered the principle of the rebel system of signals, which enabled him to interpret what was transpiring along the enemy's lines. The discovery and key to the system were made known to some of our signal officers and often through them and by this means valuable information has been secured concerning the designs of the enemy.[35]

Keim was probably the most surprised man in the press corps when he was called to headquarters a few days later and shown a dispatch from Washington stating that the *Herald* had printed over his own signature information about the key to the enemy's signal code.

Although Sherman ordered Keim to be placed under arrest and delivered to Thomas for trial as a spy, neither Thomas nor McPherson was eager to impose the extreme penalty. McPherson, in fact, had seen the letter before it was mailed. Eventually it was decided to limit Keim's punishment to transportation North of the Ohio River, with orders not to return to Sherman's army for the duration of the war. Subsequently the reporter learned that he owed his banishment to Julian K. Larke, the telegraph editor of the *Herald.* Larke mistakenly had opened the letter addressed to Bennett and, thinking the contents worth printing, had published a part of the letter along with Keim's dispatches.[36]

Eight days after the Confederate army crossed the Chattahoochee, Sherman followed, ready to begin the concluding phase of the movement against Atlanta. Contrary to the impression given by some of the Northern journalists, the terrain South of the river was almost as rough and wooded as the country around Kennesaw Mountain. From the Atlanta papers the army learned on July 19 of a change of commanders on the Confederate side. Never a great favorite of the Confederate president, Johnston had been replaced by a "fighting general," John B. Hood. Assuming the offensive, Hood lashed out at Sherman in three separate battles on July 20, 22, and 28. In these he suffered heavy losses without any compensating advantage.

The Battle of Peach Tree Creek on July 20 received fuller and probably better news coverage than either of the other actions. On the second morning after that battle, a staff officer rode in to the headquarters of Palmer's Fourteenth Corps with a report that Atlanta had fallen. Rumors based on this report quickly spread through the whole army. Without taking the trouble to verify what he had heard, Furay of the Cincinnati *Gazette* started for Nashville at once, hoping to be first with the news. As soon as he reached Nashville, he sent off a telegram to his own paper and one to the Louisville *Journal* as well, reporting that Sherman's army had entered Atlanta. To make his story more convincing, Furay added the statement that he actually had seen the flag of the Union floating over Atlanta. In spite of the fact that there was no confirmation of this report, certain correspondents in Nashville, whose proper function was to forward dispatches from the field, straightway concocted full and elaborate accounts of the "great event," which occasioned celebrations throughout the North. There was, of course, no basis for the story, and after hanging around Nashville for a week or so Furay slunk back to the army, considerably shamefaced.[37]

As a result of his premature journey to Nashville, Furay missed the bloody fighting of July 22 and 28. A Cincinnati *Commercial* reporter, who inspected the battlefield of Ezra Church after the conclusion of the fighting on the twenty-eighth, found the dead:

> yet scattered as they had fallen . . . in all the attitudes of fierce despair, of agony, or placid repose. . . . All along a little rivulet of muddy water the poor wretches had crawled down into it, in their dying agony, to quench their thirst, and made its banks bloody from their wounds. One had snatched in his feeble hand a bunch of dry leaves with which he had vainly attempted to staunch the blood with which his life was flowing slowly but certainly away.[38]

Furay's blundering report and the wild statements of the telegraph reporters at Nashville inspired a flood of ridicule. "I see by the papers that the *correspondents* captured it [Atlanta] a week or ten days ago," observed an army major in a letter to his wife written on July 31, "but the *army* hasn't got that far yet."[39] The Cincinnati *Times* correspondent, W. L. Bearrie, noted that the same kind of premature announcements had been made frequently during the campaign:

> At Pine Mountain it was announced we had Marietta, while the battles around Kenesaw were yet to be fought. At Kenesaw we were told the Rebels were driven to the Chattahoochee, while we were under fire of their guns in daily and desperate battle. At the Chattahoochee we were before Atlanta when our main forces were yet on the South bank of the river, and Department headquarters occupying "Signal Hill."[40]

After the Confederate repulse of July 28, Hood abandoned his expensive policy of attacking Sherman in his entrenchments, and for a whole month siege guns and cavalry raids were the principal topics of army reporting. "We ride, walk, sit down, write, eat, sleep, and do everything else under fire," wrote Elias Smith to his newspaper on August 6.[41] A New York *Times* correspondent, looking on while the batteries dueled, was amused by the picturesque reactions of the soldiers. "Look out for that cart-wheel," "There comes an anchor," "Look out for that blacksmith's shop," he heard them chant as sixty-four-pound shells from Confederate eight-inch guns came screaming over the lines.[42]

In most cases the reporters overestimated the effectiveness of the Federal cavalry raids, and when the Nashville correspondent of the Cincinnati *Gazette* described one of them as a "disaster," he was accused of attempting to injure the military reputation of the general in command of the raid.[43] Having little news to write about, several newspapermen left the army in mid-August, among them the able W. L. Bearrie of the Cincinnati *Times*, who was going home to write a history of the Georgia campaign.[44]

About this time, Hood sent Wheeler with the major part of his cavalry around Sherman's rear to harass his railroad communications. After being beaten off at Dalton, Wheeler galloped on into Eastern Tennessee, thereby depriving Hood of the eyes of his army at a critical moment. After a countermove by Kilpatrick, Sherman's cavalry leader, had failed, Sherman began moving his troops to the South of Atlanta on the night of August 25, leaving the Twentieth Corps behind to safeguard his railroad communication with Chattanooga. Thinking at first that Sherman was withdrawing, Hood realized too late that his adversary was striking for the Macon and Western Railroad, the city's main supply artery.

On the third day of the movement, as Miller of the Cincinnati *Commercial* was watching an endless line of troops hurrying by, Sherman with a small escort rode up to a fence, near which the reporter was standing. Miller noticed that the General's uniform was neither new nor old and saw nothing remarkable in his face except the nose, "high, thin, and planted with a curve as vehement as the curl of a Malay cutlass." Seating himself on a stick of cordwood, the reddish-haired general drew a pencil stub from his pocket and, spreading a piece of note paper on his knee, wrote with great rapidity. The reporter watched him for half an hour without being able to detect any signs of the strain which might have been expected. Presently a mail arrived. Tearing open some letters, Sherman glanced at them hastily. Then, with characteristic suddenness and a smiling countenance, he rode off down the road, past the thousands of men whose lives had been confided to his keeping.[45]

On the thirty-first of August, Schofield reached the Macon and Western Railroad near Rough and Ready Station, and Stanley's Fourth Corps struck it a little farther South. Before night the whole line of railway as far as the New York *Tribune* reporter could see was "one mass of seething, crackling, smoking pyramids of fire."[46] At Jonesboro, on the following day, one of Hood's corps commanders, Hardee, unsuccessfully fought for the railway. Hood then had to evacuate Atlanta and to retreat southward to rejoin Hardee. Between midnight of September 1-2 and daybreak, Slocum's Twentieth Corps moved southeastward into Atlanta's empty trenches just as the retreating Confederates were leaving the South end of the city.

At 11:00 A.M. the morning of September 2 Miller of the Cincinnati *Commercial* and Conyngham of the *Herald*, hoping to be the first of the army correspondents to enter the Gate City, left the main body of Sherman's army twenty miles South of Atlanta. No direct communication with Slocum's troops had yet been established, but a cavalry unit of forty men was furnished the correspondents by Brigadier General Kenner Garrard so that they made their journey without serious danger. North of Rough and Ready Station, about halfway to Atlanta, they overtook an ancient Negro riding a mule and forced him to haul up. The Negro was almost overcome with terror. In answer to a query as to whom he belonged he could only gasp: "mmmm - m - m - mmm Mr.

Ferguson." The mule also belonged to that gentleman. Taking the Negro in tow, the cavalcade rode on up the road to the Ferguson homestead. There the Negro was requested to dismount and turn his animal over to one of the troopers. Another trooper had the Negro tighten his horse's girth.

About four and a half miles out of Atlanta the party halted at an unpretentious house for dinner and found there an elderly and exceedingly garrulous lady, whose manner was suspiciously friendly.

"God bless you Yankees!" she breathed. "Why didn't you let me know? Should have had a hot meal." Then dropping her voice mysteriously, she added, "I've got two little boys with you-uns—nice little boys—Union boys. Didn't you ever meet any of the McCools?"

None of them had ever met the McCools, but one noticed that the bedspread in the next room had a peculiar appearance. Turning it down, he discovered five guns loaded and capped; two more guns were concealed in another bed. The hostess was questioned about why there were so many small arms about the premises. Without a moment's hesitation she replied, with a voice whose honeyed accents would have been irresistible in one younger and prettier:

"Oh, dear, now! My youngest—Johnny—did you never meet Johnny McCool?—was sich a great hand to hunt. Nay, do now have some more butter."

Breaking the young Nimrod's armory to pieces, the party continued on into Atlanta, where they found Slocum's men already in possession.[47] Meanwhile, Captain John C. Van Duzer, Superintendent of Military Telegraphs, had run his lines through to the city and had instructed an operator to transmit the glad news to Washington via Cumberland Gap since Wheeler had destroyed the wires between Nashville and Chattanooga. At one of the repeating stations the operator interrupted the message by asking if this were another "Furay!" He was assured emphatically that it was not. The dispatch continued on its way, and an answer was received from the War Department four hours after the Union forces entered the city.[48]

Later that day the Associated Press agent at Louisville wired Sherman, asking for details of his success. The General telegraphed back "Atlanta is ours, and fairly won," following up the expression with a brief but graphic account of the flanking movement around Atlanta and the Battle of Jonesboro. Reporter Shanks was so much impressed with the account that he wrote a long letter to the *Herald,* which the newspaper never printed, endeavoring to show that, successful as he had been as a general, Sherman would have been an even better war correspondent.[49] In an editorial published soon after the fall of Atlanta, the New York *Times* also contended that General Sherman had surpassed all the newspaper correspondents in writing about military matters, and continued:

> He is not as picturesque, nor as effective, in a popular point of view, as some of the gentlemen connected with journalism; but for conciseness, perspicacity and comprehensiveness, with brevity, he is a perfect model. The congratulatory order . . . issued to his army . . . on the 8th instant, is a superb example of this.[50]

From Chattanooga, on September 5, Miller telegraphed the Cincinnati *Commercial* the first newspaper account of the capture of Atlanta which appeared in print. It was fully ten days after that before a complete story of the city's fall appeared in any of the large Eastern newspapers. No one newspaper account of this important event stands out above the others. Probably the best of the lot were the work of Miller, Ben Truman, and Elias Smith.[51] At least one army correspondent must have cursed his fate as he pored over these accounts of the biggest news story of the campaign. The Cincinnati *Gazette*'s "well-known correspondent," William S. Furay, who had reported every important success of the Army of the Cumberland since the beginning of the war, had left the army and returned home just eight days before Atlanta fell!

* * *

While Sherman was on the march, fighting and flanking, from Chattanooga to Atlanta, the two biggest naval stories of 1864 hit the front page. The first was the sinking of the Confederate cruiser "Alabama" off Cherbourg, France, in June. Farragut's victory at Mobile Bay on August 5, 1864, followed, seven weeks later.

The "Alabama," was the most famous of all English-built Confederate war vessels. She had been at sea, preying on Northern commerce, almost two years when she sailed into Cherbourg harbor for repairs the night of June 9. During that time, under the command of Raphael Semmes, she had captured sixty-nine prizes worth $6,548,000. Together with her sister raiders, she had virtually driven the United States merchant marine from the seas. While the "Alabama" was in port, the United

States sloop of war "Kearsarge," commanded by Captain John A. Winslow, arrived off Cherbourg from a Dutch anchorage. Winslow took station outside the three-mile limit and waited for the "Alabama" to come out.

Apparently no newspapermen were on either ship when the "Alabama," capable of employing both steam and sail, got under way soon after nine o'clock on Sunday morning, June 19, and headed directly for the "Kearsarge." The hills and other observation points along the French coast were swarming with spectators, however, and arrangements had been made for special wires to Paris to report each stage of the fight to excited throngs in the French capital. Altogether, some fifteen thousand people witnessed the battle, among them the masters of several merchant vessels that had been destroyed by the "Alabama."[52]

At 10:57 A.M. when the vessels were still eighteen hundred yards apart, the "Alabama" opened fire with a broadside which, aimed too high, did little damage. Two more ineffectual broadsides were fired by the Confederate cruiser as the "Kearsarge" approached head on. Then Winslow's vessel sheared around and seemed to be heading across the "Alabama" 's stern. Consequently, Semmes started off so that the two ships soon were steaming clockwise in a common circular path, separated from each other by half the circumference of this circle, firing with their starboard batteries and gradually reducing the diameter of their circular course.

The gunnery of the "Kearsarge" proved exceptionally good. Whereas the "Alabama" fired rapidly and quite inaccurately, registering twenty-eight hits out of three hundred seventy shots fired, nearly all of the one hundred seventy-three shots fired by the "Kearsarge" took effect. Within an hour the "Alabama" was sinking and virtually helpless. Ceasing fire, she hoisted sail and attempted to run inshore. But Winslow had anticipated such a maneuver. Steering so as to cross her bow, he was about to pour in a raking fire when the "Alabama" hauled down her flag. While the small boats from the "Kearsarge" and the English yacht "Deerhound" were picking up the survivors, the "Alabama" settled by the stern and sank, her bowsprit disappearing last of all.[53]

It was over two weeks before the news of her destruction reached New York by way of "The City of Baltimore." For hours the streets in front of the principal newspaper offices in Printing House Square were crowded with people eager to learn every detail of the spectacular encounter. Along Ann Street a local reporter of the New York *Times* caught sight of an admiral and a captain with an extra between them, each reading the account of the fight as he walked along and then handing the paper to the other. Around Park Row, down Beekman, into Nassau, up Ann, and around Park Row again, they trudged, reading and exchanging the paper at intervals. After about an hour of this the admiral insisted on keeping the sheet altogether, "a new beginning being indispensable every time he got to the end of the story." Apparently the captain managed to secure an extra for himself, for they were later observed passing up Ann Street still engrossed in the story of the fight.[54]

Although he was not an eyewitness of the battle, the Paris correspondent of the *Times,* Dr. William E. Johnston, managed to piece together a description based on the statements of two members of the American legation who had been on the "Kearsarge." Editorially the *Times* boasted that Johnston's account was "the most comprehensive of the histories of the affair" and "the only account received from loyal sources."[55] In the stories of the fight published by various English and French newspapers wide discrepancies appeared. Said the London *Daily News*:

> The sceptic who called history a matter-of-fact romance should have lived in our day, when a naval action is fought off Cherbourg on Sunday, and reported in the London and Paris newspapers on the Monday following, no two reports agreeing in any single fact except in the result.[56]

A New York *Herald* reporter who spent a day on board the "Kearsarge" gathering details of the action from the ship's officers also was critical of the way the European press reported the battle. In a lengthy analysis of its shortcomings, he stated:

> The English and French papers in the Southern interest are endeavoring to create the impression that the loss of the Alabama was caused by greatly superior advantages in size and calibre of guns on the part of her adversary. This, however, is not the fact. The tonnage of the Alabama was a little greater than that of the Kearsarge, and . . . the calibre of the latter was in all but sixty-two pounds more than the former. The Kearsarge owes her success greatly, it is true, to her two heavy Dahlgrens, but principally to her superior concentration of fire, and her more thorough training and discipline. . . .

> It is reported in most of the papers that the Alabama was disabled by a shot striking and breaking her screw. This the officers of the Kearsarge state is not the fact, but that she went down simply because the water ran with too great rapidity into the holes made by their shot and shell. It is also reported that if she had not been disabled just as she was she would have taken the Kearsarge by boarding. If this were so she certainly gave no evidence of it, and all these "ifs" prove nothing in the matter.... All the stories about Capt. Winslow having sent a challenge and arranged the conditions of the fight with Semmes are without foundation. The only thing in the form of a challenge came from Capt. Semmes, and was in substance what I gave you yesterday....
>
> One of the Paris journals states that Capt. Winslow and Semmes are brothers-in-law. They are not related to each other, but have long been personal and intimate friends each having a high opinion of the other's personal courage, determination, skill, and personal honor.[57]

There were other inaccuracies in the press accounts of the battle about the number of guns, the size of crews, and the number of casualties suffered by each vessel; whether or not the "Kearsarge" was an "ironclad"; and the supposed collusion of Joseph Lancaster, the owner of the "Greyhound," with Captain Semmes.

Comparatively few newspapermen were on hand on August 5, 1864, to report Admiral Farragut's great triumph at Mobile Bay. Oscar G. Sawyer of the New York *Herald* was on board the "Hartford" as secretary to the Admiral.[58] A New York *Times* reporter was on the "Winnebago." A New York *Tribune* "special" watched the thrilling struggle from the deck of the "Oneida." Somewhere in the squadron was another *Herald* correspondent, Tom Cook, who had been transferred during the summer from the service of General Sickles to the Department of the Gulf.

An attack on Mobile, the second port of the Confederacy, had been under consideration at one time or another ever since New Orleans fell. After the capture of Vicksburg, Grant had planned to land an army at Mobile with cooperation from Farragut and advance from there against Atlanta. But the plan had been shelved by Grant's superiors, and nothing had come of subsequent projects for a movement against Mobile. Still the harbor remained open for blockade running, and Farragut was unprepared to force his way in, even with assistance from the army, until the ironclads for which he had been importuning the navy for months finally reached the Gulf in July, 1864.

It was approximately 6:10 on the morning of August 5 when Farragut's fleet of eighteen vessels headed by the "Brooklyn" entered Mobile Bay in the face of crisscrossing fire from the three Confederate forts (Powell, Gaines, and Morgan) which stood guard over the entrance to the harbor. The water was swarming with torpedoes, and behind Mobile Point with three partly armored light gunboats was the great ironclad ram "Tennessee," the most powerful vessel ever to fly the Confederate flag, waiting to join battle.

One of the best accounts of the action was written by the New York *Tribune* reporter on the "Oneida":

> We had not long been engaged when the "Tecumseh" was seen to be lifted out of the water to the height of about 20 feet; a tremendous explosion followed, and she was seen no more. She had struck a torpedo which, we were subsequently informed, contained little less than *ten tons* of powder. . . .
>
> By this time this ship [the "Oneida"] had got nearly abreast of the fort when a rifle shell struck the side, passing through the chain cable armor as easily as if it had been paper, and entering the starboard boiler *exploded in it.* The effect produced was appalling; the ship was instantly enveloped in the escaping steam, and all the engineers, firemen and coal heavers, with the exception of two or three, were horribly scalded. But this did not prevent us from working our guns; the presence of mind of a few prevented any thing more than a momentary confusion, and the firing was continued as rapidly as before. We, being the sternmost ships, were exposed to a much longer and heavier fire than any of the other vessels, for there was nothing astern of us to draw the fire of the enemy, and long after the fleet had passed by the fort and entered the bay, a tremendous raking fire was kept up on us by the fort and water-batteries.

Eventually all the ships under Farragut's command, except the "Tecumseh," were safely past the forts. Then the "Tennessee," flying the flag of Admiral Buchanan, onetime commander of the "Virginia," stood forth with its gunboats to fight it out with the Northern fleet. Closely pursued by the Union monitor, "Winnebago," the "Tennessee" made for the "Oneida," whose crippled condition was obvious to those on board the Confederate ram. Said the *Tribune* correspondent:

> The ram approached to within 200 yards of us, intending to fire into us and run us down at the same time, but we were saved by what I am sure was nothing but a direct interposition of Divine Providence in our behalf.
>
> *Three times* we could distinctly hear the primers of her guns snap without exploding the charges in them; and then, upon her preparing to run into us, she found she was so closely pressed by the Winnebago that had she done so and sunk us she would undoubtedly have sunk herself also. . . .
>
> Getting astern of us she gave us two or three raking shots . . . but she was gallantly met by our fleet; first the Monongahela, then the Lackawanna, each heavy ships of fifteen or sixteen hundred tons, ran with all their force under a full head of steam right into her. . . .
>
> Notwithstanding this, no breach was effected in the massive sides of our huge opponent. The Brooklyn, the Hartford and the Richmond came next, each in their turn running full tilt against her and pouring broadside after broadside into her; the three monitors also discharging their 11-inch and 15-inch guns into her, or rather against her, without any apparent effect. At length a broadside from the Brooklyn carried away her smoke-stack and her fire began to slacken, and soon, finding further resistance useless, she hauled down her colors and ran up the white flag in token of surrender.[59]

Discouraged by the loss of the "Tennessee" and the "Selma," which likewise had surrendered after a sturdy resistance, the other Confederate ships fled up the river as fast as steam could take them. Fort Morgan managed to hold out for another two weeks, until amphibious landings in her rear had severed her connections with the mainland.

Farragut's bluejackets had suffered heavy losses in the desperate fight of August 5. In addition to the one hundred twenty men drowned or blown up on the "Tecumseh," the Union forces had lost fifty-two killed and one hundred seventy wounded, the heaviest casualty lists being on the "Hartford" and the "Brooklyn."[60]

According to one of the *Herald* reporters, when Farragut was asked if he would go to pay a call on the wounded Confederate admiral, he looked about his decks and replied:

> With these brave men before me killed and mangled by him, I consider him but my enemy. I want nothing to do with him.[61]

Not until August 8, three days after the fight, did the first news of Farragut's great victory reach Washington. The news came from General Butler, who had obtained the information from an official dispatch to the Confederate Secretary of War which Butler had seen in the Richmond newspapers of August 8. The dispatch announced that Farragut's fleet had passed Fort Morgan with the loss of the "Tecumseh" and that the "Tennessee" had been captured. The additional statement that the "Tecumseh" had been sunk by the guns of Fort Morgan was doubted at the Navy Department and was subsequently found to be incorrect. The news of the victory did not appear in the Northern papers, however, until the following day, when it was prominently featured with front-page headlines.

On August 6, the *Herald* had tried to scoop the other papers by publishing a story indicating that Farragut's fleet had passed the forts below Mobile on July 30. The *Herald* story credited Farragut with double the number of ironclads he really had and stated, quite without basis, that the attacking force included mortars. At that very time, according to the *Herald* account, Farragut was hammering away at the city of Mobile! In a letter, written about two weeks later to a friend, Captain Drayton of the "Hartford" commented derisively:

> What a canard. Who says we are not a hopeful people? The fall of Mobile is no doubt hourly looked for, and if twenty thousand men take it, they will do well . . . our force is three [thousand], and to get this New Orleans has been left almost defenceless.[62]

Fortunately for the *Herald* its correspondents were on hand to give a realistic account of the fight when it really occurred. Tom Cook's story of Farragut's victory, printed in the *Herald* on August 20, 1864, was rated by the Assistant Secretary of the Navy as "the best account of the Mobile Bay fight."[63]

* * *

Relatively few army reporters—probably not more than eight or ten at the outside[64]—accompanied Sherman on his march from Atlanta to the sea. Although Sherman made no attempt to keep reporters from going along on this expedition, his previous comments about the press and his unpleasant attitude toward its representatives kept many reporters away. Moreover, the army newspapermen were well aware that they would have little or no opportunity to supply their newspapers with copy from the time Sherman cut all communications with the North until he reached the coast. Some may have felt that the risks involved in such a desperate venture were too great.

Sherman's decision to march to the coast was no sudden inspiration. When his inspector general had asked him on the opening day of the spring campaign what he would do if and when he captured Atlanta, he had answered tersely but significantly as he snapped the ashes from his cigar: "Salt water."[65] After Atlanta fell, his army needed rest, however, and he had still to reckon with Hood. Hoping to draw Sherman northward out of Georgia in pursuit of him, the Confederate commander crossed the Tennessee River on October 30 after attacking several points along the railroad. The reporters noted that Sherman, who had followed him as far as Gaylesville, Alabama, held Hood in profound contempt, saying, "Damn him, if he will go to the Ohio River, I'll give him rations. . . . Let him go north, my business is down South."[66] Leaving Thomas to keep watch on Hood, Sherman started back to Atlanta to embark on his big gamble of splitting the Confederacy and destroying its material resources.

On November 9, six days before the great march commenced, the Indianapolis *Journal* published a news dispatch under a Cincinnati date line giving a reasonably accurate estimate of Sherman's strength and intentions. Official Washington buzzed with indignation as the New York *Times* and the other Northern newspapers picked up the story, hitting even closer to the truth. From City Point, Grant wired Secretary Stanton that the story in the *Times* was "the most contraband news I have seen published during the war."[67] Stanton was inclined to think that the disclosure was very largely Sherman's own fault. "There is reason to believe he has not been very guarded in his own talk," Stanton told Grant:

> I saw to-day, in a paymaster's letter to another officer, his plans as stated by himself. Yesterday I was told full details given by a member of his staff to a friend in Washington. Matters not spoken of aloud in the Department are bruited by officers coming from Sherman's army in every Western printing office and street. If he cannot keep from telling his plans to paymasters, and his staff are permitted to send them broadcast over the land, the Department cannot prevent their publication.[68]

Learning of the news break from Dana, Sherman advised the Assistant Secretary of War to counteract its effect by planting other stories designed to mislead the enemy. He was to say, for example, that "Sherman's army has been much re-enforced, especially in the cavalry, and he will soon move . . . to catch Hood's army" and also that "Sherman's destination is not Charleston, but Selma, where he will meet an army from the Gulf."[69]

In accordance with the plan which had leaked to the press, all communication with the rear was broken November 12, and on the fourteenth and fifteenth of that month the army began moving eastward from Atlanta, sixty-two thousand strong. The last troops to leave the city belonged to Davis' Fourteenth Corps, which had remained behind to carry out orders for the complete destruction of all public buildings. On the evening of the fifteenth the Engineer Corps fired the downtown debris; fanned by a high wind, the conflagration spread, continuing throughout the night. From a hill overlooking the city "Jep" Doyle of the New York *Herald* watched the fire sweep from house to house and block to block until half the city was in flames. So bright was the glare that soldiers a mile distant from the city could read their last letters from home by the reflected light. On the following morning, the *Herald* correspondent rode through the ruined section of the city:

> where nothing remained to tell the tale but tottering walls and blackened chimneys, that, like gravestones, stood there as monuments of departed glory.[70]

At first the army marched in two columns, the right wing feinting at Macon, the left at Augusta. Never before during this war had the army newspapermen seen such a march as this. Foraging, rather than fighting, was the order of the day. Operating along a front sixty miles wide, Sherman's "bummers" reduced the collecting of supplies to a science. In the opinion of one of the *Herald* correspondents:

> To draw the line between capturing and stealing, when permission is given troops to take everything which will sustain life or assist military operations, would puzzle the keenest practitioner. . . . Such things cannot be avoided. An army passes along a road. A planter's house stands by the wayside; without a halt the whole premises are overrun as if by ants, the heads of sorghum barrels are knocked in and tin cupsfulls scooped out; beehives are knocked in pieces, and wild grabs are made for the last vestige of

> "comb," sweet potato caches are broken in, and the contents packed in pockets, in handkerchiefs, in anything that will hold that esculent; hogs are bayoneted, quartered with the hair on and hung on the ends of muskets to bleed; chickens, geese, turkeys, &c., knocked over with sticks, and strung in garlands around the necks of sweaty warriors. This is the work of fighting men who cannot stop their march to ransack. The "mule" brigade and the "bummers" follow in the course of time, when the "loot hunting" commences, if ever. A column ten miles long generally furnished men enough to pick the premises clean. . . . General Sherman's army has so far lived off the country, and lived well, as soldiers should live if the land produces. If the people along the line of march have suffered loss it has been the fortune of a war they voted for. The policy of our Commanding General has been to take nothing but that which would benefit the enemy. The balance of the evils are but natural consequences of a military expedition like this.[71]

On the evening of November 22, the advance guard of the left wing entered Milledgeville, then the state capital. E. D. Westfall of the *Herald,* who also represented the Associated Press on Sherman's march, accompanied the first echelon of troops that invaded the State House and watched them scoop up large quantities of Georgia paper money. He told his newspaper:

> Being rather short of decent paper on which to write this communication, I have the honor to forward it to you on the back of the rebel "grayback notes." I have been somewhat surprised to find that I have used up over a million dollars in this way already, with my task only half finished. I have plenty, however.[72]

Before they left Milledgeville, the reporters viewed a mock session of the State Legislature in which a number of Union officers took part, with Theodore Davis, the *Harper's* artist, acting as one of the pages.[73] After a lengthy session, punctuated by some humorous exchanges between the gallery and the "Speaker," Georgia's ordinance of secession was solemnly "repealed" by the mock legislature.

On the day before the occupation of Milledgeville, the right wing of the army under General Howard had arrived at Gordon, twenty miles South of the state capital, and had begun a systematic destruction of the Georgia Central Railroad. Two reporters, convinced that Brigadier General John M. Corse's advance column would reach Clinton on the twenty-second, had pushed on ahead of the army and stopped overnight at the home of an elderly woman, whose widowed daughter had aroused their interest. The representative of the Cincinnati *Commercial* was clad in the hateful blue uniform, but his brother of the New York *Tribune* was garbed in gray. Naturally the ladies wanted to know what position the *Tribune* man held in the army.

"None," he answered.

"Why are you with it?" they inquired.

"Oh, it's my business."

"Are you a sutler?"

"No, indeed."

"An army correspondent," put in the *Commercial* man at that point, not wishing to prolong their suspense any further.

"Please tell me for what paper?" pleaded the young widow.

Before the *Commercial* reporter could reply, his colleague informed her that it was the New York *World.*

"Indeed!" exclaimed the widow with sparkling eyes. "I'm *so* glad to meet you! It's seldom one gets a word of cheer these days. You'll stay until all the troops pass through—won't you?"

"Thank you!" he replied. "You know—'A little word, kindly spoken—.' "

Before he could finish the quotation, the widow supplied the missing words: "Relieves a heart that's almost broken."

From that moment on, the newspaper guests were assured the most bountiful hospitality that the house could afford. They enjoyed a sumptuous dinner that night, counterpointed with gay conversation and laughter. Afterwards they were entertained with pianoforte music. But the next morning after breakfast, the *Tribune* man concluded that he had better acknowledge the deception which he had practiced.

"I can not," he announced, "I can not deceive you, ladies, longer. Allow me to say that I am *not* a correspondent for the New York World, *but for the New York Tribune, that great apostolic Abolition sheet!*"

"Oh, it can make no difference to us," the widow quickly answered, but her face and manner told a different story. And when her mother asked what was the difference between the papers, remarking that she had never read either, the daughter exclaimed with some surprise: "Why, Ma, don't you know the World sympathizes with us!"[74]

On November 24, the left wing of the army marched eastward from Milledgeville, crossed the Ogeechee River, and headed for Savannah, one hundred seventy-five miles distant. On the twenty-eighth, there was a stiff cavalry fight near Waynesboro, during which the correspondent of the Philadelphia *Inquirer* narrowly escaped capture, along with General Kilpatrick and his staff, when an enemy force, firing their pistols as they came, advanced within twenty-five yards of the reporter's party.[75] Five days later, railroad communication between Augusta and Savannah was severed by the Federal occupation of Millen.

Meanwhile the North was in a fever of curiosity about the fate of Sherman's army and its destination. Ever since November 12, when all telegraph communication between the army and the North had ceased, neither the Government nor the public at large had had any information of Sherman's movements other than what was reported in the Southern press. Some time elapsed before the Richmond newspapers awoke to the fact that the only means the North had of getting news from Sherman was through Southern news channels. From then on they maintained a strict silence about military movements in Georgia, coupled with hints that their editors knew much more about the situation than they could print. The Georgia newspapers continued, however, to give information, much of it highly confused and extremely unreliable, about Sherman's coastward progress.[76]

Rumors and speculation vied for space in the Northern press with what few facts were available. Since they all added up to success, editorial optimism reflected itself in the news columns. "Sherman's Grandest Campaign," "Piercing the Heart of the Rebellion," and "The Gallop Through Georgia" were typical of the headlines which appeared in the New York *Herald*.[77] Both the *Times* and the *Tribune* were more restrained in their comments. As late as December 10, when Hardee could muster only seventeen thousand troops for the defense of Savannah, the *Tribune* warned its readers of "A Formidable Army in His [Sherman's] Front." And when, on December 26, the other newspapers were exulting over Sherman's "Christmas gift" to the nation, the *Tribune* saw fit to emphasize in a prominent subhead: "Hardee's Army Make Their Escape."

As Sherman's army neared the sea, the Northern press rushed correspondents to Hilton Head and other points along the coast to meet Sherman as he emerged from the interior. At the War Department where he had gone to obtain a pass, however, Stillson of the New York *World* met a stinging rebuff. Identifying himself as "Mr. Jerome B. Stillson, of the *World* newspaper, who was introduced to you in the Wilderness at Gen. Grant's headquarters," Stillson explained to Dana that he was eager to be placed where he could meet Sherman or "failing in that to get speedily to some point on the coast where I shall be likely to hear the first reliable tidings from his army."

"You say you have been acting as correspondent of the *World*?" asked Dana.

"Yes sir," the *World* man assured him.

"Are you now going forth in that capacity?"

"Yes sir."

At that point Dana announced abruptly that "the Secretary of War refuses to give any passes to correspondents of the *World*. He does not consider that paper a proper one to receive such facilities."

"Indeed!" ejaculated Stillson. "Is this not a new arrangement?"

"The Secretary has so directed."

"Does the Secretary revoke passes already given?"

"He has issued no orders on that subject."

With a "Good afternoon, sir," the baffled *World* reporter withdrew from the Assistant Secretary's presence and resolved to drop the whole Sherman matter.[78]

More successful than Stillson, J. W. Miller of the Cincinnati *Commercial* was at Hilton Head, thirty miles North of Savannah, when the first direct news from Sherman reached that place. For days the blockading fleet had been on the lookout for boats issuing from the streams South of the Head, being advised that word from Sherman might come in that way. And so there was considerable excitement in Miller's vicinity when the Federal gunboat "Flag" came steaming up from the South in the early morning hours of Monday, December 12, with three of Sherman's scouts on board. The three men had left Sherman's lines five miles East of Savannah the previous Friday evening, carrying with them dispatches from Sherman for Brigadier General John G. Foster. Taking advantage of a rainstorm, they had slipped past Fort McAllister in a dugout on Saturday night and had been picked up in Ossabaw Sound by the "Flag" the following day.[79] Within three days, the reports brought by the scouts, establishing beyond doubt the safety of Sherman's command, were in the news columns of every important Northern newspaper.

Before Sherman could establish a line of communication with the fleet, it was necessary for him to seize Fort McAllister, which lay on the right bank of the Ogeechee. The task of storming the fort was assigned to Hazen's division of the Fifteenth Corps, formerly commanded by Sherman himself. At one o'clock in the afternoon of Tuesday, December 13, *Herald* reporter Doyle sat on the roof of a rice mill, on the opposite side of the river from the fort, with Sherman and several other officers, waiting for the attack to begin. As yet Sherman had had no word from the fleet; his face lighted up, therefore, when his keen eye detected smoke on the seaward horizon, and Doyle heard him exclaim, "Look! Howard; there is the gunboat!" A half hour passed, and the vessel became visible, but still there was no signal from either the ship or Hazen. As all eyes were focused on the Confederate stronghold, a signal was reported from the gunboat.

"Can we run up? Is Fort McAllister ours?" came the question across the water from Foster and Dahlgren.

"No," the reply was flagged back. "Hazen is just ready to storm it. Can you assist?"

Before Sherman could tell the Admiral what was expected of him, the guns of the fort opened simultaneously with puffs of smoke that rose a few hundred yards away, and a moment later came the signal from Hazen, "I have invested the fort and will assault immediately." Sitting flat on the roof with field glass in hand, the army commander watched the scene intently. "There they go grandly, not a waver," Doyle heard him remark. Twenty seconds passed, and again he exclaimed,

"See that flag in the advance, Howard; how steadily it moves; not a man falters. There they go still; see the roll of musketry. Grand, grand!"

There was a pause for a moment as the thin line of Union soldiers struggled to open a way through the obstacles that the ingenious Confederates had strewed in their path.

"Look!" exclaimed Sherman, "It has halted. They waver. No! It's the parapet! There they go again; now they scale it; some are over. Look! there's a flag on the works! Another, another. It's ours. The fort's ours!"[80]

Hardly more than ten minutes had elapsed from the time the signal for the attack was given before Hazen's tattered colors were floating over the fort. In the opinion of the correspondent of the New York *Evening Post*, no more striking example of quick, determined action had occurred any time during the war.[81]

The news that Sherman's army had reached the sea coast came to the

Army of the Potomac in the columns of a Washington newspaper. As the newsboys galloped along the lines of entrenchments before Petersburg, they were hailed with tumultous shouts, until it seemed as if the whole army were cheering in unison. The Confederate pickets were anxious to know what all the cheering was about, and when they were informed, a great silence descended on Lee's camp. Very little musketry was heard around Petersburg that night, and not a single cannon shot disturbed the slumbers of the opposing camps.[82]

On December 21, the same day that Savannah fell, two New York *Herald* correspondents from widely separated theaters of warfare walked into the *Herald* office in New York only a few minutes apart. Exactly forty days before, these two reporters, Doyle and Conyngham, had bidden farewell to each other in Atlanta and had set forth, the one to join Sherman in his march to the sea, the other to head North with Thomas in pursuit of Hood. On the fourteenth of December, after four weeks of steady marching, Doyle had been on hand to watch the junction of Sherman's forces with General Foster at the seaboard. Four days later, he had left Hilton Head in the "Fulton" with what the *Herald* styled "a full budget of stirring intelligence" and had arrived in New York just in time to meet Conyngham, who had come in that day from Nashville with the tidings of Thomas' smashing success over Hood. The two men greeted each other heartily and exchanged congratulations on their fortunate escapes from many perils since they had last seen each other.[83]

In their accounts of Sherman's march, the army correspondents made no attempt to conceal their jubilant feelings. One of the *Herald* correspondents boasted that Sherman had achieved his objective "without the loss of a wagon or mule, a gun or a pound of ammunition."[84] Hayes of the New York *Tribune,* who had witnessed all the operations of "Sherman's grand army" since the preceding May, was overcome with admiration for "such noble self-sacrificing men" and asserted his belief that nothing could withstand their progress.

Probably the best newspaper account of Sherman's march was published by the New York *Evening Post* in its issue of December 22, 1864. Its author, Major George W. Nichols, was one of Sherman's staff officers who also functioned as a special correspondent of the *Post.* Nichols' account was widely reprinted in other newspapers and was later expanded into a war book which had some popular success.[85] On the same day that Nichols' story appeared in the *Post,* the Philadelphia

Bulletin published a nine-column account of the march, the first to appear in any of the Philadelphia papers. Although the *Bulletin's* account purported to issue from a special correspondent of the paper who had been with Sherman during the march, its content and phraseology were remarkably similar to that of the narrative which Doyle furnished to the *Herald.*

Not having sent a correspondent with Sherman, the New York *Times* had to rely upon a review of the campaign pieced together from miscellaneous sources, and reprints from other papers. The best coverage the *Tribune* could provide was a belated and rather disappointing letter from its special correspondent, Hayes, whose haversack, containing his entire account of the campaign together with the note books upon which his account was based, had been stolen by "some rascally thief." In a letter describing his misfortune in detail, Hayes declared that:

> nothing since my connection with the press as a correspondent has ever so disheartened me as this disaster. The campaign has been a hard one, my health has been very poor part of the time . . . and then to consider that all my efforts have been wasted and brought . . . to naught by the dishonesty of some vile wretch. Between discouragement, chagrin, mortification and fear [of being beaten by the *Herald*], I am unwell physically, mentally, and morally.[86]

Some fairly interesting narratives of the march appeared in other newspapers—the Cincinnati *Gazette,* the Chicago *Tribune,* and the New York *World* among them.[87]

At Savannah, as at Atlanta, the army correspondents were received in a way that must have convinced them that the war was drawing near its end. On the day Williams' Twentieth Corps marched into Savannah, the reporter for the Cincinnati *Gazette* could distinguish:

> none of the rank bitterness . . . which our army encountered at Nashville, Memphis, Vicksburg and New Orleans. . . . The route over which Gen. Sherman rode was jammed by the inhabitants as closely as ever the Boulevards of Paris were when Napoleon rode through them.[88]

The end of the war was indeed clearly in sight. Only one more campaign remained to try the reporters who had followed that magnificent Western army from Atlanta to the sea.

22

"If All . . . Battles . . . Were as Well Described"

ALTHOUGH civilians were common around City Point, Virginia, during the latter part of June, 1864, *Herald* reporter William H. Merriam still must have been surprised when, shortly after noon of June 21, he saw a long, gaunt, bony man, dressed in black, enter General Grant's tent. The stranger had just come in from Washington on "The City of Baltimore" without giving any advance notice. Mistaking him for a member of the Sanitary Commission, the sentinel had refused to admit him to the General's presence until, after some parleying, the stranger had identified himself as Abraham Lincoln, President of the United States!

While Reporter Merriam looked on, Grant and his unexpected guest carried on a "brief, but as I observed it, an exceedingly animated conversation, in which the Presidential gestures were both numerous and awkward," following which "the distinguished party retired to the mess tent for dinner."[1] During the meal, according to Merriam's colleague Cadwallader, Lincoln "managed to ring in three favorite jokes . . . under the plea of illustrating the topics discussed" and kept everybody in good humor until the party rose.[2] About four o'clock he rode out to the front with the General and his staff past long lines of weather-beaten veterans eager to catch a glimpse of "Old Abe." After a visit to Butler's headquarters on the following day, the President returned to Washington, apparently well satisfied that the army was in good hands.

Since the establishment of the army's new advanced base at City Point, the *Herald* had hit on another scheme to bypass the censors in the War and Post Office departments. Blair, the Postmaster General, had the irritating habit of holding back the mails just when the reporters were most eager to use them. By using messengers sent from City Point by steamer at ten o'clock each morning, however, the *Herald* had packages of unopened correspondence delivered at its New York office early in the evening of the following day. To the surprise of Bennett and Cadwallader, it actually cost less, when the volume of correspondence was large, to transmit news by messenger than to telegraph that same news from Washington to New York.

When the other New York papers learned of the *Herald's* new arrangement, several of them sent an agent to Meade's headquarters to obtain authorization for a similar line to be used jointly by the *Tribune, Times, World,* and Philadelphia *Inquirer*. To eliminate such competition, Cadwallader secured an interview with Brigadier General Rufus Ingalls, the army's chief quartermaster. Within a few days, General Ingalls issued a new regulation requiring all civilians traveling on military steamboat lines between City Point, Fortress Monroe, Washington, and Baltimore to pay fifteen cents per mile for transportation, one dollar per day for a stateroom, and one dollar for each meal. The regulation also prohibited them from obtaining meals or staterooms until all officers and privates on board had first been accommodated. After several weeks, during which the *Herald* paid these exorbitant charges without a murmur, the other newspapers withdrew from the contest and went back to the old system. Then, evidently by prearrangement, General Ingalls revoked the order, leaving the *Herald* to enjoy the benefits of its monopoly undisturbed.[3]

June that year was hot and dry. Soldiers and correspondents alike growled about the weather when they were not complaining about their food, enemy snipers, the idiosyncracies of generals and fleas, and the other torments that war invents to try men's souls. During the last week of June, Charles A. Page of the *Tribune* suffered a sun stroke. While he was recuperating in the hospital, Page composed a letter to the *Tribune* which was at once a masterpiece of whimsy and a remarkable portrayal of the trials of the army correspondent:

> Invalids are proverbially querulous and unreasonable, and because they are invalids it is forgiven them. Their whims and vagaries are humored. They may fret and scold, abuse their toast and their friends, scatter their maledictions and the furniture, and who shall cry them "Nay?" The reader of this, if any there be, is informed respectfully but firmly that the writer, being an invalid, proposes to avail himself of all the privileges which attach to the character. Released from the bonds of the proprieties, for him there are no improprieties. Careless of consequences, careless in rhetoric, altogether careless of everything, this letter

that is to be shall write itself. I am an invalid. If any thin stratum of sense or news should happen to crop out between underlying and overlying strata of nonsense, such formation will be accidental, abnormal, unaccountable.

Imprimis: It is hot. It is hotter than yesterday. Yesterday was hotter than the day before. The day before hotter than its immediate predecessor, and *it* than *its,* and so on indeterminately. . . . How hot it is now, no thermometer of words will begin to indicate. The boy who extended the comparison of the adjective from hot to hottest, then began again with Hottentot and ended with Hottentotest, made a creditable effort, but failed. In other climates he may be thought to have succeeded. But in the light and heat of this locality I denounce the ambitious youth as unequal to his attempt. It is hot. Has the lower world invaded the confines of this, or is Virginia a part of that world?

This indescribable hotness is a part of the misery of correspondents.

It is dusty. I wrote the de-apotheosis of dust the other day (did you see it in the "Daily——"?), but failed in the deep damnation commensurate with the subject. Did you ever smile and smile, and feel like a villain? We down here do, whenever we come in dusty from a long ride. Did you ever grit your teeth in rage? We do, whenever we shut our mouths—else we shouldn't shut 'em. Water, I adore thee; soap, thou art my benefactor; towels, ye are blessed! . . .

Dust is a part of the misery of correspondents.

A Scene: Three "specials" of metropolitan journals, smoking meerschaums, and conning letters yet to be. Mail arrives with New-York papers. Each reads one of his own letters.

Reading their own letters is a part of the misery of correspondents.

"Herald" special swears oaths both loud and deep: "They have rewritten my despatch!" "Times" special finds something he spoke of as "impudent" pronounced "important." "Tribune" special is amused. He had said certain troops were "handled skilfully;" he is made to say that they "were travelled skilfully." In another place, where he had described foliage as of the "densest, deepest green," it appears that it was of the *direst* green! "Magnificent" is transformed into "magnified" and destroys the point of a quarter of a column of elaborate rhetoric.

Verily, reading their own letters is a part of the misery of correspondents.

Mr. Winser of "The Times" had his horse shot under him at Cold Harbor. Mr. Anderson of "The Herald" was hit in the arm at Wilderness. Richardson and Browne of "The Tribune" have been sixteen months in Rebel prisons. All have had their hair-breadth 'scapes.

Constant danger, without the soldier's glory, is a part of the misery of correspondents.

Abstractly considered, horseback exercise is a good thing. I have known it to be recommended by physicians. Taken in moderate quantities not too long after sunrise, or not too long before sunset, I have myself found it not unpleasant. In imagination I see myself, September next, indulging in flowing rein on smooth beach roads to the murmur of ocean waves, or in the back country where the foliage is crimson and there are cider-presses in the orchards, following where there are

"Old roads winding, as old roads will
Here to a ferry, and there to a mill."

This is one picture. Now look on this: Virginia wastes, where only desolation dwells, arid with summer heats, and now four weeks without sprinkle of rain. The sky is brass, heated to a white fervor; the air you breathe heated like the blast of a furnace, and laden with dust that chokes you. A fierce, pitiless sun sheds rays like heated daggers; these impalpable daggers stab you. You boil; you pant; you thirst; your temples throb with thrills of mighty pain; you are threatened with *coup de soleil;* you wish yourself anywhere—anywhere out of such torment.

Pooh, man! You forget that you are a "special," and therefore not supposed to be subject to the laws which govern other mortals. You are a Salamander. You are Briareus. You are Argus. You are Hercules. You are Mark Tapley. Be jolly. Ride your ten, fifteen hours; your twenty, thirty, forty, fifty miles. Fatigue is your normal condition. Sleeplessness ditto. "Tired nature" is yours; the "sweet restorer" somebody else's. "Balmy sleep" is for babies. You are a "special," I tell you.

Incessant riding in the sun is a part of the misery of correspondents.

Composition is pleasant, sometimes. I don't mean the mighty joy of creation of the great author, but the simple pleasure of ordinary mortals writing ordinary things. With dressing-gown elegance, and beslippered ease, a fair prospect out of the window, fragrance stealing through from the garden beneath, tempered by the fragrance of a rich Havana between your lips, a well-ordered desk before you, quill pens, and clear, white paper, a snug bookcase in the corner, a basket of fruit and a bouquet at your elbow, a good dinner in prospect, and a drive at sunset with somebody, your friends to see in the evening, and only a column to write—under such circumstances, "by St. Paul, the work goes bravely on!"

But you are a "special." It is far into the night when you begin. You rode all day and a part of the night, and have only now had your ablution and your supper. You begin, — "squat like a toad" before a camp-fire; a stumpy lead-pencil, and smoke in your eyes, dingy paper, and ashes puffed in your face; no part of you that has not its own special pain and torment. Your brain is in a state of "confusion worse confounded." Your eyes will shut, your pencil will drop from nerveless fingers, but I say unto you, Write! Do you forget that you are a "special," and must write? Force yourself to the rack, tug away, bear on hard, and when you are done, do not read it over, or you will throw it into the fire. Now arrange with the guard to have yourself awakened at daybreak, an hour or two hence, and then lie down, wondering who wouldn't be a "special."

The necessity of writing just so much every day is a part of the misery of correspondents.

You will inevitably write things that will offend somebody. Somebody will say harsh things of you, and perhaps seek you out to destroy you. Never mind. Such is a part of the misery of correspondents.

Was your horse stolen last night? Are your saddle-bags and all that they contain missing this morning? No matter. It is a thing of course. It is a part of the misery of correspondents.

You are a "special," and who wouldn't be?[4]

During July the campaign in Virginia took a startling new turn for the reporters. Still confident of his ability to hold the Army of the Potomac in check, Lee placed Lieutenant General Jubal A. Early in command of the Confederate forces in the Shenandoah Valley and sent reinforcements to enable him to clear the Valley of Union troops. Early was more than equal to his assignment. After driving Hunter, the Union commander, over the mountains into West Virginia, he crossed the Potomac into Maryland on July 6 and moved eastward toward Frederick. One of the *Herald* correspondents, who was stationed at Harper's Ferry, sent his paper a glowing account of an engagement between Hunter's command and Early's Confederates, thereby scooping the reporters who had actually been present at the battle. Unfortunately for his reputation as a reliable correspondent, the *Herald* man made two bad errors: he said that the battle occurred two days earlier than it did; he located it sixteen miles from where it really happened. That performance pretty well "cooked his goose."[5]

At Ellery Mills, three and a half miles East of Frederick, Early was temporarily halted by a force of less than six thousand "hundred days'" troops and Sixth Corpsmen, commanded by General Lew Wallace. While a New York *World* reporter, trapped in Frederick by Early's rapid advance, looked on from the Confederate side,[6] Early defeated Wallace in the ensuing Battle of the Monacacy and prepared to march on Washington the following day, Sunday, July 10.

On the morning of the ninth, George F. Williams, who had been covering the Shenandoah Valley campaign for the New York *Times*, had reached Baltimore, intent on finding the best means of getting to the scene of the fighting. At Baltimore he had learned that the government had taken over the Baltimore and Ohio Railroad during the period of the emergency and had forbidden all civilian travel over it. Meanwhile, the most absurd bulletins based on news current at Frederick were coming in over the wires at Baltimore. In desperation, Williams jumped on board a train bound for Washington and rode as far as the Relay House, where the line for Frederick branched off. He was now six miles nearer to the battlefield, but for all the good it augured, he might as well have remained in Baltimore. Just as he was about to climb aboard the 5:00 P.M. local from Washington to go back to Baltimore, a military train loaded with wounded came in from the battlefield. This was the very opportunity he had been looking for. Climbing aboard, Williams went from boxcar to boxcar, collecting the names of the soldiers and putting together a roster of the troops which had taken part in the battle.

In one of the cars was a farmer who lived near the battlefield and who had volunteered to come along to help take care of the wounded. Although he knew very little about military matters, he had been an eyewitness of most of the fighting that day. Williams persuaded him to go over to a hotel room and talk in his rambling fashion about what he had seen that day. Although the farmer was unable to identify the commands that had figured in an important charge which had occurred at a critical moment in the fighting, he was able to describe the colors of the different generals. From this and similar information, Williams was able to reconstruct most of the happenings of the day, and being familiar with the ground, he was able to form a reasonably correct idea of the whole battle.

Handing his informant a ten-dollar bill to repay him for his trouble, the *Times* man rushed over to the telegraph office and sent through a column-length story of the battle, together with a list of casualties. The next day the *Times* was the only newspaper in New York which contained anything about the battle except a brief statement authorized by the Government. Furthermore, Williams' account of the battle was so accurate that General Wallace was quoted as having said it was strange he had not noticed the New York *Times* correspondent on the field as the reporter must have been in his immediate vicinity most of the day.[7]

In Washington, toward which Early was marching with all possible speed, no one seemed to be excited. For days the newspapers had been filled with rumors of Confederate invasion. Every few hours a newspaper "extra" would come out with the announcement that the Confederates had entered Maryland in force and that the capital would be attacked in twelve hours. The next issue would then declare that this was nothing more than an "idle scare" and that the only Confederates North of the Potomac were a few cavalrymen on a raid. At nine o'clock on that Sunday morning, July 10, the Washington correspondent of the Chicago *Journal,* Benjamin F. Taylor, heard that the enemy was within sixteen miles of Baltimore. But there was still no evidence, other than the cries of the newsboys and some additional activity around the hotels, that Washington was perturbed.

As the day advanced, the city gradually began to shake off some of its lethargy. Taylor's letter to the Chicago *Journal,* published more than a week later, gave an excellent picture of Washington's transformation that momentous Sunday:

> Bands of music, bodies of infantry and little clouds of cavalry begin to pass across the city; hard riders dash through the streets; engines are harnessed to the trains; steamers draw heavy breaths and give symptoms of waking; the treble of the newsboys flaunting their second extra, and singing out, "rebels a marchin' on to Washin'ton!" again startles you, and at last the city brushes the poppy leaves off its eyelids and is broad awake. It leans out of windows; it comes fairly out of doors; it ties itself in knots on street corners; it buys "extras" and reads them; it hears rumors and believes them; it whistles a little and tries to look unconcerned. We have the defeat of Wallace at Monocacy yesterday; we know that

> the pirate Florida is off the mouth of Chesapeake Bay, and in mischief; a dragging anchor parts the telegraph cable at Fortress Monroe, and leaves us "no sign" from the Lieutenant General; the enemy is advancing toward Laurel, sixteen miles from Washington, on the Baltimore and Ohio Railroad; he appears at Rockville on the Frederick turnpike, sixteen miles distant. . . .

Strolling along Pennsylvania Avenue that night, Taylor could hear everybody from tight-lipped gentlemen with beaver hats and silver-handled canes to frightened Negroes huddled in small groups muttering "trenches—cavalry—defenses—rebels."[8]

On the following morning, a Confederate raiding party under the command of Major Harry Gilmor burned the railroad bridge over the Gunpowder River and temporarily severed all rail communications between Baltimore, Washington, and the North. One of the *Herald* correspondents, Charles Hannam, had the misfortune to be on a northbound train which was stopped near the bridge by Gilmor's men. They relieved Hannam of his dispatches and some other valuables but left the envelopes minus the dispatches at Magnolia, together with a penciled notation consigning them to the *Herald* with "Harry Gilmor's respects." The *Herald* was very philosophical about the whole matter, mainly because Hannam had been able to reproduce from memory most of the material contained in the dispatches "of which our readers have had the benefit long since."[9]

At two o'clock on Monday afternoon, an employee of the American Telegraph Company rode into Baltimore on a handcar with the news that the last remaining telegraph link between Baltimore and the North had been cut. When the telegraph went dead, the reporters in Baltimore were at a standstill. Just as they were about to leave the telegraph office, a dispatch was received from Washington stating that a cavalry fight was going on near the Blair residence at Silver Spring within six miles of the capital. The Baltimore agent of the Associated Press, Charles C. Fulton, showed the dispatch to General Wallace and suggested that by sending a tug to Havre de Grace communication with the North might be re-established. The General promptly ordered out a tug to carry dispatches and permitted Fulton and the *Times* reporter Williams to go along with the staff officer who had been detailed as bearer of dispatches.

At the mouth of the Susquehanna within sight of their destination, the little tug boat "Ella" ran aground after a quick five-hour run up the coast. The reporters had expected to reach Philadelphia by ten o'clock that night in ample time to telegraph their budget of news before midnight. But this was now plainly out of the question. Following the example of Major William M. Estes, the *Times* reporter fell asleep on the deck, but Fulton remained standing at the bow and gazing at the lights on shore—the very picture of frustration. Awaking around midnight, Williams found that Fulton and the Major had eased their little craft off the obstruction and had brought it safely to its destination. On the track nearby was a train filled with passengers, all ready to start to Philadelphia. Seizing the dispatches for the Associated Press, the two reporters swung aboard as the train moved off. But because of the great length of the train and heavy rail traffic, it was nearly 5:00 A.M. before they reached Philadelphia with the latest news from Baltimore and Washington.[10]

By that time reinforcements from the Army of the Potomac and the Department of the Gulf[11] had reached the Capital. Coffin of the Boston *Journal* had learned that the Army of the Potomac was to move several hours before the movement began. He hastened to City Point therefore to embark for Washington. To his surprise, nobody at Grant's headquarters seemed very much disturbed by the news about Early's invasion. Grant's adjutant general, Lieutenant Colonel Theodore S. Bowers, spoke lightly about the "little scare" they were having at Washington and expressed the opinion that the scare would do them good.

"How large a force is it supposed the Rebels have in Maryland?" Coffin wanted to know.

"Somewhere about twenty-five thousand—possibly thirty. Breckenridge[12] has gone, with his command. And Early has raked and scraped all the troops possible which were outside Richmond. Mosby is with him, and the irregular bands of the upper Potomac, and the troops which met Hunter at Lynchburg. It will not affect operations here. Lee undoubtedly expected to send Grant post-haste to Washington; but the siege will go on."[13]

Nonetheless, Coffin reached Washington in time to hear the cheers that greeted Wright's two divisions of the Sixth Corps as they marched down Pennsylvania Avenue, followed by Emory's Nineteenth Corps from New Orleans. It was then five o'clock in the afternoon, Monday, July 11.

Edward A. Paul of the New York *Times* had left Washington the day before to return to the army in front of Petersburg. About noon, Monday, Paul's wife and children, who were living in a rented house on the Seventh Street Pike approximately five miles North of Washington, saw long lines of armed men, dressed in gray, creeping along the fence rows on either side of the pike. Very much startled, Mrs. Paul, who had received no warning that the enemy was in the vicinity, exclaimed:

"Who are these men? Can they be rebels?"

At that instant an officer straightened up and said: "Yes, madam, we are rebels."

"Do you intend to injure us?" queried the reporter's wife in great alarm.

"No," was the reply. "We shall not injure you, but your friends may."

At that moment the Confederates were in plain sight of and within easy gun range of Fort Stevens, which was not more than a mile away. Having passed the house, Early's men formed a skirmish line at right angles to the road, and within a few minutes some real fighting commenced. During the next hour, Generals Early, Breckenridge, and nearly all the other Confederate general officers with their staffs occupied the yard surrounding the Paul home. Several times it was suggested to Mrs. Paul that she and her family go to the rear. But this she refused to do until one of her little girls had been injured by a shell from the fort and assurance had been given her that in her absence a guard would be posted to watch the house. The promise was not kept, however, and when her husband returned from Petersburg later in the week he found that his home had been completely gutted by the raiders.

Paul was convinced that the marauders knew very well whose house they were plundering. One of them, in fact, had informed Paul's wife that the *Times* reporter had done the Confederate cause more harm than any ten of Lincoln's soldiers. Still another remarked: "We have tried twenty times to catch that fellow [Paul], but we will catch and hang him yet."[14]

Just before they left, several of Early's men primed the house with kerosene and were about to set it on fire when they were put to flight by a party of Union soldiers. After some further fighting on Tuesday, Early retreated across the Potomac on Wednesday morning, carrying with him a large amount of plunder.

In reporting the raid, the Northern press generally overestimated the size of the invading force and gave Wallace all too little credit for checking the speed of Early's advance. Although Ben Taylor estimated the size of Early's army at only thirty thousand, Wilkeson placed it at fifty to fifty-five thousand, and a New York *World* reporter talked wisely about a second force of forty-five to sixty thousand Confederates under A. P. Hill, somewhere along the South bank of the Potomac, acting in conjunction with Early's force of thirty-four to thirty-eight thousand men.[15] Subjecting Wilkeson's estimate to an elaborate analysis, Whitelaw Reid found it based on extremely dubious evidence. It was Reid's opinion that the invading column:

> did not number over twenty five thousand; that scarcely one third of this number came even within supporting distance, while their skirmish line laid siege to Washington; [and] that the remainder were engaged in gathering supplies & in carrying to the river what they had plundered. . . .[16]

Reid's estimate was considerably nearer the truth than those of most of the other Washington newspaper correspondents. It is now generally conceded that the number of troops under Early's command did not exceed seventeen thousand.[17]

The New York *Times* reporter Swinton by this time was back in Washington after further difficulties with the military authorities. Throughout the campaign in Virginia, so a *Herald* correspondent charged, he had "persistently misrepresented" the operations of Burnside's Ninth Corps. In writing of the Battle of Bethesda Church of May 31, for example, Swinton had claimed that the Ninth Corps had participated with artillery only and did not engage the enemy at short range. Yet the official report showed that over twelve hundred members of the Corps had been killed or wounded in the battle.[18] Burnside's eyes had flashed fire when he scrutinized Swinton's Bethesda Church letter. Pronouncing it "a libel upon the Ninth Corps, as well as . . . myself," Burnside also had accused the *Times* reporter of having obtained access to confidential military correspondence through the connivance of the telegraph operator or otherwise. It was Burnside's opinion that for these infractions Swinton should either be disciplined as Crapsey had been or turned over to Burnside himself for appropriate punishment. Acting in the spirit of this suggestion, Grant issued an order on July 1 directing that the *Times* man be expelled from the lines of the Army of the Potomac.[19]

Raymond was highly indignant at this cavalier treatment of his ace correspondent:

> Gen. Meade and the "Corps Commanders" need not distress themselves about Mr. Swinton's return. There is nothing so exces-

sively attractive in the service, or in their official society . . . to lead any gentleman to thrust his personal presence or his literary attentions upon them against so emphatic a protest as that of Gen. Meade. We shall have no difficulty in finding quite as agreeable and as useful a field for the exercise of Mr. Swinton's abilities as that which the above order invites him to leave.

Major-Gen. Meade accuses Mr. Swinton of having "forwarded for publication *incorrect statements* respecting the operations of the troops." What these statements were, —in what respect they were incorrect, or what means were afforded of correcting them, we are not informed. Gen. Meade must have a very vague idea of the duties of a correspondent, and of the difficulties which attend their performance, if he requires perfect and exact accuracy in regard to all the details of army operations, as the condition of remaining within his lines. He has not always found it easy to be thus exact in his own official reports, even after he had taken weeks to compile and prepare them. Possibly he may, at some future day, condescend to specify the particular default which has led to Mr. Swinton's exclusion from the limits of his army, — though it is, after all, a matter of very little consequence. Judging from Gen. Meade's previous action in similar cases, and from the general temper he exhibits toward the press, Mr. Swinton is quite as likely to have been excluded for being *too* accurate as for any other offence.

We believe our readers will generally concur with us in the belief that in losing Mr. Swinton the public lose one of the most intelligent, impartial and competent of the many correspondents who have given the record of this war to the world. If he had been a little more disposed to pander to the personal vanity and the uneasy jealousy of Officers, he might have had a longer career as a correspondent, but it would scarcely have been more honorable to himself or more serviceable to the country.[20]

Toward the end of July, the deadlock at Petersburg temporarily was enlivened by an episode which provided sensational copy for the army newspapermen. On June 25, the Forty-Eighth Pennsylvania Volunteers, nearly all of them coal miners from the anthracite district, had begun working on a tunnel to be used for exploding a mine under the Confederate fortifications. The idea originally had been conceived by Colonel Henry Pleasants of the Forty-Eighth Pennsylvania. It had been enthusiastically endorsed by Pleasants' division commander, Brigadier General Robert B. Potter, and by the corps commander, Burnside. Meade had been skeptical from the very outset, however, and only with reluctance had he permitted it to go ahead. In fact, he gave so little help to the enterprise that some observers thought he really hoped the tunneling would fail.

By July 23, the excavation was completed, however, and after some further delays Meade directed that the mine should be exploded at 3:30 A.M., Saturday, July 30. Burnside already had been asked to furnish troops from the Ninth Corps to exploit the breach in the enemy's lines. To spearhead the assault, he had planned, without specific authorization from Meade, to use Ferrero's division of Negro troops, who for several weeks had been specially trained for this action. Meade finally decided against the use of the Negro troops for this purpose, however, on the ground that they were without previous battle experience and that charges of racial discrimination might be made in case the assault failed. Learning only a few hours beforehand that his battle order had been countermanded, the harassed Burnside did a peculiar thing. He was unable to decide which of his three white divisions should be used, and so he permitted the three division commanders to draw lots for the assignment. The lot fell to Ledlie's First Division of the Ninth Corps, an extremely poor choice.

Precisely on schedule, at half-past three in the morning, the fuse was lighted. A stream of fire passed rapidly through the gallery, but there was no explosion. An investigation disclosed that the fire had gone out, one hundred feet from the gallery entrance, at a point where the fuse had been spliced together. The fire was relighted, and finally at 4:45 A.M. a blinding flash shot a mountain of earth, men, timber, and cannons skyward. When the smoke cleared away, it could be seen that a gaping hole over two hundred feet long, fifty feet wide, and twenty-five feet deep had been quarried out of the Confederate line.

The surprise of the enemy was complete. Had the advantage thus gained been exploited rapidly, Cemetery Hill, the key to the Petersburg defenses, might have been quickly occupied. Very little support was given to the Ninth Corps, however, by the other corps of the Army of the Potomac. Moreover, the cowardice of Burnside's division commanders —Ledlie, Wilcox, and Ferrero—compromised the potential success of the assault. These men remained in a bomb-proof shelter to the rear of the mine opening throughout the action. Recovering from their initial panic, the Confederates brought up artillery to enfilade the crater and began pouring a deadly fire into the confused mass of Federals, who still were attempting to press forward without adequate leadership. Meade recognized the futility of the struggle, and about 9:15 A.M. he dispatched to Burnside a peremptory order, calling for him to withdraw his attacking force. Yet within those few hours nearly five thousand Federal troops, killed, wounded, and missing, had been sacrificed.[21]

On their way to the mail boat at City Point the following morning, Reporters Grey and Thaddeus S. Seybold of the New York *Tribune* were frustrated by a peculiar setback of their own. Grey's mount, a vicious animal, shied at the sight of a dead horse lying in a deep gorge through which the two correspondents had to pass. Coaxing was of no avail, the animal refused to budge, and the reporters missed their boat. Apologizing in a letter to Gay for the twenty-four hour delay in the *Tribune*'s report of the fighting on Saturday, Seybold expressed the pious hope that the delay would "not be noticed by your readers as much as it is vexatious to us."[22]

So far as the press was concerned, the construction of the Petersburg mine had been a well-kept secret. It was tacitly acknowledged in the army that the mine was an improper subject of conversation, and no indication was given that any reporter had been in it before it was exploded. On the day of the assault a correspondent of the Philadelphia *Inquirer* informed his newspaper that:

> The existence of this mine has for several weeks been generally known and spoken of in the army, yet I am not aware that it has been once mentioned in any newspaper, and I presume the majority of people had heard nothing of it until the news of its explosion was forwarded for publication this morning.[23]

Newspaper accounts of the failure generally fell into two categories: (1) those minimizing it as a small affair which would not particularly affect the outcome of the campaign and (2) those which portrayed it as an overwhelming disaster which might cause the campaign against Richmond to be abandoned. Both the New York *Times* and the Philadelphia *Inquirer* preferred to suspend judgment until a court of inquiry had thoroughly investigated the cause of the failure.[24] But Sam Wilkeson, the old war-horse of the New York *Tribune*, now back in the field again, would not permit himself to be muzzled by considerations of military security, real or supposed. In a vehement letter to his paper he wrote:

> Twilight yesterday was not dark enough to hide the shame of the true soldiers of the Army of the Potomac, kindled by the reading

of the first accounts in the New-York city papers of the last attempt made to take Petersburg by storm. The displayed headings—"Explosion of a Mine under the Rebel Works!" "A Battery of Sixteen Guns Blown Up!" "The Grand Assault on the Rebel Defenses!" "Three Tiers of Earthworks Carried!"[25]—provoked exclamations of astonishment muffled under mortification and sorrow. Glorious news from Petersburg! Why, O swindled people! the ink, that made the lie that gave the false journalism in New-York its last sensation, was not yet spread on the types, while every drummer-boy and mule-driver in the Army of the Potomac knew that a crowning disaster and a crowning disgrace had happened to it, and the number of our killed, wounded, and missing was whispered among them to be five thousand. "Three tiers of earthworks carried!" Aye, carried as Pharaoh's cavalry and war charioteers carried the Red Sea—carried precisely in that way. . . .

I tell no secret when I say that Grant wrapped himself in silence on Monday, and that his heart was gnawed at by disgust and rage—and the statement of this fact is the measure of a great soldier's appreciation of the misconduct which turned an accomplished victory into a disgraceful and ruinous disaster.

What was the affair of Saturday? I shall tell it only in the outlines, for it is my desire to do no wrong, yet my determination to tell the truth. So, until I gather the sure facts of the case, I will only say generally that the commander of the corps charged with the duty and intrusted with the coveted honor of making the assault [Burnside], did not accompany the troops that led it; that not a commander of a division of the corps accompanied the troops; that the work which their absence thus discredited and impaired was left entirely to brigade commanders; that the charge made by the leading force *was not supported for three-quarters of an hour;* that when the support came up to and entered in the crater produced by the explosion of the mine, it found it full of the advance, in a necessarily disordered state; that the delay in supporting the leading charge gave the Rebels time to recover from the confusion and terror caused by the explosion, to gather opposite the breach all their available force, to drive back into the crater the force that had advanced beyond it, to train upon the fatal pit all their artillery, to rain into it a fire of musketry, grape and canister, that tore remorselessly, and without the possibility of error of aim, the solid mass of wriggling, heaving, twisting, crawling, helpless soldiers, black and white, that, inextricably intermingled, defied all attempts to tactically extricate them.[26]

This was strong language but none too strong. One of the other *Tribune* correspondents with the Army of the Potomac assured Gay that "Wilkeson's letter in today's Trib. is fact every word of it.—I could not state it so sweepingly without being expelled—but *he* may."[27] In the opinion of the man who had planned and helped to carry out the gigantic sapping operation, the failure of July 30 was the melancholy fruit of "individual personal jealousy; bungling incompetence; deliberate lack of co-operation, and . . . rank cowardice."[28]

Yet Wilkeson was hardly fair to either Burnside or Robert B. Potter, the only Ninth Corps division commander who accompanied his troops into battle. It is true that Burnside later was relieved of his command after a court of inquiry held him responsible, along with four other officers, for the failure.[29] But it hardly could have escaped Wilkeson's notice that Meade first had tried, and failed, to have Burnside court martialed, and that the court of inquiry which later sat in judgment upon Burnside, in spite of his protest, had been packed with Meade's friends.[30]

During the next three months, developments in the Shenandoah Valley furnished the principal theme of war reporting in the East. Lincoln had become dissatisfied with the failure of the Federal commanders in that area to hold Early in check after his retreat across the Potomac. Consequently, on August 7, 1864, the President had issued an order consolidating the four separate commands operating against Early into one and placing Sheridan at the head of it.[31] Grant instructed Sheridan to take whatever measures were necessary to make the Valley useless as a supply center for Lee's army.

Although they worked under the double handicaps of faulty communications and military censorship, the army reporters did a fairly creditable job of reporting the campaign that followed. Once E. A. Paul (whose house Early's men had almost destroyed) saved Custer from a trap by making a circuit of the Confederate lines to warn him. Custer was understandably grateful for the warning, but Paul received no thanks from Sheridan, who by this time was hardly less antagonistic toward the army newspapermen than Sherman was.[32]

Following a sharp clash with Early's rear guard at Berryville, Virginia, on September 3, Sheridan dressed down another *Times* reporter, George F. Williams, for the way in which he had reported the engagement. Using erroneous information from "those who ought to know better," Williams had placed the Federal loss at three hundred. He had further intimated that the ambulance train recently captured from the enemy had been recaptured by Early.[33] In reality the Federals had lost no more than a third of Williams' figure, and all but one of the ambulances had been recovered.

"So you have been making fun of me in your damned newspaper!" were Sheridan's opening words.

"Fun, General?"

"Yes; you told all about those confounded ambulances and paid no sort of respect to the commander of the army in which you are suffered to live."

"There was no exaggeration in my story, sir; you must admit that!"

"Admit hell!" cried Sheridan. "This business has got to stop. You are ordered to leave my department within twenty-four hours!"

"Well, General," retorted Williams, "you have just been made Commander of the United States Military Department. Even if I go back to New York, I shall still be within the lines of your command."

"Oh, go to the devil if you like!" shot back Sheridan. "I don't care where you go."

"All right, General," said the reporter nonchalantly as he turned to go, "but I am afraid I shall not be out of your department even with his Satanic Majesty!"[34]

The affair at Berryville was only a minor action, however, and since there were no general engagements, the army reporters had little to write about. Most of them had gone up to Harper's Ferry and were caught napping when Sheridan suddenly took the offensive on the morning of September 19. Battle was joined with the Confederates early that morning at the crossing of Opequon Creek, about two miles East of Winchester. After a hard fight, during which Emory's Nineteenth Corps was temporarily forced to give ground, Crook's West Virginia troops were successfully used to turn the Confederate left flank. Through the streets of Winchester and beyond, the routed Confederates streamed, continuing their flight until they reached Fisher's Hill, about twenty miles below Winchester. There another fight occurred on the twenty-second, in which the Confederates were again defeated. Had the cavalry been able to get to Early's rear, his entire command would have been captured before it could reach New Market.

The first of the army reporters to reach Washington with an account of the Battle of Winchester was the *Times* correspondent, Williams. Consequently, he was invited to the White House at two o'clock in the morning to give details of the fighting to the President. To express his appreciation for this service, Lincoln gave Williams a red-letter pass, which permitted him to pass all army lines and picket guards without presenting any other credentials.[35]

One of the few other newspaper accounts of the Battle of Winchester was contributed by Jerome B. Stillson of the New York *World,* who, during this campaign, completely justified Croly's good opinion of him. Although his account was substantially accurate, Stillson made the performance of the Federal troops appear more heroic than it actually was:

> Here is no cowardly fear of what is in a soberer time called death. This tremendous work and excitement of fighting has crushed out *all* fear. Every eye that looks forward from these ranks, looks with a hope and an expectation of something in the achievement of which, the accident of death is held as nothing.[36]

Nor did Stillson give any indication in his letter of the demoralized condition of the Nineteenth Corps: when Crook tried to lead some of them into battle, the others would "flop down again and wouldn't fire a shot." One of Emory's division commanders, Brigadier General Emory Upton, pled with Crook to prefer charges against Emory, saying that:

> he [Emory] was a damned old coward, that he [Upton] had tried to get him to go in to enfilade those fences, and he said he wouldn't do it without orders from Gen. Sheridan, etc. Upton was nearly crying, he was so mad.[37]

After their victory at Fisher's Hill, Sheridan's Army of the Shenandoah followed the retreating Confederates beyond New Market all the way to Port Republic. Near there, Early's men made their escape into the Luray Valley through a gap in the Blue Ridge. Francis C. Long of the New York *Herald* decided at that time to leave the army and to ride back to Harper's Ferry, more than one hundred and twenty-five miles away. There he planned to telegraph the news of Early's escape to New York. At the Ferry, he met his former *Tribune* colleague, T. C. Grey, who just had gotten back from Washington. Grey already had managed to pick up some general information about Early's retreat from Long's cavalry escort, but he realized that information was most inadequate. He was determined to go to any length, however, to keep the *Herald* man from scooping him.

Hurrying to the telegraph office, Grey began sending off what little news he had as "furnished by an intelligent contraband." Fully aware that Grey had nothing of real importance to send, Long, begging him to surrender the wire, stressed that he had been in the saddle almost continuously for nearly a week and greatly needed rest. Grey merely laughed at this and vowed he would hold the wire until midnight at any cost. He then produced a pocket-sized edition of the Bible and announced that he would telegraph the whole book of Genesis before he would give way to any other reporter.

Long lost no time in further protest, for he well knew that his *Tribune* rival would do exactly as he had said. Without speaking to the operators, who obviously were enjoying the situation, Long left the telegraph office. From the post quartermaster, he borrowed a horse and rode the seventeen miles to Frederick. In spite of his weariness, he reached Frederick in time to send a full account of Sheridan's operations to the *Herald* before the telegraph office closed. Thus, the first full account of Early's retreat reached the *Herald* before all the other newspapers.[38]

But a bigger news story, of a smashing Federal success, was about to break. Thomas Buchanan Read's poem (published for the first time in the New York *Tribune* of November 8, 1864) did more than did any army reporter to immortalize Sheridan's ride to the battlefield of Cedar Creek and shape the legend of a spectacular victory, which the Federal commander achieved almost single-handed.[39] The press did full justice to Sheridan's dashing performance, however, and although Northern newspaper readers hardly could have known that Early had attacked with inferior numbers, the New York papers did an effective job of reporting the Cedar Creek action.

Soon after Early's escape into the Luray Valley in late September, Sheridan had pulled back his army North of the Shenandoah to Cedar Creek, about nineteen miles South of Winchester. On October 15, he had been called to Washington for a conference with Stanton and Halleck. While Sheridan was away from his army, Early had unleashed a surprise attack at early dawn on October 19 and had driven the Union left and center from their positions. How Early's dawn attack had caught the Federal command completely unprepared was vividly but not altogether accurately described by the New York *World* correspondent Stillson:

> Just before daybreak this morning Early began his movement. An impenetrable fog enveloped the whole region, favoring his

> designs. . . . Just as the first gleam of day began to mingle with the dim moonlight, the advance of Lee's division[40] was preceded and covered by an unimportant and feint attack on our extreme right. As this attack began, the sentinels of the enemy, along our whole front, fired signal muskets from right to left. Immediately afterward the three rebel divisions, under Pegram, Ramseur, and Gordon, advanced in solid columns without skirmishers, and assaulted General Crook's position in front and flank. The warning given by our pickets was not, it seemed, timely enough to secure an adequate manning of the breastworks. The result was that the rebels, firing rapid and terrific volleys of musketry, swept over the works almost without opposition. . . . Nearly all the encampments of the command were overrun by the enemy, numbers of our soldiers being taken prisoners while not yet arisen from slumber. Shelter tents were in some instances pulled from soldiers lying in their blankets. . . . General Crook and his division commanders did their best, under the circumstances, to meet the shock, and constantly opposed a half organized front against the enemy.[41]

Manifestly, Stillson was striving for emotional effect here, and with some success. But in the process he neglected completely some other attributes of good reporting. How, for example, could anyone, reporter or soldier, see "dim moonlight" through an "impenetrable fog"? Were the signal muskets fired from right to left from Stillson's point of view or from the point of view of the advancing Confederates? And what about those "solid columns" of Confederate gray whose "rapid and terrific volleys of musketry" would have wiped out their own men if they had remained in that formation as they swept over the Union breastworks?

Elias Smith of the New York *Tribune,* who had recently come up from Atlanta, was sleeping about a quarter of a mile away from Cedar Creek when the tumult started. Saddling his horse, Smith rode up to the center of the line where Emory's Nineteenth Corpsmen were crouched low, nervously fingering their guns as they awaited the enemy's onslaught. Less than five minutes after he reached the field, the *Tribune* correspondent saw the left of Emory's line begin to double up as the enemy's fire, issuing from front, flank, and rear, rattled like hail along the inside of the breastworks. Turning his horse about, Smith made off at top speed, running the gauntlet of bullets which whizzed all about him.[42]

By that time General Wright, who commanded the army in Sheridan's absence, had received word of the desperate situation of the Union left and center. Off rode a staff officer with instructions from Wright. The Sixth Corps (connected with the right of the Nineteenth) was to pivot on its left and check the enemy's advance. Stillson's battle report praised the resolute manner in which these veterans swung around and confronted the advancing Confederates:

> These orders had scarcely been received before General Ricketts, with the Sixth corps, and General Torbert, with the two divisions of cavalry mentioned, were in motion. As the solid marching columns of the Sixth corps swung round and up to the scene of conflict in the center, nobody who saw them but felt hope revive within him. At this time the Nineteenth corps, very much broken and weakened . . . was fast retreating before the fierce onset of the rebels. . . . The Sixth corps, moving by the left flank, came up a short distance in rear of what had been General Sheridan's headquarters; opened the right of its line to permit the stragglers from the left of the Nineteenth corps to pass through, and then, in conjunction with the remainder of the Nineteenth corps . . . repulsed a tremendous charge of the enemy and held them at bay.[43]

Here is another example of Stillson's striving for effect coupled with his carelessness of fact. To permit the stragglers of the Nineteenth Corps to pass through its lines, the Sixth Corps would have had to open not the *right* but the *left* of its line. Nor is it the only instance in which a possible change in point of view led Stillson to say just the opposite of what he meant.

Sheridan had stayed all night in Winchester on his way back from Washington. When he received reports of heavy firing from the direction of Middletown, however, he had started out from Winchester about eight-thirty the morning of October 19 to rejoin his army. After a two-hour ride he reached the battlefield, where he was greeted by a storm of cheers and cries of "Sheridan!" "Sheridan!" Stillson asked one of Sheridan's aides, who had ridden on up to the skirmish line, if the General had arrived yet.

"He is here," replied the aide, Major George A. Forsyth.

"Well? What is he going to do about it?"

"He's going to whale hell out of them."

"He can't do it."

"Wait, and you'll see."

"I wish I may," said Stillson, "but I doubt it," and turning away, he rode back to find the General.[44]

Before the battle was over, Stillson would have reversed his opinion. Whatever his previous evaluation of Sheridan might have been, whatever he may still have thought of him, the *World* man was too good a reporter to do less than full justice to the part Sheridan had played in turning defeat into victory. In view of the conversation Stillson had with Forsyth, his description of Sheridan's return to the battlefield is especially interesting:

> At 10 o'clock, just as the last retreat alluded to was about completed, and as the army was getting into its new position, a faint hurrah from the rear, along the pike, announced his coming. He rode his famous black horse, and asked questions as he rode, of those along the line.
>
> "Where is the Nineteenth corps?" he inquired of a mounted officer near one of the batteries in rear of the cavalry.
>
> "On the right, general, in those woods," was the reply.
>
> Riding on still farther, he said to another whom he recognized, "Now, all I want, by God, is to get those men up in the rear and whip these rascals back."
>
> One of his staff officers, coming out to meet him, announced that the situation of the army was "awful."
>
> "Pshaw!" said Sheridan, "it's nothing of the sort. It's all right, or we'll fix it right!"
>
> The general rode on with his staff and escort, which soon became in the distance a mass of dust and gleaming hoofs. Galloping past the batteries to the extreme left of the line held by the cavalry, he rode to the front, took off his hat and waved it, while a cheer went up from the ranks not less hearty and enthusiastic than that which greeted him after the battle of Winchester. Generals rode out to meet him, officers waved their swords, men threw up their hats in an extremity of glee. General Custer, discovering Sheridan at the moment he arrived, rode up to him, threw his arms around his neck, and kissed him on the cheek. Waiting for no other parley than simply to exchange greeting, and to say, "This retreat must be stopped, by God," Sheridan broke loose, and began galloping down the lines, along the whole front of the army. Everywhere the enthusiasm caused by his appearance was the same. It increased at last until that part of the army in line of battle became a new being, having twice its previous will to fight, and until that part of the army in rear, hearing

of it, became partially ashamed of secession, and came back.[45]

In no part of his battle report was Stillson more effective than in his description of the arrival of Sheridan. Yet overanxiety to reach an emotional climax limited its effectiveness. From Stillson's report it is difficult to know what Sheridan really intended to do with the men in the rear. It hardly seems likely, moreover, that the same general who made use of the expression, "By God," would utter only a feeble "Pshaw" when one of his own staff officers had told him that the army's situation was "awful."

Although Wright already had checked the enemy and had given orders for a counterattack, it was not until 4:00 P.M. that the Army of the Shenandoah advanced to the attack, in the face of a fire so deadly that it seemed as if the assault must fail. Just before sundown, however, one of the Sixth Corps divisions breached the Confederate line. Panic spread to other parts of the line, and Custer's cavalry, swooping down from the right, drove the Southerners in wild confusion across Cedar Creek. Pressing vigorously after them, Custer's horsemen put the finishing touches on one of the most decisive victories of the war.

Scores of officers were rehashing the events of the battle at Sheridan's headquarters that night when Custer came in about nine o'clock. According to Stillson, the excited Custer, upon arriving, grabbed Sheridan in a bear hug immediately. As he lifted Sheridan into the air and whirled him around and around, Custer shouted, "By Jesus, we've cleaned them out and got the guns!" Catching sight of General Torbert, Custer embraced him too until Torbert was obliged to cry out, "There, there, old fellow. Don't capture me!"[46]

From the standpoint of its emotional effect, Stillson's report was the best newspaper account of Cedar Creek and one of the outstanding battle accounts of the war. Commenting upon Stillson's performance, the New York *World* stated editorially:

> Without disparagement to . . . other . . . gentlemen who have written letters from the field, we think our readers will agree with us that none . . . have shown more talent for descriptive writing than . . . Stillson. . . . If all the battles of the war were as well described, the work of the military annalist would be comparatively easy.[47]

Editorially this statement was perfectly justified. Stillson's battle story could be expected to sell newspapers and to please the public at the same time. That it would materially facilitate the work of the military historian is not so easy to demonstrate. Any historian trying to use it as a source for what happened at Cedar Creek will find contradictions and non sequiturs that must be cleared up elsewhere. Some other members of the *World* staff shared the opinion of the editorial writer, however. In a letter to Croly, the paper's Washington correspondent remarked enthusiastically:

> What a magnificent success Stillson has made. Everybody here is talking about him & his account. Every paper here copied it—the *Chronicle* much against its will.[48]

Most of the other Northern Republican newspapers, also much against their will, reprinted Stillson's battle story, generally without comment. Since it originally had appeared in the Copperhead *World*, near the end of a bitter presidential campaign, this was high if grudging praise.

Not all the contemporary reactions to the reporting of the battle, however, were complimentary. Although Sheridan must have been pleased by what the reporters had to say about him, some of his subordinates—Crook in particular—were considerably irritated by newspaper statements which indicated that Early's attack had taken them by surprise. One of the officers in Crook's command dashed off a letter to the Cincinnati *Commercial*. In it he objected strenuously to the "vile slanders" in Stillson's battle account which imputed cowardice to Crook's men. The statements to which the officers objected nevertheless were corroborated by the other reporters, and there seems to be good reason to think that the facts of the "surprise" were substantially as Stillson reported them.[49]

Another reporter, E. A. Paul of the New York *Times*, was criticized for giving Custer's division the credit for capturing the great majority of the forty-five guns taken from the enemy. In a letter to the editor, one of the *Times*'s readers alleged that Custer was not even present at the charge when the greater part of the guns was captured. He further asserted that Brigadier General Thomas Devin, who commanded a brigade in Merritt's First Cavalry Division, was the commanding officer of the forces engaged and as such entitled to the chief credit.[50] In a letter replying to these strictures, Paul admitted that Devin should have received credit for capturing twenty-one of the captured guns, but he denied any intention of attempting to deprive Devin of what rightfully was his due.[51] From information which has since come to light, it seems likely that Paul was more nearly correct when he first assigned to Custer the credit for the lion's share of the captures.[52]

The Battle of Cedar Creek was the last important action fought in the Shenandoah Valley during 1864. Since the failure of the Petersburg mine there had also been little on the Petersburg front to break the routine for either the army reporters or the forces there. In a letter written on October 11 to the New York *Times*, George F. Williams told how an officer "pretty well up among the stars" had berated the army correspondents for their failure to write more about the day-to-day happenings of the siege of Petersburg. Williams retorted:

> He forgot that nearly every bullet whistles alike, and that shells and mortar bombs only differ from each other in their voices. . . .
>
> Besides, one becomes so habituated to the sound of shot and shell, that anything less than a general bombardment, or a regular fusilade along our lines, fails to elicit comment, and the monotonous crack of the picket's rifle or the occasional boom of cannon are passed by with as little comment as the roar of vehicles in Broadway.[53]

Williams, in recognition of his scoop of the Battle of Winchester, had been sent to City Point at the end of September to act as the chief correspondent of the New York *Times* with the Army of the Potomac. On the day he arrived at City Point he learned that Meade was extending his line to the left and that a fierce struggle already had begun. Eager for a news story, the *Times* reporter hurried to the Provost Marshal's tent, exhibited his red-letter pass, and requested a local pass authorizing train travel in that sector. The clerk examined the red-letter pass with some curiosity and then observed in a flippant manner that no passes were issued while the troops were in motion and, therefore, Williams would have to wait until the next day. Determined to reach the battlefield at all hazards, the new arrival borrowed a horse from a fellow *Times* correspondent and, without much difficulty, eluded the Provost. A sharp gallop of twelve miles brought him to Preble's farm in time to witness the closing scenes of the day and to write a long description of it for the *Times*.

As soon as the issue of the *Times* which contained his letter came back to the Army, Williams was hauled up before the Provost Marshal and called to account for what he had written. Following a hot exchange of arguments, the Provost Marshal terminated the discussion by haling his victim before General Grant, who was sitting by the fire at the door of his hut and smoking a cigar. After listening to what the Provost Marshal had to say, Grant glanced at the correspondent's pass, blew a large ring of smoke into the air, and then asked the Provost Marshal whether there was anything wrong with Mr. Williams' description of the fight.

"No, sir," stammered the Provost. "It seems correct enough, but he had no business passing through my lines without my pass."

"I suppose you considered it your duty to reach the left that day," said Grant, eying the correspondent.

"Most assuredly I did, sir. With the pass I carried I believed I had the right to do so."

"Had you any difficulty in passing the Provost lines?" the General inquired.

"None at all, sir. My pass was shown, and the way was at once opened for me."

"How did you get back to the Point?" Grant wanted to know.

"Rode back the next day."

"And the guards accepted your pass?"

"Yes, sir."

"Well, General," said Grant, turning to his Provost Marshal, "I don't see that you can blame Mr. Williams. The fault lays with your system. The clerk should have given him his local pass when asked for it. Then there would have been none of this trouble."

"But, General," expostulated the Provost Marshal, "this correspondent had no right to transgress the rule once it was made known to him."

"Perhaps not; but he thought he was right. And, after all, the President's pass should count for something. Your description of the battle, Mr. Williams, was a very good one. I read it with a great deal of interest."

The Provost Marshal took the hint and withdrew. After some further conversation, Williams also left, but in this accidental way be had laid the basis for what was to be a lasting friendship with the General.[54]

Early in October, and shortly after Williams' arrival, Edward Crapsey, the victim of Meade's vengeance, had returned to the Army of the Potomac.[55] On the eighteenth of that month, he wrote to Painter, suggesting that one of the *Inquirer* men in the field be entrusted with the functions of chief correspondent. He protested:

> While I am not inordinately solicitous for the position, I still think that I can do better in getting news through and in organizing the work here and in getting it done than either of the others.

There is no reason in the world why you should not have had full files of the Richmond papers every day for the last three months or ever since the army has been in front of Petersburg. If you see fit to give me the position of chief I shall see to it that in the future you get these papers and without costing a cent either. . . .

If you are going to re-call MacDuff[56] I wish you would do it immediately. He will be buying horses and performing other feats shortly. At the same time I dont think you have too many here for the work that will be at hand in a few days or whenever this last struggle for Richmond commences.[57]

Possibly as a result of this transparent proposal, Crapsey was appointed chief correspondent for the *Inquirer* soon afterward. On November 1 he wrote to Painter again, recommending that Rhoads, another of the *Inquirer* correspondents, be dismissed as soon as the presidential election was over:

Since the movement last week I have come to the conclusion that he [Rhoads] has not the knack of telling what he knows—You must have been as much disappointed in what he wrote about the move as I was. He is industrious however and if he will accept the position of messenger between Peters & the mail boat he will do very well.

In the last paragraph of his letter, Crapsey made an oblique reference to a time-honored practice of military men the world over:

The losses during what Grant calls his reconnoissance I see he puts down to 200. I was told at his Hd Qrs before I sent my despatch that my estimate was a little higher than the reports Showed. I think still that our losses are about what I stated then but it will be well enough to say that further and more definate [sic] information has materially reduced them. . . . The movement was not called by anybody a reconnoissance until after it failed and I am certain it was not so intended.[58]

Active campaigning for the year was now practically at an end. The year 1864 had been a difficult year for the army correspondents in Virginia, partly because of the increasing severity of army regulations. One correspondent had noted:

All that can be recorded . . . for publication . . . is a plain narrative of accomplished facts, without comments, deductions, or inquiries into and disclosures of the inner history of events.[59]

To another correspondent it seemed that most of the better class of reporters already had left the army and that those who remained behind were compelled to hang around the back entrance of the General's headquarters or depend upon the charity of a senior officer who expected favorable press notices.[60] Possibly Henry J. Winser of the New York *Times* echoed the sentiments of a significant number of his confreres when he wrote in an army letter:

> I am strongly in favor of abolishing altogether the present veteran class of newspaper correspondents, and putting in recruits of new material. The infusion of young blood would result in a change, and the public would be regaled with high-flavored, spicy dishes of description, instead of the homely food which is becoming insipid if not nauseating to them. Now that the rebellion is so nearly "crushed out," let its dying moments pass amid a rhetorical blaze of glory, not in the tame, stereotyped phrases which are the offspring of a sort of mental cowardice begotten by the restrictions which the military authorities, all through the progress of the war, have imposed upon the representatives of the press.[61]

23

The Grand Finale

DURING the twenty months following their capture near Vicksburg in May, 1863, the New York *Tribune* reporters A. D. Richardson and Junius Browne endured the stench and starvation of seven different Confederate prisons. Colburn of the New York *World*, who was with them at the time of their capture, was turned loose by the Confederate authorities within a month. But repeated efforts—by Greeley, Stanton, Ben Butler, Governor Brough of Ohio, even Lincoln himself—failed to win the release of the two *Tribune* reporters. The Confederate exchange agents claimed that they were being held in retaliation for citizens arrested and held by the Federals, and refused even to discuss their exchange except in connection with a blanket exchange of all civilian and noncombatant prisoners held by both sides. In an unguarded moment, Robert Ould, the Confederate Commissioner of Exchange, told the U. S. Commissioner that:

> *The Tribune* did more than any other agency to bring on the war. It is useless for you to ask the exchange of its correspondents. They are just the men we want, and just the men we are going to hold.[1]

After an attempt by Stanton to exchange a Georgia newspaper editor[2] for Richardson had failed, Edward A. Pollard of the Richmond *Examiner* was permitted to return to Richmond as a paroled prisoner to negotiate for the release of Richardson and Browne.[3] Pollard had been captured off Wilmington, North Carolina, in April, 1864, while endeavoring to reach England in a blockade-runner. On January 17, 1865, while Pollard was in Richmond seeking to carry out his mission, the press published an exciting story. From Tennessee's capital city came the news of Richardson's and Browne's safe arrival there the previous day after a spectacular jail break. In the company of another journalist, William

E. Davis of the Cincinnati *Gazette,* the two *Tribune* correspondents had escaped from Salisbury Prison in Western North Carolina on the night of December 18. To reach the Union lines at Knoxville, they had come three hundred forty miles over difficult roads. They had concealed themselves in barns or thickets by day and had followed secluded pathways by night. Sometimes they were helped by Negroes, sometimes by Union sympathizers. For a part of the distance they were piloted by a young Tennessee girl whom they alluded to in their newspaper narratives as the "Nameless Heroine."[4]

From Nashville they went on up to Cincinnati where Murat Halstead spoke for the local press at a banquet in their honor. After the reporters had recounted some of their thrilling experiences, Thomas Buchanan Read recited the first draft of a poem, "The Walk of the Journalists," he had written in honor of the occasion. Following a trip to Washington to urge prompt relief measures for the prisoners at Salisbury, Richardson went on a lecture tour, speaking almost every night until a lung ailment caused his collapse early in March, in Albany, New York.[5]

On the day after the *Tribune* had carried the news of the escape of Richardson and Browne, the last big naval news story of the war—the fall of Fort Fisher—was made public. Only two important ports, Charleston and Wilmington, had remained in Confederate hands after Mobile Bay was sealed off in August, 1864. During the autumn, plans for an operation against Wilmington began to take shape. Planned originally for October, the attack was postponed two months because of the War Department's lack of interest. By the time the expedition, jointly commanded by Porter and Butler, was ready to sail, December was half over.

Before the Wilmington expedition could achieve its objective, its approximate scope and purpose were revealed to the public in a story published in several newspapers.[6] Investigation by the Federal authorities disclosed that these newspapers had obtained their information from the former *Herald* reporter, B. S. Osbon, who now was operating a news syndicate in New York. Osbon had sent out a form letter to fifteen or twenty different newspapers on October 27 offering to furnish them with a list of the vessels in the expedition, the number of guns they mounted, a descriptive sketch of the enemy's defenses, and an abstract of Admiral Porter's sailing, fighting, and divisional orders — "a full & accurate epitome," as he described it, "of the grand movement against Wilmington." Osbon explained:

> I will supply this in *advance,* so that upon receipt of the telegram announcing the attack, you can publish, thereby being in advance of the New York papers.[7]

Unfortunately, several of Osbon's customers did not stick to the agreement. On December 19, five days before the attack took place, both the Boston *Daily Advertiser* and the Philadelphia *Press* published articles based on the information released to them by Osbon. Other newspapers followed. Three days later Osbon's story appeared in the Richmond press. From Assistant Secretary Fox, Commodore John Rodgers received instructions on December 25 to "tell Porter his whole plan, copied from our newspapers, was published in Richmond Thursday last."[8] Lincoln and Stanton were even more exasperated by this syndicated "leak" because the Porter-Butler expedition had made such a poor showing.

Everything had gone wrong with the expedition, including Butler's powder ship, a contraption which he had foisted upon the navy as the price of his assistance. Butler hoped to destroy Fort Fisher, at the entrance to Wilmington Harbor, by exploding his powder ship and its two-hundred fifteen tons of gunpowder near the fort. As the ordnance experts had predicted, the tremendous concussion the General and his army friends expected simply did not materialize. Watching the experiment from ten miles away, W. H. Whittemore of the New York *Times* heard a deep, heavy sound "not unlike that produced by the discharge of a 100-pounder."[9] A few minutes after the explosion, his Associated Press colleague saw a huge cloud of dense, black smoke appear above the horizon. It was sharply defined against the clear, starlit sky:

> and as it rose rapidly in the air, and came swiftly toward us on the wings of the wind, [it] presented a most remarkable appearance, assuming the shape of a monstrous water-spout, its tapering base seemingly resting on the sea.
>
> In a very few minutes it passed us, filling the atmosphere with its sulphurous odor, as if a spirit from the infernal regions had swept by us.
>
> Thus passed off and vanished in smoke this anxiously awaited event.[10]

The shock was hardly felt in the fleet, however, which stood in to the attack shortly after daylight that morning of December 24. Before the action commenced, the press correspondents who accompanied the expedition were transferred to the steam gunboat "Montgomery" from the various ships in which they had come down from Hampton Roads. The "Montgomery" had orders from Porter to move about during the fight so that the reporters could view what occurred from the most advantageous angle.[11]

What they saw hardly could have pleased them. Although Porter's two-day bombardment of the fort was a thunderous spectacle of flame and smoke, Butler's ineptitude defeated the operation. He had failed to arrive at the rendezvous point until three days after the time agreed upon. Moreover, even though he then landed twenty-five hundred men, he re-embarked them within a few hours and returned to Hampton Roads. As a result, W. W. Vaughan of the New York *World* heard Butler denounced by a naval officer, "whose name is familiar in every household of the land," as "either black-hearted traitor or an arrant coward." Another officer, equally well known, remarked in Vaughan's hearing that:

> He [Butler] forced himself into the expedition, and I believe . . . came down with the deliberate purpose of defeating the enterprise. He was determined to have his own way, and, seeing that he could not, was bent on thwarting everything.[12]

Grant had never intended that Ben Butler should command the land forces in the expedition. Moreover, the sudden return of Butler and his men to Fortress Monroe was a direct violation of the orders of the General in Chief. To Porter's great joy, Lincoln's Executive Order No. 1 for 1865 removed Butler from the command of the Army of the James and made provision for a second attack on Fort Fisher under another army commander. Butler's political influence probably was the only reason he escaped court martial.[13]

From an inside source, Cadwallader, the *Herald* correspondent at the headquarters of the Army of the Potomac, received early information of the change in command in the Army of the James. While Wilkeson and the other Washington reporters tried in vain for three consecutive days to telegraph the information to their newspapers, the censors permitted Cadwallader to send a full account with extended comments to his newspaper in New York, an important scoop.

Wilkeson was so annoyed with this favoritism toward the *Herald* that he presented a petition to Congress requesting that the censorship of the telegraph be abolished.[14]

Butler was annoyed with the *Herald* too, but for a different reason. To Grant's friend Rawlins, he wrote a letter which expressed dissatisfaction with the way in which the story had become public. The letter in part is also an interesting commentary on the relations of the General in Chief with Cadwallader:

> My Dear Rawlins: You know that I like to see a thing well done, if done at all, and I must say my enemies about your headquarters are very bungling in their malice and will bring the general into remark. Take the article in the Herald by Cadwallader, and it will appear to have been dictated at headquarters, where I know the general had nothing to do with it. It was not telegraphed, and to have reached Tuesday's Herald must have left in the mail-boat at 10 a.m., when the order for my removal was not served on me till 12 m. of the same day, Sunday. Unless the orders of the general are disclosed before they are made public, how could the "news of General Butler's removal excite much comment; but as far as I can learn but little or no animadversion". . . . Again, Cadwallader could never have written this sentence:
>
> *It has been General Butler's misfortune to appoint too many of (these) selfish and irresponsible persons to official positions of trust and responsibility. Their indiscretions have cost him dearly, &c.*
>
> Now, as I appointed Cadwallader himself as a lieutenant in the U. S. Volunteers, as I supposed and believed at the wish of General Grant, for the selfish reason on Cadwallader's part that he wished to escape the draft which would take him away from general headquarters as a reporter, and as he is wholly "irresponsible," and as not only I but General Grant is "suffering from his indiscretion," although he had this piece of news in advance of anybody else, I do not believe he would wish to communicate it to the Herald. Now, wasn't the fellow who got up this dispatch a bungler?[15]

On January 13, 1865, the same day this letter was written, a second attack was launched against Fort Fisher. This time, however, the reporters were not provided with a press steamer and were, therefore, scattered about among the various ships in the squadron.[16] After a vigorous three-day bombardment, Brigadier General Alfred H. Terry's soldiers, aided by two thousand bluejackets and marines, cracked the defenses of Fort Fisher. By ten o'clock that night the victory was complete. The reporter for the New York *Tribune,* who visited the fort the next day, "breakfasting on horrors, that I might know of what I speak," found many large guns:

> dismounted and tumbled down. Among these are entangled Rebel dead in almost every shape and position, some standing on their feet and others on their heads, all glaring and grinning . . . upon the passerby.[17]

Hardly had Fort Fisher fallen before a friendly competition to be first with the news of the victory developed between the army and navy commanders. While Terry worked feverishly at his report in his drab tent on Federal Point, a large group of reporters, naval officers, and others watched from outside, close to the campfire. By seven-thirty the following morning the army dispatch ship "Atlantic" was underway for Fortress Monroe sufficiently in advance of the Admiral's "Vanderbilt" to reach its destination four hours earlier. In less than an hour from the time that the "Atlantic" hove in sight of Old Point Comfort (the peninsula on which Fortress Monroe is located), Grant at his breakfast table was reading the news of the fall of Fort Fisher.[18] Although William H. Merriam of the New York *Herald* was on board the "Atlantic" when it docked at Fortress Monroe, the *Herald* failed to scoop the other newspapers as it had when Butler was removed. Indeed by publishing twenty-four hours earlier a full two-page story of the great success as reported by its three correspondents with the expedition, the *Tribune* managed to beat the *Herald.*[19] One of the best newspaper accounts of the victory was written by Henry M. Stanley, who watched the fight from the deck of the "Moses H. Stuyvesant." Stanley's lucid and vigorous story of the fall of Fort Fisher was the beginning of an outstanding career in journalism.[20]

Meanwhile, Assistant Secretary Fox had taken advantage of Osbon's slip to satisfy his long-standing grudge against Osbon. On the first of January, 1865, the reporter had been arrested at his New York office and hustled to Washington for confinement in the Old Capitol Prison. On January 24, 1865, he was brought before a military commission headed by General Abner Doubleday and, according to his own statement, "commanded" to plead guilty. His case was held over for a few days to permit him to procure the services of an attorney and witnesses. By the thirtieth, however, he was so seriously ill that his case was postponed indefinitely, and he was returned to his cell. On March 27, after he had repeatedly attempted to get a speedy trial or, in lieu of that, release on parole, Osbon was removed to New York for trial by court martial. Presiding over the court was Brigadier General Fitz-Henry Warren, formerly the Washington correspondent of the New York *Tribune.* Osbon's objection that his case was not subject to the jurisdiction of a military court was overruled, and the trial dragged on until June 5, when the court returned a verdict of not guilty.

At the outset, it had been generally understood that the President would intervene to prevent the death penalty's being carried out should Osbon be convicted. Lincoln's assassination occurred while the trial was in progress, however, so Osbon must have had some uneasy moments. Even after the verdict was rendered, he was not released from custody. On June 20, 1865, he addressed a letter, which later was placed in the War Department files along with the record of the court martial proceedings, to President Andrew Johnson asking the President to use his good offices to bring about prompt action in the case:

> I now appeal to you and your sense of justice to direct that my case no longer meets with any more delay than is necessary. My family are suffering and in actual want; my business has been broken up and ruined; my detention has been unreasonably long and severe; and my health sadly undermined by my peculiar and close incarceration.
>
> I have thus frankly written you, Mr. President, conscious of my innocence, and *if* I did wrong it surely was unintentional. I have always endeavored to do right, and in fighting for the Union and Liberty I have suffered enough in honorable wounds recieved [sic] in battle—to have exempted me from the miseries of the past *six months* of my prison existence.[21]

After three more weeks, enough military red tape had been untied that Osbon was a free man once more.

* * *

Approximately a month from the time that Osbon first appeared before the Doubleday Commission, Wilmington fell. By that time the press had given out the information that Sherman was on the move again, this time in a northerly direction. On the morning of February 1 the movement began. While the left wing of Sherman's army under Slocum threatened Augusta, the right wing with Howard commanding feinted in the direction of Charleston. Westfall, Conyngham, and Doyle, three of the *Herald*'s veteran correspondents, and two reporters each from the *Times* and *Tribune* accompanied Sherman on his four-hundred-mile march through the Carolinas. A third *Tribune* reporter also was to have made the march, but by the time Elias Smith received his instructions from Gay to join Sherman the General already had cut loose from his base at Savannah and was completely out of reach.[22]

The Confederate commanders, unable to determine where their Federal adversary would strike first, tried to hold a hundred-mile line from Augusta to Charleston. But Sherman neatly eluded the defenders and, crossing into South Carolina Southeast of Augusta, moved on the state capital, Columbia.

At times the marchers ploughed through swamps filled waist-high with icy water. A *Herald* correspondent looking about for the headquarters of the Twentieth Corps one damp night heard some one shout, "Hello, old fellow, is that you? You had better come up and secure a roosting place." Looking up, he discovered the corps commander, General Williams, perched in the forks of a tree, with his staff members nearby. They were all swathed in sheets and blankets foraged from the Georgia countryside. Williams was smoking a cigar and "looking as quiet and serene as if he had been in his tent on dry ground."[23]

Among the troops there was great bitterness toward the state which they were entering for the first time.

"Come with me," General Williams had said to Charles Carleton Coffin as the army prepared to leave Savannah. "You will see high old times, I reckon. My soldiers are crazy to get into South Carolina."[24]

Westfall of the *Herald* reported that during the first part of the march through the Palmetto State:

> houses were burned as they were found. Whenever a view could be had from high ground black columns of smoke were seen rising here and there within a circuit of twenty or thirty miles.[25]

And Conyngham once overheard General Hazen remark to Sherman:

"There goes the bridge," one over which the army had just passed.

"I am sorry," replied Sherman. Then after gazing a few moments at a thick column of smoke rising above a clump of trees in the distance, he exclaimed: "No, Hazen, no; that's a house; it is not the bridge. A bridge would not emit such a dense smoke."

It was the accuracy of Sherman's perception rather than any feeling of surprise that the house should have been set on fire which prompted the reporter to jot down this conversation.[26]

The two wings of Sherman's army reached the outskirts of Columbia on February 16, and on the following day the Confederates evacuated the city without making any attempt to defend it. On the morning that Sherman's army marched into Columbia, Conyngham stood on a high bluff overlooking the Saluda River. Alongside him was a group of generals, also watching the morning sun light up the housetops:

> There was General Sherman, now pacing up and down in the midst of the group, all the time with an unlit cigar in his mouth, and now and then abruptly halting to speak to some of the generals around him. Again, he would sit down, whittle a stick, and soon nervously start up to resume his walk. Above all the men I have ever met, that strange face of his is the hardest to be read. It is a sealed book even to his nearest friends.
>
> Sitting on a log beside him was Howard, reading a newspaper, and occasionally stopping to answer some questions of Sherman's or make some comment on some passages.
>
> Howard always looks the same—the kind, courteous general, the Christian soldier.
>
> Another of the group was Frank P. Blair, with his strongly marked features, indicative both of talent, energy and ability.
>
> John A. Logan, too, was there, with his dark, almost bronzed countenance, and fiery, commanding eye, the true type of the dashing general.
>
> Not least was General Hazen, the hero of McAllister, with his frank, expressive and finely moulded head, betokening the warm-hearted gentleman, the soldier of mind and brains.
>
> These, with several other generals, with a host of gay officers and orderlies in the back ground, formed a group worthy the pencil of a Reubens [sic] or Vandyke.[27]

It is a pity that Conyngham left no record of the conversation among the generals, for it would be interesting to know whether Sherman dropped any unguarded hints of his intentions toward the Carolina capital. Never has it been proven whether Columbia's fire resulted from the Confederate General Hampton's order on the fourteenth of February, which directed the citizens of Columbia to place their cotton where it could be burned rather than let it fall into the hands of the enemy; or whether the city was wantonly destroyed by Sherman's army either under his orders or without his consent.[28] Most of the army correspondents described the event with a certain degree of reluctance, attributing it variously to the whiskey which was passed out freely to the Yankee soldiers by the women of Columbia, to Wheeler's cavalry which set fire to the abandoned cotton, and to pillaging gangs of escaped prisoners, soldiers, and Negroes.

The position of the Confederates in Charleston became untenable after Columbia fell. At nine o'clock on the morning of February 18, just before the steamer "Fulton" was scheduled to leave Hilton Head for New York, the rumor that "Charleston is evacuated!" ran through the crowd along the wharf. James Redpath of the New York *Tribune,* who happened to be among the crowd, immediately began to buttonhole every officer and captain within reach to establish the truth of this startling tale.

"Gen. Gilmore left this morning at half past two," said one informant.

"The Provost-Marshal has gone too," added another.

"Oh, there's no doubt that James Island is evacuated anyhow," replied a third. "I just see the captain of a steamer that's come down, and he says it's true."

A visit to the General's headquarters and to the headquarters of the Provost Marshal, the Adams Express Office, and the Quartermaster's Office unearthed further evidence that the rumor was true or at least the precursor of the actual event. Redpath therefore decided to go down to Charleston at once to see for himself what was happening.

The "Fulton," he learned, had received instructions from the department commander, General Gillmore, to make for the lightship off Charleston Harbor in order to take on dispatches. Redpath made arrangements to go aboard the steamer and to accompany her on this special mission. Although the "Fulton" was under orders to sail precisely at ten, it was nearly eleven o'clock before she fired her "signal gun" and got fairly underway. All the passengers were on deck that morning, straining their eyes for the first view of the birthplace of secession. In good weather the trip from Port Royal to Charleston ordinarily required no more than four hours. So great, however, was the anxiety of the "Fulton" 's passengers to learn the fate of the great Confederate seaport that the journey seemed much longer.

Shortly after three o'clock in the afternoon, a ship sighting was reported. About the same time some of the passengers were able to distinguish through their field glasses clouds of smoke in the direction of Charleston. Gradually the ship became plainly visible, riding at anchor, and presently the "Fulton" received a signal to approach within speaking distance. The helm was put hard to port. As the distance grew less, excitement on board the "Fulton" reached fever pitch. At length an officer appeared on the port gangway of the blockader and in a clear loud voice announced, "Charleston and all its defenses are evacuated, and in our possession." There were hearty cheers from the passengers as the "Fulton" drew alongside the Charleston lightship where it anchored to await the arrival of General Gillmore.

It was nearly six o'clock in the evening before the "W. W. Coit," flying the headquarters flag of the department commander, pulled alongside the "Fulton" and a member of General Gillmore's staff came aboard with dispatches for Washington. Redpath grasped at the opportunity to go on board the headquarters boat, for he hoped to be the first reporter to reach Charleston. But, considerably to his disappointment, instead of re-entering the harbor the "Coit" made off at full speed for Hilton Head. As a result of his miscalculation, Redpath had to lay over there another day before he could go down to Charleston with a numerous delegation of the press on the "U. S. Grant."[29]

Whereas several other reporters had entrusted their dispatches to the purser, Coffin gave his to a passenger on board the "Fulton." This unofficial courier had agreed to leap onto the pier as soon as the vessel docked in New York, ride to the telegraph office, and put the *Journal* dispatch on the wire for Boston. As Coffin had anticipated, the purser did not trouble to deliver the dispatches consigned to his care until the steamer docked and his duties were completed. As a result, the people of Boston received the news of the fall of Charleston within an hour after the "Fulton" docked in New York and before it was published in any New York newspaper. Moreover, Coffin's story was telegraphed back to New York and broadcast throughout the country before any other newspaper account appeared. In this way the *Journal* registered one of the most successful news scoops of the war.[30]

It was with a note of grim satisfaction that the Yankee reporters dated their letters from the fountainhead of the secessionist movement. In a letter subsequently published in the *Journal,* Coffin wrote:

> The city is a ruin. The tall rank weeds of last year's growth, dry and withered now, rattle in every passing breeze in the very heart of that city which, five years ago, was so proud and lofty in spirit. Lean and hungry dogs skulk amid the tenantless houses. . . . Spiders spin their webs in counting houses. Such is the lower half of Charleston today.[31]

Redpath agreed:

> No imagination can conceive of the utter wreck, the universal ruin, the stupendous desolation. . . . Hardly a building in all this part of the city—and this the business part—has escaped the terrible crashing and smashing of the shells.[32]

That "retribution had overtaken this proud sinner" was the theme of many a newspaper paragraph. Both Coffin and Redpath visited the old office of the Charleston *Mercury* on Broad Street. In the last hours before the city's fall, Rhett, the editor of the *Mercury*, had fled, taking with him his printing press and types. Among the "dead matter" in the standing galley of the print shop were three lines of type which attracted the attention of the two reporters. The lines were so characteristic of what they had come to regard as Southern bluster and brag: "There are no indications that our authorities have the first intention of abandoning Charleston, as I have ascertained by careful inquiry." Over the mantelpiece, however, was a penciled inscription—probably the handiwork of some passing soldier:

> For President in 1868,
> Wendell Phillips, of Massachusetts;
> For Vice-President,
> Frederick Douglass, of New-York.[33]

On the same day that Coffin and Redpath visited the *Mercury* office, another Charleston newspaper, the *Courier*, was seized by the Provost Marshal and placed under the editorial supervision of W. H. Whittemore of the New York *Times* and George W. Johnson of the Port Royal *New South*.[34]

Four days after Charleston fell, several representatives of the press accompanied General Gillmore and some other officers on a visit to Fort Sumter. While Gillmore and his party were inspecting the famous ruins, two of *Frank Leslie's* army artists made sketches of the interior of the Fort.[35] That evening Washington's birthday was celebrated in Charleston in fitting fashion. Coffin, Redpath, Kane O'Donnell of the Philadelphia *Press*, and another reporter were guests at a dinner to which General Joseph D. Webster, Sherman's chief of staff, and several other army and navy officers were also invited. They feasted on a sumptuous meal including canned fruits run through the blockade from England. Following the dinner, Lloyd's Concert Band, an organization of colored musicians, played "Yankee Doodle," "Hail Columbia," and many other songs which had not been heard in Charleston for years. Toasts were offered and speeches also were made which in the days before the war the townspeople would have regarded as incendiary. "Henceforth," declared Coffin emphatically in his report of the celebration, "there shall be free speech in Charleston."[36]

Meanwhile Sherman's army was pushing steadily northward from Columbia. At Cheraw, the army's last stop in South Carolina, someone handed Sherman a copy of the New York *Tribune* which revealed the location of his supply rendezvous at Morehead City, North Carolina. Anyone—Sherman's new adversary, Joe Johnston included—could deduce from the *Tribune* story that Sherman was heading for Goldsboro. So bitter was Sherman about this disclosure, leading as it did to a fight he had hoped to avoid, that he is said at a later time to have refused an introduction to Greeley.[37]

On March 8, Sherman's army crossed into North Carolina. Up to the time it had reached Columbia, the movements of that army had been freely reported by the Southern press. Now the Yankee invaders were operating without even that doubtful medium of publicity. On March 14, the Boston *Journal* editorialized that:

> there never was probably a time when so little was known about the various movements of the Union armies as at present. Columns of infantry or cavalry plunge into the depths of the enemy's country at various points, and then we lose sight of them, and then the rebel papers endeavor to conceal their operations, till some exploit more important than usual brings them momentarily to view.

This editorial was hardly twenty-four hours old when Stanton released to the press a dispatch from Sherman stating that all was well with the army, which was then at Laurel Hill, about thirty miles Southwest of Fayetteville. By the time the dispatch was in print Sherman was already at Fayetteville and had established communication with Generals Terry and Schofield at Wilmington.

Several of the correspondents who had marched with Sherman from Savannah to Fayetteville went down to Wilmington on the steam tug "Davidson" to forward their stories of the march through South Carolina. The "Davidson" had run the gauntlet of enemy fire all the way up the Cape Fear River from Wilmington. On the return trip, however, the "Davidson" had in convoy a mail boat with two guns, a sufficient deterrent to Confederate fire. According to Conyngham, all newspapermen on board were in gay spirits, for "it was like waking to a new life, after being so long shut out from the outer world."[38]

Pausing at Fayetteville only momentarily, Sherman continued northward, fighting small engagements with Johnston on March 16 and 19. On the twenty-third, he made a junction with Schofield's forces at Goldsboro.[39] In the opinion of the *Tribune* reporter Elias Smith, who had arrived in Goldsboro just ahead of Sherman, the entry of Sherman's barefoot soldiery into Goldsboro was one of the most interesting events of the war. Smith's portrayal of the notorious "bummers" was hardly less interesting:

> In rear of each Division followed the foragers, or "bummers," as they are called by the soldiers, constituting a motley group which strongly recalls the memory of Falstaff's ragged army, though they are by no means men in buckram. The men having worn out all their clothing and shoes during the march, were obliged to provide themselves the best way they could as they went along.
>
> Here came men strutting in mimic dignity in an old swallow-tailed coat, with plug hats, the tops knocked in; there a group in seedy coats and pants of Rebel grey, with arms and legs protruding beyond all semblance of fit or of fashion; short jackets, long-tailed surtouts, and coats of every cast with broad tails, narrow tails, and no tails at all—all of the most antiquated styles. Some wore women's bonnets, or young ladies' hats, with streamers of faded ribbons floating fantastically in the wind.
>
> The procession of vehicles and animals was of the most grotesque description. There were donkeys large and small, almost smothered, under burdens of turkeys, geese and other kinds of poultry, ox carts, skinny horses pulling in the fills of some parish doctors, old sulkies, farm wagons and buggies, hacks, chaises, rockaways, aristocratic and family carriages, all filled with plunder and provisions.
>
> There was bacon, hams, potatoes, flour, pork, sorghum, and freshly slaughtered pigs, sheep, and poultry dangling from saddle tree and wagon, enough, one would suppose, to feed the army for a fortnight.[40]

On the evening of March 25, Sherman, leaving Goldsboro to go up to City Point, remarked in the presence of a *Herald* reporter that he was "going up to see Grant for five minutes and have it all chalked out for me and then come back and pitch in."[41] Coffin was in the Adjutant General's headquarters at City Point the morning after Sherman's arrival.

The reporter was poring over some military maps when he saw Grant approaching, with President Lincoln close behind. Sherman was next in line, talking rapidly and gesticulating as he talked. As they entered the Adjutant General's office, Lincoln instantly recognized Coffin. Extending his hand the President asked smilingly, "What news have you?" Coffin informed him that he had just returned from Charleston and Savannah.

"Indeed!" observed Lincoln in a tone indicating that he was pleasantly surprised. "Well, I am right glad to see you. How do the people like being back in the Union again?"

Coffin said he thought some of them were reconciled to it:

> if we may draw conclusions from the action of one planter, who, while I was there, came down the Savannah River with his whole family—wife, children, negro woman and her children, of whom he was father—and with his crop of cotton, which he was anxious to sell at the highest price.

"Oh, yes, I see," laughed the President. "Patriarchal times once more; Abraham, Sarah, Isaac, Hagar and Ishmael, all in one boat!" He paused, then added with a chuckle, "I reckon they'll accept the situation now that they can sell their cotton."[42]

"We shall be in position to catch Lee between our two thumbs," exulted Sherman as his chief bent low over the maps that had been placed for their inspection. Before the conferees parted, it was settled that Grant should immediately open his spring drive against Petersburg and Richmond. Sherman was to march against Johnston at Raleigh on April 10.

* * *

While Sherman had been advancing northward during February and March, siege operations against Richmond and Petersburg had continued, with small benefit, so far as news was concerned, to the correspondents attached to the Army of the Potomac. Crapsey of the Philadelphia *Inquirer* had observed in a letter published during January:

> Only those who have lain with an army in winter quarters can have an idea of the desolation it works. All of us who started with the army from Culpeper and Brandy Station last spring, can remember the wilderness we left behind us there—a vast expanse of country denuded of trees, fences and habitations, with roads twining and twisting in every direction. In precisely such a condition is the country around Petersburg fast becoming. Those

> who saw these lands when they first became the theatre of active operations, would now have difficulty in recognizing a single field. The houses are nearly all still remaining, but every other trace of the old inhabitants has disappeared. A large portion of the section we occupy was densely wooded with pine when we came; it has now become a question whether there is wood enough in the army lines to last much longer, so nearly have the forests disappeared.[43]

Early in March, quick thinking by a correspondent of the New York *Herald* had saved General Grant from capture by the enemy. At the time, the Army of the Potomac was making one of a series of attempts to cut Lee's railroad communications South of Petersburg. During this particular movement, since known as the second Hatcher's Run or Boydton Plank Road engagement, William J. Starks of the *Herald* left Warren's Fifth Corps on the extreme right of the line and rode off to the left, where Hancock's guns could be heard pounding away.

As he jogged along, the *Herald* man noticed that the left flank of Warren's line was unprotected. In following the course of Hatcher's Creek, Warren had shifted gradually away to the right, leaving a considerable gap in the line, into which Mahone's Confederate division had infiltrated. Starks, who was riding along one of the narrow horse paths then common to all Virginia woods, could hear the chattering of an unusually large number of squirrels in the treetops over his head. Having learned from experience that these noisy little rodents never took to the trees en masse unless large bodies of armed men were near, he decided that some of Lee's troops must have slipped through Meade's line. Therefore, as he came around a bend in the narrow path, he was surprised to see General Grant before him, accompanied only by two orderlies.

"Excuse me, General," said Starks as he reined up. "I don't think it's quite safe for you to go any further on this path."

"Why not?"

"Because General Warren has gone away off to the right in following the creek, and I believe there's a serious gap in our line."

"I thought Warren was getting lost," mused Grant. Then, turning to the correspondent, he continued, "Well, suppose there *is* a gap for the time being, where's the danger?"

"I believe, sir, that a strong force of the enemy has got in here, somewhere."

"What makes you think so?"

"My principal reason is the presence of those squirrels in the treetops."

The General peered upward at the chattering squirrels, eyed the correspondent again, and remarked:

"You may be right, sir. We will go back."

They had not ridden more than two or three hundred yards to the rear before a volley of rifle shots fell among them. One of the orderlies was struck by a bullet, as was the other orderly's horse. Without waiting for a second warning, all four riders clapped spurs to their horses and were soon out of range. In the excitement, however, the *Herald* correspondent lost his hat and was obliged to wear a spare cap of one of the General's aides for the rest of the day.[44]

In accordance with the decisions that had been reached in the conference at City Point, Grant gave orders for the advance to begin on Wednesday, March 29. That day Starks announced in a dispatch to the *Herald:*

> The Army of the Potomac is again in motion. The campaign of 1865 is opened, and, under the leadership of the indomitable and tenacious Grant, is about to commence that series of blows which will result in the death of this most unrighteous rebellion.[45]

Yet Starks probably had little idea how near they all were to the finale.

During the first two days of the campaign, the army was held back by heavy rains. Then on the thirty-first, the advance was resumed. On the following day Sheridan won a smashing victory at Five Forks on the Confederate right, capturing three thousand two hundred twenty-four of Pickett's men and four guns.[46] On April 2, Grant renewed his attack on the Confederate right, breaking their line and forcing it back. Lee now had the choice of abandoning Petersburg and Richmond or of seeing his army entrapped and eventually forced to surrender. Perhaps it was already too late for him to make that choice.

Among the Northern newspaper correspondents who had gathered below Petersburg to report the spring campaign of 1865 was George Alfred Townsend, who now was reporting for the New York *World.* Townsend had but recently returned from a long holiday of twenty-two months in Europe. Back in journalism once more, he had contributed to the *World* a description of an execution on Governor's Island. Around the *World* office it was whispered that Marble wanted the man who wrote that sketch "to go to the seat of war." Townsend had no idea that he could get a pass to go to the army, since Stanton's hatred of the *World* was well known. But one fine spring day the pass arrived, and Townsend arrived at the front just in time to achieve a splendid success.[47]

On the day of the Battle of Five Forks, Townsend left his post on the Federal right and rode some twenty or twenty-five miles to the left, tardily as it proved, for he did not realize that he had just missed seeing a great battle until he was forced off the road by a long line of Confederate prisoners who marched steadily past him for a period of more than a half hour. Both Townsend and an old army chaplain who had ridden with him for some distance gazed at the spectacle in amazement.

It was evening when the *World* reporter rode into the Five Forks and halted before a large circle of officers. One of them, Brigadier General Joshua L. Chamberlain, Townsend had met only the day before. Chamberlain told him that an important battle had been fought that day, that a whole division of enemy troops had been captured, and that General Warren had been removed from the command of the Fifth Corps and replaced by Brigadier General Simon G. Griffin. He (Chamberlain) had been temporarily assigned to the command of Griffin's division.

"Where is Sheridan?" asked Townsend.

"There he sits, down there," chorused Griffin and the others, pointing to a little man with a red face who was sitting under a tree and gnawing on some cheese. Upon being introduced to Sheridan, Townsend said:

"General, you have done a great day's work here, and if you could help me for a minute or two to form some idea of what it is, I would start tonight from this field and go to New York with it to put it in the papers."

Greatly to his delight, Sheridan produced a map upon which the roads and parks around Five Forks were sketched against a reddish-brown background, and during the next twenty minutes the General carefully explained to Townsend the significance of the movement and the reasons for its success. Among other things he discussed the relation of the enemy on that flank to the cavalry force which he, Sheridan, had brought to the army from the Shenandoah Valley; the number and classification of his cavalry and the different commanders; the number of infantry in the Fifth Corps which had been loaned to him by Grant; and the character of their cooperation. Townsend later observed:

> Most generals would have made a great secret of these numbers, or have lectured me at the expense of interesting details about

> the enormity of printing army news. But this really great soldier only said once when I asked him point blank how many men were in the Fifth Corps: "I will tell you for your own information, but do not print it. There were about ten thousand men."

No doubt Sheridan, whom correspondents had not always found so approachable, was mellowed by the afterglow of his success. Although Townsend jotted down a few names on scraps of envelopes and bits of paper, he took hardly any notes on the conversation lest he inhibit the free flow of the General's ideas:

> When I had thanked General Sheridan, however, and turned away I rapidly ran over in my mind his talk, and dashed down such points as I might forget by a word or two here and there. I then picked out the surrounding officers . . . and had them explain to me some things I had not fully questioned Sheridan about, and describe to me the movement of a command in eschelon as the Fifth Corps was moved so as to hem the rebels in their works.

By this time it was almost midnight, and the *World* reporter was thoroughly tired out. He would have been only too happy to get some sleep, but thinking that his might be an exclusive account of the battle, he started out to find the railroad to City Point. After a series of adventures of the kind that usually befell correspondents going in from the field, he succeeded in reaching New York with his account of the victory. When his battle account finally appeared in the *World* other important events were crowding hard on the heels of Sheridan's success. Nevertheless, Townsend's story of Five Forks was widely read and in his own opinion was largely instrumental in establishing his reputation as a first-class reporter.[48]

Both Petersburg and Richmond had fallen before Townsend got to New York. At about three o'clock on Monday morning, April 3, J. R. Hamilton of the New York *Times* left an army hospital below Petersburg, where he had been compiling a list of the wounded, and walked outside to see what was going on. A dead silence hung over the front. From time to time during the night Hamilton had heard loud cheers from the Union lines which he had interpreted as expressions of delight at having repelled another enemy attack. But the cheers had now ceased, and not a single musket shot had been fired for some time. In the direction of Petersburg he could see a huge fire lighting the dark. Just as dawn was breaking, he heard the sound of cheering from the Federal lines again, first very loud, then growing fainter. The cheers came from the Federal troops entering Petersburg, which had been evacuated by the Confederates during the night.

One of the first reporters to enter the city was Hamilton's *Times* colleague H. H. Young, who made off "like a streak of greased lightning," leaving Hamilton at Hancock's Station to look after the mailing of the news matter that had been accumulated during the night.[49] Two *Herald* reporters who also accompanied the Ninth Corps into Petersburg that morning were soon comfortably lodged in the Jarratt House, Petersburg's principal hotel.[50] Arriving at the same hotel a little later, the *Tribune* reporters Page and Grey presented their breakfast requests to a Negro man who was apparently the chief steward. After some hesitation which was diminished by the promise of liberal remuneration, the steward prepared a meal of dry bread and some indigestible scraps of bacon for the correspondents. In return for this meager repast, they offered the steward a handful of Confederate currency.

"Lord bress ye, massas," he exclaimed with astonishment, "I got heaps o' dat ar' stuff, more as a mule can tote; hasn't ye got any Yankee money?"

"But see here, John," Page replied with mock seriousness, "here is over five hundred dollars for our breakfast; that surely ought to pay you!"

"I know it's a heap o' money, but I don't want it, massas; you alls is welcome to your breakfast, if dat's all de money you's got."

"John's" customers finally produced a five-dollar bill of the "Union persuasion," with which he was appeased.[51] Several other reporters, after trying in vain to find anything to eat in Petersburg, left for City Point to satisfy their hunger.[52]

On that same Monday morning the first contingents of the Army of the James entered Richmond. As Coffin rode into the Confederate capital soon after sunrise, troops were pouring into the city from all directions, cheering, swinging their caps, helping themselves to tobacco, and making ready to start off toward Danville in pursuit of Lee.[53] Shortly after 9:30 that morning, the Washington telegraph operators were startled by what seemed a foolish demand from the operator at Fortress Monroe—"to turn down for Richmond, quick." Then came the question:

"Do you get me well?"

"All right. Here's the first message for four years."

Then the following information came over the wire from Richmond:

Hon. E. M. Stanton, Secretary of War.
We entered Richmond at 8 o'clock this morning.
G. Weitzel, Brigadier-General Commanding.

The operator who took the message was a fifteen-year old named William E. Kettles. According to a story[54] published long after the war, Kettles jumped up from his chair with the message in his hand and, upsetting inkstand and instrument, rushed into the next room where allegedly President Lincoln was talking with Charles A. Tinker, the cipher clerk. Kettles was about to hand the message to Tinker when the President sighted its contents and "with one motion and two strides" disappeared, clutching the message, on his way to Secretary Stanton's office. Within fifteen minutes from the time it reached Washington the news of Richmond's fall had gone out over the telegraph wires to all parts of the country.[55] The story was true only in part. Lincoln was not in Washington on April 3; he was down at City Point observing army operations at first-hand.

For reasons best known to Stanton, the War Department promptly canceled all newspaper passes and issued strict orders forbidding any newspaper correspondent to go down to the army. Disregarding Stanton's wishes, three prominent newspapermen, Whitelaw Reid, Lorenzo L. Crounse, and Charles A. Page, together left Washington for City Point around noon that day. Assistant Secretary of War Dana sent telegram after telegram after the three reporters directing that they be stopped, but by shifting from one steamer to another they managed to evade his directive.[56] Arriving at City Point late in the afternoon, the reporters barely had time to transfer to the Varina boat—so little time in fact that Crounse failed to get aboard before the boat pulled away. Up the James River the small craft containing the other two men warped its way and reached Varina Landing, fifteen miles from Richmond, at sunset.

The only vehicle at the wharf was a mail ambulance. After attempting to steal it, the correspondents were about to continue their journey on foot when a four-horse wagon drove up with a party of ladies from General Weitzel's headquarters in Richmond. Since Major Eugene E. Graves, their escort, was an acquaintance of Page, it was speedily arranged for the correspondents to have seats in the wagon for transportation back to Richmond. Presently, however, they ran into difficulty. Even the contents of flask and pocketbook could not tempt the driver to travel after dark. Under questioning he explained that in the darkness he might stray from the well-marked path through the enemy fortifications and detonate an enemy land mine—thereby killing his horses! As a result of their driver's solicitude for his horses, Reid and Page were forced to put up for the night at a village of log cabins about ten miles outside Richmond. The next morning they rode on into town and obtained accommodations in Richmond's finest hotel, the Spottswood House.[57] Crounse arrived in Richmond twenty-four hours later on the same vessel that brought his nemesis Dana up the river from City Point! Dana was on his way to Richmond with orders from Stanton to gather up the Confederate archives.[58]

By the time Reid and Page reached Richmond on Tuesday the heart of the city, some thirty squares in all, was burned out. In accordance with General Ewell's order, the retreating Confederates had set fire to the government buildings and tobacco warehouses at daylight on Monday, just before the Union troops marched in. Richmond's business district was virtually a sea of flame by Monday afternoon. Along both sides of Main Street the fire was roaring and the walls were tumbling as Reporter Coffin rode up to the Capitol and then bore off along a side street toward the Spottswood House.

"Can you accommodate me with a room?" he asked the desk clerk at the Spottswood.

"I reckon we can, sir," the clerk told him, "but like enough you will be burned out before morning."[59]

Somehow the hotel managed to escape the fire, however, and a little past noon on Tuesday, Coffin saw an amazing sight. As he was standing by the river bank and viewing the desolation, he noticed a boat pulled by ten rowers coming upstream with President Lincoln and his little son, Admiral Porter, and three other naval officers aboard. Coffin remarked to a Negro woman as the boat approached the landing:

"There is the man who made you free."

"What, massa?"

"That is President Lincoln."

"Dat President Linkum?"

"Yes."

She gazed at the strange, tall figure in amazement mingled with joy and rapture, then clapped her hands together, shouting "Glory! Glory! Glory!"

Some Negroes who had been working along the canal nearby threw down their shovels and crowded around the President, throwing their hats in the air and shouting their delight. There was no carriage in sight, and so the President walked to General Weitzel's headquarters, accompanied by Coffin, the Admiral, and twelve sailors armed with navy carbines. Before the presidential party reached their destination, the streets became so crowded with onlookers that soldiers had to be summoned to clear the way. Coffin's description of this historic scene appeared in due course in the Boston *Journal,* and from Coffin, Thomas Nast obtained the necessary verbal information to paint his famous picture of Lincoln in Richmond.[60]

Another reporter had participated in a different type of scene the day before. Entering the Confederate House of Delegates on Monday afternoon, the Negro correspondent of the Philadelphia *Press,* J. Morris Chester, had seated himself in the Speaker's chair and had begun to compose a letter to the *Press.* At that moment a captured Confederate officer who had been placed on parole passed the doorway and caught sight of Chester in the Speaker's chair.

"Come out of there, you black cuss," shouted the irate military man. The reporter looked up, eyed the Confederate officer calmly, and went on with his writing.

"Get out of there or I'll knock your brains out," the officer bellowed, adding some especially choice epithets.

Still Chester did not move but continued writing as if nothing had happened. The other man then rushed up the steps to seize him by the collar. A well-aimed blow sent him sprawling down the aisle. Springing to his feet, the exponent of white supremacy called upon a Union officer who came up just then to lend him a sword so that he might "cut the damned nigger's heart out!"

"I'll do nothing of the sort," retorted Captain Hutchins, the Union officer, "but if you want to try a fair fight, I'll have a ring made for you here, and see that there's no interference. You'll get more damnably thrashed," he added cheerfully, "than ever you were in your life before."

The Confederate officer left the hall in disgust while the Negro correspondent continued to write on, sitting in the chair of the Speaker of the House of Delegates of the State of Virginia.[61]

While some army correspondents lingered in Richmond, the others were with Grant and Meade pushing southwestward after Lee. On April 5, Sheridan cut the Richmond and Danville Railroad and forced Lee to substitute Lynchburg for Danville as his marching objective. On the following day, Ewell's Corps, which formed Lee's rear guard, was cut off and surrounded at Sailor's Creek. Some eight thousand Confederates with Ewell among them were captured that day.[62] Yet the newspapers had comparatively little to say about it. Years afterward, Sheridan told George Alfred Townsend that:

> there was one battle during the pursuit of Lee which some of you young fellows ought to have had a chance to describe. It was Sailor's Creek. The people had so much to read about at that time that the battle never got a full description.[63]

On Friday, April 6, a wave of rejoicing swept over the nation as a result of a premature report, which had originated in Philadelphia, of Lee's surrender.[64] Lee's situation, however, was fast becoming hopeless. On the morning of April 9, after some previous negotiation, Grant agreed to a meeting with Lee to discuss surrender terms. The interview between the two generals took place at the brick house of Wilmer McLean in the little village of Appomattox Court House. Lee, accompanied by a Federal officer, Colonel Francis Price, and two or three of his own aides, rode up to the McLean House about two-thirty that afternoon. To make sure of Lee's identity, Seybold of the New York *Tribune* asked an aide of the Confederate General Armistead L. Long who the distinguished-looking officer was.

"That," said the aide with considerable emphasis, "is the greatest man the country ever produced, Gen. Robt. E. Lee."[65]

In the opinion of Cadwallader, the *Herald* correspondent:

> Lee looked very much jaded and worn, but, nevertheless, presented the same magnificent *physique* for which he has always been noted. He was neatly dressed in gray cloth, without embroidery or any insignia of rank, except three stars worn on the turned portion of his coat collar. His cheeks were very much bronzed by exposure, but still shone ruddy underneath it all. He is growing quite bald, and wears one of the sidelocks of his hair thrown across the upper portion of his forehead, which is as white and fair as a woman's. . . . During the whole interview he was retired and dignified to a degree bordering on taciturnity, but was free from all exhibition of temper or mortification. His demeanor was that of a thoroughly possessed gentleman who had a very disagreeable duty to perform, but was determined to get through it as well and as soon as he could.[66]

No newspaper reporter was present during the interview between Grant and Lee.[67] Shortly before four o'clock, however, the reporters waiting outside the McLean house learned that the Army of Northern Virginia had surrendered unconditionally. Henry E. Wing of the New York *Tribune* previously had made an arrangement with one of Grant's staff officers that as soon as the surrender had been agreed to the staff officer should come out of the house where the generals were in conference, remove his hat, and stroke his forehead three times with a handkerchief. In the event of some other development, an appropriate signal was to be given.

While the conference between Grant and Lee was in progress, Wing remained outside the house, anxiously awaiting the outcome. Finally the door opened. A federal officer stepped out, doffed his hat, and drew his handkerchief across his forehead three times. Without a moment's delay, the *Tribune* correspondent was in the saddle, riding like mad for the telegraph station to beat the correspondent of the New York *Herald.* By eleven o'clock that night Wing's enterprise had paid off. Before Greeley had finished reading his dispatch, cheer after cheer rang through the night air as the word spread along the streets outside the *Tribune* office that "Lee has surrendered." It was Wing's last dispatch.[68] The war was over.

24

"Thirty"

ALTHOUGH Edwin Lawrence Godkin had represented the London *Daily News* in the bloody Crimean War of the eighteen-fifties, in his opinion it did not begin to compare with the American Civil War. In fact:

> There never was a war which afforded such materials for "special correspondence" of the best kind as this one—no matter in what way we look at it. It is vast, grandiose, sanguinary, checkered, full of brilliant episodes, of striking situations, of strange and varied incidents of all kinds. In the two things which most impress the imagination, the size of the forces engaged, and the desperation of the fighting, there has been nothing like it since Napoleon's campaign in Russia.[1]

In comparison, the Mexican War was remote, and the War of 1812 had occurred at a time when American journalism was as yet incapable of achieving comprehensive coverage. Never before in our history had the press been called upon to depict from day to day so moving a spectacle. Clearly this tragic conflict offered unusual opportunities for outstanding achievement in the reporting field. How successfully did the journalistic profession meet the challenge?

Any over-all judgment of Northern press performance during Civil War days depends in large part upon the answers to a number of related questions: How extensive was the news coverage? With what degree of accuracy and objectivity did the correspondents report battles and campaigns? How readable were their accounts—how descriptive and understandable to civilians and military? To what extent did the reporters display critical judgment in selecting material that was really newsworthy and in interpreting the causes and effects of the events about which they wrote? And in what measure did their reporting have a propaganda, as well as an objective, value for the men in the service and the "folks back home"?

In both World Wars I and II, the facilities for rapid dissemination of news, the sheer volume of news wordage, and the degree of accuracy in the output of the various wire services clearly has exceeded even the optimum in Civil War reporting. Yet Frank Luther Mott was substantially correct when he said that no great war has ever been so thoroughly covered by eyewitness reporters as the American Civil War.[2] Literally hundreds of reporters followed the movements of the U.S. armed forces. From the Washington telegraph office alone as many as fifty-eight thousand words passed over the wires to the nation's press in a single day during 1864. At the time of a great battle whole pages of extra editions were devoted to the reports of army or navy correspondents whose observations were made while they were under fire from the enemy.

In general, the best news coverage was given to the campaigns in the East, although even there at times military defeat resulted in a temporary tightening of the censorship and limited the possibilities of truthful reporting. The public was probably least well informed about the campaigns West of the Mississippi and in the Department of the Gulf. Speaking of the Gulf area, the *Army and Navy Journal* complained that:

> Contradictory despatches arrive by each steamer, and on turning for explanation to letters of public reporters, these in most cases furnish only a string of leisurely mendacity. . . . In case of our loss, it is safe to double all the figures of the Gulf reporters.[3]

Much greater space was given in the Northern press to army news than to news of naval operations, proportionately greater space than even the disparity in size of the two services would seem to have warranted. This, however, was not entirely the fault of the press. Tighter news control was exercised by the officers of the regular navy and their civilian superiors; the reporters naturally looked for their feature stories to the political generals in the army. Moreover, the South never was able to create a navy that could meet the United States fleet on anything like equal, and newsworthy, terms.

Although most correspondents presented the strictly military aspects of the war in their letters, Coffin, Ben Taylor, and others gave some attention to what one editor characterized as "the inner life of the army."[4] Almost all reporters told at one time or another how the soldiers felt, talked, and lived; how they were fed, clothed, and otherwise cared for in a material way, especially when they were sick or wounded; and how the chaplains ministered to their spiritual needs. In the opinion of a St. Louis editor, the emphatic denunciation of abuses in army administration was fully as much the business of an army reporter as the description of a battle scene.[5] Although the army newspapermen brought to light no major scandals, their exposures of graft and medical mismanagement were salutary.

Contemporary judgments of Southern war reporting varied. As a Northern newspaper saw it:

> Aside from their intense malice toward the North, and their boastfulness, and habitual extravagance in the employment of language, they [the Southern newspapers] have often given tolerably fair accounts of the events of the war. Their defeats at Mill Spring, Fort Donelson, Newbern, New Orleans, Hilton Head, Malvern Hill, and Corinth, were pretty fairly acknowledged, and in the disputed actions of Pea Ridge, Baton Rouge, Fair Oaks, Antietam, Perryville and Stone River, it was possible to discern the substantial truth through the haze of fiction.[6]

The Richmond *Whig*, on the other hand, was inclined to ask why the Southern reporting of a battle:

> by telegraph, by letter, or by word of mouth, should deprive a man of every particle of common sense, or every spark of principle. . . . A battle is no sooner begun, than we are notified by a "reliable" dispatch that the "whole army of the enemy will certainly be killed or captured". . . . It has been claimed that the people of the North are liars, and that we of the South are truthful—This is a delusion. . . . Everybody knows that "the whole army of the enemy will certainly be killed or captured" means that the Confederates will be defeated the next day. . . .
>
> The country is sick of the ineffable nonsense of the knaves and fools who pretend to report our battles.[7]

The *Whig* might well have been commenting on many efforts of the Northern reporters. Sensationalism and exaggeration, outright lies, puffery, slander, faked eyewitness accounts, and conjectures built on pure imagination cheapened much that passed in the North for news: McDowell drunk at Bull Run and Hooker in a similar condition at Chancellorsville; Rosecrans' addiction to drugs;[8] and General Lee's leaving the Confederate army in disgust, and his being eager to return to his old position in the Federal army.[9] There were detailed accounts of battles that never were fought and repeated stories of the fall of Richmond, Atlanta, Vicksburg, Savannah, Petersburg, and Mobile. To judge from the number of times his death was reported in the Northern press Stonewall Jackson must have been the target of extraordinary reportorial animosity. Even the Associated Press enlivened the details of Pope's second Bull Run campaign with a cock-and-bull story about General Sigel's having shot General McDowell through the head on the battlefield at Warrenton.[10]

In a letter to the New York *Times* written from London in October, 1861, Henry Adams expressed the opinion that nothing had done the Union cause so much harm abroad as the exaggerations and misrepresentations of the Northern press:

> People have become so accustomed to the idea of disbelieving everything that is stated in the American papers that all confidence in us is destroyed; and how can we wonder at it, when we see daily accounts of "masterly movements" of regiments which turn out to have run away without firing a gun, and "glorious victories" which result in disastrous defeats?[11]

Most of the unfounded rumors which had their brief day of glory in the press were disseminated by the telegraph, even though the telegraphic reporters were subjected to a hit-or-miss censorship which became somewhat more effective after Stanton entered the War Department in January, 1862. To the Boston *Post*, it seemed, as early as June, 1861, that the appearance of a telegram relating to almost any subject warranted the inference that the contrary was true. "The country is supposed to expect 'success at all points,' " echoed the New York *Tribune*, "and it seems to be the business of the telegraph to gratify it."[12] From all sides criticism was directed at the news which came over the wires from Cairo, Nashville, Memphis, Baltimore, and Philadelphia—"the great mother of false intelligence, windy rumors, and sidewalk stories."[13] During the Vicksburg campaign, one of the New York *Tribune* reporters commented on the enterprising newspapers in the North and East, which, not content with such news from Vicksburg as they received from their correspondents on the ground, habitually published absurd rumors from Murfreesboro, Pittsburgh, and any number of other places which entirely lacked facilities for obtaining news from Vicksburg:

> The men who send dispatches from Memphis and Cairo are doubtless very industrious, worthy men but their labors, it seems to me must result in greatly befogging the public . . . as they forward every statement of every crew on a northbound steamer passing these points, whether it is old or new, false or true. We can afford here to laugh at the ridiculous stuff purporting to be news from Vicksburg to which you are daily treated; but we still think it unfair that you should be so trifled with.[14]

In the early part of the war the greatest amount of criticism was reserved for the Washington reporters of the New York press and their original wire versions of the latest news. The Cincinnati *Commercial* commented:

> The fact is, with these gentlemen it is . . . sensation or nothing. They hang about the Department offices; they button-hole the unhappy ushers; they besiege goers and comers; they read physiognomies; they absorb the contents of all leaky vessels like a sponge; they study hotel registers as faithfully as a monk his breviary; they "spot" "distinguished arrivals" as quickly as a detective, and pursue them like Death in the Apocalypse. And if these resources fail, there is a bank that never fails, a supply that never gives out, in their fertile imaginations. Rumors are recorded as facts with an amazing indifference, and, like the Fate that unravels in the night what she knits in the day, they contradict as flatly as they publish confidently. . . .
>
> We have had Fremont removed, superseded and transferred, all in the same day; nay within the same hour all these statements contradicted. As if this feat were not sufficiently enormous, they must supersede McClellan in the same breath, and elevate General Halleck to his pedestal. . . . They have killed Jeff. Davis and Beauregard a dozen times at least since the opening of the war, and insisted in slaughtering Gen. Gustavus Smith, at Leesburg, though he was not in command of the rebel forces there. When Col. Baker fell, they assure us a hundred guns were pointed at him —how precise is the statement!—and that he was pierced by six balls, and today we are informed that an irrepressible rebel rode up to him, and discharged his revolver five times, each shot taking effect in the distinguished Senator.[15]

Typical of the "howlers" in the telegraphic columns of the press was a news item in the Louisville *Journal* during December, 1862: "A sharp skirmish took place on the Franklin Pike yesterday, between some of Gen. Negley's troops and the enemy. Nobody hurt."[16] The real story about the "skirmish," as later established by a reporter for the Cincinnati *Commercial,* was that a foraging column in brigade strength had gone out along the Franklin Pike from Nashville. The column had been halted when some one sighted something glistening like bayonets in the sunlight about two miles ahead. The foragers hastily wheeled a cannon into position and hurled a few shells toward the "bayonets." The enemy—a badly frightened Negro, mounted on an only slightly less frightened mule, and carrying a shiny ax—turned and fled. "I see many such ludicrous mistakes in the telegraph reports," commented the *Commercial* reporter.[17]

The press's tendency to fabricate war news extended beyond wire stories. A correspondent of the Cincinnati *Commercial* informed his newspaper that the "small-pox maps" of the New York *Herald* were a standing jest in the army,[18] and the St. Louis *Democrat* characterized such maps, improvised by sensational newspapers, as "striking and lifelike pictures of a drunkard's stomach."[19]

Similar remarks were directed at the sketches of the army artists. Many of the battle scene representations which appeared in *Harper's Weekly* and the other illustrated newspapers were, to quote a Cincinnati *Times* correspondent, "little better than a sensational farce."[20] When Joe Wheeler's cavalry set fire to some Federal army trains near Chattanooga in October, 1863, *Harper's Weekly* carried sketches of the scene from its artist "on the spot," although the artist had been in bed twenty miles away from the burning when it actually took place. Only a few weeks before, the same magazine had used an old Potomac cut to represent the Battle of Chickamauga, another "on the spot" performance.[21] Satirizing such practices, the popular humor magazine *Vanity Fair* earlier had printed a cartoon which showed "Our Own Artist" using tin soldiers for models in sketching a view of General Banks's army "on the spot!"[22]

Much of the inaccuracy in Civil War reporting, however, was accidental, or at least unintentional; comparatively few war reporters were chronic liars. In many cases the misstatements which cropped up in news stories were not so much a matter of willful misrepresentation as they were the result of the haste and confusion involved in newsgathering, especially after a battle.

Moreover, the reporter's news sources were of varying reliability. The people best able to provide him with an accurate picture were the very people who were the least willing to talk. Under the circumstances, army reporters were forced to pick up news wherever they could find it—from "weak-kneed, watery-eyed young quartermaster clerks," from sick or disabled soldiers, from returned prisoners, Union refugees, "intelligent contrabands," deserters, and, as a last resort, from "reliable gentlemen."[23] A reporter for the Philadelphia *Inquirer* decided that there were three general categories of army news: news based on orders made known at headquarters, which in his opinion was the most reliable news; "chin news," which he defined as "somebody hearing something from somebody else, which somebody told him he got from somebody who heard from some reliable source"; and "cook house news," which consisted of such impossible exaggerations that no one but a cook would have been capable of spreading them.[24]

Since much of the fighting took place in wooded country, the army reporter usually could see only the merest segment of the action. He therefore had to rely on the descriptions of a large number of eyewitnesses posted in various parts of the field, and often it was not easy to reconcile their discrepancies.

Working as he did under difficulties of this kind, the reporter was tempted to fall back on stereotyped descriptions of advancing battle lines, dashing cavalry charges, brilliant officers with drawn swords, and riderless horses careering over the plains. Some reporters habitually portrayed the army on all occasions as "burning to be led against the foe" and "eager for the fray." Charles A. Page declared:

> Writers who indulge in the use of such phrases, know nothing of armies . . . or rather state what they do not know, unless indeed they know it to be false. . . . The man who affects any of this fine frenzy is a coward. Let it be understood that troops never "rush frantically to the front" for the love of the thing—at least not after they have been in one fight. After that, they are sure to know better.[25]

To some extent, the dishonest practices of the army reporters were the natural result of their managing editors' low ethical standards. The editors were more likely to censure a reporter for being scooped by an enterprising rival than for including items of doubtful authenticity. A Philadelphia *Press* correspondent wrote:

> Of all the great newspaper establishments that send out special correspondents, but two proprietors give positive instructions to tell the plain truth and criticise matters without fear or favor.[26]

One of the greatest offenders was the New York *Herald,* a paper with a reputation based not on ethics but on enterprise. In a letter written to Manton Marble from New Orleans in July, 1863, Philip Ripley of the New York *World* described at some length the way the fighting at Port Hudson was being reported from New Orleans. In the course of his letter, Ripley asked the editor of the *World* whether he had noticed how widely the *Herald's* account of the assault of June 14 had been reprinted by other newspapers:

> It is because it was dated "near Port Hudson", and gives the scene from a reporter "up a tree" & bears apparently every evidence of being the narrative of an eye witness. Now that letter was written by Johnson of the Herald, Cash's then assistant, & at the time of the events described he was actually in the Gulf on his way from New York to this city. This is private of course; but he arrived in time to bone some one who was there & sent the account. He has never been I believe to P. Hudson. The letter was shown to me "as a good joke" before it was mailed.[27]

In some cases what passed for special telegraphic dispatches to the *Herald* were manufactured in the *Herald's* Fulton Street office or were scissored together from material which came to the newspaper office through the mail.[28]

In its own defense, the press was quick to point out that the official reports of commanding officers were by no means invariably accurate. Although they might be more factually correct than newspaper letters, in the opinion of the New York *Evening Post,* they were "not so faithful as to impressions."[29] A writer for the St. Louis *Democrat* stated:

> Unless I very much mistake the humor of your readers, they will much prefer to learn the impression produced upon the mind of an actual eye witness of a great battle field, to a general summary of statistics, which will come in a much more authentic and complete form, through an official channel. . . . A diagram of the situation and strategy will represent a great game with human chess men, but they tell you nothing of the desperate rancor, the heroism, or the closing desolation and gloom, which make up the tragedy of the battle field.[30]

Moreover, such reports were slow in coming through. Meade's official report of the Battle of Gettysburg did not appear in the newspapers until four months after the battle, and McClellan's report of the Peninsular Campaign was even longer delayed.

In fact, the public was willing to accept, even to expect, a certain amount of inaccurate reporting as the price of insight into the everyday life of the army. When the newsmen were driven from the army, the public was compelled to depend upon official reports for information about happenings at the front. They found these reports quite as distorted as the correspondents', since the military covered for each other. As the Cincinnati *Commercial* phrased it, "West Point takes care of her own."[31] Furthermore, to some extent, newspaper errors canceled out each other. Although the press spread all the exciting rumors of the day, the New York *Times* was convinced that rumors would be ten times as numerous and far more mischievous if there were no newspapers. "Where the Press starts one false report, it kills a dozen—and its constant issues render it impossible that any *canard* should have a long life."[32]

Although the news writing of the sixties was more direct than that of the previous decade, the stilted rhetoric which even the best army reporters commonly employed contrasts sharply with the simpler journalistic style of the present day. Letters from the front abounded with such expressions as "night's sable mantle,"[33] "the grim blood-dripping visage of war,"[34] and "the proud, towering rebel edifice of folly, fraud and reckless passions."[35] Yet the war reporting of these years contained some effective figures of speech, such as the "volleys of musketry, which rattled and crackled like a canebrake on fire"[36] and "the whole centre of the rebel line . . . crushed down as a field of ripe wheat through which a tornado has passed."[37]

"Opening the ball" was a phrase commonly used by reporters to refer to the firing of the first gun in a battle. The hasty and disorderly flight of a body of troops amounted to a "skedaddle" or a "scyugle." Employing army slang, the reporters alluded to Confederate soldiers as "Secesh," "Confeds," "Graybacks," or "Johnnies." "Foraging" was the army term, and consequently the army reporters' term, for stealing. As the war dragged on, the newspapermen learned to distinguish between a skirmish, an affair, an action, an engagement, and a battle—the names given by military men to conflicts varying in the order of their magnitude. Prisoners were commonly "bagged" or "gobbled up" rather than captured; dissent was expressed in the remark, "I don't see it"; Negroes usually were spoken of as "contrabands," as a result of General Butler's famous dictum, placing Negroes in the category of "contraband of war." Even the expression "doughboy" was used to describe an infantryman in the letter of a Philadelphia *Inquirer* reporter.[38]

Euphemisms, such as to "retire" or to "make a change of base," were commonly used to gloss over a retreat or reverse. Some reporters moreover were addicted to superlatives which were not always warranted by the facts. Samuel Fiske, the "Dunn Browne" of the Springfield (Massachusetts) *Republican,* in a letter to his newspaper referred to a newspaper account of some recent fighting in which the statement was made that the musketry firing was the most terrific the writer had ever seen. Later in the account, the unnamed reporter admitted that this was the first action of any kind that he had ever witnessed. "It occurred to me," said Browne drily, "that, considering the last-mentioned fact, the first statement was not very strange."[39]

Yet, in many instances, the letters of the Civil War correspondents were highly descriptive. There is an unforgettable quality in Franc Wilkie's description of ravaged Missouri in the autumn of 1861,[40] in Whitelaw Reid's realistic picture of a volunteer camp in midwinter,[41] or in George F. Williams' clever portrait of an army sutler with "that great hat, and 'those boots'... cigar in mouth... the restless spirit of peculation rife in his eye."[42] There were no news photographers at Bull Run and Antietam, at Shiloh, Gettysburg, or Chickamauga. Yet each of those battles was portrayed by able news writers only less vividly than the news camera might have done. Widely reprinted in both the American and European press, such battle accounts gave a very real picture of what this terrible war was like.

Curiously enough, the news-hungry public seemed to read about disastrous defeats with the same relish that it read the details of great victories. In fact, the worse a defeat was made to appear, the more eager the public seemed to be to hear about it. Over a period of four years the reading public might be supposed to have wearied of newspaper accounts of wholesale bloodshed and slaughter. Nevertheless, what the Cincinnati *Enquirer* described as an "insatiable appetite for horrible news and rumors" continued unabated throughout the war:

> To satisfy this morbid appetite the flippant newspaper correspondent has but to work up a skirmish into a column of gore, and his efforts are successful; the miserable imposition is greedily swallowed and no questions asked.[43]

To some extent, a note of grim pleasantry ran through the writings of the army reporters, which may have made their tales of death and disaster less forbidding.

On the other hand, for comprehensive analysis and interpretation of the strategy of the campaigns, news correspondents had to rely on native good sense, talks with well-informed officers, and a hastily acquired familiarity with writings on military subjects. The New York *Times* correspondent Swinton was so successful in this field that after he left the army in 1864 the *Times* kept him in Washington to write letters about the grand strategy of the campaign in Virginia.

Insofar as this sort of reporting involved judging the qualifications of commanding officers, the authors exposed themselves to reprisals from the officers they criticized. In some cases, therefore, reporters avoided giving their own opinions in letters for publication. Instead they wrote private letters for their editors to use as a basis for editorials dealing with the military situation. Nonetheless, the reporters' ability to grasp the significance of what was happening, even when they did not see fit to write freely about it, is indicated by their success in predicting army movements and in being on the spot when important news stories were breaking.

Complete objectivity from the reporters was too much to expect, since the building of both civilian and military morale generally was considered an essential part of their work. With few exceptions they built well. It is hardly surprising, therefore, that a New York *Tribune* reporter should refer to a dead Confederate soldier as "sacrificed to the devilish ambition of his implacable masters, Davis and Lee."[44] Even the correspondents of such anti-Administration dailies as the New York *World* and the Chicago *Times* commonly used a pro-Northern slant in their reporting. In the South, the reporters were, if anything, even more partisan.

Yet the most serious criticism of the Northern press, both during the war and since, was that the press consistently printed information vital to the national security.[45] In spite of the censorship, which was haphazard at best, the leakage of such information through the press was well-nigh scandalous. Lee and other Confederate generals regularly read the Northern newspapers, for even the casualty lists often gave full information about the position of brigades and regiments, the arrival of reinforcements, and the location and strength of battery units.[46]

These premature announcements of troop movements caused unnecessary battles and the needless expenditure of human lives.

In the great majority of cases, however, the fault lay not with the reporters, but with their editors. It was the reporter's duty to provide his newspaper with all the information he could obtain about army or navy operations and leave to the discretion of the editor what could safely be published. In exercising the prerogatives of office censorship, editors were not always prudent and far-sighted. And when they were called to account for improper disclosures, they were prone to argue that by establishing an official censorship the government had relieved them of the responsibility of censoring their own news columns.[47]

During this country's earlier wars there had been some governmental interference with the freedom of the press. It was not until the Civil War, however, that the Federal government imposed upon the press an official censorship, beginning in April, 1861, at the time of the Baltimore riots. In general the censorship was of news sent by telegraph, although at times the restrictions were made to apply to mail and express dispatches as well.

At the beginning of the war, most of the censors were novices at their task, but by 1863 a Washington correspondent of the *Tribune* was writing to Gay and urging him to use caution in heading as "special dispatches" the material obtained by cipher. The correspondent explained that "these operators and censors are too sharp—too sharp by half," and that one of them, named House, "being one of the craft knows where the *leaks* are and how to 'whip the devil around the stump.' "[48]

Although in the early days the censors also frequently had rejected entire dispatches which contained a single censorable fact, they later learned to scissor and hack the correspondents' dispatches. These mutilated fragments the censors then sent on, frequently without bothering to show them to the reporters.

It is questionable which practice angered the reporters more. At any rate, many of them paid—with arbitrary arrests, military commission trials, and even expulsion from the lines—for evading the censorship code in one way or another. Among the reporters who achieved this peculiar distinction were Knox, Winser, Osbon, McCullagh, Swinton, Crapsey, Denyse, and Deming.

The effectiveness of the censorship itself was variable. Perhaps it was most effective at times of military defeat—on the Peninsula, at Fredericksburg, and at Chancellorsville—when the mechanisms for news suppression were most tightly applied. Even then, however, the censorship was better able to curb news from Washington than to stop the flow of news from the field. Chiefly it managed to delay stories of disaster rather than to kill them outright.

Although at such times the censorship may have been overly severe, and certainly it was continuously unpopular with most people outside of the armed services, it was most often utterly ineffectual. Administrative confusion made a really effective censorship almost an impossibility. At different times during the war the censorship was administered by the State, Treasury, and War departments, sometimes by two of them simultaneously. Furthermore, the commanding generals might exercise their own discretion. They could censor dispatches originating in their own commands, or they could relax censorship to favor individual reporters and their newspapers.

Moreover, the agencies charged with the censorship often failed to make any distinction between preventing military information from reaching the enemy and interdicting wholesome criticism of the general conduct of the war and of Administration policy. This failure gave the press an opening, and editorial complaints resulted in an investigation by the Judiciary Committee of the House of Representatives. The investigators found that there were inequities in the censorship and expressed the opinion that its measures had been carried too far.

In spite of irresponsible editors and overzealous reporters, however, in spite of erratic censorship and temperamental generals, there was some excellent reporting during the Civil War. In Henry Villard's opinion, the best reporting of the war on the Northern side occurred during the year 1862. From that time on, but more especially after 1863, he felt, there was a marked decline in the quality of Civil War reporting as the more competent and high-minded correspondents gradually withdrew, leaving their places to be filled by men who possessed neither the native intelligence, the education, nor the character to offer adequate replacement. As Villard expressed it:

> Men turned up in the army as correspondents more fit to drive cattle than to write for newspapers. With a dull or slow perception, incapable of logical arrangement of facts, innocent of grammatical English, they were altogether out of place in the positions they tried to fill.[49]

To the Chicago *Tribune,* on the other hand, it seemed in 1864 that:

> one thing is to be noticed as the war progresses. The judgment of our reporters not only becomes better, but their candor improves also. It is much more common now to find our own losses fairly stated than in the early years of the war, as well as those of the enemy.[50]

For one of the leading correspondents of the Civil War, writing thirty years afterward, the first requisites of good war reporting were accuracy and absolute truthfulness "written without fear, favor, or affection." He went on to say:

> It should be as minute and detailed as possible . . . . penned under the excitement and inspiration of battle surroundings, when practicable, and in the fewest words that will convey a pen picture of the battlefield and its attendants. . . .
>
> A great battle possesses an absorbing, terrible interest to the typical correspondent who witnesses it, [and] exerts a fascination wholly indescribable and superior to any other on earth. His whole soul will be thrown into his account of it, and he will find neither time nor inclination to garnish a pretty story.
>
> The zip and ping of minie balls, the rattling, rolling, swelling and falling musketry fire, the trembling, thundering roar of heavy artillery, the shouting and yelling of contending hosts, the groans of wounded men, the screaming of crippled horses, the blinding sulphurous smoke, the horrible scenes of destruction and death which cover a field of battle are all legitimate subjects for description and afford play for every natural and artificial faculty. . . .
>
> The master of the art, however, never allows these minor delineations to become the chief features of his correspondence, and never so exhausts himself on a skirmish that he cannot describe a battle. He weaves them into his account as bits of coloring, to set off stupendous facts. He remembers that the chief interest will always center on the heroic deeds of those engaged, the responsibility of each for failure or success and the paramount question of whether the field was lost or won. . . .
>
> That I was often misinformed or mistaken about many details need scarcely be stated, but . . . I can truthfully affirm that I never knowingly wrote an untruth for publication. . . .
>
> My faults were those of being a slow penman—of spending

> too much time in gathering material, and verifying statements—of condensing much that deserved elaboration—and the very common fault of overlooking, or omitting, many small details which seemed to me at the time too insignificant to mention.[51]

Such were the standards of the best reporters—Reid, Coffin, Smalley, and Cadwallader. Within the limitations which continually circumscribe the reporter in time of war, they labored to keep the public fully, and on the whole accurately, informed of what was going on at the front. Although much of what they wrote was ephemeral from a historical point of view, to at least one contemporary observer it seemed that writing "with a precision, a dignity, and an eloquence that rises in many cases to the level of the historian," they were bringing to light the "true material for the historian of this war."[52] Some such thought seems to have been in the mind of the biographer of Samuel Bowles as he leafed through the daily pages of the Civil War newspaper files twenty years after the war had ended:

> There it all stands vividly out—the four years' experience which so deeply impressed the lives of all who shared it. There is the first eager and passionate rush against the foe; there are the first defeats, the disappointments, the perplexities, the evergrowing sacrifices; then the deep breath of anticipated triumph when one week saw Gettysburg won at the east and Vicksburg captured at the west; the brightening hope; then the industries of peace recovering and multiplying themselves in the midst of war; the dogged, desperate rally for the last tug of the Wilderness and Petersburg; the equal valor of North and South; the myriads of lives lost and homes desolated; the new manliness wrought by heroic endurance into North and South alike; the birth of a race into freedom, the restoration of a people to unity.[53]

Viewed through the eyes of the reporters who pictured the great drama of those years, the Civil War takes on a deeper, a more personal meaning. We stand beside George Alfred Townsend near Culpeper on an August afternoon in 1862 and watch Banks's men marching along the road in open order, singing and jesting as they march. We see Osbon kneeling on the deck of the "Hartford" as it runs the gauntlet to New Orleans and hear Farragut call out reprovingly, "Come, sir, this is no time for prayer." With Villard we enter the White House on the second night after the Battle of Fredericksburg and sense the anxiety in

Lincoln's mind as he listens to the *Tribune* correspondent's description of Burnside's plight.

To compensate for the erratic and ill-informed writing of inferior pens, there was great reporting in full measure. The blood-soaked battlefields of Gettysburg, Antietam, Shiloh, and Chickamauga; the dingy telegraph offices of Washington, Louisville, and Cairo; the guerilla-infested country between, through which the reporters, striving to be first with the news, trekked by rail, on horseback, or even on foot; and the poorly-lighted editorial rooms, where special dispatches from the front were carefully scrutinized for their news value—these were the proving grounds for distinguished journalism, both during the war and in the years to come.

Notes

1
THE REPORTER AND THE FORT
Pages 1-5

1. L. A. Gobright, *Recollections of Men and Things at Washington during the Third of a Century* (Philadelphia, 1869), pp. 312-314. For enthusiastic editorial comment on this "welcome revelation of the government's purpose to defend its property and maintain the laws," see the New York *Evening Post,* April 10, 1861.
2. New York *World,* April 19, 1861.
3. New York *Times,* May 5, 1861.
4. F. G. De Fontaine, "The First Day of Real War," *Southern Bivouac,* II (July, 1886), 77.
5. The frigate "Powhatan," the flagship of the expedition, which Secretary Seward had diverted to Fort Pickens on the Florida coast, and the "Pocahontas," which did not arrive at the rendezvous point off Charleston until the afternoon of April 13.
6. New York *Morning Express,* May 17, 1865.
7. A. B. Paine, *A Sailor of Fortune* (New York, 1906), p. 120; T. W. Sheridan, "The Navy and the Press during the Civil War," *United States Naval Institute Proceedings,* LXIII (May, 1937), 709-711.
8. I. M. Tarbell, *The Life of Abraham Lincoln* (New York, 1909), II, 33.
9. J. G. Nicolay and John Hay, *Abraham Lincoln, A History* (New York, *ca.* 1914), IV, 44-45, 70.
10. New York *Times,* April 15, 1861.
11. Paine, *op. cit.,* p. 126.
12. *Ibid.,* p. 128.

2
THE PRESS GIRDS FOR THE CONFLICT
Pages 6-34

1. J. D. Reid, *The Telegraph in America* (New York, 1886), p. 419; A. F. Harlow, *Old Wires and New Waves* (New York and London, 1936), pp. 247, 257; A. H. Shaw, *The Plain Dealer* (New York, 1942), p. 354. The two principal telegraph companies in 1861 were the American Telegraph Company with headquarters in New York and the Western Union system, which blanketed the region west of the Alleghenies and made connections with the American Telegraph system at Albany, Philadelphia, Pittsburgh, and Cincinnati.
2. W. H. Smith, "The Press as a News Gatherer," *Century Magazine,* XLII (August, 1891), 530.
3. W. F. G. Shanks, "How We Get Our News," *Harper's New Monthly Magazine,* XXXIV (March, 1867), 520.
4. R. L. Thompson, *Wiring a Continent* (Princeton, New Jersey, 1947), p. 224; Frederic Hudson, *Journalism in the United States* (New York, 1873), p. 610.
5. Reid, *op. cit.,* p. 415; Harlow, *op.*

cit., pp. 112-113.

6. See e.g., Cincinnati *Daily Commercial*, July 9, 1861.
7. F. L. Mott, *American Journalism* (New York, 1941), pp. 350, 658; St. Louis *Daily Missouri Republican*, September 5, 1861. The selling price of the *Times* in 1861 was reported to be $23,000. Chicago *Daily Journal*, April 22, 1924. The New York *Sun* brought only $35,000 at public auction in October, 1861, although in 1852 when it passed into the sole possession of Moses Beach it had been valued at $250,-000. F. M. O'Brien, *The Story of the Sun* (New York, 1918), p. 171.
8. G. F. Williams, "Bennett, Greeley and Raymond," *Journalist*, IV (October 2, 1886), 2.
9. During the 1850's the local reporters of the New York papers rarely received more than $20 a week. In Philadelphia the local reporters were so poorly paid at the outbreak of the war that the more ambitious felt obliged to work simultaneously for two or three different newspapers.
10. Adams S. Hill to Darwin Ware, November 23, 1857, Miscellaneous MSS in the possession of Arthur Hill, Esq., Boston, Massachusetts.
11. Allen Johnson and Dumas Malone, *Dictionary of American Biography* (New York, 1928-1944), VII, 529; H. L. Stoddard, *Horace Greeley* (New York, 1946), p. 60.
12. J. F. Rhodes, *History of the United States from the Compromise of 1850* (New York and London, 1928), II, 27.
13. Miscellaneous scrapbooks, Horace Greeley Papers, Library of Congress.
14. Murat Halstead, "Breakfasts with Horace Greeley," *Cosmopolitan*, XXXVI (April, 1904), 699-700.
15. New York *Times*, September 18, 1851.
16. Augustus Maverick, *Henry J. Raymond and the New York Press* (Hartford, 1870), p. 170. For a more recent as well as a more scholarly treatment of Raymond, see Francis Brown, *Raymond of the Times* (New York, 1951).
17. From a newspaper clipping in the George Alfred Townsend Scrapbooks, George Alfred Townsend Papers, in the possession of the Townsend family, New York City.
18. Horace Greeley, *Recollections of a Busy Life* (New York, 1869), p. 138.
19. Thurlow Weed, *Autobiography* (Boston, 1883-1884), II, 280-281.
20. *Dictionary of American Biography*, XV, 409; Elmer Davis, *History of the New York Times* (New York, 1921), p. 46; Meyer Berger, *The Story of the New York Times, 1851-1951* (New York, 1951), pp. 21-22.
21. *Dictionary of American Biography*, III, 205. Bryant's journalistic career is treated at greater length in Parke Godwin, *A Biography of William Cullen Bryant* (New York, 1883), I, 230-265; H. H. Peckham, *Gotham Yankee: A Biography of William Cullen Bryant* (New York, 1952), pp. 88-98, 135-154.
22. New York *Times*, February 28, 1860.
23. Allan Nevins, *The Evening Post, A Century of Journalism* (New York, 1922), pp. 359-361; John Bigelow, *Retrospections of an Active Life*, I (New York, 1909), 320-321.
24. *Dictionary of American Biography*, II, 195; D. C. Seitz, *The James Gordon Bennetts* (Indianapolis, 1928), p. 17; Oliver Carlson, *The Man Who Made News, James Gor-*

don Bennett (New York, 1942), p. 34.

25. S. R. Fiske, *Off-Hand Portraits of Prominent New Yorkers* (New York, 1884), p. 86.

26. Adam Gurowski, *Diary* (Boston, New York, and Washington, D.C., 1862-1866), I, 81. In June, 1863, however, Lincoln's secretary, John G. Nicolay, informed one of the editors of the Chicago *Tribune* that "excepting the Washington City dailies, in which he carefully reads the telegraphic dispatches, the President rarely ever looks at any papers, simply for want of leisure to do so." Helen Nicolay, *Lincoln's Secretary* (New York, 1949), pp. 185-186. For evidence supporting Nicolay's statement, see F. B. Carpenter, *Six Months at the White House* (New York, 1866), pp. 153-154.

27. J. R. Young, *Men and Memories* (New York and London, 1901), I, 208-209.

28. Davis, *op. cit.*, pp. 53-54. An item in the New York *Daily Tribune* of April 17, 1861, indicates that the Boston *Post* also had a correspondent in Charleston at that time.

29. Nevins, *op. cit.*, p. 317; R. B. Rhett, Jr., to John Bigelow, November 14, 1860, in Bigelow, *op. cit.*, I, 305.

30. Philadelphia *Press*, December 15, 1862.

31. G. F. Williams, "How a Reporter Faced Danger in Disguise," *Independent*, LIII (August 8, 1901), 1860-1862; *Journalist*, II (January 9, 1886), 4.

32. A. D. Richardson, *The Secret Service, the Field, the Dungeon, and the Escape* (Hartford, 1865), pp. 122-123; E. R. Jewett to Hon. J. Holt, February 21, 1861, Office of the Secretary of War, Letters Received, National Archives.

33. Richardson, *op. cit.*, p. 124.

34. See e.g., New York *Times*, April 15, 1861. During January or February, 1861, the managing editor of the *Tribune* told Richardson that "we have six [correspondents] still in the South" and that two others the week before had come home after "narrow escapes."

35. Richardson, *op. cit.*, p. 19.

36. *Journalist*, II (March 28, 1885), 5; *ibid.* (October 10, 1885), p. 1.

37. New York *Times*, April 15, 16, 17, 1861.

38. New York *Herald*, April 27, 1861.

39. Hudson, *op. cit.*, p. 715; New York *Herald*, May 2, 1861.

40. Williams, *op. cit.*, p. 1862.

41. New York *Times*, May 16, 1861.

42. Hudson, *op. cit.*, p. 705.

43. Henry Villard, "Army Correspondence," *Nation*, I (August 3, 1865), 146. To cut expense, newspapers sometimes shared their special correspondence with other papers. In 1864, for example, the Philadelphia *Inquirer* subscribed for the Southern news service of the Cincinnati *Gazette* at a cent and a half a word plus $15 a week for the services of a correspondent in Cincinnati who forwarded dispatches to Philadelphia. Richard Smith to Uriah H. Painter, March 3, 1864, Uriah Hunt Painter Papers, in the possession of the Painter family, West Chester, Pennsylvania.

44. See e.g., Henry Villard, *Memoirs of Henry Villard, Journalist and Financier* (Boston and New York, 1904), I, 163; A. B. Paine, *A Sailor of Fortune* (New York, 1906), pp. 95, 132; Washington *Evening Star*, October 16, 1896; Shanks, *op. cit.*, p. 512; W. G. Bleyer, *Main Currents in the History of American Journalism* (Boston and New York,

1927), pp. 200-201.

45. Shanks, *op. cit.*, p. 519. The large turnover of army correspondents, together with editorial statements by the *Herald*, June 7, 1863, and June 8, 1864, makes Shanks's estimate appear conservative.

46. Hudson, *op. cit.*, pp. 483, 717; New York *Herald*, May 7, 1916. The *Herald* claimed on August 14, 1861, that its bill for special telegraphic material, exclusive of news furnished by the AP, for the preceding week was over $1,000.

47. James Parton, "The New York Herald," *North American Review*, CII (April, 1866), 401. During the Petersburg campaign, Sylvanus Cadwallader of the *Herald* had a locomotive standing ready day and night for his exclusive use. Washington *Evening Star*, October 16, 1896.

48. Hudson, *op. cit.*, p. 483; New York *Herald*, May 7, 1916.

49. Shanks, *op. cit.*, pp. 518-519.

50. Thomas W. Knox to James Gordon Bennett, June 28, 1862, James Gordon Bennett Papers, Library of Congress.

51. L. A. Whitely to James Gordon Bennett, September 9, 1862, Bennett Papers.

52. Mott, *op. cit.*, p. 332. At one time in 1862, the *Tribune* had from five to eight "specials" with the Army of the Potomac and no less than a dozen in the Western war zone.

53. New York *Times*, March 27, 1898.

54. J. H. Wilson, *The Life of Charles A. Dana* (New York and London, 1927), p. 171; D. C. Seitz, *Horace Greeley, Founder of the New York Tribune* (Indianapolis, 1926), pp. 207-208; O'Brien, *op. cit.*, pp. 214-215.

55. H. W. Baehr, Jr., *The New York Tribune Since the Civil War* (New York, 1936), p. 26.

56. *Dictionary of American Biography*, XII, 267; XIII, 548; Nevins, *op. cit.*, pp. 315-317, 319-320.

57. G. A. Townsend, "Recollections and Reflections," *Lippincott's Monthly Magazine*, XXXVIII (November, 1886), 521. Corroborative evidence appears in a rate table, issued by the Magnetic Telegraph Company some time during the Civil War period, which the author found in the Painter Papers. At five cents a word, a column of Washington dispatches would cost one of the New York papers about $130.

58. Philadelphia *Inquirer*, March 3, 1862. The single exception was, of course, the *Herald*.

59. E. P. Oberholtzer, *Jay Cooke, Financier of the Civil War* (Philadelphia, 1907), I, 232. After 1862, the *Inquirer*, because of necessary economies, was less active in war reporting.

60. Henry Watterson to E. A. Muschamp, January 12, 1921, Miscellaneous MSS, Historical Society of Pennsylvania, Philadelphia.

61. George Alfred Townsend Scrapbooks.

62. J. T. Scharf, *History of Baltimore City and County* (Philadelphia, 1881), p. 611; R. H. Spencer, *Genealogical and Memorial Encyclopedia of the State of Maryland* (New York, 1919), I, 4-12; Baltimore *American and Commercial Advertiser*, June 8, 1883.

63. New York *Times*, June 23, 1861.

64. St. Louis *Daily Missouri Republican*, January 4, 1863. Forney himself subsequently remarked: "But what a change the war has made in the Washington newspapers. *The Sunday Chronicle*, which was the first of its class ever seen at the capital . . . gave more news and telegrams in one number than all the old-time dailies did . . . in

a week." J. W. Forney, *Anecdotes of Public Men*, I (New York, 1873), 383.

65. Chicago *Daily Tribune*, May 19, 1863.

66. G. M. Roe, *Cincinnati, The Queen City of the West* (Cincinnati, 1895), pp. 265-268; Roe, "Newspapers and Literature," *New England Magazine*, VI (September, 1888), 451; New York *Daily Graphic*, September 24, 1875.

67. For biographical details concerning Halstead, see *Dictionary of American Biography*, VIII, 163; *National Cyclopedia of American Biography* (New York, 1893-1952), I, 270; Albert Shaw, "Murat Halstead, Journalist," *American Review of Reviews*, XIII (April, 1896), 439-443; Mott, *op. cit.*, p. 459.

68. Richardson, *op. cit.*, p. 157.

69. Buffalo *Commercial Advertiser*, as quoted in Chicago *Daily Tribune*, June 15, 1863.

70. Chicago *Daily Tribune*, November 20, 1861.

71. *Ibid.*, August 22, 1864.

72. Mark Skinner to Edwin M. Stanton, October 20, 1862, Edwin M. Stanton Papers, Library of Congress.

73. C. S. Diehl, *The Staff Correspondent* (San Antonio, Texas, 1931), p. 53.

74. Chicago *Times*, November 10, 1863.

75. Chicago *Daily Journal*, April 22, 1924.

76. D. B. Sanger, "The Chicago Times and the Civil War," *Mississippi Valley Historical Review*, XVII (March, 1931), 560-561; Chicago *Daily Tribune*, June 3, 1861; F. W. Scott, *Newspapers and Periodicals of Illinois, 1814-1879*, *Collections of the Illinois State Historical Library*, VI, (1910), 65-66.

77. W. J. Abbot, "Chicago Newspapers and Their Makers," *American Review of Reviews*, XI (June, 1895), 651; J. M. Lee, *History of American Journalism* (New York, 1917), p. 286.

78. The Cincinnati *Daily Commercial* of July 1, 1863, gave another explanation for the increasing popularity of the *Times*: "We read the Chicago Times. It is the best of a bad class of newspapers in the West."

79. Chicago *Daily Journal*, April 22, 1924.

80. Joe Skidmore, "The Copperhead Press and the Civil War," *Journalism Quarterly*, XVI (December, 1939), 349; Galusha Anderson, *The Story of a Border City during the Civil War* (Boston, 1908), p. 144.

81. Oliver Gramling, *AP, The Story of News* (New York and Toronto, 1940), p. 42.

82. Victor Rosewater, *History of Coöperative News-Gathering in the United States* (New York and London, 1930), p. 99.

83. *Ibid.*, p. 106. For some of the reasons for the Indianapolis meeting, see St. Louis *Daily Missouri Republican*, November 18, 1862.

84. Further information on Craig appears in *Dictionary of American Biography*, IV, 494-495; Reid, *op. cit.*, pp. 794-795; Hudson, *op. cit.*, pp. 611-613.

85. *Frank Leslie's Illustrated Newspaper*, XIX (November 26, 1864), 146.

86. St. Louis *Daily Missouri Republican*, June 27, 1861.

87. Horace Greeley to Mrs. Margaret Allen, June 17, 1861, Greeley Papers, Library of Congress.

88. New York *Daily Tribune*, October

1, 1861. During September, 1861, the New York *World* was said to be running behind at the rate of $1,500 a week.

89. During the eighteen-month period ending February 29, 1864, the St. Louis *Republican* realized over $95,000 from its advertising. At the height of the conflict, the Cincinnati *Gazette* distributed an annual dividend of 65 per cent.
90. One of the chief factors in the price rise was the paper shortage, which caused the price of newsprint to soar from the prewar ten cents a pound to as much as thirty cents a pound in 1864.
91. J. T. Scharf and Thompson Westcott, *History of Philadelphia, 1609-1884* (Philadelphia, 1884), III, 1994; G. A. Sala, *My Diary in America in the Midst of War* (London, 1865), I, 289.
92. Lee, *op. cit.*, pp. 311-312.
93. Mott, *op. cit.*, p. 401.
94. Chicago *Daily Tribune,* June 10, 1897.
95. Anderson, *op. cit.*, p. 144.
96. Justin Winsor, *The Memorial History of Boston* (Boston, 1881), III, 629.
97. New York *Times,* September 25, 1901.
98. Havilah Babcock, "The Press and the Civil War," *Journalism Quarterly,* VI (March, 1929), 1-5.

3
"GENTLEMEN OF THE RAVENOUS PEN"
Pages 35-59

1. T. W. Knox, *Camp-Fire and Cotton-Field* (Philadelphia and Cincinnati, 1865), p. 486.
2. Cincinnati *Daily Gazette,* March 23, 1865.
3. W. H. Russell, *My Diary, North and South* (Boston, 1863), p. 45.
4. J. F. Essary, *Covering Washington* (Boston and New York, 1927), p. 21; F. L. Mott, *American Journalism* (New York, 1941), p. 198.
5. Essary, *op. cit.*, pp. 22-23; B. P. Poore, *Perley's Reminiscences* (Philadelphia, 1886), I, 56-58, 107.
6. Cabell Phillips, *Dateline: Washington* (New York, 1949), p. 14.
7. Frederic Hudson, *Journalism in the United States* (New York, 1873), p. 286.
8. L. A. Gobright, *Recollections of Men and Things at Washington* (Philadelphia, 1869), pp. 400-401. Among the outstanding Washington reporters of the 1850's were James E. Harvey of the Philadelphia *North American* and James S. Pike of the New York *Daily Tribune.*
9. Chicago *Daily Tribune,* May 18, 1861. For a more lengthy account of life in the national capital during Civil War days, see Margaret Leech, *Reveille in Washington* (New York and London, 1941).
10. New York *Times,* May 9, 1861.
11. *Dictionary of American Biography,* XX, 149; Frances Winwar, *American Giant* (New York and London, 1941), pp. 253-262.
12. Philadelphia *Inquirer,* October 19, 1861.
13. Chicago *Times,* October 28, 1862. For other evidence about the indifferent attitude of old Washingtonians toward the war, see St. Louis *Daily Missouri Republican,* October 24, 1862.
14. Chicago *Times,* November 11, 1863.
15. G. A. Townsend, *Campaigns of a Non-Combatant* (New York, 1866), p. 219.
16. M. C. Ames, *Ten Years in Washington* (Cincinnati, 1874), p. 68.
17. J. E. Pollard, *The Presidents and*

the Press (New York, 1947), p. 353; D. C. Seitz, *Horace Greeley* (Indianapolis, 1926), p. 238.

18. H. v. N. Boynton, "The Press and Public Men," *Century Magazine*, XLII (October, 1891), p. 853. Seventy-two years later, there were 504 accredited newspaper and magazine correspondents in Washington, a group almost as large as the two houses of Congress combined. L. C. Rosten, *The Washington Correspondents* (New York, 1937), p. 3.

19. Chicago *Daily Tribune*, August 20, 1861. For a list of the reporters who were entitled to sit in the Reporter's Gallery of the House of Representatives at this time, see *Official Congressional Directory*, 37 Cong., 2 sess. (Washington, D.C., 1861), p. 33.

20. Chicago *Daily Tribune*, February 27, 1862.

21. Washington *National Republican*, November 12, 1863. Twelve representatives of the newspaper press signed the resolutions adopted at a meeting of Washington newspapermen, August 2, 1861. Two of the twelve signers were newspaper editors. The other ten apparently were accredited reporters of the various out-of-town newspapers which were then represented at the national capital. Report of the House Committee on Judiciary, March 20, 1862, *House Report No. 64*, House Executive Documents, 37 Cong., 2 sess., p. 2.

22. Essary, *op. cit.*, p. 31.

23. Henry Villard, *Memoirs* (Boston and New York, 1904), I, 339; New York *Tribune*, December 26, 1910.

24. Villard, *op. cit.*, I, 153; *National Cyclopedia of American Biography*, V, 355-356.

25. *Dictionary of American Biography*, XV, 73.

26. W. E. Griffis, *Charles Carleton Coffin* (Boston, 1898), p. 106; A. T. Rice, *Reminiscences of Abraham Lincoln* (New York, 1888), pp. 622-623.

27. Philadelphia *Weekly Times*, April 23, 1887.

28. E. V. Smalley, *History of the Northern Pacific Railroad* (New York, 1883), p. 283.

29. *Harper's Weekly*, XXXIII (December 14, 1889), 1003-1004; Buffalo *Express*, December 3, 8, 1889; New York *Tribune*, December 3, 1889. Wilkeson's conflict with Weed is discussed at some length in G. G. Van Deusen, *Thurlow Weed, Wizard of the Lobby* (Boston, 1947), pp. 207-208, 231-232, 295. For Wilkeson's activity in bond sales, see H. M. Larson, *Jay Cooke, Private Banker* (Cambridge, Massachusetts, 1936), p. 170; E. P. Oberholtzer, *Jay Cooke, Financier of the Civil War* (Philadelphia, 1907), I, 480.

30. W. B. Wilson, *From the Hudson to the Ohio* (Philadelphia, 1902), p. 47; S. R. Kamm, *The Civil War Career of Thomas A. Scott* (Philadelphia, 1940), p. 83.

31. Samuel Wilkeson to Edwin M. Stanton, February 16, 1862, Stanton Papers.

32. For biographical information about Wikoff, see *Dictionary of American Biography*, XX, 197-198; New York *Times*, May 3, 1884; J. W. Forney, *Anecdotes of Public Men*, I (New York, 1873), 366-371; F. M. Anderson, *The Mystery of a Public Man* (Minneapolis, 1948), pp. 126-129.

33. Richard Hooker, *Story of an Independent Newspaper* (New York, 1924), pp. 81-82. Although Bartlett commonly was known as "D. W.," his real name was David V. G. Bartlett.

34. Washington *Evening Star,* October 11, 1886.

35. *Ibid.,* October 11, 1886.

36. New York *Citizen,* January 19, 1867.

37. New York *World,* October 14, 1886.

38. *Dictionary of American Biography,* XX, 104-105.

39. Whitelaw Reid to William Henry Smith, August 6, 1863, William Henry Smith Papers, Ohio State Archaeological and Historical Society, Columbus.

40. In another letter to the same correspondent, Reid expressed his surprise at being "actually complimented (with a genial smile and in manifest good faith) by old Thad Stevens!" He added, "I'd as soon have expected compliments from a vinegar barrel – or father Wickliffe!" Whitelaw Reid to William Henry Smith, February 15, 1863, Smith Papers, Ohio State Archaeological and Historical Society.

41. Hooker, *op. cit.,* p. 81. Reid's career as a Washington correspondent is adequately treated in Royal Cortissoz, *The Life of Whitelaw Reid* (New York, 1921), I, 99-117. For other estimates of Reid, see S. R. Fiske, *Off-Hand Portraits of Prominent New Yorkers* (New York, 1884), pp. 265-270; "Whitelaw Reid," *Scribner's Monthly,* VIII (August, 1874), 444-451.

42. Isabel Ross, *Ladies of the Press* (New York and London, 1936), p. 323. This was five years before Greeley astounded the newspaper world by appointing a woman, Margaret Fuller Ossoli, literary critic of the New York *Tribune.*

43. *Dictionary of American Biography,* XI, 288-289.

44. *Ibid.,* XVI, 534. In 1862, Miss Redden published *Notable Men in the House* (Privately printed), based on her work as a Congressional correspondent.

45. Chicago *Daily Tribune,* June 24, 1863; New York *Daily Tribune,* June 25, 1863.

46. S. C. Chollis to Uriah H. Painter, April 13, 1863, Painter Papers. In the papers of Whitelaw Reid there is also an undated memorandum from the Washington office of Jay Cooke & Co. notifying Reid of the sale of fifty shares of Pittsburgh, Fort Wayne & Chicago Railroad stock belonging to his account. Reid made a profit of over $200 on the transaction. Whitelaw Reid Papers (formerly in the possession of the Reid family), Library of Congress.

47. Townsend, *op. cit.,* p. 220.

48. From a letter addressed by Whitelaw Reid to an unidentified editorial staff member of the Cincinnati *Gazette,* December 9, 1865, Reid Papers.

49. J. Barclay Harding to Uriah H. Painter, December 1, 1862, Painter Papers.

50. J. M. Lee, *History of American Journalism* (New York, 1917), pp. 291-292.

51. D. W. Bartlett to Uriah H. Painter, no date, Painter Papers.

52. *Journalist,* I (November 15, 1884), 7; B. P. Poore, "Washington News," *Harper's New Monthly Magazine,* XLVIII (January, 1874), 234. For comments about the Washington news bureaus of particular newspapers, see Villard, *op. cit.,* I, 339; Chicago *Daily Tribune,* December 16, 1862; St. Louis *Daily Missouri Democrat,* December 23, 1862.

53. Washington *Sunday Morning Chronicle,* June 16, 1861. The expression "gentlemen of the ravenous pen" was not original with

Forney. Charles Dickens had applied it earlier to the London reporters.

54. Cincinnati *Daily Commercial,* December 29, 1862.
55. *Ibid.,* September 19, 1861.
56. New York *Times,* August 23, 1861.
57. Jerome B. Stillson, one of the army correspondents of the New York *World.*
58. George W. Adams to Manton Marble, June 30, 1864, Manton Marble Papers, Library of Congress.
59. Pollard, *op. cit.,* p. 365.
60. *Journalist,* V (April 9, 1887), 14; Rice, *op. cit.,* pp. 227-228.
61. Pollard, *op. cit.,* pp. 370-371; Emanuel Hertz, *Lincoln Talks* (New York, 1939), pp. 272-273. Lincoln was sometimes unwilling, however, to place complete trust in the newspapermen, Gobright, *op. cit.,* pp. 337-339, describes an instance in which Lincoln refused to provide the Washington agent of the Associated Press with an advance copy of an important political document, only to see it appear in print prematurely as a result of a breach of confidence by an editorial friend.
62. J. T. Morse, Jr., *Diary of Gideon Welles* (Boston and New York, 1911), II, 131.
63. *Dictionary of American Biography,* III, 82.
64. The New York *World* correspondent, Adams, was in the audience at Ford's Theater on the night of the assassination but was not, of course, included in the presidential party. For a more extensive treatment of Lincoln's relations with the press, see Pollard, *op. cit.,* pp. 348-390.
65. Villard, *op. cit.,* I, 171-172. It was the regular practice of the *Herald* to lighten the labors of its correspondents by "puffing" various public officials in its editorial columns. The lengths to which it went in its flattery of Mrs. Lincoln are described in Oliver Carlson, *The Man Who Made News* (New York, 1942), pp. 336-338; Chicago *Daily Tribune,* August 20, 1861.
66. Villard, *op. cit.,* I, 172. A letter from Asa McFarland to Simon Cameron, April 1, 1861, contains a significant allusion to "your known regard for members of the Newspaper Press, and your ability to appreciate, by personal experience, their trials and imperfectly rewarded services." Simon Cameron Papers, Library of Congress.
67. Simon Cameron to H. E. Thayor, October 5, 1861, as reprinted in the Cincinnati *Daily Commercial,* March 27, 1862.
68. Noah Brooks, *Washington in Lincoln's Time* (New York, 1895), p. 33; R. S. West, Jr., "The Navy and the Press during the Civil War," *United States Naval Institute Proceedings,* LXIII (January, 1937), 40.
69. Brooks, *op. cit.,* p. 29.
70. L. A. Whitely to Frederic Hudson, March 30, 1863, Bennett Papers.
71 The main facts of Ives's early life are given in the Chicago *Daily Tribune,* February 11, 13, 1862; New York *Daily Tribune,* February 12, 1862.
72. William B. Shaw, a member of the *Herald*'s Washington staff.
73. Cincinnati *Daily Gazette,* February 10, 1862; Chicago *Daily Tribune,* February 11, 1862.
74. The best newspaper account of Ives's strange performance at the War Department appeared in the Philadelphia *Inquirer,* February 12, 1862. This account was reprinted with some minor omissions in the New York *Tribune* the fol-

lowing day. Ives's version of what happened is to be found in a letter to Bennett which the *Herald* published February 14. Ives admitted in this letter that the frankness, cordiality, and apparent confidence which the Secretary had displayed toward him on previous occasions had encouraged him to speak with "perfect unrestraint." For further evidence of Ives's earlier intimacy with Stanton, see his letter of January 15, 1862, to James Gordon Bennett, Bennett Papers.

75. Published in various newspapers February 11, 1862.
76. New York *Herald*, February 11, 1862.
77. Washington *Daily National Intelligencer*, February 12, 1862.
78. Ives's release from Fort McHenry was announced in the New York *Herald* on May 21, 1862. According to the Boston *Daily Journal*, April 14, 1862, Ives remained on the payroll of the *Herald* after he went to jail. On June 10, 1862, however, the *Herald* announced that Ives no longer had any connection with the paper.
79. H. v. N. Boynton, "The Press and Public Men," *Century Magazine*, XLII (October, 1891), 854.
80. From the Philadelphia *Press*, as quoted in the New York *Times*, August 1, 1861. To a Washington correspondent of the *Tribune* who on one occasion began a column of trivia with the solemn pronouncement that "these are grand and awful times," Dana is said to have remarked caustically that the fact stated was already known in New York and therefore he thought it was hardly worthwhile to pay the telegraph charges for sending it! Buffalo *Express*, as quoted in the St. Louis *Daily Missouri Republican*, June 23, 1861.
81. Essay, *op. cit.*, pp. 28-29.

4
THE MEN IN THE FIELD
Pages 60-75

1. J. R. Gilmore, *Letters of a War Correspondent* (Boston, 1899), p. v.
2. On the monument to the war correspondents of the Civil War which George Alfred Townsend erected on South Mountain are inscribed the names of 147 correspondents and artists who reported the war from the field, but this is hardly more than half the number who actually participated.
3. Philadelphia *Press*, August 21, 1862. In the opinion of Ben Perley Poore, the majority of the correspondents were "mere newsscavengers" who had to remain in the rear of the armies, "gathering up such information as they could." Ben Perley Poore, *Perley's Reminiscences* (Philadelphia, 1886), II, 127.
4. William Painter to Uriah H. Painter, August 3, 1862, Painter Papers.
5. For his hazardous exploit House received only $75 from the *Tribune*. When he mentioned his disappointment to Nordhoff, the managing editor of the *Post*, the latter bleakly remarked, "Why, he [Dana] ought to have made it a hundred!"
6. McCullagh and Joel Cook each were nineteen in 1861. Finley Anderson was one year younger; McGahan and Sawyer, seventeen. Joe Robinson of the Philadelphia *Inquirer* was probably the youngest war correspondent of all; he was only sixteen years old at the outbreak of the war.
7. Finley Anderson, Conyngham, Cooney, Forrest, Halpine, McCullagh, and John Russell Young were Irish-born. Redpath and Swinton were of Scottish origin; Boweryem

and Richard T. Colburn had been born in England. Stanley was Welsh; Villard, Bavarian. Winser was a product of Bermuda. Williams had perhaps the most cosmopolitan background of all: he was born of English parents at the Rock of Gibraltar. His early life was spent in both the East and West Indies, the Gold Coast of Africa, Nova Scotia, and Canada before he came to the United States in 1850 at the age of thirteen.

8. *Dictionary of American Biography,* VI, 423.
9. Cincinnati *Commercial Gazette,* May 26, 1889.
10. New York *Tribune,* January 13, 1884.
11. I. M. Tarbell, *A Reporter for Lincoln* (New York, 1927), p. 20. According to the London *Times* correspondent Russell, General McDowell tried unsuccessfully during the first Bull Run campaign to induce the newspapermen with the army to wear white uniforms "to indicate the purity of their character." W. H. Russell, *My Diary, North and South* (London, 1863), p. 424.
12. New York *Times,* April 30, 1862.
13. Russell, *op. cit.,* p. 427; Russell, "Recollections of the Civil War," *North American Review,* CLXVI (May, 1898), 627. J. H. Browne, *Four Years in Secessia* (Hartford, 1865), pp. 205-207, and G. A. Townsend, *Campaigns of a Non-Combatant* (New York, 1866), pp. 230-231, further illustrate the difficulties of the army reporters in getting mounts.
14. A. D. Richardson, *The Secret Service, the Field, the Dungeon, and the Escape* (Hartford, 1865), p. 257; New York *Daily Tribune,* June 4, 1862. To alter the appearance of the stolen animals, professional horse thieves shaved manes, removed tails, and utilized chemicals so that when a stolen animal reappeared he was indeed a "horse of another color."
15. Henry Villard, *Memoirs* (Boston and New York, 1904), I, 335. The more important sources on Smalley's career as a war correspondent are the biographical sketches in the *Dictionary of American Biography,* XVII, 223-224, and the *National Cyclopedia of American Biography,* III, 454; G. W. Smalley, *Anglo-American Memories,* 1st Ser. (New York and London, 1911), pp. 129-160; G. W. Smalley, "Chapters in Journalism," *Harper's New Monthly Magazine,* LXXXIX (August, 1894), 426-435.
16. U. S. Grant, *Personal Memoirs* (New York, 1885-1886), II, 145. For details of Swinton's wartime career, see *Dictionary of American Biography,* XVIII, 252-253; *Appletons' Cyclopaedia of American Biography* (New York, 1900-1928), VI, 13; *Appletons' Annual Cyclopaedia,* New Ser. XVII (New York, 1892), 576; New York *Times,* October 26, 1892. In the Robert T. Lincoln Papers, Library of Congress, is a letter from Henry J. Raymond to President Lincoln, April 4, 1864, which describes Swinton as "a gentleman of ability & intelligence . . . fully worthy of any confidence you may place in him."
17. Elmer Davis, *History of the New York Times* (New York, 1921), p. 58.
18. New York *Times,* September 18, 1901. Biographical information on Crounse also may be found in New York *Citizen,* January 19, 1867; Milwaukee *Republican,* July 12, 1881; and an undated clipping from a Kingston (New York) paper

in the possession of the Crounse family.

19. L. A. Whitely to Frederic Hudson, November 30, 1863, Bennett Papers.

20. Wilkie, *op. cit.*, pp. 203-208; B. A. Weisberger, *Reporters for the Union* (Boston, 1953), p. 132; Letter to the author from the Rev. Lynn Townsend White, January 20, 1953. For a denial from Cadwallader that his intimacy with Grant was traceable to his activities as a press agent, see Washington *Evening Star,* October 16, 1896.

21. New York *Herald,* May 24, 1914. It was Keim's failure to receive a letter sent him in Ceylon by the younger Bennett which let Stanley, rather than Keim, draw the assignment to search for David Livingstone. During Grant's administration, Keim was said to be the only Washington correspondent who had access to the White House to interview the President. These interviews, which always took place on Sundays, were well paid for by the newspapers which employed Keim.

22. F. L. Mott, *American Journalism* (New York, 1941), p. 338; O. G. Villard, *Fighting Years* (New York, 1939), p. 16.

23. Troy (New York) *Daily Times,* November 20, 1875. A letter from Merriam to General Butler, November 5, 1864, in which the *Herald* representative avowed his desire "beyond all other things to be attached to your fortunes so long as I remain with the *Herald*" is included in the *Private and Official Correspondence of Gen. Benjamin F. Butler* (Privately printed, 1917), V, 317-318.

24. William H. Stiner to Frederic Hudson, April 21, 1864, Bennett Papers.

25. Russell, *My Diary, North and South,* p. 440.

26. B. F. Taylor, *Mission Ridge and Lookout Mountain* (New York and Chicago, 1872), p. 171; Chicago *Evening Journal,* May 5, 1864.

27. Mott, *op. cit.*, p. 332.

28. T. W. Knox, *Camp-Fire and Cotton-Field* (Philadelphia and Cincinnati, 1865), p. 486. Bickham and Reid were both aides de camp on the staff of General Rosecrans. Shanks performed similar service for General Rousseau. John Russell Young was on Banks's staff during the Red River campaign. There were many others.

29. "An Interviewer Interviewed," *Lippincott's Monthly Magazine,* XLVIII (November, 1891), 634.

30. Laura Stedman and G. M. Gould, *Life and Letters of Edmund Clarence Stedman* (New York, 1910), I, 254; E. C. Stedman to Laura Stedman, November 10, 1861, Edmund Clarence Stedman Papers, Columbia University Library.

31. R. S. West, Jr., "The Navy and the Press during the Civil War," *United States Naval Institute Proceedings,* LXIII (January, 1937), 38.

32. Thomas M. Cook to Frederic Hudson, November 3, 1864, Bennett Papers.

33. For biographical information about Sawyer, see New York *Herald,* August 1, 1887; New York *Tribune,* August 1, 1887; *Journalist,* I (April 19, 1884), IV (August 6, 1887). For similar details about Winser, see *National Cyclopedia of American Biography,* X, 394-395; *Appletons' Cyclopaedia of American Biography,* VI, 565; New York *Times,* August 24, 1896; C. G. Halpine, *Baked Meats of the Funeral* (New York, 1866), p. 189.

34. Knox, *op. cit.*, p. 489.

35. Henry Villard, "Army Correspondence," *Nation,* I (August 3, 1865), 145; Richardson, *op. cit.,* p. 304. Ordinarily military business and the AP reports took precedence over the effusions of the "specials" on the army telegraph.

36. In July, 1864, newspaper letters from Sherman's army in Georgia commonly took fifteen days to reach Chicago. Such delays were in large part the result of an inefficient army mail service. In some cases army mail was intercepted by enemy guerillas. In July, 1862, the New York *Tribune* declared that more than half its letters from its various army correspondents were lost in transit to New York.

37. Frederic Hudson, *Journalism in the United States* (New York, 1873), p. 484; J. M. Lee, *History of American Journalism* (New York, 1917), p. 294.

38. New York *Herald,* December 27, 1864.

39. New York *Times,* August 13, 1862.

40. Finley Anderson to Frederic Hudson, March 28, 1864, Bennett Papers.

41. Stedman and Gould, *op. cit.,* I, 229.

5
THE FIRST FRUITS OF THE CENSORSHIP
Pages 76-101

1. Everett's essay, "The Dark Day," from which this extract is taken, first appeared in the New York *Ledger,* September 21, 1861. For similar editorial comment, see New York *Daily Tribune,* August 3, 1861.

2. Henry Villard expressed himself vigorously on this subject in an article for the *Nation,* July 27, 1865. See also J. F. Rhodes, *Historical Essays* (New York, 1909), p. 92.

3. A. K. McClure, *Old Time Notes of Pennsylvania* (Philadelphia, 1905), I, 578.

4. Allan Nevins, *The Evening Post,* (New York, 1922), p. 441.

5. Villard had contributed occasional letters to the local German paper while he was still in Belleville. He had also published letters descriptive of Chicago and the West in several New York German weeklies before he became a regular correspondent of the *Staats Zeitung.*

6. Henry Villard, *Memoirs* (Boston and New York, 1904), I, 96.

7. *Ibid.,* pp. 163-165.

8. From a letter written by Henry Villard to C. H. Ray and Joseph Medill of the Chicago *Tribune* editorial staff, April 27, 1861, Charles H. Ray Papers, HM RY 204, The Huntington Library, San Marino, California. By April 30 telegraphic communication between Washington and Baltimore had been restored.

9. For further information about House's connection with the death of Ellsworth, see Carl Sandburg, *Abraham Lincoln, The War Years* (New York, 1939), I, 264-265. Apparently House was granted a special favor in being permitted to accompany the expedition. A similar courtesy was withheld from a Washington correspondent of the Chicago *Tribune,* who was under the impression that Senator Chandler was the only civilian allowed to cross the Potomac with the troops. Chicago *Daily Tribune,* May 25, 1861.

10. Chicago *Daily Tribune,* May 30, 1861. The Confederate flag used to cover Ellsworth's body was divided piecemeal by the newspaper reporters, who were among the first

to reach the scene. One of the reporters who shared this strange trophy was E. C. Stedman of the New York *World.*

11. Theodore Winthrop, "New York Seventh Regiment, Our March to Washington," *Atlantic Monthly,* VII (June, 1861), 744-756. Winthrop's career received appropriate notice in *ibid.,* VIII, 242-251.
12. New York *Herald,* June 12, 1861.
13. Cincinnati *Daily Commercial,* June 17, 1861.
14. Bullard, Mott, and other writers have stated that Coffin was the only war correspondent who remained in the field throughout the war. Similar statements have been made about other reporters, however. Charles F. Horner, e.g., in *The Life of James Redpath* (New York and Newark, 1926, p. 112) states that Redpath remained active as a newspaper correspondent throughout the war, and *Appletons' Annual Cyclopaedia* for 1891 (New Ser. XVI, 651) says explicitly that "He [Redpath] was one of the earliest war correspondents at the front, and remained in the field, principally with the armies of Gens. Sherman and Thomas, till the close of the war." Homer Byington of the New York *Tribune* and L. A. Hendricks of the *Herald* are other reporters for whom the same claim has been made.
15. W. E. Griffis, *Charles Carleton Coffin* (Boston, 1898), p. 59.
16. *Ibid.,* pp. 72-75; A. T. Rice, *Reminiscences of Abraham Lincoln* (New York, 1888), pp. 164-171.
17. F. L. Bullard, *Famous War Correspondents* (Boston, 1914), p. 381.
18. Griffis, *op. cit.,* p. 94; *Dictionary of American Biography,* IV, 265.
19. Griffis, *op. cit.,* p. 89.
20. C. C. Coffin, *The Boys of '61* (Boston, 1896), p. 28.
21. C. W. Elliott, *Winfield Scott, The Soldier and the Man* (New York, 1937), p. 727.
22. Statement of Donn Piatt, a Union officer at Bull Run, Thomas S. Townsend Scrapbooks, LXXXVIII, 259, Thomas S. Townsend Library of National, State, and Individual Civil War Records, Columbia University (a compilation of newspaper and magazine articles with manuscript notes and letters relating to the Civil War and bearing dates from 1860 to 1901).
23. Laura Stedman and G. M. Gould, *Life and Letters of Edmund Clarence Stedman* (New York, 1910), I, 230; E. C. Stedman to Laura Stedman, July 17, 1861, Stedman Papers.
24. W. H. Russell, "Recollections of the Civil War," *North American Review,* CLXVI (February, 1898), 234; The Times (London), *The History of the Times* (New York, 1935-1947), II, 363. Russell left Queenstown on the "Arabic" the day before Lincoln's inauguration and arrived in New York on March 16.
25. W. H. Russell, *My Diary, North and South* (London, 1863), pp. 424 ff.
26. Villard, *Memoirs,* I, 185-186.
27. Stedman and Gould, *op. cit.,* I, 231; E. C. Stedman to Laura Stedman, July 20, 1861, Stedman Papers.
28. Cincinnati *Daily Gazette,* July 25, 1861. There apparently was no telegraphic connection between Washington and Centreville at the time, and therefore the army newspapermen were relying upon couriers "who are rapidly passing to and fro." Chicago *Daily Tribune,* July 20, 1861.
29. Emma Brace, *The Life of Charles Loring Brace* (New York, 1894), p.

242. The letters written for the *Times* during the first Bull Run campaign were signed "Civilian."

30. New York *Times,* July 24, 1861.

31. New York *World,* July 24, 1861. Haggerty lost his life in the battle which followed. *War of the Rebellion: A Compilation of the Official Records of the Union and Confederate Armies* (Washington, D.C.), Ser. I, vol. iii, p. 371, hereinafter referred to as *O.R.* (Army).

32. New York *Daily Tribune,* July 26, 1861.

33. Croffut erred here. Either the photographer was jesting (his real name was Mathew B. Brady) or Croffut was mistaken in his recollection of the conversation.

34. W. A. Croffut, *An American Procession* (Boston, 1931), p. 50; Thomas S. Townsend Scrapbooks, LXXXVIII, 526. For further information about Brady's activities at first Bull Run, see Roy Meredith, *Mr. Lincoln's Camera Man, Mathew B. Brady* (New York, 1946), pp. 8-14.

35. Thomas S. Townsend Scrapbooks, LXXXVIII, 526.

36. New York *World,* July 24, 1861; New York *Daily Tribune,* July 26, 1861.

37. Cincinnati *Daily Gazette,* July 27, 1861.

38. Russell, *My Diary, North and South,* pp. 447-449.

39. London *Times,* August 6, 1861.

40. Philadelphia *Inquirer,* July 23, 1861.

41. This battle description draws upon the narratives of Geer, Rhodes, Ropes and others, as well as the official reports of the generals on both sides as presented in the *Official Records.* The most detailed treatment of the first Bull Run campaign is R. M. Johnston's *Bull Run, Its Strategy and Tactics* (Boston and New York, 1913).

42. Philadelphia *Inquirer,* July 23, 1861.

43. *Ibid.,* July 23, 1861. Stedman makes no mention of the incident in his account of the battle.

44. New York *Herald,* July 24, 1861.

45. Ely's release from prison occurred during the latter part of December, 1861. Chicago *Daily Tribune,* December 27, 1861; Charles Lauman, *Journal of Alfred Ely, A Prisoner of War in Richmond* (New York, 1862), pp. 262-263. On July 30, 1861, the Philadelphia *Inquirer* noted that "a Boston reporter, who was a silent observer at the Bull's Run battle, is missing." The *Inquirer* did not identify the reporter by name, however, and nothing further was published to indicate whether he had fallen into the hands of the Confederates.

46. Thomas S. Townsend Scrapbooks, LXXXVIII, 526; Croffut, *op. cit.,* p. 52.

47. Cincinnati *Daily Gazette,* July 27, 1861.

48. New York *Times,* July 24, 1861.

49. L. A. Gobright, *Recollections of Men and Things at Washington* (Philadelphia, 1869), pp. 316-317; Oliver Gramling, *AP, The Story of News* (New York and Toronto, 1940), p. 40.

50. Russell, *My Diary, North and South,* p. 465; Chicago *Daily Tribune,* July 23, 1861.

51. Raymond's editorial comments about this appeared in the New York *Times,* July 24, 1861. See also Elmer Davis, *History of the New York Times* (New York, 1921), pp. 55-56.

52. Stedman and Gould, *op. cit.,* I, 233.

53. E. P. Oberholtzer, *Jay Cooke, Fin-*

ancier of the Civil War (Philadelphia, 1907), I, 146-147; *One Hundred Years of the Philadelphia Inquirer,* pp. 20-21.

54. Stedman and Gould, *op. cit.,* I, 234.
55. Villard, *Memoirs,* I, 196-199.
56. F. L. Mott, *American Journalism* (New York, 1941), p. 338; C. P. Stone, "Washington in March and April, 1861," *Magazine of American History,* XIV (July, 1885), 14-17.
57. *O.R.* (Army), Ser. III, vol. i, p. 324.
58. Cincinnati *Daily Gazette,* July 17, 1861; New York *World,* July 13, 1861.
59. Oberholtzer, *op. cit.,* I, 147.
60. New York *Times,* July 24, 1861.
61. Gobright, *op. cit.,* pp. 316-318. That same day Daniel H. Craig, General Agent of the AP, relayed to the War Department a dispatch, which had been sent from Richmond via New Orleans to the AP New York office, containing brief details of the battle as viewed from the Southern side up to the time the "federalists" left the field.
62. George Alfred Townsend Scrapbooks.
63. Fitz Hugh Ludlow, a prominent New York writer and a member of Stedman's literary circle.
64. Stedman and Gould, *op. cit.,* I, 235. Stedman's triumph must have been all the sweeter in view of the letter, addressed to him earlier in the campaign by Marble, complaining that his reporting had not been "up to the mark" and admonishing him to "have the canvass & the paint pot ready when the smoke-puffs and the white wreaths begin the bloody day." Manton Marble to E. C. Stedman, June 4, 1861, Stedman Papers.
65. Pennsylvania Central Railroad, subsequently renamed the Pennsylvania Railroad.
66. G. B. P. Ringwalt to John Russell Young, July 26, 1861, John Russell Young Papers, Library of Congress.
67. New York Express, as quoted in the St. Louis *Daily Missouri Republican,* July 31, 1861.
68. St. Louis *Daily Missouri Republican,* August 9, 1861. The Louisville *Courier,* e.g., gave the impression that General Patterson's army had joined McDowell in time to participate in the Battle of Bull Run.
69. Cincinnati *Daily Gazette,* July 31, 1861.
70. New York *Daily Tribune,* July 26, 1861.
71. For this and other stories critical of Miles's conduct at Bull Run, see Philadelphia *Inquirer,* July 23, 1861; Chicago *Daily Tribune,* July 26, 1861. These charges later were substantiated by the findings of a court of inquiry, set forth in *O.R.* (Army), Ser. I, vol. ii, pp. 438-439.
72. See e.g., St. Louis *Daily Missouri Democrat,* October 23, 1861.
73. Philadelphia *Inquirer,* July 23, 1861.
74. It was Samuel J. Rea, a special correspondent of the New York *Herald* and also a telegraphic agent of the AP, who fell afoul of General Patterson. For a sample of the newspaper abuse heaped upon Patterson in connection with first Bull Run, see Cincinnati *Daily Commercial,* July 31, 1861. Curiously enough, Patterson seems to have received his first notification of McDowell's defeat from the columns of a Philadelphia newspaper!
75. New York *Times,* July 26, 1861. Raymond's version of Scott's intentions is confirmed by McDowell's testimony before the Committee

on the Conduct of the War. Report of the Joint Committee on the Conduct of the War, *Senate Report No. 108,* 1863, Pt. II, p. 37.

76. *National Cyclopedia of American Biography,* XII, 228; R. R. Fahrney, *Horace Greeley and the Tribune* (Cedar Rapids, Iowa, 1936), pp. 83, 88; F. M. O'Brien, *The Story of the Sun* (New York, 1918), pp. 213-214.

77. St. Louis *Daily Missouri Republican,* August 8, 1861.

78. Chicago *Daily Tribune,* August 23, 1861.

79. See e.g., St. Louis *Daily Missouri Democrat,* August 31, 1861. In the opinion of James Ford Rhodes, Russell's letter would have been regarded as "the best written account of the affair [first Battle of Bull Run] if it had appeared in the Northern press immediately after the battle." J. F. Rhodes, *Lectures on the American Civil War* (New York, 1913), p. 159.

80. New York *Daily Tribune,* July 30, 1861.

6

THE CURTAIN SLOWLY RISES

Pages 102-134

1. Henry Villard, "Army Correspondence," *Nation,* I (July 20, 1865), 80. The prolonged inactivity of the armies was also a source of dissatisfaction to the newspaper owners, who were expending thousands of dollars for news without adequate return.

2. Laura Stedman and G. M. Gould, *Life and Letters of Edmund Clarence Stedman* (New York, 1910), I, 239; E. C. Stedman to Laura Stedman, October 2, 1861, Stedman Papers.

3. Cincinnati *Daily Gazette,* July 22, 1861. Throughout the campaign the New York press gave considerable space to correspondence reprinted from the Cincinnati newspapers. For the difficulties the New York *World* had in finding a reporter for the campaign in Western Virginia, see Manton Marble to E. C. Stedman, July 3, 1861, Stedman Papers.

4. Royal Cortissoz, *The Life of Whitelaw Reid* (New York, 1921), I, 74; Cincinnati *Daily Gazette,* June 8, 1861.

5. Cincinnati *Daily Gazette,* June 29, 1861. Another reference to Lovie appears in *ibid.,* July 22, 1861.

6. The biographical literature about McClellan is more extensive than that for any other Union general except Grant. McClellan's early life is treated at some length in H. J. Eckenrode and Byran Conrad, *George B. McClellan* (Chapel Hill, North Carolina, 1941), pp. 1-25; C. E. N. Macartney, *Little Mac* (Philadelphia, 1940), pp. 19-47; P. S. Michie, *General McClellan* (New York, 1901), pp. 1-68; W. S. Myers, *A Study in Personality, General George B. McClellan* (New York and London, 1934), pp. 1-156.

7. New York *Daily Tribune,* June 19, 1861.

8. Whitelaw Reid to Gavin Reid, June 27, 1861, Reid Papers.

9. McClellan's campaign in Western Virginia is described at greater length in Michie, *op. cit.,* pp. 79-92; R. U. Johnson and C. C. Buel, *Battles and Leaders of the Civil War* (New York, 1884-1888), I, 126-148; G. B. McClellan, *Report on the Organization and Campaigns of the Army of the Potomac* (New York, 1864), pp. 5-36.

10. Cincinnati *Daily Commercial,* July 19, 1861.

11. Cincinnati *Daily Gazette,* July 27, 1861. A few weeks earlier there had been similar criticism of the

Wheeling *Intelligencer's* account of the Phillippi affair, which had given greater prominence to the performance of the Virginia troops than some thought was warranted.

12. Cincinnati *Daily Times,* July 19, 1861; Cincinnati *Daily Gazette,* July 15, 22, 1861.
13. Cincinnati *Daily Commercial,* July 18, 1861; Cincinnati *Daily Gazette,* July 20, 1861; Cortissoz, *op. cit.,* I, 77-78.
14. Cincinnati *Daily Gazette,* June 27, 1861.
15. *Ibid.,* July 22, 1861. For editorial criticism of the army reporters' readiness to unmake military reputations, see *ibid.,* July 19, 1861.
16. Probably Albert D. Richardson of the New York *Tribune.* See A. D. Richardson, *The Secret Service, the Field, the Dungeon, and the Escape* (Hartford, 1865), pp. 173-179.
17. J. D. Cox, *Military Reminiscences of the Civil War* (New York, 1900), I, 76-78, 78n; Johnson and Buel, *op. cit.,* I, 141-142. For samples of this obnoxious reporting of the Cox expedition, see the New York *Times,* August 2, 8, 1861; New York *Daily Tribune,* August 7, 1861.
18. See e.g., the comments of the special correspondent of the Cincinnati *Gazette,* August 3, 1861.
19. *Ibid.,* August 23, 1861.
20. *Ibid.,* August 16, 1861.
21. *Ibid.,* September 16, 1861.
22. Rosecrans' autumn campaign in Western Virginia receives adequate treatment in Comte de Paris, *History of the Civil War in America,* I (Philadelphia, 1875), 372-387. An interesting description of the campaign from the Southern point of view is in D. S. Freeman, *R. E. Lee, A Biography* (New York and London, 1935), I, 554-604.
23. Cincinnati *Daily Gazette,* September 18, 1861.
24. Cincinnati *Daily Commercial,* September 20, 1861; Cincinnati *Daily Gazette,* September 21, 1861.
25. Cincinnati *Daily Commercial,* September 25, 1861; New York *Times,* September 26, 1861.
26. Cincinnati *Daily Commercial,* September 23, 1861.
27. Cincinnati *Daily Gazette,* September 16, 1861; Frank Moore, *The Rebellion Record* (New York, 1861-1873), III, 44-49.
28. Cincinnati *Daily Gazette,* September 30, 1861.
29. Cincinnati *Daily Commercial,* September 30, 1861.
30. Cincinnati *Daily Times,* October 11, 1861.
31. Whitelaw Reid, *Ohio in the War* (Columbus, 1893), I, 61. An excellent description of widespread abuses in feeding and clothing the volunteers may be found in F. A. Shannon, *The Organization and Administration of the Union Army, 1861-1865* (Cleveland, 1928), I, 53-103.
32. Richardson, *op. cit.,* pp. 163-164.
33. Henry Villard, *Memoirs* (Boston and New York, 1904), I, 200, 203.
34. New York *Times,* October 3, 1861.
35. J. B. Spore, "Sherman and the Press," *Infantry Journal,* LXIII (October, 1948), 28.
36. This version of the conversation between Sherman and the *Commercial* reporter follows that given in Lloyd Lewis, *Sherman, Fighting Prophet* (New York, 1932), pp. 190-191. Other versions of this conversation may be found in Reid, *op. cit.,* I, 428, and the Cincinnati *Daily Commercial,* September 26, 1861.
37. W. F. G. Shanks, *Personal Recol-*

lections of Distinguished Generals (New York, 1866), p. 38.

38. Villard, *Memoirs,* I, 203-204; Oliver Gramling, *AP, The Story of the News* (New York and Toronto, 1940), p. 44.

39. Shanks, *op. cit.,* p. 32. In his *Memoirs* (New York, 1875), I, 203, Sherman contended that what he had actually told Cameron was that "for the purpose of defense, we should have sixty thousand men at once, and for offense, would need two hundred thousand, before we were done." Still another account, "prepared under his [Sherman's] eye" quotes Sherman as having said "sixty thousand [men] to drive the enemy out of Kentucky, two hundred thousand to finish the war in this section." Reid, *op. cit.,* I, 429n. For further data on Sherman's use of the controversial figure "two hundred thousand," see Lewis, *op. cit.,* p. 194.

40. Villard, *Memoirs,* I, 212.

41. Lewis, *op. cit.,* p. 195.

42. *Ibid.,* p. 202.

43. Villard, *Memoirs,* I, 212.

44. Freeman Cleaves, *Rock of Chickamauga, The Life of General George H. Thomas* (Norman, Oklahoma, 1948), p. 91.

45. Cincinnati *Daily Commercial,* January 30, 1862; Cincinnati *Daily Gazette,* January 31, 1862. Reid's biographer, Royal Cortissoz, makes no reference to the incident.

46. New York *Times,* November 25, 1861.

47. B. J. Lossing, *Pictorial History of the Civil War* (Hartford, 1868), II, 86.

48. St. Louis *Daily Missouri Republican,* October 29, 1861.

49. Adam Badeau, *Military History of Ulysses S. Grant* (New York, 1885), I, 16.

50. U. S. Grant, *Personal Memoirs* (New York, 1895), I, 227; *O.R.* (Army), Ser. I, vol iii, p. 271.

51. New York *Herald,* November 19, 1861.

52. St. Louis *Daily Missouri Republican,* November 10, 1861.

53. Moore, *op. cit.,* III, 288.

54. L. A. Coolidge, *Ulysses S. Grant* (Boston and New York, 1922), p. 63.

55. T. W. Knox, *Camp-Fire and Cotton-Field* (Philadelphia and Cincinnati, 1865), p. 24; F. B. Wilkie, *Pen and Powder* (Boston, 1888), p. 23.

56. Knox, *op. cit.,* pp. 25-26.

57. J. G. Randall, *The Civil War and Reconstruction* (Boston and New York, 1937), p. 326.

58. Knox, *op. cit.,* p. 46.

59. Richardson, *op. cit.,* p. 154; Knox, *op. cit.,* pp. 50-51.

60. St. Louis *Daily Missouri Democrat,* June 27, 1861.

61. *Ibid.,* June 24, 1861; St. Louis *Daily Missouri Republican,* June 27, 1861.

62. Fremont's career is described in full detail in Allan Nevins, *Fremont, Pathmarker of the West* (New York and London, 1939), and C. L. Goodwin, *John Charles Fremont* (Stanford, California, 1930). See also *Dictionary of American Biography,* VII, 19-23.

63. Knox, *op. cit.,* p. 71.

64. For the official reports of the Battle of Wilson Creek, see *O.R.* (Army), Ser. I, vol. iii, pp. 53-130. Satisfactory accounts of the battle will also be found in Paris, *op. cit.,* I, 332-338, and Johnson and Buel, *op. cit.,* I, 289-297.

65. Knox, *op. cit.*, pp. 81-82. One of the reporters who was also a telegraph operator took special pains to conceal the fact, even leaving his pocket instrument behind in Springfield. His reason for so doing was a rumor that the enemy were prepared to show no quarter to any telegraph operator who fell into their hands.
66. Wilkie, *op. cit.*, pp. 32-33.
67. See e.g., New York *Herald*, August 14, 1861; St. Louis *Daily Missouri Democrat*, August 14, 1861. Inaccurate reports of McCulloch's death continued to crop up. Said a Rolla correspondent of the St. Louis *Daily Missouri Republican*, October 10, 1861: "The rumors from the Southwest in relation to the death of Ben McCulloch still come to us . . . . The more we hear on this intricate question, the worse we are confounded . . . . In either event, his army is yet in existence, and, in all probability, will be just as effective . . . without as with him."
68. One of the erroneous statements in the Fairchild account indicated that Sigel's command had remained in Springfield on the morning of the battle and had not been brought into action until two o'clock in the afternoon. A Chicago *Tribune* reporter, August 21, 1861, labeled the Fairchild account "a complete humbug," highly amusing to anyone who had participated in the battle.
69. St. Louis *Daily Missouri Republican*, August 21, 1861. See also Cincinnati *Gazette*, same date, for a discussion among the soldiers about various newspaper misstatements – overheard by a *Gazette* reporter.
70. New York *Herald*, August 19, 1861; New York *Daily Tribune*, August 19, 1861; Chicago *Post*, August 20, 1861. The *Post*'s battle story was rated by the New York *Times*, August 26, 1861, as "the clearest and most intelligible account of the battle . . . that we have seen.
71. Wilkie, *op. cit.*, pp. 37-38.
72. C. S. Diehl, *The Staff Correspondent* (San Antonio, Texas, 1931), p. 53.
73. Cincinnati *Daily Gazette*, August 29, 1861.
74. Chicago *Daily Tribune*, August 28, 1861.
75. *Ibid.*, August 29, 1861; Cincinnati *Daily Gazette*, September 14, 1861.
76. One of the members of this California "ring," according to the Chicago *Tribune* of October 10, 1861, was the editor of the Chicago *Journal*, John L. Wilson.
77. Tyler Dennett, *Lincoln and the Civil War* (New York, 1939), p. 26.
78. Wilkie, *op. cit.*, pp. 40-42; Knox, *op. cit.*, p. 94; Francis Brown, *Raymond of the Times* (New York, 1951), p. 216.
79. At this time Wilkie was being paid $7.50 a column. Since his letter ran to five columns, he could expect $37.50 for his story.
80. Wilkie, *op. cit.*, pp. 43-45.
81. New York *Times*, October 3, 1861.
82. Nevins, *op. cit.*, p. 525; St. Louis *Daily Evening News*, September 25, 1861.
83. In its issue of September 30, 1861, the St. Louis *Missouri Democrat* described the New York *Times* as the most antagonistic toward General Fremont of all Eastern newspapers. "This . . . we think is attributable to the editorial position held in the *Times* office by Mr. A. S. Mitchell, formerly of the *Evening News* of this city. Mr. Mitchell is a gentleman of large editorial experience, but in this

case, we are persuaded, has been unduly influenced by the appeals of some of his old friends from this city, who are engaged in the malignant warfare upon Gen. Fremont."

84. *O.R.* (Army), Ser. I, vol. iii, p. 184.
85. Cincinnati *Daily Commercial,* October 9, 1861.
86. Richardson, *op. cit.,* pp. 189-191; J. H. Browne, *Four Years in Secessia,* (Hartford, 1865), p. 28; Knox, *op. cit.,* pp. 95-97.
87. St. Louis *Daily Missouri Democrat,* October 11, 1861.
88. *Ibid.,* October 15, 1861.
89. Wilkie, *op. cit.,* pp. 70-71.
90. Richardson, *op. cit.,* p. 197; Knox, *op. cit.,* p. 100; New York *Times,* November 4, 1861.
91. Carl Sandburg, *Abraham Lincoln, The War Years* (New York, 1939), I, 350.
92. See e.g., New York *Herald,* October 3, 1861; also S. P. Hanscom to James Gordon Bennett, October 6, 1861, Bennett Papers.
93. Chicago *Daily Tribune,* October 23, 1861; St. Louis *Daily Missouri Democrat,* November 5, 1861. The St. Louis correspondent of a Columbus (Ohio) newspaper believed "the unmilitary condition of both himself [Thomas] and his right-hand man (Wilkinson [*sic*] of the New York *Tribune*) entirely unfitted them, during most of their trip to Tipton . . . for doing justice to anyone, much less to one already under the ban of their biased judgment." Columbus *Daily Ohio State Journal,* November 7, 1861.
94. St. Louis *Daily Missouri Republican,* November 6, 1861.
95. New York *Herald,* November 8, 1861.
96. St. Louis *Daily Missouri Republican,* November 9, 1861.
97. Richard Smith to Salmon P. Chase, November 7, 1861, Salmon P. Chase Papers, Library of Congress.
98. New York *Times,* November 7, 1861.
99. *Ibid.,* November 22, 1861.
100. New York *World,* July 13, 1861.
101. St. Louis *Daily Missouri Republican,* November 16, 1861. For similar disclaimers by other army correspondents, see St. Louis *Evening News,* November 20, 1861.
102. New York *Times,* November 22, 1861.

7
THE FIRST TIDINGS FROM THE FLEET
Pages 135-157

1. Out of commission.
2. J. R. Soley, *The Blockade and the Cruisers* (London, 1898), p. 86.
3. New York *Daily Tribune,* June 1, 1861.
4. New York *Times,* June 5, 1861.
5. New York *Daily Tribune,* September 14, 1861.
6. *Ibid.,* September 11, 1861.
7. *Ibid.,* November 11, 1861.
8. New York *Times,* August 3, 1861.
9. New York *Daily Tribune,* October 1, 1861.
10. New York *Times,* September 30 1861.
11. "Flag officer" in 1861 meant the commanding officer of a squadron.
12. E. S. Maclay, *A History of the United States Navy, from 1775 to 1898* (New York, 1898), II, 176-177.
13. B. F. Butler, *Private and Official Correspondence of Gen. Benjamin F. Butler* (Privately printed, 1917), I, 227-228; C. H. Metcalf, *A History of the United States Marine Corps* (New York, 1939), p. 199.

14. New York *Times,* September 2, 1861.
15. New York *Daily Tribune,* September 3, 1861.
16. *Ibid.,* September 3, 1861.
17. Maclay, *op. cit.,* II, 178.
18. New York *Times,* September 3, 1861.
19. Evidently confused by either Welles or Osbon with the Fifty-Seventh Article of War, which provided court martial, with a possible sentence of death, for imparting military information to the enemy either directly or indirectly.
20. A. B. Paine, *A Sailor of Fortune* (New York, 1906), pp. 133-134.
21. Francis Brown, *Raymond of the Times* (New York, 1951), p. 217.
22. Boston *Daily Journal,* March 11, 1862.
23. The actual number of ships in the expedition, including transports, was forty-six. *Report of the Secretary of the Navy for 1861* (Washington, 1862), p. 7.
24. New York *Herald,* November 14, 1861.
25. New York *Daily Tribune,* November 14, 1861.
26. *Ibid.,* November 14, 1861.
27. New York *Evening Post,* November 14, 1861. That a correspondent of the London *Daily News* accompanied the expedition to Port Royal is mentioned in R. U. Johnson and C. C. Buel, *Battles and Leaders of the Civil War* (New York, 1884-1888), I, 685.
28. New York *Times,* November 14, 1861.
29. J. T. Headley, *Farragut and Our Naval Commanders* (New York, 1867), pp. 128-130. See also *Official Records of the Union and Confederate Navies in the War of the Rebellion,* Ser. I, vol. xii, pp. 233-235, hereinafter referred to as *O.R.* (Navy).
30. Gideon Welles to Edgar T. Welles, November 3, 1861, Gideon Welles Papers, Library of Congress.
31. New York *Herald,* November 14, 1861.
32. Maclay, *op. cit.,* II, 191-192.
33. New York *Evening Post,* November 14, 1861.
34. New York *Herald,* November 14, 1861.
35. Frank Moore, *The Rebellion Record* (New York, 1861-1873), III, 115-117.
36. *O.R.* (Navy), Ser. I, vol. xii, 266.
37. For statements crediting the *Post* correspondent, W. C. Church, with a beat, see F. M. O'Brien, *The Story of the Sun* (New York and London, 1918), p. 137; *Dictionary of American Biography,* IV, 104-105. Most of the principal newspaper accounts of the capture of Port Royal were published November 14.
38. Philadelphia *Press,* July 27, 1861. Apparently the editor of the New York *World* viewed McClellan somewhat differently at this time. "Give us a good pen & ink portrait of McClellan," he wrote to one of his Washington correspondents three days after Forney's article appeared in print. "If the people believe him a Demi-god, the war will get a new impetus after our disaster. I am astonished at the blind faith people are reposing in him." Manton Marble to E. C. Stedman, July 30, 1861, Stedman Papers.
39. See e.g., Washington *Evening Star,* August 5, 1861; New York *World,* August 7, 1861.
40. C. C. Coffin, *The Boys of '61* (Boston, 1925), p. 54. For another version of the origin of the sobri-

quet, see James Longstreet, *From Manassas to Appomattox,* (Philadelphia, 1896), p. 63.

41. Chicago *Daily Tribune,* August 16, 1861.
42. *O.R.* (Army), Ser. III, vol. i, pp. 390, 454-455.
43. Henry Villard, "Army Correspondence," *Nation,* I (July 20, 1865), 80.
44. B. J. Lossing, *Pictorial History of the Civil War,* (Hartford, 1868), II, 133.
45. Coffin, *op. cit.,* p. 56.
46. See e.g., Washington column, New York *Herald,* August 29, 1861.
47. Cincinnati *Daily Gazette,* September 12, 1861. In the Cincinnati *Daily Commercial,* September 17, 1861, appears an allusion to "the incessant war cry of the New York reporters."
48. *Vanity Fair,* October 12, 1861.
49. The news of Scott's resignation and of McClellan's appointment to succeed him was released to the press on November 1. Scott's retirement was the culmination of a series of acrimonious exchanges between the two men.
50. S. P. Hanscom to James Gordon Bennett, October 6, 1861, Bennett Papers.
51. New York *Herald,* October 11, 1861; Chicago *Daily Tribune,* October 16, 1861.
52. Lossing, *op. cit.,* p. 133.
53. Allan Pinkerton, chief of McClellan's secret service.
54. H. M. Smith to C. H. Ray, no date, Ray Papers. Although there is nothing but the heading "Sunday eve" to indicate when the letter was written, it is evident from its content that it was mailed some time during the early part of October, 1861.
55. Coffin, *op. cit.,* pp. 56-57; A. T. Rice's *Reminiscences of Abraham Lincoln,* (New York, 1888), pp. 171-173.
56. For a more detailed analysis of what happened at Ball's Bluff, see Johnson and Buel, *op. cit.,* II, 123-124; Comte de Paris, *History of the Civil War in America,* I (Philadelphia, 1875), 367-421; Report of the Joint Committee on the Conduct of the War, *Senate Report No. 108,* 1863, Pt. II, pp. 252-510.
57. Stedman's five-column account was published in the *World,* October 29, 1861. For editorial praise of his effort, see St. Louis *Daily Missouri Republican,* November 1, 1861. Said the editor of the *World,* "No account so full and so authentic has hitherto appeared in this or any other journal." New York *World,* October 29, 1861. See also Manton Marble to E. C. Stedman, October 29, 1861, Stedman Papers.
58. On October 25, 1861, Ainsworth Spofford, the Washington correspondent of the Cincinnati *Daily Commercial,* stated in a letter published October 29: "There is a general murmur of dissatisfaction here, not loud, but deep, on account of the course of the authorities in suppressing all dispatches concerning the battle at Edward's Ferry [Ball's Bluff]. The State Department, it is said, out of motives of 'policy,' connected with the New York Stock market and our foreign diplomacy, sent to the telegraph office in Washington positive orders to withhold all dispatches respecting that engagement, save one prepared or supervised by the Government. So the public were left, for days, in doubt whether the troops of the Union had met a defeat or a victory, while the most exaggerated rumors of the carnage

. . . were spread from mouth to mouth. . . ." Outspoken criticism of the suppression of facts may be found as well in the New York *Times* and the Chicago *Daily Tribune*, November 2, 1861. See also, E. C. Stedman Diary, October 27, 1861, and E. C. Stedman to Richard Henry Stoddard, October 29, 1861, both Stedman Papers.

59. New York *Daily Tribune*, November 5, 1861.

60. *Dictionary of American Biography*, XVIII, 72.

61. For newspaper comment on the Potomac blockade, see Washington letter, Chicago *Daily Tribune*, November 7, 1861. To mitigate the food shortage, dray service was temporarily instituted between Baltimore and Washington, thereby relieving the pressure on the single-track Washington branch of the Baltimore and Ohio Railroad.

62. Brown, *op. cit.*, p. 218. Also George B. McClellan to Simon Cameron, December 9, 1861; Simon Cameron to Henry J. Raymond, December 11, 1861; Henry J. Raymond to Simon Cameron, December 13, 1866, all Henry J. Raymond Papers, New York Public Library.

63. Thomas Bailey Aldrich to Sarah A. Aldrich, October 30, 1861, as reprinted in Ferris Greenslet, *The Life of Thomas Bailey Aldrich* (Boston and New York, 1908), p. 56.

64. J. C. Ropes and W. L. Livermore, *The Story of the Civil War* (New York and London, 1894-1913), Pt. I, p. 183.

65. Perhaps the most impressive of these reviews was one which took place at Bailey's Cross Roads on November 20 and in which 70,000 soldiers participated. The review was described at some length in the Washington letter, New York *Times*, November 23. In somewhat more flamboyant style the Chicago *Tribune*, November 25, characterized this as being "the greatest review the world ever saw!"

8
AN AFFRAY WITH GENERAL HALLECK
Pages 158-188

1. Boston *Daily Journal*, May 15, 1862.

2. F. B. Wilkie, *Pen and Powder* (Boston, 1888), pp. 172-173.

3. *Ibid.*, pp. 81-82; New York *Times*, January 31, 1862.

4. C. C. Coffin to Senator Henry Wilson, January 18, 1862. This letter was subsequently turned over to the War Department and is now in the letter file of the War Department, National Archives. See also Boston *Daily Journal*, January 29, 1862.

5. Department of the Ohio, with headquarters at Louisville.

6. See e.g., an allusion to the Mill Springs affair in a Chicago *Tribune* army letter, January 22, 1862, as "the most brilliant victory yet achieved by the Federal land forces in this war." In a letter written to his brother from Cincinnati, January 21, 1862, Whitelaw Reid stated: "We [i.e., the Cincinnati *Gazette*] had a splendid account of Zollicoffer's Defeat. It was in the form of a private letter to me, but I struck out the 'Dear Reid' & a few other things of the sort. It is from my old friend Tom Fullerton." Reid Papers.

7. For unflattering descriptions of Cairo at this time by army correspondents, see Cincinnati *Daily Gazette*, January 16, 1862; New York *Times*, January 18, 1862; Boston *Daily Journal*, January 20, 1862.

8. A. D. Richardson, *The Secret Service, the Field, the Dungeon, and the Escape* (Hartford, 1865), p. 213.
9. A band of Union soldiers or guerrillas disguised as Confederates, named in honor of Fremont's wife, Jessie Benton.
10. New York *Daily Tribune,* February 14, 1862.
11. Richardson, *op. cit.,* p. 217; New York *Daily Tribune,* February 14, 1862.
12. Richardson, *op. cit.,* p. 218.
13. New York *Daily Tribune,* March 8, 1862.
14. J. H. Browne, *Four Years in Secessia* (Hartford, 1865), p. 67.
15. *Dictionary of American Biography,* XII, 5.
16. Wilkie, *op. cit.,* pp. 54-55.
17. Cincinnati *Daily Commercial,* May 16, 1862.
18. James Morgan, *Charles H. Taylor* (Boston, 1923), p. 103.
19. From an account of the experience written by McCullagh many years later for the St. Louis *Globe-Democrat,* as reprinted in the New York *Sun,* March 5, 1893. See also W. B. Stevens, "Joseph B. McCullagh," *Missouri Historical Review,* XXV (October, 1930), 7-9.
20. Chicago *Daily Tribune,* February 19, 1862.
21. Walter Geer, *Campaigns of the Civil War* (New York, 1926), p. 58.
22. Browne, *op. cit.,* pp. 84-85.
23. Boston *Daily Journal,* February 24, 1862. The lackluster attitude of the Tennesseans was ascribed by the New York *Times* reporter to the fact that a majority of the Tennessee regiments had not received a cent of pay since they were mustered into the service. New York *Times,* February 22, 1862.
24. New York *Daily Tribune,* February 22, 1862.
25. Since the capture of Fort Donelson was the first large-scale Northern success, it was the occasion for celebration throughout the North. In both houses of Congress, news of the victory caused frantic excitement and the announcement that Floyd "stole away" produced hearty laughter. At a large gathering in Chicago, one of the editors of the *Tribune,* Charles H. Ray, after reading aloud to a large crowd in front of the *Tribune* office the dispatch containing this momentous news, added: "Friends, 'Deacon' Bross [a member of the *Tribune* staff whose puritanical views were well known] authorized me to say that any man who goes to bed sober tonight is a traitor to the government." The Tribune (Chicago), *The W.G.N.* (Chicago, 1922), pp. 35-36. A good description of these victory demonstrations is given in J. B. McMaster, *History of the People of the U.S. during Lincoln's Administration* (New York and London, 1927), pp. 196-197.
26. W. E. Griffis, *Charles Carleton Coffin* (Boston, 1898), pp. 110-114.
27. Note e.g., a complaint in the St. Louis *Republican,* March 8, 1862, that "Chicago papers . . . are . . . enthusiastic at the capture of Fort Donelson and at the part the troops from Illinois had in it in *particular,* but they seem to have ignored the presence of other regiments who fought at that place except by an occasional hasty mention of them." See also New York *Times,* February 28, 1862.
28. Cincinnati *Daily Commercial,* March 18, 1862. In the Whitelaw Reid Papers is an undated letter, from Grant's father to a publishing house in Cincinnati, attributing the

origin of the story of Grant's being a drunkard to the agreement described in the text. It is quite probable that Frank Chapman of the *Herald* was the New York reporter to whom Grant's father was referring. According to the Cincinnati *Daily Commercial,* May 24, 1862, Chapman was arrested by Halleck some time during the advance upon Corinth because in conversation with some friends Chapman "said he knew that Gen. Grant was so drunk that he had to be helped on his horse, just before the battle of Fort Donelson."

29. Whitelaw Reid to G. W. Reid, February 18, 1862, Reid Papers. By March 10, the *Gazette* had five correspondents in and around Nashville, three with the various divisions of General Buell's army and two at large. Cincinnati *Daily Gazette,* March 15, 1862.
30. Frank Moore, *The Rebellion Record* (New York, 1861-1873), IV, 186; Wilkie, *op. cit.,* pp. 139-140.
31. Henry Villard, *Memoirs* (Boston and New York, 1904), I, 228. For another interesting journalistic description of the occupation of Nashville, see St. Louis *Missouri Republican,* March 3, 4, 1862.
32. C. C. Coffin, *My Days and Nights on the Battle-Field,* (Boston, 1887), p. 233.
33. George P. Upton to C. H. Ray, March 4, 1862, Ray Papers, HM RY 199.
34. Chicago *Daily Tribune,* February 26, 1862; St. Louis *Daily Missouri Republican,* February 27, 1862; Cincinnati *Daily Gazette,* March 5, 1862; New York *Daily Tribune,* March 8, 1862; Philadelphia *Inquirer,* March 12, 1862. Cullom was replaced by General William K. Strong, supplanted in turn a month later by H. E. Thayer, who formerly had acted as telegraphic censor in Washington.
35. New York *Times,* April 4, 1862; Cincinnati *Daily Gazette,* May 13, 1862.
36. St. Louis *Daily Missouri Democrat,* April 21, 1862; New York *Times,* May 10, 1862.
37. St. Louis *Daily Missouri Democrat,* April 3, 1862.
38. *The W.G.N.,* p. 35.
39. Richardson, *op. cit.,* pp. 249-250.
40. R. U. Johnson and C. C. Buel, *Battles and Leaders of the Civil War* (New York, 1884-1888), I, 491-492.
41. Whitelaw Reid stated flatly (Cincinnati *Daily Gazette,* May 3, 1862) that there were not more than five newspaper correspondents in Grant's army on the eve of Shiloh: two accredited to the New York *Herald,* and one each to the Philadelphia *Inquirer,* the Cincinnati *Gazette,* and the Cincinnati *Times.* A letter in the Cincinnati *Times,* April 10, 1862, refers, however, to M. C. Misener of the Chicago *Times* and a correspondent of the Louisville *Journal* as being in the vicinity of Pittsburg Landing at the time of the battle. For an indication that at least two other correspondents were within forty miles of the battle zone, see Ben Truman's letter from Nashville, New York *Times,* November 28, 1864.
42. *O.R.* (Army), Ser. I, vol. x, Pt. 1, pp. 385-386; J. C. Ropes and W. L. Livermore, *The Story of the Civil War* (New York and London, 1894-1913), Pt. II, pp. 63-64.
43. Philadelphia *Inquirer,* April 15, 1862; Cincinnati *Daily Commercial,* April 21, 1862.
44. Royal Cortissoz, *The Life of Whitelaw Reid* (New York, 1921), I, 85; Lewis Wallace, *Autobiography*

(New York and London, 1906), I, 462, 501.

45. S. F. Horn, *The Army of Tennessee* (Indianapolis, 1941), p. 134.

46. Villard, *op. cit.*, I, 243.

47. *Ibid.*, pp. 245-246.

48. Cincinnati *Daily Times*, April 10, 1862.

49. *O.R.* (Army), Ser. I, vol. x, Pt. 1, pp. 293-296, 325, 387-388.

50. Philadelphia *Inquirer*, April 14, 1862; Cincinnati *Daily Commercial*, April 21, 1862.

51. Villard, *op. cit.*, I, 249-253.

52. Wilkie, *op. cit.*, pp. 153-154.

53. Cincinnati *Daily Times*, April 10, 1862. Chapman's connection with the *Herald*'s Shiloh scoop was made public by George Alfred Townsend in a series of articles published in the San Francisco *Chronicle* during the spring and summer of 1882.

54. *Congressional Globe*, 37 Congress, 2 sess., Vol. XXXII, Pt. 2, p. 1581.

55. *Ibid.*, p. 1584; New York *Herald*, April 10, 1862. In the Bennett Papers is a letter from W. H. Stiner to Frederic Hudson, April 12, 1862, offering congratulations on the *Herald*'s "complete victory in beating the other papers on the Pittsburg Landing fight."

56. "We have lost in killed and wounded and missing from eighteen to twenty thousand," stated Chapman. "That of the enemy is estimated at from thirty-five to forty thousand." Final estimates of the losses on both sides as officially reported in Johnson and Buel, *op. cit.*, I, 538-539, were: Federal, 13,047 (killed 1,754; wounded, 8,408; captured or missing, 2,885); Confederate, 10,699 (killed, 1,728; wounded, 8,012; missing, 959). In its issue of May 7, 1862, the Boston *Journal* noted the discrepancy between Chapman's estimate and the official return, saying, "This is certainly rather nearer the truth than the *Herald* usually comes, but a statement so wide of the mark would damage the reputation of almost any other newspaper."

57. New York *Herald*, April 9, 1862.

58. U. S. Grant, *Personal Memoirs* (New York, 1895), I, 288-289; *O.R.* (Army), Ser. I, vol. x, Pt. 1, pp. 108-111; Cincinnati *Daily Commercial*, April 21, May 9, 1862.

59. Andrew Hickenlooper, "The Battle of Shiloh," in W. H. Chamberlin and G. A. Thayer, *Sketches of War History* (Cincinnati, 1903), V, 447. For a further indication of the doubtful character of the *Herald* man's story, see Edwin D. Judd to Gideon Welles, May 28, 1862, Welles Papers.

60. The usually reliable Franc Wilkie said in a letter to the New York *Times*, published May 17, 1862: "Another correspondent . . . in speaking of the battle of Shiloh, says that the muzzle of the Southern rifle was crossed by . . . Northern bayonets, showing that the conflict was a desperate hand-to-hand struggle, in which the antagonists bayoneted, throttled, gouged and pistoled each other, in a sort of indiscriminate, terrific mob fight . . . .

There has never been a battle in the West where a hand-to-hand conflict occurred—there has never been a battle in which one party waited to receive a bayonet charge, or did receive a bayonet charge from the other . . . .

The only case of any one killed by a bayonet thrust in the battle of Shiloh, was that of one man found in a tent. He was probably sick or asleep and in that condition was killed by a stab from behind."

61. See e.g., a letter from a special correspondent, St. Louis *Daily Missouri Republican,* April 18, 1862.

62. Three days after the Battle of Shiloh, the Philadelphia *Inquirer* reported that Corinth was in Federal hands and that the Union cavalry had even advanced beyond it! See also Cincinnati *Daily Times,* April 10, 1862.

63. Henry Villard, "Army Correspondence," *Nation,* I (July 27, 1865), 115. A flagrant example of faked eyewitness reporting had appeared at the battle of Pea Ridge (March 6-7, 1862). Knox of the New York *Herald* and William Fayel of the St. Louis *Democrat* were the only correspondents present at the battle. After the fighting was over, they rode almost 200 miles on horseback to reach the railroad at Rolla and then, well satisfied at having the only accounts of the action, continued on to St. Louis. Since their newspapers were too widely separated geographically to be rivals in any sense, they cooperated in writing up their reports. To their utter amazement they found when they reached St. Louis that a copy of the New York *Tribune* had just arrived there with a full-page account of the Battle of Pea Ridge. Junius H. Browne had reached St. Louis several days previously, had heard rumors that a great battle had been fought in Arkansas, and had gone down to Springfield or Rolla with Richard Colburn of the New York *World* to gather information from officers returning from the fight. Not a single regiment of infantry or cavalry, no battery by name was mentioned; yet Browne's account, dated at Pea Ridge and purporting to relate personal observations from the battle field, was widely read in this country and was acclaimed in the London *Times* as "the ablest and best battle account which had been written during the American war." Richardson, *op. cit.,* 271; Wilkie, *op. cit.,* pp. 124-129; St. Louis *Daily Missouri Democrat,* April 17, 23, 1862.

64. See e.g., St. Louis *Daily Missouri Republican,* April 11, 1862.

65. Cincinnati *Daily Commercial,* May 3, 1862. These stories were picked up by the AP and given a wider circulation than they would otherwise have received. Cincinnati *Daily Gazette,* May 8, 1862.

66. Chicago *Daily Tribune,* April 30, 1862.

67. Lloyd Lewis, *Sherman, Fighting Prophet* (New York, 1932), I, 233-234. See also W. T. Sherman, *Memoirs* (New York, 1875), I, 246.

68. Elihu B. Washburne to C. H. Ray, April 25, 1862, Ray Papers, HM RY 210. The "slanderous article" referred to in the text was probably the editorial on Grant in the Cincinnati *Gazette,* April 21, 1862.

69. Chicago *Daily Tribune,* June 16, 1862. The author of this letter was probably Joseph A. Ware, subsequently one of the editors of Forney's Washington *Chronicle.*

70. Allan Nevins, *The Evening Post* (New York, 1922), p. 318; New York *Evening Post,* April 16, 1862. For contemporary estimates of Reid's reportorial achievement, see Knox, *op. cit.,* 150; St. Louis *Daily Missouri Democrat,* April 16, 1862; Chicago *Times,* April 16, 1862; Baltimore *American and Commercial Advertiser,* April 17, 1862.

71. For material on the controversy, see Cortissoz, *op. cit.,* II, 336-337; New York *Daily Tribune,* April 8, 9, 1881.

72. Not simply did "all the correspondents of Northern newspapers . . .

[declare] that our army was surprised." B. C. Truman, "A Spectacular Battle and Its 'If's'," *Overland Monthly,* New Ser. XXXIV (August, 1899), 156. Grant himself stated in a dispatch to General Halleck, April 5, 1862, that he had "scarcely the faintest idea of an attack being made upon us." Sherman said substantially the same thing in a dispatch to Grant of the same date. *O.R.* (Army), Ser. I, vol. x, Pt. 2, pp. 93-94.

73. Cortissoz, *op. cit.,* I, 88. A somewhat different version of Grant's remark appears in Cincinnati *Daily Gazette,* April 14, 1862.
74. Savannah *Republican,* April 14, 1862.
75. W. B. Stevens, "Joseph B. McCullagh," *Missouri Historical Review,* XXV (April, 1931), 425.
76. Halleck's army took more than a month to advance the twenty-three miles from Pittsburg Landing to Corinth.
77. Cincinnati *Daily Gazette,* May 9, 1862; St. Louis *Daily Missouri Democrat,* May 17, 1862. According to a special correspondent of the Chicago *Times,* there were approximately fifty newspaper correspondents in Halleck's camp on May 17. Chicago *Times,* May 24, 1862.
78. St. Louis *Daily Missouri Republican,* May 13, 1862.
79. Wilkie, *op. cit.,* p. 178.
80. Brigadier General Thomas J. Wood, one of Halleck's division commanders.
81. Chicago *Times,* May 20, 1862.
82. New York *Times,* May 26, 1862.
83. The full text of the order was given in New York *Daily Tribune,* May 17, 1862.
84. From an unpublished letter to the *Gazette* in the Reid Papers dated at Cairo, May 21, 1862. Although Reid was evidently its author, the *Gazette* was probably unwilling to publish it because of the strong language.
85. Cincinnati *Daily Commercial,* May 24, 1862.
86. New York *Daily Tribune,* May 26, 1862.
87. Cincinnati *Daily Times,* May 27, 1862.
88. Although most of the newspaper correspondents dismissed the spy angle as a mere pretext, there were rumors that valuable information had leaked to Beauregard through the Irwin family at Savannah, whose five fascinating daughters had frequent callers, one of them an unnamed newspaper correspondent. Later (June 11, 1863) the Chicago *Tribune* intimated that the correspondent was Warren P. Isham of the Chicago *Times.* For another theory, see the Cincinnati *Daily Times,* May 26, 1862.
89. St. Louis *Daily Missouri Republican,* May 23, 1862; Cortissoz, *op. cit.,* I, 89-91; Cincinnati *Daily Times,* May 27, 1862; Cincinnati *Daily Gazette,* May 28, 1862; St. Louis *Daily Missouri Democrat,* May 24, 1862. For the text of a statement issued by the excluded correspondents presenting their side of the case, see New York *Times,* May 26, 1862. Fourteen correspondents representing nine different newspapers signed the statement.
90. Cincinnati *Daily Times,* May 27, 1862.
91. See e.g., editorials in the Cincinnati *Daily Commercial,* May 22, 1862; St. Louis *Daily Missouri Democrat,* May 23, 1862; Cincinnati *Daily Gazette,* May 24, 1862; Chicago *Daily Tribune,* May 21, 22, 24, 1862.

92. New York *Daily Tribune,* May 26, 1862.
93. New York *Herald,* May 23, 1862.
94. Cincinnati *Daily Gazette,* September 1, 1862.
95. New York *Times,* May 26, 1862.
96. Mobile *News,* May 31, 1862; St. Louis *Daily Missouri Republican,* June 8, 1862; *O.R.* (Army), Ser. I, vol. x, Pt. 2, p. 543.
97. J. F. Rhodes, *History of the U.S. from the Compromise of 1850* (New York, 1928), III, 515.
98. Chicago *Daily Tribune,* June 6, 1862.
99. Moore, *op. cit.,* V, 156.
100. Chicago *Daily Tribune,* June 3, 1862. Also *O.R.* (Army), Ser. I, vol. x, Pt. 1, pp. 771-772; the Cincinnati *Commercial* reporter (*ibid,* pp. 772-773) referred to "the old joke of quaker guns . . . (having) been played off on us. They were real wooden guns, with stuffed 'paddies' for gunners. I saw them." Grant, *op. cit.,* I, 315, confirmed the existence of the "Quaker guns" in the Corinth fortifications.

9

THE PRESS GOES TO THE PENINSULA

Pages 189-217

1. Joseph Medill to Edwin M. Stanton, January 21, 1862, Stanton Papers.
2. M. H. Taylor, *On Two Continents* (New York, 1905), p. 115.
3. New York *Times,* March 14, 15, 1862.
4. New York *Daily Tribune,* March 15, 1862; E. A. Pollard, *The Lost Cause* (New York, 1866), pp. 262-263. Upon his return from Manassas, Taylor was summoned before a Senate committee to testify about what he had seen there. R. C. Beatty, *Bayard Taylor, Laureate of the Gilded Age* (Norman, Oklahoma, 1936), p. 223.
5. Taylor, *op. cit.,* p. 116.
6. Chicago *Daily Tribune,* April 9, 1862. For further press comment about the "Quaker guns," see Cincinnati *Daily Commercial,* March 25, 1862; Chicago *Daily Tribune,* March 26, 1862; Baltimore *American and Commercial Advertiser,* April 14, 1862. See also K. P. Williams, *Lincoln Finds a General* (New York, 1949), I, 124, 153.
7. W. C. H. Wood, *Captains of the Civil War* (New Haven, 1921), p. 198; New York *Daily Tribune,* April 9, 1862; Chicago *Times,* April 15, 1862.
8. The popular name given to one of the regiments in the Pennsylvania Reserve Corps because of their badge, the tail of a deer, worn on the caps of both officers and privates.
9. Evidently the poet Nathaniel Hawthorne, who was in Washington at the time. He later made a short trip to Fortress Monroe, described in "Chiefly about War Matters," *Atlantic Monthly,* X (July, 1862), 43-61.
10. Taylor, *op. cit.,* p. 117.
11. *Ibid.,* pp. 117-118.
12. From an undated newspaper clipping in the George Alfred Townsend Scrapbooks. On April 23, 1862, the discerning Washington correspondent of the St. Louis *Republican,* Laura C. Redden, informed her newspaper that a map had appeared in the New York *Herald* on the previous day purporting to represent the Confederate defenses at Yorktown. She added: "If Bennet [sic] knew how this gross imposition is received by all military men, as well as sensible civilians, he would certainly *quit his tricks at fabricating*

defenses that don't exist and plans that never entered any head except his own. The Confederate entrenchments on the peninsula are strong, but that they are of such character as the above map represents is preposterous." St. Louis *Daily Missouri Republican,* April 28, 1862.

13. W. M. Wallington to Uriah H. Painter, March 27, 31, 1862, Painter Papers.
14. *O.R.* (Army), Ser. II. vol. ii, p. 246; *ibid.,* Ser. III, vol. i, p. 899; F. A. Flower, *Edwin McMasters Stanton* (Akron, Ohio, 1905), p. 208; Oliver Gramling, *AP, The Story of News* (New York and Toronto, 1940), pp. 45-46; Chicago *Daily Tribune,* March 7, 1862. Stanton was said to have told a United States Senator that his newspaper order was intended to apply only to present or future movements of the army and, when asked why he had phrased it to cover past movements also, he replied, "So that they can't drive a coach and six through it!"
15. Chicago *Daily Tribune,* March 29, 1862. For the text of the Postmaster General's order, see *ibid.,* March 25, 1862.
16. Horace White to Charles H. Ray, March 26, 1862, Ray Papers, HM RY 223.
17. Washington *Sunday Chronicle,* March 16, 1862; New York *Herald,* March 18, 1862; Philadelphia *Inquirer,* March 18, 1862; E. B. Robinson, "The Public Press of Philadelphia during the Civil War" (unpublished doctoral dissertation, Western Reserve University, Cleveland, 1936), p. 155. Both the Chicago *Tribune* of March 18, 1862, and the Cincinnati *Gazette* of the following day claimed that the proceedings against the *Chronicle* were instigated by the Washington correspondent of the *Herald,* who insisted on telegraphing the story in the *Chronicle* unless the War Department took some action in the matter.
18. Boston *Daily Journal,* March 22, 1862; Philadelphia *Inquirer,* March 25, 26, 1862; New York *Times,* March 25, 1862. The New York *Journal of Commerce* and the New York *Sunday Mercury* likewise were called on the carpet for having reprinted the *Journal* article.
19. Washington *Evening Star,* April 2, 1862; New York *Daily Tribune,* April 5, 1862; Cincinnati *Daily Gazette,* April 5, 1862.
20. Tyler Dennett, *Lincoln and the Civil War* (New York, 1939), p. 39. The Philadelphia *Inquirer,* April 7, 1862, told at some length how Russell had fitted up a wagon at heavy expense with a liberal supply of champagne, cooking utensils, sleeping conveniences; and how he was all ready to embark with several friends when the order of ejectment was served.
21. W. H. Russell, *My Diary, North and South* (Boston, 1863), II, 432-442; Russell, "Recollections of the Civil War," *North American Review,* CLXVI (June, 1898), 750; St. Louis *Daily Missouri Republican,* May 13, 1862; William H. Russell to Edwin M. Stanton, March 27, April 2, 1862, Stanton Papers. Russell attributed his exclusion from the expedition to Fortress Monroe to Stanton's jealousy of McClellan and his desire to curry favor with certain elements in the North. However the London *Times* correspondent had become increasingly unpopular among the friends of the administration because of the hostile attitude of his newspaper, and he also was embarrassed by charges that he had used confidential information from

the British Embassy to promote a Wall Street speculation. In this connection see The Times (London), *The History of the Times* (New York, 1935-1947), II; Report of the House Committee on Judiciary, March 20, 1862, *House Report No. 64,* 37 Cong., 2 sess., pp. 9-10; J. C. Derby, *Fifty Years among Authors, Books, and Publishers* (New York, 1886), p. 75.

22. New York *Daily Tribune,* April 11, 1862; New York *Times,* April 11, 1862; Philadelphia *Inquirer,* April 12, 1862; W. H. Stiner to Frederic Hudson, April 13, 1862, Bennett Papers; E. S. Sanford to Edwin M. Stanton, April 13, 1862, Office of Secretary of War, Letters Received, National Archives. Stiner, who was one of the *Herald* staff on the Peninsula, informed Hudson that he had ridden to headquarters in the midst of a terrible storm to lodge a stiff protest against the action of General Wool in permitting publication of the *Inquirer* article.

23. Cincinnati *Daily Commercial,* April 14, 1862; Philadelphia *Inquirer,* April 19, 1862; Cincinnati *Daily Gazette,* April 25, 1862.

24. Joel Cook, *The Siege of Richmond* (Philadelphia, 1862), p. 10. Later (May 6, 1864) the New York *Times* accused McClellan of having neglected to safeguard important military information during the Peninsular Campaign. "The conclusive evidence of this is found in the fact that the letters of the army correspondents at the time constantly prefigured every movement before it was made—General McClellan neither stopping their communicativeness, nor closing up their sources of information."

25. Thomas S. Townsend Scrapbooks, LXXXIV, 392. The New York *Tribune,* however, did not succeed in getting permission from the War Department to use a tugboat for transmitting news from the Peninsula to Baltimore or Cherrystone. In this connection, see a letter from Samuel Wilkeson to Edwin M. Stanton, April 28, 1862, Office of the Secretary of War, Letters Received, National Archives.

26. This letter was published in the New York *Herald,* May 16, 1862, with the explanation that it had been picked up with some other documents by a *Herald* reporter after the evacuation of Yorktown. The *Tribune* did not deny that the letter was authentic but accused the *Herald* of having stolen it from the saddlebags of the *Tribune* reporter, Thomas Butler Gunn, to whom it had been written. New York *Daily Tribune,* May 17, 1862, February 16, 1863, January 19, 1865; T. B. Gunn to Sydney Howard Gay, no date, Sydney Howard Gay Papers, Columbia University Library.

27. J. H. Harper, *The House of Harper* (New York and London, 1912), pp. 181-182; Derby, *op. cit.,* p. 104. The New York *Times,* May 3, 1862, claimed that within two days after the offending issue of *Harper's* reached the army, McClellan was shelled out of his camp by the enemy.

28. Report of the Joint Committee on the Conduct of the War, *Senate Report No. 108,* 1863, Pt. I, p. 284.

29. New York *Times,* May 8, 1862. Actually the number of Confederate troops defending Yorktown did not exceed 25,000.

30. Frank Moore, *The Rebellion Record* (New York, 1861-1873), V, 21.

31. L. L. Crounse, "The Army Correspondent," *Harper's New Monthly Magazine,* XXVII (October, 1863), 629.

32. New York *World,* May 17, 1862.

33. New York *Daily Tribune,* May 15, 1862.

34. *Ibid.,* May 19, 1862. The letter to which the chaplain referred had appeared in *ibid.,* May 10, 1862, and had been written by Wilkeson. For another complaint later in the month concerning the reporting of the campaign, see A. L. Castleman, *The Army of the Potomac* (Milwaukee, 1863), pp. 126-127.

35. G. A. Townsend, *Campaigns of a Non-Combatant* (New York, 1866), p. 73. Newspaper correspondents were prone to exaggerate the extent to which the bayonet was used in the battles of the Civil War. In this connection, see J. B. Gordon, *Reminiscences of the Civil War* (New York, 1903), pp. 5-6.

36. Laura Stedman and G. M. Gould, *Life and Letters of Edmund Clarence Stedman* (New York, 1910), I, 276.

37. See e.g., Fitz John Porter to Manton Marble, April 26, June 20, 1862, Marble Papers; typical of the tone of these letters was the statement in the April 26 letter: "Such an ass as Stanton would ruin any cause but ours in such good hands as is here."

38. New York *Times,* May 17, 1862; Cincinnati *Daily Commercial,* May 29, 1862; *O.R.* (Army), Ser. I, vol. xi, Pt. 3, p. 167. Later orders were issued forbidding any army correspondent to make a balloon ascension. Philadelphia *Inquirer,* June 28, 1862.

39. Philadelphia *Inquirer,* May 13, 1862; St. Louis *Daily Missouri Democrat,* May 13, 1862. One of the "specials" who led the vanguard into Norfolk was attached to the staff of a New York illustrated paper; the other was a Fortress Monroe correspondent of the *Inquirer.*

40. Crounse, *op. cit.,* pp. 629-630. A slightly different version of the incident, written by S. T. Bulkley of the New York *Herald,* may be found in an undated newspaper clipping in the Stedman Papers. According to Bulkley, the general who put the reporters under arrest was William Sprague, also governor of Rhode Island.

41. New York *Times,* June 1, 1862.

42. Crounse, *op. cit.,* p. 632. For a similar experience in which Townsend was the victim, see Townsend, *Campaigns of a Non-Combatant,* pp. 86-102.

43. Comment of William D. Bickham in the Cincinnati *Daily Commercial,* June 7, 1862.

44. *O.R.* (Army), Ser. I, vol. xi, Pt. 3, p. 194.

45. *Ibid.,* p. 214.

46. The famous Chicago detective, Allan Pinkerton, was still in charge of McClellan's intelligence during this campaign. For critical comment about Pinkerton's efforts, see D. S. Freeman, *R. E. Lee, A Biography* (New York and London, 1935), II, 237; Williams, *op. cit.,* I, 128-129; R. W. Rowan, *The Pinkertons* (Boston, 1931), pp. 145, 182-183.

47. New York *Times,* June 3, 1862.

48. *O.R.* (Army), Ser. I, vol. xi, Pt. 1, p. 816.

49. More detailed information concerning the Battle of Fair Oaks may be found in R. U. Johnson and C. C. Buel, *Battles and Leaders of the Civil War* (New York, 1884-1888), II, 220-263; J. C. Ropes and W. L. Livermore, *The Story of the Civil War* (New York and London, 1894-1913), Pt. II, 133-157. The battle was variously styled by the press "The Battle before Richmond," "The Battle of the Chickahominy," "The Battle of the Pines," "The Battle of the Seven

Pines," and "The Battle of Bottom's Bridge."

50. Thomas S. Townsend Scrapbooks, LXXXIV, 392. During the Battle of Fair Oaks the War Department in Washington was in direct communication by telegraph with the battlefield. A telegraph operator installed in the basket of an observation balloon transmitted reports of the fighting to Washington at fifteen-minute intervals direct from the balloon. F. S. Haydon, *Aeronautics in the Union and Confederate Armies* (Baltimore, 1941), I, 325.
51. New York *Herald,* June 7, 1862.
52. New York *Times,* June 3, 1862.
53. New York *Herald,* June 5, 1862.
54. Philadelphia *Press,* June 4, 1862.
55. New York *World,* June 3, 1862.
56. New York *Times,* June 4, 1862.
57. New York *Herald,* June 5, 1862.
58. Cincinnati *Daily Commercial,* June 23, 1862.
59. New York *Times,* June 3, 1862.
60. For an outstanding Southern newspaper account of the battle, see Charleston *Mercury,* June 9, 1862.
61. New York *Daily Tribune,* June 2, 1862. For examples of the widespread criticism which the *Tribune* editorial evoked, see New York *Times,* June 3, 1862; New York *World,* June 3, 1862; Philadelphia *Inquirer,* June 5, 1862.
62. New York *Daily Tribune,* June 5, 1862. On the basis of preliminary reports, McClellan himself had informed the Secretary of War, June 1, 1862, that Casey's division had given way "unaccountably and discreditably." Subsequently he admitted that this comment, to which the press had given wide publicity, had not done full justice to the men in Casey's command. For McClellan's official report of the Battle of Fair Oaks, see U.S. House Executive Documents, *Exec. Doc. 15,* 38 Cong., 1 sess., pp. 107-113.
63. Wilkeson referred to the fact that Birney had been relieved of his command and placed under arrest by General Heintzelman for disobedience of orders and cowardice, and he indicated that in his opinion the punishment was well merited. Birney presented his side of the case in a letter to the New York *Times* published March 28, 1863, more than nine months after the battle. See also Philadelphia *Inquirer,* June 7, 1862; New York *Times,* April 10, 1863; *Dictionary of American Biography,* II, 290-291.
64. Cook, *op. cit.,* pp. 286-287.
65. From an undated item in the George Alfred Townsend Scrapbooks.
66. "An Interviewer Interviewed, A Talk with 'Gath'," *Lippincott's Monthly Magazine,* XLVIII (November, 1891), 634.
67. This series of battles—Mechanicsville, Gaines's Mill, Savage's Station, Glendale, and Malvern Hill—is generally referred to collectively as the Battles of the Seven Days. Extensive accounts of them appear in Walter Geer, *Campaigns of the Civil War* (New York, 1926), pp. 105-124; Johnson and Buel, *op. cit.,* II, 347-428; Williams, *op. cit.,* I, 223-241; Freeman, *op. cit.,* II, 122-219.
68. At the suggestion of Lee, who was well aware of McClellan's habit of reading the Richmond newspapers, the Richmond editors printed stories on the eve of the Battles of the Seven Days indicating that troops were being withdrawn from the Richmond area to reinforce Jackson in the Shenandoah Valley. J. G. Randall, "The Newspaper Problem in Its Bearing upon

Military Secrecy during the Civil War," *American Historical Review*, XXIII (January, 1918), 314. Even as late as June 30, Barclay Harding reported to his newspaper (the Philadelphia *Inquirer*) from Fortress Monroe that "it is not believed that Jackson has yet reached Richmond." Barclay Harding to W. W. Harding, June 30, 1862, Office of Secretary of War, Telegrams Received, National Archives.

69. Townsend, *Campaigns of a Non-Combatant,* p. 171.
70. Cook, *op. cit.,* p. 320.
71. *Vide infra,* pp. 219-226.
72. Townsend, *Campaigns of a Non-Combatant,* pp. 183-184.
73. Chicago *Times,* July 9, 1862.
74. Crounse, *op. cit.,* pp. 631-632.
75. Townsend, *Campaigns of a Non-Combatant,* p. 210.
76. Philadelphia *Press,* June 30, 1862.
77. New York *Times,* June 30, 1862; New York *World,* June 30, 1862; Boston *Daily Journal,* July 4, 1862. All telegraphic communication with McClellan had ceased shortly before noon on Saturday, June 28, at the time of the Confederate seizure of White House. On June 29, however, Stanton informed Major General Benjamin F. Butler that "information has reached the Department that General McClellan has met with a serious reverse in front of Richmond. Though the details have not transpired, it is quite certain that the published accounts are very much exaggerated. The Army has changed its base with comparatively little loss to a much stronger position . . . on the James River, and will, it is confidently expected, very soon march on, and into Richmond." Stanton Papers.
78. Cincinnati *Daily Commercial,* July 4, 1862. In a telegram to Frederic Hudson, June 30, 1862, the chief Washington correspondent of the *Herald* stated: "I tried to send last night an accurate statement of facts but not one word is allowed to go." Bennett Papers.
79. Baltimore *American and Commercial Advertiser,* July 1, 2, 3, 1862; New York *World,* July 2, 1862; New York *Evening Post,* July 3, 1862; Cincinnati *Daily Commercial,* July 3, 1862; S. T. Matthews, "Control of the Baltimore Press during the Civil War," *Maryland Historical Magazine,* XXXVI (June, 1941), 158; *O.R.* (Army), Ser. II, vol. iv, pp. 108-109. Abraham Lincoln to William H. Seward, June 29, 1862, in J. G. Nicolay and John Hay, *Abraham Lincoln, Complete Works* (New York, 1905), VII, 243-244. The complete text of the offending dispatch was as follows:

    "I am writing for the *American* a detailed account of events at the White House, before Richmond and on the peninsula, during the last four days, including facts obtained from Washington, having been sent for by special train to communicate with the President.

    "If you desire it, and will give due credit, I will send it to you. It will make four or five thousand words.

    "We have the grandest military triumph over the enemy, and Richmond must fall."
80. New York *Times,* July 4, 1862.
81. Boston *Daily Journal,* July 7, 1862. The Cincinnati *Commercial* reporter, Bickham, traveled all the way from the Peninsula to Cincinnati without stopping, arriving there with his account of the battles on the afternoon of July 4.
82. A. B. Paine, *A Sailor of Fortune* (New York, 1906), pp. 217-220. There is some conflict between Osbon's story and that of Town-

send, who also claimed credit for a *Herald* scoop. In his *Campaigns of a Non-Combatant* (pp. 214-217), Townsend told of reaching New York the evening of July 3 in time to meet the deadline for the morning edition of July 4. He further stated that his story covered five pages of the *Herald* and included forty columns of material. Osbon did not specify the exact time of his arrival in New York. According to his own statement, he left Fortress Monroe soon after the Battle of Malvern Hill (July 1) and arrived in Baltimore in time to catch the morning train for New York. The two correspondents evidently were not on the same train, for Osbon did not reach Philadelphia until evening, while Townsend stated that he arrived there at noon and made connections with the New York ferry. Hudson's willingness to provide Osbon with a special engine indicates that Townsend had not put in an appearance at the *Herald* office up to the time that Osbon's wire was received. It is the author's opinion that Osbon arrived in New York early on the morning of July 3 with an abbreviated account which he had worked up at Fortress Monroe and that Townsend came in later that day with a more complete account of the fighting direct from the Army of the Potomac. The two accounts probably were pieced together to make up the *Herald*'s big story of July 4.

83. In the Cincinnati *Daily Gazette*, September 4, 1862, an editorial accused unnamed reporters who were with the Army of the Potomac during the Battles of the Seven Days of having deliberately falsified the record:

"We remember that the . . . New York Herald's correspondent wrote . . . on that terrible Tuesday, after the doubly decimated army had changed its base and reached Malvern Hill . . . that the soldiers were recovering from their fatigues and were in the jolliest of spirits, and unbounded in their confidence in their General.

"Unfortunately for this picture . . . on all that Tuesday the exhausted but heroic army was fighting the desperate battle of Malvern Hill, and the correspondent had taken flight the day before and was drawing on his imagination for the army's repose and confidence in McClellan. A set of correspondents were engaged by the World and Times in the same business. The army's confidence in Gen. McClellan was required to be put in at stated intervals in their letter. So in the Herald office it was kept standing, to be inserted into the correspondence at stated intervals, that Gen. McClellan was on the field in the thickest of the fight, inspiring the troops with the utmost enthusiasm . . . ."

84. Chicago *Daily Tribune*, July 14, 1862.

85. From a newspaper clipping furnished the author by R. I. Linton, Ravenna, Ohio.

86. In connection with the reprint of Wilkeson's letter that appeared in its columns on July 8, 1862, the Chicago *Times* expressed the opinion that the letter "must have been admitted into that paper [the New York *Tribune*] by mistake. It is, however, all the more valuable coming from the source that it does."

87. New York *Daily Tribune*, July 3, 1862. In a letter to Gay from Fortress Monroe, Wilkeson declared that his only motive in denouncing the administration was to frighten it into reinforcing the army. "I do not care the snap of

my finger for McClellan. But I do care for the army and the cause." Samuel Wilkeson to Sydney Howard Gay, July 5, 1862, Gay Papers.

88. On July 15, 1862 the St. Louis *Republican* contained a news item that Sam Wilkeson of the *Tribune*, "whose recent letters from the army of the Potomac have so much surprised his friends and the journal he represents, has been granted leave of absence. He is in Washington, on his way to his farm in the interior of New York." For a later comment about Wilkeson's reporting of the Battles of the Seven Days, see New York *Daily Tribune*, May 13, 1863.

89. Painter seems to have been the only army correspondent who had any accurate knowledge of the size of the Confederate army. In this connection, see his testimony before the Joint Committee on the Conduct of the War, Report of the Joint Committee on the Conduct of the War, *Senate Report No. 108*, 1863, Pt. I, p. 283; Philadelphia *Inquirer*, June 25, 1862. Lee's total offensive strength on the eve of the Battles of the Seven Days is estimated by Freeman at approximately 67,000.

90. For outstanding Southern newspaper narratives of the Battles of the Seven Days, see Savannah *Republican*, July 17-19, 1862; *Daily Richmond Examiner*, July 4, 1862. According to the New York *Times*, August 25, 1862, the *Examiner's* account was "copied all over Europe."

91. Senator Henry Wilson of Massachusetts expressed this feeling in a speech before the United States Senate, July 9, 1862, saying: "We have had a censorship of the press during the last few weeks that I believe has been most disastrous to the interests of the country .... Sir, it appears to me that we have an organized system of lying in this country that is calculated to degrade and deceive and delude the American people. I hope that this is to be changed, and that we are to deal frankly with the people . . . [for] in their sober second thought I have the fullest confidence." *Congressional Globe*, 37 Cong., 2 sess., Vol XXXII, Pt. 4, p. 3202.

92. St. Louis *Daily Missouri Democrat*, July 12, 1862. In spite of the War Department's refusal to permit Russell to accompany McClellan's army to the Peninsula, several English newspaper correspondents viewed the Battles of the Seven Days from the Northern side, among them Frederick M. Edge of John Bright's London *Morning Star* and Coates, the representative of a Yorkshire newspaper.

93. Henry Villard, "Army Correspondence," *Nation*, I (July 27, 1865), 115.

10
"COME, SIR, THIS IS NO TIME FOR PRAYER"
Pages 218-251

1. New York *Daily Tribune*, October 21, 1862.
2. Philadelphia *Inquirer*, February 17, 1862.
3. Chicago *Daily Tribune*, January 15, 1862; New York *World*, January 17, 1862.
4. Philadelphia *Inquirer*, February 17, 1862.
5. New York *Daily Tribune*, January 31, 1862.
6. New York *Times*, January 29, 1862.
7. Chicago *Daily Tribune*, January 31, 1862.
8. John Tucker, transportation agent for the War Department.

9. Horace White to editors of Chicago *Tribune,* January 31, 1862, Ray Papers, HM RY 219.
10. New York *Daily Tribune,* February 15, 1862.
11. Philadelphia *Inquirer,* February 15, 1862.
12. New York *Times,* February 15, 1862.
13. *O.R.* (Navy), Ser. I, vol. vi, p. 552.
14. J. T. Headley, *Farragut and Our Naval Commanders* (New York, 1867), p. 203.
15. *Ibid.,* p. 204; *O.R.* (Navy), Ser. I, vol. vi, p. 557.
16. *O.R.* (Navy), Ser. I, vol. vi, p. 559.
17. Frank Moore, *The Rebellion Record* (New York, 1861-1873), IV, 102.
18. R. U. Johnson and C. C. Buel, *Battles and Leaders of the Civil War* (New York, 1884-1888), I, 668; *O.R.* (Army), Ser. I, vol. ix, p. 77.
19. B. P. Poore, *The Life and Public Services of Ambrose E. Burnside* (Providence, Rhode Island, 1882), p. 132.
20. New York *Times,* February 15, 1862.
21. *O.R.* (Navy), Ser. I, vol. vi, p. 554.
22. New York *Times,* February 15, 1862.
23. *O.R.* (Navy), Ser. I, vol. vi, p. 554.
24. Moore, *op. cit.,* IV, 115.
25. Philadelphia *Inquirer,* February 15, 1862.
26. E. S. Maclay, *A History of the United States Navy, from 1775 to 1898* (New York, 1898), II, 207-208.
27. Philadelphia *Weekly Times,* July 9, 1881; New York *Times,* February 12, 1862.
28. Philadelphia *Inquirer,* February 17, 1862. For a grudging reference to the way "Smith of the *Times* beat us all in the Burnside matter," see Manton Marble to E. C. Stedman, February 28, 1862, Stedman Papers.
29. A. B. Paine, *A Soldier of Fortune* (New York, 1906), pp. 159-161.
30. New York *Times,* March 14, 1862.
31. *Ibid.,* March 14, 1862.
32. New York *Herald,* March 11, 1862.
33. St. Louis *Daily Missouri Republican,* March 15, 1862.
34. R. S. West, Jr., *Gideon Welles, Lincoln's Navy Department* (Indianapolis and New York, 1943), p. 156.
35. Baltimore *American and Commercial Advertiser,* March 12, 1862.
36. This is evidently an error. The correct time was approximately 7:30 A.M., Sunday morning.
37. By this Fulton apparently meant a 13-inch shell. Neither of the "Monitor" 's two heavy guns, however, were larger than 11-inch.
38. This figure likewise is incorrect. The armament of the "Virginia" consisted of ten heavy guns (six 9-inch Dahlgrens and four rifled guns).
39. *Baltimore American and Commercial Advertiser,* March 12, 1862; Moore, *op. cit.,* IV, 275-276.
40. D. W. Knox, *A History of the United States Navy* (New York, 1936), p. 220; Maclay, *op. cit.,* II, 225.
41. *O.R.* (Navy), Ser. I, vol. vii, p. 11.
42. New York *Times,* March 14, 1862.
43. *Ibid.,* March 14, 1862.
44. New York *Herald,* March 11, 1862.
45. Moore, *op. cit.,* IV, 229.
46. New York *Daily Tribune,* March 11, 1862.
47. J. P. Baxter, *The Introduction of the Ironclad Warship* (Cambridge, Massachusetts, 1933), p. 295.

48. J. R. Spears, *The History of Our Navy* (New York, 1899), IV, 232.
49. New York *Herald,* March 18, 1862.
50. *O.R.* (Navy), Ser. I, vol. vii, pp. 39-40. The letter was dated April 24, 1862, and was signed "The Monitors Boys."
51. James Parton, *General Butler in New Orleans* (New York, 1864), p. 195.
52. Paine, *op. cit.,* p. 168.
53. West, *op. cit.,* p. 166.
54. Philadelphia *Inquirer,* May 9, 1862.
55. *Vide supra,* p. 3.
56. Paine, *op. cit.,* p. 171.
57. Loyall Farragut, *The Life of David Glasgow Farragut* (New York, 1891), p. 217.
58. West, *op. cit.,* p. 175.
59. New York *Times,* May 8, 1862. A New York *Herald* correspondent at Key West was making use about this same time of a nineteen-foot boat to board vessels for late news. New York *Herald,* June 17, 1862.
60. C. L. Lewis, *David Glasgow Farragut, Our First Admiral* (Annapolis, Maryland, 1943), II, 38-40.
61. New York *Times,* May 8, 1862.
62. New York *Herald,* May 10, 1862. The Navy Department apparently had planned at one time to send the "Monitor" to join the expedition against New Orleans, but the news of the approaching completion of the "Virginia" at Norfolk caused this plan to be changed. W. C. Church, *The Life of John Ericsson* (New York, 1891), p. 278.
63. New York *Evening Post,* May 8, 1862.
64. Fewer than ten guns out of the one hundred twenty-six in the two forts were disabled by the six-day bombardment, and the casualties among the garrison were no more than fourteen killed and thirty-nine wounded. One mortar schooner was sunk and one of the steamers disabled by rifled shot from the fort. The Baltimore *American and Commercial Advertiser,* May 15, 1862, estimated that the cost of the mortar shells used in the bombardment was "nearly $20 each."
65. Paine, *op. cit.,* p. 183.
66. *Ibid.,* p. 186.
67. *Ibid.,* p. 193.
68. *Ibid.,* pp. 196-197.
69. New York *Times,* May 8, 1862.
70. Lewis, *op. cit.,* II, 62. See also *O.R.* (Navy), Ser. I, vol. xviii, pp. 177-180.
71. Philadelphia *Inquirer,* May 13, 1862.
72. *O.R.* (Navy), Ser. I, vol. xviii, p. 150. For the manner in which Farragut's victory was reported by the New Orleans press, see T. E. Dabney, *One Hundred Great Years, The Story of the Times-Picayune from Its Founding to 1940* (Baton Rouge, Louisiana, 1944), p. 151.
73. Paine, *op. cit.,* pp. 209-210.
74. *National Cyclopedia of American Biography,* X, 395. Subsequently (May 9) the *Times* accused the New York *Express* of reprinting Winser's battle story without giving due credit to the *Times.*
75. Lewis, *op. cit.,* II, 76; New York *Daily Tribune,* April 28, 1862; *O.R.* (Navy), Ser. I, vol. xviii, p. 195.
76. Baltimore *American and Commercial Advertiser,* April 28, 1862.
77. New York *Daily Tribune,* April 28, 1862.
78. David D. Porter to Gustavus Fox, June 2, 1862, as quoted in R. M. Thompson and Richard Wainwright, *Confidential Correspondence of Gustavus Vasa Fox* (New

York, 1920), II, 113. For Butler's side of the story, see B. F. Butler, *Autobiography* (Boston, 1892), pp. 371-372.

79. See e.g., New York *Herald*, April 30, 1862; New York *Daily Tribune*, April 30, 1862; New York *World*, April 30, 1862; Washington *Daily National Intelligencer*, May 1, 1862.
80. *O.R.* (Navy), Ser. I, vol. xviii, pp. 195-196.
81. Farragut, *op. cit.*, p. 261.
82. J. H. Browne, *Four Years in Secessia* (Hartford, 1865), p. 179.
83. Boston *Daily Journal*, June 12, 1862.
84. C. C. Coffin, *The Boys of '61* (Boston, 1886), p. 103.
85. T. W. Knox, *Camp-Fire and Cotton-Field* (Philadelphia and Cincinnati, 1865), pp. 180-181; Moore, *op. cit.*, V, 179; Cincinnati *Daily Commercial*, June 11, 1862; St. Louis *Daily Missouri Republican*, June 10, 1862.
86. Boston *Daily Journal*, June 12, 1862. Coffin's statement that not a man on the Federal gunboats had been injured nor any of the gunboats hit was not strictly accurate. In his detailed report of the action, Flag Officer Davis asserted, "Three men only of the flotilla were wounded, and those slightly; but one ship was struck by shot." *O.R.* (Navy), Ser. I, vol. xxiii, p. 121.
87. Spears, *op. cit.*, IV, 301; *O.R.* (Navy), Ser. I, vol. xxiii, p. 140.
88. *O.R.* (Navy), Ser. I, vol. xxiii, p. 134.
89. New York *Daily Tribune*, June 11, 1862.
90. New York *Herald*, June 12, 1862.
91. New York *Daily Tribune*, June 11, 1862.
92. Boston *Daily Journal*, June 12, 1862.
93. New York *Daily Tribune*, June 11, 1862.
94. Boston *Daily Journal*, June 12, 1862.
95. Browne, *op. cit.*, p. 189.
96. Knox, *op. cit.*, p. 190; A. D. Richardson, *The Secret Service, the Field, the Dungeon, and the Escape* (Hartford, 1865), p. 265.

11

BATTLE REPORTING AT ITS BEST

Pages 252-285

1. John A. Gurley, a prominent Republican Congressman from Ohio.
2. Horace White to Joseph Medill, March 3, 1862, Ray Papers, HM RY 220.
3. *O.R.* (Army), Ser. I, vol xii, Pt. 3, p. 129; F. H. Harrington, *Fighting Politician, Major General N. P. Banks* (Philadelphia, 1948), p. 66.
4. *O.R.* (Army), Ser. I, vol. xii, Pt. 3, p. 122.
5. Cincinnati *Daily Times*, May 22, 1862; Cincinnati *Daily Commercial*, May 23, 1862; D. S. Freeman, *Lee's Lieutenants, A Study in Command*, I (New York, 1942), 356.
6. Harrington, *op. cit.*, p. 72.
7. New York *Times*, May 27, 1862.
8. New York *Herald*, May 26, 1862; Allen Tate, *Stonewall Jackson, The Good Soldier* (New York, 1928), pp. 151-152. For a complete analysis of the panic in Washington and the extent to which it was reflected in the press, see Freeman, *op. cit.*, I, 410 n.
9. Philadelphia *Inquirer*, May 30, 1862; Cincinnati *Daily Gazette*, May 30, 1862.
10. New York *World*, May 28, 1862.
11. Harrington, *op. cit.*, p. 76.
12. L. A. Sigaud, *Belle Boyd, Confederate Spy* (Richmond, Virginia,

1944), pp. 47, 57. The *Herald* also had a correspondent with Fremont whom Whitely described to Bennett in a letter dated June 17, 1862, as being a "good man." Bennett Papers.

13. *O.R.* (Army), Ser. I, vol. xii, Pt. 1, p. 643.
14. Horace White to C. H. Ray, May 28, 1862, Ray Papers, HM RY 224.
15. New York *Times,* June 14, 1862.
16. *Ibid.,* June 14, 1862.
17. See *ibid.,* May 31, 1862, for complete text of AP dispatch dated at Williamsport, May 28.
18. New York *Daily Tribune,* June 12, 1862.
19. New York *Herald,* June 10, 1862. This was Clarke's version of his experience. A correspondent of the Cincinnati *Times* reported to his newspaper that Clarke had pled hard for his release, informing his captors that the *Herald* had always favored the secessionist cause as much as it ever had the Union. A colonel of a New York regiment was quoted as saying that he had heard Clarke make this remark but that he appeared to be so frightened that he didn't know what he was saying. Cincinnati *Daily Times,* June 21, 1862. For Clarke's denial of the accusation, see Philadelphia *Inquirer,* June 12, 1862. No reference to Clarke's interview appears in any biography of Jackson.
20. New York *Times,* June 16, 20, 1862. For statements strongly critical of Webb's reporting of the Battle of Cross Keys, see George W. Smalley's letter, New York *Daily Tribune,* June 30, 1862. Apparently Smalley's account of the Cross Keys engagement never reached the *Tribune.*
21. K. P. Williams, *Lincoln Finds a General* (New York, 1949), I, 210.
22. New York *Times,* June 26, 1862.
23. *O.R.* (Army), Ser. I, vol. xii, Pt. 1, p. 653; J. F. Rhodes, *History of the United States from the Compromise of 1850* (New York, 1928), IV, 22.
24. *Vide supra,* pp. 209-211.
25. New York *Times,* June 16, 1862.
26. Chicago *Daily Tribune,* June 19, 1862.
27. New York *Daily Tribune,* June 27, 1862; July 6, 1863. For comment in the Southern press about Jackson's spectacular success in the Valley, see Charleston *Mercury,* May 29, 1862; *Daily Richmond Examiner,* June 2, 1862; Richmond *Enquirer,* June 5, 1862.
28. W. H. Stiner to Frederic Hudson, July 25, 1862, Bennett Papers; New York *Times,* July 19, 1862.
29. New York *Herald,* July 28, 1862.
30. E. V. D. Bangs to Manton Marble, July 20, 1862, Marble Papers.
31. L. A. Whitely to James Gordon Bennett, July 29, 1862, Bennett Papers.
32. Chicago *Daily Tribune,* July 25, 1862. This probably was not altogether true, for in his letter to Bennett of July 29, 1862, Whitely mentioned that a *Herald* correspondent named Wilson recently had been "smuggled into the Army of the Potomac by General Marcy." He further stated that "Talcott [another *Herald* correspondent] has got through the blockade and will take care of himself." In this connection, see also W. H. Stiner to Frederic Hudson, July 25, 1862, Bennett Papers.
33. New York *Times,* August 1, 1862.
34. *O.R.* (Army), Ser. I, vol. xii, Pt. 3, p. 435.
35. Pope's vainglorious address to his new command stated in part: "I have come to you from the West,

where we have always seen the backs of our enemies; from an army whose business it has been to seek the adversary and to beat him when he was found; whose policy has been attack and not defense." For evidence of the unfriendly attitude of the McClellan clique toward Pope at the outset of the second Bull Run campaign, see Franc Wilkie's letter published in the Chicago *Times,* August 15, 1862; Fitz John Porter to Manton Marble, August 3, 1862, Marble Papers.

36. George Alfred Townsend Scrapbooks.
37. Williams, *op. cit.,* I, 253.
38. Rhodes, *op. cit.,* IV, 115; Walter Geer, *Campaigns of the Civil War* (New York, 1926), p. 129.
39. G. A. Townsend, "Campaigning with General Pope," *Cornhill Magazine,* VI (December, 1862), 765.
40. *Ibid.,* p. 766.
41. For futher information about the Battle of Cedar Mountain, see Harrington, *op. cit.,* pp. 80-84; G. F. R. Henderson, *Stonewall Jackson and the American Civil War* (London and New York, 1919), II, 90-98; Freeman, *op. cit.,* II, 16-51.
42. Philadelphia *Press,* August 21, 1862. Townsend, Nathaniel Paige of the New York *Tribune,* and an unidentified third reporter.
43. G. A. Townsend, *Campaigns of a Non-Combatant* (New York, 1866), pp. 274-276; New York *Herald,* August 13, 1862.
44. George Alfred Townsend Scrapbooks.
45. Williams, *op. cit.,* I, 270. Judging by a censored dispatch to the *Tribune* from Cedar Mountain, August 11, 1862, some of the *Tribune*'s reporting was not favorably regarded by the censors. Among the passages disallowed were: (a) "About 500 of Gen Milroys men are engaged in burying the dead the leaders are very much swollen & the stench arising from the battle field almost unendurable." (b) "586 of our wounded are now in the Hospital at Culpepper three churches two hotels five warehouses and ten or fifteen Private residences have been taken for the wounded." (c) "The troops on the battle field are suffering much for the want of water. Much disease is feared from the drinking of thick mud." Office of Secretary of War, Telegrams Received, National Archives.
46. Williams, *op. cit.,* I, 259. Rhodes, *op. cit.,* IV, 112, disagrees, saying that after August 4, the day McClellan received Halleck's order to withdraw to Aquia Creek, "his operations were marked by promptness, order, and zeal." According to General Cox, Halleck apparently believed, however, that ten days was sufficient for the transfer of McClellan's army with the means at his disposal. J. D. Cox, *Military Reminiscences of the Civil War* (New York, 1900), I, 225.
47. Philadelphia *Inquirer,* August 21, 1862. See also Philadelphia *Press,* August 18, 1862; New York *World,* August 21, 1862; Cincinnati *Daily Commercial,* August 21, 1862; C. D. Brigham to Sydney Howard Gay, August 15, 1862, Gay Papers. Yet Lee knew as early as August 5 that McClellan's army was about to be withdrawn from the Peninsula. C. W. Russell, *The Memoirs of Colonel John S. Mosby* (Boston, 1917), pp. 129-133. Other newspapers were hardly less culpable than the three mentioned above. The New York *Express,* August 12, had published a letter from its correspondent at Harrison's Landing stating that "a movement is now

on foot, which the uninitiated cannot comprehend, but which, from particular circumstances, is deemed extremely important." The day before, Whitely had telegraphed Frederic Hudson from Washington that Stanton and Halleck "commend the prudence of the Herald & request the further suppression of the news from the peninsula. The papers that have published are to be severely delt [sic] with."

48. Geer, *op. cit.*, p. 130.
49. N. Paige to Adams S. Hill, August 19, 1862, Lincoln Papers.
50. *O.R.* (Army), Ser. I, vol. xii, Pt. 2, p. 29.
51. Geo. W. Smalley to Adams S. Hill, August 19, 1862, Lincoln Papers.
52. New York *World*, August 26, 1862; New York *Herald*, August 29, 1862.
53. The second Battle of Bull Run is described in some detail in Geer, *op. cit.*, pp. 136-143; J. C. Ropes and W. L. Livermore, *The Story of the Civil War* (New York and London, 1894-1913), Pt. II, pp. 275-298; D. S. Freeman, *R. E. Lee, A Biography* (New York and London, 1935), II, 317-349; Williams, *op. cit.*, I, 333-355.
54. Although the text of this order is not given in the Official Records, it appears from various newspaper statements that Pope issued such an order, August 22, 1862.
55. G. W. Smalley, "Chapters in Journalism," *Harper's New Monthly Magazine*, LXXXIX (August, 1894), 426-427; *O.R.* (Army), Ser. I, vol. xii, Pt. 3, p. 602.
56. Chicago *Daily Tribune*, August 28, 1862.
57. Philadelphia *Inquirer*, August 21, 1862; Chicago *Times*, August 21, 27, 1862; New York *Herald*, August 21, 24, 1862; Williams, *op. cit.*, I, 290.
58. Philadelphia *Inquirer*, August 25, 1862; New York *Herald*, May 17, 1863.
59. L. L. Crounse, "The Army Correspondent," *Harper's New Monthly Magazine*, XXVII (October, 1863), 633.
60. Chicago *Times*, August 28, 1862. The figures quoted for the number of reporters present at the second Battle of Bull Run are probably inaccurate. Both Smalley and Charles A. Page of the New York *Tribune* witnessed the battle. Two other army correspondents, John T. Jacobs of the New York *Express* and a Philadelphia *Inquirer* reporter, fell into Confederate hands near Manassas Junction at the time of the battle or shortly before.
61. Said the Washington correspondent of the New York *Commercial Advertiser*, August 25, 1862: "Nothing relating either to the enemy or our forces is allowed to pass the censorship at the present time. This is the most strict rule put in force since the war." The Washington newspapers were still permitted, however, to publish substantially what they pleased about military operations.
62. Philadelphia *Press*, September 1, 1862. See also New York *Evening Post*, September 2, 1862, for an editorial commenting that General Halleck had readmitted to his lines the correspondents whom his orders previously had excluded.
63. Chicago *Times*, September 4, 1862.
64. New York *Times*, September 2, 1862; J. T. Scharf and Thompson Westcott, *History of Philadelphia* (Philadelphia, 1884), I, 802. According to Allan Nevins, *The Evening Post* (New York, 1922), p. 322, a similar panic was precipitated in New York the same day by a false report that Pope had

been driven back to Alexandria and defeated by the Confederates within sight of Washington.

65. New York *Daily Tribune*, September 8, 1862.

66. J. T. Morse, Jr., *Diary of Gideon Welles* (Boston and New York, 1911), I, 100-105; S. P. Chase, *Diary and Correspondence*, In *American Historical Association, Annual Report for 1902*, II (Washington, D.C., 1903), 62-65.

67. From an extract of a letter from Sydney Howard Gay to Adams S. Hill cited in Rhodes, *op. cit.*, IV, 137n. On September 5, 1862, an editorial in the Chicago *Tribune* stated that the newspaper had refrained from publishing a highly interesting letter from its Washington correspondent. The editorial went on to say that the letter accused an unnamed general of "wilfully withholding aid from his own friends in their dire extremity—aid which he had been ordered three days before to send forward." Subsequently (September 16) the *Tribune* revealed that the general was McClellan.

68. Even the Washington correspondent of the Chicago *Tribune*, no friend of McClellan, testified to his popularity in the army at this time. "I have disbelieved the reports of the army's affection for McClellan, being entirely unable to account for the phenomenon," he asserted. "I cannot account for it to my satisfaction now, but I accept it as a fact." Chicago *Daily Tribune*, September 9, 1862.

69. Freeman, *R. E. Lee*, II, 354-355.

70. New York *Herald*, August 23, 1862. See also Boston *Daily Journal*, August 25, 1862; St. Louis *Daily Missouri Republican*, August 25, 1862.

71. C. C. Coffin, *The Boys of '61* (Boston, 1896), pp. 140-141; Washington *Evening Star*, September 6, 1862; Philadelphia *Inquirer*, September 8, 1862; Boston *Daily Journal*, September 10, 1862.

72. G. W. Smalley, *Anglo-American Memories* (New York and London, 1911), 1st Ser., p. 138; Smalley, "Chapters in Journalism," *Harper's New Monthly Magazine*, LXXXIX (August, 1894), 427; A. D. Richardson, *The Secret Service, the Field, the Dungeon, and the Escape* (Hartford, 1865), p. 278.

73. W. W. Harding to Uriah H. Painter, September 8, 1862, Painter Papers.

74. L. A. Whitely to Frederic Hudson, September 10, 1862, Bennett Papers. In all probability the *Herald* staff was using a cipher to circumvent the censorship. An ingenious cipher utilized by the Washington office of Jay Cooke's banking firm to provide the Philadelphia office with war news during the Antietam campaign is described in E. P. Oberholtzer, *Jay Cooke, Financier of the Civil War* (Philadelphia, 1907), I, 207. For the simple substitution cipher used by the New York *World* during the Antietam campaign, see Manton Marble to E. C. Stedman, September 1, 1862, Stedman Papers.

75. Chicago *Times*, September 19, 1862. Samples of newspaper speculation on Lee's destination will be found in New York *Daily Tribune*, September 12, 1862; Boston *Daily Journal*, September 15, 1862; H. M. Flint to Frederic Hudson, September 10, 1862, Bennett Papers.

76. R. U. Johnson and C. C. Buel, *Battles and Leaders of the Civil War* (New York, 1884-1888), II, 603. The most likely explanation for this blunder is that General D. H. Hill, whose division was

operating as an independent command, received two copies of the order, one from general headquarters and the other from General Jackson, who apparently thought that Hill was attached to his command. The copy received from general headquarters was permitted to go astray; the other was retained.

77. Crounse, *op. cit.*, pp. 632-633.
78. Smalley, *Anglo-American Memories*, 1st Ser., p. 140.
79. T. L. Livermore, *Numbers and Losses in the Civil War in America, 1861-1865* (Boston and New York, 1900), pp. 90-91.
80. J. W. Forney to John R. Young, September 15, 1862, Young Papers.
81. Geer, *op. cit.*, p. 158.
82. Boston *Daily Journal*, September 19, 1862. The correspondent of the New York *World* at Frederick telegraphed his newspaper Tuesday evening, September 16, that 10,000 Union troops had surrendered to the enemy at Harper's Ferry. According to an editorial published in the *World*, September 18, the government censor marked out the "ten" and replaced it with a "six." On the same evening the Washington correspondent of the *World* was permitted to telegraph that only 4,000 Federal troops had been captured. The number surrendered was actually 11,200. *O.R.* (Army), Ser. I, vol. xix, Pt. 1, p. 519.
83. New York *Daily Tribune*, September 18, 1862. A military commission headed by Major General David Hunter subsequently determined that Harper's Ferry had been surrendered largely because of the "incapacity, amounting to almost imbecility" of the commanding officer, Colonel Dixon S. Miles. The commission also decided that Maryland Heights, the key to the position, "was prematurely surrendered." *O.R.* (Army), Ser. I, vol. xix, Pt. 1, p. 799.
84. New York *Times*, September 18, 1862.
85. Richardson, *op. cit.*, pp. 280-282.
86. W. H. Hebert, *Fighting Joe Hooker* (Indianapolis and New York, 1944), p. 140; New York *Times*, September 20, 1862.
87. Thomas S. Townsend Scrapbooks, LXXXVI, 526. Key later was dismissed from the service for having said that it "was not the game" to bag the enemy after the Sharpsburg engagement and that the true policy for preserving the Union was to "tire the rebels . . . and ourselves" in order that fraternal feeling might be restored and slavery saved. J. G. Nicolay and John Hay, *Abraham Lincoln, Complete Works* (New York, 1905), VIII, 46-47. For a contrasting view of Key, see Cox, *op. cit.*, I, 354-355.
88. Coffin, *op. cit.*, p. 115.
89. C. C. Coffin, "Antietam Scenes," *Century Magazine*, New Ser. X (June, 1886), p. 316; W. E. Griffis, *Charles Carleton Coffin* (Boston, 1898), pp. 120-121.
90. *O.R.* (Army) Ser. I, vol. xix, Pt. 1, p. 55.
91. Ropes and Livermore, *op. cit.*, Pt. II, p. 377; U.S. House Executive Documents, *Exec. Doc. 15*, 38 Cong., 1 sess., p. 214.
92. *Wilkes' Spirit of the Times*, VII (February 7, 1863), 360.
93. Smalley, *Anglo-American Memories*, 1st Ser., pp. 146-147.
94. Coffin, *The Boys of '61*, p. 149.
95. Boston *Daily Journal*, September 23, 1862.
96. Smalley, "Chapters in Journalism," pp. 428-429.
97. The exact time Burnside received the order to advance has been the

subject of considerable controversy. Both Burnside's and McClellan's official reports of Antietam agree in fixing the time that the order was communicated to Burnside as "10 o'clock" A.M. In his official report of the operations of the Army of the Potomac under his command, submitted almost a year later, however, McClellan stated that the order for Burnside to carry the bridge in his front was first sent to him "at 8 o'clock." From the text of the order published in *O.R.* (Army), Ser. I, vol. li, Pt. 1, p. 844, dated "September 17, 1862 —9:10 A.M.," it would appear that Burnside's estimate was substantially correct.

98. The Confederate loss was probably in excess of 13,000 men, killed, wounded, and missing; that of the Union army was placed at 12,410. Livermore, *op. cit.,* pp. 92-93.

99. Richardson, *op. cit.,* p. 286.

100. Smalley, *Anglo-American Memories,* 1st Ser., pp. 150-152; Smalley, "Chapters in Journalism," pp. 429-430.

101. Smalley's battle account was reprinted in the New York *Times,* September 20, 1862; Baltimore *American and Commercial Advertiser,* September 22, 1862; Cincinnati *Daily Commercial,* September 22, 1862; St. Louis *Daily Missouri Democrat,* September 25, 1862, and in approximately 1,400 other newspapers throughout the country. A special correspondent of the Cincinnati *Daily Commercial,* September 25, 1862, wrote "whoever has read the account of it [Antietam] published in the New York Tribune will have as clear and accurate a conception of its general features as can or will be given." For further enthusiastic comments about Smalley's work, see New York *Evening Post,* September 19, 1862; Chicago *Tribune,* September 28, 1862.

102. Henry Villard, *Memoirs* (Boston and New York, 1904), I, 335; Richardson, *op. cit.,* p. 286. For an adverse comment on Smalley's reporting, see W. H. Hebert, *op. cit.,* p. 140.

103. New York *Daily Tribune,* September 23, 1862.

104. Coffin, *The Boys of '61,* p. 159. For an enthusiastic appraisal of Coffin's Antietam story, see Chicago *Daily Tribune,* October 23, 1862.

105. New York *Herald,* September 19, 1862. J. P. Dunn of the *Herald* was with Burnside's Ninth Corps on the Union left. Sawyer, Hendricks, Talcott, Hosmer, and Ward were other *Herald* correspondents at Antietam.

106. Ben Perley Poore, Boston *Daily Journal,* September 17, 1862.

107. The apologia of the *Inquirer* correspondent at Antietam appeared in the Philadelphia *Inquirer,* September 22, 1862.

108. New York *World,* September 20, 1862.

109. Boston *Daily Journal,* September 24, 1862.

110. Richmond *Enquirer,* September 23, 1862; Frank Moore, *The Rebellion Record* (New York, 1861-1873), V, 476.

111. Charleston *Daily Courier,* September 29, 1862; Moore, *op. cit.,* V, 475.

112. *Daily Richmond Whig,* October 4, 1862.

113. New York *Herald,* September 18, 1862.

114. Philadelphia *Press,* September 18, 1862; Philadelphia *Inquirer,* September 19, 1862.

115. St. Louis *Daily Missouri Democrat,* September 22, 1862.

116. New York *Herald,* September 20, 1862.
117. George Meade, *Life and Letters* (New York, 1913), I, 315.
118. A newspaper correspondent for the Philadelphia *Press.*
119. Meade, *op. cit.,* I, 312.
120. See e.g., New York *Herald,* September 20, 1862.
121. Cincinnati *Daily Gazette,* October 2, 1862; T. C. Grey to Sydney Howard Gay, June 2, 1863, Gay Papers. No reference to misconduct by Meagher at Antietam appears in the sketch of his life given in the *Dictionary of American Biography* or in any of the biographies of Meagher. McClellan's official report of the battle, *O.R.* (Army), Ser. I, vol. xix, Pt. 1, p. 59, states specifically that Meagher was "disabled by the fall of his horse, shot under him." For a statement by another correspondent about Meagher's cowardice in a subsequent battle, *vide infra* pp. 327-328.
122. In his article on army reporting published in the *Nation,* I (July 27, 1865), 115, Henry Villard expressed the opinion that the Antietam campaign "gave occasion to the greatest successes accomplished by the correspondents." He added, "The quickness and range of comprehension, fulness of correct information, and expeditious working up for publication displayed by a representative of one of the New York papers were truly admirable."
123. S. W. Fiske, *Mr. Dunn Browne's Experiences in the Army* (Boston and New York, 1866), p. 47. Among the dead, however, were two Union corps commanders, Mansfield and Jesse L. Reno, and two division commanders, Richardson and Isaac P. Rodman.
124. *O.R.* (Army), Ser. I, vol. xix, Pt. 2, p. 322.
125. New York *Daily Tribune,* September 26, 1862.

12
ON THE MARCH WITH BUELL AND ROSECRANS
Pages 286-314

1. W. F. G. Shanks, *Personal Recollections of Distinguished Generals* (New York, 1866), p. 246; *O.R.* (Army), Ser. I, vol. xvi, Pt. 1, p. 107. In a letter published in the Chicago *Tribune,* September 5, 1862, an army correspondent of that newspaper stated that Buell "is very bitter on them [the correspondents]. I suppose it is because they are so bitter on him."
2. William S. Furay to Richard Smith, July 6, 1862, Office of the Secretary of War, Letters Received, National Archives. Furay's letter appeared as an enclosure in a letter from Smith to Congressman John A. Gurley, who promptly forwarded it to the War Department.
3. Henry Villard, *Memoirs* (Boston and New York, 1904), I, 292; H. M. Cist, *The Army of the Cumberland* (New York, 1882), pp. 43-45.
4. New York *Herald,* July 25, 1862.
5. *Ibid.,* August 1, 1862.
6. Philadelphia *Press,* August 12, 1862.
7. J. B. Fry, *Operations of the Army under Buell* (New York, 1884), pp. 37-38.
8. The fight at Richmond is described at greater length in N. S. Shaler, *Kentucky, A Pioneer Commonwealth* (Boston and New York, 1888), pp. 291-293; T. D. Clark, *History of Kentucky* (New York, 1937), pp. 457-458.
9. Cincinnati *Daily Commercial,* September 6, 1862; Cincinnati *Daily Gazette,* September 6, 8, 1862; T. W. Knox, *Camp-Fire and Cotton-Field* (Philadelphia and Cincinnati, 1865), p. 487.

10. Cincinnati *Daily Gazette,* September 5, 1862; New York *Daily Tribune,* September 5, 1862; H. A. and K. B. Ford, *History of Cincinnati, Ohio* (Cleveland, 1881), p. 117.
11. New York *Daily Tribune,* September 12, 1862.
12. New York *Herald,* September 15, 1862.
13. Fry, *op. cit.,* pp. 45-47; Cist, *op. cit.,* pp. 57-59.
14. Villard, *op. cit.,* I, 304-305.
15. Chicago *Times,* September 26, 30, 1862.
16. Cincinnati *Daily Gazette,* September 25, 1862.
17. Philadelphia *Inquirer,* September 23, 1862.
18. New York *Daily Tribune,* September 26, 1862.
19. Identified by McCullagh (Cincinnati *Daily Commercial,* September 30, 1862) as Henry Villard. However, Villard, *op. cit.,* I, 305, indicates that he was with McCook's corps marching northward toward Louisville at the time this incident supposedly occurred. It is difficult to understand how McCullagh could have confused Villard with some other reporter since he mentions Villard's name several times in the course of his narrative, which he composed within a day or two after the experience. Villard's memoirs, on the other hand, are the recollections of an elderly man written many years later and may not be altogether trustworthy in time element. I have therefore included the incident as told by McCullagh, reserving judgment whether it was actually Villard or someone else who accompanied the Cincinnati *Commercial* reporter on the trip to Elizabethtown.
20. Cincinnati *Daily Times,* September 30, 1862; Chicago *Times,* October 3 1862; Villard, *op. cit.,* I, 308-309. See also J. B. Fry, *Military Miscellanies* (New York, 1889), pp. 486-505; W. D. Foulke, *Life of Oliver P. Morton* (Indianapolis and Kansas City, 1899), I, 194-195. *Dictionary of American Biography,* V, 131; XVII, 426.
21. Freeman Cleaves, *Rock of Chickamauga* (Norman, Oklahoma, 1948), pp. 112-113; New York *Times,* October 10, 1862.
22. Chicago *Times,* October 10, 1862.
23. Fry, *Operations of the Army under Buell,* pp. 57-59.
24. Villard, *op. cit.,* I, 312.
25. *O.R.* (Army), Ser. I, vol. xvi, Pt. 1, p. 1023; P. H. Sheridan, *Personal Memoirs* (New York, 1888), I, 199; J. C. Ropes and W. L. Livermore, *The Story of the Civil War* (New York and London, 1894-1913), Pt II, p. 409.
26. Cincinnati *Daily Gazette,* October 13, 1862; Frank Moore, *The Rebellion Record* (New York, 1861-1873), V, 528.
27. Villard, *op. cit.,* I, 317-318.
28. Shanks, *op. cit.,* pp. 249-250.
29. Villard, *op. cit.,* I, 319.
30. For a more comprehensive treatment of the Battle of Perryville, see Hambleton Tapp, "The Battle of Perryville, 1862," *Filson Club History Quarterly,* IX (July, 1935), 158-181; R. U. Johnson and C. C. Buel, *Battles and Leaders of the Civil War* (New York, 1884-1888), III, 14-18, 47-49, 52-59; Ropes and Livermore, *op. cit.,* II, 407-410. Official reports of Buell and Bragg, *O.R.* (Army), Ser. I, vol. xvi, Pt. 1, 1022-1032, 1087-1094.
31. Alfred Burnett, *Incidents of the War* (Cincinnati, 1863), pp. 17-18.
32. New York *Times,* October 17, 1862.
33. Cincinnati *Daily Commercial,* October 18, 1862.

34. Cincinnati *Daily Times,* October 13, 1862.
35. Chicago *Times,* October 15, 1862.
36. Chicago *Daily Tribune,* October 28, 1862.
37. *Ibid.,* October 24, 1862.
38. New York *Daily Tribune,* October 25, 1862.
39. Royal Cortissoz, *The Life of Whitelaw Reid* (New York, 1921), I, 92; Cincinnati *Daily Gazette,* October 16, 1862. See also two letters from Whitelaw Reid to his brother G. W. Reid, October 13, 16, 1862, Reid Papers.
40. Philadelphia *Press,* October 16, 1862. See also S. F. Horn, "Nashville during the Civil War," *Tennessee Historical Quarterly,* IV (March, 1945), 13-15.
41. Philadelphia *Press,* January 5, 1863.
42. R. W. Winston, *Andrew Johnson, Plebeian and Patriot* (New York, 1928), pp. 236-237.
43. New York *Herald,* November 22, 1862; Philadelphia *Press,* October 8, 1862.
44. Cist, *op. cit.,* p. 81.
45. New York *Herald,* November 27, 1862.
46. Walter Geer, *Campaigns of the Civil War* (New York, 1926), p. 199.
47. New York *Herald,* November 27, 1862.
48. Cincinnati *Daily Commercial,* December 20, 1862.
49. *Vide infra* pp. 323-327.
50. New York *Herald,* January 7, 1863.
51. Cincinnati *Daily Commercial,* January 5, 1863.
52. Cleaves, *op. cit.,* p. 124.
53. Cincinnati *Daily Commercial,* January 5, 1863.
54. New York *Herald,* January 7, 1863. In a letter to the author, October 13, 1954, Professor Bell I. Wiley, Emory University, expressed the opinion that the *Herald* reporter who made this statement was "grossly distorting the facts." He added: "I have found nothing that would indicate a willful neglect of the wounded by either side."
55. See e.g., Philadelphia *Inquirer,* January 2, 1863.
56. Cist, *op. cit.,* p. 99.
57. T. B. Van Horne, *The Life of Major-General George H. Thomas* (New York, 1882), pp. 91-92.
58. New York *Herald,* January 9, 1863.
59. Sill had been killed earlier that morning.
60. Cincinnati *Daily Gazette,* January 8, 1863.
61. Cleaves, *op. cit.,* p. 127.
62. New York *Herald,* January 9, 1863.
63. Philadelphia *Press,* January 9, 1863.
64. Cleaves, *op. cit.,* p. 129.
65. Cincinnati *Daily Times,* January 10, 1863. This was the second account of the battle transmitted by the *Times* reporter, his first having been intercepted by the enemy.
66. St. Louis *Daily Missouri Republican,* January 9, 1863.
67. For a more detailed analysis of the Battle of Murfreesboro, see Cist, *op. cit.,* pp. 102-135; Johnson and Buel, *op. cit.,* III, 613-634; Geer, *op. cit.,* pp. 199-205.
68. Chicago *Times,* January 9, 1863.
69. St. Louis *Daily Missouri Republican,* January 24, 1863.
70. New York *Times,* January 5, 1863.
71. New York *Herald,* January 10, 1863.
72. Philadelphia *Press,* January 16, 1863.
73. New York *Daily Tribune,* January 5, 1863.
74. Chicago *Daily Tribune,* January 9, 1863.

75. Cincinnati *Daily Gazette,* January 8, 1863.
76. New York *Herald,* January 9, 1863; Cincinnati *Daily Commercial,* January 8, 1863.
77. New York *Daily Tribune,* January 5, 9, 1863; New York *Times,* January 6, 9, 1863.
78. Cincinnati *Daily Commercial,* January 15, 1863.
79. Chicago *Daily Tribune,* January 9, 1863.
80. W. W. Harding to Uriah H. Painter, January 7, 1863, Painter Papers.
81. Chicago *Daily Tribune,* January 15, 1863.
82. The Union casualties (killed, wounded, and missing) amounted to 12,267, approximately 28 per cent of the total force engaged. The Confederates lost over 10,000 men, roughly 25 per cent of their number. Johnson and Buel, *op. cit.,* III, 632; W. F. Fox, *Regimental Losses in the American Civil War* (Albany, New York, 1898), pp. 544, 550.

13

"DON'T TREAT . . . FREDERICKSBURG AS A DISASTER"

Pages 315-336

1. An army correspondent of the New York *Herald.*
2. Finley Anderson to Frederic Hudson, September 26, 1862. Bennett Papers.
3. F. A. Macartney to Horace Greeley, September 30, 1862. This letter was forwarded to the Secretary of War, along with a letter from Greeley to Stanton, dated October 2, 1862, Office of Secretary of War, Letters Received, National Archives.
4. L. A. Whitely to James Gordon Bennett, September 24, 1862, Bennett Papers.
5. J. F. Rhodes, *History of the U.S. from the Compromise of 1850* (New York and London, 1928), IV, 184-185.
6. J. M. Winchell to William C. Church, September 29, 1862, William Conant Church Papers, Library of Congress.
7. New York *Daily Tribune,* October 4, 1862.
8. *O.R.* (Army), Ser. I, vol. xix, Pt. 1, p. 72.
9. Walter Geer, *Campaigns of the Civil War* (New York, 1926), p. 175.
10. A. B. Talcott to Frederic Hudson, October 19, 1862, Bennett Papers.
11. Sydney Howard Gay to S. Draper, October 28, 1862, Stanton Papers.
12. Chicago *Daily Tribune,* October 29, 1862. See also St. Louis *Daily Missouri Republican,* October 27, 1862; New York *Herald,* October 28, 1862.
13. New York *Herald,* October 31, 1862; New York *Daily Tribune,* November 3, 1862. A reference to an order, issued by McClellan on or just before November 2, threatening to penalize certain Baltimore and Philadelphia newspapers "unless they cease from divulging every movement of our army" appeared in the New York *Times,* November 6, 1862.
14. New York *Times,* October 30, 1862.
15. Rhodes, *op. cit.,* IV, 188; J. G. Nicolay and John Hay, *Abraham Lincoln, A History* (New York, *ca.* 1914), VI, 188-189.
16. Philadelphia *Inquirer,* November 11, 1862; Chicago *Times,* November 19, 1862; George W. Adams to Manton Marble, November 10, 1862, Marble Papers.
17. Chicago *Daily Tribune,* November 12, 1862; New York *Daily Tribune,* November 14, 1862; A. D. Rich-

ardson, *The Secret Service, the Field, the Dungeon, and the Escape* (Hartford, 1865), p. 303. McClellan had the officers placed under arrest and subsequently apologized to Richardson for what he termed a "cowardly and shameful act."

18. New York *Times*, November 13, 1862.
19. *Ibid.*, November 13, 1862.
20. Henry Villard, *Memoirs* (Boston and New York, 1904), I, 338. Villard's colleague Richardson informed Gay, however, that "I am very sure of one thing: Whenever he [Burnside] gets a positive order to Go, he will Go if it breaks his neck." Albert D. Richardson to Sydney Howard Gay, *ca.* December 5, 1862, Gay Papers.
21. Hooker had acquired this nickname, through a typesetter's error, during the Peninsular Campaign of 1862. At three o'clock one morning, as the New York papers were about to go to press, a last-minute dispatch from the AP came in with additional news of the fighting involving Hooker's division. At the top of the dispatch was written "Fighting – Joe Hooker." Several typesetters, not realizing that this dispatch was to be added on to the previous copy, printed it separately under the heading "Fighting Joe Hooker." The expression caught on and, much to his distaste, Hooker was known as "Fighting Joe" thereafter. W. F. G. Shanks, *Personal Recollections of Distinguished Generals* (New York, 1866), pp. 189-190.
22. E. D. Townsend, *Anecdotes of the Civil War in the United States* (New York, 1884), p. 87. W. H. Hebert in his *Fighting Joe Hooker* (Indianapolis and New York, 1944), p. 148, likewise states: "It was generally conceded in the army that if McClellan were removed Hooker would succeed him."
23. Villard, *op. cit.*, I, 347.
24. *Ibid.*, p. 348.
25. William A. Babcock to Uriah H. Painter, December 7, 1862, Painter Papers. Hooker's willingness to grant an interview to Babcock is rather surprising, for, three days earlier he had written Stanton: "I send herewith a slip from the Philadelphia Enquirer [sic] of yesterday's date." Hooker went on to say: "I wish that you could chalk the newspapers. They are a nuisance in their effects on certain minds. . . . I have no doubt but that Burnside would have permitted me to have marched from Warrenton to Fredericksburgh on the south bank of the Rappahannock but from my newspaper connection with the command of this Army." Gen. Joseph Hooker to Edwin M. Stanton, December 4, 1862, Stanton Papers.
26. *O.R.* (Army), Ser. I, vol. xix, Pt. 2, p. 579.
27. New York *Daily Tribune*, November 21, 1862.
28. K. P. Williams, *Lincoln Finds a General* (New York, 1949), II, 511-512.
29. *O.R.* (Army), Ser. I, vol xxi, p. 1035.
30. New York *Daily Tribune*, November 22, 1862. A garbled version of this dialogue appears in Carl Sandburg, *Abraham Lincoln, The War Years* (New York, 1939), I, 626, based apparently on Richardson's statement, *op. cit.*, pp. 303-304. There is a discrepancy, however, between the quotation reproduced in Richardson three years after the conversation allegedly took place and the Sandburg version. For an account given by an unnamed Southern war correspondent of a

similar conversation between Union and Confederate pickets, see F. G. De Fontaine, *Marginalia* (Columbia, South Carolina, 1864), pp. 113-114.

31. C. C. Coffin, *The Boys of '61* (Boston, 1896), p. 139; Chicago *Daily Tribune,* November 30, 1862.
32. B. P. Poore, *The Life and Public Services of Ambrose E. Burnside* (Providence, Rhode Island, 1882), p. 186; Coffin, *op. cit.,* pp. 139-140.
33. New York *Times,* December 5, 1862.
34. *Ibid.,* November 27, 1862.
35. Cincinnati *Daily Commercial,* December 18, 1862.
36. William Swinton, *Campaigns of the Army of the Potomac* (New York, 1866), pp. 238-239.
37. Coffin, *op. cit.,* p. 186; Boston *Daily Journal,* December 16, 1862.
38. *O.R.* (Army), Ser. I, vol. xxi, pp. 89, 167-168, 169-171.
39. New York *Times,* December 13, 1862.
40. Cincinnati *Daily Commercial,* December 18, 1862.
41. New York *Daily Tribune,* December 13, 1862; Chicago *Daily Tribune,* December 13, 1862; Chicago *Times,* December 19, 1862. At this time Fredericksburg was connected with Washington by only a single telegraph wire, mainly used for government business.
42. Villard, *op. cit.,* I, 363.
43. *O.R.* (Army), Ser. I, vol. xxi, pp. 450, 511.
44. Boston *Daily Journal,* December 17, 1862.
45. Williams, *op. cit.,* II, 532-533; R. U. Johnson and C. C. Buel, *Battles and Leaders of the Civil War* (New York, 1884-1888), III, 111.
46. Cincinnati *Daily Commercial,* December 18, 1862.
47. Johnson and Buel, *op. cit.,* III, 79-81.
48. Frank Moore, *The Rebellion Record* (New York, 1861-1873), VI, 107.
49. Williams, *op. cit.,* II, 532.
50. Villard, *op. cit.,* I, 371.
51. Nathaniel Paige, J. Warren Newcomb, and R. D. Francis.
52. One of the army correspondents of the Philadelphia *Inquirer.*
53. William A. Babcock to Uriah H. Painter, December 14, 1862, Painter Papers.
54. Villard, *op. cit.,* I, 385-388.
55. J. T. Morse, Jr., *Diary of Gideon Welles* (Boston and New York, 1911), I, 192. See also St. Louis *Daily Missouri Republican,* December 22, 1862.
56. Villard, *op. cit.,* I, 389.
57. New York *Times,* December 17, 1862.
58. Cincinnati *Daily Commercial,* December 18, 1862.
59. Villard, *op. cit.,* I, 389.
60. *Ibid.,* p. 390.
61. *Ibid.,* p. 391.
62. Herman Haupt, *Reminiscences* (Milwaukee, 1901), p. 177.
63. New York *Times,* December 18, 1862.
64. Noah Brooks, *Washington in Lincoln's Time* (New York, 1895), p. 40.
65. New York *Evening Post,* December 16, 1862.
66. New York *Times,* December 27, 1862.
67. New York *Herald,* December 23, 1862.
68. L. A. Gobright, *Recollections of Men and Things at Washington* (Philadelphia, 1869), p. 318.
69. Cincinnati *Daily Gazette,* December 22, 1862. See also various

Baltimore newspapers, December 18, 1862.

70. An army correspondent of the Philadelphia *Inquirer*.

71. George C. Bower to Uriah H. Painter, December 17, 1862, Painter Papers.

72. George C. Bower to Uriah H. Painter, December 15, 1862, Painter Papers.

73. New York *Times*, December 17, 1862. In a letter written to his brother from Washington, December 18, 1862, Stedman remarked: "The papers (. . . — the *Times* account is the best) will tell you the sickening details." Laura Stedman and G. M. Gould, *Life and Letters of Edmund Clarence Stedman* (New York, 1910), I, 299. A similar characterization of Swinton's account will be found in the Lancaster (Pennsylvania) *Daily Express*, December 18, 1862.

74. New York *Daily Tribune*, December 16, 1862. Villard's account appeared in only a part of the *Tribune*'s morning edition, December 15.

75. Boston *Daily Journal*, December 18, 1862.

76. Cincinnati *Daily Commercial*, December 18, 1862. See also Moore, *op. cit.*, VI, 94-101.

77. "Our Historical Writers," *Historical Magazine and Notes and Queries*, New Ser. XVI (November, 1869), 296.

78. New York *Herald*, December 14, 1862.

79. George G. Meade to Mrs. George G. Meade, December 17, 1862. G. G. Meade, *Life and Letters* (New York, 1913), I, 338-339.

80. David B. Birney to James Gordon Bennett, March 28, 1864, Bennett Papers. Birney had been charged with failing to support Meade adequately during the Battle of Fredericksburg, but a careful investigation of these charges cleared Birney.

81. John W. Forney to John R. Young, December 16, 1862, Young Papers.

82. Philadelphia *Press*, December 17, 1862.

83. New York *World*, December 17, 1862; New York *Herald*, December 16, 17, 19, 1862; R. R. Fahrney, *Horace Greeley and the Tribune in the Civil War* (Cedar Rapids, Iowa, 1936), p. 138.

84. Sandburg, *op. cit.*, I, 632.

85. Albert D. Richardson to Sydney Howard Gay, December 17, 1862, Gay Papers.

86. Johnson and Buel, *op. cit.*, III, 84.

14

BY-LINES BY GENERAL ORDER

Pages 337-373

1. An army supply base on the West bank of the Potomac estuary below Aquia Creek.

2. H. W. Raymond, "Extracts from the Journal of Henry J. Raymond," *Scribner's Monthly*, XIX (January 1880), 419-420; A. D. Richardson, *The Secret Service, the Field, the Dungeon, and the Escape* (Hartford, 1865), p. 307.

3. Boston *Daily Journal*, December 24, 1862.

4. William A. Babcock to Uriah H. Painter, December 23, 1862, Painter Papers.

5. S. M. Carpenter to Frederic Hudson, January 21, 1863, Bennett Papers. See also Washington *Evening Star*, January 22, 1863; New York *Times*, January 23, 24, 1863; St. Louis *Daily Missouri Republican*, January 29, 1863. On February 4, 1863, W. W. Harding wired his brother: "Sid Deming says there is not a word of truth in Painter's Special about his being interested

in any contracts since the peninsula campaign & this could not be the reason of the order for the arrest. He wants Inquirer to retrace [retract?] the statement." W. W. Harding to J. B. Harding, February 4, 1863, Painter Papers.

6. Raymond, *op. cit.*, p. 422.
7. *Ibid.*, p. 424. The Swinton letter to which Burnside referred appeared in the New York *Times*, January 16, 1863.
8. Raymond, *op. cit.*, p. 705.
9. New York *Times*, February 12, 1863.
10. S. M. Carpenter to Frederic Hudson, February 2, 1863, Bennett Papers.
11. Walter Geer, *Campaigns of the Civil War* (New York, 1926), p. 208; W. H. Hebert, *Fighting Joe Hooker* (Indianapolis and New York, 1944), pp. 183-184.
12. Noah Brooks, *Washington in Lincoln's Time* (New York, 1895), p. 52.
13. *Ibid.*, p. 53.
14. Hooker, of course, was removed from command the same year. His letter first was published in the Providence *Journal*, May 6, 1879. The complete text of the letter is also to be found in J. G. Nicolay and John Hay, *Abraham Lincoln, Complete Works* (New York, 1905), VIII, 206-207.
15. L. A. Whitely to Frederic Hudson, March 16, 1863, Bennett Papers; L. A. Whitely to S. M. Carpenter, March 17, 1863; A. H. Caldwell to Thomas T. Eckert, March 18, 1863, Office of Secretary of War, Telegrams Received, National Archives; Philadelphia *Inquirer*, March 18, 23, 1863; New York *Times*, March 23, 1863.
16. R. S. West, Jr., *Gideon Welles* (Indianapolis and New York, 1943), p. 218; Report of the Joint Committee on the Conduct of the War, *Senate Report No. 108*, 1863, Pt. III, p. 421.
17. A. K. McClure, *Old Time Notes of Pennsylvania* (Philadelphia, 1905), II, 77.
18. Henry Villard, *Memoirs* (Boston and New York, 1904), II, 12.
19. *Ibid.*, p. 13.
20. New York *Times*, March 2, 1863. According to *O.R.* (Army), Ser. II, vol. vi, p. 62, Gladding was still in Federal custody at Hilton Head as late as June 29, 1863.
21. S. R. Glen to an unidentified member of the *Herald* staff (probably Bennett), February 23, 1863, Bennett Papers.
22. A. B. Paine, *A Sailor of Fortune* (New York, 1906), p. 224.
23. *O.R.* (Navy), Ser. I, vol. xiii, p. 549. For a general order later issued by Rear Admiral Porter, October 21, 1864, stating that naval officers under his command were forbidden to act as newspaper correspondents, see *ibid.*, vol. x, p. 576.
24. Paine, *op. cit.*, p. 245.
25. Villard, *op. cit.*, II, 13; Henry Villard to Murat Halstead, February 18, 1863, Murat Halstead Papers, Historical and Philosophical Society of Ohio, Cincinnati.
26. J. T. Morse, Jr., *Diary of Gideon Welles* (Boston and New York, 1911), I, 236-237. Apparently Lincoln's estimate of DuPont was similar to that of Welles. See *ibid.*, I, 259, 265; M. V. Dahlgren, *Memoir of John A. Dahlgren* (Boston, 1882), p. 389.
27. R. M. Thompson and Richard Wainwright, *Confidential Correspondence of Gustavus Vasa Fox* (New York, 1920), I, 187.
28. Philadelphia *Inquirer*, April 16, 1863.

29. New York *Times,* April 14, 1863.
30. New York *Daily Tribune,* April 14, 1863; Villard, *op. cit.,* II, 47.
31. Boston *Daily Journal,* April 15, 1863. According to the New York *Times,* April 16, 1863, the London *Times* correspondent Charles Mackay went on board the "Circassian" off Hilton Head "to be a spectator of our Monitors' attack on Charleston." No eyewitness account of the fight appeared in the London *Times,* however.
32. New York *Times,* April 15, 1863.
33. So called in honor of its builder, C. W. Whitney.
34. *O.R.* (Navy), Ser. I, vol. xiv, pp. 8-9; G. E. Belknap, "Reminiscent of the Siege of Charleston," *Naval Actions and History, 1799-1898, Papers of the Military Historical Society of Massachusetts,* XII (1902), 157-207.
35. New York *Times,* April 14, 1863.
36. *O.R.* (Navy), Ser. I, vol. xiv, p. 6.
37. Baltimore *American and Commercial Advertiser,* April 15, 1863.
38. *O.R.* (Navy), Ser. I, vol. xiv, p. 28.
39. New York *Times,* April 14, 1863.
40. Boston *Daily Journal,* April 15, 1863; W. E. Griffis, *Charles Carleton Coffin* (Boston, 1898), pp. 135-136.
41. C. C. Coffin, *The Boys of '61* (Boston, 1886), pp. 255-256.
42. New York *Daily Tribune,* April 14, 1863.
43. New York *Times,* April 15, 1863.
44. D. W. Knox, *A History of the United States Navy* (New York, 1936), p. 269. More detailed reports of the damage sustained by the monitors are given in *O.R.* (Navy), Ser. I, vol. xiv, pp. 9-24.
45. New York *Times,* April 14, 1863.
46. Boston *Daily Journal,* April 15, 1863; Baltimore *American and Commercial Advertiser,* April 17, 1863.
47. Stimers was acquitted by the court martial but later resigned from the Navy after a disagreement with Welles, explained at some length in Morse, *op. cit.,* II, 349-351. For a critical view of Stimers' opinion, see H. A. Du Pont, *Rear-Admiral Samuel Francis Du Pont, United States Navy, A Biography* (New York, 1926), pp. 220-221.
48. Boston *Daily Journal,* April 15, 1863.
49. Baltimore *American and Commercial Advertiser,* April 15, 1863.
50. *Ibid.,* April 15, 1863.
51. *O.R.* (Navy), Ser. I, vol. xiv, p. 56. In his letter to DuPont, April 22, 1863, Boutelle informed the Admiral that "Mr. Fulton said it was his practice to use a 'manifold letter writer' in writing his notes, making several copies. One was mailed to his brother at Baltimore, and another copy was sent by the mail to Mr. Fox, Assistant Secretary of the Navy. Mr. Fulton went on to say that his brother did not publish the letter until sufficient time had elapsed for Mr. Fox to receive and examine the manuscript and telegraph to Baltimore if he objected to any portion thereof."
52. *O.R.* (Navy), Ser. I, vol. xiv, pp. 51-56.
53. *Ibid.,* p. 64.
54. *Ibid.,* pp. 63-64.
55. *Ibid.,* p. 111. The statement about "two embrasures being knocked into one" appeared in the *Herald's* April 14, 1863, account of the battle.
56. According to the *Herald* reporter, "no less than three hundred guns of the largest calibre concentrated their fire upon the eight assailants . . . ." In his official report of the

action, Beauregard attested that 76 guns of various caliber answered the fire of the fleet. Whereas the *Times* reporter estimated that "not less than thirty-five hundred round could have been fired by the rebels during the brief engagement," the correct figure was 2,209. In the opinion of the *Herald* reporter "the real instruments of our defeat were the apparently insignificant and contemptible barricades of rope-work and netting suspended across the channel . . . ." For evidence indicating that they really were insignificant, see J. R. Spears, *The History of Our Navy* (New York, 1899), IV, 469-470, 485; John Johnson, *The Defense of Charleston Harbor, 1863-1865* (Charleston, South Carolina, 1890), p. 60.

57. Baltimore *American and Commercial Advertiser,* April 15, 1863.

58. The armament of the "New Ironsides" consisted of fourteen 11-inch Dahlgren smooth-bore guns and two 150-pounder Parrott rifles of 8-inch caliber.

59. *O.R.* (Navy), Ser. I, vol. xiv, p. 27.

60. Charles Nordhoff, "Two Weeks at Port Royal," *Harper's New Monthly Magazine,* XXVII (June, 1863), 113. See also New York *Evening Post,* May 30, 1863.

61. Thomas M. Newbould to John W. Forney, April 14, 1863, Lincoln Papers. Newbould formerly had worked for Forney on the Philadelphia *Press.*

62. Geer, *op. cit.,* pp. 208-209. Estimates of the size of the two armies vary. Rhodes placed the total strength of Hooker's army at 130,000. Geer, however, estimates that not more than 105,000 men were available for combat on the Union side. See also John Bigelow, *The Campaign of Chancellorsville* (New Haven, 1910), pp. 132-134; D. S. Freeman, *R. E. Lee, A Biography* (New York and London, 1935), II, 506.

63. *O.R.* (Army), Ser. I, vol. xxv, Pt. 2, p. 239. For an explanation of how the Surgeon General's Office came to permit the copying of its report by the *Chronicle* reporter, see *ibid.,* pp. 240-241. Jonathan Letterman, *Medical Recollections of the Army of the Potomac* (New York, 1866), makes no mention of the incident.

64. Edwin M. Stanton to Major General Hooker, April 30, 1863 (1:10 P.M.), *O.R.* (Army), Ser. I, vol. xxv, Pt. 2, pp. 300-301.

65. New York *Herald,* May 2, 1863.

66. *O.R.* (Army), Ser. I, vol. xxv, Pt. 1, p. 171.

67. See Freeman, *op. cit.,* II, 514-516, for a discussion of the factors which led to Lee's decision.

68. J. F. Rhodes, *History of the United States from the Compromise of 1850* (New York, 1928), IV, 260.

69. G. F. R. Henderson, *Stonewall Jackson and the American Civil War* (London and New York, 1919), II, 432; Freeman, *op. cit.,* II, 520-524.

70. Geer, *op. cit.,* pp. 217-218. At 9:30 A.M. on May 2, however, Hooker sent a dispatch to Howard advising him to examine the ground to determine his position in case an attack were made on his flank; see Bigelow, *op. cit.,* pp. 266-267.

71. New York *Herald,* May 2, 1863; New York *Times,* May 2, 1863. For Vosburg's account of his visit to Libby Prison, see New York *Herald,* May 9, 1863.

72. Thomas S. Townsend Scrapbooks, LXXXVII, 41.

73. Cincinnati *Daily Gazette,* May 5, 1863.

74. New York *Herald,* May 7, 1863.

75. Cincinnati *Daily Gazette,* May 5, 1863.
76. New York *Herald,* May 6, 1863.
77. *O.R.* (Army), Ser. I, vol. xxv, Pt. 2, pp. 365-366.
78. New York *Times,* May 6, 1863.
79. Frank Moore, *The Rebellion Record* (New York, 1861-1873), VI, 598.
80. Hebert, *op. cit.,* p. 216.
81. New York *Times,* May 8, 1863.
82. K. P. Williams, *Lincoln Finds a General* (New York, 1949), II, 600.
83. New York *Herald,* May 9, 1863.
84. New York *Times,* May 11, 1863.
85. W. A. Croffut, *An American Procession* (Boston, 1931), p. 96.
86. Chicago *Daily Tribune,* May 7, 1863. The army correspondents of both the New York *Times* and *Tribune* evidently were instructed to use cipher dispatches in evading censorship. In the Crounse Papers is an undated key, presumably for use during the Chancellorsville campaign. For "Hooker will fight today" Crounse was instructed to say, "Will send you twelve pages tonight"; for "Hooker will fight tomorrow," "I must have another reporter." "Swinton's horse stolen long ago" was understood to mean "Battle nearly through. Enemy giving way everywhere. We will win great victory." For the *Tribune* code, see Josiah R. Sypher to Adams S. Hill, April 7, 1863, Gay Papers.
87. New York *Daily Tribune,* May 5, 1863.
88. New York *Times,* May 4, 1863.
89. Philadelphia *Press,* May 6, 1863. Swinton's account of the Battle of Chancellorsville subsequently appeared in revised form in his *Campaigns of the Army of the Potomac* (New York, 1866), pp. 267-307.
90. J. R. Gilmore, *Personal Recollections of Abraham Lincoln and the Civil War* (Boston, 1898), p. 103.
91. New York *Daily Tribune,* May 6, 1863.
92. New York *World,* May 8, 1863. Several newspapers reported the capture of large numbers of Confederate prisoners, and the Philadelphia *Bulletin* circulated a story, utterly without basis, that 30,000 men under General Heintzelman were being sent to reinforce Hooker. On May 6, the Washington correspondent of the Philadelphia *Press,* to prepare his readers for what was to follow, offered the remarkable opinion that even if Fredericksburg were recaptured by the enemy, the result would not necessarily be disastrous to the Union cause. "Our soldiers could easily return to this side of the Rappahannock," pontificated the *Press* man, "and as our guns planted on Falmouth Heights command the whole town, the place would soon be made too hot for the enemy." The *Press* did not explain why these same guns were not used for this highly desirable purpose before Sedgwick ever crossed the Rappahannock.
93. W. W. Harding to J. B. Harding, May 6, 1863, Painter Papers.
94. New York *Times,* May 8, 1863. The New York *Tribune,* still smarting from the indignity of having been beaten by the *Times,* already had succeeded, by use of its cipher, in slipping past the censor the news of Hooker's recrossing. Adams S. Hill to Sydney Howard Gay, May 7, 1863, Gay Papers.
95. Chicago *Daily Tribune,* May 19, 1863.
96. Pittsburgh *Evening Chronicle,* May 7, 1863; Pittsburgh *Post,* May 8, 1863. Hooker was so angry about Sypher's criticism that he ordered

the correspondent's arrest. Sypher, who was beyond the General's reach, dared not return to the Army of the Potomac until Hooker was removed from command.

97. Approximately a week after the Battle of Chancellorsville, Forney apologized to Lincoln because "my editor in chief in Philadelphia, usually discreet, fell into the grievous blunder of allowing a most ungenerous criticism upon Generals Halleck and Hooker to appear. I have not been surprised to hear that you were astonished to learn of these untimely and improper fault-findings." Forney went on to assure the President that "the instructions I have always given to the gentlemen connected with me, never to criticise the Government in its hours of peril and trouble, are now and hereafter will be, faithfully followed." John W. Forney to Abraham Lincoln, May 12, 1863, Lincoln Papers.

98. Boston *Daily Journal,* May 8, 1863.

99. A Washington correspondent of the New York *Times* declared that nothing so false had been published since the war began as "the military canards sent to New York on Saturday by two Philadelphia newspaper offices." Various explanations of the episode were given by the Cincinnati *Daily Gazette,* May 15, 1863, and the New York *Commercial Advertiser,* May 19, 1863. See also San Francisco *Bulletin,* May 11, 1863.

100. New York *Times,* May 28, 1863; Carl Schurz, *Reminiscences* (New York, 1907), II, 433, 438; S. W. Williams to Mr. Crounse, correspondent New York *Times,* May 11, 1863, Lorenzo Livingston Crounse Papers, in the possession of the Crounse family, Washington, D. C.

101. New York *Times,* May 28, 1863.

102. New York *Herald,* May 30, 1863. See also New York *Daily Tribune,* June 6, 1863, for an exposure of the *Herald's* attempt to shift the blame to the *Tribune.* Captain Samuel Fiske, the army correspondent of the Springfield *Republican,* likewise was criticized for the way he reported the battle. In a letter printed in the *Republican* he stated flatly that the Union officers had exhibited much greater courage at Chancellorsville than had the men in the ranks. Furthermore, he declared that he had seen very little real fighting at Chancellorsville and that Hooker's army had been driven from a position of its own choosing by a vastly inferior force. According to Fiske, "scores of newspapers came down with fury upon my poor little articles . . . and my sincerest friends chided me for my injudicious strictures." S. W. Fiske, *Mr. Dunn Browne's Experiences in the Army* (Boston and New York, 1866), pp. 151-152, 167, 169, 266.

103. William Swinton, "Hooker's Campaign Reviewed," *Historical Magazine and Notes and Queries,* II, (September, 1867), 161.

104. "Our Historical Writers," *Historical Magazine and Notes and Queries,* New Ser. VI (November, 1869), p. 296; Adam Gurowski, *Diary* (Boston, New York, and Washington, 1862-1866), II, 233.

105. Hooker evidently showed the effects of dissipation, however. In a letter to John C. Gray, May 30, 1863, the historian John C. Ropes remarked that "Shattuck [a Boston attorney] has seen Smalley, who wrote up Hooker in the *Tribune* last fall. He says Hooker is the mere wreck of what he was last fall. He has been played out by wine and women." J. C. Gray and J. C. Ropes, *War Letters, 1862-*

1865 (Boston and New York, 1927), p. 117.

106. G. W. Smalley, *Anglo-American Memories* (New York and London, 1911), 1st Ser., pp. 155-160.

15

SOME "CASUALTIES" AMONG THE BOHEMIANS

Pages 374-405

1. Walter Wellman, "Of De B. Randolph Keim," *The Keim and Allied Families,* No. 23 (October, 1900), 720.
2. Major General Earl Van Dorn, then in charge of the defense of Vicksburg.
3. Thomas W. Knox to James Gordon Bennett, August 19, 1862, Bennett Papers.
4. U. S. Grant, *Personal Memoirs* (New York, 1895), I, 358-359; W. T. Sherman, *Memoirs* (New York, 1875), I, 281-282.
5. Junius H. Browne of the Cincinnati *Times* and New York *Tribune.*
6. Edward Betty to William H. Smith, December 9, 1862, Smith Papers.
7. *O.R.* (Army), Ser. I, vol. xvii, Pt. 1, pp. 619-620.
8. Chicago *Times,* January 13, 1863.
9. T. W. Knox, *Camp-Fire and Cotton-Field* (Philadelphia and Cincinnati, 1865), pp. 245-247.
10. F. B. Wilkie, *Pen and Powder* (Boston, 1888), pp. 238-239.
11. St. Louis *Daily Missouri Democrat,* January 15, 1863.
12. R. S. Thorndike, *The Sherman Letters* (New York, 1894), p. 189.
13. New York *Times,* January 20, 1863.
14. Knox, *op. cit.,* p. 254; A. D. Richardson, *The Secret Service, the Field, the Dungeon, and the Escape* (Hartford, 1865), pp. 317-318.
15. *O.R.* (Army), Ser. I, vol. xvii, Pt. 2, p. 896.
16. *Ibid.,* pp. 580-581.
17. *Ibid.,* p. 889. In a letter to his wife, January 28, 1863, he had stated, however, "I have ordered the arrest of one [newspaper reporter], shall try him, and if possible execute him as a spy." M. A. D. W. Howe, *Home Letters of General Sherman* (New York, 1909), p. 238.
18. This account of the court martial proceedings against Knox is based upon his own narrative as set forth in *Camp-Fire and Cotton-Field;* upon material in *O.R.* (Army), Ser. I, vol. xvii, Pt. 2, pp. 889-892; upon the documentary record of the court martial in the War Department Records of the National Archives; and upon contemporary newspaper accounts. See e.g., Cincinnati *Daily Commercial,* February 14, 1863, and St. Louis *Daily Missouri Democrat,* February 28, 1863; also Lloyd Lewis, *Sherman, Fighting Prophet* (New York, 1932), pp. 263-267. There is no reference to the Knox court martial in Sherman's *Memoirs.*
19. *O.R.* (Army), Ser. I, vol. xvii, Pt. 2, pp. 892-893.
20. Richardson, *op. cit.,* p. 319.
21. In a letter to Knox dated at Vicksburg, April 17, 1863, Sherman announced his refusal of Knox's petition in no uncertain terms: "Come with a sword or musket in your hand, prepared to share with us our fate in sunshine and storm . . . and I will welcome you as a brother and associate; but come as you now do, expecting me to ally the reputation and honor of my country and my fellow-soldiers with you, as the representative of the press, which you yourself say makes so slight a difference between truth and falsehood, and my

answer is, Never." *O.R.* (Army), Ser. I, vol. xvii, Pt. 2, p. 895.

22. New York *Times,* February 23, 1863. In an editorial on Wilkie's letter, the editor of the St. Louis *Republican* commented: "This statement, appearing as it does, in the *Times,* cannot be supposed to have been made without a full conviction of its truth . . . . If it is not [true], we marvel at the audacity of a newspaper correspondent, who would send from within the lines of an army untruths so discreditable to any of its officers, and the sooner he is sent without the lines the better." St. Louis *Daily Missouri Republican,* March 1, 1863; for other statements by reporters indicating a large amount of sickness in the army, see *ibid.,* March 4, 1863; Chicago *Times,* February 20, 26, 1863.
23. For a public statement by James Yeatman, president of the Western Sanitary Commission, describing the results of his fact-finding mission to Grant's army, see St. Louis *Daily Missouri Republican,* March 14, 1863. In a letter to Congressman Washburne, March 10, 1863, Grant already had signified that "the health of this command is a subject that has been very much exaggerated by the press." J. G. Wilson, *General Grant's Letters to a Friend, 1861-1880* (New York and Boston, 1897), p. 25.
24. Cincinnati *Daily Commercial,* March 11, 1863.
25. Cincinnati *Daily Times,* January 9, 1863.
26. Cincinnati *Daily Commercial,* April 7, 1863.
27. This letter is missing from the Chase Papers at the Library of Congress and the Historical Society of Pennsylvania. What purported to be a facsimile copy was published in the Cincinnati *Enquirer* on September 27, 1885. Halstead later admitted that he had written to Chase in this manner, but defended himself on the basis of his war record as a whole. Another letter from Halstead to Chase lambasted Grant even more violently, calling him a "poor drunken imbecile" and predicting that he would fail "miserably, hopelessly, eternally . . . . Anybody would be an improvement on Grant!" Murat Halstead to Salmon P. Chase, April 1, 1863, Lincoln Papers. For information indicating that the medical department in Grant's army was reasonably efficient during the Vicksburg campaign, see G. W. Adams, *Doctors in Blue* (New York, 1952), pp. 93-94.
28. I. M. Tarbell, "Charles A. Dana in the Civil War," *McClure's Magazine,* IX (October, 1897), 1087.
29. C. A. Dana, *Recollections of the Civil War* (New York, 1898), p. 30. Dana was not the first representative of the War Department to give day-by-day reports of the operations of the Western army, however. During 1862, Thomas A. Scott, then Assistant Secretary of War, made several visits to the Western army and sent back extensive reports of his observations to Stanton. S. R. Kamm, *The Civil War Career of Thomas A. Scott* (Philadelphia, 1940), pp. 83-133.
30. Wilkie, *op. cit.,* pp. 283-286.
31. Finley Anderson to Frederic Hudson, February 10, 1863, Bennett Papers.
32. W. B. Stevens, "Joseph B. McCullagh," *Missouri Historical Review,* XXV (January, 1931), 252; St. Louis *Daily Missouri Republican,* February 10, 1863.
33. New York *Herald,* March 6, 1864. See also *ibid.,* March 6, 1863;

Philadelphia *Inquirer,* March 7, 1863.

34. Cincinnati *Daily Commercial,* March 4, 1863.

35. Thomas M. Cash to Frederic Hudson, March 5, 1863, Bennett Papers.

36. C. L. Lewis, *David Glasgow Farragut, Our First Admiral* (Annapolis, Maryland, 1943), II, 171; T. S. Bacon, "The Fight at Port Hudson, Recollections of an Eyewitness," *Independent,* LIII (March 14, 1901), 589.

37. New York *Herald,* March 31, 1863.

38. Lewis, *op. cit.,* p. 181; *O.R.* (Army), Ser. I, vol. xix, pp. 670, 676, 682-684, 688-689.

39. New York *Times,* March 31, 1863.

40. Wilkie, *op. cit.,* pp. 310-311.

41. *Ibid.,* p. 317; New York *Times,* April 24, 1863. Earlier, before the armada moved, Wilkie was on board one of several steam boats which came loose from their moorings during the night and were carried down the river toward Vicksburg. None of the stampeding craft had any steam up. Fortunately, however, one of them still had some fire in her furnace and was able to build up sufficient steam to check the progress of the flotilla by the time it had floated within three miles of Vicksburg.

42. New York *World,* May 28, 1863.

43. Accounts of the capture of the three correspondents may be found in J. H. Browne, *Four Years in Secessia* (Hartford, 1865), pp. 231-239, and Richardson, *op cit.,* pp. 337-346, as well as in the issue of the New York *World* cited above. Sherman is reported to have remarked sardonically upon hearing that the three correspondents had been killed, "That's good! We'll have dispatches now from hell before breakfast." Browne, *op. cit.,* p. 238.

44. New York *Daily Tribune,* May 23, 1863.

45. Chicago *Daily Tribune,* June 10, 1863. The *Tribune* man was probably more nearly correct than McCullagh. According to the general summary of casualties in the Vicksburg campaign, *O.R.* (Army), Ser. I, vol. xxiv, Pt. 2, p. 167, the number of Union casualties at the Battle of Port Gibson was almost double that at Raymond.

46. New York *Times,* June 2, 1863.

47. Cincinnati *Daily Commercial,* June 1, 1863; Frank Moore, *The Rebellion Record* (New York, 1861-1873), VI, 616-620.

48. Cincinnati *Daily Commercial,* June 4, 1863.

49. New York *Daily Tribune,* May 25, 1863; Philadelphia *Inquirer,* May 25, 1863; New York *Times,* May 25, 28, 1863; Cincinnati *Commercial,* June 10, 1863.

50. L. A. Gobright, *Recollections of Men and Things in Washington* (Philadelphia, 1869), pp. 335-336.

51. F. G. De Fontaine, *Marginalia* (Columbia, South Carolina, 1864), p. 121.

52. Chicago *Evening Journal,* June 30, 1863. For evidence confirming the *Journal* reporter's accusations against McClernand, see Cincinnati *Daily Gazette,* June 3, 1863.

53. Chicago *Daily Tribune,* July 14, 1863.

54. Cincinnati *Daily Commercial,* July 8, 1863; Cincinnati *Daily Gazette,* July 9, 1863; St. Louis *Daily Missouri Democrat,* July 9, 1863; Baltimore *American and Commercial Advertiser,* July 13, 1863.

55. Wilkie, *op. cit.,* pp. 349-351; Wilkie, *Personal Reminiscences of Thirty-five Years of Journalism*

(Chicago, 1891), p. 90. Raymond was very understanding about Wilkie's failure, expressing only mild regret that he had made such an unfortunate choice of a subordinate.

56. New York *Daily Tribune,* July 15, 1863.
57. Thomas M. Cash to Frederic Hudson, July 10, 1863, Bennett Papers.
58. Chicago *Daily Tribune,* June 23, 1863.
59. Chicago *Evening Journal,* June 17, 1863. For other evidence from the reporters themselves on the unreliable character of much of the Vicksburg campaign reporting, see Chicago *Times,* May 16, 1863; St. Louis *Daily Missouri Republican,* March 22, April 1, 17, June 10, 1863.
60. New York *Times,* June 12, 1863.

16

GETTYSBURG AS THE NEWSMEN SAW IT

Pages 406-436

1. Boston *Daily Journal,* June 29, 1863.
2. Nearly 25 per cent of the forces in the battle on both sides were casualties. T. L. Livermore, *Numbers and Losses in the Civil War in America, 1861-65* (Boston and New York, 1900), pp. 102-103.
3. Joseph Medill to Major William H. Medill, May 24, 1863, Joseph Medill Papers, Chicago Historical Society.
4. A. R. Hancock, *Reminiscences of Winfield Scott Hancock by His Wife* (New York, 1887), p. 94. For a letter, to an editor of the New York *Evening Post* from one of its Washington correspondents, reflecting the disillusionment in Washington, see M. C. Ames to Parke Godwin, June 3, 1863, William Cullen Bryant (—Godwin) Papers, New York Public Library.
5. Philadelphia *Inquirer,* May 20, 1863.
6. The cavalry action at Brandy Station is described in K. P. Williams, *Lincoln Finds a General* (New York, 1949), II, 623-624; D. S. Freeman, *Lee's Lieutenants,* III (New York, 1944), 8-12.
7. See e.g., *Daily Richmond Enquirer,* June 13, 1863; *Daily Richmond Examiner,* June 12, 1863.
8. Philadelphia *Inquirer,* June 22, 1863. Frederick was occupied by a Confederate raiding force from June 20 to June 22, however. S. M. Carpenter of the *Herald* was marooned there until the morning of June 21, when he escaped on a handcar to Monocacy along with an army captain. New York *Herald,* June 25, 1863.
9. G. G. Meade, *Life and Letters* (New York, 1913), II, 19-20; James Longstreet, *From Manassas to Appomattox* (Philadelphia, 1896), p. 344.
10. New York *Herald,* June 19, 1863.
11. New York *Times,* June 20, 1863.
12. New York *Daily Tribune,* June 25, 1863.
13. *O.R.* (Army), Ser. I, vol. xxvii, Pt. 3, p. 192.
14. *Ibid.,* Pt. 1, p. 52.
15. New York *Daily Tribune,* June 23, 1863; New York *Herald,* June 23, 1863. Shepherd's incriminating letter was published in the *Tribune* on June 18.
16. Pittsburgh *Evening Chronicle,* June 25, July 7, 1863.
17. New York *Daily Tribune,* June 24, 1863.
18. *Ibid.,* June 24, 1863.
19. New York *Herald,* June 24, 25, 1863; Chicago *Daily Tribune,* June 29, 1863.

20. C. C. Coffin, *Four Years of Fighting* (Boston, 1866), p. 261.
21. New York *Herald*, July 2, 1863. See also T. C. Grey to Sydney Howard Gay, June 29, 1863, Gay Papers.
22. Pittsburgh *Evening Chronicle*, June 18, 1863.
23. Philadelphia *Press*, June 26, 1863; Harrisburg *Evening Telegraph*, June 26, 1863; New York *Times*, June 30, 1863.
24. New York *Times*, July 1, 1863.
25. Philadelphia *Inquirer*, May 3, 1862; Philadelphia *Press*, June 26, 1863; New York *Daily Tribune*, June 26, 1863; Lancaster *Daily Express*, June 26, 1863.
26. New York *Times*, June 29, 1863.
27. Harrisburg *Evening Telegraph*, June 29, 1863; Lancaster *Daily Express*, July 2, 1863.
28. Harrisburg *Evening Telegraph*, July 1, 1863; Philadelphia *Daily Evening Bulletin*, July 1, 1863; Philadelphia *Inquirer*, July 4, 1863. The *Bulletin* claimed, however, that notwithstanding the order a New York *Herald* correspondent by subterfuge had succeeded in crossing the river.
29. D. S. Freeman, *R. E. Lee, A Biography* (New York and London, 1935), III, 60-61.
30. Freeman, *Lee's Lieutenants*, III, 34.
31. Royal Cortissoz, *Life of Whitelaw Reid* (New York, 1921), I, 93; Cincinnati *Daily Gazette*, July 8, 1863.
32. New York *Times*, July 21, 1863.
33. C. C. Coffin, *Marching to Victory* (New York, 1888), p. 195.
34. Cincinnati *Daily Gazette*, July 8, 1863; G. F. Williams, "Important Services Rendered by War Correspondents," *Independent*, LIV (January 23, 1902), 212.
35. Coffin, *Marching to Victory*, pp. 231-233; Coffin, *The Boys of '61*, p. 289.
36. For information about the Meade–Sickles controversy, see Williams, *op. cit.*, II, 721; Edgcumb Pinchon, *Dan Sickles* (New York, 1945), pp. 195ff.; R. W. Johnson and C. C. Buel, *Battles and Leaders of the Civil War* (New York, 1884-1888), III, 413-419.
37. New York *World*, June 29, 1913.
38. New York *Herald*, July 6, 1863.
39. Cincinnati *Daily Gazette*, July 8, 1863.
40. J. G. Randall, *The Civil War and Reconstruction* (Boston and New York, 1937), p. 521; Johnson and Buel, *op. cit.*, III, 313-314.
41. J. B. McMaster, *A History of the People of the United States during Lincoln's Administration* (New York and London, 1927), p. 396; various newspapers, July 3, 1863.
42. Office of the Secretary of War, Telegrams Received, National Archives. At the bottom of the telegram appeared the notation, "Send to Mr. Lynch." S. G. Lynch, the censor, was described by the New York *Commercial Advertiser* of June 22, 1863, as "a very young man, whose profession prior to being installed as censor, a month since, was to manipulate a telegraph key in a country telegraph office." For a vastly different estimate of the censor, see Adams S. Hill to Sydney Howard Gay, June 21, 1863, Gay Papers.
43. Johnson and Buel, *op. cit.*, III, 369-370.
44. New York *Times*, July 6, 8, 1863; Cincinnati *Daily Gazette*, July 8, 1863; Coffin, *Marching to Victory*, pp. 217-218; Johnson and Buel, *op. cit.*, III, 281n.
45. Cincinnati *Daily Gazette*, July 8, 1863.
46. New York *Times*, July 6, 1863;

J. R. Sypher, *History of the Pennsylvania Reserve Corps* (Lancaster, Pennsylvania, 1865) p. 467n.

47. New York *World,* July 7, 1863.
48. New York *Times,* July 8, 1863.
49. Coffin, *The Boys of '61,* p. 247. For a vivid Southern account of Pickett's charge, see *Daily Richmond Enquirer,* July 22, 1863.
50. New York *Times,* July 8, 1863.
51. Cincinnati *Daily Gazette,* July 8, 1863.
52. J. T. Morse, Jr., *Diary of Gideon Welles* (Boston and New York, 1911), I, 357.
53. W. A. Croffut, *An American Procession* (Boston, 1931), pp. 98-101; New York *Daily Tribune,* July 7, 1863; *Journalist,* II (November 28, 1885), 4. A. H. Byington to Sydney Howard Gay, July 5, 1863, Gay Papers. The New York *Times* claimed on the other hand that L. L. Crounse's dispatch to that paper received at the *Times* office at 4:00 A.M. on July 2 was the first information of the first day's battle to reach New York
54. New York *Herald,* May 7, 1916.
55. W. E. Griffis, *Charles Carleton Coffin* (Boston, 1898), pp. 145-146.
56. *Ibid.,* pp. 147-148; F. L. Bullard, *Famous War Correspondents* (Boston, 1914), pp. 382-383. See *Boston Daily Journal,* July 7, 1863, for Coffin's full-length account of the battle.
57. New York *Times,* July 6, 1863.
58. J. F. Rhodes, *History of the United States from the Compromise of 1850* (New York and London, 1928), IV, 294-295; McMaster, *op. cit.,* pp. 397-398.
59. New York *Herald,* July 7, 1863. A correspondent of the Philadelphia *Evening Journal* was responsible for a widely spread and ridiculous story about the capture of 20,000 rebel prisoners and 118 guns.
60. New York *Herald,* July 8, 1863.
61. Johnson and Buel, *op. cit.,* III, 384n.
62. McMaster, *op. cit.,* pp. 398-399; Savannah *Republican,* July 8, 1863. See also Freeman, *Lee's Lieutenants,* III, 168.
63. New York *Times,* July 11, 1863.
64. J. H. Taggart to Uriah H. Painter, July 13, 1863, Painter Papers.
65. Coffin, *The Boys of '61,* p. 255.
66. Noah Brooks, *Washington in Lincoln's Time* (New York, 1895), pp. 93-94.
67. J. H. Taggart to Uriah H. Painter, July 15, 1863, Painter Papers. For J. R. Sypher's account of how he galloped 24 miles to Chambersburg with the news of the crossing, see J. R. Sypher to Sydney Howard Gay, July 14, 1863, Gay Papers.
68. The literature of the Gettysburg campaign is quite extensive. The official reports of Meade and Lee appear in *O.R.* (Army), Ser. I, vol. xxvii, Pt. 1, pp. 114-119; Pt. 2, pp. 305-325. Good briefer accounts will be found in Walter Geer, *Campaigns of the Civil War* (New York, 1926), pp. 229-263; Williams, *op. cit.,* II, 618-759; Freeman, *R. E. Lee,* II, 29-161. Of the larger-scale studies, F. A. Haskell, *The Battle of Gettysburg* (Madison, Wisconsin, 1908), and J. B. Young, *The Battle of Gettysburg, A Comprehensive Account* (New York and London, 1913), are of particular value.
69. Dr. Frederick Marbut, department of journalism, Pennsylvania State University, has expressed the opinion to the author that "Bonaparte" was the Washington correspondent of the *World,* George W. Adams.
70. See Cortissoz, *op. cit.,* I, 94-96, for an able critique of Reid's re-

porting of the Battle of Gettysburg. E. C. Stedman, a good judge of such matters, rated Reid's account of Gettysburg as "the best group of battle letters made up during the war, without exception." Even the Cincinnati *Enquirer,* no friend of the newspaper by which Reid was employed, referred to his story (July 9, 1863) as "the best written and most connected account that we have yet seen of the great battles at Gettysburg."

71. *Daily Richmond Enquirer,* July 22, 1863; Frank Moore, *The Rebellion Record* (New York, 1861-1873), VII, 108-115; Richmond *Sentinel,* July 14, 1863.
72. New York *Times,* July 21, 1863.
73. Charles Francis Adams, Jr., to John Quincy Adams, July 12, 1863, in W. C. Ford, *A Cycle of Adams Letters, 1861-1865* (Boston and New York, 1920), II, 44-45.
74. New York *Times,* July 9, 1863.
75. The full text of the letter was printed in the *Adams Sentinel,* a Gettysburg newspaper, July 14, 1863, and in the New York *Tribune,* July 24, 1863. The *Times* did not print the letter.
76. New York *Times,* July 24, 1863; Philadelphia *Press,* July 25, 1863.

17

"SHAMBLING SHANKS AND THE FUGACIOUS FURAY"

Pages 437-463

1. J. R. Gilmore, *Personal Recollections of Abraham Lincoln and the Civil War* (Boston, 1898), p. 142.
2. Henry Villard, *Memoirs* (Boston and New York, 1904), II, 64. For an indication of the Western press's increasing impatience with Rosecrans, however, see Chicago *Daily Tribune,* May 21, 1863.
3. Villard, *op. cit.,* II, 66-67.
4. *Ibid.,* 67.
5. Gilmore, *op cit.,* pp. 127-128.
6. *Ibid.,* p. 128. The first of Gilmore's series of war letters from Murfreesboro appeared in the New York *Tribune,* July 6, 1863.
7. New York *Times,* June 25, 1863. For subsequent comment about his Tennessee war reporting, see William Swinton, *The Twelve Decisive Battles of the War* (New York, 1867), p. 223; William Swinton to Major Finley Anderson, October 17, 1865, Miscellaneous MSS, New York Public Library.
8. Villard, *op. cit.,* II, 73-76.
9. Chicago *Times,* July 15, 1863; New York *Times,* June 29, 1863.
10. *O.R.* (Army), Ser. I, vol. xxiii, Pt. 1, p. 424.
11. Cincinnati *Daily Commercial,* July 22, 1863; New York *Daily Tribune,* July 24, 1863.
12. New York *Herald,* July 13, 1863.
13. *Ibid.,* July 8, 1863.
14. *Ibid.,* August 13, 1863.
15. A dispatch from Headquarters to McCook at 9:30 P.M., June 25, signed by one of Rosecrans' aides, Frank S. Bond, e.g., quotes Rosecrans as saying that "he hopes that the demonstration will result in convincing the enemy that the main attack will be made by your force." *O.R.* (Army), Ser. I, vol. xxiii, Pt. 2, p. 457. In his official report of the campaign, however, Rosecrans indicated that McCook's corps was expected to "seize and hold Liberty Gap." *O.R.* (Army), Ser. I, vol. xxiii, Pt. 1, p. 405.
16. New York *Daily Tribune,* July 15, 1863; Philadelphia *Inquirer,* July 15, 1863. No mention of Swinton's story appeared in the New York *Times.*
17. New York *Daily Tribune,* July 21, 1863.

18. See various newspapers, July 25, 1863.
19. New York *Herald,* August 7, 1863.
20. Cincinnati *Enquirer,* March 16, 1882.
21. Dana made these charges in the columns of the New York *Sun.* For Garfield's side of the story, see T. C. Smith, *The Life and Letters of James Abram Garfield* (New Haven, 1925), I, 309-312.
22. *Ibid.,* p. 316. See also Freeman Cleaves, *Rock of Chickamauga* (Norman, Oklahoma, 1948), pp. 146-147.
23. For an excellent description of Burnside's march to Knoxville, see a letter from army correspondent Edward Crapsey to the Cincinnati *Commercial,* September 16, 1863.
24. W. F. G. Shanks, "Chattanooga and How We Held It," *Harper's New Monthly Magazine,* XXXVI (January, 1868), 142.
25. Shanks's article, based on his interview with Rosecrans, appeared in the New York *Herald,* September 3, 1863.
26. Cincinnati *Daily Commercial,* September 9, 1863. The crossing of the Tennessee by Negley's division also was described in the Cincinnati *Daily Gazette,* September 12, 1863.
27. *O.R.* (Army), Ser. I, vol. xxx, Pt. 4, p. 600. Bragg also forwarded to the Confederate War Department a copy of the New York *Times* which fell into his hands at this time, considerably less informative than its Chicago namesake.
28. Smith, *op. cit.,* I, 319.
29. S. F. Horn, *The Army of the Tennessee* (Indianapolis and New York, 1941), p. 248.
30. New York *Herald,* September 20, 1863.
31. New York *World,* September 21, 1863.
32. *Vide supra,* pp. 384-385.
33. At that time the Nashville and Chattanooga Railroad was not operating East of Bridgeport, 123 miles by rail from Nashville and 28 miles West of Chattanooga.
34. C. A. Dana, *Recollections of the Civil War* (New York, 1898), pp. 106-107; W. F. G. Shanks, *Personal Recollections of Distinguished Generals* (New York, 1866), p. 263. Sutlers had none too good a reputation in the army, a result of high prices and the generally mediocre quality of their wares.
35. Chicago *Evening Journal,* September 18, 1863.
36. Cincinnati *Daily Gazette,* September 22, 1863.
37. *Ibid.,* September 29, 1863.
38. *O.R.* (Army), Ser. I, vol. xxx, Pt. 3, pp. 570, 607.
39. Horn, *op. cit.,* pp. 249-254.
40. Cincinnati *Daily Gazette,* September 25, 1863.
41. H. M. Cist, *The Army of the Cumland* (New York, 1882), pp. 193-195.
42. New York *Herald,* September 27, 1863.
43. Cincinnati *Daily Gazette,* September 25, 1863.
44. Chicago *Evening Journal,* October 6, 1863.
45. Frank Moore, *The Rebellion Record* (New York, 1861-1873), VII, 366.
46. Shanks, *Personal Recollections,* p. 267.
47. Cincinnati *Daily Commercial,* September 28, 1863.
48. *Ibid.,* September 28, 1863. As usual, reports were conflicting about the time the fighting of the second day's battle began. According to Bragg's official report of Chickamauga, the action on the Confederate right began "about 10

A.M." But Breckenridge, who commanded the advance Confederate division, stated that it went into action shortly after 9:30. According to Rosecrans, however, "fighting began on the extreme Union left at 8:30 a.m."

49. T. R. Hay, "The Campaign and Battle of Chickamauga," *Georgia Historical Quarterly,* VII (September, 1923), 232; E. T. Wells, "The Campaign and Battle of Chickamauga," *United Service Magazine,* New Ser. XVI (September, 1896), 226; P. H. Sheridan, *Personal Memoirs* (New York, 1888), I, 281-283; Cist, *op. cit.,* pp. 205-207.

50. Louisville *Daily Journal,* October 10, 1863.

51. Among them were "Sidney" of the New York *Tribune,* "Quill" of the Louisville *Journal,* and Miller of the Cincinnati *Commercial.*

52. Shanks, *Personal Recollections,* pp. 67-69; New York *Herald,* September 27, 1863.

53. Chicago *Evening Journal,* October 6, 1863.

54. Shanks, *Personal Recollections,* pp. 263-265. Curiously enough, in the New York *Herald,* September 29, 1863, Shanks accused Dana of working in collusion with Halleck to play down the fact that a defeat had occurred.

55. W. F. G. Shanks, "How We Get Our News," *Harper's New Monthly Magazine,* XXXIV (March, 1867), 519-520.

56. *O.R.* (Army), Ser. I, vol. xxx, Pt. 1, pp. 192-193. Four hours later, though, Dana admitted in a second dispatch to the War Department that his previous telegram had given an exaggerated picture of the Federal disaster and that "having been myself swept bodily off the battle-field by the panic-struck rabble into which the divisions of Davis and Sheridan were temporarily converted, my own impressions were naturally colored by the aspect of that part of the field." *Ibid.,* pp. 193-194.

57. In a dispatch to Major Thomas T. Eckert, dated at Chattanooga, October 11, 1863, Dana remarked, "It is rather curious . . . that the agent of the Associated Press at Louisville, in a private printed circular, quoted me as authority for reporting the battle as a total defeat. . . ." *O.R.* (Army), Ser. I, vol. xxx, Pt. 1, p. 214. In a letter to the editor of the Cincinnati *Gazette,* however, the AP reporter alleged that his information was based on "a dispatch . . . from an officer at Nashville to an officer at Louisville." Cincinnati *Daily Gazette,* September 25, 1863.

58. For the text of the AP report from Louisville, see various newspapers, September 21, 1863.

59. New York *Daily Tribune,* September 22, 1863; Cincinnati *Daily Times,* September 22, 1863. The size of both armies at Chickamauga was actually about the same (slightly in excess of 60,000) in spite of the fact that Bragg had been substantially reinforced.

60. Cincinnati *Daily Gazette,* September 22, 1863. For a warm endorsement of the *Gazette* editor's position, see Chicago *Daily Tribune,* September 24, 1863.

61. Cincinnati *Daily Gazette,* September 25, 1863.

62. See e.g., *O.R.* (Army), Ser. I, vol. xxx, Pt. 1, pp. 149-150.

63. Cincinnati *Daily Gazette,* September 25, 1863; Moore, *op. cit.,* VII, 409-417.

64. Chicago *Evening Journal,* September 26, 1863.

65. Different versions of this story ap-

peared in the Cincinnati *Enquirer,* September 30, 1863, and the New York *Herald,* October 8, 1863. The *Herald's* account would seem to be more nearly correct. See also Henry Villard's statement published in the Cincinnati *Commercial,* September 30, 1863, defending himself and the New York *Tribune* against charges set forth in the Cincinnati *Gazette,* September 29, 1863, that: (1) Villard had lifted his account of the battle from the columns of the *Gazette;* (2) the *Tribune* had published Villard's letter without giving proper credit to the *Gazette.*

66. New York *Herald,* October 12, 1863.

67. This incident was related to the author by Clarence E. Miller, Librarian of the St. Louis Mercantile Library Association and a son of the *Commercial's* army correspondent.

68. Cincinnati *Daily Commercial,* September 28, 1863.

69. *Ibid.,* September 30, 1863. Hostile feeling toward Shanks and Furay in the army was indicated in a letter mailed to the *Commercial* from Chattanooga on October 5 by its army correspondent, Joe McCullagh: "There is a feeling of intense indignation in this army, against the correspondent of the New York Herald, who rushed into telegraphic notoriety in Cincinnati, at the expense of the reputation of our bravest and best men and officers. The correspondent of the Gazette is in bad odor too. To what extent these gentlemen are martyrs to the cause of truth I can not say. I only know that since my arrival here, I have heard the Herald's correspondent denounced in most unqualified terms, and at least twenty times have the errors of his pretended statement of facts been pointed out to me." Cincinnati *Daily Commercial,* October 16, 1863. A similar picture was given in the Chicago *Times,* October 23, 1863.

70. See e.g., St. Louis *Daily Missouri Democrat,* September 26, 1863; Louisville *Daily Journal,* September 29, 1863.

71. *O.R.* (Army), Ser. I, vol. xxx, Pt. 1, p. 62; Pt. 2, p. 35.

72. New York *Herald,* Cincinnati *Gazette,* Cincinnati *Commercial,* Chicago *Journal,* and Louisville *Journal.*

73. Villard, *op. cit.,* II, 172. For contemporary journalistic criticism of inaccuracies in the newspaper accounts of Chickamauga, see Cincinnati *Daily Commercial,* October 21, 27, 1863; Chicago *Daily Tribune,* October 21, 1863. Probably the most complete analysis of the Battle of Chickamauga, written from the Southern point of view, is Archibald Gracie, *The Truth about Chickamauga* (Boston and New York, 1911).

74. Richmond *Dispatch,* September 29, 1863; Atlanta *Daily Intelligencer,* September 24, 1863; Savannah *Republican,* September 28, 1863; Mobile *Tribune,* September 29, 1863; Moore, *op. cit.,* VII, 362-370.

75. W. S. Furay and G. C. Kniffen, *The Real Chickamauga* (Privately printed, 1888), pp. 2-3.

18

GRIM DAYS AT CHATTANOOGA

Pages 464-495

1. Chicago *Daily Tribune,* October 20, 1863. On the same theme, a New York *Tribune* correspondent also stressed the hostile feeling in the army toward Shanks: "Among those particularly unfortunate [is] the correspondent of *The New-York Herald,* who would now find

the army an unwholesome place." New York *Daily Tribune,* October 21, 1863.

2. Cincinnati *Daily Commercial,* October 5, 7, 1863. McCullagh also was reporting for the New York *Tribune.* He had made an arrangement with Villard before leaving Cincinnati to contribute occasional letters to the *Tribune* at $5 a column. Henry Villard to Sydney Howard Gay, October 5, 6, 1863, Gay Papers.
3. New York *Herald,* October 19, 1863. Writing from Chattanooga late in October, a veteran *Tribune* correspondent informed Gay: "I find it almost impossible to live here. Coffee & crackers is about all that can be had now." Henry Villard to Sydney Howard Gay, October 20, 1863, Gay Papers.
4. J. F. Rhodes, *History of the United States from the Compromise of 1850* (New York and London, 1928), IV, 399.
5. Henry Villard, *Memoirs* (Boston and New York, 1904), II, 177.
6. Noah Brooks, *Washington in Lincoln's Time* (New York, 1895), pp. 61-62; Philadelphia *Sunday Dispatch,* September 27, 1863.
7. New York *Evening Post,* September 28, 1863.
8. Villard, *op. cit.,* II, 178-179; W. H. Hebert, *Fighting Joe Hooker* (Indianapolis and New York, 1944), pp. 251-252; Thomas A. Scott to Edwin M. Stanton, September 30, 1863, Edwin M. Stanton to D. H. Watson, October 2, 1863, both Stanton Papers.
9. Chicago *Daily Tribune,* October 7, 1863.
10. B. F. Taylor, *Mission Ridge and Lookout Mountain* (New York and Chicago, 1872), p. 16.
11. W. F. G. Shanks, "Chattanooga and How We Held It," *Harper's New Monthly Magazine,* XXXVI (January, 1868), 146-147; C. E. Fairman, *Art and Artists of the Capitol of the United States of America* (Washington, D.C., 1927), p. 212.
12. Chicago *Daily Tribune,* October 20, 1863.
13. *Ibid.,* October 26, 1863. Bodman also told of being summoned before the Provost Marshal, on the basis of information furnished by Dana, and of being required to hand over a list of regiments which he had compiled for his own personal use and which as a courtesy he had shown to the Assistant Secretary of War earlier in the day.
14. The favorite theme of the deserters was the destitute, even mutinous state of Bragg's army. Whereas the *Herald* reporters were generally inclined to credit such stories and make use of them in their correspondence, the Cincinnati *Times* correspondent Doggett put them down as "lies." "Bragg's army is well clothed, has plenty to eat, and is in good discipline," he insisted. "Stories that they are desirous of deserting and that they won't fight will do to tell, but in every battle we find out the contrary." Cincinnati *Daily Times,* November 16, 1863.
15. Cincinnati *Daily Commercial,* October 16, 1863.
16. New York *Daily Tribune,* October 29, 1863.
17. Villard, *op. cit.,* II, 184-185.
18. *Ibid.,* p. 186. Having been nominated for Congress in a district which was comfortably Republican, Garfield expected to leave the army soon.
19. *Ibid.,* p. 188.
20. The text of McCook's parting address to his troops was given in full in the New York *Herald,* Oc-

tober 24, 1863. For an indication of McCook's feeling toward Shanks, see Cincinnati *Daily Commercial,* October 20, 1863.

21. *Ibid.,* October 16, 1863. See also various newspapers, October 13, 1863.
22. Except Banks's Department of the Gulf.
23. Thomas W. Knox (to James Gordon Bennett ?), October 22, 1863, Bennett Papers. Knox informed his correspondent that "my private opinion has all along been favorable to Rosecrans but Shanks dont [*sic*] appear to appreciate him highly. Of course you are aware that Halleck & Stanton were his personal & military enemies. They were determined to remove him at the earliest opportunity." How Shanks learned of Rosecrans' removal was described in New York *Herald,* October 23, 1863.
24. Cincinnati *Daily Commercial,* November 3, 1863. For the testimony of another army reporter about the apathetic reaction of the Army of the Cumberland to the change of command, see Cincinnati *Daily Times,* November 3, 1863. "The boys are more interested in a good supply of bread and bacon, and without it will get up little enthusiasm," was the conclusion of Doggett, the *Times* reporter.
25. Villard, *op. cit.,* II, 212; Henry Villard to Sydney Howard Gay, October 21, 1863, Gay Papers.
26. Villard, *op. cit.,* II, 216.
27. Whitelaw Reid to Horace Greeley, November 2, 1863, Reid Papers; William S. Rosecrans to Charles A. Dana, March 17, 1882, Charles A. Dana Papers, Library of Congress.
28. Reid may very well have obtained some of the information for his article from Garfield. On November 2, the same day he wrote the letter to Greeley, Reid was in conference with Garfield and "Pig Iron" Kelley. Tyler Dennett, *Lincoln and the Civil War* (New York, 1939), p. 114.
29. See e.g., the statements of C. D. Brigham and Furay in New York *Daily Tribune,* November 23, 1863; Cincinnati *Daily Gazette,* November 18, 1863. A brigadier general in the Army of the Cumberland noted in his wartime diary on November 15, 1863: "Have read Whitelaw Reid's statement of the causes of Rosecrans' removal. He is, I presume, in the main correct. Investigation will show that the army could have gotten into Chattanooga without a battle on the Chickamauga. There would have been a battle here, doubtless, and defeat would have result probably in our destruction; yet it seems reasonable to suppose that, if able to hold Chattanooga after defeat, we would have been able to do so before." John Beatty, *The Citizen-Soldier* (Cincinnati, 1879), p. 355.
30. Washington *Evening Star,* November 17, 1863.
31. Whitelaw Reid's pen name.
32. Richard Smith to W. H. Smith, November 15, 1863, Smith Papers, Ohio State Historical and Archaeological Society, Columbus. Subsequently Editor Smith made a public denial of the truth of the *Star's* charges. Cincinnati *Daily Gazette,* November 26, 1863.
33. Chicago *Times,* October 27, 1863. Wilkie had attempted to go down to the Army of the Cumberland during the first week of October to represent the *Times.* Finding it impossible to get any father than Bridgeport, he returned to Nashville.
34. Villard, *op. cit.,* II, 221.

35. New York *Times,* November 5, 1863.
36. New York *Daily Tribune,* November 11, 1863.
37. New York *Times,* February 12, 1899. See also Thomas S. Townsend Scrapbooks, XCI, 181.
38. See various newspapers, October 31, 1863. Both the New York *Herald* and *Times* stated in identical language: "Lookout Mountain was yesterday taken by our forces, the enemy falling back without resistance. Our troops occupy the south bank of the river from Bridgeport to Chattanooga, and the river and railroad are unobstructed."
39. Major General Joseph Hooker to L. L. Crounse, December 14, 1863, Crounse Papers. According to the *Tribune* correspondent Brigham, the Northern press was deceived by "a false dispatch to 'the leading journal of the country' [the *Herald*], . . . by a correspondent who subsequently gave a graphic description of Hooker's fight, with a map of equal faithfulness, but which no one here detects as resembling any locality in all this region." New York *Daily Tribune,* November 23, 1863.
40. New York *Daily Tribune,* November 14, 1863.
41. Cincinnati *Daily Commercial,* November 4, 1863. McCullagh's offending letter had been published in *ibid.,* October 16, 1863.
42. Cincinnati *Daily Gazette,* November 11, 1863; Cincinnati *Daily Times,* November 13, 1863; New York *Daily Tribune,* November 18, 1863.
43. Chicago *Daily Tribune,* November 5, 1863.
44. Charles A. Dana to Edwin M. Stanton, October 29, 1863, Stanton Papers.
45. Lloyd Lewis, *Sherman, Fighting Prophet* (New York, 1932), p. 316; U. S. Grant, *Personal Memoirs* (New York, 1895), I, 523.
46. Villard, *op. cit.,* II, 237-238.
47. As a result, Jefferson C. Davis' division was transferred from Thomas' command to Sherman's; Howard's corps was then ordered to report to Thomas in place of Davis' division.
48. Cincinnati *Daily Times,* November 30, 1863.
49. J. A. Connolly, "Major Connolly's Letters to His Wife, 1862-1866," *Transactions of the Illinois State Historical Society,* XXIX (1928), 294.
50. Taylor, *op. cit.,* p. 30, Chicago *Evening Journal,* December 5, 1863.
51. New York *World,* December 4, 1863.
52. Cincinnati *Daily Gazette,* December 2, 1863.
53. Villard, *op. cit.,* II, 251.
54. Taylor, *op. cit.,* pp. 41-42; Chicago *Evening Journal,* December 7, 1863.
55. New York *Herald,* December 2, 1863.
56. Cincinnati *Daily Gazette,* December 2, 1863.
57. The phrase first appeared in an unofficial dispatch from Meigs to Secretary Stanton, November 26, 1863. Meigs's dispatch was released to the press a few days later and subsequently was reprinted in pamphlet form. Said the editor of the Philadelphia *Press,* December 3, 1863: "The brief but very accurate and interesting account of Grant's victory, telegraphed by Quartermaster General Meigs, gives a far better idea of the battle than any report yet published, if we except the extended and spirited narrative of Mr. Shanks, to the New York *Herald.*"

58. J. R. Young, *Around the World with General Grant* (New York, 1879), II, 306.
59. W. F. G. Shanks, "Lookout Mountain and How We Won It," *Harper's New Monthly Magazine,* XXXVII (June, 1868), 5; New York *Daily Tribune,* August 9, 1878; Chicago *Times,* December 1, 1863.
60. Washington *Evening Star,* October 16, 1896.
61. Taylor, *op. cit.,* p. 52; Chicago *Evening Journal,* December 12, 1863.
62. New York *Herald,* December 2, 1863.
63. New York *Daily Tribune,* December 4, 1863.
64. Taylor, *op. cit.,* p. 56; Chicago *Evening Journal,* December 12, 1863.
65. New York *Herald,* December 2, 1863.
66. Taylor, *op. cit.,* pp. 68-69; Chicago *Evening Journal,* December 12, 1863.
67. New York *Times,* December 8, 1863. Of the three divisions that took part in the assault on Missionary Ridge, only 366 men were killed during the five-day period November 23-27. *O.R.* (Army), Ser. I, vol. xxxi, Pt. 2, pp. 80-90.
68. New York *World,* December 4, 1863.
69. Cincinnati *Daily Gazette,* December 2, 1863.
70. This account of Cadwallader's adventurous journey northward following the three-day battle at Chattanooga is based on his own narrative as it appeared in the Washington *Evening Star,* October 16, 1896. Although Shanks did not refer to his part in the experience in any of his published writings, there is no reason to believe that the Cadwallader narrative is not substantially correct.
71. New York *Daily Tribune,* December 2, 1863.
72. Frank Moore, *The Rebellion Record* (New York, 1861-1873), VIII, 237; Richmond *Dispatch,* December 4, 1863. The *Dispatch* account was almost identical with P. W. Alexander's battle narrative published in the Savannah *Republican,* November 30, December 1, 1863.
73. See e.g., Cadwallader's comments in his account of the battle, Chicago *Times,* December 1, 1863.
74. Hebert, *op. cit.,* p. 266.
75. Joseph Hooker to L. L. Crounse, December 14, 1863, Crounse Papers.
76. Joseph Hooker to Edwin M. Stanton, February 25, 1864, in *O.R.* (Army), Ser. I, vol. xxxii, Pt. 2, pp. 467-469.
77. The existence of such a "league" was affirmed in a letter from W. F. G. Shanks (to James Gordon Bennett ?), December 18, 1863, Bennett Papers. According to Shanks, the chief agent of the league was Assistant Secretary Dana, whom he characterized as "a sneaking, lying dog." Shanks further alleged that "the chief oracle [of the league] is the *Tribune* and the articles which you have seen in the *Tribune* of late as coming from their correspondent Villiard [*sic*] were concocted by that worthy, Dana, Wood and Brannon [*sic*], with some assistance perhaps from Baldy Smith."
78. New York *Daily Tribune,* December 23, 1863.
79. M. H. Hunter, *Report of the Military Services of Gen. David Hunter, U.S.A., during the War of the Rebellion* (New York, 1892), pp. 44-45; R. C. Schenck, "Major-General David Hunter," *Magazine of*

American History, XVII (February, 1887), 149.

80. Chicago *Daily Tribune,* October 7, 1863.

81. Baltimore *American and Commercial Advertiser,* April 22, 1863.

82. *O.R.* (Army), Ser. I, vol. xxviii, Pt. 2, p. 41; Philadelphia *Inquirer,* August 31, 1863. The disclosure which precipitated this drastic order was an item about the Confederate works on Morris Island supposedly given to the Boston *Transcript* by Colonel John H. Jackson, Third New Hampshire Volunteers. Jackson denied that he had supplied this information to the *Transcript* reporter.

83. M. V. Dahlgren, *Memoir of John A. Dahlgren* (Boston, 1882), p. 418. See also New York *Herald,* October 7, 1863.

84. Dahlgren, *op. cit.,* p. 421.

85. *Ibid.,* p. 435. Gillmore apparently was playing a two-faced role. At a conference held on October 19, 1863, the General, according to Dahlgren, "very good-naturedly disclaimed any idea of disagreement, or that there had been any but the best understanding between us," saying that the idea of disagreement "came from the reporters and the discontented officers." *Ibid.,* pp. 418-419. Yet five days later, Secretary Welles conferred with two officers who came direct from Gillmore to denounce the Admiral as "incompetent, imbecile, and insane . . . . totally unfit for his position." J. T. Morse, Jr., *The Diary of Gideon Welles* (Boston and New York, 1911), I, 474-475.

86. *Vide supra,* pp. 177-178.

87. Philadelphia *Weekly Times,* April 23, 1887. The map referred to by Long appeared in the New York *Herald,* December 5, 1863. See also A. H. Byington to Sydney Howard Gay, December 3, 1863, Gay Papers.

88. New York *Herald,* December 3, 1863. For a fitting rejoinder to Chapman, see New York *Daily Tribune,* December 9, 1863.

19

STRANGE TALES FROM THE RED RIVER COUNTRY

Pages 496-521

1. John W. Forney to John Russell Young, February 26, 1864, Young Papers.

2. M. D. R. Young, *Men and Memories* (New York and London, 1901), I, 23-24.

3. Philadelphia *Press,* April 12, 1864.

4. *O.R.* (Army), Ser. I, vol. xxvi, Pt. 1, pp. 664, 673; F. H. Harrington, *Fighting Politician, Major General N. P. Banks* (Philadelphia, 1948), p. 130.

5. New York *Herald,* September 20, 1863.

6. A. J. H. Duganne, *Camps and Prisons* (New York, 1865), p. 259.

7. J. G. Randall, *The Civil War and Reconstruction* (Boston and New York, 1937), p. 592.

8. J. K. Hosmer, *Outcome of the Civil War* (New York and London, 1907), p. 78.

9. New York *Daily Tribune,* March 28, 1864.

10. St. Louis *Daily Missouri Republican,* March 26, 1864.

11. New York *Daily Tribune,* April 4, 1864.

12. R. W. Johnson and C. C. Buel, *Battles and Leaders of the Civil War* (New York, 1884-1888), IV, 350.

13. New York *Times,* April 14, 1864.

14. New York *Herald,* April 16, 1864.

15. New York *Daily Tribune,* April 6, 1864.
16. *Ibid.,* April 11, 1864.
17. D. D. Porter, *Incidents and Anecdotes of the Civil War* (New York, 1885), pp. 218-219.
18. New York *Times,* April 16, 1864.
19. Much of Banks's attention during his stay at Alexandria was given to administering the oath of allegiance to all who would thus attest their allegiance to the new government; also, to holding an election for delegates to a state constitutional convention.
20. New York *World,* April 16, 1864.
21. *Ibid.,* April 21, 1864.
22. St. Louis *Daily Missouri Republican,* April 17, 1864.
23. New York *Times,* April 16, 1864.
24. New York *Evening Post,* April 21, 1864.
25. New York *Herald,* April 11, 1864.
26. R. S. West, Jr., *The Second Admiral* (New York, 1937), p. 248.
27. St. Louis *Daily Missouri Republican,* April 17, 1864.
28. New York *World,* April 16, 1864.
29. Philadelphia *Press,* April 25, 1864.
30. New York *Herald,* May 1, 1864.
31. St. Louis *Daily Missouri Republican,* April 20, 1864.
32. New York *Herald,* May 1, 1864; see also New York *Evening Post,* April 21, 1864; and John E. Hayes to Sydney Howard Gay, April 25, 1864, Gay Papers.
33. St. Louis *Daily Missouri Republican,* April 6, 1864. Yet on April 7, the *Republican* reporter at Alexandria informed his newspaper that General Steele's forces from Arkansas had arrived "in the rear of Shreveport" and were ready to cooperate with General Banks in the capture of that place. On that same date, April 7, General Steele was still in Southern Arkansas, approximately 100 miles from Shreveport.
34. Johnson and Buel, *op. cit.,* IV, 361-362, 374.
35. See e.g., St. Louis *Daily Missouri Democrat,* April 5, 1864; St. Louis *Daily Missouri Republican,* April 6, 21, 1864; New York *World,* April 23, 1864; New York *Evening Post,* April 25, 1864.
36. St. Louis *Daily Missouri Republican,* April 21, 1864.
37. Philadelphia *Press,* April 25, 1864.
38. Frank Moore, *The Rebellion Record* (New York, 1861-1873), VIII, 558; Chicago *Daily Tribune,* April 25, 1864.
39. Philadelphia *Press,* April 25, 1864.
40. This is based in part on the tabulation presented by General Lee to the Joint Committee on the Conduct of the War, Report of the Joint Committee on the Conduct of the War, *Senate Report No. 108,* 1863, Pt. II, pp. 58, 62. Banks indicated, however, in his testimony before the committee (*ibid.,* p. 25) that Lee's wagon train consisted of 156 wagons, same figure as that given by Lee for the number captured.
41. New York *Herald,* April 24, 1864.
42. St. Louis *Daily Missouri Republican,* April 25, 1864. For more complete and more authentic data on Union losses during the Red River campaign, see *O.R.* (Army), Ser. I, vol. xxxiv, Pt. 1, p. 208.
43. Johnson and Buel, *op. cit.,* IV, 372.
44. New York *Herald,* April 24, 1864.
45. John Homans, "The Red River Expedition," *The Mississippi Valley – Tennessee, Georgia, Alabama, 1861-1864, Papers of the Military Historical Society of Mass.,* VIII (1910), 85-86.
46. There were at least five General Smiths in the Federal army; two

of them (A. J. Smith and T. Kilby Smith) were attached to the Red River expedition. The similarity of T. Kilby Smith's name to that of the Confederate General E. Kirby Smith was even more confusing.

47. St. Louis *Daily Missouri Democrat,* May 10, 1864.
48. St. Louis *Daily Missouri Republican,* April 21, 1864.
49. New York *World,* April 25, 1864.
50. New York *Daily Tribune,* April 30, 1864.
51. John E. Hayes to Sydney Howard Gay, April 15, 1864, Gay Papers.
52. New York *Times,* May 14, 1864.
53. *Ibid.,* May 14, 1864.
54. St. Louis *Daily Missouri Democrat,* May 10, 1864.
55. St. Louis *Daily Missouri Republican,* May 8, 1864.
56. The New York *World,* May 14, 1864, described it as "the most complete and humiliating disaster of the whole war." For a similar characterization, see St. Louis *Daily Missouri Republican,* May 8, 1864.
57. New York *Times,* April 25, 1864.
58. In a letter written from Natchitoches, April 11, a New York *World* reporter remarked with some exaggeration that half of Banks's army was kept busy feeding and transporting the other half. According to Porter (*Incidents and Anecdotes,* p. 217), only two wagons were used to transport supplies for A. J. Smith's whole command.
59. New York *Daily Tribune,* April 25, 1864.
60. Cincinnati *Daily Gazette,* April 30, 1864.
61. St. Louis *Daily Missouri Democrat,* May 7, 1864. For Lee's testimony concerning his part in the campaign, see Report of the Joint Committee on the Conduct of the War, *Senate Report No. 108,* 1863, Pt. II, pp. 57-66.
62. Cincinnati *Daily Gazette,* May 18, 1864.
63. The injustice to which Stone was subjected by his military superiors throughout most of his war career is brought out in the short biographical sketch in the *Dictionary of American Biography,* XVIII, 72.
64. St. Louis *Daily Missouri Republican,* April 25, 1864. In an earlier letter published in this issue, the same correspondent had commented on the lack of ostentation or "parade" by General Banks and had depicted him standing on the forecastle of the "Black Hawk" the day he left Alexandria, in the midst of deck hands and soldiers, "as unpretending as the humblest individual aboard."
65. New York *Times,* May 10, 1864.
66. St. Louis *Daily Missouri Republican,* May 7, 1864.
67. *Ibid.,* May 7, 1864.
68. *Ibid.,* June 7, 1864. For a seemingly unwarranted charge that the radical press was out to "get" Banks because of alleged mistreatment of the Negro, see a letter from its New Orleans correspondent published in New York *Herald,* May 28, 1864.
69. New York *World,* April 26, 1864.
70. St. Louis *Daily Missouri Republican,* May 29, 1864.
71. Chicago *Daily Tribune,* July 23, 1864.
72. *Congressional Globe,* 38 Cong., 1 sess., Vol. XXXIV, Pt. 2, p. 1946.
73. St. Louis *Daily Missouri Republican,* May 10, 1864.
74. Chicago *Daily Tribune,* May 5, 1864; Nathaniel P. Banks to Manton Marble, June 8, 1864, Marble Papers.

75. John Russell Young to Nathaniel P. Banks, May 31, 1864, Nathaniel P. Banks Papers, Essex Institute, Salem, Massachusetts.
76. New Orleans *Times,* May 18, 1864,
77. New Orleans *Era,* May 17, 1864.
78. New York *Daily Tribune,* June 3, 1864.
79. St. Louis *Daily Missouri Republican,* June 10, 1864. The *Republican's* information was based on hearsay. For a refutation of its accuracy, see Philadelphia *Press,* June 14, 1864.
80. St. Louis *Daily Missouri Republican,* June 10, 1864.
81. Report of the Joint Committee on the Conduct of the War, *Senate Report No. 108,* 1863, Pt. II, pp. iii-xv.
82. *Ibid.,* pp. xvi-xlix.
83. Porter, *op. cit.,* pp. 227-230.
84. For conflicting estimates of the Red River campaign, see H. L. Landers, "Wet Sand and Cotton—Banks' Red River Campaign," *Louisiana Historical Quarterly,* XIX (January, 1936), 150-195; D. B. Sanger, "Red River—A Mercantile Expedition," *Tyler's Quarterly Historical and Genealogical Magazine,* XVII (October, 1935), 70-81; Harrington, *op cit.,* pp. 151-162.

20

INTO THE WILDERNESS AGAIN

Pages 522-551

1. New York *Daily Tribune,* March 9, 1864. For the story of how the photographer Mathew Brady was called in to help Reporters Crounse and Hanscom identify Grant at the railroad station, see Roy Meredith, *Mr. Lincoln's Camera Man* (New York, 1946), p. 162.
2. Noah Brooks, *Washington in Lincoln's Time* (New York, 1895), p. 146.
3. G. A. Sala, *My Diary in America* (London, 1865), I, 278.
4. *Ibid.,* p. 280.
5. New York *Times,* March 15, 1864.
6. *Ibid.,* March 7, 1864. A brief description of Kilpatrick's raid is given in R. U. Johnson and C. C. Buel, *Battles and Leaders of the Civil War* (New York, 1884-1888), IV, 95-96.
7. New York *Times,* March 14, 1864. The AP story was based on a statement appearing in the Washington *National Republican,* March 11, 1864, which the *National Intelligencer* contradicted three days later.
8. I. M. Tarbell, *A Reporter for Lincoln* (New York, 1927), p. 41
9. *Ibid.,* pp. 42-43
10. Jerome B. Stillson, subsequently one of the *World's* best army correspondents.
11. David G. Croly to Manton Marble, March 21, 1864, Marble Papers.
12. John W. Forney to Edwin M. Stanton, May 21, 1864, Office of Secretary of War, Letters Received, National Archives. On July 2, 1864, the Adjutant General made the following indorsement on a formal request by Sam Wilkeson for permission to send an additional *Tribune* correspondent to the Army of the Potomac: "It appears that the New York *Tribune* has seven correspondents registered as being with the army and the Comdg. Genl. does not approve of an increase of this number." Samuel Wilkeson to Marcellus R. Patrick, June 27, 1864, Office of Secretary of War, Letters Received, National Archives. See also *O.R.* (Army), Ser. I, vol. xl, Pt. 3, p. 62.
13. Thomas S. Townsend Scrapbooks, LXXXVI, 200.
14. New York *Herald,* April 13, 1864; *U. S. Army and Navy Journal,* I

(April 23, 1864), 583. Unnumbered circular, Headquarters of the Army of the Potomac, Office of Provost Marshal General, April 9, 1864, National Archives.

15. J. R. Gilmore, *Letters of a War Correspondent by Charles A. Page* (Boston, 1899), p. 314.
16. Sylvanus Cadwallader to Frederic Hudson, May 3, 1864, Bennett Papers.
17. Thomas S. Townsend Scrapbooks, LXXXVI, 200.
18. *O.R.* (Army), Ser. I, vol. xxxiii, pp. 827-829; Walter Geer, *Campaigns of the Civil War* (New York, 1926), p. 329.
19. New York *Daily Tribune,* May 9, 1864; Gilmore, *op. cit.,* p. 50.
20. Washington *Evening Star,* October 16, 1896.
21. Boston *Daily Journal,* May 13, 1864.
22. Thomas S. Townsend Scrapbooks, LXXXVI, 200.
23. Boston *Daily Journal,* May 13, 1864; New York *Times,* May 13, 1864; New York *Daily Tribune,* May 9, 10, 1864. For a detailed analysis of the Battles of the Wilderness, see W. B. Wood and J. E. Edmonds, *The Civil War in the United States with Special Reference to the Campaigns of 1864 and 1865* (London, 1937), pp. 81-91; D. S. Freeman, *R. E. Lee* (New York and London, 1935), III, 269-297; Morris Schaff, *The Battle of the Wilderness* (Boston and New York, 1910).
24. *U. S. Army and Navy Journal,* I (May 21, 1864), 649.
25. *Dictionary of American Biography,* XVIII, 252-253; U. S. Grant, *Personal Memoirs* (New York, 1895), II, 69-70; Elmer Davis, *History of the New York Times* (New York, 1921), p. 56.
26. Tarbell, *op. cit.,* pp. 2-8; New York *Daily Tribune,* May 10, 1864; Chicago *Daily Tribune,* May 11, 1864; J. T. Morse, Jr., *The Diary of Gideon Welles* (Boston and New York, 1911), II, 25. The claim is made in the *Memoirs of Henry Villard* (Boston and New York, 1904), II, 267, however, that Villard was the first army reporter to reach Washington with the news of the bloody drawn battles in the Wilderness. Villard had left the *Tribune* at the end of 1863 and was functioning as an army correspondent for a news agency which he had formed with Horace White and Adams S. Hill.
27. Oliver Gramling, *AP—The Story of News* (New York and Toronto, 1940), p. 51.
28. Wing also was carrying a dispatch for Coffin which he had agreed to forward to the Boston *Journal.* The transmission of the *Journal's* dispatch from Washington to Boston was forbidden by the censor, however, even after the *Tribune* dispatch had been published in New York and sent back to Washington to be reprinted in the evening newspapers at the Capital. W. E. Griffis, *Charles Carleton Coffin* (Boston, 1898), p. 168; Boston *Daily Journal,* May 10, 1864.
29. For a more detailed account of Wing's adventurous exploit, see Tarbell, *op. cit.,* pp. 4-28; H. E. Wing, *When Lincoln Kissed Me* (New York and Cincinnati, 1913).
30. Public anxiety in the North remained unabated, nevertheless. In a letter written four days after Wing's arrival in Washington, the Chicago *Tribune* editor, Medill, told Congressman Washburne that "we are terribly alarmed here for the result of the struggle between Grant & Lee. . . . Every possible man ought to be sent [to Grant].

No troops should be kept back." He added that he had written to Lincoln in February, 1864, recommending that reinforcements be sent to the Army of the Potomac from the various scattered commands along the Southern coast, but "I suppose I might have addressed the letter to a side of sole leather and produced an equal impression." Joseph Medill to Elihu B. Washburne, May 11, 1864, Elihu B. Washburne Papers, Library of Congress.

31. New York *Herald,* May 11, 1864; Philadelphia *Inquirer,* May 10, 1864.
32. Philadelphia *Inquirer,* May 13, 1864; New York *Herald,* May 15, 1864.
33. C. C. Coffin, *The Boys of '61* (Boston, 1896), p. 353-354.
34. New York *Times,* May 18, 1864.
35. Thomas S. Townsend Scrapbooks, LXXXVI, 57, 200; Cincinnati *Daily Gazette,* May 16, 1864.
36. W. W. Harding to U. H. Painter, May 13, 1864, Painter Papers. In the Painter Papers for this period are almost daily telegrams from Harding to Painter indicating Harding's desire to get ahead of the other newspapers. On May 8, e.g., Harding told Painter: "Send all you can and get the American Telegraph Co. to keep three or four wires on all news you can get or you may perhaps get the other Telegraph Co. [the Independent Lines] to help you out with it. Keep it up with full details even if it is up to four o'clock in morning. Try to beat all others and when done send good night."
37. New York *Herald,* May 15, 1864.
38. New York *Daily Tribune,* May 20, 1864.
39. *O.R.* (Army), Ser. I, vol. xxxvi, Pt. 1, p. 337.
40. Charleston *Daily Courier,* June 2, 1864.
41. Thomas S. Townsend Scrapbooks, LXXXVI, 70. In a letter to the business manager of the *Tribune* giving an account of his expenditures while on a ten-day trip to the Army of the Potomac, Sam Wilkeson had indicated that all the horses in the army were down to five pounds of forage a day, "and there was daily danger of our animals wholly breaking down." Samuel Wilkeson to Thomas McElrath, May 21, 1864, Samuel Wilkeson Papers, New York Public Library.
42. *O.R.* (Army), Ser. I, vol. xxxvi, Pt. 1, p. 20.
43. William H. Stiner to Frederic Hudson, May 22, 1864, Bennett Papers.
44. Oscar G. Sawyer to Frederic Hudson, May 26, 1864, William H. Stiner to Frederic Hudson, June 3, 1864, Bennett Papers. For an example of Stiner's "lickspittle style," see New York *Herald,* May 27, 1864. Before the campaign even had begun, Stiner had signified to the *Herald* that "as General Butler takes *chief command* of operations in this Department, it might be better not to offend him." William H. Stiner to Frederic Hudson, April 21, 1864, Bennett Papers.
45. Gustavus V. Fox to Benjamin F. Butler, May 31, 1864, in *Private and Official Correspondence of Gen. Benjamin F. Butler* (Privately printed, 1917), IV, 290.
46. Chicago *Daily Tribune,* May 23, 1864. For similar comment about the reporting of the campaign, see St. Louis *Daily Missouri Republican,* June 8, 1864; Charles A. Page to Sydney Howard Gay, May 19, 1864, Gay Papers; G. R. Agassiz, *Meade's Headquarters, 1863-1865* (Boston, 1922), pp. 100, 124. "Do not, for a moment, look

for the 'annihilation,' the 'hiving,' or the 'total rout,' of Lee," Colonel Lyman of Meade's staff told his wife in a letter written May 24. "Such things exist only in the New York *Herald.*"

47. F. A. Flower, *Edwin McMasters Stanton* (Akron, Ohio, 1905), pp. 214-215; New York *Times,* May 9, 1864. On May 16, 1864, it was announced in the Philadelphia *Inquirer* that thenceforth bulletins from the War Department also would be sent to General Cadwalader in Philadelphia for distribution to the Philadelphia newspapers.

48. See e.g., New York *Times,* May 12, 1864; Cincinnati *Daily Commercial,* May 13, 1864; Chicago *Daily Tribune,* May 17, 1864.

49. New York *Herald,* May 31, 1864.

50. On August 3, 1864, the *Herald* published an editorial commenting that Stanton had abandoned the practice of issuing daily war bulletins. "We want daily bulletins from the War Office," declared the Herald. "In the name of the people, we demand them."

51. L. A. Whitely to Frederic Hudson, May 22, 1864, Bennett Papers.

52. David G. Croly to Manton Marble, May 23, 1864, Marble Papers.

53. Probably George Harding, a brother of the *Inquirer* editor.

54. George P. Bower to Uriah H. Painter, May 23, 1864, Painter Papers. Bower had written to Painter the day before, apprising him that "I got cut off from the army yesterday thinking the whole line was moving in this direction. Peters [another *Inquirer* reporter] is with me. I shall get back as soon as our line is opened."

55. William Swinton, *Campaigns of the Army of the Potomac* (New York, 1866), p. 487.

56. E. P. Alexander, *Military Memoirs of a Confederate* (New York, 1907), p. 541. See also J. B. Gordon, *Reminiscences of the Civil War* (New York, 1903), p. 298.

57. Grant, *op. cit.,* II, 171-172.

58. Boston *Daily Journal,* June 9, 1864.

59. Philadelphia *Inquirer,* June 2, 1864.

60. F. B. Wiener, "Decline of a Leader, The Case of General Meade," *Infantry Journal,* XLV (November-December, 1938), 538; Horace Porter, *Campaigning with Grant* (New York, 1906), pp. 83-84; Charles A. Dana to Edwin M. Stanton, July 7, 1864, Stanton Papers.

61. Wiener, *op. cit.,* p. 539; St. Louis *Daily Missouri Republican,* March 5, 1864; Boston *Daily Advertiser,* April 4, 1864; New York *Daily Tribune,* April 6, 1864. For a statement calculated to arouse Meade's bile, made by a Washington correspondent of one of the New York papers before the campaign had even begun, see *U. S. Army and Naval Journal,* I (April 2, 1864), 537.

62. Porter, *op. cit.,* p. 191; *O.R.* (Army), Ser. I, vol. xxxvi, Pt. 1, p. 94; *ibid.,* Pt. 3, p. 722.

63. *O.R.* (Army), Ser. I, vol. xxxvi, Pt. 3, p. 670; G. G. Meade, *Life and Letters* (New York, 1913), II, 202-203; B. P. Poore, *Perley's Reminiscences* (Philadelphia, 1886), II, 151-152; Philadelphia *Inquirer,* June 10, 1864; New York *Times,* June 10, 1864; Cincinnati *Daily Gazette,* June 10, 13, 1864; New York *Daily Tribune,* June 14, 1864; Cincinnati *Daily Commercial,* June 15, 1864. Subsequently Meade admitted to Cadwallader, the *Herald* correspondent, that it had been a great mistake to inflict on Crapsey such a degrading form of punishment. Washington *Evening Star,* October 16, 1896.

64. From a letter in the Whitelaw Reid Papers entitled "An Instance of the Chivalric & Honor Command of an Army sometimes breeds," marked "Unpublished," and dated at Washington, June 11, 1864. The letter was signed "Agate." Apparently Count Gurowski had heard the same story about Meade as Reid and Crapsey had. Opposite the date May 8, 1864, appears the following entry in Gurowski's diary: "It is said that after the first two days' fighting Meade advised Grant to retreat. I do not doubt that it is true." Adam Gurowski, *Diary* (Boston, New York, and Washington, D.C., 1862-1866), III, 221. For a conflicting estimate of the authenticity of this report, see C. A. Dana, *Recollections of the Civil War* (New York, 1898), p. 215. Dana did not reach Grant's headquarters until some time during the morning of May 7, however.

65. This account of the newspaper conspiracy against Meade is based upon three sources: (1) a special dispatch to the Boston *Daily Journal* from Washington (signed "Perley" and published in the June 11, 1864, issue of the *Journal*) stating that "newspaper correspondents here are somewhat exercised by the report of the treatment of several members of the press by military officers, and have taken measures to have a thorough investigation"; (2) a letter written by Sylvanus Cadwallader to one of Meade's staff officers in 1894 and reprinted on p. 318 of I. S. Pennypacker's life of General Meade (New York, 1901); (3) a letter addressed to the Philadelphia *Weekly Times* by an individual who signed himself "W." and which was published in the August 24, 1878, *Times*. Cadwallader was in Washington at the time of Crapsey's punishment but returned to Grant's headquarters soon afterward. In his letter to the *Times*, "W." (who may have been Sam Wilkeson) asserted that although he had never seen any allusion to the meeting of the correspondents in print many besides himself were cognizant of it. He went on to say: "I have always thought and often said . . . that Crapsey's punishment made General Grant President of the United States and that the resolution of the meeting referred to had a very unjust and injurious effect upon the estimation of the people of the United States upon the character of General Meade."

66. Tarbell, *op. cit.*, pp. 46-54.

67. J. G. Randall, *The Civil War and Reconstruction* (Boston and New York, 1937), p. 549.

68. Boston *Daily Journal*, June 8, 1864.

69. In his *R. E. Lee*, III, 399-404, Freeman gives evidence to show that Lee had foreseen the possibility that Grant might cross the James but admits that Lee was unaware that Grant actually had crossed to the South bank of the James until the evening of June 17. See also note in Wood and Edmonds, *op. cit.*, pp. 111-113.

70. New York *Times*, June 23, 1864.

71. Washington *Evening Star*, October 16, 1896; *O.R.* (Army), Ser. I, vol. xl, Pt. 1, p. 307.

72. New York *Daily Tribune*, June 27, 1864.

73. B. F. Butler, *Autobiography* (Boston, 1892), pp. 700-701; *O.R.* (Army), Ser. I, vol. xl, Pt. 2, pp. 567, 583, 593.

21

"ATLANTA IS OURS, AND FAIRLY WON"

Pages 552-584

1. Walter Wellman, "Of De B. Ran-

dolph Keim," *The Keim and Allied Families,* No. 23 (October, 1900), p. 722; New York *Herald,* March 15, 1864. Sherman likewise exhibited a certain amount of favoritism toward the army reporters of his good friend Prentice's Louisville *Journal.* See Hamilton Busbey, "Recollections of Abraham Lincoln and the Civil War," *Forum,* XLV (March, 1911), 285.

2. M. A. D. W. Howe, *Home Letters of General Sherman* (New York, 1909), p. 285.
3. W. F. G. Shanks, *Personal Recollections of Distinguished Generals* (New York, 1866), pp. 21-22.
4. T. M. Cook to Frederic Hudson, May 3, 1864, Bennett Papers.
5. Cincinnati *Daily Commercial,* May 9, 1864; St. Louis *Daily Missouri Republican,* June 4, 1864.
6. Cincinnati *Daily Commercial,* May 11, 1864.
7. Joseph Hooker to L. L. Crounse, February 2, 1864, Crounse Papers.
8. New York *Daily Tribune,* May 20, 1864.
9. Shanks, *op. cit.,* pp. 311-314; New York *Herald,* May 22, 1864.
10. Cincinnati *Daily Commercial,* May 19, 1864; Louisville *Daily Journal,* May 21, 1864.
11. New York *Herald,* December 27, 1864.
12. New York *Times,* May 21, 1864; St. Louis *Daily Missouri Republican,* June 4, 1864.
13. B. C. Truman, "Anecdotes of Andrew Johnson," *Century Magazine,* LXXXV (January, 1913), 437. For a different explanation of Sickles' mission, see Edgcumb Pinchon, *Dan Sickles* (New York, 1945), pp. 206-209.
14. *O.R.* (Army), Ser. I, vol. xxxviii, Pt. 4, p. 272. The text of the circular was also given in various newspapers such as the Cincinnati *Daily Gazette,* May 23, 1864.
15. Cincinnati *Daily Gazette,* June 15, 1864. For other editorial reactions to the circular, see New York *Times,* June 6, 1864; Cincinnati *Daily Commercial,* June 10, 1864.
16. D. P. Conyngham, *Sherman's March through the South* (New York, 1865), pp. 74-75.
17. Elias Smith to Sydney Howard Gay, May 31, 1864, Gay Papers.
18. Chicago *Daily Tribune,* June 12, 16, 1864.
19. Cincinnati *Daily Commercial,* June 7, 1864; Chicago *Daily Tribune,* June 8, 1864.
20. New York *Herald,* June 19, 1864.
21. *Ibid.,* July 1, 1864. The idea that the Northern army consisted in very large part of foreign troops apparently was widely disseminated among the civil population of Georgia. As Sherman's army was marching through Jonesboro during a later stage of the campaign, a Cincinnati *Gazette* reporter overhead an old lady express surprise at being able to understand the Yankee tongue! She had been led to believe, she intimated, that the Northern army was made up entirely of foreigners. Cincinnati *Daily Gazette,* September 13, 1864.
22. New York *Daily Tribune,* June 2, 1864. A similar comment by the same reporter appeared in *ibid.,* July 14, 1864.
23. Chicago *Daily Tribune,* June 12, 1864.
24. New York *Daily Tribune,* June 23, 1864.
25. New York *Herald,* July 1, 1864.
26. Cincinnati *Daily Times,* June 28, 1864.
27. New York *Daily Tribune,* July 14, 1864.

28. Louisville *Daily Journal,* June 28, 1864; New York *Daily Tribune,* July 12, 14, 1864; O. O. Howard, *Autobiography* (New York, 1907), I, 563-564.
29. Donn Piatt, *Memories of the Men Who Saved the Union* (New York and Chicago, 1887), pp. 254-255.
30. Cincinnati *Daily Commercial,* July 4, 1864.
31. Lloyd Lewis, *Sherman, Fighting Prophet* (New York, 1932), p. 378.
32. Cincinnati *Daily Commercial,* July 4, 1864.
33. Cincinnati *Daily Gazette,* July 4, 1864.
34. *Ibid.,* July 4, 1864; W. F. G. Shanks, "How We Get Our News," *Harper's New Monthly Magazine,* XXXIV (March, 1867), 520.
35. New York *Herald,* June 23, 1864.
36. Wellman, *op. cit.,* pp. 722-723; *O.R.* (Army), Ser. I, vol. xxxviii, Pt. 4, pp. 637, 642; Cincinnati *Daily Commercial,* July 8, 1864; Washington *Evening Star,* October 16, 1896. According to the New York *Tribune,* July 12, 1864, the Confederates already had changed their signal code by the time the disclosure was made. In the *Tribune*'s opinion, however, the publication of such information, whether true or false, marked the *Herald* reporter as either a "blockhead" or a "copperhead" and therefore an unsafe person to be in the army.
37. Cincinnati *Daily Gazette,* July 25, 26, 1864; Louisville *Daily Journal,* July 25, 1864; Cincinnati *Daily Commercial,* July 29, August 9, 1864; New York *Times,* August 10, 1864; New York *Daily Tribune,* August 12, 1864; Chicago *Daily Tribune,* August 1, 12, 1864.
38. Cincinnati *Daily Commercial,* August 5, 1864.
39. J. A. Connolly, "Major Connolly's Letters to His Wife, 1862-1865," *Transactions of Illinois State Historical Society,* XXIX (1928), 354.
40. Cincinnati *Daily Times,* August 1, 1864. For examples of some of these premature announcements, see *U. S. Army and Navy Journal,* I (June 4, 1864), 676; New York *Daily Tribune,* June 28, 1864. A false report of a Confederate retreat across the Chattahoochee, emanating from the Louisville office of the AP, was commented on in Cincinnati *Daily Gazette,* June 28, 1864.
41. New York *Daily Tribune,* August 19, 1864.
42. New York *Times,* August 27, 1864.
43. Cincinnati *Daily Commercial,* August 18, 1864.
44. Chattanooga *Daily Gazette,* August 14, 1864; Philadelphia *Inquirer,* August 17, 1864; New York *Daily Tribune,* August 31, 1864.
45. Cincinnati *Daily Commercial,* September 13, 1864.
46. New York *Daily Tribune,* September 15, 1864.
47. Cincinnati *Daily Commercial,* September 13, 1864.
48. *Ibid.,* September 3, 1864; New York *Times,* September 4, 1864; Chicago *Daily Tribune,* September 14, 1864.
49. Shanks, *Personal Recollections,* pp. 30-31.
50. New York *Times,* September 19, 1864.
51. Cincinnati *Daily Commercial,* September 13, 1864; New York *Times,* September 15, 1864; New York *Daily Tribune,* September 15, 1864. At some time during the campaign, Truman left the employment of the Philadelphia *Press* and shifted to the New York *Times.*
52. E. S. Maclay, *A History of the United States Navy, from 1775 to 1898* (New York, 1898), II, 524.

53. J. R. Spears, *The History of Our Navy* (New York, 1899), IV, 437-442; Maclay, *op. cit.*, II, 524-527; J. R. Soley, *The Blockade and the Cruisers* (London, 1898), pp. 206-213; W. M. Robinson, Jr., "The Alabama–Kearsarge Battle, A Study in Original Sources," *Essex Institute Historical Collections*, LX (April, 1924), 97-120, (July, 1924), 209-218.
54. New York *Times*, July 6, 1864.
55. *Ibid.*, July 6, 1864. The claim made in the New York *Herald*, May 7, 1916, that a *Herald* correspondent cabled the first news of the sinking of the "Alabama" is inaccurate. At no time in 1864 was the Atlantic cable in use.
56. Frank Moore, *The Rebellion Record* (New York, 1861-1873), IX, 235; London *Daily News*, June 24, 1864.
57. New York *Herald*, July 9, 1864.
58. New York *Daily Tribune*, August 1, 1887.
59. *Ibid.*, September 2, 1864.
60. C. L. Lewis, *David Glasgow Farragut* (Annapolis, Maryland, 1943), II, 280-281.
61. New York *Herald*, August 20, 1864.
62. Percival Drayton to Alexander Hamilton, Jr., August 19, 1864, in Percival Drayton, *Naval Letters from Captain Percival Drayton, 1861-1865* (New York, 1906), pp. 67-68.
63. *Vide supra*, p. 70.
64. The New York *Herald* had two reporters, the New York *Tribune*, the New York *Evening Post*, the Philadelphia *Inquirer* and *Bulletin*, the Cincinnati *Commercial*, and Chicago *Tribune* one each. Neither Conyngham of the *Herald* nor James Redpath of the Boston *Journal* accompanied Sherman on the march to the sea in spite of statements to that effect in J. B. Spore, "Sherman and the Press," *Infantry Journal*, LXIII (December, 1948), 31, and C. F. Horner, *The Life of James Redpath* (New York and Newark, 1926), p. 112.
65. B. H. Liddell Hart, *Sherman, The Genius of the Civil War* (London, 1933), p. 326.
66. Lewis, *Sherman*, p. 430.
67. *O.R.* (Army), Ser. I, vol. xxxix, Pt. 3, p. 740.
68. *Ibid.*, p. 740; F. A. Flower, *Edwin McMasters Stanton* (Akron, Ohio, 1905), p. 210. For an editorial slap at Stanton for loose talk about Sherman's future movements, see Cincinnati *Daily Commercial*, September 8, 1864.
69. *O.R.* (Army), Ser. I, vol. xxxix, Pt. 3, p. 727. Significantly enough all Northern papers of November 10, 1864, which had been brought to Butler's Army of the James were ordered burned to keep them from falling into the hands of the enemy. E. T. Peters to Uriah H. Painter, November 13, 1864, Painter Papers.
70. New York *Herald*, December 22, 1864.
71. *Ibid.*, December 28, 1864.
72. *Ibid.*, December 28, 1864.
73. Frequent references to Davis appear in the campaign diaries of George W. Nichols and Henry Hitchcock. To his wife, Major Hitchcock, Sherman's personal secretary, wrote on December 13, 1864: "You must take 'Harper's Weekly' now. Their special artist, Theo. R. Davis, has been with us all the time . . . with our own party and mess. His sketches are good and truthful. . . . Davis is a pleasant fellow, quite young—twenty-three—and has real talent . . . ." Henry Hitchcock, *Marching with Sherman* (New Haven, 1927), pp. 186-187.

74. Cincinnati *Daily Commercial,* December 24, 1864.
75. Philadelphia *Inquirer,* December 23, 1864.
76. See F. Y. Hedley, *Marching through Georgia* (Chicago, 1890), p. 314, for the comment of a Union officer about the "scandalous narratives of robbery, rapine, and murder" by Sherman's soldiers with which the columns of the Southern press teemed.
77. For an interesting analysis of the New York *Herald's* headline treatment of the campaign, see Spore, *op. cit.,* p. 33.
78. Jerome B. Stillson to David G. Croly, December 8, 1864, Marble Papers. In his letter to Croly, Stillson voiced the opinion that the "absurd and wretched stuff" written for publication by the *World's* Baltimore correspondent, Henry M. Flint, had been largely responsible for this discrimination against the *World.*
79. Cincinnati *Daily Commercial,* December 21, 1864.
80. New York *Herald,* December 22, 1864.
81. New York *Evening Post,* December 22, 1864.
82. G. F. Williams, "Lights and Shadows of Army Life," *Century Magazine,* XXVIII (October, 1884), 807.
83. New York *Herald,* December 22, 1864.
84. *Ibid.,* December 22, 1864. Although this was probably an exaggerated statement, Sherman's losses during the march from Atlanta to the sea (531 killed and wounded and 1,616 missing) were remarkably light.
85. G. W. Nichols, *The Story of the Great March* (New York, 1865); Allan Nevins, *The Evening Post* (New York, 1922), p. 318. Harpers had difficulty manufacturing enough copies of the Nichols volume to meet the demand. It was one of the most financially remunerative of all Civil War books published in the decade following the war. J. H. Harper, *The House of Harper* (New York and London, 1912), p. 243. An interesting scrapbook of reviews of the Nichols volume is in the possession of the Historical and Philosophical Society of Ohio, Cincinnati.
86. John E. Hayes to Sydney Howard Gay, December 15, 1864, Gay Papers; New York *Daily Tribune,* December 30, 1864.
87. Cincinnati *Daily Gazette,* January 2, 1865; Chicago *Daily Tribune,* December 22, 1865; New York *World,* December 28, 1864.
88. Cincinnati *Daily Gazette,* January 2, 1865.

22

"IF ALL . . . BATTLES . . . WERE AS WELL DESCRIBED"

Pages 585-612

1. New York *Herald,* June 25, 1864.
2. *Ibid.,* June 25, 1864.
3. Washington *Evening Star,* October 16, 1896.
4. J. R. Gilmore, *Letters of a War Correspondent by Charles A. Page* (Boston, 1899), pp. 143-146; New York *Daily Tribune,* June 29, 1864.
5. *Journalist,* II (October 31, 1885), 6.
6. New York *World,* July 14, 1864.
7. *Journalist,* II (October 31,1885), 6.
8. Chicago *Evening Journal,* July 20, 1864.
9. New York *Herald,* July 13, 25, 1864.
10. New York *Times,* July 13, 1864.
11. Emory's Nineteenth Corps had left New Orleans before anything was known about Early's raid and had arrived off Fortress Monroe just in

time to be dispatched to the relief of Washington.

12. After an earlier assignment in the Shenandoah Valley, Breckenridge had joined Lee's army, commanding a division at the Battle of Cold Harbor. At the time of Early's raid on Washington, Breckenridge was second in command of the raiding force.
13. C. C. Coffin, *The Boys of '61* (Boston, 1886), p. 386.
14. New York *Times,* July 22, 1864.
15. New York *World,* July 14, 1864.
16. "Letters from Washington, The 'Siege of Washington,' and the Responsibility. Was it a Large or Little Force that did it? A Careful Resumé of the Facts," July 15, 1864, Reid Papers. Apparently the *Gazette* did not see fit to publish Reid's lengthy resumé.
17. W. B. Wood and J. E. Edmonds, *The Civil War in the United States* (London, 1937), p. 199; Noah Brooks, *Washington in Lincoln's Time* (New York, 1895), p. 175. Early's estimate of 8,000 infantrymen in his command by the time he reached Washington was much too low. *Dictionary of American Biography,* V, 599.
18. New York *Herald,* July 13, 1864. In his official report of the Ninth Corps's performance during the action, Burnside stated: "On the 31st the entire line was advanced from one-fourth to three-fourths of a mile under a brisk fire of the enemy. Several detached lines of skirmish pits were carried, and our people took position close up to the enemy's main line." *O.R.* (Army), Ser. I, vol. xxxvi, Pt. 1, p. 913.
19. *O.R.* (Army), Ser. I, vol. xxxvi, Pt. 3, p. 751; vol. xl, Pt. 2, pp. 559-560, 582. Also Philadelphia *Inquirer,* July 14, 1864; "Our Historical Writers," *Historical Magazine and Notes and Queries,* New Ser. VI (November, 1869), 296.
20. New York *Times,* July 14, 1864. Raymond erred in supposing that Meade issued the order for Swinton's expulsion from the Army of the Potomac. Meade simply indorsed Grant's order and forwarded it to the Provost Marshal for execution.
21. R. U. Johnson and C. C. Buel, *Battles and Leaders of the Civil War* (New York, 1884-1888), IV, 559; T. L. Livermore, *Numbers and Losses in the Civil War* (Boston and New York, 1900), p. 116; Henry Pleasants, Jr., *The Tragedy of the Crater* (Boston, 1938), pp. 32 *passim; O.R.* (Army), Ser. I, vol. xl, Pt. 1, pp. 526-530.
22. T. S. Seybold to Sydney Howard Gay, August 1, 1864; T. C. Grey to Sydney Howard Gay, August 2, 1864, Gay Papers.
23. Philadelphia *Inquirer,* August 2, 1864.
24. New York *Times,* August 2, 1864; Philadelphia *Inquirer,* August 6, 1864.
25. These headlines had appeared on the first page of the New York *Herald,* August 1, 1864.
26. New York *Daily Tribune,* August 6, 1864.
27. Charles A. Page to Sydney Howard Gay, August 5 [6 ?], 1864, Gay Papers.
28. Pleasants, *op. cit.,* p. 14.
29. *Dictionary of American Biography,* III, 313; Report of the Joint Committee on the Conduct of the War, *Senate Report No. 108,* 1863, Pt. I, pp. 216-217.
30. Pleasants, *op. cit.,* p. 105; B. P. Poore, *Life and Public Services of General Ambrose E. Burnside,* (Providence, Rhode Island, 1882), p. 251. Subsequently, August 10, 1864, the New York *Tribune* came

to Burnside's defense with a lengthy statement of his side of the case.

31. Walter Geer, *Campaigns of the Civil War* (New York, 1926), p. 409; P. H. Sheridan, *Personal Memoirs* (New York, 1888), I, 466.
32. G. F. Williams, "Important Services Rendered by War Correspondents," *Independent*, LIV (January 23, 1902), 212.
33. New York *Times*, September 7, 1864.
34. "The Rise and Fall of the War Correspondent," *Macmillan's Magazine*, XC (August, 1904), 306. What appears to have been the same incident was referred to by Williams in the New York *Times*, September 15, 1864, without any indication that he was the reporter who was hauled over the coals. Williams quite possibly told, and colored, this anecdote to the author of the Macmillan article, whoever he was.
35. *Journalist*, II (October 31, 1885), 6; New York *Times*, January 1, 1921.
36. New York *World*, September 24, 1864.
37. M. F. Schmitt, *General George Crook, His Autobiography* (Norman, Oklahoma, 1946), p. 128. Yet Sheridan did not censure Emory in his official report of the battle. *O.R.* (Army), Ser. I, vol. xliii, Pt. 1, pp. 46-47. For other shortcomings in the reporting of the Battle of Winchester, see New York *Daily Tribune*, October 20, 1864.
38. Thomas S. Townsend Scrapbooks, LXXXVII, 74. The army reporters with Sheridan were not permitted to use the military telegraph at this time. A Washington correspondent of the New York *World* informed the managing editor, September 25: "Stillson is very innocent, if he thinks that his dispatches can go *through the War. Dept.* military telegraph to the *World*. In fact they won't let the *Tribune* use the line, no matter who in the field *approves dispatches*." George W. Adams to David G. Croly, September 25, 1864, Marble Papers.
39. A brief but informative analysis of the Sheridan "legend" may be found in Wood and Edmonds, *op. cit.*, p. 225n. See also J. G. Randall, *The Civil War and Reconstruction* (New York, 1937), p. 570.
40. Evidently Rosser's division, formerly commanded by Fitzhugh Lee. Lee had been seriously wounded at the Battle of Winchester and was not able to return to duty until January, 1865.
41. New York *World*, October 22, 1864.
42. New York *Daily Tribune*, October 26, 1864.
43. New York *World*, October 22, 1864.
44. G. A. Forsyth, *Thrilling Days in Army Life* (New York and London, 1900), p. 147.
45. New York *World*, October 22, 1864.
46. *Ibid.*, October 22, 1864.
47. *Ibid.*, October 22, 1864.
48. George W. Adams to David G. Croly, October 26, 1864, Marble Papers.
49. Cincinnati *Daily Commercial*, November 11, 1864. According to Crook, his cavalry pickets had been shifted by higher authority from the fords where the enemy crossed, before the attack, to the rear and left of his command where they were of no use. Schmitt, *op. cit.*, pp. 132-133, 134.
50. New York *Times*, October 28, 1864.

51. *Ibid.*, November 8, 1864.

52. A. C. Hamlin, "Who Recaptured the Guns at Cedar Creek, October 19, 1864?" *The Shenandoah Campaigns of 1862, and 1864, and the Appomattox Campaign, 1865, Papers of Military Historical Society of Mass.*, VI (1907), 183-208. Paul originally had given Custer's division the credit for capturing all but seven or eight pieces of artillery. For some interesting comment about the Confederate reporting of Cedar Creek, see New York *Times,* November 1, 1864.

53. New York *Times,* October 14, 1864.

54. *Journalist,* II (October 31, 1885), 6; New York *Times,* October 7, 1864.

55. Meade's reaction to Crapsey's return was indicated by a letter to his wife, September 16, 1864, in which he remarked: "I have this evening a letter from Mr. Cropsey [*sic*], asking permission to return to the army. I do not altogether like its tone or spirit, but shall not take any other notice of it than to send him a pass." G. G. Meade, *Life and Letters* (New York, 1913), II, 228.

56. One of the *Inquirer* correspondents.

57. Edward Crapsey to Uriah H. Painter, October 18, 1864, Painter Papers. The methods employed by Williams to procure Richmond papers for the New York *Times* at this time are described in *Journalist,* IX (July 13, 1889), 6.

58. Edward Crapsey to Uriah H. Painter, November 1, 1864, Painter Papers.

59. Chicago *Daily Tribune,* July 11, 1864.

60. *Ibid.*, June 28, 1864.

61. New York *Times,* September 10, 1864.

23
THE GRAND FINALE
Pages 613-637

1. A. D. Richardson, *The Secret Service, the Field, the Dungeon, and the Escape* (Hartford, 1865), p. 421, Cf. *O.R.* (Army), Ser. II, vol. vi, p. 59.

2. James P. Hambleton of the Atlanta *Southern Confederacy.*

3. *O.R.* (Army), Ser. II, vol. viii, pp. 88-89, 1035; New York *Daily Tribune,* January 9, 1865.

4. Richardson, *op. cit.*, pp. 501-502; J. H. Browne, *Four Years in Secessia* (Hartford, 1865), pp. 421-426; New York *Daily Tribune,* January 17, February 8, 1865.

5. New York *Herald,* January 23, 1865; New York *Daily Tribune,* January 24, February 17, 1865; Albert D. Richardson to E. R. Perkins, March 22, 1865, Miscellaneous MSS, The New-York Historical Society.

6. A. B. Paine, *A Sailor of Fortune* (New York, 1906), p. 249.

7. Communication A, Osbon Court Martial Records, Office of the Secretary of War, National Archives.

8. *O.R.* (Navy), Ser. I, vol. xi, p. 205.

9. New York *Times,* December 30, 1864.

10. See various newspapers, December 30, 1864.

11. New York *World,* December 31, 1864; New York *Daily Tribune,* January 20, 1865; *O.R.* (Navy), Ser. I, vol. xi, p. 251.

12. New York *World,* December 31, 1864.

13. W. B. Wood and J. E. Edmonds, *The Civil War in the United States* (London, 1937), p. 247; T. H. Williams, *Lincoln and His Generals* (New York, 1952), pp. 347-348. An earlier attempt by Grant

to get rid of Butler had backfired when Lincoln refused to take the responsibility for ousting him. Williams, *op. cit.*, pp. 321-323.

14. New York *Daily Tribune*, January 12, 1864; Philadelphia *Inquirer*, January 14, 1865; New York *Herald*, January 16, 1865; *Congressional Globe*, 38 Congress, 2 sess., Vol. XXXV, p. 257.
15. *O.R.* (Army), Ser. I, vol. xlvi, Pt. 2, pp. 120-121.
16. New York *Daily Tribune*, January 20, 1865. One of the *Tribune*'s reporters on this expedition was T. S. Seybold. For his totally inaccurate prediction of its objective, see T. S. Seybold to Sydney Howard Gay, January 6, 1865, Gay Papers.
17. R. S. West, Jr., *The Second Admiral* (New York, 1937), pp. 287-288. West inaccurately attributes this statement to a reporter for the Baltimore *American*. In reality the *American* copied it from the *Tribune*.
18. New York *Herald*, January 19, 1865.
19. New York *Daily Tribune*, January 18, 1865; Edward H. Hall to Charles A. Dana, January 17, 1865, Stanton Papers.
20. Dorothy Stanley, *The Autobiography of Sir Henry Morton Stanley* (Boston and New York, 1909), pp. 220-221; Frank Hird, *H. M. Stanley, The Authorized Life* (London, 1935), pp. 43-44.
21. Osbon Court Martial Records. See also, New York *Daily Tribune*, January 25, 1865; B. S. Osbon to Manton Marble, January 25, 1865, Marble Papers; Paine, *op. cit.*, pp. 250-251.
22. Elias Smith to Sydney Howard Gay, February 3, 1865; A. H. Byington to Sydney Howard Gay, February 8, 1865, Gay Papers.
23. O. O. Howard, *Autobiography* (New York, 1907), II, 113.
24. C. C. Coffin, *The Boys of '61* (Boston, 1886), p. 437.
25. New York *Herald*, March 18, 1865.
26. *Ibid.*, March 18, 1865.
27. *Ibid.*, March 18, 1865.
28. The evidence for the various hypotheses is summarized in J. F. Rhodes, *Historical Essays* (New York, 1909), pp. 301-313.
29. New York *Daily Tribune*, February 22, 1865.
30. W. E. Griffis, *Life of Charles Carleton Coffin* (Boston, 1898), pp. 178-181.
31. Boston *Daily Journal*, March 3, 1865.
32. New York *Daily Tribune*, March 2, 1865. For adverse editorial comment about Redpath's account, see *Daily Richmond Examiner*, March 7, 1865.
33. New York *Daily Tribune*, March 2, 1865.
34. New York *Herald*, February 28, 1865.
35. New York *Daily Tribune*, March 2, 1865.
36. Coffin, *op. cit.*, p. 481.
37. W. T. Sherman, *Memoirs* (New York, 1875), II, 292; Lloyd Lewis, *Sherman, Fighting Prophet* (New York, 1932), p. 508; J. G. Randall, "The Newspaper Problem in its Bearing upon Military Secrecy during the Civil War," *American Historical Review*, XXIII (January, 1918), 311.
38. New York *Herald*, March 18, 1865; G. W. Nichols, *Story of the Great March* (New York, 1865), p. 249.
39. Schofield's Twenty-Third Corps had been moved from Tennessee to Washington during January, 1865, to take over the newly organized Department of North Carolina and to cooperate with Sherman.
40. New York *Daily Tribune*, April 1, 1865.

41. Lewis, *op. cit.*, p. 521.
42. A. T. Rice, *Reminiscences of Abraham Lincoln* (New York, 1888), pp. 175-177.
43. Philadelphia *Inquirer*, January 20, 1865.
44. G. F. Williams, "Important Services Rendered by War Correspondents," *Independent*, LIV (January 23, 1902), 210-211.
45. New York *Herald*, April 1, 1865.
46. Walter Geer, *Campaigns of the Civil War* (New York, 1926), p. 416.
47. Cincinnati *Enquirer*, April 28, 1882.
48. New York *World*, April 4, 1865; San Francisco *Chronicle*, July 23, 1882; George Alfred Townsend Scrapbooks.
49. New York *Times*, April 7, 1865.
50. New York *Herald*, April 6, 1865.
51. J. R. Gilmore, *Letters of a War Correspondent by Charles A. Page* (Boston, 1899), pp. 309-310.
52. Charles H. Woodwell Scrapbooks, Charles H. Woodwell Papers, in the possession of the Woodwell family, Tamaqua, Pennsylvania.
53. Coffin, *op. cit.*, p. 499.
54. From the Detroit *News-Tribune*, as reprinted in New York *Tribune*, October 25, 1896. The story in the Detroit paper was based on a little volume of telegraph tales by W. J. Johnson which must have been privately printed.
55. As late as April 5 the New Yorkers were still very skeptical about Richmond having fallen, nevertheless. According to the New York *Times*, April 6, 1865, they interpreted the lack of direct news from Richmond in the morning papers as indicating that the story was "false or at least quite premature."
56. Gilmore, *op. cit.*, p. 314. Cortissoz claims, however, that Reid had a pass from the War Department to Richmond direct, "a boon so rare just then that speculative persons offered him a hundred dollars and more for the precious bit of paper." Royal Cortissoz, *The Life of Whitelaw Reid* (New York, 1921), I, 114.
57. Gilmore, *op. cit.*, pp. 315-317; New York *Daily Tribune*, April 10, 1865.
58. New York *Times*, April 10, 1865; F. M. O'Brien, *The Story of the Sun* (New York, 1918), p. 224.
59. Coffin, *op. cit.*, p. 508.
60. *Ibid.*, pp. 510-514; C. C. Coffin to Thomas Nast, July 19, 1866, "Lincoln's Visit to Richmond, April 4, 1865," *Moorsfield Antiquarian*, I (May, 1937), 27-29.
61. Differing versions of the incident are given in the Boston *Daily Journal*, April 11, 1865; Coffin, *op cit.*, p. 519; and Gilmore, *op. cit.*, pp. 326-327. Chester's account of the fall of Richmond appeared in Philadelphia *Press*, April 6, 1865.
62. Wood and Edmonds, *op. cit.*, pp. 300-301.
63. George Alfred Townsend Scrapbooks.
64. Cincinnati *Daily Gazette*, April 8, 1865.
65. New York *Daily Tribune*, April 15, 1865.
66. New York *Herald*, April 14, 1865.
67. According to the New York *Times* correspondent L. L. Crounse, the only civilian present during the conference between Grant and Lee was a telegraph engineer named Tal. P. Shaffner. New York *Times*, April 14, 1865.
68. I. M. Tarbell, *A Reporter for Lincoln* (New York, 1927), p. 77; New York *Daily Tribune*, April 10, 1865.

24
"THIRTY"
Pages 638-653

("Thirty" is printers' slang for "the end." It is said of, or written on, the final sheet or line of copy for an edition of a newspaper.)

1. Rollo Ogden, *Life and Letters of Edwin Lawrence Godkin* (New York and London, 1907), I, 204-205.
2. F. L. Mott, *American Journalism* (New York, 1941), p. 329.
3. *U. S. Army and Navy Journal,* I (May 7, 1864), 609.
4. New York *Herald,* March 19, 1865.
5. St. Louis *Daily Missouri Democrat,* March 11, 1863.
6. Cincinnati *Daily Commercial,* May 14, 1863. Cf. M. A. D. W. Howe, *Home Letters of General Sherman* (New York, 1909), p. 241.
7. *Daily Richmond Whig,* April 14, 1862. See also Havilah Babcock, "The Press and the Civil War," *Journalism Quarterly,* VI (March, 1929), 3-4.
8. *Vide supra,* p. 471.
9. Philadelphia *Press,* June 28, 1861.
10. See various newspapers, August 28, 1862. Apparently the story originated in Baltimore. For a more favorable judgment of the performance of the AP in Civil War reporting, see Oliver Gramling, *AP—The Story of News* (New York and Toronto, 1940), p. 44.
11. New York *Times,* November 7, 1861.
12. Boston *Post,* as quoted in St. Louis *Daily Missouri Democrat,* June 26, 1861; New York *Daily Tribune,* May 15, 1862.
13. New York *Daily Tribune,* March 8, 1865. The telegraph reporters at Cairo had an especially bad reputation. See e.g., the reference in the Cincinnati *Commercial,* April 10, 1863, to "the magnificent fictions that find their way over the wires from Cairo."
14. New York *Daily Tribune,* June 29, 1863.
15. Cincinnati *Daily Commercial,* October 25, 1861.
16. Louisville *Daily Journal,* as quoted in Cincinnati *Daily Commercial,* January 5, 1863.
17. Cincinnati *Daily Commercial,* January 5, 1863.
18. *Ibid.,* April 30, 1862.
19. St. Louis *Daily Missouri Democrat,* April 1, 1863.
20. Cincinnati *Daily Times,* June 2, 1862.
21. *Ibid.,* November 10, 1863.
22. *Vanity Fair,* September 14, 1861.
23. Writing in defense of the " 'intelligent contraband,' whose narratives were given to the press by war correspondents," a soldier author expressed the point of view that "his news was usually reliable in its general terms, although ignorance led him into exaggerations whenever a numerical force was in question." F. Y. Hedley, *Marching through Georgia* (Chicago, 1890), p. 302.
24. Philadelphia *Inquirer,* as quoted in Boston *Daily Journal,* March 10, 1865.
25. J. R. Gilmore, *Letters of a War Correspondent by Charles A. Page* (Boston, 1899), p. 208.
26. Philadelphia *Press,* August 21, 1862.
27. Philip Ripley to Manton Marble, July 16, 1863, Marble Papers.
28. See J. C. Derby, *Fifty Years among Authors, Books, and Publishers* (New York, 1886), pp. 480-481; A. K. McClure, *Old Time Notes of Pennsylvania* (Philadelphia, 1905), I, 573-574.

29. New York *Evening Post,* May 27, 1862.
30. St. Louis *Daily Missouri Democrat,* April 14, 1862.
31. Cincinnati *Daily Commercial,* September 11, 1862.
32. New York *Times,* January 3, 1862.
33. *Ibid.,* June 21, 1864.
34. *Ibid.,* April 16, 1864.
35. *Ibid.,* May 21, 1864.
36. Cincinnati *Daily Commercial,* April 25, 1862.
37. New York *Times,* April 25, 1864.
38. Philadelphia *Inquirer,* April 3, 1865.
39. S. W. Fiske, *Mr. Dunn Browne's Experiences in the Army* (Boston, 1866), pp. 200-201.
40. New York *Times,* November 4, 1861.
41. Cincinnati *Daily Gazette,* February 11, 1862.
42. New York *Times,* February 1, 1865.
43. Cincinnati *Enquirer,* September 28, 1863.
44. Gilmore, *op. cit.,* p. 309.
45. J. G. Randall, "The Newspaper Problem in its Bearing upon Military Secrecy during the Civil War," *American Historical Review,* XXIII (January, 1918), 310.
46. *Ibid.,* pp. 311-312.
47. See e.g., New York *Times,* December 29, 1862.
48. Adams S. Hill to Sydney Howard Gay, June 21, 1863, Gay Papers.
49. Henry Villard, "Army Correspondence," *Nation,* I (July 27, 1865), 116. For evidence tending to confirm Villard's statement about the departure of the better-type reporters from the field, see J. H. Browne, *Four Years in Secessia* (Hartford, 1865), pp. 19-20.
50. Chicago *Daily Tribune,* July 12, 1864. In an earlier stage of the war, a New York *Tribune* reporter had attributed the numerous errors which appeared in the newspaper lists of killed and wounded to "the itching of vain men to figure in bulletins" and "the prudent taste of officers conscious of having behaved badly, to cover themselves with the false testimony of courage before the charge of cowardice shall be made or proven against them." New York *Daily Tribune,* June 14, 1862.
51. Washington *Evening Star,* October 16, 1896.
52. Philadelphia *Press,* May 28, 1864.
53. G. S. Merriam, *The Life and Times of Samuel Bowles* (New York, 1885), I, 363.

Acknowledgments

ATOP South Mountain at Gapland near Frederick, Maryland, is a gigantic memorial arch, dedicated to the war correspondents and newspaper artists of the American Civil War. It was built more than a half century ago by the noted war correspondent, George Alfred Townsend, out of stones quarried from the mountain side, and patterned, so the story goes, after a Hagerstown fire house. In a sense this book is a memorial, too, albeit of a markedly different kind, to the newspapermen who from 1861 to 1865 covered the operations of the Northern army and navy.

Like most historical works, this volume is a product of composite authorship. It has been more than a decade since Professor Arthur Meier Schlesinger of Harvard University suggested to me the idea out of which this book has taken shape. I am enormously indebted to Professor Schlesinger for his continuing interest in the project and for his critical comment at various stages in the preparation of the manuscript. I should like also to acknowledge my indebtedness to Professor Robert L. Zetler of the Pennsylvania College for Women, whose expert advice in matters of style and presentation has been available, always and readily; to Professor Russell S. Ferguson of the University of Pittsburgh, who shared his intimate knowledge of the Civil War period; and to Mr. David Rankin Barbee of Washington, D. C., whose thorough acquaintanceship with Civil War newspapers enabled him to open up many new avenues to me during the early phases of my research.

For the opportunity to use manuscript material in private collections, I especially should like to express my appreciation to Mrs. Helen Rogers Reid, chairman of the board of the New York Herald Tribune Inc.; as well as to Mr. E. P. Bonaventure, New York City; Mrs. Ellen P. Cunningham, West Chester, Pennsylvania; Arthur Hill, Esq., Boston, and Mrs. Henry L. Milmore, Washington, D. C.

Libraries and librarians everywhere have been unfailing in cooperation. I owe a special debt of gratitude to the Library of Congress for the opportunity to examine its extensive manuscript and newspaper collections and for the assistance offered by Dr. St. George L. Sioussat, Dr.

C. P. Powell, and Dr. Elizabeth McPherson of the Manuscripts Division. For their many helpful suggestions in research I wish to thank Mr. Robert C. Ballantine and Mr. Nelson M. Blake of the National Archives staff; Miss Margaret Scriven and Miss Elizabeth Baughman of the Chicago Historical Society; Mrs. Alice P. Hook of the Historical and Philosophical Society of Ohio in Cincinnati; Miss Anne C. Dever, onetime Document Librarian of the Pennsylvania State Library in Harrisburg; and Miss Martha Barnes and other members of her staff at the Carnegie Library of Pittsburgh.

In addition, the Columbia University Library made it possible for me to examine the Edmund Clarence Stedman papers and the Sydney Howard Gay papers, both of them collections of the greatest importance to the student of Civil War reporting.

The Huntington Library of San Marino, California, has permitted me to quote from the Charles Henry Ray papers in their collection, including HM RY 199, 204, 210, 219, 220, 223, and 224; and I have used pertinent manuscript materials in the Essex Institute of Salem, Massachusetts; New York Public Library; University of Rochester Library; Ohio State Archaeological and Historical Society, Columbus; Widener Library, Harvard University; and the Illinois State Historical Society, Springfield.

Howard N. Ziegler, senior in The College, University of Pittsburgh, drew the maps as a special research project in cartography under the direction of Dr. John A. Bradley, assistant professor of geography; and T. Ward Hunter drew the picture for the title page.

Many people have given me family photographs and papers to illustrate this book: Mrs. Ellen P. Cunningham, the picture of her father, Uriah Hunt Painter; Mrs. Charles W. Kutz, the picture of her father, De Benneville Randolph Keim; C. C. Fulton Leser, the picture of his grandfather, Charles Carroll Fulton; Mrs. Albert McBride, the picture of war bulletins at the Pittsburgh *Dispatch,* edited during the Civil War by her great-grandfather, Joseph Singerly Lare; Mrs. Henry L. Milmore, the picture of her father-in-law, Lorenzo Livingston Crounse, and the reporter's pass issued to him; Oswald Garrison Villard, the picture of his father, Henry Villard; and Miss Nathalie E. Winser, the picture of her father, Henry Jacob Winser.

James T. White & Co. has granted permission to reproduce the photograph of William W. Harding which appears in *The National Cyclo-*

pedia of American Biography; and G. P. Putnam's Sons, the picture of George Washburn Smalley which appears in the 1911 edition of Smalley's *Anglo-American Memories.* The L. C. Handy-Studios in Washington, D. C., successor of the original Mathew B. Brady studio, graciously made available to me a number of pictures from the original Brady negatives: James Gordon Bennett, Sr., J. Whitelaw Reid, Lawrence A. Gobright, George Alfred Townsend, and the newspaper wagon in the Army of the Potomac.

Other pictures from original Brady negatives were made available to me by the National Archives; these include the picture of Samuel Wilkeson and that of the New York *Herald* headquarters in the field. The Huntington Library has permitted me to reproduce the Charles Henry Ray photograph and part of a letter to him (HM RY 223), both in the Ray papers; the Library of Congress, letters and a telegram to Frederic Hudson, all in the James Gordon Bennett papers; the New York Public Library, the picture of Printing House Square.

Various historical societies have supplied me with illustrations: the Chicago Historical Society, the picture of Wilbur F. Storey; the Historical and Philosophical Society of Ohio, Cincinnati, the pictures of Richard Smith and Murat Halstead; and The New-York Historical Society, New York City, the picture of Henry J. Raymond.

The Social Science Research Council awarded me a grant-in-aid which made possible a year's leave of absence from teaching to carry on research in various libraries. Special mention should be made of my secretary, Mrs. Norman H. Dawes, who gave invaluable aid in manuscript preparation. I am very grateful to the editors of the University of Pittsburgh Press for their liberal use of the blue pencil and to The Buhl Foundation of Pittsburgh for making the publication of this work possible.

J. Cutler Andrews
Pennsylvania College for Women
Pittsburgh, March 1, 1955

Northern Reporters

Adams, George W.
New York *World*

"Agate" (*See* Reid, J. Whitelaw)

Aldrich, Thomas Bailey
New York *Tribune*

Ames, Mary Clemmer
New York *Evening Post*

Anderson, Finley
New York *Herald*

Anderson, William
Philadelphia *Inquirer*

Armstrong, J.
New York *Times*

Ashbrook, Sam [uel?] C.
Philadelphia *Inquirer*

Ashley, James Nye
New York *Herald*

Atcheson, Thomas
New York *Tribune*

Austen, J. A.
Chicago *Tribune*

Avery, R. B.
Chicago *Times*

Babcock, Charles T.
New York Associated Press

Babcock, William A.
Philadelphia *Inquirer*

Badeau, Adam
New York *Times*

Baker, William ("Umbra")
New York *Tribune*

Barnard, Theodore
New York Associated Press

Barnes, Lucien J.
New York *Tribune;*
St. Louis *Missouri Democrat*

Barrett, Edwin Shepard
Boston *Traveller*

"Bartlett" (*See* Hammond, James Bartlett)

Bartlett, David V. G.
New York *Evening Post;*
Springfield (Massachusetts) *Republican*

Beaman, George W.
St. Louis *Missouri Democrat*

Bearrie, W. L.
Cincinnati *Times*

Bellew, Frank H.
New York *Tribune*

Bentley, Henry
Philadelphia *Inquirer*

Berford, ———
New York *Times*

"Berwick" (*See* Redpath, James)

Betty, Edward
Cincinnati *Gazette*

Bickham, William Denison
Cincinnati *Commercial*

Bingham, ———
New York *Herald*

"Bod." (*See* Bodman, Albert H.)

Bodman, Albert H. ("Bod.")
Chicago *Tribune;* New York *Herald*

Bower, George C., Jr.
Philadelphia *Inquirer*

Boweryem, George
New York *Tribune;* Philadelphia *Press*

Brace, Charles L.
New York *Times*

Bradford, Joseph
New York *Tribune*

Brady, John A.
New York *Herald*

Brigham, Charles D.
New York *Tribune*

Brittingham, J. W.
St. Louis *Missouri Republican*

Brooks, Noah
Sacramento (California) *Union*

Brown, George W.
New York *Herald*

"Browne, Dunn"
(*See* Fiske, Samuel Wheelock)

Browne, Junius Henri
Cincinnati *Gazette;*
New York *Tribune;*
St. Louis *Missouri Republican*

Buckingham, Lynde Walter
New York *Herald*

Buell, George P.
Cincinnati *Times*

Bulkley, Solomon T.
New York *Herald*

Burnett, Alfred
Cincinnati *Commercial, Times*

Burritt, Ira N.
Cincinnati *Gazette*

Buxton, Frank Lacy
New York *Tribune*

Byington, Aaron Homer
New York *Tribune*

Cadwallader, Sylvanus
Chicago *Times;* New York *Herald*

"Carleton" (*See* Coffin, Charles Carleton)

Carpenter, S. M.
New York *Herald*

Carroll, William
New York *Times*

Carson, Irving
Chicago *Tribune*

Carson, John Miller
New York *Times*

Cash, Thomas M.
New York *Herald*

Cazaran, Augustus
Boston *Traveller*

Chadwick, James B.
New York *Tribune*

Chamberlin, W. H.
Cincinnati *Gazette*

Chapman, Frank G.
New York *Herald*

Chester, Thomas Morris ("Rollin")
Philadelphia *Press*

Chounce, ———
Cincinnati *Commercial*

Church, Francis Pharcellus
New York *Times*

Church, William Conant ("Pierrepont")
New York *Evening Post, Times*

Clark, G. C.
Chicago *Tribune*

Clark, Thomas H.
Philadelphia *Inquirer*

Clarke, George W.
New York *Herald*

Coffin, Charles Carleton ("Carleton")
Boston *Journal*

Colburn, C. C.
New York *Times*

Colburn, Richard T.
New York *World*

Colston, ———
New York *Tribune*

"Con Ihnan" (*See* Wheeler, Charles L.)

Conyngham, David Power
New York *Herald*

Cook, Joel
Philadelphia *Press*

Cook, Thomas M.
New York *Herald*

Cooney, Myron A.
New York *Herald*

Coscorran, ———
Chicago *Post*

Crapsey, Edward ("Esey")
Cincinnati *Commercial, Gazette;*
Philadelphia *Inquirer*

Creighton, F.
New York *World*

Crippen, William G. ("Invisible Green")
Cincinnati *Times*

Croffut, William Augustus
New York *Tribune*

Crounse, Lorenzo Livingston
New York *Times, World*

Crounse, Silas Hilton
New York *Times*

Cummins, Thomas J.
New York *Herald*

Cunnington, William H.
Philadelphia *Inquirer*

Cureau, ———
New York Associated Press

Curry, Lewellan
Chicago *Tribune*

Davenport, John I.
New York *Tribune*

Davidson, A.
New York *Herald*

Davidson, Nathaniel
New York *Herald*

Davis, R. Stewart
Philadelphia *Inquirer*

Davis, William E.
Cincinnati *Gazette*

Dawson, J. J.
New York *Herald*

Deming, Sid [ney?]
New York Associated Press

Denyse, Edwin F.
New York *Herald*

"Doesticks" (*See* Thompson, Mortimer)

Doyle, John Edward Parker
New York *Herald*

Driscoll, F.
New York *Tribune*

"Druid" (*See* Flint, Henry Martyn)

Dugan, James
Cincinnati *Commercial*

Dunglison, J. Robly
Philadelphia *Inquirer*

"Dunn Browne"
(*See* Fiske, Samuel Wheelock)

Dunn, John P.
New York *Herald*

Eaton, B. D. M.
New York *Herald*

Elliott, James
Cincinnati *Gazette*

Elliott, Thomas H.
Philadelphia *Inquirer*

"Esey" (*See* Crapsey, Edward)

Evans, John
New York *Tribune*

Everett, ———
New York *Herald*

Farrell, Charles H.
New York *Herald*

Fawcette, ———
New York *Times*

Fayel, William A.
St. Louis *Missouri Democrat*

Fiske, Samuel Wheelock
("Dunn Browne")
Springfield (Massachusetts) *Republican*

Fiske, Stephen Ryder
New York *Herald*

Fitzpatrick, James C.
New York *Herald*

Flint, Henry Martyn ("Druid")
New York *World*

Forrest, Joseph K. C.
Chicago *Tribune*

Foss, G. W.
Philadelphia *Inquirer*

Foster, F. E.
Chicago *Tribune*

Francis, R. D.
New York *Herald, Tribune, World*

Fuller, Arthur B.
Boston *Journal*

Fulton, Albert
Baltimore *American*

Fulton, Charles Carroll
Baltimore *American*

Fulton, Edington
Baltimore *American*

Furay, William S. ("Y.S.")
Cincinnati *Gazette*

"Galway" (*See* Wilkie, Franc Bangs)

Gatchell, William
New York *Herald*

George, William
New York *Times*

Gilbert, Curtis F.
Cincinnati *Gazette;* New York *Tribune*

Gilden, van, G. P.
New York *Times;* Philadelphia *Press*

Gilden, van, Ira
New York *Times*

Gilmore, James Roberts
New York *Tribune*

Glen, Samuel R.
New York *Herald*

Glenn, Joseph
Cincinnati *Gazette*

Glenn, W.
New York *Herald*

Glover, Thaddeus B.
New York *Herald*

"Glyndon, Howard" (*See* Redden, Laura)

Gobright, Lawrence Augustus
New York Associated Press

"Grace Greenwood"
(*See* Lippincott, Sara)

Graffan, Charles H.
New York *Herald*

Green, John H.
Cincinnati *Enquirer*

"Green, Invisible"
(*See* Crippen, William G.)

"Greenwood, Grace"
(*See* Lippincott, Sara)

Grey, T. C.
New York *Tribune*

Groves, ———
St. Louis *Missouri Republican*

Gunn, Thomas Butler
New York *Tribune*

Hall, E. H.
New York *Tribune*

Halpine, Charles Graham
New York *Herald*

Halstead, Murat
Cincinnati *Commercial*

Hamilton, John R. ("Nemo")
New York *Times*

Hammond, James Bartlett ("Bartlett")
New York *Tribune, World*

Hannam, Charles
New York *Herald*

Hanscom, Simon P.
New York *Herald*

Hardenbrook, John A.
New York *Tribune*

Hart, Charles H.
New York *Times*

Hart, George H.
New York *Herald*

Harwood, J. H.
New York *Times*

Hasson, John
New York Associated Press

Hayes, John E.
Boston *Traveller;* New York *Tribune*

Henderson, Thomas J.
New York *Tribune*

Hendricks, Leonard A.
New York *Herald*

Henry, Arthur
New York *Tribune*

Henry, Frank
New York *Times, Herald*

Hickox, Volney
Chicago *Tribune;*
Cincinnati *Commercial*

Hill, Adams S.
New York *Tribune*

Hills, Alfred Clark
New York *Herald*

Hills, William H.
Boston *Journal*

Hinton, Richard Josiah
Chicago *Tribune*

Homans, Phineas
New York *Herald*

Hosmer, George Washington
New York *Herald*

House, Edward Howard
New York *Tribune*

Houston, Alexander
New York *Herald*

"Howard Glyndon" (*See* Redden, Laura)

Northern Reporters

Howard, Joseph, Jr.
New York *Times*

Howe, O. P.
New York *Herald*

Hudson, Henry Norman
New York *Evening Post*

"Ihnan, Con" (*See* Wheeler, Charles L.)

"Illinoien" (*See* Seybold, Thaddeus S.)

"Invisible Green"
(*See* Crippen, William G.)

Isham, Warren P. ("Shiloh")
Chicago *Times*

Ives, Malcolm
New York *Herald*

"Jack" (*See* Miller, John C.)

Jacobs, John T.
New York *Express*

Johnson, ———
New York *Herald*

Johnson, ———
Philadelphia *Inquirer*

Johnston, George W.
New York *Herald*

Judd, David Wright
New York *Times*

Kaw, Ralph
Chicago *Tribune*

Keim, De Benneville Randolph
New York *Herald*

Kelly, Henry C.
St. Louis *Missouri Democrat*

Kennedy, ———
Philadelphia *Inquirer*

Kent, William H.
New York *Tribune*

"Kerr, Orpheus C."
(*See* Newell, Robert Henry)

Kinney, D. J.
New York *Tribune*

Knox, Thomas Wallace
New York *Herald*

Landon, Melville D.
New York *Tribune*

Latham, James
New York *Herald*

Law, W. B. S.
New York *Herald*

"Leo" (*See* Swain, James Barrett)

Lippincott, Sara ("Grace Greenwood")
New York *Times, Tribune*

Long, Francis C.
New York *Herald, Tribune*

McAran, C. S.
Philadelphia *Inquirer*

McBride, R. H.
Philadelphia *Press*

McCormick, Richard Cunningham
New York *Evening Post, Commercial Advertiser*

McCracken, W. B.
New York *Herald*

McCullagh, Joseph Burbridge ("Mack")
Cincinnati *Commercial, Enquirer, Gazette*

McDevitt, J. F.
Philadelphia *Press*

MacDuff, J.
Philadelphia *Inquirer*

McElrath, Thompson P.
New York *Times*

McGahan, Januarius A.
St. Louis *Missouri Democrat*

McGregor, William D.
New York Associated Press, *Herald, Times, Tribune*

"Mack" (*See* McCullagh, Joseph Burbridge)

McKee, Henry
St. Louis *Missouri Democrat*

McKenna, John L.
New York *Tribune*

McQuillan, Milton P.
Cincinnati *Gazette*

Mason, Samuel W.
New York *Herald*

Matteson, Andre
Chicago *Post*

Maverick, Augustus
New York *Evening Post*
Maynard, E. L.
New York *Herald*
Meader, William H.
Philadelphia *Press*
Medberry, W. H.
Cincinnati *Gazette*
Merriam, William H.
New York *Herald*
Millar, Constantine D.
Cincinnati *Commercial*
Miller, John C. ("Jack")
Chicago *Journal*
Miller, Joseph W.
Cincinnati *Commercial*
Miller, Wilson
New York *Tribune*
Misener, M. C.
Chicago *Times*
Mitchell, Abram S. ("York")
New York *Times*
Moore, William D.
Columbus *Ohio State Journal*
Murdock, D.
Philadelphia *Inquirer*
Murrell, Hower
New York *Herald*
Myers, ———
New York Associated Press

"Nemo" (*See* Hamilton, John R.)
Newbould, Thomas M.
New York *Tribune*
Newcomb, J. Warren
New York *Herald*
Newell, Robert Henry
("Orpheus C. Kerr")
New York *Herald*
Nichols, George Ward
New York *Evening Post*
Norcross, John
Philadelphia *Press*
Noyes, James Oscar
New York Associated Press
Nuneville, ———
Philadelphia *Inquirer*

O'Donnell, Kane
Philadelphia *Press*
Olcott, Henry S.
New York *Tribune*
"Orpheus C. Kerr"
(*See* Newell, Robert Henry)
Osbon, Bradley Sillick
New York *Herald, World*
Osborne, Galen H.
New York *Herald*

"P." (*See* Plympton, Florus B.)
Page, ———
St. Louis *Missouri Democrat*
Page, Charles A.
New York *Tribune*
Paige, Nathaniel
New York *Tribune*
Painter, Uriah Hunt
Philadelphia *Inquirer*
Paul, Edward Alexander
New York *Times*
Pedrick, A. K.
Philadelphia *Inquirer*
Peters, E. T.
Philadelphia *Inquirer*
"Pierrepont"
(*See* Church, William Conant)
Plympton, Florus B. ("P.")
Cincinnati *Commercial*
Pollock, ———
New York *Tribune*
Poore, Benjamin Perley
Boston *Journal*
Post, Truman A.
New York *Tribune;*
St. Louis *Missouri Democrat*
"Prescott" (*See* Woodwell, Charles H.)
Puleston, J. H.
Philadelphia *North American*

Quigg, John Travis
New York *World*

Rathbone, John F.
New York *World*

Northern Reporters

Ray, Charles H.
Chicago *Tribune*

Raymond, ———
New York *Herald*

Raymond, Henry J.
New York *Times*

Rea, Samuel J.
New York Associated Press; Philadelphia *Inquirer*

Redden, Laura C. ("Howard Glyndon")
St. Louis *Missouri Republican*

Redfield, W. R.
Chicago *Journal*

Redpath, James ("Berwick")
Boston *Journal;* New York *Tribune*

Reid, J. Whitelaw ("Agate")
Cincinnati *Gazette*

Reilly, Frank W.
Chicago *Tribune;* Cincinnati *Times*

Rhoads, J. S.
Philadelphia *Inquirer*

Richardson, Albert Deane
New York *Tribune*

Ricks, ———
Cincinnati *Commercial*

Ripley, Philip
New York *World, Evening Post*

Robinson, Joseph
Philadelphia *Inquirer*

Rogers, George M.
New York *Times*

"Rollin" (*See* Chester, Thomas Morris)

Runkle, ———
New York *Herald*

Rust, George W.
Chicago *Times*

Salter, George H. C.
New York *Times*

Sawyer, Oscar G.
New York *Herald*

Schenk, ———
New York *Herald*

School, Charles E.
Philadelphia *Press*

Schrick, Julius
St. Louis *Missouri Republican*

"Scout" (*See* Stanley, Nehemiah)

Seward, ———
Philadelphia *Inquirer*

Seybold, Thaddeus S. ("Illinoien")
New York *Tribune*

Shanahan, Charles S.
New York *Herald*

Shanks, William Franklin Gore
New York *Herald*

Shelly, R. L.
New York Associated Press

Shepherd, Nathaniel Graham
New York *Tribune, World*

"Shiloh" (*See* Isham, Warren P.)

Shoaff, James
Chicago *Times*

Shore, W. W.
New York *Tribune, World*

Shrick, Ernest
St. Louis *Missouri Republican*

"Sigma" (*See* Spofford, Ainsworth)

Silsby, ———
Cincinnati *Gazette*

Simonton, James
New York *Times*

Slack, ———
New York *Herald*

Slocum, J. D.
New York *Herald*

Smalley, George Washburn
New York *Tribune*

Smith, Elias
New York *Times, Tribune*

Smith, Henry M.
Chicago *Tribune*

Snell, James
New York *Herald*

Sparks, William J.
New York *Herald*

Spenser, E. M. (Ned)
Cincinnati *Times*

Spofford, Ainsworth ("Sigma")
Cincinnati *Commercial*

Stafford, ———
St. Louis *Missouri Democrat*

Stanley, Henry Morton
———

Stanley, Nehemiah ("Scout")
Boston *Journal*

Stark, William J.
New York *Herald*

Stedman, Edmund Clarence
New York *World*

Stillson, Jerome B.
New York *World*

Stiner, William H.
New York *Herald*

Surface, D.
Cincinnati *Gazette;*
Philadelphia *Inquirer*

Swain, James Barrett ("Leo")
New York *Times*

Swinton, William
New York *Times*

Swisshelm, Jane Grey
New York *Tribune*

Sypher, Josiah Rhinehart
New York *Tribune*

Taggart, John H.
Philadelphia *Inquirer*

Talcott, Alfred B.
New York *Herald*

Tallman, Pelegg
Chicago *Times;* New York *Herald*

Taylor, Bayard
New York *Tribune*

Taylor, Benjamin Franklin
Chicago *Journal*

Thompson, Henry
New York *Herald*

Thompson, Mortimer ("Doesticks")
New York *Tribune*

Townsend, George Alfred
New York *Herald, World*

Tracey, ———
St. Louis *Missouri Republican*

Trembly, J. R.
New York *Herald*

Truman, Benjamin Cummings
New York *Times;*
Philadelphia *Inquirer, Press*

Tyler, George W.
New York Associated Press

"Umbra" (*See* Baker, William)

Upton, George Putnam
Chicago *Tribune*

Vaughan, W. W.
New York *World*

Villard, Henry
New York *Herald, Tribune*

Vosburg, J. H.
New York *Herald*

Wallazz, Lawrence W.
New York *Herald;* Philadelphia *Press*

Wallington, William M.
Philadelphia *Inquirer*

Ward, Ulysses B.
New York *Herald*

Wardell, James
New York *Herald*

Warden, W. W.
Cincinnati *Enquirer*

Ware, Joseph A.
Philadelphia *Press;*
Washington *Chronicle*

Warner, James C.
Philadelphia *Press*

Warren, Fitz-Henry
New York *Tribune*

Wayland, H. L.
New York *World*

Webb, Charles Henry
New York *Times*

Webb, William E.
St. Louis *Missouri Republican*

Weed, ———
New York *Herald*

Weik, John
Philadelphia *Press*

Wells, William H.
New York *Herald, Tribune*

Northern Reporters

Westfall, E. D.
New York Associated Press, *Herald*

Wheeler, Charles L. ("Con Ihnan")
St. Louis *Missouri Republican*

Whipple, T. Herbert
New York *Herald*

"Whit" (*See* Whittemore, W. H.)

White, Horace
Chicago *Tribune*

Whitely, L. A.
New York *Herald*

Whittemore, W. H. ("Whit")
New York *Times*

Wikoff, Henry
New York *Herald*

Wilkes, George
New York *Tribune*

Wilkeson, Samuel
New York *Times*, *Tribune*

Wilkie, Franc Bangs ("Galway")
New York *Times*

Williams, George Forrester
New York *Times*

Williams, Walter F.
New York *Evening Post*

Williamson, D. B.
Philadelphia *Inquirer*

Wilson, John R.
Chicago *Journal*

Wilson, Theodore C.
New York *Herald*

Winchell, James M.
New York *Times*

Wing, Henry Ebeneser
New York *Tribune*

Winser, Henry Jacob
New York *Times*

Woodal, A. T.
Cincinnati *Gazette*

Woods, George Z.
Boston *Daily Advertiser*

Woodwell, Charles H.
Boston *Post*

"York" (*See* Mitchell, Abram S.)

Young, Harry H.
New York *Times*, *World*

Young, John Russell
Philadelphia *Press*

Young, William
Boston *Herald;* New York *Herald*

"Y.S." (*See* Furay, William S.)

Bibliography

I. BIBLIOGRAPHICAL AIDS

Beers, Henry Putney, *Bibliographies in American History, Guide to Materials for Research* (New York, 1942).

Cannon, Carl L., *Journalism: A Bibliography* (New York, 1924).

Channing, Edward, and others, *Guide to the Study and Reading of American History* (Boston and London, 1912).

Ely, Margaret, *Some Great American Newspaper Editors* (White Plains, New York, and New York City, 1916).

Ginsburg, Claire E., *A Newspaperman's Library*, University of Missouri Bulletin, Vol. XXII, No. 19 (Columbia, 1921).

Graham, Robert Xavier, *A Bibliography in the History and Backgrounds of Journalism* (Pittsburgh, Pennsylvania, 1940).

Gregory, Winifred (ed.), *American Newspapers, 1821-1936, A Union List of Files Available in the United States and Canada* (New York, 1937).

Griffin, Grace Gardner, and others, *Writings on American History, 1906-1940, 1948,* In *American Historical Association, Annual Reports* (Washington, D.C., 1908-1943, 1950).

Mineau, Georgia, *Famous War Correspondents* (Madison, Wisconsin, 1915).

Mott, Frank Luther, *Selected Lists of Books on Journalism,* State University of Iowa Extension Bulletin No. 292 (Iowa City, 1932).

The Tribune (New York), *Index to the Daily Tribune, 1875-1888, 1890-1906* (New York, 1876-1907).

Peet, Hubert W., *A Bibliography of Journalism, A Guide to the Books about the Press and Pressmen* (London, 1915).

Poole, William Frederick, and Fletcher, William I., *Poole's Index to Periodical Literature,* 6 vols. in 7 (New York, 1938).

Stockett, Julia Carson, *Masters of American Journalism* (White Plains, New York, and New York City, 1916).

II. MANUSCRIPT SOURCES

Nathaniel P. Banks Papers, Essex Institute, Salem, Massachusetts.

James Gordon Bennett Papers, Library of Congress.

William Cullen Bryant (-Godwin) Papers, New York Public Library.

Simon Cameron Papers, Library of Congress.

Salmon P. Chase Papers, Library of Congress.

William Conant Church Papers, Library of Congress.

Lorenzo Livingston Crounse Papers, in the possession of the Crounse family, Washington, D.C.

Charles A. Dana Papers, Library of Congress.
Sydney Howard Gay Papers, Columbia University Library.
Louis M. Goldsborough Papers, Library of Congress.
Ulysses S. Grant Papers, Library of Congress.
Horace Greeley Papers, Library of Congress.
Horace Greeley Papers, New York Public Library.
Murat Halstead Papers, Historical and Philosophical Society of Ohio, Cincinnati.
De Benneville Randolph Keim Papers, Library of Congress.
Robert T. Lincoln Papers, Library of Congress.
George B. McClellan Papers, Library of Congress.
Manton Marble Papers, Library of Congress.
Joseph Medill Papers, Chicago Historical Society.
Uriah Hunt Painter Papers, in the possession of the Painter family, West Chester, Pennsylvania.
David Dixon Porter Papers, Library of Congress.
Charles Henry Ray Papers, The Huntington Library, San Marino, California.
Henry J. Raymond Papers, New York Public Library.
J. Whitelaw Reid Papers (formerly in the possession of the Reid family), Library of Congress.
William H. Seward Papers, University of Rochester Library.
William T. Sherman Papers, Library of Congress.
William Henry Smith Papers, Indiana State Library, Indianapolis.
William Henry Smith Papers, Ohio State Archaeological and Historical Society, Columbus.
Ainsworth Spofford Papers, Library of Congress.
Edwin M. Stanton Papers, Library of Congress.
Edmund Clarence Stedman Papers, Columbia University Library.
George Alfred Townsend Papers, in the possession of the Townsend family, New York City.
Thomas S. Townsend Library of National, State, and Individual Civil War Records, Columbia University.
Henry Villard Papers, Widener Library, Harvard University.
Elihu B. Washburne Papers, Library of Congress.
Gideon Welles Papers, Library of Congress.
Horace White Papers, Illinois State Historical Library, Springfield.
Samuel Wilkeson Papers, New York Public Library.
Charles H. Woodwell Papers, in the possession of the Woodwell family, Tamaqua, Pennsylvania.
John Russell Young Papers, Library of Congress.

III. NEWSPAPERS

Atlanta *Daily Intelligencer*
Baltimore *American and Commercial Advertiser*
Boston *Daily Advertiser*
Boston *Daily Journal*
Boston *Traveller*
Buffalo *Express*
Charleston *Daily Courier*
Charleston *Mercury*
Daily Chicago Post
Chicago *Daily Tribune*
Chicago *Evening Journal*
Chicago *Times*
Cincinnati *Daily Commercial*
Cincinnati *Daily Gazette*
Cincinnati *Daily Times*

Cincinnati *Enquirer*
Columbus *Daily Ohio State Journal*
Harrisburg (Pennsylvania) *Evening Telegraph*
Lancaster (Pennsylvania) *Daily Express*
London *Daily News*
London *Times*
Louisville *Courier*
Louisville *Daily Journal*
Milwaukee *Republican*
Mobile *News*
Mobile *Tribune*
New Orleans *Era*
New Orleans *Times*
New York *Citizen*
New York *Commercial Advertiser*
New York *Daily Tribune*
New York *Evening Post*
New York *Herald*
New York *Ledger*
New York *Morning Express*
New York *Sun*
New York *Times*
New York *World*
Philadelphia *Daily Evening Bulletin*
Philadelphia *Inquirer*
Philadelphia *Press*
Philadelphia *Sunday Dispatch*
Philadelphia *Weekly Times*
Pittsburgh *Evening Chronicle*
Pittsburgh *Gazette*
Pittsburgh *Post*
Daily Richmond Enquirer
Daily Richmond Examiner
Daily Richmond Whig
Richmond *Dispatch*
Richmond *Sentinel*
St. Louis *Daily Evening News*
St. Louis *Missouri Democrat*
St. Louis *Missouri Republican*
San Francisco *Bulletin*
San Francisco *Chronicle*
Savannah *Republican*
Troy (New York) *Daily Times*
Washington *Chronicle*
Washington *Daily National Intelligencer*
Washington *Evening Star*
Washington *National Republican*
Wheeling (West Virginia) *Intelligencer*

IV. GOVERNMENT DOCUMENTS

A. Published

Congressional Globe, 37, 38 Congs., 1861-1865.

Official Records of the Union and Confederate Navies in the War of the Rebellion, 30 vols. (Washington, D.C., 1894-1922).

Organization of the Army of the Potomac, 1863, *Executive Document No. 15,* House Executive Documents, 38 Cong., 1 sess.

Report of the House Committee on Judiciary, March 20, 1862, *House Report No. 64,* House Executive Documents, 37 Cong., 2 sess.

Report of the Joint Committee on the Conduct of the War, 1863, *Senate Report No. 108,* Senate Reports, 37 Cong., 3 sess.

Reports of the Secretary of the Navy (annual), 1861-1865.

Reports of the Secretary of War (annual), 1861-1865.

U.S. Congress, *Official Congressional Directory,* 37 cong., 2 sess. (Washington, D.C., 1861).

War of the Rebellion: A Compilation of the Official Records of the Union and Confederate Armies, 128 vols. (Washington, D.C., 1880-1901).

B. Unpublished

National Archives, The Naval Records Collection of the Office of Naval Records and Library: Miscellaneous Letters.

National Archives, Office of Judge Advocate General: Court Martial Records.

National Archives, Office of the Secretary of War: Letters Sent, Letters Received, Telegrams Sent, Telegrams Received.

V. BOOKS AND ARTICLES WRITTEN BY CIVIL WAR CORRESPONDENTS

Ames, Mary Clemmer, *Ten Years in Washington, Life and Scenes in the National Capital, as a Woman Sees Them* (Cincinnati, 1874).

Badeau, Adam, *Military History of Ulysses S. Grant, from April, 1861, to April, 1865,* 3 vols. (New York, 1885).

Barrett, Edwin Shepard, *What I Saw at Bull Run* (Boston, 1886).

Bickham, William Denison, *Rosecrans' Campaign with the Fourteenth Army Corps of the Army of the Cumberland: A Narrative of Personal Observations with . . . Official Reports of the Battle of Stone River* (Cincinnati, 1863).

Brooks, Noah, *Washington in Lincoln's Time* (New York, 1895).

Browne, Junius Henri, *Four Years in Secessia* (Hartford, 1865).

———, *The Great Metropolis* (Hartford, 1869).

———, "Horace Greeley," *Harper's New Monthly Magazine,* XLVI (April, 1873), 734-741.

Burnett, Alfred, *Incidents of the War* (Cincinnati, 1863).

Church, William Conant, *The Life of John Ericsson* (New York, 1891).

Coffin, Charles Carleton, *Four Years of Fighting: A Volume of Personal Observation with the Army and Navy, from the first Battle of Bull Run to the Fall of Richmond* (Boston, 1866).

———, *The Boys of '61, or Four Years of Fighting* . . . . (Boston, 1881; 1886; 1896; 1925).

———, "Antietam Scenes," *Century Magazine,* New Ser. X (June, 1886), 315-319.

———, *My Days and Nights on the Battlefield* (Boston, 1887).

———, *Marching to Victory* (New York, 1888).

———, "Lincoln's Visit to Richmond, April 4, 1865," *Moorsfield Antiquarian,* I (May, 1937), 27-29.

Conyngham, David Power, *Sherman's March through the South with Sketches and Incidents of the Campaign* (New York, 1865).

Cook, Joel, *The Siege of Richmond, A Narrative of the Military Operations of Major-General George B. McClellan during the Months of May and June, 1862* (Philadelphia, 1862).

Croffut, William Augustus, "Horace Greeley Knows His Business," *Atlantic Monthly,* CXLV (February, 1930), 228-239.

———, *An American Procession, 1855-1914, A Personal Chronicle of Famous Men* (Boston, 1931).

Crounse, Lorenzo Livingston, "The Army Correspondent," *Harper's New Monthly Magazine,* XXVII (October, 1863), 627-633.

De Fontaine, Felix Gregory, *Marginalia, or Gleanings from an Army Notebook* (Columbia, South Carolina, 1864).

———, "The First Day of Real War," *Southern Bivouac,* II (July, 1886), 73-79.

———, *Army Letters of "Personne," 1861-1865,* issued monthly, I, Nos. 1-2 (Columbia, 1896-1897).

Fiske, Samuel Wheelock, *Mr. Dunn Browne's Experiences in the Army* (Boston and New York, 1866).

Fiske, Stephen Ryder, "Gentlemen of the Press," *Harper's New Monthly Magazine,* XXVI (February, 1863), 361-367.

———, *Off-Hand Portraits of Prominent New Yorkers* (New York, 1884).

Furay, William S., and Kniffen, G. C., *The Real Chickamauga* (Privately printed, 1888).

Gallenga, Antonio, *Episodes of My Second Life,* 2 vols. (London, 1884).

Bibliography

Gilmore, James Roberts (ed.), *Personal Recollections of Abraham Lincoln and the Civil War* (Boston, 1898).

———, *Letters of a War Correspondent by Charles A. Page, Special Correspondent of the New York "Tribune" during the Civil War* (Boston, 1899).

Gobright, Lawrence Augustus, *Recollections of Men and Things at Washington during the Third of a Century* (Philadelphia, 1869).

Halpine, Charles Graham, *Baked Meats of the Funeral* (New York, 1866).

Halstead, Murat, "Some Reminiscences of Mr. Villard," *American Review of Reviews*, XXIII (January, 1901), 60-63.

———, "Breakfasts with Horace Greeley," *Cosmopolitan*, XXXVI (April, 1904), 698-702.

Hosmer, George Washington, *The Battle of Gettysburg* (New York, 1913).

Judd, David Wright, *The Story of the Thirty-Third N.Y.S. Vols.: or Two Years Campaigning in Virginia and Maryland* (Rochester, New York, 1864).

Knox, Thomas Wallace, *Camp-Fire and Cotton-Field: Southern Adventure in Time of War. Life with the Union Armies and Residence on a Louisiana Plantation* (Philadelphia and Cincinnati, 1865).

Mackay, Charles, *Forty Years' Recollections of Life, Literature, and Public Affairs from 1830 to 1870*, 2 vols. (London, 1877).

Mayo, Lida (ed.), *Rustics in Rebellion, A Yankee Reporter on the Road to Richmond, 1861-1865* (Chapel Hill, North Carolina, 1950).

Newell, Robert Henry, *The Orpheus C. Kerr Papers, First Series* (New York, 1866).

Nichols, George Ward, *The Story of the Great March from the Diary of a Staff Officer* (New York, 1865).

Paine, Albert Bigelow, *A Sailor of Fortune, Personal Memoirs of Captain B. S. Osbon* (New York, 1906).

Poore, Benjamin Perley, "Washington News," *Harper's New Monthly Magazine*, XLVIII (January, 1874), 225-236.

———, *The Life and Public Services of Ambrose E. Burnside, Soldier–Citizen–Statesman* (Providence, Rhode Island, 1882).

———, *Perley's Reminiscences of Sixty Years in the National Metropolis*, 2 vols. (Philadelphia, 1886).

Redden, Laura C., *Notable Men in the House* (Privately printed, 1862).

Reid, J. Whitelaw, *Ohio in the War; Her Statesmen, Generals, and Soldiers*, 2 vols. (Columbus, 1893).

Richardson, Albert Deane, *The Secret Service, the Field, the Dungeon, and the Escape* (Hartford, 1865).

Russell, William Howard, *My Diary, North and South* (Boston, 1863).

———, "Recollections of the Civil War," *North American Review*, CLXVI (February-June, 1898), 234-249, 362-373, 490-502, 618-630, 740-750.

Sala, George Augustus, *My Diary in America in the Midst of War*, 2 vols. (London, 1865).

———, *The Life and Adventures of George Augustus Sala Written by Himself*, 2 vols. (New York, 1895).

Sears, Louis M., "The London Times' American Correspondent in 1861; Unpublished Letters of William H. Russell in the First Year of the Civil War," *Historical Outlook*, XVI (October, 1925), 251-257.

Shanks, William Franklin Gore, *Personal Recollections of Distinguished Generals* (New York, 1866).

Shanks, William Franklin Gore, "How We Get Our News," *Harper's New Monthly Magazine,* XXXIV (March, 1867), 511-522.

———, "Chattanooga and How We Held It," *Harper's New Monthly Magazine,* XXXVI (January, 1868), 137-149.

———, "Lookout Mountain and How We Won It," *Harper's New Monthly Magazine,* XXXVII (June, 1868), 1-15.

Smalley, George Washburn, "Chapters in Journalism," *Harper's New Monthly Magazine,* LXXXIX (August, 1894), 426-435.

———, "Notes on Journalism," *Harper's New Monthly Magazine,* XCVII (July, 1898), 213-223.

———, *Anglo-American Memories,* 1st Ser. (New York and London, 1911); 2d Ser. (London, 1912).

Stanley, Dorothy (ed.), *The Autobiography of Sir Henry Morton Stanley* (Boston and New York, 1909).

Swinton, William, *Campaigns of the Army of the Potomac* (New York, 1866).

———, "Hooker's Campaign Reviewed," *Historical Magazine and Notes and Queries,* II (September, 1867), 160-166.

———, *The Twelve Decisive Battles of the War, A History of the Eastern and Western Campaigns in Relation to the Actions that Decided Their Issue* (New York, 1867).

———, *History of the [New York] Seventh Regiment* (New York, 1870).

Sypher, Josiah Rhinehart, *History of the Pennsylvania Reserve Corps* (Lancaster, Pennsylvania, 1865).

Taylor, Benjamin Franklin, *Mission Ridge and Lookout Mountain, with Pictures of Life in Camp and Field* (New York and Chicago, 1872).

Townsend, George Alfred, "Campaigning with General Pope," *Cornhill Magazine,* VI (December, 1862), 758-770.

———, "An American War Correspondent in England," *Harper's New Monthly Magazine,* XXX (January, 1865), 229-235.

———, *Campaigns of a Non-Combatant and His Romaunt Abroad during the War* (New York, 1866).

———, "Recollections and Reflections," *Lippincott's Monthly Magazine,* XXXVIII (November, 1886), 515-524.

Truman, Benjamin Cummings, "A Spectacular Battle and Its 'Ifs'," *Overland Monthly,* New Ser. XXXIV (August, 1899), 154-159.

———, "Old Time Editors and Newspapers I Have Known," *Pacific Printer,* VI (December, 1911), 338-340, 368.

———, "Anecdotes of Andrew Johnson," *Century Magazine,* LXXV (January, 1913), 435-440.

Tuckerman, Charles Keating, "The London Times, A Personal Reminiscence," *Magazine of American History,* XXVII (April, 1892), 290-296.

Villard, Henry, "Army Correspondence," *Nation,* I (July 20, 27, August 3, 1865), 79-81, 114-116, 144-146.

———, *Memoirs of Henry Villard, Journalist and Financier, 1835-1900,* 2 vols. (Boston and New York, 1904).

Webb, Charles Henry, *John Paul's Book* (New York and Chicago, 1874).

Wilkes, George, *The Great Battle Fought at Manassas between the Federal Forces, under General McDowell, and the Rebels, under General Beauregard, Sunday, July 21, 1861, from Notes Taken on the Spot* (New York, 1861).

Wilkeson, Samuel, *The Battle of Gettysburg* (Privately printed, 1863).

Wilkie, Francis Bangs, *Walks about Chicago, 1871-1881. And Army and Miscellaneous Sketches* (Chicago, 1882).
———, *Pen and Powder* (Boston, 1888).
———, *Personal Reminiscences of Thirty-five Years of Journalism* (Chicago, 1891).
———, "The Battle of Wilson's Creek," *Palimpsest,* IX (August, 1928), 291-310.
Williams, George Forrester, "Lights and Shadows of Army Life," *Century Magazine,* XXVIII (October, 1884), 803-819.
———, "Bennett, Greeley and Raymond, A Glimpse of New York Journalism Twenty-five Years Ago," *Journalist,* IV (October 2, 1886), 1-2.
———, "How a Reporter Faced Danger in Disguise," *Independent,* LIII (August 8, 1901), 1860-1862.
———, "Important Services Rendered by War Correspondents," *Independent,* LIV (January 23, 1902), 210-212.
Winchell, James M., "Three Interviews with President Lincoln," *Galaxy,* XVI (July, 1873), 33-41.
Wing, Henry Ebeneser, *When Lincoln Kissed Me, A Story of the Wilderness Campaign* (New York and Cincinnati, 1913).
Young, John Russell, *Around the World with General Grant,* 2 vols. (New York, 1879).
———, "Men Who Reigned: Bennett, Greeley, Raymond, Prentice, Forney," *Lippincott's Monthly Magazine,* LI (February, 1893), 185-197.
Young, May Dow Russell (ed.), *Men and Memories, Personal Reminiscences by John Russell Young,* 2 vols. (New York and London, 1901).

VI. BIOGRAPHIES, AUTOBIOGRAPHIES, DIARIES, AND LETTERS

Agassiz, George R. (ed.), *Meade's Headquarters, 1863-1865; Letters of Colonel Theodore Lyman from the Wilderness to Appomattox* (Boston, 1922).
Alexander, Edward Porter, *Military Memoirs of a Confederate* (New York, 1907).
Atkins, John Black, *Life of Sir William Howard Russell: The First Special Correspondent,* 2 vols. (London, 1911).
Beatty, John, *The Citizen-Soldier or Memoirs of a Volunteer* (Cincinnati, 1879).
Beatty, Richard Croom, *Bayard Taylor, Laureate of the Gilded Age* (Norman, Oklahoma, 1936).
Bigelow, Donald Nevius, *William Conant Church and the Army and Navy Journal* (New York, 1952).
Bigelow, John, *Retrospections of an Active Life,* 5 vols. (New York, 1909-1913).
Biographical Cyclopedia of Representative Men of Maryland and District of Columbia (Baltimore, 1879).
Brace, Emma (ed.), *The Life of Charles Loring Brace Chiefly Told in His Own Letters* (New York, 1894).
Brown, Francis, *Raymond of the Times* (New York, 1951).
Brown, John Howard (ed.), *Lamb's Biographical Dictionary of the United States,* 7 vols. (Boston, 1900-1903).
Bullard, Frederic Lauriston, *Famous War Correspondents* (Boston, 1914).
Butler, Benjamin Franklin, *Autobiography and Personal Reminiscences of Major-General Benj. F. Butler; Butler's Book* (Boston, 1892).
———, *Private and Official Correspondence of Gen. Benjamin F. Butler, during the Period of the Civil War,* 5 vols. (Privately printed, 1917).
Carlson, Oliver, *The Man Who Made News, James Gordon Bennett* (New York, 1942).

Carpenter, Francis Bicknell, *Six Months at the White House with Abraham Lincoln, The Story of a Picture* (New York, 1866).

Castleman, Alfred L., *The Army of the Potomac .... A Diary of Unwritten History from the Organization of the Army to the Close of the Campaign in Virginia, about the First Day of January, 1863* (Milwaukee, 1863).

Chase, Salmon P., *Diary and Correspondence,* In *American Historical Association, Annual Report for 1902,* Vol. II (Washington, D.C., 1903).

Childs, George William, *Recollections* (Philadelphia, 1890).

Cleaves, Freeman, *Rock of Chickamauga, The Life of General George H. Thomas* (Norman, Oklahoma, 1948).

Congdon, Charles Taber, *Reminiscences of a Journalist* (Boston, 1880).

Connolly, James Austin, "Major Connolly's Letters to His Wife, 1862-1865," *Transactions of the Illinois State Historical Society,* XXIX (1928), 215-438.

Coolidge, Louis Arthur, *Ulysses S. Grant* (Boston and New York, 1922).

Cortissoz, Royal, *The Life of Whitelaw Reid,* 2 vols. (New York, 1921).

Cox, Jacob Dolson, *Military Reminiscences of the Civil War,* 2 vols. (New York, 1900).

Cummins, Thomas J., *My Irish Colleagues of New York, Reminiscences and Experiences of a Journalist, 1861 to 1901* (New York, 1901).

Dahlgren, Madeleine Vinton, *Memoir of John A. Dahlgren, Rear-Admiral United States Navy by His Widow* (Boston, 1882).

Dana, Charles Anderson, *Recollections of the Civil War* (New York, 1898).

Dennett, Tyler (ed.), *Lincoln and the Civil War in the Diaries and Letters of John Hay* (New York, 1939).

Derby, James Cephas, *Fifty Years among Authors, Books, and Publishers* (New York, 1886).

Dix, Morgan (ed.), *Memoirs of John Adams Dix,* 2 vols. (New York, 1883).

Downes, William Howe, *The Life and Works of Winslow Homer* (Boston and New York, 1911).

Drayton, Percival, *Naval Letters from Captain Percival Drayton, 1861-1865* (New York, 1906).

Drell, Muriel Bernett (ed.), "Letters by Richard Smith of the Cincinnati Gazette," *Mississippi Valley Historical Review,* XXVI (March, 1940), 535-554.

Duganne, Augustine J. H., *Camps and Prisons. Twenty Months in the Department of the Gulf* (New York, 1865).

Du Pont, Henry Algernon, *Rear-Admiral Samuel Francis Du Pont, United States Navy, A Biography* (New York, 1926).

Eckenrode, Hamilton J., and Conrad, Bryan, *George B. McClellan, The Man Who Saved the Union* (Chapel Hill, North Carolina, 1941).

Elliott, Charles Winslow, *Winfield Scott, The Soldier and the Man* (New York, 1937).

Farragut, Loyall, *The Life of David Glasgow Farragut, First Admiral of the United States Navy, Embodying His Journal and Letters* (New York, 1891).

Flower, Frank Abial, *Edwin McMasters Stanton, The Autocrat of Rebellion, Emancipation, and Reconstruction* (Akron, Ohio, 1905).

Ford, Worthington Chauncey (ed.), *A Cycle of Adams Letters, 1861-1865,* 2 vols. (Boston and New York, 1920).

Forney, John Wien, *Anecdotes of Public Men,* 2 vols. (New York, 1873-1881).

Forsyth, George Alexander, *Thrilling Days in Army Life* (New York and London, 1900).

Foulke, William Dudley, *Life of Oliver P. Morton, including his Important Speeches,* 2 vols. (Indianapolis and Kansas City, 1899).

Freeman, Douglas Southall, *R. E. Lee, a Biography,* 4 vols. (New York and London, 1935).

Fuller, Richard Frederick, *Chaplain Fuller: Being a Life Sketch of a New England Clergyman and Army Chaplain* (Boston, 1863) .

Godwin, Parke, *A Biography of William Cullen Bryant, with Extracts from His Private Correspondence,* 2 vols. (New York, 1883).

Goodwin, Cardinal Leonidas, *John Charles Fremont* (Stanford, California, 1930).

Gordon, John Brown, *Reminiscences of the Civil War* (New York, 1903).

Gorham, George Congdon, *Life and Public Services of Edwin M. Stanton* (Boston and New York, 1899).

Grant, Ulysses Simpson. *Personal Memoirs,* 2 vols. (New York, 1885-1886); 2 vols. in 1 (New York, 1894); 2d ed., 2 vols. (New York, 1895); 2 vols. (New York, 1909); 2 vols. (New York, 1917).

Gray, John Chipman, and Ropes, John Codman, *War Letters, 1862-1865* (Boston and New York, 1927).

Greeley, Horace, *Recollections of a Busy Life* (New York, 1869).

Greenslet, Ferris, *The Life of Thomas Bailey Aldrich* (Boston and New York, 1908).

Griffis, William Elliott, *Charles Carleton Coffin, War Correspondent, Traveller, Author, and Statesman* (Boston, 1898).

Gurowski, Adam, *Diary,* 3 vols. (Boston, New York, and Washington, D.C., 1862-1866).

Hale, William Harlan, *Horace Greeley, Voice of the People* (New York, 1950).

Hancock, Almira Russell, *Reminiscences of Winfield Scott Hancock by His Wife* (New York, 1887).

Harrington, Fred Harvey, *Fighting Politician, Major General N. P. Banks* (Philadelphia, 1948).

Haupt, Herman, *Reminiscences of General Herman Haupt* (Milwaukee, 1901).

Hebert, Walter H., *Fighting Joe Hooker* (Indianapolis and New York, 1944).

Headley, Joel Tyler, *Farragut and Our Naval Commanders* (New York, 1867).

Hedley, Fenwick Y., *Marching through Georgia, Pen-Pictures of Every-Day Life in General Sherman's Army, from the Beginning of the Atlanta Campaign until the Close of the War* (Chicago, 1890).

Henderson, George Francis Robert, *Stonewall Jackson and the American Civil War,* 2 vols. (London and New York, 1919).

Hill, Jim Dan, *Sea Dogs of the Sixties: Farragut and Seven Contemporaries* (Minneapolis, 1935).

Hindes, Ruthanna, *George Alfred Townsend* (Wilmington, Delaware, 1946).

Hird, Frank, *H. M. Stanley, The Authorized Life* (London, 1935).

Hitchcock, Henry, *Marching with Sherman* (New Haven, 1927).

Hoppin, James Mason, *Life of Andrew Hull Foote, Rear Admiral United States Navy* (New York, 1874).

Horner, Charles F., *The Life of James Redpath and the Development of the Modern Lyceum* (New York and Newark, 1926).

Howard, John Raymond, *Remembrance of Things Past, A Familiar Chronicle of Kinsfolk and Friends Worth While* (New York, 1925).

Howard, Oliver Otis, *Autobiography of Oliver Otis Howard, Major General, United States Army,* 2 vols. (New York, 1907).

Howe, Mark Antony De Wolfe (ed.), *Home Letters of General Sherman* (New York, 1909).

Howe, Mark Anthony De Wolfe (ed.), *Touched with Fire; Civil War Letters and Diary of Oliver Wendell Holmes, Jr., 1861-1864* (New York, 1946).

Johnson, Allen, and Malone, Dumas (eds.), *Dictionary of American Biography*, 21 vols. (New York, 1928-1944).

Kamm, Samuel Richey, *The Civil War Career of Thomas A. Scott* (Philadelphia, 1940).

Larson, Henrietta M., *Jay Cooke, Private Banker* (Cambridge, Massachusetts, 1936).

Lauman, Charles (ed.), *Journal of Alfred Ely, A Prisoner of War in Richmond* (New York, 1862).

Letterman, Jonathan, *Medical Recollections of the Army of the Potomac* (New York, 1866).

Lewis, Charles Lee, *David Glasgow Farragut, Our First Admiral*, 2 vols. (Annapolis, Maryland, 1943).

Lewis, Lloyd, *Sherman, Fighting Prophet* (New York, 1932).

Liddell Hart, Basil Henry, *Sherman, The Genius of the Civil War* (London, 1933).

Longstreet, James, *From Manassas to Appomattox* (Philadelphia, 1896).

Macartney, Clarence Edward Noble, *Little Mac, The Life of General George B. McClellan* (Philadelphia, 1940).

Maverick, Augustus, *Henry J. Raymond and the New York Press for Thirty Years* (Hartford, 1870).

Meade, George Gordon (ed.), *The Life and Letters of George Gordon Meade, Major-General United States Army*, 2 vols. (New York, 1913).

Meredith, Roy, *Mr. Lincoln's Camera Man, Mathew B. Brady* (New York, 1946).

Merriam, George Spring, *The Life and Times of Samuel Bowles*, 2 vols. (New York, 1885).

Michie, Peter Smith, *General McClellan* (New York, 1901).

Morgan, James, *Charles H. Taylor, Builder of the Boston Globe* (Boston [?], 1923).

Morse, John T., Jr. (ed.), *The Diary of Gideon Welles, Secretary of the Navy under Lincoln and Johnson*, 3 vols. (Boston and New York, 1911).

Myers, William Starr, *A Study in Personality, General George B. McClellan* (New York and London, 1934).

National Cyclopedia of American Biography, 37 vols. (New York, 1893-1952).

Nevins, Allan, *Fremont, Pathmarker of the West* (New York and London, 1939).

Nicolay, Helen, *Lincoln's Secretary* (New York, 1949).

Nicolay, John George, and Hay, John, *Abraham Lincoln, A History*, 10 vols. (New York, *ca.* 1914).

———, *Abraham Lincoln, Complete Works*, 12 vols. (New York, 1905).

Noyes, George Freeman, *The Bivouac and the Battle-Field; or, Campaign Sketches in Virginia and Maryland* (New York, 1863).

Oberholtzer, Ellis Paxson, *Jay Cooke, Financier of the Civil War*, 2 vols. (Philadelphia, 1907).

Ogden, Rollo, *Life and Letters of Edwin Lawrence Godkin*, 2 vols. (New York and London, 1907).

Palmer, George Thomas, *A Conscientious Turncoat, The Story of John M. Palmer, 1817-1900* (New Haven, 1941).

Pease, Theodore Calvin, and Randall, James Garfield, *The Diary of Orville Hickman Browning, Illinois State Historical Library Collections*, Vols. XX, XXII (1925, 1933).

Peckham, Harry Houston, *Gotham Yankee: A Biography of William Cullen Bryant* (New York, 1952).

Pennypacker, Isaac Rusling, *General Meade* (New York, 1901).
Piatt, Donn, *Memories of the Men Who Saved the Union* (New York and Chicago, 1887).
Pinchon, Edgcumb, *Dan Sickles, Hero of Gettysburg and "Yankee King of Spain"* (New York, 1945).
Porter, David Dixon, *Incidents and Anecdotes of the Civil War* (New York, 1885).
Porter, Horace, *Campaigning with Grant* (New York, 1906).
Randall, James Garfield, *Lincoln, the President,* 3 vols. (New York, 1945-1952).
Raymond, Henry W., "Extracts from the Journal of Henry J. Raymond," *Scribner's Monthly,* XIX (November, 1879; January, March, 1880), 57-61, 419-424, 703-710; XX (June, 1880), 275-280.
Rice, Allen Thorndike (ed.), *Reminiscences of Abraham Lincoln by Distinguished Men of His Time* (New York, 1888).
Romilly, Henry, *Letters on the Civil War in America* (London, 1889).
Ross, Isabel, *Ladies of the Press; The Story of Women in Journalism by an Insider* (New York and London, 1936).
Rowan, Richard Wilmer, *The Pinkertons, A Detective Dynasty* (Boston, 1931).
Russell, Charles Wells, *The Memoirs of Colonel John S. Mosby* (Boston, 1917).
Sandburg, Carl, *Abraham Lincoln, The War Years,* 4 vols. (New York, 1939).
Schmitt, Martin Ferdinand (ed.), *General George Crook, His Autobiography* (Norman, Oklahoma, 1946).
Schofield, John McAllister, *Forty-six Years in the Army* (New York, 1897).
Schurz, Carl, *The Reminiscences of Carl Schurz,* 3 vols. (New York, 1907).
Seitz, Don Carlos, *Braxton Bragg, General of the Confederacy* (Columbia, South Carolina, 1924).
———, *Horace Greeley, Founder of the New York Tribune* (Indianapolis, 1926).
———, *The James Gordon Bennetts, Father and Son, Proprietors of the New York Herald* (Indianapolis, 1928).
Sheridan, Philip H., *Personal Memoirs of P. H. Sheridan, General, United States Army,* 2 vols. (New York, 1888).
Sherman, William Tecumseh, *Memoirs of General William T. Sherman by Himself,* 2 vols. (New York, 1875).
Sigaud, Louis Adrien, *Belle Boyd, Confederate Spy* (Richmond, Virginia, 1944).
Smith, Theodore Clarke, *The Life and Letters of James Abram Garfield,* 2 vols. (New Haven, 1925).
Smyth, Albert Henry, *Bayard Taylor* (Boston, 1896).
Stedman, Laura, and Gould, George M., *Life and Letters of Edmund Clarence Stedman,* 2 vols. (New York, 1910).
Stewart, Alexander Morrison, *Camp, March and Battle-Field; or, Three Years and a Half with the Army of the Potomac* (Philadelphia, 1865).
Stewart, Kenneth, and Tebbel, John, *Makers of Modern Journalism* (New York, 1952).
Stoddard, Henry Luther, *Horace Greeley, Printer, Editor, Crusader* (New York, 1946).
Tarbell, Ida Minerva, *The Life of Abraham Lincoln,* 2 vols. (New York, 1909).
———, *A Reporter for Lincoln: Story of Henry E. Wing, Soldier and Newspaperman* (New York, 1927).
Tate, Allen, *Stonewall Jackson, The Good Soldier* (New York, 1928).
Taylor, Marie Hansen, *On Two Continents, Memories of Half a Century* (New York, 1905).

Taylor, Marie Hansen, and Scudder, Horace E., *Life and Letters of Bayard Taylor,* 2 vols. (Boston, 1895).

Thompson, Robert Means, and Wainwright, Richard (eds.), *Confidential Correspondence of Gustavus Vasa Fox, Assistant Secretary of the Navy, 1861-1865,* 2 vols. (New York, 1920).

Thorndike, Rachel Sherman (ed.), *The Sherman Letters, Correspondence between General and Senator Sherman from 1837 to 1891* (New York, 1894).

Townsend, Edward Davis, *Anecdotes of the Civil War in the United States* (New York, 1884).

Van Deusen, Glyndon Garlock, *Thurlow Weed, Wizard of the Lobby* (Boston, 1947).

Van Horne, Thomas Budd, *The Life of Major-General George H. Thomas* (New York, 1882).

Villard, Oswald Garrison, *Fighting Years, Memoirs of a Fighting Editor* (New York, 1939).

Wallace, Lewis, *Lew Wallace, an Autobiography,* 2 vols. (New York and London, 1906).

Weed, Harriet A., and Barnes, Thurlow Weed, *Life of Thurlow Weed including his Autobiography and a Memoir,* 2 vols. (Boston, 1883-1884).

West, Richard Sedgwick, Jr., *The Second Admiral, A Life of David Dixon Porter, 1813-1891* (New York, 1937).

———, *Gideon Welles, Lincoln's Navy Department* (Indianapolis and New York, 1943).

"Whitelaw Reid," *Scribner's Monthly,* VIII (August, 1874), 444-451.

Who's Who in America, A Biographical Dictionary of Notable Living Men and Women of the United States (Chicago, 1899-1900 ——).

Wilson, James Grant (ed.), *General Grant's Letters to a Friend, 1861-1880* (New York and Boston, 1897).

Wilson, James Grant, and Fiske, John (eds.), *Appleton's Cyclopaedia of American Biography,* 11 vols. (New York, 1900-1928).

Wilson, James Harrison, *The Life of Charles A. Dana* (New York and London, 1927).

Winston, Robert Watson, *Andrew Johnson, Plebeian and Patriot* (New York, 1928).

Winwar, Frances [pseud.], *American Giant, Walt Whitman and His Times* (New York and London, 1941).

Yount, Charles Allen, *William Bross, 1813-1890* (Lake Forest, Illinois, 1940).

VII. BOOKS AND ARTICLES DEALING WITH THE PRESS

Abbot, Willis John, "Chicago Newspapers and Their Makers," *American Review of Reviews,* XI (June, 1895), 646-665.

"The American Newspaper Press," *Leisure Hour,* XIII (July 23, 30, 1864), 477-480, 493-495.

Andrews, J. Cutler, "The Pennsylvania Press during the Civil War," *Pennsylvania History,* IX (January, 1942), 22-36.

Babcock, Havilah, "The Press and the Civil War," *Journalism Quarterly,* VI (March, 1929), 1-5.

Baehr, Harry William, Jr., *The New York Tribune Since the Civil War* (New York, 1936).

Baker, Ray Stannard, "How the News of the War is Reported," *McClure's Magazine,* XI (September, 1898), 491-495.

Beamish, Richard Joseph, *The History of the Philadelphia Inquirer, 1829-1924* (Privately printed, 1924).

Bibliography

Berger, Meyer, *The Story of the New York Times, 1851-1951* (New York, 1951).

Bleyer, Willard Grosvenor, *Main Currents in the History of American Journalism* (Boston and New York, 1927).

Boynton, Henry van Ness, "The Press and Public Men," *Century Magazine,* XLII (October, 1891), 853-862.

Byars, William Vincent, "The Century of Journalism in Missouri," *Missouri Historical Review,* XV (October, 1920), 53-73.

Carroll, Thomas F., "Freedom of Speech and of the Press during the Civil War," *Virginia Law Review,* IX (May, 1923), 516-551.

Clark, Delbert, *Washington Dateline* (New York and Toronto, 1941).

Clement, Edward Henry, "19th Century Boston Journalism," *New England Magazine,* New Ser. XXXV (November, 1906-February, 1907), 277-281, 415-421, 523-528, 707-713; XXXVI (March-August, 1907), 41-49, 170-176, 321-330, 462-467, 558-564, 729-735; XXXVII (September, 1907), 92-98.

Congdon, Charles Taber, *Tribune Essays: Leading Articles Contributed to the New York Tribune from 1857 to 1863; with an Introduction by Horace Greeley* (New York, 1869).

Dabney, Thomas Ewing, *One Hundred Great Years, The Story of the Times-Picayune from Its Founding to 1940* (Baton Rouge, Louisiana, 1944).

Davis, Elmer, *History of the New York Times, 1851-1921* (New York, 1921).

Diehl, Charles Sanford, *The Staff Correspondent, How the News of the World is Collected and Dispatched by a Body of Trained Press Writers* (San Antonio, Texas, 1931).

Essary, Jesse Frederick, *Covering Washington, Government Reflected to the Public in the Press, 1822-1926* (Boston and New York, 1927).

Fahrney, Ralph Ray, *Horace Greeley and the Tribune in the Civil War* (Cedar Rapids, Iowa, 1936).

Glicksberg, Charles Irving, "Henry Adams and the English and American Press in 1861," *Journalism Quarterly,* XVI (September, 1939), 245-252.

Gramling, Oliver, *AP, The Story of News* (New York and Toronto, 1940).

"A Great American Journalist, Murat Halstead," *American Review of Reviews,* XXXVIII (August, 1908), 191-192.

"Henry Villard," *Nation,* LXXI (November 15, 1900), 380-383.

Hooker, Richard, *The Story of an Independent Newspaper, One Hundred Years of the Springfield Republican, 1824-1924* (New York, 1924).

Hudson, Frederic, *Journalism in the United States from 1690 to 1872* (New York, 1873).

Hyde, William, "Newspapers and Newspaper People of Three Decades," *Missouri Historical Society Collections,* I, 5-24.

"An Interviewer Interviewed, a Talk with 'Gath'," *Lippincott's Monthly Magazine,* XLVIII (November, 1891), 630-638.

Johnson, Gerald White, and others, *The Sunpapers of Baltimore, 1837-1937* (New York, 1937).

Jones, Robert W., *Journalism in the United States* (New York, 1947).

Kinsley, Philip, *The Chicago Tribune, Its First Hundred Years,* 3 vols. (New York, 1943-1946).

Lee, Alfred McClung, *The Daily Newspaper in America, The Evolution of a Social Instrument* (New York, 1937).

Lee, James Melvin, *History of American Journalism* (New York, 1917).

McKenzie, Ralph M., *Washington Correspondents, Past and Present* (New York, 1903).

McNamara, John, *Extra! U.S. War Correspondents in Action* (Boston, 1945).

Matthews, Sidney T., "Control of the Baltimore Press during the Civil War," *Maryland Historical Magazine,* XXXVI (June, 1941), 150-170.

Mott, Frank Luther, *American Journalism, A History of Newspapers in the United States through 250 Years, 1690 to 1940* (New York, 1941).

———, "Evidences of Reliability in Newspapers and Periodicals in Historical Studies," *Journalism Quarterly,* XXI (December, 1944), 304-310.

Munday, Eugene H., "The Press of Philadelphia in 1870," *Proof-Sheet,* III-VI (March, 1870-November, 1872): III, 65-71, 81-85; IV, 1-10, 21-25, 37-42, 53-56, 69-76, 85-88; V, 1-5, 17-23, 33-38, 49-52, 65-66; VI, 3-5, 26-29.

Nevins, Allan, *The Evening Post, A Century of Journalism* (New York, 1922).

"Newspapers and the War," *The Knickerbocker Monthly Magazine,* LX (October, 1862), 350-351.

O'Brien, Frank Michael, *The Story of the Sun, New York: 1833-1918* (New York and London, 1918).

"Our Historical Writers—William Swinton," *Historical Magazine and Notes and Queries,* New Ser. VI (November, 1869), 295-298.

Palmer, Frederick, "A War Correspondent's Story of Gettysburg," *Hearst's Magazine,* XXIV (July, 1913), 70-83.

Parton, James, "The New York Herald," *North American Review,* CII (April, 1866), 373-419.

Payne, George Henry, *History of Journalism in the United States* (New York and London, 1920).

Penniman, Thomas D., "The Early History of the 'Baltimore American'," *Maryland Historical Magazine,* XXVIII (September, 1933), 272-278.

Perry, Edwin A., *The Boston Herald and Its History* (Boston, 1878).

Philips, Melville (ed.), *The Making of a Newspaper, Experiences of Certain Representative American Journalists Related by Themselves and Edited by Melville Philips* (New York, 1893).

Phillips, Cabell, *Dateline: Washington, The Story of National Affairs Journalism in the Life and Times of the National Press Club* (New York, 1949).

Pollard, James Edward, *The Presidents and the Press* (New York, 1947).

"The Press in the United States," *Continental Monthly,* II (November, 1862), 604-609.

Putnam, George Haven, "The London *Times* and the American Civil War," *Magazine of History with Notes and Queries,* XXII (April, 1916), 131-144.

K.R., "The Newspaper Press of America," *Temple Bar,* VII (January, 1863), 190-201.

Randall, James Garfield, "The Newspaper Problem in Its Bearing upon Military Secrecy during the Civil War," *American Historical Review,* XXIII (January, 1918), 303-323.

Richardson, Francis A., "Recollections of a Washington Newspaper Correspondent," *Records of the Columbia Historical Society,* VI (1903), 24-42.

Rideing, William H., "The Metropolitan Newspaper," *Harper's New Monthly Magazine,* LVI (December, 1877), 43-59.

"The Rise and Fall of the War-Correspondent," *Macmillan's Magazine,* XC (August, 1904), 301-310.

Robinson, Elwyn Burns, "The Public Press of Philadelphia during the Civil War" (unpublished doctoral dissertation, Western Reserve University, Cleveland, 1936).

———, "The Dynamics of American Journalism from 1787 to 1865," *Pennsylvania Magazine of History and Biography*, LXI (October, 1937), 435-445.

———, "*The Press:* President Lincoln's Philadelphia Organ," *Pennsylvania Magazine of History and Biography*, LXV (April, 1941), 157-170.

Roe, George Mortimer, "Newspapers and Literature," *New England Magazine*, VI (September, 1888), 447-454.

Rosewater, Victor, *History of Cooperative News-Gathering in the United States* (New York and London, 1930).

Rosten, Leo Calvin, *The Washington Correspondents* (New York, 1937).

Salmon, Lucy, *The Newspaper and the Historian* (New York, 1923).

Sanger, Donald Bridgman, "The Chicago Times and the Civil War," *Mississippi Valley Historical Review*, XVII (March, 1931), 557-580.

Scott, Franklin William, *Newspapers and Periodicals of Illinois, 1814-1879, Illinois State Historical Library Collections*, VI (1910).

Shaw, Albert, "Murat Halstead, Journalist," *American Review of Reviews*, XIII (April, 1896), 439-443.

Shaw, Archer H., *The Plain Dealer, One Hundred Years in Cleveland* (New York, 1942).

Sheridan, T. W., "The Navy and the Press during the Civil War," *United States Naval Institute Proceedings*, LXIII (May, 1937), 709-711.

Skidmore, Joe, "The Copperhead Press and the Civil War," *Journalism Quarterly*, XVI (December, 1939), 345-355.

Smith, William Henry, "The Press as a News Gatherer," *Century Magazine*, XLII (August, 1891), 524-536.

Snyder, Louis Leo, and Morris, Richard Brandon, *A Treasury of Great Reporting, "Literature under Pressure" from the Sixteenth Century to Our Own Time* (New York, 1949).

Spore, John B., "Sherman and the Press," *Infantry Journal*, LXIII (October, 1948), 28-32; (November, 1948), 31-35; (December, 1948), 30-35.

Starr, Louis M., *Bohemian Brigade, Civil War Newsmen in Action* (New York, 1954).

Stevens, Walter B., "Joseph B. McCullagh," *Missouri Historical Review*, XXV (October, 1930-July, 1931), 3-9, 245-253, 425-431, 576-584; XXVI (October, 1931-July, 1932), 40-53, 153-162, 256-266, 374-386; XXVII (October, 1932-July, 1933), 50-62, 151-156, 257-261, 337-343; XXVIII (October, 1933-April, 1934), 38-42, 125-129, 206-210.

Swinton, John, "The New York Daily Papers and Their Editors," *Independent*, LII (January 18, 25, 1900), 168-171, 237-240.

Tebbel, John, *An American Dynasty, The Story of the McCormicks, Medills, and Pattersons* (New York, 1947).

The Times (London), *The History of the Times*, 4 vols. (New York, 1935-1947), Vol. II.

The Tribune (Chicago), *The W.G.N., A Handbook of Newspaper Administration—Editorial, Advertising, Production, Circulation,—Minutely Depicting in Word and Picture, "How It's Done" by the World's Greatest Newspaper* (Chicago, 1922).

Weisberger, Bernard A., *Reporters for the Union* (Boston, 1953).

Wellman, Walter, "Of De B. Randolph Keim," *The Keim and Allied Families*, No. 23 (October, 1900), 719-724.

West, Richard Sedgwick, Jr., "The Navy and the Press during the Civil War," *United States Naval Institute Proceedings,* LXIII (January, 1937), 33-41.

White, Z. L., "Western Journalism," *Harper's New Monthly Magazine,* LXXVII (October, 1888), 678-699.

Wilson, Quintus C., "Confederate Press Association: A Pioneer News Agency," *Journalism Quarterly,* XXVI (June, 1949), 160-166.

Wingate, Charles Frederick, *Views and Interviews on Journalism* (New York, 1875).

Wykoff, George S., "Charles Mackay: England's Forgotten Civil War Correspondent," *South Atlantic Quarterly,* XXVI (January, 1927), 50-62.

VIII. BOOKS AND ARTICLES PERTAINING TO THE CIVIL WAR

Adams, George Worthington, *Doctors in Blue, The Medical History of the Union Army in the Civil War* (New York, 1952).

Bacon, Thomas Scott, "The Fight at Port Hudson, Recollections of an Eyewitness," *Independent,* LIII (March 14, 1901), 589-598.

Baxter, James Phinney, *The Introduction of the Ironclad Warship* (Cambridge, Massachusetts, 1933).

Belknap, George E., "Reminiscent of the Siege of Charleston," *Naval Actions and History, 1799-1898, Papers of the Military Historical Society of Massachusetts,* XII (1902), 157-207.

Bigelow, John, *The Campaign of Chancellorsville* (New Haven, 1910).

Bill, Ledyard, *Pen Pictures of the War* (New York, 1864).

Busbey, Hamilton, "Recollections of Abraham Lincoln and the Civil War," *Forum,* XLV (March, 1911), 282-290.

Catton, Bruce, *Mr. Lincoln's Army* (New York, 1951).

———, *Glory Road* (New York, 1952).

———, *A Stillness at Appomattox* (New York, 1953).

Chamberlin, William Henry, and Thayer, G. A. (eds.), *Sketches of War History, 1861-1865,* 5 vols. (Cincinnati, 1903).

Cist, Henry Martyn, *The Army of the Cumberland* (New York, 1882).

Commager, Henry Steele, *The Blue and the Gray, The Story of the Civil War as Told by Participants,* 2 vols. (Indianapolis and New York, 1950).

Eisenschiml, Otto, and Newman, Ralph, *The American Iliad, The Epic Story of the Civil War as Narrated by Eyewitnesses and Contemporaries* (Indianapolis and New York, 1947).

Fox, William Freeman, *Regimental Losses in the American Civil War* (Albany, New York, 1898).

Freeman, Douglas Southall, *Lee's Lieutenants, A Study in Command,* 3 vols. (New York, 1942-1944).

Fry, James Barnet, *Operations of the Army under Buell from June 10th to October 30, 1862* (New York, 1884).

———, *Military Miscellanies* (New York, 1889).

Geer, Walter, *Campaigns of the Civil War* (New York, 1926).

Gosnell, Harpur Allen, *Guns on the Western Waters, The Story of River Gunboats in the Civil War* (Baton Rouge, Louisiana, 1949).

Gracie, Archibald, *The Truth about Chickamauga* (Boston and New York, 1911).

Hamlin, A. C., "Who Recaptured the Guns at Cedar Creek, October 19, 1864?," *The Shenandoah Campaigns of 1862, and 1864, and the Appomattox Campaign, 1865, Papers of the Military Historical Society of Massachusetts,* VI (1907), 183-208.

Bibliography

Haskell, Franklin Aretas, *The Battle of Gettysburg* (Madison, Wisconsin, 1908).

Hawthorne, Nathaniel, "Chiefly about War Matters," *Atlantic Monthly,* X (July, 1862), 43-61.

Hay, Thomas Robson, "The Campaign and Battle of Chickamauga," *Georgia Historical Quarterly,* VII (September, 1923), 213-250.

Haydon, Frederick Stansbury, *Aeronautics in the Union and Confederate Armies, with a Survey of Military Aeronautics Prior to 1861* (Baltimore, 1941).

Homans, John, "The Red River Expedition," *The Mississippi Valley—Tennessee, Georgia, Alabama, 1861-1864, Papers of the Military Historical Society of Massachusetts,* VIII (1910), 67-97.

Horn, Stanley Fitzgerald, *The Army of Tennessee, A Military History* (Indianapolis and New York, 1941).

———, "Nashville during the Civil War," *Tennessee Historical Quarterly,* IV (March, 1945), 3-22.

Hosmer, James Kendall, *Outcome of the Civil War, 1863-1865* (New York and London, 1907).

Hunter, Moses Hoge (ed.), *Report of the Military Services of Gen. David Hunter, U.S.A., during the War of the Rebellion made to U.S. War Department, 1873* (New York, 1892).

Johnson, John, *The Defense of Charleston Harbor, 1863-1865* (Charleston, South Carolina, 1890).

Johnson, Robert Underwood, and Buel, Clarence Clough (eds.), *Battles and Leaders of the Civil War,* 4 vols. (New York, 1884-1888).

Johnston, Robert Matteson, *Bull Run, Its Strategy and Tactics* (Boston and New York, 1913).

Kizer, John H., "Federal Government Propaganda in Great Britain during the Civil War," *Historical Outlook,* XIX (May, 1928), 204-209.

Landers, H. L., "Wet Sand and Cotton—Banks' Red River Campaign," *Louisiana Historical Quarterly,* XIX (January, 1936), 150-195.

Leech, Margaret, *Reveille in Washington, 1860-1865* (New York and London, 1941).

Livermore, Thomas Leonard, *Numbers and Losses in the Civil War in America, 1861-65* (Boston and New York, 1900).

Lossing, Benson John, *Pictorial History of the Civil War in the United States of America,* 3 vols. (Hartford, 1868).

McClellan, George Brinton, *Report on the Organization and Campaigns of the Army of the Potomac* (New York, 1864).

McCordock, Robert Stanley, *The Yankee Cheese Box* (Philadelphia, 1938).

Maclay, Edgar Stanton, *A History of the United States Navy, from 1775 to 1898,* 2 vols. (New York, 1898), Vol. II.

McMaster, John Bach, *History of the People of the United States during Lincoln's Administration* (New York and London, 1927).

Mahan, Alfred Thayer, *The Gulf and Inland Waters* (New York, 1883).

Meneeley, Alexander Howard, *The War Department, 1861, A Study in Mobilization and Administration* (New York and London, 1928).

Military History Society of Massachusetts, Papers of the, 14 vols. (1881-1918).

Moore, Frank (ed.), *The Rebellion Record, A Diary of American Events, with Documents, Narratives, Illustrative Incidents, Poetry, etc.,* 12 vols. (New York, 1861-1873).

Nordhoff, Charles, "Two Weeks at Port Royal," *Harper's New Monthly Magazine,* XXVII (June, 1863), 110-118.

Paris, Louis Philippe Albert d'Orleans, Comte de, *History of the Civil War in America,* 4 vols. (Philadelphia, 1875-1888).

Parton, James, *General Butler in New Orleans* (New York, 1864).

Pleasants, Henry, Jr., *The Tragedy of the Crater* (Boston, 1938).

Randall, James Garfield, *The Civil War and Reconstruction* (Boston and New York, 1937).

Rhodes, James Ford, *Lectures on the American Civil War Delivered Before the University of Oxford, 1912* (New York, 1913).

———, *History of the United States from the Compromise of 1850 to the End of the Roosevelt Administration,* 9 vols. (New York and London, 1928), Vols. II-V.

Robinson, William M., Jr., "The Alabama–Kearsarge Battle, A Study in Original Sources," *Essex Institute Historical Collections,* LX (April-July, 1924), 97-120, 209-218.

Roman, Alfred, *The Military Operations of General Beauregard in the War between the States 1861 to 1865,* 2 vols. (New York, 1884).

Ropes, John Codman, and Livermore, W. L., *The Story of the Civil War,* 3 Pts. in 4 vols. (New York and London, 1894-1913).

Sanger, Donald Bridgman, "Red River—A Mercantile Expedition," *Tyler's Quarterly Historical and Genealogical Magazine,* XVII (October, 1935), 70-81.

Schaff, Morris, *The Battle of the Wilderness* (Boston and New York, 1910).

Schenck, Robert C., "Major-General David Hunter," *Magazine of American History,* XVII (February, 1887), 138-152.

Shannon, Fred Albert, *The Organization and Administration of the Union Army, 1861-1865,* 2 vols. (Cleveland, 1928).

Soley, James Russell, *The Blockade and the Cruisers* (London, 1898).

Spears, John Randolph, *The History of Our Navy from Its Origin to the Present Day, 1775-1897,* 5 vols. (New York, 1897-1899), Vol. IV.

Steele, Matthew Forney, *American Campaigns,* 2 vols. (Washington, 1909).

Stone, Charles Pomeroy, "Washington in March and April, 1861," *Magazine of American History,* XIV (July, 1885), 1-24.

Tapp, Hambleton, "The Battle of Perryville, 1862," *Filson Club History Quarterly,* IX (July, 1935), 158-181.

Tarbell, Ida Minerva, "Charles A. Dana in the Civil War," *McClure's Magazine,* IX (October, 1897), 1085-1088.

Watson, Elmo Scott, "Mathew B. Brady, the First Man to 'Cover' a War with a Camera," *Quill,* XXV (September, 1937), 10-11, 21.

Wells, E. T., "The Campaign and Battle of Chickamauga," *United Service Magazine,* New Ser. XVI (September, 1896), 205-233.

Wiener, Frederick Bernays, "Decline of a Leader, The Case of General Meade," *Infantry Journal,* XLV (November-December, 1938), 535-542.

Wiley, Bell I., *Life of Billy Yank: Common Soldier of the Union* (Indianapolis and New York, 1952).

Williams, Kenneth Powers, *Lincoln Finds a General, A Military Study of the Civil War,* 2 vols. (New York, 1949).

Williams, Thomas Harry, *Lincoln and His Generals* (New York, 1952).

Winthrop, Theodore, "New York Seventh Regiment, Our March to Washington," *Atlantic Monthly,* VII (June, 1861), 744-756.

Wood, Walter Birbeck, and Edmonds, James E., *The Civil War in the United States with Special Reference to the Campaigns of 1864 and 1865* (London, 1937).

Wood, William Charles Henry, *Captains of the Civil War, A Chronicle of the Blue and Gray* (New Haven, 1921).
Young, Jesse Bowman, *The Battle of Gettysburg, A Comprehensive Narrative* (New York and London, 1913).

IX. MISCELLANEOUS BOOKS AND ARTICLES

Anderson, Frank Maloy, *The Mystery of a Public Man, A Historical Detective Story* (Minneapolis, 1948).
Anderson, Galusha, *The Story of a Border City during the Civil War* (Boston, 1908).
Appleton's Annual Cyclopaedia and Register of Important Events, 1876-1902, 27 vols. (New York, 1886-1903).
Bristed, Charles Astor, "A New Theory of Bohemians," *The Knickerbocker Monthly Magazine,* LVII (March, 1861), 311-317.
Clark, Thomas Dionysius, *A History of Kentucky* (New York, 1937).
Cole, Arthur Charles, *The Irrepressible Conflict, 1850-1865* (New York, 1934).
Fairman, Charles Edwin, *Art and Artists of the Capitol of the United States of America* (Washington, D.C., 1927).
Flick, Alexander Clarence (ed.), *History of the State of New York,* 10 vols. (New York, 1933-1937), Vol. IX.
Ford, Henry Allen, and Kate B., *History of Cincinnati, Ohio with Illustrations and Biographical Sketches* (Cleveland, 1881).
Greve, Charles Theodore, *Centennial History of Cincinnati and Representative Citizens,* 2 vols. (Chicago, 1904).
Hall, Clayton Colman, *Baltimore, Its History and Its People,* 3 vols. (New York and Chicago, 1912).
Harlow, Alvin Fay, *Old Wires and New Waves, The History of the Telegraph, Telephone, and Wireless* (New York and London, 1936).
Harper, Joseph Henry, *The House of Harper, A Century of Publishing in Franklin Square* (New York and London, 1912).
Hertz, Emanuel, *Lincoln Talks* (New York, 1939).
Hyde, William, and Conard, Howard L., *Encyclopedia of the History of St. Louis,* 4 vols. (New York, Louisville, and St. Louis, 1899).
Ingersoll, Lurton Dunham, *A History of the War Department of the United States with Biographical Sketches of the Secretaries* (Washington, D.C., 1880).
The Journalist, Vols. I-XXXVIII (New York, 1884-1904).
Knox, Dudley Wright, *A History of the United States Navy* (New York, 1936).
McClure, Alexander Kelly, *Old Time Notes of Pennsylvania,* 2 vols. (Philadelphia, 1905).
Metcalf, Clyde Hill, *A History of the United States Marine Corps* (New York, 1939).
Morgan, George, *The City of Firsts* (Philadelphia, 1926).
Pierce, Bessie Louise, *A History of Chicago,* 2 vols. (New York, 1940), Vol. II.
Reid, James D., *The Telegraph in America and Morse Memorial* (New York, 1886).
Rhodes, James Ford, *Historical Essays* (New York, 1909).
Roe, George Mortimer, *Cincinnati, The Queen City of the West* (Cincinnati, 1895).
Scharf, John Thomas, *History of Baltimore City and County, from the Earliest Period to the Present Day* (Philadelphia, 1881).
Scharf, John Thomas, and Westcott, Thompson, *History of Philadelphia, 1609-1884,* 3 vols. (Philadelphia, 1884).
Shaler, Nathaniel Southgate, *Kentucky, A Pioneer Commonwealth* (Boston and New York, 1888).

Smalley, Eugene Virgil, *History of the Northern Pacific Railroad* (New York, 1883).
Smith, Henry Bascom, *Between the Lines, Secret Service Stories Told Fifty Years After* (New York, 1911).
Spencer, Richard Henry (ed.), *Genealogical and Memorial Encyclopedia of the State of Maryland,* 2 vols. (New York, 1919).
Thompson, Robert Luther, *Wiring a Continent, The History of the Telegraph Industry in the United States, 1832-1866* (Princeton, New Jersey, 1947).
United States Army and Navy Journal, I-II (August 29, 1863-April 9, 1865).
Wilkes' Spirit of the Times, Vols. IV-XII (New York, 1861-1865).
Wilson, William Bender, *From the Hudson to the Ohio—A Region of Historic, Romantic and Scenic Interest, and Other Sketches* (Philadelphia, 1902).
Winsor, Justin (ed.), *The Memorial History of Boston Including Suffolk County, Massachusetts, 1630-1880,* 4 vols. (Boston, 1881).

Index

Index

Index

Index

Index

DATE DUE			
2/16/12			

FRAMINGHAM CAMPUS
MASS BAY COMMUNITY COLLEGE
19 FLAGG DRIVE
FRAMINGHAM MA 01701-5914